Tolley's Company Law Handbook 2015

by

Janet Rosser, Solicitor

AF896344

81402365

LexisNexis®

Members of the LexisNexis Group worldwide

United Kingdom	Reed Elsevier (UK) Limited trading as LexisNexis, 1-3 Strand, London WC2N 5JR
Australia	LexisNexis Butterworths, Chatswood, New South Wales
Austria	LexisNexis Verlag ARD Orac GmbH & Co KG, Vienna
Benelux	LexisNexis Benelux, Amsterdam
Canada	LexisNexis Canada, Markham, Ontario
China	LexisNexis China, Beijing and Shanghai
France	LexisNexis SA, Paris
Germany	LexisNexis Deutschland GmbH, Munster
Hong Kong	LexisNexis Hong Kong, Hong Kong
India	LexisNexis India, New Delhi
Italy	Giuffrè Editore, Milan
Japan	LexisNexis Japan, Tokyo
Malaysia	Malayan Law Journal Sdn Bhd, Kuala Lumpur
New Zealand	LexisNexis NZ Ltd, Wellington
Singapore	LexisNexis Singapore, Singapore
South Africa	LexisNexis Butterworths, Durban
USA	LexisNexis, Dayton, Ohio

© Reed Elsevier (UK) Ltd 2015

Published by LexisNexis
This is a Tolley title

All rights reserved. No part of this publication may be reproduced in any material form (including photocopying or storing it in any medium by electronic means and whether or not transiently or incidentally to some other use of this publication) without the written permission of the copyright owner except in accordance with the provisions of the Copyright, Designs and Patents Act 1988 or under the terms of a licence issued by the Copyright Licensing Agency Ltd, Saffron House, 6–10 Kirby Street, London EC1N 8TS. Applications for the copyright owner's written permission to reproduce any part of this publication should be addressed to the publisher.
Warning: The doing of an unauthorised act in relation to a copyright work may result in both a civil claim for damages and criminal prosecution.

Crown copyright material is reproduced with the permission of the Controller of HMSO and the Queen's Printer for Scotland. Parliamentary copyright material is reproduced with the permission of the Controller of Her Majesty's Stationery Office on behalf of Parliament. Any European material in this work which has been reproduced from EUR-lex, the official European Communities legislation website, is European Communities copyright.
A CIP Catalogue record for this book is available from the British Library.

ISBN for this volume: 9781405794916

Visit LexisNexis at www.lexisnexis.co.uk

LIBRARY
8140265
346
410
66
Ros.

About This Book

Tolley's Company Law Handbook is intended to be a first book of reference for accountants, solicitors, company secretaries and all those involved in company law.

The twenty third edition includes full coverage of the Companies Act 2006 (CA 2006). CA 2006 replaced the company law provisions of the Companies Act 1985, the Companies Act 1989 and the Companies (Audit, Investigations and Community Enterprise) Act 2004, except for the self-standing provisions on community interest companies and provisions on investigations (which go wider than companies). The Act extends to the whole of the UK, so that there is no separate regime for Northern Ireland.

This edition covers, in alphabetical order, the relevant topics of CA 2006. The contents of this edition have been updated as follows:

changes throughout the chapters to reflect amendments to the amount of daily default fines for certain offences

for public companies changes have been made to the UK Corporate Governance Code, to the Listing Rules to reflect their major review in 2014, to the Takeover Code and to the insider dealing and market abuse regime

for private companies changes have been made to the way in which and how much, cash can be used to redeem or purchase own shares and

company name provisions have been amended.

The major changes however are to reflect the Small Business, Enterprise and Employment Act 2015 which is being brought into force through a series of enabling measures. This Act:

will replace annual returns with annual 'confirmation statements'

adds an additional requirement to include the aggregate amount unpaid on shares in returns

requires all directors to be natural persons (subject to some exceptions)

adds two new grounds for directors' disqualification

amends and extends the definition of, and duties of, shadow directors

prohibits the issue of share warrants to bearer after May 2015 (with additional requirements for how existing share warrants must be dealt with) and

requires all companies to keep a register of people with 'significant interests'

The book also covers other relevant company law provisions (excluding insolvency), case law and other important information, including the Listing Rules, Prospectus Rules, Disclosure and Transparency Rules and the UK Corporate Governance Code.

Chapters are in alphabetical order for ease of reference to a particular subject and cross-references, an index and a table of statutes provide further ways of quickly finding the matter required.

Comments on the publication and suggestions for improvement of future editions are always welcome.

Contents

PAGE

About This Book iii

Abbreviations and References vii

CHAPTER

1 Introduction 1

2 Accounts (general) and Accounting Reference Dates and Periods 3

3 Accounts: Large Companies 29

4 Accounts: Medium-sized Companies 97

5 Accounts: Small Companies 103

6 Accounts: Summary Financial Statements 167

7 Annual Returns 173

8 Audit 181

9 Class Rights 223

10 Community Interest Companies 229

11 Companies not Formed under the Companies Acts 259

12 Company formation and types of companies 265

13 Company Secretaries 275

14 Constitution - Memorandum and Articles 279

15 Corporate Governance 295

16 Dealings with Third Parties 337

17 Debt finance-Debentures and Other Borrowing 357

18 Directors 365

19 Directors' Remuneration Reports 439

20 Directors' Reports 465

21 Dissolution and Restoration 483

22 Distributions 507

23 Insider Dealing and Market Abuse 529

24 Interests in Public Company Shares 553

25 Investigations 563

26 Members 583

27 Names and Business Names 605

28 Northern Ireland 629

29 Offences and Legal Proceedings 631

30 Overseas Companies 645

31 Political Donations 745

32 Prospectuses 755

33 Public and Listed Companies 785

34 Purchase of Own Shares 889

35 Reconstructions and Mergers 925

36 Records 975

37 Registered Office 983

38 Registers 985

39 Registrar of Companies 1009

40 Registration of Charges 1035

41 Re-Registration 1055

42 Resolutions and Meetings 1069

43 Scotland 1113

44 Securities: Certification and Transfers 1119

45 Security for Company Borrowing 1133

46 Share Premium 1141

47 Shares 1145

Contents

48 Takeovers 1199
App 1 Definitions 1283
App 2 Forms 1299
App 3 Fees 1305
App 4 Standard Articles of Association 1315
Table of Statutes 1385
Table of Statutory Instruments 1407
Table of EU Material 1423
Table of Cases 1425
Index 1435

Abbreviations and References

Abbreviations

AGM	=	Annual General Meeting
AIM	=	Alternative Investment Market
Art	=	Article
BNA 1985	=	Business Names Act 1985
CA 1948	=	Companies Act 1948
CA 1985	=	Companies Act 1985
CA 1989	=	Companies Act 1989
CA 2006	=	Companies Act 2006
C(AICE)A 2004	=	Companies (Audit, Investigations and Community Enterprise) Act 2004
CC(CP)A 1985	=	Companies Consolidation (Consequential Provisions) Act 1985
CDDA 1986	=	Company Directors Disqualification Act 1986
Ch	=	Chapter
CS(ID)A 1985	=	Company Securities (Insider Dealing) Act 1985
EA 2002	=	Enterprise Act 2002
EC	=	European community
ECUs	=	European Currency Units
EEA	=	European Economic Area
EEC	=	European Economic Community
EGM	=	Extraordinary General Meeting
FRS	=	Financial Reporting Standard
FSA	=	Financial Services Authority
FSA 1986	=	Financial Services Act 1986
FSMA 2000	=	Financial Services and Markets Act 2000
FTA 1973	=	Fair Trading Act 1973
IA 1985	=	Insolvency Act 1985
IA 1986	=	Insolvency Act 1986
IA 2000	=	Insolvency Act 2000
IAS	=	International Accounting Standards
ICTA 1988	=	Income and Corporation Taxes Act 1988
LLP	=	Limited Liability Partnership
LLPA 2000	=	Limited Liability Partnership Act 2000
LLPR 2001	=	Limited Liability Partnership Regulations 2001
NI	=	Northern Ireland
No	=	Number
Para	=	Paragraph
POS Regulations	=	Public Offers of Securities Regulations 1995
PPERA 2000	=	Political Parties, Elections and Referendum Act 2000
Pt	=	Part
Reg	=	Regulation
RIE	=	Recognised Investment Exchange
RIS	=	Regulatory Information Service
s(s)	=	Section(s)
Sec	=	Section
Sch	=	Schedule [*4 Sch 10* = 4th Schedule, paragraph 10]
SFS	=	Summary Financial Statement
SI	=	Statutory Instrument
SSAP	=	Standard Statement of Accounting Practice
STA 1963	=	Stock Transfer Act 1963

STA 1982	=	Stock Transfer Act 1982
VAT	=	Value Added Tax

References

AC	=	Law Reports, Appeal Cases
All ER	=	All England Law Reports (1936 onwards)
App Cas	=	Law Reports Appeal Cases (1875–90)
BCC	=	British Company Law Cases (CCH Editions Ltd)
BCLC	=	Butterworths Company Law Cases
[1891] Ch	=	Law Reports, Chancery (1891 onwards)
ChD	=	Law Reports, Chancery Division (1876–90)
CLR	=	Commonwealth Law Reports (1903 onwards)
CPD	=	Common Pleas Division (1875–80)
E & B	=	Ellis and Blackburn's Queen's Bench Reports (1852–58)
Ex D	=	Exchequer Division (1875–80)
Hare	=	Hare's Vice-Chancellor's Reports (1841–53)
HL Cas	=	House of Lords Cases (Clark) (1847–66)
[1901] KB	=	Law Reports, King's Bench (1901 onwards)
Lloyd's Rep	=	Lloyd's List Law Reports
LR CP	=	Law Reports, Common Pleas (1865–75)
LR Eq	=	Law Reports, Equity (1865–75)
LR Ex	=	Law Reports, Exchequer (1865–75)
LR HL	=	Law Reports, English and Irish Appeal Cases (1865–75)
LR QB	=	Law Reports, Queen's Bench (1865–75)
LT	=	Law Times (1843 onwards)
Macq	=	Macqueen's Scotch Appeal Cases (1851–65)
[1891] QB	=	Law Reports, Queen's Bench (1891 onwards)
QBD	=	Law Reports, Queen's Bench Division (1876–90)
[1907] SC	=	Court of Session Cases (1907 onwards)
TLR	=	Times Law Reports (1885 onwards)
WLR	=	Weekly Law Reports
WN	=	Weekly Notes (1886 onwards)

1 Introduction

1.1 Territorial extent
1.2 Meaning of 'company' and 'Companies Acts'

1.1 TERRITORIAL EXTENT

The *Companies Act 2006* (*CA 2006*) creates a single company law regime which applies to the whole of the UK and unless the context otherwise requires, the provisions of the '*Companies Acts*' (see **1.2**) as described in this book apply to the whole of the UK.

[*CA 2006, s 1299*].

Northern Ireland. Before *CA 2006*, the provisions of GB company law were generally replicated in separate Northern Ireland legislation. However, as the provisions of *CA 2006* were commenced, they were extended to Northern Ireland and the separate Northern Ireland legislation was repealed.

[*CA 2006, s 1284*].

See **28** NORTHERN IRELAND.

1.2 MEANING OF 'COMPANY' AND 'COMPANIES ACTS'

Unless the context requires otherwise, '*company*' means a company formed and registered under *CA 2006*, ie

- a company so formed and registered after 1 October 2009; or
- a company that immediately before that date
  - (i) was formed and registered under *CA 1985* or the *Companies (Northern Ireland) Order 1986* (*SI 1986 No 1032*); or
  - (ii) was an existing company for the purposes of that *Act* or that *Order*,

  (which is to be treated on commencement as if formed and registered under *CA 2006*).

Certain provisions of the 'Companies Acts' apply to

- companies registered, but not formed, under *CA 2006* (see **11** COMPANIES NOT FORMED UNDER THE COMPANIES ACTS); and
- bodies incorporated in the UK but not registered under *CA 2006*.

[*CA 2006, s 1*].

See **12** COMPANY FORMATIONS AND TYPES OF COMPANIES for types of companies which can be formed and registered under *CA 2006* and **30** OVERSEAS COMPANIES for the provisions applying to companies incorporated outside the UK.

1.2 Introduction

Any reference to the '*Companies Acts*' is a reference to

(a) the company law provisions of *CA 2006*, ie *CA 2006, Pts 1–39* together with *CA 2006, Pts 45–47* in so far as they apply for the purposes of those *Parts*;

(b) *C(AICE)A 2004, Pt 2* (community interest companies); and

(c) the provisions of *CA 1985* and *CC(CP)A 1985* that remain in force.

The provisions under (*b*) and (*c*) above are extended to Northern Ireland by *CA 2006, s 1284*.

[*CA 2006, s 2*].

2 Accounts (general) and Accounting Reference Dates and Periods

2.1 **Introduction**
2.2 **Preparation, approval and signing of accounts**
2.3 **Publication of accounts and reports**
2.4 Name of signatory to be stated in published copies of accounts and reports
2.5 Requirements in connection with publication of accounts
2.6 Circulation to members, debenture holders, etc
2.7 Right to demand copies
2.8 Quoted companies: availability of accounts and reports on website
2.9 **Laying of accounts and reports before general meeting**
2.10 **Filing accounts and reports with the Registrar of Companies**
2.11 Period allowed for filing accounts
2.12 **Revision of defective accounts and reports**
2.13 Small and medium-sized companies
2.14 Powers of the Secretary of State and authorised persons
2.15 **Accounting standards**
2.16 **True and fair view**
2.17 **Accounting reference dates and periods**
2.18 **Accounting reference date**
2.19 Alteration of an accounting reference date
2.20 **Overseas companies**

Cross-references. See 3 ACCOUNTS: LARGE COMPANIES; 4 ACCOUNTS: MEDIUM-SIZED COMPANIES; 5 ACCOUNTS: SMALL COMPANIES; 6 ACCOUNTS: STRATEGIC REPORTS; 8 AUDIT; 20 DIRECTORS' AND STRATEGIC REPORTS; 36.5–36.8 RECORDS.

Background. The provisions in this chapter apply, unless otherwise stated, to accounts and reports for financial years beginning on or after 6 April 2008. [*SI 2007 No 3495, Sch 4 para 6*]. The corresponding provisions of *CA 1985* continue to apply to accounts and reports for financial years beginning before 6 April 2008. There is no historical information for pre 6 April 2008 in the text of this chapter. The *Companies Act 2006 (Strategic Report and Directors' Report) Regulations 2013* ("the *2013 Regulations*") which are referred to in various parts of this chapter, brought into force the requirement for a company to produce a strategic report for financial years ending on or after 30 September 2013. [*SI 2013 No 1970*].

2.1 INTRODUCTION

The provisions described in this chapter cover the requirements which relate to accounts generally, whether individual or group including accounting reference dates and periods.

2.2 PREPARATION, APPROVAL AND SIGNING OF ACCOUNTS

The directors of every company must prepare accounts for the company for each of its financial years unless the company is exempt from that requirement under *Companies Act 2006 (CA 2006), s 394A* (dormant subsidiaries). The accounts must be approved by the board of directors and signed on behalf of the board by a director of the company. The signature must be on the balance sheet. If the accounts are prepared in accordance with the small companies regime (see **5** ACCOUNTS: SMALL COMPANIES), the balance sheet must contain in a prominent position above the signature

- in the case of individual accounts prepared in accordance with the micro-entity provisions, a statement to that effect or
- in the case of accounts not prepared in accordance with those provisions, a statement to the effect that the accounts have been prepared in accordance with the provisions applicable to companies subject to the small companies' regime.

If annual accounts are approved that do not comply with the requirements of *CA 2006* (or, where applicable, the requirements of adopted International Accounting Standards), every director of the company who

- knew that they did not comply, or was reckless as to whether they complied, and
- failed to take reasonable steps to secure compliance with those requirements or, as the case may be, to prevent the accounts from being approved,

commits an offence. A person guilty of such an offence is liable (i) on conviction on indictment, to a fine; and (ii) on summary conviction, to a fine not exceeding the statutory maximum. See **29.1** Offences and Legal Proceedings for the statutory maximum.

[*CA 2006, ss 394, 414; SI 2013 No 3008, Reg 5(4); SI 2012 No 2301, Reg 8*].

Corporate governance statements. In relation to financial years beginning on or after 29 June 2008 and which did not end before 27 June 2009, any separate corporate governance statement must be approved by the board of directors and signed on behalf of the board by a director or the secretary of the company. [*CA 2006, s 419A; SI 2009 No 1581, Reg 2*].

2.3 PUBLICATION OF ACCOUNTS AND REPORTS

There are a number of provisions which must be complied with in *CA 2006* in connection with the publication of accounts and reports. These are considered in 2.4–2.8. Note also that, in certain circumstances, a company could, before 30 September 2013 provide a, summary financial statement instead of the full accounts and reports. The *2013 Regulations* substitute the option to send a summary financial statement with an option to send a copy of a strategic report with supplementary material. See 6 Accounts: Strategic Reports.

2.4 Name of signatory to be stated in published copies of accounts and reports

Every copy of the following document that is 'published' by or on behalf of a company must state the name of the person who signed it on behalf of the board under 2.2.

- In the case of an unquoted company,

  (i) the company's balance sheet;

  (ii) the strategic report; and

  (iii) the directors' report.

- In the case of a quoted company,
  - (i) the company's balance sheet;
  - (ii) the directors' remuneration report;
  - (iii) the strategic report; and
  - (iv) the directors' report.

A quoted company is defined in *CA 2006, s 385* as a company whose equity share capital is either included in the UK official list or is officially listed in an EEA state or is admitted to trading on Nasdaq or New York Stock Exchange. A company is regarded as '*publishing*' a document if it publishes, issues or circulates it or otherwise makes it available for public inspection in a manner calculated to invite members of the public generally, or any class of members of the public, to read it.

If a copy is published without the required statement of the signatory's name, an offence is committed by the company and every officer of the company who is in default. A person guilty of such an offence is liable, on summary conviction, to a fine not exceeding level 3 on the standard scale. See **29.1 Offences and Legal Proceedings** for the standard scale.

[*CA 2006, s 433; SI 2013 No 1970, Schedule, para 6*].

2.5 Requirements in connection with publication of accounts

(1) *Statutory accounts*

If a company publishes any of its 'statutory accounts', they must be accompanied by the auditor's report on those accounts (unless the company is exempt from audit and the directors have taken advantage of that exemption).

A company that prepares statutory group accounts for a financial year must not publish its statutory individual accounts for that year without also publishing with them its statutory group accounts.

'*Statutory accounts*' are a company's accounts for a financial year as required to be delivered to the Registrar of Companies (see **2.10**). They include

(i) abbreviated accounts delivered to the Registrar of Companies under the provisions for small companies (see **5.46** and **5.76 Accounts: Small Companies**) and medium-sized companies (see **4.5 Accounts: Medium-Sized Companies**), in which case references to the auditor's report are to be read as references to the special auditor's report required under those provisions; and

(ii) any additional copy of the annual accounts delivered in euros (see **2.10**).

In the case of an unlimited company, the statutory accounts are the accounts as prepared in accordance with *CA 2006* and approved by the board of directors.

If a company contravenes any of the above provisions, an offence is committed by the company and by every officer of the company who is in default. A person guilty of such an offence is liable on summary conviction to a fine not exceeding level 3 on the standard scale. See **29.1 Offences and Legal Proceedings** for the standard scale.

[*CA 2006, ss 434, 448(4)(a), 449(5), 469(4)*].

(2) *Non-statutory accounts*

A company must not publish with 'non-statutory accounts' the auditor's report on the company's statutory accounts. But it must publish with non-statutory accounts a statement indicating

- that they are not the company's statutory accounts;
- whether statutory accounts dealing with any financial year with which the non-statutory accounts purport to deal have been delivered to the Registrar of Companies (or in the case of an unlimited company, that the company is exempt from the requirement to deliver statutory accounts); and
- whether an auditor's report has been made on the company's statutory accounts for any such financial year, and if so whether the report

  (i) was qualified or unqualified, or included a reference to any matters to which the auditor drew attention by way of emphasis without qualifying the report; or

  (ii) contained a statement under *CA 2006, s 498(2)* (accounting records or returns inadequate or accounts or directors' remuneration report not agreeing with records and returns), or *CA 2006, s 498(3)* (failure to obtain necessary information and explanations).

If abbreviated accounts are delivered to the Registrar of Companies under the provisions for small companies (see **5.46** and **5.76** ACCOUNTS: SMALL COMPANIES) or medium-sized companies (see **4.5** ACCOUNTS: MEDIUM-SIZED COMPANIES), references above to the auditor's report are to be read as references to the special auditor's report required under those provisions.

See (1) above for '*statutory accounts*'.

'*Non-statutory accounts*' means either of the following which is published otherwise than as part of the company's statutory accounts.

(i) Any balance sheet or profit and loss account relating to, or purporting to deal with, a financial year of the company.

(ii) An account in any form purporting to be a balance sheet or profit and loss account for 'a group headed by the company' relating to, or purporting to deal with, a financial year of the company.

A '*group headed by the company*' means a group consisting of the company and any other undertaking (regardless of whether it is a subsidiary undertaking of the company) other than a parent undertaking of the company.

If a company contravenes any of the above provisions, an offence is committed by the company, and by every officer of the company who is in default. A person guilty of such an offence is liable on summary conviction to a fine not exceeding level 3 on the standard scale. See **29.1** OFFENCES AND LEGAL PROCEEDINGS for the standard scale.

[*CA 2006, ss 435, 448(4)(b), 449(5), 469(4)*].

For the purposes of both (1) and (2) above, a company is regarded as publishing a document if it publishes, issues or circulates it or otherwise makes it available for public inspection in a manner calculated to invite members of the public generally, or any class of members of the public, to read it. [*CA 2006, s 436*].

2.6 Circulation to members, debenture holders, etc

Subject (for financial years ending on or after 30 September 2013) to the provisions relating to strategic reports (see **6 Accounts: Strategic reports**) a company must send a copy of its 'annual accounts and reports' for each financial year to

- every member of the company;
- every holder of the company's debentures; and
- every person who is entitled to receive notice of general meetings.

See **Appendix 1 Definitions** for the meaning of '*annual accounts and reports*'.

Exceptions. Copies need not be sent to the following persons.

(a) A person for whom the company does not have a 'current address'. It has a current address for a person if

 (i) an address has been notified to the company by the person as one at which documents may be sent to him; and

 (ii) the company has no reason to believe that documents sent to him at that address will not reach him.

 As a result of (ii) above, a company does not have a current address if previous correspondence has been returned marked not known at this address (or its electronic equivalent).

(b) In the case of a company not having a share capital, copies need not be sent to anyone who is not entitled to receive notices of general meetings of the company.

See **16.32 Dealings With Third Parties** for general provisions about supplying documents to joint holders.

[*CA 2006, s 423(1)–(4), (6)*].

Where copies are sent out over a period of days, references in the *Companies Acts* to the day on which copies are sent out are to be read as references to the last day of that period. [*CA 2006, s 423(5)*].

Time allowed for sending out copies of accounts and reports.

- *A public company* must comply with the above provisions at least 21 days before the date of the general meeting of the company at which the accounts and reports in question are to be laid in accordance with **2.9**. If copies are sent out later than this, they will still be deemed to have been duly sent if all the members entitled to attend and vote at that meeting so agree.
- *A private company* must comply with the above provisions not later than

 (i) the end of the period for filing accounts and report (see **2.11**), or

 (ii) if earlier, the date on which it actually delivers its accounts and reports to the Registrar of Companies.

Whether the time allowed is that for a private company or a public company is determined by reference to the company's status immediately before the end of the accounting reference period by reference to which the financial year for the accounts in question was determined.

[*CA 2006, s 424*].

2.6 Accounts (general): Accounting Reference (Dates/Periods)

Offences. In default in complying with any of the above provisions, an offence is committed by the company and every officer of the company who is in default. A person guilty of such an offence is liable (i) on conviction on indictment, to a fine; and (ii) on summary conviction, to a fine not exceeding the statutory maximum. See **29.1 Offences and Legal Proceedings** for the statutory maximum. [*CA 2006, s 425*].

Method of sending accounts. For the provisions explaining how a company can communicate with members, etc. (including in electronic form and by means of a website) see **16.28–16.32 Dealings With Third Parties.**

2.7 Right to demand copies

In addition to any copy to which a person is entitled under **2.6**, a member or debenture holder of a company is entitled to be provided, on demand and without charge, with a single copy of

- the company's last annual accounts;
- the strategic report (if any) for the last financial year;
- the last directors' report;
- in the case of a quoted company, the last directors' remuneration report; and
- the auditor's report on those accounts (including the report on the directors' report and, where applicable, the directors' remuneration report *and* (where applicable) on the strategic report).

If a demand made under these provisions is not complied with within seven days of receipt by the company, an offence is committed by the company and by every officer of the company who is in default. A person guilty of such an offence is liable (i) on summary conviction, to a fine not exceeding level 3 on the standard scale, and (ii) for continued contravention, a daily default fine not exceeding one-tenth of level 3 on the standard scale. See **29.1 Offences and Legal Proceedings** for the standard scale.

[*CA 2006, ss 431, 432; SI 2013 No 1970, Schedule, para 4*]

2.8 Quoted companies: availability of accounts and reports on website

A quoted company (see **2.4** for a definition) must ensure that its annual accounts and reports are made available on a website and remain so available until the annual accounts and reports for the company's next financial year are made available on the website.

If the directors' remuneration policy is revised in accordance with *CA 2006, s 422A* (see **19.19**) the company must ensure that the revised policy is made available on the website on which its annual accounts and reports are made available.

Website availability. The accounts and reports must be made available on a website that is maintained by, or on behalf of, the company and identifies the company in question. They must be made available as soon as reasonably practicable, must be kept available until the report and accounts for the company's next financial year are made available and, where *CA 2006, s 430(2A)* applies (quoted company's revised remuneration policy), the material in question must also be made available as soon as reasonably practicable and must be kept available until the next directors' remuneration report is made available on the website. Access to the materials made available under *CA 2006, s 230*, and the ability to obtain a hard copy of such material from the website, must not be conditional on the payment of a fee or otherwise restricted (except so far as necessary to comply with any enactment or regulatory requirement in the UK or elsewhere).

A failure to make the material available on a website throughout the period mentioned in *CA 2006, s 420(4)* or *(4A)* as the case may be, is disregarded if

- it is made available on the website for part of that period; and
- the failure is wholly attributable to circumstances that it would not be reasonable to have expected the company to prevent or avoid.

Offences. In default in complying with the above provisions, an offence is committed by every officer of the company who is in default. A person guilty of such an offence is liable, on summary conviction, to a fine not exceeding level 3 on the standard scale. See **29.1 Offences and Legal Proceedings** for the standard scale.

[*CA 2006, s 430; ERRA, ss 81(6), (7), (8), (9)*].

2.9 LAYING OF ACCOUNTS AND REPORTS BEFORE GENERAL MEETING

(1) Public companies

The directors of a public company must lay before the company in general meeting copies of its annual accounts and reports. They must do so not later than the end of the period for filing the accounts and reports in question (see **2.11**).

If these requirements are not complied with before the end of the period allowed, every person who immediately before the end of that period was a director of the company commits an offence. A person guilty of such an offence is liable (i) on summary conviction, to a fine not exceeding level 5 on the standard scale, and (ii) for continued contravention, a daily default fine not exceeding one-tenth of the greater of £5,000 or level 4 on the standard scale. See **29.1 Offences and Legal Proceedings** for the standard scale. It is a defence for a person charged with such an offence to prove that he took all reasonable steps for securing that those requirements would be complied with before the end of that period. It is not a defence to prove that the documents in question were not in fact prepared as required.

[*CA 2006, ss 437, 438; SI 2015 No 664, Sch 3*].

(2) Private companies

Private companies are no longer under a statutory obligation to hold an AGM or to lay accounts and reports in general meeting (although they may be required to do so under the articles). This applies to financial years ending on or after 1 October 2007 [*SI 2007 No 2194 Sch 3 Para 49*]. If a private company's articles require it to lay accounts and reports in general meeting, a special resolution can be passed to amend the articles and remove the requirement.

2.10 FILING ACCOUNTS AND REPORTS WITH THE REGISTRAR OF COMPANIES

The directors of a company must deliver to the Registrar of Companies for each financial year a copy of its accounts and reports unless it is exempt from filing because it is an unlimited company or a dormant subsidiary See **12 Company Formation and Types of Companies** for the exemption from this requirement for certain unlimited companies and dormant subsidiaries.

[*CA 2006, s 441; SI 2008 No 393, Reg 6(6); SI 2012 No 2301, Reg 10*].

2.10 Accounts (general): Accounting Reference (Dates/Periods)

(1) **Companies subject to the small companies regime**

The directors of a company subject to the small companies' regime (see **5.2** ACCOUNTS: SMALL COMPANIES)

(a) must deliver to the Registrar of Companies for each financial year a copy of a balance sheet drawn up as at the last day of that year;

(b) may also deliver to the Registrar of Companies

(i) a copy of the company's profit and loss account for that year; and

(ii) a copy of the directors' report for that year; and

(c) must also deliver to the Registrar of Companies a copy of the auditor's report on the accounts (and any directors' report) that it delivers unless the company is exempt from audit and the directors have taken advantage of that exemption.

Subject to *CA 2006, s 444(3A)* (provisions for abbreviated accounts to be delivered) the copies of accounts and reports delivered to the Registrar of Companies must be copies of the company's annual accounts and reports. The abbreviated accounts provisions in *CA 2006, s 444(3A)* apply:

- where a company prepares Companies Act accounts
- where *CA 2006, s 444(3B)* (micro-entity provisions) do not apply
- and allow the directors to deliver a copy of the balance sheet drawn up in accordance with regulations made by the Secretary of State and a profit and loss account with such items omitted as may be specified by the regulations.

If abbreviated accounts are delivered, the obligation to deliver a copy of the auditor's report on the accounts is to deliver a copy of the special auditor's report required by *CA 2006, s 449* (**8.31** AUDIT).

The abbreviated accounts provisions in *CA 2006, s 444(3A)* do not apply if the company qualifies as a micro –entity in relation to a financial year and those accounts are prepared for that year in accordance with any of the micro-entity provisions (see **5** ACCOUNTS :SMALL COMPANIES).

Where the directors of a company subject to the small companies regime deliver to the Registrar of Companies either IAS accounts or Companies Act accounts that are not abbreviated accounts and take the option under (*b*) above of not delivering a copy of the company's profit and loss account or directors' report, the copy of the balance sheet delivered to the Registrar of Companies must contain, in a prominent position, a statement that the company's annual accounts and reports have been delivered in accordance with the provisions applicable to companies subject to the small companies regime.

The copies of the balance sheet and any directors' report delivered to the Registrar of Companies under these provisions must state the name of the person who signed it on behalf of the board.

The copy of the auditor's report delivered to the Registrar of Companies under these provisions must

- state the name of the auditor and (where the auditor is a firm) the name of the person who signed it as senior statutory auditor; or

- if the conditions is *CA 2006, s 506* are met (circumstances in which names may be omitted, see **8.34 Audit**), state that a resolution has been passed and notified to the Secretary of State in accordance with those provisions.

[*CA 2006, s 444; SI 2008 No 393, Reg 12; S I2013 No 3008, Reg 6*].

(2) **Companies entitled to the small companies' exemption in relation to the directors' report**

Where a company is entitled to the small companies exemption in relation to its directors' report for a financial year but does not fall within (1) above (because it is a member of an ineligible group, see **20.18 Directors' Reports**), the directors of the company

- must deliver to the Registrar of Companies a copy of the company's annual accounts for that year;
- may also deliver to the Registrar of Companies a copy of the directors' report; and
- must also deliver to the Registrar of Companies a copy of the auditor's report on the accounts (and any directors' report) that it delivers unless the company is exempt from audit and the directors have taken advantage of that exemption.

The copies of the balance sheet and any directors' report delivered to the Registrar of Companies under these provisions must state the name of the person who signed it on behalf of the board.

The copy of the auditor's report delivered to the Registrar of Companies under these provisions must

- state the name of the auditor and (where the auditor is a firm) the name of the person who signed it as senior statutory auditor; and
- if the conditions in *CA 2006, s 506* (circumstances in which names may be omitted, see **8.34 Audit**) are met, state that a resolution has been passed and notified to the Secretary of State in accordance with that section.

[*CA 2006, s 444A; SI 2008 No 393, Reg 6(7); SI 2009 No 1581, Reg 10*].

(3) **Medium-sized companies**

The directors of a company that qualifies as a medium-sized company (other than a company within (1) above) in relation to a financial year (see **4.2 Accounts: Medium-Sized Companies**) must deliver to the Registrar of Companies a copy of

- the company's annual accounts;
- the strategic report;
- the directors' report;
- the auditor's report on those accounts (and on the strategic report and directors' report) unless the company is exempt from audit and the directors have taken advantage of that exemption.

Where the company prepares Companies Act accounts, the directors may deliver abbreviated accounts. See **4.5 Accounts: Medium-Sized Companies**. If such abbreviated accounts are delivered, the obligation to deliver a copy of the auditor's report on the accounts is to deliver a copy of the special auditor's report required by *CA 2006, s 449* (**8.31 Audit**).

The copies of the balance sheet and strategic report and directors' report delivered to the Registrar of Companies under these provisions must state the name of the person who signed it on behalf of the board.

The copy of the auditor's report delivered to the Registrar of Companies under these provisions must

- state the name of the auditor and (where the auditor is a firm) the name of the person who signed it as senior statutory auditor; or
- if the conditions is *CA 2006, s 506* are met (circumstances in which names may be omitted, see **8.34** AUDIT), state that a resolution has been passed and notified to the Secretary of State in accordance with those provisions.

[*CA 2006, s 445, SI 2008 No 393, Reg 6(8); SI 2013 No 1970, Schedule, para 9*].

(4) **Unquoted companies**

The directors of an unquoted company (which does not fall within (1)–(3) above) must deliver to the Registrar of Companies for each financial year of the company a copy of

- the company's annual accounts;
- the strategic report;
- the directors' report;
- any separate corporate governance statement; and
- the auditor's report on those accounts, the strategic report (where this is covered by the auditor's report) (and the directors' report and any separate corporate governance statement) unless the company is exempt from audit and the directors have taken advantage of that exemption.

The copies of the balance sheet, and strategic report and directors' report and any separate corporate governance statement delivered to the Registrar of Companies under these provisions must state the name of the person who signed it on behalf of the board.

The copy of the auditor's report delivered to the Registrar of Companies under these provisions must

- state the name of the auditor and (where the auditor is a firm) the name of the person who signed it as senior statutory auditor; or
- if the conditions is *CA 2006, s 506* are met (circumstances in which names may be omitted, see **8.34** AUDIT), state that a resolution has been passed and notified to the Secretary of State in accordance with that section.

[*CA 2006, s 446; SI 2008 No 393, Reg 6(9) and 6(9)(a); SI 2009 No 1581, Reg 3(2), 3(3) and 3(6); SI 2013 No 1970, Schedule, para 10*].

(5) **Quoted companies**

The directors of a quoted company must deliver to the Registrar of Companies for each financial year of the company a copy of

- the company's annual accounts;
- the strategic report;
- the directors' remuneration report;

- the directors' report;
- any separate corporate governance statement; and
- the auditor's report on those accounts and on the directors' remuneration report, the strategic report (where this is covered by the auditor's report) the directors' report and any separate corporate governance statement.

The copies of the balance sheet, directors' remuneration report, *the strategic report and* directors' report and any separate corporate governance statement delivered to the Registrar of Companies under these provisions must state the name of the person who signed it on behalf of the board.

The copy of the auditor's report delivered to the Registrar of Companies under these provisions must

- state the name of the auditor and (where the auditor is a firm) the name of the person who signed it as senior statutory auditor; or
- if the conditions is *CA 2006, s 506* are met (circumstances in which names may be omitted, see **8.34** AUDIT), state that a resolution has been passed and notified to the Secretary of State in accordance with that section.

[*CA 2006, s 447; SI 2009 No 1581, Reg 4(2), 4(3) and 4(6); SI 2013 No 1970, Schedule, para 11*].

Failure to file accounts and reports. There are three possible consequences of failing to comply with the requirements under (1) to (5) above (as the case may be) before the end of the period for filing those accounts and reports (see **2.11**).

(a) *Offences*. Every person who immediately before the end of that period was a director of the company commits an offence. A person guilty of such an offence is liable (i) on summary conviction, to a fine not exceeding level 5 on the standard scale; and (ii) for continued contravention, to a daily default fine not exceeding one-tenth of the greater of £5,000 or level 4 on the standard scale. See **29.1** OFFENCES AND PENALTIES for the standard scale. It is a defence for a person charged with such an offence to prove that he took all reasonable steps for securing that those requirements would be complied with before the end of that period. It is not a defence to prove that the documents in question were not in fact prepared as required. [*CA 2006, s 451; SI 2015 No 664, Sch 3*].

(b) *Court orders*. If the directors of the company fail to make good the default within 14 days after the service of a notice on them requiring compliance, the court may, on the application of any member or creditor of the company or of the Registrar of Companies, make an order directing the directors (or any of them) to make good the default within such time as may be specified in the order. The court's order may provide that all costs (in Scotland, expenses) of, and incidental to, the application are to be borne by the directors. [*CA 2006, s 452*].

(c) *Civil penalty (the late filing penalty)*. In addition to any liability of the directors under (*a*) above, the company is liable to a civil penalty. The amount of the penalty depends upon the length of the period between the end of the period for filing the accounts and reports in question and the date of eventual compliance and on whether the company is a private or public company, as follows.

Accounts filed on or after 1 February 2009

Note. If there was a failure to comply with the filing requirements in relation to the previous financial year of the company, and that previous financial year began on or after 6 April 2008, the penalties in the table below are doubled.

2.10 Accounts (general): Accounting Reference (Dates/Periods)

Length of period	*Public company*	*Private company*
Not more than 1 month	£750	£150
More than 1 month but not more than 3 months	£1,500	£375
More than 3 months but not more than 6 months	£3,000	£750
More than 6 months	£7,500	£1,500

Whether a company is a public company or a private company depends upon its status at the end of the financial year in question.

It is not a defence in proceedings under these provisions to prove that the documents in question were not in fact prepared.

[*CA 2006, s 453; SI 2008 No 497*].

Filing of accounts in euros. The amounts set out in the annual accounts of a company may also be shown in the same accounts translated into euros. When complying with (1) to (4) above, the directors may deliver to the Registrar of Companies an additional copy of the company's annual accounts in which the amounts have been translated into euros. In both cases, the amounts must have been translated at the exchange rate prevailing on the date to which the balance sheet is made up and the rate must be disclosed in the notes to the accounts. The requirement to disclose the rate in the notes to the accounts does not apply to the individual accounts of a company for a financial year in which the company qualifies as a micro-entity. For the meaning of 'micro-entity' see **5.3A**,

[*CA 2006, ss 469(1)–(3), (3A); SI 2013 No 3008, Reg 7(2)*].

For the form, authentication and manner of delivery of accounts sent to the Registrar of Companies. See **39.6 Registrar of Companies**.

2.11 Period allowed for filing accounts

Subject to below, the period allowed for the directors of a company to deliver accounts and reports for a financial year to the Registrar of Companies under **2.10** is

- *for a private company*, nine months after the end of the relevant accounting reference period; and
- *for a public company*, six months after the end of the relevant accounting reference period.

The '*relevant accounting reference period*' is the accounting reference period by reference to which the financial year for the accounts in question was determined (see **2.17**).

Whether the period allowed is that for a private company or a public company is determined by reference to the company's status immediately before the end of the relevant accounting reference period.

Exceptions.

(1) If the relevant accounting reference period is the company's first and is a period of more than twelve months, the period is

- nine months or six months, as the case may be, from the first anniversary of the incorporation of the company; or

- three months after the end of the accounting reference period;

whichever expires last.

(2) If the relevant accounting reference period is treated as shortened by virtue of a notice given by the company under 2.19, the period is

- that applicable in accordance with the above provisions; or
- three months from the date of the notice;

whichever expires last.

(3) Applying for extra time to file. If for any special reason the Secretary of State thinks fit, he may, on an application made before the expiry of the period otherwise allowed, give notice in writing to a company extending that period by such further period as may be specified in the notice.

An application for such an extension, giving reasons why the extension should be granted, should be sent before the normal filing deadlines. The application must be in writing (by e-mailing the enquiries section at Companies House) or in hard copy (for companies incorporated in England and Wales) to Companies House, Crown Way, Cardiff, CF14 3UZ or (for companies incorporated in Scotland) to Companies House, 4th Floor, Edinburgh Quay 2, 139 Fountainbridge, Edinburgh, EH1 9FF. (Companies House Guidance Booklet GP2 Life of a company, Ch 5, para 9.)

Calculation of the period allowed. For the purposes of calculating the period for filing a company's accounts and reports which is expressed as a specified number of months from a specified date (or after the end of a specified previous period), the period ends with the date in the appropriate month corresponding to the specified date or the last day of the specified previous period. For example, if the end of the accounting reference period is 5 June, six months from then is 5 December. But this is overridden in two circumstances.

(a) If the specified date (or the last day of the specified previous period) is the last day of a month, the period ends with the last day of the appropriate month (whether or not that is the corresponding date). For example, if the end of the accounting reference period is 30 June, six months from then is 31 December (not 30 December).

(b) If the specified date (or the last day of the specified previous period) is not the last day of a month but is the 29th or 30th, and the appropriate month is February, the period ends with the last day of February. For example, if the end of the accounting reference period is 29 or 30 August, six months from then is the last day of the following February.

[*CA 2006, ss 442, 443*].

Companies House policy. Companies House rigidly applies the deadline. If a filing deadline expires on a Sunday or Bank Holiday, the accounts must still be filed by that date and therefore should be posted in time to arrive before such a deadline.

Companies House cannot accept accounts until they meet the requirements of *CA 2006*. If, for example, a signature is missing, the accounts will be returned for amendment. This might result in a penalty if the corrected accounts are delivered late and it is therefore recommended that accounts are delivered as soon as they are completed and as far in advance as possible of the last date for delivery.

(Companies House Guidance Booklets GP2 – Life of a company – Part 1 Annual Requirements and GP5 – Late Filing Penalties).

2.12 REVISION OF DEFECTIVE ACCOUNTS AND REPORTS

If it appears to the directors of a company that

- the annual accounts or
- strategic report or
- directors' report, or
- directors' remuneration report

did not comply with the requirements of *CA 2006* (or, where applicable, adopted international accounting standards), they may prepare revised accounts or a revised report. Where copies of the previous accounts or report have been sent out to members, delivered to the Registrar of Companies or (in the case of a public company) laid before the company in general meeting, the revisions must do no more than correct those respects in which the previous accounts, etc did not comply with the said requirements and make any necessary consequential alterations.
[*CA 2006, s 454(1) (2); SI 2013 No 1970, Reg 1(3), Schedule, paras 12(b), 12(c)*].

For provisions relating to defective reports, see **19.20–19.25** Directors' Remuneration Reports and **20.19–20.24** Directors' Reports and Strategic Reports.

(1) **Contents of revised accounts**

The provisions of *CA 2006* (and, where applicable, *IAS Regulations*) as to the matters to be included in a company's annual accounts apply to revised accounts as if they had been prepared and approved by the directors as at the date of approval of the original accounts. In particular,

- the revised accounts must show a true and fair view as at the date of the original accounts; and
- the requirement to deal in the accounts with liabilities arising between the balance sheet date and the date the accounts are signed is to be treated as a reference to the date of the original accounts.

Where the accounts provisions in *CA 2006* are amended after the date of approval of the original accounts but before the date of revision, it is the provisions before amendment that apply. [*SI 2008 No 373, Regs 2, 3(1)–(3), 19(1)*]. See **2.16** for '*true and fair view*'.

(2) **Approval and signature**

The provisions under **2.2** as regards the approval and signing of accounts apply equally to revised accounts, but if the revision is by way of '*supplementary note*' (ie a note indicating corrections to be made to the original accounts or reports), it is that note rather than the balance sheet which must be signed. The approved revised accounts (or supplementary note) must state the date of approval. Where copies of the original accounts have been sent out to members, etc under **2.6**, laid before the company in general meeting under **2.9** or delivered to the Registrar of Companies under **2.10**, the directors must, before approving the revised accounts, cause the following matters to be made in a prominent position in the revised accounts (or the supplementary note).

- In the case of revisions by replacement (ie where revision is by way of a replacement set of accounts in substitution for the originals):

  (i) that the revised accounts replace the original annual accounts for the specified financial year;

(ii) that they are now the company's statutory accounts for that financial year;

(iii) that they have been prepared as at the date the original accounts were approved and not as at the date the revised accounts were approved and so do not deal with events between those dates;

(iv) the respects in which the original accounts did not comply with the requirements of *CA 2006*; and

(v) any significant amendments made as a consequence of remedying those defects.

- In the case of revision by supplementary note:

(i) that the note revises in certain respects the original annual accounts and is to be treated as forming part of those accounts; and

(ii) that the annual accounts have been revised as at the date the original accounts were approved and not as at the date of the revised accounts were approved and so do not deal with events between those dates.

The penalty provisions in **2.2** apply in the case of non-compliance.

[*SI 2008 No 373, Regs 2, 4*].

(3) **Effect of revision and publication of accounts**

Upon the directors approving revised accounts, the provisions of *CA 2006* have effect as if the revised accounts were, as from the date of their approval, the annual accounts of the company in place of the original annual accounts. This applies in particular for the purposes of

- *CA 2006, ss 431, 432* (the right to demand copies of accounts, see **2.7**);
- *CA 2006, s 434(3)* (meaning of 'statutory accounts', see **2.5**); and
- *CA 2006, s 423* (persons entitled to receive copies, see **2.6**), *CA 2006, s 437* (accounts, etc of public company to be laid before company in general meeting, see **4.9**) and *CA 2006, s 441* (accounts, etc to be delivered to Registrar of Companies, see **2.10**) if the requirements of those provisions have not been complied with prior to the date of revision.

Where the directors have prepared a revised report and copies of the original report have been sent to any person under *CA 2006, s 423* (persons entitled to receive copies, see **2.6**) or *CA 2006, s 146* (traded companies: nomination of persons to enjoy information rights, see **26.4 Members**), the directors must send to any such person

- in the case of a revision by replacement, a copy of the revised accounts, together with a copy of the auditor's report on those accounts; or
- in the case of revision by supplementary note, a copy of that note together with a copy of the auditor's report on the revised accounts.

This must be done not more than 28 days after the date of the revision (ie the date on which the revised report is approved by the directors).

The directors must also, not more than 28 days after the revision, send a copy of the revised accounts and auditor's report on those accounts to any person who is not entitled to receive a copy under the above provisions but who is, as at the date of revision,

(a) a member of the company,

(b) a holder of the company's debentures, or

(c) a person who is entitled to receive notice of general meetings

unless the company would be entitled at that date to send to that person a strategic report and supplementary material.

The exceptions from the requirement to send copies of the annual accounts and reports in **2.6** equally apply to sending out copies of the revised directors' report.

References in *CA 2006* to the day on which the accounts are sent out refer to the original accounts (with *CA 2006, s 423(5)* – see **2.6** – applying where necessary) in cases where the sending out of the original accounts has been completed prior to the date of the directors' approval of the revised accounts. In other cases, such references are to the day, or the last day, on which the revised accounts are sent out.

In default in complying with the above provisions, an offence is committed by each of the directors who approved the revised accounts. A person guilty of such an offence is liable (i) on conviction on indictment, to a fine; and (ii) on summary conviction, to a fine not exceeding the statutory maximum. See **29.1 Offences and Legal Proceedings** for the statutory maximum.

[*SI 2008 No 373, Regs 10, 12; SI 2013 No 2224, Reg 11*].

(4) **Laying of revised accounts**

Where the directors of a public company have prepared revised accounts and copies of the original annual accounts have been laid before a general meeting under **2.9**, a copy of the revised accounts (together with the auditor's report thereon) must be laid at the next general meeting held (after the date of the directors' approval to the revised accounts) at which the annual accounts for a financial year are laid (unless the revised accounts have already been laid before an earlier general meeting). The same penalty provisions as in **2.9** apply, except that the reference to 'the period allowed' was a reference to the period between the date of approval of the revised accounts and the date of the, next general meeting, referred to above. [*SI 2008 No 373, Reg 13*].

(5) **Delivery to Registrar of Companies**

Where the directors have prepared revised accounts and a copy of the original accounts has been delivered to the Registrar of Companies, the directors must deliver, within 28 days of their approval of the revised accounts, a copy of the revised accounts (or supplementary note) together with the auditor's report on the revised accounts. The same offences apply as in **2.10**(*a*) (Failure to file accounts and reports) for failure to deliver the replacement accounts in the period of 28 days referred to above. [*SI 2008 No 373, Reg 14*].

2.13 Small and medium-sized companies

The following rules apply where the directors have prepared revised accounts and the company has, prior to the date of revision, delivered to the Registrar of Companies accounts (the '*abbreviated accounts*') that took advantage of the exemptions for small companies under **5.46** and **5.76** ACCOUNTS: SMALL COMPANIES or medium-sized companies under **4.5** ACCOUNTS: MEDIUM-SIZED COMPANIES.

(a) Where the abbreviated accounts so delivered would, if they had been prepared by reference to the revised accounts, not comply with the provisions of *CA 2006* because either the company would not have qualified as 'small' or 'medium-sized' or because the accounts have been revised in a manner that affects the content of the abbreviated accounts, the directors must cause the company to either

- deliver to the Registrar of Companies a copy of the revised accounts (with a copy of the directors' report and auditor's report on the revised accounts); or
- (if on the basis of the revised accounts they would be entitled under *CA 2006* to do so), prepare further abbreviated accounts and deliver them to the Registrar of Companies together with a statement as to the effect of the revisions made.

(b) Where the abbreviated accounts would, if they had been prepared by reference to the revised accounts, comply with the requirements of *CA 2006*, the directors of the company must cause the company to deliver to the Registrar of Companies

- a note stating that the annual accounts for the relevant specified financial year have been revised in a respect which has no bearing on the abbreviated accounts already delivered for that year; and
- a copy of the auditor's report on the revised accounts.

Where the directors have delivered to the Registrar of Companies abbreviated accounts which do not comply with the provisions of *CA 2006* for reasons other than under (*a*) above, the directors must cause the company to prepare further abbreviated accounts and deliver them to the Registrar of Companies together with a statement as to the effect of the revisions made.

In each of the above cases, delivery of revised accounts, etc must be made within 28 days of the date of the directors' approval of the revised accounts, with the same penalty provisions applying as in **2.10**(*a*) (Failure to file accounts and reports) for failure to deliver within the 28 days.

Where, after delivery of the original abbreviated accounts but before the date of the directors' approval of the revised accounts, the provisions relating to 'small' and 'medium-sized' companies are amended, reference above to the provisions of *CA 2006* are to be taken as references to the provisions at the date of delivery of the original abbreviated accounts.

[*SI 2008 No 373, Regs 15, 16, 19(2)*].

2.14 Powers of the Secretary of State and authorised persons

Where

- copies of a company's annual accounts strategic report or directors' report have been sent out in accordance with **2.6**, or

- a copy of a company's annual accounts strategic report or directors' report has been laid before the company in general meeting under **2.9** or delivered to the Registrar of Companies under **2.10**

the Secretary of State (or a person authorised by him for these purposes, see below) may apply to the court for a declaration (or declarator) that the annual accounts of the company do not comply (or a strategic report or directors' report do not comply) with the requirements of *CA 2006*.

If at the end of the period specified in the notice (which must be at least one month), it appears to the Secretary of State that the directors have not

- given a satisfactory explanation of the accounts or report, or
- revised the accounts or report so as to comply with the requirements of *CA 2006*,

the Secretary of State (or a person authorised by him for these purposes, see below) may apply to the court for a declaration (or declarator) that the annual accounts of the company do not comply (or a directors' report does not comply) with the requirements of *CA 2006* and for an order requiring the directors to prepare revised accounts (or a revised report).

The applicant must give notice of the application, together with a general statement of the matters at issue, to the Registrar of Companies for registration. At the end of the proceedings, he must similarly give the Registrar of Companies a copy of the court order for registration or, where applicable, notice that the application has either failed or been withdrawn.

If the court orders revised accounts to be prepared, it may give directions with respect to

- auditing of the accounts;
- the revision of any directors' report strategic report or directors' remuneration report or summary financial statement (see **2.3** above for provisions replacing the summary financial statement)
- the taking of steps by the directors to bring the order to the notice of those person likely to rely on the previous accounts; and
- any other matters which it thinks fit.

If the court orders a revised strategic report or directors' report to be prepared, it may give directions with respect to

- the review of the directors' report by the auditor;
- the revision of any summary financial statement (*see* **2.3** above for provisions replacing the summary financial statement)
- the taking of steps by the directors to bring the order to the notice of persons likely to rely on the previous report; and
- any other matters which it thinks fit.

If the court finds that the accounts or report did not comply with the requirements of *CA 2006* (or, where applicable, adopted international accounting standards), it may order that those directors who were party to the approval of the defective accounts, etc should bear all or part of both the costs (in Scotland, expenses) of the application (including incidental costs) and any reasonable expenses incurred by the company in connection with, or in consequence of, the preparing of the revised accounts, etc.

Every director of the company at the time of the approval of the annual reports and accounts is deemed to have been party to the approval unless he shows that he took all reasonable steps to prevent that approval. The court may, however, take account of whether the directors party to the approval knew, or ought to have known, that the accounts, etc did not comply with the requirements of *CA 2006* (or, where applicable, adopted international accounting standards) and may exclude one or more directors from the order or order the payment of different amounts by different directors.

Revised accounts. The above provisions apply equally to revised annual accounts revised strategic reports and revised directors' reports, in which case they have effect as if the references to revised accounts or reports were references to further revised accounts or reports.

Authorised person. The Secretary of State can authorise persons to act on his behalf for the purposes of the above provisions and has authorised the body known as the Financial Reporting Review Panel (established under the articles of association of The Financial Reporting Review Panel Ltd) to do so.

[*CA 2006, ss 455–457; SI 2008 No 623; SI 2013 No 1970, Schedule, para 14*].

Disclosure of tax information by HM Revenue and Customs (HMRC). HMRC can disclose information to a person authorised under the above provisions to facilitate his application to the court for a declaration that a company's accounts do not comply with the legislation. Any personal data cannot be disclosed in contravention of the *Data Protection Act 1998*. The authorised person can only use the information to determine whether there are grounds for an application, to determine whether or not to make an application, and in any court proceedings. The authorised person cannot further disclose the information except to the person to whom it relates or in connection with court proceedings.

In contravention of use or disclosure, a person is guilty of an offence and liable (i) on conviction on indictment, to imprisonment for a term not exceeding two years or a fine (or both); and (ii) on summary conviction, to imprisonment for a term not exceeding 12 months (in Scotland and Northern Ireland, six months) or a fine up to the statutory maximum (or both). See **29.1 Offences and Legal Proceedings** for the statutory maximum. It is a defence for a person charged with such an offence to prove he did not know, and had no reason to suspect, that the information has been disclosed under these provisions or that he took all reasonable steps and exercised all due diligence to avoid the commission of the offence. Where such an offence is committed by a body corporate, every officer of the body who is in default also commits the offence. For this purpose, any person who purports to act as a director, manager or secretary of the body is treated as an officer of the company and is, if the body is a company, any shadow director (see **18.1(2) Directors**). [*CA 2006, s 458*]. Proceedings for such an offence can only be brought with the consent of the Secretary of State or the Director of Public Prosecutions (in Northern Ireland the Director of Public Prosecutions for Northern Ireland). [*CA 2006, s 1126*; the *2013 Regulations, Schedule, para 16*].

Powers of an authorised person to require documents, information and explanations. Where it appears to an authorised person that a company's annual accounts, strategic report or directors' report may not comply with the requirements of *CA 2006* (or, where applicable, *IAS Regulation, Art 4*) he may require

(a) the company,

(b) any officer, employee or auditor of the company, and

(c) any person who fell within (*b*) above at the time to which the document or information relates

to produce any document (which includes information recorded in any form, eg on computer) or provide him with any information or explanations that he may reasonably require for the purposes of discovering whether there are grounds for an application to the court or determining whether or not to make such an application. A statement made by any person under these provisions cannot be used in evidence against him in any criminal proceedings. Nothing in the above provisions compels any person to disclose documents or information in respect of which a claim to legal professional privilege (in Scotland, a claim to confidentiality of communications) could be maintained. Subject to this, on failure to comply, a court can grant an order directing that the information or explanations are provided.

Information relating to the private affairs of an individual can only be disclosed, during the lifetime of that individual, with his consent. Similarly, any information which relates to any particular business can only be disclosed, so long as that business continues to be carried on, with the consent of the person for the time being carrying on the business. These restrictions do not apply to the disclosure of information

- that is or has been available to the public from another source;
- for the purposes of facilitating the carrying out by the authorised person of his functions under *CA 2006, s 456*;
- to the Secretary of State, the Department of Enterprise, Trade and Investment for Northern Ireland, the Treasury, the Bank of England, the Financial Services Authority, or the Commissioners of Revenue and Customs;
- for certain specified circumstances including

  (i) assisting the Financial Reporting Council to exercise its functions under *CA 2006, Pt 42* (statutory auditors);

  (ii) facilitating the carrying out of inspections under *CA 2006, Sch 10, para 23* (arrangements for independent monitoring of auditors of listed companies and other major bodies);

  (iii) disciplinary proceedings relating to the performance of his professional duties by an accountant or auditor;

  (iv) enabling the Secretary of State or Treasury to exercise any of their functions under the *Companies Acts*, *CJA 1993, Pt 5* (insider dealing), *IA 1986* (or the *Insolvency (Northern Ireland) Order 1989*), *CDDA 1986* (or the *Company Directors Disqualification (Northern Ireland) Order 2002*), and *FSMA 2000*;

  (v) enabling the Department of Enterprise, Trade and Investment for Northern Ireland to exercise any powers conferred on it relating to companies, directors' disqualification or insolvency;

  (vi) enabling the Bank of England or the Commissioners of Revenue and Customs to exercise their functions;

  (vii) enabling the FCA to exercise its functions under the *Building Societies Act 1986*, *CA 1989, Part 7*, *FSMA 2000*, or the legislation relating to friendly societies or to industrial and provident societies; or

  (viii) in pursuance of any EU obligation.

- to a body that exercises functions of a public nature under legislation in any country or territory outside the UK similar in function to those of the authorised person and which is made for the purpose of enabling or assisting that body to exercise those functions.

But this does not authorise the making of a disclosure in contravention of the *Data Protection Act 1998*.

A person who discloses information in contravention of the above provisions commits an offence and is liable (i) on conviction on indictment, to imprisonment for two years or a fine (or both); and (ii) on summary conviction, to imprisonment for a term not exceeding 12 months (in Scotland and Northern Ireland, six months) or a fine up to the statutory maximum (or both). See **29.1 Offences and Legal Proceedings** for the statutory maximum. It is a defence for a person charged with such an offence to show that he did not know, and had no reason to suspect, that the information has been disclosed under these powers or that he took all reasonable steps and exercised all due diligence to avoid the commission of the offence. Where such an offence is committed by a body corporate, every officer of the body who is in default also commits the offence. For this purpose, any person who purports to act as a director, manager or secretary of the body is treated as an officer of the company and is, if the body is a company, any shadow director (see **18.1**(2) **Directors**).

[*CA 2006 ss 459–461; SI 2008 No 948, Sch 1, paras 245, 246; SI 2013 No 1970, Schedule, para 16*].

Proceedings for such an offence can only be brought with the consent of the Secretary of State or the Director of Public Prosecutions (in Northern Ireland the Director of Public Prosecutions for Northern Ireland). [*CA 2006, s 1126*].

2.15 ACCOUNTING STANDARDS

Companies Act accounts. Accounts of large companies must disclose by way of note that they have been prepared in accordance with applicable accounting standards. This requirement does not apply to small and medium-sized companies.

The following accounting standards are currently in issue.

SSAP 4	Accounting for government grants
SSAP 5	Accounting for value added tax
SSAP 9	Stocks and long term contracts
SSAP 13	Accounting for research and development
SSAP 17	Accounting for post balance sheet events
SSAP 19	Accounting for investment properties
SSAP 20	Foreign currency translation
SSAP 21	Accounting for leases and hire purchase contracts
SSAP 24	Accounting for pension costs
SSAP 25	Segmental reporting
FRS 1	Cash flow statements
FRS 2	Accounting for subsidiary undertakings
FRS 3	Reporting financial performance
FRS 4	Capital instruments

FRS 5	Reporting the substance of transactions
FRS 6	Acquisitions and mergers
FRS 7	Fair values in acquisition accounting
FRS 8	Related party disclosures
FRS 9	Associates and joint ventures
FRS 10	Goodwill and intangible assets
FRS 11	Impairment of fixed assets and goodwill
FRS 12	Provisions, contingent liabilities and contingent assets
FRS 13	Derivatives and other financial instruments: disclosures
FRS 14	Earnings per share
FRS 15	Tangible fixed assets
FRS 16	Current tax
FRS 17	Retirement benefits
FRS 18	Accounting policies
FRS 19	Deferred tax
FRS 20 (IFRS 2)	Share-based payment
FRS 21 (IAS 10)	Events after the balance sheet date
FRS 22 (IAS 33)	Earnings per share
FRS 23 (IAS 21)	The effects of changes in foreign exchange rates
FRS 25 (IAS 32)	Financial instruments: presentation
FRS 26 (IAS 39)	Financial instruments: recognition and measurement
FRS 27	Life assurance
FRS 28	Corresponding amounts
FRS 29 (IFRS 7)	Financial instruments: disclosures
FRS 30	Heritage Assets
FRS 100	Application of Financial Reporting Requirements
FRS 101	Reduced Disclosure Framework
FRS 102	The Financial Reporting Standard applicable in the UK and Republic of Ireland
FRS 103	Insurance Contracts

IAS accounts. Where a company must, or (as the case may be) opts to, prepare IAS accounts rather than Companies Act accounts, its accounts must be prepared on the basis of the accounting standards issued by the International Accounting Standard Board (IASB) which is the standard setting body of the IFRS. The international accounting standards currently in issue are as follows.

IFRS 1	First-time adoption of international financial reporting standards
IFRS 2	Share-based payment
IFRS 3	Business combinations
IFRS 4	Insurance contracts

IFRS 5	Non-current assets held for sale and discontinued operations
IFRS 6	Exploration for and evaluation of mineral resources
IFRS 7	Financial Instruments: disclosures
IRFS 8	Operating segments
IRFS 9	Financial Instruments
IRFS 10	Consolidated financial statements
IRFS 11	Joint arrangements
IRFS 12	Disclosure of interests in other entities
IRFS 13	Fair value measurement
IAS 1	Presentation of financial statements
IAS 2	Inventories
IAS 7	Statements of cash flow
IAS 8	Accounting policies, changes in accounting estimates and errors
IAS 10	Events after the reporting period
IAS 11	Construction contracts
IAS 12	Income taxes
IAS 16	Property, plant and equipment
IAS 17	Leases
IAS 18	Revenue
IAS 19	Employee benefits
IAS 20	Accounting for government grants and disclosure of government assistance
IAS 21	The effects of changes in foreign exchange rates
IAS 23	Borrowing costs
IAS 24	Related party disclosures
IAS 26	Accounting and reporting by retirement benefit plans
IAS 27	Separate financial statements
IAS 28	Investments in associates and joint ventures
IAS 29	Financial reporting in hyperinflationary economies
IAS 32	Financial instruments: presentation
IAS 33	Earnings per share
IAS 34	Interim financial reporting
IAS 36	Impairment of assets
IAS 37	Provisions, contingent liabilities and contingent assets
IAS 38	Intangible assets
IAS 39	Financial instruments: recognition and measurement
IAS 40	Investment property
IAS 41	Agriculture

2.16 TRUE AND FAIR VIEW

The directors of a company must not approve annual accounts unless they are satisfied that they give a true and fair view of the assets, liabilities, financial position and profit or loss

- in the case of the company's individual accounts, of the company; and

- in the case of the company's group accounts, of the undertakings included in the consolidation as a whole so far as concerns the members of the company.

The auditor of a company, in carrying out his functions in relations to the company's annual accounts must have regard to the directors' duty under the above provisions.

Where a company qualifies as a micro-entity in relation to a financial year (see **5 Accounts: Small Companies**) the following applies to the directors in their consideration of whether the individual accounts of the company for that year give a true and fair view

- where the accounts comprise only micro-entity minimum accounting items, the directors must disregard any provision of an accounting standard which would require the accounts to contain information additional to those items
- in relation to a micro-entity minimum accounting item contained in the accounts, the directors must disregard any provision of an accounting standard which would require the accounts to contain further information in relation to that item and
- where the accounts contain an item of information additional to the micro-entity minimum accounting items, the directors must have regard to any provision of an accounting standard which relates to that item.

[*CA 2006, s 393; SI 2013 No 3008, Reg 5*].

Counsels' opinions on the meaning of 'true and fair view'. There is no definition of 'true and fair view' in *CA 2006* (or earlier legislation) and the courts have never attempted to define it although there has been some commentary in case law. In 2008 the FRC took counsel's opinion. A copy of the 2008 opinion given by Martin Moore QC is available on the FRC website together with his 2013 commentary on an opinion given by George Bompas QC. Martin Moore's 2008 Opinion confirms that the introduction of IFRS did not change the fundamental requirement for accounts to give a true and fair view. The FRC believe that this 2008 Opinion is an important confirmation of a key contributor to the integrity of financial reporting in the UK. In 2014 the FRC published a paper 'True and Fair' which confirms that the concept of true and fair remains of fundamental importance in both UK GAAP and IFRS.

2.17 ACCOUNTING REFERENCE DATES AND PERIODS

A company must prepare accounts for each financial year. The financial year is determined by the company's 'accounting reference period' which, in turn, is determined according to its 'accounting reference date' in each calendar year (see **2.18**). [*CA 2006, s 391(1)*]. This date can only be altered in certain defined circumstances (see **2.19**).

A company's first accounting reference period is the period of more than six months, but not more than 18 months, beginning with its date of incorporation and ending with its accounting reference date. Its subsequent accounting reference periods are successive periods of 12 months beginning immediately after the end of the previous accounting reference period and ending with its accounting reference date. [*CA 2006, s 391(5), (6)*].

2.18 ACCOUNTING REFERENCE DATE

The '*accounting reference date*' is the date on which a company's accounting reference period ends in each calendar year. Subject to **2.19**, the accounting reference date of a company is determined as follows.

For companies incorporated in Great Britain before 1 April 1996, the accounting reference date is

- the date specified by notice to the Registrar of Companies in accordance with *CA 1985, s 224(2)* (notice specifying accounting reference date given within nine months of incorporation); or
- failing such notice
  - (i) in the case of a company incorporated before 1 April 1990, 31 March; and
  - (ii) in the case of a company incorporated on or after 1 April 1990, the last day of the month in which the anniversary of its incorporation falls.

For companies incorporated in Northern Ireland before 22 August 1997, the accounting reference date is

- the date specified by notice to the Registrar of Companies in accordance with *Companies (Northern Ireland) Order 1986, Art 232(2)* (notice specifying accounting reference date given within nine months of incorporation); or
- failing such notice
  - (i) in the case of a company incorporated before the coming into operation of *Companies (Northern Ireland) Order 1990, Art 5*, 31 March; and
  - (ii) in the case of a company incorporated after the coming into operation of that *Article*, the last day of the month in which the anniversary of its incorporation falls.

For companies incorporated in Great Britain after 31 March 1996 or Northern Ireland after 21 August 1997, the accounting reference date is the last day of the month in which the anniversary of its incorporation falls.

[*CA 2006, s 391(2)–(4), (7)*].

2.19 Alteration of an accounting reference date

A company may, by notice to the Registrar of Companies, specify a new accounting reference date having effect in relation to either

- its current and subsequent accounting reference periods; or
- its immediately preceding and subsequent accounting reference periods. This option is not available if the period for filing accounts and reports for the financial year determined by reference to the immediately preceding accounting reference period has already expired (normally six months after the end of the relevant accounting reference period for public companies and nine months for private companies).

The notice must state whether the current or immediately preceding accounting reference period is to be shortened or extended (ie whether it is to end on the first or second occasion on which the new accounting reference date falls).

Notice to shorten. A company may give notice to shorten the current or immediately preceding accounting reference period as often as it likes.

Notice to extend. A notice to extend a company's current or immediately preceding accounting reference period is not effective if given less than five years after the end of an earlier accounting reference period of the company which was extended under these provisions unless

(a) it is given by a company that is a 'subsidiary undertaking' or 'parent undertaking' (see APPENDIX 1 DEFINITIONS) of another 'EEA undertaking' and the new accounting reference date coincides with that of the other EEA undertaking (or, where that undertaking is not a company, the last day of its financial year);

(b) the company is in administration under *IA 1986, Pt II* or *Insolvency (Northern Ireland) Order 1989, Pt III*; or

(c) the Secretary of State directs otherwise.

But in any case, unless (*b*) above applies, an accounting reference period may not be extended so as to exceed 18 months and any notice attempting to do this is ineffective.

'*EEA undertaking*' means an undertaking established under the law of any part of the UK or any other EEA State.

[*CA 2006, s 392*].

EEA States. See Appendix 1 Definitions for the current EEA States.

Listed companies. See 33 PUBLIC AND LISTED COMPANIES for additional requirements for listed companies.

2.20 OVERSEAS COMPANIES

With effect from 1 October 2009, see 30 OVERSEAS COMPANIES.

3 Accounts: Large Companies

3.1 **Introduction**
3.2 **Individual accounts: duty to prepare**
3.3 **Individual accounts: form and content of Companies Act accounts**
3.4 Balance sheet formats
3.5 Profit and loss account formats
3.6 Accounting principles
3.7 Historic cost accounting rules
3.12 Alternative accounting rules
3.15 Fair value accounting
3.16 Notes to the accounts: general
3.17 Notes to the accounts: information supplementing the balance sheet
3.26 Notes to the accounts: information supplementing the profit and loss account
3.32 **Individual accounts: related undertakings**
3.33 Subsidiary undertakings
3.38 Significant holdings in undertakings other than subsidiary undertakings
3.39 Membership of certain undertakings
3.40 Parent undertaking drawing up accounts for larger group
3.41 **Individual accounts: directors' remuneration and benefits**
3.42 Directors' remuneration, etc.
3.48 Directors' benefits: advances, credit and guarantees
3.49 **Individual accounts: employee numbers and costs**
3.50 **Individual accounts: auditor's remuneration and liability limitation agreements**
3.51 **Individual accounts: off-balance sheet arrangements**
3.52 **Group accounts: introduction**
3.53 **Group accounts: duty to prepare**
3.54 Exemption for parent companies included in accounts of larger groups
3.55 Exclusion of subsidiary undertakings from consolidation
3.56 **Group accounts: treatment of individual profit and loss account where group accounts prepared**
3.57 **Group accounts: form and content of Companies Act group accounts**
3.58 Elimination of group transactions
3.59 Acquisition and merger accounting
3.60 Minority interests
3.61 Joint ventures
3.62 Associated undertakings
3.63 Related party transactions
3.64 **Group accounts: related undertakings**
3.65 Subsidiary undertakings
3.69 Joint ventures
3.70 Associated undertakings
3.71 Other significant holdings of parent company or group
3.72 Parent company's or group's membership of certain undertakings
3.73 Information where parent company is a subsidiary undertaking
3.74 **Group accounts: directors' remuneration and benefits**

Cross-references. See 2 ACCOUNTS: (GENERAL) AND ACCOUNTING REFERENCE DATES; 4 ACCOUNTS; MEDIUM-SIZED COMPANIES; 5 ACCOUNTS: SMALL COMPANIES; 6 ACCOUNTS: STRATEGIC REPORTS; 19 DIRECTORS' REMUNERATION-QUOTED COMPANIES; APPENDIX 1 DEFINITIONS.

Background. The provisions as described in this chapter are, unless otherwise stated, taken from *CA 2006* and supporting Regulations which apply to accounts for financial years beginning on or after 6 April 2008.

3.1 Accounts: Large Companies

3.1 INTRODUCTION

The provisions described in this chapter relate to the requirements for accounts of all companies other than those that are subject to the small companies regime which can prepare abbreviated accounts (see **5 Accounts: Small Companies**) and where a company qualifies as 'medium-sized' in relation to a financial year, although it is not entitled to prepare individual accounts in abbreviated form in the same way as a company subject to the small companies regime, it is entitled to certain exemptions with respect to its accounts. See **4 Accounts: Medium-Sized Companies** for the definition of 'medium-sized' and the provisions relating to accounts of medium-sized companies generally.

3.2 INDIVIDUAL ACCOUNTS: DUTY TO PREPARE

The directors of every company must prepare accounts for the company for each of its financial years unless the company is exempt under *CA 2006, s 394A* (dormant subsidiaries). Those accounts are referred to in this chapter as the company's 'individual accounts'. [*CA 2006, s 394; SI 2012 No 2301, Reg 8*].

Subject to below, these accounts may be prepared in accordance with

- *CA 2006, s 396* ('*Companies Act individual accounts*'); or
- international accounting standards ('*IAS individual accounts*').

But

- the individual accounts of a company that is a charity *must* be Companies Act individual accounts; and
- after the first financial year in which the directors of a company prepare IAS individual accounts ('*the first IAS year*'), all subsequent individual accounts of the company must be prepared in accordance with international accounting standards unless there is a '*relevant change of circumstance*'. This is subject to the right to change to Companies Act accounts set out in *CA 2006, s 395(4A)* (see below) A relevant change of circumstance occurs if, at any time during or after the first IAS year
  - (i) the company becomes a subsidiary undertaking of another undertaking that does not prepare IAS individual accounts;
  - (ii) the company ceases to be a subsidiary undertaking;
  - (iii) the company ceases to be a company with securities admitted to trading on a regulated market in an EEA State; or
  - (iv) a parent undertaking of the company ceases to be an undertaking with securities admitted to trading on a regulated market in an EEA State.

  After a financial year in which IAS individual accounts are prepared, the directors may change to preparing Companies Act individual accounts for a reason other than a relevant change of circumstance, provided they have not changed to Companies Act accounts in the five years preceding the first day of that financial year.

  If, having changed to preparing Companies Act individual accounts, the directors again prepare IAS individual accounts for the company, the above provisions apply again as if the first financial year for which such accounts are again prepared were the first IAS year.

[*CA 2006, s 395; SI 2008 No 393, Reg 9; SI 2012 No 2301, Reg 12*].

See APPENDIX 1 DEFINITIONS for the current EEA States.

Companies Act individual accounts. Companies Act individual accounts must comprise

- a balance sheet as at the last day of the financial year; and
- a profit and loss account.

The balance sheet must give a true and fair view of the state of affairs of the company as at the end of the financial year and the profit and loss account must give a true and fair view of the profit or loss of the company for the financial year. See **2.16** ACCOUNTS: GENERAL for the interpretation of '*true and fair view*'.

Companies Act individual accounts must comply with the *Large and Medium Sized Companies and Groups (Accounts and Reports) Regulations 2008 (SI 2008 No 410)* as amended by the *Large and Medium-Sized Companies and Groups (Amendment) Regulations 2013* and are set out in **3.3** to **3.31**. They describe the form and content of the balance sheet and profit and loss account and additional information to be provided by way of notes to the accounts. If compliance with those provisions, and other provisions made by or under *CA 2006* (see **3.32** to **3.51**) as to the matters to be included in a company's individual accounts or in notes to those accounts, would not be sufficient to give a true and fair view, the necessary additional information must be given in the accounts or notes. If, in special circumstances, compliance with any of those provisions is inconsistent with the requirement to give a true and fair view, the directors must depart from that provision to the extent necessary to give a true and fair view. Particulars of any such departure, the reasons for it and its effect must be given in a note to the accounts.

[*CA 2006, s 396*].

IAS individual accounts. The provisions as described in **3.3** to **3.31** do not apply to IAS individual accounts. Instead, individual accounts must be prepared on the basis of the accounting standards issued by the International Accounting Standard Board (IASB). [*EC Council Regulation 1606/2002, Art 4*]. In place of the profit and loss account and balance sheet, companies must prepare primary financial statements and supporting notes as required under international accounting standards. See **2.15** ACCOUNTS: GENERAL for a list of standards.

However, the provisions relating to

- related undertakings (see **3.32** to **3.40**),
- directors' remuneration and benefits (see **3.41** to **3.48**),
- employee numbers and costs (see **3.49**),
- auditor's remuneration, etc (see **3.50**), and
- off balance sheet arrangements (see **3.51**)

continue to apply where IAS individual accounts are prepared, as do aspects of *CA 2006* that deal with matters outside the scope of international accounting standards (eg the requirements relating to directors' reports, publication (as opposed to preparation) of accounts, and audit).

Where the directors of a company prepare IAS individual accounts, they must state in the notes to the accounts that the accounts have been prepared in accordance with international accounting standards. [*CA 2006, s 397*].

3.2 Accounts: Large Companies

Consistency of accounts within a group. Subject to the exceptions below, the directors of a parent company must secure that the individual accounts of

(a) the parent company, and

(b) each of its subsidiary undertakings

are all prepared using the same financial reporting framework (ie Companies Act or IAS), except to the extent that in their opinion there are good reasons for not doing so. BIS indicated, in their 2008 guidance to companies on the introduction of IAS accounts, that 'good reasons' could include the following.

- Where a group using IAS acquires a subsidiary undertaking that had not been using IAS, in the first year of acquisition it might not be practical for the newly acquired company to switch to IAS straight away.
- Where a group contains subsidiary undertakings that are themselves publicly traded, market pressures or regulatory requirements to use IAS might come into play, without necessarily justifying a switch to IAS by the non-publicly traded subsidiaries.
- Where a subsidiary undertaking or the parent is planning to list and so might wish to convert to IAS in advance, but the rest of the group is not listed.
- Where the group contains minor or dormant subsidiaries and the costs of switching accounting framework would outweigh the benefits.

Exceptions. The general requirement to prepare individual accounts using the same financial framework is subject to the following specific exceptions, It:

- does not apply if the directors do not prepare group accounts for the parent company;
- only applies to the accounts of subsidiary undertakings that are required to be prepared under *CA 2006*;
- does not require accounts of undertakings that are charities to be prepared using the same financial reporting framework as accounts of undertakings which are not charities; and
- does not apply where the directors of a parent company prepare both group accounts and individual accounts under IAS. In this case the parent company is not required to ensure that all its subsidiary undertakings also use IAS. However it must ensure that all its subsidiary undertakings use the same accounting framework, unless there are good reasons for not doing so.

[*CA 2006, s 407(2)–(4)* and *(5)*].

3.3 INDIVIDUAL ACCOUNTS: FORM AND CONTENT OF COMPANIES ACT ACCOUNTS

The directors of a company

- for which they are preparing Companies Act individual accounts, and
- which is not a banking company or an insurance company,

must comply with the provisions in this paragraph and in 3.4 to 3.31 as to the form and content of the balance sheet and profit and loss account, and additional information to be provided by way of notes to the accounts. The only exception is that medium-sized companies need not comply with the disclosure requirements relating to accounting standards (see **3.16**) or related party transactions (see **3.32**).

[*SI 2008 No 410, Regs 3(1), 4(2)*].

Every balance sheet of a company must show the items listed in either of the balance sheet formats in **3.4** and every profit and loss account must show the items listed in any one of the profit and loss account formats in **3.5**, in both cases in the order and under the headings and sub-headings given in the format used, but subject to the following.

(1) The notes to the formats may permit alternative positions for any particular items.

(2) The heading or sub-heading for any item does not have to be distinguished by any letter or number assigned to that item in the format used.

(3) Any item required to be shown in a company's balance sheet or profit and loss account may be shown in greater detail than required by the particular format used.

(4) A heading or sub-heading corresponding to an item in the balance sheet or profit and loss account format used must not be included if there is no amount to be shown for that item for the financial year in question unless an amount must be disclosed for the immediately preceding financial year (see below).

(5) The balance sheet or profit and loss account may include an item representing or covering the amount of any asset or liability, income or expenditure not otherwise covered by any of the items listed in the format used, except that none of the following may be treated as assets in any balance sheet.

- Preliminary expenses.
- Expenses of, and commission on, any issue of shares or debentures.
- Costs of research.

(6) Where the special nature of the company's business requires it, the company's directors

   (a) *must* adapt the arrangement, headings and sub-headings otherwise required in respect of items given an Arabic number in the balance sheet or profit and loss account format used; and

   (b) *may* combine items to which Arabic numbers are given in any of the formats if

      (i) their individual amounts are not material to assessing the state of affairs or profit or loss of the company for the financial year in question; or

      (ii) the combination facilitates that assessment (but in this case the individual amounts of any items which have been combined must be disclosed in a note to the accounts).

[*SI 2008 No 410, Sch 1 paras 1, 3–5*].

Consistency in use of formats. Where a company's balance sheet or profit and loss account for any financial year has been prepared by reference to one of the said formats, the company's directors must use the same format in preparing Companies Act individual accounts for subsequent financial years, unless in their opinion there are special reasons for a change. Particulars of any such change must be given in a note to the accounts in which the new format is first used, and the reasons for the change must be explained. [*SI 2008 No 410, Sch 1 para 2*].

Profit before taxation. Every profit and loss account must show the amount of a company's profit or loss on ordinary activities before taxation.

[*SI 2008 No 410, Sch 1 para 6*].

Preceding financial year. For every item shown in the balance sheet or profit and loss account the corresponding amount for the immediately preceding financial year must also be shown. Where that corresponding amount is not comparable with the figure for the current year, the former amount may be adjusted, in which case particulars of the non-comparability and of any adjustment must be disclosed in a note to the accounts.

[*SI 2008 No 410, Sch 1 para 7*].

Set-offs. Amounts in respect of items representing assets or income may not be set off against amounts in respect of items representing liabilities or expenditure, or vice versa.

[*SI 2008 No 410, Sch 1 para 8*].

Presentation in accordance with accounting principles. The company's directors must, in determining how amounts are presented within items in the profit and loss account and balance sheet, have regard to the substance of the reported transaction or arrangement, in accordance with generally accepted accounting principles or practice.

[*SI 2008 No 410, Sch 1 para 9*].

Materiality. Amounts which in the particular context are not material may be disregarded for the purposes of that provision.

[*SI 2008 No 410, Sch 10 para 10*].

Accounts in euros. The amounts set out in the annual accounts of a company may also be shown in the same accounts translated into euros. If so, the amounts must have been translated at the exchange rate prevailing at the balance sheet date and that rate must be disclosed in the notes to the accounts.

[*CA 2006, s 469(1)(3)*].

Listed companies. In addition to the requirements of *CA 2006* and supporting Regulations, listed companies must also comply with the requirements of the FCA Listing Rules as to the content of annual accounts (annual financial report). See **33.28** PUBLIC AND LISTED COMPANIES.

3.4 Balance sheet formats

The two balance sheet formats set out in *SI 2008 No 410, Sch 1* and referred to in **3.3** are reproduced below, and are followed by the notes also set out in the *Regulations*.

Format 1

A. Called up share capital not paid (see note (1))

B. Fixed assets (see below)

  I Intangible assets

    1. Development costs

2. Concessions, patents, licences, trademarks and similar rights and assets (see note (2))
3. Goodwill (see note (3))
4. Payments on account

II Tangible assets
1. Land and buildings
2. Plant and machinery
3. Fixtures, fittings, tools and equipment
4. Payments on account and assets in course of construction

III Investments
1. Shares in group undertakings
2. Loans to group undertakings
3. Participating interests
4. Loans to undertakings in which the company has a participating interest
5. Other investments other than loans
6. Other loans
7. Own shares (see note (4))

C. Current assets (see below)

I Stocks
1. Raw materials and consumables
2. Work in progress
3. Finished goods and goods for resale
4. Payments on account

II Debtors (see note (5))
1. Trade debtors
2. Amounts owed by group undertakings
3. Amounts owed by undertakings in which the company has a participating interest
4. Other debtors
5. Called up share capital not paid (see note (1))
6. Prepayments and accrued income (see note (6))

III Investments
1. Shares in group undertakings
2. Own shares (see note (4))
3. Other investments

IV Cash at bank and in hand

D. Prepayments and accrued income (see note (6))

E. Creditors: amounts falling due within one year
1. Debenture loans (see note (7))
2. Bank loans and overdrafts
3. Payments received on account (see note (8))
4. Trade creditors
5. Bills of exchange payable

6. Amounts owed to group undertakings
7. Amounts owed to undertakings in which the company has a participating interest
8. Other creditors including taxation and social security (see note (9))
9. Accruals and deferred income (see note (10))

F. Net current assets (liabilities) (see note (11))

G. Total assets less current liabilities

H. Creditors: amounts falling due after more than one year
1. Debenture loans (see note (7))
2. Bank loans and overdrafts
3. Payments received on account (see note (8))
4. Trade creditors
5. Bills of exchange payable
6. Amounts owed to group undertakings
7. Amounts owed to undertakings in which the company has a participating interest
8. Other creditors including taxation and social security (see note (9))
9. Accruals and deferred income (see note (10))

I. Provisions for liabilities (see below)
1. Pensions and similar obligations
2. Taxation, including deferred taxation
3. Other provisions

J. Accruals and deferred income (see note (10))

K. Capital and reserves

I Called up share capital (see note (12))

II Share premium account

III Revaluation reserve

IV Other reserves
1. Capital redemption reserve
2. Reserve for own shares
3. Reserves provided for by the articles of association
4. Other reserves

V Profit and loss account

Format 2

ASSETS

A. Called up share capital not paid (see note (1))

B. Fixed assets (see below)

I Intangible assets
1. Development costs
2. Concessions, patents, licences, trademarks and similar rights and assets (see note (2))
3. Goodwill (see note (3))
4. Payments on account

II Tangible assets

1. Land and buildings
2. Plant and machinery
3. Fixtures, fittings, tools and equipment
4. Payments on account and assets in course of construction

III Investments

1. Shares in group undertakings
2. Loans to group undertakings
3. Participating interests
4. Loans to undertakings in which the company has a participating interest
5. Other investments other than loans
6. Other loans
7. Own shares (see note (4))

C. Current assets (see below)

I Stocks

1. Raw materials and consumables
2. Work in progress
3. Finished goods and goods for resale
4. Payments on account

II Debtors (see note (5))

1. Trade debtors
2. Amounts owed by group undertakings
3. Amounts owed by undertakings in which the company has a participating interest
4. Other debtors
5. Called up share capital not paid (see note (1))
6. Prepayments and accrued income (see note (6))

III Investments

1. Shares in group undertakings
2. Own shares (see note (4))
3. Other investments

IV Cash at bank and in hand

D. Prepayments and accrued income (see note (6))

LIABILITIES

A. Capital and reserves

I Called up share capital (see note (12))

II Share premium account

III Revaluation reserve

IV Other reserves

1. Capital redemption reserve
2. Reserve for own shares
3. Reserves provided for by the articles of association

4. Other reserves

V Profit and loss account

B. Provisions for liabilities (see below)

1. Pensions and similar obligations
2. Taxation, including deferred taxation
3. Other provisions

C. Creditors (see note (13))

1. Debenture loans (see note (7))
2. Bank loans and overdrafts
3. Payments received on account (see note (8))
4. Trade creditors
5. Bills of exchange payable
6. Amounts owed to group undertakings
7. Amounts owed to undertakings in which the company has a participating interest
8. Other creditors including taxation and social security (see note (9))
9. Accruals and deferred income (see note (10))

D. Accruals and deferred income (see note (10))

Notes

(1) *Called up share capital not paid.* This item may be shown in either of the two positions given in each format.

(2) *Concessions etc.* Amounts in respect of assets are to be included under this item only if the assets in question either were acquired for valuable consideration (and are not required to be shown under 'goodwill') or were created by the company itself.

(3) *Goodwill.* Amounts representing goodwill are to be included only to the extent that the goodwill was acquired for valuable consideration.

(4) *Own shares.* The nominal value of the shares held must be shown separately.

(5) *Debtors.* The amount falling due after more than one year must be shown separately for each item included under debtors.

(6) *Prepayments and accrued income.* This item may be shown in either of the two positions given in each format.

(7) *Debenture loans.* The amount of any convertible loans must be shown separately.

(8) *Payments received on account.* Payments received on account of orders must be shown in so far as they are not shown as deductions from stocks.

(9) *Other creditors including taxation and social security.* The amount for creditors in respect of taxation and social security must be shown separately from the amount for other creditors.

(10) *Accruals and deferred income.* The two positions given for this item in Format 1 at E.9 and H.9 are an alternative to the position at J, but if the item is not shown in a position corresponding to that at J it may be shown in either or both of the other two positions (as the case may require). The two positions given for this item in Format 2 are alternatives.

(11) *Net current assets (liabilities).* In determining the amount to be shown for this item, any amounts shown under 'prepayments and accrued income' must be taken into account wherever shown.

(12) *Called up share capital.* The amount of allotted share capital and the amount of called up share capital which has been paid up must be shown separately.

(13) *Creditors.* Amounts falling due within one year and after one year must be shown separately for each of these items and for the aggregate of all of these items.

[*SI 2008 No 410, Sch 1 Part 1 Section B*].

'*Fixed assets*' means assets of a company which are intended for use on a continuing basis in the company's activities. [*SI 2008 No 410, Sch 10 para 4*].

'*Current assets*' means assets not intended for use as fixed assets. [*SI 2008 No 410, Sch 10 para 4*].

Provision for liabilities. A provision for liabilities means any amount retained as reasonably necessary for the purpose of providing for any liability the nature of which is clearly defined and which is either likely to be incurred, or certain to be incurred but uncertain as to amount or as to the date on which it will arise. [*SI 2008 No 410, Sch 9 para 2*].

3.5 Profit and loss account formats

The four profit and loss account formats set out in *SI 2008 No 410, Sch 1* and referred to in **3.3** are reproduced below, and are followed by the notes also set out in the *Regulations*.

Format 1 (see note (4))

1. Turnover
2. Cost of sales (see note (1))
3. Gross profit or loss
4. Distribution costs (see note (1))
5. Administrative expenses (see note (1))
6. Other operating income
7. Income from shares in group undertakings
8. Income from participating interests
9. Income from other fixed asset investments (see note (2))
10. Other interest receivable and similar income (see note (2))
11. Amounts written off investments
12. Interest payable and similar charges (see note (3))
13. Tax on profit or loss on ordinary activities
14. Profit or loss on ordinary activities after taxation
15. Extraordinary income
16. Extraordinary charges

17. Extraordinary profit or loss
18. Tax on extraordinary profit or loss
19. Other taxes not shown under the above items
20. Profit or loss for the financial year

Format 2

1. Turnover
2. Change in stocks of finished goods and in work in progress
3. Own work capitalised
4. Other operating income
5. (*a*) Raw materials and consumables
   (*b*) Other external charges
6. Staff costs:
   (*a*) wages and salaries (see below)
   (*b*) social security costs (see below)
   (*c*) other pension costs (see below)
7. (*a*) Depreciation and other amounts written off tangible and intangible fixed assets (see below)
   (*b*) Exceptional amounts written off current assets
8. Other operating charges
9. Income from shares in group undertakings
10. Income from participating interests
11. Income from other fixed asset investments (see note (2))
12. Other interest receivable and similar income (see note (2))
13. Amounts written off investments
14. Interest payable and similar charges (see note (3))
15. Tax on profit or loss on ordinary activities
16. Profit or loss on ordinary activities after taxation
17. Extraordinary income
18. Extraordinary charges
19. Extraordinary profit or loss
20. Tax on extraordinary profit or loss
21. Other taxes not shown under the above items
22. Profit or loss for the financial year.

Format 3 (see note (4))

A. Charges
   1. Cost of sales (see note (1))
   2. Distribution costs (see note (1))
   3. Administrative expenses (see note (1))
   4. Amounts written off investments
   5. Interest payable and similar charges (see note (3))
   6. Tax on profit or loss on ordinary activities
   7. Profit or loss on ordinary activities after taxation
   8. Extraordinary charges

9. Tax on extraordinary profit or loss
10. Other taxes not shown under the above items
11. Profit or loss for the financial year

B. Income
1. Turnover
2. Other operating income
3. Income from shares in group undertakings
4. Income from participating interests
5. Income from other fixed asset investments (see note (2))
6. Other interest receivable and similar income (see note (2))
7. Profit or loss on ordinary activities after taxation
8. Extraordinary income
9. Profit or loss for the financial year

Format 4

A. Charges
1. Reduction in stocks of finished goods and work in progress
2. (*a*) Raw materials and consumables
   (*b*) Other external charges
3. Staff costs:
   (*a*) wages and salaries (see below)
   (*b*) social security costs (see below)
   (*c*) other pension costs (see below)
4. (*a*) Depreciation and other amounts written off tangible and intangible fixed assets (see below)
   (*b*) Exceptional amounts written off current assets
5. Other operating charges
6. Amounts written off investments
7. Interest payable and similar charges (see note (3))
8. Tax on profit or loss on ordinary activities
9. Profit or loss on ordinary activities after taxation
10. Extraordinary charges
11. Tax on extraordinary profit or loss
12. Other taxes not shown under the above items
13. Profit or loss for the financial year

B. Income
1. Turnover
2. Increase in stocks of finished goods and in work in progress
3. Own work capitalised
4. Other operating income
5. Income from shares in group undertakings
6. Income from participating interests
7. Income from other fixed asset investments (see note (2))

8. Other interest receivable and similar income (see note (2))
9. Profit or loss on ordinary activities after taxation
10. Extraordinary income
11. Profit or loss for the financial year

Notes

(1) *Cost of sales: distribution costs: administrative expenses.* These items must be stated after taking into account any necessary provisions for depreciation or diminution in value of assets.

(2) *Income from other fixed asset investments: other interest receivable and similar income.* Income and interest derived from group undertakings must be shown separately from income and interest derived from other sources.

(3) *Interest payable and similar charges.* The amount payable to group undertakings must be shown separately.

(4) *Formats 1 and 3.* Where either of these formats is used, the amount of any provisions for depreciation and diminution in value of tangible and intangible fixed assets falling to be shown under items 7(*a*) and A.4(*a*) respectively in Formats 2 and 4 must be disclosed in a note to the accounts.

[*SI 2008 No 410, Sch 1 Part 1, Section B*].

Staff costs.

- '*Social security costs*' means any contributions by the company to any state social security or pension scheme, fund or arrangement.
- '*Pension costs*' includes
  (i) any costs incurred by the company in respect of any pension scheme established for the purpose of providing pensions for persons currently or formerly employed by the company;
  (ii) any sums set aside for the future payment of pensions directly by the company to current or former employees; and
  (iii) any pensions paid directly to such persons without having first been set aside.

Any amount stated in respect of the item 'social security costs' or in respect of the item 'wages and salaries' in the company's profit and loss account must be determined by reference to payments made or costs incurred in respect of all persons employed by the company during the financial year under contracts of service.

[*SI 2008 No 410, Sch 10 para 14*].

Depreciation, etc. Any reference in the profit and loss account formats (or the notes to them) to the depreciation of, or amounts written off, assets of any description is to any provision for depreciation or diminution in value of assets of that description. [*SI 2008 No 410, Sch 9 para 1(2)*].

'*Fixed assets*' means assets of a company which are intended for use on a continuing basis in the company's activities. [*SI 2008 No 410, Sch 10 para 4*].

3.6 Accounting principles

The amounts to be included in respect of all items shown in a company's accounts must be determined in accordance with the principles set out in (*a*)–(*e*) below. But if it appears to the directors that there are special reasons for departing from any of those principles in preparing the company's accounts for any financial year, they may do so, in which case particulars of the departure, the reasons for it and its effect must be given in a note to the accounts.

(a) The company is presumed to be carrying on business as a going concern.

(b) Accounting policies must be applied consistently within the same accounts and from one financial year to the next.

(c) The amount of any item must be determined on a prudent basis, and in particular

- (i) only profits realised at the balance sheet date are to be included in the profit and loss account; and
- (ii) all liabilities which have arisen in respect of the financial year to which the accounts relate or a previous financial year must be taken into account. This includes those which only become apparent between the balance sheet date and the date on which it is signed on behalf of the board of directors (see **2.2 Accounts: General**). Where revised accounts are prepared (see **2.12 Accounts: General**) it is the date on which the original accounts were signed that is taken into account for this purposes.

(d) All income and charges relating to the financial year to which the accounts relate must be taken into account, without regard to the date of receipt or payment.

(e) In determining the aggregate amount of any item, the amount of each individual asset or liability that falls to be taken into account must be determined separately.

[*SI 2008 No 410, Sch 1 paras 10–15*].

3.7 Historic cost accounting rules

Subject to

- the alternative accounting rules in **3.12** to **3.14**, and
- the fair value accounting provisions in **3.15**

the amounts to be included in respect of all items shown in a company's accounts must be determined in accordance with the rules set out in **3.8** to **3.11**. [*SI 2008 No 410, Sch 1 para 16*].

3.8 *Fixed assets*

General rules. Fixed asset (ie assets of a company which are intended for use on a continuing basis in the company's activities) must be included at their 'purchase price' or 'production cost' (see **3.11**). [*SI 2008 No 410, Sch 1 para 17, Sch 10 para 4*].

Rules for depreciation and diminution in value.

(a) In the case of any fixed asset which has a limited useful economic life, its purchase price or production cost, less the amount of any estimated residual value at the end of the asset's useful economic life, must be reduced by provisions for depreciation calculated to write off that amount systematically over the asset's useful economic life. [*SI 2008 No 410, Sch 1 para 18*].

(b) Where a fixed asset investment falling to be included under item B.III of either of the balance sheet formats set out in **3.4** has diminished in value, provisions for diminution in value may be made in respect of it and the amount to be included in respect of it may be reduced accordingly. Such provisions must be made in respect of *any* fixed asset which has diminished in value if the reduction in its value is expected to be permanent (whether it's useful economic life is limited or not), and the amount to be included in respect of it must be reduced accordingly. [*SI 2008 No 410, Sch 1 para 19*].

(c) Where the reasons for which any provision was made have ceased to apply to any extent, that provision must be written back to the extent that it is no longer necessary. [*SI 2008 No 410, Sch 1 para 20(1)*].

Any provisions made or amounts written back which are not shown in the profit and loss account must be disclosed (either separately or in aggregate) in a note to the accounts. [*SI 2008 No 410, Sch 1 para 20(2).*]

Goodwill. Where goodwill is treated as an asset, the application of the general rules above is subject to the following.

- The amount of the consideration for any goodwill acquired by a company must be reduced by provisions for depreciation calculated to write off that amount systematically over a period chosen by the directors of the company although the period chosen must not exceed the useful economic life of the goodwill in question.
- Where any goodwill acquired by a company is shown or included as an asset in the company's balance sheet, there must be disclosed in a note to the accounts
  (i) the period chosen for writing off the consideration for that goodwill; and
  (ii) the reasons for choosing that period.

[*SI 2008 No 410, Sch 1 para 22*].

Development costs. Despite the fact that an item in respect of 'development costs' is included under 'fixed assets' in the balance sheet formats in **3.4**, an amount may only be included in the balance sheet in respect of development costs in special circumstances. If any amount is so included, there must be given in a note to the accounts the reasons for capitalising the development costs in question and the period over which the amount of those costs originally capitalised is being (or is to be) written off. [*SI 2008 No 410, Sch 1 para 21*].

3.9 *Current assets*

The amount to be included in respect of any current asset must be its 'purchase price' or 'production cost' (see **3.11**) or, if lower, its net realisable value. Where the reasons for which any provision for diminution in value has been made (ie to reduce the assets to its net realisable value) have ceased to apply to any extent, that provision must be written back to the extent that it is no longer necessary. [*SI 2008 No 410, Sch 1 paras 23, 24*].

3.10 *Miscellaneous provisions*

(1) *Excess of money owed over value received*

Where the amount repayable on any debt owed by a company is greater than the value of the consideration received in the transaction giving rise to the debt, the amount of the difference may be treated as an asset. But in the case of such treatment, the amount of the difference must be written off by reasonable amounts each year and must be completely written off before repayment of the debt. If the current amount is not shown as a separate item in the company's balance sheet, it must be disclosed in a note to the accounts. [*SI 2008 No 410, Sch 1 para 25*].

(2) *Assets included at a fixed amount*

Assets which fall to be included either amongst the

- fixed assets of a company under the item 'tangible assets', or
- current assets of a company under the item 'raw materials and consumables',

may be included at a fixed quantity and value where the assets are of a kind which are constantly being replaced and where their

- overall value is not material to assessing the company's state of affairs; and
- quantity, value and composition are not subject to material variation.

[*SI 2008 No 410, Sch 1 para 26*].

3.11 *Determination of purchase price or production cost*

The '*purchase price*' of an asset is the actual price paid plus any expenses incidental to its acquisition.

'*Purchase price*', in relation to an asset of a company or any raw materials or consumables used in the production of such an asset, includes any consideration (whether in cash or otherwise) given by the company in respect of that asset or those materials or consumables, as the case may be.

The '*production cost*' of an asset is the purchase price of the raw materials and consumables used plus the costs incurred by the company which are directly attributable to the production of that asset. In addition, there may be included

- a reasonable proportion of the costs so incurred by the company which are only indirectly attributable to the production of that asset, but only to the extent that they relate to the period of production; and
- interest on capital borrowed to finance the production of that asset, to the extent that it accrues in respect of the period of production. The inclusion of interest in determining the cost and the amount of the interest so included must be disclosed in a note to the accounts.

In the case of current assets, production costs must not include distribution costs. [*SI 2008 No 410, Sch 1 para 27, Sch 10 para 12*].

Where

- there is no record of the purchase price or production cost of any asset (of any price, expenses or costs relevant to its determination), or
- any such record cannot be obtained without unreasonable expense or delay,

the purchase price or production cost of the asset must be taken to be the value ascribed to it in the earliest available record of its value made on or after its acquisition or production by the company. [*SI 2008 No 410, Sch 1 para 29*].

Stocks and fungible assets. The purchase price or production cost of

- any assets which fall to be included under any item shown in a company's balance sheet under the general item 'stocks', and
- any assets which are 'fungible assets' (including investments),

may be determined by applying any of the following methods in relation to any such assets of the same class, provided that the method chosen is one which appears to the directors to be appropriate in the circumstances of the company.

(1) 'First in, first out' (FIFO).

(2) 'Last in, first out' (LIFO).

(3) A weighted average price.

(4) Any other method similar to any of the above.

'*Fungible assets*' means assets of any description which are substantially indistinguishable one from another.

But where the result of such determination differs materially from the 'relevant alternative amount', the difference must be disclosed in a note to the accounts.

The '*relevant alternative amount*' is the amount which would have been shown in respect of the item in question if assets of any class included under that item had instead been included at their replacement cost as at the balance sheet date. If, however, the directors consider it a more appropriate standard of comparison in the case of assets of a particular class, the relevant alternative amount may instead be determined by reference to the most recent actual purchase price or production cost before the balance sheet date of assets of that class.

[*SI 2008 No 410, Sch 1 para 28, Sch 10 para 5*].

3.12 Alternative accounting rules

Any of the accounting rules set out below may be used (as alternatives to the historical cost accounting rules in **3.7** to **3.11**) to determine the amounts to be included in respect of the assets in question.

(a) *Intangible fixed assets*, other than goodwill, may be included at their current cost.

(b) *Tangible fixed assets* may be included at a market value (determined as at the date of their last valuation) or at their current cost.

(c) *Investments of any description falling to be included under item B III* of either of the balance sheet formats in **3.4** may be included either at

   (i) market value determined as at the date of their last valuation; or

   (ii) a value determined on any basis which appears to the directors to be appropriate in the circumstances of the company (but in this case particulars of the method of valuation adopted and of the reasons for adopting it must be disclosed in a note to the accounts).

(d) *Investments of any description falling to be included under item C III* of either of the balance sheet formats in **3.4** may be included at their current cost.

(e) *Stocks* may be included at their current cost.

Application of the depreciation rules. Where the value of any asset is determined on any basis within (*a*)–(*e*) above, that value (instead of the purchase price, production cost or any value previously so determined for that asset) must be (or, as the case may require, must be the starting point for determining) the amount to be included in respect of that asset in the accounts. The historic cost depreciation rules in **3.8** to **3.10** above apply accordingly in relation to any such asset with the substitution for any reference to its purchase price or production cost of a reference to the value most recently determined for that asset under (*a*)–(*e*) above (the '*adjusted depreciation rules*').

In the case of a fixed asset, any provision for depreciation in respect of that asset which is

- included in any item shown in the profit and loss account in respect of amounts written off assets of the description in question, or
- taken into account as required by note (1) to the profit and loss account formats in 3.5

will normally be included or taken into account at the amount calculated under the adjusted depreciation rules above. It may, however, be included or taken in account under the historic cost depreciation rules instead of the adjusted depreciation rules, provided that the amount of any difference between the two is shown separately in the profit and loss account or in a note to the accounts.

[*SI 2008 No 410, Sch 1 paras 30–33*].

3.13 *Additional information to be provided in case of departure from historical cost accounting rules*

Where the amounts to be included in respect of assets covered by any items shown in the accounts have been determined on any basis in **3.12**(*a*)–(*e*), the following additional information must be disclosed in a note to the accounts or alternatively, in the case of (*b*) below, shown separately in the balance sheet.

(a) The items affected and the basis of valuation adopted in determining the amounts of the assets in question in the case of each such item.

(b) In the case of each balance sheet item affected (except stocks), either

- the 'comparable amounts determined according to the historical cost accounting rules'; or
- the differences between those amounts and the corresponding amounts actually shown in the balance sheet in respect of that item.

The '*comparable amounts determined according to the historical cost accounting rules*' are

- the aggregate amount which would be required to be shown in respect of that item if the amounts to be included in respect of all the assets covered by that item were determined according to the historical cost accounting rules; and
- the aggregate amount of the cumulative provisions for depreciation or diminution in value which would be permitted or required in determining those amounts according to those rules.

[*SI 2008 No 410, Sch 1 para 34*].

3.14 *Revaluation reserve*

The amount of any profit or loss arising from the determination of the value of an asset on any basis mentioned in 3.12(*a*)–(*e*) (after allowing, where appropriate, for any provisions for depreciation or diminution in value) must be credited or, as the case may be, debited to a separate reserve, the 'revaluation reserve'.

The amount of the revaluation reserve must be shown in the balance sheet under a separate sub-heading in the position given for the item 'revaluation reserve' in either of the balance sheet formats in **3.4**, although it need not be shown under that name.

The revaluation reserve must be reduced to the extent that the amounts transferred to it are no longer necessary for the purposes of the valuation method used. In addition, an amount may be transferred

- from the revaluation reserve to the profit and loss account, if the amount was previously charged to that account or represents realised profit;
- from the revaluation reserve on capitalisation (ie by applying the amount in wholly or partly paying up unissued shares in the company to be allotted to members as fully or partly paid shares); and
- to or from the revaluation reserve in respect of the taxation relating to any profit or loss credited or debited to the reserve.

The revaluation reserve must not be reduced except as mentioned above.

The treatment for taxation purposes of amounts credited or debited to the revaluation reserve must be disclosed in a note to the accounts.

[*SI 2008 No 410, Sch 1 para 35*].

3.15 Fair value accounting

(1) *Financial instruments*

Financial instruments (including 'derivatives') may be included at fair value with the following exceptions.

- Financial instruments which constitute liabilities unless
  - (i) they are held as part of a 'trading portfolio';
  - (ii) they are derivative; or
  - (iii) they are financial instruments that, under international accounting standards adopted by the European Commission before 6 September 2006 in accordance with the IAS Regulation, may be included in accounts at fair value, provided that the disclosures required by such accounting standards are made.
- Any of the following, namely
  - (i) financial instruments (other than derivatives) 'held to maturity',
  - (ii) loans and 'receivables' originated by the company and not 'held for trading purposes',
  - (iii) interests in subsidiary undertakings, associated undertaking (see **3.62**) and joint ventures (see **3.61**),
  - (iv) 'equity instruments' issued by the company,

(v) contracts for contingent consideration in a 'business combination',

(vi) other financial instruments with such special characteristics that the instruments, according to generally accepted accounting principles or practice, should be accounted for differently from other financial instruments,

unless they are financial instruments that, under international accounting standards adopted by the European Commission before 6 September 2006 in accordance with the IAS Regulation, may be included in accounts at fair value, provided that the disclosures required by such accounting standards are made.

- If the fair value of a financial instrument cannot be determined reliably under the rules set out below.

'*Derivatives*' include 'commodity-based contracts' that give either contracting party the right to settle in cash or in some other financial instrument, except when such contracts

- were entered into for the purpose of, and continue to meet, the company's expected purchase, sale or usage requirements;
- were designated for such purpose at their inception; and
- are expected to be settled by delivery of the commodity.

Determination of fair value. The fair value of a financial instrument is determined as follows.

(a) If a 'reliable market' can readily be identified for the financial instrument, its fair value is determined by reference to its market value.

(b) If a reliable market cannot readily be identified for the financial instrument but can be identified for its components or for a similar instrument, its fair value is determined by reference to the market value of its components or of the similar instrument.

(c) If neither (*a*) or (*b*) above applies, the fair value of the financial instrument is a value resulting from generally accepted valuation models and techniques which ensure a reasonable approximation of the market value.

Hedged items. A company may include any assets and liabilities, or identified portions of such assets or liabilities, that qualify as hedged items under a 'fair value hedge accounting system' at the amount required under that system.

The expressions '*business combination*', '*commodity-based contracts*', '*derivative*', '*equity instrument*', '*fair value hedge accounting system*', '*financial instrument*', '*hedge accounting*', '*hedge accounting system*', '*hedged items*', '*held for trading purposes*', '*held to maturity*', '*receivables*', '*reliable market*' and '*trading portfolio*' have the same meaning as they have in *Council Directive 78/660/EEC* on the annual accounts of certain types of companies (as amended).

(2) *Investment property*

Investment property that, under international accounting standards, may be included in accounts at fair value may be included at fair value, provided that all such investment property is so included where its fair value can reliably be determined. For these purposes, 'fair value' means fair value determined in accordance with relevant international accounting standards.

(3) *Living animals and plants*

Living animals and plants that, under international accounting standards, may be included in accounts at fair value may be included at fair value, provided that all such living animals and plants are so included where their fair value can reliably be determined. For these purposes, 'fair value' means fair value determined in accordance with relevant international accounting standards.

Accounting for changes in value. Where a financial instrument or asset is valued in accordance with (1) to (3) above, a change in the value of the financial instrument or asset must be included in the profit and loss account. But

(A) where

(i) the financial instrument accounted for is a 'hedging instrument' under a hedge accounting system that allows some or all of the change in value not to be shown in the profit and loss account, or

(ii) the change in value relates to an 'exchange difference' arising on a 'monetary item' that forms part of a company's net investment in a 'foreign entity',

the amount of the change in value *must* be credited to or (as the case may be) debited from a separate reserve ('*the fair value reserve*'); and

(B) where the instrument accounted for

(i) is an 'available for sale financial asset', and

(ii) is not a derivative,

the change in value *may* be credited to or (as the case may be) debited from the fair value reserve.

The expressions '*available for sale financial asset*', '*exchange difference*', '*financial instrument*', '*foreign entity*', '*hedge accounting*', '*hedge accounting system*', '*hedging instrument*', and '*monetary item*' have the same meaning as they have in *Council Directive 78/660/EEC* on the annual accounts of certain types of companies (as amended).

The fair value reserve. The fair value reserve must be adjusted to the extent that the amounts shown in it are no longer necessary for the purposes of (A) or (B) above.

The treatment for taxation purposes of amounts credited or debited to the fair value reserve must be disclosed in a note to the accounts.

[*SI 2008 No 410, Sch 1 paras 36–41, Sch 10 paras 2, 3*].

3.16 Notes to the accounts: general

Reserves and dividends. There must be stated

(a) any amount set aside or proposed to be set aside to, or withdrawn or proposed to be withdrawn from, reserves;

(b) the aggregate amount of dividends paid in the financial year (other than those for which a liability existed at the immediately preceding balance sheet date);

(c) the aggregate amount of dividends that the company is liable to pay at the balance sheet date; and

(d) the aggregate amount of dividends that are proposed before the date of approval of the accounts, and not otherwise disclosed under (*b*) or (*c*) above.

Disclosure of accounting policies. The accounting policies adopted in determining the profit or loss and the amounts of balance sheet items (including policies with respect to the depreciation and diminution in value of assets) must be stated.

Accounting standards. It must be stated whether the accounts have been prepared in accordance with applicable accounting standards. Particulars of any material departure from those standards, and the reasons for it, must also be given.

Foreign currency translation. Where any sums originally denominated in foreign currencies have been brought into account under any items shown in the balance sheet or profit and loss account, the basis on which those sums have been translated into sterling (or the currency in which the accounts are drawn up) must be stated.

Dormant companies acting as agents. Where the directors of a company take advantage of the exemption from audit conferred on dormant companies by *CA 2006, s 480* (see **8.28 Audit**) and the company has during the financial year in question acted as an agent for any person, the fact that it has so acted must be stated.

[*SI 2008 No 410, Sch 1 paras 42–45, 70, 71*].

Listed companies. In addition to the requirements of *CA 2006* and supporting Regulations, listed companies must also comply with the requirements of the FCA Listing Rules as to content of annual accounts. See **33.28 Public and Listed Companies**.

3.17 Notes to the accounts: information supplementing the balance sheet

The information required, as set out in **3.18** to **3.25**, being information which either supplements that given with respect to particular items in the balance sheet or is otherwise relevant to assessing the company's state of affairs, must be given by way of notes to the accounts (if not given in the accounts themselves). [*SI 2008 No 410, para 46*].

3.18 *Share capital and debentures*

(1) *Share capital*

The following information must be given with respect to the company's share capital.

- Where shares of more than one class have been allotted, the number and aggregate nominal value of shares of each class allotted.
- Where shares are held as treasury shares, the number and aggregate nominal value of the treasury shares and, where shares of more than one class have been allotted, the number and aggregate nominal value of the shares of each class held as treasury shares.

If any part of the allotted share capital consists of redeemable shares, the following information must be given.

- The earliest and latest dates on which the company has power to redeem those shares.
- Whether those shares must be redeemed in any event or are liable to be redeemed at the option of the company or of the shareholder.
- Whether any (and, if so, what) premium is payable on redemption.

If the company has allotted any shares during the financial year, the following information must be given.

- The classes of shares allotted.

- As respects each class of shares, the number allotted, their aggregate nominal value, and the consideration received by the company for the allotment.

[*SI 2008 No 410, Sch 1 paras 47, 48*].

With respect to any contingent right to the allotment of shares in the company (meaning any option to subscribe for shares and any other right to require the allotment of shares to any person whether arising on the conversion into shares of securities of any other description or otherwise), the following particulars must be given.

- The number, description and amount of the shares in relation to which the right is exercisable.
- The period during which it is exercisable.
- The price to be paid for the shares allotted.

[*SI 2008 No 410, Sch 1 para 49*].

(2) *Debentures*

If the company has issued any debentures during the financial year, the following information must be given.

- The classes of debentures issued.
- As respects each class of debentures, the amount issued and the consideration received by the company for the issue.

Where any of the company's debentures are held by a nominee of, or trustee for, the company, the nominee amount of the debentures and the amount at which they are stated in the company's accounting records must be stated.

[*SI 2008 No 410, Sch 1 para 50*].

3.19 *Fixed assets*

The information set out below must be given for each item which is shown under the general item 'fixed assets' in the balance sheet (or which would be shown there were it not for **3.3**(6)(*b*)(ii)).

(a) The 'appropriate amounts' in respect of that item as at both the beginning of the financial year and at the balance sheet date.

(b) The effect on any amount shown in the balance sheet in respect of that item of

   (i) any revision of the amount in respect of any assets included under that item made during that year on any basis in **3.12**(*a*)–(*e*);

   (ii) acquisitions and disposals during that year of any assets; and

   (iii) any transfers of assets of the company to and from that item during that year.

(c) In respect of each item

   - the cumulative amount of provisions for depreciation or diminution in value of assets included under that item both as at the beginning of the financial year and at the balance sheet date;
   - the amount of any such provisions made in respect of the financial year; and

- the amount of any adjustments made in respect of any such provisions during that year, distinguishing between adjustments made in consequence of disposals and other adjustments.

For the purposes of (*a*) above, the '*appropriate amounts*' in respect of any item as at either of the dates there mentioned are the aggregate amounts determined, as at that date, in respect of assets falling to be included under that item, either on the basis of purchase price or production cost (see **3.11**) or on any basis in **3.12**(*a*)–(*e*) but in either case leaving out of account in either case any provisions for depreciation or diminution in value. [*SI 2008 No 410, Sch 1 para 51*].

Assets included at valuation. The following additional information must be given where any fixed assets (other than listed investments, see **3.20**) are included under any balance sheet item at an amount determined on any basis in **3.12**(*a*)–(*e*).

(i) The years (so far as they are known to the directors) in which the assets were severally valued, and the several values.

(ii) In the case of assets valued during the financial year, the bases of valuation used and either the names or qualifications of the valuers.

[*SI 2008 No 410, Sch 1 para 52*].

Land and buildings. In relation to any amount shown in the balance sheet in respect of the item 'land and buildings' (or which would be shown there but for 3.3(6)(*b*)(ii)), the following must be stated.

- How much of that amount is ascribable to land of freehold tenure and how much to land of leasehold tenure (in Scotland, land in respect of which the company is the owner and land of which the company is the tenant under a lease).
- How much of the amount ascribable to land of leasehold tenure (in Scotland, land of which the company is the tenant under a lease) is ascribable to land held on 'long lease' and how much to land held on 'short lease'. '*Long lease*' means a lease with an unexpired term at the end of the financial year of not less than 50 years and '*short lease*' means a lease which is not a long lease. '*Lease*' includes an agreement for a lease.

[*SI 2008 No 410, Sch 1 para 53, Sch 10 paras 7, 15*].

3.20 *Investments*

In respect of the amount of each item shown in the balance sheet under the general item 'investments' (whether as fixed or current assets) (or which would be shown there were it not for **3.3**(6)(*b*)(ii)) there must be stated how much is ascribable to 'listed investments'.

Where the amount of any listed investments is stated (as required above), there must also be stated

- their aggregate market value where this differs from the amount so stated; and
- both the market value and the stock exchange value of any investments of which the former value is, for the purposes of the accounts, taken as being higher than the latter.

A '*listed investment*' is an investment which has been granted a listing either on a recognised investment exchange other than an overseas investment exchange (which terms have the same meaning as in *FSMA 2000, Pt 18*) or on any stock exchange of repute outside the UK.

[*SI 2008 No 410, Sch 1 para 54, Sch 10 para 8*].

See also **3.32** to **3.40** for disclosure of shares in related undertakings.

3.21 *Fair value of assets and liabilities*

(1) *Financial instruments*

Financial instrument included at fair value. Where financial instruments have been valued in accordance with **3.15**(1), the following must be stated.

(a) Where the fair value of the instruments has been determined in accordance with **3.15**(1)(*c*), the significant assumptions underlying the valuation models and techniques used.

(b) For each category of financial instrument, the fair value of the instruments in that category and the changes in value

(i) included in the profit and loss account, or

(ii) credited to or (as the case may be) debited from the fair value reserve,

in respect of those instruments.

(c) For each class of 'derivatives', the extent and nature of the instruments, including significant terms and conditions that may affect the amount, timing and certainty of future cash flows.

(d) Where any amount is transferred to or from the fair value reserve during the financial year, there must be stated in tabular form

(i) the amount of the reserve as at the beginning of the financial year and the balance sheet date;

(ii) the amount transferred to or from the reserve during that year; and

(iii) the source and application respectively of the amounts so transferred.

Derivatives not included at fair value. Where the company has derivatives that it has not included at fair value, there must be stated for each class of such derivatives

- the fair value of the derivatives in that class, if such a value can be determined in accordance with **3.15**(1), and
- the extent and nature of the derivatives.

Financial fixed assets. If

- the company has 'financial fixed assets' that could be included at fair value by virtue of **3.15**(1),
- the amount at which those items are included under any item in the company's accounts is in excess of their fair value, and
- the company has not made provision for diminution in value of those assets in accordance with **3.8**,

there must be stated

- the amount at which either the individual assets or appropriate groupings of those individual assets are included in the company's accounts;
- the fair value of those assets or groupings; and

- the reasons for not making a provision for diminution in value of those assets, including the nature of the evidence that provides the basis for the belief that the amount at which they are stated in the accounts will be recovered.

[*SI 2008 No 410, Sch 1 paras 55–57*].

See **3.15** for the meaning of '*derivatives*'.

(2) *Investment property*

Where the amounts to be included in the accounts in respect of investment property have been determined in accordance with **3.15**(2), the balance sheet items affected and the basis of valuation adopted in determining the amounts of the assets in question in the case of each such item must be disclosed in a note to the accounts.

For each balance sheet item affected there must be shown, either separately in the balance sheet or in a note to the accounts

- the 'comparable amounts' determined according to the historical cost accounting rules; or
- the differences between those amounts and the corresponding amounts actually shown in the balance sheet in respect of that item.

'*Comparable amounts*' mean

- the aggregate amount which would be required to be shown in respect of that item if the amounts to be included in respect of all the assets covered by that item were determined according to the historical cost accounting rules; and
- the aggregate amount of the cumulative provisions for depreciation or diminution in value which would be permitted or required in determining those amounts according to those rules.

[*SI 2008 No 410, Sch 1 para 58*].

(3) *Living animals and plants*

Where the amounts to be included in the accounts in respect of living animals and plants have been determined in accordance with **3.15**(3), the balance sheet items affected and the basis of valuation adopted in determining the amounts of the assets in question in the case of each such item must be disclosed in a note to the accounts.

[*SI 2008 No 410, Sch 1 para 58*].

3.22 *Reserves and provisions*

Where any amount is transferred

- to or from any reserves,
- to any 'provisions for liabilities', or
- from any such provision for liabilities, otherwise than for the purpose for which the provision was established,

and the reserves or provisions are shown as separate items in the balance sheet (or would be so shown were it not for **3.3**(6)(*b*)(ii)), the following information must be given in respect of the aggregate of reserves or provisions included in the same item.

- The amount of the reserves or provisions at the beginning of the financial year and at the balance sheet date.
- Any amounts transferred to or from the reserves or provisions during the year.
- The source and application of the amounts so transferred.

Where the amount of the provision is material, particulars must be given of each provision included in the item 'other provisions' in the balance sheet.

References to '*provisions for liabilities*' are to any amount retained as reasonably necessary for the purpose of providing for any liability the nature of which is clearly defined and which is either likely to be incurred, or certain to be incurred but uncertain as to amount or as to the date on which it will arise.

[*SI 2008 No 410, Sch 1 para 59, Sch 9 para 2*].

Provision for deferred taxation. The amount of any provision for deferred taxation must be stated separately from the amount of any provision for other taxation. [*SI 2008 No 410, Sch 1 para 60*].

3.23 *Details of indebtedness*

In respect of each item shown in the balance sheet under 'creditors' (or which would be shown there were it not for 3.3(6)(*b*)(ii)), the following information is required.

(a) The aggregate amount of any debts included under that item which are payable or repayable otherwise than by instalments and which fall due for payment or repayment after the end of a five-year period beginning with the day after the end of the financial year.

(b) In the case of any debts so included which are payable or repayable by instalments, the aggregate amount of any instalments which fall due for payment after the end of the period specified in (*a*) above.

(c) The aggregate amount of any debts included under that item in respect of which any security has been given by the company.

(d) An indication of the nature of the securities so given.

In relation to each debt falling to be taken into account under (*a*) and (*b*) above, the terms of payment or repayment and the rate of any interest payable on the debt must be stated. But if the number of debts is such that, in the opinion of the directors, compliance with this requirement would result in a statement of excessive length, it is sufficient to give a general indication of the terms of payment or repayment and the rates of any interest payable on the debts.

Where a distinction is made in the balance sheet between amounts falling due to creditors within one year and those falling due after more than one year, (*a*) and (*b*) above apply only to items shown under the latter of those categories and (*c*) above applies to items shown under either category.

[*SI 2008 No 410, Sch 1 para 61*].

Fixed cumulative dividends. If any fixed cumulative dividends on the company's shares are in arrear, there must be stated the amount of the arrears and the period for which the dividends (or, if there is more than one class, each class of them) are in arrear. [*SI 2008 No 410, Sch 1 para 62*].

3.24 *Guarantees and other financial commitments*

The following information must be given.

(a) Particulars of any charge on the assets of the company to secure the liabilities of any other person, including, where practicable, the amount secured.

(b) With respect to any other contingent liability not provided for

(i) the amount or estimated amount of that liability;

(ii) its legal nature; and

(iii) whether any valuable security has been provided by the company in connection with that liability and if so, what.

(c) Where practicable, the aggregate amount or estimated amount of contracts for capital expenditure, so far as not provided for.

(d) Particulars of any pension commitments included under any provision shown in the company's balance sheet, and any such commitments for which no provision has been made, giving separate particulars of any commitment so far as it relates to pensions payable to past directors.

(e) Particulars of any other financial commitments that have not been provided for and are relevant to assessing the company's state of affairs.

[*SI 2008 No 410, Sch 1 para 63*].

Guarantees and other financial commitments in favour of group undertakings. Commitments within any of (*a*)–(*e*) above which are undertaken on behalf of or for the benefit of

(i) any parent undertaking or fellow subsidiary undertaking, or

(ii) any subsidiary undertaking of the company,

must be stated separately from the other commitments within each of (*a*)–(*e*) above, distinguishing commitments within (i) from those within (ii) above.

[*SI 2008 No 410, Sch 1 para 73*].

3.25 *Miscellaneous matters*

The following information must be given.

(a) Particulars of any case where the purchase price or production cost of any asset is for the first time determined *SI 2008 No 410, Sch 1 para 29* (see **3.11**).

(b) The aggregate amount, for each item in question, of any outstanding loans made under the authority of *CA 2006, s 682(2)(b), (c)* or *(d)* (various cases of financial assistance by a company for purchase of its own shares, see **34.21**(*i*)(*j*)(*k*) **PURCHASE OF OWN SHARES**) included under any item shown in the company's balance sheet.

[*SI 2008 No 410, Sch 1 para 64*].

3.26 Notes to the accounts: information supplementing the profit and loss account

The information required, as set out in **3.27** to **3.31**, being information which either supplements that given with respect to particular items in the profit and loss account or otherwise provides particulars of income or expenditure or of circumstances affecting items shown in the profit and loss account, must be given by way of notes to the accounts (if not given in the accounts themselves). [*SI 2008 No 410, Sch 1 para 65*]. See **3.56** for exemption from these provisions for companies preparing group accounts in accordance with *CA 2006*.

3.27 *Separate statement of loan interest*

The amount of the interest on (or any similar charges in respect of)

- bank loans and overdrafts, and
- loans of any other kind made to the company

must be stated.

This does not apply to interest or charges on loans to the company from group undertakings, but, with that exception, it applies to interest or charges on all loans, whether made on the security of debentures or not.

[*SI 2008 No 410, Sch 1 para 66*].

3.28 *Particulars of tax*

Particulars must be given of any special circumstances which affect liability in respect of taxation of profits, income or capital gains for the financial year in question and/or succeeding financial years.

In respect of each of the amounts shown under the items 'tax on profit or loss on ordinary activities' and 'tax on extraordinary profit or loss' in the profit and loss account (or which would be shown were it not for **3.3**(6)(*b*)(ii)), the following must be stated.

- The amount of the charge for UK corporation tax.
- If that amount would have been greater but for double taxation relief, the amount which it would have been but for such relief.
- The amount of the charge for UK income tax.
- The amount of the charge for taxation imposed outside the UK of profits, income and (so far as charged to revenue) capital gains.

[*SI 2008 No 410, Sch 1 para 67*].

3.29 *Particulars of turnover*

If, in the course of the financial year, the company has

- carried on business of two or more classes that, in the directors' opinion, differ substantially from each other, there must be stated in respect of each class
  (i) a description of the class concerned; and
  (ii) the amount of the turnover attributable to it; and
- supplied different markets ('market' meaning a market delimited by geographical bounds) that, in the directors' opinion, differ substantially from each other, there must be stated the amount of the turnover attributable to each such market.

Where, in the directors' opinion, the disclosure of any information required above would be seriously prejudicial to the interests of the company, that information need not be disclosed, but the fact that any such information has not been disclosed must be stated.

In analysing for the above purposes the source (in terms of either business or market) of turnover, the directors must have regard to the manner in which the company's activities are organised. Classes of business and markets which, in the opinion of the directors, do not differ substantially from each other must be treated as one class or one market respectively. Any amounts properly attributable to one class of business or (as the case may be) to one market which are not material may be included in the amount stated in respect of another.

[*SI 2008 No 410, Sch 1 para 68*].

3.30 *Miscellaneous matters*

Prior year adjustments. Where any amount relating to any preceding financial year is included in any profit and loss account item, the effect must be stated.

Extraordinary items. Particulars must be given of any extraordinary income or charges arising in the financial year.

Exceptional items. The effect of any exceptional transactions (by virtue of size or incidence) must be stated, even though they fall within the ordinary activities of the company.

[*SI 2008 No 410, Sch 1 para 69*].

3.31 *Related party transactions*

Particulars *may* be given of transactions which the company has entered into with 'related parties' and *must* be given if such transactions are material and have not been concluded under normal market conditions.

The particulars of transactions required to be disclosed must include

- the amount of such transactions;
- the nature of the related party relationship; and
- other information about the transactions necessary for an understanding of the financial position of the company.

Information about individual transactions may be aggregated according to their nature, except where separate information is necessary for an understanding of the effects of related party transactions on the financial position of the company.

Particulars need not be given of transactions entered into between two or more members of a group, provided that any subsidiary undertaking which is a party to the transaction is wholly-owned by such a member.

'*Related party*' has the same meaning as in international accounting standards.

[*SI 2008 No 410, Sch 1 para 72*].

3.32 INDIVIDUAL ACCOUNTS: RELATED UNDERTAKINGS

Where a company is not preparing group accounts, its Companies Act or IAS individual accounts must comply with the provisions in 3.33 to 3.40 as to the information about related undertakings to be given in notes to the company's accounts. There are two exceptions.

Exception 1 - Statutory

(1) **Exemption**

The information (other than that in 3.37 and 3.39) need not be disclosed with respect to an undertaking that

- is established under the law of a country outside the UK, or
- carries on business outside the UK,

but only if

- in the opinion of the directors of the company, the disclosure would be seriously prejudicial to the business of
  - (i) that undertaking;
  - (ii) the company;
  - (iii) any of the company's subsidiary undertakings; or
  - (iv) any other undertaking which is included in the consolidation; and
- the Secretary of State agrees that the information need not be disclosed.

Where advantage is taken of this exemption, a note to that effect must be included in the company's accounts.

[*CA 2006, s 409(4)(5); SI 2008 No 410, Reg 7*].

Exception 2

(2) **Alternative compliance in cases of excessive length**

Where the directors are of the opinion that the number of undertakings in respect of which the company is required to disclose information under any provision described in **3.33** to **3.40** is such that compliance would result in information of excessive length being given in the notes to the accounts, information need only be given in respect of the undertakings whose results or financial position, in the directors' opinion, principally affected the figures shown in the company's annual accounts.

If advantage is taken of this, then

(i) the notes to the company's annual accounts must include a statement that the information is given only with respect to undertakings whose results or financial position, in the directors' opinion, principally affected the figures shown; and

(ii) the full information (ie both that which is disclosed and that which is not) must be annexed to the next annual return delivered to the Registrar of Companies after the accounts in question have been approved by the board.

If a company fails to comply with (ii) above, an offence is committed by the company and every officer of the company who is in default. A person guilty of such an offence is liable, on summary conviction, to a fine not exceeding level 3 on the standard scale and, for continued contravention, a daily default fine not exceeding one-tenth of level 3 on the standard scale. See **29.1 Offences and Legal Proceedings** for the standard scale.

[*CA 2006, s 410*].

3.33 Subsidiary undertakings

Subject to **3.32**, where, at the end of the financial year, the company has subsidiary undertakings, there must be stated in respect of each one of them

- its name;
- if it is incorporated outside the UK, the country in which it is incorporated;
- if it is unincorporated, the address of its principal place of business.

[*SI 2008 No 410, Sch 4 para 1*].

Reason for not preparing group accounts. There must also be stated the reason why the company is not required to prepare group accounts. If the reason is that all the company's subsidiary undertakings fall within the exclusions in *CA 2006, s 405* (see 3.55), there must be stated, for each subsidiary undertaking, which of those exclusions applies.

[*SI 2008 No 410, Sch 4 para 10*].

3.34 *Holdings in subsidiary undertakings*

Subject to **3.32**, in relation to shares of each class 'held by the company' in a subsidiary undertaking, there must be stated

- the identity of the class; and
- the proportion of the nominal value of the shares of that class represented by those shares.

The shares held by or on behalf of the company itself must be distinguished from those attributed to the company which are held by or on behalf of a subsidiary undertaking.

[*SI 2008 No 410, Sch 4 para 11*].

In ascertaining the shares '*held by the company*',

- there must be attributed to the company any shares held by a subsidiary undertaking, or by a person acting on behalf of the company or a subsidiary undertaking. Any shares held on behalf of a person other than the company or a subsidiary undertaking must be treated as not held by the company; and
- shares held by way of security must be treated as held by the person providing the security where
  - (i) the rights attached to the shares are exercisable only in accordance with his instructions; and
  - (ii) the shares are held in connection with the granting of loans as part of normal business activities and the rights attached to the shares are exercisable only in his interests

  disregarding, in each case, any right to exercise the rights for the purpose of preserving the value of the security, or of realising it.

[*SI 2008 No 410, Sch 4 para 14*].

3.35 *Financial information about subsidiary undertakings*

Subject to **3.32** and the exceptions below, there must be disclosed with respect to each subsidiary undertaking not included in consolidated accounts by the company

- the aggregate amount of its capital and reserves as at the end of its 'relevant financial year'; and
- its profit or loss for that year.

For this purposes, the '*relevant financial year*' of a subsidiary undertaking is, if its financial year ends with that of the company, that year and, if it does not, its financial year ending last before the end of the company's financial year.

Exceptions. The above information need not be given if

- the company is exempt under **3.54** from the requirement to prepare group accounts (parent company included in accounts of larger group);
- the company's investment in the subsidiary undertaking is included in the company's accounts by way of the equity method of valuation;
- the subsidiary undertaking is not required by any provision of the *CA 2006* to deliver a copy of its balance sheet for its relevant financial year and does not otherwise publish that balance sheet in the UK or elsewhere *and* the shares '*held by the company*' (see **3.34**) are less than 50% of the nominal value of the shares in the undertaking; or
- it is not material.

[*SI 2008 No 410, Sch 4 para 2*].

3.36 *Financial years of subsidiary undertakings*

Where disclosure is made under **3.35** with respect to a subsidiary undertaking and that undertaking's financial year does not end with that of the company, there must be stated in relation to that undertaking the date on which its last financial year ended (ie last before the end of the company's financial year).

[*SI 2008 No 410, Sch 4 para 12*].

3.37 *Shares and debentures of company held by subsidiary undertakings*

Subject to **3.32**, the number, description and amount of shares in the company held by, or on behalf of, its subsidiary undertakings must be disclosed. This does not apply in relation to shares in the case of which the subsidiary undertaking is concerned as

- personal representative; or
- trustee unless the company, or any subsidiary undertaking of the company, is 'beneficially interested under the trust', otherwise than by way of security only for the purposes of a transaction entered into by it in the ordinary course of a business which includes the lending of money.

[*SI 2008 No 410, Sch 4 para 3*].

In determining whether the company is '*beneficially interested under the trust*', certain residual interests under pension and employees' share schemes, employer's charges and other rights of recovery under such schemes, and a trustee's right to expenses, remuneration, indemnity, etc are disregarded. See *SI 2008 No 410, Sch 4 paras 24–27* for full details.

3.38 Significant holdings in undertakings other than subsidiary undertakings

Subject to **3.32**, where at the end of the financial year the company has a 'significant holding' in an undertaking which is not a subsidiary undertaking, the following must be stated.

(a) The name of the undertaking.

(b) If the undertaking is incorporated outside the UK, the country in which it is incorporated

(c) If it is unincorporated, the address of its principal place of business.

(d) The identity of each class of shares in the undertaking held by the company.

(e) The proportion of the nominal value of the shares of that class represented by those shares.

(f) Subject to the exemption below, the aggregate amount of the capital and reserves of the undertaking as at the end of its 'relevant financial year'.

(g) Subject to the exemption below, its profit or loss for that year.

A '*significant holding*' is a holding which amounts to 20% or more of the nominal value of any class of shares in the undertaking *or* the amount of which (as stated or included in the company's individual accounts) exceeds one-fifth of the amount (as so stated) of the company's assets.

The '*relevant financial year*' of an undertaking for these purposes is, if its financial year ends with that of the company, that year, and if it does not, its financial year ending last before the end of the company's financial year.

Exemption. The information in (*f*) and (*g*) above need not be given in respect of an undertaking if

- the undertaking is exempt under **3.54** from the requirement to prepare group accounts (parent company included in accounts of larger group) *and* the investment of the company in all undertakings in which it has a significant holding is shown, in aggregate, in the notes to the accounts by way of the equity method of valuation;
- the undertaking in question is not required by any provision of *CA 2006* to deliver a copy of its balance sheet for its relevant financial year and does not otherwise publish that balance sheet in the UK or elsewhere *and* the company's holding is less than 50% of the nominal value of the shares in the undertaking; or
- it is not material.

[*SI 2008 No 410, Sch 4 paras 4–6, 13*].

In ascertaining, for any of the above purposes, the company's holding,

- there must be attributed to the company shares held on its behalf by any person but any shares held on behalf of a person other than the company must be treated as not held by the company; and
- shares held by way of security must be treated as held by the person providing the security where

  (i) the rights attached to the shares are exercisable only in accordance with his instructions; and

  (ii) the shares are held in connection with the granting of loans as part of normal business activities and the rights attached to the shares are exercisable only in his interests

  disregarding, in each case, any right to exercise the rights for the purpose of preserving the value of the security, or of realising it.

[*SI 2008 No 410, Sch 4 para 14*].

3.39 Membership of certain undertakings

Subject to **3.32**, where at the end of the financial year a company is a member of a 'qualifying undertaking' the following must be stated.

- The name and legal form of the undertaking (unless it is not material).
- The address (whether in or outside the UK) of its registered office or, if it does not have such an office, its head office (unless it is not material).
- Where the undertaking is a qualifying partnership, either
  - (i) a statement that a copy of the latest accounts of the undertaking has been or is to be appended to the copy of the company's accounts sent to the Registrar of Companies; or
  - (ii) the name of at least one body corporate (which may be the company) in whose group accounts the undertaking has been or is to be dealt with on a consolidated basis. This information need not be given if the notes to the company's accounts disclose that advantage has been taken of the exemption in *regulation 7* of the *Partnerships (Accounts) Regulations 2008*.

A '*qualifying undertaking*' means

(a) a qualifying partnership; or

(b) an unlimited company each of whose members is

(i) a limited company;

(ii) another unlimited company each of whose members is a limited company; or

(iii) a Scottish partnership each of whose members is a limited company,

and, for these purposes, references to a limited company, another unlimited company and a Scottish partnership include a comparable undertaking incorporated in, or formed under, the law of a country or territory outside the UK.

[*SI 2008 No 410, Sch 4 para 7; SI 2008 No 569, Reg 17*].

3.40 Parent undertaking drawing up accounts for larger group

Subject to 3.32, where the company is a subsidiary undertaking, the following information must be given.

(a) Particulars as follows with respect to the parent undertaking of the largest and smallest group of undertakings for which group accounts are drawn up and of which the company is a member.

(i) The name of the parent undertaking.

(ii) If the undertaking is incorporated outside the UK, the country in which it is incorporated.

(iii) if it is unincorporated, the address of its principal place of business.

(iv) If copies of the group accounts referred to above are available to the public, the addresses from which copies of the accounts can be obtained.

(b) Particulars as follows with respect to the company (which includes any body corporate) regarded by the directors as being the company's ultimate parent company.

(i) Its name.

(ii) If that company is incorporated outside the UK, the country in which it is incorporated (if known to the directors).

[*SI 2008 No 410, Sch 4 paras 8, 9*].

3.41 INDIVIDUAL ACCOUNTS: DIRECTORS' REMUNERATION AND BENEFITS, UNQUOTED COMPANIES

The information as described in **3.42** to **3.48** must be given in the notes to a company's individual accounts, except that the information in **3.44** to **3.47** only applies to unquoted companies. (Quoted companies must instead prepare a directors' remuneration report. See **19 Directors' Remuneration Reports**.)

The provisions apply whether the company is preparing Companies Act or IAS accounts.

[*SI 2008 No 410, Reg 8*].

Listed companies. In addition to the requirements of *CA 2006* and supporting Regulations, listed companies must also comply with the requirements of the FCA Listing Rules. See **33.28(*q*) Public and Listed Companies**.

3.42 Directors' remuneration

The information on directors' remuneration as described in **3.43** to **3.47** must be given in the notes to a company's annual accounts. [*CA 2006, s 412(1)*]. It is the duty of

- any director of a company, and
- any person who is or has at any time in the preceding five years been a director of the company

to give notice to the company of such matters relating to himself as may be necessary for these purposes. A person in default commits an offence and is liable, on summary conviction to a fine not exceeding level 3 on the standard scale. See **29.1 Offences and Legal Proceedings** for the standard scale.

[*CA 2006, s 412(5)(6)*].

Information is to be given only so far as it is contained in the company's books and papers or the company has the right to obtain it from the persons concerned. [*SI 2008 No 410, Sch 5 para 6(1)*].

Where it is necessary for the purpose of making any distinction required in **3.43** to **3.47**, the directors may apportion payments between the matters in respect of which they have been paid or are receivable in such manner as they think appropriate. [*SI 2008 No 410, Sch 5 para 7(6)*].

Meaning of 'subsidiary undertakings'. Any reference in these provisions to a subsidiary undertaking of the company, in relation to a person who is or was, while a director of the company, a director also, by virtue of the company's nomination (direct or indirect) of any other undertaking, includes that undertaking (whether or not it is or was in fact a subsidiary undertaking of the company). [*SI 2008 No 410, Sch 5 para 14(1)*].

3.43 *Total amount of directors' remuneration, etc*

The following must be shown. Any information is treated as being shown if it is capable of being readily ascertained from other information which is shown.

(a) The aggregate amount of 'remuneration' paid to or receivable by directors in respect of 'qualifying services'.

'*Remuneration*' of a director includes

- salary, fees and bonuses;
- sums paid by way of expenses allowance (so far as they are chargeable to UK income tax); and
- the estimated money value of any other benefits received by the director otherwise than in cash

but does not include

- the value of any share options granted to the director or the amount of any gains made on the exercise of any such options;
- any company contributions paid, or treated as paid, under any pension scheme or any benefits to which the director is entitled under any such scheme; or
- any money or other assets paid to or received or receivable by the director under any 'long term incentive scheme'.

(b) For quoted companies and companies whose equity share capital is listed on the AIM only, the aggregate of the amount of gains made by directors on the exercise of share options in shares of the company or a group undertaking.

(c) The aggregate of

(i) the amount of money paid to or receivable by directors under 'long-term incentive schemes' in respect of 'qualifying services'; and

(ii) the 'net value' of assets (other than money and share options and, in the case of a company which is not a quoted company and whose equity share capital is not listed on the market known as AIM, shares in the company or any group undertaking) received or receivable by directors under long-term incentive schemes in respect of qualifying services. '*Net value*' means the value after deducting any money paid or other value given by the director in respect of those assets.

(d) The aggregate value of any 'company contributions' paid, or treated as paid, to a pension scheme in respect of directors' 'qualifying services', being contributions by reference to which the rate or amount of any 'money purchase benefits' that may become payable will be calculated.

'*Company contributions*' mean any payments (including insurance premiums) made, or treated as made, to the scheme in respect of the director by any person other than the director.

'*Money purchase benefits*' are retirement benefits payable under a pension scheme, the rate or amount of which is calculated by reference to payments made, or treated as made, by the director or by any other person in respect of the director and which are not average salary benefits.

(e) The number of directors (if any) to whom retirement benefits are accruing in respect of 'qualifying services' under each of

(i) '*money purchase schemes*' (ie, pension schemes under which all of the benefits that may become payable to, or in respect of, the director are 'money purchase benefits', see (*d*) above); and

(ii) '*defined benefit schemes*' (ie any pension scheme which is not a money purchase scheme).

(f) In the case of a company which is not a quoted company and whose equity share capital is not listed on the market known as AIM, both the number of directors

(i) who exercised share options in shares in the company or a group undertaking; and

(ii) in respect of whose 'qualifying services' shares in the company or a group undertaking were received or receivable under 'long-term incentive schemes'.

'*Qualifying services*' in respect of any person means

- his services as director of the company; and
- his services while director of the company

(i) as director of any of its subsidiary undertakings; or

(ii) otherwise in connection with the management of the company's affairs or those of any of its subsidiary undertakings.

Reference to a subsidiary undertaking of the company is to an undertaking which is a subsidiary undertaking at the time the services were rendered.

A '*long term incentive scheme*' means any agreement or arrangement under which money or other assets may become receivable by a director and which includes one or more qualifying conditions with respect to service or performance which cannot be fulfilled in a single financial year, but disregarding

- bonuses determined by reference to service or performance in a single financial year;
- compensation for loss of office, payments for breach of contract and other termination payments; and
- retirement benefits.

Notes

(1) Remuneration paid or receivable or share options granted in respect of a person's accepting office as director are treated as remuneration paid or receivable or share options granted in respect of his services as director.

(2) For the purpose of determining whether a pension scheme is a money purchase scheme or defined benefit scheme, any death in service benefits provided are to be disregarded.

(3) Where a pension scheme provides for any benefits that may become payable to or in respect of any director to be whichever are the greater of money purchase benefits and defined benefits (in each case as determined under the scheme), the company may assume that those benefits will be whichever appears more likely at the end of the financial year.

(4) Amounts paid to or receivable by a person include amounts paid to or receivable by a connected person or a body corporate controlled by him (both to be construed in accordance with *CA 2006, ss 252–255*, see **18 Directors**), but not so as to require an amount to be counted twice.

(5) The amounts to be shown include all relevant sums paid by or receivable from the company, its subsidiary undertakings and any other person. They do not, however, include sums to be accounted for

- to the company or any of its subsidiary undertakings; or
- under 18 **Directors** (payments in connection with shares transfers, duty to account) to persons who sold their shares as a result of the offer made.

(6) The amounts to be shown for any financial year are the sums receivable in respect of that financial year (whenever paid) or, in the case of sums not payable in respect of a period, the sums paid during the year. However, in either of the two circumstances set out below, the sums in question must be shown (and distinguished as such), to the extent appropriate, in a note to the first accounts in which it is practicable to show them. The said circumstances are where

(i) any sums are not shown for the relevant financial year on the grounds that the person receiving them is liable to account for them as mentioned above, but the liability is later released (wholly or partly) or is not enforced within a period of two years; or

(ii) sums paid by way of expenses allowances are charged to UK income tax after the end of the relevant financial year.

[*SI 2008 No 410, Sch 5 paras 1, 6(2), 7(2)–(5), 8, 9, 11, 12, 13(3)(4)(6)(7), 14(2), 15*].

3.44 *Details of highest paid director's emoluments, etc*

Note. The provisions in this paragraph only apply to unquoted companies.

Where the aggregates shown under **3.43**(*a*)–(*c*) is £200,000 or more, the following information must be shown. Any information is treated as being shown if it is capable of being readily ascertained from other information which is shown.

(a) So much of the total of the aggregate of **3.43**(*a*)–(*c*) which is attributable to the '*highest paid director*' (ie the director to whom is attributable the greatest part of that aggregate).

(b) So much of the aggregate in **3.43**(*d*) attributable to the 'highest paid director'.

(c) If the highest paid director has performed 'qualifying services' during the financial year by reference to which the rate or amount of any 'defined benefits' that may become payable will be calculated,

(i) the amount at the end of the year of his 'accrued pension'; and

(ii) where applicable, the amount at the end of the year of his 'accrued lump sum'.

'*Accrued pension*' and '*accrued lump sum*' mean respectively the amount of the annual pension and the amount of the lump sum which would be payable under the pension scheme on his attaining normal pension age under the scheme if

- he had left the company's service at the end of the financial year;
- there were no increases in the general level of prices in the UK from the end of the financial year until his attaining that age;
- no question arose of any commutation of the pension or inverse commutation of the lump sum; and
- any amounts attributable to voluntary contributions paid by the director to the scheme, and any 'money purchase benefits' which would be payable under the scheme, were disregarded.

(d) In the case of a company which is not a listed company, whether

(i) the highest paid director exercised any share options in the shares of the company or any group undertaking; and

(ii) any shares were received or receivable by that director in respect of qualifying services under a long term incentive scheme.

If the highest paid director has not been involved in any of the transactions specified in (i) or (ii) above, that fact need not be stated.

See **3.43** for the definitions of '*qualifying services*', '*defined benefits*', '*money purchase benefits*' and '*long-term incentive scheme*'.

Notes (1)–(6) in **3.43** equally apply for the above purposes.

[*SI 2008 No 410, Sch 5 paras 2, 6(2), 7(2)–(5), 8, 10, 11, 12, 13(2)(4)(6)(7), 15)*].

3.45 *Excess retirement benefits of directors and past directors*

Note. The provisions in this paragraph only apply to unquoted companies.

Subject to below, there must be shown the aggregate amount of

(a) so much of 'retirement benefits' paid to or receivable by directors under 'pension schemes', and

(b) so much of retirement benefits paid to or receivable by past directors under such schemes,

as (in each case) is in excess of the retirement benefits to which they were respectively entitled on the date on which the benefits first became payable (or 31 March 1997, if later). The amounts shown must include the estimated money value of any benefits paid otherwise than in cash, and the nature of any such benefit must also be disclosed.

Amounts paid or receivable under a pension scheme need not be included in the aggregate amount if

(i) the funding of the scheme was such that the amounts were or, as the case may be, could have been paid without recourse to additional contributions; and

(ii) amounts were paid to or receivable by all pensioner entitled to the present payment of retirement benefits under the scheme on the same basis.

Notes (4)–(6) in **3.43** equally apply for the above purposes.

[*SI 2008 No 410, Sch 5 paras 3, 7(2)-(5), 8, 13(1), 15(2)*].

3.46 *Compensation to directors for loss of office*

Note. The provisions in this paragraph only apply to unquoted companies.

There must be shown the aggregate amount of any compensation to directors or past directors in respect of loss of office. The amount shown must include the estimated money value of any benefits paid otherwise than in cash, and the nature of any such compensation must be disclosed. The necessary information is treated as shown if it can be readily ascertained from other information which is shown.

There must be included compensation received or receivable for

(a) loss of office as director of the company; or

(b) loss, while director of the company or on (or in connection with) his ceasing to be a director of it, of

  (i) any other office in connection with the management of the company's affairs; or

  (ii) any office (as director or otherwise) in connection with the management of the affairs of any subsidiary undertaking of the company.

References above to compensation for loss of office include

- compensation in consideration for (or in connection with) a person's retirement from office; and
- where such a retirement is occasioned by a breach of the person's contract with the company or with a subsidiary undertaking of the company

  (i) payments made by way of damages for the breach; or

  (ii) payments made by way of settlement or compromise of any claim in respect of the breach.

Reference to a subsidiary undertaking of the company is to a subsidiary undertaking immediately before the loss of office as director.

Notes (4)–(6) in **3.43** equally apply for the above purposes.

[*SI 2008 No 410, Sch 5 paras 4, 6(2), 7(2)–(5), 8, 14(2), 15(2)*].

3.47 *Sums paid to third parties in respect of directors' services*

Note. The provisions in this paragraph only apply to unquoted companies.

There must be shown the aggregate amount of any consideration paid to or receivable by 'third parties' for making available the services of any person

- as a director of the company; or
- while director of the company

  (i) as director of any of its subsidiary undertakings; or

  (ii) otherwise in connection with the management of the affairs of the company or any of its subsidiary undertakings.

The amount shown must include the estimated money value of benefits paid otherwise than in cash, and the nature of any such consideration must be disclosed.

A '*third party*' means a person other than

- the director himself or a person connected with him or a body corporate controlled by him; or
- the company or any of its subsidiary undertakings.

Notes (4)–(6) in **3.43** equally apply for the above purposes.

[*SI 2008 No 410, Sch 5 paras 5, 7(2)–(5), 8, 15(2)*].

3.48 Directors' benefits: advances, credit and guarantees

In the case of a company that does not prepare group accounts, the notes to its individual accounts must show the following.

(a) In respect of any advance or credit granted by the company to a director, details of

(i) its amount;

(ii) an indication of the interest rate;

(iii) its main conditions; and

(iv) any amounts repaid.

(b) In respect of any guarantee of any kind entered into by the company on behalf of a director, details of

(i) its main terms;

(ii) the amount of the maximum liability that may be incurred by the company; and

(iii) any amount paid and any liability incurred by the company for the purpose of fulfilling the guarantee (including any loss incurred by reason of enforcement of the guarantee).

There must also be stated in the notes to the accounts the totals of amounts stated under (*a*)(i), (*a*)(iv), (*b*)(ii) and (*b*)(iii).

The provisions apply to

- persons who were directors of the company at any time in the financial year to which the accounts relate; and
- every advance, credit or guarantee subsisting at any time in the financial year to which the accounts relate

(i) whenever it was entered into; and

(ii) whether or not the person concerned was a director of the company in question at the time it was entered into.

[*CA 2006, s 413(1), (3)–(7)*].

3.49 INDIVIDUAL ACCOUNTS: EMPLOYEE NUMBERS AND COSTS

The notes to the accounts of a company not subject to the small companies regime must state

(a) the 'average number of persons employed' by the company in the financial year; and

(b) the average number of persons so employed within each category of persons employed by the company (the categories being such as the directors may select, having regard to the manner in which the company's activities are organised).

The '*average number of persons employed*' is calculated by the formula

$$A \div B$$

where

A = the sum of the number of persons employed under contracts of service by the company in each month (whether throughout it or not) in the financial year or, as the case may be, the numbers of persons so employed within a particular category

B = the number of months in the financial year

In respect of all persons employed by the company during the financial year who are taken into account in determining the relevant annual number for the purposes of (*a*) above, there must also be stated (unless stated elsewhere in the accounts) the aggregate amounts of each of the following.

- Wages and salaries paid or payable in respect of that year to those persons.
- '*Social security costs*' incurred by the company on their behalf, ie any contributions by the company to any state social security or pension scheme, fund or arrangement.
- Other 'pension costs' incurred by the company on their behalf. '*Pension costs*' includes any costs incurred by the company in respect of
  - (i) any pension scheme set up for current and formerly employed employees;
  - (ii) any sums set aside for the future payment of pensions directly by the company to current or former employees; and
  - (iii) any pensions paid directly to such persons without having first been set aside.

[*CA 2006, s 411(1)–(6)*].

3.50 INDIVIDUAL ACCOUNTS: AUDITOR'S REMUNERATION AND LIABILITY LIMITATION AGREEMENTS

Remuneration. The following must be disclosed in the notes to the annual accounts.

(a) The amount of any 'remuneration' receivable by the company's auditor or any associate of the company's auditors for the auditing of the accounts.

(b) The amount of any remuneration receivable by in respect of the period to which the accounts relate by

- the company's auditor, or
- any person who was, at any time during the period to which the accounts relate, an 'associate of the company's auditor'

for the supply of other services to the company or any 'associates of the company'.

This requirement is subject to two exceptions.

(i) Disclosure is not required of remuneration receivable for the supply of services falling within *SI 2008 No 489, Sch 2, para 10* (ie all other auditing services) supplied by a 'distant associate' of a company's auditor where the total remuneration receivable for all those services supplied by that associate does not exceed either

- £10,000; or
- 1% of the 'total audit remuneration received' by the company's auditor in the most recent 'financial year of the auditor' which ended no later than the end of the financial year of the company to which the accounts relate.

'*Total audit remuneration received*' means the total remuneration received for auditing pursuant to legislation (including that of countries and territories outside the UK) of any accounts of any person.

'*Financial year of the auditor*' means the period of not more than 18 months in respect of which the auditor's profit and loss account is required to be made up *or*, failing any such requirement, the period of 12 months beginning with 1 April.

(ii) The notes to the individual accounts of

- a 'parent company' which is required to prepare (and does prepare) group accounts in accordance with *CA 2006*, and
- a 'subsidiary company' where its parent is required to prepare (and does prepare) group accounts in accordance with *CA 2006* and the subsidiary company is included in the consolidation

need not disclose this information if the group accounts are required to disclose it and the individual accounts state that the group accounts are so required.

Types of services in respect of which separate disclosure is required. Separate disclosure is required in respect of the auditing of the accounts in question and of each of the following types of service.

(1) The auditing of accounts of associates of the company pursuant to legislation (including that of countries and territories outside the UK).

(2) Other services supplied pursuant to such legislation.

(3) Other services relating to taxation.

(4) Services relating to information technology.

(5) Internal audit services.

(6) Valuation and actuarial services.

(7) Services relating to litigation.

(8) Services relating to recruitment and remuneration.

(9) Services relating to corporate finance transactions entered into or proposed to be entered into by or on behalf of the company or any of its associates.

(10) All other services.

It is not necessary to disclose separately each service falling within a type of service listed above.

Separate disclosure is required

- in respect of services supplied to the company and its subsidiaries on the one hand and to 'associated pension schemes' on the other; and
- where more than one person has been appointed as a company's auditor during the period to which the accounts relate, in respect of the remuneration of each such person and his associates.

Duty of auditor to supply information. The auditor must supply the directors of the company with such information as is necessary to enable the disclosure required by (*b*) above.

3.50 Accounts: Large Companies

Definitions.

(1) *Remuneration*

Remuneration includes payments in respect of expenses and benefits in kind. Where it includes benefits in kind, the nature and estimated money value must also be disclosed in the notes.

(2) *Associate of a company's auditor*

(a) Each of the following is regarded as an associate of a company's auditor.

(i) Any person controlled by the company's auditor or by any associate of the company's auditor (whether alone or through two or more persons acting together to secure or exercise control). This only applies if that control does *not* arise solely by virtue of the company's auditor or any associate of the company's auditor acting as an insolvency practitioner in relation to any person *or* acting in the capacity of a receiver, or a receiver or manager, of the property of a company or other body corporate (including a receiver or, as the case may be, a receiver or manager, of part only of that property) *or* acting as a judicial factor on the estate of any person.

(ii) Any person who, or group of persons acting together which, has control of the company's auditor.

(iii) Any person using a trading name which is the same as or similar to a trading name used by the company's auditor, but only if the company's auditor uses that trading name with the intention of creating the impression of a connection between him and that other person.

(iv) Any person who is party to an arrangement with the company's auditor, with or without any other person, under which costs, profits, quality control, business strategy or significant professional resources are shared.

(b) Where a company's auditor is a partnership, each of the following is also regarded as an associate of the auditor.

(i) Any other partnership which has a partner in common with the company's auditor.

(ii) Any partner in the company's auditor.

(iii) Any body corporate which is in the same group as a body corporate which is a partner in the company's auditor.

(iv) Any body corporate which is in the same group as a body corporate which is a partner in a partnership which has a partner in common with the company's auditor.

(v) Any body corporate of which a partner in the company's auditor is a director.

(c) Where a company's auditor is a body corporate (other than one which is also a partnership as defined for these purposes below), each of the following is also regarded as an associate of the auditor.

(i) Any other body corporate which has a director in common with the company's auditor.

(ii) Any director of the company's auditor.

(iii) Any body corporate which is in the same group as a body corporate which is a director of the company's auditor.

(iv) Any body corporate which is in the same group as a body corporate which has a director in common with the company's auditor.

(v) Any partnership in which a director of the company's auditor is a partner.

(vi) Any body corporate which is in the same group as the company's auditor.

(vii) Any partnership in which any body corporate which is in the same group as the company's auditor is a partner.

A '*distant associate*' of the company's auditor is a person who is an associate of that auditor by reason only that that person is an associate within one or more of

- (*a*)(i) above where the person in question is controlled by a distant associate of the company's auditor but not by the auditor or by an associate who is not a distant associate;
- (*b*)(i)(iv) or (v); or
- (*c*)(i)(iv) or (v).

For these purposes, '*partner*' includes a member of an LLP and '*partnership*' includes an LLP and a partnership constituted under the law of a country or a territory outside the UK.

A person able, directly or indirectly, to control or materially to influence the operating and financial policy of another person is to be treated as having control of that other person.

A body corporate is in the same group as another body corporate if it is a parent or subsidiary of that body corporate, or a subsidiary of a parent of that body corporate.

(3) *Associate of a company*

References to an associate of a company are references to

- any subsidiary of that company, other than a subsidiary in respect of which severe long-term restrictions substantially hinder the exercise of the rights of the company over the assets or management of the subsidiary; and
- any scheme which is an 'associated pension scheme' in relation to that company.

(4) *Parent/subsidiary*

See APPENDIX 1 DEFINITIONS.

(5) *Associated pension scheme*

Associated pension scheme means, in relation to a company, a scheme for the provision of benefits for or in respect of directors or employees (or former directors or employees) of the company or any subsidiary of the company where

- the benefits consist of or include any pension, lump sum, gratuity or other like benefit given or to be given on retirement or on death or in anticipation of retirement or, in connection with past service, after retirement or death; and
- either
  - (i) a majority of the trustees are appointed by (or by a person acting on behalf of) the company or a subsidiary of the company; or
  - (ii) the company, or a subsidiary of the company, exercises a dominant influence over the appointment of the auditor (if any) of the scheme.

[*SI 2008 No 489, Regs 3, 5, 6(2), (3), 7, Sch 1, Sch 2*].

Liability limitation agreements. A company is able to enter into a liability limitation agreement with its auditors, the effect of which is to limit the auditor's liability to not less than such amount as it is fair and reasonable in all the circumstances of the case having regard in particular to

- the auditor's responsibilities under *CA 2006*
- the nature and purpose of the auditor's contractual obligations to the company; and
- the professional standards expected of an auditor.

A company which has entered into a liability limitation agreement must have it approved by its shareholders (unless it is a private company whose shareholders have waived the need for approval) and must disclose the following in a note to its annual accounts for the financial year to which the agreement relates.

- Its principal terms.
- The date of the resolution approving the agreement or the agreement's principal terms or, in the case of a private company, the date of the resolution waiving the need for such approval.

The annual accounts in which the required disclosure must be made are those for the financial year to which the agreement relates unless the agreement was entered into too late for it to be reasonably practicable for the disclosure to be made in those accounts. In such a case, the disclosure must be made in a note to the company's next following annual accounts.

[*CA 2006, ss 534–538*; *SI 2008 No 489, Reg 8*; *SI 2011 No 2198, Reg 2*].

3.51 INDIVIDUAL ACCOUNTS: OFF-BALANCE SHEET ARRANGEMENTS

If in any financial year

- the company is, or has been, party to arrangements that are not reflected in its balance sheet, and

- at the balance sheet date the risks or benefits arising from those arrangements are material,

the following information must be given in notes to the company's annual accounts.

(a) The nature and business purpose of the arrangements.

(b) The financial impact of the arrangements on the company.

The information need only be given to the extent necessary for enabling the financial position of the company to be assessed.

[*CA 2006, s 410A(1)–(3); SI 2008 No 393, Reg 8*].

3.52 GROUP ACCOUNTS: INTRODUCTION

The provisions in 3.53 to 3.73 relate to the general requirements for accounts of groups of companies. Unless otherwise stated, the provisions apply whether the groups' accounts concerned are Companies Act group accounts or IAS group accounts (see 3.54).

3.53 GROUP ACCOUNTS: DUTY TO PREPARE

If, at the end of a financial year, a company is a parent company (see APPENDIX 1 DEFINITIONS) the directors, as well as preparing individual accounts for the year *must* prepare group accounts for the year. This does not apply where

- the company is subject to the small companies regime under 5.2 ACCOUNTS: SMALL COMPANIES; or
- exemption applies under 3.54 (company included in group accounts of a larger group) or 3.55 (exclusion of subsidiary undertakings from consolidation)

but a company to which these provisions apply and which is exempt from the requirement to prepare group accounts, *may* nevertheless do so.

[*CA 2006, s 399*].

Applicable accounting framework. Subject to below

(a) companies, governed by the law of a Member State (ie incorporated in a Member State), whose securities (including debt securities) are admitted to trading on a regulated market in any EEA State *must* prepare their group accounts in accordance with international accounting standards ('*IAS group accounts*', see below); and

(b) companies not falling within (*a*) above may

(i) prepare their group accounts in accordance with *CA 2006, s 404* ('*Companies Act group accounts*', see below); or

(ii) prepare IAS group accounts.

But

- the group accounts of a parent company that is a charity must be Companies Act group accounts; and
- after the first financial year in which the directors of a parent company prepare IAS group accounts ('*the first IAS year*'), all subsequent group accounts of the company must be prepared in accordance with international accounting stan-

dards unless there is a *'relevant change of circumstance'*. This is subject to the right to change to Companies Act accounts set out in *CA 2006, s 403(5A)* (see below) A relevant change of circumstance occurs if, at any time during or after the first IAS year

(i) the company becomes a subsidiary undertaking of another undertaking that does not prepare IAS group accounts;

(ii) the company ceases to be a company with securities admitted to trading on a regulated market in an EEA State; or

(iii) a parent undertaking of the company ceases to be an undertaking with securities admitted to trading on a regulated market in an EEA State.

After a financial year in which IAS group accounts are prepared, the directors may change to preparing Companies Act individual accounts for a reason other than a relevant change of circumstance, provided they have not changed to Companies Act accounts in the five years preceding the first day of that financial year

If, having changed to preparing Companies Act group accounts, the directors again prepare IAS group accounts for the company, the above provisions again apply as if the first financial year for which such accounts are again prepared were the first IAS year.

[*CA 2006, s 403; SI 2012 No 2301, Reg 15, 16, 17*].

See APPENDIX 1 DEFINITIONS for the current EEA States.

Companies Act group accounts. Companies Act group accounts must comprise

- a consolidated balance sheet dealing with the state of affairs of the parent company and its 'subsidiary undertakings' (see APPENDIX 1 DEFINITIONS); and
- a consolidated profit and loss account dealing with the profit or loss of the parent company and its subsidiary undertakings.

The accounts must give a true and fair view of the state of affairs as at the end of the financial year, and the profit or loss for the financial year, of the undertakings included in the consolidation as a whole, so far as concerns members of the company.

Companies Act group accounts must comply with the provisions made by Regulations as described in **3.57** to **3.63** as to the form and content of the consolidated balance sheet and consolidated profit and loss account and additional information to be provided by way of notes to the accounts. If compliance with the those provisions, and any other provisions made by or under *CA 2006*, as to the matters to be included in a company's group accounts or in notes to those accounts would not be sufficient to give a true and fair view, the necessary additional information must be given in the accounts or notes. If, in special circumstances, compliance with any of those provisions is inconsistent with the requirement to give a true and fair view, the directors must depart from that provision to the extent necessary to give a true and fair view. Particulars of any such departure, the reasons for it and its effect must be given in a note to the accounts.

[*CA 2006, s 404*].

See **2.16** ACCOUNTS: GENERAL for 'true and fair view'.

IAS group accounts. The provisions described in **3.57** to **3.63** do not apply to IAS group accounts. Instead, consolidated accounts must be prepared on the basis of the accounting standards issued by the International Accounting Standard Board (IASB) that are adopted by the European Commission. [*EC Council Regulation 1606/2002, Art 4*]. Instead of the profit and loss account and balance sheet required under *CA 2006*, a company must prepare primary financial statements and supporting notes as required under international accounting standards. See **2.15 ACCOUNTS: GENERAL** for a list of accounting standards.

Where the directors of a company prepare IAS group accounts, they must state in the notes to those accounts that the accounts have been prepared in accordance with international accounting standards. [*CA 2006, s 406*].

3.54 Exemption for parent companies included in accounts of larger group

(1) *Where a company's immediate parent undertaking is established under the law of an EEA State*

Subject to *all* the conditions below being fulfilled, a company is exempt from the requirement to prepare group accounts if

- it is itself a subsidiary undertaking;
- its immediate parent undertaking is established under the law of an EEA State; and
- either

(i) the company is a wholly-owned subsidiary of that parent undertaking; or

(ii) that parent undertaking holds more than 50% of the company's allotted shares and no notice requesting the preparation of group accounts has been served on the company by shareholders with aggregate holdings amounting to either more than half of the remaining allotted shares in the company or 5% of the total allotted shares in the company. Such notice must be served not later than six months after the end of the financial year *before that* to which it relates.

For the purposes of (ii) above, shares held by a wholly-owned subsidiary of the parent undertaking are attributed to the parent undertaking, as are shares held on behalf of the parent undertaking or a wholly-owned subsidiary of it.

The conditions are as follows.

(i) The company must be included in consolidated accounts for a larger group drawn up to the same date, or to an earlier date in the same financial year, by a parent undertaking established under the law of an EEA State.

(ii) Those accounts must be drawn up and audited, and the parent undertaking's annual report must be drawn up, according to that law, in accordance with the *EC 7th Directive (83/349/EEC)* or in accordance with international accounting standards.

(iii) The company must disclose in its individual accounts that it is exempt from the obligation to prepare and deliver group accounts.

(iv) The company must state in its individual accounts the name of the parent undertaking that draws up the group accounts referred to above and

- if it is incorporated outside the UK, the country in which it is incorporated; and
- if it is unincorporated, the address of its principal place of business.

(v) The company must deliver to the Registrar of Companies under **2.10** ACCOUNTS: GENERAL, and within the period allowed for delivering its individual accounts under **2.11** ACCOUNTS: GENERAL, copies of the group accounts and the parent undertaking's annual report, together with the auditor's report on them.

(vi) If any document comprised in accounts and reports delivered under (v) above is in a language other than English, there must be annexed thereto a certified translation of it into English.

(vii) None of the 'securities' of the company must be admitted to trading on a regulated market in an EEA State.

Shares held by directors of a company for the purpose of complying with any share qualification requirement are disregarded for the above purposes in determining whether the company is a wholly-owned subsidiary.

[*CA 2006, s 400(1)–(5)*].

(2) *Where a company's parent undertaking is not established under the law of an EEA State*

Subject to *all* the conditions below being fulfilled, a company is exempt from the requirement to prepare group accounts if

- it is itself a subsidiary undertaking;
- its parent undertaking is not established under the law of an EEA State; and
- either

  (i) the company is a wholly-owned subsidiary of that parent undertaking; or

  (ii) that parent undertaking holds more than 50% of the company's allotted shares and no notice requesting the preparation of group accounts has been served on the company by shareholders with aggregate holdings amounting to either more than half of the remaining allotted shares in the company or 5% of the total allotted shares in the company. Such notice must be served not later than six months after the end of the financial year *before that* to which it relates.

  For the purposes of (ii) above, shares held by a wholly-owned subsidiary of the parent undertaking are attributed to the parent undertaking, as are shares held on behalf of the parent undertaking or a wholly-owned subsidiary of it.

The conditions are as follows.

(i) The company and all of its subsidiary undertakings must be included in consolidated accounts for a larger group drawn up to the same date, or to an earlier date in the same financial year, by a parent undertaking.

(ii) Those accounts and, where appropriate, the group's annual report, must be drawn up in accordance with the provisions of the *EC 7th Directive (83/349/EEC)* or in a manner equivalent to consolidated accounts and consolidated annual reports so drawn up.

(iii) The consolidated accounts must be audited by one or more persons authorised to audit accounts under the law under which the parent undertaking which draws them up is established.

(iv) The company must disclose in its individual accounts that it is exempt from the obligation to prepare and deliver group accounts.

(v) The company must state in its individual accounts the name of the parent undertaking which draws up the group accounts referred to above and

- if it is incorporated outside the UK, the country in which it is incorporated; and
- if it is unincorporated, the address of its principal place of business.

(vi) The company must deliver to the Registrar of Companies under **2.10 Accounts: General**, and within the period allowed for delivering its individual accounts under **2.11 Accounts: General**, copies of the group accounts and, where appropriate, the consolidated annual report, together with the auditor's report on them.

(vii) If any document comprised in accounts and reports delivered under (vi) above is in a language other than English, there must be annexed thereto a translation of it into English.

(viii) None of the 'securities' of the company must be admitted to trading on a regulated market in an EEA State.

Shares held by directors of a company for the purpose of complying with any share qualification requirement are disregarded for the above purposes in determining whether the company is a wholly-owned subsidiary.

[*CA 2006, s 401(1)–(5)*].

For the purpose of (1)(vii) and (2)(viii) above, '*securities*' includes

- shares and stock;
- debentures, including debenture stock, loan stock, bonds, certificates of deposit and other instruments creating or acknowledging indebtedness;
- warrants or other instruments entitling the holder to subscribe for securities falling within either of the above; and
- certificates or other instruments which confer
  - (i) property rights in respect of a security falling within any of the above;
  - (ii) any right to acquire, dispose of, underwrite or convert a security, being a right to which the holder would be entitled if he held any such security to which the certificate or other instrument relates; or
  - (iii) a contractual right (other than an option) to acquire any such security otherwise than by subscription.

[*CA 2006, ss 400(6), 401(6)*].

3.55 Exclusion of subsidiary undertakings from consolidation

Where a parent company prepares Companies Act group accounts (see **3.53**) all subsidiary undertakings of the company must normally be included in the consolidation. There are, however, exclusions, as listed below. If *all* of a parent company's subsidiary undertakings could be excluded from consolidation in Companies Act group accounts, the parent company need not prepare group accounts.

(a) A subsidiary undertaking may be excluded from consolidation if its inclusion is not material for the purpose of giving a true and fair view (see **2.16 Accounts: General**). Two or more undertakings can be excluded only if they are not material taken together.

(b) A subsidiary undertaking may be excluded from consolidation where

(i) severe long-term restrictions substantially hinder the exercise of the parent company's rights over the assets or management of the undertaking; or

(ii) the information necessary to prepare group accounts cannot be obtained without disproportionate expense or undue delay; or

(iii) the interest of the parent company is held exclusively with a view to subsequent resale.

The references in (i) and (iii) above to, respectively, the rights and the interest of the parent company are references to rights and interests held by or attributed to it for the purposes of the definition of 'parent undertaking' (see **Appendix 1 Definitions**) in the absence of which it would not be the parent company.

[*CA 2006, ss 402, 405*].

3.56 GROUP ACCOUNTS: TREATMENT OF INDIVIDUAL PROFIT AND LOSS ACCOUNT WHERE GROUP ACCOUNTS PREPARED

Where a company prepares group accounts in accordance with *CA 2006* and the notes to its individual balance sheet show the company's profit or loss for the financial year (determined in accordance with *CA 2006*), its individual profit and loss account

- need not contain the information specified in

  (i) *CA 2006, s 411* (information about employee numbers and costs, see **3.49**); or

  (ii) *SI 2008 No 410, Sch 1 paras 65–69* (information supplementing the profit and loss, see **3.26** to **3.30**); and

- may be omitted from the company's annual accounts, although it must still be approved in accordance with *CA 2006, s 414(1)* (see **2.2 Accounts: General**).

The above exemption is conditional upon the company's annual accounts disclosing the fact that the exemption applies.

[*CA 2006, s 408; SI 2008 No 393, Reg 10; SI 2008 No 410, Reg 3(2)*].

3.57 GROUP ACCOUNTS: FORM AND CONTENT OF COMPANIES ACT GROUP ACCOUNTS

Where the directors of a parent company

- prepare Companies Act group accounts, and
- the company is not a banking company or an insurance company,

the accounts must comply with the provisions in this paragraph and in **3.58** to **3.63** as to the form and content of the consolidated balance sheet and consolidated profit and loss account, and additional information to be provided by way of notes to the accounts. [*SI 2008 No 410, Reg 9(1)*].

The group accounts must comply, so far as practicable, with the provisions of

- *SI 2008 No 410, Sch 1* (see **3.3** to **3.31**),
- *CA 2006, s 411* (employee numbers and cost, see **3.49**),
- *SI 2008 No 489, Reg 5(1)(b)* (disclosure of auditor's remuneration, see **3.50**(*b*)), and
- *CA 2006 s 410A* (off-balance sheet arrangements, see **3.51**)

as if the '*group*' (meaning, for these purposes, all the undertakings included in the consolidation) were a single company.

[*CA 2006, ss 410A(5), 411(7), SI 2008 No 393, Reg 11; SI 2008 No 410, Sch 6 para 1; SI 2008 No 489, Reg 6(1)*].

The consolidated balance sheet and profit and loss account must incorporate in full the information contained in the individual accounts of the undertakings included in the consolidation, subject to the adjustments authorised or required by under this paragraph and **3.58** to **3.63** and to such other adjustments (if any) that are appropriate in accordance with generally accepted accounting principles or practice.

Subsidiaries with different financial years. If the financial year of a subsidiary undertaking included in the consolidation does not end with that of the parent company, the group accounts must be made up

- from the accounts of the subsidiary undertaking for its financial year last ending before the end of the parent company's financial year (provided that year ended no more than three months before that of the parent company); or
- from interim accounts prepared by the subsidiary undertaking as at the end of the parent company's financial year.

[*SI 2008 No 410, Sch 6 para 2*].

But note that the directors of a parent company must secure that, except where in their opinion there are good reasons against it, the financial year of each of its subsidiary undertakings coincides with the company's own financial year. [*CA 2006, s 390(5)*].

Assets and liabilities. Where assets and liabilities to be included in the group accounts have been valued or otherwise determined by undertakings according to accounting rules differing from those used for the group accounts, the values or amounts must be adjusted so as to accord with the rules used for the group accounts (unless such adjustments are not material for the purpose of giving a true and fair view). If it appears to the parent company's directors that there are special reasons for doing so, they may depart from this requirement, but particulars of the departure, the reasons for it and its effect must be given in a note to the accounts. [*SI 2008 No 410, Sch 6 para 3*].

Accounting rules. Any differences between the accounting rules used for a parent company's individual accounts for a financial year and those used for its group accounts must be disclosed in a note to the group accounts. The reasons for the difference must be given. [*SI 2008 No 410, Sch 6 para 4*].

Materiality. Amounts that in the particular context of any provision in this paragraph and **3.58** to **3.63** are not material may be disregarded for the purposes of that provision. [*SI 2008 No 410, Sch 6 para 5*].

Accounts in euros. The amounts set out in the annual accounts of a company may also be shown in the same accounts translated into euros. If so, the amounts must have been translated at the exchange rate prevailing at the balance sheet date and that rate must be disclosed in the notes to the accounts. [*CA 2006, s 469(1), (3)*].

3.58 Elimination of group transactions

In preparing group accounts, the following must be eliminated (unless the amounts concerned are not material for the purpose of giving a true and fair view, see **2.16** ACCOUNTS: GENERAL).

- Debts and claims between undertakings included in the consolidation.
- Income and expenditure relating to transactions between such undertakings.
- Profits and losses resulting from transactions between such undertakings and included in the book value of assets. This may be effected in proportion to the group's interest in the shares of the undertakings concerned.

[*SI 2008 No 410, Sch 6 para 6*].

3.59 Acquisition and merger accounting

The following provisions apply where an undertaking becomes a subsidiary undertaking of the parent company, such an event being referred to as an '*acquisition*'. An acquisition must be accounted for by the 'acquisition method of accounting' unless the conditions for accounting for it as a merger are met and the 'merger method of accounting' is adopted. [*SI 2008 No 410, Sch 6 paras 7, 8*].

(1) **Acquisition method of accounting**

Under the '*acquisition method of accounting*'

- the identifiable assets and liabilities of the undertaking acquired must be included in the consolidated balance sheet at their fair values as at the date of acquisition;
- the income and expenditure of the undertaking acquired must be brought into the group accounts only as from the date of the acquisition; and
- the interest of the parent company and its subsidiary undertakings in the adjusted capital and reserves of the undertaking acquired must be set off against the acquisition cost of the interest in the shares of the undertaking held by the parent company and its subsidiary undertakings. The resulting amount, if positive, must be treated as goodwill and, if negative, as a negative consolidation difference.

[*SI 2008 No 410, Sch 6 para 9*].

Where a group is acquired, references above to shares of the undertaking acquired should be read as references to shares of the parent undertaking of the group acquired. Other references to the undertaking acquired should be read as references to the group acquired. References to the assets and liabilities, income and expenditure and capital and reserves of the undertaking acquired should be read as references to those of the group acquired, after making the set-offs and other adjustments required by **3.57** to **3.63** in the case of group accounts. [*SI 2008 No 410, Sch 6 para 12*].

(2) **Merger method of accounting**

The '*merger method of accounting*' can only be used if the following conditions are satisfied.

- At least 90% of the nominal value of the 'relevant shares' in the undertaking acquired (excluding any shares in the undertaking held as treasury shares) is held by, or on behalf of, the parent company and its subsidiary undertakings.

  '*Relevant shares*' are those carrying unrestricted rights to participate both in distributions and in the assets of the undertaking upon liquidation.
- That proportion was attained pursuant to an arrangement providing for the issue of equity shares by the parent company or one or more of its subsidiary undertakings.
- The fair value of any consideration other than the issue of equity shares given pursuant to the arrangement by the parent company and its subsidiary undertakings did not exceed 10% of the nominal value of the equity shares issued.
- Adoption of the merger method of accounting accords with generally accepted accounting principles or practice.

[*SI 2008 No 410, Sch 6 para 10*].

Where the above conditions are satisfied

- the assets and liabilities of the undertaking acquired must be brought into the group accounts at the figures at which they stand in the undertaking's accounts, subject to any adjustment authorised or required by the provisions in **3.57** to **3.63**;
- the income and expenditure of the undertaking acquired must be included in the group accounts for the entire financial year, including the period before the acquisition;
- the group accounts must show comparative figures for the previous financial year as if the undertaking acquired had been included in the consolidation throughout that year; and
- the nominal value of the issued share capital of the undertaking acquired held by the parent company and its subsidiary undertakings must be set off against the aggregate of

  (i) the appropriate amount in respect of 'qualifying shares' issued by the parent company or its subsidiary undertakings in consideration for the acquisition of shares in the undertaking acquired; and

  (ii) the fair value of any other consideration for the acquisition of shares in the undertaking acquired, determined as at the date when those shares were acquired.

The resulting amount must be shown as an adjustment to the consolidated reserves.

'*Qualifying shares*' means

- shares to which *CA 1985, s 131* or *CA 2006, s 612* applies (merger relief, see **46.2 Share Premium**), in respect of which the appropriate amount is the nominal value; or

- shares to which *CA 1985, s 132* or *CA 2006, s 611* applies (relief in respect of group reconstructions, see **46.3 Share Premium**), in respect of which the appropriate amount is the nominal value together with any 'minimum premium value' as there defined.

[*SI 2008 No 410, Sch 6 para 11*].

Where a group is acquired, references above to shares of the undertaking acquired should be read as references to shares of the parent undertaking of the group acquired. Other references to the undertaking acquired should be read as references to the group acquired. References to the assets and liabilities and to income and expenditure of the undertaking acquired should be read as references to those of the group acquired, after making the set-offs and other adjustments required by **3.57** to **3.63** in the case of group accounts. [*SI 2008 No 410, Sch 6 para 12*].

(3) **Information to be given in the notes to the accounts**

Subject to below, the following information with respect to acquisitions taking place in the financial year must be given in a note to the accounts (although the information in (*c*) and (*d*) below need only be given in relation to an acquisition which significantly affects the figures shown in the group accounts).

(a) The name of the undertaking acquired or, where a group was acquired, the name of the parent undertaking of that group.

(b) Whether the acquisition has been accounted for by the acquisition or the merger method of accounting.

(c) The composition and fair value of the consideration for the acquisition given by the parent company and its subsidiary undertakings.

(d) Where the acquisition method of accounting has been adopted, the book values immediately prior to the acquisition, and the fair values at the date of acquisition, of each class of assets and liabilities of the undertaking (or group) acquired in tabular form. This must include a statement of the amount of any goodwill or negative consolidation difference arising on the acquisition, together with an explanation of any significant adjustments made.

In ascertaining for these purposes the profit or loss of a group, the book values and fair values of assets and liabilities of a group or the amount of the assets and liabilities of a group, the set-offs and other adjustments required by **3.57** to **3.63** in the case of group accounts must be made.

[*SI 2008 No 410, Sch 6 para 13*].

Subject to below, the following information must also be stated in a note to the accounts.

(i) The cumulative amount of goodwill resulting from acquisitions in that and earlier financial years which has been written off otherwise than in the consolidated profit and loss account for that or any earlier financial year. That figure must be shown net of any goodwill attributable to subsidiary undertakings or businesses disposed of prior to the balance sheet date.

(ii) Where, during the financial year, there has been a disposal of an undertaking or group which significantly affects the figure shown in the group accounts, the name of that undertaking (or parent undertaking of that group) and the extent to which the profit or loss shown in the group accounts is attributable to profit or loss of that undertaking or group.

[*SI 2008 No 410, Sch 6 paras 14, 15*].

The information required by (*a*) to (*d*) and (i) and (ii) above need not be disclosed with respect to an undertaking which is either

- established under the law of a country outside the UK, or
- carries on business outside the UK

if, in the opinion of the directors of the parent company, the disclosure would be seriously prejudicial to the business of that undertaking or to the business of the parent company or any of its subsidiary undertakings *and* the Secretary of State agrees that the information should not be disclosed.

[*SI 2008 No 410, Sch 6 para 16*].

3.60 Minority interests

The formats for the balance sheet (see **3.4**) and profit and loss account (see **3.5**) have effect in relation to group accounts with the following additions.

(1) *Balance sheet formats*

There must be shown, as a separate item and under an appropriate heading, the amount of capital and reserves attributable to shares in subsidiary undertakings included in the consolidation held by or, on behalf of, persons other than the parent company and its subsidiary undertakings.

For the purposes of *SI 2008 No 410, Sch 1 para 4(1)(2)* (power of directors to adapt or combine items, see **3.3**(6)), this additional item is treated as one to which a letter is assigned (and not an Arabic number).

(2) *Profit and loss account formats*

There must be shown, as a separate item and under an appropriate heading,

- the amount of any profit or loss on ordinary activities, and
- the amount of any profit or loss on extraordinary activities,

attributable to shares in subsidiary undertakings included in the consolidation held by, or on behalf of, persons other than the parent company and its subsidiary undertakings.

For the purposes of *SI 2008 No 410, Sch 1 para 4(1)(2)* (power of directors to adapt or combine items, see **3.3**(6)), these additional items are treated as ones to which an Arabic number is assigned.

[*SI 2008 No 410, Sch 6 para 17*].

3.61 Joint ventures

Where an undertaking included in the consolidation manages another undertaking (the 'joint venture') jointly with one or more undertakings not included in the consolidation, the joint venture may, if it is not

- a body corporate, or
- a subsidiary undertaking of the parent company,

be dealt with in the group accounts by the method of proportional consolidation.

The provisions in **3.57** to **3.63** relating to the preparation of consolidated accounts apply, with any necessary modifications, to proportional consolidation under this provisions. [*SI 2008 No 410, Sch 6 para 18*].

3.62 Associated undertakings

Definition. An '*associated undertaking*' means an undertaking in which an undertaking included in the consolidation has a 'participating interest' (see **Appendix 1 Definitions**) and over whose operating and financial policy it exercises a significant influence, and which is not

- a subsidiary undertaking of the parent company; or
- a joint venture dealt with in **3.61**.

Where an undertaking holds 20% or more of the voting rights in another undertaking, it is presumed to exercise such an influence over it unless the contrary is shown. The voting rights in an undertaking means the rights conferred on shareholders in respect of their shares (or, if the undertaking does not have a share capital, on members) to vote at general meetings of the undertaking on all (or substantially all) matters.

In determining whether 20% or more of the voting rights are held, the provisions in **Appendix 1 Definitions** apply.

Disclosure requirements. The balance sheet and profit and loss account formats in **3.4** and **3.5** respectively are modified as below in relation to group accounts to give information in respect of associated undertakings.

(1) *Balance sheet formats*

The item 'Participating interests' in each of the two formats (item B.III.3 in Format 1 and item B.III.3 under 'ASSETS' in Format 2) is replaced by two items, 'Interests in associated undertakings' and 'Other participating interests'.

(2) *Profit and loss account formats*

The item 'Income from participating interests' in each of the four formats (item 8 in Format 1, item 10 in Format 2, item B.4 in Format 3 and item B.6 in Format 4) is replaced by two items, 'Income from interests in associated undertakings' and 'Income from other participating interests'.

The interest of an undertaking in an associated undertaking, and the amount of profit or loss attributable to such an interest, must be shown by the equity method of accounting (including dealing with any goodwill arising in accordance with **3.8**. But the equity method of accounting need not be applied if the amounts in question are not material for the purpose of giving a true and fair view.

Where the associated undertaking is itself a parent undertaking, the net assets and profits or losses to be taken into account are those of the parent and its subsidiary undertakings (after making any consolidation adjustments).

[*SI 2008 No 410, Sch 6 paras 19–21*].

3.63 Related party transactions

Particulars must be given of transactions (other than intra-group transactions) which the parent company, or other undertakings included in the consolidation, have entered into with 'related parties' if these transactions are material and have not been concluded under normal market conditions.

The particulars must include

- the amounts of such transactions;
- the nature of the related party relationship; and
- other information about the transactions necessary for an understanding of the financial position of the undertakings included in the consolidation taken as a whole.

Information about individual transactions may be aggregated according to their nature, except where separate information is necessary for an understanding of the effects of related party transaction on the financial position of the undertakings included in the consolidation taken as a whole.

'*Related party*' has the same meaning as in international accounting standards.

[*SI 2008 No 410, Sch 6 para 22*].

3.64 GROUP ACCOUNTS: RELATED UNDERTAKINGS

Where a company is preparing group accounts, its Companies Act or IAS accounts must comply with the provisions in **3.65** to **3.73** as to the information about related undertakings to be given in the notes to the company's accounts. There are two exceptions.

Exception 1 - Statutory

(1) **Exemption**

The information (other than that in **3.68** and **3.72**) need not be disclosed with respect to an undertaking that

- is established under the law of a country outside the UK, or
- carries on business outside the UK,

but only if

- in the opinion of the directors of the company, the disclosure would be seriously prejudicial to the business of
  - (i) that undertaking;
  - (ii) the company;
  - (iii) any of the company's subsidiary undertakings; or
  - (iv) any other undertaking which is included in the consolidation; and
- the Secretary of State agrees that the information need not be disclosed.

Where advantage is taken of this exemption, a note to that effect must be included in the company's accounts.

[*CA 2006, s 409(5); SI 2008 No 410, Reg 7*].

Exception 2

(2) **Alternative compliance in cases of excessive length**

Where the directors are of the opinion that the number of undertakings in respect of which the company is required to disclose information under any provision described in **3.65** to **3.73** is such that compliance would result in information of excessive length being given in the notes to the accounts, information need only be given in respect of

(a) the undertakings whose results or financial position, in the directors' opinion, principally affected the figures shown in the company's annual accounts; and

(b) undertakings excluded from consolidation under **3.55**(*b*).

If advantage is taken of this, then

(i) the notes to the company's annual accounts must include a statement that the information is given only with respect to undertakings of the type mentioned in (*a*) and (*b*) above; and

(ii) the full information (ie both that which is disclosed and that which is not) must be annexed to the next annual return delivered to the Registrar of Companies after the accounts in question have been approved by the board.

If a company fails to comply with (ii) above, an offence is committed by the company and every officer of the company who is in default. A person guilty of such an offence is liable, on summary conviction, to a fine not exceeding level 3 on the standard scale and, for continued contravention, a daily default fine not exceeding one-tenth of level 3 on the standard scale. See **29.1 Offences and Legal Proceedings** for the standard scale. [*CA 2006, s 410*].

In the above provisions, and in **3.65** to **3.73**:

- '*The group*' means the group consisting of the parent company and its subsidiary undertakings. [*SI 2008 No 410, Sch 4 para 15*].
- References to shares held by the group are to any shares held by or on behalf of the parent company or any of its subsidiary undertakings. But any shares held on behalf of a person other than the parent company or any of its subsidiary undertakings are not to be treated as held by the group. [*SI 2008 No 410, Sch 4 para 22(3)*].
- Shares held by way of security must be treated as held by the person providing the security

(i) where the rights attached to the shares are exercisable only in accordance with that person's instructions (disregarding any right to exercise them in order to preserve the value of, or realise, the security); and

(ii) as regards shares held in connection with the granting of loans as part of normal business activities, where the rights attached to the shares are exercisable only in that person's interests (disregarding any right to exercise them in order to preserve the value of, or realise, the security).

[*SI 2008 No 410, Sch 4 para 22(4)*].

3.65 Subsidiary undertakings

Subject to **3.64**, where, at the end of the financial year, the company has subsidiary undertakings the following must be stated in respect of each of them.

(a) Its name.

(b) If the undertaking is incorporated outside the UK, the country in which it is incorporated.

(c) If it is unincorporated, the address of its principal place of business.

(d) Whether the subsidiary undertaking is included in the consolidation and, if it is not, the reasons for excluding it.

(e) Which of the conditions in **Appendix 1**(*a*)–(*f*) **Definitions** applies to make it a subsidiary undertaking of its immediate parent undertaking But that information need not be given if the relevant condition is that specified in **Appendix 1**(*a*) **Definitions** (holding of a majority of the voting rights) and the immediate parent undertaking holds the same proportion of the shares in the undertaking as it holds voting rights.

[*SI 2008 No 410, Sch 4 paras 1, 16*].

3.66 *Holdings in subsidiary undertakings*

Subject to **3.64**, with respect to the shares of a subsidiary undertaking held by

- the parent company, and
- the group,

there must be stated

- the identity of each class of shares held, and
- the proportion of the nominal value of the shares of that class represented by those shares.

This information must (if different) be shown separately as regards the parent company and group.

[*SI 2008 No 410, Sch 4 para 17*].

For the above purposes, there must be attributed to the parent company shares held on its behalf by any person. But shares held on behalf of a person other than the parent company must be treated as not held by that company. [*SI 2008 No 410, Sch 4 para 22(2)*].

3.67 *Financial information about subsidiary undertakings not included in the consolidated accounts*

Subject to **3.64**, with respect to each subsidiary undertaking not included in the consolidated accounts, there must be shown

- the aggregate amount of its capital and reserves as at the end of its relevant financial year; and
- its profit or loss for that year.

This information need not be given if

- the company is exempt under **3.54** from the requirement to prepare group accounts (parent company included in the accounts of a larger group);

- the company's investment in the subsidiary undertaking is included in the company's accounts by way of the equity method of valuation;
- the company's holding is less than 50% of the nominal value of the shares in the undertaking *and* the subsidiary undertaking is not required by any provision of *CA 2006* to deliver to the Registrar of Companies a copy of its balance sheet for its 'relevant financial year' and does not otherwise publish that balance sheet in the UK or elsewhere; or
- it is not material.

The '*relevant financial year*' of a subsidiary undertaking is

- if its financial year ends with that of the company, that year; and
- if not, its financial year ending last before the end of the company's financial year.

[*SI 2008 No 410, Sch 4 para 2*].

3.68 *Shares and debentures of company held by subsidiary undertakings*

Subject to **3.64**, the number, description and amount of the shares in the company held by, or on behalf of, its subsidiary undertakings must be disclosed. This does not apply in relation to shares in the case of which the subsidiary undertaking is concerned as

- personal representative; or
- trustee, unless the company, or any of its subsidiary undertakings is 'beneficially interested under the trust', otherwise than by way of security only for the purposes of a transaction entered into by it in the ordinary course of a business which includes the lending of money.

[*SI 2008 No 410, Sch 4 para 3*].

In determining whether the company is '*beneficially interested under the trust*', certain residual interests under pension and employees' share schemes, employer's charges and other rights of recovery under such schemes, and a trustee's right to expenses, remuneration, indemnity, etc are disregarded. See *SI 2008 No 410, Sch 4 paras 24–27* for full details.

3.69 Joint ventures

Subject to **3.64**, where an undertaking is dealt with in the consolidated accounts by the method of proportional consolidation (in accordance with **3.61**), the following information must be given in respect of the undertaking.

- Its name.
- The address of its principal place of business.
- The factors on which joint management of the undertaking is based.
- The proportion of its capital held by undertakings included in the consolidation.
- Where its financial year did not end with that of the company, the date on which a financial year of the undertaking last ended before that date.

[*SI 2008 No 410, Sch 4 para 18*].

3.70 Associated undertakings

Subject to **3.64**, the following information must be given where an undertaking included in the consolidation has an interest in an associated undertaking.

(a) The name of the associated undertaking.

(b) If that undertaking is incorporated outside the UK, the country in which it is incorporated.

(c) If it is unincorporated, the address of its principal place of business.

(d) With respect to the shares of the undertaking held by the parent company and by the group,

- the identity of each class of shares held, and
- the proportion of the nominal value of the shares of that class represented by those shares,

giving details for the parent company and group separately.

'*Associated undertaking*' has the same meaning as in **3.63** and the information required above must be given notwithstanding that the amounts of net assets, profits or losses attributable to the interests held in the associated undertaking are not material in relation to the accounts themselves.

[*SI 2008 No 410, Sch 4 para 19*].

For the above purposes, there must be attributed to the parent company shares held on its behalf by any person. But shares held on behalf of a person other than the parent company must be treated as not held by that company. [*SI 2008 No 410, Sch 4 para 22(2)*].

3.71 Other significant holdings of parent company or group

Parent company holdings. Subject to **3.64**, where at the end of the financial year the parent company has a 'significant holding' in an undertaking which is not one of its subsidiary undertakings and does not fall within **3.69** or **3.70**, the following must be stated.

(a) The name of the undertaking.

(b) If the undertaking is incorporated outside the UK, the country in which it is incorporated.

(c) if it is unincorporated, the address of its principal place of business.

(d) The identity of each class of shares of the undertaking held by the parent company.

(e) The proportion of the nominal value of the shares of that class represented by those shares.

(f) The aggregate amount of the capital and reserves of the undertaking as at the end of its 'relevant financial year'.

(g) Its profit or loss for that year.

A '*significant holding*' is a holding which amounts to 20% or more of the nominal value of any class of shares in the undertaking *or* the amount of which (as stated or included in the parent company's individual accounts) exceeds one-fifth of the amount (as so stated) of the parent company's assets.

The '*relevant financial year*' of an undertaking for these purposes is, if its financial year ends with that of the company, that year, and if it does not, its financial year ending last before the end of the company's financial year.

Exemption. The information in (*f*) and (*g*) above need not be given if

- the undertaking in question is not required by any provision of *CA 2006* to deliver a copy of its balance sheet for its relevant financial year and does not otherwise publish that balance sheet in the UK or elsewhere *and* the company's holding is less than 50% of the nominal value of the shares in the undertaking; or
- it is not material.

[*SI 2008 No 410, Sch 4 paras 4–6*].

For the above purposes, there must be attributed to the parent company shares held on its behalf by any person. But shares held on behalf of a person other than the parent company must be treated as not held by that company. [*SI 2008 No 410, Sch 4 para 22(2)*].

Group holdings. Subject to **3.64**, where at the end of the financial year the group has a 'significant holding' in an undertaking which is not a subsidiary undertaking of the parent company and does not fall within **3.69** or **3.70**, the same information must be given as under (*a*) to (*g*) above (and with the same exemption as above), substituting 'group' for 'parent company' in (*d*) and in the definition of 'significant holding'. [*SI 2008 No 410, Sch 4 para 20*].

3.72 Parent company's or group's membership of certain undertakings

Where, at the end of the financial year, the company or group is a member of a 'qualifying undertaking' the following must be stated.

(a) The name and legal form of the undertaking.

(b) The address of its registered office (whether in or outside the UK) or, if it does not have such an office, its head office (whether in or outside the UK).

(c) Where the undertaking is a qualifying partnership, either

  (i) a statement that a copy of the latest accounts of the partnership has been or is to be appended to the copy of the company's accounts sent to the Registrar of Companies; or

  (ii) the name of at least one body corporate (which may be the company itself) in whose group accounts the undertaking has been, or is to be, dealt with on a consolidated basis.

The information required by (*a*) and (*b*) above need not be given if not material and the information required by (*c*)(ii) above need not be given if the notes to the company's accounts disclose that advantage has been taken of the exemption in *regulation 7* of the *Partnerships (Accounts) Regulations 2008*.

A '*qualifying undertaking*' means

(a) a qualifying partnership; or

(b) an unlimited company each of whose members is

  (i) a limited company;

  (ii) another unlimited company each of whose members is a limited company; or

  (iii) a Scottish partnership each of whose members is a limited company,

and, for these purposes, references to a limited company, another unlimited company and a Scottish partnership include a comparable undertaking incorporated in, or formed under, the law of a country or territory outside the UK.

[*SI 2008 No 410, Sch 4 paras 7, 21*].

3.73 Information where parent company is a subsidiary undertaking

Subject to **3.64**, where the parent company is itself a subsidiary undertaking, the following information must be given.

(a) Particulars, as follows, with respect to the parent undertaking of the largest and smallest group of undertakings for which group accounts are drawn up and of which that company is a member.

  (i) The name of the parent undertaking.

  (ii) If the undertaking is incorporated outside the UK (in relation to accounts for financial years beginning before 6 April 2008, GB), the country in which it is incorporated.

  (iii) If it is unincorporated, the address of its principal place of business.

  (iv) If copies of the above-mentioned group accounts are available to the public, the addresses from which copies of the accounts can be obtained.

(b) Particulars, as follows, with respect to the company (which includes any body corporate) regarded by the directors as being that company's ultimate parent company.

  (i) Its name.

  (ii) If that company is incorporated outside the UK, the country in which it is incorporated (if known to the directors).

[*SI 2008 No 410, Sch 4 paras 8, 9*].

3.74 GROUP ACCOUNTS, UNQUOTED COMPANIES: DIRECTORS' REMUNERATION AND BENEFITS

Directors' remuneration. Companies Act and IAS group accounts for unquoted companies must comply with the provisions in **3.41** to **3.47**. [*SI 2008 No 410, Reg 8*].

Directors' benefits: advances, credits and guarantees. In the case of a parent company that prepares group accounts, the notes to the group accounts must show the following.

(a) In respect of any advance or credit granted to the directors of the parent company, by that company or by any of its subsidiary undertakings, details of

(i) its amount;

(ii) an indication of the interest rate;

(iii) its main conditions; and

(iv) any amounts repaid.

(b) In respect of any guarantee of any kind entered into on behalf of the directors of the parent company, by that company or by any of its subsidiary undertakings, details of

(i) its main terms;

(ii) the amount of the maximum liability that may be incurred by the company (or its subsidiary); and

(iii) any amount paid and any liability incurred by the company (or its subsidiary) for the purpose of fulfilling the guarantee (including any loss incurred by reason of enforcement of the guarantee).

There must also be stated in the notes to the accounts the totals of amounts stated under (*a*)(i), (*a*)(iv), (*b*)(ii) and (*b*)(iii).

The provisions apply to

- persons who were directors of the company at any time in the financial year to which the accounts relate; and
- every advance, credit or guarantee subsisting at any time in the financial year to which the accounts relate

(i) whenever it was entered into; and

(ii) whether or not the person concerned was a director of the company in question at the time it was entered into; and

(iii) in the case of an advance, credit or guarantee involving a subsidiary undertaking of that company, whether or not that undertaking was such a subsidiary undertaking at the time it was entered into.

[*CA 2006, s 413(2)–(7)*].

For the reporting requirements of directors' remuneration in quoted companies, see **19** **Directors' Remuneration Reports: Quoted Companies.**

4 Accounts: Medium-sized Companies

4.1 **Introduction**
4.2 **Meaning of 'medium-sized'**
4.3 Companies excluded from being treated as medium-sized
4.4 **Form and content of individual accounts**
4.5 **Accounts delivered to the Registrar of Companies**

Background. The provisions in this chapter apply, unless otherwise stated, to accounts for financial years beginning on or after 6 April 2008. The *Companies Act 2006 (Strategic Report and Directors' Report) Regulations 2013* ('the *2013 Regulations*') which are referred to in various parts of this chapter brought into force the requirement for a company to produce a strategic report for financial years ending on or after 30 September 2013.

4.1 INTRODUCTION

A company which qualifies as 'medium-sized' (see **4.2**) is, for most purposes, treated the same as a large company so that the provisions in **3 Accounts: Large Companies** and **2 Accounts: General** apply to it as for a large company. But this is subject to the following exceptions.

- In preparing its accounts, the company
  - (i) need not comply with the provisions relating to disclosure with respect to compliance with accounting standards or related party transactions;
  - (ii) need not comply with the full requirements relating to off-balance sheet arrangements; and
  - (iii) need not disclose the more detailed information on auditor's remuneration as requirements by larger companies.

  See **4.4**.
- The directors of the company may deliver abbreviated accounts to the Registrar of Companies. See **4.5**.

4.2 MEANING OF 'MEDIUM-SIZED'

(1) *Companies qualifying as medium-sized: general*

Subject to (2) below, a company qualifies as medium-sized

(a) in relation to its first financial year if the qualifying conditions below are met in that year; and

(b) in relation to a subsequent financial year if

- (i) the qualifying conditions are met in that year and the preceding financial year;
- (ii) the qualifying conditions are met in that year and the company qualified as medium-sized in relation to the preceding financial year; or
- (iii) the qualifying conditions were met in the preceding financial year and the company qualified as medium-sized in relation to that year.

The qualifying conditions are met by a company in a year in which it satisfies two or more of the following requirements.

Turnover	Not more than £25.9m
'Balance sheet total'	Not more than £12.9m
'Number of employees'	Not more than 250

Notes.

- For a period that is a company's financial year but not in fact a year, the maximum figures for turnover must be proportionately adjusted.
- The '*balance sheet total*' means the aggregate of the amounts shown as assets in the company's balance sheet.
- The '*number of employees*' means the average number of persons employed by the company in the year, calculated as

$$A \div B$$

where

A = the sum of the number of persons employed under contracts of service by the company for each month in the financial year (whether throughout the month or not)
B = the number of months in the financial year

- In determining under (*b*) above whether a company qualifies as medium-sized, the company is treated as having qualified as medium-sized in any previous financial year in which it would have so qualified if the amendments made to the qualifying conditions above for financial years *beginning* on or after 6 April 2008 had been in force.

[*CA 2006, s 465; SI 2008 No 393, Regs 2, 4*].

(2) *Companies qualifying as medium-sized: parent companies*

A parent company qualifies as a medium-sized company in relation to a financial year only if the group headed by it qualifies as a medium-sized group. A group qualifies as medium-sized

(a) in relation to the parent company's first financial year if the qualifying conditions below are met in that year; and

(b) in relation to a subsequent financial year of the parent company if

(i) the qualifying conditions are met in that year and the preceding financial year;

(ii) the qualifying conditions are met in that year and the group qualified as medium-sized in relation to the preceding financial year; or

(iii) the qualifying conditions were met in the preceding financial year and the group qualified as medium-sized in relation to that year.

The qualifying conditions are met by a group in a year in which it satisfies two or more of the following requirements.

Aggregate turnover	Not more than £25.9 million net (or £31.1m gross)
Aggregate balance sheet total	Not more than £12.9m net (or £15.5m gross)
Aggregate number of employees	Not more than 250

Notes.

- The aggregate figures are ascertained by aggregating the relevant figures determined as under (1) above for each member of the group.
- In relation to the aggregate figures for turnover and balance sheet total, 'net' means after any set-offs and other adjustments made to eliminate group transactions and 'gross' means without those set-offs and other adjustments.

  A company may satisfy any relevant requirement on the basis of either the net or the gross figure.
- The figures for each subsidiary undertaking are those included in its individual accounts for the relevant financial year, ie
  (i) if its financial year ends with that of the parent company, that financial year; and
  (ii) if not, its financial year ending last before the end of the financial year of the parent company.

  If those figures cannot be obtained without disproportionate expense or undue delay, the latest available figures can be taken.
- In determining under (*b*) above whether a group qualifies as medium-sized, the group is treated as having qualified as medium-sized in any previous financial year in which it would have so qualified if the amendments made to the qualifying conditions above for financial years *beginning* on or after 6 April 2008 had been in force.

[*CA 2006, s 466, SI 2008 No 393, Regs 2, 4*].

4.3 Companies excluded from being treated as medium-sized

A company is not entitled to take advantage of any of the provisions relating to medium-sized companies if it was at any time within the financial year in question

(a) a public company;

(b) a company that has permission under *FSMA 2000, Pt 4* to carry on a regulated activity or carries on insurance market activity; or

(c) a member of an 'ineligible group'.

A group is an '*ineligible group*' if any of its members is

(i) a public company;

(ii) a body corporate (other than a company) whose shares are admitted to trading on a regulated market;

(iii) a person (other than a small company) who has permission under *FSMA 2000, Pt 4* to carry on a regulated activity;

(iv) a small company that is an authorised insurance company, a banking company, an e-money issuer, a 'MiFID investment firm' or a UCITS management company; or

(v) a person who carries on insurance market activity;

and a company is a small company for these purposes if it qualified as small in relation to its last financial year ending on or before the end of the financial year in question.

The above provisions do not prevent a company from taking advantage of *CA 2006, s 417(7)* (business review: non-financial information, see **20.5 Directors' Reports**) by reason only of its having been a member of an ineligible group at any time within the financial year in question.

See **Appendix 1 Definitions** for the meaning of 'MiFID investment firm'.

[*CA 2006, s 467; SI 2008 No 393, Reg 7*].

4.4 FORM AND CONTENT OF INDIVIDUAL ACCOUNTS

Apart from the exceptions below, there are no special provisions for the form and content of the individual accounts of 'medium-sized' companies. Such companies must therefore prepare individual accounts complying with the full requirements in **3 Accounts: Large Companies**.

The exceptions to this general are as follows.

(1) Where the directors of the company are preparing Companies Act individual accounts, those individual accounts *need not* comply with the requirements of

- *SI 2008 No 410, Sch 1 para 45* (disclosure with respect to compliance with accounting standards, see **3.16 Accounts: Large Companies**);
- *SI 2008 No 410, Sch 1 para 72* (related party transactions, see **3.31 Accounts: Large Companies**); or
- *CA 2006, s 410A(2)(b)* (financial impact of off-balance sheet arrangements on the company, see **3.51**(*b*) **Accounts: Large Companies**).

(2) The accounts do not have to comply with the more detailed requirements on disclosure of auditor's remuneration required by larger companies (see **3.50 Accounts: Large Companies**).

Instead, a note to the annual accounts of a medium-sized company must disclose

- the amount of any remuneration receivable by the company's auditor for the auditing of those accounts;
- where the remuneration includes benefits in kind, the nature and estimated money-value of those benefit; and

Where more than one person has been appointed as a company's auditor in respect of the period to which the accounts relate, separate disclosure is required in respect of the remuneration of each such person.

Note, however, that a medium-sized company must stillcomply with the requirements on disclosure of liability limitation agreements. See **3.50 Accounts: Large Companies**.

[*CA 2006, s 410A(4); SI 2008 No 393, Reg 8; SI 2008 No 410, Reg 4(1), (2); SI 2008 No 489, Reg 4*].

4.5 ACCOUNTS DELIVERED TO THE REGISTRAR OF COMPANIES

Accounts generally. Unless they deliver abbreviated accounts (see below), the directors of a company that qualifies as a medium-sized company in relation to a financial year must deliver to the Registrar of Companies

- the company's annual accounts,
- the strategic report;
- the directors' report, and
- unless the company is exempt from audit and the directors have taken advantage of that exemption, the auditor's report on those accounts (and on the *strategic report* and directors' report).

But the above provisions do not apply to companies within

- *CA 2006, s 444* (filing obligations of companies subject to the small companies regime, see **2.10**(1) **Accounts: General**), or
- *CA 2006, s 444A* (filing obligations of companies entitled to small companies exemption in relation to the directors' report, see **2.10**(2) **Accounts: General**

[*CA 2006, s 445(1)–(3), (7); SI 2008 No 393, Reg 6(8); SI 2013 No 1970, Schedule, para 9*].

Abbreviated accounts. Where a company prepares Companies Act accounts, the directors *may* deliver to the Registrar of Companies a copy of its annual accounts for the year

(a) which includes a profit and loss account in which the following items listed in the profit and loss account formats set out in **3.5 Accounts: Large Companies** are combined as one item:

Format 1 — items 2, 3 and 6

Format 2 — items 2 to 5

Format 3 — items A.1 and B.2

Format 4 — items A.1, A.2 and B.2 to B.4

(b) which does not contain the information required by *SI 2008 No 410, Sch 1 para 68*, (particulars of turnover, see **3.29 Accounts: Large Companies**).

Such accounts are referred to as 'abbreviated accounts'.

If abbreviated accounts are delivered, the obligation to deliver a copy of the auditor's report on the accounts is to deliver a copy of the special auditor's report required by *CA 2006, s 449* (see **8.31 Audit**).

Approval and signing of abbreviated accounts. Abbreviated accounts must be approved by the board of directors and signed on behalf of the board by a director of the company. The signature must be on the balance sheet.

The balance sheet must contain, in a prominent position above the signature, a statement to the effect that it is prepared in accordance with the special provisions relating to medium-sized companies.

If abbreviated accounts are approved that do not comply with the relevant requirements, every director of the company who

- knew that they did not comply, or was reckless as to whether they complied, and
- failed to take reasonable steps to prevent them from being approved,

commits an offence.

A person guilty of such an offence is liable (i) on conviction on indictment, to a fine; and (ii) on summary conviction, to a fine not exceeding the statutory maximum. See **29.1** OFFENCES AND LEGAL PROCEEDINGS for the statutory maximum.

[*CA 2006, ss 445(3), (4), 450; SI 2008 No 410, Reg 4(1), (3)*].

Names appearing on accounts. The copies of the balance sheet and strategic report and directors' report delivered to the Registrar of Companies under these provisions must state the name of the person who signed it on behalf of the board.

The copy of the auditor's report delivered to the Registrar of Companies under these provisions must either

- state the name of the auditor and (where the auditor is a firm) the name of the person who signed it as senior statutory auditor; or
- if the conditions is *CA 2006, s 506* are met (circumstances in which names may be omitted, see **8.34** AUDIT), state that a resolution has been passed and notified to the Secretary of State in accordance with those provisions.

[*CA 2006, s 445(5), (6); SI 2013 No 1970, Schedule, para 9*].

5 Accounts: Small Companies and Micro-entities

5.1 **Introduction**
5.2 **Meaning of 'small'**
5.3 Companies excluded from the small companies regime
5.3A Companies qualifying as micro-entities
5.3B Companies excluded from being treated as micro-entities
5.4 **Individual accounts: duty to prepare**
5.5 **Individual accounts: form and content of Companies Act accounts**
5.6 Balance sheet formats
5.7 Profit and loss account formats
5.8 Accounting principles
5.9 Historic cost accounting rules
5.14 Alternative accounting rules
5.17 Financial instruments
5.18 Notes to the accounts: general
5.19 Notes to the accounts: information supplementing the balance sheet
5.28 Notes to the accounts: information supplementing the profit and loss account
5.31 **Individual accounts: information on related undertakings**
5.32 Subsidiary undertakings
5.36 Significant holdings in undertakings other than subsidiary undertakings
5.37 Membership of certain undertakings
5.38 Parent undertaking drawing up accounts for larger group
5.39 **Individual accounts: directors' remuneration and benefits**
5.40 Directors' remuneration
5.44 Directors' benefits: advances, credits and guarantees
5.45 **Individual accounts: auditor's remuneration and liability limitation agreements**
5.46 **Individual accounts: abbreviated Companies Act accounts for delivery to the Registrar of Companies**
5.47 Balance sheet format
5.48 Notes to the accounts
5.56 **Group accounts**
5.57 Exclusion of subsidiary undertakings from consolidation
5.58 **Group accounts: treatment of individual profit and loss account where group accounts prepared**
5.59 **Group accounts: form and content of Companies Act group accounts where prepared**
5.60 Elimination of group transactions
5.61 Acquisition and merger accounting
5.62 Minority interests
5.63 Joint ventures
5.64 Associated undertakings
5.65 **Group accounts: information about related undertakings where group accounts prepared**
5.66 Subsidiary undertakings
5.70 Joint ventures
5.71 Associated undertakings
5.72 Other significant holdings of parent company or group
5.73 Parent company's or group's membership of certain undertakings
5.74 Information where parent company is a subsidiary undertaking
5.75 **Group accounts: directors' remuneration and benefits**
5.76 **Group accounts: abbreviated Companies Act group accounts for delivery to the Registrar of Companies**

Cross-references. See 2 ACCOUNTS: GENERAL; 3 ACCOUNTS: LARGE COMPANIES; 4 ACCOUNTS: MEDIUM-SIZED COMPANIES; APPENDIX 1 DEFINITIONS.

5.1 INTRODUCTION

A company which qualifies as 'small' (see **5.2**) in relation to a financial year is entitled to various exemptions with respect to

(a) the preparation of individual accounts (see **5.4** to **5.45**);

(b) abbreviated Companies Act individual accounts which may be delivered to the Registrar of Companies (see **5.46** to **5.55**);

(c) the requirement to prepare group accounts (see **5.56**);

(d) the content of group accounts where prepared (see **5.59** to **5.75**); and

(e) abbreviated Companies Act group accounts which may be delivered to the Registrar of Companies (see **5.76**).

A small company is also exempt from certain of the requirements as to the contents of the directors' and strategic reports. See **20 Directors' and Strategic Reports**.

Certain very small companies which are classed as micro-entities are also exempt from some financial reporting requirements and are referred to where relevant in this chapter.

See also

- **8.31 Audit** for the special auditor's report required where small companies take advantage of the exemptions conferred by (*b*) or (*e*) above; and
- **8.25** to **8.27 Audit** for the audit exemptions available to small companies satisfying certain conditions.

5.2 MEANING OF 'SMALL'

The small companies regime applies to a company for a financial year in relation to which the company

- qualifies as small (see (1) and (2) below); and
- is not excluded from the regime (see **5.3**).

[*CA 2006, s 381; SI 2008 No 393, Reg 6(1)*].

(1) **Companies qualifying as small: general**

Subject to (2) below, a company qualifies as small

(a) in relation to its first financial year if the qualifying conditions below are met in that year;

(b) subject to the provision set out in (c) in relation to a subsequent financial year if the qualifying conditions are met in that year and the preceding financial year; and

(c) in relation a subsequent financial year where on its balance sheet date a company meets or ceases to meet the qualifying conditions, that affects its qualification as a small company only if it occurs in two consecutive financial years.

The qualifying conditions are met by a company in a year in which it satisfies two or more of the following requirements.

Turnover	Not more than £6.5m
'Balance sheet total'	Not more than £3.26m
'Number of employees'	Not more than 50

Notes.

- For a period that is a company's financial year but not in fact a year, the maximum figures for turnover must be proportionately adjusted.
- The '*balance sheet total*' means the aggregate of the amounts shown as assets in the company's balance sheet.
- The '*number of employees*' means the average number of persons employed by the company in the year, calculated as

  $$A \div B$$

  where

  A = the sum of the number of persons employed under contracts of service by the company for each month in the financial year (whether throughout the month or not)

  B = the number of months in the financial year
- In determining under (*b*) above whether a company qualifies as small, the company is treated as having qualified as small in any previous financial year in which it would have so qualified if the amendments made to the qualifying conditions above for financial years *beginning* on or after 6 April 2008 had been in force.

[*CA 2006, s 382; SI 2008 No 393, Regs 2, 3; SI 2013 No 3008, Reg 4(2)*].

(2) Companies qualifying as small: parent companies

A parent company qualifies as a small company in relation to a financial year only if the group headed by it qualifies as a small group. A group qualifies as small

(a) in relation to the parent company's first financial year if the qualifying conditions below are met in that year;

(b) subject to the provision in (c) in relation to a subsequent financial year of the parent company if the qualifying conditions are met in that year; and

(c) in relation to a subsequent financial year of the parent company, where on the parent company's balance sheet date the group meets or ceases to meet the qualifying conditions, that affects the group's qualification as a small group only if it occurs in two consecutive financial years.

The qualifying conditions are met by a group in a year in which it satisfies two or more of the following requirements.

Aggregate turnover	Not more than £6.5m net (or £7.8m gross)
Aggregate balance sheet total	Not more than £3.26m net (or £3.9m gross)
Aggregate number of employees	Not more than 50

Notes.

- The aggregate figures are ascertained by aggregating the relevant figures determined as under (1) above for each member of the group.
- In relation to the aggregate figures for turnover and balance sheet total, 'net' means after any set-offs and other adjustments made to eliminate group transactions and 'gross' means without those set-offs and other adjustments.

  A company may satisfy any relevant requirement on the basis of either the net or the gross figure.
- The figures for each subsidiary undertaking are those included in its individual accounts for the relevant financial year, ie

  (i) if its financial year ends with that of the parent company, that financial year; and

  (ii) if not, its financial year ending last before the end of the financial year of the parent company.

  If those figures cannot be obtained without disproportionate expense or undue delay, the latest available figures can be taken.
- In determining under (*b*) above whether a group qualifies as small in relation to a financial year *ending* on or after 6 April 2008, the group is treated as having qualified as small in any previous financial year in which it would have so qualified if the amendments made to the qualifying conditions above for financial years *beginning* on or after 6 April 2008 had been in force.

  [*CA 2006, s 383; SI 2008 No 393, Regs 2, 3; SI 2013 No 3008, Reg 4(3)*.]

5.3 Companies excluded from the small companies regime

The small companies regime does not apply to a company that is, or was at any time within the financial year to which the accounts relate,

(a) a public company;

(b) a company that

(i) is an authorised insurance company, a banking company, an e-money issuer, a 'MiFID investment firm' (for financial years ending before 1 November 2007, an ISD investment firm) or a UCITS management company; or

(ii) carries on insurance market activity; or

(c) a member of an 'ineligible group'.

A group is an '*ineligible group*' if any of its members is

(i) a public company;

(ii) a body corporate (other than a company) whose shares are admitted to trading on a regulated market in an EEA State;

(iii) a person (other than a small company) who has permission under *FSMA 2000, Pt 4* to carry on a regulated activity;

(iv) a small company that is an authorised insurance company, a banking company, an e-money issuer, a 'MiFID investment firm' (for financial years ending before 1 November 2007, an ISD investment firm) or a UCITS management company; or

(v) a person who carries on insurance market activity;

and a company is a small company for these purposes if it qualified as small in relation to its last financial year ending on or before the end of the financial year to which the accounts relate.

[*CA 2006, s 384; SI 2007 No 2932, Reg 3*].

See **Appendix 1 Definitions** for the meaning of '*MiFID investment firm*'.

5.3A Companies qualifying as micro-entities

A company qualifies as a micro-entity

(a) in relation to its first financial year if the qualifying conditions below are met in that year;

(b) subject to the provision set out in (c) in relation to a subsequent financial year if

the qualifying conditions are met in that year; and

(c) in relation a subsequent financial year where on its balance sheet date a company meets or ceases to meet the qualifying conditions, that affects its qualification as a micro-entity only if it occurs in two consecutive financial years.

The qualifying conditions are met by a company in a year in which it satisfies two or more of the following requirements.

Turnover	Not more than £632,000
'Balance sheet total'	Not more than £316,000
'Number of employees'	Not more than 10

Notes

- For a period that is a company's financial year but not in fact a year the maximum figures for turnover must be proportionately adjusted.
- The balance sheet total means the aggregate of the amounts shown as assets in the company's balance sheet.
- The number of employees means the average number of persons employed by the company in the year determined as follows

(i) find for each month in the financial year the number of persons employed under contracts of service by the company in that month (whether throughout the month or not)

(ii) add together the monthly totals and

(iii) divide by the number of months in the financial year.

- In the case of a company which is a parent company ,the company qualifies as a micro-entity in relation to a financial year only if the company qualifies as a micro-entity in relation to that year as determined by the provisions in this section and the group headed by the company qualifies as a small group as determined by the provisions set out in 5(2)

[*CA 2006, s 384A; SI 2013 No 3008, Reg 4(4)*]

5.3B Companies excluded from being treated as micro-entities

The micro- entity provisions do not apply in relation to a company's accounts for a particular financial year if the company was at any time within that year

(a) a company excluded from the small companies regime by virtue of *CA 2006, s 384* (see **5.2**);

(b) an investment undertaking as defined in *Article 2(14)* of *Directive 2013/34/EU* (1) on the annual financial statements etc of certain types of undertakings

(c) a financial holding undertaking as defined in *Article 2(15)* of the above *Directive*

(d) a credit institution as defined in *Article 4* of *Directive 2006/48/EC* relating to the taking up and pursuit of the business of credit institutions, other than one referred to in *Article 2* of that *Directive*

(e) an insurance undertaking as defined in *Article 2(1)* of *Council Directive 91/674/EEC* on the annual accounts of insurance undertakings or

(f) a charity.

The micro-entity provisions also do not apply in relation to a company's accounts for a financial year if

(a) the company is a parent company which prepares group accounts for that year as permitted by *CA 2006, s 398* (see **5.56**) or

(b) the company is not a parent company but its accounts are included in consolidated group accounts for that year.

[*CA 2006, ss 384A, 384B; SI 2013 No 3008, Reg 4*]

5.4 INDIVIDUAL ACCOUNTS: DUTY TO PREPARE

The directors of every company, including a small company, must prepare accounts for the company for each of its financial years. Those accounts are referred to in this chapter as the company's '*individual accounts*'. [*CA 2006, s 394*]. Subject to below, these accounts may be prepared in accordance with

- *CA 2006, s 396* ('*Companies Act individual accounts*'); or
- international accounting standards ('*IAS individual accounts*').

But

- the individual accounts of a company that is a charity *must* be Companies Act individual accounts; and
- after the first financial year in which the directors of a company prepare IAS individual accounts (*'the first IAS year'*), all subsequent individual accounts of the company must be prepared in accordance with international accounting standards unless there is a *'relevant change of circumstance'*. This is subject to the right to change to Companies Act accounts set out in *CA 2006, s 395(4A)* (see below) A relevant change of circumstance occurs if, at any time during or after the first IAS year,

  (i) the company becomes a subsidiary undertaking of another undertaking that does not prepare IAS individual accounts;

  (ii) the company has ceased to be a subsidiary undertaking;

  (iii) the company ceases to be a company with securities admitted to trading on a regulated market in an EEA State; or

  (iv) a parent undertaking of the company ceases to be an undertaking with securities admitted to trading on a regulated market in an EEA State.

  After a financial year in which IAS individual accounts are prepared, the directors may change to preparing Companies Act individual accounts for a reason other than a relevant change of circumstance, provided they have not changed to Companies Act accounts in the five years preceding the first day of that financial year.

  If, having changed to preparing Companies Act individual accounts, the directors again prepare IAS individual accounts for the company, the above provisions apply again as if the first financial year for which such accounts are again prepared were the first IAS year.

[*CA 2006, s 395; SI 2008 No 393, Reg 9; SI 2012 No 2301, Reg 13*].

See **Appendix 1 Definitions** for the current EEA States.

Companies Act individual accounts. Companies Act individual accounts must comprise

(a) a balance sheet as at the last day of the financial year; and

(b) a profit and loss account.

The balance sheet must give a true and fair view of the state of affairs of the company as at the end of the financial year and the profit and loss account must give a true and fair view of the profit or loss of the company for the financial year. See **2.16 Accounts: General** for the interpretation of *'true and fair view'*.

Where a company qualifies as a micro- entity in relation to a financial year (see **5.3A**) , the micro-entity minimum accounting items included in the company's accounts for the year are presumed to give a true and fair view required by *CA 2006, s 396(2)*.

Where a company qualifies as 'small' in relation to the financial year (see **5.2**) and its individual accounts for the year are Companies Act individual accounts, its accounts may either

- be prepared in compliance with the provisions in **5.5** to **5.30** as to form and content of the balance sheet and profit and loss account and additional information to be provided by way of notes to the accounts; or

- comply with the fuller provisions as described in **3.3** to **3.31** ACCOUNTS: LARGE COMPANIES.

If compliance with the chosen method would not be sufficient to give a true and fair view, the necessary additional information must be given in the accounts or notes. If, in special circumstances, compliance with any of those provisions is inconsistent with the requirement to give a true and fair view, the directors must depart from that provision to the extent necessary to give a true and fair view. Particulars of any such departure, the reasons for it and its effect must be given in a note to the accounts. These requirements do not apply in relation to the micro-entity minimum accounting items included in the individual accounts of a company for a financial year in relation to which the company qualifies as a micro-entity.

"Micro-entity minimum accounting item" means an item of information required by *CA 2006, Part 15* or by regulations made under those provisions to be contained in *CA 2006* individual accounts of a company for a financial year in relation to which it qualifies as a micro-entity.

[*CA 2006, s 396, s 393(2A), s 474(1)(a); SI 2013 No 3008, Reg 5*]

IAS individual accounts. The provisions relating to the individual accounts of small companies as described in **5.5** to **5.30** do not apply to IAS individual accounts. Instead:

- Individual accounts must be prepared on the basis of the accounting standards issued by the International Accounting Standard Board (IASB) that are adopted by the European Commission. [*EC Council Regulation 1606/2002, Art 4*]. In place of the profit and loss account and balance sheet, companies must prepare primary financial statements and supporting notes as required under international accounting standards. See **2.15** ACCOUNTS: GENERAL for a list of standards.
- The provisions relating to

  (i) related undertakings (see **5.31** to **5.38**),

  (ii) directors' remuneration and benefits (see **5.39** to **5.44**), and

  (iii) auditor's remuneration, etc (see **5.45**),

  continue to apply where IAS individual accounts are prepared, as do aspects of *CA 2006* that deal with matters outside the scope of international accounting standards (eg the requirements relating to directors' reports, publication (as opposed to preparation) of accounts, and audit).

Where the directors of a company prepare IAS individual accounts, they must state in the notes to the accounts that the accounts have been prepared in accordance with international accounting standards. [*CA 2006, s 397*].

Consistency of accounts within a group. Subject to the exceptions below, the directors of a parent company must secure that the individual accounts of

(a) the parent company, and

(b) each of its subsidiary undertakings

are all prepared using the same financial reporting framework (ie Companies Act or IAS), except to the extent that in their opinion there are good reasons for not doing so. BIS indicated, in their 2008 guidance to companies on the introduction of IAS accounts, that 'good reasons' could include the following.

- Where a group using IAS acquires a subsidiary undertaking that had not been using IAS, in the first year of acquisition it might not be practical for the newly acquired company to switch to IAS straight away.
- Where a group contains subsidiary undertakings that are themselves publicly traded, market pressures or regulatory requirements to use IAS might come into play, without necessarily justifying a switch to IAS by the non-publicly traded subsidiaries.
- Where a subsidiary undertaking or the parent is planning to list and so might wish to convert to IAS in advance, but the rest of the group is not listed.
- Where the group contains minor or dormant subsidiaries and the costs of switching accounting framework would outweigh the benefits.

Exceptions. The general requirement to prepare individual accounts using the same financial framework is subject to the following specific exceptions. It

- does not apply if the directors do not prepare group accounts for the parent company;
- only applies to the accounts of subsidiary undertakings that are required to be prepared under *CA 2006*;
- does not require accounts of undertakings that are charities to be prepared using the same financial reporting framework as accounts of undertakings which are not charities; and
- does not apply where the directors of a parent company prepare both group accounts and individual accounts under IAS. In this case the parent company is not required to ensure that all its subsidiary undertakings also use IAS. However it must ensure that all its subsidiary undertakings use the same accounting framework, unless there are good reasons for not doing so.

[*CA 2006, s 407(2)–(4) and (5)*].

5.5 INDIVIDUAL ACCOUNTS: FORM AND CONTENT OF COMPANIES ACT ACCOUNTS

Subject to *regulations 3* and *5A* of *SI 2008 No 409* (the *Small Companies and Groups (Accounts and Directors' Reports) Regulations 2008*), Companies Act individual accounts for small companies must comply with the provisions of that SI described in this paragraph and in **5.6** to **5.30** as to the form and content of the balance sheet and profit and loss account, and additional information to be provided by way of notes to the accounts. However, accounts are treated as having complied with those provisions if they comply instead with the corresponding provision of *SI 2008 No 410, Sch 1* (see **3.3** to **3.31 Accounts: Large Companies**). *Sections C* (alternative accounting rules) and *D* (fair value accounting) in *SI 2008 No 409, Schedule 1, Part 2* do not apply to a company which qualifies as a micro-entity in relation to a financial year and whose accounts for that year are prepared in accordance with the exemption permitted by *SI 2008 No 409, Reg 5A* or *section A, Part 1, Schedule 1, para 1(1A).*

Every balance sheet of a small company must show the items listed in either of the balance sheet formats in **5.6** and every profit and loss account must show the items listed in any one of the profit and loss account formats in **5.7**, subject to the requirements for micro-entities set out in **5.7** and **5.7A** (below) in the order and under the headings and sub-headings given in the particular format used, but subject to the following.

(1) The notes to the formats may permit alternative positions for any particular items.

(2) The heading or sub-heading for any item does not have to be distinguished by any letter or number assigned to that item in the format used.

(3) Any item required to be shown in a company's balance sheet or profit and loss account may be shown in greater detail than required by the particular format used.

(4) A heading or sub-heading corresponding to an item in the balance sheet or profit and loss account format used must not be included if there is no amount to be shown for that item for the financial year in question unless an amount must be disclosed for the immediately preceding financial year (see below).

(5) The balance sheet or profit and loss account may include an item representing or covering the amount of any asset or liability, income or expenditure not otherwise covered by any of the items listed in the format used, except that none of the following may be treated as assets in any balance sheet.

- Preliminary expenses.
- Expenses of, and commission on, any issue of shares or debentures.
- Costs of research.

(6) Where the special nature of the company's business requires it, the company's directors

(a) *must* adapt the arrangement, headings and sub-headings otherwise required in respect of items given an Arabic number in the balance sheet or profit and loss account format used; and

(b) *may* combine items to which Arabic numbers are given in any of the formats if

(i) their individual amounts are not material to assessing the state of affairs or profit or loss of the company for the financial year in question; or

(ii) the combination facilitates that assessment (but in this case the individual amounts of any items which have been combined must be disclosed in a note to the accounts).

(7) In relation to a company which qualifies as a micro-entity in relation to a financial year, the only items which must be shown in the company's balance sheet for that year are those listed in either of the balance sheet formats in **5.7A** and the only items which must be shown in the company's profit and loss account for that year are those listed in the profit and loss format in **5.7A**.

[*SI 2008 No 409, Reg 3, 5, Sch 1 paras 1, 3–5; SI 2013 No 3008, Reg 9, 10*].

Consistency in use of formats. Where a company's balance sheet or profit and loss account for any financial year has been prepared by reference to one of the said formats, the company's directors must use the same format in preparing Companies Act individual accounts for subsequent financial years, unless in their opinion there are special reasons for a change. Particulars of any such change must be given in a note to the accounts in which the new format is first used, and the reasons for the change must be explained. [*SI 2008 No 409, Sch 1, para 2; SI 2013 No 3008, Reg 10*].

Profit before taxation. Every profit and loss account, other than one prepared by reference to the format in **5.7A**, must show the amount of a company's profit or loss on ordinary activities before taxation. [*SI 2008 No 409, Sch 1, para 6; SI 2013 No 3008, Reg 10*].

Preceding financial year. For every item shown in the balance sheet or profit and loss account the corresponding amount for the immediately preceding financial year must also be shown. Where that corresponding amount is not comparable with the figure for the current year, the former amount may be adjusted, in which case particulars of the non-comparability and of any adjustment must be disclosed in a note to the accounts. [*SI 2008 No 409, Sch 1 para 7*].

Set-offs. Amounts in respect of items representing assets or income may not be set off against amounts in respect of items representing liabilities or expenditure, or vice versa. [*SI 2008 No 409, Sch 1 para 8*].

Presentation in accordance with accounting principles. The company's directors must, in determining how amounts are presented within items in the profit and loss account and balance sheet, have regard to the substance of the reported transaction or arrangement, in accordance with generally accepted accounting principles or practice. [*SI 2008 No 409, Sch 1 para 9*].

Materiality. Amounts which in the particular context of any provision of *SI 2008 No 409, Sch 1* (see above and **5.6** to **5.30**) are not material may be disregarded for the purposes of that provision. [*SI 2008 No 409, Sch 8 para 7*].

Accounts in euros. The amounts set out in the annual accounts of a small company may also be shown in the same accounts translated into euros. If so, the amounts must have been translated at the exchange rate prevailing at the balance sheet date and that rate must be disclosed in the notes to the accounts. The requirement to disclose the rate in the notes to the accounts does not apply to the individual accounts of a company for a financial year in which the company qualifies as a micro-entity. For the meaning of 'micro-entity' see **5.3A**. [*CA 2006, s 469(1) (3) (3A); SI 2013 No 3008, Reg 7 (2)*].

5.6 Balance sheet formats for companies other than micro-entities

The three balance sheet formats set out in *SI 2008 No 409, Sch 1* and in *SI 2013 No 3008* and referred to in **5.5** are reproduced below and in **5.7A**, and are followed by the notes also set out in the relevant SI.

Format 1 – the required format for companies other than micro-entities

A. Called up share capital not paid (see note (1))

B. Fixed assets

- I Intangible assets
  - 1. Goodwill (see note (2))
  - 2. Other intangible assets (see note (3))
- II Tangible assets
  - 1. Land and buildings
  - 2. Plant and machinery etc.
- III Investments
  - 1. Shares in group undertakings and participating interests
  - 2. Loans to group undertakings and undertakings in which the company has a participating interest

3. Other investments other than loans
4. Other investments (see note (4))

C. Current assets

I Stocks

1. Stocks
2. Payments on account

II Debtors (see note (5))

1. Trade debtors
2. Amounts owed by group undertakings and undertakings in which the company has a participating interest
3. Other debtors (see notes (1) and (6))

III Investments

1. Shares in group undertakings
2. Other investments

IV Cash at bank and in hand

D. Prepayments and accrued income (see note (6))

E. Creditors: amounts falling due within one year

1. Bank loans and overdrafts
2. Trade creditors
3. Amounts owed to group undertakings and undertakings in which the company has a participating interest
4. Other creditors (see note (7))

F. Net current assets (liabilities) (see note (8))

G. Total assets less current liabilities

H. Creditors: amounts falling due after more than one year

1. Bank loans and overdrafts
2. Trade creditors
3. Amounts owed to group undertakings and undertakings in which the company has a participating interest
4. Other creditors (see note (7))

I. Provisions for liabilities

J. Accruals and deferred income (see note (7))

K. Capital and reserves

I Called up share capital (see note (9))

II Share premium account

III Revaluation reserve

IV Other reserves

V Profit and loss account

Format 2

A. Called up share capital not paid (see note (1))

B. Fixed assets

I Intangible assets

1. Goodwill (see note (2))
2. Other intangible assets (see note (3))

II Tangible assets
1. Land and buildings
2. Plant and machinery etc.

III Investments
1. Shares in group undertakings and participating interests
2. Loans to group undertakings and undertakings in which the company has a participating interest
3. Other investments other than loans
4. Other investments (see note (4))

C. Current assets

I Stocks
1. Stocks
2. Payments on account

II Debtors (see note (5))
1. Trade debtors
2. Amounts owed by group undertakings and undertakings in which the company has a participating interest
3. Other debtors (see notes (1) and (6))

III Investments
1. Shares in group undertakings
2. Other investments

IV Cash at bank and in hand

D. Prepayments and accrued income (see note (6))

LIABILITIES

A. Capital and reserves

I Called up share capital (see note (9))

II Share premium account

III Revaluation reserve

IV Other reserves

V Profit and loss account

B. Provisions for liabilities

C. Creditors (see note (10))
1. Bank loans and overdrafts
2. Trade creditors
3. Amounts owed to group undertakings and undertakings in which the company has a participating interest
4. Other creditors (see note (7))

D. Accruals and deferred income (see note (7))

Notes

(1) *Called up share capital not paid.* This item may be shown at item A or included under item C.II.3 in format 1 or 2.

(2) *Goodwill.* Amounts representing goodwill must be included only to the extent that the goodwill was acquired for valuable consideration.

(3) *Other intangible assets.* Amounts in respect of concessions, patents, licences, trademarks and similar rights and assets must only be included under this item if the assets in question were either acquired for valuable consideration (and are not required to be shown under 'goodwill') or created by the company itself.

(4) *Own shares.* Where this item includes own shares, the nominal value of the shares held must be shown separately.

(5) *Debtors.* The amount falling due after more than one year must be shown separately for each item included under debtors unless the aggregate amount of debtors falling due after more than one year may be disclosed in the notes to the accounts.

(6) *Prepayments and accrued income.* This may be shown at item D or included under item C.II.3 in format 1 or 2.

(7) *Other creditors.*

(a) The amount of any convertible loans must be shown separately.

(b) The amount for creditors in respect of taxation and social security must be shown separately.

(c) Payments received on account of orders must be included in so far as they are not shown as deductions from stocks.

(d) In format 1, accruals and deferred income may be shown under item J or included under item E.4 or H.4, or both (as the case may require). In format 2, accruals and deferred income may be shown under item D or within item C.4 under Liabilities.

(8) *Net current assets (liabilities).* In determining the amount to be shown under this item, any 'prepayments and accrued income' (see note (6) above) are to be taken into account wherever shown.

(9) *Called up share capital.* The amount of allotted share capital and the amount of called up share capital which has been paid up must be shown separately.

(10) *Creditors.* In format 2, amounts falling due within one year and after one year must be shown separately for each item under this heading and for the aggregate of all these items unless the aggregate amount of creditors falling due within one year and the aggregate amount of creditors falling due after more than one year is disclosed in the notes to the accounts.

[*SI 2008 No 409, Sch 1 Section B*].

5.7 Profit and loss account formats for companies other than micro-entities

The five profit and loss account formats set out in *SI 2008 No 409, Sch 1* and in *SI 2013 No 3008, Reg 10* and referred to in **5.5** are reproduced below and in **5.7A**, and are followed by the notes also set out in the relevant SI.

Format 1 (see note (4)) – formats for companies other than micro-entities

1. Turnover
2. Cost of sales (see note (1))
3. Gross profit or loss
4. Distribution costs (see note (1))
5. Administrative expenses (see note (1))

6. Other operating income
7. Income from shares in group undertakings
8. Income from participating interests
9. Income from other fixed asset investments (see note (2))
10. Other interest receivable and similar income (see note (2))
11. Amounts written off investments
12. Interest payable and similar charges (see note (3))
13. Tax on profit or loss on ordinary activities
14. Profit or loss on ordinary activities after taxation
15. Extraordinary income
16. Extraordinary charges
17. Extraordinary profit or loss
18. Tax on extraordinary profit or loss
19. Other taxes not shown under the above items
20. Profit or loss for the financial year

Format 2

1. Turnover
2. Change in stocks of finished goods and in work in progress
3. Own work capitalised
4. Other operating income
5. (a) Raw materials and consumables
   (b) Other external charges
6. Staff costs:
   (a) wages and salaries (see below)
   (b) social security costs (see below)
   (c) other pension costs (see below)
7. (a) Depreciation and other amounts written off tangible and intangible fixed assets
   (b) Exceptional amounts written off current assets
8. Other operating charges
9. Income from shares in group undertakings
10. Income from participating interests
11. Income from other fixed asset investments (see note (2))
12. Other interest receivable and similar income (see note (2))
13. Amounts written off investments
14. Interest payable and similar charges (see note (3))
15. Tax on profit or loss on ordinary activities
16. Profit or loss on ordinary activities after taxation
17. Extraordinary income
18. Extraordinary charges
19. Extraordinary profit or loss
20. Tax on extraordinary profit or loss
21. Other taxes not shown under the above items
22. Profit or loss for the financial year

Format 3 (see note (4))

A. Charges

1. Cost of sales (see note (1))
2. Distribution costs (see note (1))
3. Administrative expenses (see note (1))
4. Amounts written off investments
5. Interest payable and similar charges (see note (3))
6. Tax on profit or loss on ordinary activities
7. Profit or loss on ordinary activities after taxation
8. Extraordinary charges
9. Tax on extraordinary profit or loss
10. Other taxes not shown under the above items
11. Profit or loss for the financial year

B. Income

1. Turnover
2. Other operating income
3. Income from shares in group undertakings
4. Income from participating interests
5. Income from other fixed asset investments (see note (2))
6. Other interest receivable and similar income (see note (2))
7. Profit or loss on ordinary activities after taxation
8. Extraordinary income
9. Profit or loss for the financial year

Format 4

A. Charges

1. Reduction in stocks of finished goods and in work in progress
2. (a) Raw materials and consumables
   (b) Other external charges
3. Staff costs:
   (a) wages and salaries (see below)
   (b) social security costs (see below)
   (c) other pension costs (see below)
4. (a) Depreciation and other amounts written off tangible and intangible fixed assets
   (b) Exceptional amounts written off current assets
5. Other operating charges
6. Amounts written off investments
7. Interest payable and similar charges (see note (3))
8. Tax on profit or loss on ordinary activities
9. Profit or loss on ordinary activities after taxation
10. Extraordinary charges

11. Tax on extraordinary profit or loss
12. Other taxes not shown under the above items
13. Profit or loss for the financial year

B. Income

1. Turnover
2. Increase in stocks of finished goods and in work in progress
3. Own work capitalised
4. Other operating income
5. Income from shares in group undertakings
6. Income from participating interests
7. Income from other fixed asset investments (see note (2))
8. Other interest receivable and similar income (see note (2))
9. Profit or loss on ordinary activities after taxation
10. Extraordinary income
11. Profit or loss for the financial year

Notes

(1) *Cost of sales: distribution costs: administrative expenses.* These items must be stated after taking into account any necessary provisions for depreciation or diminution in value of assets.

(2) *Income from other fixed asset investments: other interest receivable and similar income.* Income and interest derived from group undertakings must be shown separately from income and interest derived from other sources.

(3) *Interest payable and similar charges.* The amount payable to group undertakings must be shown separately.

(4) *Formats 1 and 3.* Where either of these formats is used, the amount of any provisions for depreciation and diminution in value of tangible and intangible fixed assets falling to be shown under items 7(*a*) and A.4 (*a*) respectively in Formats 2 and 4 must be disclosed in a note to the accounts.

[*SI 2008 No 409, Sch 1 Section B*].

Staff costs.

- '*Social security costs*' means any contributions by the company to any state social security or pension scheme, fund or arrangement.
- '*Pension costs*' includes

  (i) any costs incurred by the company in respect of any pension scheme established for the purpose of providing pensions for persons currently or formerly employed by the company;

  (ii) any sums set aside for the future payment of pensions directly by the company to current or former employees; and

  (iii) any pensions paid directly to such persons without having first been set aside.

Any amount stated in respect of the item 'social security costs' or in respect of the item 'wages and salaries' in the company's profit and loss account must be determined by reference to payments made or costs incurred in respect of all persons employed by the company during the financial year under contracts of service.

[*SI 2008 No 409, Sch 8 para 14*].

Depreciation, etc. Any reference in the profit and loss account formats (or the notes to them) to the depreciation of, or amounts written off, assets of any description is to any provision for depreciation or diminution in value of assets of that description. [*SI 2008 No 409, Sch 7 para 1(2)*].

'*Fixed assets*' means assets of a company which are intended for use on a continuing basis in the company's activities. [*SI 2008 No 409, Sch 8 para 3*].

[*SI 2013 No 3008, Reg 10(4)*]

5.7A Balance sheet and profit and loss formats for micro-entities

Format 1 –Balance sheet

A.	Called up share capital not paid
B.	Fixed assets
C.	Current assets
D.	Prepayments and accrued income
E.	Creditors: amounts falling due within one year
F.	Net current assets (liabilities)
G.	Total assets less current liabilities
H.	Creditors: amounts falling due after more than one year
I.	Provisions for liabilities
J.	Accruals and deferred income (see note (7))
K.	Capital and reserves

Format 2 –Balance sheet

A.	Called up share capital not paid
B.	Fixed assets
C.	Current assets
D.	Prepayments and accrued income

LIABILITIES

A.	Capital and reserves
B.	Fixed assets
C.	Creditors[1]
D.	Accruals and deferred income

Format 1 –profit and loss account format

A.	Turnover
B.	Other income
C.	Cost of raw materials and consumables
D.	Staff costs
E.	Depreciation and other amounts written off assets
F.	Other charges
G.	Tax
H.	Profit or loss

1 Creditors. In format 2, amounts falling due within one year and after one year must be shown separately

5.8 Accounting principles

The amounts to be included in respect of all items shown in a company's accounts must be determined in accordance with the principles set out in (*a*)–(*e*) below. But if it appears to the directors that there are special reasons for departing from any of those principles in preparing the company's accounts for any financial year, they may do so, in which case particulars of the departure, the reasons for it and its effect must be given in a note to the accounts.

(a) The company is presumed to be carrying on business as a going concern.

(b) Accounting policies must be applied consistently within the same accounts and from one financial year to the next.

(c) The amount of any item must be determined on a prudent basis, and in particular

(i) only profits realised at the balance sheet date are to be included in the profit and loss account; and

(ii) all liabilities which have arisen in respect of the financial year to which the accounts relate or a previous financial year must be taken into account. This includes those which only become apparent between the balance sheet date and the date on which it is signed on behalf of the board of directors (see **2.2 Accounts: General**). Where revised accounts are prepared (see **2.12 Accounts: General**) it is the date on which the original accounts were signed that is taken into account for this purposes.

(d) All income and charges relating to the financial year to which the accounts relate must be taken into account, without regard to the date of receipt or payment.

(e) In determining the aggregate amount of any item, the amount of each individual asset or liability that falls to be taken into account must be determined separately.

[*SI 2008 No 409, Sch 1 paras 10–15*].

5.9 Historic cost accounting rules

Subject to

- the alternative accounting rules in **5.14** to **5.16**, and

- the fair value accounting provisions in **5.17**

the amounts to be included in respect of all items shown in a company's accounts must be determined in accordance with the rules set out in **5.10** to **5.13**. [*SI 2008 No 409, Sch 1 para 16*].

5.10 *Fixed assets*

General rules. Fixed asset (ie assets of a company which are intended for use on a continuing basis in the company's activities) must be included at their 'purchase price' or 'production cost' (see **5.13**). [*SI 2008 No 409, Sch 1 para 17, Sch 8 para 3*].

Rules for depreciation and diminution in value.

(a) In the case of any fixed asset which has a limited useful economic life, its purchase price or production cost, less the amount of any estimated residual value at the end of the asset's useful economic life, must be reduced by provisions for depreciation calculated to write off that amount systematically over the asset's useful economic life. [*SI 2008 No 409, Sch 1 para 18*].

(b) Where a fixed asset investment falling to be included under item B.III of either of the balance sheet formats set out in **5.6** has diminished in value, provisions for diminution in value may be made in respect of it and the amount to be included in respect of it may be reduced accordingly. Such provisions must be made in respect of *any* fixed asset which has diminished in value if the reduction in its value is expected to be permanent (whether it's useful economic life is limited or not), and the amount to be included in respect of it must be reduced accordingly. [*SI 2008 No 409, Sch 1 para 19*].

(c) Where the reasons for which any provision was made have ceased to apply to any extent, that provision must be written back to the extent that it is no longer necessary. [*SI 2008 No 409, Sch 1 para 20(1)*].

Any provisions made or amounts written back which are not shown in the profit and loss account must be disclosed (either separately or in aggregate) in a note to the accounts. [*SI 2008 No 409, Sch 1 para 20(2)*].

Goodwill. Where goodwill is treated as an asset, the application of the general rules above is subject to the following.

- The amount of the consideration for any goodwill acquired by a company must be reduced by provisions for depreciation calculated to write off that amount systematically over a period chosen by the directors of the company although the period chosen must not exceed the useful economic life of the goodwill in question.
- Where any goodwill acquired by a company is shown or included as an asset in the company's balance sheet, there must be disclosed in a note to the accounts
  - (i) the period chosen for writing off the consideration for that goodwill; and
  - (ii) the reasons for choosing that period.

[*SI 2008 No 409, Sch 1 para 22*].

Development costs. Development costs may only in special circumstances be included in 'other intangible assets' under 'fixed assets' in the balance sheet formats set out in **5.6**. If any amount is so included, there must be given in a note to the accounts the reasons for capitalising the development costs in question and the period over which the amount of those costs originally capitalised is being (or is to be) written off. [*SI 2008 No 409, Sch 1 para 21; SI 2013 No 3008, Reg 11*].

5.11 *Current assets*

The amount to be included in respect of any current asset must be its 'purchase price' or 'production cost' (see **5.13**) or, if lower, its net realisable value. Where the reasons for which any provision for diminution in value has been made (ie to reduce the assets to its net realisable value) have ceased to apply to any extent, that provision must be written back to the extent that it is no longer necessary. [*SI 2008 No 409, Sch 1 paras 23, 24*].

5.12 *Miscellaneous provisions*

(1) *Excess of money owed over value received*

Where the amount repayable on any debt owed by a company is greater than the value of the consideration received in the transaction giving rise to the debt, the amount of the difference may be treated as an asset. But in the case of such treatment, the amount of the difference must be written off by reasonable amounts each year and must be completely written off before repayment of the debt. If the current amount is not shown as a separate item in the company's balance sheet, it must be disclosed in a note to the accounts.

[*SI 2008 No 409, Sch 1 para 25*].

(2) *Assets included at a fixed amount*

Assets which fall to be included either amongst the

- fixed assets of a company under the item 'tangible assets', or
- current assets of a company under the item 'raw materials and consumables',

may be included at a fixed quantity and value in the balance sheet formats set out in **5.6** where the assets are of a kind which are constantly being replaced and where their

- overall value is not material to assessing the company's state of affairs; and
- quantity, value and composition are not subject to material variation.

[*SI 2008 No 409, Sch 1 para 26; SI 2013 No 3008, Reg 11*].

5.13 *Determination of purchase price or production cost*

The '*purchase price*' of an asset is the actual price paid plus any expenses incidental to its acquisition.

'*Purchase price*', in relation to an asset of a company or any raw materials or consumables used in the production of such an asset, includes any consideration (whether in cash or otherwise) given by the company in respect of that asset or those materials or consumables, as the case may be.

The '*production cost*' of an asset is the purchase price of the raw materials and consumables used plus the costs incurred by the company which are directly attributable to the production of that asset. In addition, there may be included

- a reasonable proportion of the costs so incurred by the company which are only indirectly attributable to the production of that asset, but only to the extent that they relate to the period of production; and
- interest on capital borrowed to finance the production of that asset, to the extent that it accrues in respect of the period of production. The inclusion of interest in determining the cost and the amount of the interest so included must be disclosed in a note to the accounts.

In the case of current assets, production costs must not include distribution costs.

[*SI 2008 No 409, Sch 1 para 27; Sch 8 para 9*].

Where

- there is no record of the purchase price or production cost of any asset (of any price, expenses or costs relevant to its determination), or
- any such record cannot be obtained without unreasonable expense or delay,

the purchase price or production cost of the asset must be taken to be the value ascribed to it in the earliest available record of its value made on or after its acquisition or production by the company. [*SI 2008 No 409, Sch 1 para 29*].

Stocks and fungible assets. The purchase price or production cost of

- any assets which by virtue of *SI 2008 No 409, reg 3* (see **5.5**) and the balance sheet formats set out in 5.6 fall to be included under any item shown in a company's balance sheet under the general item 'stocks', and
- any assets which are 'fungible assets' (including investments),

may be determined by applying any of the following methods in relation to any such assets of the same class, provided that the method chosen is one which appears to the directors to be appropriate in the circumstances of the company.

(1) 'First in, first out' (FIFO).

(2) 'Last in, first out' (LIFO).

(3) A weighted average price.

(4) Any other method similar to any of the above.

'*Fungible assets*' means assets of any description which are substantially indistinguishable one from another.

[*SI 2008 No 409, Sch 1 para 28*].

5.14 Alternative accounting rules

Any of the accounting rules set out below may be used (as alternatives to the historical cost accounting rules in **5.9** to **5.13**) to determine the amounts to be included in respect of the assets in question.

(a) *Intangible fixed assets*, other than goodwill, may be included at their current cost.

(b) *Tangible fixed assets* may be included at a market value (determined as at the date of their last valuation) or at their current cost.

(c) *Investments of any description falling to be included under item B III* of either of the balance sheet formats in **5.6** may be included either at

 (i) market value determined as at the date of their last valuation; or

 (ii) a value determined on any basis which appears to the directors to be appropriate in the circumstances of the company (but in this case particulars of the method of valuation adopted and of the reasons for adopting it must be disclosed in a note to the accounts).

(d) *Investments of any description falling to be included under item C III* of either of the balance sheet formats in **5.6** may be included at their current cost.

(e) *Stocks* may be included at their current cost.

Application of the depreciation rules. Where the value of any asset is determined on any basis within (*a*)–(*e*) above, that value (instead of the purchase price, production cost or any value previously so determined for that asset) must be (or, as the case may require, must be the starting point for determining) the amount to be included in respect of that asset in the accounts. The historic cost depreciation rules in **5.10** to **5.12** apply accordingly in relation to any such asset with the substitution for any reference to its purchase price or production cost of a reference to the value most recently determined for that asset under (*a*)–(*e*) above (the '*adjusted depreciation rules*').

In the case of a fixed asset, any provision for depreciation in respect of that asset which is

- included in any item shown in the profit and loss account in respect of amounts written off assets of the description in question, or
- taken into account as required by note (1) to the profit and loss account formats in **5.7**

will normally be included or taken into account at the amount calculated under the adjusted depreciation rules above. It may, however, be included or taken in account under the historic cost depreciation rules instead of the adjusted depreciation rules, provided that the amount of any difference between the two is shown separately in the profit and loss account or in a note to the accounts.

[*SI 2008 No 409, Sch 1 paras 30–33*].

5.15 *Additional information to be provided in case of departure from historical cost accounting rules*

Where the amounts to be included in respect of assets covered by any items shown in the accounts have been determined on any basis in **5.14**(*a*)–(*e*), the following additional information must be disclosed in a note to the accounts or alternatively, in the case of (*b*) below, shown separately in the balance sheet.

(a) The items affected and the basis of valuation adopted in determining the amounts of the assets in question in the case of each such item.

(b) In the case of each balance sheet item affected (except stocks), either

- the 'comparable amounts determined according to the historical cost accounting rules'; or
- the differences between those amounts and the corresponding amounts actually shown in the balance sheet in respect of that item.

The '*comparable amounts determined according to the historical cost accounting rules*' are

- the aggregate amount which would be required to be shown in respect of that item if the amounts to be included in respect of all the assets covered by that item were determined according to the historical cost accounting rules; and
- the aggregate amount of the cumulative provisions for depreciation or diminution in value which would be permitted or required in determining those amounts according to those rules.

[*SI 2008 No 409, Sch 1 para 34*].

5.16 *Revaluation reserve*

The amount of any profit or loss arising from the determination of the value of an asset on any basis mentioned in **5.14**(*a*)–(*e*) (after allowing, where appropriate, for any provisions for depreciation or diminution in value) must be credited or, as the case may be, debited to a separate reserve, the 'revaluation reserve'.

The amount of the revaluation reserve must be shown in the balance sheet under a separate sub-heading in the position given for the item 'revaluation reserve' in either of the balance sheet formats in **5.6**, although it need not be shown under that name.

The revaluation reserve must be reduced to the extent that the amounts transferred to it are no longer necessary for the purposes of the valuation method used. In addition, an amount may be transferred

- from the revaluation reserve to the profit and loss account, if the amount was previously charged to that account or represents realised profit;
- from the revaluation reserve on capitalisation (ie by applying the amount in wholly or partly paying up unissued shares in the company to be allotted to members as fully or partly paid shares); and
- to or from the revaluation reserve in respect of the taxation relating to any profit or loss credited or debited to the reserve.

The revaluation reserve must not be reduced except as mentioned above.

The treatment for taxation purposes of amounts credited or debited to the revaluation reserve must be disclosed in a note to the accounts.

[*SI 2008 No 409, Sch 1 para 35*].

5.17 Financial instruments

(1) *Financial instruments*

Financial instruments (including 'derivatives') may be included at fair value with the following exceptions.

- Financial instruments which constitute liabilities unless
  - (i) they are held as part of a 'trading portfolio';
  - (ii) they are derivative; or
  - (iii) they are financial instruments that, under international accounting standards adopted by the European Commission before 6 September 2006 in accordance with the IAS Regulation, may be included in accounts at fair value, provided that the disclosures required by such accounting standards are made.
- Any of the following, namely
  - (i) financial instruments (other than derivatives) 'held to maturity',
  - (ii) loans and 'receivables' originated by the company and not 'held for trading purposes',
  - (iii) interests in subsidiary undertakings, associated undertaking (see **5.64**) and joint ventures (see **5.63**),

(iv) 'equity instruments' issued by the company,

(v) contracts for contingent consideration in a 'business combination',

(vi) other financial instruments with such special characteristics that the instruments, according to generally accepted accounting principles or practice, should be accounted for differently from other financial instruments,

unless they are financial instruments that, under international accounting standards adopted by the European Commission before 6 September 2006 in accordance with the IAS Regulation, may be included in accounts at fair value, provided that the disclosures required by such accounting standards are made.

- If the fair value of a financial instrument cannot be determined reliably under the rules set out below.

'*Derivatives*' include 'commodity-based contracts' that give either contracting party the right to settle in cash or in some other financial instrument, except when such contracts

- were entered into for the purpose of, and continue to meet, the company's expected purchase, sale or usage requirements;
- were designated for such purpose at their inception; and
- are expected to be settled by delivery of the commodity.
- *Determination of fair value*. The fair value of a financial instrument is determined as follows.

(a) If a 'reliable market' can readily be identified for the financial instrument, its fair value is determined by reference to its market value.

(b) If a reliable market cannot readily be identified for the financial instrument but can be identified for its components or for a similar instrument, its fair value is determined by reference to the market value of its components or of the similar instrument.

(c) If neither (*a*) or (*b*) above applies, the fair value of the financial instrument is a value resulting from generally accepted valuation models and techniques which ensure a reasonable approximation of the market value.

Hedged items. A company may include any assets and liabilities that qualify as hedged items under a 'fair value hedge accounting system', or identified portions of such assets or liabilities, at the amount required under that system.

The expressions '*business combination*', '*commodity-based contracts*', '*derivative*', '*equity instrument*', '*fair value hedge accounting system*', '*financial instrument*', '*hedge accounting*', '*hedge accounting system*', '*hedged items*', '*held for trading purposes*', '*held to maturity*', '*receivables*', '*reliable market*' and '*trading portfolio*' have the same meaning as they have in *Council Directive 78/660/EEC* on the annual accounts of certain types of companies (as amended).

(2) *Investment property*

Investment property that, under international accounting standards, may be included in accounts at fair value may be included at fair value, provided that all such investment property is so included where its fair value can reliably be determined. For these purposes, 'fair value' means fair value determined in accordance with relevant international accounting standards.

(3) *Living animals and plants*

Living animals and plants that, under international accounting standards, may be included in accounts at fair value may be included at fair value, provided that all such living animals and plants are so included where their fair value can reliably be determined. For these purposes, 'fair value' means fair value determined in accordance with relevant international accounting standards.

Accounting for changes in value. Where a financial instrument or asset is valued in accordance with (1) to (3) above, a change in the value of the financial instrument or asset must be included in the profit and loss account. But

(A) where

(i) the financial instrument accounted for is a 'hedging instrument' under a hedge accounting system that allows some or all of the change in value not to be shown in the profit and loss account, or

(ii) the change in value relates to an 'exchange difference' arising on a 'monetary item' that forms part of a company's net investment in a 'foreign entity',

the amount of the change in value *must* be credited to or (as the case may be) debited from a separate reserve ('*the fair value reserve*'); and

(B) where the instrument accounted for

(i) is an 'available for sale financial asset', and

(ii) is not a derivative,

the change in value *may* be credited to or (as the case may be) debited from the fair value reserve.

The expressions '*available for sale financial asset*', '*exchange difference*', '*financial instrument*', '*foreign entity*', '*hedge accounting*', '*hedge accounting system*', '*hedging instrument*', and '*monetary item*' have the same meaning as they have in *Council Directive 78/660/EEC* on the annual accounts of certain types of companies (as amended).

The fair value reserve. The fair value reserve must be adjusted to the extent that the amounts shown in it are no longer necessary for the purposes of (A) or (B) above.

The treatment for taxation purposes of amounts credited or debited to the fair value reserve must be disclosed in a note to the accounts.
[*SI 2008 No 409, Sch 1 paras 36–41, Sch 8 paras 1, 2*].

5.18 Notes to the accounts: general

Reserves and dividends. There must be stated

(a) any amount set aside or proposed to be set aside to, or withdrawn or proposed to be withdrawn from, reserves;

(b) the aggregate amount of dividends paid in the financial year (other than those for which a liability existed at the immediately preceding balance sheet date);

(c) the aggregate amount of dividends that the company is liable to pay at the balance sheet date; and

(d) the aggregate amount of dividends that are proposed before the date of approval of the accounts, and not otherwise disclosed under (*b*) or (*c*) above.

Disclosure of accounting policies. The accounting policies adopted in determining the profit or loss and the amounts of balance sheet items (including policies with respect to the depreciation and diminution in value of assets) must be stated.

Foreign currency translation. Where any sums originally denominated in foreign currencies have been brought into account under any items shown in the balance sheet or profit and loss account, the basis on which those sums have been translated into sterling (or the currency in which the accounts are drawn up) must be stated.

Dormant companies acting as agents. Where the directors of a company take advantage of the exemption from audit conferred on dormant companies by *CA 2006, s 480* (see AUDIT) and the company has during the financial year in question acted as an agent for any person, the fact that it has so acted must be stated.

[*SI 2008 No 409, Sch 1 paras 43, 44, 62, 63*].

5.19 Notes to the accounts: information supplementing the balance sheet

The information required, as set out in **5.20** to **5.27**, being information which either supplements that given with respect to particular items in the balance sheet or is otherwise relevant to assessing the company's state of affairs, must be given by way of notes to the accounts (if not given in the accounts themselves). [*SI 2008 No 409, Sch 1 paras 42, 45*].

5.20 *Share capital*

The following information must be given with respect to the company's share capital.

- Where shares of more than one class have been allotted, the number and aggregate nominal value of shares of each class allotted.
- If any part of the allotted share capital consists of redeemable shares,
  - (i) the earliest and latest dates on which the company has power to redeem those shares;
  - (ii) whether those shares must be redeemed in any event or are liable to be redeemed at the option of the company or of the shareholder; and
  - (iii) whether any (and, if so, what) premium is payable on redemption.
- If the company has allotted any shares during the financial year,
  - (i) the classes of shares allotted; and
  - (ii) as respects each class of shares, the number allotted, their aggregate nominal value, and the consideration received by the company for the allotment.

[*SI 2008 No 409, Sch 1 paras 46, 47*].

5.21 *Fixed assets*

The information set out below must be given for each item which is shown under the general item 'fixed assets' in the balance sheet (or which would be shown there were it not for **5.5**(6) (*b*) (ii)).

(a) The 'appropriate amounts' in respect of that item as at both the beginning of the financial year and at the balance sheet date.

(b) The effect on any amount shown in the balance sheet in respect of that item of

(i) any revision of the amount in respect of any assets included under that item made during that year on any basis in **5.14**(*a*)–(*e*);

(ii) acquisitions and disposals during that year of any assets; and

(iii) any transfers of assets of the company to and from that item during that year.

(c) In respect of each item

- the cumulative amount of provisions for depreciation or diminution in value of assets included under that item both as at the beginning of the financial year and at the balance sheet date;
- the amount of any such provisions made in respect of the financial year; and
- the amount of any adjustments made in respect of any such provisions during that year, distinguishing between adjustments made in consequence of disposals and other adjustments.

For the purposes of (*a*) above, the '*appropriate amounts*' in respect of any item as at either of the dates there mentioned are the aggregate amounts determined, as at that date, in respect of assets falling to be included under that item, either on the basis of purchase price or production cost (see **5.13**) or on any basis in **5.14**(*a*)–(*e*) but in either case leaving out of account in either case any provisions for depreciation or diminution in value.

[*SI 2008 No 409, Sch 1 para 48*].

Assets included at valuation. The following additional information must be given where any fixed assets (other than listed investments, see **5.22**) are included under any balance sheet item at an amount determined on any basis in **5.14**(*a*)–(*e*).

(i) The years (as far as they are known to the directors) in which the assets were severally valued, and the several values.

(ii) In the case of assets valued during the financial year, the bases of valuation used and either the names or qualifications of the valuers.

[*SI 2008 No 409, Sch 1 para 49*].

5.22 *Investments*

In respect of the amount of each item shown in the balance sheet set out in **5.6** under the general item 'investments' (whether as fixed or current assets) (or which would be shown there were it not for **5.5**(6)(*b*)(ii)) there must be stated how much is ascribable to 'listed investments'.

Where the amount of any listed investments is stated (as required above), there must also be stated

- their aggregate market value where this differs from the amount so stated; and
- both the market value and the stock exchange value of any investments of which the former value is, for the purposes of the accounts, taken as being higher than the latter.

A '*listed investment*' is an investment which has been granted a listing either on a recognised investment exchange other than an overseas investment exchange (which terms have the same meaning as in *FSMA 2000, Pt 18*) or on any stock exchange of repute outside the UK.

[*SI 2008 No 409, Sch 1 para 50, Sch 8 para 5; SI 2013 No 3008, Reg 13*].

See also **5.31** to **5.38** for disclosure of holdings in related undertakings.

5.23 *Fair value of assets and liabilities*

(1) *Financial instruments*

Financial instrument included at fair value. Where financial instruments have been valued in accordance with **5.17**(1), the following must be stated.

(a) Where the fair value of the instruments has been determined in accordance with **5.17**(1) (*c*), the significant assumptions underlying the valuation models and techniques used.

(b) For each category of financial instrument, the fair value of the instruments in that category and the changes in value

  (i) included in the profit and loss account, or

  (ii) credited to or (as the case may be) debited from the fair value reserve,

  in respect of those instruments.

(c) For each class of 'derivatives', the extent and nature of the instruments, including significant terms and conditions that may affect the amount, timing and certainty of future cash flows.

(d) Where any amount is transferred to or from the fair value reserve during the financial year, there must be stated in tabular form

  - the amount of the reserve as at the beginning of the financial year and the balance sheet date;
  - the amount transferred to or from the reserve during that year; and
  - the source and application respectively of the amounts so transferred.

Financial fixed assets. If

- the company has 'financial fixed assets' that could be included at fair value by virtue of **5.17**(1),
- the amount at which those items are included under any item in the company's accounts is in excess of their fair value, and
- the company has not made provision for diminution in value of those assets in accordance with **5.10**,

there must be stated

- the amount at which either the individual assets or appropriate groupings of those individual assets are included in the company's accounts;
- the fair value of those assets or groupings; and
- the reasons for not making a provision for diminution in value of those assets, including the nature of the evidence that provides the basis for the belief that the amount at which they are stated in the accounts will be recovered.

[*SI 2008 No 409, Sch 1 paras 51, 52*].

See **5.17** for the meaning of '*derivatives*'.

(2) *Investment property*

Where the amounts to be included in the accounts in respect of investment property have been determined in accordance with **5.17**(2), the balance sheet items affected and the basis of valuation adopted in determining the amounts of the assets in question in the case of each such item must be disclosed in a note to the accounts.

For each balance sheet item affected there must be shown, either separately in the balance sheet or in a note to the accounts

- the 'comparable amounts' determined according to the historical cost accounting rules; or
- the differences between those amounts and the corresponding amounts actually shown in the balance sheet in respect of that item.

'*Comparable amounts*' mean

- the aggregate amount which would be required to be shown in respect of that item if the amounts to be included in respect of all the assets covered by that item were determined according to the historical cost accounting rules; and
- the aggregate amount of the cumulative provisions for depreciation or diminution in value which would be permitted or required in determining those amounts according to those rules.

[*SI 2008 No 409, Sch 1 para 53*].

(3) *Living animals and plants*

Where the amounts to be included in the accounts in respect of living animals and plants have been determined in accordance with **5.17**(3), the balance sheet items affected and the basis of valuation adopted in determining the amounts of the assets in question in the case of each such item must be disclosed in a note to the accounts.

[*SI 2008 No 409, Sch 1 para 53*].

5.24 *Reserves and provisions*

Where any amount is transferred

- to or from any reserves,
- to any 'provisions for liabilities', or
- from any such provision for liabilities, otherwise than for the purpose for which the provision was established,

and the reserves or provisions are shown as separate items in the balance sheet (or would be so shown were it not for **5.5**(6) (*b*) (ii)), the following information must be given in respect of the aggregate of reserves or provisions included in the same item.

- The amount of the reserves or provisions at the beginning of the financial year and at the balance sheet date.
- Any amounts transferred to or from the reserves or provisions during the year.
- The source and application of the amounts so transferred.

Where the amount of the provision is material, particulars must be given of each provision included in the item 'other provisions' in the balance sheet.

References to '*provisions for liabilities*' are to any amount retained as reasonably necessary for the purpose of providing for any liability the nature of which is clearly defined and which is either likely to be incurred, or certain to be incurred but uncertain as to amount or as to the date on which it will arise.

[*SI 2008 No 409, Sch 1 para 54, Sch 7 para 2*].

5.25 *Details of indebtedness*

In respect of each item shown in the balance sheet under 'creditors' (or which would be shown there were it not for 5.5(6) (*b*) (ii)), the following information is required.

(a) The aggregate amount of any debts included under that item which are payable or repayable otherwise than by instalments and which fall due for payment or repayment after the end of a five-year period beginning with the day after the end of the financial year.

(b) In the case of any debts so included which are payable or repayable by instalments, the aggregate amount of any instalments which fall due for payment after the end of the period specified in (*a*) above.

(c) The aggregate amount of any debts included under that item in respect of which any security has been given by the company.

Where a distinction is made in the balance sheet between amounts falling due to creditors within one year and those falling due after more than one year, (*a*) and (*b*) above apply only to items shown under the latter of those categories and (*c*) above applies to items shown under either category.

[*SI 2008 No 409, Sch 1 para 55*].

Fixed cumulative dividends. If any fixed cumulative dividends on the company's shares are in arrear, there must be stated the amount of the arrears and the period for which the dividends (or, if there is more than one class, each class of them) are in arrear. [*SI 2008 No 409, Sch 1 para 56*].

5.26 *Guarantees and other financial commitments*

The following information must be given.

(a) Particulars of any charge on the assets of the company to secure the liabilities of any other person, including, where practicable, the amount secured.

(b) With respect to any other contingent liability not provided for

(i) the amount or estimated amount of that liability;

(ii) its legal nature; and

(iii) whether any valuable security has been provided by the company in connection with that liability and if so, what.

(c) Where practicable, the aggregate amount or estimated amount of contracts for capital expenditure, so far as not provided for.

(d) Particulars of any pension commitments included under any provision shown in the company's balance sheet, and any such commitments for which no provision has been made, giving separate particulars of any commitment so far as it relates to pensions payable to past directors.

(e) Particulars of any other financial commitments that have not been provided for and are relevant to assessing the company's state of affairs.

Guarantees and other financial commitments in favour of group undertakings. Commitments within any of (*a*)–(*e*) above which are undertaken on behalf of or for the benefit of

(i) any parent undertaking or fellow subsidiary undertaking, or

(ii) any subsidiary undertaking of the company,

must be stated separately from the other commitments within each of (*a*)–(*e*) above, distinguishing commitments within (i) from those within (ii) above.

[*SI 2008 No 409, Sch 1 para 57*].

5.27 *Miscellaneous matters*

Particulars of any case where the purchase price or production cost of any asset is for the first time determined *SI 2008 No 409, Sch 1 para 29* (see **5.13**). [*SI 2008 No 409, Sch 1 para 58*].

5.28 Notes to the accounts: information supplementing the profit and loss account

The information required, as set out in **5.29** and **5.30**, being information which either supplements that given with respect to particular items in the profit and loss account or otherwise provides particulars of income or expenditure or of circumstances affecting items shown in the profit and loss account, must be given by way of notes to the accounts (if not given in the accounts themselves). [*SI 2008 No 409, Sch 1 paras 42, 59*]. See **5.58** for exemption from these provisions for companies preparing group accounts in accordance with *CA 2006*.

5.29 *Particulars of turnover*

If the company has supplied geographical markets outside the UK during the financial year in question, the percentage of turnover attributable, in the opinion of the directors, to those markets must be stated. In analysing the source of turnover, the directors must have regard to the manner in which the company's activities are organised. [*SI 2008 No 409, Sch 1 para 60*].

5.30 *Miscellaneous matters*

Prior year adjustments. Where any amount relating to any preceding financial year is included in any profit and loss account item, the effect must be stated.

Extraordinary items. Particulars must be given of any extraordinary income or charges arising in the financial year.

Exceptional items. The effect of any exceptional transactions (by virtue of size or incidence) must be stated, even though they fall within the ordinary activities of the company.

[*SI 2008 No 409, Sch 1 para 61*].

5.31 INDIVIDUAL ACCOUNTS: INFORMATION ON RELATED UNDERTAKINGS

Subject to the provisions of *SI 2008 No 409, regulation 5A* where a small company is not preparing group accounts, it's Companies Act or IAS individual accounts must comply with the provisions in **5.32** to **5.38** as to the information about related undertakings to be given in notes to the company's accounts. There are three exceptions.

(1) **Exemption**

The information (other than that in **5.35** and **5.37**) need not be disclosed with respect to an undertaking that

- is established under the law of a country outside the UK, or
- carries on business outside the UK,

but only if

- in the opinion of the directors of the company, the disclosure would be seriously prejudicial to the business of
  - (i) that undertaking;
  - (ii) the company;
  - (iii) any of the company's subsidiary undertakings; or
  - (iv) any other undertaking which is included in the consolidation; and
- the Secretary of State agrees that the information need not be disclosed.

Where advantage is taken of this exemption, a note to that effect must be included in the company's accounts.

[*CA 2006, s 409(4) (5); SI 2008 No 409, Reg 4*].

(2) **Alternative compliance in cases of excessive length**

Where the directors are of the opinion that the number of undertakings in respect of which the company is required to disclose information under any provision described in **5.32** to **5.38** is such that compliance would result in information of excessive length being given in the notes to the accounts, information need only be given in respect of the undertakings whose results or financial position, in the directors' opinion, principally affected the figures shown in the company's annual accounts.

If advantage is taken of this, then

(i) the notes to the company's annual accounts must include a statement that the information is given only with respect to undertakings whose results or financial position, in the directors' opinion, principally affected the figures shown; and

(ii) the full information (ie both that which is disclosed and that which is not) must be annexed to the next annual return delivered to the Registrar of Companies after the accounts in question have been approved by the board.

If a company fails to comply with (ii) above, an offence is committed by the company and every officer of the company who is in default. A person guilty of such an offence is liable, on summary conviction, to a fine not exceeding level 3 on the standard scale and, for continued contravention, a daily default fine not exceeding one-tenth of level 3 on the standard scale. See **29.1** OFFENCES AND LEGAL PROCEEDINGS for the standard scale.

[*CA 2006, s 410*].

(3) Micro entities

Nothing in the Schedules to *SI 2008 No 409* requires the Companies Act individual accounts of a company for a year in which the company qualifies as a micro-entity, to contain any information by way of notes to the accounts, except that the company is required to disclose by way of notes to the accounts the information required by *SI 2008 No 409, Schedule 1, paragraph 57*(guarantees and other financial commitments).

[*SI 2013 No 3008, Reg 9(5)*]

5.32 Subsidiary undertakings

Subject to **5.31**, where, at the end of the financial year, the company has subsidiary undertakings, there must be stated in respect of each one of them

- its name;
- if it is incorporated outside the UK, the country in which it is incorporated;
- if it is unincorporated, the address of its principal place of business.

[*SI 2008 No 409, Sch 2 para 1*].

5.33 *Holdings in subsidiary undertakings*

Subject to **5.31**, in relation to shares of each class 'held by the company' in a subsidiary undertaking, there must be stated

- the identity of the class; and
- the proportion of the nominal value of the shares of that class represented by those shares.

The shares held by or on behalf of the company itself must be distinguished from those attributed to the company which are held by or on behalf of a subsidiary undertaking.

[*SI 2008 No 409, Sch 2 para 2*].

In ascertaining the shares '*held by the company*',

- there must be attributed to the company any shares held by a subsidiary undertaking, or by a person acting on behalf of the company or a subsidiary undertaking. Any shares held on behalf of a person other than the company or a subsidiary undertaking must be treated as not held by the company; and
- shares held by way of security must be treated as held by the person providing the security where
  - (i) the rights attached to the shares are exercisable only in accordance with his instructions; and
  - (ii) the shares are held in connection with the granting of loans as part of normal business activities and the rights attached to the shares are exercisable only in his interests

  disregarding, in each case, any right to exercise the rights for the purpose of preserving the value of the security, or of realising it.

[*SI 2008 No 409, Sch 2 para 11*].

5.34 *Financial information about subsidiary undertakings*

Subject to **5.31** and the exceptions below, there must be disclosed with respect to each subsidiary undertaking not included in consolidated accounts by the company

- the aggregate amount of its capital and reserves as at the end of its 'relevant financial year'; and
- its profit or loss for that year.

For this purposes, the *'relevant financial year'* of a subsidiary undertaking is, if its financial year ends with that of the company, that year and, if it does not, its financial year ending last before the end of the company's financial year.

Exceptions. The above information need not be given if

- the company would (if it were not subject to the small companies regime) be exempt by virtue of *CA 2006, s 400* or *401* (parent company included in accounts of larger group, see **3.54 Accounts: Large Companies**) from the requirement to prepare group accounts;
- the company's investment in the subsidiary undertaking is included in the company's accounts by way of the equity method of valuation;
- the subsidiary undertaking is not required to deliver a copy of its balance sheet for its relevant financial year and does not otherwise publish that balance sheet in the UK or elsewhere *and* the shares '*held by the company*' (see **5.33**) are less than 50% of the nominal value of the shares in the undertaking; or
- it is not material.

[*SI 2008 No 409, Sch 2 para 3*].

5.35 *Shares of company held by subsidiary undertakings*

Subject to **5.31**, the number, description and amount of shares in the company held by, or on behalf of, its subsidiary undertakings must be disclosed. This does not apply in relation to shares in the case of which the subsidiary undertaking is concerned as

- personal representative; or
- trustee unless the company, or any subsidiary undertaking of the company, is 'beneficially interested under the trust', otherwise than by way of security only for the purposes of a transaction entered into by it in the ordinary course of a business which includes the lending of money.

[*SI 2008 No 409, Sch 2 para 4*].

In determining whether the company is '*beneficially interested under the trust*', certain residual interests under pension and employees' share schemes, employer's charges and other rights of recovery under such schemes, and a trustee's right to expenses, remuneration, indemnity, etc are disregarded. See *SI 2008 No 409, Sch 2 paras 12–17* for full details.

5.36 Significant holdings in undertakings other than subsidiary undertakings

Subject to **5.31**, where at the end of the financial year the company has a 'significant holding' in an undertaking which is not a subsidiary undertaking, the following must be stated.

(a) The name of the undertaking.

(b) If the undertaking is incorporated outside the UK, the country in which it is incorporated.

(c) If it is unincorporated, the address of its principal place of business.

(d) The identity of each class of shares in the undertaking held by the company.

(e) The proportion of the nominal value of the shares of that class represented by those shares.

(f) Subject to the exemption below, the aggregate amount of the capital and reserves of the undertaking as at the end of its 'relevant financial year'.

(g) Subject to the exemption below, its profit or loss for that year.

A '*significant holding*' is a holding which amounts to 20% or more of the nominal value of any class of shares in the undertaking *or* the amount of which (as stated or included in the company's individual accounts) exceeds one-fifth of the amount (as so stated) of the company's assets.

The '*relevant financial year*' of an undertaking for these purposes is, if its financial year ends with that of the company, that year, and if it does not, its financial year ending last before the end of the company's financial year.

Exemption. The information in (*f*) and (*g*) above need not be given in respect of an undertaking if

- the company would (if it were not subject to the small companies regime) be exempt by virtue of *CA 2006, s 400* or *401* (parent company included in accounts of larger group, see **3.54 Accounts: Large Companies**) from the requirement to prepare group accounts *and* the investment of the company in all undertakings in which it has a significant holding is shown, in aggregate, in the notes to the accounts by way of the equity method of valuation;
- the undertaking in question is not required to deliver to the Registrar of Companies a copy of its balance sheet for its relevant financial year and does not otherwise publish that balance sheet in the UK or elsewhere *and* the company's holding is less than 50% of the nominal value of the shares in the undertaking; or
- it is not material.

[*SI 2008 No 409, Sch 2 paras 5–7*].

In ascertaining, for any of the above purposes, the company's holding,

- there must be attributed to the company shares held on its behalf by any person but any shares held on behalf of a person other than the company must be treated as not held by the company; and
- shares held by way of security must be treated as held by the person providing the security where

  (i) the rights attached to the shares are exercisable only in accordance with his instructions; and

  (ii) the shares are held in connection with the granting of loans as part of normal business activities and the rights attached to the shares are exercisable only in his interests

  disregarding, in each case, any right to exercise the rights for the purpose of preserving the value of the security, or of realising it.

[*SI 2008 No 409, Sch 2 para 11*].

5.37 Membership of certain undertakings

Subject to **5.31**, where at the end of the financial year a company is a member of a 'qualifying undertaking' the following must be stated.

- The name and legal form of the undertaking (unless it is not material).
- The address (whether in or outside the UK) of its registered office or, if it does not have such an office, its head office (unless it is not material).
- Where the undertaking is a qualifying partnership, either
  - (i) a statement that a copy of the latest accounts of the undertaking has been or is to be appended to the copy of the company's accounts sent to the Registrar of Companies; or
  - (ii) the name of at least one body corporate (which may be the company) in whose group accounts the undertaking has been or is to be dealt with on a consolidated basis. This information need not be given if the notes to the company's accounts disclose that advantage has been taken of the exemption in *regulation 7* of the *Partnerships (Accounts) Regulations 2008*.

A '*qualifying undertaking*' means

(a) a qualifying partnership; or

(b) an unlimited company each of whose members is

- (i) a limited company;
- (ii) another unlimited company each of whose members is a limited company; or
- (iii) a Scottish partnership each of whose members is a limited company,

and, for these purposes, references to a limited company, another unlimited company and a Scottish partnership include a comparable undertaking incorporated in, or formed under, the law of a country or territory outside the UK.

[*SI 2008 No 409, Sch 2 para 8; SI 2008 No 569, Reg 17*].

5.38 Parent undertaking drawing up accounts for larger group

Subject to **5.31**, where the company is a subsidiary undertaking, the following information must be given.

(a) Particulars as follows with respect to the parent undertaking of the largest and smallest group of undertakings for which group accounts are drawn up and of which the company is a member.

- (i) The name of the parent undertaking.
- (ii) If the undertaking is incorporated outside the UK, the country in which it is incorporated.
- (iii) if it is unincorporated, the address of its principal place of business.
- (iv) If copies of the group accounts referred to above are available to the public, the addresses from which copies of the accounts can be obtained.

(b) Particulars as follows with respect to the company (which includes any body corporate) regarded by the directors as being the company's ultimate parent company.

 (i) Its name.

 (ii) If that company is incorporated outside the UK, the country in which it is incorporated (if known to the directors).

[*SI 2008 No 409, Sch 2 paras 9, 10*].

5.39 INDIVIDUAL ACCOUNTS-UNQUOTED COMPANIES: DIRECTORS' REMUNERATION AND BENEFITS

The information as described in **5.40** to **5.44** must be given in the notes to a company's individual accounts. The provisions apply whether the company is preparing Companies Act or IAS accounts.

5.40 Directors' remuneration

Subject to the provisions of *SI 2008 No 409, regulation 5A*, the information on directors' remuneration as described in **5.41** to **5.43** must be given in the notes to a company's annual accounts. [*CA 2006, s 412(1); SI 2008 No 409, Reg 5*].

It is the duty of

- any director of a company, and
- any person who is or has at any time in the preceding five years been a director of the company

to give notice to the company of such matters relating to himself as may be necessary for these purposes. A person in default commits an offence and is liable, on summary conviction to a fine not exceeding level 3 on the standard scale. See **29.1 Offences and Legal Proceedings** for the standard scale.

[*CA 2006, s 412(5) (6)*].

Information is to be given only so far as it is contained in the company's books and papers or the company has the right to obtain it from the persons concerned. [*SI 2008 No 409, Sch 3 para 4(1)*].

Where it is necessary for the purpose of making any distinction required in **5.41** to **5.43**, the directors may apportion payments between the matters in respect of which they have been paid or are receivable in such manner as they think appropriate. [*SI 2008 No 409, Sch 3 para 5(6)*].

Micro entities

Nothing in the Schedules to *SI 2008 No 409* requires the Companies Act individual accounts of a company for a year in which the company qualifies as a micro-entity, to contain any information by way of notes to the accounts, except that the company is required to disclose by way of notes to the accounts the information required by *SI 2008 No 409 ,Schedule 1, paragraph 57*(guarantees and other financial commitments).

[*SI 2013 No 3008, Reg 9(5)*]

Meaning of 'subsidiary undertakings'. Any reference in these provisions to a subsidiary undertaking of the company, in relation to a person who is or was, while a director of the company, a director also, by virtue of the company's nomination (direct or indirect) of any other undertaking, includes that undertaking (whether or not it is or was in fact a subsidiary undertaking of the company). [*SI 2008 No 409, Sch 3 para 11(1)*].

5.41 *Total amount of directors' remuneration, etc*

The following must be shown. Any information is treated as being shown if it is capable of being readily ascertained from other information which is shown.

(a) The amount of 'remuneration' paid to or receivable by directors in respect of 'qualifying services'.

'*Remuneration*' of a director includes

- salary, fees and bonuses;
- sums paid by way of expenses allowance (so far as they are chargeable to UK income tax); and
- the estimated money value of any other benefits received by the director otherwise than in cash, but does not include
  - the value of any share options granted to the director or the amount of any gains made on the exercise of any such options;
  - any company contributions paid, or treated as paid, under any pension scheme or any benefits to which the director is entitled under any such scheme; or
  - any money or other assets paid to or received or receivable by the director under any 'long term incentive scheme'.

(b) The aggregate of

(i) the amount of money paid to or receivable by directors under 'long-term incentive schemes' in respect of 'qualifying services'; and

(ii) the 'net value' of assets (other than money, share options and shares (whether allotted or not) in the company or any group undertaking) received or receivable by directors under long-term incentive schemes in respect of qualifying services. '*Net value*' means the value after deducting any money paid or other value given by the director in respect of those assets.

(c) The value of any 'company contributions' paid, or treated as paid, to a pension scheme in respect of directors' 'qualifying services', being contributions by reference to which the rate or amount of any 'money purchase benefits' that may become payable will be calculated.

'*Company contributions*' mean any payments (including insurance premiums) made, or treated as made, to the scheme in respect of the director by any person other than the director.

'*Money purchase benefits*' are retirement benefits payable under a pension scheme, the rate or amount of which is calculated by reference to payments made, or treated as made, by the director or by any other person in respect of the director and which are not average salary benefits.

(d) The number of directors (if any) to whom retirement benefits are accruing in respect of 'qualifying services' under each of

(i) '*money purchase schemes*' (ie pension schemes under which all of the benefits that may become payable to, or in respect of, the director are 'money purchase benefits', see (*c*) above); and

(ii) '*defined benefit schemes*' (ie any pension scheme which is not a money purchase scheme).

'*Qualifying services*' in respect of any person means

- his services as director of the company; and
- his services while director of the company
  - (i) as director of any of its subsidiary undertakings; or
  - (ii) otherwise in connection with the management of the company's affairs or those of any of its subsidiary undertakings.

Reference to a subsidiary undertaking of the company is to an undertaking which is a subsidiary undertaking at the time the services were rendered.

A '*long term incentive scheme*' means any agreement or arrangement under which money or other assets may become receivable by a director and which includes one or more qualifying conditions with respect to service or performance which cannot be fulfilled in a single financial year, but disregarding

- bonuses determined by reference to service or performance in a single financial year;
- compensation for loss of office, payments for breach of contract and other termination payments; and
- retirement benefits.

Notes

(1) Remuneration paid or receivable or share options granted in respect of a person's accepting office as director are treated as remuneration paid or receivable or share options granted in respect of his services as director.

(2) For the purpose of determining whether a pension scheme is a money purchase scheme or defined benefit scheme, any death in service benefits provided are to be disregarded.

(3) Where a pension scheme provides for any benefits that may become payable to or in respect of any director to be whichever are the greater of money purchase benefits and defined benefits (in each case as determined under the scheme), the company may assume that those benefits will be whichever appears more likely at the end of the financial year.

(4) Amounts paid to or receivable by a person include amounts paid to or receivable by a connected person or a body corporate controlled by him, but not so as to require an amount to be counted twice.

(5) The amounts to be shown include all relevant sums paid by or receivable from the company, its subsidiary undertakings and any other person. They do not, however, include sums to be accounted for

- to the company or any of its subsidiary undertakings; or
- by virtue of *CA 2006, s 219* and *222(3)* (payments in connection with shares transfers, duty to account) to persons who sold their shares as a result of the offer made.

(6) The amounts to be shown for any financial year are the sums receivable in respect of that financial year (whenever paid) or, in the case of sums not payable in respect of a period, the sums paid during the year. However, in either of the

two circumstances set out below, the sums in question must be shown (and distinguished as such), to the extent appropriate, in a note to the first accounts in which it is practicable to show them. The said circumstances are where

(i) any sums are not shown in a note to the accounts for the relevant financial year on the grounds that the person receiving them is liable to account for them as mentioned above, but the liability is later released (wholly or partly) or is not enforced within a period of two years; or

(ii) sums paid by way of expenses allowances are charged to UK income tax after the end of the relevant financial year.

[*SI 2008 No 409, Sch 3 paras 1, 4–12*].

5.42 *Compensation to directors for loss of office*

There must be shown the aggregate amount of any payments made to directors or past directors for loss of office. For this purpose, '*payment for loss of office*' has the same meaning as in *CA 2006, s 215* (see **18.47 Directors**). Reference to a subsidiary undertaking of the company in those provisions is to a subsidiary undertaking immediately before the loss of office as director.

The necessary information is treated as shown if it can be readily ascertained from other information which is shown.

Notes (4)–(6) in **5.41** equally apply for the above purposes.

[*SI 2008 No 409, Sch 3 paras 2, 4, 5, 11(2)*].

5.43 *Sums paid to third parties in respect of directors' services*

There must be shown the aggregate amount of any consideration paid to or receivable by 'third parties' for making available the services of any person

- as a director of the company; or
- while director of the company
  (i) as director of any of its subsidiary undertakings; or
  (ii) otherwise in connection with the management of the affairs of the company or any of its subsidiary undertakings.

The amount shown must include the estimated money value of benefits paid otherwise than in cash, and the nature of any such consideration must be disclosed.

A '*third party*' means a person other than

- the director himself or a person connected with him or a body corporate controlled by him; or
- the company or any of its subsidiary undertakings.

Notes (4)–(6) in **5.41** equally apply for the above purposes.

[*SI 2008 No 409, Sch 3 paras 3, 5*].

For the reporting requirements of directors' remuneration in quoted companies, see **19 Directors' Remuneration – Quoted Companies**.

5.44 DIRECTORS' BENEFITS: ADVANCES, CREDIT AND GUARANTEES

In the case of a company that does not prepare group accounts, the notes to its individual accounts must show the following.

(a) In respect of any advance or credit granted by the company to a director, details of

- (i) its amount;
- (ii) an indication of the interest rate;
- (iii) its main conditions; and
- (iv) any amounts repaid.

(b) In respect of any guarantee of any kind entered into by the company on behalf of a director, details of

- (i) its main terms;
- (ii) the amount of the maximum liability that may be incurred by the company; and
- (iii) any amount paid and any liability incurred by the company for the purpose of fulfilling the guarantee (including any loss incurred by reason of enforcement of the guarantee).

There must also be stated in the notes to the accounts the totals of amounts stated under (*a*) (i), (*a*) (iv), (*b*) (ii) and (*b*) (iii).

The provisions apply to

- persons who were directors of the company at any time in the financial year to which the accounts relate; and
- every advance, credit or guarantee subsisting at any time in the financial year to which the accounts relate
  - (i) whenever it was entered into; and
  - (ii) whether or not the person concerned was a director of the company in question at the time it was entered into.

[*CA 2006, s 413(1) (3)–(7)*].

5.45 INDIVIDUAL ACCOUNTS: AUDITOR'S REMUNERATION AND LIABILITY LIMITATION AGREEMENTS

Remuneration. The following must be disclosed in the notes to the annual accounts.

- The amount of any remuneration receivable by the company's auditor for the auditing of those accounts.
- Where the remuneration includes benefits in kind, the nature and estimated money-value of those benefits.

Where more than one person has been appointed as a company's auditor in respect of the period to which the accounts relate, separate disclosure is required in respect of the remuneration of each such person.

[*SI 2008 No 489, Reg 4*].

Liability limitation agreements. A company is able to enter into a liability limitation agreement with its auditors, the effect of which is to limit the auditor's liability to not less than such amount as is fair and reasonable in all the circumstances of the case having regard in particular to

- The auditor's responsibilities under *CA 2006*;
- The nature and purpose of the auditor's contractual obligations to the company; and
- The professional standards expected of an auditor.

A company which has entered into a liability limitation agreement must have it approved by shareholders (unless it is a private company and the shareholders have waived the need for approval) and must disclose the following in a note to its annual accounts for the financial year to which the agreement relates.

- Its principal terms;
- the date of the resolution approving the agreement or the agreement's principal terms or, in the case of a private company, the date of the resolution waiving the need for such approval.

The annual accounts in which the required disclosure must be made are those for the financial year to which the agreement relates unless the agreement was entered into too late for it to be reasonably practicable for the disclosure to be made in those accounts. In such a case, the disclosure must be made in a note to the company's next following annual accounts.
[*SI 2007 No 489, Reg 8*].

5.46 INDIVIDUAL ACCOUNTS: ABBREVIATED COMPANIES ACT ACCOUNTS FOR DELIVERY TO THE REGISTRAR OF COMPANIES

Accounts generally. For each financial year, the directors of a company subject to the small companies regime

(a) *must* deliver to the Registrar of Companies a copy of a balance sheet drawn up as at the last day of that year;

(b) *may* also deliver to the Registrar of Companies

   (i) a copy of the company's profit and loss account for that year; and

   (ii) a copy of the directors' report for that year; and

(c) *must* deliver to the Registrar of Companies a copy of the auditor's report on the accounts (and any directors' report) unless the company is exempt from audit and the directors have taken advantage of that exemption.

The copies of accounts and reports delivered to the Registrar of Companies must be copies of the company's annual accounts and reports, except that where the company prepares Companies Act accounts, the directors may deliver abbreviated accounts (see below).

Where the accounts delivered to the Registrar of Companies are either

- IAS accounts, or
- Companies Act accounts that are not abbreviated accounts

and the directors take the option under (*b*) above of not delivering a copy of the company's profit and loss account or directors' report, the copy of the balance sheet delivered to the Registrar of Companies must contain, in a prominent position, a statement that the company's annual accounts and reports have been delivered in accordance with the provisions applicable to companies subject to the small companies regime.

[*CA 2006, s 444(1)–(3), (5); SI 2008 No 393, Reg 12*].

For the above purposes, a company is entitled to small companies exemption in relation to the directors' report for a financial year if

- it is entitled to prepare accounts for the year in accordance with the small companies regime; or
- it would be so entitled but for being or having been a member of an ineligible group.

[*CA 2006, s 415A; SI 2008 No 393, Reg 6*].

Abbreviated accounts. Where a company prepares Companies Act individual accounts, its accounts delivered to the Registrar of Companies need only comply with the following requirements.

(1) Instead of the balance sheet formats in **5.6**, one of the formats in **5.47** may be used.

(2) The company in not obliged to send a copy of its profit and loss account to the Registrar of Companies (see under *Accounts generally* above).

(3) The accounting principles and rules in **5.8** to **5.17** still apply to the accounts.

(4) Instead of the supporting notes in **5.18** to **5.30**, only the notes in **5.48** to **5.55** are required.

(5) The information required by *SI 2008 No 409, Sch 2* on related undertaking in **5.31** to **5.38** must still be given in the accounts apart from that required by *SI 2008 No 409, Sch 2 para 4* (shares of company held by subsidiary undertakings) in **5.35**.

(6) The information required by *SI 2008 No 409, Sch 3* on directors' remuneration in **5.39** to **5.43** need *not* be given.

(7) The information in **5.44** (directors benefits: advances, credits and guarantees) and **5.45** (auditor's remuneration, etc) must still be given.

Such accounts are referred to as 'abbreviated accounts'.

Where abbreviated accounts are delivered, the obligation to deliver a copy of the auditor's report on the accounts is to deliver a copy of the special auditor's report under *CA 2006, s 449* (see **8.31** Audit).

Approval and signing of abbreviated accounts. Abbreviated accounts must be approved by the board of directors and signed on behalf of the board by a director of the company. The signature must be on the balance sheet.

The balance sheet must contain, in a prominent position above the signature, a statement to the effect that it is prepared in accordance with the small companies regime.

If abbreviated accounts are approved that do not comply with the relevant requirements, every director of the company who

- knew that they did not comply, or was reckless as to whether they complied, and
- failed to take reasonable steps to prevent them from being approved,

commits an offence.

A person guilty of such an offence is liable (i) on conviction on indictment, to a fine; and (ii) on summary conviction, to a fine not exceeding the statutory maximum. See **29.1 Offences and Legal Proceedings** for the statutory maximum.

[*CA 2006, ss 444(3) (4), 450; SI 2008 No 409, Reg 6, Sch 4 para 1*].

Names appearing on accounts. The copies of the balance sheet and any directors' report delivered to the Registrar of Companies under these provisions must state the name of the person who signed it on behalf of the board. *Before 1 October 2009*, they also had to be signed on behalf of the board by a director or, in the case of the directors' report, a director or the secretary.

The copy of the auditor's report delivered to the Registrar of Companies under these provisions must either

- state the name of the auditor and (where the auditor is a firm) the name of the person who signed it as senior statutory auditor; or
- if the conditions in *CA 2006, s 506* are met (circumstances in which names may be omitted, see **8.34 Audit**), state that a resolution has been passed and notified to the Secretary of State in accordance with those provisions.

[*CA 2006, s 444(6) (7); SI 2007 No 3495, Sch 1 para 6; SI 2008 No 2860, Art 6*].

5.47 Balance sheet format

A company may deliver to the Registrar of Companies a copy of the balance sheet showing the items listed in either of the balance sheet formats set out below, in the order and under the headings and sub-headings given in the format adopted, but in other respects corresponding to the full balance sheet.

Format 1

A. Called up share capital not paid
B. Fixed assets
   I Intangible assets
   II Tangible assets
   III Investments
C. Current assets
   I Stocks
   II Debtors (note (1))
   III Investments
   IV Cash at bank and in hand
D. Prepayments and accrued income
E. Creditors: amounts falling due within one year
F. Net current assets (liabilities)
G. Total assets less current liabilities
H. Creditors: amounts falling due after more than one year
I. Provisions for liabilities
J. Accruals and deferred income
K. Capital and reserves
   I Called up share capital

II Share premium account
III Revaluation reserve
IV Other reserves
V Profit and loss account

Format 2

ASSETS

A. Called up share capital not paid

B. Fixed assets
- I Intangible assets
- II Tangible assets
- III Investments

C. Current assets
- I Stocks
- II Debtors (note (1))
- III Investments
- IV Cash at bank and in hand

D. Prepayments and accrued income

LIABILITIES

A. Capital and reserves
- I Called up share capital
- II Share premium account
- III Revaluation reserve
- IV Other reserves
- V Profit and loss account

B. Provisions for liabilities

C. Creditors (note (2))

D. Accruals and deferred income

Notes

(1) *Debtors.* The aggregate amount of debtors falling due after more than one year must be shown separately (unless disclosed in the notes to the accounts).

(2) *Creditors.* The aggregate amount of creditors falling due within one year and after more than one year must be shown separately (unless disclosed in the notes to the accounts).

[*SI 2008 No 409, Sch 4 para 1*].

5.48 Notes to the accounts

The information set out in **5.49** to **5.55** must be given by way of note to the accounts (if not given in the accounts themselves). [*SI 2008 No 409, Sch 4 para 2*].

5.49 *Disclosure of accounting policies*

The accounting policies adopted by the company in determining the amounts to be included in respect of items shown in the balance sheet and in determining the profit or loss of the company (including policies with respect to the depreciation and diminution in value of assets) must be stated. [*SI 2008 No 409, Sch 4 para 3*].

5.50 *Share capital*

The following information must be given with respect to the company's share capital.

(a) Where shares of more than one class have been allotted, the number and aggregate nominal value of shares of each class allotted.

(b) If any part of the allotted share capital consists of redeemable shares,

- (i) the earliest and latest dates on which the company has power to redeem those shares;
- (ii) whether those shares must be redeemed in any event or are liable to be redeemed at the option of the company or of the shareholder; and
- (iii) whether any (and, if so, what) premium is payable on redemption.

(c) If the company has allotted any shares during the financial year,

- (i) the classes of shares allotted; and
- (ii) as respects each class of shares, the number allotted, their aggregate nominal value, and the consideration received by the company for the allotment.

[*SI 2008 No 409, Sch 4 paras 4, 5*].

5.51 *Fixed assets*

The information set out below must be given for each item to which a letter or Roman number is shown under the general item 'fixed assets' in the balance sheet.

(a) The 'appropriate amounts' in respect of that item as at both the beginning of the financial year and at the balance sheet date.

(b) The effect on any amount shown in the balance sheet in respect of that item of

- (i) any revision of the amount in respect of any assets included under that item made during that year on any basis in **5.14**(*a*)–(*e*);
- (ii) acquisitions and disposals during that year of any assets; and
- (iii) any transfers of assets of the company to and from that item during that year.

(c) In respect of each item

- the cumulative amount of provisions for depreciation or diminution in value of assets included under that item both as at the beginning of the financial year and at the balance sheet date;
- the amount of any such provisions made in respect of the financial year; and
- the amount of any adjustments made in respect of any such provisions during that year, distinguishing between adjustments made in consequence of disposals and other adjustments.

For the purposes of (*a*) above, the '*appropriate amounts*' in respect of any item as at either of the dates there mentioned are the aggregate amounts determined, as at that date, in respect of assets falling to be included under that item, either on the basis of purchase price or production cost (see **5.13**) or on any basis in **5.14**(*a*)–(*e*) but in either case leaving out of account in either case any provisions for depreciation or diminution in value.

[*SI 2008 No 409, Sch 4 para 6*].

5.52 *Financial fixed assets*

If

- the company has 'financial fixed assets' that could be included at fair value by virtue of **5.17**(1),
- the amount at which those items are included under any item in the company's accounts is in excess of their fair value, and
- the company has not made provision for diminution in value of those assets in accordance with **5.10**,

there must be stated

- the amount at which either the individual assets or appropriate groupings of those individual assets are included in the company's accounts;
- the fair value of those assets or groupings; and
- the reasons for not making a provision for diminution in value of those assets, including the nature of the evidence that provides the basis for the belief that the amount at which they are stated in the accounts will be recovered.

[*SI 2008 No 409, Sch 4 para 7*].

5.53 *Details of indebtedness*

In respect of each item shown in the balance sheet under 'creditors', the following information is required.

(a) The aggregate amount of any debts included under that item which are payable or repayable otherwise than by instalments and which fall due for payment or repayment after the end of a five-year period beginning with the day after the end of the financial year.

(b) In the case of any debts so included which are payable or repayable by instalments, the aggregate amount of any instalments which fall due for payment after the end of the period specified in (*a*) above.

(c) The aggregate amount of any debts included under that item in respect of which any security has been given by the company.

Where a distinction is made in the balance sheet between amounts falling due to creditors within one year and those falling due after more than one year, (*a*) and (*b*) above apply only to items shown under the latter of those categories and (*c*) above applies to items shown under either category.

[*SI 2008 No 409, Sch 4 para 8*].

5.54 *Foreign currency translation*

Where any sums originally denominated in foreign currencies have been brought into account under any items shown in the balance sheet or profit and loss account, the basis on which those sums have been translated into sterling (or the currency in which the accounts are drawn up) must be stated. [*SI 2008 No 409, Sch 4 para 9*].

5.55 *Dormant companies acting as agents*

Where the directors of a company take advantage of the exemption from audit conferred on dormant companies by *CA 2006, s 480* (see **8.28** Audit) and the company has during the financial year in question acted as an agent for any person, the fact that it has so acted must be stated. [*SI 2008 No 409, Sch 4 para 10*].

5.56 GROUP ACCOUNTS

If, at the end of a financial year, a company subject to the small companies regime is a parent company, the directors, as well as preparing individual accounts for the year may prepare group accounts.

[*CA 2006, s 398*]

Where group accounts are prepared, the provisions below and in **5.57** to **5.76** apply to the accounts.

Applicable accounting framework. Subject to below, the group accounts may be prepared in accordance with

- *CA 2006, s 404* ('*Companies Act individual accounts*'); or
- international accounting standards ('*IAS individual accounts*').

But

- the group accounts of a parent company that is a charity must be Companies Act group accounts; and
- after the first financial year in which the directors of a parent company prepare IAS group accounts ('*the first IAS year*'), all subsequent group accounts of the company must be prepared in accordance with international accounting standards unless there is a '*relevant change of circumstance*'. This is subject to the right to change to Companies Act accounts in *CA 2006, s 403(5A)* (see below). A relevant change of circumstance occurs if, at any time during or after the first IAS year

  (i) the company becomes a subsidiary undertaking of another undertaking that does not prepare IAS group accounts;

  (ii) the company ceases to be a company with securities admitted to trading on a regulated market in an EEA State; or

  (iii) a parent undertaking of the company ceases to be an undertaking with securities admitted to trading on a regulated market in an EEA State.

  After a financial year in which IAS group accounts are prepared, the directors may change to preparing Companies Act group accounts for a reason other than a relevant change of circumstance, provided they have not changed to Companies Act group accounts in the five years preceding the first day of that financial year.

  If, having changed to preparing Companies Act group accounts the directors again prepare IAS group accounts for the company, the above provisions again apply as if the first financial year for which such accounts are again prepared were the first IAS year.

[*CA 2006, s 403; SI 2012 No 2301, Reg 15, 16, 17*].

See APPENDIX 1 DEFINITIONS for the current EEA States.

Companies Act group accounts. Companies Act group accounts must comprise

- a consolidated balance sheet dealing with the state of affairs of the parent company and its 'subsidiary undertakings' (see APPENDIX 1 DEFINITIONS); and
- a consolidated profit and loss account dealing with the profit or loss of the parent company and its subsidiary undertakings.

The accounts must give a true and fair view of the state of affairs as at the end of the financial year, and the profit or loss for the financial year, of the undertakings included in the consolidation as a whole, so far as concerns members of the company.

Companies Act group accounts must comply with the provisions in **5.59** to **5.64** as to the form and content of the consolidated balance sheet and consolidated profit and loss account and additional information to be provided by way of notes to the accounts. If compliance with the those provisions, and any other provisions made by or under *CA 2006*, as to the matters to be included in a company's group accounts or in notes to those accounts would not be sufficient to give a true and fair view, the necessary additional information must be given in the accounts or notes. If, in special circumstances, compliance with any of those provisions is inconsistent with the requirement to give a true and fair view, the directors must depart from that provision to the extent necessary to give a true and fair view. Particulars of any such departure, the reasons for it and its effect must be given in a note to the accounts.

[*CA 2006, s 404*].

See **2.16** ACCOUNTS: GENERAL for 'true and fair view'.

IAS group accounts. The provisions described in **5.59** to **5.64** do not apply to IAS group accounts. Instead, consolidated accounts must be prepared on the basis of the accounting standards issued by the International Accounting Standard Board (IASB) that are adopted by the European Commission. [*EC Council Regulation 1606/2002, Art 4*]. Instead of the profit and loss account and balance sheet required under *CA 2006*, a company must prepare primary financial statements and supporting notes as required under international accounting standards. See **2.15** ACCOUNTS: GENERAL for a list of standards.

Where the directors of a company prepare IAS group accounts, they must state in the notes to those accounts that the accounts have been prepared in accordance with international accounting standards. [*CA 2006, s 406*].

5.57 Exclusion of subsidiary undertakings from consolidation

Where a parent company prepares Companies Act group accounts (see **5.56**) all subsidiary undertakings of the company must normally be included in the consolidation. There are, however, exclusions, as listed below. If *all* of a parent company's subsidiary undertakings could be excluded from consolidation in Companies Act group accounts, the parent company need not prepare group accounts.

(a) A subsidiary undertaking may be excluded from consolidation if its inclusion is not material for the purpose of giving a true and fair view (see **2.16** ACCOUNTS: GENERAL). Two or more undertakings can be excluded only if they are not material taken together.

(b) A subsidiary undertaking may be excluded from consolidation where

(i) severe long-term restrictions substantially hinder the exercise of the parent company's rights over the assets or management of the undertaking; or

(ii) the information necessary to prepare group accounts cannot be obtained without disproportionate expense or undue delay; or

(iii) the interest of the parent company is held exclusively with a view to subsequent resale.

The references in (i) and (iii) above to, respectively, the rights and the interest of the parent company are references to rights and interests held by or attributed to it for the purposes of the definition of 'parent undertaking' (see **APPENDIX 1 DEFINITIONS**) in the absence of which it would not be the parent company.

[*CA 2006, ss 402, 405*].

5.58 GROUP ACCOUNTS: TREATMENT OF INDIVIDUAL PROFIT AND LOSS ACCOUNT WHERE GROUP ACCOUNTS PREPARED

Where a small company prepares group accounts in accordance with *CA 2006* and the notes to its individual balance sheet show the company's profit or loss for the financial year (determined in accordance with *CA 2006*), its individual profit and loss account

- need not contain the information specified in *SI 2008 No 409, Sch 1 paras 59–61* (information supplementing the profit and loss, see **5.28** to **5.30**) or information about employee numbers and costs; and
- may be omitted from the company's annual accounts, although it must still be approved in accordance with *CA 2006, s 414(1)* (see **2.2 ACCOUNTS: GENERAL**).

The above exemption is conditional upon the company's annual accounts disclosing the fact that the exemption applies.

[*CA 2006, s 408; SI 2008 No 393, Reg 10; SI 2008 No 409, Reg 3(2)*].

5.59 GROUP ACCOUNTS: FORM AND CONTENT OF COMPANIES ACT GROUP ACCOUNTS WHERE PREPARED

Where the directors of a parent company which

- is subject to the small companies regime, and
- has prepared Companies Act individual accounts

prepare Companies Act group accounts, those accounts must comply with the provisions in this paragraph and in **5.60** to **5.64** as to the form and content of the consolidated balance sheet and consolidated profit and loss account, and additional information to be provided by way of notes to the accounts. Accounts are treated as having complied with any of those provisions if they comply instead with the corresponding provision in **3.58** to **3.64 ACCOUNTS: LARGE COMPANIES**. [*SI 2008 No 409, Reg 8*].

The group accounts must comply, so far as practicable, with the provisions of *SI 2008 No 409, Sch 1* (see **5.5** to **5.30**) as if the '*group*' (meaning, for these purposes, all the undertakings included in the consolidation) were a single company, except that

(a) for item B.III in each balance sheet format in **5.6** substitute:

B.III. Investments

(1) Shares in group undertakings

(2) Interests in associated undertakings

(3) Other participating interests

(4) Loans to group undertakings and undertakings in which a participating interest is held

(5) Other investments other than loans

(6) Others

(b) In the profit and loss account formats in **5.7**, in

- format 1, item 8,
- format 2, item 10,
- format 3, item B.4, and
- format 4, item B.6,

replace the items headed 'Income from participating interests' by two items: 'Income from interests in associated undertakings' and 'Income from other participating interests'.

[*SI 2008 No 409, Sch 6, para 1*].

The consolidated balance sheet and profit and loss account must incorporate in full the information contained in the individual accounts of the undertakings included in the consolidation, subject to the adjustments authorised or required by under this paragraph and **5.60** to **5.64** and to such other adjustments (if any) that are appropriate in accordance with generally accepted accounting principles or practice.

Subsidiaries with different financial years. If the financial year of a subsidiary undertaking included in the consolidation does not end with that of the parent company, the group accounts must be made up

- from the accounts of the subsidiary undertaking for its financial year last ending before the end of the parent company's financial year (provided that year ended no more than three months before that of the parent company); or
- from interim accounts prepared by the subsidiary undertaking as at the end of the parent company's financial year.

[*SI 2008 No 409, Sch 6, para 2*].

But note that the directors of a parent company must secure that, except where in their opinion there are good reasons against it, the financial year of each of its subsidiary undertakings coincides with the company's own financial year. [*CA 2006, s 390(5)*].

Assets and liabilities. Where assets and liabilities to be included in the group accounts have been valued or otherwise determined by undertakings according to accounting rules differing from those used for the group accounts, the values or amounts must be adjusted so as to accord with the rules used for the group accounts (unless such adjustments are not material for the purpose of giving a true and fair view). If it appears to the parent company's directors that there are special reasons for doing so, they may depart from this requirement, but particulars of the departure, the reasons for it and its effect must be given in a note to the accounts. [*SI 2008 No 409, Sch 6, para 3*].

Accounting rules. Any differences between the accounting rules used for a parent company's individual accounts for a financial year and those used for its group accounts must be disclosed in a note to the group accounts. The reasons for the difference must be given. [*SI 2008 No 409, Sch 6, para 4*].

Materiality. Amounts that in the particular context of any provision in this paragraph and **5.60** to **5.64** are not material may be disregarded for the purposes of that provision. [*SI 2008 No 409, Sch 6, para 5*].

Accounts in euros. The amounts set out in the annual accounts of a company may also be shown in the same accounts translated into euros. If so, the amounts must have been translated at the exchange rate prevailing at the balance sheet date and that rate must be disclosed in the notes to the accounts. The requirement to disclose the rate in the notes to the accounts does not apply to the individual accounts of a company for a financial year in which the company qualifies as a micro-entity. For the meaning of 'micro-entity' see **5.3A**,

[*CA 2006, ss 469(1)–(3) (3A); SI 2013 No 3008, Reg 7(2)*].

5.60 Elimination of group transactions

In preparing group accounts, the following must be eliminated (unless the amounts concerned are not material for the purpose of giving a true and fair view, see **2.16** ACCOUNTS: GENERAL).

- Debts and claims between undertakings included in the consolidation.
- Income and expenditure relating to transactions between such undertakings.
- Profits and losses resulting from transactions between such undertakings and included in the book value of assets. This may be effected in proportion to the group's interest in the shares of the undertakings concerned.

[*SI 2008 No 409, Sch 6, para 6*].

5.61 Acquisition and merger accounting

The following provisions apply where an undertaking becomes a subsidiary undertaking of the parent company, such an event being referred to as an '*acquisition*'. An acquisition must be accounted for by the 'acquisition method of accounting' unless the conditions for accounting for it as a merger are met and the 'merger method of accounting' is adopted. [*SI 2008 No 409, Sch 6, paras 7, 8*].

(1) **Acquisition method of accounting**

Under the '*acquisition method of accounting*'

- the identifiable assets and liabilities of the undertaking acquired must be included in the consolidated balance sheet at their fair values as at the date of acquisition;
- the income and expenditure of the undertaking acquired must be brought into the group accounts only as from the date of the acquisition; and
- the interest of the parent company and its subsidiary undertakings in the adjusted capital and reserves of the undertaking acquired must be set off against the acquisition cost of the interest in the shares of the undertaking held by the parent company and its subsidiary undertakings. The resulting amount, if positive, must be treated as goodwill and, if negative, as a negative consolidation difference.

[*SI 2008 No 409, Sch 6, para 9*].

Where a group is acquired, references in (1) above to shares of the undertaking acquired should be read as references to shares of the parent undertaking of the group acquired. Other references to the undertaking acquired should be read as references to the group acquired. References to the assets and liabilities, income and expenditure and capital and reserves of the undertaking acquired should be read as references to those of the group acquired, after making the set-offs and other adjustments required by **5.59** to **5.64** in the case of group accounts. [*SI 2008 No 409, Sch 6, para 12*].

(2) **Merger method of accounting**

The '*merger method of accounting*' can only be used if the following conditions are satisfied.

- At least 90% of the nominal value of the 'relevant shares' in the undertaking acquired (excluding any shares in the undertaking held as treasury shares) is held by, or on behalf of, the parent company and its subsidiary undertakings.

  '*Relevant shares*' are those carrying unrestricted rights to participate both in distributions and in the assets of the undertaking upon liquidation.
- That proportion was attained pursuant to an arrangement providing for the issue of equity shares by the parent company or one or more of its subsidiary undertakings.
- The fair value of any consideration other than the issue of equity shares given pursuant to the arrangement by the parent company and its subsidiary undertakings did not exceed 10% of the nominal value of the equity shares issued.
- Adoption of the merger method of accounting accords with generally accepted accounting principles or practice.

[*SI 2008 No 409, Sch 6, para 10*].

Where the above conditions are satisfied

- the assets and liabilities of the undertaking acquired must be brought into the group accounts at the figures at which they stand in the undertaking's accounts, subject to any adjustment authorised or required by the provisions in **5.59** to **5.64**;
- the income and expenditure of the undertaking acquired must be included in the group accounts for the entire financial year, including the period before the acquisition;
- the group accounts must show comparative figures for the previous financial year as if the undertaking acquired had been included in the consolidation throughout that year; and
- the nominal value of the issued share capital of the undertaking acquired held by the parent company and its subsidiary undertakings must be set off against the aggregate of

  (i) the appropriate amount in respect of 'qualifying shares' issued by the parent company or its subsidiary undertakings in consideration for the acquisition of shares in the undertaking acquired; and

(ii) the fair value of any other consideration for the acquisition of shares in the undertaking acquired, determined as at the date when those shares were acquired.

The resulting amount must be shown as an adjustment to the consolidated reserves.

'*Qualifying shares*' means

- shares to which *CA 2006, s 612* applies (merger relief, see **46.2 Share Premium**), in respect of which the appropriate amount is the nominal value; or
- shares to which *CA 2006, s 611* applies (relief in respect of group reconstructions, see **46.3 Share Premium**), in respect of which the appropriate amount is the nominal value together with any 'minimum premium value' as there defined.

[*SI 2008 No 409, Sch 6, para 11*].

Where a group is acquired, references above to shares of the undertaking acquired should be read as references to shares of the parent undertaking of the group acquired. Other references to the undertaking acquired should be read as references to the group acquired. References to the assets and liabilities and to income and expenditure of the undertaking acquired should be read as references to those of the group acquired, after making the set-offs and other adjustments required by **5.59** to **5.64** in the case of group accounts. [*SI 2008 No 410, Sch 6, para 12*].

(3) **Information to be given in the notes to the accounts**

Subject to below, the following information with respect to acquisitions taking place in the financial year must be given in a note to the accounts (although the information in (*c*) and (*d*) below need only be given in relation to an acquisition which significantly affects the figures shown in the group accounts).

(a) The name of the undertaking acquired or, where a group was acquired, the name of the parent undertaking of that group.

(b) Whether the acquisition has been accounted for by the acquisition or the merger method of accounting.

(c) The composition and fair value of the consideration for the acquisition given by the parent company and its subsidiary undertakings.

(d) Where the acquisition method of accounting has been adopted, the book values immediately prior to the acquisition, and the fair values at the date of acquisition, of each class of assets and liabilities of the undertaking (or group) acquired in tabular form. This must include a statement of the amount of any goodwill or negative consolidation difference arising on the acquisition, together with an explanation of any significant adjustments made.

In ascertaining for these purposes the profit or loss of a group, the book values and fair values of assets and liabilities of a group or the amount of the assets and liabilities of a group, the set-offs and other adjustments required by **5.59** to **5.64** in the case of group accounts must be made.

[*SI 2008 No 409, Sch 6, para 13*].

Subject to below, the following information must also be stated in a note to the accounts.

(i) The cumulative amount of goodwill resulting from acquisitions in that and earlier financial years which has been written off otherwise than in the consolidated profit and loss account for that or any earlier financial year. That figure must be shown net of any goodwill attributable to subsidiary undertakings or businesses disposed of prior to the balance sheet date.

(ii) Where, during the financial year, there has been a disposal of an undertaking or group which significantly affects the figure shown in the group accounts, the name of that undertaking (or parent undertaking of that group) and the extent to which the profit or loss shown in the group accounts is attributable to profit or loss of that undertaking or group.

[*SI 2008 No 409, Sch 6, paras 14, 15*].

The information required by (*a*) to (*d*) and (i) and (ii) above need not be disclosed with respect to an undertaking which is either

- established under the law of a country outside the UK, or
- carries on business outside the UK

if, in the opinion of the directors of the parent company, the disclosure would be seriously prejudicial to the business of that undertaking or to the business of the parent company or any of its subsidiary undertakings *and* the Secretary of State agrees that the information should not be disclosed.

[*SI 2008 No 409, Sch 6, para 16*].

5.62 Minority interests

The formats for the balance sheet (see 5.6) and profit and loss account (see 5.7) have effect in relation to group accounts with the following additions.

(1) *Balance sheet formats*

There must be shown, as a separate item and under an appropriate heading, the amount of capital and reserves attributable to shares in subsidiary undertakings included in the consolidation held by or, on behalf of, persons other than the parent company and its subsidiary undertakings.

For the purposes of *SI 2008 No 409, Sch 1 para 4* (power of directors to adapt or combine items, see 5.5(6)), this additional item is treated as one to which a letter is assigned.

(2) *Profit and loss account formats*

There must be shown, as a separate item and under an appropriate heading,

- the amount of any profit or loss on ordinary activities, and
- the amount of any profit or loss on extraordinary activities,

attributable to shares in subsidiary undertakings included in the consolidation held by, or on behalf of, persons other than the parent company and its subsidiary undertakings.

For the purposes of *SI 2008 No 409, Sch 1 para 4* (power of directors to adapt or combine items, see **5.5**(6)), these additional items are treated as ones to which an Arabic number is assigned.

[*SI 2008 No 409, Sch 6, para 17*].

5.63 Joint ventures

Where an undertaking included in the consolidation manages another undertaking (the 'joint venture') jointly with one or more undertakings not included in the consolidation, the joint venture may, if it is not

- a body corporate, or
- a subsidiary undertaking of the parent company,

be dealt with in the group accounts by the method of proportional consolidation.

The provisions in **5.59** to **5.64** relating to the preparation of consolidated accounts apply, with any necessary modifications, to proportional consolidation under this provision.

[*SI 2008 No 409, Sch 6, para 18*].

5.64 Associated undertakings

Definition. An '*associated undertaking*' means an undertaking in which an undertaking included in the consolidation has a 'participating interest' (see **Appendix 1 Definitions**) and over whose operating and financial policy it exercises a significant influence, and which is not

- a subsidiary undertaking of the parent company; or
- a joint venture dealt with in **5.63**.

Where an undertaking holds 20% or more of the voting rights in another undertaking, it is presumed to exercise such an influence over it unless the contrary is shown. The voting rights in an undertaking means the rights conferred on shareholders in respect of their shares (or, if the undertaking does not have a share capital, on members) to vote at general meetings of the undertaking on all (or substantially all) matters.

In determining whether 20% or more of the voting rights are held, the provisions in **Appendix 1 Definitions** apply.

Disclosure requirements. The interest of an undertaking in an associated undertaking, and the amount of profit or loss attributable to such an interest, must be shown by the equity method of accounting (including dealing with any goodwill arising in accordance with **5.10**. But the equity method of accounting need not be applied if the amounts in question are not material for the purpose of giving a true and fair view.

Where the associated undertaking is itself a parent undertaking, the net assets and profits or losses to be taken into account are those of the parent and its subsidiary undertakings (after making any consolidation adjustments).

[*SI 2008 No 409, Sch 6, paras 19, 20*].

5.65 GROUP ACCOUNTS: INFORMATION ABOUT RELATED UNDERTAKINGS WHERE GROUP ACCOUNTS PREPARED

Where a company is preparing group accounts, it's Companies Act or IAS accounts must comply with the provisions in **5.66** to **5.74** as to the information about related undertakings to be given in the notes to the company's accounts. There are two exceptions.

5.65 Accounts: Small Companies and Micro-entities

(1) **Exemption**

The information (other than that in **5.69** and **5.73**) need not be disclosed with respect to an undertaking that

- is established under the law of a country outside the UK, or
- carries on business outside the UK,

but only if

- in the opinion of the directors of the company, the disclosure would be seriously prejudicial to the business of
  - (i) that undertaking;
  - (ii) the company;
  - (iii) any of the company's subsidiary undertakings; or
  - (iv) any other undertaking which is included in the consolidation; and
- the Secretary of State agrees that the information need not be disclosed.

Where advantage is taken of this exemption, a note to that effect must be included in the company's accounts.

[*CA 2006, s 409(5)*; *SI 2008 No 409, Reg 10*].

(2) **Alternative compliance in cases of excessive length**

Where the directors are of the opinion that the number of undertakings in respect of which the company is required to disclose information under any provision described in **5.66** to **5.74** is such that compliance would result in information of excessive length being given in the notes to the accounts, information need only be given in respect of

(a) the undertakings whose results or financial position, in the directors' opinion, principally affected the figures shown in the company's annual accounts; and

(b) undertakings excluded from consolidation under **5.57**(*b*).

If advantage is taken of this, then

(i) the notes to the company's annual accounts must include a statement that the information is given only with respect to undertakings of the type mentioned in (*a*) and (*b*) above; and

(ii) the full information (ie both that which is disclosed and that which is not) must be annexed to the next annual return delivered to the Registrar of Companies after the accounts in question have been approved by the board.

If a company fails to comply with (ii) above, an offence is committed by the company and every officer of the company who is in default. A person guilty of such an offence is liable, on summary conviction, to a fine not exceeding level 3 on the standard scale and, for continued contravention, a daily default fine not exceeding one-tenth of level 3 on the standard scale. See **29.1 Offences and Legal Proceedings** for the standard scale.

[*CA 2006, s 410*].

In the above provisions, and in **5.66** to **5.74**:

- '*The group*' means the group consisting of the parent company and its subsidiary undertakings. [*SI 2008 No 409, Sch 6, para 21*].
- References to shares held by the group are to any shares held by or on behalf of the parent company or any of its subsidiary undertakings. But any shares held on behalf of a person other than the parent company or any of its subsidiary undertakings are not to be treated as held by the group. [*SI 2008 No 409, Sch 6, para 37(3)*].
- Shares held by way of security must be treated as held by the person providing the security

  (i) where the rights attached to the shares are exercisable only in accordance with that person's instructions (disregarding any right to exercise them in order to preserve the value of, or realise, the security); and

  (ii) as regards shares held in connection with the granting of loans as part of normal business activities, where the rights attached to the shares are exercisable only in that person's interests (disregarding any right to exercise them in order to preserve the value of, or realise, the security).

  [*SI 2008 No 409, Sch 6, para 37(4)*].

5.66 Subsidiary undertakings

Subject to **5.65**, the following information must be given with respect to each of the subsidiary undertakings of the parent company at the end of the financial year.

(a) Its name.

(b) If the undertaking is incorporated outside the UK, the country in which it is incorporated.

(c) If it is unincorporated, the address of its principal place of business.

(d) Whether the subsidiary undertaking is included in the consolidation and, if it is not, the reasons for excluding it.

(e) Which of the conditions in **Appendix 1 Definitions** applies to make it a subsidiary undertaking of its immediate parent undertaking. But that information need not be given if the relevant condition is that specified in **Appendix 1 Definitions** (holding of a majority of the voting rights) and the immediate parent undertaking holds the same proportion of the shares in the undertaking as it holds voting rights.

[*SI 2008 No 409, Sch 6, para 22*].

5.67 *Holdings in subsidiary undertakings*

Subject to **5.65**, with respect to the shares of a subsidiary undertaking held by

- the parent company, and
- the group,

there must be stated

- the identity of each class of shares held, and

- the proportion of the nominal value of the shares of that class represented by those shares.

This information must (if different) be shown separately as regards the parent company and group.

[*SI 2008 No 409, Sch 6, para 23*].

For the above purposes, there must be attributed to the parent company shares held on its behalf by any person. But shares held on behalf of a person other than the parent company must be treated as not held by that company. [*SI 2008 No 409, Sch 6, para 37(2)*].

5.68 *Financial information about subsidiary undertakings not included in the consolidated accounts*

Subject to **5.65**, with respect to each subsidiary undertaking not included in the consolidated accounts, there must be shown

- the aggregate amount of its capital and reserves as at the end of its relevant financial year; and
- its profit or loss for that year.

This information need not be given if

- the company's investment in the subsidiary undertaking is included in the company's accounts by way of the equity method of valuation;
- the company's holding is less than 50% of the nominal value of the shares in the undertaking *and* the subsidiary undertaking is not required to deliver to the Registrar of Companies a copy of its balance sheet for its 'relevant financial year' and does not otherwise publish that balance sheet in the UK or elsewhere; or
- it is not material.

The '*relevant financial year*' of a subsidiary undertaking is

- if its financial year ends with that of the company, that year; and
- if not, its financial year ending last before the end of the company's financial year.

[*SI 2008 No 409, Sch 6, para 24*].

5.69 *Shares of company held by subsidiary undertakings*

Subject to **5.65**, the number, description and amount of the shares in the company held by, or on behalf of, its subsidiary undertakings must be disclosed. This does not apply in relation to shares in the case of which the subsidiary undertaking is concerned as

- personal representative; or
- trustee, unless the company, or any of its subsidiary undertakings is 'beneficially interested under the trust', otherwise than by way of security only for the purposes of a transaction entered into by it in the ordinary course of a business which includes the lending of money.

[*SI 2008 No 409, Sch 6, para 25*].

In determining whether the company is '*beneficially interested under the trust*', certain residual interests under pension and employees' share schemes, employer's charges and other rights of recovery under such schemes, and a trustee's right to expenses, remuneration, indemnity, etc are disregarded. See *SI 2008 No 409, Sch 2, paras 12–17* for full details.

5.70 Joint ventures

Subject to **5.65**, where an undertaking is dealt with in the consolidated accounts by the method of proportional consolidation (in accordance with **5.63**), the following information must be given in respect of the undertaking.

- Its name.
- The address of its principal place of business.
- The factors on which joint management of the undertaking is based.
- The proportion of its capital held by undertakings included in the consolidation.
- Where its financial year did not end with that of the company, the date on which a financial year of the undertaking last ended before that date.

[*SI 2008 No 409, Sch 6, para 26*].

5.71 Associated undertakings

Subject to **5.65**, the following information must be given where an undertaking included in the consolidation has an interest in an associated undertaking.

(a) The name of the associated undertaking.

(b) If that undertaking is incorporated outside the UK, the country in which it is incorporated.

(c) If it is unincorporated, the address of its principal place of business.

(d) With respect to the shares of the undertaking held by the parent company and by the group,

- the identity of each class of shares held, and
- the proportion of the nominal value of the shares of that class represented by those shares,

giving details for the parent company and group separately.

'*Associated undertaking*' has the same meaning as in **5.64** and the information required by this **5.71** must be given notwithstanding that disclosure is not required under **5.64** because the amounts of net assets, profits or losses attributable to the interests held in the associated undertaking are not material for the purpose of giving a true and fair view.

[*SI 2008 No 409, Sch 6, para 27*].

For the above purposes, there must be attributed to the parent company shares held on its behalf by any person. But shares held on behalf of a person other than the parent company must be treated as not held by that company. [*SI 2008 No 409, Sch 6, para 37(2)*].

5.72 Other significant holdings of parent company or group

Parent company holdings. Subject to **5.65**, where at the end of the financial year the parent company has a 'significant holding' in an undertaking which is not one of its subsidiary undertakings and does not fall within **5.70** or **5.71**, the following must be stated.

(a) The name of the undertaking.

(b) If the undertaking is incorporated outside the UK, the country in which it is incorporated.

(c) if it is unincorporated, the address of its principal place of business.

(d) The identity of each class of shares of the undertaking held by the parent company.

(e) The proportion of the nominal value of the shares of that class represented by those shares.

(f) The aggregate amount of the capital and reserves of the undertaking as at the end of its 'relevant financial year'.

(g) Its profit or loss for that year.

A '*significant holding*' is a holding which amounts to 20% or more of the nominal value of any class of shares in the undertaking *or* the amount of which (as stated or included in the parent company's individual accounts) exceeds 20% of the amount (as so stated) of the parent company's assets.

The '*relevant financial year*' of an undertaking for these purposes is, if its financial year ends with that of the parent company, that year, and if it does not, its financial year ending last before the end of the parent company's financial year.

Exemption. The information in (*f*) and (*g*) above need not be given if

- the undertaking in question is not required to deliver a copy of its balance sheet for its relevant financial year and does not otherwise publish that balance sheet in the UK or elsewhere *and* the company's holding is less than 50% of the nominal value of the shares in the undertaking; or
- it is not material.

[*SI 2008 No 409, Sch 6, paras 28–30*].

For the above purposes, there must be attributed to the parent company shares held on its behalf by any person. But shares held on behalf of a person other than the parent company must be treated as not held by that company. [*SI 2008 No 409, Sch 6, para 37(2)*].

Group holdings. Subject to **5.65**, where at the end of the financial year the group has a 'significant holding' in an undertaking which is not a subsidiary undertaking of the parent company and does not fall within **5.70** or **5.71**, the same information must be given as under (*a*) to (*g*) above (and with the same exemption as above), substituting 'group' for 'parent company' in (*d*) and in the definition of '*significant holding*'. [*SI 2008 No 409, Sch 6, paras 31–33*].

5.73 Parent company's or group's membership of certain undertakings

Where, at the end of the financial year, the company or group is a member of a 'qualifying undertaking' the following must be stated.

(a) The name and legal form of the undertaking.

(b) The address of its registered office (whether in or outside the UK) or, if it does not have such an office, its head office (whether in or outside the UK).

(c) Where the undertaking is a qualifying partnership, either

(i) a statement that a copy of the latest accounts of the partnership has been or is to be appended to the copy of the company's accounts sent to the Registrar of Companies; or

(ii) the name of at least one body corporate (which may be the company itself) in whose group accounts the undertaking has been, or is to be, dealt with on a consolidated basis.

The information required by (*a*) and (*b*) above need not be given if not material and the information required by (*c*) (ii) above need not be given if the notes to the company's accounts disclose that advantage has been taken of the exemption in *Regulation 7* of the *Partnerships (Accounts) Regulations 2008*.

A '*qualifying undertaking*' means

(a) a qualifying partnership; or

(b) an unlimited company each of whose members is

(i) a limited company;

(ii) another unlimited company each of whose members is a limited company; or

(iii) a Scottish partnership each of whose members is a limited company,

and, for these purposes, references to a limited company, another unlimited company and a Scottish partnership include a comparable undertaking incorporated in, or formed under, the law of a country or territory outside the UK.

[*SI 2008 No 409, Sch 6, para 34; SI 2008 No 569, Reg 17*].

5.74 Information where parent company is a subsidiary undertaking

Subject to **5.65**, where the parent company is itself a subsidiary undertaking, the following information must be given.

(a) Particulars, as follows, with respect to the parent undertaking of the largest and smallest group of undertakings for which group accounts are drawn up and of which that company is a member.

(i) The name of the parent undertaking.

(ii) If the undertaking is incorporated outside the UK, the country in which it is incorporated.

(iii) If it is unincorporated, the address of its principal place of business.

(iv) If copies of the above-mentioned group accounts are available to the public, the addresses from which copies of the accounts can be obtained.

(b) Particulars, as follows, with respect to the company (which includes any body corporate) regarded by the directors as being that company's ultimate parent company.

(i) Its name.

(ii) If that company is incorporated outside the UK, the country in which it is incorporated (if known to the directors).

[*SI 2008 No 409, Sch 6, paras 35, 36*].

5.75 GROUP ACCOUNTS: DIRECTORS' REMUNERATION AND BENEFITS

Directors' remuneration and benefits. Companies Act or IAS group accounts must comply with the provisions of **5.40** to **5.43** as to information about directors' remuneration to be given in notes to the company's accounts. [*SI 2008 No 409, Reg 9*].

In the case of a parent company that prepares group accounts, the notes to the group accounts must also show the following.

(a) In respect of any advance or credit granted to the directors of the parent company, by that company or by any of its subsidiary undertakings, details of

(i) its amount;

(ii) an indication of the interest rate;

(iii) its main conditions; and

(iv) any amounts repaid.

(b) In respect of any guarantee of any kind entered into on behalf of the directors of the parent company, by that company or by any of its subsidiary undertakings, details of

(i) its main terms;

(ii) the amount of the maximum liability that may be incurred by the company (or its subsidiary); and

(iii) any amount paid and any liability incurred by the company (or its subsidiary) for the purpose of fulfilling the guarantee (including any loss incurred by reason of enforcement of the guarantee).

There must also be stated in the notes to the accounts the totals of amounts stated under (*a*) (i), (*a*) (iv), (*b*) (ii) and (*b*) (iii).

The provisions apply to

- persons who were directors of the company at any time in the financial year to which the accounts relate; and
- every advance, credit or guarantee subsisting at any time in the financial year to which the accounts relate

(i) whenever it was entered into; and

(ii) whether or not the person concerned was a director of the company in question at the time it was entered into; and

(iii) in the case of an advance, credit or guarantee involving a subsidiary undertaking of that company, whether or not that undertaking was such a subsidiary undertaking at the time it was entered into.

[*CA 2006, s 413(2)–(7)*].

5.76 GROUP ACCOUNTS: ABBREVIATED COMPANIES ACT GROUP ACCOUNTS FOR DELIVERY TO THE REGISTRAR OF COMPANIES

Companies Act group accounts delivered to the Registrar of Companies need not give the information required by

- *SI 2008 No 409, Sch 3* (directors' remuneration, see **5.40** to **5.43**); or
- *SI 2009 No 409, Sch 6, para 25* (shares of company held by subsidiary, see **5.69**).

[*SI 2009 No 409, Reg 11*].

6 Accounts: Strategic Reports

6.1	**Introduction**	6.5	Relevant consultation
6.2	**Conditions for sending out strategic reports**	6.6	**Form and content of strategic report and supplementary material**
6.3	Ascertainment of wishes	6.7	**Defective reports**
6.4	Consultation by notice		

Background. The *Companies Act 2006 (Strategic Report and Directors' Report) Regulations 2013* ("the *2013 Regulations*") which are referred to in various parts of this chapter, bring into force the requirement for a company to produce a strategic report for financial years ending on or after 30 September 2013. It replaces the requirement to produce a summary financial statement.

6.1 INTRODUCTION

Chapter 20 (Directors' reports and strategic reports) sets out the requirements to prepare a strategic report for each year of the company. Once prepared a company may send a copy of the strategic report together with supplementary material instead of copies of the full accounts and reports to

(a) a person specified as entitled to receive those accounts in *CA 2006, s 423*, ie
- every member of the company;
- every holder of the company's debentures; and
- every person who is entitled to receive notice of general meetings; and

(b) a person nominated by a member to enjoy information rights under *CA 2006, s 146* (see **26.4 Members**).

But copies of the full reports and accounts must be sent to any person entitled to be sent them under those provisions and who wishes to receive them. See **6.3** for the manner in which this is determined.

A strategic report and supplementary material must comply with the minimum requirements as to form and content in **6.6** to **6.9** but this does prevent a company from including additional information derived from its annual accounts and reports.

[*CA 2006, ss 426(1) (2) (4), 427(3), 428(3); SI 2013 No 1970, Regs 9, 10, 11· SI 2013 No 1973, Reg 4*].

Offences. In case of a failure to comply with the requirements to prepare a strategic report, an offence is committed by every person who was a director of the company immediately before the end of the period for filing accounts and reports for the financial year in question and failed to take all reasonable steps for securing compliance with that requirement. A person guilty of such an offence is liable, on summary conviction, to a fine not exceeding the statutory maximum and on conviction on indictment to a fine. See **29.1 Offences and Legal Proceedings.**

[*CA 2006, s 414A(5) (6); SI 2013 No 1970, Reg 3*]

6.2 CONDITIONS FOR SENDING OUT STRATEGIC REPORTS

A company may not send a copy of its strategic report and supplementary material to any person within **6.1** in the following circumstances.

- It is prohibited from doing because
  - (i) of any relevant provision of its constitution, or
  - (ii) in the case of a debenture-holder, a relevant provision in any instrument constituting or otherwise governing any of the company's debentures of which that person is a holder or
  - (iii) in the case of any such person (whether or not a debenture holder) where it is prohibited from sending a summary financial statement to any such person by any relevant provision of its constitution.
- Where, in relation to the financial year in question, no auditor's report has been made in respect of
  - (i) the annual accounts of the company under *CA 2006, s 495*;
  - (ii) the *strategic report (if any) and the* directors' report under *CA 2006, s 496*; or
  - (iii) the auditable part of the directors' remuneration report (where relevant) under *CA 2006, 497*.
- Where, in relation to the financial year, the period for filing accounts and reports for that year under *CA 2006, s 442* (see **2.11 Accounts: General**) has expired.
- Where the strategic report in respect of that financial year has not been approved by the board of directors and the original statement has not been signed on behalf of the board by a director of the company.
- Where it has not ascertained the wishes of that person under **6.3**.

[*SI 2013 No 1973, Reg 5; SI 2013 No 1970, Schedule, para 21*].

6.3 Ascertainment of wishes

A company may not send a copy of the strategic report with supplementary material to any person within **6.1** unless it has ascertained that the person does not wish to receive copies of its full accounts and reports. In ascertaining this:

- Where such a person has expressly notified the company either
  - (i) that he wishes to receive copies of the full accounts and reports, or
  - (ii) that he wishes, instead of copies of those documents, to receive a copy of the strategic report

  the company must send copies of the full accounts and reports or copies of the strategic report with supplementary material, as appropriate, to that person in respect of the financial years to which the notification applies.

  For these purposes, a notification has effect in relation to a financial year if it relates to that year (whether or not it has been given at the invitation of the company) and if it has been received by the company not later than 28 days before the first date on which copies of the full accounts and reports for that year are sent out to the person specified in **6.1**.

- Where there has been no such express notification to the company by such a person, that person may be taken to have elected to receive SFSs if he fails to respond to an opportunity to elect to receive copies of the full accounts and reports given to him either
  - (i) by a consultation notice under **6.4**, or
  - (ii) as part of a relevant consultation of his wishes by the company under **6.5**.

The company communications provisions (see **16.22 Dealings With Third Parties**) apply to any notice or other communication required or authorised to be sent to or by the company under the above provisions.
[*SI 2013 No 1973, Reg 6*].

6.4 Consultation by notice

A consultation notice is notice given by a company to a person within **6.1** (or a person who is entitled to become such a person but who has not yet become one) which complies with the following requirements.

- It must state that for the future, so long as he is such a person he will be sent a copy of the strategic report with supplementary material for each financial year instead of a copy of the company's full accounts and reports, unless he notifies the company that he wishes to receive full accounts and reports.
- It must be accompanied by a card or form so worded as to enable the person to notify the company (by marking a box and returning the card or form) that he wishes to receive full accounts and reports for the next financial year for which he is entitled to receive them and for all future financial years thereafter.

  If sent by post, any postage for the return of the card or form has been or will be paid by the company unless the address of a person concerned is not within an EEA State (see **Appendix 1 Definitions**).
- It must state that the card or form accompanying the notice must be returned by a date set out in the notice, being a date at least 21 days after service of the notice and not less than 28 days before the first date on which copies of the full accounts and reports for the next financial year for which that person is entitled to receive them are sent out.
- It must include a statement in a prominent position to the effect that a copy of the strategic report with supplementary material will not contain sufficient information to allow as full an understanding of the results and state of affairs of the company or group as would be provided by the full annual accounts and reports and that persons requiring more detailed information have the right to obtain, free of charge, a copy of the company's last full accounts and reports.

The company communications provisions (see **16.22 Dealings With Third Parties**) apply to any notice or other communication required or authorised to be sent to or by the company under the above provisions.
[*SI 2013 No 1973, Regs 7, 9*].

6.5 Relevant consultation

A company may conduct a 'relevant consultation' to ascertain the wishes of a person within **6.1** or a person who is entitled to become such a person but who has not yet become one.

For these purposes, a '*relevant consultation*' of the wishes of such a person is a notice given to that person which complies with the following requirements.

- It states that for the future, so long as he is a such a person, he will be sent a copy of the strategic report with supplementary material instead of the full accounts and reports of the company, unless he notifies the company that he wishes to continue to receive full accounts and reports.
- It accompanies a copy of the full accounts and reports.
- It accompanies a copy of the strategic report with supplementary material for the same financial year covered by those full accounts and reports and which is identified in the notice as an example of the document which that person will receive for the future, so long as he is a such a person, unless he notifies the company to the contrary.
- It is accompanied by a card or form so worded as to enable the person to notify the company (by marking a box and returning the card or form) that he wishes to receive full accounts and reports for the next financial year for which he is entitled to receive them and for all future financial years after that.

  If sent by post, any postage for the return of the card or form must be paid by the company unless the address of a person concerned is not within an EEA State (see **Appendix 1 Definitions**).

The company communications provisions (see **16.22 Dealings With Third Parties**) apply to any notice or other communication required or authorised to be sent to or by the company under the above provisions.

[*SI 2013 No 1973, Regs 8, 9*].

6.6 FORM AND CONTENT OF STRATEGIC REPORTS AND SUPPLEMENTARY MATERIAL

The purpose of the strategic report is to inform members of the company and help them assess how the directors have performed their duty under *CA 2006, s 172* (Duty to promote the success of the company) (see **18.24**). The strategic report must:

- contain a fair review of the company's business ie a balanced and comprehensive analysis of the development and performance of the company's business during the financial year and the position of the business at the end of that year
- contain a description of the principal risks and uncertainties facing the company
- to the extent necessary for an understanding of the development, performance or position of the company's business include analysis using key performance indicators and where appropriate analysis using other key performance indicators including information relating to environmental and employee matters. For these purposes " key performance indicators" means factors by reference to which the development, performance or position of the company's business can be measured effectively. If a company qualifies as a medium-sized company in relation to a financial year (see **4 Accounts: Medium –sized Companies**), the strategic report for that year does not need to comply with this requirement so far as it relates to non-financial information.
- where appropriate include references to, and additional explanations of, amounts included in the company's annual accounts

- contain such of the matters otherwise required by regulations made under CA 2006 s 416(4) to be disclosed in the directors' report as the directors consider are of strategic importance to the company

The company is not required to disclose information in the strategic report about impending developments or matters in the course of negotiation if the disclosure would, in the opinion of the directors, be seriously prejudicial to the interests of the company.

For further information see **20 Directors' reports and strategic reports**

Supplementary material. The supplementary material referred to in *CA 2006, s 426A* must:

- Contain a statement that the strategic report is only a part of the company's annual accounts and reports
- State how a person entitled to them can obtain a full copy of the company's annual report and accounts
- State whether the auditor's report on the annual accounts was unqualified or qualified and, if the latter, set out the report in full together with any further material needed to understand the qualification.
- State whether, in that auditor's report, the auditor's statements under *CA 2006, s 496* (whether strategic report and the directors' report consistent with the accounts see **8.30 Audit**) was qualified or unqualified and, if qualified, set out the qualified statement in full together with any further material needed to understand the qualification.
- In the case of a quoted company contain a copy of that part of the directors' remuneration report which sets out the single total figure table in respect of the company's directors' remuneration in accordance with the requirements of SI 2008 No 410 Schedule 8 (as amended)

[*CA 2006, s 426A; SI 2013 No 1970, Reg 12*].

Strategic reports

For the requirements relating to the contents and signing of strategic reports and the relationship between the strategic and directors' report see **20 Directors' reports and strategic reports.**

6.7 SAVING PROVISION FOR DEFECTIVE SUMMARY FINANCIAL STATEMENTS

Where a summary financial statement has been sent to any person within **6.1**(*a*) or (*b*) which

- does not comply with the provision in this chapter, or
- if it had been prepared by reference to revised accounts or a revised report would not have complied with those requirements,

the directors of the company must prepare a further summary financial statement, or a supplementary note indicating the corrections to the original summary financial statement, and send it to

(a) any person who received the original summary financial statement; and

(b) any person to whom the company would be entitled, as at the date of preparation of the revised summary financial statement, to send a summary financial statement for the current year.

A revised summary financial statement must contain a short statement of the revisions made and their effect and a supplementary note must contain a statement that it revises the original summary financial statement in certain respects and is to be treated as forming part of that statement.

Where the summary financial statement would, if it had been prepared by reference to the revised accounts or revised report, comply with the requirements in **6.1** to **6.9**, the company must send a note to the persons in *(a)* and *(b)* above stating that the annual accounts of the company for the relevant financial year (specifying it) or, as the case may be, the directors' report or directors' remuneration report for that year have or has been revised in a way that has no bearing on the summary financial statement for that year. If the auditor's report on the revised accounts or revised report is qualified, a copy of that report must be attached to the note sent out.

The revised summary financial statement or note prepared under the above provisions must be sent out within 28 days after the date of revision of the revised accounts or revised report.

Where the provisions of this chapter as to the matters to be included in a summary financial statement have been amended after the date of the sending out of the original summary financial statement but prior to the date of the revision of the accounts or report, references above to those requirements are to the requirements in force at the date of the sending out of the original summary financial statement .

If default is made in complying with any of the above provisions, each of the directors of the company who approved the revised accounts or report is in default. A person guilty of such an offence is liable, on summary conviction, to a fine not exceeding level 3 on the standard scale. See **29.1 OFFENCES AND LEGAL PROCEEDINGS** for the standard scale.

These provisions continue to apply to financial years ending before 1 October 2013.

[*SI 2008 No 373, Reg 17, 19(3); SI 2013 No 1970, Reg 13*].

7 Annual Returns

7.1 Duty to deliver
7.2 Contents
7.3 Method of filing
7.4 Failure to deliver annual return
7.5 Reform – annual confirmation statements

Background. The provisions in *CA 2006, Pt 24* (as amended) which are considered in this chapter apply, unless otherwise stated, to returns made up to a date on or after 1 October 2009.

7.1 DUTY TO DELIVER

An annual return is a snapshot of general information about such matters as a company's directors, registered office address, shareholders and share capital. There are different requirements for shareholder details and the company's principal business activities (SIC codes) depending on whether the annual return is made up to 30 September 2011 or 1 October 2011 or later. Companies House sends a letter to the company's registered office reminding the company when it's annual return is due and advising how to file the return. See 7.3.

Every company must deliver successive annual returns to the Registrar of Companies. Each such return must contain all the required information in 7.2 and be submitted to the Registrar of Companies within 28 days of the date to which it is made up. A filing fee is payable. See APPENDIX 3 COMPANIES HOUSE FEES.

The return must be made up to a date not later than:

- in the case of a new company, the anniversary of incorporation; or
- in any other case, the anniversary of the previous return.

[*CA 2006, s 854*].

7.2 CONTENTS

Every annual return must state the date to which it is made up and contain the following information.

(a) Name, registered number and address of the company's registered office and the address (single alternate inspection location (SAIL)) where the company keeps certain records if they are not kept at the registered office.

(b) Business. Its principal business activities as described by SIC 2007 which is the UK Standard Industrial Classification of Economic Activities.

(c) The type of company it is according to the following classifications.

T1	Public limited company
T2	Private company limited by shares
T3	Private company limited by guarantee
T4	Private company limited by shares exempt from the requirement to use 'limited' as part of its name

T5 Private company limited by guarantee exempt from the requirement to use 'limited' as part of its name

T6 Private unlimited company with share capital

T7 Private unlimited company without share capital

(d) Directors.

(i) where the director is an individual, the particulars required by *CA 2006, s 163* to be entered in the register of directors (except that the former name of a director is required in relation to an annual return only if the director was known by the name for business purposes during the period covered by the return); and

(ii) where the director is a body corporate or a firm that is a legal person under the law by which it is governed, the particulars required by *CA 2006, s 164* to be entered in the register of directors.

See **38.2 Registers** for *CA 2006, ss 163, 164*.

(e) Company Secretary. In the case of a private company with a secretary or a public company,

(i) where the secretary is an individual, the particulars required by *CA 2006, s 277* to be entered in the register of secretaries (except that the former name of a secretary is required in relation to an annual return only if the secretary was known by the name for business purposes during the period covered by the return); and

(ii) where the secretary is a body corporate or a firm that is a legal person under the law by which it is governed, the particulars required by *CA 2006, s 278(1)* to be entered in the register of directors.

See **38.4 Registers** for *CA 2006, ss 277, 278(1)*.

Where all the partners in a firm are joint secretaries, the required particulars are those that would be required to be entered in the register of secretaries if the firm were a legal person and the firm had been appointed secretary.

(f) Company Records. If any company records are kept at a place other than the company's registered office, the address of that place (the single alternative inspection location (SAIL) and the records that are kept there.

(g) Traded Company. If the return is made up to 30 September 2011 whether the company was a 'traded company' at any time during the period covered by the return. If the return is made up to 1 October 2011 or later, whether the company's shares have been admitted to trading on a "relevant market" at any time during the return period.

A '*traded company*' is a company any of whose shares are shares admitted to trading on a regulated market (so that a '*non-traded company*' means a company none of whose shares are admitted to trading on a regulated market). For these purposes an AIM company is not a 'traded company'. '*Relevant market*' is one of the current UK recognised investment exchanges and regulated markets found on the FCA Financial Services register.

(h) Details of share capital. In the case of a company having a share capital, a statement of capital stating with respect to the company's share capital at the date to which the return is made up:

(i) The total number of shares of the company.

(ii) The aggregate nominal value of those shares.

(iii) For each class of shares

- the voting rights attached to the shares;
- the total number of shares of that class; and
- the aggregate nominal value of shares of that class; and

(iv) The amount paid up and the amount (if any) unpaid on each share (whether on account of the nominal value of the share or by way of premium). If a company has converted shares into stock, it must give the corresponding information in relation to that stock, stating the amount of stock instead of the number and nominal value of the shares.

(i) *Shares and shareholdings Private and Non-traded public companies (or for returns made up to 1 October 2011 or later a company whose shares have not been admitted to trading on a "relevant market" (see above for the meaning))*. If the company was a private or a non-traded public company throughout the period covered by the return, the company has to provide a "full list" of shareholders ie the information in (i)–(iv) in the first annual return following incorporation and in every third annual return after the company has provided a full list. The intervening two annual returns only need to report any changes during that year ie shares transferred and details of people who have become or ceased to be shareholders.

(i) The name (as it appears in the company's register of members) of every person who was a member or joint member of the company at the made-up date.

To enable the entries relating to any given person to be easily found, either the entries must be listed in alphabetical order by name or the return must have annexed to it an index that is sufficient to enable the name of the person in question to be easily found. Joint shareholders should be listed consecutively. Companies House recommends that private and non-traded public companies with a large number of shareholders may find it more convenient to provide a full list of shareholders with each annual return but in that case the list must not include the shareholders' addresses. Companies that file paper returns may provide this information on a CD Rom if the list is 50 pages or more.

(ii) The name of every person who became or ceased to be a shareholder or joint shareholder during the period covered by the return (or in the case of a first return since the incorporation of the company).

(iii) The number of shares of each class held by each shareholder at the made up date.

(iv) The date of registration and the number of shares of each class transferred by each shareholder or past shareholder during the period covered by the return (or in the case of the first return since the date of incorporation of the company).

Shareholder addresses must not be included on paper returns or the form will be returned to the company.

(j) *Shares and Shareholdings—Traded companies/shares traded on a "relevant market".* If the company was a traded public company at any time during the period covered by the return, the following information must be given for returns made up to 30 September 2011 or earlier.

(i) The name and address (as they appear on the company's register of members) of every shareholder or joint holder who held at least 5% of the issued shares of any class of the company at any time during the period covered by the return.

To enable the entries relating to any given person to be easily found, *either* the entries must be listed alphabetical order by name *or* the return must have annexed to it an index that is sufficient to enable the name of the person in question to be easily found. Joint shareholders should be listed consecutively.

(ii) The number of shares of each class held at the end of the date to which the return is made up.

(iii) The number of shares of each class transferred during the period coved by the return by or to each person who held at least 5% of the issued shares of any class of the company at any time during the period covered by the return.

(iv) The dates of registration of those transfers.

If either of the two immediately preceding annual returns has given the full particulars required by (i)–(iv) above, the return need only give such particulars as relate to

- persons who came to hold, or ceased to hold, at least 5% of the issued shares of any class of the company during the period covered by the return; and
- shares transferred during that period.

If the company's shares were admitted to trading on a relevant market (see above) at any time during the period covered by the return, the following information must be given for returns made up to 1 October 2011 or later.

The names and addresses (as they appear on the company's register of members) of every person or joint holder who hold 5% or more of the company's issued share capital of any class of the company as at the made-up date of the return. There is an exception for a company whose shares were admitted to trading on a relevant market throughout the period covered by the return and which were subject to the Vote Holder and Issuer Notification Rules in Chapter 5 of the FCA Disclosure and Transparency Rules. See 33 Public and Listed Companies for references to those Rules. In this case shareholder details (ie other than their names and addresses) do not have to be provided.

For shareholders who hold less than 5% of the company's issued share capital of any class,

(i) Returns made up to 30 September 2011 or earlier- no details must be given of members who hold or continue to hold less than 5% of shares of any class during the return period.

(ii) Returns made up to 1 October 2011 or later – the names and addresses of members who held less than 5% of the company's issued share capital at the made up date of the return must not be given. If a company shares were subject to the FCA Disclosure and Transparency Rules no shareholder details are required.

Companies with a class of shares that are traded and a class of shares that are not traded.

(i) Returns made up to 30 September 2011 or earlier – if shares are traded on a regulated market during the period of the annual return, the box marked "traded" on the annual return must be ticked and on paper annual returns Schedule B must be completed for all classes of shares whether or not that class of shares is traded.

(ii) Returns made up to 1 October 2011 or later – if shares have been traded on a relevant market at any time during the period covered by the return, for each person who held at least 5% of the issued shares of any class of the company at the made-up date of the return, the annual return must show the person's name and address (as they appear in the company's register of members) and the number of shares of each class held by the person at that time. The entries must be listed in alphabetical order by name or an index must be annexed to the return that is sufficient to enable the name of the person to be easily found.

[*CA 2006, ss 855, 855A, 856, 856A, 856B*; *SI 2008 No 3000, Regs 2–7, Schs 1, 2*; *SI 2011 No 1487*].

Companies House will reject the annual return if it does not include all the above required information. If the information is completed but does not match their records Companies House may accept the annual return but mark it 'inconsistent with the public register'. If you need any further help see Companies House guide GP6 Registrar's Rules and Powers.

Non-disclosure of subsidiaries in the accounts. In relation to financial years beginning on or after 6 April 2008, a company need not disclose full particulars of all its subsidiaries in its annual accounts if it would result in a statement of excessive length. In such a case, it must annex the full information required (ie both that which has been disclosed in the notes to the accounts and that which has not) in the next annual return following the approval of the accounts in question. See 3.32 ACCOUNTS: LARGE COMPANIES for full details.

[*CA 2006, ss 410(3)*].

7.3 METHOD OF FILING

Annual returns may be delivered electronically using Companies House Software Filing or Webfiling services. For more information, see the Companies House website at:

www.companieshouse.gov.uk

If the company does not have the facility to file online, it can download a hard copy form AR01 which can be completed and delivered by hand (personally or by courier), including outside office hours, bank holidays and weekends to the Registrar at Cardiff or Edinburgh (see below) or London. Companies which file paper returns may provide shareholder information on a CD-ROM if the list is 50 pages or more.

Alternatively, the completed hard copy annual return can also be sent by post, by DX or (in Scotland) by LP to

7.3 Annual Returns

For companies incorporated in England and Wales

Companies House
Crown Way
Cardiff CF14 3UZ

DX33050 Cardiff 1 (Documents Exchange Service)

For companies incorporated in Scotland:

Companies House
4th Floor
Edinburgh Quay 2
139 Fountainbridge
Edinburgh EH1 9FF

DX ED235 Edinburgh 1 (Documents Exchange Service)

LP–4 Edinburgh 2 (Legal Post)

Companies House
4 Abbey Orchard Street
Westminster
London SW1P 2HT

Documents are only acknowledged if a copy of the covering letter and a prepaid addressed return envelope are provided.

Additional security for directors' and registered office addresses and shareholder details (Companies House PROOF system). Electronic delivery of directors' details and registered office address. Companies House offers companies a free, fully electronic and secure system for notifying changes of directors, changes to the registered office address and annual returns. If a company opts to notify these electronically, it (or its authorised agents) will need a company authentication code and Companies House will not accept notices from the company delivered in any other format. The service is voluntary and the company may opt-out at any time. Companies House will then revert to accepting notices from the company delivered electronically or on paper returns.

Change of information: The annual return should confirm the information already held by Companies House but if any of the following specific information needs to be changed the relevant forms must also be sent (either electronically as above or in hard copy). The following changes have to be notified separately:

- change of registered office (Form AD01);
- appointment of company director or secretary (Forms AP01, AP02, AP03 or AP04);
- change of details of director or secretary (Form CH01. CH02, CH03 or CH04);
- termination of appointment of director or secretary (Form TM01 or TM02);
- notification of address or change of address where company records are available for inspection (SAIL) (Form AD02). If a SAIL notification has been given, the annual return will need to show the SAIL address;
- notification of company records held at an alternate address or if they are being returned to the registered office (Form AD0301 or AD04);

- allotment of new shares (Form SH01);
- change to the company's total share capital.

(Companies House Guidance GP2 Life of a Company – Part 1 Annual Requirements Annual Return, Chapter 1, para 5).

7.4 FAILURE TO DELIVER ANNUAL RETURN

If a company fails to deliver a fully completed annual return within the 28 days allowed, an offence is committed by

- the company,
- subject to below, every director (including shadow director, see **18.1 Directors**) of the company and, in the case of a private company with a secretary or a public company, every secretary of the company; and
- every other officer of the company who is in default.

A person guilty of such an offence is liable, on summary conviction, to a fine not exceeding level 5 on the standard scale and, for continued contravention, a daily default fine not exceeding one-tenth of level 5 on the standard scale until such time as the return is delivered. See **29.1 Offences and Legal Proceedings** for the standard scale. It is a defence for a director or secretary to show that he took all reasonable steps to avoid the commission or continuation of the offence. It is not a defence that another person was required to make the return (*Gibson v Barton* (1875) LR 10 QB 329).

In the case of continued contravention, an offence is also committed by every officer of the company who did not commit an offence in relation to the initial contravention but is in default in relation to the continued contravention. A person guilty of such an offence is liable, on summary conviction, to a fine not exceeding one-tenth of the greater of £5,000 or level 4 on the standard scale for each day on which the contravention continues and he is in default.

[*CA 2006, s 858; SI 2008 No 3000, Reg 8*; *SI 2015 No 664, Sch 3*].

See also **39.16 Registrar of Companies** for the Registrar's powers of enforcement.

REFORM – ANNUAL CONFIRMATION STATEMENTS

The following is a summary only of new provisions which are not (as at May 2015) in force. Full details are set out in the Small Business, Enterprise and Employment Act 2015 (SBEE 2015) which provides that instead of an annual return, companies will be required to deliver a 'confirmation statement' to the Registrar of Companies which confirms that all information required to be delivered either has been delivered or is being delivered at the same time as the confirmation statement. The confirmation statement and any information as is necessary to ensure that the company is able to make the statement must be delivered before the end of the period of 14 days after the end of each 'review period'.

A review period is

- the period of 12 months beginning with the day of incorporation; or
- each period beginning with the day after the end of the previous review period.

7.4 Annual Returns

The confirmation statement relates to the 'confirmation period' concerned under duties set out in *SBEE 2015*.

At the same time as delivering a confirmation statement a company with share capital must deliver a statement of capital (as defined) and must notify the trading status of its shares.

Non-traded companies (as defined) must deliver certain shareholder information and traded companies must deliver details of each person who at the end of the confirmation period held at least 5% of the issued shares of any class of the company and the number of shares of each class held by each such person.

New requirements to deliver details about people with significant control annually ('PSC's' – see 38.14) are also included in *SBEE 2015*.

It is anticipated that these new requirements will come into force before the end of 2016.

[CA 2006, *s 853 A–L; SBEE 2015, s 92*].

8 Audit

8.1 **Appointment of auditor**
8.2 Appointment by private companies
8.4 Appointment by public companies
8.6 Default appointment by the Secretary of State
8.7 Disclosure of terms of audit appointment and auditors' remuneration
8.8 **Eligibility for appointment as auditor**
8.9 Independence requirement
8.10 Effect of ineligibility or lack of independence
8.11 Power to require second audit
8.12 Effect of appointment of partnership
8.13 Register of auditors
8.14 Registered third country auditors
8.15 **Fixing of auditor's remuneration**
8.16 **Removal of auditor from office**
8.17 Failure to re-appoint auditor: special procedure required for written resolution
8.18 Failure to re-appoint auditor: special notice required for resolution at general meeting
8.19 **Resignation of auditor**
8.20 Rights of resigning auditor
8.21 **Statement by auditor ceasing to hold office**
8.22 Notification to the appropriate audit authority and the accounting authorities
8.23 **Effect of casual vacancies where joint auditors**
8.24 **Requirement for audited accounts**
8.25 Exemption from audit: small companies
8.27 Small companies exemption in case of a group company
8.28 Exemption from audit: dormant companies
8.29 Exemption from audit: other circumstances
8.30 **Auditor's report**
8.31 Special auditor's report where abbreviated accounts delivered to the Registrar of Companies
8.32 Auditor's report following defective accounts or reports
8.33 Duties of auditor in connection with report
8.34 Signature of auditor's report
8.35 Offences in connection with auditors' reports
8.36 **Auditor's right to information**
8.37 **Auditor's rights in relation to resolutions and meetings**
8.38 **Auditor's liability**
8.39 Provisions protecting auditor from liability
8.40 Indemnity for costs of defending proceedings
8.41 Liability limitation agreements
8.45 **Quoted companies: members' power to require website publication of audit concerns**

Cross-references. See **6.6 Accounts: Strategic Reports** for auditor's report on summary financial statements; **22.4 Distributions** for report when qualified accounts are relevant for the purposes of a proposed distribution; **34.12 Purchase of Own Shares** for report when a private company wishes to redeem or purchase its own shares out of capital; **41.4 Re-Registration** for report when a private company wishes to re-register as a public company.

The *Companies Act 2006 (Strategic Report and Directors' Report) Regulations 2013* ("the *2013 Regulations*") which are referred to in this chapter, bring into force the requirement for a company to produce a strategic report for financial years ending on or after 30 September 2013.

8.1 Audit

8.1 APPOINTMENT OF AUDITOR

Every company must appoint an auditor or auditors except where exemption from audit applies (see **8.25** to **8.29**).

8.2 Appointment by private companies

A private company must appoint an auditor or auditors for each financial year of the company, unless the directors reasonably resolve otherwise on the grounds that audited accounts are unlikely to be required.

For each financial year for which an appointment is made (other than the company's first financial year), the appointment must be made before the end of the period of 28 days beginning with

- the end of the time allowed for sending out copies of the company's annual accounts and reports for the previous financial year under *CA 2006, s 424* (see **2.6 Accounts: General**); or
- if earlier, the day on which copies of the company's annual accounts and reports for the previous financial year are sent out under *CA 2006, s 423* (see **2.6 Accounts: General**).

This is the 'period for appointing auditors'.

Without prejudice to any deemed re-appointment under **8.3**, an auditor or auditors of a private company may only be appointed by the directors or members as below or, in default, by the Secretary of State under **8.6**.

(a) *Appointment by directors.* The directors may appoint an auditor or auditors of the company

- at any time before the company's first period for appointing auditors;
- following a period during which the company did not have any auditor (because it was exempt from audit) at any time before the company's next period for appointing auditors; or
- to fill a casual vacancy in the office of auditor.

(b) *Appointment by members.* The members may appoint an auditor or auditors by ordinary resolution (see **42.2 Resolutions and Meetings**)

- during a period for appointing auditors;
- if the company should have appointed an auditor or auditors during a period for appointing auditors but failed to do so; or
- where the directors could have appointed as above but have failed to do so.

[*CA 2006, s 485*].

8.3 *Term of office of auditors of private company*

An auditor or auditors of a private company hold office in accordance with the terms of their appointment, subject to the requirements that

- they do not take office until any previous auditor or auditors cease to hold office, and
- they cease to hold office at the end of the next period for appointing auditors unless re-appointed.

This is without prejudice to the provisions as to removal and resignation of auditors.

An auditor's term of office will therefore typically run from the end of the 28-day period following the circulation of the accounts until the end of the corresponding period in the following year.

Deemed re-appointment. Where no auditor has been appointed by the end of the next 'period for appointing auditors' (see 8.2), any auditor in office immediately before that time is deemed to be re-appointed at that time unless

(a) he was appointed by the directors;

(b) the company's articles require actual re-appointment;

(c) the deemed re-appointment is prevented by the members (see below);

(d) the members have resolved that he should not be re-appointed; or

(e) the directors have resolved that no auditor or auditors should be appointed for the financial year in question.

No account is to be taken of any loss of the opportunity of deemed re-appointment under the above provisions in determining the amount of any compensation or damages payable to an auditor on his ceasing to hold office for any reason.

Prevention by members of deemed re-appointment. An auditor of a private company is not deemed to be re-appointed if the company has received notices from members representing at least 5% (or such lower percentage as is specified in the company's articles) of the total voting rights of all members who would be entitled to vote on a resolution that the auditor should not be re-appointed.

Such a notice may be in hard copy or electronic form. It must be authenticated by the person or persons giving it and must be received by the company before the end of the accounting reference period immediately preceding the time when the deemed re-appointment would have effect (ie before the end of the financial year the accounts for which he is auditing).

[*CA 2006, ss 487, 488; SI 2007 No 2194, Sch 1 para 18, Sch 3 para 44*].

Transitional provisions–the effect of resolutions in force before 1 October 2007

(1) Where a private company elected under *CA 1985, s 386* to dispense with the annual appointment of auditors and that election was in force immediately before 1 October 2007, (*a*) above does not prevent the deemed re-appointment of auditors first appointed before 1 October 2007.

(2) Where, immediately before 1 October 2007, a resolution of a private company under *CA 1985, s 390A* (auditors' remuneration) was in force and was expressed to continue to have effect so long as a resolution under *CA 1985, s 386* continued in force, the repeal of *CA 1985, s 386* does not affect the continued operation of the resolution which continues to have effect until

- it is revoked or superseded by a further resolution,
- the auditors to which it applied cease to hold office; or
- it otherwise ceases to have effect in accordance with its terms.

[*SI 2007 No 2194, Sch 3 paras 44, 45*].

8.4 Audit

8.4 Appointment by public companies

A public company must appoint an auditor or auditors for each financial year of the company, unless the directors reasonably resolve otherwise on the ground that audited accounts are unlikely to be required.

For each financial year for which an appointment is made (other than the company's first financial year), the appointment must be made before the end of the accounts meeting of the company at which the company's annual accounts and reports for the previous financial year are laid.

An auditor or auditors of a public company may only be appointed by the directors or members as below or, in default, by the Secretary of State under **8.6**.

(a) *Appointment by directors*. The directors may appoint an auditor or auditors of the company

- at any time before the company's first accounts meeting;
- following a period during which the company did not have any auditor (because it was exempt from audit), at any time before the company's next accounts meeting; or
- to fill a casual vacancy in the office of auditor.

(b) *Appointment by members*. The members may appoint an auditor or auditors by ordinary resolution

- at an accounts meeting;
- if the company should have appointed an auditor or auditors at an accounts meeting but failed to do so; or
- where the directors could have appointed as above but failed to do so.

[*CA 2006, s 489*].

See APPENDIX 1 DEFINITIONS for the meaning of "accounts meeting".

8.5 *Term of office of auditors of public company*

The auditor or auditors of a public company hold office in accordance with the terms of their appointment, subject to the requirements that

- they do not take office until the previous auditor or auditors have ceased to hold office; and
- they cease to hold office at the conclusion of the accounts meeting next following their appointment, unless re-appointed.

This is without prejudice to the provisions as to removal and resignation of auditors.

[*CA 2006, s 491*].

8.6 Default appointment by the Secretary of State

Where

- a private company fails to appoint an auditor or auditors before the end of the 'period for appointing auditors' in accordance with **8.2**, or
- a public company fails to appoint an auditor or auditors before the end of the accounts meeting in accordance with **8.4**

the company must, within one week of the end of that period/meeting, give notice to the Secretary of State of his power having become exercisable to appoint one or more persons to fill the vacancy.

If a company fails to give the required notice, an offence is committed by the company and every officer of the company who is in default. A person guilty of such an offence is liable, on summary conviction, to a fine not exceeding level 3 on the standard scale and, for continued contravention, a daily default fine not exceeding one-tenth of level 3 on the standard scale. See **29.1 Offences and Legal Proceedings** for the standard scale. [*CA 2006, ss 486, 490*].

8.7 Disclosure of terms of audit appointment and auditors' remuneration

SI 2007 No 3495 provides that the Secretary of State may make regulations for the disclosure of the terms on which a company's auditor is appointed, remunerated or performs his duties. [*CA 2006, s 493; SI 2007 No 3495, Sch 4 para 11*; *SI 2011 No 2198*].

For disclosure of remuneration the *Companies (Disclosure of Auditor Remuneration and Liability Limitation Agreements) Regulations 2008 (SI 2008 No 489)* provide that

- for small and medium-sized companies the amount of any remuneration receivable by the auditor for auditing the accounts must be disclosed in a note to the annual accounts and where the remuneration includes benefits in kind, the nature and estimated money-value of those benefits must also be disclosed; and
- for any other companies the notes to the accounts must disclose remuneration receivable for auditing the accounts and also any remuneration receivable by the auditor or any associate of that auditor for the supply of any other services to both the company and any associate of the company. The provision for benefits in kind (above) also applies here. The types of services for which disclosure has to be made are set out in *Schedule 2A* [*SI 2007 No 3495* as amended by *SI 2011 No 2198*].

8.8 ELIGIBILITY FOR APPOINTMENT AS AUDITOR

The main purposes of *CA 2006, Pt 42* (statutory auditors) are to secure that

- only persons who are properly supervised and appropriately qualified are appointed as statutory auditors; and
- audits by persons so appointed are carried out properly, with integrity and with a proper degree of independence.

[*CA 2006, s 1209*].

8.8 Audit

(1) **Eligibility for appointment**

An individual or 'firm' is eligible for appointment as a statutory auditor if the individual or firm is

(a) a member of a recognised 'supervisory body' (see (2) below), *and*

(b) eligible for appointment under the rules of that body. A person cannot be eligible for appointment unless

(i) in the case of an individual, he holds an 'appropriate qualification'; and

(ii) in the case of a firm, each individual responsible for statutory audit work on behalf of the firm is eligible for appointment as a statutory auditor *and* the firm is controlled by qualified persons. A firm is to be treated as controlled by qualified persons if, and only if, both a majority of the members of the firm are qualified persons *and* (where the firm's affairs are managed by a board of directors, committee or other management body) a majority of that body are qualified persons. If the body consists of two persons only, at least one of them must be a qualified person.

In the case of an individual who is an '*EEA auditor*' (ie an individual approved by a competent authority in another EEA state to carry out audits), he must *either* hold an appropriate qualification *or* have been authorised before 6 April 2008 to practise the profession of company auditor under *EC (Recognition of Professional Qualifications) Regs 2005* (*SI 2005 No 18*) *or* have passed an aptitude test.

A firm which has ceased to comply with the conditions in (*b*)(ii) above may be permitted to remain eligible for appointment as a statutory auditor for a period of not more than three months.

'*Firm*' means any entity, whether or not a legal person, which is not an individual and includes a body corporate, a corporation sole and a partnership or other unincorporated association.

[*CA 2006, ss 1212(1), 1261, Sch 10 paras 6, 7; SI 2007 No 3494, Regs 17, 18; SI 2011 No 1856, Reg 5*].

(2) **Supervisory body**

A '*supervisory body*' means a body 'established in the UK' which maintains and enforces binding rules as to eligibility of persons for appointment as a statutory auditor and the conduct of statutory audit work. [*CA 2006, s 1217; SI 2007 No 3494, Reg 4*].

See *CA 2006, Sch 10* for provisions on the recognition of supervisory bodies.

Part 1 covers the grant and revocation of recognition.

Part 2 deals with the requirements for recognition including rules for

- holding of appropriate qualifications by auditors;
- the necessity for auditors to be fit and proper persons;
- professional integrity and independence;
- technical standards;

- technical standards for group audits;
- public interest entity reporting requirements;
- public interest entity independence requirements;
- procedures for maintaining competence;
- monitoring and enforcement of compliance;
- monitoring of audits;
- membership, eligibility and discipline;
- investigation of complaints;
- independent investigation of disciplinary purposes of public interest cases;
- transfer papers to third countries;
- meeting of claims arising out of audit work;
- maintenance of a register of auditors;
- taking account of costs of compliance; and
- the promotion and maintenance of standards.

Part 3 covers arrangements in which recognised supervisory bodies are required to participate, including those for

- setting standards in relation to professional integrity and independence;
- setting technical standards;
- setting standards relating to public interest entity reporting requirements;
- setting standards relating to public interest entity independence requirements;
- independent monitoring of audits of listed and other major bodies; and
- independent investigation for disciplinary purposes of public interest cases.

For these purposes, a body is to be regarded as '*established in the UK*' if and only if it is incorporated or formed under the law of the UK (or a part of the UK) or its central management and control are exercised in the UK. [*CA 2006, s 1261(2)*].

(3) **Appropriate qualification**

A person holds an '*appropriate qualification*' in the following circumstances.

(a) He holds a 'recognised professional qualification' obtained in the UK.

See *CA 2006, Sch 11* for provisions relating to 'recognised professional qualifications'.

Part 1 covers the grant and revocation of recognition of a professional qualification.

Part 2 deals with the requirements for recognition. The qualification must only be open to persons who have attained university entrance level or have a sufficient period of professional expertise. It must be restricted to persons who have completed a course of theoretical instruction and passed an examination (at least part of which is in writing) testing theoretical knowledge and the ability to put that knowledge into practice and requiring a standard of attainment at least equivalent to that required to obtain a degree in the UK.

The subjects for theoretical instruction are prescribed by Regulations made by the Professional Oversight Board.

The qualification may be awarded to a person without his theoretical knowledge of a subject being tested by examination if he has passed a university or other examination of equivalent standard in that subject or holds a university degree or equivalent qualification in it. The qualification may also be awarded to a person without his ability to apply his theoretical knowledge of a subject in practice being tested by examination if he has received practical training in that subject which is attested by an examination or diploma recognised by the Professional Oversight Board for these purposes.

The qualification must also be restricted to persons who have completed at least three years' practical training, part of which must be spent being trained in statutory audit work by a person qualified for appointment as a statutory auditor.

(b) Immediately before 6 April 2008, he held (or was treated as holding) an appropriate qualification for the purposes of *CA 1989, Part 2* (eligibility for appointment as company auditor) by virtue of *CA 1989, s 31*.

(c) Immediately before 6 April 2008, he held (or was treated as holding) an appropriate qualification for the purposes of *Companies (Northern Ireland) Order 1990 (SI 1990 No 593) Pt 3* by virtue of *Article 34* of that *Order*.

(d) Before 1 January 1990, he began a course of study or practical training leading to a professional qualification in accountancy offered by a body 'established in the UK' (see above); he obtained that qualification on or after that date and before 1 January 1996; and the Professional Oversight Board approves his qualification as an appropriate qualification for these purposes.

(e) He is regarded as holding an approved overseas qualification as a result of a declaration by the Professional Oversight Board under *CA 2006, s 1221*.

[*CA 2006, ss 1219, 1220; SI 2007 No 3494, Reg 5*].

A person whose only appropriate qualification is based upon his retention of an authorisation granted by the Board of Trade or the Secretary of State under the CA 1967, s 13(1) is eligible only for appointment as auditor of an unquoted company. For these purposes, a company is unquoted if, at the time of the person's appointment, neither the company, nor any parent undertaking of which it is a subsidiary undertaking, is a quoted company (see APPENDIX 1 DEFINITIONS). [*CA 2006, ss 1212(2), 1222; SI 2005 No 2337*].

8.9 Independence requirement

A person may not act as statutory auditor of an audited person if

(a) he is an 'officer' or employee of the audited person;

(b) he is a partner or employee of a person within (*a*) above or a partnership of which such a person is a partner;

(c) he is an officer or employee of an 'associated undertaking' of the audited person;

(d) he is a partner or employee of a person within (*c*) above or a partnership of which such a person is a partner; or

(e) there exists between

(i) the person or an 'associate' of his, and

(ii) the audited person or an associated undertaking of the audited person,

a connection of any such description as may be specified by Regulations made by the Secretary of State.

An auditor of an audited person is not to be regarded as an officer or employee of that person for the purposes of (*a*)–(*d*) above.

'*Officer*', in relation to a body corporate, includes a director, a manager, a secretary or, where the affairs of the body are managed by its members, a member.

'*Associated undertaking*' for these purposes, in relation to an audited person, means

- a parent undertaking or subsidiary undertaking of the audited person; or
- a subsidiary undertaking of a parent undertaking of the audited person.

'*Associate*', in relation to a person, for these purposes means

- in relation to an individual,

  (i) that individual's spouse, civil partner or minor child or step-child;

  (ii) any body corporate of which that individual is a director; and

  (iii) any employee or partner of that individual;
- in relation to a body corporate,

  (i) any body corporate of which that body is a director;

  (ii) any body corporate in the same group as that body; and

  (iii) any employee or partner of that body or of any body corporate in the same group;
- in relation to a partnership constituted under the law of Scotland, or any other country or territory in which a partnership is a legal person,

  (i) any body corporate of which that partnership is a director;

  (ii) any employee of or partner in that partnership; and

  (iii) any person who is an associate of a partner in that partnership; and
- in relation to a partnership constituted under the law of England and Wales or Northern Ireland, or the law of any other country or territory in which a partnership is not a legal person, any person who is an associate of any of the partners. [*CA 2006, ss 1214, 1260*].

8.10 Effect of ineligibility or lack of independence

If at any time during his term of office a statutory auditor becomes

- ineligible for appointment as a statutory auditor under **8.8**, or
- prohibited from acting through lack of independence under **8.9**

he must immediately resign his office (with immediate effect) and give notice in writing to the audited person that he has resigned by reason of becoming ineligible for appointment or, as the case may be, lack of independence.

A person is guilty of an offence if he

(a) acts as a statutory auditor in contravention of the above; or

(b) fails to give the required notice.

A person guilty of such an offence is liable (i) on conviction on indictment, to a fine; and (ii) on summary conviction, to a fine not exceeding the statutory maximum. See **29.1** OFFENCES AND LEGAL PROCEEDINGS for the statutory maximum.

A person is also guilty of an offence if, having been convicted of an offence under (*a*) or (*b*) above, he continues to act as a statutory auditor (when still ineligible or prohibited through lack of independence) or continues to fail to give the required notice. A person guilty of such an offence is liable (i) on conviction on indictment, to a fine; and (ii) on summary conviction, to a fine not exceeding one-tenth of the greater of £5,000 or level 4 on the standard scale for each day on which the act or the failure continues.

In proceedings against a person for an offence under these provisions it is a defence for him to show that he did not know and had no reason to believe that he was, or had become, ineligible for appointment as a statutory auditor or, as the case may be, prohibited from acting through lack of independence.

[*CA 2006, ss 1213, 1215; SI 2015 No 664, Sch 3*].

8.11 Power to require second audit

Where a person appointed as statutory auditor of a company was not an 'appropriate' person for any part of the period during which the audit was conducted, the Professional Oversight Board for Accountancy may direct the company concerned to retain an appropriate person to

- conduct a second audit of the relevant accounts; or
- review the first audit and to report (giving his reasons) whether a second audit is needed.

For the above purposes, a person is '***appropriate***' if he is eligible for appointment as a statutory auditor under **8.8** and is not ineligible under **8.9** through lack of independence.

The FRC must send a copy of any direction made to the Registrar of Companies. The company must

(i) comply with the direction within 21 days of it being given;

(ii) send a copy of any report from the second auditor to the Registrar of Companies within 21 days of receipt; and

(iii) if that report states that a second audit is needed, take such steps as are necessary for the carrying out of that audit.

The company is guilty of an offence if it

(a) fails to comply with the direction within the 21-day period;

(b) fails to send a copy of a report from the second auditor to the Registrar of Companies within the 21-day period;

(c) where (iii) above applies, fails to take the necessary steps to carry out the audit immediately it receives the report; and

(d) has been convicted of a previous offence under *(a)*–*(c)* above and the failure which led to the conviction continues after the conviction.

A company guilty of such an offence is liable, on summary conviction, in a case within *(a)*–*(c)* above to a fine not exceeding level 5 on the standard scale and in a case within *(d)* above to a fine not exceeding one-tenth of the greater of £5,000 or level 4 on the standard scale for each day on which the failure continues. See **29.1 OFFENCES AND LEGAL PROCEEDINGS** for the standard scale.

If a person accepts an appointment, or continues to act, as statutory auditor of a company when he knows he is not an appropriate person, the company may recover from him any costs incurred by it in complying with the above requirements.

Where a second audit is carried out, any statutory or other provision applying in relation to the first audit applies also, in so far as practicable, in relation to the second audit.

A direction under these provisions is, on the application of the Board, enforceable by injunction or, in Scotland, by an order under *Court of Session Act 1988, s 45*.

[*CA 2006, ss 1248, 1249; SI 2015 No 664, Sch 3*].

8.12 Effect of appointment of partnership

The appointment of a partnership constituted under the law of

- England and Wales,
- Northern Ireland, or
- any other country or territory in which a partnership is not a legal person

as statutory auditor is, unless a contrary intention appears, the appointment of the partnership as such and not of the partners.

Where the partnership ceases, the appointment is treated as extending to

- any partnership which succeeds to the practice of that partnership provided the membership of the successor partnership is substantially the same as that of the former partnership; or
- any other person who succeeds to that practice having previously carried it on in partnership.

In each case, the succeeding partnership or other person must

(a) be eligible for the appointment as a statutory auditor;

(b) not be prohibited from acting as the statutory auditor because of lack of independence (see **8.10**); and

(c) succeed to the whole, or substantially the whole, of the business of the former partnership.

Where a partnership ceases and no person succeeds under the above rules, the appointment may, with the consent of the audited company, be treated as extending to a partnership or person satisfying the conditions in (*a*) and (*b*) above who succeeds to the business of the former partnership or such part of it as is agreed by the audited person as comprising the appointment.

[*CA 2006, s 1216*].

8.13 Register of auditors

The Secretary of State must make regulations requiring the keeping of a register of persons eligible for appointment as a statutory auditor (see below) and, with effect from 6 April 2008, third country auditors who apply to be registered (see 8.14). [*CA 2006, s 1239; SI 2007 No 3494, Reg 30*].

Register to be kept from 29 June 2009

The FRC has been empowered, by the Secretary of State, to make regulations requiring the keeping of a register of the persons eligible for appointment as a statutory auditor. Under these regulations, the recognised supervisory bodies (see 8.8) must keep a register of persons eligible for appointment as a statutory auditor in electronic form.

Contents of the register. The register must contain the following information.

(a) In relation to a person eligible for appointment as a statutory auditor who is an individual,

- (i) his name and address;
- (ii) his registered number;
- (iii) the name and address of the recognised supervisory body under whose rules he is eligible for appointment as a statutory auditor;
- (iv) if he is responsible for statutory audit work on behalf of any firm, the firm's name, address, registered number, and if it has a website, its address; and
- (v) the name of any EEA competent authority or third country authority with whom he is registered for audit purposes and any registration number which such an authority has allocated to him.

(b) In relation to a person eligible for appointment as a statutory auditor which is a firm,

- (i) its name and address;
- (ii) its registered number;
- (iii) the address of each of its offices in which it carries out statutory audit work;
- (iv) information as to how the firm is to be contacted, the primary contact person and, if it has a website, its address;
- (v) the name, business address and registration number of each individual responsible for statutory audit work on behalf of the firm;
- (vi) in the case of a limited liability partnership, the name and business address of each member of the partnership;

(vii) in the case of a body corporate, other than a limited liability partnership, the name and business address of each person who is a director of the body or holds any shares in it;

(viii) in the case of a corporation sole, the name and address of the individual for the time being holding the office by the name of which he is the corporation sole;

(ix) in the case of a partnership, the name and business address of each partner

(x) the name and address of the recognised supervisory body under whose rules it is eligible for appointment as a statutory auditor;

(xi) in the case of a firm which is a member of a 'network', the name of the network, a list of the names and addresses of the other members of that network and of the affiliates of all the members of that network or a reference to the address of a website or any other place where that information is available to the public; and

(xii) the name of any EEA competent authority or third country authority with whom it is registered for audit purposes and any registration number which such an authority has allocated to it.

References under (vi)–(ix) above to a limited liability partnership, a body corporate, a corporation sole or a partnership include references to any comparable undertaking incorporated in or formed under the law of any country or territory outside the UK.

'*Network*' means a larger structure to which the firm belongs and which is aimed at co-operation and either

- is clearly aimed at profit- or cost-sharing;
- shares common ownership, control or management;
- has common quality control policies and procedures;
- has a common business strategy;
- has the use of a common name; or
- shares significant professional resources.

Maintenance. One of the supervisory bodies must be responsible for keeping the register and making it available for inspection by electronic means ('*the maintaining body*'). It must ensure that the information contained in the register may be inspected

- alphabetically by name of person;
- by reference to individuals or firms;
- by reference to registration numbers;
- by reference to recognised supervisory bodies; and
- by address.

Information on the register relating to a person may be excluded from being made available for inspection if to do so would create a serious risk that an individual, or any other person, would be subject to violence or intimidation.

Any supervisory body which is not the maintaining body must send that body in electronic form for entry on the register

- before 29 June 2009, the information specified in (*a*) and (*b*) above; and
- thereafter, any changes to that information, including that relating to persons who become eligible for appointment as statutory auditors, within 10 business days of becoming aware of the relevant change.

Inspection. Each recognised supervisory body must provide at its principal office in the UK facilities by which any person may inspect the register by electronic means, at any reasonable time during a business day. Any person inspecting the register may require a copy of any entry on the register relating to a particular individual or firm. A charge may be made but not exceeding £1 per copy of an entry.

Duty to provide updated information. Any person eligible for appointment as a statutory auditor must take all reasonable steps to notify the recognised supervisory body, by virtue of whose rules the person is eligible for appointment as statutory auditor, without undue delay, of any information necessary to ensure that the information in the register relating to that person is correct.

[*CA 2006, s 1239; SI 2007 No 3494, Reg 30*]

8.14 Registered third country auditors

A '*third country auditor*' means a person, other than a person eligible for appointment as a statutory auditor, who is eligible to conduct audits of the accounts of bodies corporate incorporated or formed under the law of a third country (ie a country which is not part of the EEA) in accordance with the laws of that country. A '*registered third country auditor*' means a third country auditor who is entered in the register (see below). [*CA 2006, s 1241; SI 2007 No 3494, Reg 31*].

CA 2006, ss 1242–1247 contain provisions relating to registered third country auditors. *Section 1242* is amended by *SI 2011 No 1856* (the *Statutory Auditors and Third Country Auditors (Amendment) Regulations 2011*).

A registered third country auditor who audits the accounts of a 'UK-traded non-EEA company' is subject to arrangements for independent monitoring of audits and investigations for disciplinary purposes in the UK in accordance with *CA 2006, Sch 12*. These provisions are similar to supervision arrangements for statutory auditors under 8.8. The Secretary of State may direct in writing that these provisions are not to apply, in whole or in part, in relation to a particular registered third country auditor or class of registered third country auditors. [*CA 2006, s 1242; SI 2007 No 3494, Reg 32*]. He may do this, for example, if satisfied that the third company auditor is already subject to equivalent supervision in his home country.

A '*UK-traded non-EEA company*' means a body corporate

- which is incorporated or formed under the law of a third country;
- whose transferable securities are admitted to trading on a regulated market situated or operating in the UK; and
- which has not been excluded from the definition by the Secretary of State. A large debt securities issuer (ie a body corporate whose only issued transferable securities admitted to trading are debt securities with a denomination of not less than 50,000 euros or its equivalent) has been excluded.

[*CA 2006, s 1241(2); SI 2007 No 3494, Regs 31, 43*].

Register of third country auditors. The FRC must keep a register of third country auditors containing specified information. The register must be kept in electronic form and the information on it must be available for inspection by any person by electronic means (unless making the information so available would create a serious risk that the individual, or any other person, would be subject to violence or intimidation). [*SI 2007 No 3494, Regs 29, 34; SI 2008 No 2639*].

Application for registration. A third country auditor may apply to the FRC in writing for registration. The application must comply with the requirements in *SI 2007 No 3494, Regs 35, 36* which include an application statement that he holds the necessary qualifications, is a fit and proper person to conduct audits and conducts audits under the necessary standards. If satisfied with the application, the FRC will duly register him and allocate him a registered number. If it refuses registration, the FRC must give him written notice to that effect stating the reason for the refusal. [*SI 2007 No 3494, Regs 37, 38*].

Duty to provide updated information. Once registered a third country auditor must take all reasonable steps to notify the FRC without undue delay of any change or addition to the information specified in *Reg 35(3A)(a)* (the name, registered number, third country or territory in which it is incorporated or under the law of which it is formed and the accounting period to which the audit relates in respect of each UK traded non EEA company for which the third country auditor provides a service), any information or event which may lead the FRC to consider that the application statement required by *Reg 36* made by the third country auditor is not correct, and any information necessary to ensure that the information in the register relating to the third country auditor is correct. [*SI 2007 No 3494, Reg 39*; *SI 2008 No 2639*; *SI 2011 No 1856, Reg 7(6)*; *SI 2012 No 1471*].

8.15 FIXING OF AUDITOR'S REMUNERATION

The 'remuneration' of an auditor appointed by the members of a company must be fixed by the members by ordinary resolution (or in such manner as the members may by ordinary resolution determine). The remuneration of an auditor appointed by the directors or the Secretary of State must be fixed by the directors or Secretary of State (as the case may be).

'*Remuneration*' includes sums paid in respect of expenses and the provisions apply to benefits in kind as to payments of money.

[*CA 2006, s 492*].

8.16 REMOVAL OF AUDITOR FROM OFFICE

Notices of intended resolutions to remove auditor given to company. The members of a company can remove an auditor from office at any time. This power is exercisable only by ordinary resolution at a meeting and in accordance with the procedure set out below. Nothing in these provisions is to be taken as depriving the person removed of compensation or damages payable to him in respect of the termination

- of his appointment as auditor; or
- of any appointment terminating with that as auditor.

Procedure. Special notice (see **42.18 Resolutions and Meetings**) is required for a resolution at a general meeting of a company removing an auditor from office. On receipt of notice of such an intended resolution, the company must immediately send a copy of it to the person proposed to be removed. That person may then make written representations to the company, not exceeding a reasonable length, and request their notification to the members. The company must then, unless the representations are received too late to do so, state the fact that representations have been made in the notice of any resolution to the members and send a copy of the representations to every member to whom notice of the meeting is or has been sent.

If a copy of the representations is not sent because it is received too late or because of the company's default, the auditor can, without prejudice to his right to be heard orally, require that the representations be read out at the meeting.

Copies of the representations need not be sent out, and the representations need not be read at the meeting if, on the application either of the company or of any other person claiming to be aggrieved, the court is satisfied that the auditor is using these provisions to secure needless publicity for defamatory matter. The court may order the company's costs (in Scotland, expenses) on the application to be paid in whole or in part by the auditor, notwithstanding that he is not a party to the application.

Notice to the Registrar of Companies. Where a resolution removing an auditor is passed under the above provisions, the company must give notice of that fact to the Registrar of Companies within 14 days. If it fails to do so, an offence is committed by the company and every officer of it who is in default. A person guilty of such an offence is liable, on summary conviction, to a fine not exceeding level 3 on the standard scale and, for continued contravention, a daily default fine not exceeding one-tenth of level 3 on the standard scale. See **29.1** Offences and Legal Proceedings for the standard scale.

Rights of auditor who has been removed from office. An auditor who has been removed by a resolution as above still has the right under **8.37** to attend the general meeting of the company at which

- his term of office would otherwise have expired; or
- it is proposed to fill the vacancy caused by his removal.

[*CA 2006, ss 510–513; SI 2007 No 3495, Sch 4 para 13*].

8.17 Failure to re-appoint auditor: special procedure required for written resolution

Where:

- a resolution is proposed as a written resolution of a private company, the effect of which would be to appoint a person as auditor in place of a person (the '*outgoing auditor*') whose term of office has expired, or is to expire, at the end of the 'period for appointing auditors' (see **8.2**), and
- either
  - (i) no period for appointing auditors has ended since the outgoing auditor ceased to hold office, or
  - (ii) such a period has ended and an auditor or auditors should have been appointed but were not,

the company must send a copy of the proposed resolution to the person proposed to be appointed and to the outgoing auditor. The outgoing auditor may, within 14 days of receiving the notice, make representations in writing to the company (not exceeding a reasonable length) about the proposed resolution and request their circulation to members of the company.

The company must circulate the representations together with the copy or copies of the written resolution circulated in accordance with *CA 2006, s 291* (resolution proposed by directors, see **42.7 Resolutions and Meetings**) or, as the case may be, *CA 2006, s 293* (resolution proposed by members, see **42.8 Resolutions and Meetings**). Where the latter applies, the period allowed for service of copies of the proposed resolution is 28 days (instead of 21 days).

Application to the court. Copies of the representations need not be circulated if, on the application either of the company or of any other person claiming to be aggrieved, the court is satisfied that the auditor is using these provisions to secure needless publicity for defamatory matter. The court may order the company's costs (in Scotland, expenses) on the application to be paid in whole or in part by the auditor, notwithstanding that he is not a party to the application.

If any of the requirements above are not complied with, the resolution is ineffective.

[*CA 2006, s 514*].

8.18 Failure to re-appoint auditor: special notice required for resolution at general meeting

The following provisions apply to a resolution at a general meeting of a company the effect of which would be to appoint a person as auditor in place of a person (the '*outgoing auditor*') whose term of office has ended, or is to end

- in the case of a private company, at the end of the 'period for appointing auditors' (see **8.2**); or
- in the case of a public company, at the end of the next accounts meeting.

Special notice (see **42.18 Resolutions and Meetings**) is required of such a resolution if

(a) in the case of a private company

 (i) no period for appointing auditors has ended since the outgoing auditor ceased to hold office; or

 (ii) such a period has ended and an auditor or auditors should have been appointed but were not; and

(b) in the case of a public company

 (i) there has been no accounts meeting of the company since the outgoing auditor ceased to hold office; or

 (ii) there has been an accounts meeting at which an auditor or auditors should have been appointed but were not.

On receipt of notice of such an intended resolution, the company must immediately send a copy of it to the person proposed to be appointed and to the outgoing auditor. The outgoing auditor may then make written representations to the company, not exceeding a reasonable length, and request their notification to the members. The company must then, unless the representations are received too late to do so, state the fact that representations have been made in the notice of any resolution to the members and send a copy of the representations to every member to whom notice of the meeting is or has been sent.

If a copy of the representations is not sent because it is received too late or because of the company's default, the auditor can, without prejudice to his right to be heard orally, require that the representations be read out at the meeting.

Application to the court. Copies of the representations need not be sent out, and the representations need not be read at the meeting if, on the application either of the company or of any other person claiming to be aggrieved, the court is satisfied that the auditor is using these provisions to secure needless publicity for defamatory matter. The court may order the company's costs (in Scotland, expenses) on the application to be paid in whole or in part by the auditor, notwithstanding that he is not a party to the application.

[*CA 2006, s 515*].

8.19 RESIGNATION OF AUDITOR

An auditor may resign his office by depositing a notice in writing to that effect at the company's registered office. To be effective, it must be accompanied by a statement required under **8.21**. His term of office then ends on the date on which the notice is deposited or on such later date as may be specified in the notice.

Notice to Registrar of Companies. Where an auditor resigns, the company must within 14 days of the deposit of a notice of resignation send a copy of the notice to the Registrar of Companies. In default, an offence is committed by the company and every officer of the company who is in default.. A person guilty of such an offence is liable (i) on conviction on indictment, to a fine; and (ii) on summary conviction, to a fine not exceeding the statutory maximum and, for continued contravention, a daily default fine not exceeding one-tenth of the greater of £5,000 or level 4 on the standard scale. See **29.1 Offences and Legal Proceedings** for the statutory maximum.

[*CA 2006, ss 516, 517; SI 2015 No 664, Sch 3*].

8.20 Rights of resigning auditor

Where an auditor's notice of resignation is accompanied by a statement of the circumstances connected with his resignation (see **8.21**), he may deposit with the notice a signed requisition calling on the directors to convene a general meeting of the company for the purpose of receiving and considering such explanation of the circumstances connected with his resignation as he may wish to place before the meeting.

He may also request the company to circulate to members

(a) before the meeting convened on his requisition, or

(b) before any general meeting at which his term of office would otherwise have expired or at which it is proposed to fill the vacancy caused by his resignation

a written statement of reasonable length of the circumstances connected with his resignation.

The company must then, unless the statement is received too late for it to comply, state the fact of the statement having been made in any notice of the meeting to the members and send a copy of the statement to every member to whom notice of the meeting is or has been sent.

The directors must then, within 21 days from the date of the deposit of the requisition, proceed to convene a meeting for a day not more than 28 days after the date on which the notice convening the meeting is given. In default, every director who failed to take all reasonable steps to secure that a meeting was convened commits an offence. A person guilty of such an offence is liable (i) on conviction on indictment, to a fine; and (ii) on summary conviction, to a fine not exceeding the statutory maximum. See **29.1 Offences and Legal Proceedings** for the statutory maximum.

Where a copy of the statement is not sent out because it was received too late or because of the company's default, the auditor can, without prejudice to his right to be heard orally, require that the statement be read out at the meeting.

Application to the court. Copies of a statement need not be sent out and the statement need not be read out at the meeting if, on the application either of the company or of any other person who claims to be aggrieved, the court is satisfied that the auditor is using these provisions to secure needless publicity for defamatory matter. The court may order the company's costs (in Scotland, expenses) on such an application to be paid in whole or in part by the auditor, notwithstanding that he is not a party to the application.

An auditor who has resigned still has the right to receive notices of, attend and be heard at, any general meeting mentioned in (*a*) or (*b*) above.

[*CA 2006, s 518*].

8.21 STATEMENT BY AUDITOR CEASING TO HOLD OFFICE

Auditors ceasing to hold office

Deposit of statement by auditor with company. An auditor who ceases to hold office for any reason (ie whether removed or by resignation) *must* deposit at the company's registered office

(a) a statement of the circumstances connected with his ceasing to hold office; or

(b) in the case of the auditor of an unquoted company, if he considers that there are no circumstances in connection with his ceasing to hold office that need to be brought to the attention of members or creditors of the company, a statement to that effect.

The statement must be deposited

- in the case of resignation, along with the notice of resignation;
- in the case of failure to seek re-appointment, not less than 14 days before the end of the time allowed for appointing the next auditor; and
- in any other case, not later than 14 days after he ceases to hold office.

If a person ceasing to hold office as auditor fails to comply with these provisions, he commits an offence. A person guilty of such an offence is liable (i) on conviction on indictment, to a fine; and (ii) on summary conviction, to a fine not exceeding the statutory maximum. See **29.1 Offences and Legal Proceedings** for the statutory maximum. However, it is a defence for the person charged to show that he took all reasonable steps and exercised all due diligence to avoid the commission of the offence. Where such an offence is committed by a body corporate, every officer of the body (which includes any person who purports to act as a director, manager or secretary of the body and, if the body is a company, any shadow director) who is in default also commits an offence.

[*CA 2006, s 519*].

Company's duties in relation to the statement. If the statement falls within (*a*) above, the company must, within 14 days of the deposit of the statement, either send a copy of it to every person entitled to receive copies of the accounts (see **2.6 Accounts: General**) or apply to the court and notify the auditor of the application.

If the court is satisfied that the auditor is using the statement to secure needless publicity for a defamatory matter, it must direct that copies of the statement need not be sent out. It may also order the company's costs (in Scotland, expenses) on the application to be paid in whole or part by the auditor (even if he is not a party to the application). The company must then, within 14 days of the court's decision, send to every person entitled to receive the accounts as above a statement setting out the effect of the order.

In the event of default in complying with these provisions, an offence is committed by every officer of the company who is in default. A person guilty of such an offence is liable (i) on conviction on indictment, to a fine; and (ii) on summary conviction, to a fine not exceeding the statutory maximum. See **29.1 Offences and Legal Proceedings** for the statutory maximum. However, it is a defence for the person charged to show that he took all reasonable steps and exercised all due diligence to avoid the commission of the offence.

[*CA 2006, s 520*].

Copy of statement to be sent to the Registrar of Companies. Unless, within 21 days of the day on which he deposited the statement with the company, the auditor receives notice of an application to the court as above, he must within a further seven days send a copy of the statement to the Registrar of Companies.

Where an application to the court is made and the auditor subsequently receives notice that no direction has been made, he must within seven days of receiving the notice send a copy of the statement to the Registrar of Companies.

An auditor who fails to comply with these provisions commits an offence. A person guilty of such an offence is liable (i) on conviction on indictment, to a fine; and (ii) on summary conviction, to a fine not exceeding the statutory maximum. See **29.1 Offences and Legal Proceedings** for the statutory maximum. However, it is a defence for the person charged to show that he took all reasonable steps and exercised all due diligence to avoid the commission of the offence. Where such an offence is committed by a body corporate, every officer of the body (which includes any person who purports to act as a director, manager or secretary of the body and, if the body is a company, any shadow director) who is in default also commits an offence.

[*CA 2006, s 521*].

8.22 Notification to the appropriate audit authority and the accounting authorities

Duty of auditor to notify appropriate audit authority. Where

- in the case of a 'major audit', an auditor ceases for any reason to hold office, or
- in the case of any other audit, an auditor ceases to hold office before the end of his term of office,

the auditor ceasing to hold office must notify the 'appropriate audit authority'.

The notice must inform the appropriate audit authority that he has ceased to hold office and be accompanied by

- a copy of the statement deposited by him at the company's registered office under **8.21**; and
- if that statement is to the effect that he considers that there are no circumstances in connection with his ceasing to hold office that need to be brought to the attention of members or creditors of the company, a statement of the reasons for his ceasing to hold office.

The auditor must comply with these provisions

(a) in the case of a major audit, at the same time as he deposits a statement at the company's registered office under **8.21**; and

(b) in the case of any other audit, at such time (not being earlier than the time mentioned in (*a*) above) as the appropriate audit authority may require.

'*Appropriate audit authority*' means (i) in the case of a major audit (other than one conducted by an Auditor General), the Secretary of State or, if the Secretary of State has delegated functions under *CA 2006, s 1252* to a body whose functions include receiving the notice in question, that body. The FRC has delegated functions given by *SI 2012 No 1741*; (ii) in the case of any other audit (other than one conducted by an Auditor General), the relevant supervisory body (see **8.8**); and (iii) in the case of an audit conducted by an Auditor General, the Professional Oversight Body.

'*Major audit*' means a statutory audit of a listed company or any other company in which there is a major public interest.

A person ceasing to hold office as auditor who fails to comply with these provisions commits an offence. If that person is a firm an offence is committed by the firm and every officer of the firm who is in default. A person guilty of such an offence is liable (i) on conviction on indictment, to a fine; and (ii) on summary conviction, to a fine not exceeding the statutory maximum. See **29.1 Offences and Legal Proceedings** for the statutory maximum. However, it is a defence for the person charged to show that he took all reasonable steps and exercised all due diligence to avoid the commission of the offence.

[*CA 2006, ss 522, 525; SI 2007 No 3494, Reg 41; 2012 No 1741, Reg 8*].

Duty of company to notify appropriate audit authority. Where an auditor ceases to hold office before the end of his term of office, the company must notify the appropriate audit authority (see above). The notice must

- inform the appropriate audit authority that the auditor has ceased to hold office; and
- be accompanied by
  - (i) a statement by the company of the reasons for his ceasing to hold office; or
  - (ii) if the copy of the statement deposited by the auditor at the company's registered office under **8.21** contains a statement of circumstances in connection with his ceasing to hold office that need to be brought to the attention of members or creditors of the company, a copy of that statement.

The company must give this notice not later than 14 days after the date on which the auditor's statement under **8.21** is deposited at the company's registered office.

If a company fails to comply with these provisions, an offence is committed by the company and every officer of the company who is in default. A person guilty of such an offence is liable (i) on conviction on indictment, to a fine; and (ii) on summary conviction, to a fine not exceeding the statutory maximum. See **29.1 Offences and Legal Proceedings** for the statutory maximum. However, it is a defence for the person charged to show that he took all reasonable steps and exercised all due diligence to avoid the commission of the offence.

[*CA 2006, s 523*].

Information to be given to accounting authorities. The appropriate audit authority (see above) on receiving notice from the auditor or company under the above provisions must inform the 'accounting authorities'. It may also, if it thinks fit, forward to those authorities a copy of the statement or statements accompanying the notice.

The '*accounting authorities*' are the Secretary of State and any person authorised by the Secretary of State for the purposes of *CA 2006, s 456* to apply to the court in respect of the revision of defective accounts (currently the Financial Reporting Review Panel).

If either of the accounting authorities is also the appropriate audit authority, it is only necessary to comply with these provisions as regards any other accounting authority.

If the court has made an order under **8.21** directing that copies of the statement need not be sent out by the company, the accounting authorities must treat the statement as confidential.

[*CA 2006, s 524*].

8.23 EFFECT OF CASUAL VACANCIES WHERE JOINT AUDITORS

If an auditor ceases to hold office for any reason, any surviving or continuing auditor or auditors may continue to act. [*CA 2006, s 526*]. The effect of this is that when one out of two or more joint auditors cease to be an auditor of the company, the remaining auditors can continue in office.

8.24 REQUIREMENT FOR AUDITED ACCOUNTS

A company's annual accounts for a financial year beginning on or after 6 April 2008 must be audited in accordance with *CA 2006, Pt 16* unless the company is

(a) exempt from audit under the provisions relating to

- small companies (see **8.25** to **8.27**) or subsidiary companies (see **8.27A**);;
- dormant companies (see **8.28**); or
- charitable companies (see **8.29**); or

(b) exempt from the requirements under the provisions relating to non-profit-making companies subject to public sector audit (see **8.29**).

The provisions relating to exemption from audit for small and subsidiary companies were amended by *SI 2012 No 2301* (the *Companies and Limited Liability Partnerships (Accounts and Audit Exemptions and Change of Accounting Framework) Regulations 2012*) which came into force on 1 October 2012 and apply to financial years ending on or after that date.

Statement on the balance sheet confirming exemption. A company is not entitled to any exemption

- under (*a*) or (*b*) above unless its balance sheet contains a statement by the directors to that effect; or
- under (a) above unless its balance sheet also contains a statement by the directors to the effect that

  (i) the members have not required the company to obtain an audit of its accounts for the year in question under the provisions below; and

(ii) the directors acknowledge their responsibilities for complying with the requirements of *CA 2006* with respect to accounting records and the preparation of accounts.

The statement required must appear on the balance sheet above the signature of the director of the company who signs the company's accounts on behalf of the board.

[*CA 2006, s 475*; *SI 2012 No 2301, Reg 6*].

Right of members to require audit. The members of a company that would otherwise be entitled to exemption from audit under any of the provisions in (*a*) above may by notice require it to obtain an audit of its accounts for a financial year. The notice must be given by

- members representing not less in total than 10% in nominal value of the company's issued share capital, or any class of it; or
- if the company does not have a share capital, not less than 10% in number of the members of the company.

The notice may not be given before the financial year to which it relates and must be given not later than one month before the end of that year. [*CA 2006, s 476*].

8.25 Exemption from audit: small companies

Subject to the

- requirement for a statement on the balance sheet (see **8.24**),
- right of members to require an audit (see **8.24**),
- companies excluded from small companies exemption (see **8.26**), and
- availability of small companies exemption in case of a group company (see **8.27**)

a company that qualifies as a small company in relation to a financial year is exempt from the requirements of *CA 2006* relating to the audit of accounts for that year.

[*CA 2006, s 477; SI 2012 No 2301, Reg 4*].

8.26 *Companies excluded from small companies exemption*

A company is not entitled to the exemption under **8.25** if it was at any time in the financial year in question

(a) a public company (see **33.1 Public and Listed Companies**);

(b) a company that

(i) is an authorised insurance company, a banking company, an e-money issuer, a 'MiFID firm' or a UCITS management company; or

(ii) carried on an insurance market activity; or

(c) a special register body or an employers' association as defined by, respectively, the *Trade Union and Labour Relations (Consolidation) Act 1992, s 117(1)* and *s 122.*

See **Appendix 1 Definitions** for the meaning of '*MiFID investment firm*'

[*CA 2006, s 477; SI 2012 No 2301, Reg 4*].

8.27 *Small companies exemption in case of a group company*

A company is not entitled to the exemption under **8.25** unless the group qualifies as a small group in relation to that financial year and was not at any time in that year an ineligible group (see **5.2** and **5.3** ACCOUNTS: SMALL COMPANIES) or throughout the whole of the period or periods during the financial year when it was a group company, it was both a subsidiary undertaking and dormant.

'*Group company*' means a company that is a parent company or a subsidiary undertaking.

'*The group*', in relation to a group company, means that company together with all its associated undertakings. For this purpose undertakings are associated if one is a subsidiary undertaking of the other or both are subsidiary undertakings of a third undertaking.

[*CA 2006, s 479; SI 2012 No 2301, Reg 5*].

8.27A Subsidiary companies: conditions for exemption from audit

A company is exempt from the requirements of CA 2006 relating to the audit of individual accounts for a financial year if

(a) it is a subsidiary undertaking, and

(b) its parent undertaking is established under the law of an EEA State.

Exemption is however conditional upon compliance with all the following conditions

(a) all members of the company must agree to the exemption in respect of the financial year in question;

(b) the parent undertaking must give a guarantee in respect of that year (see **8.27B**)

(c) the company must be included in the consolidated accounts drawn up for that year or to an earlier date in that year by the parent undertaking in accordance with the provisions of the Seventh Directive (83/349/EEC) or international accounting standards

(d) the parent undertaking must disclose in the notes to the consolidated accounts that the company is exempt from the requirements of CA 2006 relating to the audit of individual accounts by virtue of *CA 2006, s 479A* and

(e) the directors of the company must deliver to the Registrar of Companies on or before the date that they file the accounts for that year

    (i) a written notice of the agreement referred to in (a) (above)

    (ii) a statement of guarantee (see **8.27B** below)

    (iii) a copy of the consolidated accounts referred to in (c) (above) and a copy of the auditor's report on those accounts

    (iv) a copy of the consolidated account drawn up by the parent undertaking.

A company is not entitled to the subsidiary company exemption above if it was at any time within the financial year in question a quoted company (as defined in *CA 2006, s 385(2)*), an authorised insurance company, a banking company, an e-money issuer, a MiFID investment firm, a UCITS management company, or if it carries on insurance market activity or is a special register body as defined in *s 117(1)* of the *Trade Union and Labour Relations (Consolidation) Act 1992* or an employers' association as defined in *s 122* of that *Act* or *Article 4* of the *Industrial Relations (Northern Ireland) Order 1992*

[*CA 2006 s 479A, 479B; SI 2012 No 2301, Reg 7*]

8.27B Parent undertaking guarantee

A guarantee is only given by a parent undertaking when the subsidiary company delivers to the Registrar of Companies a statement by the parent undertaking that it guarantees the subsidiary company under CA 2006 s 479C. The statement must be authenticated by the parent and must specify

(a) the name of the parent undertaking

(b) if the parent is incorporated in the United Kingdom, its registered number (if any)

(c) if the parent is incorporated outside the United Kingdom and registered in the country in which it is incorporated, the identity of the register on which it is registered and the number with which it is registered

(d) the name and registered number of the subsidiary company in respect of which the guarantee is being given

(e) the date of the statement and

(f) the financial year to which the guarantee relates.

The guarantee given under *CA 2006, s 479C* has the effect that the parent guarantees all outstanding liabilities to which the subsidiary company is subject at the end of the financial year to which the guarantee relates until they are satisfied in full and the guarantee is enforceable against the parent by any person to whom the subsidiary is liable in respect of those liabilities.

[*CA 2006, s 479C; SI 2012 No 2301, Reg 7*]

8.28 Exemption from audit: dormant companies

Subject to the

- requirement for a statement on the balance sheet (see **8.24**),
- right of members to require an audit (see **8.24**), and
- companies excluded from dormant companies exemption (see below)

a company is exempt from the requirements relating to the audit of accounts in respect of a financial year if

(a) it has been 'dormant' since its formation, or

(b) it has been dormant since the end of the previous financial year and

   (i) as regards its individual accounts for the financial year in question, it is entitled to prepare accounts in accordance with the small companies regime or would be so entitled but for having been a public company or a member of an ineligible group (see **5.3 Accounts: Small Companies**); and

   (ii) is not required to prepare group accounts for that year.

[*CA 2006, s 480*].

See **Appendix 1 Definitions** for the meaning of 'dormant company'.

Excluded companies. A company is not entitled to the above exemption if it was at any time within the financial year in question a company that

- is an authorised insurance company, a banking company, an e-money issuer, a 'MiFID investment firm' or a UCITS management company; or
- carries on insurance market activity.

[*CA 2006, s 481*].

See **Appendix 1 Definitions** for the meaning of 'MiFID investment firm'.

8.29 Exemption from audit: other circumstances

(1) *Public sector audits*

Subject to the requirement for a statement on the balance sheet (see **8.24**), the requirements of *CA 2006, Pt 16* as to audit of accounts do not apply to a company for a financial year if it is non-profit-making and its accounts

- are subject to audit by
  - (i) the Comptroller and Auditor General by virtue of an order under *Government Resources and Accounts Act 2000, s 25(6)*; or
  - (ii) the Auditor General for Wales by virtue of *Government of Wales Act 1998, s 96* or an order under *Government of Wales Act 1998, s 144*;
- are accounts
  - (i) in relation to which *Public Finance and Accountability (Scotland) Act 2000, s 21* applies; or
  - (ii) that are subject to audit by the Auditor General for Scotland by virtue of an order under *CA 2006, s 483* (see below); or
- are subject to audit by the Comptroller and Auditor General for Northern Ireland by virtue of an order under *Audit and Accountability (Northern Ireland) Order 2003 (SI 2003 No 418), Art 5(3)*.

In the case of a company that is a parent company or a subsidiary undertaking, the above provisions apply only if every group undertaking is non-profit-making. [*CA 2006, s 482*].

(2) *Scottish public sector companies: audit by Auditor General for Scotland*

The Scottish Ministers may, by *Order*, provide for the accounts of a company having its registered office in Scotland to be audited by the Auditor General for Scotland. Such an *Order* may be made in relation to a company only if it appears to the Scottish Ministers that the company

- exercises in or as regards Scotland functions of a public nature none of which relate to reserved matters (within the meaning of the *Scotland Act 1998*); or
- is entirely or substantially funded from a body having accounts
  - (i) in relation to which *S* applies; or
  - (ii) which are subject to audit by the Auditor General for Scotland by virtue of an order under these provisions. [*CA 2006, s 483*].

(3) *Charitable companies*

A charitable company is one which is formed and registered under *CA 2006* and is established for exclusively charitable purposes.

England and Wales. Financial years beginning on or after 1 April 2008. From April 2008 the specific audit requirements for charitable companies were removed from *CA 1985*. A charitable company (from that date) only requires a *CA 2006* audit if it exceeds the audit thresholds set out in *CA 2006* (see **8.24**). A charitable company which is a small company (see **5.2**) is not required to have a *CA 2006* audit. Instead it is required to have its accounts audited only if (for accounts periods ending on or after 1 April 2009) gross income exceeds £500,000 or gross assets exceed £3.26 million and gross income exceeds £250,000. Charitable companies may also (unless their articles of association otherwise require an audit) opt for an independent examination instead of an audit where gross income does not exceed £500,000 and where gross income exceeds £250,000, gross assets do not exceed £3.26 million.

[*CA 2006, s 1175, Sch 9 Pt 1; SI 2008 No 674, Art 3; SI 2008 No 629; Charities Act 2011*].

8.30 AUDITOR'S REPORT

A company's auditor must make a report to the company's members on all annual accounts of the company of which copies are, during his tenure of office

- in the case of a private company, to be sent out to members under *CA 2006, s 423*, see **2.6 ACCOUNTS: GENERAL**; or
- in the case of a public company, to be laid before the company in general meeting under *CA 2006, s 437*, see **2.9 ACCOUNTS: GENERAL**.

Despite this obligation to report to the *members*, the auditor's obligation is satisfied by forwarding the signed report to the company secretary, leaving him or the directors to convene the meeting and send copies of the account and report to the members (*Re Allen, Craig & Co (London) Ltd* [1934] Ch 483, 103 LJ Ch 193).

The report must specifically deal with the following matters.

Annual accounts. The report must

(a) include an introduction identifying the annual accounts that are the subject of the audit and the financial reporting framework that has been applied in their preparation;

(b) include a description of the scope of the audit identifying the auditing standards in accordance with which the audit was conducted;

(c) state clearly whether, in the auditor's opinion, the annual accounts

  (i) give a 'true and fair view'

  - in the case of an individual balance sheet, of the state of affairs of the company as at the end of the financial year;
  - in the case of an individual profit and loss account, of the profit or loss of the company for the financial year;
  - in the case of group accounts, of the state of affairs as at the end of the financial year and of the profit or loss for the financial year of the undertakings included in the consolidation as a whole, so far as concerns the company;

- in the case of a company which qualifies as a micro- entity in relation to a financial year (see **5.3A**) ,
  - where the accounts comprise only micro-entity minimum accounting items ,the auditors must disregard any provision of an accounting standard which would require the accounts to contain information additional to those items
  - in relation to a micro-entity minimum accounting item contained in the accounts the auditors must disregard any provision of an accounting standard which would require the accounts to contain further information in relation to those items and
  - where the accounts contain an item of information additional to the micro-entity minimum accounting items, the auditors must have regard to any provision of an accounting standard which relates to that item.

(ii) have been properly prepared in accordance with the relevant financial reporting framework; and

(iii) have been prepared in accordance with the requirements of *CA 2006* (and, where applicable, *IAS Regulation, Art 4*).

(d) be either unqualified or 'qualified', and must include a reference to any matters to which the auditor wishes to draw attention by way of emphasis without qualifying the report.

'Qualified' in relation to an auditor's report (or statement contained in an auditor's report) means that the report or statement does not state the auditor's unqualified opinion that the accounts have been properly prepared in accordance with *CA 2006* or, in the case of an undertaking not required to prepare accounts in accordance with *CA 2006*, under any corresponding legislation under which it is required to prepare accounts.

For the meaning of 'micro-entity minimum accounting item' and 'micro-entity provisions' see **App 1**.

[*CA 2006, ss 495, 539; SI 2013 No 3008, Reg 8*].

Strategic report and Directors' report. The auditor must state in his report on the company's annual accounts whether, in his opinion, the information given in the strategic report or the directors' report for the financial year for which the accounts are prepared is consistent with those accounts. [*CA 2006, s 496; SI 2007 No 3495, Sch 4 para 12*; the *2013 Regulations, Schedule, para 21*].

Directors' remuneration report. In the case of a quoted company, the auditor, in his report on the company's annual accounts for the financial year, must

- report to the company's members on the *'auditable part'* of the directors' remuneration report (see **19.9** to **19.15 Directors' Remuneration Reports**); and
- state whether in his opinion that part of the directors' remuneration report has been properly prepared in accordance with *CA 2006*.

See **2.16 Accounts: General** for *'true and fair view'*.

[*CA 2006, s 497*].

Corporate governance statement. Where a company prepares a separate corporate governance statement (see **15.5(2) CORPORATE GOVERNANCE**) in respect of a financial year, the auditor must state in his report on the company's accounts for that year whether, in his opinion, the information given in the statement is in accordance with Disclosure and Transparency

- rule 7.2.5 (a description of the main features of the issuer's internal control and risk management systems in relation to the financial reporting process); and
- rule 7.2.6 (information about share capital where the issuer is subject to those requirements)

is consistent with those accounts.

Where a company is required to prepare a corporate governance statement and no such statement is included in the directors' report, the auditor when preparing his report on the company's accounts

- must ascertain whether a corporate governance statement has been prepared and
- if it appears to the auditor that no such statement has been prepared he must state that fact in his report.

[*CA 2006, ss 497A, 498A; SI 2009 No 1581, Reg 6* and *7*].

8.31 Special auditor's report where abbreviated accounts delivered to the Registrar of Companies

Where

- the directors of a company deliver abbreviated accounts to the Registrar of Companies prepared in accordance with *CA 2006, s 444* (small companies) or *CA 2006, s 445* (medium-sized companies), see **2.10 ACCOUNTS: GENERAL**, and
- the company is not exempt from audit (or the directors have not taken advantage of any such exemption)

the directors must also deliver to the Registrar of Companies a copy of a special report of the company's auditor stating that in his opinion

- the company is entitled to deliver abbreviated accounts in accordance with the *section* in question; and
- the abbreviated accounts to be delivered are properly prepared in accordance with regulations under that *section*.

In such a case, a copy of the auditor's report required under **8.30** need not be delivered to the Registrar of Companies but

- if that report was 'qualified' (see **8.30**), the special report must set out that report in full together with any further material necessary to understand the qualification; and
- if that report contained a statement that the company has failed to comply with **8.33**(*a*)(i) or (ii) or (*b*), the special report must set out that statement in full.

The provisions of **8.34** (signature of report) and **8.35** (offences in connection with report) also apply to a special report. [*CA 2006, s 449*].

8.32 Auditor's report following defective accounts or report

The annual accounts, directors' report or directors' remuneration report of a company may, in certain circumstances, be replaced or partially revised because the original was defective. See **2.12** ACCOUNTS: GENERAL. A special auditor's report is then required (unless the company is exempt from audit). [*SI 2008 No 373, Reg 18*] and in those circumstances the following provisions apply.

(1) *Auditor's Report on either revised accounts or revised strategic report or directors' report or* revised remuneration report

Who can prepare the auditor's report – a company's current auditor must make a report or (as the case may be) further report to the company's members on any revised accounts prepared. But if the auditor's report on the original annual accounts was not made by the company's current auditor, the directors of the company may resolve that the report is to be made by the person or persons who made that report, provided that that person or those persons agree to do so and would be qualified for appointment as auditor of the company.

What must be included in the report – the provisions in **8.33** also apply to this report and the report must state whether in the auditor's opinion:

- The revised accounts have been properly prepared in accordance with *CA 2006* (and, where applicable, *IAS Regulations, Art 4*) and in particular whether a true and fair view, seen as at the date the original annual accounts were approved, is given by the revised accounts with respect to the matters set out in **8.30(*c*)(i)**. For this purpose, where any provision of *CA 2006* as to matters to be included in the annual accounts or report have been amended after the date of the original annual accounts or report but before the date of revision, the relevant provisions are those in force at the date of the original accounts or report.
- The original annual accounts failed to comply with the requirements of *CA 2006* (and, where applicable, IAS Regulations, Art 4) in the respects identified by the directors
  - (i) in the case of a revision by replacement, in the statement the directors are required to make in the revised accounts as to how the original accounts failed to comply; or
  - (ii) in the case of a revision by supplementary note, in the supplementary note.

The auditor must also state whether the information contained in the strategic report or directors' report for the financial year for which the annual accounts are prepared (which is, if the report has been revised under these provisions, that revised report) is consistent with those accounts.

Signature – The provisions in **8.34** relating to signature of the auditor's report also apply to the auditor's report under these provisions (with any necessary modifications) which, as from the date that report is signed, becomes the auditor's report on the annual accounts of the company in place of the report on the original annual accounts.

[*SI 2008 No 373, Regs 7, 19(1); SI 2013 No 2224, Reg 8,9*].

(2) *Report where company ceases to be exempt from audit*

Where, as a result of the revisions to its accounts, a company is no longer entitled to exemption from audit, the company must cause an auditor's report on the revised accounts to be prepared. The auditor's report must be delivered to the Registrar of Companies within 28 days after the date of revision of the accounts. If the report is not delivered within the 28 day period then every person who immediately before the end of that period was a director of the company commits an offence. A person guilty of such an offence is liable (i) on summary conviction, to a fine not exceeding level 5 on the standard scale; and (ii) for continued contravention, to a daily default fine not exceeding one-tenth of level 5 on the standard scale. See **29.1 Offences and Penalties** for the standard scale. It is a defence for a person charged with such an offence to prove that he took all reasonable steps for securing that those requirements would be complied with before the end of that period. It is not a defence to prove that the documents in question were not in fact prepared as required. [*CA 2006, s 451*].

If the directors of the company fail to make good the default within 14 days after the service of a notice on them requiring compliance, the court may, on the application of any member or creditor of the company or of the Registrar of Companies, make an order directing the directors (or any of them) to make good the default within such time as may be specified in the order. The court's order may provide that all costs (in Scotland, expenses) of, and incidental to, the application are to be borne by the directors. [*CA 2006, s 452*].

[*SI 2008 No 373, Reg 8*].

(3) *Auditor's report on revised directors' report alone*

A company's current auditor must make a report or (as the case may be) further report to the company's members on any revised report prepared if the relevant annual accounts have not been revised at the same time. But where the auditor's report on the annual accounts for the financial year covered by the revised report was not made by the company's current auditor, the directors of the company may resolve that the required report should be made by the person or persons who made that report, provided that that person or those persons agree to do so and would be qualified for appointment as auditor of the company.

Where a revised strategic report or directors' report is prepared, the auditor's report must state whether in his opinion the information given in that revised report is consistent with the annual accounts for the relevant year and must specify the relevant year.

Where a revised directors' remuneration report is prepared, the auditor's report must state whether in his opinion any 'auditable part' (see **19.2 Directors' Remuneration Reports**) of that revised report has been properly prepared.

The provisions in **8.34** relating to signature of the auditor's report also apply to the auditor's report under these provisions (with any necessary modifications).

[*SI 2008 No 373, Reg 9; SI 2013 No 2224, Reg 9*].

8.33 Duties of auditor in connection with report

In relation to auditors' reports on accounts and reports for financial years beginning on or after 6 April 2008, an auditor of a company must have regard to the directors' duty under *CA 2006, s 393(1)* (ie that the directors must not approve annual accounts unless they are satisfied that they give a true and fair view).

8.33 Audit

An auditor of a company, in addition to the matters which he must deal with in his report under **8.30**, also has a duty to consider and include the following in his report where relevant.

(a) The auditor must carry out such investigations as will enable him to form an opinion as to

(i) whether adequate accounting records have been kept by the company and returns adequate for their audit have been received from branches not visited by him;

(ii) whether the company's individual accounts are in agreement with the accounting records and returns; and

(iii) in the case of a quoted company, whether the auditable part of the company's directors' remuneration report (see **19.9** to **19.15 Directors' Remuneration Reports**) is in agreement with the accounting records and returns.

If the auditor is of the opinion that (i), (ii) or (iii) above has not been complied with he must state that fact in his report.

(b) If the auditor fails to obtain all the information and explanations which, to the best of his knowledge and belief, are necessary for the purposes of his audit, he must state that fact in his report.

(c) If

(i) the requirements of regulations under *CA 2006, s 412* (disclosure of directors' benefits: remuneration, pensions and compensation for loss of office, see **3.42 Accounts: Large Companies** or **5.40 Accounts: Small Companies**) are not complied with in the annual accounts, or

(ii) in the case of a quoted company, the requirements of regulations under *CA 2006, s 421* as to information forming the auditable part of the directors' remuneration report are not complied with in that report (see **19.9** to **19.15 Directors' Remuneration Report**)

the auditor must include in his report, so far as he is reasonably able to do so, a statement giving the required particulars.

(d) If the directors of the company have

(i) prepared accounts in accordance with the small companies regime, or

(ii) have taken advantage of small companies exemption from the requirement to prepare a *strategic report* or in preparing the directors' report

and in the auditor's opinion they were not entitled so to do, the auditor must state that fact in his report.

[*CA 2006, s 498; SI 2008 No 393, Reg 6*; the *2013 Regulations, Schedule, para 22*].

Case law explaining auditor's standard of care

In *Re London and General Bank (No 2)* [1895] 2 Ch 673, CA, the court held that an auditor is not bound to do more than exercise reasonable care and skill in making enquiries and investigations. What is reasonable care in any particular case must depend upon the circumstances of that case. Where suspicion is aroused more care is necessary. An auditor is a watch-dog not a bloodhound (*Re Kingston Cotton Mill Co (No 2)* [1896] 2 Ch 279, CA).

However, the standard of skill and care may be more exacting since these earlier cases were decided and, where suspicion ought emphatically to be aroused, the auditor should take steps to investigate in depth and cannot make such excuses as shortage of time (*Re Thomas Gerrard & Son Ltd* [1968] Ch 455, [1967] 2 All ER 525). In *Lloyd Cheyham & Co Ltd v Littlejohn & Co* [1987] BCLC 303, [1986] PCC 389 the court adopted the test of whether the defendant had acted in accordance with a practice accepted as proper by a body of responsible and skilled opinion. Current accounting standards (see below) were relied upon by the court as setting the appropriate standards and must now be considered of paramount importance.

In applying the necessary standard of care, the auditor should be aware of the content of the company's articles. See *Leeds Estate, Building and Investment Co v Shepherd* (1887) 36 Ch D 787 where dividends were paid out of capital. As to whether auditor should rely on a bank certificate, etc for verification of ownership of securities, see *Re City Equitable Fire Insurance Co Ltd* [1925] Ch 407, 94 LJ Ch 445, CA.

Auditing standards. Auditing standards are mainly set by the International Auditing and Assurance Standards Board. These are then adopted by the Auditing Practices Board (APB) and known as International Standards of Auditing (ISAs). (Previously the APB issued its own Statements of Auditing Practice (SASs).) ISAs set out the basic principles which auditors are expected to follow.

The APB also issues Practice Notes and other explanatory material. These give guidance on the procedures by which ISAs may be applied and deal with current auditing techniques and particular auditing problems.

8.34 Signature of auditor's report

The auditor's report must state the name of the auditor and be signed and dated. Where the auditor is an individual, the report must be signed by him. Where the auditor is a firm, the report must be signed by the 'senior statutory auditor' in his own name, for and on behalf of the auditor.

'*Senior statutory auditor*' means the individual identified by the firm as senior statutory auditor in relation to the audit in accordance with standards issued by the European Commission (or, if there is no applicable standard so issued, any relevant guidance issued by the Secretary of State or a body appointed by order of the Secretary of State).The FRC is the body appointed for this purpose. The person identified as senior statutory auditor must be eligible for appointment as auditor of the company in question (see **8.8** and **8.9**).

The senior statutory auditor is not, by reason of being named or identified as senior statutory auditor or by reason of his having signed the auditor's report, subject to any civil liability to which he would not otherwise be subject.

[*CA 2006, ss 503, 504; SI 2012 No 1741, Reg 15*].

Statement of names in published copies of auditor's report. Every copy of the auditor's report that is published by or on behalf of the company must

- state the name of the auditor and (where the auditor is a firm) the name of the person who signed it as senior statutory auditor; or
- if that information may be omitted (see below), state that a resolution has been passed and notified to the Secretary of State in accordance with those provisions.

For these purposes, a company is regarded as publishing the report if it publishes, issues or circulates it or otherwise makes it available for public inspection in a manner calculated to invite members of the public generally, or any class of members of the public, to read it.

If a copy of the auditor's report is published without the required statement, an offence is committed by the company and every officer of the company who is in default. A person guilty of such an offence is liable on summary conviction to a fine not exceeding level 3 on the standard scale. See **29.1 Offences and Legal Proceedings** for the standard scale.

Circumstances in which names may be omitted. The auditor's name and, where the auditor is a firm, the name of the person who signed the report as senior statutory auditor, may be omitted from published copies of the report and the copy of the report delivered to the Registrar of Companies for filing if the following conditions are met.

- The company, considering on reasonable grounds that statement of the name would create or be likely to create a serious risk that the auditor or senior statutory auditor (or any other person) would be subject to violence or intimidation, has resolved that the name should not be stated.
- The company has given notice of the resolution to the Secretary of State, stating
  - (i) the name and registered number of the company;
  - (ii) the financial year of the company to which the report relates; and
  - (iii) the name of the auditor and (where the auditor is a firm) the name of the person who signed the report as senior statutory auditor.

[*CA 2006, ss 505, 506*].

8.35 Offences in connection with auditors' reports

The following offences apply in relation to auditors' reports on accounts:

(a) where the auditor is an individual, to that individual and any employee or agent of his who is eligible for appointment as auditor of the company; and

(b) where the auditor is a firm, to any director, member, employee or agent of the firm who is eligible for appointment as auditor of the company.

A person within (*a*) or (*b*) above commits an offence if he knowingly or recklessly causes an auditor's report on a company's annual accounts to

- include any matter that is misleading, false or deceptive in a material particular; or
- omit a statement required by **8.33**(*a*)(ii), (*b*) or (*d*).

A person guilty of such an offence is liable (i) on conviction on indictment, to a fine; and (ii) on summary conviction, to a fine not exceeding the statutory maximum. See **29.1 Offences and Legal Proceedings** for the statutory maximum.

[*CA 2006, s 507*].

Guidance for regulatory and prosecuting authorities. The Secretary of State (in Scotland, the Lord Advocate) may issue guidance about handling matters where the same behaviour by an auditor could give rise to prosecution under the above provisions and disciplinary proceedings by a certain regulatory body. [*CA 2006, ss 508, 509*].

8.36 AUDITOR'S RIGHT TO INFORMATION

(1) *General right to information*

An auditor of a company

- has a right of access at all times to the company's books, accounts and vouchers (in whatever form they are held); and
- can require such information or explanations as he thinks necessary for the performance of his duties as auditor from
  - (i) any officer or employee of the company;
  - (ii) any person holding or accountable for any of the company's books, accounts or vouchers;
  - (iii) any subsidiary undertaking of the company which is a body corporate incorporated in the UK;
  - (iv) any officer, employee or auditor of any such subsidiary undertaking or any person holding or accountable for any books, accounts or vouchers of any such subsidiary undertaking; and
  - (v) any person who fell within any of (i)–(iv) above at a time to which the information or explanations required by the auditor relates.

A company cannot rely on any of its regulations which restricts the rights of auditors to information to which they are entitled under these provisions (*Newton v Birmingham Small Arms Co Ltd* [1906] 2 Ch 378, 75 LJ Ch 627).

A statement made by a person in response to a requirement under the above provisions may not be used in evidence against him in any criminal proceedings except proceedings for an offence as below.

Offences. A person commits an offence who knowingly or recklessly makes a statement (oral or written) to an auditor of a company that

- conveys or purports to convey any information or explanations which the auditor requires, or is entitled to require; under the above provisions; and
- is misleading, false or deceptive in a material particular.

A person guilty of such an offence is liable (i) on conviction on indictment, to imprisonment for a term not exceeding two years or a fine (or both); and (ii) on summary conviction, to imprisonment for a term not exceeding 12 months (in Scotland or Northern Ireland, 6 months) or a fine up to the statutory maximum (or both). See **29.1 Offences and Legal Proceedings** for the statutory maximum.

A person who fails to comply with a requirement under the above provisions without delay commits an offence unless it was not reasonably practicable for him to provide the required information or explanations. A person guilty of such an offence is liable, on summary conviction, to a fine not exceeding level 3 on the standard scale. See **29.1 Offences and Legal Proceedings** for the standard scale.

[*CA 2006, ss 499(1)–(3), 501(1)–(3)(5)*].

(2) *Overseas subsidiaries*

Where a parent company has a subsidiary undertaking that is not a body corporate incorporated in the UK, the auditor of the parent company may require it to obtain such information or explanations as he may reasonably require for the purposes of his duties as auditor from

(a) the undertaking;

(b) any officer, employee or auditor of the undertaking;

(c) any person holding or accountable for any of the undertaking's books, accounts or vouchers; and

(d) any person who fell within (*b*) or (*c*) above at a time to which the information or explanations relates.

If so required, the parent company must take all such steps as are reasonably open to it to obtain the information or explanations from the person concerned.

A statement made by a person in response to a requirement under the above provisions may not be used in evidence against him in any criminal proceedings except proceedings for an offence as below.

Offences. If a parent company fails to comply with the above provisions, an offence is committed by the company and every officer of it who is in default. A person guilty of such an offence is liable, on summary conviction, to a fine not exceeding level 3 on the standard scale. See **29.1 Offences and Legal Proceedings** for the standard scale.

[*CA 2006, ss 500(1)–(4), 501(4)(5)*].

(3) *Professional privilege*

Nothing in the above provisions compels any person to disclose information in respect of which a claim to legal professional privilege (in Scotland, to confidentiality of communications) could be maintained in legal proceedings. [*CA 2006, ss 499(4), 500(5), 501(6)*].

8.37 AUDITOR'S RIGHTS IN RELATION TO RESOLUTIONS AND MEETINGS

A company's auditor is entitled to

- receive all notices of, and other communications relating to, any general meeting of the company which a member is entitled to receive;
- attend any general meeting of the company; and
- be heard at any general meeting which he attends on any part of the business which concerns him as auditor.

Where a written resolution has been proposed by a private company (see **42.5 Resolutions and Meetings**) the company's auditor is entitled to receive all such communications relating to the resolution which must be supplied to members.

Where the auditor is a firm, the right to attend or be heard at a meeting is exercisable by an individual authorised by the firm in writing to act as its representative at the meeting.

[*CA 2006, s 502*].

8.38 AUDITOR'S LIABILITY

In addition to the cases listed in **8.33**, liability of the auditors to the members has been considered in *London Oil Storage Co Ltd v Seear Hasluck & Co* (1904) 30 Acct LR 93 (verification of assets); *AE Green & Co v Central Advance and Discount Corpn Ltd* (1920) 63 Acct LR 1 (bad debts provision); and *Pendleburys Ltd v Ellis Green & Co* (1936) 80 Acct LR 39 (insufficient internal control in a private company where the directors were the sole shareholders).

In *Hedley Byrne & Co Ltd v Heller & Partners Ltd* [1964] AC 465, [1963] 2 All ER 575, HL, the House of Lords approved of the dissenting judgment of Denning LJ in *Candler v Crane, Christmas and Co* [1951] 2 KB 164, [1951] 1 All ER 426, CA, which included the comment that '. . . accountants owe a duty of care not only to their own clients, but also to those whom they know will rely on their accounts in the transactions for which the accounts are prepared'. On this basis, an auditor could be held liable for negligence to third parties (eg investors) where he knows, or ought to know, that his work is liable to be relied upon by such a person and that person suffers a financial loss as a result. Subsequent cases have, however, tended to restrict this liability. In *Caparo Industries plc v Dickman* [1990] 2 AC 605, [1990] BCLC 273, HL, the House of Lords considered the auditor's duty of care to shareholders and potential shareholders. It held that the purpose of the audit report was to enable shareholders to exercise their proprietary powers as shareholders by giving them reliable intelligence on the company's affairs, sufficient to allow them to scrutinise the management's conduct and to exercise their collective powers to control the management through general meetings. To meet the requirements for a duty of care to exist, the report must be used for the purpose for which it was intended and the precise purpose for which the accounts are required must be known to the wrongdoer. In the circumstances of a shareholder (or potential shareholder) simply dealing in the company's shares on the basis of the report, these requirements were not met.

Liability for false or misleading statements in directors' reports, etc. No person (including therefore an auditor) can be subject to any liability to a person other than the company resulting from reliance, by that person or another, on information in the directors' report, the directors' remuneration report or a summary financial statement so far as it is derived from either of those reports This does not affect liability for a civil penalty or a criminal offence. [*CA 2006. s 463(4)(6)*].

8.39 Provisions protecting auditor from liability

Except as permitted under **8.40** and **8.41** below, any provision (whether contained in the company's articles or in any contract with the company or otherwise)

- exempting an auditor of a company (to any extent) from any liability that would otherwise attach to him, or
- by which a company (directly or indirectly) provides an indemnity (to any extent) for an auditor of the company, or of an associated company, against any liability attaching to him

in connection with any negligence, default, breach of duty or breach of trust in relation to the company occurring in the course of the audit of accounts is void.

For these purposes, companies are associated if one is a subsidiary of the other or both are subsidiaries of the same body corporate.

[*CA 2006, s 532*].

Before 6 April 2008, any provision (whether contained in the company's articles or in any contract with the company or otherwise) exempting any person employed by a company as auditor from, or indemnifying him against, any liability was, subject to **8.40**, void. This applied to any liability which by virtue of any rule of law would otherwise attach to that person in respect of any negligence, default, breach of duty or breach of trust of which he might be guilty in relation to the company. [*CA 1985, s 310(1)(2)*].

8.40 Indemnity for costs of defending proceedings

The provisions in **8.39** do not prevent a company from indemnifying an auditor against any liability incurred by him

- in defending proceedings (whether civil or criminal) in which judgment is given in his favour or he is acquitted; or
- in connection with an application under *CA 2006, s 1157* or, before 1 October 2008, *CA 1985, s 727* (power of court to grant relief in case of honest and reasonable conduct, see **29.9 Offences and Legal Proceedings**) in which relief is granted to him by the court.

[*CA 2006, s 533*].

Before 6 April 2008, the provisions in **8.39** did not prevent a company from

- purchasing and maintaining for any such auditor insurance against any such liability; or
- from indemnifying any such auditor against any liability incurred by him
  - (i) in defending any proceedings (whether civil or criminal) in which judgment was given in his favour or he was acquitted; or
  - (ii) in connection with any application under *CA 1985, s 727* (general power to grant relief in case of honest and reasonable conduct) in which relief was granted to him by the court.

[*CA 1985, s 310; CA 1989, s 137; C(AICE)A 2004, s 19*].

8.41 **Liability limitation agreements**

The provisions in **8.39** do not affect the validity of a liability limitation agreement that

- complies with the terms in **8.42**; and
- is authorised by the members of the company as in **8.43**.

Such an agreement is not subject

- in England and Wales or Northern Ireland, to *Unfair Contract Terms Act 1977, s 2(2)* or *3(2)(a)*; or
- in Scotland, to *Unfair Contract Terms Act 1977, s 16(1)(b)* or *17(1)(a)*.

A '*liability limitation agreement*' is an agreement that purports to limit the amount of a liability owed to a company by its auditor in respect of any negligence, default, breach of duty or breach of trust, occurring in the course of the audit of accounts, of which the auditor may be guilty in relation to the company.

[*CA 2006, s 534*].

Disclosure of agreement by company. A company which has entered into a liability limitation agreement must make such disclosure in connection with the agreement as the Secretary of State may require by Regulations. [*CA 2006, s 538*].

8.42 *Terms of liability limitation agreement*

A liability limitation agreement must

- not apply in respect of acts or omissions occurring in the course of the audit of accounts for more than one financial year; and
- specify the financial year in relation to which it applies.

Subject to the above, it is immaterial how a liability limitation agreement is framed. In particular, the limit on the amount of the auditor's liability need not be a sum of money, or a formula, specified in the agreement.

[*CA 2006, s 535*].

8.43 *Authorisation of agreement by members of the company*

A liability limitation agreement must be authorised by the members of the company in one of the following ways for each financial year of the company.

Private companies. A liability limitation agreement auditor may be authorised—

(i) by the company passing an ordinary resolution, before it enters into the agreement, waiving the need for approval;

(ii) by the company passing an ordinary resolution, before it enters into the agreement, approving the agreement's 'principal terms'; or

(iii) by the company passing an ordinary resolution, after it enters into the agreement, approving the agreement;

Public companies. A liability limitation agreement may be authorised—

(i) by the company passing an ordinary resolution in general meeting, before it enters into the agreement, approving the agreement's principal terms; or

(ii) by the company passing an ordinary resolution in general meeting, after it enters into the agreement, approving the agreement.

The '*principal terms*' of an agreement are terms specifying, or relevant to the determination of

- the kind (or kinds) of acts or omissions covered;
- the financial year to which the agreement relates; or
- the limit to which the auditor's liability is subject.

Withdrawal of authorisation. Authorisation may be withdrawn by the company passing an ordinary resolution to that effect

(a) at any time before the company enters into the agreement; or

(b) if the company has already entered into the agreement, before the beginning of the financial year to which the agreement relates. This applies notwithstanding anything in the agreement.

[*CA 2006, s 536*].

8.44 *Effect of liability limitation agreement*

A liability limitation agreement is not effective to limit the auditor's liability to less than such amount as is fair and reasonable in all the circumstances of the case having regard (in particular) to

- the auditor's responsibilities under *CA 2006, Pt 16*;
- the nature and purpose of the auditor's contractual obligations to the company; and
- the professional standards expected of him.

A liability limitation agreement that purports to limit the auditor's liability to less than such an amount has effect as if it limited his liability to that amount.

In determining what is fair and reasonable in all the circumstances of the case, no account is to be taken of

- matters arising after the loss or damage in question has been incurred; or
- matters (whenever arising) affecting the possibility of recovering compensation from other persons liable in respect of the same loss or damage.

[*CA 2006, s 537*].

8.45 QUOTED COMPANIES: MEMBERS' POWER TO REQUIRE WEBSITE PUBLICATION OF AUDIT CONCERNS

Requests from members. The members of a 'quoted company' may require the company to publish on a website a statement setting out any matter relating to

- the audit of the company's accounts (including the auditor's report and the conduct of the audit) that are to be laid before the next accounts meeting, or
- any circumstances connected with an auditor of the company appointed for such a year ceasing to hold office since the previous accounts meeting,

that the members propose to raise at the next accounts meeting of the company. A request from a member may be sent to the company in hard copy or electronic form and must identify the statement to which it relates. It must be authenticated by the person or persons making it and must be received by the company at least one week before the meeting to which it relates.

See **Appendix 1 Definitions** for the meaning of '*quoted company*' which applies for these purposes and definition of '*accounts meeting*'.

[*CA 2006, ss 527(1)(4), 531*].

Duties of company. Unless the court directs otherwise (see below), the company must publish the statement, on a website that is maintained by or on behalf of the company and which identifies the company in question, once it has received requests to that effect from

- members representing at least 5% of the total voting rights of all the members who have a 'relevant right to vote' (excluding any voting rights attached to any shares in the company held as treasury shares); or
- at least 100 members who have a relevant right to vote and hold shares in the company on which there has been paid up an average sum, per member, of at least £100.

See **26 Members** for different criteria where members have exercised their rights in relation to shares held on behalf of others.

A '*relevant right to vote*' means a right to vote at the accounts meeting.

Access to the information on the website, and the ability to obtain a hard copy of the information from the website, must not be conditional on the payment of a fee or otherwise restricted.

The statement must be made available within three working days of the company being required to publish it on a website and must be kept available until after the meeting to which it relates. A failure to make the information available on a website throughout this period is disregarded if

- the information is made available on the website for part of that period; and
- the failure is wholly attributable to circumstances that it would not be reasonable to have expected the company to prevent or avoid.

Application to court. A quoted company is not required to place a statement on a website if, on an application by the company or another person who claims to be aggrieved, the court is satisfied that the rights conferred by these provisions are being abused. The court may order the members requesting website publication to pay the whole or part of the company's costs (in Scotland, expenses) on such an application, even if they are not parties to the application.

[*CA 2006, ss 527(2), (3), (5), (6), 528*].

Supplementary duties of company. The quoted company must in the notice it gives of the accounts meeting draw attention to

- the possibility of a statement being placed on a website in pursuance of members' requests;
- the fact that the company must pay its expenses in complying with these requirements;
- the fact that it must (and has) forwarded the statement to the company's auditor not later than the time when it makes the statement available on the website; and
- the fact that the business which may be dealt with at the accounts meeting includes any statement that the company has been required to publish on a website.

[*CA 2006, s 529*].

Offences. In the event of the company defaulting in complying with its above duties, an offence is committed by every officer of the company who is in default. A person guilty of such an offence is liable (i) on conviction on indictment, to a fine; and (ii) on summary conviction, to a fine not exceeding the statutory maximum. See **29.1 Offences and Legal Proceedings** for the statutory maximum.

[*CA 2006, s 530*].

9 Class Rights

9.1 **Variation of class rights: companies with a share capital**
9.2 Right to object to variation
9.3 Registration of particulars
9.4 **Variation of class rights: companies without shares**
9.5 Right to object to variation
9.6 Registration of particulars
9.7 **Powers of the court**

Background. The provisions in this chapter apply, unless otherwise stated, with effect from 1 October 2009. They retain the earlier provisions in *CA 1985* (with some simplification) but notably extend them to cover companies without a share capital.

9.1 VARIATION OF CLASS RIGHTS: COMPANIES WITH A SHARE CAPITAL

Where a company's share capital is divided into different classes (eg ordinary shares and preference shares), there are special provisions concerned with the 'variation' of the rights attached to any class of shares in a company. Class rights might cover such matters as voting rights, rights to dividends and right to a return of capital on a winding up. Where all the shares in a company fall within one class, there are no class rights, only shareholder rights.

Classes of shares. For the purposes of the *Companies Acts*, shares are of one class if the rights attached to them are in all respects uniform. The rights attached to shares are not regarded as different from those attached to other shares by reason only that they do not carry the same rights to dividends in the twelve months immediately following their allotment. [*CA 2006, s 629*]. Apart from this, what amounts to a 'class' is not defined in the legislation.

Meaning of variation. For these purposes, and (except where the context requires otherwise) in any provision in a company's articles for the variation of rights attached to a class of shares, references to the '*variation*' of those rights includes references to their abrogation. [*CA 2006, s 630(6)*]. Otherwise, the meaning of 'variation' has been strictly construed by the courts, so that where the value of the rights of a class of shareholders has effectively been reduced, but those rights themselves have not been affected as such, this has been held not to be a variation (see *Greenhalgh v Arderne Cinemas Ltd* [1946] 1 All ER 512, 90 Sol Jo 248, CA). See also *White v Bristol Aeroplane Co Ltd* [1953] Ch 65, [1953] 1 All ER 40, CA; *Re John Smith's Tadcaster Brewery Co Ltd, John Smith's Tadcaster Brewery Co Ltd v Gresham Life Assurance Society Ltd* [1953] Ch 308, [1953] 1 All ER 518, CA; *Re Saltdean Estate Co Ltd* [1968] 3 All ER 829, [1968] 1 WLR 1844; and *House of Fraser plc v ACGE Investments Ltd* [1987] AC 387, [1987] BCLC 478, HL.

For a right to be a class right, it must be given to members of a class in their capacity as members, although such a right need not be attached to particular shares. See *Cumbrian Newspapers Group Ltd v Cumberland and Westmorland Herald Newspaper and Printing Co Ltd* [1987] Ch 1, [1986] BCLC 286.

Any amendment of a provision contained in a company's articles for the variation of the rights attached to a class of shares, or the insertion of any such provision into the articles, is itself to be treated as a variation of those rights. [*CA 2006, s 630(5)*].

9.1 Class Rights

Conditions for variation. Subject to **9.7**, the rights attached to a class of a company's shares may only be varied

- in accordance with provisions in the company's articles for variation of the rights; or
- where the company's articles contain no such provision, if the holders of shares of that class consent to the variation.

The consent must take the form of either

- consent in writing from the holders of at least three-quarters in nominal value of the issued shares of that class (excluding any shares held as treasury shares); or
- a special resolution passed at a separate general meeting of the holders of that class sanctioning the variation.

This is without prejudice to any other restrictions on the variation of the rights. Thus, if the company has adopted a more onerous regime in its articles for the variation of class rights (eg a higher percentage) it must comply with the more onerous regime. Also, if and to the extent that the company has protected class rights by making provisions for entrenchment of those rights under *CA 2006, s 22* (see **14.7 CONSTITUTION – MEMORANDUM AND ARTICLES**) that protection cannot be circumvented by changing the class rights under these provisions.

[*CA 2006, s 630(2)–(4)*].

9.2 Right to object to variation

Where the rights attached to any class of shares in a company are varied under **9.1**, the holders of not less than 15% of the issued shares of the class in question (being persons who did not consent to, or vote in favour of, the resolution for variation) may apply to the court to have the variation cancelled. The application must be made within 21 days after the date on which the consent to the variation was given or the resolution for the variation was passed (as the case may be). Such application may be made, on behalf of the shareholders entitled to make it, by such one or more of their number as they may appoint in writing for the purpose.

If such an application is made, the variation has no effect unless and until it is confirmed by the court.

In determining whether any application is made by the holders of 15% of the issued shares of the class in question, any of the company's share capital held as treasury shares is disregarded.

[*CA 2006, s 633(1)–(4)*].

The court may disallow the variation if satisfied that, having regard to all the circumstances of the case, the variation would unfairly prejudice the shareholders of the class represented by the applicant. If the court is not so satisfied, it must confirm the variation. The decision of the court is final. [*CA 2006, s 633(5)*].

For an example of what could constitute unfair prejudice in this context, see *Re Holders Investment Trust Ltd* [1971] 2 All ER 289, [1971] 1 WLR 583, a case on reduction of capital.

The company must, within 15 days after the court makes an order by the court, forward a copy of the order to the Registrar of Companies. In default, an offence is committed by the company and every officer of the company who is in default. A person guilty of such an offence is liable, on summary conviction, to a fine not exceeding level 3 on the standard scale and, for continued contravention, a daily default fine not exceeding one-tenth of level 3 on the standard scale. [*CA 2006, s 635*]. See **29.1 Offences and Legal Proceedings** for the standard scale.

9.3 Registration of particulars

Under certain circumstances, a company is required to provide the Registrar of Companies with particulars of the rights attaching to its shares.

(a) **Variation of rights**. Where the rights attached to any shares of a company are varied, the company must, within one month from the date on which the variation is made, deliver to the Registrar of Companies a notice giving particulars of the variation. [*CA 2006, s 637(1)*].

(b) **Name or other designation of class of shares**. Where a company assigns a name or other designation, or a new name or other designation, to any class or description of its shares, it must, within one month from doing so deliver to the Registrar of Companies a notice giving particulars of the name or designation so assigned. [*CA 2006, s 636(1)*].

If default is made in complying with either (*a*) or (*b*) above, an offence is committed by the company and every officer of the company who is in default. A person guilty of such an offence is liable, on summary conviction, to a fine not exceeding level 3 on the standard scale and, for continued contravention, a daily default fine not exceeding one-tenth of level 3 on the standard scale. [*CA 2006, ss 636(2)(3), 637(2)(3)*]. See **29.1 Offences and Legal Proceedings** for the standard scale.

Allotment of shares. Under *CA 2006, s 555*,

- a company limited by shares, or
- a company limited by guarantee and having a share capital

must, within one month of allotting shares, deliver to the Registrar of Companies a statement of capital which, amongst other things, gives details, for each class of shares, of prescribed particulars of the rights attached to the share. See **47.12 Shares**.

Similarly, under *CA 2006, s 556*, if an unlimited company allots shares with rights which are not in all respects uniform with shares previously allotted, it must, within one month of the allotting the shares, deliver to the Registrar of Companies a return of allotments containing prescribed particulars of those rights. See **47.12 Shares**.

9.4 VARIATION OF CLASS RIGHTS: COMPANIES WITHOUT SHARES

Where a company does not have a share capital but has different classes of members, there are special provisions concerned with the variation of the rights attached to any class of members in the company. These might apply, for example, where a company limited by guarantee has different classes of members with different voting rights. Where all the members in a company fall within one class, there are no class rights, only members' rights.

Meaning of variation. For these purposes, and (except where the context requires otherwise) in any provision in a company's articles for the variation of the rights of a class of members, references to the variation of those rights includes reference to their abrogation.

9.4 Class Rights

Any alteration of a provision contained in a company's articles for the variation of the rights of a class of members, or the insertion of any such provision into the articles, is itself to be treated as a variation of those rights.

[*CA 2006, s 631(5)(6)*].

Conditions for variation. Subject to **9.7**, rights of a class of members may only be varied

- in accordance with provisions in the company's articles for variation of the rights; or
- where the company's articles contain no such provision, if the members of that class consent to the variation.

The consent must take the form of either

- consent in writing from at least three-quarters of the members of the class; or
- a special resolution passed at a separate general meeting of the members of that class sanctioning the variation.

This is without prejudice to any other restrictions on the variation of the rights. Thus, if the company has adopted a more onerous regime in its articles for the variation of class rights (eg a higher percentage) it must comply with the more onerous regime. Also, if and to the extent that the company has protected class rights by making provisions for entrenchment of those rights under *CA 2006, s 22* (see **14.5 CONSTITUTION – MEMORANDUM AND ARTICLES**) that protection cannot be circumvented by changing the class rights under these provisions.

[*CA 2006, s 631(2)–(4)*].

9.5 Right to object to variation

Where the rights attaching to any class of members of a company are varied under **9.4**, members amounting to not less than 15% of the members of the class in question (being persons who did not consent to, or vote in favour of, the resolution for variation) may apply to the court to have the variation cancelled. The application must be made within 21 days after the date on which the consent to the variation was given or the resolution for the variation was passed (as the case may be). The application may be made, on behalf of the members entitled to make it, by such one or more of their number as they may appoint in writing for the purpose.

If an application is made, the variation has no effect unless and until it is confirmed by the court.

[*CA 2006, s 634(1)–(4)*].

The court may disallow the variation if satisfied that, having regard to all the circumstances of the case, the variation would unfairly prejudice the members of the class represented by the applicant. If the court is not so satisfied, it must confirm the variation. The decision of the court is final. [*CA 2006, s 634(5)*].

The company must, within 15 days after the court makes an order, forward a copy of the order to the Registrar of Companies. In default, an offence is committed by the company and every officer of the company who is in default. A person guilty of an offence under these provisions is liable, on summary conviction, to a fine not exceeding level 3 on the standard scale and, for continued contravention, a daily default fine not exceeding one-tenth of level 3 on the standard scale. [*CA 2006, s 635*]. See **29.1 OFFENCES AND LEGAL PROCEEDINGS** for the standard scale.

9.6 Registration of particulars

Under certain circumstances, a company is required to provide the Registrar of Companies with particulars of the rights attaching to any class of members.

The following apply after 1 October 2009.

(a) **Creation of a new class of members.** If, a company creates a new class of members, the company must, within one month from the date on which the new class is created, deliver to the Registrar of Companies a notice containing particulars of the rights attached to that class. [*CA 2006, s 638(1)*].

(b) **Variation of class rights.** If the rights of any class of members are varied, the company must, within one month from the date on which the variation is made, deliver to the Registrar of Companies a notice (Form SH 10) containing particulars of the variation. [*CA 2006, s 640(1)*].

(c) **Name or other designation of class of members.** Where a company assigns a name or other designation, or a new name or other designation, to any class of its members, it must, within one month of doing so, deliver to the Registrar of Companies a notice (Form SH08) giving particulars of the name or designation so assigned. [*CA 2006, s 639(1)*].

If default is made in complying with (*a*)–(*c*) above, an offence is committed by the company and every officer of the company who is in default. A person guilty of such an offence is liable, on summary conviction, to a fine not exceeding level 3 on the standard scale and, for continued contravention, a daily default fine not exceeding one-tenth of level 3 on the standard scale. [*CA 2006, ss 638(2)(3), 639(2)(3), 640(2)(3)(6)*]. See **29.1 Offences and Legal Proceedings** for the standard scale.

9.7 POWERS OF THE COURT

Nothing in **9.1** or **9.4** (variation of class rights) affects the power of the court under the following provisions.

- *CA 2006, s 98* (application to cancel resolution for public company to be re-registered as private). See **41.9 Re-Registration**.
- *CA 2006, Pt 26* (arrangements and reconstructions). See **35 Reconstructions and Mergers**.
- *CA 2006, Pt 30* (protection of members against unfair prejudice). See **26.5 Members**.

[*CA 2006, s 632*].

10 Community Interest Companies

10.1 **Introduction**
10.2 **Eligible companies**
10.3 **Becoming a community interest company**
10.4 Requirements for new companies
10.5 Requirements for existing companies to become CICs
10.6 Charities
10.7 **Restrictions on the transfer of assets (distributions and interest)**
10.8 Declaration of dividends
10.9 Dividend cap
10.10 The Interest cap
10.11 Redemption and purchase of shares
10.12 Reduction of share capital
10.13 **Articles of association**
10.14 Alteration of objects
10.15 **Names**
10.16 **Report on activities**
10.17 **The Regulator and his powers**
10.18 Conditions for exercising powers
10.19 Investigation of the affairs of a CIC
10.20 Audit of annual accounts
10.21 Appointment and removal of directors
10.22 Appointment of a manager
10.23 Powers in relation to property
10.24 Transfers of shares
10.25 Dissolution and striking off
10.26 **Appeals**
10.27 **Change of status – re-registration**
10.28 **Ceasing to be a CIC**
10.29 Distribution of assets on a winding up
10.30 Becoming a charity
10.31 Becoming an industrial and provident society
10.32 **Disclosure of information**
10.33 **Offences**

10.1 INTRODUCTION

With effect from 1 July 2005 (6 April 2007 for Northern Ireland), a community interest company ('CIC') was created by *Companies (Audit, Investigations and Community Enterprise) Act 2004*. [*C(AICE)A 2004, s 26(1)*]. CICs can be used by non-profit-distributing enterprises providing benefit to a community in areas such as childcare, social housing, leisure and community transport. The special characteristics of the CIC make it a particularly suitable vehicle for social enterprises that wish to work for community benefit within the relative freedom of the non-charitable company form, but with a clear assurance of non-profit-distribution status.

Companies that are formed as, or become, CICs are formed under *CA 2006* and continue to be subject to the general framework of company law. In particular, CICs and directors of CICs have to comply with their obligations and duties under the *CA 2006* and the common law. CICs must register as companies with the Registrar of Companies in the usual way, and are subject to the usual regulatory constraints and powers associated with company status (including the oversight of the BIS Companies Investigation Branch).

The distinguishing features of a CIC are as follows.

- In order to become a CIC, a company must satisfy a community interest test, confirming that it will pursue purposes beneficial to the community and will not serve an unduly restricted group of beneficiaries. Certain companies may be excluded from CIC status. See **10.2**.
- Even if a CIC is established for charitable purposes, it is not treated as being established for such purposes, and therefore is not a charity. [*C(AICE)A 2004, s 26(3); SI 2006 No 242*]. This means that CICs are not subject to the benefits

or obligations of charitable status; nor are they subject to regulation by the Charity Commission or the charitable jurisdiction of the High Court. CICs, and outright bequests to them, are not eligible for any tax reliefs or exemptions which are only available to charities or for charitable giving. However, a donation to a charitable trust of which a CIC is trustee will be eligible for relief. The charitable status of the trust is unaffected by the status of the trustee.

Charities (and all other organisations except political parties) are able to establish CICs as subsidiaries.

- Every CIC is required to produce an annual community interest company report containing key information relevant to CIC status. The report must be placed on the public register of companies. See **10.16**.
- CICs have an asset lock, ie they are ordinarily prohibited from distributing any profits they make to their members. See **10.7**. However, CICs limited by shares can issue dividend-paying 'investor shares' although the dividend payable on such shares is subject to a cap. See **10.9**.
- When a CIC is wound up, its surplus residual assets are not distributed to its members but pass to another suitable organisation that has restrictions on the distribution of its profits (eg another CIC or a charity). See **10.30**.
- A Regulator (see **10.17**) must approve applications for CIC status, receive copies of the community interest company reports and police the requirements of CIC status, including compliance with the asset lock. He has powers to investigate abuses of CIC status and to take action where necessary (eg to remove directors, freeze assets or apply to the courts for a CIC to be wound up). He also sets the cap on CIC dividends.

10.2 ELIGIBLE COMPANIES

Community interest test. A '*community interest test*' is used to determine the eligibility of a company to be formed as a CIC (see **10.4**) or to become a CIC if already incorporated (see **10.5**). The Regulator can also exercise certain supervisory powers if a CIC ceases to satisfy the community interest test (see **10.18**).

A company satisfies the community interest test if

- it is not an excluded company; and
- a reasonable person might consider that its activities are being carried on for the benefit of the 'community'.

  '*Community*' includes a 'section of the community' (whether in the UK or anywhere else). For the purposes of the CIC test, any group of individuals may constitute a '*section of the community*' if

  (i) they share a common characteristic which distinguishes them from other members of the community; and

  (ii) a reasonable person might consider that they constitute a section of the community.

[*C(AICE)A 2004, s 35; SI 2005 No 1788, Reg 5*].

Excluded companies. The following are excluded companies.

- A company which is (or when formed would be) a 'political party' or a 'political campaigning organisation'.

- A company which is (or when formed would be) a subsidiary of a political party or of a political campaigning organisation.

A '*political party*' includes any person standing, or proposing to stand, as a candidate at any 'election', and any person holding public office following his election to that office. '*Election*' means any election to public office held in the UK or elsewhere.

A '*political campaigning organisation*' means any person carrying on, or proposing to carry on, activities

- to promote or oppose
  - (i) changes in any law applicable in the UK or elsewhere, or
  - (ii) any policy of a 'governmental authority' or 'public authority', or
- which could reasonably be regarded as intended
  - (i) to affect public support for a political party, or
  - (ii) to influence voters in relation to any election or 'referendum'

unless, in either case, such activities are incidental to other activities carried on by that person.

'*Governmental authority*' includes

- any national, regional or local government in the UK or elsewhere,
- the European Community,
- any inter-governmental organisation, and
- any organisation which is able to make rules or adopt decisions which are legally binding on any governmental authority falling within either of the above three categories

or any of their organs, institutions or agencies.

'*Public authority*' includes a court or tribunal and any person certain of whose functions are functions of a public nature whether in the UK or elsewhere.

'*Referendum*' includes any national or regional referendum or other poll held in pursuance of any provision made by or under the law of any state on one or more questions or propositions specified in or in accordance with any such provision.

[*SI 2005 No 1788, Regs 2, 6*].

Activities not treated as for the benefit of the community. For the purposes of the community interest test, subject to below, the following activities are to be treated as *not* being activities which a reasonable person might consider are activities carried on for the benefit of the community.

(a) The promotion of, or the opposition to, changes in

  (i) any law applicable in the UK or elsewhere; or

  (ii) the policy adopted by any 'governmental authority' or 'public authority' (see above) in relation to any matter.

(b) The promotion of, or the opposition (including the promotion of changes) to, the policy which any governmental authority or public authority proposes to adopt in relation to any matter.

(c) Activities which can reasonably be regarded as intended or likely to

(i) provide or affect support (whether financial or otherwise) for a 'political party' or 'political campaigning organisation' (see above); or

(ii) influence voters in relation to any 'election' or 'referendum' (see above).

(d) Activities to the extent that a reasonable person might consider that they benefit only the members of a particular body or the 'employees' of a particular 'employer'.

But activities within (*a*) to (*c*) above *are* to be treated as being activities which a reasonable person might consider are activities carried on for the benefit of the community if

- they can reasonably be regarded as incidental to other activities, which a reasonable person might consider are being carried on for the benefit the community; and
- those other activities cannot reasonably be regarded as incidental to activities within (*a*) to (*c*) above.

'*Employee*' means a person who has entered into or works under (or, where the employment has ceased, worked under)

- a contract of service or apprenticeship; or
- a contract for services under which it is agreed that a specified individual is to perform services

whether express or implied, and (if it is express) whether oral or in writing.

'*Employer*' means the person by whom an employee is (or, where the employment has ceased, was) employed.

[*SI 2005 No 1788, Regs 1, 3, 4*].

10.3 BECOMING A COMMUNITY INTEREST COMPANY

A new organisation applying to be incorporated as a CIC can be incorporated as a public or private company and either

- a company limited by shares; or
- a company limited by guarantee and not having a share capital.

An existing registered company can also apply to be converted into a CIC if it is currently

- limited by shares;
- limited by guarantee and not having a share capital; or
- limited by guarantee having a share capital.

[*C(AICE)A 2004, s 26(2); CA 2006, s 6*].

10.4 Requirements for new companies

Since CICs are companies under the *Companies Acts*, the normal company formation provisions apply, together with additional provisions specific to CICs.

If a company is to be formed as a CIC, the documents delivered to the Registrar of Companies under *CA 2006, s 9* (see **12 Company Formation and Types of Company**) must be accompanied by the 'prescribed formation documents'. [*C(AICE)A 2004, s 36(1), (2)*].). Note that the articles of a CIC must comply with the requirements of *CA 2006, s 18* and *C(AICE)A 2004* and the regulations made under that *Act* (See **10.13**). A CIC cannot rely on the default articles under *CA 2006, s 20*. Model constitutional documents are available on the Regulator's website at www.cicregulator.gov.uk on the guidance page. A filing fee of £35 is payable. See **Appendix 3 Fees**.

The '*prescribed formation documents*' are

(a) a community interest statement (Form CIC36) (signed by each person who is to be a first director of the company) in a form approved by the Regulator and which

  (i) contains a declaration that the company will carry on its activities for the benefit of the community or a section of the community; and

  (ii) indicates how it is proposed that the company's activities will benefit the community (or a section of the community); and

(b) a declaration made by each person who is to be a first director of the company that the company, when formed, will not be an excluded company (see **10.2**).

On receiving the documents, the Registrar of Companies must (instead of registering them) forward a copy of each of the documents to the Regulator (see **10.17**) and retain the documents pending the Regulator's decision. Same day registration service is not available for a CIC.

The Regulator must decide whether the company is eligible to be formed as a CIC, ie whether

- the articles comply with the requirements under **10.13**;
- the company's name complies with the provisions in **10.15**; and
- having regard to the documents delivered and any other relevant considerations, the company will satisfy the community interest test and is not an excluded company (see **10.2**).

The Regulator must give notice of the decision to the Registrar of Companies (but the Registrar is not required to record it).

If the Regulator decides that the company is eligible to be formed as a CIC, the Registrar of Companies must proceed with the registration of the company and issue a certificate of incorporation. If the company is entered on the register, the Registrar must retain and record the prescribed formation documents. The certificate of incorporation must state that the company is a CIC and is conclusive evidence that the company is a CIC.

If the Regulator decides that the company is not eligible to be formed as a CIC, any subscriber to the memorandum may appeal against the decision (see **10.27**).

[*C(AICE)A 2004, ss 36, 36A, 36B; SI 2005 No 1788, Regs 2, 11*].

10.5 Requirements for existing companies to become CICs

If an existing company is to become a CIC, the following conditions must be satisfied.

- The company must by special resolution

(i) alter its articles to state that it is to be a CIC;

(ii) make such alterations of its articles by special resolution as it considers necessary to comply with requirements imposed under **10.13** or otherwise appropriate in connection with becoming a CIC; and

(iii) change its name by special resolution to comply with **10.15**.

- An application to become a CIC must be delivered to the Registrar of Companies, together with certain other documents (see below).

[*C(AICE)A 2004, s 37(1)(2)*].

Application to court to cancel special resolutions. Where special resolutions have been passed with a view to the company becoming a CIC, an application to the court for the cancellation of the resolutions may be made

- by the holders of not less in the aggregate than 15% in nominal value of the company's issued share capital or any class of the company's issued share capital (disregarding any shares held by the company as treasury shares),
- if the company is not limited by shares, by not less than 15% of its members, or
- by the holders of not less than 15% of the company's debentures entitling the holders to object to an alteration of its objects

but not by a person who has consented to or voted in favour of the resolutions.

The application must be made within 28 days after the date on which the resolutions are passed or made (or, if the resolutions are passed or made on different days, the date on which the last of them is passed or made). It may be made on behalf of the persons entitled to make it by such one or more of their number as they may appoint for the purpose.

On making such an application, the applicants (or the person making the application on their behalf) must immediately give notice to the Registrar of Companies. The company must also immediately give notice to the Registrar of Companies on being served with notice of such an application.

The court must make an order (on such terms as it thinks fit) either cancelling or confirming the resolutions. The order may provide (where relevant) for the purchase by the company of the shares of any of its members and for the reduction accordingly of the company's capital (making such alteration in the company's articles as may be required in consequence).

Within 15 days of the making of the court's order on the application, or such longer period as the court may at any time direct, the company must deliver to the Registrar of Companies a copy of the order.

If a company fails to comply with the above requirement to notify the Registrar of Companies of service of an application or to deliver to him a copy of the court order, an offence is committed by the company and every officer of the company who is in default. A person guilty of such an offence is liable on summary conviction to a fine not exceeding level 3 on the standard scale and, for continued contravention, a daily default fine not exceeding one-tenth of level 3 on the standard scale. See **29.1 Offences and Legal Proceedings** for the standard scale.

[*C(AICE)A 2004, ss 37A, 37B*].

Application and accompanying documents. An application to the Registrar of Companies to become a CIC must be accompanied by

- a copy of the special resolutions;
- Form NMO1-notice of change of name by CIC
- resolution fee of £25
- a printed copy of the company's articles as altered by the special resolutions; and
- Form CIC37, the community interest statement. The form contains declarations that the company will provide benefit to the community by describing its activities, who they will help and how. Form CIC 37 also contains the following
  - (a) a declaration that the company is not an excluded company (see **10.2**); and
  - (b) either
    - (i) a declaration that the company is not a charity or
    - (ii) in the case of a company that is an English charity, a declaration that the Charity Commission has consented to the change of name of the company. The company will cease to be a charity on becoming a CIC; or
    - (iii) in the case of a company that is a Scottish charity, a declaration that the Scottish Charity Regulator and, where applicable, the Charity Commission, has given the company the written consent required by *C(AICE)A 2004, s 40* (see **10.6**).

The statement under (*a*) above must be signed, and the declarations under (*b*) and (*c*) above must be made, by each person who is a director of the company and each must be in a form approved by the Regulator.

On receiving an application to become a CIC together with the other documents required to accompany it, the Registrar of Companies must (instead of recording the documents and entering a new name on the register) forward a copy of each of the documents to the Regulator and retain the documents pending the Regulator's decision.

A company is treated as complying with the requirements of *CA 2006, s 30* (copies of resolutions to be forwarded to the Registrar of Companies, see **14.8 Constitution – Memorandum and Articles**) by forwarding copies of the resolutions together with the application in accordance with the above provisions. Copies of the resolutions must not be so forwarded before the 'relevant date' and *CA 2006, s 30(1)* has effect in relation to the resolutions as if it referred to 15 days after the relevant date. The '*relevant date*' is

- if an application is made for cancellation of the special resolutions (see above)
  - (i) the date on which the court determines the application (or if there is more than one application, the date on which the last to be determined by the court is determined); or
  - (ii) such later date as the court may order; or
- if there is no such application
  - (i) if having regard to the number of members who consented to or voted in favour of the resolutions, no such application may be made, the date on which the resolutions were passed or made (or, if the resolutions were passed or made on different days, the date on which the last of them was passed or made);

(ii) in any other case, the end of the period for making such an application.

[*C(AICE)A 2004, ss 37(3)(4), 37C; SI 2005 No 1788, Regs 2, 12*].

Decision by the Regulator. The Regulator must decide whether the company is eligible to become a CIC, ie whether

- its articles as proposed to be amended comply with the requirements imposed under **10.13**;
- its proposed name complies with the provisions in **10.15**; and
- having regard to the application and accompanying documents and any other relevant considerations, the Regulator considers that the company will satisfy the community interest test and is not an excluded company (see **10.2**).

The Regulator must give notice of the decision to the Registrar of Companies (but the Registrar is not required to record it).

If the Regulator gives notice of a decision that the company is eligible to become a CIC, the Registrar of Companies must proceed in accordance with *CA 2006, s 80* (registration and issue of new certificate of incorporation on change of name, see **27.17 Names and Business Names**). If the Registrar of Companies enters the new name of the company on the register, he must retain and record the application to become a CIC together with the other documents required to accompany it. The new certificate of incorporation must state that it is issued on the company's conversion to a CIC, the date on which it is issued, and that the company is a CIC. On the issue of the certificate, the company by virtue of the issue of the certificate becomes a CIC and the changes in the company's name and articles take effect. The certificate is conclusive evidence that the company is a CIC.

If the Regulator decides that the company is not eligible to become a CIC, the company may appeal to the Appeal Officer against the decision.

[*C(AICE)A 2004, ss 38, 38A*].

10.6 Charities

English charities. A CIC must be a limited company. Therefore an unincorporated charity cannot convert to a CIC. Similar provisions apply as in **10.5** where a company which is a charity wishes to become a CIC except that the company cannot become a CIC without the prior written consent of the Charity Commission. In contravention of this requirement, the Charity Commission may apply to the High Court for an order quashing any altered certificate of incorporation issued.

If a company that is an English charity becomes a CIC, that does not affect the application of

- any property acquired under any disposition or agreement previously made otherwise than for full consideration in money or money's worth, or any property representing property so acquired,
- any property representing income which has previously accrued, or
- the income from any such property

which remains applicable to the company's original charitable purposes.

[*C(AICE)A 2004, s 39*].

Scottish charities. A company that is a Scottish charity cannot become a CIC without the prior written consent

(a) if the company's registered office is situated in Scotland, of the Scottish Charity Regulator; or

(b) if the company's registered office is situated in England and Wales (or Wales), of both the Scottish Charity Regulator and the Charity Commission.

In contravention of (*a*) above, the Scottish Charity Regulator may apply to the Court of Session for an order quashing any altered certificate of incorporation issued. In contravention of (*b*) above, the Scottish Charity Regulator or the Charity Commission may apply to the High Court for such an order.

If a company that is a Scottish charity becomes a CIC, it continues to be under a duty to apply

- any property previously acquired or any property representing property previously acquired,
- any property representing income which has previously accrued, or
- the income from any such property

in accordance with its purposes as set out in its entry in the Scottish Charity Register immediately before it become a CIC.

[*C(AICE)A 2004, s 40(3)–(9); SI 2006 No 242*].

Northern Ireland. A company that is a NI charity may not become a CIC. If such a company purports to become a CIC, HMRC may apply to the High Court for an order quashing any altered certificate of incorporation. [*C(AICE)A 2004, s 40A*].

10.7 RESTRICTIONS ON THE TRANSFER OF ASSETS (DISTRIBUTIONS AND INTEREST)

Asset lock

Section 30 of *C(AICE)A 2004* and Regulations made under the *Act* provide for asset locking by:

- a ban on distribution of assets to members. Assets must either be retained within the CIC to be used for the community purposes for which the CIC was formed or, if they are transferred out of the CIC the transfer must either be made for full consideration (ie at market value) or be transferred to another asset locked body specified in the CIC's Articles of Association or transferred to another asset locked body with the consent of the CIC Regulator or be made for the benefit of the community
- limits on the extent to which distributions may be made
- limits on the payment of interest on debentures
- provisions for caps on dividends
- regulation on the return of capital to members and
- restriction on the transfer of assets.

See **10.8** to **10.12** and, for distributions of assets on a winding up, **10.29**.

10.8 Declaration of dividends

A CIC which is either a company limited by shares or a company limited by guarantee with a share capital may only pay dividends out of distributable profits and may declare a dividend to its members only

(a) to the extent that its articles permit it to do so;

(b) if an ordinary or special resolution of the company's members has approved the declaration of the dividend; and

(c) (subject to below) if the declaration of the dividend does not cause

 (i) the total amount of dividend declared on any of the company's shares for the financial year for which it is declared to exceed the maximum dividend per share for that financial year (see **10.9**); or

 (ii) the total amount of all the dividends declared on shares in the relevant company for the financial year for which it is declared to exceed the maximum aggregate dividend for that financial year (see **10.9**).

Exempt dividends

To qualify as an exempt dividend, the conditions in each of the following (with alternatives) must be satisfied.

- the dividend is declared on a share which is held by an 'asset-locked body' (but this condition is not satisfied in respect of a share which the directors recommending the dividend are aware is being held on trust for a person who is not an asset-locked body); or
- The dividend is declared on a share which is held on behalf of an asset-locked body (or is believed by the directors recommending the dividend to be so held).
- The Regulator has consented to the declaration of the dividend; or
- The asset-locked body by or on behalf of which the share on which the dividend is declared is held (or on behalf of which the directors declaring the dividend believe that it is held) is named in the memorandum or articles of the company as a possible recipient of the assets of the company.

'*Asset-locked body*' (See APPENDIX 1 DEFINITIONS)

The benefits of an exempt dividend are:

- the dividend only needs to be authorised by the articles and approved by an ordinary or special resolution; and
- conditions (c)(i) and (ii) above do not apply to exempt dividends so that there is no limit on the sum that can be paid by way of an exempt dividend (other than the general rules on distributions).

[*SI 2005 No 1788, Regs 2, 17*].

10.9 Dividend cap

Maximum dividend per share. A dividend is subject to the dividend cap if shares are not held by an asset-locked body or they are held by an asset-locked body not specified in the CIC's articles of association and the Regulator has not consented to the payment of the dividend. The maximum dividend per share for a financial year is the dividend which a CIC declares on a share when the total amount of dividend declared on that share for that year (when expressed as a percentage of the 'paid-up value' of the share) equals that share's 'applicable share dividend cap'.

'*Paid-up value*' means, in respect of any share in a company, the sum of

- so much of the share's nominal value as has been paid up; and
- any premium on that share paid to the company.

The '*applicable share dividend cap*' of a share in a relevant company is the share dividend cap which had effect in relation to that share at the time that the share was issued or the company became a CIC, whichever is the later.

Where the expression of the applicable dividend cap includes reference to a rate or figure determined by any person other than the company, the Regulator or the Secretary of State (in NI, the Department of Enterprise, Trade and Investment for NI) (eg by reference to the Bank of England base rate), the maximum dividend per share for any financial year is calculated by reference to that rate or figure as it had effect at the beginning of the first day of that financial year.

[*SI 2005 No 1788, Regs 2, 18*].

Maximum aggregate dividend. The maximum aggregate dividend for a financial year of a relevant company is declared when the total amount of all dividends declared on its shares for that year, less the amount of any exempt dividends (see **10.8**), equals (when expressed as a percentage of the relevant company's 'distributable profits') the aggregate dividend cap which had effect in relation to that company on the first day of the financial year in respect of which the dividends are declared. Examples of how to work out dividend calculations can be found on the Community Interest Companies pages on the BIS website – www.gov.uk.

'*Distributable profits*' means, in relation to a company, its accumulated realised profits (so far as not previously utilised by distribution or capitalisation) less its accumulated realised losses (so far as not previously written off in a reduction or reorganisation of capital duly made).

[*SI 2005 No 1788, Regs 2, 19*].

Carrying forward of unused dividend capacity from previous financial years. The unused dividend capacity is the amount that could have been paid on shares in a financial year but was not paid. Notwithstanding **10.8(*c*)(i)**, but subject to **10.8(*c*)(ii)**, the total amount of dividends declared on a share in a relevant company for a financial year may, subject to the company's articles, include the whole or any part of the share's unused dividend capacity calculated by the formula

$$A - B$$

where

A = the aggregate of any sums by which, for any of the four financial years immediately preceding the financial year for which a dividend is to be declared under this provision, the total amount of dividend declared and paid on the share for that financial year was less than the maximum dividend per share for that financial year; and

B = any part of A which has already been distributed by way of a dividend declared and paid for a previous financial year.

[*SI 2005 No 1788, Reg 20*].

Rates of caps.

- For shares in issue between 1 July 2005 and 5 April 2010 the share dividend cap is that percentage of the paid-up value of a share in a relevant company which is 5% higher than the Bank of England's base lending rate. For shares in issue between 6 April 2010 and 30 September 2014, the dividend cap is 20% of the paid-up value of a share in a relevant company. From 1 October 2014 the dividend per share cap has been removed.
- The aggregate dividend cap is 35% of a relevant company's distributable profits.

The Regulator may from time to time, with the approval of the Secretary of State, set a new share dividend cap or aggregate dividend cap. Any such new cap, cannot take effect from a date less than three months after it is published.

[*SI 2005 No 1788, Reg 22*].

10.10 The interest cap

In relation to debentures issued by, and debts of, a CIC

- on which a '*performance-related rate*' (ie any rate which is linked to the company's profits or turnover or to any item in the balance sheet of the company) of interest is payable, and
- where the agreement to pay interest at a performance-related rate was entered into by the company on or after the date on which it became a CIC,

a CIC must not be liable to pay, and must not pay, interest at a higher rate than the 'applicable interest cap'.

The '*applicable interest cap*' is the interest cap which had effect at the time that the agreement to pay interest at a performance-related rate was made.

Where the expression of the interest cap includes reference to a rate or figure determined by any person other than the company, the Regulator or the Secretary of State (in NI, the Department of Enterprise, Trade and Investment for NI) (eg by reference to the Bank of England base rate), the interest payable on any debt or debenture to which the interest cap applies must be calculated by reference to that rate or figure as it had effect at the beginning of the first day of the financial year in which the interest became due.

Nothing in the above provisions is to be taken as releasing a CIC from liability to pay, or as preventing a CIC from paying

- interest which accrued before the company became a CIC; or
- arrears of interest which, if it had been paid at the time it became due, would not have breached those provisions.

[*SI 2005 No 1788, Reg 21*].

Rate of interest cap. The CIC Regulations set the first interest cap as that percentage of the average amount of a CIC's debt, or the sum outstanding under a debenture issued by it, during the 12-month period immediately preceding the date on which the interest on that debt or debenture becomes due which is 4% higher than the Bank of England's base lending rate. This applies to agreements made between 1 July 2005 and 5 April 2010. Further changes were made in 2010 and 2014.

For agreements made between 6 April 2010 and 30 September 2014 the interest cap is 10% of the average amount of a CIC's debt, or sum outstanding under a debenture issued by it, during the 12-month period immediately preceding the date on which the interest on that debt or debenture becomes due.

For agreements made on or after 1 October 2014, the interest cap is 20% of the average amount of a CIC's debt, or sum outstanding under a debenture issued by it, during the 12-month period immediately preceding the date on which the interest on that debt or debenture becomes due.

[*SI 2005 No 1788, Reg 22, Sch 4*].

10.11 Redemption and purchase of shares

A CIC may not distribute assets to its members by way of the redemption or purchase of the company's own shares unless the amount to be paid by the company in respect of any such share does not exceed the paid-up value of the share (see **10.9**). [*SI 2005 No 1788, Reg 24*].

10.12 Reduction of share capital

A CIC may not distribute assets to its members by way of a reduction of the company's share capital unless

- the reduction is made by extinguishing or reducing the liability of any of the members on any of the company's shares in respect of share capital not paid up; or
- the amount to be paid by the company to members in paying off paid-up share capital does not exceed the paid-up value (see **10.9**) of their respective shares.

[*SI 2005 No 1788, Reg 25*].

10.13 ARTICLES OF ASSOCIATION

Every CIC must have articles of association. A CIC cannot be registered without supplying articles. The articles of a CIC must state that the company is to be a CIC and must at all times include the provisions (and must also not include certain other provisions) set out in *Regulations* (see below). Subject to this and the requirements of company law, a CIC can include any other provisions in its articles it wishes.

If a CIC's constitution contains any provision which is inconsistent with the *C(AICE) Act 2004* and such Regulations, that provision will have no effect.

[*C(AICE)A 2004, s 32*].

The following Regulations set out what a CIC must include in its articles:

For companies without share capital – *SI 2005 No 1788, Regs 2, 7, 9, 10, Sch 1*; *SI 2006 No 242*; *SI 2007 No 1093, Sch 4 paras 27, 29, 42*; *SI 2008 No 948, Sch 1 para 242*; *SI 2009 No 1942, Regs 3, 6, 7, 19–22*;

For companies with share capital – *SI 2005 No 1788, Regs 2, 8–10, Schs 2, 3*; *SI 2006 No 242*; *SI 2007 No 1093, Sch 4, paras 27, 43, 44*; *SI 2008 No 948, Sch 1 para 242*; *SI 2009 No 1942, Regs 3, 6, 8, 19–22*.

10.14 Alteration of objects

As from 1 October 2009 the constitution of any company (including a CIC) is set out in its articles by virtue of *section 8* of the *CA 2006*. This includes the company's objects. So if a company wants to alter its objects unless

- a CIC ceases being a CIC by becoming a charity; and
- a special resolution to alter the articles of the company with respect to the statement of its objects is forwarded to the Registrar of Companies as required by *C(AICE)A 2004, s 54* (see **10.30**).

then any alteration of the articles of a CIC with respect to the statement of the company's objects does not have effect unless it is approved by the Regulator.

If notice under *CA 2006, s 31(2)(a)* (see **14.10 Constitution – Memorandum and Articles**) is given to the Registrar of Companies of an amendment of the articles so as to add, remove or alter a statement of the company's objects the company must also deliver

- a community interest statement; and
- a statement, in a form approved by the Regulator, of the steps that have been taken to bring the proposed alteration to the notice of persons affected by the company's activities.

Both statements must be signed by each person who is a director of the company.

On receiving these documents, the Registrar of Companies must forward a copy of each to the Regulator and retain the documents pending the Regulator's decision (but take no further action at that time).

The Regulator must decide whether to approve the proposed alteration of the articles of the CIC with respect to the statement of the company's objects. He may do so if he considers that

- the altered objects will comply with the requirements imposed on CICs under the provisions in **10.13**;
- the company will continue to satisfy the community interest test; and
- the company has taken reasonable steps to bring the proposed alteration to the notice of persons affected by its activities.

The Regulator must give notice of the decision to the Registrar of Companies (but the Registrar is not required to record it). The Registrar of Companies must not

- register the notice under *CA 2006, s 31(2)(a)*,
- register any copy of the amended articles as delivered to him, or
- cause notice of that alteration to be published in the Gazette

unless and until the Regulator has given notice of his decision to approve the proposed alteration.

If the Regulator gives such notice, the Registrar of Companies must also record the community interest statement and the statement of the steps that have been taken to bring the proposed alteration to the notice of persons affected by the company's activities.

If the Regulator does not to approve the proposed alteration, the company may appeal (see **10.26**).

[*C(AICE)A 2004, s 32(6); SI 2005 No 1788, Regs 13–16*].

10.15 NAMES

The name of a CIC which is not a public company must end with 'community interest company' or 'c.i.c.'. In the case of a Welsh company, its name may instead end with 'cwmni buddiant cymunedol' or 'c.b.c.'.

The name of a CIC which is a public company must end with 'community interest public limited company' or 'community interest p.l.c.'. In the case of a Welsh company, its name may instead end with 'cwmni buddiant cymunedol cyhoeddus cyfyngedig' or 'cwmni buddiant cymunedol c.c.c.'.

[*C(AICE)A 2004, s 33*].

10.16 REPORT ON ACTIVITIES

The directors of a CIC must prepare in respect of each financial year a report about the company's activities during the financial year (a 'CIC report'). A copy of the report must be delivered to the Registrar of Companies and the Registrar must forward a copy to the Regulator. [*C(AICE)A 2004, s 34(1)(2)(4)*]. A filing fee is payable. See APPENDIX 3 FEES.

Contents of report.

(1) *General.*

(a) Every CIC report must contain

(i) a fair and accurate description of the manner in which the company's activities during the financial year have benefited the community;

(ii) a description of the steps, if any, which the company has taken during the financial year to consult persons affected by the company's activities, and the outcome of any such consultation; and

(iii) for financial years ending on or after 1 October 2009, but subject to below, if the company is a small company, the information specified in *SI 2008 No 409, Sch 3* (directors' remuneration, etc, see **5.41–5.43** ACCOUNTS: SMALL COMPANIES). If the company is a large or medium-sized company, the report must contain the information specified in *SI 2008 No 410, Sch 5* (directors' remuneration, etc, see **3.43–3.47** ACCOUNTS: LARGE COMPANIES) except that the information in **3.44–3.47** need only be given in the case of a company which is not a quoted company.

But if a CIC has provided the information required by (iii) above in its copy of the annual accounts for the year delivered to the Registrar of Companies and its CIC report contains a statement that detail of directors' remuneration during the financial year may be found in the notes to the annual accounts, the CIC report need not contain the information required by (iii) above.

(b) If, during a financial year, a CIC has transferred any of its assets other than for full consideration

- to any 'asset-locked body' (other than by way of an 'exempt dividend'); or
- for the benefit of the community other than by way of transfer to an asset-locked body,

its community interest report for that financial year must specify the amount, or contain a fair estimate of the value, of such transfer.

See **10.8** for '*asset-locked body*' and '*exempt dividend*'.

(2) *Dividends.*

Where a CIC

- has declared (or its directors propose to declare) a dividend for the financial year to which a report relates; or
- has declared a dividend for any of the four financial years immediately preceding that financial year

its report must state

- the amount of any dividend declared, or proposed to be declared, by the company on each of its shares for the financial year to which the report relates; and
- for each of the four financial years immediately preceding the financial year to which the report relates (in so far as the company was formed and trading during that period)
  - (i) the amount of any dividend declared and paid on each of the company's shares; and
  - (ii) the maximum dividend per share (see **10.9**) in respect of each of the company's shares.

The report must also explain how the declaration or proposed declaration of any dividend declared, or proposed to be declared, by the company in respect of the financial year to which the report relates complies, or will comply, with the provisions in **10.8** and **10.9**. This explanation must include details of

- in the case of an exempt dividend (see **10.8**), why it is an exempt dividend;
- in the case of any other dividend
  - (i) the applicable share dividend cap (see **10.8**) and the maximum dividend per share (see **10.8**) for each share on which the dividend has been, or is to be, declared;
  - (ii) the amount of any unused dividend capacity (see **10.8**) distributed or to be distributed as part of the dividend declared, or proposed to be declared; and
  - (iii) the maximum aggregate dividend (see **10.8**),

  and how each of these has been determined.

(3) *Debts or debentures on which a performance-related rate is payable.*

Where a CIC has at any time during the financial year a debt outstanding, or a debenture in issue, to which the interest cap provisions in **10.10** apply, its CIC report must state

- the rate of interest payable on that debt or debenture as calculated over a 12-month period ending with the most recent date on which interest became payable in respect of that debt or debenture during the financial year; and

- the applicable interest cap (see **10.10**) applying to that debt or debenture,

and how each of these has been determined.

Where the company has at any time during the financial year a debt outstanding, or a debenture in issue, to which the interest cap provisions in **10.10** do not apply, but on which a performance-related rate (ie any rate which is linked to the company's profits or turnover or to any item in the balance sheet of the company) is payable, its CIC report must state

- the rate of interest payable on that debt or debenture as calculated over a 12-month period ending with the most recent date on which interest became payable in respect of that debt or debenture during the financial year; and
- why the interest cap provisions do not apply to that debt or debenture.

Application of provisions relating to directors' reports (and from 1 October 2013 strategic reports). The following provisions of *CA 2006* apply to the CIC report as they apply to the directors' and strategic report.

- *CA 2006, s 419* (approval and signing, see **20.18** DIRECTORS' REPORTS);
- *CA 2006, ss 423–425* (circulation, see **2.6** ACCOUNTS: GENERAL);
- *CA 2006, s 430* (quoted companies; website availability, see **2.8** ACCOUNTS: GENERAL);
- *CA 2006, ss 431–432* (right to demand copies, see **2.7** ACCOUNTS: GENERAL);
- *CA 2006, s 433, 436* (name of signatory to be stated in published copies, see **2.4** ACCOUNTS: GENERAL);
- *CA 2006, ss 437, 438* (public companies: laying of accounts and reports before general meeting, see **2.9** ACCOUNTS: GENERAL);
- *CA 2006, ss 441–443, 445(1)* and *445(5), 446(1)* and *446(3), 447(1)* and *447(3), 451–453. Sections 444(1)* and *444(6)* have effect as if the directors of a CIC subject to the small companies regime must deliver a copy of the CIC report for each financial year to the Registrar of Companies and s 444A(1) has effect as if the directors of a CIC subject to the small companies exemption in relation to the directors' report for a financial year must deliver a copy of the CIC report for that year to the Registrar of Companies (filing obligations, see **2.10**, **2.11** ACCOUNTS: GENERAL); and
- *CA 2006, s 454* (revision of defective accounts, see **2.12** ACCOUNTS: GENERAL).

[*SI 2005 No 1788, Regs 26–29; SI 2012 No 2335 Reg 2*].

10.17 THE REGULATOR AND HIS POWERS

The role of Regulator of CICs came into force at the same time as the *C(AICE) Act*. The Regulator is appointed by the Secretary of State for Business, Innovation and Skills and is an independent public office holder. Full details can be found on the CIC website at www.bis.gov.uk/cicregulator. He has such functions relating to CICs as are conferred or imposed on him by virtue of *C(AICE)A 2004* or any other enactment.

The Regulator must adopt an approach to the discharge of those functions which is based on good regulatory practice, that is an approach adopted having regard to

- the likely impact on those who may be affected by the discharge of those functions,
- the outcome of consultations with, and with organisations representing, CICs and others with relevant experience, and
- the desirability of using the Regulator's resources in the most efficient and economic way.

The Regulator may issue (or the Secretary of State may require him to issue) guidance, or otherwise provide assistance, about any matter relating to CICs.

[*C(AICE)A 2004, s 27*].

C(AICE)A 2004, Sch 3 sets out the Regulator's terms of appointment and makes provisions about his remuneration, staffing, and financial and reporting framework. The Regulator is subject to investigation by the Parliamentary Commissioner and is disqualified from membership of the House of Commons.

The Office of the Regulator of Community Interest Companies is a partner of the Department for Business, Innovation and Skills (BIS).

10.18 Conditions for exercising powers

In deciding whether and how to exercise the powers conferred on him by **10.19** to **10.25**, the Regulator must adopt an approach which is based on the principle that those powers should be exercised only to the extent necessary to maintain confidence in CICs. In particular:

- No power conferred under **10.23**, **10.24** or **10.5** is exercisable in relation to a CIC unless the 'company default condition' is satisfied in relation to the power and the company.

  The '*company default condition*' is satisfied if it appears to the Regulator necessary to exercise the power in relation to the company because

  (a) there has been misconduct or mismanagement in the administration of the company,

  (b) there is a need to protect the company's property or to secure the proper application of that property,

  (c) the company is not satisfying the community interest test, or

  (d) if the company has community interest objects, the company is not carrying on any activities in pursuit of those objects.

- The power conferred to transfer shares (see **10.24**) is not exercisable unless it appears to the Regulator that the company is an excluded company (see **10.2**).

[*C(AICE)A 2004, s 41*].

10.19 Investigation of the affairs of a CIC

The Regulator may

- investigate the affairs of a CIC; or
- appoint any person (other than a member of his staff) to investigate the affairs of a CIC on his behalf.

[*C(AICE)A 2004, s 42*].

The Regulator may also authorise members of his own staff to carry out investigations under *C(AICE)A 2004, Sch 3 para 5*.

Power to require documents and information. The investigator of a CIC may require the company or any other person to produce such documents or provide such information as the investigator may specify. Such a requirement must be complied with at such time and place as may be specified by the investigator. The production of a document does not affect any lien which a person has on the document.

The investigator may take copies of or extracts from a document produced. In relation to information recorded otherwise than in legible form, the power to require production of it includes power to require the production of a copy of it in legible form or in a form from which it can readily be produced in visible and legible form.

Privileged information. Nothing in the above requires a person to produce a document or provide information in respect of which a claim could be maintained

- in an action in the High Court, to legal professional privilege, or
- in an action in the Court of Session, to confidentiality of communications,

but a person who is a lawyer may be required to provide the name and address of his client.

A person carrying on the business of banking cannot be required to produce a document, or provide information, relating to the affairs of a customer unless a requirement to produce the document, or provide the information, has been imposed on the customer.

Use of information as evidence. A statement made by a person in compliance with a requirement imposed under the above provisions may be used in evidence against the person. But in criminal proceedings

- no evidence relating to the statement may be adduced by or on behalf of the prosecution, and
- no question relating to it may be asked by or on behalf of the prosecution,

unless evidence relating to it is adduced or a question relating to it is asked in the proceedings by or on behalf of that person.

However, this does not apply to proceedings in which a person is charged with an offence under *Perjury Act 1911, s 5*, *Criminal Law (Consolidation) (Scotland) Act 1995, s 44(2)* or *Perjury (NI) Order 1979, Art 10* (false statement made otherwise than on oath) or the provisions below relating to false information.

Failure to comply with requirement. If a person fails to comply with a requirement relating to the production of documents or information, the investigator may certify that fact in writing to the court. Where, after hearing any witnesses who may be produced against or on behalf of the alleged offender and any statement which may be offered in defence, the court is satisfied that the offender failed, without reasonable excuse, to comply with the requirement, it may deal with him as if he had been guilty of contempt of the court.

False information. A person commits an offence if in purported compliance with a requirement to provide information as above, the person

- provides information which he knows to be false in a material particular, or

- recklessly provides information which is false in a material particular.

A prosecution may be instituted in England and Wales only with the consent of the Director of Public Prosecutions (in NI only with the consent of the Director of Public Prosecutions for NI).

A person guilty of such an offence is liable,

- on conviction on indictment, to imprisonment for a term not exceeding two years or a fine or to both;
- on summary conviction in England and Wales, to imprisonment for a term not exceeding twelve months (six months before the commencement of *Criminal Justice Act 2003, s 154(1)*) or a fine of an amount not exceeding the statutory maximum or to both, and
- on summary conviction in Scotland, to imprisonment for a term not exceeding six months or a fine of an amount not exceeding the statutory maximum or to both.

See **29.1** Offences and Legal Proceedings for the statutory maximum.

[*C(AICE)A 2004, Sch 7*].

10.20 Audit of annual accounts

The Regulator may, by order, require a CIC to allow its annual accounts to be audited by a qualified auditor appointed by him. *CA 2006, ss 499–501* (auditor's rights to information, see **8.36** Audit) apply in relation to such an auditor.

On completion of the audit, the auditor must make a report to the Regulator on such matters and in such form as the Regulator specifies. The expenses of the audit, including the remuneration of the auditor, are to be paid by the Regulator.

An audit under these provisions is in addition to, and does not affect, any audit required by or by virtue of any other enactment.

[*C(AICE)A 2004, s 43*].

10.21 Appointment and removal of directors

Note. The powers conferred by this paragraph can only be exercised if the 'company default condition' in **10.18** is satisfied.

Appointment of director. The Regulator may, by order, appoint anyone he thinks fit (other than a member of his staff) to be a director of a CIC although the company may appeal against the order (see **10.26**).

A person may be appointed as a director of a company under this provision

- whether or not the person is a member of the company, and
- irrespective of any provision made by the articles of the company or a resolution of the company.

Any such order must specify the terms on which the director is to hold office; and those terms have effect as if contained in a contract between the director and the company. The terms specified must include the period for which the director is to hold office, and may include terms as to the remuneration of the director by the company.

A director appointed under this provision has all the powers of the directors appointed by the company (including powers exercisable only by a particular director or class of directors). He may not be removed by the company but may be removed by the Regulator at any time (see below).

Where a person is appointed to be a director of the company under this provision (or a person so appointed ceases to be a director), the obligation which would otherwise be imposed on the company to notify the Registrar of Companies of the change within 14 days is instead an obligation of the Regulator. But if a person so appointed ceases to be a director otherwise than by removal by the Regulator, the company must give notification of that fact to the Regulator within 14 days and the Regulator must then send a notification to the Registrar of Companies within 14 days from the date on which he receives notification from the company. If a company fails to give notice to the Regulator as required, an offence is committed by the company and every officer of the company who is in default. A person guilty of such an offence is liable, on summary conviction, to a fine not exceeding level 5 on the standard scale and, for continued contravention, a daily default fine not exceeding one-tenth of level 5 on the standard scale. See **29.1 Offences and Legal Proceedings** for the standard scale. For the purposes of this offence a shadow director (see **18.1 Directors**) is treated as an officer of the company.

[*C(AICE)A 2004, s 45*].

Removal of director. The Regulator may, by order:

(a) Remove a director of a CIC, in which case

  (i) the company may not subsequently appoint that person a director of the company, and

  (ii) any assignment to the person of the office of director of the company is of no effect (even if approved by special resolution of the company).

  The Regulator may discharge any such order. The discharge does not reinstate the person removed as a director of the company, but (i) and (ii) above then cease to apply to the person.

(b) Suspend a director of the company, for a maximum period of one year, pending a decision whether to remove him. The Regulator may then give directions in relation to the performance of the director's functions.

  The Regulator must, from time to time, review any such order and, if appropriate, discharge the order.

Before making an order under (*a*) or (*b*) above, the Regulator must give at least 14 days' notice to the director and the company. The director may appeal against the order (in England and Wales and Northern Ireland to the High Court and in Scotland to the Court of Session).

The Regulator must, before the end of the period of 14 days beginning with the date on which an order under (*a*) or (*b*) above is made, discharged or quashed on appeal (or an order under (*b*) above expires) give notification of that event to the Registrar of Companies. Where the event involves a change in the company's directors, the company is not also obliged to notify the Registrar under *CA 2006, s 167(1)(a)*.

[*C(AICE)A 2004, s 46*].

10.22 Appointment of a manager

Note. The powers conferred by this paragraph can only be exercised if the 'company default condition' in **10.18** is satisfied.

The Regulator may, by order, appoint a manager in respect of the property and affairs of a CIC although the company may appeal against any such order. The person appointed may be anyone whom the Regulator thinks appropriate, other than a member of his staff.

The Regulator must give notice of the appointment of the manager to the Registrar of Companies, specifying an address at which service of documents (including legal process) can be effected on the person appointed. The Regulator must also give notice of any subsequent change in this address.

In carrying out his functions, the manager acts as the company's agent; and a person dealing with the manager in good faith and for value need not inquire whether the manager is acting within his powers.

The appointment of the manager does not affect

- any right of any person to appoint an interim manager of the company's property (including any right under *IA 1986, s 51* – power to appoint receiver under laws of Scotland); or
- the rights of an interim manager appointed by a person other than the Regulator.

The manager's functions are to be discharged by him under the supervision of the Regulator; and the Regulator must, from time to time, review the order by which the manager is appointed and, if it is appropriate to do so, discharge it in whole or in part. In particular, the Regulator must discharge the order on the appointment of a person to act as administrative receiver, administrator, provisional liquidator or liquidator of the company.

[*C(AICE)A 2004, s 47; CA 2006, s 1154(1)–(3)*].

Remuneration. The Regulator is authorised to determine the amount of a manager's remuneration. Any remuneration is payable out of the income of the CIC in respect of which the manager was appointed.

The Regulator may disallow any amount of a manager's remuneration if, having served a notice on him for failure to give security or discharge any of his functions (see below), the time specified in the notice for replying has expired and the Regulator, having considered such representations (if any) as are duly made, is satisfied that the manager has failed in his obligations.

Security. The Regulator may require the manager to give security to him for the due discharge of the manager's functions within such time and in such form as the Regulator may specify.

Failure and removal. Where

(a) it appears to the Regulator that a manager has failed

(i) to give security within such time or in such form as the Regulator has specified; or

(ii) satisfactorily to discharge any function imposed on him; and

(b) the Regulator wishes to consider exercising his powers to disallow any amount of remuneration (see above) or remove the manager (see below), the Regulator must give the manager, in person or by post, a written notice informing him of

- any failure under (*a*) above in respect of which the notice is issued;
- the Regulator's power to authorise the disallowance of any amount of remuneration if satisfied as to any such failure;

- the Regulator's power to remove the manager if satisfied as to any such failure; and
- the manager's right to make representations to the Regulator in respect of any such alleged failure within such reasonable time as is specified in the notice.

The Regulator may remove a manager (whether or not he also exercises the power to disallow any remuneration) if, having served a notice on him for failure to give security or discharge any of his functions (see above), the time specified in the notice for replying has expired and the Regulator, having considered such representations (if any) as are duly made, is satisfied that the manager has failed in his obligations.

The Regulator must give notice of the termination of the appointment of a manager to the Registrar of Companies.

Reports. The manager must make such reports to the Regulator as the Regulator may from time to time require on such matters and in such form as the Regulator specifies.

[*CA 2006, s 1154(4); SI 2005 No 1788, Regs 30–33*].

10.23 Powers in relation to property

Note. The powers conferred by this paragraph can only be exercised if the 'company default condition' in **10.18** is satisfied.

The Regulator may

(a) by order, vest in the Official Property Holder, (who is an officer appointed by the Regulator from his own staff) any property held by or in trust for a CIC;

(b) by order, require persons in whom such property is vested to transfer it to the Official Property Holder;

(c) order a person who holds property on behalf of a CIC, or on behalf of a trustee of a CIC, not to part with the property without the Regulator's consent;

(d) order any debtor of a CIC not to make any payment in respect of the debtor's liability to the company without the Regulator's consent; and

(e) by order, restrict the transactions which may be entered into by a CIC or the nature or amount of the payments that a CIC may make.

The Regulator must, from time to time, review any order made and, if appropriate, discharge the order in whole or in part. On discharging an order made under (*a*) or (*b*) above, the Regulator may make any order as to the vesting or transfer of the property, and give any directions which he considers appropriate.

Penalties, etc. If a person fails to comply with an order under (*b*) above, the Regulator may certify that fact in writing to the court. If the court is satisfied that the offender failed without reasonable excuse to comply with the order, it may deal with him as if he had been guilty of contempt of the court.

A person who contravenes an order under (*c*) to (*e*) above commits an offence although a prosecution may be instituted in England and Wales only with the consent of the Regulator or the Director of Public Prosecutions (in NI only with the consent of the Regulator or the Director of Public Prosecutions for NI). A person found guilty of such an offence is liable on summary conviction to a fine not exceeding level 5 on the standard scale. See **29.1 Offences and Legal Proceedings** for the standard scale.

Any criminal proceedings as above do not prevent the bringing of civil proceedings in respect of a contravention of an order under (*b*) to (*e*) above.

Appeals. The company may appeal against an order under (*a*) to (*e*) above and any person to whom it is directed may appeal against an order under (*a*) to (*d*) above.

[*C(AICE)A 2004, s 48*].

10.24 Transfers of shares

Note. The power conferred under this paragraph is not exercisable unless it appears to the Regulator that the company is an excluded company (see **10.2**). [*C(AICE)A 2004, s 41(4)*].

Subject to below,

(a) if a CIC has a share capital, the Regulator may, by order, transfer specified shares in the company to specified persons; and

(b) if a CIC is a company limited by guarantee, the Regulator may by order

  (i) extinguish the interests in the company of specified members of the company (otherwise than as shareholders), and

  (ii) appoint a new member in place of each member whose interest has been extinguished.

However

(1) he may not transfer any shares under (*a*) above in respect of which

  (i) a dividend may be paid, or

  (ii) a distribution of the company's assets may be made if the company is wound up; and

(2) an order in relation to a company may only transfer shares to, and appoint as new members, persons who have consented to the transfer or appointment.

The Regulator may make an order irrespective of any provision made by the articles of the company or a resolution of the company in general meeting.

Appeals. The company, and any person from whom shares are transferred by the order, may appeal against an order under (*a*) above. The company, and any person whose interest is extinguished by the order, may appeal against an order under (*b*) above.

[*C(AICE)A 2004, s 49*].

10.25 Dissolution and striking off

If a CIC has been dissolved or struck off the register, the Regulator may apply to the court for an order restoring the company's name to the register. These powers will enable the Regulator to safeguard the assets of a CIC for the community interest where the CIC has been struck off the register without having been wound up, or where an asset has been overlooked in a winding up.

If an application is made under *CA 2006, s 1003* by the director's of a CIC which is a private company to have the company struck off the register, the directors must send a copy of the application to the Regulator.

[*C(AICE)A 2004, s 51*].

10.26 APPEALS

The Secretary of State must appoint a person to be known as the Appeal Officer for CICs ('the Appeal Officer'). He has the function of determining appeals against decisions and orders of the Regulator which under or by virtue of *C(AICE)A 2004* or any other enactment lie with him.

An appeal to the Appeal Officer against a decision or order of the Regulator may be brought on the ground that the Regulator made a material error of law or fact. On such an appeal, the Appeal Officer must dismiss the appeal, allow the appeal, or remit the case to the Regulator. In the latter case, the Regulator must reconsider it in accordance with any rulings of law and findings of fact made by the Appeal Officer.

[*C(AICE)A 2004, s 28*].

C(AICE)A 2004, Sch 4 sets out the Appeal Officer's terms of appointment, remuneration and financing and provides for the Secretary of State to make regulations about the procedures to be followed by the Appeal Officer. The Appeal Officer is subject to investigation by the Parliamentary Commissioner and is disqualified from membership of the House of Commons.

10.27 CHANGE OF STATUS – RE-REGISTRATION

A CIC is excluded from re-registering under *CA 2006, s 102* ie as an unlimited company.

If a CIC re-registers as a public company under *CA 2006, s 90* or re-registers as a private company under *CA 2006, s 97* the new certificate of incorporation must contain a statement that the company is a CIC and the fact that is does so is conclusive evidence that the company is a CIC.

[*C(AICE)A 2004, s 52(2)*].

10.28 CEASING TO BE A COMMUNITY INTEREST COMPANY

A CIC can only cease to be a CIC

- by dissolution (see **10.25** for the powers of the Regulator following a dissolution and **10.29** for distribution of assets on a winding up);
- by becoming a charity (see **10.30**); or
- by becoming an industrial and provident society (see **10.31**).

[*C(AICE)A 2004, s 53*].

10.29 Distribution of assets on a winding up

Where a CIC is wound up under *IA 1986* and some property of the company (the '*residual assets*') remains after satisfaction of the company's liabilities, the residual assets must be distributed to those members of the CIC (if any) who are entitled to share in any distribution of assets on the winding up of the company according to their rights and interests in the company. But no member must receive an amount which exceeds the 'paid-up value' of the shares which he holds in the company.

'*Paid-up value*' means, in respect of any share in a company, the sum of

- so much of the share's nominal value as has been paid up; and
- any premium on that share paid to the company.

If any residual assets remain after any such distribution to members, they must be distributed as follows.

(a) If the articles of the company specify an 'asset-locked body' to which any remaining residual assets of the company should be distributed, then, unless either of the conditions in (*b*) (ii) or (iii) below is satisfied, the remaining residual assets must be distributed to that asset-locked body in such proportions or amounts as the Regulator directs.

(b) If

(i) the articles of the company do not specify an asset-locked body to which any remaining residual assets of the company should be distributed,

(ii) the Regulator is aware that the asset-locked body to which the articles of the company specify that the remaining residual assets of the company should be distributed is itself in the process of being wound up, or

(iii) the Regulator

- has received representations from a member or director of the company stating, with reasons, that the asset-locked body to which the articles of the company specify that the remaining residual assets of the company should be distributed is not an appropriate recipient of the company's remaining residual assets; and
- has agreed with those representations,

then the remaining residual assets must be distributed to such asset-locked bodies, and in such proportions or amounts, as the Regulator directs.

'*Asset-locked body*' means

- a CIC, a charity or a permitted industrial and provident society; or
- a body established outside the UK that is equivalent to either of those.

In considering any direction to be made under these provisions, the Regulator must consult the directors and members of the company to the extent that he considers it practicable and appropriate to do so. He must also have regard to the desirability of distributing assets in accordance with any relevant provisions of the company's articles.

The Regulator must give notice of any direction under these provisions to the company and the liquidator. Any member or director of the company can appeal to the Appeal Officer against such a direction. See **10.26 Appeals**.

[*SI 2005 No 1788, Reg 23*].

10.30 Becoming a charity

If a company is to cease to be a CIC and become a charity, the following conditions must be satisfied.

- The company must by special resolution
  - (i) state that it is to cease to be a CIC;
  - (ii) make such alterations of its articles as it considers appropriate; and
  - (iii) change its name so that it no longer complies with **10.15**;

[*C(AICE)A 2004, s 54(1)(2)*].

Application to court to cancel special resolutions. Where special resolutions have been passed with a view to the company ceasing to be a CIC and becoming a charity, an application to the court for the cancellation of the resolutions may be made

- by the holders of not less in the aggregate than 15% in nominal value of the company's issued share capital or any class of the company's issued share capital (disregarding any shares held by the company as treasury shares),
- if the company is not limited by shares, by not less than 15% of its members, or
- by the holders of not less than 15% of the company's debentures entitling the holders to object to an alteration of its objects

but not by a person who has consented to or voted in favour of the resolutions.

The application must be made within 28 days after the date on which the resolutions are passed or made (or, if the resolutions are passed or made on different days, the date on which the last of them is passed or made). It may be made on behalf of the persons entitled to make it by such one or more of their number as they may appoint for the purpose.

On making such an application, the applicants (or the person making the application on their behalf) must immediately give notice to the Registrar of Companies. The company must also immediately give notice to the Registrar of Companies on being served with notice of such an application.

The court must make an order (on such terms as it thinks fit) either cancelling or confirming the resolutions. The order may provide for the purchase by the company of the shares of any of its members and for the reduction accordingly of the company's capital (making such alteration in the company's articles as may be required in consequence).

Within 15 days of the making of the court's order on the application, or such longer period as the court may at any time direct, the company must deliver to the Registrar of Companies a copy of the order.

If a company fails to comply with the above requirement to notify the Registrar of Companies of service of an application or to deliver to him a copy of the court order, an offence is committed by the company and every officer of the company who is in default. A person guilty of such an offence is liable on summary conviction to a fine not exceeding level 3 on the standard scale and, for continued contravention, a daily default fine not exceeding one-tenth of level 3 on the standard scale. See **29.1 Offences and Legal Proceedings** for the standard scale.

[*C(AICE)A 2004, ss 54A, 54B*].

Application and accompanying documents. An application to the Registrar of Companies to cease to be a CIC and become a charity must be accompanied by

- a copy of the special resolutions;
- a copy of the company's articles as proposed to be amended; and
- a statement
  - (i) where the company is to become an English charity, by the Charity Commission that, in its opinion, if the proposed changes take effect the company will be an English charity and will not be an exempt charity;
  - (ii) where the company is to become a Scottish charity, by the Scottish Charity Regulator that if the proposed changes take effect the company will be entered in the Scottish Charity Register; or
  - (iii) where the company is to become a Northern Ireland charity, by the Commissioners of Her Majesty's Revenue and Customs that the company has claimed exemption under *ICTA 1988, s 505(1)*.

On receiving an application to cease to be a CIC and become a charity, together with the other documents required to accompany it, the Registrar of Companies must (instead of recording the documents and entering a new name on the register) forward a copy of each of the documents to the Regulator and retain the documents pending the Regulator's decision.

[*C(AICE)A 2004, ss 54(3)(4), 54C*].

Decision by the Regulator. The Regulator must decide whether the company is eligible to cease being a CIC, ie whether it has complied with *C(AICE)A 2004, ss 54* and *54C* above and that *none* of the following apply.

- The Regulator has appointed an auditor to audit the company's annual accounts and the audit has not been completed.
- Civil proceedings instituted by the Regulator in the name of the company under *C(AICE)A 2004, s 44* have not been determined or discontinued.
- A director of the company holds office by virtue of an order under *C(AICE)A 2004, s* 45 (see **10.21**).
- A director of the company is suspended under *C(AICE)A 2004, s 46(3)* (see **10.21**).
- There is a manager in respect of the property and affairs of the company appointed under *C(AICE)A 2004, s 47* (see **10.22**).
- The Official Property Holder holds property as trustee for the company.
- An order under *C(AICE)A 2004, s 48(2)*, re the company's property, debtors or transactions (see **10.23**).
- A petition has been presented for the company to be wound up.

The Regulator must give notice of the decision to the Registrar of Companies (but the Registrar is not required to record it).

If the Regulator gives notice of a decision that the company is eligible to cease being a CIC and become a charity, the Registrar of Companies must proceed in accordance with *CA 2006, s 80* (registration and issue of new certificate of incorporation on change of name, see **27.17** Names and Business Names). If the Registrar of Companies enters the new name of the company on the register, he must retain and record the application to cease to become a CIC together with the other documents required to accompany it. The new certificate of incorporation must state that it is issued on the company's ceasing to be a CIC and the date on which it is issued. On the issue of the certificate, the changes in the company's name and articles take effect and the company ceases to be a CIC.

If the Regulator decides that the company is not eligible to cease being a CIC, the company may appeal to the Appeal Officer against the decision.

[*C(AICE)A 2004, ss 55, 55A*].

10.31 Becoming an industrial and provident society

Section 56 of the *C(AICE)A 2004* provides that 'unless Regulations make provision to the contrary' a CIC may not convert itself into an industrial or provident society. However *regulation 5* of the *Community Interest Companies (Amendment) Regulations 2009 (SI 2009/1942)* allows a CIC to convert itself to a permitted industrial and provident society by special resolution of its members and provided it complies with *section 53* of the *Industrial and Provident Societies Act 1965* (as modified by the *2009 Regulations*).

10.32 DISCLOSURE OF INFORMATION

A public authority may disclose to the Regulator, for any purpose connected with the exercise of the Regulator's functions, information received by it in connection with its functions.

The Regulator may disclose to a public authority any information received by him in connection with his functions

- for a purpose connected with the exercise of those functions, or
- for a purpose connected with the exercise by the authority of its functions.

The powers to disclose information are subject to

- any restriction on disclosure imposed by, or by virtue of, an enactment, and
- any express restriction on disclosure subject to which information was supplied.

A person who discloses information in contravention of a restriction imposed is guilty of an offence, but a prosecution may be instituted in England or Wales only with the consent of the Regulator or the Director of Public Prosecutions (in NI only with the consent of the Regulator or the Director of Public Prosecutions for NI). A person guilty of such an offence is liable on summary conviction to a fine not exceeding level 3 on the standard scale. See **29.1 Offences and Legal Proceedings** for the standard scale.

[*C(AICE)A 2004, s 59*].

10.33 OFFENCES

If an offence committed by a body corporate is proved

- to have been committed with the consent or connivance of an 'officer', or
- to be attributable to any neglect on the part of an officer,

the officer, as well as the body corporate, is guilty of the offence and liable to be proceeded against and punished accordingly.

'*Officer*' means a 'director', manager, secretary or other similar officer of the body corporate, or a person purporting to act in any such capacity. '*Director*' includes a shadow director and, if the affairs of a body corporate are managed by its members, means a member of the body. [*C(AICE)A 2004, s 60*].

11 Companies not Formed under the Companies Acts

11.1 **Companies not formed under the Companies Act but authorised to register**
11.2 **Registration requirements**
11.3 Consent of members
11.4 Companies other than joint stock companies
11.5 Joint stock company
11.7 Company name
11.8 Issue of Certificate of incorporation
11.9 Transfer of property, rights and liabilities
11.10 Pending legal proceedings
11.11 The Company's constitution
11.12 Power to substitute articles of association for deed of settlement
11.13 Application of the Companies Act
11.14 Capital structure

Background. The *CA 2006* provisions of this chapter apply, under otherwise stated, to applications for registration received by the Registrar of Companies on or after 1 October 2009. If a resolution was agreed to, or other thing done, before 1 October 2009 it may be relied upon for the purposes of meeting the requirements of these provisions.

[*SI 2008 No 2860, Sch 2 para 93*].

11.1 COMPANIES NOT FORMED UNDER THE COMPANIES ACTS BUT AUTHORISED TO REGISTER

Subject to the exceptions below, any company

- in existence on November 1862 (including any company registered under the *Joint Stock Companies Acts*), or
- formed after that date (whether before or after the commencement of *CA 2006*)
  (i) in pursuance of any Act of Parliament other than *CA 2006* or any of the 'former Companies Acts',
  (ii) in pursuance of letters patent, or
  (iii) that is otherwise duly constituted according to law

may, on making application, register under *CA 2006*. It may register as an unlimited company, as a company limited by shares or as a company limited by guarantee. Registration is not invalid because it has taken place with a view to the company's being wound up (in fact registration is often sought for this very purpose).

Exceptions. This procedure cannot be used

- by a company having the liability of its members limited by Act of Parliament or letters patent which is either
  (i) not a 'joint stock company'; or
  (ii) seeking to register as an unlimited company or a company limited by guarantee; or
- by a company that is not a joint stock company seeking to register as a company limited by shares.

[*CA 2006, s 1040*].

See APPENDIX 1 DEFINITIONS for the meaning of the '*Companies Acts*' and '*Former Companies Acts*'.

'*Joint stock company*' for these purposes means a company having a permanent paid-up or nominal share capital of fixed amount *either* divided into shares of fixed amount *or* held and transferable as stock *or* divided and held partly in one way and partly in the other. It must be formed on the principle of having for its members the holders of those shares or that stock and no other persons. Such a company when registered with limited liability under the *CA 2006* is deemed to be a company limited by shares. [*CA 2006, s 1041*].

11.2 REGISTRATION REQUIREMENTS

Regulations made under *CA 2006* (the *Companies (Companies Authorised to Register) Regulations 2009*) provide the registration requirements for non Companies Act companies [*CA 2006, s 1042*; *SI 2009 No 2437*].

On compliance with the registration requirements, the Registrar of Companies must register the documents delivered to him.

The following is a summary of the registration requirements.

11.3 Consent of members

A company must have the consent of a majority of members present in person or by proxy (in cases where proxies are allowed) at a general meeting summoned for the purpose of registration.

If the company wants to register as a limited company and the liability of the company's members is not limited by an enactment or letters patent, the majority required must be not less than 75% of the members present in person or by proxy at the meeting.

In computing any majority when a poll is demanded, regard is to be had to the number of votes to which each member is entitled according to the company's regulations.

Guarantee companies. Where a company wishes to register as a company limited by guarantee, the consent to its being so registered must be accompanied by a resolution by each member undertaking to contribute to the company's assets, in the event of its being wound up while he is a member or within one year after he ceases to be a member, such amount as may be required for

- payment of the company's debts and liabilities contracted before he ceases to be a member,
- payment of the costs, charges and expenses of winding up, and
- the adjustment of the rights of the contributories among themselves,

such amount as may be required, not exceeding a specified amount "(a statement of guarantee)".

[*SI 2009 No 2437 Regs 3* and *6*].

11.4 Companies other than joint stock companies

Before the registration of a company other than a 'joint stock company' (see **11.1**) an application for registration 'the application for registration' must be delivered to the Registrar of Companies together with the documents required by *regulation 4* of *SI 2009 No 2437* and a statement of compliance.

The application for registration must state.

(a) The name with which the company is proposed to be registered. See **11.7**.

(b) Whether the company's registered office is to be situated in England and Wales (or in Wales), in Scotland or in Northern Ireland.

(c) Whether the liability of the members is to be limited, and if so whether it is to be limited by shares or by guarantee and whether the company is to be a private or public company and must contain

(i) (for guarantee companies) a statement of guarantee (see above)

(ii) a statement of the company's proposed officers (directors, and, where relevant, secretary (see *Regulation 7* of *SI 2009 No 2437* for the required details)

(iii) a statement of the intended address of the company's registered office

(d) A copy of any enactment, royal charter, letters patent, deed of settlement, contract of partnership or other instrument constituting or regulating the company and must be accompanied by a statement of compliance ie a statement that the requirements of registration have been complied with. The Registrar may accept the statement of compliance as evidence of that compliance.

[*SI 2009 No 2437 Regs 4, 5, 6, 7* and *8*]

11.5 Joint stock company

Before the registration of a joint stock company, the following must be delivered to the Registrar of Companies.

(a) The application for registration and documents as for other companies and the statement of compliance (see **11.4**);

(b) A statement of capital and initial shareholdings complying with *Reg 5* of *SI 2009 No 2437.*

[*SI 2009 No 2437 Regs 4, 5, 6, 7* and *8*]

11.6 *Registration of a joint stock company as a public company*

A joint stock company may apply to be registered as a public company subject to meeting the following conditions.

(a) It must satisfy the requirements set out in

(i) *CA 2006, s 91(1)* (requirements as to share capital, see **41.3**(*a*)–(*d*) **RE-REGISTRATION**));

(ii) *CA 2006, s 92* (requirements re net assets); and

(iii) (where applicable) *CA 2006, s 93(2)(a)*, namely it must not allot shares as fully or partly paid up (as to their nominal value and any premium on them) otherwise than in cash unless the consideration for the allotment has been independently valued and the valuer's report has been made to the company in the six months immediately preceding the allotment of the shares.

(b) Before the registration, the following must be delivered to the Registrar of Companies.

- (i) All the documents required under **11.5**.
- (ii) A copy of the resolution that the company be a public company.
- (iii) A copy of the balance sheet, and other documents referred to *CA 2006, s 92(3)*.
- (iv) A copy of any valuation report prepared under (*a*)(iii) above.

[*SI 2009 No 2437 Regs 4* and *9*]

11.7 Company name

The following provisions apply with respect to the name of the company registering (whether or not it is a joint stock company).

(a) If the company is to be registered as a public company, its name must end with the words

- (i) 'public limited company', or,
- (ii) where it is stated that the company's registered office is to be situated in Wales, with those words or their equivalent in Welsh ('cwmni cyfyngedig chyoeddus')

and those words (or that equivalent) may not be preceded by the word 'limited' or its equivalent in Welsh ('cyfyngedig').

(b) In the case of a company limited by shares or by guarantee (not being a public company), the name must have as its last word

- (i) 'limited", or
- (ii) where the company's registered office is to be situated in Wales, 'cyfyngedig'

but this is subject to *CA 2006, s 60* which exempts a company, in certain circumstances, from having 'limited' as part of the name. See **27.5** Names and Business Names.

(c) If the company is registered with limited liability, then any additions to the company's name set out in the statement specifying the name with which the company is proposed to be registered must form and be registered as the last part of the company's name.

(d) Where the name of a company seeking registration is a name by which it is precluded from registration by

- *CA 2006, s 53* (prohibited names), see **27.4** Names and Business Names,
- *CA 2006, s 54* (name suggesting connection with government or public authority) or *CA 2006, s 55* (other sensitive words or expressions), see **27.7** Names and Business Names,
- *CA 2006, s 57* (permitted characters), see **27.8** Names and Business Names,
- *CA 2006, s 65* (inappropriate use of indications of company type or legal form), see **27.5** Names and Business Names, or
- *CA 2006, s 66* (name not to be the same as another in the index), see **27.6** Names and Business Names

the company may change its name with effect from the date on which it is registered. Such a change of name requires the like consent of the company's members as is required by **11.3** for registration.

[*SI 2009 No 2437, Reg 10*]

11.8 Issue of certificate of incorporation

On the registration of a company, the Registrar of Companies must give a certificate that the company is incorporated. The certificate must state

- the name and registered number of the company;
- the date of its incorporation;
- whether it is a limited or unlimited company, and if it is limited whether it is limited by shares or limited by guarantee;
- whether it is a private or a public company; and
- whether the company's registered office is situated in England and Wales (or in Wales), in Scotland or in Northern Ireland.

The certificate must be signed by the Registrar of Companies or authenticated by his official seal and is conclusive evidence that the requirements relating to registration have been complied with.

[*SI 2009 No 2437, Reg 12*]

CONSEQUENCES OF REGISTRATION

11.9 Transfer of property, rights and liabilities

All property belonging to or vested in the company at the date of its registration passes to and vests in the company on registration but registration does not affect the company's rights or liabilities in respect of any debt or obligation incurred, or contract entered into, by, to, with or on behalf of the company before registration.

[*SI 2009 No 2437, Reg 14*]

11.10 Pending legal proceedings

Subject to below, all actions and other legal proceedings which, at the time of the company's registration, are pending by or against the company, or the public officer or any member of it, may be continued in the same manner as if the registration had not taken place.

But execution cannot be issued against the effects of any individual member of the company on any judgment, decree or order obtained in such an action or proceeding. In the event of the company's property and effects being insufficient to satisfy the judgment, decree or order, an order may be obtained for winding up the company.

[*SI 2009 No 2437, Reg 15*]

11.11 The company's constitution

Although the *2009 Regulations* provide that all provisions contained in any enactment or other instrument constituting or regulating the company are deemed to be conditions and regulations of the company, as if, had the company been formed under *CA 2006*, they had been contained in registered articles of association, there are limits to the changes the company can make to its constitution.

[*SI 2009 No 2437, Regs 16 and 20*]

11.12 Power to substitute articles of association for deed of settlement

A company authorised to register may, by special resolution, alter the form of its constitution by substituting articles of association for any instrument constituting or regulating the company, other than an enactment, a royal charter or letters patent.

[*SI 2009 No 2437, Reg 17*]

11.13 Application of the Companies Act

The provisions of the *Companies Acts* apply to a registered company and to its members, contributories and creditors, in the same manner as if the company had been formed under *CA 2006*, except that

(a) the model articles of association prescribed by the Secretary of State do not apply unless adopted by special resolution; (see APPENDIX 4 MODEL ARTICLES OF ASSOCIATION) and

(b) provisions relating to the numbering of shares do not apply to any joint stock company whose shares are not numbered;

The company does not have the power

- to alter any provision contained in an enactment relating to the company
- (without the consent of the Secretary of State) to alter any provision in letters patent relating to the company; or
- to alter any provision in a royal charter or letters patent with respect to the company's objects
- and in each case does not have the power to ratify the acts of the directors which contravene such provisions.

For these purposes the *Companies Acts*' include the *Companies (Cross-Border Mergers) Regulations 2007* and do not include *Part 2* of the *C(AICE) A 2004*.

[*SI 2009 No 2437, Reg 18, 19, 20*]

11.14 Capital structure

Provisions in *CA 2006* with respect to

- the re-registration of an unlimited company as limited,
- the powers of an unlimited company on re-registration as a limited company and to provide that a portion of its share capital is not capable of being called up except in the event of winding up, and
- the power of a limited company to determine that a portion of its share capital is not capable of being called up except in that event,

of an unlimited company on re-registration as a limited company and to provide that a portion of its share capital is not capable of being called up except in the event of winding up, and

[*SI 2009 No 2437, Reg 21*]

12 Company Formation and Types of Companies

12.1	**Pre-incorporation**	12.5	Effect of registration
12.2	**Method of forming a company**	12.6	**Company as a separate legal person**
12.3	**Registration of a company**	12.7	**Types of companies formed under the Companies Act**
12.4	Certificate of incorporation		

Cross-references. See 14 CONSTITUTION – MEMORANDUM AND ARTICLES.

12.1 PRE-INCORPORATION

Promoters

A '*promoter*' is a person who undertakes to form a company with reference to a given project and to set it going, and who takes the necessary steps to accomplish that purpose (*Twycross v Grant* (1877) 2 CPD 469, CA).

A promoter has duties towards the company before it comes into existence and may continue to be in a fiduciary relation to it after incorporation (*Emma Silver Mining Co v Lewis & Son* (1879) 4 CPD 396). If he sells property to the company he is bound to take care that he sells it through the medium of the board of directors who can and do exercise an independent judgement on the transaction (*Erlanger (Emile) v New Sombrero Phosphate Co* (1878) 3 App Cas 1218, HL). Where a promoter makes any undisclosed profit, this should be handed over to the company (*Whaley Bridge Calico Printing Co v Green and Smith* (1879) 5 QBD 109). See also *Gluckstein v Barnes* [1900] AC 240, HL.

Pre-incorporation contracts

A contract that purports to be made by or on behalf of a company at a time when the company has not been formed has effect, subject to any agreement to the contrary, as one made with the person purporting to act for the company or as agent for it, and that person or agent is personally liable on the contract.

This also applies to

- the making of a deed under the law of England and Wales or Northern Ireland, and
- the undertaking of an obligation under the law of Scotland

as it applies to the making of a contract.

[*CA 2006, s 51*].

For cases involving the enforceability of pre-incorporation contracts by and against the agent or promoter, see *Kelner v Baxter* (1866) LR 2 CP 174; *Newborne v Sensolid (Great Britain) Ltd* [1954] 1 QB 45, [1953] 1 All ER 708, CA; *Black v Smallwood* (1965) 117 CLR 52, [1966] ALR 744, Aust HC; and *Phonogram Ltd v Lane* [1982] QB 938, [1981] 3 All ER 182, CA. As the company has not yet been formed, it cannot be bound by the contract (*Re English and Colonial Produce Co Ltd* [1906] 2 Ch 435, 75 LJ Ch 831, CA) and cannot sue on it (*Natal Land and Colonization Co Ltd v Pauline Colliery and Development Syndicate* [1904] AC 120, 73 LJPC 22, PC).

12.2 METHOD OF FORMING A COMPANY

For companies incorporated on or after 1 October 2009 a company is formed by one or more persons

- subscribing their names to a memorandum of association; and
- complying with the requirements as to registration.

A company may not be so formed for an unlawful purpose.

[*CA 2006, s 7*].

Any type of company can be formed by a single subscriber and can continue as a single member company. If that is the case *CA 2006, s 38* provides that any enactment or rule of law applicable to companies formed by two or more persons or having two or more members applies with any necessary modification in relation to a company formed by one person or having only one person as a member. [*CA 2006, s 38*].

12.3 REGISTRATION OF A COMPANY

A company seeking registration must deliver to the Registrar of Companies

- the memorandum of association. The memorandum of a company incorporated on or after 1 October 2009 is in a short form only and states only that the subscribers wish to form a company under *CA 2006* and agree to become members of the company and in the case of a company that is to have a share capital, to take at least one share each (see **14 Constitution – Memorandum and Articles**);
- an application for registration of the company (form INO1) including a statement of compliance and the fee (see **Appendix 3**); and
- a copy of the company's articles (unless the company decides that the relevant model articles should apply in their entirety - see **14 Constitution – Memorandum and Articles** and **Appendix 4 Standard Articles of Association**).
- additional information if the application includes a prescribed or sensitive word or expression in its name – see **27 Names and Business Names**.

Application for registration. Companies Form IN01 (Application to register a company) requires the following information.

(a) The company's proposed name and, if the proposed name contains a sensitive or restricted word or expression, confirmation that the company has requested the views of a government department or other body (see **27 Names and Business names**).

(b) Whether the company's registered office is to be situated in England and Wales, Wales, Scotland or Northern Ireland and the address of the registered office, which must be the same as the situation of the registered office.

(c) Whether the liability of the members of the company is to be limited, and if so whether it is to be limited by shares or by guarantee.

(d) Whether the company is to be private, public or unlimited company (see **Types of Company 12.7**).

(e) If the application is delivered by a person as agent for the subscribers to the memorandum of association, it must state his name and address.

(f) In the case of a company that is to have a share capital, a statement of capital and a statement of initial shareholdings. The statement of capital must

- state the total number of shares and the total aggregate nominal value of issued share capital and must set out for shares held in sterling and any shares held in other currencies);
- state for each class of shares
  - (i) particulars of any voting rights attached to the shares, including rights that arise only in certain circumstances;
  - (ii) particulars of any rights attached to the shares, as respects dividends, to participate in a distribution;
  - (iii) particulars of any rights attached to the shares, as respects capital, to participate in a distribution (including on a winding up);
  - (iv) whether the shares are to be redeemed or are liable to be redeemed at the option of the company or the shareholder and any terms or conditions relating to redemption of those shares;
  - (v) the total number of shares of that class; and
  - (vi) the aggregate nominal value of shares of that class;

  The Small Business, Enterprise and Employment Act 2015 (SBEE 2015) introduces a requirement to also include in the statement of capital the aggregate amount (if any) unpaid on those shares (whether on account of their nominal value or by way of premium). As at May 2015 this provision is not in force.
- state the amount to be paid up and the amount (if any) unpaid on each share (whether on account of the nominal value of the share or by way of premium).

  The statement of initial shareholdings must
- state the name(s) (in alphabetical order) and address of each subscriber to the memorandum of association;
- state, with respect to each subscriber to the memorandum,
  - (i) the number, nominal value (of each share), currency and class of shares to be taken by him on formation, and
  - (ii) the amount to be paid up and the amount (if any) unpaid on each share (whether on account of the nominal value of the share or by way of premium).

  Where a subscriber to the memorandum is to take shares of more than one class, the information required under (i) above is required for each class.

(g) In the case of a company that is to be limited by guarantee, a statement of guarantee. This must

- contain the name and address of each subscribers to the memorandum of association. The address does not have to be the subscriber's usual residential address;

- state that each member undertakes that, if the company is wound up while he is a member, or within one year after he ceases to be a member, he will contribute to the assets of the company such amount as may be required for
  - (i) payment of the debts and liabilities of the company contracted before he ceases to be a member;
  - (ii) payment of the costs, charges and expenses of winding up; and
  - (iii) adjustment of the rights of the contributories among themselves, not exceeding a specified amount.

(h) A statement of the company's proposed officers containing the particulars of

- the person who is, or the persons who are, to be the first director or directors of the company as will be required to be stated in the company's register of directors and register of directors' residential addresses (see **38.2** and **38.3** Registers). Private companies must appoint at least one director and public companies must appoint at least two directors. In either case one director of a company must be an individual (but see **18.2** for the effect of changes to be brought about by the SBEE 2015 in relation to corporate directors); or
- the person who is (or the persons who are) to be the first secretary (or joint secretaries) of the company as will be required to be stated in the company's register of secretaries (see **38.4 Registers**). Additional information is required if the secretary or director is a corporate secretary or director and is registered within the EEA (Companies House guidance provides full details of EEA countries). The secretary must supply a service address.

The statement must also contain a consent by each of the persons named as a director or secretary (as the case may be) to act in the relevant capacity. If all the partners in a firm are to be joint secretaries, consent may be given by one partner on behalf of all of them. The SBEE 2015, s 100, slightly amends these provisions. The consent statements will have to be made

- in the case of directors by the subscribers to the memorandum and
- in the case of the company secretary by the company.

As at May 2015, SBEE 2015, s 100 is not yet in force.

(i) Each director must supply a service address and a usual residential address. The service address is the address which will appear on the public record. When supplying the usual residential address, the director must also complete details of any *CA 2006, s 243* exemption which has been applied for or already granted (see **18 Directors**).

(j) A copy of any proposed articles of association (to the extent that these are not supplied by the default application of model articles under *CA 2006, s 20*, see **14.3 Constitution – Memorandum and Articles**).

(k) Whether a private company limited by guarantee wishes to apply to be exempt from the requirement to use "limited" or "cyfyngedig" in its name.

(l) A statement of compliance. The statement of compliance required to be delivered to the Registrar of Companies is a statement that the requirements of *CA 2006* as to registration have been complied with. The statement must be signed by all the subscribers or by an agent acting on behalf of all the subscribers. The Registrar of Companies may accept the statement of compliance as sufficient evidence of compliance.

The application must be delivered to the Registrar of Companies for England and Wales (if the registered office of the company is to be situated in England and Wales or in Wales), to the Registrar of Companies for Scotland (if the registered office of the company is to be situated in Scotland) or to the Registrar of Companies for Northern Ireland (if the registered office of the company is to be situated in Northern Ireland) together with the memorandum and articles (if relevant). If the company does not send a copy of its articles then by default the relevant model articles will apply (see *CA 2006, s 20* and **14 Constitution – Memorandum and Articles**). The application can be filed either electronically or by paper application. From 6 April 2011 an application for web incorporation can also be made via Companies House Businesslink service. See **Appendix** 3 for fees payable.
[*CA 2006, ss 9–13*].

There is also a useful checklist on Form IN01.

Registration. If the Registrar of Companies is satisfied that the above requirements have been complied with, he must register the documents delivered to him. [*CA 2006, s 14*].

12.4 Certificate of incorporation

On the registration of a company, the Registrar of Companies must give a certificate that the company is incorporated. The certificate must state

- the name and registered number of the company;
- the date of its incorporation;
- whether it is a limited or unlimited company, and if it is limited whether it is limited by shares or limited by guarantee;
- whether it is a private or a public company; and
- whether the company's registered office is situated in England and Wales, Wales) Scotland or Northern Ireland.

The certificate must be signed by the Registrar of Companies or authenticated by the Registrar's official seal.

The certificate is conclusive evidence that the requirements of *CA 2006* as to registration have been complied with and that the company is duly registered under that *Act*. [*CA 2006, s 15*].

12.5 Effect of registration

The registration of a company has the following effects as from the date of incorporation.

- The subscribers to the memorandum, together with such other persons as may from time to time become members of the company, are a body corporate by the name stated in the certificate of incorporation.
- That body corporate is capable of exercising all the functions of an incorporated company.

- The status and registered office of the company are as stated in the application for registration.
- In the case of a company having a share capital, the subscribers to the memorandum become holders of the shares specified in the statement of capital and initial shareholdings.
- A person named in the statement of proposed officers (see **12.3**(*h*)) as a director or secretary is deemed to have been appointed to that office.

[*CA 2006, s 16*].

A public company, however, cannot do business or borrow money until it receives a trading certificate from the Registrar of Companies under *CA 2006, s 761*. A trading certificate will not be issued unless the Registrar is satisfied that the company's allotted share capital is not less the authorised minimum (currently £50,000 or the prescribed equivalent). For the purposes of calculating the amount allotted, any shares allotted pursuant to an employees' share scheme must not be taken into account unless they are paid up to at least one quarter of their nominal value plus the whole of any premium. (see **33.3 Public and Listed Companies**).

12.6 COMPANY AS A SEPARATE LEGAL PERSON

Once a company has been validly formed and incorporated, it is a legal person distinct from its members. This applies even where a controlling shareholder effectively owns all the shares in the company (*Salomon v A Salomon & Co Ltd* [1897] AC 22, HL). See also *Lee v Lee's Air Farming Ltd* [1961] AC 12, [1960] 3 All ER 420, PC, where such a person may function in a dual capacity and a contractual relationship may be established between the shareholder and the company.

Once incorporated, the company is bound by the decision of a majority of its members in general meeting and the courts will not normally interfere in the internal management of a company acting within its powers (*Foss v Harbottle* (1843) 2 Hare 461).

Foss v Harbottle also established the fundamental rule that to redress a wrong done to a company or to recover moneys or damages due to it, action must *prima facie* be brought by the company itself. Subsequent case law, however, established exceptions to the rule in *Foss v Harbottle* for the protection of minority interests and *CA 2006* provides a statutory remedy for the protection of members who may take action against the directors. See **26.6 Members**.

Lifting the veil. In certain circumstances, the court may pull aside the corporate veil and look through the transactions of the company to see what really lies behind them. See *Wallersteiner v Moir* [1974] 3 All ER 217, [1974] 1 WLR 991, CA, and *Littlewoods Mail Order Stores Ltd v IRC* [1969] 3 All ER 855, [1969] 1 WLR 1241, CA. The courts have frequently done this and looked at the personal relationships of the shareholders when deciding if a family company should be wound up (see, for example, *Ebrahimi v Westbourne Galleries Ltd* [1973] AC 360, [1972] 2 All ER 492, HL); to determine whether a company is an 'enemy' at time of war (*Daimler Co Ltd v Continental Tyre and Rubber Co (Great Britain) Ltd* [1916] 2 AC 307, 85 LJKB 1333, HL); where a company is used to carry out a fraud (*Re Darby, ex p Brougham* [1911] 1 KB 95, 80 LJKB 180); and to treat a group of companies as one company (*DHN Food Distributors Ltd v Tower Hamlets London Borough Council* [1976] 1 WLR 852, [1976] 1 WLR 852, CA).

12.7 TYPES OF COMPANIES FORMED UNDER THE COMPANIES ACT

Limited and unlimited companies

A company is a '*limited company*' if the liability of its members is limited by its constitution. Liability may be limited in two ways.

- The company is '*limited by shares*' if the liability of members is limited to the amount, if any, unpaid on the shares held by them.
- The company is '*limited by guarantee*' if the liability of members is limited to such amount as the members undertake to contribute to the assets of the company in the event of its being wound up.

If there is no limit on the liability of its members, the company is an '*unlimited company*'. [*CA 2006, s 3*].

Private and public companies

A '*private company*' is any company that is not a public company.

A '*public company*' is a company limited by shares or limited by guarantee and having a share capital

- whose certificate of incorporation states that it is a public company; and
- in relation to which the requirements of the *CA 2006* or the '*former Companies Acts*' (see APPENDIX 1 DEFINITIONS) as to registration or re-registration as a public company have been complied with on or after
  - (i) in relation to registration or re-registration in Great Britain, 22 December 1980; and
  - (ii) in relation to registration or re-registration in Northern Ireland, 1 July 1983.

[*CA 2006, s 4*].

For some of the major differences between private and public companies, see 33 PUBLIC AND LISTED COMPANIES.

Companies limited by guarantee

A company limited by guarantee is a company having the liability of its members limited to such amount as the members undertake to contribute to the assets of the company in the event of its being wound up. Such companies are widely used by schools, professional and trade associations, clubs and for management companies of blocks of flats in which all the tenants are members.

A company cannot be formed as, or become, a company limited by guarantee with a share capital. Provision to this effect has been in force in Great Britain since 22 December 1980 and in Northern Ireland since 1 July 1983. Any provision in the constitution of a company limited by guarantee that purports to divide the company's undertaking into shares or interests is a provision for a share capital (whether or not the nominal value or number of the shares or interests is specified by the provision). [*CA 2006, s 5*].

As the definition of a public company only includes companies limited by guarantee which have a share capital, it follows that a guarantee company can only be formed as a private company.

12.7 Company Formation and Types of Companies

See **14.3 Constitution – Memorandum and Articles** for requirements of the articles of association; formation for requirements of the memorandum of association and registration; **27.2 Names and Business Names** for exemption from requirement as to the use of 'limited'.

Right to participate in profits otherwise than as member void

In order to prevent members of a company limited by guarantee and not having a share capital being given rights equivalent to those of shareholders, any provision in the company's articles, or in any resolution of the company, purporting to give a person a right to participate in the divisible profits of the company otherwise than as a member is void. [*CA 2006, s 37*]. In the case of a company formed before 1 October 2009, this also applies to any provision of its memorandum (which, from that date, is deemed to be part of its articles under *CA 2006, s 28*, see **14 Constitution – Memorandum and Articles**).

There is no statutory restriction on the members of such a company participating in their profits except where it has sought exemption from the use of the word 'limited' in its name (see **27 Names and Business Names**).

Unlimited companies

An unlimited company is a company having no limit on the liability of its members. Such a company can only be a private company and cannot be a public one. [*CA 2006, s 4(2)*]. This liability arises only on the company being insolvent on winding up. Whilst the company is a going concern, liability is limited to the amount unpaid on shares.

See **14 Constitution** for requirements of the articles of association; and **41 Re-Registration** for private limited company becoming unlimited, an unlimited private company becoming limited, and a public company becoming private and unlimited.

Exemption for unlimited companies from obligation to file accounts

Subject to below, the directors of an unlimited company are not required to deliver accounts and reports to the Registrar of Companies in respect of a financial year unless at any time during the 'relevant accounting reference period'

- the company was a subsidiary undertaking or a parent of an undertaking which was then limited

  Relevant accounting reference period' in relation to a financial year means the accounting reference period by reference to which the financial year was determined.

  [*CA 2006, s 448(1)–(3)(5); SI 2008 No 393, Reg 13*].

  References to an undertaking being limited at a particular time are to an undertaking (under whatever law established) the liability of whose members is at that time limited.

- the company was a banking or insurance company or the parent company of a banking or insurance group or each of the company's members was

  (i) a limited company; or

  (ii) another unlimited company or Scottish partnership, each of whose members is a limited company.

  References in (i) or (ii) above to a limited company, another unlimited company or Scottish partnership include references to any comparable undertaking incorporated in, or formed under, the law of a country or territory outside the UK.

Unregistered companies

Only specific provisions of the *Companies Act* apply to '*unregistered companies*'. See *Schedule 1* to the *Unregistered Companies Regulations 2009 (SI 2009 No 2436)* which apply provisions of *CA 1985* and *CA 2006* with modifications to unregistered companies and *Schedule 2* to that *Order* which contains transitional provisions applying to companies incorporated before 1 October 2009. The *2009 Regulations* also revoked the *Companies (Unregistered Companies) Regulations 2007.*

'*Unregistered companies*' means any body corporate, incorporated in and having a principal place of business in the UK, other than

(a) any body incorporated by or registered under, a public general Act of Parliament;

(b) any body not formed for the purpose of carrying on a business which has for its object the acquisition of gain by the body or its individual members;

(c) any body exempted by statutory instrument; and

(d) any open-ended investment company.

Section 1043 of the *CA 2006* does not repeal or revoke any enactment, Royal Charter or other instrument constituting or regulating any unregistered company or restrict the power to grant a charter in lieu of, or supplementary to, any such charter. However, the operation of any such enactment, etc which is inconsistent with any of those provisions is suspended to the extent of that inconsistency.

[*CA 2006, s 1043*].

Community interest companies

With effect from 1 October 2009, a company

- limited by shares or a company limited by guarantee and not having a share capital may be formed as or become a community interest company; and
- limited by guarantee and having a share capital may become a community interest company.

[*CA 2006, s 6*]

Such companies are intended for use by non-profit-distributing enterprises providing benefit to a community in areas such as childcare, social housing, leisure and community transport. They are subject to the general framework of company law. See **10 Community interest companies**.

Open-ended investment companies

A company can be incorporated as an open-ended investment company (OEIC). The regulations making provision for OEICs are the *Open-Ended Investment Companies Regulations 2001 (SI 2001 No 1228)*. These regulations are concerned with

- the formation and subsequent control and supervision of OEICs; and
- the corporate framework within which an OEIC operates.

Under *SI 2001 No 1228, Reg 6*, the FCA are given powers to make additional rules on both the constitution and management of OEICs and the publication of scheme particulars.

12.7 Company Formation and Types of Companies

Detailed coverage of the provisions of these rules and regulations is beyond the scope of this book.

13 Company Secretaries

13.1	**Private companies**	13.5	**Vacancy in office or secretary unable to act**
13.2	**Public companies**	13.6	**Liability of a company secretary**
13.3	**Appointment and removal**	13.7	**Powers of a company secretary**
13.4	Notification of changes to Companies House		

13.1 PRIVATE COMPANIES

As from 6 April 2008 a private company is not required to have a company secretary unless its articles expressly require it (although it may choose to do so). In the case of a private company 'without a secretary',

- anything authorised or required to be given or sent to, or served on, the company by being sent to its secretary
  - (i) may be given or sent to, or served on, the company itself; and
  - (ii) if addressed to the secretary is treated as addressed to the company; and
- anything else required or authorised to be done by or to the secretary of the company may be done by or to
  - (i) a director; or
  - (ii) a person authorised generally or specifically in that behalf by the directors.

Any reference in the *Companies Acts* to a company '*without a secretary*' is to a private company which has taken advantage of the exemption (as opposed to one which normally has a company secretary but which for some reason, such as death of the office holder, is without a secretary at a given time). References to a private company 'with a secretary' are construed accordingly.

[*CA 2006, ss 270, 271*].

If the articles of a private company immediately before 6 April 2008 expressly required it to have a secretary it is a company 'with a secretary' for the above purposes until its articles are amended to remove the requirement. For this purpose a provision

- requiring or authorising things to be done by or in relation to a secretary, or
- as to the manner in which, or terms on which, a secretary is to be appointed or removed,

is not a provision expressly requiring the company to have a secretary.

[*SI 2007 No 3495, Sch 4 para 4*].

Provisions applying to all secretaries

Acts done by person in a dual capacity. Although a director can act as secretary note that a provision requiring or authorising a thing to be done by or to a director *and* the secretary of a company is not satisfied by its being done by or to the same person acting both as director and as, or in place of, the secretary. So for example if the articles required countersignature of company documents by both a director and the secretary, the same person could not countersign in each capacity. [*CA 2006, s 280*].

Secretary not also to be auditor. It should be noted that an officer of the company (which includes the company secretary) cannot act as the statutory auditor of the company. [*CA 2006, s 1214*]. It follows from this that an existing auditor cannot be appointed company secretary.

13.2 PUBLIC COMPANIES

A public company, unlike a private one, must have a secretary. [*CA 2006, s 271*].

Qualifications of a public company secretary

The directors of a public company must take all reasonable steps to secure that the secretary (or each joint secretary) is a person who appears to them to have the requisite knowledge and experience to discharge the functions of secretary of the company and who has one or more of the following qualifications.

- He has held the office of secretary of a public company for at least three of the five years immediately preceding his appointment as secretary.
- He is a member of
  - (i) the Institute of Chartered Accountants in England and Wales;
  - (ii) the Institute of Chartered Accountants of Scotland;
  - (iii) the Chartered Association of Certified Accountants;
  - (iv) the Institute of Chartered Accountants in Ireland;
  - (v) the Institute of Chartered Secretaries and Administrators;
  - (vi) the Chartered Institute of Management Accountants; or
  - (vii) the Chartered Institute of Public Finance and Accountancy.
- He is a barrister, advocate or solicitor called or admitted in any part of the UK.
- He is a person who, by virtue of his holding or having held any other position or his being a member of any other body, appears to the directors to be capable of discharging the functions of secretary of the company.

[*CA 2006, s 273*].

Direction requiring public company to appoint secretary

If it appears to the Secretary of State that a public company is in breach of the requirement to have a company secretary, he may give the company a direction to that effect, specifying

- what it must do to comply with the direction;
- the period, which must be not less than one month or more than three months after the date on which the direction is given, in which the company must comply with the direction; and
- the consequences failing to comply.

Where the company does not have a secretary, it must make the necessary appointment and notify the Registrar of Companies of the appointment before the end of the period specified in the direction. If the company has already made the necessary appointment, it must still ensure that it notifies the Registrar of Companies before the end of the period specified.

If a company fails to comply with a direction under these provisions, an offence is committed by the company and every officer of the company who is in default. For this purpose a shadow director (see directors) is treated as an officer of the company. A person guilty of such an offence is liable on summary conviction to a fine not exceeding level 5 on the standard scale and, for continued contravention, a daily default fine not exceeding one-tenth of the greater of £5,000 or level 4 on the standard scale. See **29 Offences and Legal Proceedings** for the standard scale.

[*CA 2006, s 272; SI 2015 No 664, Sch 3*].

13.3 APPOINTMENT AND REMOVAL

Particulars of the first secretary (or joint secretaries) of a company must be given in the statement of the company's proposed officers required to be delivered to the Registrar of Companies at the time of application for formation under *CA 2006, s 12* (see **12.3**(h) **Company Formation**). On registration, the person or persons so named are deemed to be appointed. [*CA 2006, s 16(6)*].

Appointment of subsequent secretaries is regulated by the articles. Where the company has adopted standard Table A articles, see *Table A 1985 Reg 99.*

The model articles for both private and public companies made under *CA 2006* are silent on the subject of re-appointment or appointment of subsequent secretaries and so companies incorporated on after 1 October 2009 will if necessary either have to modify the model articles (if adopted) or draft bespoke articles to include such provision. Table A and the Model Articles are set out in **Appendix 4 Standard Articles of Association**.

Where the articles are silent, it is likely that analogous powers are within the board's scope of authority. In relation to listed companies, the the UK Corporate Governance Code states that any question of the removal of the secretary should be a matter for the board of directors as a whole (Code provision B.5.2).

Details of the first secretary and all subsequent changes must be recorded in the company's register of secretaries. See **38.4 Registers**.

13.4 Notification of changes to Companies House

A company must, within 14 days of

- a person becoming or ceasing to become its secretary, or
- any change in the particulars contained in its register of secretaries (see **38.4 Registers**),

give notice to the Registrar of Companies of the change and of the date on which it occurred. Notification is given on Form TM02 (Termination of appointment of secretary) or CH03 (Change of secretary's details).

Any notice of a person having become secretary (or one of joint secretaries) of the company must be accompanied by a consent by that person to act in the relevant capacity.

In default in complying with the above provisions, an offence is committed by every officer of the company who is in default. For this purpose a shadow director (see **18.1 Directors**) is treated as an officer of the company. A person guilty of such an offence is liable on summary conviction to a fine not exceeding level 5 on the standard scale and, for continued contravention, a daily default fine not exceeding one-tenth of level 5 on the standard scale. See **29.1 Offences and Legal Proceedings** for the standard scale.

[*CA 2006, s 276*].

13.5 VACANCY IN OFFICE OR SECRETARY UNABLE TO ACT

If the office of secretary is vacant, or there is for any other reason no secretary capable of acting, anything required or authorised to be done by or to the secretary may be done

- by or to an assistant or deputy secretary (if any); or
- if there is no assistant or deputy secretary or none capable of acting, by or to any person (before 1 October 2009, an officer of the company) authorised generally or specially in that behalf by the directors.

[*CA 2006, s 274*].

See also **13.2** for the power of the Secretary of State to direct a public company to appoint a secretary.

13.6 LIABILITY OF A COMPANY SECRETARY

An '*officer*' in relation to a company includes a secretary. [*CA 2006, s 1173*].

A secretary is, therefore, potentially liable for any of the penalties and fines imposed under the *Companies Acts* for default by officers. Penalties are dealt with in the appropriate part of the text but see also

- **29.2 Offences and Legal Proceedings** for the liability of the company secretary where an offence is committed by the company;
- **18.33–18.38 and 18.41 Directors** for liabilities under the *Insolvency Act 1986* and the *Theft Act 1968* which also apply to the company secretary; and
- **29.9 Offences and Legal Proceedings** for the power of the court to grant relief.

Note that the general prohibition on indemnifying directors against liabilities in *CA 2006, s 232* does not expressly include other officers (including the company secretary) so companies may provide (and often do provide in their articles) indemnities for the secretary. The company can also take out personal legal liability insurance for the benefit of the secretary.

13.7 POWERS OF A COMPANY SECRETARY

A company secretary has been held to be a mere servant whose position is to do what he is told so that he has no authority to represent anything at all (*Barnett, Hoares & Co v South London Tramways Co* (1887) 18 QBD 815, CA). But a modern company secretary is a much more important person. He is an officer of the company normally with extensive duties and responsibilities. He may regularly make representations on behalf of the board and enter into contracts on its behalf which come within the day-to-day running of the company's business. Signing contracts connected with the administrative side of the company's affairs therefore comes within his ostensible authority (*Panorama Developments (Guildford) Ltd v Fidelis Furnishing Fabrics Ltd* [1971] 2 QB 711, [1971] 3 All ER 16, CA).

14 Constitution – Memorandum and articles

14.1 **A company's constitution**
14.2 **Memorandum of association**
14.3 **Articles of association**
14.4 Form and content of articles
14.5 Alteration of articles – the law
14.6 Alteration of articles – the practical issues
14.7 Entrenched provisions of the articles
14.8 Filing requirements, etc
14.9 Effect of alteration of articles on company's members
14.10 **Resolutions and agreements affecting a company's constitution**
14.11 **Constitutional documents to be provided to members**
14.12 **Effect of company's constitution**
14.13 **Alteration of company's constitution by enactment or order**

Cross-references. See **12 Company Formation and Types of Companies** and **Appendix 4 Standard Articles of Association.**

Background. The provisions in this chapter apply, unless otherwise stated, with effect from 1 October 2009.

14.1 A COMPANY'S CONSTITUTION

Before 1 October 2009 the constitution of a company incorporated under the Companies Act was comprised in the memorandum of association and the articles of association. Articles (typically based on *Table A 1985 (SI 1985 No 805)*), were concerned with the company's internal management and as such could be changed by special resolution by the members. The memorandum of association could only be changed in ways specified by *CA 1985* given that it contained the company's objects and the basis on which the company was incorporated (for example the authorised share capital of the company).

From 1 October 2009 the constitution of a company has been defined [*CA 2006, s 17*] as;

- the company's articles; and
- any resolutions and agreements to which *CA 2006, Chapter 3* applies (see *section 29*). *Section 29* then sets out which resolutions and agreements affect a company's constitution.

Other parts of *CA 2006* give a wider meaning to "constitution"– see *CA 2006, s 257* where references to a company's constitution include resolutions and decisions made by members of the company.

Before 1 October 2009, where any provision of *CA 2006* which came into force before that date refers to the company's articles (including above), this is to be taken as including a reference to the company's memorandum. [*SI 2007 No 2194, Sch 1 para 1*].

14.2 MEMORANDUM OF ASSOCIATION

The memorandum of a company incorporated on or after 1 October 2009 is a statement that the subscribers wish to form a company under the *CA 2006* and agree to become members of the company and, in the case of a company with share capital, to take at least one share each [*CA 2006, s 8*]. It must be in a prescribed form set out in the *Companies (Registration) Regulations 2008 (SI 2008 No 3014)* in order to comply with the registration requirements of the *CA 2006* [*ss 7–12*]. It is in effect a short form, historical document used only on incorporation and thereafter not capable of alteration.

Effect on the memorandum of companies incorporated before 1 October 2009. Provisions that immediately before 1 October 2009 were contained in a company's memorandum but are not provisions of the kind to be included in the new-style memorandum under *CA 2006, s 8* (see **12 Company Formation and Types of Companies**) are treated, with effect from 1 October 2009, as provisions of the company's articles. This applies not only to substantive provisions but also to provisions for entrenchment. Where the memorandum of a company incorporated before that date contained entrenching provisions, those provisions are deemed with effect from that date, to be entrenching provisions of the company's articles .[*CA 2006, s 28*].

Objects. As from 1 October 2009 a company's objects are unrestricted unless the company's articles provide otherwise [*CA 2006, s 31(1)*]. A company incorporated on or after 1 October 2009 may adopt restricted objects which would have to be set out in the articles of association. A company incorporated before that date whose objects are restricted but which wants to have unrestricted objects will need to amend its articles.

Share capital. From 1 October 2009 companies have not been required to have an upper limit on share capital (authorised share capital). If the memorandum of a company incorporated before 1 October 2009 provides for an authorised share capital this is deemed to form a provision of its articles (see above) and can be removed by ordinary resolution.

Limitation of liability. For companies incorporated on or after 1 October 2009, the prescribed form memorandum (see above and *CA 2006, s 8*) does not include a limitation of liability statement. The statement has instead in the case of a company limited by shares or by guarantee, to be included in the articles. The Model Articles for both private and public companies (see **Appendix 4 standard articles of association**) provide for limitation of members liability. If a company's articles exclude the Model Articles it should ensure that a limited liability statement is included in its articles.

14.3 ARTICLES OF ASSOCIATION

Historically companies' articles of association adopted *Table A 1985* (or *Table A 1948* for companies incorporated before *Table A 1985* came into force) in whole or in part. *Table A 1985* was replaced on 1 October 2009 by the Model Articles for private and public companies (see *Schedules 1* and *3* to the *Companies (Model Articles) Regulations 2008 (SI 2008 No 3229)* set out in **Appendix 4**).

The Model Articles were amended with effect from 28 April 2013 to remove the provision which allowed companies to terminate a director's appointment on the grounds of mental health. The Model Articles do not duplicate provisions in *CA 2006* (for example the provisions for resolutions and meetings). It is therefore important to bear this in mind if a company incorporated on or after 1 October 2009 is either adopting the Model Articles (unamended) on incorporation or, after incorporation if it is adopting new articles based on the Model Articles. In most cases thought needs to be given whether amendments or additions need to be made to the articles whether or not a company was incorporated before 1 October 2009 and still has *Table A* or is adopting the Model Articles. (See **14.6 Alteration of articles - the practical issues**).

The starting point in law is that every company must have articles of association on incorporation. It must register the articles with the Registrar of Companies at the same time as it registers the memorandum of association. See **12.3 Company formation and types of companies**.

Articles of association registered by a company must

- be contained in a single document; and
- be divided into paragraphs numbered consecutively

[*CA 2006, s 218*].

A company's articles are rules, chosen by the members, governing the company's internal affairs and form an integral and, after 1 October 2009, the main part of the company's constitution. All the company's key internal rules on matters such as the allocation of powers between members and its directors are set out in the articles.

14.4 Form and content of articles

The form of a company's articles depends on the date of incorporation (see **14.1** and **14.3**). The important thing to note is that the articles adopted by a company (or as subsequently altered) will continue to apply to that company unless and until they are changed.

A company incorporated on after 1 October 2009 may adopt all or any of the provisions of the Model Articles which can be made by reference. This is common where a company wishes to incorporate specific provisions of the model articles. For example, a company's registered articles may read 'The Model Articles apply except for articles X, Y and Z' or 'Model Article A applies but is amended as follows'.

Default application of Model Articles. On the formation of a limited company

- if articles are not registered, or
- if articles are registered, in so far as they do not exclude or modify the relevant Model Articles,

the relevant Model Articles prescribed for a company of that description (so far as applicable) form part of the company's articles in the same manner and to the same extent as if articles in the form of those articles had been duly registered.

[*CA 2006, s 20*].

Companies not limited by shares. In the case of company incorporated between 1 July 1985 and 30 September 2009 which is

- a company limited by guarantee and not having a share capital,
- a company limited by guarantee and having a share capital, or
- an unlimited company having a share capital,

the form of the articles must be respectively in accordance with *Table C, D,* or *E* set out in *SI 1985 No 805* or as near as circumstances permit. [*CA 1985, s 8(4)* before repeal by *CA 2006*]. In the case of a company incorporated on or after 1 October 2009 as a private company limited by guarantee, the form of the model articles is in *SI 2008 No 3229, Sch 2.* None of these model articles are reproduced in this book.

Charitable companies. A model memorandum and articles of association for use by charitable companies can be downloaded from the Law Commission website at www.charity-commission.gov.uk.

14.5 Alteration of articles – the law

Alteration by special resolution of members. Subject to the rules on entrenchment in **14.7**, a company may amend its articles by special resolution (see **42.3** RESOLUTIONS AND MEETINGS). But this does not apply to the provisions of the articles (including provisions of the company's memorandum that are treated as provisions of the articles) of a company incorporated before 1 October 2009 where the articles were not capable of being so amended immediately before 1 October 2009.

The *Small Business, Enterprise and Employment Act 2015 (SBEE 2015)*, ss 84 and 85 provide (in summary) that a company may not (after May 2015) issue share warrants to bearer. If the company's articles authorise the company to issue share warrants, the articles can be amended to remove that provision without the need for a special resolution and without complying with any provision for entrenchment which is relevant to the provision for share warrants. A copy of the articles when amended must be sent to the Registrar of Companies (see **14.8**).

[*SBEE 2015, ss 84, 85, 164*].

Charities. Note also that the amendment of articles by special resolution is, in the case of a company that is

- a charity, subject to *Charities Act 2011, ss 197* and *198* (in Northern Ireland *Charities (Northern Ireland) Order 1987 (SI 1987 No 2048), Art 9*); and
- registered in the Scottish Charity Register, subject to *CA 1989, s 162* and *Charities and Trustee Investment (Scotland) Act 2005, s 16*.

[*CA 2006, s 21; SI 2008 No 2860, Sch 2 para 4*].

Private companies may also alter their articles without a special resolution in meeting by means of a written resolution. See **42.5 Resolutions and Meetings**.

Restrictions on alteration. Apart from the above restrictions and specific statutory restrictions, any requirements of the Listing Rules and the rules on entrenchment in **14.7**, a company is free to alter its articles as it wishes, and it must not nullify or restrict its ability to alter them. See *Allen v Gold Reefs of West Africa Ltd* [1900] 1 Ch 656, CA, and *Russell v Northern Bank Development Corpn Ltd* [1992] 3 All ER 161, [1992] BCLC 1016, HL. This applies even if to do so would involve a breach of contract with a third party. Such a third party would, however, be entitled to damages for the breach (*Southern Foundries (1926) Ltd v Shirlaw* [1940] AC 701, [1940] 2 All ER 445, HL).

Any alteration must be made *bona fide* for the benefit of the company as a whole. See *Allen v Gold Reefs of West Africa Ltd* above (creation of a lien on fully paid shares); *Brown v British Abrasive Wheel Co* [1919] 1 Ch 290, 88 LJ Ch 143 (compulsory purchase of minority shares); and *Sidebottom v Kershaw, Leese & Co Ltd* [1920] 1 Ch 154, 89 LJ Ch 113, CA (forced sale of shares by shareholders carrying on business in direct competition). Whether such an alteration is for the company's benefit is for the shareholders to decide, and the court will intervene only if it considers the alteration to be such that no reasonable person would consider it to be in the interests of the company (*Shuttleworth v Cox Bros & Co (Maidenhead) Ltd* [1927] 2 KB 9, 96 LJKB 104, CA). As to the meaning of '*bona fide* for the benefit of the company as a whole', see *Greenhalgh v Arderne Cinemas Ltd* [1951] Ch 286, [1950] 2 All ER 1120, CA.

See also generally *Peter's American Delicacy Co Ltd v Heath* (1939) 61 CLR 457, Aust HC.

14.6 Alteration of articles – the practical issues

The following practical issues are based on:

- the fact that pre 1 October 2009 articles based on *Table A* may not reflect changes made by *CA 2006* or any subsequent legislation; and

- the *Model Articles* are in minimal form and do not repeat or amend any provisions of *CA 2006* (for example provisions for proxies).

The practical issues are categorised for the purposes of this chapter as: 1) general issues with, where relevant, references to *Table A 1985* and/or the *Model Articles* 2) issues specific to *Table A 1985*, where relevant referring to numbered regulations in *Table A* and 3) issues specific to the *Model Articles* (again where relevant) referring to numbered articles and also whether the issue affects only the *Model Articles* for private companies or the *Model Articles* for public companies (or both).

Table A 1985 and the *Model Articles* are set out in **Appendix 4 standard articles of association**.

1. General issues

Electronic communication. Do the articles contain provision for electronic communication to and from members? Under *CA 2006* companies are able to send a wide range of documents both electronically and by posting them on a website provided that the requirements of *CA 2006 ss 308, 309, 333, 1143–1148* and *Schedules 4* and *5* are complied with and in the case of fully listed companies they comply with the electronic communication provisions in the FCA's Disclosure and Transparency Rules.

There is no statutory requirement to amend the articles to permit electronic communication but:

- a company can assume that a member has agreed to accept communications posted on a website (the so called 'deemed' agreement in *CA 2006*) if either the member has agreed to receive documents by means of a website or an ordinary resolution has been passed resolving that the company can send documents to members by means of a website or there is a provision in the articles to that effect
- there is some debate whether *CA 2006, s 1134* which sets out what can be sent to and from a company includes for example online voting as it refers only to 'documents or information'. It is preferable therefore to make this clear in the articles
- if members send documents to the company there are two relevant provisions. The first is that if the company includes an electronic address in either a notice of meeting or proxy, it is deemed to have agreed to receive documents relating to that meeting or proxy by electronic means and at the address set out. Secondly for all other documents *CA 2006, Sch 4, Part 3, para 6* provides that documents can only be sent electronically to the company if the company expressly agrees. The articles therefore could be amended to provide that only specific types of documents can be sent electronically and to set out how the company wants the sender's identity to be confirmed. If the articles do not expressly set this out then the default position is that a document is 'authenticated' if it contains or is accompanied by a statement of identity of the sender and the company has no reason to doubt the truth of the statement [*CA 2006, s 1146*].
- it is better practice to ensure the articles are consistent with *CA 2006* provisions to avoid confusion and make it clear what can or cannot be sent electronically.

2. Company objects

See **14.2** above that as from 1 October 2009 a company has unrestricted objects unless its articles provided otherwise. The *Model Articles* therefore do not include an objects clause. If a company is incorporated after 1 October 2009 and adopts the model articles but wants to have restricted objects it will have to amend its articles.

The objects of a company incorporated before 1 October 2009 and which are contained in its memorandum are deemed to form part of its articles [*CA 2006, s 28*]. If such a company whose objects are restricted wants to have unrestricted objects, the articles will need to be amended either to remove the objects altogether or to amend them.

Charitable companies. Any amendment of the articles of a charitable company to add, remove or alter the company's objects is a "regulated" alteration which requires the prior written consent of the Charity Commission and is ineffective if such consent has not been obtained. Any such regulated alteration is governed by *CA 2006, ss 26, 30* and *31* as to the requirements to notify the Registrar of Companies (see **14.8, 14.10**)

[*Charities Act 2011, s 198*]

3. Consolidation/sub-division of share capital/purchase of own shares

CA 2006 does not require a company to have shareholder approval to consolidate or sub-divide capital or purchase its own shares. If there are such restrictions in pre 1 October 2009 articles (see *Table A 1985, regulations 32* and *34*) removing them means that the articles will not need to be amended (and filed) on each change of capital. Alternatively a pre 1 October 2009 company could retain such restrictions and a post 1 October 2009 could include them as *CA 2006, s 618(5)* provides that a company's articles can exclude or restrict the power to change capital without authority and *s 690(1)* provides that a company can purchase its own shares subject to any prohibition or restriction in the company's articles.

4. Share capital reduction (private companies only)

See **47.51** Shares that as from 1 October 2008 a private company has been able to reduce share capital without the need for a court application provided it complies with *CA 2006, ss 641–644*.

This is subject to any provision of the company's articles which restricts or prohibits a reduction of capital. Any such restrictions or prohibitions would need to be removed. *Table A, regulation 32* only requires an ordinary resolution to cancel shares and diminish share capital, The Model Articles for private companies contain no restrictions or prohibitions.

5. Directors' age restrictions

Provisions which prevent a director remaining in office or being re-elected to office after a specific age are potentially discriminatory and should be removed. Neither *Table A* or the *Model Articles* contain such provisions.

6. Authorised share capital

(Formerly found in the memorandum of association but sometimes provision was, pre 1 October 2009, also included in the articles). See **47.6** Shares, that as from 1 October 2009 there is no requirement to have an upper limit on authorised share capital. Companies incorporated before that date with an upper limit in the memorandum, which is deemed as from that date to form provisions of the articles by virtue of *CA 2006, s 28* continue to be subject to that limit unless and until the articles are amended. The *Model Articles* contain no provision for authorised share capital.

7. Proxies

On a vote on a show of hands if a proxy has been appointed by more than one member the proxy has one vote 'for' and one vote 'against' the resolution provided that the proxy has been instructed by one or more of those members to vote for the resolution and by one or more of those members to vote against it [*CA 2006, s 285(2)*]. This is subject to anything in the company's articles. See *Table A, regulation 54* which only provides for single voting and note that if a company was incorporated before 1 October 2007, *regulation 54* (if not later amended) did not refer to a right for a proxy to vote on a show of hands. The *Model Articles* make no provision for how proxies should vote.

8. AGMs (private companies only)

As from 1 October 2007 *CA 2006* removed the requirement for private companies to hold an AGM. There is however nothing in *CA 2006* which prevents a private company holding an AGM. Consider whether the company needs to hold an AGM and, if not, check the articles for any provision which requires the holding of an AGM (see for example *Table A 1985* which does not require the holding of an AGM but does, pre 1 October 2007, at *regulations 36* and *38* refer to notice of AGM). If the company does not intend to hold AGMs other changes to the articles may also be needed (see for the example the need for directors to retire by rotation in pre 1 October 2007 *Table A 1985* at *regulations 73–76*).

If a company was incorporated after 1 October 2007 and adopted *Table A 1985* unamended or after 1 October 2009 and adopted the *Model Articles* unamended and wants to hold AGMs, it may need to add provisions back in to the articles to regulate both notice of AGM and the holding of an AGM. The Model Articles for public companies contain provisions which could be included in the articles of a private company where necessary.

9. Notice of general meetings

The Model Articles for private companies are silent on the issue of calling and providing notice of general meetings.

CA 2006 provides that only 14 days notice of general meetings (ie not AGMs or meetings requiring special notice to remove directors or auditors) needs to be given. Check the articles to see whether longer notice (eg 21 days) needs to be given and amend if necessary.

Traded companies. If the company is 'traded' (see **Appendix 1 Definitions** for the meaning of traded) the following conditions must be met to take advantage of the 14 day notice period

- the general meeting must not be an AGM
- the company must offer the facility for members to vote by electronic means. This condition is met if there is a facility to appoint a proxy by means of a website. ICSA guidance (ICSA Guidance on the Implementation of the Shareholder Rights Directive July 2009) suggests that offering electronic voting through CREST does not meet the 'electronic means' requirement. To comply a company would need to offer electronic proxy appointment to all their shareholders by means of a website. The facility does not necessarily have to be on the company's own website – it could be hosted for example on a registrar's website.
- a special resolution reducing the notice period to not less than 14 days has been passed either at the preceding AGM or at a general meeting held since the AGM. If the company has not held an AGM the resolution has to be passed at a general meeting (see *CA 2006, ss 307* and *307A*).

All companies: the company's articles may require a longer period of notice (see *CA 2006, s 307(3)* and *307A(6)* and *Table A 1985, regulation 85*). See **42.14 Resolutions and Meetings**.

10. Share capital redenomination

Section 622 of *CA 2006* allows a company to redenominate the whole, or any class of, share capital, into other currencies but provides that the company's articles may prohibit or restrict the power to do this.

11. Directors' conflicts of interest

The directors of a private company can authorise other directors' conflicts of interests [*CA 2006, s 175(5)(a)*] provided that

- there is nothing in the company's constitution that invalidates that authorisation (*s 175(5)(a)*)
- the quorum for the meeting is met without counting the conflicted director and any other interested director (*s 175(6)(a)*)
- the matter is agreed without the conflicted director or any other interested director voting (or would have been agreed if their votes had not been counted) (*s 175(6)(b)*).

Consider whether any limits should be imposed in the articles either on the types of conflicts which can be authorised and/or any procedures to be followed or restrictions to be imposed.

Public companies. Similar provisions (as above) apply as for private companies except that the company's constitution must positively provide for directors' authorisation of conflicts ie provision must be made in the company's articles. *Table A 1985, regulations 84* and *85* provide for limited situations in which a director may be a party to or interested in transactions or arrangements with the company but do not expressly provide for other conflicts of interest. *Regulation 94* limited the situations in which a director can vote and be counted in the quorum where he has a conflict of interest. The *Model Articles* (at *article 14* for private companies and *article 16* for public companies) provide for participation in the quorum and voting where conflicts arise.

12. Company name

CA 2006, s 77(1)(b) allows a company to change its name by any means provided for in the articles, for example by allowing the directors to change the name. This is in addition to the usual means of changing a name by special resolution of the shareholders. Neither *Table A 1985* nor the *Model Articles* contain alternate means of changing the company name.

13. Employees

CA 2006, s 247 enables the directors to make provision for employees/former employees employed either by the company or any of its subsidiaries on cessation or transfer of the company's business provided that any board resolution is authorised by the articles. *Section 247* largely reproduces *CA 1985, s 719*. *Table A 1985* made no such provision (although *regulation 87* enables the directors to provide for directors' gratuities and pensions). The *Model Articles* at *article 51* for private companies and *84* for public companies enable the directors to make such provision for employees.

14 Nomination and information rights

The articles can enable a shareholder to nominate a third party to 'enjoy or exercise all or any of the specified rights of the member' (see *CA 2006, s 145*). If a company is traded company (see Appendix 1 Definitions) members can nominate third parties to enjoy information rights ie the right to receive copies of communications that the company sends to its members and the right to require copies of accounts and reports and to require hard copies of documents provided 'in other forms' (see *CA 2006, s 146*). These statutory information rights do not depend on anything in the company's articles.

Neither *Table A 1985* or the *Model Articles* contain such provisions.

15 Conflicting provisions of *CA 2006*

Certain provisions of *CA 2006* may conflict with or override the company's articles. Check the following to determine whether the articles need amending

- appointment of proxies (see *CA 2006, s 324, 327(2)* and *330(6)*
- time for delivery of proxies (see *CA 2006, s 327(3)*)
- voting on a poll (see *CA 2006, s 285A*)
- appointment of multiple corporate representatives (see *CA 2006, s 323*)
- refusal of transfer of shares (see *CA 2006, s 771*)
- percentage of members who can requisition a general meeting of a private or non traded public company (see *CA 2006, s 303*)

16 Attendance and speaking at general meetings

The Model Articles do not, in the way that Table A attempted to, set out provisions for attending and speaking at general meetings. Instead they are permissive and allow the directors to make any arrangements appropriate to enable those attending a general meeting to exercise their rights to speak or vote at it. The Model Articles do not set out what those arrangements should be.

Issues specific to Table A 1985 (or articles based on Table A 1985)

EGMs and extraordinary resolutions. *CA 2006* refers only to AGMs and general meetings and special and ordinary resolutions (see *CA 2006, ss 281, 282* and *283*) and not to EGMs and extraordinary resolutions. *Table A 1985* refers to extraordinary resolutions (see for example *regulation 117* 'winding up') and that all general meetings other than AGMs are called EGMs (see *regulation 36*).

Although it is not strictly incorrect to continue to refer to EGMs and extraordinary resolutions, for consistency with *CA 2006* the terms should be changed. If not transitional provisions in *paragraph 23* of *Sch 3* to the *CA 2006 Third Commencement Order 2007 (SI 2007 No 2194)* expressly say that any reference to an extraordinary resolution in a company's articles continues to have effect and shall continue to be construed in accordance with *CA 1985, s 378* "as if that section had not been repealed".

Old statutory references. Old statutory references to provisions which have either been repealed or replaced by provisions of *CA 2006* need to be checked for any inconsistency/change in meaning.

Share capital (private companies only). Private companies no longer need shareholder approval to allot redeemable shares or to redeem or purchase shares out of capital. Consider removing any restrictions in the articles (see for example *regulation 3* of *Table A* which says that redeemable shares may only be issued subject to 'the Act' ie *CA 1985*).

Company secretary (private companies only). As from 6 April 2008 private companies have not been required to have a company secretary but if, at that time, the articles expressly required the company to have a secretary it must have one. *Table A 1985* does not specifically require companies to appoint a secretary.

Notice of members' meetings (private companies only). *CA 2006, s 307(6)* reduced the percentage required to consent to short notice from 95% to 90%. If the articles require 95% consent, consider reducing it to the statutory limit although this is not obligatory as *s 307(6)(a)* does say "90% or such higher percentage (not exceeding 95%) as may be specified in the company's articles".

Written resolutions (private companies only). Under *CA 2006, s 296(4)* written resolutions do not need unanimous consent to be passed but only the required majority. Consider removing the need for unanimous consent if it is included in the articles. *Table A 1985* does not refer to the majority required for written resolutions.

2007 changes. SIs *2007 No 2541* and *2007 No 2826* made substantial changes to *Table A 1985* as a consequence of which companies incorporated on or after 1 October 2007 adopted an amended *Table A*.

Issues specific to the Model Articles

Share capital (private companies only). The *Model Articles* (*Article 21.8*) for private companies assume that all shares are issued fully paid and so make no provisions for liens, calls on shares or forfeiture of shares.

Directors' meetings. The following amendments need to be considered for the *Model Articles* for both private and public companies:

- Calling the meeting. The *Model Articles* do not provide a period of notice for calling a directors meeting but do provide that the notice of meeting does not need to be in writing.
- Unanimous decisions. It is not clear whether the *Model Articles* anticipate that if directors sign multiple copies of written resolutions each copy has to be signed by each director.
- Participating in meetings. The *Model Articles* enable directors to participate in meetings wherever the directors are and however they communicate with each other.

Alternate directors (private companies only). The *Model Articles* for private companies do not provide for the appointment of alternates.

Authority to allot shares. Private companies with one class of shares incorporated after 1 October 2009 do not need authority in the articles to allot shares. The company can however choose to include in its articles an express prohibition on allotment without authority [*CA 2006, s 550*]. This type of private company incorporated before 1 October 2009 needs to 'opt in' to the new *CA 2006* regime by passing an ordinary resolution (which may also have the effect of altering the articles).

Private companies with more than one class of shares/public companies incorporated after 1 October 2009 still need to give directors authority in the articles (or by ordinary resolution) to allot shares [*CA 2006, s 551*].

Article 43 of the *Model Articles* for public companies provides that the company may issues shares with such rights or restrictions as the company may by ordinary resolution determine.

14.7 Entrenched provisions of the articles

A company's articles may contain *provisions for entrenchment* ie specified provisions of the articles may be amended or repealed only if conditions are met, or procedures are complied with, that are more restrictive than those applicable in the case of a special resolution. [*CA 2006, s 22(1)*]

Provision for entrenchment may only be made

- in the company's articles on formation; or

- by an amendment of the company's articles agreed to by *all* the members of the company. (*CA 2006, s22(2)*)

Section 22(2) has not been brought into force (see the *Companies Act 2006* and *LLPs (Transitional Provisions and Savings) (Amendment) Regulations 2009 (SI 2009 No 2476)*. See the BIS website at FAQs on Articles of Association for details of this.

Provision for entrenchment does not prevent amendment of the company's articles

(a) by agreement of all the members of the company; or

(b) by order of a court or other authority having power to alter the company's articles.

The members cannot (as in (a) above) agree to amend provisions of the articles (including provisions of the company's memorandum that are treated as provisions of the articles of a company incorporated before 1 October 2009) which were not capable of being so amended immediately before that date.

Notice to Registrar of Companies. Where a company's articles

(a) on formation contain provision for entrenchment (but see above for the non-commencement of *s 22(2)*)

(b) are amended so as to include such provision,

(c) are altered by order of a court or other authority so as to restrict or exclude the power of the company to amend its articles under (*b*),

(d) are amended so as to remove provision for entrenchment, or

(e) are altered by order of a court or other authority so as to remove

  (i) such provision under (*d*), or

  (ii) any other restriction on, or any exclusion of, the power of the company to amend its articles,

the company must give notice of that fact to the Registrar of Companies.

[*CA 2006, s 23*].

Statement of compliance where amendment of articles restricted. Where a company's articles are subject to

- provision for entrenchment, or
- an order of a court or other authority restricting or excluding the company's power to amend the articles

if the company amends its articles and is required to send to the Registrar of Companies a document making or evidencing the amendment, the company must deliver with that document a statement of compliance. This is a statement certifying that the amendment has been made in accordance with the company's articles and, where relevant, any applicable order of a court or other authority. The Registrar of Companies may rely on the statement of compliance as sufficient evidence of the matters stated in it.

[*CA 2006, s 24*].

14.8 Filing requirements, etc

Copies of amended articles to Registrar of Companies. If a company amends its articles, it must send a copy of the articles as amended to the Registrar of Companies, not later than 15 days after the amendment takes effect. If the company's articles are amended on or after 1 October 2009 (or pre 1 October 2009 amendments take effect after that date) the company can either append a copy of the old style memorandum to its articles or send a copy of the old style memorandum indicating which provisions are deemed to be part of the articles. If a company fails to comply with these provisions, an offence is committed by the company and every officer of the company who is in default. A person guilty of such an offence is liable, on summary conviction, to a fine not exceeding level 3 on the standard scale and, for continued contravention, a daily default fine not exceeding one-tenth of level 3 on the standard scale. See **29.1 Offences and Legal Proceedings** for the standard scale.

[*CA 2006, s 26; SI 2008 No 2860, Sch 2 para 6*].

The Registrar of Companies must ensure that notice of receipt of the amended articles is published (see **39.8 Registrar of Companies**). A company cannot rely on any amendment of its articles unless, at the material time, the amendment has been published or the company shows that the person concerned knew of the amendment. But if the material time falls within 15 days of publication and the person concerned can show that he was unavoidably prevented from knowing of the event at that time, the company still cannot rely on the amendment as against that person. [*CA 2006, s 1079*]. See **16.18 Dealings with Third Parties**.

Notice to comply by Registrar of Companies. If it appears to the Registrar of Companies that a company has failed to comply with the above provisions (or a similar requirement in earlier legislation) requiring it to send to him

- a document making or evidencing an alteration in the company's articles, or
- a copy of the company's articles as amended,

the Registrar of Companies may give notice to the company requiring it to comply. The notice must state the date on which it is issued and require the company to comply within 28 days from that date.

If the company complies with the notice within the specified time, no criminal proceedings may be brought in respect of the failure to comply. But if the company does not comply with the notice within the specified time, it is liable to a civil penalty of £200. This is in addition to any liability to criminal proceedings in respect of the failure.

[*CA 2006, s 27*].

14.9 Effect of alteration of articles on company's members

Unless a member agrees to the alteration in writing (before or after the alteration is made), he is not bound by an alteration to the articles if and so far as the alteration

- requires him to take or subscribe for more shares than the number held by him at the date on which the alteration is made; or
- in any way increases his liability as at that date to contribute to the company's share capital or otherwise to pay money to the company.

[*CA 2006, s 25*].

14.10 RESOLUTIONS AND AGREEMENTS AFFECTING A COMPANY'S CONSTITUTION

A copy of each of the following resolutions or agreements (or, in the case of a resolution or agreement that is not in writing, a written memorandum setting out its terms) must be forwarded to the Registrar of Companies within 15 days after it is passed or made.

- Any special resolution. (see **42.3 Resolutions and Meetings**).
- Any resolution or agreement agreed to by all the members of a company that, if not so agreed to, would not have been effective for its purpose unless passed as a special resolution.
- Any resolution or agreement agreed to by all the members of a class of shareholders that, if not so agreed to, would not have been effective for its purpose unless passed by some particular majority or otherwise in some particular manner.
- Any resolution or agreement that effectively binds all members of a class of shareholders though not agreed to by all those members.
- Any other resolution or agreement to which this paragraph applies by virtue of any enactment.

References above to a member of a company, or of a class of members of a company, do not include the company itself where it is such a member by virtue only of its holding shares as treasury shares.

If a company fails to comply with the above provisions, an offence is committed by the company and every officer of it (which for these purposes includes a liquidator) who is in default. A person guilty of such an offence is liable, on summary conviction, to a fine not exceeding level 3 on the standard scale and, for continued contravention, a daily default fine not exceeding one-tenth of level 3 on the standard scale. See **29.1 offences and legal proceedings** for the standard scale.

[*CA 2006, ss 29, 30*].

14.11 CONSTITUTIONAL DOCUMENTS TO BE PROVIDED TO MEMBERS

A company must on request send a member the following documents.

- An up-to-date copy of the company's articles.

  When complying with the obligation to send the articles, if the articles are deemed to incorporate provisions of the memorandum a company can either append a copy of the provisions of the old style memorandum which are deemed to be provisions of the articles or can send a copy of the old-style memorandum indicating which provisions are deemed to be provisions of the articles (*SI 2008 No 2860, art 5, Sch 2, para 9*).
- A copy of any resolution or agreement relating to the company to which *CA 2006, ss 29, 30* apply (see **14.10**).
- A copy of any document required to be sent to the Registrar of Companies under *CA 2006, s 34(2)* (notice where company's constitution altered by special enactment) or *CA 2006, s 35(2)(a)* (notice where order of court or other authority alters company's constitution).
- A copy of any court order under *CA 2006, s 899* (order sanctioning compromise or arrangement) or *CA 2006, s 900* (order facilitating reconstruction or amalgamation). See **35.3** and **35.4 Reconstructions and Mergers**.
- A copy of any court order under *CA 2006, s 996* (protection of members against unfair prejudice: powers of the court) that alters the company's constitution. See **26.5, Members**.
- A copy of the company's current certificate of incorporation, and of any past certificates of incorporation.

- In the case of a company with a share capital, a current statement of capital, ie
  (a) the total number of shares of the company;
  (b) the aggregate nominal value of those shares; The *SBEE 2015* introduces a requirement to also include in the statement of capital the aggregate amount (if any) unpaid on those shares (whether on account of their nominal value or by way of premium). As at May 2015 this provision is not in force.
  (c) for each class of shares
    (i) particulars of any voting rights attached to the shares, including rights that arise only in certain circumstances;
    (ii) particulars of any rights attached to the shares, as respects dividends, to participate in a distribution;
    (iii) particulars of any rights attached to the shares, as respects capital, to participate in a distribution (including on a winding up);
    (iv) whether the shares are to be redeemed or are liable to be redeemed at the option of the company or the shareholder;
    (v) the total number of shares of that class; and
    (vi) the aggregate nominal value of shares of that class; and
  (d) the amount paid up and the amount (if any) unpaid on each share (whether on account of the nominal value of the share or by way of premium).
- In the case of a company limited by guarantee, a copy of the statement of guarantee.

If a company defaults in complying with the above provisions, an offence is committed by every officer of the company who is in default. A person guilty of such an offence is liable, on summary conviction, to a fine not exceeding level 3 on the standard scale. See 29.1 OFFENCES AND LEGAL PROCEEDINGS for the standard scale.

[*CA 2006, s 32; SI 2009 No 388, Art 2*].

Inspection of the articles. Any person may inspect a copy of the articles at Companies House and may obtain a certified copy of the articles on payment of the prescribed fee. See APPENDIX 3 FEES.

14.12 EFFECT OF COMPANY'S CONSTITUTION

The provisions of a company's constitution bind the company and its members to the same extent as if there were covenants on the part of the company and of each member, to observe those provisions.

In relation to liabilities arising on or after 1 October 2009, money payable by a member to the company under its constitution is a debt due from him to the company. In England and Wales and Northern Ireland it is of the nature of an ordinary contract debt. (The provisions in *CA 1985, s 14(2)* continue to apply to liabilities arising before 1 October 2009 and for this purpose, a liability is treated as arising when the limitation period starts to run for the purposes of the *Limitation Act 1980*.)

[*CA 2006, s 33; SI 2009 No 1941, Art 11*].

The above wording (which broadly follows the earlier wording in *CA 1985, s 14(1)* except that it refers to 'a company's constitution' rather than its 'memorandum and articles') does not make very clear the nature of the relationship which it creates between one member and another and between a member and the company. As a result, there have been numerous court cases on the relationships.

Between members. The cases seem to indicate that, even if the articles do constitute a contract between the members of a company, generally the rights bestowed by the articles can only be enforced through the company or, where the company is being wound up, through the liquidator (*Welton v Saffery* [1897] AC 299, HL).

However, in some cases, the court has adopted a different approach, most notably in *Rayfield v Hands* [1960] Ch 1, [1958] 2 All ER 194 where the company's articles required the directors to be members of the company, and also required any member proposing to transfer shares in the company to inform the directors 'who will take the shares equally between them at a fair value'. It was held that a member could compel the directors to purchase his shares in accordance with this provision as the relationship was between the plaintiff as a member and the defendants not as directors but as members.

Nevertheless, the general view appears to be that *Welton v Saffery* still represents the principle which will normally be applied and the reasoning in *Rayfield v Hands* is probably only applicable where the articles give one member a personal right as against another member.

Between the company and its members. The general principle is that the articles constitute a contract between the company and its members in relation to their rights and obligations as members. In *Hickman v Kent or Romney Marsh Sheep-Breeders' Association* [1915] 1 Ch 881, 84 LJ Ch 688 the court granted the company a stay of proceedings brought against it by a member who was disputing his expulsion from the company. The articles provided that disputes between the company and its members were to go to arbitration, and by bringing the action, the member was acting contrary to the articles. Similarly, in *Wood v Odessa Waterworks Co* (1889) 42 Ch D 636, a member was granted an injunction restraining the company from acting on a resolution which was contrary to the articles.

However, the general principle applies only where the articles confer a right on a member in his capacity as a member. Thus, in *Eley v Positive Government Security Life Assurance Co Ltd* (1876) 1 Ex D 88, CA, the articles stated that the plaintiff was to be employed for life as the company's solicitor. When the company ceased to employ him, the plaintiff was held not to be entitled to damages for breach of contract, because the articles did not constitute a contract between the company and the plaintiff in a capacity other than as a member. (See also *Beattie v E & F Beattie Ltd* [1938] Ch 708, [1938] 3 All ER 214, CA.)

14.13 ALTERATION OF COMPANY'S CONSTITUTION BY ENACTMENT OR ORDER

Alteration by enactment. *In relation to any enactment coming into force on or after 1 October 2009*, where a company's constitution is altered by an enactment (other than an enactment amending the general law), the company must give notice of the alteration to the Registrar of Companies, specifying the enactment, not later than 15 days after the enactment comes into force. In the case of a 'special enactment' the notice must be accompanied by a copy of the enactment. [*CA 2006, s 34(1)(2); SI 2008 No 2860, Sch 2 para 12*].

If the enactment amends

- the company's articles, or
- a resolution or agreement under **14.10**,

the notice must be accompanied by a copy of the company's articles, or the resolution or agreement in question, as amended.

A '*special enactment*' means an enactment that is not a public general enactment, and includes

- an Act for confirming a provisional order;
- any provision of a public general Act in relation to the passing of which any of the standing orders of the House of Lords or the House of Commons relating to Private Business applied; or
- any enactment to the extent that it is incorporated or applied for the purposes of a special enactment.

[*CA 2006, s 34(3)(4)*].

In relation to any enactment coming into force before 1 October 2009, CA 1985, s 18 continues to apply.

Alteration by order. *In relation to orders made on or after 1 October 2009*, where a company's constitution is altered by an order of a court or other authority, the company must give notice to the Registrar of Companies of the alteration not later than 15 days after the alteration takes effect. The notice must be accompanied by

(a) a copy of the order; and

(b) if the order amends

(i) the company's articles, or

(ii) a resolution or agreement under **14.10**

a copy of the company's articles, or the resolution or agreement in question, as amended.

These provisions do not apply where another enactment provides for the delivery of a copy of the order in question to the Registrar of Companies.

[*CA 2006, s 35(1)(2)(5)*].

Penalties. If a company fails to comply with either of the above provisions, an offence is committed by the company and every officer of the company who is in default. A person guilty of such an offence is liable, on summary conviction, to a fine not exceeding level 3 on the standard scale and, for continued contravention, a daily default fine not exceeding one-tenth of level 3 on the standard scale. See **29.1 Offences and Legal Proceedings** for the standard scale.

[*CA 2006, ss 34(5)(6), 35(3)(4)*].

15 Corporate Governance

15.1	**Introduction**
15.2	**The UK regulatory framework**
15.2	The UK Corporate Governance Code
15.3	The UK Stewardship Code
15.4	The Listing Rules
15.5	The Disclosure and Transparency Rules
15.6	CA 2006 requirements
15.7	**Company committee structure**
15.7	The Structure
15.8	The Audit Committee
15.9	The Nomination Committee
15.10	The Remuneration Committee
15.11	The Risk Committee
15.12	Matters reserved to the board
15.13	Non-executive directors
15.14	Proposed reforms-executive remuneration and shareholder power
Appendix	**The UK Corporate Governance Code**

Cross-references. See **19 Directors' Remuneration Reports—Quoted Companies; 33 Public Companies; 42 Resolutions and Meetings.**

15.1 INTRODUCTION

Corporate Governance is not a term which is defined in *CA 2006*. but is generally accepted as meaning the system by which companies are managed and controlled. The general framework for corporate governance is:

- *CA 2006* (see **15.6** below)
- the Listing Rules (see **15.4** below) and the Disclosure and Transparency Rules (see **15.5** below) and
- the UK Corporate Governance Code (see **15.2** below) and the UK Stewardship Code for institutional shareholders ("the Stewardship Code" see **15.3** below)

The Financial Reporting Council (FRC) is responsible for corporate governance in the United Kingdom and as such also has responsibility to publish and maintain a single code of good corporate governance practice. This is now known as the UK Corporate Governance Code ("The Code") (formerly known as the Combined Code). Adherence to the Code is expected by institutional shareholders and committees of those shareholders (in particular NAPF and PIRC) publish their own best practice guidelines.

In general the system of corporate governance set out in the Code applies to larger listed companies ie companies with securities admitted to trading on the London Stock Exchange main market. Some of its provisions apply to companies in the FTSE 350 and are not obligatory for smaller listed companies. Smaller listed companies and unlisted companies (for example those companies with securities traded on the Alternative Investment Market) may choose to comply with the Code or comply with the QCA (Quoted Companies Alliance) corporate governance guidelines. Additionally the London Stock Exchange publishes a corporate governance guide 'Corporate Governance for main market and AIM companies'. On its corporate governance website page the Department for Business, Innovation and Skills (BIS) says that the most important elements of good corporate governance include:

- the timely provision by companies of good quality information;

- a clear and credible company decision making process; and
- shareholders giving proper consideration to the information provided and making considered judgements.

The FRC in its publication 'The UK approach to corporate governance' (available from the FRC website) says that the key aspects of corporate governance in the UK are:

- a single board collectively responsible for the sustainable success of the company;
- checks and balances including a separate chairman and chief executive, a balance of executive and independent non-executives, strong, independent audit and remuneration committees (see **15.8** and **15.10**) and annual evaluation by the board of its performance;
- transparency on appointments and remuneration; and
- effective rights for shareholders who are encouraged to engage with the companies in which they invest.

THE UK REGULATORY FRAMEWORK

15.2 The UK Corporate Governance Code

The Code sets out standards of good practice re board leadership and effectiveness, remuneration, accountability and relations with a company's shareholders. The Listing Rules require all companies with a premium listing of equity shares in the United Kingdom to report on how they have applied the main principles of the Code in their annual report and accounts and either to confirm that they have complied with the Code's provisions or, where they have not complied, explain why they have not (the so called "comply or explain" principle). For corporate governance systems to work effectively shareholders need rights to enable them to influence board behaviour when they are not happy with the approach the board has taken. Comply or explain therefore needs to be underpinned by a regulatory framework. This is achieved by provisions of *CA 2006* relating to voting and disclosure rights (see **42.38A Resolutions and Meetings** and **19 Directors' Remuneration Reports-Quoted Companies**) and provisions of the Listing Rules (see **15.4** below). The comply or explain principle has also been reinforced by the UK Stewardship Code (see **15.3** below) under which institutional investors report on their policies for monitoring and engaging with companies in which they invest.

The Code comprises main principles, supporting principles and framework provisions. It includes best practice in relation to:

- the role of non-executive directors ("NEDS") (see **15.13** below);
- remuneration of directors and the role of the remuneration committee (see **15.10** below);
- appointment of directors and the role of the nomination committee (see **15.9** below).

The FRC publishes guidance notes to assist companies in applying the principles of the Code. See the FRC website at www.frc.org for details. The Code is set out in full in the Appendix to this chapter. The Code is reviewed every two years and was last amended in 2014 (with changes taking effect for reporting periods beginning on or after

1 October 2014) Companies reporting on periods beginning before 1 October 2014 should continue to report against the 2012 edition of the Code although the FRC advises that they are 'encouraged to consider whether it would be beneficial to adopt some or all of the new provisions ....earlier than formally expected'.

15.3 The UK Stewardship Code

The Stewardship Code, published by the FRC, aims to:

- enhance the quality of engagement between institutional investors and companies;
- help improve the long term returns for investors; and
- help to promote the efficient exercise of governance responsibilities by setting out good practice on engagement with companies in which shareholders invest.

The FRC sees the Stewardship Code as complementary to the Code and that like the Code it should be applied on a comply or explain basis (see **15.2**). In the case of the Stewardship Code, the FRC expects signatories of the Code to publish on their website, or if they do not have a website, in another accessible form a statement that describes how the signatory has applied each of the seven principles of the Code and discloses the specific information requested in the guidance to the principles or if more than one of the principles have not been applied or the specific information requested in the guidance has not been disclosed, explains why the signatory has not complied with those elements of the Code. From October 2010 the FRC have been listing on its website all investors that have published reporting statements and encourages all institutional investors to publish on their websites a statement of the extent to which they have complied with the Stewardship Code and to notify the FRC when they have done so.

The Stewardship Code is aimed principally at those firms who manage assets on behalf of institutional investors and the Financial Services Authority (FCA) amended its Conduct of Business sourcebook to require a UK authorised firm managing investments to disclose:

- the nature of its commitment to the Stewardship Code; or
- if it does not commit to the Stewardship Code, its alternative Business Strategy (COBS 2.2.3).

The Stewardship Code comprises seven principles, each with related guidance. The principles require institutional investors to:

- publicly disclose their policy on how they will discharge their stewardship responsibilities (Principle 1);
- have a robust policy on managing conflicts of interest in relation to stewardship and publicly disclose this policy (Principle 2);
- monitor their investee companies (Principle 3);
- establish clear guidelines on when and how they will escalate their stewardship activities (Principle 4);
- be willing to act collectively with other investors where appropriate (Principle 5);
- have a clear policy on voting and disclosure of voting activity (Principle 6); and
- report periodically on their stewardship and voting activities (Principle 7).

The Stewardship Code is, like the Corporate Governance Code, reviewed regularly and was last updated in September 2012.

15.4 Corporate Governance

15.4 The Listing Rules

The Listing Rules require a UK company with a premium listing of equity shares in the UK and an overseas company with a premium listing in the UK of equity shares whose financial years begin on or after 29 June 2010 to include in its annual report:

- a statement of how the company has applied the main principles set out in the Code, in a manner that would enable shareholders to evaluate how the principles have been applied, and
- a statement as to whether the company has complied throughout the accounting period with all relevant provisions of the Code or has not complied throughout the accounting period with all relevant provisions of the Code and, if so, setting out those provisions, if any, it has not complied with and, in the case of provisions of a continuing nature, the period within which, if any, it did not comply and the company's reasons for non-compliance.

(FCA Listing Rules 9.8.6(5) and 9.8.6 (6))

For the meaning of "premium listing" and "equity shares" see the Glossary to the FCA handbook.

15.5 The Disclosure and Transparency Rules

The provisions of the Disclosure and Transparency Rules set out below apply to financial years of a company beginning on or after 29 June 2008.

(1) *Application*

The provisions in (2) below apply to an issuer:

- whose transferable securities are admitted to trading; and
- which is a company within the meaning of *CA 2006, s 1(1)*

but subject to the exception indicated in (2) below.

(FCA Disclosure and Transparency Rules, paras 1B.1.5, 1B.1.6).

(2) *Statements*

An issuer to which these provisions apply must either:

- include a corporate governance statement as a specific section of its directors' report;
- set out the required information in a separate report published together with, and in the same manner as, its annual report (in which case the corporate governance statement must contain either the information required by (c) below or a reference to the directors' report where that information is made available; or
- set out the required information by means of a reference in its directors' report to where such document is publicly available on the issuer's website.

The corporate governance statement must contain the following:

(a) Subject to the exemption below, a reference to:

(i) the corporate governance code to which the issuer is subject; and/or

(ii) the corporate governance code which the issuer may have voluntarily decided to apply; and/or

(iii) all relevant information about the corporate governance practices applied beyond the requirements under national law.

An issuer which is complying with (i) or (ii) above must:

- state in its directors' report where the relevant corporate governance code is publicly available; and
- to the extent that it departs from that corporate governance code, explain which parts of the corporate governance code it departs from and the reasons for doing so.

Where (iii) above applies, the issuer must make its corporate governance practices publicly available and state in its directors' report where they can be found.

If an issuer has decided not to apply any provisions of a corporate governance code referred to under (i) and (ii) above, it must explain its reasons for that decision.

A listed company which complies with the comply or explain rule in relation to the Code will satisfy the above requirements.

(b) A description of the main features of the issuer's internal control and risk management systems in relation to the financial reporting process.

(c) The information about share capital required by **20.17**(1)(*c*), (*d*), (*f*), (*h*) and (*i*) **Directors' Reports** where the issuer is subject to those requirements.

(d) A description of the composition and operation of the issuer's administrative, management and supervisory bodies and their committees.

In the FCA's view, the information specified in provisions A.1.1, A.1.2, B.2.4, C.3.3 and C.3.8 of the Code will satisfy these requirements.

Group directors' reports. An issuer which is required to prepare a group directors' report must include in that report a description of the main features of the group's internal control and risk management systems in relation to the process for preparing consolidated accounts. In the event that the issuer presents its own annual report and its consolidated annual report as a single report, this information must be included in the corporate governance statement in its directors' report. If the issuer elects to include its corporate governance statement in a separate report, it must provide the information in that report.

(FCA Disclosure and Transparency Rules, paras 1B.1.6, 7.2.1–7.2.11).

Approval and signing of separate corporate governance statement

15.6 *CA 2006 Requirements*

In relation to financial years beginning on or after 29 June 2008 any separate corporate governance statement must be approved by the board of directors and signed on behalf of the board by a director or the secretary of the company. [*CA 2006, s 419A; SI 2009 No 1581, Reg 2*].

See also **8.30 Duties of Auditors** in connection with the corporate governance report (*CA 2006, s 498A*).

COMPANY COMMITTEE STRUCTURE

15.7 The Structure

There are various provisions which regulate the setting up of committees which are responsible for regulating and monitoring corporate governance in a company. The Code (see **15.2**) in particular says that the company should establish formal and transparent arrangements for considering how they should apply the corporate reporting and risk management and internal control principles and for maintaining an appropriate relationship with the company's auditors through an audit committee (Code principle C3). The Code also regulates the setting up of a remuneration committee (see **15.10** below) and a nomination committee (see **15.9** below) the role generally of NEDS (see **15.13**) and those matters which are reserved wholly to the board (see **15.12**).

15.8 The Audit Committee

See **15.7** above for provisions of the Code regulating the establishment of an audit committee. Additionally the FRC has published guidance ("Guidance on Audit committees") to help companies when implementing the Code provisions on audit committees. Boards are not required to follow the Guidance, it is designed to assist them. The Guidance also assists directors serving on audit committees in carrying out their role. The 2012 edition of the Guidance is available to download from the FRC website at www.frc.org.uk or printed copies can be obtained free of charge from FRC publications.

The Code says in particular that:

- a company to which the Code applies should establish an audit committee (Code provision C.3.1);
- the committee should comprise at least three or, in the case of smaller companies outside the FTSE 350 throughout the year immediately prior to the reporting period, two independent NEDS (Code provision C.3.1). The board is required to identify in its annual report which of its NEDS are considered to be "independent" (Code provision B.1.1);
- the main roles and responsibilities of the audit committee should be set out in written terms of reference (Code provision C.3.2) and the terms of reference should be "made available" (Code provision C.3.3). Model terms of reference are published by the Institute of Chartered Secretaries and Administrators (ICSA) and further details of what the terms of reference should include are found in Code provision C.3.2;
- where requested by the board the audit committee should provide advice on whether the annual report and accounts, taken as a whole, is fair, balanced and understandable and provides the information necessary for shareholders to assess the company's performance, business model and strategy (Code provision C. 3.4)
- the audit committee must review arrangements for staff "whistleblowing" (Code provision C.3.5 and also see the FRC Guidance above at paras 4.9–4.16)
- the audit committee should monitor and review the effectiveness of the internal audit activities (Code provision C.3.6) and should have primary responsibility for making recommendations on the appointment, re-appointment and removal

of the company's external auditors. FTSE companies should put the external audit contract out to tender at least every ten years. If the board does not accept the audit committee's recommendation, it should include in the annual report and in any papers recommending appointment or reappointment a statement from the audit committee explaining the recommendation and should set out reasons why the board has taken a different position.(Code provision C.3.7); and

- a separate section of the company's annual report should describe the work of the audit committee in discharging its responsibilities and the annual report should include the significant issues that the audit committee considered in relation to the financial statements and how these issues were addressed, an explanation of how it has assessed the effectiveness of the external audit process and the approach taken to the appointment or reappointment of the external auditor, and information on the length of tenure of the current audit firm and when a tender was last conducted and how, if the auditor provides non-audit services to the company, auditor independence and objectivity is safeguarded (Code provision C.3.8).

The Disclosure and Transparency Rules also apply to audit committees in a company

- whose transferable securities are admitted to trading; and
- which is required to appoint a statutory auditor;

except for

- any issuer which is a subsidiary undertaking of a parent undertaking where the parent undertaking is required to appoint an audit committee;
- any issuer, the sole business of which is to act as the issuer of asset-backed securities, provided the entity makes a statement available to the public setting out the reasons why it considers it is not appropriate to have either an audit committee or an administrative or supervisory body entrusted to carry out the functions of an audit committee; or
- a credit institution whose shares are not admitted to trading and which has, in a continuous or repeated manner, issued only debt securities provided that
  - (i) the total nominal amount of all such debt securities remains below €100 million; and
  - (ii) the credit institution has not been subject to a requirement to publish a prospectus in accordance with *FSMA 2000, s 85*.

(FCA Disclosure and Transparency Rules, paras 1B.1.2, 1B.1.3).

An issuer falling within the above must have a relevant body which is responsible for performing the functions set out below. At least one member of that body must be independent and at least one member must have competence in accounting and/or auditing. The requirements for independence and competence may be satisfied by the same member or by different members of the relevant body.

An issuer must:

(a) ensure that, as a *minimum*, the relevant body must:

  (i) monitor the financial reporting process;

  (ii) monitor the effectiveness of the issuer's internal control, internal audit where applicable, and risk management systems;

(iii) monitor the statutory audit of the annual and consolidated accounts; and

(iv) review and monitor the independence of the statutory auditor, and in particular the provision of additional services to the issuer.

(b) base any proposal to appoint a statutory auditor on a recommendation made by the relevant body; and

(c) make a statement available to the public disclosing which body carries out the functions required by (a) above and how it is composed. This statement may be included in any corporate governance statement required under **15.5**.

In the FCA's view, compliance with the requirements of A.1.2, C.3.1, C.3.2 and C.3.3 of the Code will result in compliance with the above.

(FCA Disclosure and Transparency Rules, paras 7.1.1–7.1.7).

15.9 The Nomination Committee

In addition to the setting up of an audit committee, the Code says that there should be a formal, rigorous and transparent procedure for the appointment of new directors to the board (Code Principle B.2) and companies to which the Code applies (see above) should establish a nomination committee to lead the process for board appointments and make recommendations to the board (Code provision B.2.1). The following supporting principles to main principle B.2 should also be adhered to:

- the search for board candidates should be conducted, and appointments made, on merit, against objective criteria and with due regard for the benefits of diversity on the board including gender. Note here the Lord Davies independent review into Women on Boards published on 24 February 2011. The main recommendations were that FTSE 100 companies should be aiming for a minimum of 25% female board representation by the year 2015 and FTSE 350 companies should be setting their own challenging targets for appointing women to the board. The 2012 edition of the Code has been amended to provide that a separate section of the annual report should describe the work of the nomination committee (and) should include a description of the board's policy on diversity, including gender, any measurable objectives that it has set for implementing the policy, and progress on achieving objectives. This provision is repeated in the 2014 edn of the Code (Code provision B.2.4) and annual progress reports are published by Lord Davies; and
- the board should satisfy itself that plans are in place for orderly succession for appointments to the board and to senior management, so as to maintain an appropriate balance of skills and experience within the company and on the board and to ensure progressive refreshing of the board.

The nomination committee should:

- in the majority comprise independent NEDS (Code provision B.2.1);
- be chaired by the chairman of the company or an independent NED but the chairman should not chair the committee when it is dealing with the appointment of (his) successor. (Code provision B.2.1);
- lead the process for board appointments and make recommendations to the board (Code provision B.2.1);

- before making an appointment evaluate the balance of skills, experience, independence and knowledge of the board and, in light of this evaluation, prepare a description of the role and capabilities required for a particular appointment (Code provision B.2.2);
- have terms of reference which are made "available" for example by publication on the company's website (Code provision B.2.1). For what should be included in the terms of reference see the ICSA Model terms of reference for a nomination committee available from the ICSA website;
- in relation to all appointments be mindful of the Code main principle that all directors should be able to allocate sufficient time to the company to discharge their responsibilities effectively (Code provision B.3);
- appoint NEDS for specified terms subject to re-election and to statutory provisions relating to the removal of a director. Any term of office beyond six years should be subject to particularly rigorous review and should take into account the need for progressive refreshing of the board (Code provision B.3.1);
- for the appointment of a new chairman, prepare a job specification which includes an assessment of the time commitment expected for the role (Code provision B.3.1); and
- have sufficient resources to undertake its duties (Code provision B.5.1).

Shareholder and board access to information

The ICSA guidance referred to above provides that the chairman of the nomination committee should attend the company's annual general meeting each year to answer any questions which may be raised by shareholders on matters within the committee's area of responsibility. Additionally the Code provides that:

- a separate section of the annual report should describe the work of the committee including the process it has used in relation to board appointments. The section of the annual report should include a description of the board's policy on diversity, including gender, any measurable objectives that it has set for implementing the policy, and progress on achieving the objectives. An explanation should be given if neither an external search consultancy nor open advertising has been used in the appointment of a chairman or non executive director. Where an external search consultancy has been used, it should be identified in the report and a statement should be made as to whether it has any other connection with the company(Code provision B.2.4).
- the chairman and members of the committee should be identified in the annual report (Code provision A.1.2)
- other significant commitments of the chairman and any NEDS should be disclosed to the board before appointment and, for the chairman only, should be included in the annual report. Changes to any such commitments should be reported to the board as they arise, and, in the case of the chairman, included in the next annual report (Code provision B.3.1 and B.3.2)
- the terms of appointment of NEDS should be made available for inspection by any person at the company's registered office during normal business hours and at the annual general meeting both for fifteen minutes before the meeting and during that meeting (Code provision B.3.2).

15.10 The Remuneration Committee

The Code also requires listed companies to establish a remuneration committee to ensure the company complies with the Code principle that there should be a formal and transparent procedure for developing policy on executive remuneration and for fixing the remuneration packages of individual directors, and that no director should be involved in deciding (his) own remuneration (Code principle D.2 and Code provision D.2.1). Additionally *CA 2006* requires quoted companies to prepare a directors' remuneration report for each financial year (see **19 Directors' Remuneration Reports—Quoted Companies**).

The remuneration committee should:

- consist of three, or in the case of smaller companies outside the FTSE 350, two independent NEDS (Code provision D.2.1);
- not be chaired by the chairman of the company although (he) may serve on the committee (Code provision D.2.1);
- be given delegated responsibility for setting the remuneration of all executive directors and the chairman including pension rights and any compensation payments and be expected to recommend and monitor the level and structure of remuneration for senior management. The definition of "senior management" should be determined by the board but should normally include the first level of management below board level. (Code provision D.2.1);
- take care to recognise and manage conflicts of interest when receiving views from executive directors or senior managers or consulting the chief executive officer about their proposals relating to the remuneration of other executive directors (Supporting principles to Code main principle D.2);
- be responsible for appointing any consultants in respect of executive directors' remuneration (supporting principle to Code main principle D.2); and
- have terms of reference which are made "available" for example by publication on the company's website. Its terms of reference should explain the committee's role and the authority delegated to it by the board (Code provision D.2.1). For what should be included in the terms of reference see the ICSA Model terms of reference for a remuneration committee available from the ICSA website(these are only available to members of ICSA).

Setting levels of remuneration including performance related

The Code provides that executive directors' remuneration should be designed to promote the long-term success of the company and that performance-related elements should be transparent, stretching and rigorously applied (Code main principle D.1).

Specifically the Code says:

- remuneration committees should judge where to position their company relative to others but should use such comparisons with caution in view of the risk of an upward ratchet of remuneration levels with no corresponding increase in corporate and individual performance and should avoid paying more than is necessary and should also be sensitive to pay and employment conditions elsewhere in the group, especially when determining annual salary increases (Supporting principle to main Code principle D.1);
- levels of remuneration for NEDS should reflect the time commitment and responsibilities of the role (Code provision D.1.3);
- the board itself or, where required by the company's articles of association, the shareholders should determine the remuneration of the NEDS within the limits set out in the articles. However, where permitted by the articles, the board may delegate this responsibility to a committee, which may include the chief executive (Code provision D.2.3);
- remuneration for NEDS should not include share options or other performance related elements (although if exceptionally options are granted, shareholder approval should be sought in advance and any shares acquired by the exercise of options should be held until at least one year after the NED leaves the company) (Code provision D.1.3);
- notice or contract periods should be set at one year or less and if it is necessary to offer longer notice or contract periods to new directors recruited from outside the company, such periods should reduce to one year or less after the initial period (Code provision D.1.5). See also the *CA 2006, s 188* requirement that directors' service agreements must not exceed two years duration without shareholder approval;
- the remuneration committee should carefully consider what compensation commitments (including pension contributions and other entitlements) their directors' terms of appointment would entail in the event of early termination. The aim should be to avoid rewarding poor performance and the committee should take a robust line on reducing compensation to reflect departing directors' obligations to mitigate loss (Code provision D.1.4); and
- shareholders should be invited specifically to approve all new long-term incentive schemes and significant changes to existing schemes, save in the circumstances permitted by the Listing Rules (Code provision D.2.4). The Listing Rules require all share option and long-term incentive schemes to be approved by the shareholders (by ordinary resolution) unless participation in the scheme is offered to all or substantially all employees of the group or the scheme is established specifically to facilitate, in unusual circumstances, the recruitment or retention of a director (in which case detailed information of the special scheme must be given in the company's next annual report). (LR 9.4 1. and 9.4.2).

15.10 Corporate Governance

Shareholder and board access to information

The Code provides that:

- the annual report should identify members of the remuneration committee and set out the number of meetings held by the committee with details of each director's attendance (Code provision A.1.2) and should include a statement of how the board operates, including a high level statement of which types of decisions are to be taken by the board and which are delegated (Code provision A.1.1); and
- where remuneration consultants are appointed a statement should be made available as to whether they have any other connection with the company (Code provision D.2.1).

15.11 The Risk Committee

The Code does not expressly require a company to set up a risk committee It says in the first instance that the board is responsible for determining the nature and extent of the significant risks it is willing to take in achieving its strategic objectives and for maintaining sound risk management and internal control systems (Code Main Principle C.2) . Further guidance can be found in the Walker Review ('A review of corporate governance in UK banks and other financial industry entities 2009') and in ICSA Model terms of reference–Risk Committee (as above that these are only available to ICSA members).

Guidance suggests that:

- the board of a bank or other financial institution should establish a board risk committee separate from the audit committee (Walker recommendations 23–27). The role of the risk committee in such institutions is set out in detail in the Walker recommendations referred to;
- the chairman of the risk committee should attend the company's annual general meeting to answer any questions on the risk committee's activities (ICSA Model terms of reference);
- the committee should have access to sufficient resources to carry out its duties including access to the services of the company secretary; and
- the frequency of committee meetings will vary from company to company and may change from time to time but the ICSA Model terms of reference say that the committee should meet at least three times a year at appropriate times and otherwise as required.

15.12 Matters reserved to the board

The Code requires the board to establish a formal schedule of matters specifically reserved for their decision and to include in the annual report a statement of how the board operates which should include a high-level statement of which types of decisions are to be taken by the board and which are delegated to management (Code provision A.1.1). Apart from those general provisions the Code does not specify what should be included in the matters reserved for the board. Instead guidance can be found in the original 1992 Cadbury Report (the Cadbury Code on the financial aspects of corporate governance) and in ICSA Guidance: Matters reserved for the board (available only to ICSA members). Generally it is suggested that matters to be reserved should include:

- the acquisition and disposal of material assets of the company or its subsidiaries (Cadbury report para 4.24);

- investments, capital projects, authority levels, treasury policies and risk management policies (Cadbury report para 4.24); and
- responsibility for the overall management of the group.

15.13 Non-Executive Directors (NEDS)

The starting point for any consideration of the role of NEDS in corporate governance is the Higgs review (Review of the role and effectiveness of non-executive directors 2003). The Higgs guidance was itself reviewed in 2009 by ICSA and a Guidance on Board effectiveness was published by the FRC in March 2011. The 2011 Guidance:

- replaces "Good practice suggestions from the Higgs Report"; and
- is intended to help companies apply the provisions of the Code.

In January 2013 ICSA published guidance on the liability of non –executive directors. Entitled "ICSA guidance on liability of non-executive directors: care, skill and diligence" the guidance suggests ways in which non-executive directors can approach their work in a way which would allow them to demonstrate to a regulator (eg the FCA) or in a court of law that they had taken appropriate steps to exercise care, skill and diligence in the execution of their roles and responsibilities. The guidance expressly refers to provisions of the Code which are likely to be relevant in a court's assessment. These are mainly Code provisions A.4 and B3, B4, and B5.

The Code requires that:

- a board should include an appropriate combination of executive directors and NEDS (and in particular independent NEDS) such that no individual or small group of individuals can dominate the board's decision making (Code Main principle B.1);
- at least half the board of FTSE 350 companies, excluding the chairman, should be independent. Companies outside the FTSE 350 should have at least two independent NEDS. (Code provision B.1.2);
- the board identifies in the annual report each NED they consider is independent for the purposes of the Code (Code provision B.1.1). Code provision B.1.1 contains a non-exhaustive list of circumstances which would indicate that a director is not independent and if the board determines that a NED is independent despite one of the list of circumstances applying, it should state its reasons for finding that the NED is independent in the annual report (Code provision B.1.1);
- NEDS should constructively challenge and help develop proposals on strategy (Code main principle A.4). They are responsible for scrutinising the performance of management in meeting agreed goals and objectives, monitoring the reporting of performance, satisfying themselves on the integrity of financial information and that financial controls and systems of risk management are robust and defensible, for determining appropriate levels of remuneration of executive directors and have a prime role in appointing and where necessary removing executive directors and in succession planning. (Code supporting principles to main principle A.4);
- the board should appoint one of the independent NEDS as the senior independent director and identify that person in the company's annual report (Code provision A.4.1). Provisions A.4.1, A.4.2 and E.1.1 contain details of the role of the senior independent director; and

- NEDS fees should be decided either by the board or a committee of the board if the company's articles permit such delegation or, where required by the company's articles, the shareholders (Code provision D.2.3).

For the appointment and remuneration of NEDS see **15.10** (above).

Election and re-election

All directors should be submitted for re-election at regular intervals subject to satisfactory performance and directors of FTSE 350 companies should be subject to annual election by shareholders. All other directors should be subject to election at the first annual general meeting after their appointment and then to re-election at intervals of no more than three years. (Code main principle B.7 and provision B.7.1). There are no specific provisions for the development and training of NEDS, instead there are general provisions relating to all directors (Code main principle B.4 and provisions B.4.1 and supporting principles B.4 and B.5).

FRC Guidance

The 2011 FRC Guidance on Board Effectiveness referred to above is not intended to be prescriptive. Instead it says in the Preface that it is intended to stimulate boards' thinking on how they can carry out their role most effectively. The Guidance also does not contain all the information (for example board terms of reference) which was in the Higgs guidance. Rather the FRC Guidance provides links to information available from other organisations. In relation to NEDS (and the senior independent director) the FRC Guidance provides as follows:

Senior independent directors

- In normal times the senior independent director should act as a sounding board for the chairman, providing support for the chairman in the delivery of his or her objectives, and leading the evaluation of the chairman on behalf of the other directors, as set out in the Code. The senior independent director might also take responsibility for an orderly succession process for the chairman.
- When the board is undergoing a period of stress, however, the senior independent director's role becomes critically important. He or she is expected to work with the chairman and other directors, and/or shareholders, to resolve significant issues. Boards should ensure they have a clear understanding of when the senior independent director might intervene in order to maintain board and company stability. Examples might include where:
  - there is a dispute between the chairman and CEO;
  - shareholders or non-executive directors have expressed concerns that are not being addressed by the chairman or CEO;
  - the strategy being followed by the chairman and CEO is not supported by the entire board;
  - the relationship between the chairman and CEO is particularly close, and decisions are being made without the approval of the full board; or
  - succession planning is being ignored.

These issues should be considered when defining the role of the senior independent director, which should be set out in writing. (FRC Guidance paras 1.9-1.11)

NEDS

- A non-executive director should, on appointment, devote time to a comprehensive, formal and tailored induction which should extend beyond the boardroom. Initiatives such as partnering a non-executive director with an executive board member may speed up the process of him or her acquiring an understanding of the main areas of business activity, especially areas involving significant risk. The director should expect to visit, and talk with, senior and middle managers in these areas.
- Non-executive directors should devote time to developing and refreshing their knowledge and skills, including those of communication, to ensure that they continue to make a positive contribution to the board. Being well-informed about the company, and having a strong command of the issues relevant to the business, will generate the respect of the other directors.
- Non-executive directors need to make sufficient time available to discharge their responsibilities effectively. The letter of appointment should state the minimum time that the non-executive director will be required to spend on the company's business, and seek the individual's confirmation that he or she can devote that amount of time to the role, consistent with other commitments. The letter should also indicate the possibility of additional time commitment when the company is undergoing a period of particularly increased activity, such as an acquisition or takeover, or as a result of some major difficulty with one or more of its operations.
- Non-executive directors have a responsibility to uphold high standards of integrity and probity. They should support the chairman and executive directors in instilling the appropriate culture, values and behaviours in the boardroom and beyond.
- Non-executive directors should insist on receiving high-quality information sufficiently in advance so that there can be thorough consideration of the issues prior to, and informed debate and challenge at, board meetings. High-quality information is that which is appropriate for making decisions on the issue at hand – it should be accurate, clear, comprehensive, up-to-date and timely; contain a summary of the contents of any paper; and inform the director of what is expected of him or her on that issue.
- Non-executive directors should take into account the views of shareholders and other stakeholders, because these views may provide different perspectives on the company and its performance. (FRC Guidance paras 1.18-1.23)

15.14 Executive remuneration and shareholder power

See **19 Directors' Remuneration reports-Quoted Companies** for details of provisions which came into effect in October 2013.

CHAPTER 15: APPENDIX

UK Corporate Governance Code – The UK Corporate Governance Code (September 2014) – applicable to accounting periods beginning on or after 1 October 2014

THE UK CORPORATE GOVERNANCE CODE (SEPTEMBER 2014)

GOVERNANCE AND THE CODE

1. The purpose of corporate governance is to facilitate effective, entrepreneurial and prudent management that can deliver the long-term success of the company.
2. The first version of the UK Code on Corporate Governance (the Code) was produced in 1992 by the Cadbury Committee. Its paragraph 2.5 is still the classic definition of the context of the Code:

   'Corporate governance is the system by which companies are directed and controlled. Boards of directors are responsible for the governance of their companies. The shareholders' role in governance is to appoint the directors and the auditors and to satisfy themselves that an appropriate governance structure is in place. The responsibilities of the board include setting the company's strategic aims, providing the leadership to put them into effect, supervising the management of the business and reporting to shareholders on their stewardship. The board's actions are subject to laws, regulations and the shareholders in general meeting.'
3. Corporate governance is therefore about what the board of a company does and how it sets the values of the company, and is to be distinguished from the day to day operational management of the company by full-time executives.
4. The Code is a guide to a number of key components of effective board practice. It is based on the underlying principles of all good governance: accountability, transparency, probity and focus on the sustainable success of an entity over the longer term.
5. The Code has been enduring, but it is not immutable. Its fitness for purpose in a permanently changing economic and social business environment requires its evaluation at appropriate intervals.
6. The new Code applies to accounting periods beginning on or after 1 October 2014 and applies to all companies with a Premium Listing of equity shares regardless of whether they are incorporated in the UK or elsewhere.

PREFACE

1. Over two decades of constructive usage of the Code have contributed to improved corporate governance in the UK. The Code is part of a framework of legislation, regulation and best practice standards which aims to deliver high quality corporate governance with in-built flexibility for companies to adapt their practices to take into account their particular circumstances. Similarly, investors must take the opportunity to consider carefully how companies have decided to implement the Code. There is always scope for improvement, both in terms of making sure that the Code remains relevant and improving the quality of reporting.

2. Boards must continue to think comprehensively about their overall tasks and the implications of these for the roles of their individual members. Absolutely key in these endeavours are the leadership of the chairman of a board, the support given to and by the CEO, and the frankness and openness of mind with which issues are discussed and tackled by all directors.
3. Essential to the effective functioning of any board is dialogue which is both constructive and challenging. The problems arising from 'groupthink' have been exposed in particular as a result of the financial crisis. One of the ways in which constructive debate can be encouraged is through having sufficient diversity on the board. This includes, but is not limited to, gender and race. Diverse board composition in these respects is not on its own a guarantee. Diversity is as much about differences of approach and experience, and it is very important in ensuring effective engagement with key stakeholders and in order to deliver the business strategy.
4. One of the key roles for the board includes establishing the culture, values and ethics of the company. It is important that the board sets the correct 'tone from the top'. The directors should lead by example and ensure that good standards of behaviour permeate throughout all levels of the organisation. This will help prevent misconduct, unethical practices and support the delivery of long-term success.
5. In this update of the Code the FRC has focussed on the provision by companies of information about the risks which affect longer term viability. In doing so the information needs of investors has been balanced against setting appropriate reporting requirements. Companies will now need to present information to give a clearer and broader view of solvency, liquidity, risk management and viability. For their part, investors will need to assess these statements thoroughly and engage accordingly. In addition, boards of listed companies will need to ensure that executive remuneration is aligned to the long-term success of the company and demonstrate this more clearly to shareholders.
6. To run a corporate board successfully should not be underrated. Constraints on time and knowledge combine with the need to maintain mutual respect and openness between a cast of strong, able and busy directors dealing with each other across the different demands of executive and non-executive roles. To achieve good governance requires continuing and high quality effort.
7. Chairmen are encouraged to report personally in their annual statements how the principles relating to the role and effectiveness of the board (in Sections A and B of the Code) have been applied. Not only will this give investors a clearer picture of the steps taken by boards to operate effectively but also, by providing fuller context, it may make investors more willing to accept explanations when a company chooses to explain rather than to comply with one or more provisions.
8. While in law the company is primarily accountable to its shareholders, and the relationship between the company and its shareholders is also the main focus of the Code, companies are encouraged to recognise the contribution made by other providers of capital and to confirm the board's interest in listening to the views of such providers insofar as these are relevant to the company's overall approach to governance.

Financial Reporting Council

September 2014

The UK Corporate Governance Code (September 2014)

COMPLY OR EXPLAIN

1. The 'comply or explain' approach is the trademark of corporate governance in the UK. It has been in operation since the Code's beginnings and is the foundation of the Code's flexibility. It is strongly supported by both companies and shareholders and has been widely admired and imitated internationally.
2. The Code is not a rigid set of rules. It consists of principles (main and supporting) and provisions. The Listing Rules require companies to apply the Main Principles and report to shareholders on how they have done so. The principles are the core of the Code and the way in which they are applied should be the central question for a board as it determines how it is to operate according to the Code.
3. It is recognised that an alternative to following a provision may be justified in particular circumstances if good governance can be achieved by other means. A condition of doing so is that the reasons for it should be explained clearly and carefully to shareholders[1], who may wish to discuss the position with the company and whose voting intentions may be influenced as a result. In providing an explanation, the company should aim to illustrate how its actual practices are both consistent with the principle to which the particular provision relates and contribute to good governance and promote delivery of business objectives. It should set out the background, provide a clear rationale for the action it is taking and describe any mitigating actions taken to address any additional risk and maintain conformity with the relevant principle. Where deviation from a particular provision is intended to be limited in time, the explanation should indicate when the company expects to conform with the provision.
4. In their responses to explanations, shareholders should pay due regard to companies' individual circumstances and bear in mind, in particular, the size and complexity of the company and the nature of the risks and challenges it faces. Whilst shareholders have every right to challenge companies' explanations if they are unconvincing, they should not be evaluated in a mechanistic way and departures from the Code should not be automatically treated as breaches. Shareholders should be careful to respond to the statements from companies in a manner that supports the 'comply or explain' process and bearing in mind the purpose of good corporate governance. They should put their views to the company and both parties should be prepared to discuss the position.
5. Smaller listed companies, in particular those new to listing, may judge that some of the provisions are disproportionate or less relevant in their case. Some of the provisions do not apply to companies below the FTSE 350. Such companies may nonetheless consider that it would be appropriate to adopt the approach in the Code and they are encouraged to do so. Externally managed investment companies typically have a different board structure which may affect the relevance of particular provisions; the Association of Investment Companies' Corporate Governance Code and Guide can assist them in meeting their obligations under the Code.
6. Satisfactory engagement between company boards and investors is crucial to the health of the UK's corporate governance regime. Companies and shareholders both have responsibility for ensuring that 'comply or explain' remains an effective alternative to a rules-based system. There are practical and administrative obstacles to improved interaction between boards and shareholders. But certainly there is also scope for an increase in trust which could generate a virtuous upward spiral in attitudes to the Code and in its constructive use.

The Main Principles of the Code

Section A: Leadership

The UK Corporate Governance Code (September 2014)

Every company should be headed by an effective board which is collectively responsible for the long-term success of the company.

There should be a clear division of responsibilities at the head of the company between the running of the board and the executive responsibility for the running of the company's business. No one individual should have unfettered powers of decision.

The chairman is responsible for leadership of the board and ensuring its effectiveness on all aspects of its role.

As part of their role as members of a unitary board, non-executive directors should constructively challenge and help develop proposals on strategy.

Section B: Effectiveness

The board and its committees should have the appropriate balance of skills, experience, independence and knowledge of the company to enable them to discharge their respective duties and responsibilities effectively.

There should be a formal, rigorous and transparent procedure for the appointment of new directors to the board. All directors should be able to allocate sufficient time to the company to discharge their responsibilities effectively.

All directors should receive induction on joining the board and should regularly update and refresh their skills and knowledge.

The board should be supplied in a timely manner with information in a form and of a quality appropriate to enable it to discharge its duties.

The board should undertake a formal and rigorous annual evaluation of its own performance and that of its committees and individual directors.

All directors should be submitted for re-election at regular intervals, subject to continued satisfactory performance.

Section C: Accountability

The board should present a fair, balanced and understandable assessment of the company's position and prospects.

The board is responsible for determining the nature and extent of the principal risks it is willing to take in achieving its strategic objectives. The board should maintain sound risk management and internal control systems.

The board should establish formal and transparent arrangements for considering how they should apply the corporate reporting, risk management and internal control principles and for maintaining an appropriate relationship with the company's auditor.

Section D: Remuneration

Executive directors' remuneration should be designed to promote the long-term success of the company. Performance-related elements should be transparent, stretching and rigorously applied.

There should be a formal and transparent procedure for developing policy on executive remuneration and for fixing the remuneration packages of individual directors. No director should be involved in deciding his or her own remuneration.

Section E: Relations with Shareholders

There should be a dialogue with shareholders based on the mutual understanding of objectives. The board as a whole has responsibility for ensuring that a satisfactory dialogue with shareholders takes place.

The board should use the general meetings to communicate with investors and to encourage their participation.

Section A: Leadership

A.1 The Role of the Board

Main Principle

Every company should be headed by an effective board, which is collectively responsible for the success of the company.

Supporting Principles

The board's role is to provide entrepreneurial leadership of the company within a framework of prudent and effective controls which enables risk to be assessed and managed. The board should set the company's strategic aims, ensure that the necessary financial and human resources are in place for the company to meet its objectives and review management performance. The board should set the company's values and standards and ensure that its obligations to its shareholders and others are understood and met.

All directors must act in what they consider to be the best interests of the company, consistent with their statutory duties[2].

Code Provisions

A.1.1 The board should meet sufficiently regularly to discharge its duties effectively. There should be a formal schedule of matters specifically reserved for its decision. The annual report should include a statement of how the board operates, including a high level statement of which types of decisions are to be taken by the board and which are to be delegated to management.

A.1.2 The annual report should identify the chairman, the deputy chairman (where there is one), the chief executive, the senior independent director and the chairmen and members of the board committees[3]. It should also set out the number of meetings of the board and its committees and individual attendance by directors.

A.1.3 The company should arrange appropriate insurance cover in respect of legal action against its directors.

The UK Corporate Governance Code (September 2014)

A.2 Division of Responsibilities

Main Principle

There should be a clear division of responsibilities at the head of the company between the running of the board and the executive responsibility for the running of the company's business. No one individual should have unfettered powers of decision.

Code Provision

A.2.1 The roles of chairman and chief executive should not be exercised by the same individual. The division of responsibilities between the chairman and chief executive should be clearly established, set out in writing and agreed by the board.

A.3 The Chairman

Main Principle

The chairman is responsible for leadership of the board and ensuring its effectiveness on all aspects of its role.

Supporting Principles

The chairman is responsible for setting the board's agenda and ensuring that adequate time is available for discussion of all agenda items, in particular strategic issues. The chairman should also promote a culture of openness and debate by facilitating the effective contribution of non-executive directors in particular and ensuring constructive relations between executive and non-executive directors.

The chairman is responsible for ensuring that the directors receive accurate, timely and clear information. The chairman should ensure effective communication with shareholders.

Code Provision

A.3.1 The chairman should on appointment meet the independence criteria set out in B.1.1 below. A chief executive should not go on to be chairman of the same company. If, exceptionally, a board decides that a chief executive should become chairman, the board should consult major shareholders in advance and should set out its reasons to shareholders at the time of the appointment and in the next annual report[4].

A.4 Non-Executive Directors

Main Principle

As part of their role as members of a unitary board, non-executive directors should constructively challenge and help develop proposals on strategy.

Supporting Principle

Non-executive directors should scrutinise the performance of management in meeting agreed goals and objectives and monitor the reporting of performance. They should satisfy themselves on the integrity of financial information and that financial controls and systems of risk management are robust and defensible. They are responsible for determining appropriate levels of remuneration of executive directors and have a prime role in appointing and, where necessary, removing executive directors, and in succession planning.

Code Provisions

A.4.1 The board should appoint one of the independent non-executive directors to be the senior independent director to provide a sounding board for the chairman and to serve as an intermediary for the other directors when necessary. The senior independent director should be available to shareholders if they have concerns which contact through the normal channels of chairman, chief executive or other executive directors has failed to resolve or for which such contact is inappropriate.

A.4.2 The chairman should hold meetings with the non-executive directors without the executives present. Led by the senior independent director, the non-executive directors should meet without the chairman present at least annually to appraise the chairman's performance and on such other occasions as are deemed appropriate.

A.4.3 Where directors have concerns which cannot be resolved about the running of the company or a proposed action, they should ensure that their concerns are recorded in the board minutes. On resignation, a non-executive director should provide a written statement to the chairman, for circulation to the board, if they have any such concerns.

Section B: Effectiveness

B.1 The Composition of the Board

Main Principle

The board and its committees should have the appropriate balance of skills, experience, independence and knowledge of the company to enable them to discharge their respective duties and responsibilities effectively.

Supporting Principles

The board should be of sufficient size that the requirements of the business can be met and that changes to the board's composition and that of its committees can be managed without undue disruption, and should not be so large as to be unwieldy.

The board should include an appropriate combination of executive and non-executive directors (and, in particular, independent non-executive directors) such that no individual or small group of individuals can dominate the board's decision taking.

The value of ensuring that committee membership is refreshed and that undue reliance is not placed on particular individuals should be taken into account in deciding chairmanship and membership of committees.

No one other than the committee chairman and members is entitled to be present at a meeting of the nomination, audit or remuneration committee, but others may attend at the invitation of the committee.

Code Provisions

B.1.1 The board should identify in the annual report each non-executive director it considers to be independent[5]. The board should determine whether the director is independent in character and judgement and whether there are relationships or circumstances which are likely to affect, or could appear to affect, the director's judgement. The board should state its reasons if it determines that a director is independent notwithstanding the existence of relationships or circumstances which may appear relevant to its determination, including if the director:

- has been an employee of the company or group within the last five years;
- has, or has had within the last three years, a material business relationship with the company either directly, or as a partner, shareholder, director or senior employee of a body that has such a relationship with the company;
- has received or receives additional remuneration from the company apart from a director's fee, participates in the company's share option or a performance-related pay scheme, or is a member of the company's pension scheme;
- has close family ties with any of the company's advisers, directors or senior employees;
- holds cross-directorships or has significant links with other directors through involvement in other companies or bodies;
- represents a significant shareholder; or
- has served on the board for more than nine years from the date of their first election.

B.1.2 Except for smaller companies[6], at least half the board, excluding the chairman, should comprise non-executive directors determined by the board to be independent. A smaller company should have at least two independent non-executive directors.

B.2 Appointments to the Board

Main Principle

There should be a formal, rigorous and transparent procedure for the appointment of new directors to the board.

Supporting Principles

The search for board candidates should be conducted, and appointments made, on merit, against objective criteria and with due regard for the benefits of diversity on the board, including gender.

The board should satisfy itself that plans are in place for orderly succession for appointments to the board and to senior management, so as to maintain an appropriate balance of skills and experience within the company and on the board and to ensure progressive refreshing of the board.

Code Provisions

B.2.1 There should be a nomination committee which should lead the process for board appointments and make recommendations to the board. A majority of members of the nomination committee should be independent non-executive directors. The chairman or an independent non-executive director should chair the committee, but the chairman should not chair the nomination committee when it is dealing with the appointment of a successor to the chairmanship. The nomination committee should make available its terms of reference, explaining its role and the authority delegated to it by the board[7].

B.2.2 The nomination committee should evaluate the balance of skills, experience, independence and knowledge on the board and, in the light of this evaluation, prepare a description of the role and capabilities required for a particular appointment.

B.2.3 Non-executive directors should be appointed for specified terms subject to re-election and to statutory provisions relating to the removal of a director. Any term beyond six years for a non-executive director should be subject to particularly rigorous review, and should take into account the need for progressive refreshing of the board.

B.2.4 A separate section of the annual report should describe the work of the nomination committee[8], including the process it has used in relation to board appointments. This section should include a description of the board's policy on diversity, including gender, any measurable objectives that it has set for implementing the policy and progress on achieving the objectives. An explanation should be given if neither an external search consultancy nor open advertising has been used in the appointment of a chairman or a non-executive director. Where an external search consultancy has been used, it should be identified in the annual report and a statement made as to whether it has any other connection with the company.

B.3 Commitment

Main Principle

All directors should be able to allocate sufficient time to the company to discharge their responsibilities effectively.

B.3.1 For the appointment of a chairman, the nomination committee should prepare a job specification, including an assessment of the time commitment expected, recognising the need for availability in the event of crises. A chairman's other significant commitments should be disclosed to the board before appointment and included in the annual report. Changes to such commitments should be reported to the board as they arise, and their impact explained in the next annual report.

B.3.2 The terms and conditions of appointment of non-executive directors should be made available for inspection[9]. The letter of appointment should set out the expected time commitment. Non-executive directors should undertake that they will have sufficient time to meet what is expected of them. Their other significant commitments should be disclosed to the board before appointment, with a broad indication of the time involved and the board should be informed of subsequent changes.

B.3.3 The board should not agree to a full time executive director taking on more than one non-executive directorship in a FTSE 100 company nor the chairmanship of such a company.

B.4 Development

Main Principle

All directors should receive induction on joining the board and should regularly update and refresh their skills and knowledge.

Supporting Principles

The chairman should ensure that the directors continually update their skills and the knowledge and familiarity with the company required to fulfil their role both on the board and on board committees. The company should provide the necessary resources for developing and updating its directors' knowledge and capabilities.

To function effectively, all directors need appropriate knowledge of the company and access to its operations and staff.

Code Provisions

B.4.1 The chairman should ensure that new directors receive a full, formal and tailored induction on joining the board. As part of this, directors should avail themselves of opportunities to meet major shareholders.

B.4.2 The chairman should regularly review and agree with each director their training and development needs.

B.5 Information and Support

Main Principle

The board should be supplied in a timely manner with information in a form and of a quality appropriate to enable it to discharge its duties.

Supporting Principles

The chairman is responsible for ensuring that the directors receive accurate, timely and clear information. Management has an obligation to provide such information but directors should seek clarification or amplification where necessary.

Under the direction of the chairman, the company secretary's responsibilities include ensuring good information flows within the board and its committees and between senior management and non-executive directors, as well as facilitating induction and assisting with professional development as required.

The company secretary should be responsible for advising the board through the chairman on all governance matters.

Code Provisions

B.5.1 The board should ensure that directors, especially non-executive directors, have access to independent professional advice at the company's expense where they judge it necessary to discharge their responsibilities as directors. Committees should be provided with sufficient resources to undertake their duties.

B.5.2 All directors should have access to the advice and services of the company secretary, who is responsible to the board for ensuring that board procedures are complied with. Both the appointment and removal of the company secretary should be a matter for the board as a whole.

B.6 Evaluation

Main Principle

The board should undertake a formal and rigorous annual evaluation of its own performance and that of its committees and individual directors.

Supporting Principles

Evaluation of the board should consider the balance of skills, experience, independence and knowledge of the company on the board, its diversity, including gender, how the board works together as a unit, and other factors relevant to its effectiveness.

The chairman should act on the results of the performance evaluation by recognising the strengths and addressing the weaknesses of the board and, where appropriate, proposing new members be appointed to the board or seeking the resignation of directors.

Individual evaluation should aim to show whether each director continues to contribute effectively and to demonstrate commitment to the role (including commitment of time for board and committee meetings and any other duties).

Code Provisions

B.6.1 The board should state in the annual report how performance evaluation of the board, its committees and its individual directors has been conducted.

B.6.2 Evaluation of the board of FTSE 350 companies should be externally facilitated at least every three years. The external facilitator should be identified in the annual report and a statement made as to whether they have any other connection with the company[10].

B.6.3 The non-executive directors, led by the senior independent director, should be responsible for performance evaluation of the chairman, taking into account the views of executive directors.

B.7 Re-election

Main Principle

All directors should be submitted for re-election at regular intervals, subject to continued satisfactory performance.

Code Provisions

B.7.1 All directors of FTSE 350 companies should be subject to annual election by shareholders. All other directors should be subject to election by shareholders at the first annual general meeting after their appointment, and to re-election thereafter at intervals of no more than three years. Non-executive directors who have served longer than nine years should be subject to annual re-election. The names of directors submitted for election or re-election should be accompanied by sufficient biographical details and any other relevant information to enable shareholders to take an informed decision on their election.

B.7.2 The board should set out to shareholders in the papers accompanying a resolution to elect a non-executive director why they believe an individual should be elected. The chairman should confirm to shareholders when proposing re-election that, following formal performance evaluation, the individual's performance continues to be effective and to demonstrate commitment to the role.

Section C: Accountability

C.1 Financial And Business Reporting

Main Principle

The board should present a fair, balanced and understandable assessment of the company's position and prospects.

Supporting Principle

The board's responsibility to present a fair, balanced and understandable assessment extends to interim and other price-sensitive public reports and reports to regulators as well as to information required to be presented by statutory requirements.

The board should establish arrangements that will enable it to ensure that the information presented is fair balanced and understandable.

Code Provisions

C.1.1 The directors should explain in the annual report their responsibility for preparing the annual report and accounts, and state that they consider the report and accounts, taken a whole, is fair, balanced and understandable and provides the information necessary for shareholders to assess the company's performance, business model and strategy. There should be a statement by the auditor about their reporting responsibilities[11].

C.1.2 The directors should include in the annual report an explanation of the basis on which the company generates or preserves value over the longer term (the business model) and the strategy for delivering the objectives of the company[12].

C.1.3 In annual and half-yearly financial statements the directors should state whether they considered it appropriate to adopt the going concern basis of accounting in preparing them, and identify any material uncertainties to the company's ability to continue to do so over a period of at least 12 months from the date of approval of the financial statements.

C.2 Risk Management and Internal Control[13]

Main Principle

The board is responsible for determining the nature and extent of the significant risks it is willing to take in achieving its strategic objectives. The board should maintain sound risk management and internal control systems.

Code Provision

C.2.1 The directors should confirm in the annual report that they have carried out a robust assessment of the principal risks facing the company, including those that would threaten its business model, future performance, solvency or liquidity. The directors should describe those risks and explain how they are being managed or mitigated.

C.2.2 Taking account of the company's current position and principal risks, the directors should explain in the annual report how they have assessed the prospects of the company, over what period they have done so and why they consider that period to be appropriate. The directors should state whether they have a reasonable expectation that the company will be able to continue in operation and meet its liabilities as they fall due over the period of their assessment, drawing attention to any qualifications or assumptions as necessary.

C.2.3 The board should monitor the company's risk management and internal control systems and, at least annually, carry out a review of their effectiveness, and report on that review in the annual report. The monitoring and review should cover all material controls, including financial, operational and compliance controls.

C.3 Audit Committee and Auditors[14]

Main Principle

The board should establish formal and transparent arrangements for considering how they should apply the corporate reporting and risk management and internal control principles and for maintaining an appropriate relationship with the company's auditor.

Code Provisions

C.3.1 The board should establish an audit committee of at least three, or in the case of smaller companies[15] two, independent non-executive directors. In smaller companies the company chairman may be a member of, but not chair, the committee in addition to the independent non-executive directors, provided he or she was considered independent on appointment as chairman. The board should satisfy itself that at least one member of the audit committee has recent and relevant financial experience[16].

C.3.2 The main role and responsibilities of the audit committee should be set out in written terms of reference[17] and should include:

- to monitor the integrity of the financial statements of the company and any formal announcements relating to the company's financial performance, reviewing significant financial reporting judgements contained in them;
- to review the company's internal financial controls and, unless expressly addressed by a separate board risk committee composed of independent directors, or by the board itself, to review the company's internal control and risk management systems;
- to monitor and review the effectiveness of the company's internal audit function;
- to make recommendations to the board, for it to put to the shareholders for their approval in general meeting, in relation to the appointment, re-appointment and removal of the external auditor and to approve the remuneration and terms of engagement of the external auditor;
- to review and monitor the external auditor's independence and objectivity and the effectiveness of the audit process, taking into consideration relevant UK professional and regulatory requirements;
- to develop and implement policy on the engagement of the external auditor to supply non-audit services, taking into account relevant ethical guidance regarding the provision of non-audit services by the external audit firm, and to report to the board, identifying any matters in respect of which it considers that action or improvement is needed and making recommendations as to the steps to be taken; and to report to the board on how it has discharged its responsibilities.

C.3.3 The terms of reference of the audit committee, including its role and the authority delegated to it by the board, should be made available[18].

C.3.4 Where requested by the board, the audit committee should provide advice on whether the annual report and accounts, taken as whole is fair, balanced and understandable and provides the information necessary for shareholders to assess the company's performance, business model and strategy.

C.3.5 The audit committee should review arrangements by which staff of the company may, in confidence, raise concerns about possible improprieties in matters of financial reporting or other matters. The audit committee's objective should be to ensure that arrangements are in place for the proportionate and independent investigation of such matters and for appropriate follow-up action.

C.3.6 The audit committee should monitor and review the effectiveness of the internal audit activities. Where there is no internal audit function, the audit committee should consider annually whether there is a need for an internal audit function and make a recommendation to the board, and the reasons for the absence of such a function should be explained in the relevant section of the annual report.

C.3.7 The audit committee should have primary responsibility for making a recommendation on the appointment, reappointment and removal of the external auditor. FTSE 350 companies should put the external audit contract out to tender at least every ten years. If the board does not accept the audit committee's recommendation, it should include in the annual report, and in any papers recommending appointment or re-appointment, a statement from the audit committee explaining the recommendation and should set out reasons why the board has taken a different position.

C.3.8 A separate section of the annual report should describe the work of the committee in discharging its responsibilities. The report should include:

- the significant issues that the committee considered in relation to the financial statements, and how these issues were addressed;
- an explanation of how it has assessed the effectiveness of the external audit process and the approach taken to the appointment or reappointment of the external auditor, and information on the length of tenure of the current audit firm and when a tender was last conducted ;and
- if the external auditor provides non-audit services, an explanation of how auditor objectivity and independence is safeguarded.

The UK Corporate Governance Code (September 2014)

Section D: Remuneration

D.1 The Level and Components of Remuneration

Main Principle

Executive directors' remuneration should be designed to promote the long-term success of the company. Performance-related elements should be transparent, stretching and rigorously applied.

Supporting Principles

The remuneration committee should judge where to position their company relative to other companies. But they should use such comparisons with caution in view of the risk of an upward ratchet of remuneration levels with no corresponding improvement in corporate and individual performance and should avoid paying more than is necessary.

They should also be sensitive to pay and employment conditions elsewhere in the group, especially when determining annual salary increases.

Code Provisions

D.1.1 In designing schemes of performance-related remuneration for executive directors, the remuneration committee should follow the provisions in Schedule A to this Code. Schemes should include provisions that would enable the company to recover sums paid or withhold the payment of any sum and specify the circumstances in which it would be appropriate to do so.

D.1.2 Where a company releases an executive director to serve as a non-executive director elsewhere, the remuneration report[19] should include a statement as to whether or not the director will retain such earnings and, if so, what the remuneration is.

D.1.3 Levels of remuneration for non-executive directors should reflect the time commitment and responsibilities of the role. Remuneration for non-executive directors should not include share options or other performance-related elements. If, exceptionally, options are granted, shareholder approval should be sought in advance and any shares acquired by exercise of the options should be held until at least one year after the non-executive director leaves the board. Holding of share options could be relevant to the determination of a non-executive director's independence (as set out in provision B.1.1).

D.1.4 The remuneration committee should carefully consider what compensation commitments (including pension contributions and all other elements) their directors' terms of appointment would entail in the event of early termination. The aim should be to avoid rewarding poor performance. They should take a robust line on reducing compensation to reflect departing directors' obligations to mitigate loss.

D.1.5 Notice or contract periods should be set at one year or less. If it is necessary to offer longer notice or contract periods to new directors recruited from outside, such periods should reduce to one year or less after the initial period.

D.2 Procedure

Main Principle

There should be a formal and transparent procedure for developing policy on executive remuneration and for fixing the remuneration packages of individual directors. No director should be involved in deciding his or her own remuneration.

Supporting Principles

The remuneration committee should take care to recognise and avoid conflicts of interest when receiving views from executive directors or senior management or consulting the chief executive about its proposals. The remuneration committee should also be responsible for appointing consultants in respect of executive directors' remuneration. The chairman of the board should ensure that the company maintains contact as required with its principal shareholders about remuneration.

Code Provisions

D.2.1 The board should establish a remuneration committee of at least three, or in the case of smaller companies[20] two, independent non-executive directors. In addition the company chairman may also be a member of, but not chair, the committee if he or she was considered independent on appointment as chairman. The remuneration committee should make available its terms of reference, explaining its role and the authority delegated to it by the board[21]. Where remuneration consultants are appointed, they should be identified in the annual report and a statement made as to whether they have any other connection with the company[22].

D.2.2 The remuneration committee should have delegated responsibility for setting remuneration for all executive directors and the chairman, including pension rights and any compensation payments. The committee should also recommend and monitor the level and structure of remuneration for senior management. The definition of 'senior management' for this purpose should be determined by the board but should normally include the first layer of management below board level.

D.2.3 The board itself or, where required by the Articles of Association, the shareholders should determine the remuneration of the non-executive directors within the limits set in the Articles of Association. Where permitted by the Articles, the board may however delegate this responsibility to a committee, which might include the chief executive.

D.2.4 Shareholders should be invited specifically to approve all new long-term incentive schemes (as defined in the Listing Rules [23]) and significant changes to existing schemes, save in the circumstances permitted by the Listing Rules.

Section E: Relations with Shareholders

E.1 Dialogue with Shareholders

Main Principle

There should be a dialogue with shareholders based on the mutual understanding of objectives. The board as a whole has responsibility for ensuring that a satisfactory dialogue with shareholders takes place[24].

Supporting Principles

Whilst recognising that most shareholder contact is with the chief executive and finance director, the chairman should ensure that all directors are made aware of their major shareholders' issues and concerns.

The board should keep in touch with shareholder opinion in whatever ways are most practical and efficient.

Code Provisions

E.1.1 The chairman should ensure that the views of shareholders are communicated to the board as a whole. The chairman should discuss governance and strategy with major shareholders. Non-executive directors should be offered the opportunity to attend scheduled meetings with major shareholders and should expect to attend meetings if requested by major shareholders. The senior independent director should attend sufficient meetings with a range of major shareholders to listen to their views in order to help develop a balanced understanding of the issues and concerns of major shareholders.

E.1.2 The board should state in the annual report the steps they have taken to ensure that the members of the board, and, in particular, the non-executive directors, develop an understanding of the views of major shareholders about the company, for example through direct face-to-face contact, analysts' or brokers' briefings and surveys of shareholder opinion.

E.2 Constructive Use of General meetings

Main Principle

The board should use general meetings to communicate with investors and to encourage their participation.

Code Provisions

E.2.1 At any general meeting, the company should propose a separate resolution on each substantially separate issue, and should, in particular, propose a resolution at the AGM relating to the report and accounts. For each resolution, proxy appointment forms should provide shareholders with the option to direct their proxy to vote either for or against the resolution or to withhold their vote. The proxy form and any announcement of the results of a vote should make it clear that a 'vote withheld' is not a vote in law and will not be counted in the calculation of the proportion of the votes for and against the resolution.

E.2.2 The company should ensure that all valid proxy appointments received for general meetings are properly recorded and counted. For each resolution, where a vote has been taken on a show of hands, the company should ensure that the following information is given at the meeting and made available as soon as reasonably practicable on a website which is maintained by or on behalf of the company:

- the number of shares in respect of which proxy appointments have been validly made;
- the number of votes for the resolution;
- the number of votes against the resolution; and
- the number of shares in respect of which the vote was directed to be withheld.

When, in the opinion of the board, a significant proportion of votes have been cast against a resolution at any general meeting, the company should explain when announcing the results of voting what actions it intends to take to understand the reasons behind the vote itself.

E.2.3 The chairman should arrange for the chairmen of the audit, remuneration and nomination committees to be available to answer questions at the AGM and for all directors to attend.

E.2.4 The company should arrange for the Notice of the AGM and related papers to be sent to shareholders at least 20 working days before the meeting. For other general meetings this should be at least 14 working days in advance.

Schedule A: The design of performance-related remuneration for executive directors

Balance

The remuneration committee should determine an appropriate balance between fixed and performance-related, immediate and deferred remuneration. Performance conditions, including non-financial metrics where appropriate, should be relevant, stretching and designed to promote the long-term success of the company. Remuneration incentives should be compatible with risk policies and systems. Upper limits should be set and disclosed.

The remuneration committee should consider whether the directors should be eligible for annual bonuses and/or benefits under long-term incentive schemes.

Share-based remuneration

Traditional share option schemes should be weighed against other kinds of long-term incentive scheme. Executive share options should not be offered at a discount save as permitted by the relevant provisions of the Listing Rules.

Any new long-term incentive schemes which are proposed should be approved by shareholders and should preferably replace any existing schemes or, at least, form part of a well-considered overall plan incorporating existing schemes. The total potentially available rewards should not be excessive. For share-based remuneration the remuneration committee should consider requiring directors to hold a minimum number of shares and to hold shares for a further period after vesting or exercise, including for a period after leaving the company, subject to the need to finance any costs of acquisition and associated tax liabilities. In normal circumstances, shares granted or other forms of deferred remuneration should not vest or be paid, and options should not be exercisable, in less than three years. Longer periods may be appropriate. Grants under executive share option and other long-term incentive schemes should normally be phased rather than awarded in one large block.

Pensions

In general, only basic salary should be pensionable. The remuneration committee should consider the pension consequences and associated costs to the company of basic salary increases and any other changes in pensionable remuneration, especially for directors close to retirement.

Schedule B: Disclosure of corporate governance arrangements

Corporate governance disclosure requirements are set out in three places:

- FCA Disclosure and Transparency Rules sub-chapters 7.1 and 7.2 (which set out certain mandatory disclosures);
- FCA Listing Rules 9.8.6 R, 9.8.7 R, and 9.8.7A R (which includes the 'comply or explain' requirement); and
- The UK Corporate Governance Code (in addition to providing an explanation where they choose not to comply with a provision, companies must disclose specified information in order to comply with certain provisions).

These requirements are summarised below with the full text contained in the relevant chapters of the FCA Handbook, which can be found at www.fsa.gov.uk/handbook.

The Disclosure and Transparency Rules sub-chapters 7.1 and 7.2 apply to issuers whose securities are admitted to trading on a regulated market (this includes all issuers with a Premium or Standard listing). The Listing Rules 9.8.6 R, 9.8.7 R and 9.8.7A R and UK Corporate Governance Code apply to issuers of Premium listed equity shares only.

There is some overlap between the mandatory disclosures required under the Disclosure and Transparency Rules and those expected under the Code. Areas of overlap are summarised in the Appendix to this Schedule. In respect of disclosures relating to the audit committee and the composition and operation of the board and its committees, compliance with the relevant provisions of the Code will result in compliance with the relevant Rules.

Disclosure and Transparency Rules

Sub-chapter 7.1 of the Disclosure and Transparency Rules concerns audit committees or bodies carrying out equivalent functions.

DTR 7.1.1 R to 7.1.3 R set out requirements relating to the composition and functions of the committee or equivalent body:

- DTR 7.1.1 R states than an issuer must have a body which is responsible for performing the functions set out in DTR 7.1.3 R, and that at least one member of that body must be independent and at least one member must have competence in accounting and/or auditing.
- DTR 7.1.2 G states that the requirements for independence and competence in accounting and/or auditing may be satisfied by the same member or by different members of the relevant body.
- DTR 7.1.3 R states that an issuer must ensure that, as a minimum, the relevant body must:
  (1) monitor the financial reporting process;
  (2) monitor the effectiveness of the issuer's internal control, internal audit where applicable, and risk management systems;
  (3) monitor the statutory audit of the annual and consolidated accounts;
  (4) review and monitor the independence of the statutory auditor, and in particular the provision of additional services to the issuer.

DTR 7.1.5 R to DTR 7.1.7 G set out what disclosure is required. Specifically:

- DTR 7.1.5 R states that the issuer must make a statement available to the public disclosing which body carries out the functions required by DTR 7.1.3 R and how it is composed.
- DTR 7.1.6 G states that this can be included in the corporate governance statement required under sub-chapter DTR 7.2 (see below).

- DTR 7.1.7 G states that compliance with the relevant provisions of the UK Corporate Governance Code (as set out in the Appendix to this Schedule) will result in compliance with DTR 7.1.1 R to 7.1.5 R.

Sub-chapter 7.2 concerns corporate governance statements. Issuers are required to produce a corporate governance statement that must be either included in the directors' report (DTR 7.2.1 R); or in a separate report published together with the annual report; or on the issuer's website, in which case there must be a cross-reference in the directors' report (DTR 7.2.9 R).

DTR 7.2.2 R requires that the corporate governance statements must contain a reference to the corporate governance code to which the company is subject (for companies with a Premium listing this is the UK Corporate Governance Code). DTR 7.2.3 R requires that, to the extent that it departs from that code, the company must explain which parts of the code it departs from and the reasons for doing so. DTR 7.2.4 G states that compliance with LR 9.8.6 R (6) (the 'comply or explain' rule in relation to the UK Corporate Governance Code) will also satisfy these requirements.

DTR 7.2.5 R to DTR 7.2.10 R set out certain information that must be disclosed in the corporate governance statement:

- DTR 7.2.5 R states that the corporate governance statement must contain a description of the main features of the company's internal control and risk management systems in relation to the financial reporting process. DTR 7.2.10 R states that an issuer which is required to prepare a group directors' report within the meaning of Section 415(2) of the Companies Act 2006 must include in that report a description of the main features of the group's internal control and risk management systems in relation to the process for preparing consolidated accounts.
- DTR 7.2.6 R states that the corporate governance statement must contain the information required by paragraph 13(2)(c), (d), (f), (h) and (i) of Schedule 7 to the Large and Medium-sized Companies and Groups (Accounts and Reports) Regulations 2008 (SI 2008 No 410) where the issuer is subject to the requirements of that paragraph.
- DTR 7.2.7 R states that the corporate governance statement must contain a description of the composition and operation of the issuer's administrative, management and supervisory bodies and their committees. DTR 7.2.8 G states that compliance with the relevant provisions of the UK Corporate Governance Code (as set out in the Appendix to this Schedule) will satisfy these requirements.

Listing Rules

Listing Rules 9.8.6 R (for UK incorporated companies) and 9.8.7 R (for overseas incorporated companies) state that in the case of a company that has a Premium listing of equity shares, the following items must be included in its annual report and accounts:

- a statement of how the listed company has applied the Main Principles set out in the UK Corporate Governance Code, in a manner that would enable shareholders to evaluate how the principles have been applied;
- a statement as to whether the listed company has:
    - complied throughout the accounting period with all relevant provisions set out in the UK Corporate Governance Code; or
    - not complied throughout the accounting period with all relevant provisions set out in the UK Corporate Governance Code, and if so, setting out:
        (i) those provisions, if any, it has not complied with;
        (ii) in the case of provisions whose requirements are of a

continuing nature, the period within which, if any, it did not comply with some or all of those provisions; and

(iii) the company's reasons for non-compliance.

The UK Corporate Governance Code

In addition to the 'comply or explain' requirement in the Listing Rules, the Code includes specific requirements for disclosure which must be provided in order to comply. These are summarised below. The annual report should include:

- a statement of how the board operates, including a high level statement of which types of decisions are to be taken by the board and which are to be delegated to management (A.1.1);
- the names of the chairman, the deputy chairman (where there is one), the chief executive, the senior independent director and the chairmen and members of the board committees (A.1.2);
- the number of meetings of the board and those committees and individual attendance by directors (A.1.2);
- where a chief executive is appointed chairman, the reasons for their appointment (this only needs to be done in the annual report following the appointment) (A.3.1);
- the names of the non-executive directors whom the board determines to be independent, with reasons where necessary (B.1.1);
- a separate section describing the work of the nomination committee, including the process it has used in relation to board appointments; a description of the board's policy on diversity, including gender; any measurable objectives that it has set for implementing the policy, and progress on achieving the objectives. An explanation should be given if neither external search consultancy nor open advertising has been used in the appointment of a chairman or a non-executive director. Where an external search consultancy has been used it should be identified and a statement made as to whether it has any other connection with the company (B.2.4);
- the impact of any changes to the other significant commitments of the chairman during the year should be explained (B.3.1);
- a statement of how performance evaluation of the board, its committees and its directors has been conducted (B.6.1). Where an external facilitator has been used, they should be identified and a statement made as to whether they have any other connection to the company (B.6.2);
- an explanation from the directors of their responsibility for preparing the accounts and a statement that they consider that the annual report and accounts, taken as a whole, is fair, balanced and understandable and provides the information necessary for shareholders to assess the company's position and performance, business model and strategy. There should also be a statement by the auditor about their reporting responsibilities (C.1.1);
- an explanation from the directors of the basis on which the company generates or preserves value over the longer term (the business model) and the strategy for delivering the objectives of the company (C.1.2);
- a statement from the directors whether they considered it appropriate to adopt the going concern basis of accounting in preparing them, and identify any material uncertainties to the company's ability to continue to do so over a period of at least 12 months from the date of approval of the financial statements (C.1.3);
- the principal risks facing the company, including those that would threaten its business model, future performance, solvency or liquidity.

The directors should describe the risks and explain how they are being managed or mitigated (C.2.1);

- of the company (taking account of the company's current position and principal risks), over what period they have done so and why they consider that period to be appropriate. The directors should state whether they have a reasonable expectation that the company will be able to continue in operation and meet its liabilities as they fall due over the period of their assessment, drawing attention to any qualifications or assumptions as necessary (C.2.2);
- a report on the board's review of the effectiveness of the company's risk management and internal controls systems (C.2.3):
- where there is no internal audit function, the reasons for the absence of such a function (C.3.6);
- where the board does not accept the audit committee's recommendation on the appointment, reappointment or removal of an external auditor, a statement from the audit committee explaining the recommendation and the reasons why the board has taken a different position (C.3.7);
- a separate section describing the work of the audit committee in discharging its responsibilities, including: the significant issues that it considered in relation to the financial statements, and how these issues were addressed; an explanation of how it has assessed the effectiveness of the external audit process and the approach taken to the appointment or reappointment of the external auditor, including the length of tenure of the current audit firm and when a tender was last conducted; and, if the external auditor provides non-audit services, an explanation of how auditor objectivity and independence is safeguarded (C.3.8);
- a description of the work of the remuneration committee as required under the Large and Medium-Sized Companies and Groups (Accounts and Reports) Regulations 2008 including, where an executive director serves as a non-executive director elsewhere, whether or not the director will retain such earnings and, if so, what the remuneration is (D.1.2);
- where remuneration consultants are appointed they should be identified and a statement made as to whether they have any other connection with the company (D.2.1); and
- the steps the board has taken to ensure that members of the board, in particular the non-executive directors, develop an understanding of the views of major shareholders about their company (E.1.2).

The following information should be made available (which may be met by placing the information on a website that is maintained by or on behalf of the company):

- the terms of reference of the nomination, audit and remuneration committees, explaining their role and the authority delegated to them by the board (B.2.1, C.3.3 and D.2.1); and
- the terms and conditions of appointment of non-executive directors (B.3.2).

The board should set out to shareholders in the papers accompanying a resolution to elect or re-elect directors:

- sufficient biographical details to enable shareholders to take an informed decision on their election or re-election (B.7.1);
- why they believe an individual should be elected to a non-executive role (B.7.2); and
- on re-election of a non-executive director, confirmation from the chairman that, following formal performance evaluation, the individual's performance continues to be effective and to demonstrate commitment to the role (B.7.2).

The board should set out to shareholders in the papers recommending appointment or reappointment of an external auditor:

– if the board does not accept the audit committee's recommendation, a statement from the audit committee explaining the recommendation and from the board setting out reasons why they have taken a different position (C.3.6).

Additional guidance

The FRC publishes guidance on the strategic report, risk management, internal control, business and financial reporting and audit committees, which relate to s C of the Code. These guidance notes are available on the FRC website.

Appendix: Overlap between the Disclosure and Transparency Rules and the UK Corporate Governance Code

Disclosure and Transparency Rules	UK Corporate Governance
D.T.R 7.1.1 R	**Provision C.3.1**
Sets out minimum requirements on composition of the audit committee or equivalent body.	Sets out recommended composition of the audit committee.
D.T.R 7.1.3 R	**Provision C.3.2**
Sets out minimum functions of the audit committee or equivalent body.	Sets out the recommended minimum terms of reference for the committee.
D.T.R 7.1.5 R	**Provision A.1.2**
The composition and function of the audit committee or equivalent body must be disclosed in the annual report	The annual report should identify members of the board committees.
	Provision C.3.3
DTR 7.1.7 R states that compliance with Code provisions A.1.2, C.3.1, C.3.2 and C.3.3 will result in compliance with DTR 7.1.1 R to DTR 7.1.5 R.	The annual report should describe the work of the audit committee.
D.T.R 7.2.5 R	**Provision C.2.1**
The corporate governance statement must include a description of the main features of the company's internal control and risk management systems in relation to the financial reporting process.	The directors should confirm that they have carried out a robust assessment of the principal risks facing the company – including those that would threaten its business model, future performance, solvency or liquidity. The directors should describe those risks and explain how they are being managed or mitigated.
	Provision C.2.3
	The board should monitor the company's risk management and internal control systems and, at least annually, carry out a review of their effectiveness, and report on that review in the annual report. The monitoring and review should cover all material controls, including financial, operational and compliance controls.

While this requirement differs from the requirement in the UK Corporate Governance Code, it is envisaged that both could be met by a single internal control statement.	
DTR 7.2.7 R	
The corporate governance statement must include a description of the composition and operation of the administrative, management and supervisory bodies and their committees.	This requirement overlaps with a number of different provisions of the Code:
DTR 7.2.8 R states that compliance with Code provisions A.1.1, A.1.2, A.4.6, B.2.1 and C.3.3 with result in compliance with DTR 7.2.7 R.	**A.1.1**: the annual report should include a statement of how the board operates. **A.1.2**: the annual report should identify members of the board and board committees. **B.2.4**: the annual report should describe the work of the nomination committee. **C.3.3**: the annual report should describe the work of the audit committee. **D.2.1**: a description of the work of the remuneration committee should be made available. *[Note: in order to comply with DTR 7.2.7 R this information will need to be included in the corporate governance statement].*

---

1 References to shareholders also apply to intermediaries and agents employed to assist shareholders in scrutinising governance arrangements.

2 For directors of UK incorporated companies, these duties are set out in the Sections 170 to 177 of the Companies Act 2006.

3 Provisions A.1.1 and A.1.2 overlap with FCA Rule DTR 7.2.7 R; Provision A.1.2 also overlaps with DTR 7.1.5 R (see Schedule B).

4 Compliance or otherwise with this provision need only be reported for the year in which the appointment is made.

5 A.3.1 states that the chairman should, on appointment, meet the independence criteria set out in this provision, but thereafter the test of independence is not appropriate in relation to the chairman.

6 A smaller company is one that is below the FTSE 350 throughout the year immediately prior to the reporting year.

7 The requirement to make the information available would be met by including the information on a website that is maintained by or on behalf of the company.

8 This provision overlaps with FCA Rule DTR 7.2.7 R (see Schedule B).

9 The terms and conditions of appointment of non-executive directors should be made available for inspection by any person at the company's registered office during normal business hours and at the AGM (for 15 minutes prior to the meeting and during the meeting).

10 See footnote 7.

11 The requirement may be met by the disclosures about the audit scope and the responsibilities of the auditor included, or referred to, in the auditor's report pursuant to the requirements in paragraph 16 of ISA (UK and Ireland) 700, 'The Auditor's Report on Financial Statements'. Copies are available at: www.frc.org.uk/getattachment/3e29341c-6cc7-45c2-90e1-5b0a6cf3400d/700-The-auditor-s-report-on-financial-statements.aspx.

12 It would be desirable if the explanation were located in the same part of the annual report as the

Business Review required by Section 417 of the Companies Act 2006. Guidance as to the matters that should be considered in an explanation of a business model is provided in paragraphs 30 to 32 of the Accounting Standard Board's *Reporting Statement: Operating And Financial Review*. Copies are available at: www.frc.org.uk/FRC-Documents/ASB/Reporting-Statement-Operating-and-Financial-Review.aspx.

13 The Turnbull guidance suggests means of applying this part of the Code. Copies are available at www.frc.org.uk/getattachment/5e4d12e4-a94f-4186-9d6f-19e17aeb5351/Turnbull-guidance-October-2005.aspx.

14 The FRC Guidance on Audit Committees suggests means of applying this part of the Code. Copies are available at: www.frc.org.uk/getattachment/fd68e3e4-7c14-491e-b8ad-ce7af6fd4517/Guidance-on-Audit-Committees.aspx.

15 See footnote 6.

16 This provision overlaps with FCA Rule DTR 7.1.1 R (see Schedule B).

17 This provision overlaps with FCA Rules DTR 7.1.3 R (see Schedule C).

18 See footnote 7.

19 As required for UK incorporated companies under the Large and Medium-Sized Companies and Groups (Accounts and Reports) Regulations 2008.

20 See footnote 6.

21 This provision overlaps with FCA Rule DTR 7.2.7 R (see Schedule B).

22 See footnote 7.

23 Listing Rules LR 9.4; available at www.fsa.gov.uk/pubs/other/listing_rules.pdf.

24 Nothing in these principles or provisions should be taken to override the general requirements of law to treat shareholders equally in access to information.

This material is reproduced with the kind permission of the copyright holder, the Financial Reporting Council ('FRC'). For more information contact the FRC on 020 7492 2300 or visit www.frc.org.uk.

16 Dealings with Third Parties

16.1 **A company's capacity**
16.2 Power of directors to bind the company
16.3 Transactions involving directors and their associates
16.4 Charitable companies
16.5 **Contracts**
16.6 **Deeds and documents: Provisions applying in England and Wales and Northern Ireland**
16.7 **Execution of documents: Provisions applying in Scotland**
16.8 **Common seal**
16.9 Official seal for use abroad
16.10 Official seal for share certificates, etc
16.11 **Bills of exchange and promissory notes**
16.12 **Trading disclosures**
16.13 Display of registered name at registered office, etc
16.14 Inclusion of name and other specified information in documents and communications
16.15 Provision of information on request
16.16 Civil consequences of failure to disclose
16.17 **Effect of failure to give public notice**
16.18 **Fraudulent trading**
16.19 **Service addresses**
16.20 **Service of documents on a company**
16.21 **Service of documents on directors, secretaries and others**
16.22 **Sending documents and information (the 'company communication provisions')**
16.23 Documents and information sent or supplied to a company
16.27 Communications by a company
16.33 Right of members and debenture holders to hard copy version
16.34 Deemed delivery of documents and information

Cross references. See **12.1** Company Formation and Types of Company (for pre-incorporation contracts) and **14** Constitution – Memorandum and Articles.

16.1 A COMPANY'S CAPACITY

The basis for whether a company has capacity to carry out transactions was based historically on the objects as set out in its memorandum of association and the doctrine of ultra vires. If a company exceeded the powers given by the objects its actions were ultra vires, the transaction would be void and the officers in breach responsible for breach of duty (*Ashbury Railway Carriage and Iron Co Ltd v Riche* (1875) LR 7 HL 653, HL). Changes brought about by *CA 1985, s 35* were designed to ensure that the validity of any transactions could not be challenged on the ground of lack of corporate capacity. *CA 2006, s 39* replaced *CA 1985, s 35* as from 1 October 2009 with little change other than substituting "constitution" for "memorandum" given the other constitutional changes brought in on that date (see **14** Constitution – Memorandum and Articles). *Section 39* provides that the validity of an act done by a company cannot be called into question on the ground of lack of capacity by reason of anything in the company's constitution. But see **16.3** for certain transactions where a director (or a person connected with him) is a party to the contract and **16.4** for charitable companies.

Additionally the scope of the *ultra vires* doctrine has been further limited by the introduction of *CA 2006, s 31* which provides that a company's objects are unrestricted unless the company's articles restrict them. This means that a company incorporated on or after 1 October 2009 has unlimited capacity (unless it chooses to have some restrictions in its articles) and companies incorporated before that date the provisions of whose memorandum are deemed to form provisions of their articles (see **14 Company Constitution**) can amend or remove any restrictions by changing their articles.

16.2 Power of directors to bind the company

Although for reasons given in **16.1** a company's objects do not limit the company's capacity, they do restrict the directors' authority. If the directors exceed the authority given by the objects, the transaction will not be invalid as a consequence but only voidable and provided that the other party satisfies the 'good faith' requirement they will be protected. See below for the definition of good faith. If the third party cannot show good faith and the transaction is outside the company's objects then it will be void.

Subject to **16.3** and **16.4**, where a person 'deals with' a company in good faith, the power of the directors to bind the company, or authorise others to do so, is deemed to be free of any limitation under the company's constitution. This includes limitations deriving from

- a resolution of the company or of any class of shareholders; or
- any agreement between the members of the company or of any class of shareholders.

[*CA 2006, s 40(1), (3), (6)*].

A person '*deals with*' a company if he is a party to any transaction or other act to which the company is a party. A person dealing with a company is

- not bound to enquire as to any limitation on the powers of the directors to bind the company or authorise others to do so;
- presumed to have acted in good faith unless the contrary is proved; and
- not to be regarded as acting in bad faith by reason only of his knowing that an act is beyond the powers of the directors under the company's constitution.

[*CA 2006, s 40(2)*].

The above provisions do not affect

- any right of a member of the company to bring proceedings to restrain the doing of an action that is beyond the powers of the directors. No such proceedings can be brought if the action is done to fulfil a legal obligation arising from a previous act of the company; or
- any liability incurred by the directors, or any other person, by reason of the directors exceeding their powers.

[*CA 2006, s 40(4), (5)*].

16.3 Transactions involving directors or their associates

Where a company enters into a transaction and the validity of that transaction depends on the provisions in *CA 2006, s 40* (ie that the powers of the directors are deemed to be free of any limitations under the company's constitution) if the third party is acting in good faith and the parties to the transaction include

(i) a director of the company or of its holding company, or

(ii) a person '*connected with*' any such director,

the transaction is voidable at the instance of the company. 'Connected with' has the same meaning as in *CA 2006, s 252* (see **18.1 Directors**).

Whether or not the transaction is avoided, any party to the transaction and any director of the company who authorised the transaction, is liable to

- account to the company for any gain he has made directly or indirectly by the transaction, and
- indemnify the company for any loss or damage resulting from the transaction

except that a person other than a director of the company is not liable if he shows that, at the time the transaction was entered into, he did not know that the directors were exceeding their powers.

The transaction ceases to be voidable if

- restitution of any money or other asset which was the subject-matter of the transaction is no longer possible;
- the company is indemnified for any loss or damage resulting from the transaction;
- rights acquired *bona fide* for value and without actual notice of the directors' exceeding their powers by a person who is not party to the transaction would be affected by the avoidance; or
- the transaction is affirmed by the company (but see **16.4** where the company is a charity).

Nothing in the above provisions affects the rights of any party to the transaction not within (i) or (ii) above, but the court may, on the application of the company or any such party, make an order affirming, severing or setting aside the transaction on such terms as appear to the court to be just.

[*CA 2006, s 41*].

16.4 Charitable companies

England and Wales and Northern Ireland. The provisions in **16.1** and **16.2** do not apply to the acts of a company that is a charity except in favour of a person who

(a) does not know at the time the act is done that the company is a charity, or

(b) gives full consideration in money or money's worth in relation to the act in question and does not know that the act is not permitted by the company's constitution or, as the case may be, is beyond the powers of the directors.

In any proceedings, the burden of proof that (*a*) or (*b*) above is not satisfied lies with the person asserting that fact.

But where a company that is a charity purports to transfer or grant an interest in property, the title of a person who subsequently acquires the property or an interest in it and who satisfies the conditions in (*b*) above is not affected by the fact that the act was not so permitted or beyond the directors' powers.

[*CA 2006, s 42(1)–(3)*].

In the case of a company that is a charity the affirmation of a transaction to which **16.3** applies is ineffective without the prior written consent of

- in England and Wales, the Charity Commission; or
- in Northern Ireland, the Department for Social Development (the functions of this department have been transferred to the Charities Commission for the purposes of *CA 2006, s 42(4)(b)*)

[*CA 2006, s 42(4); Charities Act (Northern Ireland) 2013, s 5*].

Scotland. Corresponding provisions apply to charitable companies that are registered in Scotland. [*CA 1989, s 112(3)–(5)*].

16.5 CONTRACTS

Under the law of England and Wales or Northern Ireland, a contract may be made

- by a company, by writing under its common seal; or
- on behalf of a company, by a person acting under its authority, express or implied.

Unless a contrary intention appears, any formalities required by law in the case of a contract made by an individual also apply to one made by or on behalf of a company.

[*CA 2006, s 43*].

16.6 DEEDS AND DOCUMENTS: PROVISIONS APPLYING IN ENGLAND AND WALES AND NORTHERN IRELAND

(1) *Execution of documents*

A document is executed by a company in either of the following ways.

(a) By the affixing of its common seal (see **16.8**)

(b) If it is signed on behalf of the company by

  (i) two 'authorised signatories'; or

  (ii) a director of the company in the presence of a witness who attests the signature.

  '*Authorised signatories*' are every director of the company and, in the case of a private company with a secretary or a public company, the secretary (or any joint secretary) of the company.

  A document so signed and expressed, in whatever words, to be executed by the company has the same effect as if executed under the common seal of the company.

In favour of a 'purchaser', a document is deemed to have been duly executed by a company if it purports to be signed in accordance with (*b*) above. A '*purchaser*' means a purchaser in good faith for valuable consideration and includes a lessee, mortgagee or other person who, for valuable consideration, acquires an interest in property.

Where a document is to be signed by a person on behalf of more than one company, it is not duly signed by that person for the purposes of these provisions unless he signs it separately in each capacity.

References above to a document being (or purporting to be) signed by a director or secretary are to be read, in a case where that office is held by a firm, as references to its being (or purporting to be) signed by an individual authorised by the firm to sign on its behalf.

The above provisions apply to a document that is (or purports to be) executed by a company in the name of or on behalf of another person whether or not that person is also a company.

[*CA 2006, s 44*].

(2) *Execution of deeds*

A document is validly executed by a company as a deed for the purposes of *Law of Property (Miscellaneous Provisions) Act 1989, s 1(2)(b)* and the law of Northern Ireland if, and only if, it is

- duly executed by the company; and
- delivered as a deed.

A document is presumed to be delivered for these purposes upon its being executed, unless a contrary intention is proved.

[*CA 2006, s 46*].

(3) *Execution of deeds or other documents by attorney*

A company may, by instrument executed as a deed, empower a person, either generally or in respect of specified matters, as its attorney to execute deeds or other documents on its behalf. A deed or other document so executed, whether in the UK or elsewhere, has effect as if executed by the company. [*CA 2006, s 47*].

Where the power to act as a company's attorney was conferred before 1 October 2009, (including in relation to instruments executed by the attorney on behalf of the company on or after that date), *CA 1985, s 38* continues to apply.

16.7 EXECUTION OF DOCUMENTS: PROVISIONS APPLYING IN SCOTLAND

Despite the provisions of any enactment, a company need not have a company seal (see **16.8**). For the purposes of any enactment

- providing for a document to be executed by a company by affixing its common seal, or
- referring (in whatever terms) to a document so executed,

a document signed or subscribed by or on behalf of the company in accordance with the provisions of the *Requirements of Writing (Scotland) Act 1995* has effect as if so executed.

[*CA 2006, s 48*].

Except where an enactment provides otherwise, a document is signed by a company if it is signed in its behalf by a director, or by the secretary, or by a person authorised to sign the document on its behalf. [*Requirements of Writing (Scotland) Act 1995, Sch 2 para 3*].

16.8 COMMON SEAL

A company may have a common seal, but need not have one. [*CA 2006, ss 45(1), 48(2)*].

Under the law of England and Wales and Northern Ireland, a company which has a common seal must have its name engraved on it in legible characters. An offence is committed by

- the company, and every officer of the company who is in default, if the company fails to have the common seal so engraved; and
- by an officer of a company, or a person acting on behalf of a company, if he uses, or authorises the use of, a seal purporting to be a seal of the company on which its name is not engraved.

A person guilty of such an offence is liable, on summary conviction, to a fine not exceeding level 3 on the standard scale. See **29.1 OFFENCES AND LEGAL PROCEEDINGS** for the standard scale.

[*CA 2006, s 45*].

Authority to use seal. Where a company has adopted standard articles, see

- *Table A, 1985, Reg 101*
- *Model Articles, Art 49* (private companies)
- *Model Articles, Art 81* (public companies)

Set out in **APPENDIX 4** standard articles of association.

Table A 1985 provides (in summary) that the seal can only be used if the directors, or a committee of the directors, authorise its use and any instruments to which the seal is affixed shall be signed either by a director and the secretary or by two directors.

The Model Articles provide (in summary) that the seal can only be used if the directors authorise its use and that any document to which the seal is affixed must be signed by either one director or by the company secretary or by any other person authorised by the directors. The Model Articles for public companies additionally provide for the use of the official seal for use abroad (see **16.9** below) and the use of the securities seal (if any) (see **16.10** below).

16.9 Official seal for use abroad

A company which has a common seal may have an official seal for use outside the UK. It must be a facsimile of the common seal with the addition on its face of place or places where it is to be used. In England and Wales and Northern Ireland, when duly affixed to a document, the official seal has the same effect as the company's common seal.

A company which has an official seal for use outside the UK may, by writing under its common seal (or, as respects Scotland, by writing subscribed in accordance with the *Requirements of Writing (Scotland) Act 1995*), authorise any person appointed for the purposes to affix the official seal to any deed or other document to which the company is a party. As between the company and a person dealing with such an agent, the agent's authority continues

- during the period mentioned in the instrument conferring the authority; or
- if no period is mentioned, until notice of the revocation or termination of the agent's authority has been given to the person dealing with him.

The person affixing the official seal must certify in writing on the deed or other document to which the seal is affixed the date on which, and place at which, it is affixed.

[*CA 2006, s 49*].

16.10 Official seal for share certificates, etc

A company that has a common seal may have an official seal for use for sealing securities issued by the company or for sealing documents creating or evidencing securities so issued. The official seal must be a facsimile of the company's common seal, with the addition on its face of the word 'Securities'. When duly affixed to the document, it has the same effect as the company's common seal. [*CA 2006, s 50*].

The foregoing provisions are without prejudice to the right of a company to subscribe such securities and documents in accordance with the *Requirements of Writing (Scotland) Act 1995*. [*Requirements of Writing (Scotland) Act 1995, Sch 4, paras 55, 57*].

16.11 BILLS OF EXCHANGE AND PROMISSORY NOTES

A bill of exchange or promissory note is deemed to have been made, accepted or endorsed on behalf of a company if made, accepted or endorsed in the name of, or by or on behalf or on account of, the company by a person acting under its authority. [*CA 2006, s 52*].

16.12 TRADING DISCLOSURES

Regulations made under *CA 2006, s 82* require a company to disclose specified trading information [*CA 2006, s 82*] and make it a criminal offence where the company fails, without reasonable excuse, to comply with the provisions. [*CA 2006, s 84*]. These requirements fall into three categories.

- Displaying a sign with the company name and certain other information at specific locations (see **16.13**).
- Including the company name and specified other information in certain documents and communications (see **16.14**).
- Providing the company name and specified other information to those who request it in the course of business (**16.15**).

16.13 Display of registered name at registered office, etc

Every company must display its registered name at

(a) its registered office;

(b) any '*inspection place*' ie any location (other than its registered office) at which it keeps available for inspection any 'company record' which it is required under the Companies Acts to keep available for inspection; and

(c) any other location at which it carries on business unless that location is primarily used for living accommodation.

But

- (*a*) and (*b*) above do not apply to a company which has at all times since its incorporation been dormant; or

- (*a*)–(*c*) above do not apply to a registered office, inspection place or other location where
  - (i) in respect of that company, a liquidator, administrator or administrative receiver has been appointed; and
  - (ii) the registered office inspection, place or location is also a place of business of that liquidator, etc; and
- (*c*) above does not apply to any location at which business is carried on by a company of which every director is an individual in respect of whom the Registrar of Companies is required to refrain from disclosing protected information to a credit reference agency. See **18.69 Directors**.

Manner of display of registered name

Where the office, place or location is shared by no more than five companies the registered name must be so positioned that it may be easily seen by any visitor to the office, place or location and must be displayed continuously.

Where the office, place or location is shared by six or more companies, each such company must ensure that either its registered name is displayed continuously for at least 15 continuous seconds at least once in every three minutes or its registered name is available for inspection on a register by any visitor to that office, place or location.

Any display or disclosure of the company name must be in characters that can be read with the naked eye.

For permitted minor variations in the displayed name see *CA 2006, s 85*.

Where the name of a charitable company does not include the word 'charity' or 'charitable', the fact that the company is a charity must be stated in legible characters in every location required by the regulations made under *CA 2006*. [*Charities Act 2011, s 194(1)*]

There are civil consequences for failure to make the disclosures required by *Charities Act 2011, s 194*. [*Charities Act 2011. s 195*]

'*Company records*' means

- any register, index, accounting records, agreement, memorandum, minutes or other documents required to be kept by a company under the Companies Acts; and
- any register kept be a company of its debenture holders.

Penalties. Where a company fails, without reasonable excuse, to comply with the above requirements, an offence is committed by the company and every officer of the company who is in default. A person guilty of such an offence is liable, on summary conviction, to a fine not exceeding level 3 on the standard scale and, for continued contravention, a daily default fine not exceeding one-tenth of level 3 on the standard scale. See **29.1 Offences and Legal Proceedings** for the standard scale. For these purposes, a 'shadow director' (see **18.1 Directors**) is treated as an officer of the company.

[*SI 2015 No 17, Regs 20–23, 28*].

16.14 Inclusion of name and other specified information in documents and communications

Every company must:

(a) Disclose its registered name on

- (i) its business letters, notices and other official publications;
- (ii) its bills of exchange, promissory notes, endorsements, and order forms;
- (iii) cheques purporting to be signed by or on behalf of the company;
- (iv) orders for money, goods or services purporting to be signed by or on behalf of the company;
- (v) its bills of parcels, invoices and other demands for payment, receipts, letters of credit;
- (vi) its applications for licences to carry on a trade or activity;
- (vii) all other forms of its business correspondence and documentation; and
- (viii) its websites.

(b) Disclose the following particulars on its business letters, order forms, and websites.

- (i) The part of the UK in which the company is registered.
- (ii) The company's registered number.
- (iii) The address of the company's registered office.
- (iv) In the case of a limited company exempt from the obligation to use the word 'limited' as part of its name under *CA 2006, s 60* (see **27.2 Names and Business Names**), the fact that it is a limited company.
- (v) In the case of a community interest company which is not a public company, the fact that it is a limited company.
- (vi) In the case of an investment company (see **22.1 Distributions**), the fact that it is such a company.

If, in the case of a company having a share capital, there is a disclosure as to the amount of share capital, it must be to paid up share capital.

(c) Where its business letter includes the 'name' of any director of the company (other than in the text or as a signatory), the letter must disclose the name of every director of that company. '*Name*' means

- (i) in the case of a director who is an individual, Christian name (or other forename) and surname (except that in the case of a peer or individual usually known by a title, the title may be stated instead of the Christian name (or other forename) and surname or in addition to either or both of them); and
- (ii) in the case of a director who is a body corporate or a firm that is a legal person under the law by which it is governed, corporate or firm name.

A reference to any type of document is a reference to a document of that type in hard copy, electronic or any other form.

Any disclosure of information required must be in characters that can be read with the naked eye.

Charitable companies. Where the name of a charitable company does not include the word "charity" or "charitable" the fact that the company is a charity must be stated in English in legible characters in every description of document or communication in which it is required by the regulations made under *CA 2006, s 82* to state its name. This does not apply to any document that is wholly in Welsh and the company's name includes the Welsh equivalent of "charity" or "charitable".

[*Charities Act 2011, ss 194(1)* and *194(2)*]

There are civil consequences for failure to make the disclosures required by *Charities Act 2011, s 194.*

[*Charities Act 2011, s 195*]

Penalties. Similar penalties apply as under **16.13**.

[*SI 2015 No 7, Regs 20, 24, 25, 26, 28*].

16.15 Provision of information on request

A company must disclose

- the address of its registered office,
- any inspection place (see **16.13**(*b*)), and
- the type of company records kept at that office or place

to any person it deals with in the course of business who makes a written request to the company for that information. It must do so in writing within five working days of the receipt of that request.

Penalties. Similar penalties apply as under **16.13** above.

[*SI 2015 No 17, Regs 27, 28*].

16.16 Civil consequences of failure to disclose the information required by CA 2006, s 82

If a company is obliged to make statutory trading disclosures and brings legal proceedings to enforce a contract made in the course of a business and the company was at the time the time the contract was made, in breach of the trading disclosure regulations made under *s 82* (ie the *Company, Limited Liability Partnerships and Business (Names and Trading Disclosures) Regulations 2015 (SI 2015 No 17)* then

- the proceedings must be dismissed if the defendant can show that he has a claim against the company that he has been unable to pursue because of the company's breach of the regulations; and
- the defendant's claim arises from the same contract; and
- the defendant has suffered some financial loss in connection with the contract as a consequence of the company's breach of the regulations.

The proceedings will not be dismissed if the court is satisfied that it is just and equitable to permit the proceedings to continue. For Scottish proceedings read 'defender' for 'defendant' and 'pursuer' for 'claimant'.

[*CA 2006, s 83*]

16.17 EFFECT OF FAILURE TO GIVE PUBLIC NOTICE

A company is not entitled to rely against other persons on the happening of any of the following events, namely

(a) an amendment to the company's articles (before 1 October 2009, memorandum and articles),

(b) a change in the directors,

(c) (as regards the service of any document on the company) a change of the company's registered office,

(d) the making of a winding-up order in respect of the company or the appointment of a liquidator in a voluntary winding up,

unless

- that event has been 'officially notified' at the material time, or
- the company shows that the person concerned knew of the event at the material time.

Where the material time falls on or before the 15th day after the date of official notification (or, where the 15th day was not a working day, on or before the next day that was) the company is not entitled to rely on the happening of the event as against a person who shows that he was unavoidably prevented from knowing of the event at that time.

'*Officially notified*' means notified in accordance with *CA 2006, s 1077* (see **39.8** **Registrar of Companies**) or, in relation to the appointment of a liquidator in a voluntary winding up, notification in accordance with *IA 1986, s 109* or *Insolvency (NI) Order 1989, Art 95*. [*CA 2006, s 1079*].

16.18 FRAUDULENT TRADING

If any business of a company is carried on with 'intent to defraud' creditors (of the company or any other person) or for any fraudulent purpose, every person who is knowingly a 'party' to the carrying on of the business in that manner commits an offence. This applies whether or not the company has been, or is in the course of being, wound up. For the meaning of a '*party*' see *Re Maidstone Buildings Provisions Ltd* [1971] 3 All ER 363, [1971] 1 WLR 1085.

A person guilty of such an offence is liable (i) on conviction on indictment, to imprisonment for a term not exceeding 10 years or a fine (or both); and (ii) on summary conviction, to imprisonment for a term not exceeding 12 months (six months in Scotland and Northern Ireland) or to a fine not exceeding the statutory maximum (or both). See **29.1** **Offences and Legal Proceedings** for the statutory maximum.

[*CA 2006, s 993*].

In addition, if the company is in the course of winding up, the court may, on the application of the liquidator, declare that such a person is liable to make such a contribution to the company's assets as it thinks proper. [*IA 1986, s 213*]. Where the person concerned is a director, he may also be disqualified from acting as a director (see **18.12**(*c*) **Directors**).

There is '*intent to defraud*' where the company continues to carry on business and to incur debts at a time when there is to the knowledge of the directors no reasonable prospect of the creditors ever receiving payment for those debts (*William C Leitch Bros Ltd, Re* [1932] 2 Ch 71, 101 LJ Ch 380). There must be actual dishonesty involving, according to current notions of fair trading among commercial men, real moral blame (*Re Patrick & Lyon Ltd* [1933] Ch 786, 102 LJ Ch 300).

16.19 SERVICE ADDRESSES

A '*service address*' in relation to a person, means an address at which documents may be effectively served on that person.

The address must be a place where

- the service of documents can be effected by physical delivery, and
- the delivery of documents is capable of being recorded by the obtaining of an acknowledgement of delivery

and must not be a post office box number or a document exchange box number.

Any obligation to give a person's address is, unless otherwise expressly provided, to give a service address for that person.

[*CA 2006, ss 1141, 1142; SI 2008 No 3000, Reg 10*].

16.20 SERVICE OF DOCUMENTS ON COMPANY

A document may be served on

- a company registered under *CA 2006* by leaving it at, or sending it by post to, the company's registered office; and
- an overseas company whose particulars are registered under *CA 2006, s 1046*
  - (i) by leaving it at, or sending it by post to, the registered address of any person resident in the UK who is authorised to accept service of documents on the company's behalf (registered address meaning any address for the time being shown as the current address on the part of the register available for public inspection); or
  - (ii) if there is no such person, or if any such person refuses service or service cannot for any other reason be effected, by leaving it at, or sending it by post to, any place of business of the company in the UK.

Where a company registered in Scotland or Northern Ireland carries on business in England and Wales, the process of any court in England and Wales may be served on the company by leaving it at, or sending it by post to, the company's principal place of business in England and Wales, addressed to the manager or other head officer in England and Wales of the company.

Where process is served on a company under these provisions, the person issuing out the process must send a copy of it by post to the company's registered office.

[*CA 2006, s 1139*].

See also **16.22** *et seq* below.

16.21 SERVICE OF DOCUMENTS ON DIRECTORS, SECRETARIES AND OTHERS

CA 2006, s 1140 was introduced by *CA 2006* (ie there was no corresponding provision in *CA 1985*). It provides that a document may be served on any of the following persons by leaving it at, or sending it by post to, the person's registered address, ie any address for the time being shown as a current address in relation to that person in the part of the register available for public inspection (see **18.29** provisions for protecting the disclosure of directors' addresses.)

(a) A director or secretary of a company.

(b) In the case of an overseas company whose particulars are registered under *CA 2006, s 1046*, a director, secretary or permanent representative.

(c) A person appointed in relation to a company as a judicial factor (in Scotland), an interim manager appointed under *Charities Act 2011, s 76* or a manager appointed under *Companies (Audit, Investigations and Community Enterprise) Act 2004*, s 47.

This applies whatever the purpose of the document in question and is not restricted to service for purposes arising out of, or in connection with, the appointment or position mentioned or in connection with the company concerned.

Change of address. If notice of a change of address (above) is given to the Registrar of Companies, a person may validly serve a document at the address previously registered until the end of the period of 14 days beginning with the date on which notice of the change is registered.

Service cannot be effected under these provisions at an address

- if notice has been registered of the termination of the appointment in relation to which the address was registered and the address is not a registered address of the person concerned in relation to any other appointment; and
- where (*b*) above applies, if the overseas company has ceased to have any connection with the UK by virtue of which it is required to register particulars under *CA 2006, s 1046*.

[*CA 2006, s 1140; SI 2009 No 1801, Reg 75*].

See also **16.23** *et seq* below.

16.22 SENDING DOCUMENTS AND INFORMATION (THE 'COMPANY COMMUNICATION PROVISIONS')

The following provisions and those in **16.23** to **16.34** (the '*company communications provisions*') have effect for the purposes of any provision of the *Companies Acts* that authorises or requires 'documents' or information to be sent or supplied by or to a company (including documents or information sent or supplied by or to the directors of a company acting on behalf of the company). [*CA 2006, ss 1143(1), 1148(3)*].

The provisions have effect subject to any requirement imposed, or contrary provision made, by or under any enactment (but a provision is not to be treated as contrary to the company communication provisions only on the grounds that it expressly authorises a document or information to be sent in hard copy form, in electronic form or by means of a website). In particular, the provisions have effect subject to the provisions in **39 Registrar of Companies** in relation to documents and information sent or supplied to the Registrar. [*CA 2006, s 1143(2)–(4)*].

'*Document*' includes summons, notice, order or other legal process and registers. [*CA 2006, s 1148(1)*].

Documents or information to be sent or supplied

(a) *to a company*, must be sent or supplied in accordance with the provisions in **16.23** to **16.26**; and

(b) *by a company*, must be sent or supplied in accordance with the provisions in **16.27** to **16.32**.

In relation to documents or information that are to be sent or supplied by one company to another, the provisions of (*b*) apply and not the provisions in (*a*) above.

[*CA 2006, s 1144*].

Where standard articles have been adopted, see

- *Model Articles, Art 48* (private companies)
- *Model Articles, Arts 79, 80* (public companies)

set out in **Appendix 4** standard articles of association

These are expressed in very general terms and provide (in summary) that anything which is sent or supplied by or to the company under the articles can be sent or supplied in any way. *CA 2006* provides that any notice or document to be sent or supplied to a director in connection with directors' decision making can be sent by the means that director has asked for documents or notices to be sent or supplied.

16.23 Documents and information sent or supplied to a company

The provisions in **16.24** to **16.26** apply to documents and information sent or supplied to a company. They do not apply to documents or information sent or supplied by one company (eg a corporate shareholder) to another. In that case the provisions in **16.28** to **16.33** apply ie communications by a company. [*CA 2006, Sch 4 para 1*].

16.24 *Communications in hard copy form*

A document or information is validly sent or supplied to a company in '*hard copy*' form (see **Appendix 1 Definitions**) if it is sent or supplied

- by hand, or
- by posting a prepaid envelope

to

- an address specified by the company for the purpose;
- the company's registered office; or
- an address to which any provision of the *Companies Acts* authorises the document or information to be sent or supplied.

[*CA 2006, Sch 4 paras 2–4*].

Authentication. A document or information sent or supplied in hard copy form is sufficiently authenticated if it is signed by the person sending or supplying it. Despite this, where a document or information is sent or supplied by one person on behalf of another, a company's articles may require reasonable evidence of the authority of the former to act on behalf of the latter. [*CA 2006, s 1146(2)(4)*].

16.25 *Communications in electronic form*

A document or information is validly sent or supplied to a company in 'electronic form' (see **Appendix 1 Definitions**) if

- the company
  - (i) has agreed (generally or specifically) that the document or information may be sent or supplied in that form (and has not revoked that agreement); or

(ii) is deemed to have so agreed by a provision in the *Companies Acts*;

- where the document or information is sent or supplied by electronic means, it is sent or supplied to an 'address'

  (i) specified for the purpose by the company (generally or specifically); or

  (ii) deemed by a provision in the *Companies Acts* to have been so specified; and

- where the document or information is sent or supplied in electronic form by hand or by post, it is sent or supplied to an address to which it could be validly sent if it were in hard copy form (see **16.24**).

'*Address*' includes a number or address used for the purposes of sending or receiving documents or information by electronic means.

[*CA 2006, s 1148(1), Sch 4 paras 5–7*].

Authentication. A document or information sent or supplied in electronic form is sufficiently authenticated

- if the identity of the sender is confirmed in a manner specified by the company; or
- where no such manner has been specified by the company, if the communication contains, or is accompanied by, a statement of the identity of the sender and the company has no reason to doubt the truth of that statement.

Despite this, where a document or information is sent or supplied by one person on behalf of another, a company's articles may require reasonable evidence of the authority of the former to act on behalf of the latter.

[*CA 2006, s 1146(3)(4)*].

16.26 *Other agreed forms of communication*

A document or information that is sent or supplied to a company otherwise than in hard copy form (see **16.24**) or electronic form (see **16.25**) is validly sent or supplied if it is sent or supplied in a form or manner that has been agreed by the company.

[*CA 2006, Sch 4 para 8*].

16.27 Communications by a company

The provisions in **16.28** to **16.32** below apply to documents or information sent or supplied by a company. [*CA 2006, Sch 5 para 1*].

16.28 *Communications in hard copy form*

A document or information is validly sent or supplied by a company in '*hard copy*' form (see **Appendix 1 Definitions**) if it is

- handed to the intended recipient; or
- sent or supplied by hand or by posting a prepaid envelope to

  (i) an address specified for the purpose by the intended recipient;

  (ii) a company at its registered office;

  (iii) a person in his capacity as a member of the company at his address as shown in the company's register of members;

(iv) a person in his capacity as a director of the company at his address as shown in the company's register of directors;

(v) an address to which any provision of the *Companies Acts* authorises the document or information to be sent or supplied; or

(vi) where the company is unable to obtain an appropriate address falling within (i)–(v) above, the intended recipient's last address known to the company.

[*CA 2006, Sch 5 paras 2–4*].

See **16.34** below for deemed delivery of documents and information.

16.29 *Communications in electronic form*

A document or information is validly sent or supplied by a company in electronic form if

(a) it is sent or supplied to

(i) a person who has agreed (generally or specifically) that the document or information may be sent or supplied in that form (and has not revoked that agreement); or

(ii) a company that is deemed to have so agreed by a provision in the *Companies Acts*;

(b) where the document or information is sent or supplied by electronic means, it is sent or supplied to an 'address'

(i) specified for the purpose by the intended recipient (generally or specifically); or

(ii) where the intended recipient is a company, deemed by a provision of the *Companies Acts* to have been so specified; and

(c) where the document or information is sent or supplied in electronic form by hand or by post, it is

(i) handed to the intended recipient; or

(ii) sent or supplied to an address to which it could be validly sent if it were in hard copy form (see **16.28**).

'*Address*' includes a number or address used for the purposes of sending or receiving documents or information by electronic means.

[*CA 2006, s 1148(1), Sch 5 paras 5–7*].

See **16.33** below for the right of a member or debenture holder to require any document or information in hard copy form and **16.34** below for deemed delivery of documents and information.

16.30 *Communications by means of a website*

A document or information is validly sent or supplied by a company if it is made available on a website and the following conditions are satisfied.

(1) *Agreement to use of website.* A document or information may only be sent or supplied by the company to a person by being made available on a website if the person

(i) has agreed (generally or specifically) that the document or information may be sent or supplied to him in that manner; or

(ii) is taken to have so agreed under the provisions relating to deemed agreement by members or debenture holders (see below)

and has not revoked that agreement, has effect on or after that date, in relation to the matters to which it relates, as an agreement under (i) above. [*SI 2006 No 3428, Sch 5 para 5*].

(2) *Availability of document or information.* A document or information authorised or required to be sent or supplied by means of a website must be made available in a form, and by a means, that the company reasonably considers will enable the recipient to read it and to retain a copy of it. For this purpose, a document or information can be read only if

(i) it can be read with the naked eye; or

(ii) to the extent that it consists of images (eg photographs, pictures, maps, plans or drawings), it can be seen with the naked eye.

(3) *Notification of availability.* The company must notify the intended recipient of

(i) the presence of the document or information on the website;

(ii) the address of the website;

(iii) the place on the website where it may be accessed; and

(iv) how to access the document or information.

The document or information is taken to be sent on the date on which that notification is sent (or, if later, the date on which the document or information first appears on the website after that notification is sent).

(4) *Period of availability on website.* The company must make the document or information available on the website throughout

(i) the period specified by any applicable provision of the *Companies Acts*;

(ii) if no such period is specified, the period of 28 days beginning with the date on which the notification required as above is sent to the person in question.

For these purposes, a failure to make a document or information available on a website throughout the period required is disregarded if it is made available on the website for part of that period and the failure to make it available throughout that period is wholly attributable to circumstances that it would not be reasonable to have expected the company to prevent or avoid.

Deemed agreement of members of company, etc to use of website. Where a document or information is to be sent or supplied to a person

- as a member of the company,
- as a person nominated by a member (in accordance with the company's articles) to enjoy or exercise all or any specified rights of the member in relation to the company, or
- as a person nominated by the member under *CA 2006, s 146* to enjoy information rights (see **26.11 Members**)

to the extent that

- the members of the company have resolved that the company may send or supply documents or information to members by making them available on a website, or
- the company's articles contain provision to that effect,

a person is taken to have agreed that the company may send or supply documents or information to him in that manner provided the following conditions are met.

(a) The person has been asked individually by the company to agree that the company may send or supply documents or information generally, or the documents or information in question, to him by means of a website.

(b) The company has not received a response within 28 days of the date on which the request was sent.

A person is not taken to have so agreed if the company's request did not state clearly what the effect of a failure to respond would be or if it was sent less than twelve months after a previous such request was made to him in respect of the same or a similar class of documents or information.

CA 2006, ss 29, 30 (resolutions affecting a company's constitution, see **14.10** Constitution – Memorandum and Articles) apply to a resolution under these provisions.

Deemed agreement of debenture holders to use of website. Where a document or information is to be sent or supplied to a person as holder of a company's debentures, to the extent that

- the 'relevant debenture holders' have duly resolved that the company may send or supply documents or information to them by making them available on a website, or
- the instrument creating the debentures in question contains provision to that effect,

a debenture holder is taken to have agreed that the company may send or supply documents or information to him in that manner provided the following conditions are met.

(i) The debenture holder has been asked individually by the company to agree that the company may send or supply documents or information generally, or the documents or information in question, to him by means of a website.

(ii) The company has not received a response within 28 days of the date on which the request was sent.

A person is not taken to have so agreed if the company's request did not state clearly what the effect of a failure to respond would be or if it was sent less than twelve months after a previous such request was made to him in respect of the same or a similar class of documents or information.

For these purposes, the '*relevant debenture holders*' are the holders of debentures of the company ranking pari passu for all purposes with the intended recipient and a resolution of the relevant debenture holders is duly passed if they agree in accordance with the provisions of the instruments creating the debentures.

[*CA 2006, Sch 5 paras 8–14; SI 2006 No 3428, Sch 1 para 16*].

See **16.33** below for the right of a member or debenture holder to require any document or information in hard copy form and **16.34** below for deemed delivery of documents and information.

16.31 *Other agreed forms of communication*

A document or information that is sent or supplied otherwise than in hard copy (see **16.28**) or electronic form (see **16.29**) or by means of a website (see **16.0**) is validly sent or supplied if it is sent or supplied in a form or manner that has been agreed by the intended recipient.

[*CA 2006, Sch 5 para 15*].

16.32 *Supplementary provisions*

Joint holders of shares or debentures. Subject to anything in the company's articles, in relation to documents or information to be sent or supplied to joint holders of shares or debentures of a company

- anything to be agreed or specified by the holder must be agreed or specified by all the joint holders;
- anything authorised or required to be sent or supplied to the holder may be sent or supplied either
  - (i) to each of the joint holders; or
  - (ii) to the holder whose name appears first in the register of members or the relevant register of debenture holders.

[*CA 2006, Sch 5 para 16*].

Death or bankruptcy of holder of shares. Subject to anything in the company's articles, following the death or bankruptcy of a holder of a company's shares, documents or information required or authorised to be sent or supplied to the member may be sent or supplied to the persons claiming to be entitled to the shares in consequence of the death or bankruptcy

(a) by name, or

(b) by the title of representatives of the deceased, or trustee of the bankrupt, or by any like description,

at the 'address' in the UK supplied for the purpose by those so claiming.

Until such an address has been supplied, a document or information may be sent or supplied in any manner in which it might have been sent or supplied if the death or bankruptcy had not occurred.

'*Address*' includes a number or address used for the purposes of sending or receiving documents or information by electronic means.

For these purposes, bankruptcy of a person includes the sequestration of the estate of a person or a person's estate being the subject of a protected trust deed (within the meaning of the *Bankruptcy (Scotland) Act 1985*). In such a case, the reference (*b*) above to the trustee of the bankrupt is to be read as the permanent or interim trustee on the sequestrated estate or, as the case may be, the trustee under the protected deed.

[*CA 2006, s 1148(1), Sch 5 para 15*].

16.33 Right of members and debenture holders to hard copy version

Where a member of a company or a holder of a company's debentures has received a document or information from the company otherwise than in hard copy form, he is entitled to require the company to send him a version of the document or information in hard copy form.

The company must send the document or information in hard copy form within 21 days of receipt of the request. It may not make a charge for doing so.

If a company fails to comply with these provisions, an offence is committed by the company and every officer of it who is in default. A person guilty of such an offence is liable, on summary conviction, to a fine not exceeding level 3 on the standard scale and, for continued contravention, a daily default fine not exceeding one-tenth of level 3 on the standard scale. See **29.1** Offences and Legal Proceedings for the standard scale. [*CA 2006, s 1145*].

16.34 Deemed delivery of documents and information

The following provisions apply to determine when documents or information are deemed to have been delivered but subject to

- in their application to documents or information sent or supplied by a company to its members, any contrary provision of the company's articles;
- in their application to documents or information sent or supplied by a company to its debentures holders, any contrary provision in the instrument constituting the debentures; and
- in their application to documents or information sent or supplied by a company to a person otherwise than in his capacity as a member or debenture holder, any contrary provision in an agreement between the company and that person.

Items sent by post. Where

- a document or information is sent by post (whether in hard copy or electronic form) to an address in the UK, and
- the company is able to show that it was properly addressed, prepaid and posted,

it is deemed to have been received by the intended recipient 48 hours after it was posted (ignoring any part of a day that is not a working day).

Items sent by electronic means. Where

- a document or information is sent or supplied by electronic means, and
- the company is able to show that it was properly addressed,

it is deemed to have been received by the intended recipient 48 hours after it was sent (ignoring any part of a day that is not a working day).

Items sent by means of a website. Where a document or information is sent or supplied by means of a website, it is deemed to have been received by the intended recipient

- when the material was first made available on the website; or
- if later, when the recipient received (or is deemed to have received) notice of the fact that the material was available on the website. [*CA 2006, s 1147*].

17 Debt finance – Debentures and other forms of borrowing

17.1 What is "borrowing"?
17.2 Company's power to borrow generally
17.3 Directors' powers to authorise borrowing and charge company property
17.4 Types of borrowing
17.5 Fixed and floating charges
17.6 Debentures
17.7 Debenture stock and loan stock
17.8 Convertible debentures
17.9 Irredeemable and perpetual debentures
17.10 Issue of debentures
17.11 Registration of allotments
17.12 Power to re-issue redeemable debentures
17.13 Deposit of debentures to secure advances
17.14 Priorities where debentures secures by a floating charge
17.15 Liabilities of trustees of debentures
17.16 Right of debenture holders to a copy of the deed
17.17 Debentures to bearer (Scotland)

Cross-references. See **2.6 ACCOUNTS: GENERAL** for the right of debenture-holders to receive copies of the accounts; **2.7 ACCOUNTS: GENERAL** for the right of debenture holders to demand an additional copy of the accounts; **22.5 DISTRIBUTIONS** for restriction on paying up debentures out of unrealised profit; **38.12 REGISTERS** for the register of debenture holders; **40 REGISTRATION OF CHARGES**; **47.21 SHARES** for the prohibition of public offers by private companies which provisions also apply to debentures; **45 SECURITY FOR COMPANY BORROWING**.

Background. The provisions in this chapter apply, unless otherwise stated, with effect from 6 April 2008. They restate the provisions in *CA 1985* without making any change in the law.

17.1 WHAT IS "BORROWING"?

For the purposes of this chapter "borrowing" means debt obligations incurred by a company as a consequence of loans made to the company. The term "borrowing" is not defined in legislation and the interpretation of its meaning derives from common law – see for example *IRC v Port of London Authority* [1923] AC 507, 92 LJKB 655, HL, *Potts' Executors v IRC* [1951] AC 443, [1951] 1 All ER 76, HL (it is the legal nature and form of the transaction which determines whether it is "borrowing") This chapter does not therefore deal with other aspects of company financing such as:

- Share capital
- Factoring/invoice discounting
- Conditional and/or credit sales of goods (including retention of title)
- Lease financing

17.2 COMPANY'S POWER TO BORROW GENERALLY

A power to borrow for the purposes of the company's business is implied in the case of a trading or commercial company as long as the power is not expressly prohibited (see, for example, *David Payne & Co Ltd, Re, Young v David Payne & Co Ltd* [1904] 2 Ch 608, 73 LJ Ch 849, CA). A non-trading company will generally include in its articles an express power to borrow for the purposes of the business.

17.2 Debt finance – Debentures and other forms of borrowing

Restrictions on borrowing may be

- contained in a company's articles;
- imposed on the company by resolution of the members; or
- included in the terms of a contract, loan agreement or trust deed.

Even where there are limitations on a company's power to borrow, any further borrowing cannot be called into question on the grounds of lack of capacity by reason of anything in the company's constitution and, in favour of a person dealing with a company in good faith, the power of the directors to bind the company is deemed to be free of any limitation under the company's constitution. [*CA 2006, ss 39, 40*]. See **16.1** and **16.2** DEALINGS WITH THIRD PARTIES.

17.3 Directors' powers to authorise borrowing and charge company property

A company's articles will usually contain a provision allowing the directors to exercise the company's powers to borrow money (but only up to any limit in the articles, see *Irvine v Union Bank of Australia* (1877) 2 App Cas 366, PC). Where a company has adopted standard articles, see

- *Table A 1985, Art 70*
- *Model Articles, Arts 3, 4* (private companies
- *Model Articles, Arts 3, 4* (public companies)

These all provide (in summary) that the business of the company will be managed by the directors who may exercise all the powers of the company including, (although this is not expressly set out in the standard articles) the power to borrow on behalf of the company.

Where a company has the power to borrow, it also has an implied or incidental power to charge all or any part of its property to secure past or future debts (*Patent File Co, Re, ex p Birmingham Banking Co* (1870) 6 Ch App 83) including a charge by way of fixed security or by way of a floating charge (see **17.5**). The directors have authority to grant security and, notwithstanding any limitations in the company's constitution, a third party who deals with the company in good faith (*CA 2006 ss 39, 40* and *41*) is entitled to rely on the power of the directors to bind the company, free of any limit under the company's constitution.

17.4 Types of borrowing

Companies are able to borrow from a wide range of sources including banks ,venture capital companies and their own directors and shareholders. Borrowings from directors can be in the form of unsecured directors' loan accounts or more formally by the granting of a debenture. Venture capital funding is usually provided in return for an equity stake in the company.

Loan facilities (secured or unsecured) – A common type of borrowing is a loan facility (typically from a bank) which can either be

- Committed (eg term/revolving loan) ie the lender makes the funds available subject to certain specified conditions precedent, the right to demand repayment arises only on certain specific acts of default, provisions for repayment and provision is made in the agreement for draw down of the facilities and for lender's returns (for example interest and commissions). The distinction between a term loan and a revolving facility is that a term loan is provided over a specific period of time and is repayable at or by the end of that specified period. A revolving facility by contrast allows the company to draw down and repay funds as required (and as provided for in a facilities agreement); or

- On-demand (eg an overdraft/working capital facility) ie the lender makes funds available and demands repayment at its own discretion.

These types of loans can be syndicated by several lenders. In this case the loan is made by several lenders, each one puts forward a percentage of the principal sum but then one or more of them act as agent and administer the loan on behalf of the syndicate.

Project/property finance. This can used to finance large scale projects such as infrastructure. Project finance involves not only debt borrowings provided by banks but also (and typically) some equity finance and often some government funding.

Debt securities. In this category are debentures, a term which describes both the document itself and the type of transaction and includes debenture stock and bonds – see **17.6**.

Asset based lending. These are loans secured by a variety of the company's assets (liquid or fixed assets).

Loans of any description can be secured or unsecured – see **45 Security for company borrowing** and **17.5 Fixed and floating charges**)

17.5 Fixed and Floating charges

As with the term "borrowing" the terms fixed and floating charge are not defined in legislation. A fixed charge is a present charge over present or future property which fastens on the property when the charge is executed (*Illingworth v Houldsworth* [1904] AC 355, 73 LJ Ch 739, HL) or in the case of future property when the property comes into existence as long as it is capable of being ascertained (*Yorkshire Woolcombers Association Ltd, Re, Houldsworth v Yorkshire Woolcombers Association Ltd* [1903] 2 Ch 284, 72 LJ Ch 635, CA). The company cannot deal with or dispose of property subject to a fixed charge without the consent of the chargee.

A 'floating charge' is an immediate and present security which floats over a company's assets so that the company is allowed to carry on its business and is left free to manage the assets which are subject to the charge. Management of the assets continues by the borrower until some event occurs or some act is done which causes the charge to attach to specific assets which are subject to the charge (see *Re Yorkshire Woolcombers* (above) and *Brightlife Ltd, Re* [1987] Ch 200, [1986] BCLC 418). At this point the charge crystallises and:

- the chargee's rights are converted into the individual assets in the fund and any property acquired thereafter which falls within the scope of the charge;
- the company is no longer free to manage the property or deal with the property without the consent of the chargee; and
- no new charge is created and therefore no new registration at Companies House of the security under *CA 2006, s 860* is required – see **40 Registration**.

The essence of a floating charge is that it is a charge, not on any particular asset, but on a fluctuating body of assets which remain under the management and control of the company who can dispose of and deal with the charged asset and, if necessary, remove it from the security without the consent of the chargee.

The instrument creating a charge will say whether it is to take effect as a fixed or floating charge but in deciding whether a charge is fixed or floating: (1) the instrument of charge is construed to establish the intention of the parties with regard to their mutual rights and obligations in respect of the charged assets; and (2) the charge is then characterised as a matter of law (*Agnew v IRC* [2001] UKPC 28, [2001] 2 AC 710, [2001] 2 BCLC 188 followed in *Spectrum Plus Ltd, Re, National Westminster Bank plc v Spectrum Plus Ltd* [2005] UKHL 41, [2005] 2 AC 680, [2005] 2 BCLC 269.)

17.6 DEBENTURES

A company may raise capital by means of loans evidenced by 'debentures'. '*Debentures*' include debenture stock, bonds and any 'other securities' of a company, whether or not constituting a charge on the assets of the company. [*CA 2006, s 738*]. The term is thus used to cover a variety of loan transactions depending upon the circumstances and is not confined to a document actually describing itself as a debenture. In *Slavenburg's Bank NV v Intercontinental Natural Resources Ltd* [1980] 1 All ER 955, [1980] 1 WLR 1076 a debenture was held to be a document which creates or acknowledges an indebtedness. A note by which a company undertook to repay a loan but gave no security was held to be a debenture in *British India Steam Navigation Co v IRC* (1881) 7 QBD 165. The document may need to disclose an agreement to repay the advance (*Topham v Greenside Glazed Fire-Brick Co* (1887) 37 Ch D 281 and *R v Findlater* [1939] 1 KB 594, [1939] 1 All ER 82, CA). '*Other securities*' includes a guarantee (*Temperance Loan Fund Ltd v Rose* [1932] 2 KB 522, 101 LJKB 609, CA; *IRC v Henry Ansbacher & Co* [1963] AC 191, [1962] 3 All ER 843, HL).

17.7 Debenture stock and loan stock

Where money is to be borrowed from many lenders, it may be more convenient to issue 'debenture stock' or 'loan stock'.

Debenture stock. The term 'debenture stock' is normally used for stock which is secured by a mortgage or charge. The lender has a certificate which gives him a right to a certain sum, which is a proportion of a larger sum, and which may be transferred, in whole or in part, subject to the terms of the issue.

The usual charge is a floating charge (ie on unascertained assets and property of the company). For cases of debenture stock accompanied by floating charges see, for example, *Robson v Smith* [1895] 2 Ch 118 and *George Barker (Transport) Ltd v Eynon* [1974] 1 All ER 900, [1974] 1 WLR 462, CA. Where there is a fixed charge on specific assets of the company, once the charge is registered (see **40 Registration of Charges**) the holder has an immediate security over those assets so that the company may not realise them without his consent.

In the event of default by the company, the holder of secured debenture stock has, in addition to the remedies of an unsecured creditor (see below), the power to appoint a receiver or administrator and the power of sale (although in practice these powers will generally be enforced on his behalf by the trustees where there is a trust deed). See, however, **17.14** for the rights of preferential creditors in the case of a floating charge.

Loan stock. If the stock is unsecured, the term 'loan stock' is generally used. It is usual for the loan stock to be constituted by a trust deed which contains a covenant by the company for the payment of capital (either at a fixed date or on the happening of a certain event, eg a winding up) and interest. In the event of default by the company, the holder may sue for his money and present a petition for winding up.

17.8 Convertible debentures

A convertible debenture contains an option entitling the holder to convert into ordinary or preference shares of the company at stated times and in stated proportions.

17.9 Irredeemable and perpetual debentures

A condition imposed in debentures, or in a deed for securing debentures, is not invalid by reason only that the debentures are made irredeemable or redeemable only on the

- happening of a contingency (however remote), or
- expiration of a period (however long),

any rule of equity to the contrary notwithstanding.

This applies to debentures whenever issued and to deeds whenever executed. [*CA 2006, s 739*].

The company must be authorised by its articles to issue irredeemable debentures but where it has issued such stock, the stock is irredeemable only as long as the company is a going concern (*Southern Brazilian Rio Grande do Sul Rly Co Ltd, Re* [1905] 2 Ch 78, 74 LJ Ch 392).

17.10 ISSUE OF DEBENTURES

For the duties of a company as to the issue of debentures and certificates of debenture stock, see **44 Securities: Certification and Transfers.**

Debentures, unlike shares, can be issued at a discount. There must, however, be no possibility that *shares* could be issued at a discount as a result, eg because debentures are, or will be, convertible into shares (see *Moseley v Koffyfontein Mines Ltd* [1904] 2 Ch 108, 73 LJ Ch 569, CA).

Debentures may also be issued (or redeemed) at a premium.

A contract with a company to take up and pay for debentures may be enforced by an order for specific performance. [*CA 2006, s 740*]. In *Kuala Pahi Rubber Estates Ltd v Mowbray* (1914) 111 LT 1072, CA it was held that where a company had forfeited debentures it was not in a position to ask for specific performance on calls made to a shareholder and not paid.

17.11 Registration of allotments

A company must register an allotment of debentures as soon as practicable and in any event within two months after the date of allotment.

If the company fails to do so, an offence is committed by the company and every officer of the company who is in default. A person guilty of such an offence is liable, on summary conviction, to a fine not exceeding level 3 on the standard scale and, for continued contravention, a daily default fine not exceeding one-tenth of level 3 on the standard scale. See **29.1 Offences and Legal Proceedings** for the standard scale.

[*CA 2006, s 741*].

17.12 POWER TO RE-ISSUE REDEEMABLE DEBENTURES

Where a company has redeemed debentures previously issued, it has, and is always deemed to have had, power to re-issue the debentures (either by re-issuing the same debentures or issuing other debentures in their place). This is subject to the conditions that

(a) no expressed or implied provision to the contrary is contained in the company's articles or in any contract made by the company; and

(b) the company has not, by passing a resolution to that effect or by some other act, manifested its intention that the debentures should be cancelled.

On the re-issue, the person entitled to the debentures has (and is deemed always to have had) the same priorities as if the debentures had never been redeemed.

The re-issue of a debenture or the issue of another debenture in its place under these provisions is treated as the issue of a new debenture for stamp duty purposes but it is not so treated for the purposes of any provision limiting the amount or number of debentures to be issued.

A person lending money on the security of a re-issued debenture which appears to be duly stamped may give the debenture in evidence in any proceedings to enforce his security without payment of the stamp duty or any penalty in respect of it unless

(i) he had notice that the debenture was not duly stamped; or

(ii) but for his negligence he might have discovered that fact.

In that case the company is liable to pay the proper stamp duty and penalty.

[*CA 2006, s 752*].

17.13 DEPOSIT OF DEBENTURES TO SECURE ADVANCES

Where a company has deposited any of its debentures to secure advances from time to time on current account or otherwise, the debentures are not treated as redeemed by reason only of the company's account ceasing to be in debit while the debentures remain so deposited. [*CA 2006, s 753*].

17.14 PRIORITIES WHERE DEBENTURES SECURED BY A FLOATING CHARGE

See **17.5** for fixed and floating charges.

Where debentures of a company registered in England and Wales or Northern Ireland are secured by a charge that, as created, was a floating charge, then if

- possession is taken, by or on behalf of the holders of the debentures, of any property comprised in or subject to the charge, and
- the company is not at that time in the course of being wound up,

the company's preferential debts must be paid out of assets coming to the hands of the person taking possession in priority to any claims for principal or interest in respect of the debentures. Payments must be recouped, as far as possible, out of the assets of the company available for payment of general creditors.

Preferential creditors are:

- Contributions to occupational pension schemes and state scheme premiums.
- Remuneration due to employees in respect of the whole or any part of the period of four months before the 'relevant date' up to a maximum (currently £800)

- Any amount owed as accrued holiday remuneration in respect of any period of employment before the relevant date to a person whose employment has been terminated, whether before, on or after that date.
- Any money advanced to the company that has been applied in paying remuneration or accrued holiday pay which would otherwise have been preferential.

The '*relevant date*' is the date of possession being taken.

[*CA 2006, s 754; IA 1986, Sch 6; EA 2002, Sch 26*].

17.15 LIABILITIES OF TRUSTEES OF DEBENTURES

Subject to below, any provision contained in a trust deed for securing an issue of debentures (or any contract with the holders of debentures secured by a trust deed) is void in so far as it would have the effect of exempting a trustee from, or indemnify him against, liability for breach of trust where he fails to show the degree of care and diligence required of him as a trustee, having regard to the provisions of the trust deed conferring on him any powers, authorities or discretions.

The above does not, however,

(a) invalidate a release otherwise validly given in respect of anything done, or omitted to be done, by a trustee before the release is given;

(b) invalidate any provision allowing such a release to be given

   (i) on the agreement of a majority of not less than 75% in value of the debenture-holders present and voting in person or, where proxies are permitted, by proxy at a meeting summoned for the purpose; and

   (ii) either with respect to specific acts or omissions or on the trustee dying or ceasing to act;

(c) invalidate any provision in force on

   (i) 1 July 1948 in a case where *CA 1985, s 192* was in force immediately before 6 April 2008, or

   (ii) 1 July 1961 in a case when *Companies (Northern Ireland) Order 1986* then applied

   so long as any person then entitled to the benefit of that provision remains a trustee; or

(d) deprive any person of any exemption or right to be indemnified in respect of anything done or omitted to be done by him while any provision within (*c*) above was in force.

While *any* trustee remains entitled to the benefit of a provision under (*c*) or (*d*) above, the benefit may also be given to

- all trustees of the deed (present and future), or
- any named trustees or proposed trustees of it

by a resolution passed by a majority of not less than 75% in value of the debenture holders present in person or, where proxies are permitted, by proxy at a meeting summoned for the purpose. A meeting for that purpose must be summoned in accordance with the provisions of the deed or, if the deed makes no provision for summoning meetings, in a manner approved by the court.

[*CA 2006, ss 750, 751*].

17.16 RIGHT OF DEBENTURE HOLDERS TO A COPY OF THE DEED

A debenture holder is entitled, on request and on payment of a fee (see **Appendix 3A Fees payable to Companies House**), to be provided with a copy of any trust deed which secures the debentures.

See **36.2 Records** for the provisions relating to providing copies.

In default, of providing a copy, an offence is committed by every officer of the company who is in default. A person guilty of such an offence is liable, on summary conviction, to a fine not exceeding level 3 on the standard scale and, for continues contravention, a daily default fine not exceeding one-tenth of level 3 on the standard scale. See **29.1 Offences and Legal Proceedings** for the standard scale.

In the case of such a default, the court may direct that the copy required is sent to the person concerned.

[*CA 2006, s 749*].

17.17 DEBENTURES TO BEARER (SCOTLAND)

Debentures to bearer issued in Scotland are valid and binding according to the terms of their issue despite anything in the statute of the Scots Parliament of 1696, chapter 25. [*CA 2006, s 742*].

18 Directors

18.1 **Meaning of the term 'director' and other associated terms**
18.2 **Minimum number of directors**
18.3 **Director also acting as secretary**
18.4 **Changes in directors**
18.5 Appointment and retirement by rotation
18.9 Removal of directors
18.10 **Alternate directors**
18.11 **Disqualification of directors**
18.12 Disqualification for general misconduct
18.13 Disqualification for unfitness
18.17 Disqualification for competition infringements
18.18 Disqualification for participation in wrongful trading
18.19 Automatic disqualification for bankruptcy, etc
18.20 Consequences of contravention
18.21 Disqualification under the company's articles
18.22 Foreign disqualifications
18.23 **Duties of directors**
18.24 General duties
18.27 Other statutory duties
18.28 Duties to third parties
18.29 **Powers of directors**
18.30 Power to make provision for employees on cessation or transfer of business
18.31 **Directors' liabilities**
18.32 Liabilities under Companies Acts provisions
18.33 Liabilities under *IA 1986*
18.41 Criminal liability
18.42 Relief from liability by court
18.43 Indemnification and provisions protecting directors from liability
18.45 Ratification of acts of directors
18.46 **Employment, remuneration, etc**
18.47 Payments for loss of office
18.52 **Directors' service contracts**
18.53 Members' approval of long-term service contracts
18.54 Inspection of service contracts
18.55 **Interests in contracts, transactions, etc**
18.56 Declaration of interest in existing transaction or arrangement
18.57 Contracts with sole member who is also a director
18.58 **Substantial property transactions: members' approval**
18.59 Consequences of contravention
18.60 **Loans, quasi loans and credit transactions**
18.61 Members' approval of loans and quasi-loans
18.62 Members' approval of credit transactions
18.63 Members' approval of related arrangements
18.64 Exceptions
18.65 Value of transactions and arrangements
18.66 Consequences of contravention
18.67 **Directors' residential addresses: protection from disclosure**
18.68 Restriction on use or disclosure of protected information
18.69 Permitted use or disclosure by the Registrar of Companies
18.71 Disclosure under a court order
18.72 Circumstances in which the Registrar of Companies can put a usual residential address on the public record
18.73 Application to make an address unavailable for inspection

Cross-references. See **16.2** DEALINGS WITH THIRD PARTIES for the power of directors to bind a company; **16.3** DEALINGS WITH THIRD PARTIES for transactions involving directors or their associates; **39.1** REGISTRAR OF COMPANIES.

18.1 Directors

18.1 MEANING OF THE TERM 'DIRECTOR' AND OTHER ASSOCIATED TERMS

(1) The definition of a director in *Companies Act 2006 (CA 2006)* is not exhaustive – *section 250* provides that the term *Director* includes any person occupying the position of director, by whatever name called. [*CA 2006, s 250*].

In *Re Eurostem Maritime Ltd* (1987) PCC 190, Mervyn Davies J thought that the words 'occupying the position of director' (which were also used in *CA 1985*) covered any person who *de facto* acted as a director despite his appointment being invalid or whether the person had in fact been appointed at all.

However in *Lo-Line Electric Motors Ltd, Re* [1988] Ch 477, [1988] BCLC 698 Browne-Wilkinson V-C thought the words "by whatever names called" (in *CA 1985*) were merely a recognition of the use of alternative terms for 'director' in a company's constitution eg governor or manager.

Because the only definition given in *CA 2006* is not exhaustive, in practice, it is necessary to examine the function of the person, the constitution of the company, and the terms of any contract between the company and the person, to decide whether a person is occupying the position of director.

The *chairman* is a member of the board (usually acting in a non-executive capacity) who is usually elected to that position by the board. Strictly, the chairman is chairman of the board and not chairman of the company.

The *managing director/CEO* is an executive director whose duties may be prescribed by the articles and who is presumed to have authority to deal with all areas of the business.

A *de facto director* a person acting as a director whether or not that person has been validly appointed, invalidly appointed or is just assuming to act as a director without any appointment at all – see the *Re Lo-Line Electric Motors* case referred to above and see also the case *Re Paycheck Services 3 Ltd (Holland v Revenue & Customs)* [2010] UKSC 51. This latter case decide that the critical test in deciding whether a person is a de facto director is whether the person has assumed to act as a director, exercising the powers and discharging the functions of a director. See below for the link between a de facto director and a shadow director

An *Executive director* is a member of the board authorised to carry out certain day-to-day functions including entering into contracts, managing staff and assets, etc. In many cases executive directors have a full time service contract with the company and can be treated as employees.

A *Non-executive director* is a director who sits as part of the decision-making board but without executive authority and who is brought onto the board for other skills. In particular non-executives play an important part in the corporate governance of a company (see **15 Corporate Governance**).

An *alternate director* acts as a proxy for the person who appoints him and has the right to receive all documents etc (eg notices of meeting) sent to the other directors (see **18.10**). The rights of an alternate are usually set out in the company's articles of association. The Model Articles for private companies do not contain such provisions but the Model Articles for public companies do (Articles 25–27) (see **Appendix 4 Standard Articles of Association**)

(2) *Shadow director*

Companies Act 2006, s 251(1) defines a '*shadow director*', in relation to a company, as a person in accordance with whose directions or instructions the directors of the company are 'accustomed to act'. But

- so that a person is not to be deemed a shadow director by reason only that the directors act on advice given by him in a professional capacity, in accordance with instructions, a direction, guidance or advice given by that person in the exercise of a function conferred by or under an enactment or in accordance with guidance or advice given by that person in that person's capacity as a Minister of the Crown (within the meaning of the Ministers of the *Crown Act 1975*); and
- a body corporate is not to be regarded as a shadow director of any of its subsidiary companies for the purposes of

  (i) *CA 2006, ss 170–181* (general duties of directors, see **18.23** to **18.26**),

  (ii) *CA 2006, ss 188, 189* (service contracts, see **18.53**),

  (iii) *CA 2006, ss 190–196* (substantial property transactions, see **18.58** and **18.59**),

  (iv) *CA 2006, ss 197–214* (loans, quasi-loans and credit transactions, see **18.60** to **18.66**),

  (v) *CA 2006, ss 215–222* (payment for loss of office, see **18.47** to **18.51**), or

  (vi) *CA 2006, s 231* (contracts with sole member who is also a director, see **18.57**)

  only because the directors of the subsidiary are accustomed to act in accordance with its directions or instructions.

[*CA 2006, s 251; SBEE s 89, 90*].

The acts of any one of several directors in complying with the directions of an outsider cannot make that outsider a shadow director of the company. Such an outsider cannot be a shadow director unless the whole of the board, or at very least a governing majority of it, are accustomed to act on that outsider's directions. '*Accustomed to act*' refers to acts on more than one occasion, over a period of time and as a regular course of conduct (*Unisoft Group Ltd (No 3), Re* [1994] 1 BCLC 609, [1994] BCC 766). See also the *Re Paycheck* case (above) which decided that a person can be both a shadow director and a de facto director simultaneously. Before this case was decided it was always thought that the roles were mutually exclusive.

(3) *Persons connected with a director*

The following persons (and only those persons) are connected with a director of a company unless the person is himself a director of the company.

(a) Members of the director's family, ie

  (i) the director's spouse or civil partner;

  (ii) any other person (whether of a different sex or the same sex) with whom the director lives as partner in an enduring family relationship (other than the director's grandparent or grandchild, sister, brother, aunt or uncle, or nephew or niece);

  (iii) the director's children or stepchildren;

  (iv) any children or stepchildren of a person within paragraph (ii) above (and who are not children or step-children of the director) who live with the director and have not attained the age of 18;

  (v) the director's parents.

(b) A body corporate with which the director is connected (see (4) below).

(c) A person acting in his capacity as trustee of a trust,

(i) the beneficiaries of which include the director or a person who by virtue of (*a*) or (*b*) is connected with him, or

(ii) the terms of which confer a power on the trustees that may be exercised for the benefit of the director or any such person,

other than a trust for the purposes of an employees' share scheme or a pension scheme.

(d) A person acting in his capacity as partner of

(i) the director; or

(ii) a person who, by virtue of (*a*), (*b*) or (*c*) above, is connected with that director.

(e) A firm that is a legal person under the law by which it is governed and in which

(i) the director is a partner;

(ii) a partner is a person who, by virtue of (*a*), (*b*) or (*c*) above, is connected with the director; or

(iii) a partner is a firm in which the director is a partner or in which there is a partner who, by virtue of (*a*), (*b*) or (*c*) above, is connected with the director.

[*CA 2006, ss 252, 253*].

(4) *Director 'connected with' a body corporate*

A director is connected with a body corporate if, but only if, he and the persons connected with him are together

- interested in shares comprised in the equity share capital of that body corporate of a nominal value equal to at least 20% of that share capital; or
- entitled to exercise or control the exercise of more than 20% of the voting power at any general meeting of that body. This includes voting power whose exercise is controlled by a body corporate controlled by the director.

See (6) below for the interpretation of 'an interest in shares'.

Shares in a company held as treasury shares, and any voting rights attached to such shares, are disregarded for these purposes. See **34.14** for the meaning of 'treasury shares'.

For the avoidance of circularity in the application of *s 252* above (the meaning of 'connected person'),

- a body corporate with which a director is connected is not treated for these purposes as connected with him unless it is also connected with him by virtue of (3)(*c*) or (*d*) above (connection as a trustee or partner); and
- a trustee of a trust, the beneficiaries of which include (or may include) a body corporate with which a director is connected is not treated for these purposes as connected with a director by reason only of that fact.

[*CA 2006, s 254*].

(5) *Director 'controlling' a body corporate*

A director of a company is taken to control a body corporate if, but only if

- he or any person connected with him is
  - (i) interested in any part of the equity share capital of that body; or
  - (ii) entitled to exercise or control the exercise of any part of the voting power at any general meeting of that body; and
- he, the persons connected with him and the other directors of that company, together are
  - (i) interested in more than 50% of that share capital; or
  - (ii) entitled to exercise or control the exercise of more than 50% of that voting power.

'*Voting power*' includes voting power whose exercise is controlled by a body corporate controlled by the director.

See (6) below for the interpretation of 'an interest in shares'.

Shares in a company held as treasury shares, and any voting rights attached to such shares, are disregarded for these purposes.

For the avoidance of circularity in the application of *s 252* above (the meaning of connected person),

- a body corporate with which a director is connected is not treated for these purposes as connected with him unless it is also connected with him by virtue of (3)(*c*) or (*d*) above; and
- a trustee of a trust, the beneficiaries of which include (or may include) a body corporate with which a director is connected is not treated for these purposes as connected with a director by reason only of that fact.

[*CA 2006, s 255*].

(6) *Interest in shares*

The following provisions have effect for the interpretation of references to an interest in shares under (4) and (5) above. Note that although the provisions are expressed only in relation to shares they apply also to debentures.

A reference to an interest in shares includes any interest of any kind whatsoever in shares. Any restraints or restrictions to which the exercise of any right attached to the interest is or may be subject are disregarded. It is immaterial that shares in which a person has an interest are unidentifiable.

Persons having a joint interest in shares are each deemed to have that interest.

(a) *Rights to acquire shares.* A person is taken to have an interest in shares if he

- enters into a contract to acquire them;
- has a right to call for delivery of the shares to himself or to his order (whether the right or obligation is conditional or absolute); or
- has a right to acquire an interest in shares or is under an obligation to take an interest in shares (whether the right or obligation is conditional or absolute).

Rights or obligations to *subscribe* for shares are not to be taken for these purposes to be rights to acquire or obligations to take an interest in shares.

A person ceases to have an interest in shares by virtue of this provision

- on the shares being delivered to another person at his order either in fulfilment of a contract for their acquisition by him or in satisfaction of a right of his to call for their delivery;
- on a failure to deliver the shares in accordance with the terms of such a contract or on which such a right falls to be satisfied; and
- on the lapse of his right to call for the delivery of shares.

(b) *Right to exercise or control exercise of rights.* A person is taken to have an interest in shares if, not being the registered holder, he is entitled to

- exercise any right conferred by the holding of the shares, or
- control the exercise of any such right

and, for this purpose, a person is taken to be entitled to exercise or control the exercise of a right conferred by the holding of shares if he

- has a right (whether subject to conditions or not) the exercise of which would make him so entitled; or
- is under an obligation (whether or not so subject) the fulfilment of which would make him so entitled.

But a person is not taken to be interested in shares by these provisions by reason only that he has been appointed

- a proxy to exercise any of the rights attached to the shares; or
- by a body corporate to act as its representative at any meeting of a company or of any class of its members.

(c) *Bodies corporate.* A person is taken to be interested in shares if a body corporate is interested in them and

(i) the body corporate or its directors are accustomed to act in accordance with his directions or instructions; or

(ii) he is entitled to exercise or control the exercise of more than 50% of the voting power at general meetings of the body corporate.

For the purposes of (ii) above, where

- a person is entitled to exercise or control the exercise of more than 50% of the voting power at general meetings of a body corporate, and
- that body corporate is entitled to exercise or control the exercise of any of the voting power at general meetings of another body corporate,

the voting power mentioned in (ii) above is taken to be exercisable by that person.

(d) *Trusts.* Where an interest in shares is comprised in property held on trust, every beneficiary of the trust is taken to have an interest in shares, subject to the following.

- So long as a person is entitled to receive, during the lifetime of himself or another, income from trust property comprising shares, an interest in the shares in reversion or remainder or (as regards Scotland) in fee is disregarded.
- A person is treated as not interested in shares if and so long as he holds them under the law in force in any part of the UK as a bare trustee or as a custodian trustee or under the law in force in Scotland as a simple trustee.
- Any interest of a person is disregarded if subsisting by virtue of an authorised unit trust scheme (within the meaning of *FSMA 2000, s 237*); a scheme made under *Charities Act 1960, s 22* or *22A*, *Charities Act (Northern Ireland) 1964, s 25, Charities Act 1993, s 24, Charities Act 2011, s 96* or *100*, *Trustee Investments Act 1961, s 11* or *Administration of Justice Act 1982, s 42*; or the scheme set out in the *Schedule* to the *Church Funds Investment Measure 1958.*
- There is to be disregarded any interest of the Church of Scotland General Trustees or of the Church of Scotland Trust in shares held by them (and of any other person in shares held by those Trustees or that Trust otherwise than as simple trustees)

[*CA 2006, Sch 1*].

18.2 MINIMUM NUMBER OF DIRECTORS

A private company must have at least one director and a public company must have at least two directors. [*CA 2006, s 154*]. There is no longer an exception for public companies registered before 1 November 1929 to have only one director.

The articles of a company may provide for a higher minimum number. Where a company has adopted standard articles, see

- *Table A 1985, Reg 64*

set out in **APPENDIX 4 STANDARD ARTICLES OF ASSOCIATION**.

Where a public company has adopted standard articles, see

- *Model Articles (public companies), Art 28*

set out in **APPENDIX 4 STANDARD ARTICLES OF ASSOCIATION** for the power of members to call a meeting if the company has fewer than two directors and the director (if any) is unable or unwilling to appoint sufficient directors to make up the quorum or to call a general meeting to do so.

One director to be a natural person. Every company must have at least one director who is a natural person (ie an individual). This requirement is met if the office of director is held by a natural person as a corporation sole (eg the Archbishop of Canterbury) or otherwise by virtue of an office.

This provision will be replaced by provisions contained in *Small Business, Enterprise and Employment Act 2015 (SBEE 2015), ss 87 and 88* which provide (in summary) that a company will not be able to appoint a corporate director once the relevant provisions of *SBEE 2015* are in force. From that date all directors must be a natural person other than ones holding office as a corporation sole or otherwise by virtue of an office. Anyone who is a corporate director ceases to be one 12 months after *CA 2006, s 156A* (as provided for in *SBEE 2015*) comes into force. Regulations may make exceptions to these provisions. As at May 2015 the relevant provisions of *SBEE 2015* are not in force.

[*CA 2006, s 155* and *SI 2007 No 3495, Sch 4, para 46*].

Direction to make an appointment. If a company is in breach of either of the above requirements (ie number of directors or requirement to have at least one director who is a natural person), the Secretary of State may direct the company to comply within a period of not less than one month or more than three months after the date of the direction. The company must comply by making the necessary appointment or appointments (if it has not already done so) and giving the required notice of them under *CA 2006, s 167* to the Registrar of Companies (see **18.4**) before the end of the period specified in the direction.

If a company fails to comply with a direction, an offence is committed by the company and every officer of the company who is in default. A person guilty of such an offence is liable, on summary conviction, to a fine not exceeding level 5 on the standard scale and, for continued contravention, a daily default fine not exceeding one-tenth of the greater of £5,000 or level 4 on the standard scale. See **29.1** OFFENCES AND LEGAL PROCEEDINGS for the standard scale. For this purpose, a shadow director (see **18.1**(2)) is treated as an officer of the company.

[*CA 2006, s 156; SI 2015 No 664, Sch 3*].

18.3 DIRECTOR ALSO ACTING AS SECRETARY

A director may also act as secretary.

Acts done by person in a dual capacity. A provision requiring or authorising a thing to be done by or to a director *and* the secretary of a company is not satisfied by its being done by or to the same person acting both as director and as, or in place of, the secretary. [*CA 2006, s 280*]. (See **13.1**.)

18.4 CHANGES IN DIRECTORS

Whenever there is a change either of directors (appointment or removal) or a change of directors' details, the company must update its own internal registers and notify Companies House.

Notifying Companies House. A company must give notice to the Registrar of Companies of any person becoming or ceasing to become a director on forms AP01 (appointment of director) or TM01 (termination of appointment of director) or CH01 (change of director's details) within 14 days of the change. Where a person becomes a director, the notice must contain a statement of the particulars of the new director that are required to be included in the company's register of directors and its register of directors' residential addresses (see **38.2** and **38.3** REGISTERS respectively) and be accompanied by a consent, by that person, to act in that capacity.

If default is made in complying with these provisions, an offence is committed by the company and every officer of the company who is in default. A person guilty of such an offence is liable, on summary conviction, to a fine not exceeding level 5 on the standard scale and, for continued contravention, a daily default fine not exceeding one-tenth of the greater of £5,000 or level 4 on the standard scale. See **29.1** OFFENCES AND LEGAL PROCEEDINGS for the standard scale. For this purpose, a shadow director (see **18.1**(2)) is treated as an officer of the company. [*CA 2006, s 167; SI 2015 No 664, Sch 3*].

Listed companies. See **33.26 Public and Listed Companies** for requirements to notify change of details of directors to a RIS under the FCA Listing Rules.

18.5 Appointment and retirement by rotation

The first directors of a company are appointed at the time of registration of the company (see **12.3 Company Formation**). Thereafter, the appointment of directors and their retirement by rotation is determined by the company's articles. Where a company has adopted standard articles, see

- *Table A 1985, Regs 73–80, 84*
- *Model Articles, Art 17* (private companies)
- *Model Articles, Arts 20, 21* (public companies)

set out in **Appendix 4 Standard Articles of Association**.

The UK Corporate Governance Code (see **15 Corporate Governance**) requires all directors of FTSE 350 companies to be subject to annual election by shareholders. For all other companies listed on the London Stock Exchange main market, directors should be subject to election by shareholders at the first annual general meeting after their appointment and then to re-election at intervals of no more than three years (Code main principle B.7 and Code provision B.7.1).

Where a company removes a director before the expiry of his term of office under *CA 2006, s 168* (see **18.9**)

- a vacancy created by the removal, if not filled at the meeting at which he is removed, may be filled as a casual vacancy; and
- a person appointed director in place of a person removed is treated, for the purpose of determining the time at which he or any other director is to retire, as if he had become director on the day on which the person in whose place he is appointed was last appointed a director.

[*CA 2006, s 168(3)(4)*].

Appointment of directors of public company to be voted on individually. Where it is proposed to appoint two or more persons as directors at a general meeting of a public company, a motion for the appointment must not be made by a single resolution unless a resolution that it should be so made has first been agreed to by the meeting without any vote being given against it. A resolution moved in contravention of this provision is void (whether or not its being so moved was objected to at the time) but where a resolution so moved is passed, no provision for the automatic reappointment of retiring directors in default of another appointment applies.

For these purposes, a motion for approving a person's appointment, or for nominating a person for appointment, is treated as a motion for his appointment.

Nothing in these provisions applies to a resolution amending the company's articles.

[*CA 2006, s 160*].

18.6 *Restrictions on appointments*

(1) *Minimum age requirement*

A person may not be appointed a director of a company until he is 16 years old. But the appointment of a director that does not take effect until he is 16 years old is a valid appointment.

18.6 Directors

Where the office of director of a company is held by a corporation sole, or otherwise by virtue of another office, the appointment to that other office of a person who has not attained the age of 16 years is not effective also to make him a director of the company until he attains the age of 16 years.

An appointment made in contravention of the above provisions is void. But this does not affect any liability of a person under any provision of the *Companies Acts* if he purports to act as director or acts as a shadow director (see **18.1**(2)) although he could not, because of these provisions, be validly appointed as a director.

Exceptions. The Secretary of State may provide, by Regulations, for cases in which a person who has not attained the age of 16 years may be appointed a director of a company.

Transitional provisions. Where

- a person was appointed a director of a company before 1 October 2008 and was not 16 years old on that date, or
- the office of director of a company was held by a corporation sole, or otherwise by virtue of another office, and the person appointed to that other office was not 16 years old on that date,

and the case is not one excepted by Regulations, that person ceased to be a director on that date.

The company must make the necessary consequential alteration in its register of directors but need not give notice to the Registrar of Companies of the change. If it appears to the Registrar of Companies (from other information) that a person has so ceased to be a director of a company, the Registrar must note that fact on the register.

[*CA 2006, ss 157–159*].

(2) *Upper age limit*

There is no upper age restriction unless the articles provide otherwise. Neither Table A nor the Model Articles contain such restrictions. The repeal of *CA 1985, s 293(3)* (age limit of 70 for a director not affecting the validity of acts done before it is discovered that his appointment has terminated) does not affect the validity of any acts done on or after 6 April 2007 by a person who was appointed and reached the age of 70 before 6 April 2007. [*SI 2006 No 3428, Sch 5 para 7*].

(3) *Other restrictions*

A person cannot be appointed a director of a company if

- he is an undischarged bankrupt (unless the court has given him permission to act for a particular company), or
- he has been disqualified from acting as a company director (unless the court has given him permission to act for a particular company) (see **18.11** et seq), or
- he is under the age of 16

(Companies House Guidance Booklet GP 1 Incorporation and names Chapter 2).

Certain non-British or EEA nationals are under restrictions as to what work they can do whilst in the UK. Further information can be obtained from the Home Office (Visas and Immigration). Details are available on the Home Office website at www.homeoffice.gov.uk

18.7 *Validity of acts of directors*

The acts of a person acting as a director are valid even though that it is afterwards discovered that

- there was a defect in his appointment;
- he was disqualified from holding office;
- he had ceased to hold office; or
- he was not entitled to vote on the matter in question.

This applies even if the resolution for his appointment is void under *CA 2006, s 160* (appointment of directors of public company to be voted on individually, see **18.5**).

Transitional provisions. CA 2006, s 161 applies to acts done by a director on or after 1 October 2007 but *CA 1985, s 285* continues to apply to acts done by a director before that date.

[*CA 2006, s 161; SI 2007 No 2194, Sch 3 para 4*].

See *Morris v Kanssen* [1946] AC 459, [1946] 1 All ER 586, HL, where a distinction was drawn between a defective appointment and no appointment at all.

18.8 *Appointment of managing directors/ other executive appointments*

Although the power to run a company is vested in the board as a whole, in practice the day to day decision making is delegated to committees of the board and/or the managing director or other executive officers usually under provisions in the company's articles of association- see for example *Table A 1985, reg 84* and *Model Articles, article 5* which provide for such delegation of authority.

18.9 Removal of directors

A company may by ordinary resolution remove a director before the expiration of his period of office, despite anything in any agreement between it and the director. Special notice (see **42.18 Resolutions and Meetings**) is required of the resolution (and of any resolution to appoint somebody at the same meeting instead of the director being removed). [*CA 2006, s 168(1)(2))*].

The provisions are not to be taken as

- depriving a person removed under them of compensation or damages payable to him in respect of the termination of his appointment as director or of any appointment terminating with that as director; or
- derogating from any power to remove a director that may exist apart from these provisions.

[*CA 2006, s 168(5)*].

It should also be noted that, although any provision in the articles requiring a special or extraordinary resolution to remove a director is overridden by *CA 2006, s 168* above, a company is not prevented from 'weighting' votes attached to shares even if the effect is to nullify the effects of *s 168*. See, for example, *Bushell v Faith* [1970] AC 1099, [1970] 1 All ER 53, HL, where the articles stated that, in the event of a resolution to remove a director, any shares held by that director carried three votes per share. This effectively increased each director's share of the votes on such a resolution from one-third to 60% so that a director could not be removed by an ordinary resolution.

Director's right to protest removal. On receipt of notice of an intended resolution to remove a director under the above provisions, the company must immediately send a copy of the notice to the director who is entitled to be heard on the resolution at the meeting (whether or not he is a member of the company). He may also make written representations of reasonable length to the company and request their notification to the members of the company. Unless received too late, the company must

- state the fact that representations have been made in any notice of the resolution given to members; and
- send a copy of the representations to every member to whom notice of the meeting is sent (whether before or after receipt of the representations by the company).

Where the representations are received too late or are not sent through the default of the company, the director may require the representations to be read out at the meeting (without affecting his right to be heard orally).

Copies of the representations need not be sent out, and the representation need not be read at the meeting, if, on application by the company or any other person claiming to be aggrieved, the court is satisfied that the rights conferred by these provisions are being abused. The court may order the company's costs (in Scotland, expenses) on the application to be paid, in whole or in part, by the director even if he is not a party to the application.

[*CA 2006, s 169*].

See also **18.21** for the possible removal of a director under the provisions of the company's articles.

18.10 ALTERNATE DIRECTORS

A company may make provision under its articles for directors to appoint alternates to act on their behalf. Where the company has adopted standard articles, see

- *Table A 1985, Regs 65–69*
- *Model Articles, Arts 25–27* (public companies)

set out in **Appendix 4 Standard Articles of Association**.

The Model Articles for private companies do not contain provision for the appointment etc of alternate directors. The provisions set out in the Model Articles for public companies can however be adapted as appropriate for private companies.

18.11 DISQUALIFICATION OF DIRECTORS

A court may (and in certain cases must) make a disqualification order against a person if one of the grounds in **18.12** to **18.18** is established. The effect of such an order is that, for the period specified in the order, the person must

(a) not, without the leave of the court,

 (i) be a director of a company;

 (ii) act as receiver of a company's property (which includes acting as a manager, or as both receiver and manager but does not include acting as an administrative receiver); or

(iii) in any way, directly or indirectly, be concerned or take part in the promotion, formation or management of a company. In *R v Campbell* (1984) 78 Cr App Rep 95, [1984] BCLC 83, CA, the Court of Appeal held that a person subject to a disqualification order who, as a management consultant, advised on the financial management and restructuring of a company, could be (and, on the facts of the case, was) 'concerned . . . in the management' of that company, and thereby in breach of the order; and

(b) not act as an insolvency practitioner.

Where a disqualification order is made against a person who is already subject to such an order or a disqualification undertaking, the periods specified in the orders (or the order and undertaking) run concurrently.

[*CDDA 1986, ss 1(1)(3), 22(10); IA 2000, s 5, Sch 4 para 2; EA 2002, s 204(3)*].

Similar provisions apply in Northern Ireland where a person is subject to a disqualification order or undertaking under *Companies Directors Disqualification (Northern Ireland) Order 2002*. [*CDDA 1986, ss 12A, 12B; IA 2000, s 7(1); SI 2004 No 1941, Art 2; SI 2009 No 1941, Sch 1 para 85*].

Where a court contemplates making a compensation order against a director, it must be careful not to reduce or inhibit his means to pay such an order. See *R v Holmes* [1991] BCC 394 where the Court of Appeal held that a compensation order made against a director in the Crown Court was inconsistent with the disqualification order also made since the latter order would seriously diminish his ability to earn the means with which to pay the compensation.

In addition to the above, a person is automatically disqualified, without the need for a disqualification order, in the circumstances in **18.19** and may be disqualified under the provisions of the company's articles where **18.21** applies.

Building societies and friendly societies. The provisions above and in **18.12** to **18.19** apply to a building society or an incorporated friendly society as they apply to a company.

[*CDDA 1986, ss 22A, 22B; CA 1989, s 211; Friendly Societies Act 1992, Sch 21 para 8; SI 2008 No 948, Sch 1 para 106; SI 2009 No 1941, Sch 1 para 85*].

Open-ended investment companies. The provisions above and in **18.12** to **18.19** apply to open-ended investment companies with modifications. [*CDDA 1986, s 22E; SI 2009 No 1941, Sch 1 para 85*].

18.12 Disqualification for general misconduct

A court may make a disqualification order against a person in the following circumstances.

(a) *He is convicted of an indictable offence* (whether on indictment or summarily) in connection with

- the promotion, formation, management, liquidation or striking off of a company;
- the receivership of a company's property; or
- his being an administrative receiver of a company.

The maximum period of disqualification is five years where the disqualification order is made by a court of summary jurisdiction and 15 years in any other case. For the wide interpretation given to 'in connection with the management of the company' see *R v Goodman* [1993] 2 All ER 789, [1994] 1 BCLC 349, CA.

An order under this provision may be made by

(i) any court having jurisdiction to wind up the company involved;

(ii) the court by or before which the person is convicted of the offence; or

(iii) in the case of a summary conviction in England and Wales, any other magistrates' court acting in the same local justice area.

[*CDDA 1986, s 2; Deregulation and Contracting Out Act 1994, Sch 11 para 6; IA 2000, Sch 4 para 3; Courts Act 2003, Sch 8 para 300*].

(b) *He has been 'persistently in default' in relation to provisions of the 'companies legislation'* requiring any return, account or other document to be filed with, delivered or sent, or notice of any matter to be given, to the Registrar of Companies.

'*Persistently in default*' may (without prejudice to its proof in any other matter) be conclusively proved by showing that, in the five years ending with the date of the application to the court, he has been 'adjudged guilty' (whether or not on the same occasion) of three or more defaults in relation to such provisions. See also *Arctic Engineering Ltd (No 2), Re* [1986] 2 All ER 346, [1986] BCLC 253.

'*Companies legislation*' means the Companies Acts and *IA 1986, Pts 1–7* (insolvency and winding up).

A person is treated as being '*adjudged guilty*' of a default in relation to any such provision if *either* he is convicted of an offence for contravention or failure to comply with that provision *or* a default order is made against him under

(i) *CA 2006, s 452* (order requiring delivery of company's accounts, see **2.10 Accounts: General** under the heading *Failure to file accounts and reports*);

(ii) *CA 2006, s 456* (order requiring preparation of revised accounts, see **2.14 Accounts: General**);

(iii) *CA 2006, s 1113* (enforcement by the Registrar of Companies of company's filing obligations);

(iv) *IA 1986, s 41* (enforcement of receiver's or manager's duty to make returns); or

(v) *IA 1986, s 170* (corresponding provision for liquidator in winding up).

The maximum period of disqualification is five years.

An order may be made by any court having jurisdiction to wind up any of the companies involved.

[*CDDA 1986, s 3; CA 1989, Sch 10 para 35; SI 2008 No 948, Sch 1 para 106; SI 2009 No 1941, Sch 1 para 85*].

(c) *In the course of the winding up of a company* it appears that he has

(i) been guilty of an offence for which he is liable (whether he has been convicted or not) under *CA 2006, s 993* (fraudulent trading, see **16.18 Dealings With Third Parties**); or

(ii) otherwise been guilty, while an officer or liquidator of the company, receiver of the company's property or administrative receiver of the company, of any fraud in relation to the company or any breach of duty as such officer, etc.

The maximum period of disqualification is 15 years.

An order may be made by any court having jurisdiction to wind up any of the companies involved.

[*CDDA 1986, s 4; IA 2000, Sch 4 para 4; SI 2007 No 2194, Sch 4 para 46*].

(d) *He is convicted of a 'summary offence'* (either on indictment or summarily) in consequence of a contravention of any provision of the 'companies legislation' requiring a return, account or other document to be filed with, delivered or sent, or notice of any matter to be given, to the Registrar of Companies where

(i) during the five years ending with the date of the conviction, he has been convicted of a similar offence or offences or has had made against him one or more default orders under the provisions listed in (*b*)(i)–(v) above; and

(ii) the number of convictions and/or default orders made against him (including the current summary conviction) totals three or more.

The maximum period of disqualification is five years.

An order may be made by the court by which he is convicted (or in England and Wales by any other magistrates' court acting in the same local justice area).

'*Companies legislation*' means the Companies Acts and *IA 1986, Pts 1–7* (insolvency and winding up).

[*CDDA 1986, s 5; Courts Act 2003, Sch 8 para 300; SI 2009 No 1941, Sch 1 para 85*].

New grounds for disqualification – disqualification for convictions abroad

Section 104 of the *SBEE 2015* inserts a new *Company Directors Disqualification Act (CDDA), s 55A* which provides (in summary) that a court may make a disqualification order against a person who has been convicted of a 'relevant foreign offence'.

A relevant foreign offence is an offence committed outside Great Britain in connection with the promotion, formation, management, liquidation or striking off of a company (or any similar procedure) or the receivership of a company's property (or any similar procedure) in each case which corresponds to an indictable offence in Great Britain. These provisions are not, as at May 2015, in force.

An application (to a court with jurisdiction to wind up companies) for the making against any person of a disqualification order under (*a*) to (*c*) above may be made by the Secretary of State; the official receiver; the liquidator; or any past or present member or creditor of any company in relation to which that person has committed, or is alleged to have committed, an offence or other default. [*CDDA 1986, s 16(2); IA 2000, Sch 4 para 11*].

18.13 Disqualification for unfitness

There are both mandatory grounds (18.14) and discretionary grounds (18.15) whereby a court can make a disqualification order against a person as being unfit to act as a director. In either case the court must have regard to the provisions of 18.16 in determining his unfitness.

18.14 *Mandatory grounds*

A court *must* make a disqualification order against a person if it is satisfied that

(a) he is or has been a director (or shadow director, see **18.1(2)**) of a company which has at any time become insolvent (whether while he was a director or subsequently); and

(b) his conduct as a director of that company (whether taken alone or taken together with his conduct as a director of any other company or companies) makes him unfit to be concerned in the management of a company. References to a person's conduct as a director of any company include, where that company has become insolvent, that person's conduct in relation to the insolvency.

A person may be included under (*a*) above where he has acted as a director even though not validly appointed or not appointed at all. To be disqualified as a *de facto* director, there must be clear evidence that either he had been the sole person directing the affairs of the company or, if there were others who were true directors, he acted on an equal footing with them in directing the affairs of the company. Where it is unclear whether his actions are referable to an assumed directorship or some other capacity (eg shareholder or consultant) the person must be given the benefit of doubt (*Re Richborough Furniture Ltd* [1996] 1 BCLC 507, [1996] BCC 155).

The minimum period of disqualification is two years and the maximum is 15 years.

A company becomes insolvent for these purposes if

- it goes into liquidation at a time when its assets are insufficient for the payment of its debts and other liabilities and the expenses of winding up;
- it enters administration; or
- an administrative receiver of the company is appointed.

An application for the making of a disqualification order against any person may be made by the Secretary of State or, if he so directs, the official receiver in the case of a director or former director of a company which is being or has been wound up by the court in England and Wales. Except with the leave of the court, such an application cannot be made more than two years from the date on which the company became insolvent. In deciding whether an application can be made out of time, the court will consider the length of, and reasons for, the delay, the strength of the case against the director and the degree of prejudice caused to the director by the delay (*Probe Data Systems Ltd (No 3), Re* [1992] BCLC 405, [1992] BCC 110, CA). See also, *inter alia*, *Re Lo-Line Electric Motors Ltd* [1988] Ch 477, [1988] BCLC 698, [1988] 2 All ER 692 and *Re Crestjoy Products Ltd* [1990] BCLC 677, [1990] BCC 23.

If it appears, as the case may be, to the official receiver, liquidator, administrator or administrative receiver that the conditions for making an order under these provisions are satisfied, he must report that fact to the Secretary of State. See the *Insolvent Companies (Reports on Conduct of Directors) Rules 1996* (*SI 1996 No 1909*) and the *Insolvent Companies (Reports on Conduct of Directors) (Scotland) Rules 1996* (*SI 1996 No 1910*) for the form and content of such a report.

[*CDDA 1986, ss 6, 7; IA 2000, Sch 4 paras 5, 6; EA 2002, Sch 17 paras 40–42*].

In *Re Deaduck Ltd (in liq), Baker v Secretary of State for Trade and Industry* [2000] 1 BCLC 148, Neuberger J held that, in considering disqualification applications under *CDDA 1986, s 6* where the director had not been guilty of dishonest or commercially flagrantly culpable behaviour, there were two competing factors to be balanced:

- the protection of the public against someone who had been found liable in respect of a charge which constituted conduct as a director which made him unfit to be concerned in the management of a company as against

- the consideration that it would involve going further than *CDDA 1986* or relevant authorities contemplated, if every time a director was found to have failed in his duty, he was liable to be disqualified.

In *Cathie v Secretary of State for Business, Innovation and Skills* [2012] 2All ER (D) 86 the court at first instance said that once misconduct is found, a finding of unfitness (to be concerned in the management of a company) must necessarily follow unless there are "exceptional circumstances" and the burden is on the director to establish those exceptional circumstances. The Court of Appeal disagreed saying that the phrase "exceptional circumstances" should be avoided. The correct approach is for the court to consider the evidence as a whole including any extenuating circumstances and to decide whether the director has fallen below the standards of probity and competence appropriate for a director of a company.

Disqualification undertakings. Instead of applying for a disqualification order, the Secretary of State, if it appears to him to be expedient in the public interest that he should do so, may accept a 'disqualification undertaking' from any person that, for the period specified in the undertaking, he will comply with the conditions in **18.11**(*a*) and (*b*). The maximum period which may be specified in such an undertaking is 15 years and the minimum period is seven years. Where a disqualification undertaking is accepted by a person who is already subject to such an undertaking or to a disqualification order, the periods specified in those undertakings and orders run concurrently. In determining whether to accept a disqualification undertaking by any person, the Secretary of State

- may take account of matters other than criminal convictions; and
- as respects the person's conduct as a director of any company concerned, must have regard to the matters listed in **18.16**.

The court may, on the application of a person who is subject to a disqualification undertaking, reduce the period for which it is to be in force or provide for it to cease altogether.

[*CDDA 1986, ss 1A, 7, 8A (1), 9; IA 2000, s 6, Sch 4 para 6; EA 2002, Sch 17 paras 40, 42*].

18.15 *Discretionary grounds*

If it appears to the Secretary of State from investigation material, ie

- a report made by inspectors under *CA 1985, s 437* (see **25.4 Investigations**) or *FSMA 2000, ss 167, 168, 169* or *284*, or
- information or documents obtained under *CA 1985, ss 437, 446E, 447, 448, 451A* or *453A* (see **25 Investigations**), *Criminal Justice Act 1987, s 2, Criminal Law (Consolidation) (Scotland) Act 1995, s 28, CA 1989, s 83*, or *FSMA 2000, ss 165, 171, 172, 173 or 175*

that it is expedient in the public interest for a disqualification order to be made against any director, former director or shadow director of the company, he may apply to the High Court (in Scotland, the Court of Sessions) for such an order to be made against that person. The court may make a disqualification order where it is satisfied that the person's conduct in relation to the company makes him unfit to be concerned in the management of the company.

The maximum period of disqualification is 15 years.

[*CDDA 1986, s 8(1)(1A)(2); C(AICE)A 2004, Sch 2 para 28; CA 2006, s 1039; SI 2001 No 3649, Art 39; SI 2009 No 1941, Sch 1 para 85*].

Disqualification undertakings. Instead of applying for a disqualification order, the Secretary of State, if it appears to him to be expedient in the public interest that he should do so, may accept a 'disqualification undertaking' from any person that his conduct in relation to a company of which he is or has been a director or shadow director makes him unfit to be concerned in the management of a company and, for the period specified in the undertaking, he will comply with the conditions in **18.11**(*a*) and (*b*) above. The maximum period which may be specified in such an undertaking is 15 years. Where a disqualification undertaking is accepted by a person who is already subject to such an undertaking or to a disqualification order, the periods specified in those undertakings and orders run concurrently. In determining whether to accept a disqualification undertaking by any person, the Secretary of State

- may take account of matters other than criminal convictions; and
- as respects the person's conduct as a director of any company concerned, must have regard to the matters listed in **18.16**.

The court may, on the application of a person who is subject to a disqualification undertaking, reduce the period for which it is to be in force or provide for it to cease altogether.

[*CDDA 1986, ss 1A, 8(2A), 8A, 9(1A); IA 2000, s 6; EA 2002, s 204*].

New provision – disqualification of persons who instruct unfit directors

Section 105 of the *SBEE 2015* inserts new *CDDA, ss 8ZA–E.* They provide (in summary) that a court may make a disqualification order against a person ('P') if it is satisfied that either a disqualification order under *CDDA, s 6* or *s 8* has been made against a person who is, or has been, a director or that the Secretary of State has accepted a disqualification undertaking from such a person, and that P exercised the requisite amount of influence over that person. 'Requisite amount of influence' is defined in *CDDA, s 8ZA (2)–(3)*. Disqualification undertakings may also be accepted in either case. As at May 2015 the relevant provisions of *SBEE* are not in force.

18.16 *Matters for determining unfitness of directors*

In determining whether a person's conduct as a director of any particular company or companies makes him unfit to be concerned in the management of a company, the court must have regard 'in particular' to the following matters.

Matters applicable in all cases

- Any misfeasance or breach of any fiduciary or other duty by the director in relation to the company, including in particular any breach by the director of a duty under *CA 2006, Pt 10, Ch 2* (general duties of directors, see **18.23–18.26**).
- Any misapplication or retention by the director of, or any conduct by the director giving rise to an obligation to account for, any money or other property of the company.
- The extent of the director's responsibility for the company entering into any transaction liable to be set aside under *IA 1986, Pt XVI* (provisions against debt avoidance).
- The extent of the director's responsibility for any failure by the company to comply with any of the requirements of:

CA 2006, s 113 (register of members, see **38.5 Registers**);

CA 2006, s 114 (register to be kept available for inspection, see **38.6 Registers**);

CA 2006, s 162 (register of directors, see **38.2 Registers**);

CA 2006, s 165 (register of directors' residential addresses, see **38.3 Registers**);

CA 2006, s 167 (duty to notify registrar of changes: directors, see **38.2 Registers**);

CA 2006, s 275 (register of secretaries, see **38.4 Registers**);

CA 2006, s 276 (duty to notify registrar of changes: secretaries, see **38.4 Registers**);

CA 2006, s 386 (duty to keep accounting records, see **36.5 Records**);

CA 2006, s 388 (where and for how long records to be kept, see **36.6** and **36.7 Records**);

CA 2006, s 854 (duty to make annual return, see **7.1 Annual Returns**);

CA 2006, ss 860, 878 (company's duty to register the charges it creates, see **40.2** and **40.11 Registration of Charges**).

- The extent of the director's responsibility for any failure by the directors of the company to comply with
  - (i) *CA 2006, s 394* or *s 399* (duty to prepare individual and group accounts respectively);
  - (ii) *CA 2006, s 414* (approval and signing of accounts) or *CA 2006, s 450* (approval and signing of abbreviated accounts); or
  - (iii) *CA 2006, s 433* (name of signatory to be stated in published copy of accounts).

Matters applicable where company has become insolvent

- The extent of the director's responsibility for the causes of the company becoming insolvent.
- The extent of the director's responsibility for any failure by the company to supply goods or services which have been paid for (in whole or part).
- The extent of the director's responsibility for the company entering into any transaction or giving any preference liable to be set aside under *IA 1986, ss 238–240* or challenged under *IA 1986, ss 242* and *243* or under any rule of law in Scotland.
- The extent of the director's responsibility for any failure by the directors of the company to comply with *IA 1986, s 98* (duty to call creditors' meeting in creditors' voluntary winding up).
- Any failure by the director to comply with any obligation imposed on him by or under

  IA 1986, Sch B1 para 47 (company's statement of affairs in administration);

  IA 1986, s 47 (statement of affairs to administrative receiver);

  IA 1986, s 66 (statement of affairs in Scottish receivership);

  IA 1986, s 99 (directors' duty to attend meetings; statement of affairs in creditors' voluntary winding up);

  IA 1986, s 131 (statement of affairs in winding up by court);

IA 1986, s 234 (duty of anyone with company property to deliver it up); or

IA 1986, s 235 (duty to co-operate with the liquidator etc).

[*CDDA 1986, s 9, Sch 1; CA 1989, s 139, Sch 10 para 35; IA 2000, Sch 4 para 7; SI 1996 No 2827, Sch 8 para 10; SI 2001 No 1228, Sch 7 para 9; SI 2003 No 2096, Sch 1 para 12; SI 2008 No 948, Sch 1 para 106; SI 2009 No 1941, Sch 1 para 85*].

In considering the question of unfitness, the court is concerned with the director's conduct generally and is not restricted in making a finding of unfitness to cases where the director could be disqualified on some other ground. The words '*in particular*' suggest that the court is not confined to looking at the matters set out in the legislation (*Re Bath Glass Ltd* [1988] BCLC 329, 4 BCC 130).

The court is required to have regard to a person's conduct as a director regardless of whether he has been validly appointed or is merely assuming to act as a director. The conduct relevant to his future suitability to act depends on his past record irrespective of the circumstances in which he came to act as a director (*Re Lo-Line Electric Motors Ltd* [1988] Ch 477, [1988] BCLC 698).

18.17 Disqualification for competition infringements

The High Court (in Scotland, the Court of Session) must make a disqualification order against a person if the following two conditions are satisfied in relation to him.

(1) A company of which he is a director commits a breach of competition law.

A company commits a breach of competition law if it engages in conduct which infringes any of the following.

- The Chapter 1 prohibition (within the meaning of the *Competition Act 1998*) (prohibition on agreements, etc preventing, restricting or distorting competition).
- The Chapter 2 prohibition (within the meaning of that *Act*) (prohibition on abuse of a dominant position).
- *Article 81* of the Treaty establishing the European Community (prohibition on agreements, etc preventing, restricting or distorting competition).
- *Article 82* of that Treaty (prohibition on abuse of a dominant position).

(2) The court considers that his conduct as a director makes him unfit to be concerned in the management of a company.

For these purpose the court

- *must* have regard to whether, as a director of the company,

  (i) his conduct contributed to the breach of competition law mentioned in (1) above (and for this purpose it is immaterial whether the person knew that the conduct of the company constituted the breach);

  (ii) his conduct did not contribute to the breach but he had reasonable grounds to suspect that the conduct of the company constituted the breach and he took no steps to prevent it; or

  (iii) he did not know, but ought to have known, that the conduct of the company constituted the breach;

- *may* have regard to his conduct as a director of a company in connection with any other breach of competition law; and
- *must not* have regard to the matters mentioned in *CDDA 1986, Sch 1* (see 18.16).

For the above purposes, 'conduct' includes omission and 'director' includes shadow director (see 18.1(2)).

The maximum period of disqualification is 15 years.

An application under these provisions for a disqualification order may be made by the OFT or by a '*specified regulator*', ie each of the following for the purposes of a breach of competition law in relation to a matter in respect of which he or it has a function, namely

- the Office of Communications;
- the Gas and Electricity Markets Authority;
- the Water Services Regulation Authority;
- the Office of Rail Regulation; and
- the Civil Aviation Authority.

Competition undertakings. Instead of applying for a disqualification order, the OFT or the specified regulator (as the case may be) may accept a 'disqualification undertaking' from any person that, for the period specified in the undertaking, he will not

(a) be a director of a company,

(b) act as receiver of a company's property,

(c) in any way, whether directly or indirectly, be concerned or take part in the promotion, formation or management of a company, or

(d) act as an insolvency practitioner

but a disqualification undertaking may provide that a prohibition falling within (*a*) to (*c*) above does not apply if the person obtains the leave of the court.

The maximum period which may be specified in a disqualification undertaking is 15 years. Where a disqualification undertaking is accepted from a person who is already subject to such an undertaking or to a disqualification order, the periods specified in those undertakings or the undertaking and the order (as the case may be) run concurrently.

Competition investigations. If the OFT or a specified regulator has reasonable grounds for suspecting that a breach of competition law has occurred, it or he (as the case may be) may carry out an investigation for the purpose of deciding whether to make an application for a disqualification order (in which case, for the purposes of such an investigation, *Competition Act 1998, ss 26–30* apply as they apply to the OFT for the purposes of an investigation under *Competition Act 1998, s 25*). Where, as a result of such an investigation, the OFT or a specified regulator proposes to apply for a disqualification order under the above provisions, before making the application the OFT or regulator (as the case may be) must

- give notice to the person likely to be affected by the application; and
- give that person an opportunity to make representations.

18.17 Directors

[*CDDA 1986, ss 9A–9E; EA 2002, s 204; Communications Act 2003, Sch 17 para 83; Railway and Transport Safety Act 2003, Sch 2 para 19; Water Act 2003, Sch 7 para 25*].

18.18 Disqualification for participation in wrongful trading

Where the court makes a declaration under *IA 1986, ss 213* (fraudulent trading) or *214* (wrongful trading) that a person is liable to contribute to a company's assets, then the court may also make a disqualification order against the person to whom the declaration relates. This applies whether or not an application for such an order is made by any person.

The maximum period of disqualification is 15 years.

[*CDDA 1986, s 10; SI 2009 No 1941, Sch 1 para 85*].

18.19 Automatic disqualification for bankruptcy etc

A person may not act as a director of, or directly or indirectly take part in or be concerned in the promotion, formation or management of, a company (including a company incorporated outside Great Britain that has a an established place of business in Great Britain) in the following circumstances.

(a) Either

- he is an undischarged bankrupt,
- a moratorium period under a debt relief order applies in relation to him, or
- a bankruptcy restriction order or a debt relief restrictions order is in force in respect of him

and the court by which he was adjudged bankrupt (or, in Scotland, by which sequestration of his estates was awarded) has not given leave for him so to act, etc. See *R v Brockley* (1993) 99 Cr App Rep 385, [1994] 1 BCLC 606, CA.

In England and Wales, the court must not give leave unless notice of intention to apply for it has been served on the official receiver, who has a duty to attend the hearing and oppose the application if he considers that it is contrary to the public interest that the application should be granted.

[*CDDA 1986, s 11; EA 2002, Sch 21 para 5; Tribunals, Courts and Enforcement Act 2007, Sch 20 para 16; SI 2009 No 1941, Sch 1 para 85*].

(b) A county court revokes an administration order made in respect of that person because either

- he failed to make two payments (whether consecutive or not) required by the order, or
- at the time the order was made, the total amount of his qualifying debts was more than the prescribed maximum for the purposes *IA 1986, Pt 6* but because of information provided, or not provided, by him, that amount was thought to be less than, or the same as, the prescribed maximum,

and the court, at the time it revokes the administration order, makes an order directing that he shall not act, etc for such period (not exceeding one year) as may be specified in the order. [*CDDA 1986, s 12; Tribunals, Courts and Enforcement Act 2007, Sch 16 para 5; SI 2009 No 1941, Sch 1 para 85*].

18.20 Consequences of contravention

Criminal penalties. A person who acts in contravention of a disqualification order or disqualification undertaking or in contravention of the provisions of **18.19** is guilty of an offence and liable (i) on conviction on indictment, to imprisonment for not more than two years or a fine (or both); and (ii) on summary conviction, to imprisonment for not more than 6 months or a fine (or both). [*CDDA 1986, s 13; IA 2000 Sch 4 para 8; SI 2004 No 1941, Art 2*].

Where a body corporate is guilty of an offence of acting in contravention of a disqualification order or disqualification undertaking, a director, manager, secretary, or other similar official of the body corporate is also guilty of the offence if it is proved that the offence occurred with the consent or connivance of, or was attributable to any neglect on the part of, that person. [*CDDA 1986, s 14(1); IA 2000, Sch 4 para 9; SI 2004 No 1941, Art 2*]. Similarly, where the affairs of a body corporate are managed by its members, a member will be liable for his acts and defaults in connection with his functions of management as if he were a director of the body corporate. [*CDDA 1986, s 14(2)*].

Personal liability. Where a person, in contravention of a disqualification order or disqualification undertaking or of **18.19**(*a*), is a director of, or is concerned or takes part in the management of, a company, he is personally responsible for such debts and other liabilities of the company as are incurred while he is so involved.

In addition, where a person (A) involved in the management of a company acts (or is willing to act) on instructions given, without leave of the court, by another person (B) whom A knows at that time to be the subject of a disqualification order or disqualification undertaking or to be an undischarged bankrupt, then A is personally responsible for such debts and other liabilities of the company as are incurred while he is acting (or willing to act) on such instructions. For these purposes, where A has at any time acted on instructions given, without the leave of the court, by B, and A knew at that time that B was the subject of a disqualification order or disqualification undertaking or to be an undischarged bankrupt, then A is presumed to have been willing to act on B's instructions at any time thereafter, unless the contrary is shown.

Where a person is personally responsible, he is jointly and severally liable for the debts referred to above with

- the company; and
- any other person who is so liable, whether under these provisions or otherwise.

[*CDDA 1986, s 15; IA 2000, Sch 4 para 10; SI 2004 No 1941, Art 2; SI 2009 No 1941, Sch 1 para 85*].

Register of orders. The Secretary of State is required to keep a register of disqualification orders and undertakings and can require court officers to furnish him with certain particulars. See *CDDA 1986, s 18* and the *Companies (Disqualification Orders) Regulations 2009 (SI 2009 No 2471)*.

18.21 Disqualification under the company's articles

Generally, a company's articles will contain provisions either for the removal of a director (see **18.9**) or requiring a director to vacate office on grounds additional to those set out in **18.12** to **18.19**. Where a company has adopted standard articles, see

- *Table A 1985, Reg 81*
- *Model Articles, Art 18* (private companies)

18.21 Directors

- *Model Articles, Art 22* (public companies)

set out in **Appendix 4 standard articles of association.**

18.22 FOREIGN DISQUALIFICATIONS

The Secretary of State may make Regulations disqualifying a person 'subject to foreign restrictions' from

(a) being a director of a 'UK company';

(b) acting as receiver of a UK company's property; or

(c) in any way, whether directly or indirectly, being concerned or taking part in the promotion, formation or management of a UK company.

'*UK company*' means a company registered under *CA 2006*.

[*CA 2006, s 1184*].

A person is '*subject to foreign restrictions*' if under the law of a country or territory outside the UK

- he is, by reason of misconduct or unfitness, disqualified to any extent from acting in connection with the affairs of a company incorporated or formed under the law of that country or territory;
- he is, by reason of misconduct or unfitness, required to

  (i) obtain permission from a court or other authority, or

  (ii) meet any other condition,

  before acting in connection with the affairs of a company incorporated or formed under the law of that country or territory; or
- he has, by reason of misconduct or unfitness, given undertakings to a court or other authority of a country or territory outside the UK

  (i) not to act in connection with the affairs of a company incorporated or formed under the law of that country or territory; or

  (ii) restricting the extent to which, or the way in which, he may do so.

The references to '*acting in connection with the affairs of a company*' are to doing anything within (*a*)–(*c*) above.

[*CA 2006, s 1182*].

18.23 DUTIES OF DIRECTORS

The general duties specified in **18.24** (modified, in the case of charitable companies, as in **18.26**) are owed by a director of a company to the company. Even where a person ceases to be a director, on or after 1 October 2008 he continues to be subject to the duty to

- to avoid conflicts of interest (see **18.24**(5)) as regards the exploitation of any property, information or opportunity of which he became aware at a time when he was a director; and

- not to accept benefits from third parties (see **18.24**(6)) as regards things done or omitted by him before he ceased to be a director.

To that extent those duties apply to a former director as to a director (subject to any necessary adaptations).

These general duties

- are based on certain common law rules and equitable principles as they apply in relation to directors and have effect in place of those rules and principles as regards the duties owed to a company by a director;
- are to be interpreted and applied in the same way as common law rules or equitable principles, so that regard must be had to the corresponding common law rules and equitable principles in interpreting and applying the general duties; and
- apply to shadow directors (see **18.1**(2)) where, and to the extent that either, the corresponding common law rules or equitable principles apply or regulations to be made under *SBEE 2015, s 89* provide how the general duties will apply to shadow directors. *Section 89* of the *SBEE 2015* came into force in May 2015 but regulations made under that section have not been made.

[*CA 2006, s 170; SBEE 2015, ss 89, 164; SI 2007 No 2194, Sch 1 para 6; SI 2007 No 3495, Art 10*].

Civil consequences of breach of general duties. The consequences of breach (or threatened breach) of any of the general duties in **18.24** are the same as would apply if the corresponding common law rule or equitable principle applied. The duties (with the exception of **18.24**(4)) are, accordingly, enforceable in the same way as any other fiduciary duty owed to a company by its directors. [*CA 2006, s 178*]. In the case of fiduciary duties, the consequences of breach may include

- damages or compensation where the company has suffered loss;
- restoration of the company's property;
- an account of profits made by the director; and
- rescission of a contract where the director fails to disclose an interest.

18.24 General duties

(1) *Duty to act within powers*

A director of a company must act in accordance with the 'company's constitution' and only exercise powers for the purposes for which they are conferred. [*CA 2006, s 171*].

(2) *Duty to promote the success of the company*

A director of a company must act in the way he considers, in good faith, would be most likely to promote the success of the company for the benefit of its members as a whole. In doing so, he must have regard (amongst other matters) to

- the likely consequences of any decision in the long term;
- the interests of the company's employees;
- the need to foster the company's business relationships with suppliers, customers and others;

- the impact of the company's operations on the community and the environment;
- the desirability of the company maintaining a reputation for high standards of business conduct; and
- the need to act fairly as between members of the company.

Where (or to the extent that) the purposes of the company consist of or include purposes other than the benefit of its members (eg charitable companies and community interest companies), the above provisions have effect as if the reference to promoting the success of the company for the benefit of its members were to achieving those purposes.

The duty imposed by these provisions has effect subject to any enactment or rule of law requiring directors, in certain circumstances, to consider or act in the interests of creditors of the company (see, for example, *IA 1986, s 214* at **18.39**).

[*CA 2006, s 172*].

In having regard to the factors listed, the duty to exercise reasonable care, skill and diligence (see (4) below) will apply.

(3) *Duty to exercise independent judgment*

A director of a company must exercise independent judgment. This duty is not infringed by his acting

- in accordance with an agreement duly entered into by the company that restricts the future exercise of discretion by its directors; or
- in a way authorised by the 'company's constitution'.

[*CA 2006, s 173*].

(4) *Duty to exercise reasonable care, skill and diligence*

A director of a company must exercise reasonable care, skill and diligence. This means the care, skill and diligence that would be exercised by a reasonably diligent person with the general knowledge, skill and experience that

- may reasonably be expected of a person carrying out the functions carried out by the director in relation to the company; and
- the director has.

[*CA 2006, s 174*].

(5) *Duty to avoid conflicts of interest*

A director of a company must avoid a situation in which he has, or can have, a direct or indirect interest that conflicts, or possibly may conflict, with the interests of the company. This applies, in particular, to the exploitation of any property, information or opportunity (and it is immaterial whether the company could take advantage of the property, information or opportunity).

This duty

(a) does not apply to a conflict of interest arising in relation to a transaction or arrangement with the company; and

(b) is not infringed if the situation cannot reasonably be regarded as likely to give rise to a conflict of interest or if the matter has been authorised by the directors.

For these purposes, a conflict of interest includes a conflict of interest and duty and a conflict of duties.

Authorisation by the directors. Authorisation may be given by the directors

(i) where the company is a private company and nothing in the company's constitution invalidates such authorisation, by the matter being proposed to and authorised by the directors; and

(ii) where the company is a public company and its constitution includes provision enabling the directors to authorise the matter, by the matter being proposed to and authorised by them in accordance with the constitution.

For the authorisation to be effective, any requirement as to the quorum at the meeting at which the matter is considered must be met without counting the director in question or any other interested director. The matter must then be agreed to without their voting (or, where they vote, would still have been agreed to if their votes had not been counted).

Transitional provisions

1. In relation to conflicts of interest situations which arose before 1 October 2008, the law that applied before that date continues to apply; and

2. In relation to companies incorporated before 1 October 2008, (i) (above) applies where the members of a private company resolved (before, on or after that date) that authorisation could be given in accordance with *CA 2006, s 175*.

[*CA 2006, s 175*].

(6) *Duty not to accept benefits from third parties*

A director of a company must not accept a benefit from a 'third party' conferred by reason of his being a director or his doing (or not doing) anything as director

'*Third party*' means a person other than the company, an associated body corporate or a person acting on behalf of the company or an associated body corporate. For these purposes, bodies corporate are associated if one is a subsidiary of the other or both are subsidiaries of the same body corporate.

This duty is not infringed if

- benefits are received by a director from a person by whom his services (as a director or otherwise) are provided to the company; or
- the acceptance of the benefit cannot reasonably be regarded as likely to give rise to a conflict of interest. For these purposes, a conflict of interest includes a conflict of interest and duty and a conflict of duties.

[*CA 2006, ss 176, 256*].

(7) *Duty to declare interest in proposed transaction or arrangement*

If a director of a company is in any way, directly or indirectly, interested in a proposed transaction or arrangement with the company, he must declare the nature and extent of that interest to the other directors. The declaration may (but need not) be made at a meeting of the directors or by notice to the directors in accordance with *CA 2006, s 184* (notice in writing) or *CA 2006, s 185* (general notice). See **18.58**. It must be made before the company enters into the transaction or arrangement in question.

If a declaration of interest as above proves to be, or becomes, inaccurate or incomplete, a further declaration must be made.

These provisions do not require a declaration of an interest

- where the director is not aware of the interest or is not aware of the transaction or arrangement in question (and for this purpose a director is treated as being aware of matters of which he ought reasonably to be aware);
- if it cannot reasonably be regarded as likely to give rise to a conflict of interest;
- if, or to the extent that, the other directors are already aware of it (and for this purpose the other directors are treated as aware of anything of which they ought reasonably to be aware); or
- if, or to the extent that, it concerns terms of his service contract that have been or are to be considered
  - (i) by a meeting of the directors; or
  - (ii) by a committee of the directors appointed for the purpose under the 'company's constitution'.

[*CA 2006, s 177*].

Transitional provisions

(1) *CA 1985, s 317* continues to apply in relation to a duty arising before 1 October 2008.

(2) A declaration of interest in a proposed transaction or arrangement made before 1 October 2008 which proves to be, or becomes, inaccurate or incomplete on or after 1 October 2008, is treated as made on or after that date for the purposes of any further declaration that must be made.

[*SI 2007 No 3495, Sch 4, para 48*].

Company's constitution. For the above purposes, a company's constitution includes

- the company's articles;
- any resolutions and agreements to which *CA 2006, ss 29, 30* apply (see **14.9** CONSTITUTION – MEMORANDUM AND ARTICLES);
- any resolution or other decision come to in accordance with the constitution; and
- any decision by the members of the company, or a class of members, that is treated by virtue of any enactment or rule of law as equivalent to a decision by the company (eg a decision taken by the informal unanimous consent of all the members).

[*CA 2006, s 257*].

Cases within more than one of the general duties. Except as otherwise provided, more than one of the general duties may apply in any given case. [*CA 2006, s 179*]. It is therefore necessary to comply with every duty that applies in any given case. For example, the duty to promote the success of the company under (2) above will not authorise a director to breach his duty to act within his powers under (1) above, even if he considers that it would be most likely to promote the success of the company.

The one exception relates to the duty to avoid conflicts of interest under (5) above which does not apply to a conflict of interest arising in relation to a transaction or arrangement with the company. In such cases, the duty to declare interests in proposed transactions or arrangements under (7) above or the requirement to declare interests in existing transactions or arrangements under **18.56** will apply instead.

18.25 *Consent, approval or authorisation by members*

In a case where a duty to avoid a conflict of interest is authorised by the directors or the director declares an interest in a proposed transaction or arrangement with the company, the transaction or arrangement is not liable to be set aside by virtue of any common law rule or equitable principle requiring the consent or approval of the members of the company. This is without prejudice to any enactment, or provision of the 'company's constitution', requiring such consent or approval.

Where a particular case falls within the transactions with directors requiring approval of members under

- *CA 2006, ss 188, 189* (service contracts, see **18.53**),
- *CA 2006, ss 190–196* (substantial property transactions, see **18.58** and **18.59**),
- *CA 2006, ss 197–214* (loans, quasi-loans and credit transactions, see **18.60** to **18.66**), or
- *CA 2006, ss 215–222* (payment for loss of office, see **18.47** to **18.51**), or
- *CA 2006, ss 226A–226F* (payments for loss of office-quoted companies, see **18.51A**)

then

(a) the application of the general duties is not affected except that it is not necessary also to comply with **18.24(5)** or **18.24(6)**

(i) where any of the above provisions apply and the necessary approval is given (including approval given by a resolution passed before 1 October 2007 if it complies with the requirements of those provisions); or

(ii) the matter is one for which approval is not needed; and

(b) compliance with the general duties does not remove the need for approval under the appropriate provision.

The general duties have effect (except as otherwise provided or the context otherwise requires) notwithstanding any enactment or rule of law, except that

- they have effect subject to any rule of law enabling the company to give authority, specifically or generally, for anything to be done (or omitted) by the directors, or any of them, that would otherwise be a breach of duty; and
- where the company's articles contain provisions for dealing with conflicts of interest, the general duties are not infringed by anything done (or omitted) by the directors, or any of them, in accordance with those provisions.

[*CA 2006, s 180; SI 2007 No 2194, Sch 3 paras 6(2), 7(2), 8(2), 12(2); SI 2007 No 3495, Sch 4 para 49*].

Company's constitution. For the purposes of **18.23(7)**, **18.25** and **18.26** (below), a company's constitution includes

- the company's articles;
- any resolutions and agreements to which *CA 2006, ss 29, 30* apply (see **14.1** CONSTITUTION – MEMORANDUM AND ARTICLES);
- any resolution or other decision come to in accordance with the constitution; and

- any decision by the members of the company, or a class of members, that is treated by virtue of any enactment or rule of law as equivalent to a decision by the company (eg a decision taken by the informal unanimous consent of all the members).

[*CA 2006, s 257*].

18.26 *Charitable companies*

In England and Wales and Northern Ireland, the provisions in **18.23** to **18.25** also apply to a company that is a charity, but with the following modifications.

(a) Conflicts of interest arising in relation to a transaction or arrangement with the company are excluded from the duty only if, or to the extent that, the charitable company's articles so allow. The articles must describe the transactions or arrangements which are excluded from the duty.

(b) Authorisation by the directors may only be given where the 'company's constitution' includes provision enabling the directors to authorise the matter and by the matter being proposed to and authorised by them in accordance with the constitution.

(c) If the matter falls within **18.25** (transactions requiring approval of members) matters not needing approval must be set out it the company's articles and only to the extent that the articles allow those duties to be disapplied.

[*CA 2006, s 181*].

18.27 Other statutory duties

In addition to the general duties in **18.24**, other statutory provisions extend and modify the general principles that directors must not abuse their positions and must deal fairly in certain transactions with the company or its shares. In particular, these arise in connection with the following.

- Payments for loss of office (see **18.47** to **18.51**).
- Service contracts (see **18.52**).
- Disclosure of interests in contracts (see **18.55**).
- Substantial property transactions (see **18.58**).
- Loans, quasi-loans and credit transactions (see **18.60**).
- Insider dealing (see **23 Insider Dealing and Market Abuse**).

Duties of internal management under the *CA 2006*. A director has a considerable number of duties under *CA 2006* which he must perform or ensure are performed. To a large extent they relate to matters of internal management and are dealt with in the appropriate chapters of this book. They include provisions relating to the keeping of accounting records, the preparation of annual accounts, the filing of documents with the Registrar of Companies, and the keeping of the statutory books of the company. The company is punishable for failure by a fine and in some cases a daily default fine; directors can suffer fines, daily default fines, and, in some cases, imprisonment.

18.28 Duties to third parties

Although a director in his capacity as such owes his duties to the company, he may in the course of carrying out those duties find that he puts himself in a position where he also owes obligations to other persons. These include:

- Shareholders and employees of the company.
- Subscribers for, and purchasers of, securities. Subscribers for listed securities are protected by *FSMA 2000, s 90*. This provides that the persons responsible for any listing particulars or a prospectus are liable to pay compensation to any person who has acquired any of the securities in question and suffered loss in respect of them as a result of any untrue or misleading statements in them or the omission of any matter required to be included in them.
- Customers, suppliers and other contracting parties.

18.29 POWERS OF DIRECTORS

Subject to any provision to the contrary in the *Companies Acts* or the company's articles, the directors are responsible for the management of the company and they may exercise all the powers of the company.

Where a company has adopted standard articles, see

(a) for general powers of directors,

- *Table A, Regs 70, 71*
- *Model Articles, Art 3* (private companies)
- *Model Articles, Art 3* (public companies);

(b) for delegation of powers

- *Table A, Reg 72*;
- *Model Articles, Arts 5, 6* (private companies)
- *Model Articles, Arts 5, 6* (public companies);

(c) for discretion to make further rules

- *Model Articles, Art 16* (private companies)
- *Model Articles, Art 19* (public companies);

set out in APPENDIX 4 STANDARD ARTICLES OF ASSOCIATION.

Where the articles give the directors the authority to manage the business of the company, the shareholders cannot, by ordinary resolution, give directions to the board or overrule a decision without first altering the articles (*Automatic Self-Cleansing Filter Syndicate Co Ltd v Cunninghame* [1906] 2 Ch 34, 75 LJ Ch 437, CA, and *John Shaw & Sons (Salford) Ltd v Shaw* [1935] 2 KB 113, 104 LJKB 549, CA).

Assignment of office. A director of a company may be empowered by the articles to assign his office to another person. *Before 1 October 2009*, an assignment had to be approved by a special resolution of the company; otherwise the assignment had no effect despite anything to the contrary in the provision. [*CA 1985, s 308*]. *Section 308* of *CA 1985* has not been reproduced in *CA 2006*.

18.30 Power to make provision for employees on cessation or transfer of business

The powers of the directors of a company include (if they would not otherwise do so) power to make provision for the benefit of persons employed (or formerly employed)

- by the company, or

- any of its subsidiaries

in connection with the cessation or the transfer to any person of the whole or part of the undertaking of the company or that subsidiary. This power is exercisable notwithstanding

- the general duty imposed by *CA 2006, s 173* (duty to promote the success of the company, see **18.24**); and
- in the case of a company that is a charity, any restrictions on the directors' powers (or the company's capacity) flowing from the objects of the company.

The power may be exercised by complying with any requirement of the company's articles and, only then, by being sanctioned by

(a) resolution of the company; or

(b) a resolution of the directors if specifically authorised by the company's articles. But a resolution of the directors is not sufficient sanction for payments to or for the benefit of directors, former directors or shadow directors.

Any payment under these provisions must be made before the commencement of any winding up of the company and out of profits of the company that are available for dividend.

[*CA 2006, s 247; SI 2008 No 2860, Sch 2 para 40*].

Where a company has adopted standard articles, see

- *Model Articles, Art 51* (private companies)
- *Model Articles, Art 84* (public companies)

set out in **Appendix 4 Standard Articles of Association** which authorise the provision for the benefit of employees (and so enable the directors to pass a resolution to sanction the exercise of the power).

18.31 DIRECTORS' LIABILITIES

A director is not liable for the acts of co-directors and company officers solely by virtue of his position, although he will be if he participates in the wrong. Merely signing minutes approving a misapplication of property attracts liability (*Re Lands Allotment Co* [1894] 1 Ch 616, CA) as does unquestioningly signing a cheque for an unauthorised payment (*City Equitable Fire Insurance Co Ltd, Re* [1925] Ch 407, 94 LJ Ch 445, CA). A director is liable for, though actually ignorant of, another's wrong where he ought to have supervised the activity or ought to have known that it was wrong (*Selangor United Rubber Estates Ltd v Cradock (a bankrupt) (No 3)* [1968] 2 All ER 1073, [1968] 1 WLR 1555).

18.32 Liabilities and offences under Companies Acts provisions

There are a large number of offences for failure to comply with the requirements of the *Companies Acts*. These are dealt with in the appropriate part of the text. See also **29.2 Offences and Legal Proceedings** for directors' liabilities where a body corporate is guilty of certain offences.

18.33 Liabilities and offences under IA 1986

In addition to offences under the *Companies Acts*, *IA 1986, ss 206–217* contain a number of other offences for malpractice before and during winding up. These are considered in **18.34** to **18.40**.

18.34 *Fraud in anticipation of winding up*

Where company is

- ordered to be wound up by the court, or
- passes a resolution for voluntary winding up,

any past or present officer of a company (including a shadow director, see **18.1**(2)) is deemed to have committed an offence if, within the twelve months immediately preceding the commencement of winding up or any time thereafter, he has

(a) concealed or fraudulently removed company property valued at £500 or more;

(b) concealed any debt due to or from the company;

(c) concealed, destroyed, mutilated, falsified or made any false entry in any books or papers relating to the company;

(d) fraudulently parted with, altered or made an omission in any document relating to the company;

(e) pawned, pledged or disposed of property of the company obtained on credit and not paid for (unless done in the normal course of business); or

(f) been privy to the doing by others of any act within (*c*) or (*d*) above.

Where appropriate, it is a defence to prove there was no intent to defraud or conceal.

A person guilty of an offence under the above provisions is liable (i) on indictment, to imprisonment for a period of up to seven years or a fine (or both); and (ii) on summary conviction, to imprisonment for a period of up to six months or a fine up to the statutory maximum (or both). See **29.1 Offences and Legal Proceedings** for the statutory maximum.

[*IA 1986, s 206, Sch 10; SI 1986 No 1996*].

18.35 *Transactions in fraud of creditors*

Where company is

- ordered to be wound up by the court, or
- passes a resolution for voluntary winding up,

an officer of the company is deemed to have committed an offence if he has

- made (or caused to be made) any gift or transfer of, or charge on, or has caused or connived at the levying of any execution against, the company's property in the five years before winding up; or
- concealed or removed any part of the company's property since, or in the two months before, the date an unsatisfied judgment or order for payment of money has been obtained against the company.

It is a defence to prove that there was no intent to defraud the company's creditors.

A person guilty of an offence under the above provisions is liable (i) on indictment, to imprisonment for a period of up to two years or a fine (or both); and (ii) on summary conviction, to imprisonment for a period of up to six months or a fine up to the statutory maximum (or both). See **29.1 Offences and Legal Proceedings** for the statutory maximum.

[*IA 1986, s 207, Sch 10*].

18.36 *Misconduct in the course of winding up*

When a company is being wound up, an officer of the company commits an offence if he

(a) does not to the best of his knowledge give the liquidator details of all the company's property and any disposals of that property not in the ordinary course of business;

(b) does not deliver up to the liquidator any of the company's property or books in his custody;

(c) fails to inform the liquidator as soon as practicable if he knows that a false debt has been proved;

(d) prevents the production of any books or papers relating to the company's property or affairs;

(e) attempts to account for any of the company's property by fictitious losses or expenses (and he is deemed to have committed that offence if he so attempted at any meeting of the company's creditors within the 12 months immediately preceding the commencement of winding up);

(f) destroys, mutilates, alters or falsifies any of the company's books or papers or is privy to the making of a false entry therein;

(g) makes any material omission in any statement relating to the company's affairs (including any such omission in the period from the date the company is ordered to be wound up by the court or has passed a resolution for voluntary winding up until the date of winding up); or

(h) makes any false representation or commits any other fraud (whether before or after the date of winding up) to obtain the consent of any of the company's creditors to an agreement in connection with the company's affairs or the winding up.

The provisions also apply, except for (*f*), to past officers and shadow directors (see **18.1**(2)).

It is a defence under (*a*), (*b*), (*d*) and (*g*) to prove that there was no intent to defraud or conceal.

A person guilty of an offence under the above provisions is liable (i) on indictment, to imprisonment for a period of up to seven years or a fine (or both); and (ii) on summary conviction, to imprisonment for a period of up to six months or a fine up to the statutory maximum (or both). See **29.1 Offences and Legal Proceedings** for the statutory maximum.

[*IA 1986, ss 208–211, Sch 10*].

18.37 *Summary remedy against delinquent officers*

If in the course of winding up it appears that a past or present officer of the company has

- misapplied or retained, or become accountable for, any money or other property of the company, or
- been guilty of any misfeasance or breach of fiduciary or other duty in relation to the company,

the court may examine the conduct of the person concerned and compel him to

- repay, restore or account for the money or property with interest; or
- contribute such sum to the company's assets by way of compensation as the court thinks fit.

[*IA 1986, s 212; EA 2002, Sch 17 para 18*].

The above is a procedural remedy only and does not give any additional right of action so that it cannot be invoked where the director has been negligent only (*Re B Johnson & Co (Builders) Ltd* [1955] Ch 634, [1955] 2 All ER 775, CA). However, 'misfeasance' comprehends any breach of duty involving a misapplication or wrongful retention of the company's assets and does not necessarily involve moral turpitude (see *Selangor United Rubber Estates Ltd v Cradock* [1967] 2 All ER 1255, [1967] 1 WLR 1168).

18.38 *Fraudulent trading*

If in the course of the winding up of a company it appears that any business has been carried on 'with intent to defraud creditors' (whether of the company or any other person) or for any fraudulent purpose, the court may declare that any persons knowingly involved are liable to make such contributions to the company's assets as the court thinks proper. [*IA 1986, s 213*].

For a consideration of the phrase '*with intent to defraud creditors*' see *Re William C Leitch Bros Ltd* [1932] 2 Ch 71, 101 LJ Ch 380 and for '*fraudulent purposes*' see *Re Patrick & Lyon Ltd* [1933] Ch 786, 102 LJ Ch 300. It does not matter that only one creditor was defrauded (*Re Gerald Cooper Chemicals Ltd* [1978] Ch 262, [1978] 2 All ER 49).

18.39 *Wrongful trading*

If a company has gone into insolvent liquidation and before that time a director (or shadow director) knew, or ought to have concluded, that there was no reasonable prospect that the company would avoid such liquidation, the court may declare that that person is liable to make such contribution to the company's assets as it thinks proper. The court must not make such a declaration if satisfied that, once the director knew, etc, he took every step which a reasonably diligent person having both

- the general knowledge, skill and experience that may be reasonably expected of a person carrying out his functions, and
- the general knowledge, skill and experience that the director himself has

would have taken to minimise the potential loss to the company's creditors.

[*IA 1986, s 214*].

18.40 *Re-use of company name*

Where a company goes into insolvent liquidation, a director or shadow director of that company is prohibited from

- being a director of another company,
- in any way being involved in the promotion, formation or management of another company, or

- in any way being concerned in the carrying on of a business

using the same, or a similar, name to that used by the company at any time in the 12 months before it went into liquidation. Except with the leave of the court, the prohibition applies to any person who was a director or shadow director within that twelve-month period and continues to apply to him for the five years beginning with the date that the company went into liquidation.

A person guilty of an offence under the above provisions is liable (i) on indictment, to imprisonment for a period of up to two years or a fine (or both); and (ii) on summary conviction, to imprisonment for a period of up to six months or a fine up to the statutory maximum (or both). See **29.1 Offences and Legal Proceedings** for the statutory maximum.

[*IA 1986, s 216*].

If, in contravention of the above provisions, a person is involved in the 'management' of a company re-using the name, he is personally responsible for the debts of the company incurred when so involved. Additionally, any other person involved in the management of the company who acts, or is willing to act, on instructions given by a person whom he knows at the time to be in contravention of the provisions, is also personally responsible for debts incurred when so acting.

For these purposes, a person is involved in the '*management*' of a company if he is a director of the company or if he is concerned, whether directly or indirectly, or takes part, in the management of the company.

[*IA 1986, s 217*].

18.41 Criminal liability

Where any officer of a company (or person purporting to act as such) publishes or concurs in publishing a written statement which to his knowledge is or may be misleading, false or deceptive in a material particular, he is liable on conviction on indictment, to imprisonment for up to seven years if he acted with intent to deceive the members or creditors about the company's affairs. [*Theft Act 1968, s 19*].

Malpractice discovered during winding up. If it appears in the course of a winding up that any past or present officer of the company has been guilty of an offence in relation to the company for which he is criminally liable, then the liquidator must report the matter to the official receiver in a winding up by the court or the Secretary of State (Lord Advocate in Scotland) in a voluntary liquidation. [*IA 1986, ss 218, 219; IA 2000, s 10*].

18.42 Relief from liability by court

If a director is or will be liable for negligence, default, breach of duty or breach of trust, a court may relieve him wholly or partly from liability under *CA 2006, s 1157*. See **29.9 Offences and Legal Proceedings**.

18.43 Indemnification and provisions protecting directors from liability

Sections 232–237 of *CA 2006* allow (to a limited extent) a company to indemnify its directors and to provide insurance against certain liabilities. The general prohibition in *s 232* (provisions for exemption of liability and indemnification are void) is then qualified by *sections 233–237* which allow the company to purchase insurance for directors and for directors to be indemnified against liabilities to a "qualifying third party" and against liabilities incurred in connection with the company's activities as trustee of a "qualifying pension scheme" but not against liabilities to the company itself. There is no specific prohibition against providing indemnities to former directors or other officers of the company.

[*CA 2006, ss 232, 256*].

(1) **Provision of insurance**

A company is not prevented from purchasing and maintaining for a director of the company, or of an associated company, insurance against liabilities for negligence, default, breach of duty or breach of trust in relation to the company. [*CA 2006, s 233*].

A company is an associated company of another company if one of the companies is a subsidiary of the other or both are subsidiaries of the same body corporate [*CA 2006, s 256*].

(2) **Qualifying third party indemnity provision**

The provisions against providing an indemnity above do not apply to 'qualifying third party indemnity provision'. 'Third party indemnity provision' means provision for indemnity against liability incurred by the director to a person other than the company or an associated company (see above). Such provision is '*qualifying third party indemnity provision*' if the following requirements are met.

- The provision must not provide any indemnity against any liability of the director to pay
  - (i) a fine imposed in criminal proceedings; or
  - (ii) a sum payable to a regulatory authority by way of a penalty in respect of non-compliance with any requirement of a regulatory nature (however arising).
- The provision must not provide any indemnity against any liability incurred by the director
  - (i) in defending any criminal proceedings in which he is convicted;
  - (ii) in defending any civil proceedings brought by the company, or an associated company (see above), in which judgment is given against him; or
  - (iii) in connection with any application under *CA 2006, s 1157* (general power of court to grant relief in case of honest and reasonable conduct, see **29.9 Offences and Legal Proceedings**) or *CA 2006, s 661(3)(4)* own in which the court refuses to grant him relief.

References in (i)–(iii) above to a conviction, judgment or refusal of relief are to the final decision in the proceedings. This occurs, if not appealed against, at the end of the period for bringing an appeal or, if appealed against, at the time when the appeal (or any further appeal) is disposed of. An appeal is disposed of if it is determined and the period for bringing any further appeal has ended or if it is abandoned or otherwise ceases to have effect.

[*CA 2006, s 234; SI 2007 No 2194, Sch 1 para 12; SI 2007 No 3495, Art 10; SI 2008 No 674, Sch 3 paras 1, 5; SI 2008 No 2860, Art 6*].

(3) **Qualifying pension scheme indemnity provision**

The general prohibition referred to above in *CA 2006, s 232* does not apply to 'qualifying pension scheme indemnity provision'. 'Pension scheme indemnity provision' means provision indemnifying a director of a company that is a trustee of an occupational pension scheme (as defined in *FA 2004, s 150(5)*) against liability incurred in connection with the company's activities as trustee of the scheme. Such provision is '*qualifying pension scheme indemnity provision*' if the following requirements are met.

- The provision must not provide any indemnity against any liability of the director to pay

  (i) a fine imposed in criminal proceedings; or

  (ii) a sum payable to a regulatory authority by way of a penalty in respect of non-compliance with any requirement of a regulatory nature (however arising).

- The provision must not provide any indemnity against any liability incurred by the director in defending criminal proceedings in which he is convicted.

  The reference to a conviction is to the final decision in the proceedings. For this purpose a conviction becomes final, if not appealed against, at the end of the period for bringing an appeal or, if appealed against, at the time when the appeal (or any further appeal) is disposed of. An appeal is disposed of if it is determined and the period for bringing any further appeal has ended or if it is abandoned or otherwise ceases to have effect.

[*CA 2006, s 235*].

Standard articles. Where a company has adopted standard articles, see

- *Table A, Reg 118* (which provides for indemnification only)
- *Model Articles, Arts 52, 53* (private companies) (which provide for both indemnity and insurance)
- *Model Articles, Arts 85, 86* (public companies) (which provide for both indemnity and insurance)

set out in **Appendix 4 Standard Articles of Association**.

18.44 *Inspection of qualifying indemnity provision*

Where a qualifying indemnity provision (or a variation of the provision) is made for a director of a company the company or (in the case of an associated company), as the case may be, each of them must keep available for inspection a copy of the qualifying indemnity provision. If the provision is not in writing, a written memorandum setting out its terms must be kept

Inspection. The copy (or memorandum) must be kept available for inspection at the company's registered office or a place specified in the regulations made under *CA 2006, s 1136* (see **36.2 Records**) for details.

The copy (or memorandum) must be open to inspection by any member of the company without charge. Any member of the company is also entitled, on request and on payment of such fee as may be prescribed, to be provided with a copy of any such copy (or memorandum) within seven days after the request is received by the company.

Availability for inspection and copying. See **36.2 Records**.

Retention. The copy (or memorandum) must be retained by the company for at least one year from the date of termination or expiry of the provision and must be kept available for inspection during that time.

Notice to Registrar of Companies. The company must, within 14 days, give notice to the Registrar of Companies of the place at which the copy or memorandum is kept available for inspection and any change in that place (unless it has at all times been kept at the company's registered office).

Offences. If inspection is refused or default is made in complying with the above provisions, an offence is committed by every officer of the company who is in default. A person guilty of such an offence is liable, on summary conviction, to a fine not exceeding level 3 on the standard scale and, for continued contravention, a daily default fine not exceeding one-tenth of level 3 on the standard scale. See **29.1 Offences and Legal Proceedings** for the standard scale.

In the case of any such refusal or default, the court may by order compel an immediate inspection or, as the case may be, direct that the copy required be sent to the person requiring it.

[*CA 2006, ss 237, 238, 256*].

18.45 Ratification of acts of directors

In addition to any indemnity or insurance which the company may provide, or any statutory authorisation by the directors of conflicts of interest (see **18.24**(5)) or any common law approval by members of such conflicts of interest (whether by provision in the company's articles or in shareholder meeting), *s 239* of *CA 2006* also preserves the common law rule that breaches of directors' duties can be ratified by the company's members. Neither the director in breach nor any person connected with him (and for the extended definition of "connected" see **18.1**(3)) can, as a member, vote on the ratification. "Ratification" in this context means a release of a claim for breach of duty against a director. *CA 2006, s 239* provides that any decision of a company to ratify any acts or omissions by a director (including a former director or a shadow director) amounting to negligence, default, breach of duty or breach of trust in relation to the company must be made by resolution of the members of the company. Where the resolution is

- proposed as a written resolution, neither the director (if a member of the company) nor any member 'connected' with him is an eligible member; and
- proposed at a meeting, it is passed only if the necessary majority is obtained disregarding votes in favour of the resolution by the director (if a member of the company) and any member connected with him. But this does not prevent the director or any such member from attending, being counted towards the quorum and taking part in the proceedings at any meeting at which the decision is considered.

The above provisions do not affect

- the validity of a decision taken by unanimous consent of the members of the company;
- any power of the directors to agree not to sue, or to settle or release a claim made by them on behalf of the company; or
- any other enactment or rule of law imposing additional requirements for valid ratification or any rule of law as to acts that are incapable of being ratified by the company.

[*CA 2006, s 239*].

18.46 EMPLOYMENT, REMUNERATION, ETC

The remuneration, etc of directors is determined in accordance with the articles. Where a company has adopted standard articles,

(a) for remuneration, see

- *Table A, Reg 82*
- *Model Articles, Art 19* (private companies)
- *Model Articles, Art 23* (public companies);

(b) for pensions and gratuities, see

- *Table A, Reg 87*; and

(c) for expenses, see

- *Table A, Reg 83*
- *Model Articles, Art 20* (private companies)
- *Model Articles, Art 24* (public companies)

set out in APPENDIX 4 STANDARD ARTICLES OF ASSOCIATION.

18.47 Payments for loss of office

Subject to the exceptions in **18.50** below, any 'payment for loss of office'

- by a company to a director of the company or its holding company,
- by any person to a director of a company in connection with the transfer of the undertaking or property of the company or a subsidiary of the company, or
- by any person to a director of a company in connection with the transfer of shares in the company or in a subsidiary company resulting from a takeover bid

requires approval by the appropriate members. See **18.48** to **18.50** for full details. Where approval by the members is required under more than one set of provisions (see **18.48–18.50**), the requirements of each applicable provision must be met but a separate resolution for each provision is not required. [*CA 2006, s 225*].

Meaning of payment for loss of office. *Payment for loss of office*' means a payment made to a director or past director of a company

(a) by way of compensation for loss of office as director of the company;

(b) by way of compensation for loss, while director of the company or in connection with his ceasing to be a director of it, of

 (i) any other office or employment in connection with the management of the affairs of the company; or

 (ii) any office (as director or otherwise) or employment in connection with the management of the affairs of any subsidiary undertaking of the company;

(c) as consideration for, or in connection with, his retirement from his office as director of the company; or

(d) as consideration for, or in connection with, his retirement, while director of the company or in connection with his ceasing to be a director of it, from

(i) any other office or employment in connection with the management of the affairs of the company; or

(ii) any office (as director or otherwise) or employment in connection with the management of the affairs of any subsidiary undertaking of the company.

The references to 'compensation' and 'consideration' include benefits otherwise than in cash. [*CA 2006, s 215(1)(2)*].

18.48 *Approval by members of payment*

Subject to the exceptions in **18.50**, a company cannot make a payment for loss of office or payment for loss of office in connection with the transfer of the whole or part of the undertaking of the company to

(a) a director of the company unless the payment has been approved by a resolution of the members of the company; or

(b) a director of its holding company (or in the case of a transfer of undertaking to a director of a subsidiary) unless the payment has been approved by a resolution of the members of each of those companies.

No approval is required on the part of the members of a body corporate that is a wholly-owned subsidiary of another body corporate or is not a UK-registered company.

Director for these purposes includes shadow director but loss of office as a director does not apply in relation to loss of a person's status as a shadow director.

Memorandum of particulars. The resolution must not be passed unless a memorandum setting out particulars of the proposed payment (including its amount) is made available to the members of the company.

- Where members' approval is sought by way of a written resolution, the memorandum must be sent or submitted to every eligible member at or before the time at which the proposed resolution is sent or submitted to him. Any accidental failure to send or submit the memorandum to one or more members is disregarded for the purpose of determining whether the requirement has been met (subject to any provision of the company's articles).
- Where members' approval is sought by a resolution at a meeting, the memorandum must be made available for inspection by the members both

  (i) at the company's registered office for not less than 15 days ending with the date of the meeting; and

  (ii) at the meeting itself.

Payment. For the above purposes,

- payment to a person connected with a director (see **18.1**(3)) is treated as payment to the director;
- payment to any person at the direction of, or for the benefit of, a director or a person connected with him is treated as payment to the director; and
- payment by a person includes payment by another person at the direction of, or on behalf of, the person referred to.

And in relation to a transfer of undertaking "payment" also means

- payment made in pursuance of an arrangement

  (i) entered into as part of the agreement for the transfer in question, or within one year before or two years after that agreement, and

  (ii) to which the company whose undertaking or property is transferred, or any person to whom the transfer is made, is privy,

  is presumed, except in so far as the contrary is shown, to be a payment to which these provisions apply; and

- where a director is to cease to hold office or is to cease to be the holder of

  (i) any other office or employment in connection with the management of the affairs of the company, or

  (ii) any office (as director or otherwise) or employment in connection with the management of the affairs of any subsidiary undertaking of the company,

  payment for loss of office includes

  (a) the excess of the price to be paid to the director for any shares in the company held by him over the price which could at the time have been obtained by other holders of like shares; and

  (b) the money value of any valuable consideration given to the director by a person other than the company.

[*CA 2006, ss 215(3)(4), 216, 217, 218, 223, 224*].

Charitable companies. Where a company is a charity in England and Wales, any approval given by the members of the company for the above purposes is ineffective without the prior written permission of the Charity Commission. Such written permission is also required where the payment for loss of office would require approval but for the exemption on the part of the members of a body corporate that is a wholly-owned subsidiary of another body corporate. [*Charities Act 2011, ss 201, 202; CA 2006, s 226*].

18.49 *Payment in connection with share transfer resulting from takeover bids*

Subject to the exceptions in **18.50**, no payment for loss of office may be made by any person to a director of a company in connection with a transfer of shares in

- the company, or
- a subsidiary of the company,

resulting from a takeover bid unless the payment has been approved by a resolution of the relevant shareholders. The relevant shareholders are the holders of the shares to which the bid relates and any holders of shares of the same class as any of those shares.

Director for these purposes includes shadow director but loss of office as a director does not apply in relation to loss of a person's status as a shadow director.

No approval is required on the part of the members of a body corporate that is a wholly-owned subsidiary of another body corporate or is not a UK-registered company.

Memorandum of particulars. The resolution must not be passed unless a memorandum setting out particulars of the proposed payment (including its amount) is made available to the members of the company.

- Where members' approval is sought by way of a written resolution, the memorandum must be sent or submitted to every eligible member at or before the time at which the proposed resolution is sent or submitted to him. Any accidental failure to send or submit the memorandum to one or more members is disregarded for the purpose of determining whether the requirement has been met (subject to any provision of the company's articles).
- Where members' approval is sought by a resolution at a meeting, the memorandum must be made available for inspection by the members both
  - (i) at the company's registered office for not less than 15 days ending with the date of the meeting; and
  - (ii) at the meeting itself.

Voting on the resolution. Neither the person making the offer, nor any associate of his, is entitled to vote on the resolution, but

- where the resolution is proposed as a written resolution, they are entitled (if they would otherwise be so entitled) to be sent a copy of it; and
- at any meeting to consider the resolution they are entitled (if they would otherwise be so entitled) to be given notice of the meeting, to attend and speak and if present (in person or by proxy) to count towards the quorum.

Deemed approval where no quorum. If at a meeting to consider the resolution a quorum is not present, and after the meeting has been adjourned to a later date a quorum is again not present, the payment is deemed to have been approved.

Payment. For the above purposes,

- payment to a person connected with a director (see **18.1**(3)) is treated as payment to the director;
- payment to any person at the direction of, or for the benefit of, a director or a person connected with him is treated as payment to the director;
- payment by a person includes payment by another person at the direction of, or on behalf of, the person referred to;
- payment made in pursuance of an arrangement
  - (i) entered into as part of the agreement for the transfer in question, or within one year before or two years after that agreement, and
  - (ii) to which the company whose undertaking or property is transferred, or any person to whom the transfer is made, is privy,

  is presumed, except in so far as the contrary is shown, to be a payment to which these provisions apply; and
- where a director is to cease to hold office or is to cease to be the holder of
  - (i) any other office or employment in connection with the management of the affairs of the company, or
  - (ii) any office (as director or otherwise) or employment in connection with the management of the affairs of any subsidiary undertaking of the company,

  payment for loss of office includes

(a) the excess of the price to be paid to the director for any shares in the company held by him over the price which could at the time have been obtained by other holders of like shares; and

(b) the money value of any valuable consideration given to the director by a person other than the company.

[*CA 2006, ss 215(3), (4), 216, 219, 223, 224*].

18.50 *Exceptions*

Approval is not required under **18.47** to **18.49** for the following payments.

(1) *Payments in discharge of legal obligations, etc*

Approval is not required for a payment made in good faith:

(a) In discharge of an '*existing legal obligation*', ie

(i) in relation to a payment within **18.47**, an obligation of the company, or any body corporate associated with it, that was not entered into in connection with, or in consequence of, the event giving rise to the payment for loss of office; or

(ii) in relation to a payment within **18.49**, an obligation of the person making the payment that was not entered into for the purposes of, in connection with or in consequence of, the transfer in question.

In the case of a payment within both **18.47** or both **18.47** and **18.49**, then (i) applies and not (ii).

(b) By way of damages for breach of such an obligation.

(c) By way of settlement or compromise of any claim arising in connection with the termination of a person's office or employment.

(d) By way of pension in respect of past services.

A payment part of which falls within *(a)*–*(d)* above and part of which does not is treated as if the parts were separate payments.

For these purposes, bodies corporate are associated if one is a subsidiary of the other or both are subsidiaries of the same body corporate.

[*CA 2006, ss 220, 256*].

(2) *Small payments*

Approval is not required if

- the payment in question is made by the company or any of its subsidiaries; and
- the amount or value of the payment, together with the amount or value of any 'other relevant payments', does not exceed £200.

'*Other relevant payments*' are payments for loss of office in relation to which the following conditions are met.

- Where the payment in question is one to which **18.47** applies, the other payment was or is paid

(i) by the company making the payment in question or any of its subsidiaries;

(ii) to the director to whom that payment is made; and

(iii) in connection with the same event.

- Where the payment in question is one to which 18.49 applies, the other payment was (or is) paid in connection with the same transfer

  (i) to the director to whom the payment in question was made; and

  (ii) by the company making the payment or any of its subsidiaries.

[*CA 2006, s 221*].

Payment. For the above purposes,

- payment to a person connected with a director (see 18.1(3)) is treated as payment to the director;
- payment to any person at the direction of, or for the benefit of, a director or a person connected with him is treated as payment to the director; and
- payment by a person includes payment by another person at the direction of, or on behalf of, the person referred to.

[*CA 2006, s 215(3), (4)*].

18.51 *Civil consequences of payments made without approval*

The following consequences apply where payments are made in contravention of 18.47 to 18.49 above.

(a) If a payment is made in contravention of *CA 2006, s 217* (payment by a company to a director)

(i) it is held by the recipient on trust for the company making the payment; and

(ii) any director who authorised the payment is jointly and severally liable to indemnify the company that made the payment for any loss resulting from it.

(b) If a payment is made in contravention of *CA 2006, s 218* (payment in connection with the transfer of an undertaking) it is held by the recipient on trust for the company whose undertaking or property is or is proposed to be transferred.

(c) If a payment is made in contravention of *CA 2006, s 219* (payment in connection with share transfers)

(i) it is held by the recipient on trust for persons who have sold their shares as a result of the offer made; and

(ii) the expenses incurred by the recipient in distributing that sum amongst those persons is borne by him and not retained out of that sum.

(d) If a payment is made in contravention of both *ss 217* and *218*, then (*b*) above applies rather than (*a*) above.

(e) If a payment is made in contravention of both *ss 217* and *219*, then (*c*) above applies rather than (*a*) above, unless the court directs otherwise.

[*CA 2006, s 222*].

PAYMENTS FOR LOSS OF OFFICE- QUOTED COMPANIES

18.51A

A quoted company may not make a remuneration payment to a person who is, or is to be or has been, a director of the company unless—

(a) the payment is consistent with the approved directors' remuneration policy, or

(b) the payment is approved by resolution of the members of the company.

'Remuneration payment' means any form of payment or other benefit made to or otherwise conferred on a person as consideration for the person holding, agreeing to hold or having held, office as director of a company or holding, agreeing to hold or having held during a period when the person is or was such a director any other office or employment in connection with the management of the affairs of the company or any office (as director or otherwise) or employment in connection with the management of the affairs of any subsidiary undertaking of the company, other than a payment for loss of office.

For details of remuneration policy requirements see **19**.

Payment for loss of office

No payment for loss of office may be made by any person to a person who is, or has been, a director of a quoted company unless—

(a) the payment is consistent with the 'approved directors' remuneration policy', or

(b) the payment is approved by resolution of the members of the company.

The approved directors' remuneration policy is the most recent remuneration policy to have been approved by a resolution passed by the members of the company in general meeting.

A resolution approving a payment for loss of office must not be passed unless a memorandum setting out particulars of the proposed payment (including its amount) is made available for inspection by the members of the company

(a) at the company's registered office for not less than 15 days ending with the date of the meeting at which the resolution is to be considered, and

(b) at that meeting itself.

The memorandum must explain the ways in which the payment is inconsistent with the approved directors' remuneration policy (see above for its meaning) and .the company must ensure that the memorandum is made available on the company's website from the first day on which the memorandum is made available for inspection until its next accounts meeting. Failure to comply with this requirement does not affect the validity of the meeting at which a resolution is passed approving a payment to which the memorandum relates or the validity of anything done at the meeting .See **Appendix 1** for the meaning of 'accounts meeting'.

Nothing in the above either

- authorises a payment for loss of office in contravention of the articles of the company concerned. or
- applies in relation to a remuneration payment or (as the case may be) a payment for loss of office made to a person who is, or is to be or has been, a director of a quoted company before the earlier of

(a) the end of the first financial year of the company to begin on or after the day on which it becomes a quoted company, and

(b) the date from which the company's first directors' remuneration policy to be approved under *CA 2006, s 439A* takes effect.

The "company's website" is the website on which the company makes material available under *CA 2006, s 430.*

Civil consequences of contravention

(a) An obligation (however arising) to make a payment which would be in contravention of the above has no effect.

(b) If a payment is made in contravention of the above provisions

  (i) it is held by the recipient on trust for the company or other person making the payment, and

  (ii) in the case of a payment by a company, any director who authorised the payment is jointly and severally liable to indemnify the company that made the payment for any loss resulting from it.

(c) If a payment for loss of office is made in contravention of *CA 2006, s 226C* to a director of a quoted company in connection with the transfer of the whole or any part of the undertaking or property of the company or a subsidiary of the company

  (i) (b) above does not apply, and

  (ii) the payment is held by the recipient on trust for the company whose undertaking or property is or is proposed to be transferred.

(d) If in proceedings against a director for the enforcement of a liability under (b)(ii)

  (i) the director shows that he or she has acted honestly and reasonably, and

  (ii) the court considers that, having regard to all the circumstances of the case, the director ought to be relieved of liability,

  the court may relieve the director, either wholly or in part, from liability on such terms as the court thinks fit.

[*CA 2006, ss 226A–226F; Enterprise and Regulatory Reform Act 2013, s 80*]

18.52 DIRECTORS' SERVICE CONTRACTS

Definition of director's service contract. A director's '*service contract*', in relation to a company, means a contract under which

(a) a director of the company undertakes personally to perform services (as director or otherwise) for the company, or for a subsidiary of the company; or

(b) services (as director or otherwise) that a director of the company undertakes personally to perform are made available by a third party to the company, or to a subsidiary of the company.

[*CA 2006, s 227(1)*].

Provisions relating to directors' service contracts apply to the terms of a person's appointment as a director of a company. They are not restricted to contracts for the performance of services outside the scope of the ordinary duties of a director. [*CA 2006, s 227(2)*].

Execution formalities. It is essential that, prior to the execution of a director's service contract on behalf of the company, the correct formalities are followed. Where a company has adopted standard articles,

(i) for general powers of directors, see

- *Table A, Reg 70*
- *Model Articles, Art 3* (private companies)
- *Model Articles, Art 3* (public companies); and

(ii) for directors powers to enter into agreements regarding directors employment, see

- *Table A, Reg 84*

set out in **Appendix 4 Standard Articles of Association**.

However, it is not uncommon for companies to have specialised articles which require the consent of members. See also **18.53** below for members' approval of long-term service contracts.

The effect of *CA 2006, s 39*, see **16.1 Dealings With Third Parties**, is that there should be no question of entry into the contract being beyond the company's capacity. However, the articles of the company should be checked to ascertain whether or not the matter requires the approval of shareholders.

Where the board of directors does have sufficient authority, any quorum and voting requirements of the articles in respect of directors' meetings should be checked. See **42.39 Resolutions and Meetings**.

Listed companies: periods of notice. Listed companies must consider the provisions of the Combined Code. Notice or contract periods should be set at one year or less. If it is necessary to offer longer notice or contract periods to new directors recruited from outside, such periods should reduce to one year or less after the initial period. (Combined Code, para B.1.6).

Compensation, etc for termination. Where a resolution is passed removing a director from office under *CA 2006, s 168* (see **18.9**), such action is not to be taken as depriving the person removed of compensation or damages in respect of the termination of his appointment as director or of any appointment terminating with that as director. [*CA 2006, s 168(5)*]. Where a company has adopted standard articles, see also

- *Table A, Reg 84*

set out in **Appendix 4 Standard Articles of Association**.

18.53 Members' approval of long-term service contracts

CA 2006, ss 188 and *189* apply to agreements made on or after 1 October 2007. If however a resolution had been passed before that date approving a long term service agreement, the resolution is effective for the purposes of *sections 188* and *189* if it complies with those sections and *CA 1985, s 319* continues to apply to agreements made before that date.

[*SI 2007 No 2194, Sch 3 para 6*].

Where the 'guaranteed term' of a director's employment under a service contract

- with the company of which he is a director, or
- where he is the director of a holding company, within the group consisting of that company and its subsidiaries,

is, or may be, longer than two years, the company cannot agree to such provision unless it has been approved

- by resolution of the members of the company; and
- in the case of a director of a holding company, by resolution of the members of that company.

No approval is required under these provisions on the part of the members of a body corporate that is a wholly-owned subsidiary of another company or is not a UK-registered company.

Director for these purposes includes shadow director (see 18.1(2)).

Guaranteed term. The '*guaranteed term*' of a director's employment is

(a) the period (if any) during which the director's employment

  (i) is to continue, or may be continued otherwise than at the instance of the company (whether under the original agreement or under a new agreement entered into in pursuance of it); and

  (ii) cannot be terminated by the company by notice, or can be so terminated only in specified circumstances; or

(b) in the case of employment terminable by the company by notice, the period of notice required to be given,

or, in the case of employment having a period within (*a*) above and a period within (*b*) above, the aggregate of those periods.

If, more than six months before the end of the guaranteed term of a director's employment, the company enters into a further service contract (otherwise than in pursuance of a right conferred by or under the original contract on the other party to it), these provisions apply as if there were added to the guaranteed term of the new contract the unexpired period of the guaranteed term of the original contract. This applies whether the original contract was entered into before or on or after 1 October 2007. (This is intended to cover the situation where, for example, at the end of the first year of a two-year contract, a director enters into another two-year contract commencing on the expiry of the original two-year contract. In these circumstances the period for which he is to be employed would be three years.)

Memorandum of proposed contract. The resolution must not be passed unless a memorandum setting out the proposed contract is made available to the members of the company.

- Where members' approval is sought by way of a written resolution, the memorandum must be sent or submitted to every eligible member at or before the time at which the proposed resolution is sent or submitted to him. Any accidental failure to send or submit the memorandum to one or more members is disregarded for the purpose of determining whether the requirement has been met (subject to any provision of the company's articles).
- Where members' approval is sought by a resolution at a meeting, the memorandum must be made available for inspection by the members both

(i) at the company's registered office for not less than 15 days ending with the date of the meeting; and

(ii) at the meeting itself.

[*CA 2006, ss 188, 223, 224*].

Civil consequences of contravention. If a company agrees to provision of a service contract in contravention of the above provisions, the provision is void to the extent of the contravention. The contract is deemed to contain a term entitling the company to terminate it at any time by the giving of reasonable notice. [*CA 2006, s 189*].

Charitable companies. Where a company is a charity in England and Wales, any approval given by the members of the company for the above purposes is ineffective without the prior written permission of the Charity Commission. Such written permission is also required where the payment would require approval but for the exemption on the part of the members of a body corporate that is a wholly-owned subsidiary of another body corporate.

[*Charities Act 2011, ss 201, 202; CA 2006, s 226*].

18.54 Inspection of service contracts

A company must keep available for inspection

- a copy of every director's service contract (or a variation of that contract) with the company or with a subsidiary of the company; or
- if the contract is not in writing, a written memorandum setting out the terms of the contract.

All the copies and memoranda must be kept available for inspection at the company's registered office or at one other location. That location must be notified to the Registrar of Companies (see *Companies (Company Records) Regulations 2008 (SI 2008 No 3006)*.

The copy (or memorandum) must be open to inspection by any member of the company without charge. Any member of the company is also entitled, on request and on payment of such fee as may be prescribed, to be provided with a copy of any such copy (or memorandum) within seven days after the request is received by the company.

Availability for inspection and copying. See **36.2 Records**.

Retention. The copy (or memorandum) must be retained by the company for at least one year from the date of termination or expiry of the contract and must be kept available for inspection during that time.

Notice to Registrar of Companies. The company must, within 14 days, give notice to the Registrar of Companies of the place at which the copy or memorandum is kept available for inspection and any change in that place (unless it has at all times been kept at the company's registered office).

Offences. If inspection is refused or default is made in complying with the above provisions, an offence is committed by every officer of the company who is in default. A person guilty of such an offence is liable, on summary conviction, to a fine not exceeding level 3 on the standard scale and, for continued contravention, a daily default fine not exceeding one-tenth of level 3 on the standard scale. See **29.1 Offences and Legal Proceedings** for the standard scale.

In the case of any such refusal or default, the court may by order compel an immediate inspection or, as the case may be, direct that the copy required be sent to the person requiring it.

Shadow directors. A shadow director is treated as a director for the above.

[*CA 2006, ss 228–230*].

Transitional provisions. The above provisions apply to

- contracts within *CA 2006, s 227(1)* (see **18.52**) entered into on or after 1 October 2007;
- appointments within *CA 2006, s 227(2)* (see **18.52**) made on or after 1 October 2007; and
- contracts to which the earlier provisions in *CA 1985, s 318(1)* applied immediately before that date.

The provisions of *CA 1985, s 318* continue to apply in relation to

- any default before 1 October 2007 in complying with *CA 1985, s 318(1)* or *(5)*;
- any request for inspection under *CA 1985, s 318(7)* made before that date; and
- any duty to give notice under to the Registrar of Companies under *CA 1985, s 318(4)* arising before that date.

[*SI 2007 No 2194, Sch 3 para 13*].

18.55 INTERESTS IN CONTRACTS, TRANSACTIONS, ETC

Sections 177 and *182* of *CA 2006* provide that if a director is interested in a proposed transaction or arrangement with the company (*s 177*) or an existing transaction or arrangement (*s 182*) he must declare both the nature and extent of that interest to the other directors. Subject to making such a declaration and to anything to the contrary in *CA 2006* or the company's articles, a director may have an interest in such a transaction or arrangement.

The distinctions between *ss 177* and *182* are:

- *section 177* is expressly categorised as a statutory duty whereas *section 182* (which replaced *CA 1985, s 317*) is expressed as an obligation to make a declaration
- breach of *section 182* is a criminal offence
- *section 177* is expressly subject to *section 180* of *CA 2006* which provides that so long as a director has complied with *s 177* the transaction cannot be set aside" by virtue of any common law rule or equitable principle requiring the consent or approval of the members of the company". In other words if the board authorises a transaction it cannot be set aside simply because the members have not given their consent (subject to anything in law or the company's constitution which may otherwise require that consent).

18.56 Declaration of interest in existing transactions and arrangements

Subject to the exemptions below, where a director of a company is in any way, directly or indirectly, interested in a transaction or arrangement that has been entered into by the company, he must declare the nature and extent of the interest to the other directors in accordance with the following provisions. The provisions do not apply if, or to the extent that, the interest has been declared under the general duty to declare interest in *a proposed* transaction or arrangement.

The declaration must be made

- at a meeting of the directors, or
- by notice in writing or by general notice (see below)

and if a declaration proves to be, or becomes, inaccurate or incomplete, a further declaration must be made.

Any required declaration must be made as soon as is reasonably practicable, but failure to comply with this requirement does not affect the underlying duty to make the declaration.

Exemptions. A declaration is not required

- of an interest of which the director is not aware or where the director is not aware of the transaction or arrangement in question (and, for this purpose, a director is treated as being aware of matters of which he ought reasonably to be aware);
- if it cannot reasonably be regarded as likely to give rise to a conflict of interest;
- if, or to the extent that, the other directors are already aware of it (and for this purpose the other directors are treated as aware of anything of which they ought reasonably to be aware); or
- if, or to the extent that, it concerns terms of his service contract that have been or are to be considered
  - (i) by a meeting of the directors; or
  - (ii) by a committee of the directors appointed for the purpose under the 'company's constitution'.

[*CA 2006, s 182; SI 2007 No 3495, Sch 4 para 50*].

For the above purposes, a '*company's constitution*' includes

- the company's articles;
- any resolutions and agreements to which *CA 2006, ss 29, 30* apply (see **14.1** CONSTITUTION – MEMORANDUM AND ARTICLES);
- any resolution or other decision come to in accordance with the constitution; and
- any decision by the members of the company, or a class of members, that is treated by virtue of any enactment or rule of law as equivalent to a decision by the company (eg a decision taken by the informal unanimous consent of all the members).

[*CA 2006, s 257*].

Offence of failure to declare interest. A director who fails to comply with the above requirements commits an offence. If found guilty, he is liable (i) on conviction on indictment, to a fine; and (ii) on summary conviction, to a fine not exceeding the statutory maximum. See **29.1** OFFENCES AND LEGAL PROCEEDINGS for the statutory maximum.

[*CA 2006, s 183; SI 2007 No 3495, Sch 4 para 50*].

Declaration made by notice in writing. A declaration made by notice in writing must be sent to the other directors. It may be sent

- in hard copy form by hand or by post; or
- if the recipient has agreed to receive it in electronic form, in an agreed electronic form by an agreed electronic means.

Where a director declares an interest by notice in writing, the making of the declaration is deemed to form part of the proceedings at the next meeting of the directors after the notice is given. The provisions of *CA 2006, s 248* (minutes of meetings of directors, see **42.40** RESOLUTIONS AND MEETINGS) apply as if the declaration had been made at that meeting.

[*CA 2006, s 184; SI 2007 No 3495, Sch 4 para 50*].

General notice. General notice is notice given to the directors of a company to the effect that a director

- has an interest (as member, officer, employee or otherwise) in a specified body corporate or firm and is to be regarded as interested in any transaction or arrangement that may, after the date of the notice, be made with that body corporate or firm; or
- is connected with a specified person (other than a body corporate or firm) and is to be regarded as interested in any transaction or arrangement that may, after the date of the notice, be made with that person. See **18.1**(3) for persons connected with a director.

General notice must state the nature and extent of the director's interest in the body corporate or firm or (as the case may be) the nature of his connection with the person. It is then sufficient declaration of interest in relation to the matters to which it relates provided

- it is given at a meeting of the directors; or
- the director takes reasonable steps to secure that it is brought up and read at the next meeting of the directors after it is given.

[*CA 2006, s 185; SI 2007 No 3495, Sch 4 para 50*].

Company with sole director. A sole director need not comply with the above requirements (as there are no other directors to whom he can declare his interests). But where a company is required to have more than one director (eg because it is a public company) and has only a sole director, a declaration is required and

- the declaration must be recorded in writing;
- the making of the declaration is deemed to form part of the proceedings at the next meeting of the directors after the notice is given; and
- the provisions of *CA 2006, s 248* (minutes of meetings of directors, see **42.40** RESOLUTIONS AND MEETINGS) apply as if the declaration had been made at that meeting.

This requirement does not affect the operations of the provisions in **18.57** below.

[*CA 2006, s 186; SI 2007 No 3495, Sch 4 para 50*].

Shadow directors. The above provisions apply to a shadow director (see **18.1**(2)) as to a director, but with the following adaptations.

- The requirement for the declaration to be made at a meeting of directors does not apply.

- In the requirements for general notice, the requirement for general notice to be given at a meeting of directors or brought up and read at the next meeting of directors does not apply. Instead, general notice by a shadow director is not effective unless given by notice in writing in accordance with the provisions of *CA 2006, s 185* above.

[*CA 2006, s 187; SI 2007 No 3495, Sch 4 para 50*].

Non-compliance with the above provisions makes the contract voidable not void (*Hely-Hutchinson v Brayhead Ltd* [1968] 1 QB 549).

Listed companies. See **33.28(*h*)** PUBLIC AND LISTED COMPANIES for disclosure of significant contracts in the annual accounts.

Transitional provisions at 1 October 2008.

(1) *CA 1985, s 317* continues to apply in relation to transactions and arrangements entered into before 1 October 2008.

(2) For the purposes *CA 2006, s 182(1)* above (declaration of interest in existing transaction not previously declared under *CA 2006, s 177*), a declaration of interest made before 1 October 2008 under *CA 1985, s 317* is treated on and after that date as if made under *CA 2006, s 177.*

(3) For the purposes of *CA 2006, s 182(3)* above (previous declaration under that section proving or becoming inadequate), a declaration of interest made before 1 October 2008 under *CA 1985, s 317* is treated on and after that date as if made under *CA 2006, s 182.*

[*SI 2007 No 3495, Sch 4 para 50*].

18.57 Contracts with sole member who is also a director

Where

- a limited company having only one member enters into a contract with the sole member,
- the sole member is also a director (or shadow director, see **18.1(2)**) of the company, and
- the contract is not entered into in the ordinary course of the company's business

the company must, unless the contract is in writing, ensure that the terms of the contract are either set out in a written memorandum or recorded in the minutes of the first meeting of the directors of the company following the making of the contract.

If a company fails to comply with these provisions, an offence is committed by every officer of the company who is in default. A person guilty of such an offence is liable, on summary conviction, to a fine not exceeding level 5 on the standard scale. See **29.1** OFFENCES AND LEGAL PROCEEDINGS for the standard scale. But failure to comply the provisions in relation to a contract does not affect the validity of the contract.

Nothing in these provisions is to be read as excluding the operation of any other enactment or rule of law applying to contracts between a company and a director of the company.

[*CA 2006, s 231; SI 2007 No 2194, Sch 3 para 14*].

18.58 SUBSTANTIAL PROPERTY TRANSACTIONS: MEMBERS' APPROVAL

Sections 190–196 of *CA 2006* apply to arrangements or substantial property transactions entered into on or after 1 October 2007. A resolution passed before that date approving an arrangement or transaction is effective for the purposes of *CA 2006 ss 190–196* if it complies with the requirements of those provisions. *CA 1985, ss 320–322* continue to apply in relation to substantial property transactions entered into before that date.

[*SI 2007 No 2194, Sch 3 para 7*].

Subject to the exceptions below, a company must not enter into an arrangement under which

(a) a director of the company or of its holding company, or a person connected with such a director, acquires (or is to acquire) a 'substantial' non-cash asset from the company (directly or indirectly), or

(b) the company acquires (or is to acquire) a substantial non-cash asset (directly or indirectly) from such a director or a person so connected,

unless the arrangement has been approved by a resolution of the members of the company or is conditional on such approval being obtained. If the director or connected person is a director of the company's holding company or a person connected with such a director, the arrangement must also have been approved by a resolution of the members of the holding company or be conditional on such approval being obtained.

For these purposes, a shadow director is treated as a director.

'*Substantial*' non-cash asset. An asset is a substantial asset in relation to a company if its value, determined as at the time the arrangement is entered into, exceeds

- 10% of the company's 'asset value' and is more than £5,000; or
- £100,000.

A company's '*asset value*' at any time is the value of its net assets determined by reference to its most recent annual accounts or, if no annual accounts have been prepared, the amount of the company's called-up share capital. The most recent annual accounts are those in relation to which the time for sending them out to members is most recent.

An arrangement involving more than one non-cash asset or an arrangement that is one of a series involving non-cash assets is treated as if it involved a non-cash asset of a value equal to the aggregate value of all the non-cash assets involved in the arrangement or, as the case may be, the series.

Exceptions to the above are as follows.

- No approval is required on the part of the members of a body corporate that is a wholly-owned subsidiary of another body corporate or is not a UK-registered company.
- The provisions do not apply to a transaction so far as it relates to
  - (i) anything to which a director of a company is entitled under his service contract; or
  - (ii) to payment for loss of office as defined in **18.47**.
- No approval is required for a transaction between

(i) a company and a person in his character as a member of that company; or

(ii) a holding company and its wholly-owned subsidiary; or

(iii) two wholly-owned subsidiaries of the same holding company.

- Where a company is being wound up (unless the winding up is a members' voluntary winding up) or is in administration (within the meaning of *IA 1986, Sch B1* or *Insolvency (Northern Ireland) Order 1989 (SI 1989 No 2405)*), no approval is required

  (i) on the part of the members of a company to which these provisions apply; or

  (ii) for an arrangement entered into by a company to which these provisions apply.

- No approval is required for a transaction on a recognised investment exchange effected by a director, or a person connected with him, through the agency of a person who, in relation to the transaction, acts as an independent broker.

[*CA 2006, ss 190–194, 223*].

Listed companies. In addition to the requirements of *CA 2006*, listed companies must also comply with the requirements of the Listing Rules on related party transactions. See **33.33 Public and Listed Companies**.

Charitable companies. Where a company is a charity in England and Wales, any approval given by the members of the company for the above purposes is ineffective without the prior written permission of the Charity Commission. Such written permission is also required where the payment would require approval but for the exemption on the part of the members of a body corporate that is a wholly-owned subsidiary of another body corporate.

[*Charities Act 2011, ss 201, 202; CA 2006, s 226*].

18.59 Consequences of contravention

Where a company enters into an arrangement which has not been approved by members or is conditional on such approval, the company is not subject to any liability by reason of a failure to obtain the required approval. [*CA 2006, s 190(3)*]. But the arrangement, and any transaction entered into in pursuance of the arrangement (whether by the company or any other person), is voidable at the instance of the company, unless

- restitution of any money or other asset that was the subject-matter of the arrangement or transaction is no longer possible;
- the company has been indemnified by any other persons for the loss or damage suffered by it; or
- rights acquired in good faith, for value and without actual notice of the contravention by a person who is not a party to the arrangement or transaction would be affected by the avoidance.

Whether or not the arrangement or any such transaction has been avoided, each of the following persons is liable to account to the company for any gain that he has made (directly or indirectly) by the arrangement or transaction, and (jointly and severally with any other person so liable) to indemnify the company for any loss or damage resulting from the arrangement or transaction.

(a) Any director of the company or of its holding company with whom the company entered into the arrangement in contravention of the provisions in **18.58**.

(b) Any person with whom the company entered into the arrangement in contravention of those provisions who is connected with a director of the company or of its holding company.

(c) The director of the company or of its holding company with whom any such person is connected.

(d) Any other director of the company who authorised the arrangement or any transaction entered into in pursuance of such an arrangement.

For these purposes, director includes shadow director.

This is subject to two exceptions.

(1) In the case of an arrangement entered into by a company in contravention of *s 190* (which has not been approved by members) with a person connected with a director of the company or of its holding company, that director is not liable if he shows that he took all reasonable steps to secure the company's compliance with *s 190*.

(2) In any case,

- a person connected with a director of the company or of its holding company is not liable by virtue of (*b*) above (ie a connected person with whom the company entered into a transaction which was not approved), and
- a director is not liable by virtue of (*d*) above (ie a director who authorised the arrangement),

if he shows that, at the time the arrangement was entered into, he did not know the relevant circumstances constituting the contravention.

Nothing in the above provisions is to be read as excluding the operation of any other enactment or rule of law by virtue of which the arrangement or transaction may be called in question or any liability to the company may arise.

[*CA 2006, s 195*].

Effect of subsequent affirmation. Where a transaction or arrangement is entered into by a company in contravention of the substantial property transactions set out in **18.58** but, within a reasonable period, it is affirmed by resolution of the members of the company (and also, where appropriate, by resolution of the members of the holding company) the transaction or arrangement may no longer be avoided under *CA 2006, s 195* above. [*CA 2006, s 196*].

Charitable companies. Where a company is a charity in England and Wales, any affirmation given by the members of the company for the above purposes is ineffective without the prior written permission of the Charity Commission.

[*Charities Act 2011, s 201; CA 2006, s 226*].

18.60 LOANS, QUASI LOANS AND CREDIT TRANSACTIONS

The provisions in **18.61** to **18.66** below require, with certain exceptions, members' approval for loans, quasi-loans, credit transactions and related guarantees or security made by a company for directors and connected persons.

18.61 Members' approval of loans and quasi-loans

Loans and quasi-loans to directors and connected persons

Subject to the exceptions in **18.64**,

(a) any company may not

(i) make a loan to a director of the company or of its holding company, or

(ii) give a guarantee or provide security in connection with a loan made by any person to such a director, and

(b) a public company or a company associated with a public company may not

(i) make a 'quasi-loan' to a director or to a person connected with a director of the company or of its holding company, or

(ii) give a guarantee or provide security in connection with a quasi-loan made by any person to such a director or to a person connected with such a director,

unless the transaction has been approved by a resolution of the members of the company. If the director is a director of the company's holding company, the transaction must also have been approved by a resolution of the members of the holding company.

No approval is required under these provisions on the part of the members of a body corporate that is a wholly-owned subsidiary of another body corporate or is not a UK-registered company.

For these purposes, a shadow director is treated as a director.

'Quasi-loan'. A 'quasi-loan' is a transaction under which one party ('the creditor') agrees to pay, or pays otherwise than in pursuance of an agreement, a sum for another ('the borrower') or agrees to reimburse, or reimburses otherwise than in pursuance of an agreement, expenditure incurred by another party for another ('the borrower')

- on terms that the borrower (or a person on his behalf) will reimburse the creditor; or
- in circumstances giving rise to a liability on the borrower to reimburse the creditor.

Any reference to the person to whom a quasi-loan is made is a reference to the borrower. The liabilities of the borrower under a quasi-loan include the liabilities of any person who has agreed to reimburse the creditor on behalf of the borrower.

Memorandum of loan. The resolution must not be passed unless a memorandum setting out

- the nature of the transaction,
- the amount of the loan/quasi-loan and the purpose for which it is required, and
- the extent of the company's liability under any transaction connected with the loan/quasi-loan

is made available to members.

Where members' approval is sought by way of a written resolution, the memorandum must be sent or submitted to every eligible member at or before the time at which the proposed resolution is sent or submitted to him. Any accidental failure to send or submit the memorandum to one or more members is disregarded for the purpose of determining whether the requirement has been met (subject to any provisions in the company's articles).

Where members' approval is sought by a resolution at a meeting, the memorandum must be made available for inspection by the members both

(i) at the company's registered office for not less than 15 days ending with the date of the meeting; and

(ii) at the meeting itself.

[*CA 2006, ss 197–199, 200, 223, 224*].

Charitable companies. Where a company is a charity in England and Wales, any approval given by the members of the company for the above purposes is ineffective without the prior written permission of the Charity Commission. Such written permission is also required where the loan or guarantee would require approval but for the exemption on the part of the members of a body corporate that is a wholly-owned subsidiary of another body corporate.

[*Charities Act 2011, ss 201, 202; CA 2006, s 226*].

18.62 Members' approval of credit transactions

Subject to the exceptions in **18.64**, a public company or a company associated with a public company may not

(a) enter into a 'credit transaction' as creditor for the benefit of a director of the company or of its holding company, or a person connected with such a director, or

(b) give a guarantee or provide security in connection with a credit transaction entered into by any person for the benefit of such a director, or a person connected with such a director,

unless the transaction (that is, the credit transaction, the giving of the guarantee or the provision of security, as the case may be) has been approved by a resolution of the members of the company. If the director or connected person is a director of its holding company or a person connected with such a director, the transaction must also have been approved by a resolution of the members of the holding company.

No approval is required under these provisions on the part of the members of a body corporate that is a wholly-owned subsidiary of another body corporate or is not a UK-registered company.

For these purposes, a shadow director is treated as a director.

'Credit transaction'. A 'credit transaction' is a transaction under which one party ('the creditor')

- supplies any goods or sells any land under a hire-purchase agreement or a conditional sale agreement;
- leases or hires any land or goods in return for periodical payments; or
- otherwise disposes of land or supplies goods or services on the understanding that payment (whether in a lump sum or instalments or by way of periodical payments or otherwise) is to be deferred.

Any reference to the person for whose benefit a credit transaction is entered into is to the person to whom goods, land or services are supplied, sold, leased, hired or otherwise disposed of under the transaction.

Memorandum of credit transaction, etc. The resolution must not be passed unless a memorandum setting out

(1) the nature of the transaction,

(2) the value of the credit transaction and the purpose for which the land, goods or services sold or otherwise disposed of, leased, hired or supplied under the credit transaction are required, and

(3) the extent of the company's liability under any transaction connected with the credit transaction

is made available to the members of the company.

- Where members' approval is sought by way of a written resolution, the memorandum must be sent or submitted to every eligible member at or before the time at which the proposed resolution is sent or submitted to him. Any accidental failure to send or submit the memorandum to one or more members is disregarded for the purpose of determining whether the requirement has been met (subject to any provision of the company's articles).
- Where members' approval is sought by a resolution at a meeting, the memorandum must be made available for inspection by the members both
  - (i) at the company's registered office for not less than 15 days ending with the date of the meeting; and
  - (ii) at the meeting itself.

[*CA 2006, s 201, 202, 223, 224*].

Charitable companies. Where a company is a charity in England and Wales, any approval given by the members of the company for the above purposes is ineffective without the prior written permission of the Charity Commission. Such written permission is also required where the transaction would require approval but for the exemption on the part of the members of a body corporate that is a wholly-owned subsidiary of another body corporate.
[*Charities Act 2011, ss 201, 202; CA 2006, s 226*].

18.63 Members' approval of related arrangements

A company may not

(a) take part in an arrangement under which

- (i) another person enters into a transaction that, if it had been entered into by the company, would have required approval under **18.61** or **18.62**, and
- (ii) that person, in pursuance of the arrangement, obtains a benefit from the company or a body corporate associated with it, or

(b) arrange for the assignment to it, or assumption by it, of any rights, obligations or liabilities under a transaction that, if it had been entered into by the company, would have required such approval,

unless the arrangement in question has been approved by a resolution of the members of the company. If the director or connected person for whom the transaction is entered into is a director of its holding company or a person connected with such a director, the arrangement must also have been approved by a resolution of the members of the holding company.

No approval is required under these provisions on the part of the members of a body corporate that is a wholly-owned subsidiary of another body corporate or is not a UK-registered company.

For these purposes, a shadow director is treated as a director and bodies corporate are associated if one is a subsidiary of the other or both are subsidiaries of the same body corporate.

Memorandum of arrangement, etc. The resolution must not be passed unless a memorandum setting out

(1) the matters that would have to be disclosed if the company were seeking approval of the transaction to which the arrangement relates,

(2) the nature of the arrangement, and

(3) the extent of the company's liability under the arrangement or any transaction connected with it

is made available to the members of the company.

- Where members' approval is sought by way of a written resolution, the memorandum must be sent or submitted to every eligible member at or before the time at which the proposed resolution is sent or submitted to him. Any accidental failure to send or submit the memorandum to one or more members is disregarded for the purpose of determining whether the requirement has been met (subject to any provision of the company's articles).
- Where members' approval is sought by a resolution at a meeting, the memorandum must be made available for inspection by the members both

  (i) at the company's registered office for not less than 15 days ending with the date of the meeting; and

  (ii) at the meeting itself.

In determining for these purposes whether a transaction is one that would have required approval under **18.61** or **18.62** if it had been entered into by the company, the transaction is to be treated as having been entered into on the date of the arrangement.

[*CA 2006, ss 203, 223, 224, 256*].

Charitable companies. Where a company is a charity in England and Wales, any approval given by the members of the company for the above purposes is ineffective without the prior written permission of the Charity Commission. Such written permission is also required where the arrangement would require approval but for the exemption on the part of the members of a body corporate that is a wholly-owned subsidiary of another body corporate.

[*Charities Act 2011, ss 201, 202; CA 2006, s 226*].

18.64 Exceptions

Approval is not required for the following payments.

(1) **Expenditure on company business**

Approval is not required for anything done by a company when making a loan or quasi loan or entering into a credit transaction

- to provide a director of the company or of its holding company, or a person connected with any such director, with funds to meet expenditure incurred or to be incurred by him for the purposes of

  (i) the company; or

  (ii) enabling him properly to perform his duties as an officer of the company; or

- to enable any such person to avoid incurring such expenditure.

But this does not authorise a company to enter into a transaction if the aggregate of the value of the transaction in question and the value of any 'other relevant transactions or arrangements' (see below) exceeds £50,000.

[*CA 2006, s 204*].

(2) **Expenditure on defending proceedings, etc**

Approval is not required for anything done by a company when making a loan or quasi loan or entering into a credit transaction

(a) to provide a director of the company or of its holding company with funds to meet expenditure incurred or to be incurred by him

  (i) in defending any criminal or civil proceedings in connection with any alleged negligence, default, breach of duty or breach of trust by him in relation to the company or associated company; or

  (ii) in connection with an application for relief under CA 2006, s 1157 (general power of court to grant relief in case of honest and reasonable conduct, see **29.9 Offences and Legal Proceedings**) or *CA 2006, s 661(3)(4)*; or

(b) to enable any such director to avoid incurring such expenditure,

if it is done on the following terms.

The terms are

- that the loan is to be repaid, or (as the case may be) any liability of the company incurred under any transaction connected with the thing done is to be discharged, in the event of

  (i) the director being convicted in the proceedings;

  (ii) judgment being given against him in the proceedings; or

  (iii) the court refusing to grant him relief on the application; and

- that it is to be so repaid or discharged not later than

  (i) the date when the conviction becomes final;

  (ii) the date when the judgment becomes final; or

  (iii) the date when the refusal of relief becomes final.

  For these purposes, a conviction, judgment or refusal of relief becomes final, if not appealed against, at the end of the period for bringing an appeal and, if appealed against, when the appeal (or any further appeal) is disposed of. An appeal is disposed of if it is determined and the period for bringing any further appeal has ended or if it is abandoned or otherwise ceases to have effect.

[*CA 2006, s 205; SI 2007 No 2194, Sch 1 para 11; SI 2007 No 3495, Art 10; SI 2008 No 674, Sch 3 paras 1, 5; SI 2008 No 2860, Art 6*].

(3) **Expenditure in connection with regulatory action or investigation**

Approval is not required for anything done by a company when making a loan or quasi loan or entering into a credit transaction

(a) provide a director of the company or of its holding company with funds to meet expenditure incurred or to be incurred by him in defending himself

(i) in an investigation by a regulatory authority, or

(ii) against action proposed to be taken by a regulatory authority,

in connection with any alleged negligence, default, breach of duty or breach of trust by him in relation to the company or associated company; or

(b) enable any such director to avoid incurring such expenditure.

[*CA 2006, s 206*].

(4) **Minor and business transactions**

Approval is not required for a company to make a loan or quasi-loan, or to give a guarantee or provide security in connection with a loan or quasi-loan, if the aggregate of

- the value of the transaction, and
- the value of any 'other relevant transactions or arrangements' (see below),

does not exceed £10,000.

Approval is not required for a company to enter into a credit transaction, or to give a guarantee or provide security in connection with a credit transaction, if the aggregate of

- the value of the transaction (that is, of the credit transaction, guarantee or security), and
- the value of any 'other relevant transactions or arrangements' (see below),

does not exceed £15,000, or if

- the transaction is entered into by the company in the ordinary course of the company's business; and
- the value of the transaction is not greater, and the terms on which it is entered into are not more favourable, than it is reasonable to expect the company would have offered to, or in respect of, a person of the same financial standing but unconnected with the company.

[*CA 2006, s 207*].

(5) **Intra-group transactions**

Approval is not required for

- the making of a loan or quasi-loan to an associated body corporate; or

- the giving of a guarantee or provision of security in connection with a loan or quasi-loan made to an associated body corporate.

Approval is not required

- to enter into a credit transaction as creditor for the benefit of an associated body corporate; or
- to give a guarantee or provide security in connection with a credit transaction entered into by any person for the benefit of an associated body corporate.

For these purposes, bodies corporate are associated if one is a subsidiary of the other or both are subsidiaries of the same body corporate.

[*CA 2006, ss 208, 256*].

(6) **Money-lending companies**

Approval is not required for the making of a loan or quasi-loan, or the giving of a guarantee or provision of security in connection with a loan or quasi-loan, by a 'money-lending company' if

(a) the transaction (that is, the loan, quasi-loan, guarantee or security) is entered into by the company in the ordinary course of its business; and

(b) (subject to below) the value of the transaction is not greater, and its terms are not more favourable, than it is reasonable to expect the company would have offered to a person of the same financial standing but unconnected with the company.

A '*money-lending company*' means a company whose ordinary business includes the making of loans or quasi-loans, or the giving of guarantees or provision of security in connection with loans or quasi-loans.

The condition specified in (*b*) above does not of itself prevent a company from making a 'home loan' to

- a director of the company or of its holding company, or
- an employee of the company,

if loans of that description are ordinarily made by the company to its employees and the terms of the loan in question are no more favourable than those on which such loans are ordinarily made. A '*home loan*' means a loan

(i) for the purpose of facilitating the purchase, for use as the only or main residence of the person to whom the loan is made, of the whole or part of any dwelling-house together with any land to be occupied and enjoyed with it;

(ii) for the purpose of improving a dwelling-house or part of a dwelling-house so used or any land occupied and enjoyed with it; or

(iii) in substitution for any loan made by any person and falling within (i) or (ii) above.

[*CA 2006, s 209*].

'Other relevant transactions or arrangements'. For the purposes of the above exceptions, '*other relevant transactions or arrangements*' are those previously entered into, or entered into at the same time as the transaction or arrangement in question, in relation to which the following conditions are met.

- Where the transaction or arrangement in question is entered into
  - (i) for a director of the company entering into it, or
  - (ii) for a person connected with such a director,

  the conditions are that the transaction or arrangement was (or is) entered into for that director, or a person connected with him, by virtue of the relevant exception by that company or by any of its subsidiaries.
- Where the transaction or arrangement in question is entered into
  - (i) for a director of the holding company of the company entering into it, or
  - (ii) for a person connected with such a director,

  the conditions are that the transaction or arrangement was (or is) entered into for that director, or a person connected with him, by virtue of the relevant exception by the holding company or by any of its subsidiaries.

A transaction or arrangement entered into by a company that at the time it was entered into

- was a subsidiary of the company entering into the transaction or arrangement in question, or
- was a subsidiary of that company's holding company,

is not a relevant transaction or arrangement if, at the time the question arises whether the transaction or arrangement in question falls within a relevant exception, it is no longer such a subsidiary.

[*CA 2006, s 210*].

18.65 Value of transactions and arrangements

For the purposes of loans, quasi loans, credit transactions and related arrangements, the value of a transaction or arrangement is determined as follows. The value of any other relevant transaction or arrangement is taken to be the value so determined reduced by any amount by which the liabilities of the person for whom the transaction or arrangement was made have been reduced.

- The value of a loan is the amount of its principal.
- The value of a quasi-loan is the amount, or maximum amount, that the person to whom the quasi-loan is made is liable to reimburse the creditor.
- The value of a credit transaction is the price that it is reasonable to expect could be obtained for the goods, services or land to which the transaction relates if they had been supplied (at the time the transaction is entered into) in the ordinary course of business and on the same terms (apart from price) as they have been supplied, or are to be supplied, under the transaction in question.
- The value of a guarantee or security is the amount guaranteed or secured.
- The value of an arrangement to which **18.63** applies is the value of the transaction to which the arrangement relates.

- If the value of a transaction or arrangement is not capable of being expressed as a specific sum of money
  - (i) whether because the amount of any liability arising under the transaction or arrangement is unascertainable, or for any other reason; and
  - (ii) whether or not any liability under the transaction or arrangement has been reduced,

  its value is deemed to exceed £50,000.

[*CA 2006, s 211*].

18.66 Consequences of contravention

Where a company enters into a transaction or arrangement in contravention of the provisions set out in **18.61** to **18.63**, the transaction or arrangement is voidable at the instance of the company, unless

- restitution of any money or other asset that was the subject-matter of the transaction or arrangement is no longer possible;
- the company has been indemnified for any loss or damage resulting from the transaction or arrangement; or
- rights acquired in good faith, for value and without actual notice of the contravention by a person who is not a party to the transaction or arrangement would be affected by the avoidance.

Whether or not the transaction or arrangement has been avoided, each of the following persons is liable to account to the company for any gain that he has made (directly or indirectly) by the transaction or arrangement and (jointly and severally with any other person so liable) to indemnify the company for any loss or damage resulting from the transaction or arrangement.

(a) Any director of the company or of its holding company with whom the company entered into the transaction or arrangement in contravention of the provisions in **18.61** to **18.63**.

(b) Any person with whom the company entered into the transaction or arrangement in contravention of any of those provisions who is connected with a director of the company or of its holding company.

(c) The director of the company or of its holding company with whom any such person is connected.

(d) Any other director of the company who authorised the transaction or arrangement.

For these purposes, director includes shadow director.

This is subject to two exceptions.

(1) In the case of a transaction or arrangement entered into by a company in contravention of the provisions in **18.61** to **18.63** with a person connected with a director of the company or of its holding company, that director is not liable by virtue of (*c*) above if he shows that he took all reasonable steps to secure the company's compliance with the provisions concerned.

(2) In any case,

- a person connected with a director of the company or of its holding company is not liable by virtue of (*b*) above, and
- a director is not liable by virtue of (d) above,

if he shows that, at the time the transaction or arrangement was entered into, he did not know the relevant circumstances constituting the contravention.

Nothing in the above provisions is to be read as excluding the operation of any other enactment or rule of law by virtue of which the transaction or arrangement may be called in question or any liability to the company may arise.

[*CA 2006, ss 213, 223*].

Effect of subsequent affirmation. Where a transaction or arrangement is entered into by a company in contravention of the provisions in **18.61** to **18.63** but, within a reasonable period, it is affirmed by resolution of the members of the company (and also, where appropriate, by resolution of the members of the holding company) the transaction or arrangement may no longer be avoided under *CA 2006, s 213* above.

[*CA 2006, s 214*].

Charitable companies. Where a company is a charity in England and Wales, any affirmation given by the members of the company for the above purposes is ineffective without the prior written permission of the Charity Commission.

[*Charities Act 1993, s 66; CA 2006, s 226*].

18.67 DIRECTORS' RESIDENTIAL ADDRESSES: PROTECTION FROM DISCLOSURE

Because directors are obliged to give both a service address and a usual residential address to Companies House, details of a director's address is on public record at both the Registrar of Companies and in the register of directors which all companies must keep. Directors have the option of

- providing their residential addresses (as the service address) for the public record (which the vast majority do); or
- providing both a service address and a residential address, with the service address being on the public record and the residential address being on a separate secure register to which access is restricted.

The provisions in **18.68** to **18.72** protect, in the case of a company director who is an individual,

- information as to his usual residential address; and
- the information that his service address is his usual residential address.

From 1 October 2009 that information is referred to as '*protected information*'. Addresses already on the public register at that time continue to be available for public inspection unless the director had applied for a confidentiality order (see below).

Information does not cease to be protected information on the individual ceasing to be a director of the company. To that extent, references to a director include a former director.

[*CA 2006, s 240*].

18.67 Directors

Before 1 October 2009, under *CA 1985, ss 723B–723E* the only effective way that a director at risk of violence or intimidation could protect his address was to apply for a confidentiality order. A director with a confidentiality order provided a single service address in addition to his usual residential address. The service address was entered on the public record. The usual residential address was kept on a secure register to which access was restricted to specified enforcement authorities.

Companies incorporated before **1 October 2009**. In the case of a company incorporated before 1 October 2009, on or after that date the service address for a director of the company is deemed to be

(a) the service address for that director that appeared in the company's register of directors and secretaries and in the register of companies as having been notified under a confidentiality order; or

(b) if no such address appeared, the address that immediately before that date appeared as his usual residential address.

Where (*b*) applies, that address is not protected information for the purposes of the provisions in **18.68** to **18.72**.

[*SI 2008 No 2860, Sch 2 para 33*].

18.68 Restriction on use or disclosure of protected information

(1) *By the company*

A company must not use or disclose 'protected information' (see **18.67**) about any of its directors, except

- for communicating with the director concerned;
- in order to comply with any requirement of the *Companies Acts* as to particulars to be sent to the Registrar of Companies; or
- to comply with a court order (see **18.71**).

But this does not prohibit any use or disclosure of protected information with the consent of the director concerned.

[*CA 2006, s 241*].

(2) *By the Registrar of Companies*

(a) The Registrar of Companies must omit 'protected information' (see **18.67**) from the material on the register that is available for inspection where

(i) it is contained in a document delivered to him in which such information is required to be stated, and

(ii) in the case of a document having more than one part, it is contained in a part of the document in which such information is required to be stated.

(b) The Registrar is not obliged

(i) to check other documents or (as the case may be) other parts of the document to ensure the absence of protected information; or

(ii) to omit from the material that is available for public inspection anything registered before 1 October 2009;

but otherwise must not use or disclose protected information except as permitted under **18.69** or **18.71**.

[*CA 2006, s 242*].

Transitional provisions.

- The provisions in (*a*) above do not apply to
  - (i) material delivered to the Registrar of Companies before 1 October 2009; or
  - (ii) material delivered to him on or after that date but which related to notification of changes to directors particulars occurring before that date.
- In (*b*)(ii) above, the material available for public inspection registered before 1 October 2009 is treated as including changes to directors particulars notified on or after that date in respect of changes occurring before that date.

But these transitional provisions are subject to the continuation of protection afforded by a confidentiality order under *SI 2008 No 2860, Sch 2 para 36.*

[*SI 2008 No 2860, Sch 2 para 34*].

18.69 Permitted use or disclosure by the Registrar of Companies

The Registrar of Companies may use 'protected information' (see **18.67**) in the following ways.

(1) **Directors**

For communicating with the director in question.

[*CA 2006, s 243(1)*].

(2) **Disclosure to specified public authorities**

To disclose the protected information to the public authorities specified in regulations made under *CA 2006* where the conditions set out in those regulations are satisfied For full details of the specified public authorities and conditions see the *Companies (Disclosure of Address) Regulations 2009 (SI 2009 No 214).*

[*CA 2006, s 243(2); SI 2009 No 214, Reg 2, Sch 1, Sch 2 paras 1–4, 11*].

(3) **Disclosure to credit agencies**

To disclose the protected information to a '*credit reference agency*' (ie a person carrying on a business comprising the furnishing of information relevant to the financial standing of individuals, being information collected by the agency for that purpose) where the conditions set out in regulations referred to in **18.69**(2) are satisfied. The Registrar must however refrain from disclosing protected information to a credit reference agency if the information relates to a "section 243 beneficiary" or a "section 243 applicant". See **18.70** for the meaning of section 243 beneficiary.

[*CA 2006, s 243(2)(7); SI 2009 No 214, Regs 3, 4, Sch 2 paras 6–10*].

18.70 *Application not to disclose protected information to credit reference agencies*

An application can be made to the Registrar of Companies requiring the Registrar to refrain from disclosing protected information relating to a director. The application can be made:

18.70 Directors

(1) *By an individual who is, or proposes to become, a director* on the grounds that the individual making the application

(a) considers that there is a serious risk that he, or a person who lives with him, will be subjected to violence or intimidation as a result of the activities of at least one of

(i) the companies of which he is, or proposes to become, a director;

(ii) the companies of which he was a director;

(iii) the overseas companies of which he is or has been a director, secretary or permanent representative; or

(iv) the limited liability partnerships of which he is or has been a member; or

(b) is or has been employed by a 'relevant organisation'.

The application on form SRO4 (together with a fee of £100) must contain

- a statement of the grounds on which the application is made;
- the name and any former name of the applicant;
- the date of birth of the applicant;
- the usual residential address of the applicant;
- where the Registrar of Companies has allocated a unique identifier to the applicant, that unique identifier;
- the name and registered number of each company of which the applicant is, or proposes to become, a director;
- where the grounds of the application are those described in (*a*)(ii), (iii) or (iv), the name and registered number of the company, overseas company or limited liability partnership.

Where the grounds of the application are those described in (*a*) above, the application must be accompanied by evidence which supports the applicant's statement of the grounds of the application. See Companies House Guidance GR7 for examples of evidence which could be supplied. The Registrar of Companies may request additional information or evidence and may also refer to a 'relevant body' any question relating to an assessment of the nature and extent of any risk of violence or intimidation.

Where the grounds of the application are that the applicant is or has been employed by a "relevant organisation", the application must be accompanied by evidence which establishes that the applicant is or has been employed by a relevant organisation. The Registrar of Companies may request additional information or evidence and may also refer to a 'relevant body' any question relating to an assessment of whether the applicant is or has been employed by a relevant organisation.

The Registrar of Companies may accept any answer from a relevant body as sufficient evidence of the matter referred to it.

A '*relevant organisation*' means the Government Communications Headquarters, the Secret Intelligence Service, the Security Service or a police force.

A '*relevant body*' means any police force and any other person whom the Registrar of Companies considers may be able to assist in answering a question referred to that person by him.

The Registrar of Companies must determine the application and send the applicant notice of the decision to the applicant's usual residential address, as stated in his application, within five working days of the determination being made.

(2) *By a company on behalf of any of its directors who are individuals* on the grounds that the company making the application considers that there is a serious risk that the director on behalf of whom the application is made, or a person who lives with that director, will be subjected to violence or intimidation as a result of the activities of the company making the application.

The application on form SRO5 (together with a fee of £100) must contain

- a statement of the grounds on which the application is made;
- the name and registered number of the applicant;
- the name and any former name of each director on behalf of whom the application is made;
- the date of birth of each such director;
- the usual residential address of each such director;
- where the Registrar of Companies has allocated a unique identifier to any such director, that unique identifier; and
- the name and registered number of each company of which each such director is a director.

The application must be accompanied by evidence which supports the applicant's statement of the grounds of the application.

The Registrar of Companies may request additional information or evidence. He may also refer to a 'relevant body' (see (1) above) any question relating to an assessment of the nature and extent of any risk of violence or intimidation and may accept any answer as sufficient evidence of that risk.

The Registrar of Companies must then determine the application and send notice of the decision to the company's registered office and to each director concerned (to his usual residential address as stated in the application) within five working days of the determination being made.

(3) *By a subscriber to a memorandum of association on behalf of any of the proposed directors of a proposed company who are individuals* on the grounds that the subscriber considers that there is a serious risk that those directors on behalf of whom the application is made, or persons who live with them, will be subjected to violence or intimidation as a result of the proposed activities of that proposed company.

The application must contain

- a statement of the grounds on which the application is made;
- the name of the applicant;
- the address of the applicant;

- the name of the proposed company;
- the name and any former name of each of the proposed directors on behalf of whom the application is made;
- the date of birth of each such proposed director;
- the usual residential address of each such proposed director; and
- the name and registered number of each company of which each such proposed director is a director.

The application must be accompanied by evidence which supports the applicant's statement of the grounds of the application.

The Registrar of Companies may request additional information or evidence. He may also refer to a 'relevant body' (see (1) above) any question relating to an assessment of the nature and extent of any risk of violence or intimidation and may accept any answer as sufficient evidence of that risk.

The Registrar of Companies must then determine the application and send the applicant (to the address stated in the application) and each of the proposed directors concerned (to their usual residential address as stated in the application) notice of his determination within five working days of that determination being made.

The Registrar of Companies must not make available for public inspection any application under the above provisions or any documents provided in support of that application.

Appeals. Unsuccessful applicants may, with leave of the court, appeal to the High Court (in Scotland, the Court of Session) on the grounds that the decision is unlawful, irrational or unreasonable, or has been made on the basis of a procedural impropriety or otherwise contravenes the rules of natural justice. Any appeal must be brought within 21 days of the date of the Registrar's notice (or later with the court's permission). The court may dismiss the appeal or quash the decision. In the later case, it may refer the matter to the Registrar of Companies with a direction to reconsider it and make a determination in accordance with the findings of the court.

Duration of decision. Any decision will continue to have effect until either

- the beneficiary of the decision or his personal representative has notified the Registrar of Companies in writing that he wishes the decision to cease to apply; or
- the Registrar of Companies revokes the decision (see below),

whichever happens first.

Revocation. The Registrar of Companies may revoke a decision at any time if he is satisfied that the 'beneficiary' of that decision or any other person, in purported compliance with any of the above provisions, is found guilty of an offence under *CA 2006, s 1112* (general false statement offence). A '*beneficiary*' includes an individual in relation to whom confidentiality order was in force immediately before 1 October 2009.

If the Registrar of Companies proposes to make a revocation decision, he must send the beneficiary notice of his intention

- informing the beneficiary that he may, within 28 days of the notice, deliver representations in writing to the Registrar; and

- stating that if representations are not received by the Registrar within that period, the revocation decision will be made at the expiry of that period.

If the beneficiary delivers representations in the time allowed, the Registrar of Companies must consider them and, within five working days of making his decision, send notice of it to the beneficiary.

[*CA 2006, s 243(4)–(6); SI 2009 No 214, Regs 5–8, 14–16*].

A person who has had a decision made in their favour is known as a section 243 beneficiary. Any forms delivered to Companies House must indicate this (either paper forms or electronic filing). Failure to do so risks the protected information being disclosed to credit reference agencies.

18.71 Disclosure under a court order

The court may make an order for the disclosure of protected information by the company or by the Registrar of Companies if

- there is evidence that service of documents at a service address other than the director's usual residential address is not effective to bring them to the notice of the director; or
- it is necessary or expedient for the information to be provided in connection with the enforcement of an order or decree of the court,

and the court is otherwise satisfied that it is appropriate to make the order. An order for disclosure by the Registrar of Companies can only be made if the company does not have the director's usual residential address or has been dissolved.

A court order can be made on the application of a liquidator, creditor or member of the company, or any other person appearing to the court to have a sufficient interest.

[*CA 2006, s 244*].

18.72 Circumstances in which the Registrar of Companies can put a usual residential address on the public record

The Registrar of Companies can put a director's usual residential address on the public record if

- communications sent by the Registrar to the director and requiring a response within a specified period remain unanswered; or
- evidence comes to the Registrar's attention that service of documents at a service address provided in place of the director's usual residential address is not effective to bring them to the notice of the director.

Before doing so, the Registrar must give notice of the proposed course of action to the director and to every company of which the Registrar has been notified that the individual is a director. The notice must state the grounds for doing so and specify a period within which representations may be made. It must be sent to the director at his usual residential address, unless it appears to the Registrar that service at that address may be ineffective to bring it to the individual's notice, in which case it may be sent to any service address provided in place of that address.

On deciding that a director's usual residential address is to be put on the public record, the Registrar of Companies must proceed as if notice of a change of registered particulars had been given stating

- the usual residential address as the director's service address; and
- that the director's usual residential address is the same as his service address.

The Registrar must give notice of having done so to the director and to the company.

On receipt of the notice the company must

- enter the director's usual residential address in its register of directors as his service address; and
- state in its register of directors' residential addresses that his usual residential address is the same as his service address.

unless it has been notified by the director in question of a more recent address as his usual residential address, in which case the company must enter that address in its register of directors as the director's service address and give notice to the Registrar as on a change of registered particulars.

If a company fails to comply with these requirements, an offence is committed by the company and every officer of the company who is in default. A person guilty of such an offence is liable, on summary conviction, to a fine not exceeding level 5 on the standard scale and, for continued contravention, a daily default fine not exceeding of the greater of £5,000 or level 4 on the standard scale. See **29.1 Offences and Legal Proceedings** for the standard scale.

A director whose usual residential address has been put on the public record by the Registrar of Companies under the above provisions cannot register a service address other than his usual residential address for a period of five years from the date of the Registrar's decision.

[*CA 2006, ss 245, 246; SI 2008 No 2860, Sch 2 para 35; SI 2015 No 664, Sch 3*].

See generally Companies House Guidance GP7 "Restricting the disclosure of your address".

18.73 Application to make an address unavailable for inspection

Where the usual residential address of an individual was placed on the public register on or after 1 January 2003, the individual can, in certain circumstances, make an application to make that address unavailable for public inspection. See **39.19** for full details.

19 Directors' Remuneration Reports and Policies—Quoted Companies

19.1	**Duty to prepare and disclose**
19.2	**General provisions**
19.3	Interpretation
19.4	Consideration by the directors of matters relating to directors' remuneration
19.5	Statement of company's policy on directors' remuneration
19.6	**Contents of the company's policy on directors' remuneration**
19.7	Future policy table
19.8	Principles for remuneration package
19.9	Service contracts
19.10	How the policy will apply
19.11	Payments for loss of office
19.12	Statement of employment conditions
19.13	Statement of shareholder views
19.14	**Contents of the remuneration report**
19.15	Statement by chair of the remuneration committee
19.16	Single total figure remuneration table
19.17	Additional requirements for single total figure table
19.18	Pensions
19.19	Scheme interests including share options
19.20	Payments to past directors
19.21	Payments for loss of office
19.22	Statement of directors' shareholdings and share interests
19.23	Performance graph and table
19.24	Percentage change in remuneration of CEO
19.25	Relative importance of spend on pay
19.26	Statement of voting at general meeting
19.27	**Approval and signing of the report and policy**
19.28	**Defective reports**
19.29	Approval and signing of revised remuneration report
19.30	Effect of revision of report or policy
19.31	Publication of revised report
19.32	Laying of revised report
19.33	Delivery of revised report to the Registrar of Companies
19.34	**Liability for false or misleading statements in report**

Background. The provisions in this chapter apply, unless otherwise stated, to financial years beginning on or after 1 October 2013 in respect of the annual remuneration report (prepared that year on directors' remuneration in the preceding year) and the remuneration policy (which contains forward-looking disclosures and will be required to be submitted to shareholders for approval for the first time at a general meeting held during that year).Regulations which came into effect on 1 October 2013 are the *Large and Medium-sized Companies and Groups (Accounts and Reports) Amendment Regulations 2013*. They amend earlier regulations by substituting a new Schedule 8 into the 2008 *Large and Medium-sized Companies and Groups (Accounts and Reports) Regulations*. The amendments made by the 2013 regulations do not apply to a company in respect of a financial year ending before 30th September 2013 and the 2008 Regulations continue to apply in that case. This chapter only sets out the new provisions ie the 2008 Regulations as amended by the *2013 Regulations*.

[*SI 2013 No 1981, Reg 3* and *4*]

19.1 DUTY TO PREPARE AND DISCLOSE

The directors of a quoted company must prepare a directors' remuneration report for each financial year of the company. In the case of failure to do so, every person who

- was a director of the company immediately before the end of the period for filing accounts and reports for the financial year in question (see **2.11** Accounts: General), and
- failed to take all reasonable steps for securing compliance with that requirement,

commits an offence. A person guilty of such an offence is liable (i) on conviction on indictment, to a fine; and (ii) on summary conviction, to a fine not exceeding the statutory maximum. See **29.1** Offences and Penalties for the statutory maximum.

[*CA 2006, s 420*].

The report must contain:

- a statement by the chair of the company's remuneration committee (see 19.15),
- the company's policy on directors' remuneration (see below), and
- information on how the remuneration policy was implemented in the financial year being reported on.

Duty to disclose. It is the duty of any director of a company, and any person who is or has at any time in the preceding five years been a director of the company, to give notice to the company of such matters relating to himself as may be necessary for the purposes of a directors' remuneration report. A person who defaults in complying with this requirement commits an offence and is liable, on summary conviction, to a fine not exceeding level 3 on the standard scale. See **29.1** offences and penalties for the standard scale.

[*CA 2006, s 421(3), (4)*].

Remuneration policy to be set out in a separate part of the report.

Section 79 of the *Enterprise and Regulatory Reform Act 2013* (*E and RR Act 2013*) inserted *CA 2006, s 421(2A)*. It provides that any information about company policies with respect to the making of remuneration payments and payments for loss of office have to be set out in a separate part of the remuneration report. Regulations made under that provision are the *Large and Medium-sized Companies and Groups (Accounts and Reports) (Amendment) Regulations 2013*, Part 4 of which sets out the requirements for a directors' remuneration policy. Revisions to that policy must be approved and signed by the board of directors.

[E and RR Act 2013, s 79(1), 79(2)]

[*CA 2006, s 421(2A), 422A; E and RR Act 2013, s 79(1), 79(2); SI 2013 No 1981, Schedule, Part 4*]

19.2 GENERAL PROVISIONS

The regulations made under *s 421* of *CA 2006* referred to above regulate the contents and presentation of the directors' remuneration report and what is to be subject to audit. [See *CA 2006, s 421(1), (2)* and the *Large and Medium-sized Companies and Groups (Accounts and Reports) Regulations 2008 (SI 2008 No 410)* (the *2008 regulations*) as amended by the *Large and Medium-sized Companies and Groups (Accounts and Reports) (Amendment) Regulations 2013*].

Under *regulation 11* of the *2008 regulations*, the remuneration report which the directors of a quoted company are required to prepare must contain the information in **19.4** to **19.25** and must comply with any requirement in those paragraphs as to how information is to be set out in the report.

- The information in **19.4** relates to information about remuneration committees. The information in **19.5** relates to the remuneration policy
- The information in **19.16** to **19.21** relates to detailed information about directors' remuneration and is required to be reported upon by the auditors. It forms the 'auditable part' of a directors' remuneration report for the purposes of *CA 2006, s 497* (see **8.30 Audit**).

[*SI 2008 No 410, Reg 11; SI 2013 No 1981, Reg 2*]

Information required to be shown in the report for, or in respect of, a particular person must be shown in a manner that links the information to that person identified by name. Nothing prevents the directors setting out in the report any such additional information as they think fit and any item which may be shown in the report may be shown in greater detail than required by *Schedule 8* to the *2008 Regulations* (as amended).

Where the requirements of *Schedule 8* to the *2008 Regulations* refer to a "director" those requirements may be complied with in such manner as to distinguish between directors who perform executive functions and those who do not (see **18.1** for the meaning of executive director).

Any requirement of that Schedule to provide information in respect of a director may, in respect of those directors who do not perform executive functions be omitted or otherwise modified where that requirement does not apply to such a director. In such a case particulars of, and the reason for, the omission or modification must be given in the report.

Any requirement of that *Schedule* to provide information in respect of performance measures or targets does not require the disclosure of information which, in the opinion of the directors, is commercially sensitive in respect of the company. Where the directors rely on this provision particulars of, and the reason for the omission, must be given in the report and an indication given of when (if at all) the information is to be reported to members of the company.

Where any provision of that *Schedule* requires a sum or figure to be given in respect of any financial year preceding the relevant financial year, in the first remuneration report prepared in accordance with that *Schedule* that sum or figure may, where the sum or figure is not readily available from the reports and accounts of the company prepared for those years, be given as an estimate and a note of explanation provided in the report.

[*SI 2008 No 410, Sch 8, paras 2, 41; SI 2013 No 1981, Reg 2*].

19.3 Interpretation

(1) *Amounts to be shown*

(a) With respect to the amounts to be shown the amount in each case includes all relevant sums paid by or receivable from

(i) the company,

(ii) the company's subsidiary undertakings, and

(iii) any other person

except sums to be accounted for to the company or any of its subsidiary undertakings or any other undertaking of which any person has been a director while director of the company, by virtue of *CA 2006, s 219* (payment in connection with share transfer resulting from a takeover bid: requirement of members' approval, see **18.51 Directors**), to past or present members of the company or any of its subsidiaries or any class of those members.

Amounts paid to or receivable by a person include amounts paid to or receivable by a person connected with him or a body corporate controlled by him (but not so as to require an amount to be counted twice).

(b) The amounts to be shown for any financial year under **19.16** to **19.26** are the sums receivable in respect of that year (whenever paid) or, in the case of sums not receivable in respect of a period, the sums paid during that year. But where

(i) any sums are not shown in the directors' remuneration report for the relevant financial year on the ground that the person receiving them is liable to account for them as mentioned in (*a*) above, but the liability is thereafter wholly or partly released or is not enforced within a period of two years, or

(ii) any sums paid by way of expenses allowance are charged to UK income tax after the end of the relevant financial year (or, in the case of any such sums paid otherwise than to an individual, it does not become clear until the end of the relevant financial year that those sums would be charged to such tax were the person an individual),

those sums must, to the extent to which the liability is released or not enforced or they are charged as mentioned above (as the case may be), be shown in the first directors' remuneration report in which it is practicable to show them and must be distinguished from the amounts to be shown apart from this provision.

Where it is necessary to do so for the purposes of making any distinction required by paragraphs (a) or (b) in any amount to be shown, the directors may apportion any payments between the matters in respect of which these have been or are receivable in such manner as they think appropriate.

[*SI 2008 No 410, Sch 8, paras 46, 47, 48; SI 2013 No 1981, Reg 3*].

(2) *Compensation*

Compensation includes benefits otherwise than in cash; and in relation to such compensation references to its amount are to the estimated money value of the benefit.

[*SI 2008 No 410, Sch 8, para 44(3); SI 2013 No 1981, Reg 3*].

(3) *Compensation in respect of loss of office*

Compensation in respect of loss of office includes compensation received or receivable by a person for

(a) loss of office as director of the company;

(b) loss, while director of the company or on or in connection with his ceasing to be a director of it, of

- any other office in connection with the management of the company's affairs, or
- any office as director or otherwise in connection with the management of the affairs of any undertaking that, immediately before the loss, is a subsidiary undertaking of the company or an undertaking of which he is a director by virtue of the company's nomination (direct or indirect);

(c) compensation in consideration for, or in connection with, a person's retirement from office; and

(d) where such a retirement is occasioned by a breach of the person's contract with the company or with an undertaking that, immediately before the breach, is a subsidiary undertaking of the company or an undertaking of which he is a director by virtue of the company's nomination (direct or indirect)

- payments made by way of damages for the breach; or
- payments made by way of settlement or compromise of any claim in respect of the breach.

[*SI 2008 No 410, Sch 8, para 44(2); SI 2013 No 1981, Reg 3*].

(4) *'Pension scheme'*

Pension scheme means a retirement benefits scheme within the meaning given by *section 150(1)* of the *Finance Act 2004* which is one in which the company participates or one to which the company paid a contribution during the financial year

[*SI 2008 No 410, Sch 8, para 44(1)*].

(5) *'Performance measure'*

Performance measure is the measure by which performance is to be assessed but does not include any condition relating to service

[*SI 2008 No 410, Sch 8, para 44(1)*].

(6) 'Performance target'

Performance target is the specific level of performance to be attained in respect of that performance measure

[*SI 2008 No 410, Sch 8, para 44(1)*].

(7) *'Qualifying services'*

Qualifying services, in relation to any person, means his services as a director of the company, and his services at any time while he is a director of the company

- as a director of an undertaking that is a subsidiary undertaking of the company at that time;
- as a director of any other undertaking of which he is a director by virtue of the company's nomination (direct or indirect); or
- otherwise in connection with the management of the affairs of the company or any such subsidiary undertaking or any such other undertaking.

[*SI 2008 No 410, Sch 8, para 44(1)*].

(8) *'Remuneration committee'*

Remuneration committee means a committee of directors of the company having responsibility for considering matters related to the remuneration of directors

[*SI 2008 No 410, Sch 8, para 44(1)*].

(9) *'Retirement benefits'*

Retirement benefits means relevant benefits within the meaning given by *section 393B* of the *Income Tax (Earnings and Pensions) Act 2003* read as if *section 393B(2)* were omitted.

[*SI 2008 No 410, Sch 8, para 44(1)*].

(10) *'Scheme'*

Scheme (other than a pension scheme) means any agreement or arrangement under which money or other assets may become receivable by a person and which includes one or more qualifying conditions with respect to service or performance that cannot be fulfilled within a single financial year, and for this purpose the following must be disregarded, namely

- any payment the amount of which falls to be determined by reference to service or performance within a single financial year
- compensation in respect of loss of office, payments for breach of contract and other termination payments and
- retirement benefits

and 'scheme interest' means an interest under a scheme.

[*SI 2008 No 410, Sch 8, para 44(1)*].

(11) *Shares*

Shares means shares (whether allotted or not) in the company, or any undertaking which is a group undertaking in relation to the company, and includes a share warrant as defined by *CA 2006, s 779* (see **44.12** Securities: Certification and Transfers). Note the provisions of *SBEE 2015* (see **44.12**) which abolish share warrants to bearer.

[*SI 2008 No 410, Sch 8, para 44(1); SI 2013 No 1981, Reg 3*].

19.4 Consideration by the directors of matters relating to directors' remuneration

If a committee of the company's directors has considered matters relating to the directors' remuneration for the relevant financial year, the directors' remuneration report must

(a) name each director who was a member of the committee at any time when the committee was considering any such matter;

(b) state whether any person provided to the committee advice, or services, that materially assisted the committee in their consideration of any such matter and name any person that has done so;

(c) in the case of any person named under (b) above who is not a director of the company (other than a person who provided legal advice on compliance with any relevant legislation), state

  (i) the nature of any other services that that person has provided to the company during the relevant financial year;

  (ii) by whom that person was appointed, whether or not by the committee and how they were selected;

  (iii) whether and how the remuneration committee has satisfied itself that the advice received was objective and independent; and

  (iv) the amount of fee or other charge paid by the company to that person for the provision of advice or services referred to in (b) and the basis on which it was charged.

[*SI 2008 No 410, Sch 8, para 22; SI 2013 No 1981, Reg 3*].

19.5 Statement of company's policy on directors' remuneration

For financial years beginning on or after 1 October 2013 the directors' remuneration report must contain a statement of the company's policy on directors' remuneration for the following financial year and which must

- be set out in a separate part of the report
- set out all the matters for which the company needs approval from shareholders under *CA 2006, Part 4A* (see **18.51A** for *Part 4A* and **19.26** for shareholder approval)
- where any provision in the policy provides for the exercise by the directors of a discretion on any aspect of the policy, set out clearly the extent of that discretion in respect of any such variation, change or amendment.

The report must also contain a statement

- describing how the company intends to implement the approved policy in the financial year following the relevant financial year
- including, where applicable, the performance measures and relative weightings for each performance measure and performance targets determined for the performance measures and how awards will be calculated
- where this is not the first year of the approved remuneration policy, details of any significant changes in the way the policy will be implemented in the next financial year compared to how it was implemented in the relevant financial year and
- need not include information that is elsewhere in the report including any disclosed in the policy.

The policy may be omitted from the report for a financial year if the company does not intend, at the accounts meeting at which the report is to be laid, to move a resolution to approve the policy in accordance with *CA 2006, s 439A* (see **19.26**).

If the policy is omitted from the report in accordance with the above provision, the following information must be set out in the report

- the date of the last general meeting of the company at which a resolution was moved by the company in respect of that directors' remuneration policy and at which the policy was approved and
- where on the company's website or at some other place a copy of the policy may be inspected by members of the company.

[*SI 2008 No 410, Sch 8, para 1, 21, 24(1), (3), (4); SI 2013 No 1981, Reg 3*]

19.6 Contents of company's policy on directors' remuneration

In addition to the matters set out in **19.5** the policy must contain

- a future policy table (see **19.7**)
- the principles for a remuneration package when appointing directors (see **19.8**)
- details of service contracts (see **19.9**)

- illustrations of how the policy will apply (see **19.10**)
- policy on payments for loss of office (see **19.11**)
- statement of consideration of employment conditions elsewhere in the group (see **19.12**) and
- statement of consideration of shareholder views (see **19.13**)

[*SI 2008 No 410, Sch 8, Part 4; SI 2013 No 1981, Reg 3*]

19.7 Future policy table

A description of each of the components of the remuneration package for directors, comprised in the remuneration policy, must be set out in tabular form and where provisions apply to all directors generally, the table must also include any particular arrangements which are specific to any individual director. In respect of directors not performing an executive function, the information may be set out in a separate table which must also set out the approach of the company to the determination of the fee payable to such directors, any additional fees payable for any other duties to the company and such other items as are to be considered in the nature of remuneration.

In respect of each of the components in the table, the following information must be set out

(a) how that component supports the long and short-term strategic objectives of the company (or where the company is a parent company, the group)

(b) an explanation of how that component of the remuneration package operates

(c) the maximum that must be paid in respect of that component (which may be expressed in monetary terms or otherwise)

(d) where applicable a description of the framework used to assess performance including

- a description of any performance measures which apply and, where more than one performance measure applies, an indication of the weighting of the performance measures or group of performance measures
- details of any performance period and
- the amount (which may be expressed in monetary terms or otherwise) that may be paid in respect of the minimum level of performance under the policy and any further levels of performance set in accordance with the policy, and

(e) an explanation as to whether there are any provisions for the recovery of sums paid or the withholding of the payment of any sum.

Notes must accompany the table which set out in respect of any component

- which falls within (d) above, an explanation of why any performance measures were chosen and how any performance targets are set
- (other than salary, fees, benefits or pension) which is not subject to performance measures, an explanation of why there are no such measures
- if the component did not form part of the remuneration package in the last approved directors' remuneration policy, why that component is now contained in the remuneration package

- which did not form part of such a package, what changes have been made to it and why and
- an explanation of the difference (if any) in the company's policy on the remuneration of directors from the policy on the remuneration of employees generally (within the company or where the company is a parent company, the group).

References to 'component parts of the remuneration package' include, but are not limited to, all those items which are relevant for the purposes of the single total figure table.

[*SI 2001 No 410, Sch 8, para 25–28; SI No 2013 No 1981, Reg 3*]

19.8 Principles for remuneration package—appointing directors

The policy must contain a statement

- of the principles which would be applied by the company when agreeing the components of a remuneration package for the appointment of directors
- which sets out the various components which would be considered for inclusion in that package and the approach to be adopted by the company in respect of each component and
- which sets out the maximum level of variable remuneration which may be granted (which can be expressed in monetary terms or otherwise). This does not apply to compensation for the forfeit of any award under variable remuneration arrangements entered into with a previous employer (this is however subject to the above two requirements).

[*SI 2008 No 410, Sch 8, para 29; SI No 2013 No 1981, Reg 3*]

19.9 Service contracts

The directors' remuneration policy must contain a description of any obligation on the company which

- is contained in all directors' service contracts.
- is contained in the service contracts of any one or more existing directors or
- it is proposed would be contained in directors' service contracts to be entered into by the company.

Where the directors' service contracts are not kept available for inspection at the company's registered office, the remuneration report must give details of where the contracts are kept and, if the contracts are available on a website, a link to that website.

All of the above apply in like manner to the terms of letters of appointment of directors.

[*SI 2008 No 410, Sch 8, para 30–32; SI 2013 No 1981, Reg 3*].

19.10 Illustrations of how the policy will apply

Other than a director who is not performing an executive function, an indication of the level of remuneration that would be received by each director in accordance with the directors' remuneration policy in the first year to which the policy applies must be set out in the form of a bar chart which must contain

(a) separate bars representing minimum remuneration receivable ie including, but not limited to, salary, fees, benefits and pension

(b) separate bars representing the remuneration receivable if the director was, in respect of any performance measures or targets, performing in line with the company's expectations

(c) separate bars representing maximum remuneration receivable (not allowing for any share price appreciation)

(d) each bar divided into separate parts representing salary, fees, benefits, pension and any other item falling within (a), remuneration where performance measures or targets relate to one financial year and remuneration where performance measures or targets relate to more than one financial year

(e) each bar showing the percentage of the total comprised by each of the parts and the total value of remuneration expected for each bar

A narrative description of the basis of calculation and assumptions used to compile the bar chart must be set out to enable an understanding of the charts presented but it is not necessary for any matter to be included in the narrative description which has been set out in the future policy table (see **19.5A(1)**).

[*SI 2008 No 410, Sch 8, para 33–35; SI 2013 No 1981, Reg 3*].

19.11 Policy on payment for loss of office

The directors' remuneration policy must set out

(a) the company's policy on the setting of notice periods under directors' service contracts

(b) the principles on which the determination of payments for loss of office will be calculated including

  (i) an indication of how each component of the payment will be calculated

  (ii) whether, and if so how, the circumstances of the director's loss of office and performance during the period of qualifying services are relevant to any exercise of discretion and

  (iii) any contractual provision agreed prior to 27 June 2012 that could impact on the quantum of that payment.

[*SI 2008 No 410, Sch 8, para 36–37; SI 2013 No 1981, Reg 3*].

19.12 Statement of consideration of employment conditions elsewhere in the company

The directors' remuneration policy must

(a) contain a statement of how pay and employment conditions of employees (other than directors) of the company and, where the company is a parent company, of the group or other undertakings within the same group as the company, were taken into account when setting the policy for directors' remuneration

(b) set out whether, and if so how, the company consulted with employees when drawing up the directors' remuneration policy set out in this part of the report and whether any remuneration comparisons measurements were used and if so, what they were, and how that information was taken into account.

[*SI 2008 No 410, Sch 8, para 38–39; SI 2013 No 1981, Reg 3*].

19.13 Statement of consideration of shareholder views

The directors' remuneration policy must contain a statement of whether, and if so how, any views in respect of directors' remuneration expressed to the company by shareholders (whether at a general meeting or otherwise) have been taken into account in the formulation of the directors' remuneration policy.
[*SI 2008 No 410, Sch 8, para 40; SI 2013 No 1981, Reg 3*].

19.14 Contents of remuneration report

In addition to the provisions of the remuneration policy (above) which forms a separate part of the remuneration report, the report must also contain

- a statement by the chair of the remuneration committee (19.15)
- single total figure of remuneration for each director and some additional information (19.16 and 19.17)
- pensions (19.18)
- scheme interests (19.19)
- payments to past directors (19.20)
- payments for loss of office (19.21)
- share holdings and share interests (19.22)
- performance graph and table (19.23)
- percentage change in remuneration of director undertaking the role of CEO (19.24)
- relative importance of spend on pay (19.25)
- statement of voting at general meeting (19.26)

19.15 Statement by chair of the remuneration committee

The directors' remuneration report must contain a statement by the chair of the remuneration committee (or where there is no such person by a director nominated by the directors to make the statement) summarising for the relevant financial year the major decisions on directors' remuneration, any substantial changes relating to directors' remuneration made during the year and the context in which those changes occurred and decisions have been taken.

[*SI 2008 No 410, Sch 8, para 3; SI 2013 No 1981, Reg 3*].

19.16 Single total figure of remuneration for each director

The directors' remuneration report must for the relevant financial year show the information in respect of each person who has served as a director of the company at any time during that year set out in a table(below) ('the single total figure table'). The directors may choose to display the table using an alternative orientation, in which case references to columns in *Schedule 8* to the *2008 Regulations* are to be read as references to rows and where it is necessary to assist in the understanding of the table by the creation of sub-totals the columns headed 'a'–'e' may be set out in an order other than the one set out below.

Single figure total table						
	a	b	c	d	e	Total
Director 1						
Director 2						

In the single figure total table the sums required to be set out in the columns are

(a) In the column headed 'a' the total amount of salary and fees .The method to be used to calculate the sums required in this column is the cash paid to or receivable by the person in respect of the relevant financial year.

(b) In the column headed 'b' all taxable benefits. The method to be used to calculate the sums required in this column is the gross value before payment of tax. Taxable benefits are defined as including

(i) sums paid by way of expenses allowances that are chargeable to United kingdom income tax (or would be if the person were an individual or would be if the person were resident in the United Kingdom for tax purposes) and paid to or receivable by the person in respect of qualifying services and

(ii) any benefits received by the person, other than salary, (whether or not in cash) that are emoluments of the person and are received by the person in respect of qualifying services. A payment or other benefit received in advance of a director commencing qualifying services, but in anticipation of performing qualifying services, is to be treated as if received on the first day of performance of the qualifying services.

(c) In the column headed 'c' money or other assets received or receivable for the relevant financial year as a result of the achievement of performance measures and targets relating to a period ending in that financial year other than

- those which result from awards made in a previous financial year and where final vesting is determined as a result of the achievement of performance measures or targets relating to a period ending in the relevant financial year or

- those receivable subject to the achievement of performance measures or targets in a future financial year.

Where the performance measures or targets are substantially (but not fully) completed by the end of the relevant financial year, the sum given in the 'c' column may include sums which relate to the following financial year but where such sums are included, those sums must not be included in the corresponding column of the single total figure table prepared for that following year and a note must explain the basis of the calculation.

The method to be used to calculate the sums required in this column is the total cash equivalent including any amount deferred, other than where the deferral is subject to the achievement of further performance measures or targets in a future financial year.

(d) In the column headed 'd' money or other assets received or receivable for periods of more than one financial year where final vesting

- is determined as a result of the achievement of performance measures or targets relating to a period ending in the relevant financial year or

- is not subject to the achievement of performance measures or targets in a future financial year

The method to be used to calculate the sums required in this column is

- the cash value of any monetary award
- the value of any shares or share options awarded, calculated by multiplying the original number of shares granted by the proportion that vest (or an estimate) and multiplying that total arrived at by the market price of shares at the date on which the shares vest. Where the market price of shares at the date on which the shares vest is not ascertainable by the date on which the remuneration report is approved by the directors, an estimate of the market price of the shares shall be calculated on the basis of an average market value over the last quarter of the relevant financial year and where the award was an award of shares or share options, the cash amount the individual was or will be required to pay to acquire the shares must be deducted from the total
- the value of any additional cash or shares receivable in respect of dividends accrued (actually or notionally)

(e) In the column headed 'e' all pension related benefits including payments (whether in cash or otherwise) in lieu of retirement benefits and all benefits in year from participating in pension schemes. The method to be used to calculate the sums required in this column is, for payments in lieu of retirement benefits, the cash benefit and for all benefits in year from participating in pension schemes, what the aggregate pension input amount would be across all the pension schemes of the company or group in which the director accrues benefit, calculated using the method set out in *Finance Act 2004, s 229*. Where there has not been a company contribution to the pension scheme in respect of the director (but if such a contribution had been made it would have been measured for pension input purposes under *Finance Act 2004, s 223(1)(b)*), when calculating the pension input amount for the purposes of this provision, it should be calculated as follows. As if the cash value of any contribution notionally allocated to the scheme in respect of the person (by or on behalf of the company) including any adjustment made for any notional investment return achieved during the relevant financial year were a contribution paid by the employer in respect of the individual for the purposes of *Finance Act 2004, s 223(1)(b)*.

(f) In the column headed 'total' the total amount of the sums set out in the previous columns.

In addition columns must be included to set out any other items in the nature of remuneration which are not set out in columns 'a' to 'e' (other than payments to past directors) and columns may be included if there are any sub-totals or other items which the directors consider necessary in order to assist in the understanding of the table.

'Emoluments' of a person includes salary, fees and bonuses, sums paid by way of expenses allowance (so far as they are chargeable to UK income tax or would be if the person were an individual) but does not include the following.

- The value of any share options granted to him.
- The amount of any gains made on the exercise of any such options (ie the difference between the market price of the shares on the day on which the option was exercised and the price actually paid for the shares).

- Any 'company contributions' paid, or treated as paid, in respect of him under any pension scheme or any benefits to which he is entitled under any such scheme. 'Company contributions' means any payments (including insurance premiums) made, or treated as made, to the scheme in respect of the person by anyone other than the person.
- Any money or other assets paid to or received or receivable by him under any long-term incentive scheme.

Any emoluments paid or receivable or share options granted in respect of a person's accepting office as a director are treated as emoluments paid or receivable or share options granted in respect of his services as a director.

[*SI 2008 No 410, Sch 8, paras 4, 5, 6, 7, 8(1), 10, 11, 44, 45; SI 2013 No 1981, Reg 3*]

19.17 Additional requirements for single total figure table

Withholding and recovery. Where any money or assets are reported in the single figure table prepared in respect of any previous financial year and are the subject of a recovery of sums paid or the withholding of any sum for any reason in the relevant financial year then

- the recovery or withholding so attributable must be shown in a separate column in the table as a negative value and deducted from the column headed 'total' and
- an explanation for the recovery or withholding and the basis of the calculation must be given in a note to the table.

Negative values. Where the calculations in the table (other than in respect of a recovery or withholding) result in a negative value, the result must be expressed as zero in the relevant column in the table.

Comparisons. In order to permit a comparison, each column in the single figure table must contain two sums as follows

- the sum set out in the corresponding column in the report prepared in respect of the financial year preceding the relevant year and
- the sum for the relevant financial year.

Estimates. Where a sum is given in the column which relates to the preceding financial year and, was given as an estimated sum, then in the relevant financial year

- it must be given as an actual sum
- the amount representing the difference between the estimate and the actual must not be included in the column relating to the relevant financial year and
- details of the calculation of the revised sum must be given in a note to the table.

Value of taxable benefits. In respect of the taxable benefits sum (see **19.16**(b)) after the table a summary must be set out identifying the types of benefits the value of which is included in the sum set out in column 'b' and the value (where significant)

Money or other assets for achievement of performance measures (see 19.16(c) and (d)). For every component, the value of which is included in columns 'c' and 'd' of the table, after the table the following relevant details must be set out

- details of any performance measures and the relative weighting of each

- within each performance measure, the performance targets set out at the beginning of the performance period and the corresponding value of the award achievable
- for each performance measure, details of actual performance relative to the targets set and measured over the relevant reporting period, and the resulting level of award and
- where any discretion has been exercised in respect of the award, particulars must be given of how the discretion was exercised and how the resulting level of award was determined.

For every component, the value of which is included in columns 'c' of the table the remuneration report must state if any amount was deferred, the percentage deferred, whether it was deferred in cash or shares, if relevant, and whether the deferral was subject to any conditions other than performance measures.

Additional columns. Where additional columns are included a note to the table must set out the basis on which the sums in the column were calculated and such other details as are necessary for an understanding of the sums set out in the column, including any performance measures relating to that component of remuneration or if there are none, an explanation of why not.

[*SI 2008 No 410, Sch 8, para 8(2), 9, 10; SI 2013 No 1981, Reg 3*]

19.18 Pensions

The directors' remuneration report must, for each person who has served as a director of the company at any time during the relevant financial year and who has a prospective entitlement to defined benefits or cash balance benefits (or to benefits under a hybrid arrangement which includes such benefits) in respect of qualifying services, contain the following information in respect of pensions.

(a) details of those rights as at the end of that year, including the person's normal retirement date

(b) a description of any additional benefit that will become receivable by a director in the event that that director retires early and

(c) where a person has rights under more than one type of pension benefit identified in column 'e' of the single total figure table (see **19.16**), separate details relating to each type of pension benefit.

'Defined benefits', 'cash balance benefits' and 'hybrid arrangement' have the same meaning as in *Finance Act 2004, s 152.*

'Normal retirement date' means an age specified in the pension scheme rules (or otherwise determined) as the earliest age at which, while the individual continues to accrue benefits under the pension scheme, entitlement to a benefit arises without consent (whether of an employer, the trustees or managers of the scheme or otherwise) and without any actuarial reduction but disregarding any special provision as to early repayment on grounds of ill health, redundancy or dismissal.

[*SI 2008 No 410, Sch 8, para 13; SI 2013 No 1981, Reg 3*].

19.19 Scheme interests including share options

The directors' remuneration report must, subject to below, contain a table setting out the following information in respect of each person who has served as a director of the company at any time during the relevant financial year.

(a) Details of the 'scheme interests' awarded to the person during the relevant financial year and

(b) For each scheme interest

(i) a description of the type of interest awarded

(ii) a description of the basis on which the award is made

(iii) the face value of the award

(iv) the percentage of scheme interests that would be receivable if the minimum performance was achieved

(v) for a scheme interest that is a share option, an explanation of any difference between the exercise price per share and the price specified below

(vi) the end of the period over which the performance measures and targets for that interest have to be achieved (or if there are different periods for different measures and targets, the end of whichever of those periods ends last) and

(vii) a summary of the performance measures and targets if not set out elsewhere in the report.

Where the report sets out the face value of an award in respect of a scheme interest relating to shares or share options, the report must specify

(a) whether the face value has been calculated using the share price at date of grant or the average share price

(b) where the share price at date of grant is used, the amount of that share price and the date of grant

(c) where the average share price is used, what that price was and the period used for calculating the average.

In respect of a scheme interest relating to shares or share options 'face value' means the maximum number of shares that would vest if all performance measures and targets are met multiplied by either the share price at date of grant or the average share price used to determine the number of shares awarded.

Where the report sets out the face value of an award in respect of a scheme interest relating to shares or share options, the report must specify

(a) whether the face value has been calculated using the share price at date of grant or the average share price

(b) where the share price at date of grant is used, the amount of that share price and the date of grant and

(c) where the average share price is used, what that price was and the period used for calculating the average.

[*SI 2008 No 410, Sch 8, para 14; SI 2013 No 1981, Reg 3*].

19.20 Payments to past directors

The directors' remuneration report must for the relevant financial year contain details of any payments of money or other assets to any person who was not a director of the company at the time the payment was made but had been a director of the company before that time, excluding,

(a) any payments falling within **19.21** 'payments for loss of office'

(b) any payments shown in the single total figure table (see **19.16**)

(c) any payments which have been disclosed in a previous directors' remuneration report of the company

(d) any payments which are below a de minimis threshold set by the company and stated in the report

(e) payments by way of regular pension benefits commenced in a previous year or dividend payments in respect of scheme interests retained after leaving office and

(f) payments in respect of employment with or any other contractual service performed for the company other than as a director.

[*SI 2008 No 410, Sch 8, para 15; SI 2013 No 1981, Reg 3*].

19.21 Payments for loss of office

The directors' remuneration report must, for the relevant financial year set out, for each person who has served as a director of the company at any time during that year, or any previous year, excluding payments which are below a de minimis threshold set by the company and stated in the report

(a) the total amount of any payment for loss of office paid to or receivable by the person in respect of that financial year, broken down into each component comprised in that payment and the value of each component

(b) an explanation of how each component was calculated

(c) any other payments paid to or receivable by the person in connection with the termination of qualifying services, whether by way of compensation for loss of office or otherwise, including the treatment of outstanding incentive awards that vest on or following termination and

(d) where any discretion was exercised in respect of the payment, an explanation of how it was exercised.

[*SI 2008 No 410, Sch 8, para 16; SI 2013 No 1981, Reg 3*].

19.22 Statement of directors' shareholdings and share interests

The directors' remuneration report for the relevant financial year must contain for each person who has served as a director of the company at any time during that year

(a) a statement of any requirements or guidelines for the director to own shares in the company and state whether or not those requirements or guidelines have been met

(b) in tabular form or forms

  (i) the total number of interests in shares in the company of the director including interests of connected persons (as defined for the purposes of *FSMA 2000*)

  (ii) the total number of scheme interests differentiating between shares and share options and those with or without performance measures

  (iii) details of those scheme interests (which may exclude any details included elsewhere in the report) and

(iv) details of share options which are vested but unexercised and exercised in the relevant financial year.

[*SI 2008 No 410, Sch 8, para 17; SI 2013 No 1981, Reg 3*].

19.23 Performance graph and table

(1) The directors' remuneration report must

(a) contain a line graph that shows for each of

(i) a holding of shares of that class of the company's equity share capital whose listing, or admission to dealing, has resulted in the company falling within the definition of quoted company, and

(ii) a hypothetical holding of shares made up of shares of the same kinds and number as those by reference to which a broad equity market index is calculated,

a line drawn by joining up points plotted to represent, for each of the financial years in the relevant period, the total shareholder return on that holding; and

(b) state the name of the index selected for the purposes of the graph and set out the reasons for selecting that index.

The '*total shareholder return*' for a relevant period on a holding of shares must be calculated using a fair method that

- takes as its starting point the percentage change over the period in the market price of the holding;
- involves making the 'assumptions as to reinvestment of income' and 'assumptions as to the funding of liabilities' specified below, and
- makes provision for any replacement of shares in the holding by shares of a different description;

and the same method must be used for each of the holdings mentioned above.

The '*assumptions as to reinvestment of income*' are

(i) that any benefit in the form of shares of the same kind as those in the holding is added to the holding at the time the benefit becomes receivable; and

(ii) that any '*benefit*' in cash, and an amount equal to the value of any benefit not in cash and not falling within (i) above, is applied at the time the benefit becomes receivable in the purchase at their market price of shares of the same kind as those in the holding and that the shares purchased are added to the holding at that time;

and for this purpose 'benefit' means any benefit (including, in particular, any dividend) receivable in respect of any shares in the holding by the holder from the company of whose share capital the shares form part.

The '*assumption as to the funding of liabilities*' is that, where the holder has a 'liability' to the company of whose capital the shares in the holding form part, shares are sold from the holding

- immediately before the time by which the liability is due to be satisfied, and

- in such numbers that, at the time of the sale, the market price of the shares sold equals the amount of the liability in respect of the shares in the holding that are not being sold;

and for this purpose '*liability*' means a liability arising in respect of any shares in the holding or from the exercise of a right attached to any of those shares.

(2) The report must also set out in tabular form the following information for each of the financial years in the relevant period in respect of the director undertaking the role of chief executive officer

(a) total remuneration as set out in the single total figure table (see **19.16**)

(b) the sum set out in the table in column headed 'c' in the single total figure table expressed as a percentage of the maximum that could have been paid in respect of that component in the financial year and

(c) the sum set out in the table in column headed 'd' in the single total figure table restated as a percentage of the number of shares vesting against the maximum number of shares that could have been received, or, where paid in money and other assets, as a percentage of the maximum that could have been paid in respect of that component in the financial year.

This provision may be complied with by use of either

(a) a sum based on the information supplied in the directors' remuneration reports for those previous years or

(b) where no such report has been compiled, a suitable corresponding sum.

In each of the above '*relevant period*' means the 'specified' period of financial years of which the last is the relevant financial year. Where the relevant financial year

- is the company's first financial year for which the performance graph is prepared in accordance with these provisions, 'specified' means five
- is the company's second, third, fourth, fifth financial year in which the report is prepared in accordance with *Schedule 8* to *SI 2008 No 418* (as amended), 'specified' means six, seven, eight, nine as the case may be and
- is any financial year after the fifth financial year in which the report is prepared in accordance with *Schedule 8* to *SI 2008 No 418* (as amended), 'specified' means ten.

[*SI 2008 No 410, Sch 8, para 18; SI 2013 No 1981, Reg 3*].

19.24 Percentage change in remuneration of director undertaking the role of chief executive officer

The directors' remuneration report must set out (in a manner which permits comparison) in relation to each of the kinds of remuneration required to be set out in each of the columns headed 'a', 'b', and 'c' of the single total figure table (see **19.16**) the following information

(a) the percentage change from the financial year preceding the relevant financial year in respect of the director undertaking the role of chief executive officer and

(b) the average percentage change from the financial year preceding the relevant financial year in respect of the employees of the company taken as a whole.

Where for the purposes of (b) a comparator group comprising the employees taken as a whole is considered by the company as an inappropriate comparator group of employees, the company may use such other comparator group of employees as the company identifies, provided the report contains a statement setting out why that group was chosen.

Where the company is a parent company, the statement must relate to the group and not the company and the director reported on is the director undertaking the role of chief executive officer of the parent company, and the employees are the employees of the group.

[*SI 2008 No 410, Sch 8, para 19; SI 2013 No 1981, Reg 3*].

19.25 Relative importance of spend on pay

The directors' remuneration report must set out in a graphical or tabular form that shows in respect of the relevant financial year and the immediately preceding financial year the actual expenditure of the company, and the difference in spend between those years, on

(a) remuneration paid to or receivable by all employees of the group

(b) distributions to shareholders by way of dividend and share buyback and

(c) any other significant distributions and payments or other uses of profit or cash-flow deemed by the directors to assist in understanding the relative importance of spend on pay.

There must be set out in a note to the report an explanation in respect of (c) why the particular matters were chosen by the directors and how the amounts were calculated.

Where the matters chosen for the report in (c) in the relevant financial year are not the same as the other items set out in the report for previous years, an explanation for that change must be given.

[*SI 2008 No 410, Sch 8, para 20; SI 2013 No 1981, Reg 3*].

19.26 Statement of voting at general meeting

The directors' remuneration report must contain a statement setting out in respect of the last general meeting at which a resolution of the following kind was moved by the company

(a) in respect of a resolution to approve the directors' remuneration report, the percentage of votes cast for and against and the number of votes withheld

(b) in respect of a resolution to approve the directors' remuneration policy, the percentage of votes cast for and against and the number of votes withheld and

(c) where there was a significant percentage of votes against either such resolution, a summary of the reasons for those votes, as far as known to the directors, and any actions taken by the directors in response to those concerns.

[*SI 2008 No 410, Sch 8, para 23; SI 2013 No 1981, Reg 3*].

19.27 APPROVAL AND SIGNING OF THE REMUNERATION REPORT AND POLICY

Board approval. The directors' remuneration report must be approved by the board of directors and signed on its behalf by a director or the secretary of the company. If such a report is approved that does not comply with the requirements of *CA 2006*, every director of the company who

- knew that it did not comply, or was reckless as to whether it complied, and
- failed to take reasonable steps to secure compliance with those requirements or, as the case may be, to prevent the report from being approved,

commits an offence. A person guilty of such an offence is liable (i) on conviction on indictment, to a fine; and (ii) on summary conviction, to a fine not exceeding the statutory maximum. See **29.1 Offences and Legal Proceedings** for the statutory maximum.

[*CA 2006, s 422*].

Revisions to directors' remuneration policy

Section 79(2) of the *E and RR Act 2013* inserted a new *CA 2006, s 422A* as from 1 October 2013. It provides that the remuneration policy may be revised but that such revision must be approved by the board of directors and the policy as so revised must be set out in a document signed on behalf of the board by a director or the Company Secretary. The document setting out a revised directors' remuneration policy must contain the information specified in *SI 2008 No 410, Schedule 8, para 42* (as amended) and must be set out in the same manner as required by *part 4* of that *Schedule*.

Quoted companies: members' approval of the report. Before each "accounts meeting" (see **Appendix 1 Definitions** for the meaning) a quoted company must give to the members entitled to be sent notice of the meeting notice of the intention to move at the meeting, as an ordinary resolution, a resolution approving the directors' remuneration report for the financial year other than the part containing the directors' remuneration policy The notice may be given in any manner permitted for the service on the member of notice of the meeting (see **42.15 Resolutions and Meetings**).

The business that may be dealt with at the accounts meeting includes the resolution to approve the report despite any default in complying with the above provisions.

The existing directors (ie persons who are directors of the company immediately before the meeting) must ensure that the resolution is put to the vote of the meeting. But no entitlement of a person to remuneration is made conditional on the resolution being passed by reason only of the provisions made above.

Penalties. An offence is committed

(a) in the event of failure to give members notice of the resolution for approval of directors' remuneration report or remuneration policy (see below), by every officer of the company who is in default; and

(b) if the resolution is not put to the vote of the meeting to which it relates, by each existing director.

A person guilty of such an offence is liable, on summary conviction, to a fine not exceeding level 3 on the standard scale. See **29.1 Offences and Legal Proceedings** for the standard scale.

It is a defence for a person charged with an offence under (*b*) above to prove that he took all reasonable steps for securing that the resolution was put to the vote of the meeting.

[*CA 2006, ss 422A, 439, 440; ERRA 2013, s 81 (10); SI 2013 No 1981, Regs 2, 42, 43*].

Quoted companies: members' approval of the remuneration policy

Prior to the "accounts meeting" (see **Appendix 1 Definitions**) held in the first financial year which begins on or after the day on which the company becomes a quoted company and at an accounts or other general meeting held no later than the end of the period of three financial years beginning with the first financial year after the last accounts or other general meeting in relation to which notice is given under CA 2006, s 439A (see **Appendix 1 Definitions** for the meaning of "accounts meeting") a quoted company must give to the members entitled to be sent notice of the meeting notice of the intention to move at the meeting, as an ordinary resolution, a resolution approving the relevant directors' remuneration policy .The notice may be given in any manner permitted for the service on the member of notice of the meeting (see **42.15 Resolutions and Meetings**).

A quoted company must also give to the members entitled to be sent notice of the meeting notice of the intention to move at the meeting, as an ordinary resolution, a resolution approving the relevant directors' remuneration policy if:

(a) *a resolution required to be put to the vote under CA 2006, s 439 was not passed at the last accounts meeting of the company and*

(b) *no notice under CA 2006, s 439A was given in relation to that meeting or any other general meeting held before the next accounts meeting.*

This provision does not apply before the first meeting in relation to which a quoted company gives notice as above in relation to approval.

For the purposes of these provisions 'relevant directors' remuneration policy' is

(a) in a case where notice is given in relation to an accounts meeting, the remuneration policy contained in the directors' remuneration report in respect of which a resolution (as above) is required to be put to the vote at that accounts meeting

(b) in a case where notice is given in relation to a general meeting other than an accounts meeting

  (i) the remuneration policy contained in the directors' remuneration report in respect of which such a resolution was required to be put to the vote at the last accounts meeting to be held before that other general meeting or

  (ii) where that policy has been revised in accordance with *CA 2006, s 422A*, the policy as so revised.

Where a company intends to move a resolution to approve a directors' remuneration policy and it is intended that some or all of the provisions of the last approved policy are to continue to apply after the resolution is approved, that fact must be stated in the policy which is the subject of the resolution and it must be made clear which provisions of the last approved policy are to continue to apply and for what period of time it is intended that they shall apply.

On the first occasion that a resolution to approve a directors' remuneration policy (or revised policy) is moved after 1 October 2013, the policy must set out a date from which it is intended by the company that the policy is to take effect.

[*CA 2006, s 439A; SI 2008 No 410, Sch 8, para 24(2), 24(4)*]

19.28 DEFECTIVE REMUNERATION REPORT AND POLICY

A directors' remuneration report or policy may be replaced or partially revised because it was originally defective. See **2.12 Accounts: General**. The provisions of *CA 2006* as to the matters to be included in a directors' remuneration report or policy apply to a revised report or policy as if the revised report or policy were prepared and approved by the directors of the company as at the date of the original report or policy.

[*SI 2013 No 2224, Reg 5*].

19.29 Approval and signing of revised remuneration report and policy

The requirement that a directors' remuneration report must be approved by the board of directors and signed on its behalf by a director or the secretary of the company (see **19.27**) also applies to a revised directors' remuneration report or revised remuneration policy (see **19.27**), except that (in either case) in the case of revision by supplementary note, the provisions apply as if they required the signature to be on the supplementary note.

Where copies of the original directors' remuneration report have already been sent out to members, laid before the company in general meeting in the case of a public company, or delivered to the Registrar of Companies, the directors must, before approving the revised report, cause statements as to the following matters to be made in a prominent position in the revised report (or, in the case of revision by supplementary note, in that note).

(a) In the case of revision by replacement

- that the revised report replaces the original report for the financial year (specifying it);
- that it has been prepared as at the date of the original directors' remuneration report and not at the date of revision and accordingly does not deal with any events between those dates;
- the respects in which the original directors' remuneration report did not comply with the requirements of *CA 2006*; and
- any significant amendments made consequential upon the remedying of those defects.

(b) In the case of a revision by supplementary note

- that the note revises in certain respects the original directors' remuneration report of the company and is to be treated as forming part of that report; and
- that the directors' remuneration report has been revised as at the date of the original directors' remuneration report and not as at the date of revision and accordingly does not deal with any events between those dates.

The date of approval of the revised report must be stated on the face of the report (or, in the case of revision by supplementary note, in that note).

The penalty for failure to comply with these provisions is as in **19.27**.

[*SI 2008 No 373, Regs 6, 6A; SI 2013 No 2224, Reg 7*].

19.30 Effect of revision of report or policy

On approval of a revised report or policy by the directors, the provisions of *CA 2006* have effect as if the revised report or policy was, as from the date of its approval, the directors' remuneration report or revised remuneration policy (as the case may be) in place of the original report or policy (as the case may be). This applies in particular for the purposes of

- *CA 2006, ss 431, 432* (right to demand copies of accounts, etc, see **2.7 Accounts: General**); and

- *CA 2006, s 423* (persons entitled to receive copies, see **2.6 Accounts: General**), *CA 2006, s 437* (accounts, etc of public companies to be laid before company in general meeting, see **2.9 Accounts: General**) and *CA 2006, s 441* (accounts, etc to be delivered to Registrar of Companies, see **2.10 Accounts: General**) if the requirements of those provisions have not been complied with prior to the date of revision.

[*SI 2008 No 373, Reg 11; SI 2013 No 2224, Reg 10]*].

19.31 Publication of revised report

Where the directors have prepared a revised directors' remuneration report and copies of the original report have been sent to any person under *CA 2006, s 423* (persons entitled to receive copies, see **2.6 Accounts: General**) or *CA 2006, s 146* (traded companies: nomination of persons to enjoy information rights, see **26.4 Members**), the directors must send to any such person

- in the case of a revision by replacement, a copy of the revised report, together with a copy of the auditor's report on that report; or
- in the case of revision by supplementary note, a copy of that note, together with a copy of the auditor's report on the revised report.

This must be done not more than 28 days after the date of the revision (ie the date on which the revised report is approved by the directors).

The directors must also, not more than 28 days after the revision, send a copy of the revised report and auditor's report thereon to any person who is not entitled to receive a copy under the above provisions but who is, at the date of the revision,

(a) a member of the company,

(b) a holder of the company's debentures, or

(c) a person who is entitled to receive notice of general meetings

unless the company would be entitled at that date to send to that person a strategic report and supplementary material.

The exceptions from the requirement to send copies of the annual accounts and reports in **2.6 Accounts: General** equally apply to sending out copies of the revised directors' remuneration report.

In default in complying with the above provisions, an offence is committed by each of the directors who approved the revised report. A person guilty of such an offence is liable (i) on conviction on indictment, to a fine; and (ii) on summary conviction, to a fine not exceeding the statutory maximum. See **29.1 Offences and Legal Proceedings** for the statutory maximum.

[*SI 2008 No 373, Reg 12; SI 2013 No 2224, Reg 11*].

19.32 Laying of revised report

Where the directors of a public company have prepared a revised directors' remuneration report and the original report has already been laid before the company in general meeting, a copy of the revised report, together with a copy of the auditor's report on that report, must be laid before the next annual general meeting of the company held after the date of revision at which any annual accounts for a financial year are laid (unless they have already been laid before an earlier general meeting).

In default, every person who is a director of the company immediately before that annual general meeting commits an offence. A person guilty of such an offence is liable, on summary conviction, to a fine not exceeding level 5 on the standard scale and, for continued contravention, a daily default fine not exceeding one-tenth of level 5 on the standard scale. See **29.1 Offences and Legal Proceedings** for the standard scale. It is a defence for a person charged with such an offence to prove that he took all reasonable steps for securing that the requirements would be complied with before that annual general meeting; it is not a defence to prove that the revised report was not in fact prepared.

[*SI 2008 No 373, Reg 13*].

19.33 Delivery of revised report to the Registrar of Companies

Where the directors have prepared a revised directors' remuneration report and a copy of the original report has been delivered to the Registrar of Companies, the directors must, within 28 days of the revision, deliver to the Registrar

- in the case of a revision by replacement, a copy of the revised report, together with a copy of the auditor's report on that report; or
- in the case of a revision by supplementary note, a copy of that note, together with a copy of the auditor's report on the revised report.

CA 2006, ss 451 and *452* (offences and court order for default in filing accounts and reports, see **2.10 Accounts: General**) also apply to a failure to comply with the above requirements but as if the reference to 'the period for filing those accounts and reports' was a reference to the 28 day period above.

[*SI 2008 No 373, Reg 14*].

19.34 LIABILITY FOR FALSE OR MISLEADING STATEMENTS IN REPORT

A director of a company is liable to compensate the company for any loss suffered by it as a result of

- any untrue or misleading statement, or
- the omission of anything required to be included

in a directors' report or a directors' remuneration report or a strategic report so far as it is derived from that report. No liability arises in respect of a report or summary financial statement first sent out before 20 January 2007.

A director is so liable only if

- he knew the statement to be untrue or misleading or was reckless as to whether it was untrue or misleading; or
- he knew the omission to be dishonest concealment of a material fact.

No person can be subject to any liability to a person other than the company resulting from reliance, by that person or another, on information in a report to which CA 2006, s 463 applies. The reference to a person being 'subject to a liability' includes a reference to another person being entitled as against him to be granted any civil remedy or to rescind or repudiate an agreement.

The effect of this is that no persons (including directors) are liable to individual investors or third parties but auditors remain liable to the company for negligence in preparing their own report.

The above provisions do not affect liability for a civil penalty or liability for a criminal offence.

[*CA 2006, s 463; SI 2006 No 3428, Sch 5 para 3; SI 2013 No 1970, Schedule, para 17*].].

20 Directors' and Strategic Reports

20.1	**Contents of directors' reports and strategic report**
20.2	Names of directors
20.3	Principal activities
20.4	Dividends
20.5	Disclosure of information to auditors
20.6	Qualifying indemnity provisions
20.7	Asset values: interests in land
20.8	Political donations and expenditure
20.9	Charitable donations
20.10	Financial instruments
20.11	Miscellaneous
20.12	Acquisition or charging of own shares
20.13	Employment of disabled persons
20.14	Employee involvement
20.15	Policy and practice on the payment of creditors
20.16	Companies whose securities are admitted to trading on a regulated market
20.17	Quoted companies— disclosure of greenhouse gas emissions
20.18	**Approval and signing**
20.19	**Defective reports**
20.20	Approval and signature of revised reports
20.21	Effect of revision of report
20.22	Publication of revised report
20.23	Laying of revised report
20.24	Delivery of revised report to the Registrar of Companies
20.25	**Liability for false or misleading statements in reports**

Cross-references. See **2 Accounts: General** for publication of directors' report, laying it before members and delivery to Registrar of Companies, etc; **8.30 Audit** for the auditor's duty concerning the directors' report.

The *Companies Act 2006 (Strategic Report and Directors' Report) Regulations 2013* ("the *2013 Regulations*") which are referred to in various parts of this chapter, bring into force the requirement for a company to produce a strategic report for financial years ending on or after 30 September 2013.

20.1 CONTENTS OF DIRECTORS' AND STRATEGIC REPORTS

The directors of a company must prepare a directors' report for each financial year of the company containing specified information. Where a company chooses in accordance with CA 2006, s 414C(11) to set out in the strategic report information which is required by *Schedule 7* to the *Large and Medium-sized Companies and Groups (Accounts and Reports) Regulations 2008* (*SI 2008 No 410*) (see **20.2–20.17A**) to be disclosed in the directors' report, it must state in the directors' report that it has done so and the information in respect of which it has done so.

- **Large and medium-sized companies** must include the information in **20.2–20.15**.
- **Small companies** must include the information in **20.2, 20.3, 20.6, 20.7, 20.9, 20.10, 20.13**, and **20.14**.
- **Companies whose securities are admitted to trading on a regulated market** must additionally include the information in **20.16**.
- Quoted companies must also include the information in **20.17**.

- **Listed companies** must additionally comply with the requirements of the FCA Listing Rules as to content of annual accounts. See **33.28 Public and Listed Companies**. The additional requirements may be shown in the directors' report or the notes to the accounts.

Parent companies preparing group accounts. For a financial year in which the company is a parent company, and the directors of the company prepare group accounts, the directors' report must be a consolidated report (a '*group directors' report*') relating to the undertakings included in the consolidation. Such a group directors' report may, where appropriate, give greater emphasis to the matters that are significant to the undertakings included in the consolidation, taken as a whole.

Penalties. In the case of failure to comply with the requirement to prepare a directors' report, an offence is committed by every person who

- was a director of the company immediately before the end of the period for filing accounts and reports for the financial year in question; and
- failed to take all reasonable steps for securing compliance with that requirement.

A person guilty of such an offence is liable (i) on conviction on indictment, to a fine; and (ii) on summary conviction, to a fine not exceeding the statutory maximum. See **29.1 Offences and Legal Proceedings** for the statutory maximum.

[*CA 2006, s 415; SI 2013 No 1970, Reg 7(3)(a), (e)*].

Strategic Report

For financial years ending on or after 30 September 2013 the directors must also prepare a strategic report for each financial year of the company. Companies entitled to a small companies' exemption will not be obliged to prepare a strategic report and a company is entitled to such an exemption if it is entitled to prepare accounts for the year in accordance with the small companies regime or would be so entitled but for being or having been a member of an ineligible group (see **5 Accounts: Small Companies**)

Parent companies preparing group accounts. For a financial year in which the company is a parent company, and the directors of the company prepare group accounts, the strategic report must be a consolidated report (a 'group strategic report') relating to the undertakings included in the consolidation. Such a group strategic report may, where appropriate, give greater emphasis to the matters that are significant to the undertakings included in the consolidation, taken as a whole.

Penalties for failure to prepare a strategic report are as above for failure to prepare a directors' report.

The report must be approved by the board of directors and signed on behalf of the board by a director or the secretary of the company

Offences. If a strategic report is approved that does not comply with the requirements of CA 2006, every director of the company who

- knew that it did not comply, or was reckless as to whether it complied, and
- failed to take reasonable steps to secure compliance with those requirements or, as the case may be, to prevent the report from being approved,

commits an offence.

A person guilty of such an offence is liable (i) on conviction on indictment, to a fine; and (ii) on summary conviction, to a fine not exceeding the statutory maximum. See **29.1** OFFENCES AND PENALTIES for the statutory maximum.

[CA 2006, s 414A, 414B 414D; SI 2013 No 1970, Regulations, Reg 3]

Contents of the strategic report

The purpose of the strategic report is to inform members of the company and help them assess how the directors have performed their duty under *CA 2006, s 172* (Duty to promote the success of the company) (see **18.24**). The strategic report must:

- contain a fair review of the company's business ie a balanced and comprehensive analysis of the development and performance of the company's business during the financial year and the position of the business at the end of that year
- contain a description of the principal risks and uncertainties facing the company
- to the extent necessary for an understanding of the development, performance or position of the company's business include analysis using key performance indicators and where appropriate analysis using other key performance indicators including information relating to environmental and employee matters. For these purposes " key performance indicators" means factors by reference to which the development, performance or position of the company's business can be measured effectively. If a company qualifies as a medium-sized company in relation to a financial year (see **4** ACCOUNTS: MEDIUM –SIZED COMPANIES), the strategic report for that year does not need to comply with this requirement so far as it relates to non-financial information.
- where appropriate include references to, and additional explanations of, amounts included in the company's annual accounts
- contain such of the matters otherwise required by regulations made under *CA 2006 ,s 416(4)* to be disclosed in the directors' report as the directors consider are of strategic importance to the company.

The company is not required to disclose information in the strategic report about impending developments or matters in the course of negotiation if the disclosure would, in the opinion of the directors, be seriously prejudicial to the interests of the company.

Additional requirements for quoted companies

In addition to the matters set out above a quoted company's strategic report must also

- to the extent necessary for an understanding of the development, performance or position of the company's business include the main trends and factors likely to affect the future development, performance and position of the company's business and information about environmental matters (including the impact of the company's business on the environment), the company's employees, social, community and human rights issues including information about any policies of the company in relation to those matters and the effectiveness of those policies. If the report does not contain the information on environmental matters, employees and social, community and human rights issues, it must state which of those kinds of information it does not contain.
- include. a description of the company's strategy, a description of the company's business model,
- contain a breakdown showing at the end of the financial year the number of persons of each sex who were directors of the company, the number of persons of each sex who were senior managers of the company (other than persons who

are directors) and the number of each person of each sex who were employees of the company. For these purposes "senior manager" means a person who has responsibility for planning, directing or controlling the activities of the company or a strategically significant part of the company and is an employee of the company

Where the company is part of a group the reference to a "company" is to the parent company and the breakdown of the numbers of each sex who were senior managers of the company must include the number of persons of each sex who were the directors of the undertaking included in the consolidation.

[CA 2006, s 414C ; SI 2013 No 1970, Regulations, Reg 3]

20.2 Names of directors

The directors' report must state the names of the persons who, at any time during the financial year, were directors of the company.

[*CA 2006, s 416(1)*].

20.3 Principal activities

The directors' report must state the principal activities of the company in the course of the year. In relation to a group directors' report (see **20.1**) the reference to the company is to be taken as a reference to the undertakings included in the consolidation.

[*CA 2006, s 416(1)(b), (2)*].

This requirement is removed for financial years ending on or after 30 September 2013

[The 2013 Regulations, Reg 6]

20.4 Dividends

Unless the company is entitled to the 'small companies exemption', the directors' report must state the amount (if any) that the directors recommend should be paid by way of dividend. [*CA 2006, s 416(3); SI 2008 No 393, Reg 6*].

A company is entitled to '*small companies exemption*' in relation to the directors' report for a financial year if

- it is entitled to prepare accounts for the year in accordance with the small companies regime; or
- it would be so entitled but for being or having been a member of an ineligible group.

See **5.2** and **5.3** ACCOUNTS: SMALL COMPANIES.

[*CA 2006, s 415A; SI 2008 No 393, Reg 6*].

20.5 Disclosure of information to auditors

Unless the directors have taken advantage of the exemption from audit under *CA 2006, Pt 16* (see **8.25–8.29** AUDIT), the directors' report must contain a statement to the effect that, in the case of each of the persons who are directors at the time when the report is approved

(a) so far as the director is aware, there is no 'relevant audit information' of which the company's auditor is unaware; and

(b) he has taken all the steps that he ought to have taken as a director in order to make himself aware of any relevant audit information and to establish that the company's auditor is aware of that information.

'*Relevant audit information*' means information needed by the company's auditor in connection with preparing his report.

For the purposes of (*b*) above, a director is regarded as having taken all the steps that he ought to have taken if he has

- made such enquiries of his fellow directors and of the company's auditor for that purpose, and
- taken such other steps (if any) for that purpose

as are required by his duty as a director of the company to exercise reasonable care, skill and diligence.

Penalties. Where a directors' report containing a statement as required above is approved but the statement is false, every director of the company who

- knew that the statement was false, or was reckless as to whether it was false, and
- failed to take reasonable steps to prevent the report from being approved,

commits an offence. A person guilty of such an offence is liable (i) on conviction on indictment, to imprisonment for a term not exceeding two years or a fine (or both); and (ii) on summary conviction, to imprisonment for a term not exceeding 12 months (6 months in Scotland or Northern Ireland or a fine not exceeding the statutory maximum (or both). See **29.1 Offences and Legal Proceedings** for the statutory maximum.

[*CA 2006, s 418*].

20.6 Qualifying indemnity provisions

If

- when a directors' report is approved, any '*qualifying indemnity provision*' (whether made by the company or otherwise) is in force for the benefit of one or more directors of the company,
- at any time during the financial year to which the directors' report relates, any such provision was in force for the benefit of one or more persons who were then directors of the company,
- when a directors' report is approved, qualifying indemnity provision made by the company is in force for the benefit of one or more directors of an 'associated company', or
- at any time during the financial year to which the directors' report relates, any such provision was in force for the benefit of one or more persons who were then directors of an associated company,

the directors' report must state that such provision was in force.

'*Qualifying indemnity provision*' means either 'qualifying third party indemnity provision' or 'qualifying pension scheme indemnity provision' as defined in **18.43 Directors**.

For these purposes, companies are associated if one is a subsidiary of the other or both are subsidiaries of the same company.

[*CA 2006, ss 236, 256*].

20.7 Asset values: interests in land

Unless the company is subject to the small companies regime (see **5.2** and **5.3 Accounts: Small Companies**), in the case of such of the fixed assets of the company as consist in interests in land, the report must indicate the difference (with such degree of precision as is practicable) between their market value as at the end of the financial year and the amount at which they are included in the balance sheet where

- these figures differ substantially; and
- the difference is, in the directors' opinion, of such significance as to require being drawn to the attention of members of the company or debenture holders.

In relation to a group directors' report (see **20.1**) the above provisions have effect as if the reference to the fixed assets of the company was a reference to the fixed assets of the company and of its subsidiary undertakings included in the consolidation.

This requirement is removed for financial years ending on or after 30 September 2013

[*SI 2008 No 410, Sch 7 para 2*; *SI 2013 No 1970, Reg 7(3)(b)*].

20.8 Political donations and expenditure

If a company, other than a wholly-owned subsidiary of a company incorporated in the UK, has in the financial year

(a) made any 'political donation' to any political party or other political organisation,

(b) made any political donation to any independent election candidate, or

(c) incurred any 'political expenditure',

and the amount of the donation or expenditure (or the aggregate amount of all such donations and expenditure) exceeds £2,000, the directors' report for the year must contain the following particulars.

- Where (*a*) or (*b*) above applies,
  - (i) the name of each political party, other organisation or independent election candidate to whom any such donation has been made; and
  - (ii) the total amount given to that party, organisation or candidate by way of such donations in the financial year.
- Where (*c*) above applies, the total amount incurred by way of such expenditure in the financial year.

If

- at the end of the financial year, the company has subsidiaries which have, in that year, made any donations or incurred any such expenditure, and

- the company itself is not the wholly-owned subsidiary of a company incorporated in the UK,

the directors' report for the year is not required to contain such particulars unless the total amount of any such donations or expenditure (or both) made or incurred in that year by the company and the subsidiaries between them exceeds £2,000, in which case the directors' report for the year must contain those particulars in relation to each body by whom any such donation or expenditure has been made or incurred.

See 31.2 Political Donations for the definitions of '*political donation*' and '*political expenditure*' for these purposes.

Non-EU political parties. If a company, other than a wholly-owned subsidiary of a company incorporated in the UK, has in the financial year made any 'contribution' to a 'non-EU political party', the directors' report for the year must contain

- a statement of the amount of the contribution; or
- if it has made two or more such contributions in the year, a statement of the total amount of the contributions.

If

- at the end of the financial year the company has subsidiaries which have, in that year, made any such contributions, and
- the company itself is not the wholly-owned subsidiary of a company incorporated in the UK,

the directors' report for the year is not required to contain any such statement but it must instead contain a statement of the total amount of the contributions made in the year by the company and the subsidiaries between them.

'*Contribution*' means any gift of money to the organisation (whether made directly or indirectly); any subscription or other fee paid for affiliation to, or membership of, the organisation; or any money spent (otherwise than by the organisation or a person acting on its behalf) in paying any expenses incurred directly or indirectly by the organisation.

'*Non-EU political party*' means any political party which carries on, or proposes to carry on, its activities wholly outside the Member States.

[*SI 2008 No 409, Sch 5 paras, 2, 3; SI 2008 No 410, Sch 7 paras 3, 4*].

20.9 Charitable donations

If a company, other than a wholly-owned subsidiary of a company incorporated in UK, has in the financial year given money for charitable purposes in excess of £2,000 (but leaving out of account any money given to a person who, when it was given, was ordinarily resident outside the UK), the directors' report for the year must contain, in the case of each of the purposes for which money has been given, a statement of the amount of money given for that purpose.

If

- at the end of the financial year the company has subsidiaries which have, in that year, given money for charitable purposes, and
- the company is not itself a wholly-owned subsidiary of a company incorporated in the UK,

the directors' report for the year is not required to contain such particulars unless the amount given in that year for charitable purposes by the company and the subsidiaries between them exceeds £2,000, in which case the directors' report for the year must contain, in the case of each of the purposes for which money has been given by the company and the subsidiaries between them, a statement of the amount of money given for that purpose.

'*Charitable purposes*' means purposes which are exclusively charitable, and as respects Scotland a purpose is charitable if it is listed in *Charities and Trustees Investment (Scotland) Act 2005, s 7(2)*.

This requirement is removed for financial years ending on or after 30 September by *regulation 7(3)(b)* of the *2013 Regulations*.

[*SI 2008 No 409, Sch 5 para 4; SI 2008 No 410, Sch 7 para 5*].

20.10 Financial instruments

Unless the company is subject to the small companies regime (see **5.2** and **5.3** Accounts: Small Companies), in relation to the use of financial instruments by a company, the directors' report must contain an indication of

- the financial risk management objectives and policies of the company, including the policy for hedging each major type of forecasted transaction for which 'hedge accounting' is used, and
- the exposure of the company to 'price risk', 'credit risk', 'liquidity risk' and 'cash flow risk'

unless such information is not material for the assessment of the assets, liabilities, financial position and profit or loss of the company.

The expressions '*hedge accounting*', '*price risk*', '*credit risk*', '*liquidity risk*' and '*cash flow risk*' have the same meaning as they have in *Council Directive 78/660/EEC* on the annual accounts of certain types of companies, and in *Council Directive 83/349/EEC* on consolidated accounts (as amended).

In relation to a group directors' report (see **20.1**) the above provisions have effect as if the references to the company were references to the company and its subsidiary undertakings included in the consolidation.

[*SI 2008 No 410, Sch 7 para 6*].

20.11 Miscellaneous

Unless the company is subject to the small companies regime (see **5.2** and **5.3** Accounts: Small Companies), the directors' report must contain

(a) particulars of all important events affecting the company which have occurred since the end of the financial year;

(b) an indication of likely future developments in the business of the company;

(c) an indication of the activities (if any) of the company in the field of research and development; and

(d) (unless the company is an unlimited company) an indication of the existence of branches of the company outside the UK.

In relation to a group directors' report (see **20.1**) the above provisions in (*a*)–(*c*) above have effect as if the references to the company were references to the company and its subsidiary undertakings included in the consolidation.

[*SI 2008 No 410, Sch 7 para 7*].

20.12 Acquisition or charging of own shares

Where shares in a company are

- purchased by the company or acquired by it by forfeiture or surrender in lieu of forfeiture, or in pursuance of *CA 2006, s 659*, see **34.1** **Purchase of Own Shares**, or
- acquired by another person in the circumstances in *CA 2006, s 662(1)*, see **34.23**(*c*) or (*d*) **Purchase of Own Shares** (acquisition by a nominee of the company, or by another with financial assistance from the company, and in either case the company has a beneficial interest in the shares), or
- made subject to a lien or other charge taken (whether expressly or otherwise) by the company and permitted under *CA 2006, s 670(2)* or *(4)*, see **34.30**(*a*) or (*c*) **Purchase of Own Shares**,

the directors' report for the financial year must state

(i) the number and nominal value of the shares so purchased, the aggregate amount of the consideration paid by the company for the shares and the reason for the purchase;

(ii) the number and nominal value of the shares so acquired or charged during the financial year;

(iii) the maximum number and nominal value of shares which, having been so acquired or charged (whether or not during the year) are held at any time by the company or that other person during the year;

(iv) the number and nominal value of the shares so acquired or charged (whether or not during the year) which are disposed of by the company or that other person or cancelled by the company during the year;

(v) the percentage of called-up share capital represented by the number and nominal value of the shares of any particular description stated within (i) to (iv) above;

(vi) where any of the shares have been so charged, the amount of the charge in each case; and

(vii) where any of the shares have been disposed of by the company or person who acquired them for money or money's worth, the amount or value of the consideration in each case.

In the case of companies subject to the Small Companies and Groups (Accounts and Directors' Report) Regulations 2008, these requirements are removed for financial years ending on or after 30 September 2013.

[*SI 2008 No 409, Sch 5 para 6; SI 2008 No 410, Sch 7 paras 8, 9; SI 2013 No 1970, Reg 8(3)*].

20.13 Employment of disabled persons

Where, during the financial year, the 'average number of persons employed' in each week exceeded 250, the directors' report must contain a statement on such policy as the company has applied during the financial year for

- giving full and fair consideration to applications for 'employment' made by disabled persons, having regard to their particular aptitudes and abilities;
- continuing employment of, and arranging for appropriate training for, employees who have become disabled during the period when they were employed by the company; and
- otherwise for the training, career development and promotion of disabled persons (as defined under the *Disability Discrimination Act 1995*) employed by the company.

'*Average number of persons employed*' is calculated by the formula

$$\frac{A}{B}$$

where

A = the sum of the numbers of persons who, under contracts of service, were employed by the company in each week of the financial year (whether throughout it or not)

B = the number of weeks in the financial year

'*Employment*' means employment other than employment to work wholly or mainly outside the UK, and '*employed*' and '*employee*' are to be construed accordingly.

[*SI 2008 No 409, Sch 5 para 5; SI 2008 No 410, Sch 7 para 10*].

20.14 Employee involvement

Unless the company is subject to the small companies regime (see **5.2** and **5.3** Accounts: Small Companies), where the average number of persons employed by the company during the financial year exceeded 250 (calculated as in **20.14** but see also below), the directors' report must contain a statement describing what action has been taken during the financial year to introduce, maintain or develop arrangements aimed at

- providing 'employees' systematically with information on matters concerning them as employees;
- consulting employees or their representatives on a regular basis so that their views can be taken into account in making decisions likely to affect their interests;
- encouraging the involvement of employees in the company's performance through a share scheme or by some other means; and
- achieving a common awareness on the part of all employees of the financial and economic factors affecting the performance of the company.

'Employee' does not include a person employed to work wholly or mainly outside the UK and in calculating the average number of persons employed, any such person is to be ignored.

[*SI 2008 No 410, Sch 7 para 11*].

20.15 Policy and practice on the payment of creditors

The report of a company which at any time in the financial year

- was a public company, or
- did not qualify as a small company under *CA 2006, s 382* (see **5.2 Accounts: Small Companies**) or a medium-sized company under *CA 2006, s 465* (see **4.2 Accounts: Medium-Sized Companies**) in relation to that year and was at any time within the year a member of a group of which the parent company was a public company

must state with respect to the next following financial year:

(a) Whether, in respect of some or all of its 'suppliers', it is the company's policy to

- follow any code or standard on payment practice and, if so, the name of the code or standard, and the place where information about it and copies of it can be obtained;
- settle the terms of payment with those suppliers when agreeing the terms of each transaction;
- ensure that those suppliers are made aware of the terms of payment; and
- abide by the terms of payment.

(b) Where the company's policy does not fall within (*a*) above in respect of some or all of its suppliers, what its policy is with respect to payments to those suppliers.

(c) If the company's policy is different for different suppliers or classes of suppliers, the identity of the suppliers or classes of suppliers to which the different policies apply.

(d) The number of days calculated by the formula

$$F \times X \div Y$$

where

F = the number of days in the financial year

X = the aggregate of the amounts which were owed to trade creditors at the end of the year. This is either

(i) where the accounts are prepared in accordance with the balance sheet formats in *SI 2008 No 410, Sch 1* (see **3.4 Accounts: Large Companies**), the amount shown under the heading corresponding to item E.4 (trade creditors) in Format 1 or, as the case may be, item C.4 (trade creditors) in Format 2; or

(ii) where the accounts are prepared in accordance with *SI 2008 No 410, Sch 2* or *3* (banking and insurance companies) or the company's accounts are IAS accounts, the amount which would be shown under the heading corresponding to item E.4 in Format 1 if the accounts were prepared in accordance with *SI 2008 No 410, Sch 1*.

Y = the aggregate of the amounts invoiced by suppliers to the company during the year.

For these purposes, a person is a '*supplier*' of the company at any time if he is owed an amount in respect of goods or services supplied and that amount would be included under the heading corresponding to item E.4 (trade creditors) if accounts were prepared at that time under balance sheet Format 1 in **3.4**: ACCOUNTS: LARGE COMPANIES). For the purposes of (a) to (c) above, suppliers include any persons who are or may become its suppliers.

This requirement is removed for financial years ending on or after 30 September 2013

[*SI 2008 No 410, Sch 7 para 12*; *SI 2013 No 1970, Reg 7(3)(d)*].

20.16 Companies whose securities are admitted to trading on a regulated market

(1) *Control and share structures, etc*

If a the company has 'securities' carrying 'voting rights' admitted to trading on a regulated market at the end of a financial year, the directors' report must contain detailed information, by reference to the end of that year, on the following matters, together with any necessary explanatory material.

(a) The structure of the company's capital, including in particular

(i) the rights and obligations attaching to the shares or, as the case may be, to each class of shares in the company; and

(ii) where there are two or more such classes, the percentage of the total share capital represented by each class.

For these purposes, a company's capital includes any securities in the company that are not admitted to trading on a regulated market.

(b) Any restrictions on the transfer of 'securities' in the company, including in particular

(i) limitations on the holding of securities; and

(ii) requirements to obtain the approval of the company, or of other holders of securities in the company, for a transfer of securities.

(c) In the case of each person with a significant direct or indirect holding of securities in the company, such details as are known to the company of

(i) the identity of the person;

(ii) the size of the holding; and

(iii) the nature of the holding.

For these purposes, a person has an indirect holding of securities if they are held on his behalf or he is able to secure that rights carried by the securities are exercised in accordance with his wishes.

(d) In the case of each person who holds securities carrying special rights with regard to control of the company

(i) the identity of the person; and

(ii) the nature of the rights.

(e) Where

(i) the company has an employees' share scheme, and

(ii) shares to which the scheme relates have rights with regard to control of the company that are not exercisable directly by the employees, how those rights are exercisable

(f) Any restrictions on 'voting rights', including in particular

(i) limitations on voting rights of holders of a given percentage or number of votes;

(ii) deadlines for exercising voting rights; and

(iii) arrangements by which, with the company's co-operation, financial rights carried by securities are held by a person other than the holder of the securities.

(g) Any agreements between holders of securities that are known to the company and may result in restrictions on the transfer of securities or on voting rights.

(h) Any rules that the company has about

(i) appointment and replacement of directors; or

(ii) amendment of the company's articles of association

(i) The powers of the company's directors, including in particular any powers in relation to the issuing or buying back by the company of its shares.

(j) Any significant agreements to which the company is a party that take effect, alter or terminate upon a change of control of the company following a 'takeover bid', and the effects of any such agreements.

This does not apply to an agreement if

(i) disclosure of the agreement would be seriously prejudicial to the company; and

(ii) the company is not under any other obligation to disclose it.

(k) Any agreements between the company and its directors or employees providing for compensation for loss of office or employment (whether through resignation, purported redundancy or otherwise) that occurs because of a 'takeover bid'.

'*Securities*' means shares or debentures.

'*Takeover bid*' has the same meaning as in the *Takeovers Directive* (*Directive 2004/25/EC*).

'*Voting rights*' means rights to vote at general meetings of the company in question, including rights that arise only in certain circumstances.

[*SI 2008 No 410, Sch 7 paras 13, 14*].

(2) *Corporate governance statements*

A company whose transferable securities are admitted to trading must either

- include a corporate governance statement as a specific section of its directors' report;
- set out the required information in a separate report published together with, and in the same manner as, its annual report; or
- set out the required information by means of a reference in its directors' report to where such document is publicly available on the issuer's website.

20.16 Directors' and Strategic Reports

See **33.73** Public and Listed Companies for full details.

20.17 Quoted companies- disclosure of greenhouse gas emissions

In the case of a quoted company the directors' report must state

(a) the annual quantity of emissions in tonnes of carbon dioxide equivalent from activities for which that company is responsible including the combustion of fuel and the operation of any facility.

(b) the annual quantity of emissions in tonnes of carbon dioxide equivalent resulting from the purchase of electricity, heat, steam or cooling by the company for its own use.

both only apply to the extent that it is practical for the company to obtain the information in question. Where it is not practical, the report must state what information is not included and why.

(c) the methodologies used to calculate the information disclosed above.

(d) at least one ratio which expresses the quoted company's annual emissions in relation to a quantifiable factor associated with the company's activities.

With the exception of the first year for which the directors' report contains the information required by (a), (b) and (d), the report must state not only the information required by (a), (b) and (d) but also that information as disclosed in the report for the preceding financial year.

(e) if the period for which it is reporting the information required by (a) and (b) is different to the period in respect of which the directors' report is prepared.

"Emissions" means emissions into the atmosphere of a greenhouse gas as defined in Climate Change Act 2008, s 92 which are attributable to human activity.

"Tonne of carbon dioxide equivalent" has the meaning given in Climate Change Act 2008, s 93(2).

[*SI 2013 No 1970, Reg 15*]

20.18 APPROVAL AND SIGNING

The directors' report and *strategic report* (see **2.4**) must be approved by the board of directors and signed on behalf of the board by a director or the secretary of the company.

Small companies. If in preparing the report advantage is taken of the 'small companies exemption', it must contain a statement to that effect in a prominent position above the signature.

A company is entitled to '*small companies exemption*' in relation to the directors' report for a financial year if

- it is entitled to prepare accounts for the year in accordance with the small companies regime; or
- it would be so entitled but for being or having been a member of an ineligible group.

See **5.2** and **5.3** Accounts: Small Companies.

Offences. If a directors' report is approved that does not comply with the requirements of *CA 2006*, every director of the company who

- knew that it did not comply, or was reckless as to whether it complied, and
- failed to take reasonable steps to secure compliance with those requirements or, as the case may be, to prevent the report from being approved,

commits an offence.

A person guilty of such an offence is liable (i) on conviction on indictment, to a fine; and (ii) on summary conviction, to a fine not exceeding the statutory maximum. See **29.1** Offences and Penalties for the statutory maximum.

[*CA 2006, s 419; SI 2008 No 393, Reg 6*].

See **2.10** Accounts: General for the requirement to file a copy of the report with the Registrar of Companies.

20.19 DEFECTIVE REPORTS

In certain circumstances, a directors' report or strategic report may be replaced or partially revised because it was originally defective. See **2.12** Accounts: General. The provisions of *CA 2006* as to the matters to be included in a strategic report or directors' report, apply to a revised report as if the revised report was prepared and approved by the directors of the company as at the date of the original report

[*SI 2008 No 373, Reg 3(4); SI 2013 No 2224, Reg 5*].

20.20 Approval and signature of revised reports

The requirement that a directors' report and *strategic report* must be approved by the board of directors and signed on its behalf by a director or secretary of the company (see **20.18**) also applies to any revised directors' report or strategic report, except that in the case of revision by supplementary note, it applies as if it required the signature to be on the supplementary note.

Where copies of the original directors' report or strategic report have already been sent out to members, laid before the company in general meeting in the case of a public company, or delivered to the Registrar of Companies, the directors must, before approving the revised report cause statements as to the following matters to be made in a prominent position in the revised report (or, in the case of revision by supplementary note, in that note).

(a) In the case of revision by replacement

- that the revised report replaces the original report for the financial year (specifying it);
- that it has been prepared as at the date of the original directors' report or strategic report and not at the date of revision and accordingly does not deal with any events between those dates;
- the respects in which the original directors' report or strategic report did not comply with the requirements of the *CA 2006*; and
- any significant amendments made as a result of remedying those defects.

(b) In the case of a revision by supplementary note

- that the note revises in certain respects the original directors' report or strategic report of the company and is to be treated as forming part of that report; and

- that the directors' report or strategic report has been revised as at the date of the original directors' report or strategic report (as the case may be) and not as at the date of the revision and accordingly does not deal with events between those dates.

The date of approval of the revised report must be stated on the face of the report (or supplementary note).

The penalty for failure to comply with these provisions is as in **20.18**.

[*SI 2008 No 373, Reg 5; SI 2013 No 2224, Reg 10*].

20.21 Effect of revision of report

Subject to the provisions of the *Companies (Revision of Defective Accounts and Reports) (Amendment) (No 2) Regulations 2013* (*SI 2013 No 2224*) when the directors approve a revised report, the provisions of *CA 2006* have effect as if, the revised report was, as from the date of its approval, the strategic report or the directors' report(as the case may be) in place of the original report. This applies in particular for the purposes of

- *CA 2006, ss 431, 432* (the right to demand copies of accounts, see **2.7 Accounts: General**); and
- *CA 2006, s 423* (persons entitled to receive copies, see **2.6 Accounts: General**), *CA 2006, s 437* (accounts, etc of public company to be laid before company in general meeting, see **2.9 Accounts: General**) and *CA 2006, s 441* (accounts, etc to be delivered to Registrar of Companies, see **2.10 Accounts: General**) if the requirements of those provisions have not been complied with prior to the date of revision.

[*SI 2008 No 373, Reg 11; SI 2013 No 2224, Reg 10*].

20.22 Publication of revised report

Where the directors have prepared a revised report and copies of the original report have been sent to any person under *CA 2006, s 423* (persons entitled to receive copies, see **2.6 Accounts: General**) or *CA 2006, s 146* (traded companies: nomination of persons to enjoy information rights, see **26.2 Members**), the directors must send to any such person

- in the case of a revision by replacement, a copy of the revised report, together with a copy of the auditor's report on that report; or
- in the case of revision by supplementary note, a copy of that note together with a copy of the auditor's report on the revised report.

This must be done not more than 28 days after the date of the revision (ie the date on which the revised report is approved by the directors).

The directors must also, not more than 28 days after the revision, send a copy of the revised report and auditor's report thereon to any person who is not entitled to receive a copy under the above provisions but who is, as at the date of revision,

(a) a member of the company,

(b) a holder of the company's debentures, or

(c) a person who is entitled to receive notice of general meetings unless the company would be entitled at that date to send to that person a strategic report and supplementary material.

The exceptions from the requirement to send copies of the annual accounts and reports in **2.6 Accounts: General** equally apply to sending out copies of the revised directors' report.

In default in complying with the above provisions, an offence is committed by each of the directors who approved the revised report. A person guilty of such an offence is liable (i) on conviction on indictment, to a fine; and (ii) on summary conviction, to a fine not exceeding the statutory maximum. See **29.1 Offences and Legal Proceedings** for the statutory maximum.

[*SI 2008 No 373, Reg 12; SI 2013 No 2224, Reg 11*].

20.23 Laying of revised report

Where the directors of a public company have prepared a revised directors' report and the original report has already been laid before the company in general meeting, a copy of the revised report, together with a copy of the auditor's report on that report, must be laid before the next general meeting of the company held after the date of revision at which annual accounts for a financial year are laid (unless they have already been laid before an earlier general meeting).

In default, every person who is a director of the company immediately before that annual general meeting commits an offence. A person guilty of such an offence is liable, on summary conviction, to a fine not exceeding level 5 on the standard scale and, for continued contravention, a daily default fine not exceeding one-tenth of level 5 on the standard scale. See **29.1 Offences and Legal Proceedings** for the standard scale. It is a defence for a person charged with such an offence to prove that he took all reasonable steps for securing that the requirements would be complied with before that annual general meeting; it is not a defence to prove that the revised report was not in fact prepared.

[*SI 2008 No 373, Reg 13*].

20.24 Delivery of revised report to the Registrar of Companies

Where the directors have prepared a revised directors' report and a copy of the original report has been delivered to the Registrar of Companies, the directors must, within 28 days of the date of revision, deliver to the Registrar

- in the case of a revision by replacement, a copy of the revised report, together with a copy of the auditor's report on that report; or
- in the case of a revision by supplementary note, a copy of that note, together with a copy of the auditor's report on the revised report.

CA 2006, ss 451 and *452* (offences and court order for default in filing accounts and reports, see **2.10 Accounts: General**) also apply to a failure to comply with the above requirements but as if the reference to 'the period for filing those accounts and reports' was a reference to the 28 day period above.

[*SI 2008 No 373, Reg 14*].

20.25 LIABILITY FOR FALSE OR MISLEADING STATEMENTS IN REPORTS

A director of a company is liable to compensate the company for any loss suffered by it as a result of

- any untrue or misleading statement, or
- the omission of anything required to be included

in a strategic report or directors' report or a summary financial statement so far as it is derived from that report. No liability arises in respect of a report or summary financial statement first sent out before 20 January 2007.

A director is so liable only if

- he knew the statement to be untrue or misleading or was reckless as to whether it was untrue or misleading; or
- he knew the omission to be dishonest concealment of a material fact.

No person can be subject to any liability to a person other than the company resulting from reliance, by that person or another, on information in a directors' report (or a summary financial statement so far as it is derived from that report). The reference to a person being 'subject to a liability' includes a reference to another person being entitled as against him to be granted any civil remedy or to rescind or repudiate an agreement.

The effect of this is that no persons (including directors) are liable to individual investors or third parties but auditors remain liable to the company for negligence in preparing their own report.

The above provisions do not affect liability for a civil penalty or liability for a criminal offence.

[*CA 2006, s 463*; *SI 2013 No 1970, Schedule, para 17*].

21 Dissolution and Restoration

21.1	**Registrar of Company's power to strike off a defunct company**	21.9	**Administrative restoration to the register**
21.2	**Voluntary striking off**	21.10	**Restoration to the register by the court**
21.3	Circumstances in which application cannot be made	21.11	**Company's name on restoration**
21.4	Withdrawal of application	21.12	**Effect of restoration where property has vested as *bona vacantia***
21.5	Notification of members, employees, etc	APPENDIX	**Provisions applying before 1 October 2009**
21.6	Objections to proposed striking off and dissolution		
21.7	**Property of dissolved company**		
21.8	Disclaimer of property vesting as *bona vacantia*		

General note. The provisions in this chapter apply, unless otherwise stated, with effect from 1 October 2009. For the provisions applying before that date, see the Appendix at the end of this chapter.

21.1 REGISTRAR OF COMPANY'S POWER TO STRIKE OFF A DEFUNCT COMPANY

If the Registrar of Companies has reasonable cause to believe that a company is not carrying on business or in operation, he may send to the company by post a letter inquiring whether it is carrying on business or in operation. [*CA 2006, s 1000(1)*]. He may take this action, for example, because he has not received documents from the company which should have been delivered to him (eg annual returns and accounts) or mail sent to the registered office is returned undelivered or the company has no directors (Companies House Guidance Booklet GP4 Strike-off, Dissolution and Restoration, Chapter 2 para 1).

If the Registrar of Companies does not, within one month of sending that letter, receive any answer to it, he must within 14 days of the end of that month send to the company by post a registered letter referring to the first letter, and stating that

- no answer has been received to the first letter; and
- if an answer is not received to the second letter within one month from its date, a notice will be published in the *Gazette* with a view to striking the company's name off the register.

If the Registrar of Companies

- receives an answer to the effect that the company is not carrying on a business or in operation, or
- does not receive an answer to the second letter within one month,

a notice will be published in the *Gazette*, and sent to the company by post, to the effect that not less than three months from the date of the notice, the company will be struck off the register and the company will be dissolved unless cause is shown to the contrary.

At the expiration of the three months, unless cause to the contrary has been shown, the Registrar of Companies may strike the company name off the register and publish notice of this in the *Gazette*. On publication, the company is dissolved although

- the liability (if any) of every director, managing officer and member of the company continues and may be enforced as if the company had not been dissolved; and
- the power of the court to wind up a company whose name has been struck off the register is not affected.

[*CA 2006, s 1000(2)–(7)*].

Duty to act in the case of a company being wound up. If, in a case where a company is being wound up,

- the Registrar of Companies has reasonable cause to believe that no liquidator is acting or that the affairs of the company are fully wound up, and
- the returns required to be made by the liquidator have not been made for a period of six consecutive months,

the Registrar of Companies must publish in the *Gazette*, and send to the company or the liquidator (if any), a notice to the effect that, at the expiration of three months from the date of the notice, the name of the company mentioned in it will be struck off the register and the company will be dissolved unless cause is shown to the contrary. At the expiration of the three months, unless cause to the contrary has been previously shown, the Registrar of Companies may strike the company name off the register and publish notice of this in the *Gazette*. On publication, the company is dissolved although

- the liability (if any) of every director, managing officer and member of the company continues and may be enforced as if the company had not been dissolved; and
- the power of the court to wind up a company whose name has been struck off the register is not affected.

[*CA 2006, s 1001*].

Addresses for notices, etc. A letter or notice to be sent to a company may be addressed

- to the company at its registered office; or
- if no office has been registered, to the care of some officer of the company; or
- if there is no such officer whose name and address is known to the Registrar of Companies, to each of the persons who subscribed the memorandum.

A notice to a liquidator may be addressed to him at his last known place of business.

[*CA 2006, s 1002*].

Even where the company is struck off the register and dissolved, the company to be restored to the register in certain circumstances (see **21.9** and **21.10**).

21.2 VOLUNTARY STRIKING OFF

Subject to the restrictions in **21.3**, a company (that is any company, unlike under *CA 1985* where only private companies could make such an application) may apply to the Registrar of Companies for the company's name to be struck off the register. The application must be made on its behalf by the directors (or a majority of them) and must contain a declaration (by the directors making the application on behalf of the company) that neither *CA 2006, s 1004* nor *CA 2006, s 1005* prevents the application from being made (see **21.3**).

[*SI 2009 No 1803, Reg 2*].

Application might be made, for example, where

- a company is no longer required because the active directors wish to retire;
- the company is a subsidiary whose name is no longer needed; or
- the company was set up to exploit an idea that turned out not to be feasible.

The procedure is not an alternative to formal insolvency proceedings where these are appropriate as creditors are likely to prevent the striking off (see **21.5** and **21.6**).

(Companies House Guidance Booklet GP4 Strike-off, Dissolution and Restoration, Chapter 1 para 1).

On receiving the request, the Registrar of Companies must publish a notice in the *Gazette* stating that he may exercise the power under these provisions in relation to the company, and inviting any person to show cause why that should not be done. If no objection is received, after the expiration of three months from the publication of the notice, the Registrar must publish a further notice in the Gazette of the company's name having been struck off. On the publication of the notice in the *Gazette*, the company is dissolved although

- the liability (if any) of every director, managing officer and member of the company continues and may be enforced as if the company had not been dissolved; and
- the power of the court to wind up a company whose name has been struck off the register is not affected.

[*CA 2006, s 1003(3)–(6)*].

Even where the company is struck off the register and dissolved, the company to be restored to the register in certain circumstances (see **21.9** and **21.10**).

21.3 Circumstances in which application cannot be made

An application cannot be made under **21.2** on behalf of a company in the following circumstances.

(a) If at any time in the previous three months, the company has

(i) changed its name;

(ii) traded or otherwise carried on business;

(iii) made a disposal for value of property or rights that, immediately before ceasing to trade or otherwise carry on business, it held for disposal for gain in the normal course of trading or otherwise carrying on business. For example, a company in business to sell apples could not continue selling apples during the 3 month period but it could sell the truck it once used to deliver the apples or the warehouse where they were stored; Or

(iv) engaged in any other activity except one necessary or expedient for the purposes of making an application to strike off the company (or deciding whether to do so), concluding the affairs of the company or complying with any statutory requirement.

(b) If at the time of the application the company is the subject, or proposed subject of:

- a *section 895* (*CA 2006*) scheme (that is a compromise or arrangement with its creditors or members)
- any insolvency proceedings such as a voluntary arrangement
- an administration order
- an interim moratorium on proceedings where application to the court for an administration order has been made or notice of intention to appoint administrator has been filed, a winding up, receivership or administration by a judicial factor.

[*CA 2006, ss 1004(1)(2), 1005(1)–(3)* and Companies House Guidance Booklet GP4 Chapter 1 Para 2].

Penalties. It is an offence for a person to make an application in contravention of the above provisions. A person guilty of such an offence is liable (i) on conviction on indictment, to a fine; and (ii) on summary conviction, to a fine not exceeding the statutory maximum. See **29.1 Offences and Legal Proceedings** for the statutory maximum.

In proceedings for such an offence it is a defence for the accused to prove that he did not know, and could not reasonably have known, of the existence of the facts that led to the contravention.

[*CA 2006, ss 1004(5)–(7), 1005(4)–(6)*].

21.4 Withdrawal of application

A director of a company which has made an application under **21.2** must secure that the application is withdrawn forthwith (by giving notice to the Registrar of Companies) where, at anytime on or after the day on which the application is made and before it is finally dealt with or withdrawn:

(a) The company

- changes its name;
- trades or otherwise carries on business;
- makes a disposal for value of property or rights other than those which it was necessary or expedient for it to hold for the purposes of making, or proceeding with, the application; or
- engages in any activity except one necessary or expedient for the purposes of
  - (i) making, or proceeding with, the application;
  - (ii) concluding affairs of the company that are outstanding because of what has been necessary or expedient for the purposes of making, or proceeding with, the application; or
  - (iii) complying with any statutory requirement.

For theses purposes, a company is not treated as trading or otherwise carrying on business by virtue only of the fact that it makes a payment in respect of a liability incurred in the course of trading or otherwise carrying on business.

(b) An application to the court under *CA 2006, Pt 26* is made on behalf of the company for the sanctioning of a compromise or arrangement.

(c) A voluntary arrangement in relation to the company is proposed.

(d) An application to the court for an administration order in respect of the company is made.

(e) An administrator is appointed in respect of the company or a copy of notice of intention to appoint an administrator of the company is filed with the court.

(f) Any of the circumstances in which the company can be voluntarily wound up arise.

(g) A petition is presented for winding up of the company by the court.

(h) A receiver or manager of the company's property is appointed.

(i) A judicial factor is appointed to administer the company's estate.

Penalties. A person who fails to perform the duty imposed on him under the above provisions commits an offence. A person guilty of such an offence is liable (i) on conviction on indictment, to a fine; and (ii) on summary conviction, to a fine not exceeding the statutory maximum. See **29.1 Offences and Legal Proceedings** for the statutory maximum.

In proceedings for such an offence it is a defence for the accused to prove that at the time of the failure he was not aware of the fact that the company had made an application for voluntary striking off or that he took all reasonable steps to perform the duty.

[*CA 2006, ss 1009, 1010*].

21.5 Notification of members, employees, etc

A person who makes an application for a voluntary striking of on behalf of a company must secure that, within seven days from the date of application, a copy of it is given to every person who on that date is

(a) a member of the company;

(b) an employee of the company;

(c) a creditor of the company (including a contingent or prospective creditor);

(d) a director of the company (other than one who was a party to the application); or

(e) a manager or trustee of any employee pension fund.

Additionally, where at any time after the date of the application and before the application is finally dealt with or withdrawn, a new person falls within (*a*)–(*e*) above, a person who is a director of the company at that time must secure that a copy of the application is given to him within seven days.

The duty imposed under these provisions ceases to apply if the application is withdrawn within the seven-day period.

[*CA 2006, ss 1006(1)–(3), 1007(1)–(3), 1011*].

Service of documents. For the above purposes, a document is treated as given to a person if it is delivered to him, left at his 'proper address', or sent by post to him at that address. The '*proper address*' of a person is

- in the case of a firm incorporated or formed in the UK, its registered or principal office;
- in the case of a firm incorporated or formed outside the UK
  - (i) if it has a place of business in the UK, its principal office in the UK; or
  - (ii) if it does not have a place of business in the UK, its registered or principal office; and
- in the case of an individual, his last known address.

In the case of a creditor of the company a document is treated as given to him if it is left or sent by post to him

- at the place of business of his with which the company has had dealings by virtue of which he is a creditor of the company; or
- if there is more than one such place of business, at each of them.

[*CA 2006, s 1008*].

Penalties. A person who fails to perform the duty imposed on him by the above provisions commits an offence. A person guilty of such an offence is liable (i) on conviction on indictment, to a fine; and (ii) on summary conviction, to a fine not exceeding the statutory maximum. See **29.1** OFFENCES AND LEGAL PROCEEDINGS for the statutory maximum.

A person commits an aggravated offence if he fails to perform the duty imposed on him by the above provisions with the intention of concealing the making of the application from the person concerned. A person guilty of an aggravated offence is liable (i) on conviction on indictment, to imprisonment for a term not exceeding seven years or a fine (or both); and (ii) on summary conviction, to imprisonment for a term not exceeding 12 months (6 months in Scotland and Northern Ireland) or to a fine not exceeding the statutory maximum (or both).

In proceedings for an offence under these provisions (aggravated or otherwise) it is a defence for the accused to prove that

- he took all reasonable steps to perform the duty; or
- in the case of a duty arising after the making of the application, that at the time of the failure he was not aware of the fact that the company had made an application.

[*CA 2006, ss 1006(4)–(7), 1007(4)–(7)*].

21.6 Objections to proposed striking off and dissolution

Any interested party may object to the striking off and dissolution of a company. Any objections should be in writing and sent to the Registrar of Companies, together with supporting evidence (eg copies of invoices showing that the company is trading). Examples of grounds for objecting are that

- the company has broken any of the conditions of its application;
- the directors have not informed interested parties;
- any of the prescribed information given is false;

- some form of action is being taken, or is pending, to recover any moneys owed (eg a winding-up petition or action in the small claims court);
- other legal action is being taken against the company; or
- the directors have wrongfully traded or committed a tax fraud or some other offence.

(Companies House Guidance Booklet GP4 Strike-off, Dissolution and Restoration, Chapter 1 para 10 and 11).

21.7 PROPERTY OF DISSOLVED COMPANY

The provisions in this paragraph and **21.8** apply in relation to the property of a company dissolved on or after 1 October 2009 whether or not the company is dissolved under the Registrar's powers (see **21.1**) or is dissolved voluntarily (see **21.2**). They also apply to the property of a company dissolved before 1st October 2009 if at that date—

(a) no period has begun to run in relation to the property under *section 656(3)(a)* or *(b)* of the *1985 Act* or *article 607(3)(a)* or *(b)* of the *1986 Order* (period within which notice of disclaimer must be executed), and

(b) the right to disclaim has not ceased to be exercisable in relation to the property by virtue of *section 656(2)* of the *1985 Act* or *article 607(2)* of the *1986 Order* (waiver of right to disclaim).

[*SI 2008 No 2860, Sch 2 para 88* and *SI 2009 No 2476*].

Property of the dissolved company to be *bona vacantia*. All property and rights whatsoever vested in or held on trust for the company immediately before its dissolution (including leasehold property, but not property held on trust for another person) are deemed to be *bona vacantia* and accordingly

- if the company's registered office is in Lancashire, belong to the Duchy of Lancaster;
- if the registered office is in Cornwall, belong to the Duke of Cornwall; and
- in all other cases, belong to the Crown.

The company's bank account will be frozen and any credit balance passed to the Crown.

Except as provided for in **21.12**, the above has effect subject to any possible restoration of the company to the register under **21.9** and **21.10**.
[*CA 2006, s 1012*].

Enquiries regarding *bona vacantia* should be addressed, as appropriate, to

In England and Wales

If the company's registered office is in Lancashire:

The Solicitor to the Duchy of Lancaster
66 Lincoln's Inn Fields
London WC2A 3LH

If the company's registered office is in Cornwall or the Isles of Scilly:

The Solicitor to the Duke of Cornwall
66 Lincoln's Inn Fields
London WC2A 3LH

In all other cases:

The Treasury Solicitor 's Department
Bona Vacantia Division (BVD)
PO Box 70165
London WC1A 9HG

In Scotland

The Queen's and Lord Treasurer's Remembrancer (QLTR Unit)
Crown Office
Unit 5
14a South St Andrews Street
Edinburgh EH2 2AZ

In Northern Ireland

The Crown Solicitor
Royal Courts of Justice
Chichester Street
Belfast BT1 3JY

(Companies House Guidance Booklet GP4, Chapter 2 para 4).

21.8 Disclaimer of property vesting as bona vacantia

Where property vests in the Crown as *bona vacantia*, the Crown's title to it may be disclaimed by a notice signed by the Crown representative. The right to exercise a notice of disclaimer may be waived by or on behalf of the Crown either expressly or by taking possession.

Any notice of disclaimer must be executed within three years after the date on which the fact that the property may have vested in the Crown first comes to the notice of the Crown representative. But if ownership of the property is not established at that date, the relevant period runs from the end of the period reasonably necessary for the Crown representative to establish the ownership of the property. If an application in writing is made to the Crown representative by a person interested in the property requiring him to decide whether he will or will not disclaim, any notice of disclaimer must be executed within 12 months after the making of the application or such further period as may be allowed by the court.

Any notice of disclaimer must be delivered to the Registrar of Companies and retained and registered by him. Copies of it must be published in the *Gazette* and sent to any persons who have give notice to the Crown representative that they claim to be interested in the property.

The above provisions similarly apply to property vesting in the Duchy of Lancaster or the Duke of Cornwall.

[*CA 2006, s 1013*].

Where notice of disclaimer is executed under the above provisions, the property concerned is deemed not to have vested in the Crown, Duchy of Lancaster or Duke of Cornwall as the case may be. [*CA 2006, s 1014*].

(1) **Effect of Crown disclaimer: England and Wales and Northern Ireland**

(a) *General effect of disclaimer*

The Crown's disclaimer operates so as to terminate, as from the date of the disclaimer, the rights, interests and liabilities of the company in or in respect of the property disclaimed. It does not, except so far as is necessary for the purpose of releasing the company from any liability, affect the rights or liabilities of any other person.

(b) *Disclaimer of leaseholds*

The disclaimer of any property of a leasehold character does not take effect unless a copy of the disclaimer has been served (so far as the Crown representative is aware of their addresses) on every person claiming under the company as underlessee or mortgagee, and either

(i) no application under (*c*) below is made with respect to that property within 14 days of the day on which the last notice under this paragraph was served; or

(ii) where such an application has been made, the court directs that the disclaimer shall take effect.

Where the court gives a direction under (ii) above, it may also, instead of or in addition to any order it makes under (*d*) below, make such order as it thinks fit with respect to fixtures, tenant's improvements and other matters arising out of the lease.

(c) *Power of court to make vesting order*

The court may, on application by a person who

(i) claims an interest in the disclaimed property, or

(ii) is under a liability in respect of the disclaimed property that is not discharged by the disclaimer,

make an order for the vesting of the disclaimed property in, or its delivery, to a person entitled to it (or a trustee for such a person). It may also make such an order to a person subject to a liability as in (ii) above (or a trustee for such a person) but only where it appears to the court that it would be just to do so for the purpose of compensating that person in respect of the disclaimer.

On a vesting order being made, the property comprised in it vests in the person named without conveyance, assignment or transfer.

(d) *Protection of persons holding under a lease*

The court must not make an order under (*c*) above vesting property of a leasehold nature in a person claiming under the company as underlessee or mortgagee except on terms making that person

(i) subject to the same liabilities and obligations as those to which the company was subject under the lease; or

(ii) if the court thinks fit, subject to the same liabilities and obligations as if the lease had been assigned to him.

A person claiming under the company as underlessee or mortgagee who declines to accept a vesting order on such terms is excluded from all interest in the property.

If there is no person claiming under the company who is willing to accept an order on such terms, the court has power to vest the company's estate and interest in the property in any person who is liable (whether personally or in a representative character, and whether alone or jointly with the company) to perform the lessee's covenants in the lease. The court may vest that estate and interest in such a person freed and discharged from all estates, incumbrances and interests created by the company.

(e) *Land subject to rentcharge*

Where, in consequence of the disclaimer, land that is subject to a rentcharge vests in any person, neither he nor his successors in title are subject to any personal liability in respect of sums becoming due under the rentcharge, except sums becoming due after he, or some person claiming under or through him, has taken possession or control of the land or has entered into occupation of it.

[*CA 2006, ss 1015–1019*].

(2) **Effect of Crown disclaimer: Scotland**

(a) *General effect of disclaimer*

The Crown's disclaimer operates to determine, as from the date of the disclaimer, the rights, interests and liabilities of the company, and the property of the company, in or in respect of the property disclaimed. It does not (except so far as is necessary for the purpose of releasing the company and its property from liability) affect the rights or liabilities of any other person.

(b) *Power of court to make vesting order*

The court may, on application by a person who

(i) claims an interest in disclaimed property, or

(ii) is under a liability not discharged by *CA 2006* in respect of disclaimed property,

make an order for the vesting of the property in or its delivery to any persons entitled to it, or to whom it may seem just that the property should be delivered by way of compensation for such liability, or a trustee for him.

On a vesting order being made, the property comprised in it vests in the person named without conveyance or assignment for that purposes.

(c) *Protection of persons holding under a lease*

Where the property disclaimed is held under a lease in favour of a person claiming under the company (whether as sub-lessee or as creditor in a duly registered or, as the case may be, recorded heritable security over a lease), the vesting order must make that person subject

(i) to the same liabilities and obligations as those to which the company was subject under the lease in respect of the property; or

(ii) if the court thinks fit, only to the same liabilities and obligations as if the lease had been assigned to him.

A sub-lessee or creditor declining to accept a vesting order on such terms is excluded from all interest in and security over the property.

If there is no person claiming under the company who is willing to accept an order on such terms, the court has power to vest the company's estate and interest in the property in any person liable (either personally or in a representative character, and either alone or jointly with the company) to perform the lessee's obligations under the lease. The court may vest that estate and interest in such a person freed and discharged from all interests, rights and obligations created by the company in the lease or in relation to the lease.

[*CA 2006, ss 1020–1022*]

Liability for rentcharge on company's land in England and Wales and Northern Ireland. Where, on the dissolution, land in England and Wales or Northern Ireland that is subject to a rentcharge vests by operation of the law in the Crown or any other person (the '*proprietor*'), neither the proprietor nor his successors in title are subject to any personal liability in respect of sums becoming due under the rentcharge, except sums becoming due after the proprietor, or some person claiming under or through him, has taken possession or control of the land or has entered into occupation of it.

[*CA 2006, s 1020*].

21.9 ADMINISTRATIVE RESTORATION TO THE REGISTER

An application may be made, by a former director or former member of the company, to the Registrar of Companies to restore to the register a company that has been struck off the register under **21.1** (**Power of the registrar to strike off defunct companies**).

It follows that a company cannot be restored under this procedure if the company was struck off voluntarily under *CA 2006, s 652A* or *CA 2006, s 1004* and *s 1005* (see **21.2**) Such an application may be made whether or not the company has in consequence been dissolved. Any application must be made within six years from the date of the dissolution of the company (an application being made when it is received by the Registrar of Companies).

Procedure. On an application being made (Form RT01), the Registrar of Companies must restore the company to the register if, and only if, the following conditions are met.

- The company was carrying on business or in operation at the time of its striking off.

- If any property or right previously vested in or held on trust for the company has vested as *bona vacantia*, the Crown representative has signified to the Registrar of Companies in writing consent to the company's restoration to the register.

  It is the applicant's responsibility to obtain that consent and to pay any costs (in Scotland, expenses) of the Crown representative

(i) in dealing with the property during the period of dissolution, or

(ii) in connection with the proceedings on the application,

that may be demanded as a condition of giving consent. Companies House refer to this consent as a *bona vacantia* waiver letter.

- The applicant has

(i) delivered to the Registrar of Companies such documents relating to the company as are necessary to bring up-to-date the records kept by the Registrar of Companies, together with form RTO1 and the fee payable (for which see **Appendix 3 Companies House fees**). The most common cause for rejected applications is lack of the necessary information, and

(ii) paid any civil penalty for failure to deliver accounts under *CA 2006, s 453* (see **2.10 Accounts: General**) or corresponding earlier provisions that were outstanding at the date of dissolution or striking off.

Statement of compliance. An application must be accompanied by a statement of compliance, ie a statement that

- the person making the application has standing to apply (ie was a former director or member of the company); and
- the requirements for administrative restoration above are met.

The registrar of Companies may accept the statement of compliance as sufficient evidence of those matters.

Decision of the Registrar of Companies. The Registrar of Companies must give notice of the decision to the applicant. If the decision is that the company should be restored to the register, the restoration takes effect as from the date that notice is sent It can take up to ten days from the receipt by Companies House of the application to restore the company. No same day service for administrative restoration is available. The Registrar of Companies must then enter on the register a note of the date as from which the company's restoration to the register takes effect, and publish notice of the restoration in the Gazette. The notice must state

- the name of the company or, if the company is restored to the register under a different name (see **21.11**), that name and its former name;
- the company's registered number; and
- the date from which the restoration takes effect.

Effect of administrative restoration. The general effect of administrative restoration to the register is that the company is deemed to have continued in existence as if it had not been dissolved or struck off the register. The company is not liable to a civil penalty for failure to deliver accounts under *CA 2006, s 453* (see **2.10 Accounts: General**) or corresponding earlier provisions for a financial year in relation to which the period for filing accounts and reports ended

- after the date of dissolution or striking off; and
- before the restoration of the company to the register.

The court may give such directions and make such provision as seems just for placing the company and all other persons in the same position (as nearly as may be) as if the company had not been dissolved or struck off the register. An application to the court for such directions or provision may be made any time within three years after the date of restoration of the company to the register.

[*CA 2006, ss 1024–1028*].

21.10 RESTORATION TO THE REGISTER BY THE COURT

An application may be made to the court by any of the persons listed below to restore to the register a company that has been

- dissolved after winding up or following administration; or
- struck off the register under 21.1 (POWER TO STRIKE OFF A DEFUNCT COMPANY) or 21.2 (VOLUNTARY STRIKE OFF) (whether or not the company has in consequence also been dissolved).

Such an application may be made by

- the Secretary of State;
- any former director of the company;
- any person having an interest in land in which the company had a superior or derivative interest;
- any person having an interest in land or other property that was subject to rights vested in the company or that was benefited by obligations owed by the company;
- any person who, but for the company's dissolution, would have been in a contractual relationship with it;
- any person with a potential legal claim against the company;
- any manager or trustee of a pension fund established for the benefit of employees of the company;
- any former member of the company (or the personal representatives of such a person);
- any person who was a creditor of the company at the time of its striking off or dissolution;
- any former liquidator of the company; or
- any other person appearing to the court to have an interest in the matter.

When application to the court may be made.

(1) An application to the court for restoration of a company to the register may be made at any time for the purpose of bringing proceedings against the company for 'damages for personal injury'. No order can be made on such an application if it appears to the court that the proceedings would fail by virtue of any enactment as to the time within which proceedings must be brought. But in making that decision, the court must have regard to its power to direct that the period between the dissolution (or striking off) of the company and the making of the order is not to count for the purposes of any such enactment.

'*Personal injury*' includes any disease and any impairment of a person's physical or mental condition and '*damages for personal injury*' include

(i) any sum in respect of funeral expenses claimed by virtue of *Law Reform (Miscellaneous Provisions) Act 1934, s 1(2)(c)* or *Law Reform (Miscellaneous Provisions) Act (Northern Ireland) 1937, s 14(2)(c)*; and

(ii) damages under *Fatal Accidents Act 1976*, *Damages (Scotland) Act 1976* or *Fatal Accidents (Northern Ireland) Order 1977*.

(2) In any other case an application to the court for restoration of a company to the register may not be made after the end of the period of six years from the date of the dissolution of the company, except that where

(i) the company has been struck off the register under **21.1**,

(ii) an application for administrative restoration under **21.9** has been made within the time allowed for making such an application, and

(iii) the Registrar of Companies has refused the application,

an application to the court may be made within 28 days of notice of the Registrar's decision being issued, even if the period of six years has expired.

Decision of the court. The court may order the restoration of the company to the register if

- the company was struck off the register under **21.1** and the company was, at the time of the striking off, carrying on business or in operation;
- the company was struck off the register under **21.2** and any of the requirements of **21.3** to **21.5** was not complied with; and
- in any other case, the court considers it just to do so.

If the court orders restoration of the company to the register, the restoration takes effect on a copy of the court's order being delivered to the Registrar of Companies. The Registrar of Companies must then publish notice of the restoration in the Gazette. The notice must state

- the name of the company or, if the company is restored to the register under a different name (see **21.11**), that name and its former name;
- the company's registered number; and
- the date from which the restoration takes effect.

Effect of court order for restoration to the register. The general effect of a court order for restoration to the register is that the company is deemed to have continued in existence as if it had not been dissolved or struck off the register. The company is not liable to a civil penalty for failure to deliver accounts under *CA 2006, s 453* (see **2.10 ACCOUNTS: GENERAL**) or corresponding earlier provisions for a financial year in relation to which the period for filing accounts and reports ended

- after the date of dissolution or striking off, and
- before the restoration of the company to the register.

The court may give such directions and make such provision as seems just for placing the company and all other persons in the same position (as nearly as may be) as if the company had not been dissolved or struck off the register. The court may also give directions as to

- the delivery to the Registrar of Companies of such documents relating to the company as are necessary to bring up-to-date the records kept by the Registrar of Companies;

- the payment of the costs (in Scotland, expenses) of the Registrar of Companies in connection with the proceedings for the restoration of the company to the register; and
- where any property or right previously vested in or held on trust for the company has vested as *bona vacantia*, the payment of the costs (in Scotland, expenses) of the Crown representative

  (i) in dealing with the property during the period of dissolution; or

  (ii) in connection with the proceedings on the application.

[*CA 2006, ss 1029–1032*].

For details of where to apply for a court order see Companies House Guidance Booklet GP4 Chapter 3, paragraph 3.

Transitional provisions.

(a) The above provisions apply whether the company was dissolved or struck off the register before, on or after 1 October 2009.

(b) Where the company was dissolved or struck off the register before 1 October 2009

- no application may be made under the above provisions if an application in respect of the same dissolution or striking off has been made under the *CA 1985* provisions and has not been withdrawn;
- the six year time limit in (2) above does not enable an application to be made in respect of a company dissolved before 1 October 2007 except that

  (i) if the company was struck off under *CA 1985, s 652* or *652A* (see **21.App(1)(2)**) it does not prevent an application being made at any time before 1 October 2015 or 20 years from publication in the Gazette of notice under the relevant section, whichever occurs first; and

  (ii) the extended time limit where (2)(i)–(iii) above applies also applies to extent the time limit in (i) above.

[*SI 2008 No 2860, Sch 2 paras 90, 91*].

21.11 COMPANY'S NAME ON RESTORATION

A company is restored to the register with the name it had before it was dissolved or struck off the register, but subject to the following provisions.

If at the date of restoration the company could not be registered under its former name without contravening *CA 2006, s 66* (name not to be the same as another in the registrar's index of company names, see **27.6 Names and Business Names**), it must be restored to the register

(a) under another name specified

  (i) in the case of administrative restoration under **21.9**, in the application to the Registrar of Companies, or

  (ii) in the case of restoration by the court under **21.10**, in the court's order, or

(b) as if its registered number was also its name.

Where (*a*)(i) above applies, the provisions relating to change of name in *CA 2006, ss 80, 81* (see **27.20 Names and Business Names**) apply as if the application to the Registrar of Companies were notice of a change of name. Similarly, where (*a*)(ii) applies, those provisions apply as if the copy of the court order delivered to the Registrar of Companies were notice of a change a name.

Where (*b*) above applies, the company must change its name within 14 days after the date of the restoration. The change may be made by resolution of the directors (without prejudice to any other method of changing the company's name) and the company must give notice to the Registrar of Companies of the change. If the company fails to change its name within 14 days or notify the Registrar of Companies, an offence is committed by the company and every officer of the company who is in default. A person guilty of such an offence is liable, on summary conviction, to a fine not exceeding level 5 on the standard scale and, for continued contravention, to a daily default fine not exceeding one-tenth of level 5 on the standard scale. See **29.1 Offences and Legal Proceedings** for the standard scale.

[*CA 2006, s 1033*].

21.12 EFFECT OF RESTORATION WHERE PROPERTY HAS VESTED AS BONA VACANTIA

The person in whom any property or right is vested under *CA 2006, s 1012* (see **21.8**) may dispose of that property or right, or any interest in it, despite the fact that the company may be restored to the register under **21.9** or **21.10**. If the company is restored to the register

- the restoration does not affect the disposition; and
- the Crown (or Duke of Cornwall) must pay to the company an amount equal to
  - (i) the consideration received, or
  - (ii) the value of any such consideration at the time of the disposition

  or, if no consideration was received, an amount equal to the value of the property, right or interest disposed of, as at the date of the disposition.

There may be deducted from the amount payable the reasonable costs of the Crown representative in connection with the disposition (to the extent that they have not been paid as a condition of administrative restoration or pursuant to a court order for restoration).

[*CA 2006, s 1034*].

Transitional provisions.

(1) The above provisions apply whenever the company was dissolved.

(2) Where the company was dissolved before 1 October 2009,

- the reference to *CA 2006, s 1012* is to be read as a reference to *CA 1985, s 654* (see **21.App(8)**) or earlier provisions; and
- no deduction is to be made for reasonable costs of Crown representatives from consideration realised before 1 October 2009.

[*SI 2008 No 2860, Sch 2 para 92*].

PROVISIONS APPLYING BEFORE 1 OCTOBER 2009

NB that these pre-1 October 2009 notes refer to the old Companies House Guidance booklets. Please check with Companies House whether the old or new guidance applies (in many cases it remains substantially the same)

Striking off defunct companies at instigation of the Registrar of Companies

If the Registrar of Companies has reasonable cause to believe that a company is not carrying on business or in operation, he may send to the company by post a letter inquiring whether it is carrying on business or in operation. [*CA 1985, s 652(1)*].

He may take this action, for example, because he has not received documents from the company which should have been delivered to him (eg annual returns and accounts) or mail sent to the registered office is returned undelivered (Companies House Guidance Booklet GBW2 Strike-off, Dissolution and Restoration, Chapter 2 para 1).

If the Registrar of Companies does not, within one month of sending that letter, receive a reply, he must within 14 days send by post a registered letter referring to the first letter and stating that no answer has been received. The letter must also state that if no reply is received to the second letter within one month from its date, a notice will be published in the *London/Edinburgh Gazette* with a view to striking the company's name off the register.

Where the Registrar of Companies

- receives an answer from the company to the effect that the company is not carrying on a business or in operation, or
- does not receive a reply to the second letter above within one month,

he may publish a notice in the *London/Edinburgh Gazette* that, at the expiration of three months from the date of that notice, the company will be struck off the register and dissolved unless cause is shown to the contrary. The Registrar of Companies must send a copy of any such notice to the company (and will also place a copy on the company's public file). At the expiration of the three months, unless cause to the contrary has been shown, the Registrar of Companies may strike the company name off the register and publish notice of this in the *London/Edinburgh Gazette*. On publication, the company is dissolved (although this does not affect the power of the court to wind up the company).

The Registrar of Companies may also take this course of action where *a company is being wound up* and he has reasonable cause to believe that no liquidator is acting, or that the affairs of the company are fully wound up, and the returns required to be made by the liquidator have not been made for a period of six consecutive months.

[*CA 1985, s 652(2)–(5)(6)(b)*].

Addresses for notices etc. A letter or notice to be sent to a company may be addressed

- to the company at its registered office, or, if no office has been registered,
- to the care of some officer of the company, or if no officer is known to the Registrar of Companies,
- to each of the subscribers to the memorandum at the addresses there mentioned.

A notice to a liquidator may be addressed to him at his last known place of business.

[*CA 1985, s 652(7)*].

In England and Wales, notices are published in the Company Law Official Notifications Supplement to the *London Gazette*, published weekly on microfiche. Copies are available from The London Gazette, PO Box 7920, London SE1 5ZH (tel: 020 7394 4517). In Scotland, notices are published in the *Edinburgh Gazette*, published twice weekly. Copies are available from The Edinburgh Gazette, 73 Lothian Road, Edinburgh EH3 9AW (tel: 0870 600 5522). (Companies House Guidance Booklet GBW2, Chapter 2 para 4).

Striking off private companies on application by the company

Subject to the conditions in (3) below being satisfied, a private company may apply to the Registrar of Companies for the company's name to be struck off the register. The application must be made on its behalf by the directors (or a majority of them) and be in the prescribed form (Form 652a).

[*CA 1985, s 652A(1)(2); Deregulation and Contracting Out Act 1994, Sch 5*].

A filing fee is payable although this will be refunded if the application is rejected or withdrawn after its registration.

Application might be made, for example, where a company is no longer required because the active directors wish to retire; the company is a subsidiary whose name is no longer needed; or the company was set up to exploit an idea that turned out not to be feasible. The procedure is not an alternative to formal insolvency proceedings where these are appropriate as creditors are likely to prevent the striking off (see (5) and (6) below). (Companies House Guidance Booklet GBW2, Chapter 1 para 1).

Following receipt of the Form 652a, the Registrar of Companies will publish a notice in the *London/Edinburgh Gazette* stating that he may exercise his power under these provisions and inviting any person to show cause why he should not do so. If cause to the contrary is not shown and the application has not been withdrawn, the Registrar of Companies will strike the company off the register not less than three months after the date of the notice. The company will be formally dissolved when the Registrar of Companies publishes a notice to that effect in the *London/Edinburgh Gazette*.

[*CA 1985, s 652A(3)–(5); Deregulation and Contracting Out Act 1994, Sch 5*].

Even where the company is struck off the register and dissolved, creditors and others may apply for the company to be restored to the register (see (9) below).

Conditions for applying

A person cannot make an application to be struck off under (2) above if

(a) at any time in the previous three months, it has
- changed its name;
- traded or otherwise carried on business;
- disposed for value of any property or rights which, immediately before ceasing to trade or carry on business, it held for disposal or gain in the normal course of that business or trade; or
- engaged in any other activity except one necessary or expedient for making a striking off application, concluding the affairs of the company or complying with any statutory requirement; or

(b) the company is the subject, or proposed subject, of any insolvency proceedings or compromise or arrangement with its creditors under *CA 1985, s 425*.

For the purposes of (*a*) above, a company is not treated as trading or carrying on business by virtue only of the fact that it makes a payment in respect of a liability incurred in the course of trading or carrying on business.

[*CA 1985, s 652B(1)–(5); Deregulation and Contracting Out Act 1994, Sch 5; EA 2002, Sch 17 para 7*].

Withdrawal of application

A director must withdraw a company's application under (2) above (using Form 652c) where, at any time after application has been made and before it is finally dealt with or voluntarily withdrawn, the company

(a) changes its name;

(b) trade or otherwise carries on business;

(c) disposes for value of any property or rights (other than those which it needed to retain to make, or proceed with, the application);

(d) engages in any other activity except one necessary or expedient for

- making or proceeding with a striking off application;
- concluding the affairs of the company which are outstanding because of what was necessary or expedient to make or proceed with the application; or
- complying with any statutory requirement; or

(e) becomes the subject of any insolvency proceedings or makes a compromise or arrangement with its creditors under *CA 1985, s 425*.

For the purposes of (*b*) above, a company is not treated as trading or carrying on business by virtue only of the fact that it makes a payment in respect of a liability incurred in the course of trading or carrying on business.

[*CA 1985, s 652C(4)–(7); Deregulation and Contracting Out Act 1994, Sch 5; EA 2002, Sch 17 para 8*].

Notification

Where an application is made under (2) above, a copy of the Form 652a must be given, within seven days of the date of application, to every person who on that date was

(a) a member of the company;

(b) an employee of the company;

(c) a creditor of the company (including a contingent or prospective creditor);

(d) a director of the company who did not sign the Form 652a; or

(e) a manager or trustee of any employee pension fund.

[*CA 1985, ss 652B(6)(7), 652D(8); Deregulation and Contracting Out Act 1994, Sch 5*].

A copy of Form 652a must also be given to any person who becomes a member, employee etc under (a)–(e) above on a date subsequent to the application (within seven days of so becoming).

[*CA 1985, ss 652C(1)(2), 652D(8); Deregulation and Contracting Out Act 1994, Sch 5*].

There is no requirement to give notice if the application is withdrawn within the seven day period of notice.

[*CA 1985, ss 652B(8), 652C(3); Deregulation and Contracting Out Act 1994, Sch 5*].

For the above purposes, a copy of the Form 652a is treated as given to a person if it is delivered to, left at, or posted to his 'proper address' ie

(i) in the case of an individual, his last known address;

(ii) in the case of a company or partnership incorporated under the law outside the UK which has a place of business in the UK, its principal office in the UK;

(iii) in the case of a company or partnership not falling within (ii) above, its registered or principal office.

Where a creditor has more than one place of business, copies of Form 652a must be left at, or sent by post to, each place of business of the creditor which the company has had dealings with in relation to the debt.

[*CA 1985, s 652D(1)–(4); Deregulation and Contracting Out Act 1994, Sch 5*].

Objections to proposed striking off and dissolution

Any interested party may object to the striking off and dissolution of the company. Any objections should be in writing and sent to the Registrar of Companies, together with supporting evidence (eg copies of invoices showing that the company is trading). Examples of grounds for objecting are that

- the company has broken any of the conditions of its application under (2) above;
- the directors have not informed interested parties;
- any of the declarations on Form 652a are false;
- some form of action is being taken, or is pending, to recover any moneys owed (eg a winding up petition or action in the small claims court);
- other legal action is being taken against the company; or
- the directors have wrongfully traded or committed a tax fraud or some other offence.

(Companies House Guidance Booklet GBW2 Strike-off, Dissolution and Restoration, Chapter 1 para 8).

Offences and penalties

The following offences and penalties are imposed for breaches in connection with the provisions in (2)–(5) above.

- A person who breaches or fails to perform a duty imposed under (3) to (5) above is guilty of an offence and liable to a fine up. It is a defence for the accused to prove that

  (i) in proceedings for an offence of breach of duty under (3) above (by making an application when all the conditions were not satisfied) that he did not know, and could not reasonably have known, of the existence of the facts which led to the breach;

  (ii) in proceedings for an offence consisting of failure to give notice under *CA 1985, s 652B(6)* (see (5) above) that he took all reasonable steps to perform the duty; and

  (iii) in proceedings for an offence consisting of failure to give notice under *CA 1985, s 652C(2)* (see (5) above) or failure to withdraw an application under (4) above, either that, at the time of the failure, he was not aware that an application had been made or he took all reasonable steps to perform the duty.

- A person who fails to give notification as required under (5) above with the intention of concealing the making of the application is guilty of an offence and liable to a penalty.
- Where a company makes an application under (2) above, any person who, in connection with the application, knowingly or recklessly furnishes any information to the Registrar of Companies which is false or misleading in a material particular is guilty of an offence and liable to a penalty.
- Any person who knowingly or recklessly makes an application to the Registrar of Companies, which purports to be an application under (2) above, but which is not, is guilty of an offence and liable to a penalty.

[*CA 1985, ss 652E, 652F, Sch 24; Deregulation and Contracting Out Act 1994, Sch 5*].

Effect of dissolution

Liability of directors etc. The liability (if any) of every director, managing officer and member of the company continues and may be enforced as if the company had not been dissolved.

[*CA 1985, ss 652(6)(a), 652A(6); Deregulation and Contracting Out Act 1994, Sch 5*].

Assets of the company. All property and rights whatsoever vested in or held on trust for the company immediately before its dissolution (including leasehold property, but not property held on trust for any other person) are deemed to be *bona vacantia* and accordingly

- if the company's registered office is in Lancashire, belong to the Duchy of Lancaster;
- if the registered office is in Cornwall, belong to the Duchy of Cornwall; and
- in all other cases, belong to the Crown.

For enquiries regarding *bona vacantia* see **21.7**)

If the company's registered office is in Cornwall or the Isles of Scilly:

The property vesting as *bona vacantia* may be disclaimed by the Crown or Duchy as the case may be.

[*CA 1985, ss 654, 656*]. (Companies House Guidance Booklet GBW Strike-off, Dissolution and Restoration, Chapter 2 para 5).

See *CA 1985, s 657* and *Sch 20* for the effect of Crown disclaimer.

Liability for rentcharge on company's land in England and Wales. Where land in England and Wales vests subject to a rentcharge in the Crown or any other person (the '*proprietor*') on the dissolution of a company, the proprietor and his successors in title are not subject to any personal liability in respect of any sums becoming due under the rentcharge except sums becoming due after the proprietor, or some person claiming under or through him, has taken possession or control of the land or has entered into occupation of it.

[*CA 1985, s 658; IA 1985, Sch 6 para 47; IA 1986, Sch 13*].

Restoration to the register

Where a company has been struck off the register, the court may, on application within 20 years of dissolution, order the company's name to be restored to the register.

If the company has been struck off at the instigation of the Registrar of Companies under (1) above, the application may be made by the company (even though it does not legally exist) or any member or creditor. The court may order the company's name to be restored if it was carrying on business or in operation at the time it was struck off or if it is just to do so. For a consideration of these criteria for restoring to the register, see *Priceland Ltd, Re, Waltham Forest London Borough Council v Registrar of Companies* [1997] 1 BCLC 467, [1997] BCC 207.

If the company was struck off following an application by the company under (2) above, the application may be made by any person to whom a copy of the application was required to be given under (5) above. The court may order the company's name to be restored to the register if that person was not given a copy of the application, or the application by the company involved a breach of the conditions of the application under (3) above, or for some other reason if it is just to do so. The court may also order restoration, on application by the Secretary of State, if satisfied that it is in the public interest to do so.

[*CA 1985, s 653(1)–(2D); Deregulation and Contracting Out Act 1994, Sch 5*].

The repeal of the above provisions with effect from 1 October 2009 does not affect an application made under those provisions before that date.

[*SI 2008 No 2860, Sch 2 para 89*].

The application for restoration may be made by any person who was legally prejudiced by the dissolution of the company. This includes a person who wishes to enforce a liability of the company and does not depend on there having been an existing cause of action when the company was struck off. The provisions are also intended to provide a remedy for a person who has a claim, whether against the company or against a third party (such as the company's insurer or guarantor), which can only be enforced if the company is restored to the register (*City of Westminster Assurance Co Ltd v Registrar of Companies* [1997] BCC 960, CA).

Procedure. The Registrar of Companies will provide information to assist in an application to the court but has no power to register a company without a court order.

In England and Wales, the application can be made to the High Court by completing a Part 8 claim form. This is the standard form that starts proceedings and can be downloaded from:

www.courtservice.gov.uk

The Registrar of the Companies Court in London usually hears restoration cases in chambers once a week on Friday afternoons. Cases are also heard at the District Registries. Alternatively, an application can be made to a County Court that has the authority to wind up the company. The claim form should be served on the solicitor dealing with any *bona vacantia* (see (8) above) and the Registrar of Companies, Restoration Section, Companies House, Crown Way, Cardiff CF14 3UZ (tel 029 2038 0069; fax 029 2038 0006). The Registrar of Companies will accept delivery by post (recorded delivery is recommended) or by hand at Companies House, Cardiff or London.

In Scotland, application may be made to the Court with jurisdiction to wind up the company, i.e. the Court of Sessions or, for a company whose paid-up capital does not exceed £120,000, the Sheriff Court in the Sheriffdom in which the company has its registered office. The petition should be served on The Lord Advocate, Crown Office, 25 Chambers Street, Edinburgh EH1 1LA and the Registrar of Companies, Companies House, 37 Castle Terrace, Edinburgh EH1 2EB. The Registrar of Companies will accept service by post (recorded delivery is recommended) or by hand. The Registrar of Companies and/or the Lord Advocate may be represented at the hearing by an agent.

Evidence. The Registrar of Companies will normally ask for delivery (prior to the hearing) of any statutory documents to bring the public file of the company up to date, and the correction of any irregularities in the company's structure.

The court will require an affidavit or witness statement (in Scotland, evidence) covering

(a) service of the originating summons/petition

(b) the circumstances of the company, including

- when it was incorporated and the nature of its objects (a copy of the certificate of incorporation and memorandum and articles of association should be attached);
- its membership and officers;
- its trading activities and, if applicable, when it stopped trading;
- an explanation of any failure to deliver accounts, returns or notices to the Registrar of Companies;
- details of the striking-off and dissolution (based on information provided by the Registrar of Companies);
- comments on the company's solvency; and
- any further information necessary to explain the reason for the application.

The applicant will normally be expected to pay the Registrar of Companies' costs in relation to the hearing.

(Companies House Guidance Booklet GBW Strike-off, Dissolution and Restoration, Chapter 3 paras 2–5 and GBW2(S) Strike-off, Dissolution and Restoration, Chapter 3 paras 2–5).

Effect of court order. When an office copy of the order is delivered to the Registrar of Companies, the company is deemed to have continued in existence as if its name had not been struck off. The court may, by the order, give such directions and make such provisions as seem just for placing the company and all other persons in the same position (as nearly as possible) as if the company's name had never been struck off.

[*CA 1985, s 653(3); Deregulation and Contracting Out Act 1994, Sch 5*].

Power of court to declare dissolution of company void

Where a company has been dissolved, the court may, on an application within two years (subject to below) of the date of dissolution by the liquidator or any other interested party, make an order, on such terms as it thinks fit, declaring the dissolution to have been void. Such proceedings may then be taken as if the company had not been dissolved.

The applicant must, within seven days of the order (or such further time as the court allows), deliver an office copy of the order to the Registrar of Companies. In default, he is liable to a fine.

There is no time limit where the application is for the purposes of bringing proceedings against the company for

(a) damages in respect of 'personal injuries' including any funeral expenses claimed by virtue of the *Law Reform (Miscellaneous Provisions) Act 1934, s 1(2)(c)*, or

(b) damages under the *Fatal Accidents Act 1976* or the *Damages (Scotland) Act 1976*, although no order must be made if the proceedings would fail under a time limit in any other enactment. For the interaction of this provision in relation to personal injuries actions with the *Limitation Act 1980, s 33*, see *Workvale Ltd (in dissolution), Re* [1992] 1 WLR 416, [1991] BCLC 528, CA.

'*Personal injuries*' include any disease and any impairment of a person's physical or mental condition.

Before 1 October 2008, no application under (*a*) or (*b*) above could be made in relation to a company dissolved before 16 November 1969 [*CA 1989, s 141(4)*] but this restriction was removed from that date by *SI 2008 No 1886, Art 2*.

[*CA 1985, s 651; CA 1989, s 141*].

The repeal of the above provisions with effect from 1 October 2009 does not affect an application made under those provisions before that date.

[*SI 2008 No 2860, Sch 2 para 89*].

The interest of an applicant under *CA 1985, s 651* above in having the company revived does not have to be firmly established or likely to prevail. It is sufficient that it is not 'merely shadowy'. It follows, therefore, that an order may be made to enable a company to meet a liability which would otherwise remain unpaid. Normally a third party should not be entitled to intervene to argue that an order should not be made. However, in cases where the making of an order would directly affect the rights of a third party, irrespective of whether the applicant has any claim against the company or the company has any claim against the third party, the third party is entitled to be joined to argue that such an order should not be made (*Forte's (Manufacturing) Ltd, Re, Stanhope Pension Trust Ltd v Registrar of Companies* (1993) 69 P & CR 238, [1994] 1 BCLC 628, CA).

Effect of company's revival after dissolution

The person in whom any property or right is vested following dissolution (see (8) above under the heading *Assets of the company*) may dispose of that property or right, or any interest in it, despite the fact that an order may be made under (9) or (10) above. Where such an order is then made,

- it does not affect the disposition; and
- the Crown (or Duke of Cornwall) must repay to the company an amount equal to
  - (i) the consideration received; or
  - (ii) the value of any such consideration at the time of the disposition; or
  - (iii) if no consideration was received, the value of the property, right or interest disposed of, as at the date of the disposition.

[*CA 1985, s 655*].

22 Distributions

22.1	**Restrictions on distributions**
22.2	**Profits available for distribution**
22.3	Treatment of development costs
22.4	**Accounting requirements**
22.5	Successive distributions
22.6	Realised losses and profits and revaluation of fixed assets
22.7	Distribution in kind
22.8	**Consequences of unlawful distributions**
22.9	**Application of rules of law restricting distributions**
22.10	**Procedures, etc for payment of dividends**
22.11	Listed company requirements
22.12	Companies on LSE main market: Admission and Corporate transactions
22.13	Continuing obligations
22.14	Uncertificated Securities and CREST
22.15	LSE Dividend Procedure Timetable
22.16	AIM companies
Appendix	**Provisions applying before 6 April 2008**

Cross-references. See **47.62** Shares for bonus issues.

Background. The provisions in this chapter apply, unless otherwise stated, to distributions made on or after 6 April 2008.

[*SI 2007 No 3495, Sch 4 para 33*].

For a summary of the provisions applying to distributions made before 6 April 2008, see the Appendix at the end of the chapter.

22.1 RESTRICTIONS ON DISTRIBUTIONS

CA 2006, ss 829–851 provide for what profits a company may lawfully distribute by way, for example, of dividends to shareholders and

- Largely restate *CA 1985, Part VIII*
- Apply to distributions made after 6 April 2008 and
- Clarify the rule in *Aveling Barford Ltd v Perion Ltd* [1989] BCLC 626, 5 BCC 677 (see **22.8**)

The basic restriction is set out in *section 830* which provides that, subject to anything in the company's articles or in any enactment which restricts what distributions can be made:

(a) Any company may only make a distribution out of profits available for the purpose (see **22.2**).

[*CA 2006, s 830(1)*].

(b) A *public company* may only make a distribution

- if the amount of its 'net assets' is not less than the aggregate of its called-up share capital and 'undistributable reserves'; and
- if, and to the extent that, the distribution does not reduce the amount of those assets to less than that aggregate.

'*Net assets*' means the aggregate of the company's assets (excluding any uncalled share capital) less the aggregate of its liabilities. Liabilities here include

- where the relevant accounts are Companies Act accounts,
  - (i) any provisions for liabilities (or, in the case of insurance companies, provisions for other risks) which are reasonably necessary to provide for any liability the nature of which is clearly defined and which is either likely to be incurred, or certain to be incurred but uncertain as to amount or as date on which it will arise; and
  - (ii) in the case of insurance companies, any amount included under Liabilities items B (funds for future appropriations), C (technical provisions) and D (technical provisions for linked liabilities) in the balance sheet;
- where the relevant accounts are IAS accounts, provisions of any kind.

Distribution

Distribution means every description of distribution of a company's assets to its members, whether in cash or otherwise, except for

- an issue of shares as fully or partly paid bonus shares;
- the reduction of share capital
  - (i) by extinguishing or reducing the liability of any of the members on any of the company's shares in respect of share capital not paid up, or
  - (ii) by repaying off paid up share capital;
- the redemption or purchase of any of the company's own shares out of capital (including the proceeds of any fresh issue of shares) or out of unrealised profits in accordance with *CA 2006, Pt 18, Chapter 3, 4 or 5* (see **34.2–34.13 Purchase of Own Shares**); or
- a distribution of assets to members of the company on its winding up.

[*CA 2006, s 829; SI 2007 No 3495, Sch 1 para 14; SI 2008 No 2860, art 6*].

Undistributable reserves

A company's undistributable reserves are

(A) its share premium account;

(B) the capital redemption reserve;

(C) the amount by which its accumulated, unrealised profits (so far as not previously utilised by capitalisation) exceeds its accumulated, unrealised losses (so far as not previously written off in a reduction or reorganisation of capital duly made); and

(D) any other reserve which the company is prohibited from distributing by any other enactment or by its articles.

In (C) above, the reference to capitalisation does not include a transfer of profits of the company to its capital redemption reserve

[*CA 2006, s 831(4)*].

Capitalisation

Capitalisation, in relation to a company's profits, means any of the following operations (whenever carried out).

- Applying the profits in wholly or partly paying up unissued shares in the company to be allotted to members of the company as fully or partly paid bonus shares.
- Transferring the profits to capital redemption reserve.

[*CA 2006, s 853(3)*].

(c) [*CA 2006, s 831(1)–(3)(5)(6); SI 2008 No 410, Sch 9 paras 2, 4*].

See **22.4** to **22.6** for the company's accounts to be considered in determining whether a distribution may be made without contravening the above provisions.

(d) A company must not apply an unrealised profit in paying up debentures or unpaid amounts on its issued shares.

[*CA 2006, s 849*].

22.2 PROFITS AVAILABLE FOR DISTRIBUTION

Insofar as a company is able to make distributions then a company's profits available for distribution are, its accumulated, realised profits (so far as not previously utilised by distribution or capitalisation) less its accumulated, realised losses (so far as not previously written off in a reduction or reorganisation of capital duly made). [*CA 2006, s 830(2)(3)*].

Older profits and losses

Where the directors of a company are, after making all reasonable enquiries, unable to determine whether

- a particular profit made before the 'relevant date' is realised or unrealised, they may treat the profit as realised; and
- a particular loss made before the relevant date is realised or unrealised, they may treat the loss as unrealised.

The 'relevant date' is, for companies registered in Great Britain, 22 December 1980 and, for companies registered in Northern Ireland, 1 July 1983.

[*CA 2006, s 850*].

Profits or losses

References to profits or losses of any description

- are to profits and losses of that description made at any time; and
- except where the context otherwise requires, are to profits or losses of a revenue or capital character.

[*CA 2006, s 853(2)*].

22.2 Distributions

Realised profits and losses.

References to 'realised profits' and 'realised losses', in relation to a company's accounts, are to such profits or losses of the company as fall to be treated as realised in accordance with principles generally accepted at the time when the accounts are prepared, with respect to the determination for accounting purposes of realised profits or losses. This is without prejudice to

- the construction of any other expression (where appropriate) by reference to accepted accounting principles or practice; or
- any specific provision for the treatment of profits or losses of any description as realised.

[*CA 2006, s 853(4)(5)*].

22.3 TREATMENT OF DEVELOPMENT COSTS

Where development costs are shown or included as an asset in the company's accounts, any amount shown or included in respect of those costs is treated as

- a realised loss for the purposes of **22.2**; and
- a realised revenue loss in the case of an investment company.

This does not apply to any part of that amount representing an unrealised profit made on revaluation of those costs. It also does not apply if

(a) there are special circumstances in the company's case justifying the directors in deciding that the amount is not to be so treated;

(b) it is stated

(i) in the case of Companies Act accounts, in the note required to the accounts as to the reason for showing development costs as an asset, or

(ii) in the case of IAS individual accounts, in any note to the accounts

that the amount is not to be so treated; and

(c) the note explains the circumstances relied upon to justify the decision of the directors to that effect.

[*CA 2006, s 844*].

22.4 ACCOUNTING REQUIREMENTS

Subject to **22.7**(1), whether a distribution can be made without contravening the provisions of **22.1** is determined by reference to

(i) profits, losses, assets and liabilities,

(ii) provisions of the following kind, namely

- where the relevant accounts are Companies Act accounts,
  - — provisions for depreciation or diminution in value of assets;
  - — any provisions for liabilities (or, in the case of insurance companies, provisions for other risks) which are reasonably necessary to provide for any liability the nature of which is clearly defined and which is either likely to be incurred, or certain to be incurred but uncertain as to amount or as date on which it will arise; and

— in the case of insurance companies, any amount included under Liabilities items Ba (funds for future appropriations), C (technical provisions) and D (technical provisions for linked liabilities) in the balance sheet; and

- where the relevant accounts are IAS individual accounts, provisions of any kind, and

(iii) share capital and reserves (including 'undistributable reserves', see **22.1**)

as stated in the company's 'relevant accounts'.

The '*relevant accounts*' for these purposes are the company's last annual accounts (see (*a*) below), except that

- where the distribution would be found to contravene the provisions of this chapter by reference to the company's last annual accounts, it may be justified by reference to interim accounts (see (*b*) below); and
- where the distribution is proposed to be declared during the company's first accounting reference period, or before any accounts have been circulated in respect of that period, it may be justified by reference to initial accounts (see (*c*) below).

The requirements of (*a*), (*b*) or (*c*) below must be complied with, as and where applicable. If any applicable requirement not complied with, the accounts may not be relied on for the purposes of this chapter and the distribution is accordingly treated as contravening the requirements for distribution.

(a) **Requirements where last annual accounts used**. The company's last annual accounts means the company's individual accounts that were last circulated to members in accordance with *CA 2006, s 423* (see **2.6** ACCOUNTS: GENERAL) or, if in accordance with *CA 2006, s 426* the company provided a strategic report instead, that formed the basis of that statement (see **6.1** ACCOUNTS: SUMMARY FINANCIAL STATEMENTS). The requirements are:

- The accounts must have been 'properly prepared' in accordance with *CA 2006* or have been so prepared subject only to matters which are not material for determining, by reference to (i)–(iii) above, whether the distribution would contravene the relevant provisions.
- Unless the company is exempt from audit and the directors take advantage of that exemption, the auditor must have made his report on the accounts. If that report was qualified, the auditor must have stated in writing (either at the time of his report or subsequently) whether in his opinion the matters in respect of which his report is qualified are material for determining whether a distribution would contravene the provisions of this chapter. A copy of that statement must, in the case of a private company, have been circulated to members in accordance with *CA 2006, s 423* (see **2.6** ACCOUNTS: GENERAL), or, in the case of a public company, have been laid before the company in general meeting. An auditor's statement is sufficient for the purposes of a distribution if it relates to distributions of a description that includes the distribution in question, even if at the time of the statement it had not been proposed.

  See also *Precision Dippings Ltd v Precision Dippings Marketing Ltd* [1986] Ch 447, [1985] BCLC 385, CA.

(b) **Requirements where interim accounts used**. Interim accounts must be accounts that enable a reasonable judgment to be made as to the amounts of the items mentioned in (i)–(iii) above. Where interim accounts are prepared for a proposed distribution by a *public company*, the requirements are:

- The accounts must have been 'properly prepared', or have been so prepared subject to matters that are not material for determining, by reference to (i)–(iii) above, whether the distribution would contravene the relevant provisions.

  '*Properly prepared*' means prepared in accordance with *CA 2006, ss 395–397* (see **3.2 Accounts: Large Companies**), applying those requirements with such modifications as are necessary because the accounts are prepared otherwise than in respect of an accounting reference period.

- The balance sheet comprised in the accounts must have been signed in accordance with *CA 2006, s 414* (see **2.2 Accounts: General**).

- A copy of the accounts must have been delivered to the Registrar of Companies. Before 1 October 2009, the balance sheet must state the name of the person who signed it on behalf of the board and be signed on behalf of the board by a director of the company.

Any requirement of as to the delivery of a certified translation into English of any document forming part of the accounts must also have been met.

(c) **Requirements where initial accounts used**. Initial accounts must be accounts that enable a reasonable judgment to be made as to the amounts of the items mentioned in (i)–(iii) above. Where initial accounts are prepared for a proposed distribution by a *public company*, the requirements are:

- The accounts must have been 'properly prepared' (see (*b*) above), or have been so prepared subject to matters that are not material for determining, by reference to (i)–(iii) above, whether the distribution would contravene the relevant provisions.

- The company's auditor must have made a report stating whether, in his opinion, the accounts have been properly prepared. If that report was qualified, the auditor must have stated in writing (either at the time of his report or subsequently) whether in his opinion the matters in respect of which his report is qualified are material for determining whether a distribution would contravene the provisions of this chapter. A copy of that statement must have been laid before the company in general meeting (before 1 October 2009, in the case of a private company, have been circulated to members in accordance with *CA 2006, s 423* (see **2.6 Accounts: General**)).

- A copy of the accounts, of the auditor's report and of any auditor's statement must have been delivered to the Registrar of Companies. Before 1 October 2009, the balance sheet must state the name of the person who signed it on behalf of the board and be signed on behalf of the board by a director of the company. The auditor's report and any audit statement must state the name of the auditor and (where the auditor is a firm) the name of the person who signed it as senior statutory auditor. It must also be signed by the auditor or (where the auditor is a firm) in the name of the firm by a person authorised to sign on its behalf. Alternatively, if the conditions in *CA 2006, s 506* (circumstances in which names may be omitted, see 8.34 AUDIT) are met, the report and any statement must state that a resolution has been passed and notified to the Secretary of State in accordance with that section.

Any requirement of as to the delivery of a certified translation into English of any document forming part of the accounts must also have been met.

[*CA 2006, ss 836–839; SI 2007 No 3495, Sch 1 paras 17, 18; SI 2008 No 409, Sch 7, paras 2, 5; SI 2008 No 410, Sch 9 paras 2, 7; SI 2008 No 2860, Art 6; SI 2009 No 1941, Sch 1 para 260*].

Transitional provisions. The relevant accounts for the purposes of this paragraph and **22.5** and **22.6** may be accounts for a financial year beginning before 6 April 2008 (to which the provisions of *CA 1985* apply). In that case, the references in those paragraphs to *CA 2006* should be read as references to the corresponding provisions in *CA 1985*. See *SI 2007 No 3495, Sch 4 para 35* for full details.

22.5 Successive distributions

In determining whether a proposed distribution may be made by a company in a case where

(a) one or more previous distributions have been made in pursuance of a determination made by reference to the same relevant accounts, or

(b) relevant 'financial assistance' has been given, or other relevant payments have been made, since those accounts were prepared

the provision of this chapter apply as if the amount of the proposed distribution was increased by the amount of the previous distributions, financial assistance or other payments.

Financial assistance and other payments that are relevant for these purposes are

- financial assistance lawfully given by the company out of its distributable profits;
- financial assistance for the acquisition of shares given by a company in contravention of *CA 2006, s 678* or *CA 2006, s 679* (see **34.20 PURCHASE OF OWN SHARES**) in a case where the giving of that assistance reduces the company's 'net assets' or increases its 'net liabilities';
- payments made by a company in respect of the purchase by it of shares in the company (except a payment made lawfully otherwise than out of distributable profits); and
- payments of any description specified in *CA 2006, s 705* (before 1 October 2009, *CA 1985, s 168*) (payments apart from purchase price of shares to be made out of distributable profits, see **34.8 PURCHASE OF OWN SHARES**).

For the meaning of '*financial assistance*', see **34.20 PURCHASE OF OWN SHARES**.

'*Net assets*' means the amount by which the aggregate amount of the company's assets exceeds the aggregate amount of its liabilities, taking the amount of the assets and liabilities to be as stated in the company's accounting records immediately before the financial assistance is given.

'*Net liabilities*' means the amount by which the aggregate amount of the company's liabilities exceeds the aggregate amount of its assets, taking the amount of the assets and liabilities to be as stated in the company's accounting records immediately before the financial assistance is given. For this purpose, a company's liabilities include any amount retained as reasonably necessary to provide for any liability

- the nature of which is clearly defined, and
- which is either likely to be incurred or certain to be incurred but uncertain as to amount or as to the date on which it will arise.

[*CA 2006, s 840; SI 2007 No 3495, Sch 1 para 19; SI 2008 No 2860, Art 6*].

22.6 Realised losses and profits and revaluation of fixed assets

Provisions to be treated as realised losses. For the purposes of this chapter

(a) in the case of Companies Act accounts,

  (i) provisions for depreciation or diminution in value of assets, and

  (ii) any provision for liabilities (ie any amount retained as reasonably necessary for the purpose of providing for any liability the nature of which is clearly defined and which is either likely to be incurred or certain to be incurred but uncertain as to the amount or as to the date on which it will arise,

  except 'revaluation provisions', and

(b) in the case of IAS accounts, provisions of any kind (except revaluation provisions)

are treated as realised losses.

A '*revaluation provision*' means a provision in respect of a diminution in value of a fixed asset appearing on a revaluation of all the fixed assets of the company, or of all of its fixed assets other than goodwill.

For the above purposes, any consideration by the directors of the value at a particular time of a fixed asset is treated as a revaluation provided

- the directors are satisfied that the aggregate value at that time of the fixed assets of the company that have not actually been revalued is not less than the aggregate amount at which they are then stated in the company's accounts; and
- it is stated in a note to the accounts that

  (i) the directors have considered the value of some or all of the fixed assets of the company without actually revaluing them;

  (ii) that they are satisfied that the aggregate value of those assets at the time of their consideration was not less than the aggregate amount at which they were then stated in the company's accounts; and

  (iii) that amounts are stated in the accounts on the basis that a revaluation of fixed assets of the company is treated as having taken place at that time.

Depreciation following revaluation of fixed asset. Where

- an unrealised profit is shown to have been made on the revaluation of a fixed asset, and
- on or after the revaluation, a sum is written off or retained for depreciation of that asset over a period,

an amount equal to the amount by which that sum exceeds the sum which would have been so written off or retained for the depreciation of that asset over that period, if that profit had not been made, is treated as a realised profit made over that period.

Fixed assets for these purposes means assets which are intended for use on a continuing basis in the company's activities.

Example

	Asset value	*Depreciation at 10%*
	£	£
2005	10,000	1,000
2006	10,000	1,000
2007	15,000 (revaluation)	1,500
2008	15,000	1,500
2009	15,000	1,500

The increase of £500 in depreciation in 2007 and subsequent years following the revaluation may be treated as a realised profit and available for distribution.

Cost of asset unknown. Where there is no record of the original cost of an asset, or a record cannot be obtained without unreasonable expense or delay, then in determining whether the company has made a profit or loss on the asset, its cost is taken to be the value given to it in the earliest available record of its value made on or after its acquisition by the company.

[*CA 2006, ss 841, 842; 853(6); SI 2008 No 409, Sch 7 para 6; SI 2008 No 410, Sch 9 para 2; SI 2009 No 1581, Regs 11, 12*].

22.7 Distribution in kind

(1) *Determination of amount*

The following provisions apply for determining the amount of a distribution consisting of or including, or treated as arising in consequence of, the sale, transfer or other disposition by a company of a non-cash asset where

- at the time of the distribution the company has 'profits available for distribution'; and
- if the amount of the distribution were to be determined in accordance with this paragraph, the company could make the distribution without contravening the provisions of this chapter.

In such circumstances, the amount of the distribution (or the relevant part of it) is taken to be

- in a case where the amount or value of the consideration for the disposition is not less than the book value of the asset, zero; and
- in any other case, the amount by which the book value of the asset exceeds the amount or value of any consideration for the disposition.

The company's '*profits available for distribution*' are treated as increased by the amount (if any) by which the amount or value of any consideration for the disposition exceeds the book value of the asset.

'*Book value*', in relation to an asset, means the amount at which the asset is stated in the relevant accounts or, where the asset is not stated in those accounts at any amount, zero.

The provisions of **22.4** and **22.5** have effect subject to the above provisions.

[*CA 2006, s 845*].

This provision is intended to remove doubts to which the decision in *Aveling Barford Ltd v Perion Ltd* [1989] BCLC 626, 5 BCC 677 had given rise. Although not disturbing the decision in that case (such that where a company which does not have distributable profits makes a distribution by way of a transfer of assets at an undervalue, this will be an unlawful distribution), it clarifies the position where the company does have distributable profits and the above conditions apply.

(2) *Treatment of unrealised profits*

Where

- a company makes a distribution consisting of or including, or treated as arising in consequence of, the sale, transfer or other disposition by the company of a non-cash asset, and
- any part of the amount at which that asset is stated in the relevant accounts represents an unrealised profit

that profit is treated as a realised profit for the purposes of

- determining the lawfulness of the distribution in accordance with this chapter (whether before or after the distribution takes place); and
- the application, in relation to anything done with a view to or in connection with the making of the distribution, of any provision of Regulations under *CA 2006, s 396* under which only realised profits are to be included in or transferred to the profit and loss account.

[*CA 2006, s 846*].

22.8 CONSEQUENCES OF UNLAWFUL DISTRIBUTIONS

Where

- a distribution, or part of one, made by a company to one of its members is made in contravention of the provisions of this chapter, and
- at the time of the distribution the member knows, or has reasonable grounds for believing, that it is so made,

he is liable

- to repay it (or that part of it, as the case may be) to the company; or
- in the case of a distribution made otherwise than in cash, to pay the company a sum equal to the value of the distribution (or part) at that time.

See *Precision Dippings Ltd v Precision Dippings Marketing Ltd* [1986] Ch 447, [1985] BCLC 385, CA.

The above is without prejudice to any obligation otherwise imposed, apart from these provisions, on a member to repay a distribution unlawfully made to him but does not apply to

- financial assistance for the acquisition of shares given by a company in contravention of *CA 2006, ss 678* or *CA 2006, s 679* (before 1 October 2009, *CA 1985, s 151*) (see **34.20 Purchase of Own Shares**); or

- any payment made by a company in respect of the redemption or purchase by the company of shares in itself.

[*CA 2006, s 847; SI 2007 No 3495, Sch 1 para 20; SI 2008 No 2860, Art 6*].

Directors who are parties to the payment of an unlawful dividend are jointly and severally liable to repay the amount. This applies even if the dividend is approved by a general meeting or the company's articles. See *Exchange Banking Co, Re, Flitcroft's Case* (1882) 21 Ch D 519, CA and also *Wallersteiner v Moir* [1974] 3 All ER 217, [1974] 1 WLR 991, CA; *Selangor United Rubber Estates Ltd v Cradock (a bankrupt) (No 3)* [1968] 2 All ER 1073, [1968] 1 WLR 1555 and *Belmont Finance Corpn Ltd v Williams Furniture Ltd (No 2)* [1980] 1 All ER 393, CA.

In *Bairstow v Queens Moat Houses plc* [2000] 1 BCLC 549, [2000] BCC 1025 it was held that a director who authorised the payment of an unlawful dividend in breach of his duty as a quasi trustee would be liable to repay such a dividend if

- he knew the dividends were unlawful, whether or not that actual knowledge amounted to a fraud;
- he knew the facts that established the impropriety of the payments, even though he was unaware that such impropriety rendered the payment unlawful;
- he must be taken in all the circumstances to have known all the facts which rendered the payments unlawful; or
- he ought to have known, as a reasonably competent and diligent director, that the payments were unlawful.

The decision was upheld in the Court of Appeal ([2001] 2 BCLC 531) which also held that the liability to repay applied whether the company was solvent or insolvent and that the amount to be repaid was the full amount of the unlawful dividend, not just the excess over the dividend which could lawfully have been paid.

22.9 APPLICATION OF RULES OF LAW RESTRICTING DISTRIBUTIONS

The provisions of this chapter are without prejudice to any rule of law restricting the sums out of which, or the cases in which, a distribution may be made. However, for the purposes of any rule of law requiring distributions to be paid out of profits or restricting the return of capital to members

- 22.7(1) applies to determine the amount of any distribution or return of capital consisting of or including, or treated as arising in consequence of the sale, transfer or other disposition by a company of a non-cash asset; and
- 22.7(2) applies as it applies for the purposes of this chapter.

[*CA 2006, s 851*].

22.10 PROCEDURES, ETC FOR PAYMENT OF DIVIDENDS

Because *CA 2006* and its predecessors do not regulate the procedures for payment of dividends, provision is usually made in the company's articles.

Where a company has adopted standard articles, see the provisions in

- *Table A, Regs 102–108*

22.10 Distributions

- *Model Articles, Arts 30–35* (private companies)
- *Model Articles, Arts 70–77* (public companies)

There is no principle which compels a company to divide its profit among its shareholders. Whether the whole or part should be paid as dividend is a question for the directors and shareholders to decide (*Burland v Earle* [1902] AC 83, 71 LJPC 1, PC).

Unless the company's articles (whether standard or otherwise) contain provision for a dividend to be satisfied by the distribution of assets, a dividend must be made in cash (*Wood v Odessa Waterworks Co* (1889) 42 Ch D 636).

22.11 Listed company requirements

For the purposes of this chapter a company is listed if either

- Its securities are admitted to the Official List by the UKLA (either a standard or premium listing) and are admitted to trading on the London Stock Exchange ("LSE") main market; or
- Its shares are admitted to LSE Alternative Investment Market ("AIM")

22.12 Companies on LSE main market: Admission and Corporate transactions

To be eligible for admission to LSE main market the company seeking admission must comply with the LSE Admission and Disclosure Standards which cover both pre-admission and ongoing continuing obligations.

Payment of dividends by a company on the main market:

- A company must contact the LSE Stock Situation Analysis team in advance of announcing a timetable for any proposed action which affects the rights of existing holders of securities traded on the LSE markets
- Where applicable, dividend payments must follow the procedures set out in the guidance in Rule 3.8 of the Standards which provides (in summary) that if a dividend timetable follows the Dividend Procedure timetable it does not need to be notified to LSE in advance provided that the announcement of the dividend includes:
  - The amount of the dividend (stating whether the dividend is net or gross);
  - The record and payment dates;
  - The availability of any scrip, DRIP or dividend currency option; and
  - The election date.

Dividends outside of the guidelines must be agreed by the Stock Situation Analysis team in advance of the announcement of the dividend.

[*LSE Admission and Disclosure Standards Rules 3.5, 3.8.*]

For the purposes of the Admission and Disclosure Standards "dividend" includes all interest payments for debt securities (excluding specialist securities).

For further information on the LSE Dividend Timetable see **22.15** below **LSE DIVIDEND PROCEDURE TIMETABLE**.

22.13 Continuing obligations

The FCA Listing Rules regulate both the admission to the main market and continuing obligations which apply to all companies listed on that market. The Listing Rules require every company listed on the main market to notify a RIS (ie a service which disseminates regulatory information such as company announcements) as soon as possible after the board has approved any decision:

- To pay or make any dividend or other distribution on listed equity; or
- To withhold any dividend on listed securities giving details of:
  - The exact net amount payable per share;
  - The payment date;
  - The record date (where applicable); and
  - Any foreign income dividend election, together with any income tax treated as paid at the lower rate and not repayable.

For the meaning of listed equity and listed securities see the Glossary of definitions to the FCA Full Handbook.

In certain circumstances the FCA can authorise the omission of the dividend information required by LR 9.7A.2. This is where the FCA considers that disclosure of this information would be contrary to the public interest or seriously detrimental to the relevant listed company. If the FCA authorise omission it can only do so if the omission would not be likely to mislead the public with regard to facts and circumstances, knowledge of which is essential for the assessment of the shares.

[FCA Listing Rules, paras 9.7A.2, 9.7A.3]

Disclosure by companies on the main market

Companies listed on the main market are also obliged to comply on an ongoing basis with the Disclosure and Transparency Rules ("DTRs").

DTR 6.1.13 provides that an issuer of shares (as defined) must publish notices or distribute circulars concerning the allocation and payment of dividends.

22.14 Uncertificated Securities and CREST

The conditions for eligibility for admission to LSE main market provide that the company's securities must be capable of being traded electronically ie are capable of being admitted to and traded via CREST, the electronic settlement system for holding and transferring uncertificated securities. Once shares are being traded electronically then:

- Dividend payments can be mandated through CREST
- Shareholders can make dividend elections (for example in relation to scrip issues) through CREST; and
- Companies can combine payment of dividends and interest through CREST using tax vouchers in electronic form.

To take advantage of the use of electronic payment of dividends, the company's articles of association must not be inconsistent with the payment of dividends via CREST. Specimen wording for articles of association, payment mandates and dividend elections is available (guidance only) from Euroclear.

22.14 Distributions

Conditions for payment mandates:

- The shareholder must elect to receive dividends payment via CREST in respect of all (and not just some) holdings;
- The company is not obliged to make payments through CREST where a holder has elected to receive dividends in that way. Each company can decide whether this is the payment mechanism they want to adopt and, if so, notify its shareholders accordingly.

See Euroclear's website – www.euroclear.com.

22.15 LSE Dividend Procedure Timetable

The LSE provide a dividend procedure timetable ("DP Timetable") which sets out how and when companies listed on the main market should announce dividends (whether interim or final). Provided that a company's timetable follows the DP timetable it does not need to be notified to LSE in advance provided that:

- The dividend information is disseminated by a Primary Information Provider ("PIP"); and
- The announcement includes the amount of the dividend and whether net or gross the record date, the pay date and the availability of any scrip, DRIP, currency election or other alternative and if available the last day to elect for the alternative.

Conditions which apply are set out in the notes to the DP Timetable.

22.16 AIM companies

Payment of dividends by AIM companies is governed by the AIM rules (Rule 17) which provides that an AIM company must notify a RIS without delay of any decision to make any payments in respect of its securities (including the payment of dividends). The company must specify:

- The net amount which is payable per security;
- The payment date;
- The record date.

Information about such notifications in the past twelve months must be included on the company's website.

PROVISIONS APPLYING BEFORE 6 APRIL 2008

(1) General definitions

Capitalisation meant, in relation to a company's profits, any of the following operations (whenever carried out), ie

- applying the profits in wholly or partly paying up unissued shares to be allotted to members of the company as fully or partly paid bonus shares; or
- transferring the profits to capital redemption reserve.

[*CA 1985, s 280*].

Distribution meant every description of distribution of a company's assets to its members, in cash or otherwise, except

- an issue of shares as fully or partly paid bonus shares;
- the redemption or purchase of any of the company's own shares out of capital (including the proceeds from the fresh issue of shares) or out of unrealised profits under *CA 1985, ss 159–181*;
- the reduction of share capital by extinguishing or reducing the liability of any of the members on company shares in respect of unpaid share capital, or by paying off paid up share capital; and
- a distribution of assets to members of the company on its winding up.

[*CA 1985, s 263(2)*].

Profits and **losses** of any description were references (respectively) to profits and losses of that description made at any time and, except where the context otherwise required, were to revenue and capital profits and revenue and capital losses.

[*CA 1985, s 280(3)*].

Undistributable reserves were

- the share premium account;
- the capital redemption reserve;
- the amount by which the company's accumulated, unrealised profits (so far as not previously utilised by capitalisation other than a transfer to capital redemption reserve after 21 December 1980) exceeded its accumulated, unrealised losses (so far as not previously written off in a reduction or reorganisation of capital); and
- any other reserve which the company was prohibited from distributing by any other enactment or by its memorandum or articles.

[*CA 1985, s 264(3)*].

(2) Profits available for distribution

Profits available for distribution were accumulated, realised profits (so far as not previously utilised by distribution or capitalisation) less accumulated, realised losses (so far as not previously written off in a reduction or reorganisation of capital).

Where directors, after making reasonable enquiries, were unable to determine whether a particular profit or loss made before 22 December 1980 was realised or unrealised, they could treat the profit as realised and the loss as unrealised.

[*CA 1985, s 263(3)(5)*].

Where, before 22 December 1980 under *CA 1980*, a company was authorised by its articles to apply its *unrealised* profits to pay up unissued shares as fully or partly paid bonus shares, that provision continued (subject to any alteration of the articles) as authority after that date.

[*CA 1985, s 278*].

(3) **Treatment of development costs**

Where development costs were shown as an asset in the company's accounts, any amount shown in respect of those costs was to be treated as

- a realised loss for the purposes of (2) above; and
- a realised revenue loss

The above did not apply to any part of that amount representing an unrealised profit made on revaluation of those costs. It also did not apply if

- there were special circumstances in the company's case justifying the directors in deciding that the amount was not to be so treated;
- it was stated
  - (i) in the case of Companies Act individual accounts, in the note to the accounts under *CA 1985, Sch 4 para 20* or *Sch 8 para 20* (reasons for showing development costs as an asset), or
  - (ii) in the case of IAS individual accounts, in any note to the accounts

  that the amount was not to be so treated; and
- the note explained the circumstances relied upon to justify the decision of the directors to that effect.

[*CA 1985, s 269; SI 1997 No 220, Reg 7; SI 2004 No 2947, Sch 1 para 25*].

(4) **Restrictions on distributions**

The following provisions applied without prejudice to any law or any provision of a company's memorandum or articles restricting the sums out of which, or the cases in which, a distribution could be made.

[*CA 1985, s 281*].

A company could not

- make a distribution except out of profits available for distribution (see (2) above) although there was no rule that all profits had to be distributed (*Burland v Earle* [1902] AC 83) until the company was wound up; or
- apply an unrealised profit in paying up debentures or unpaid amounts on its issued shares.

[*CA 1985, s 263(1)(4)*].

Additionally, a *public company* could only make a distribution if

- its 'net assets' at the time of the distribution were not less than the aggregate of its called-up share capital and 'undistributable reserves'; and
- the distribution did not reduce the amount of those assets to less than that aggregate.

'*Net assets*' meant the aggregate of the company's assets (excluding any uncalled share capital) less the aggregate of its 'liabilities' (including any provision for liabilities or charges within *CA 1985, Sch 4 para 89* that was made in Companies Act accounts and any provision that was made in IAS accounts).

See (1) above for '*undistributable reserves*'.

[*CA 1985, s 264(1)(2)(4); SI 2004 No 2947, Sch 1 para 22, Sch 7 para 8*].

See (5) to (8) below for the company's accounts to be considered in determining whether a distribution could be made without contravening the above provisions.

(5) **Accounting requirements**

A distribution which could be made without contravening the provisions of (4) above was determined by reference to

(i) profits, losses, assets and liabilities,

(ii) the following provisions, namely

- in the case of Companies Act individual accounts, provisions for depreciation or diminution in value of assets plus any provisions for liabilities which were reasonably necessary to provide for any liability the nature of which was clearly defined and which was either likely to be incurred, or certain to be incurred but uncertain as to amount or as date on which it would arise; and
- in the case of IAS individual accounts, provisions of any kind, and

(iii) share capital and reserves (including 'undistributable reserves', see (1) above)

as stated in the company's 'relevant accounts'.

The '*relevant accounts*' for these purposes were:

(a) Where (*b*) or (*c*) below did not apply, its '*last annual accounts*' that is to say:

For financial years ending after 30 September 2007

- in the case of a private company, those that were last sent to members in accordance with *CA 1985, s 238(1)*; and
- in the case of a public company, those which were laid under in respect of the last preceding accounting reference period.

For financial years ending before 1 October 2007, those which were laid in respect of the last preceding accounting reference period.

In respect of a distribution of *any company*

(i) the accounts must have been 'properly prepared' or have been so prepared subject only to matters which were not material for determining, by reference to (i)–(iii) above, whether the distribution would contravene the relevant provisions. Subject to this, the accounts had to give a true and fair view of the state of the company's affairs at the balance sheet date and its profit or loss in respect of the period for which they were prepared; and

(ii) the auditors must have reported on the accounts and, if that report was qualified, they had to state in writing whether, in their opinion, the qualification was material for determining by reference to (i)–(iii) above, whether the distribution would contravene the relevant provisions. *For financial years ending after 30 September 2007*, a copy of the auditors' statement had, in the case of a private company, to have been circulated to members along with the copies of the accounts sent to them under *CA 1985, s 238(1)* and, in the case of a public company, to have been laid before the company in general meeting. *For financial years ending before 1 October 2007*, a copy of the auditors' statement must have been laid before the company in general meeting.

See also *Precision Dippings Ltd v Precision Dippings Marketing Ltd* [1986] Ch 447, [1985] BCLC 385, CA.

(b) Where the distribution would have contravened the relevant provisions if reference were made only to the last annual accounts in (*a*) above, such *interim accounts* as were necessary to enable a reasonable judgement to be made as to the amounts in (i)–(iii) above.

In respect of a proposed distribution by a *public company*

(i) the provisions of (*a*)(i) above applied (but see below for the meaning of 'properly prepared'); and

(ii) a copy of the accounts must have been delivered to the Registrar of Companies.

(c) Where the distribution was proposed to be declared during the company's first accounting reference period (or before any accounts were laid in respect of that period) such *initial accounts* as were necessary to enable a reasonable judgement to be made as to the amounts in (i)–(iii) above.

In respect of a proposed distribution by a *public company*

(i) the provisions of (*a*)(i) above applied (but see below for the meaning of 'properly prepared');

(ii) the auditors must have made a report stating whether, in their opinion, the accounts had been properly prepared and, if their report was qualified, they had to state in writing whether, in their opinion, the qualification was material for determining, by reference to (i)–(iii) above, whether the distribution would have contravened the relevant provisions; and

(iii) a copy of the accounts, auditors' report and statement (if any) must have been delivered to the Registrar of Companies.

'*Properly prepared*' for the purposes of (*a*)(i) above meant prepared in accordance with *CA 1985*. For the purposes of (*b*)(i) and (*c*)(i) above it means that the accounts had to comply with *CA 1985, ss 226, 226A* and *226B* and *Sch 4*, with necessary modifications where the accounts were prepared otherwise than in respect of an accounting reference period, and any balance sheet must have been signed in accordance with *CA 1985, s 233*.

Documents in foreign languages. Where any document within (*b*)(ii) or (*c*)(iii) above was in a language other than English, an English translation, certified as correct, also had to be delivered to the Registrar of Companies.

[*CA 1985, ss 270–273; CA 1989, Sch 10 paras 4–6; Welsh Language Act 1993, s 30; SI 2004 No 2947, Sch 1 paras 26, 27; SI 2006 No 3428, Sch 2; SI 2007 No 2194, Sch 4 para 3*].

(6) **Successive distributions**

For determining by reference to a particular set of accounts whether a proposed distribution could be made, (5) above had effect where one or more distributions had already been made by reference to those accounts as if the proposed distribution was increased by those distributions already made.

[*CA 1985, s 274(1)*].

This applied to distributions generally and also, if it would not have otherwise done so, to

- 'financial assistance' lawfully given by a public or private company out of its distributable profits where assistance was required to be given under *CA 1985, s 154* or *s 155(2)*;
- financial assistance given by a company in contravention of *CA 1985, s 151* which reduced the company's 'net assets' or increases its 'net liabilities';
- a payment made by a company for purchase of its own shares (except a payment made lawfully otherwise than out of distributable profits); and
- a payment of any description specified in *CA 1985, s 168*.

The financial assistance or payments must have been given or made after the relevant accounts were prepared and were treated as if they were distributions already made in pursuance of a determination made by reference to the accounts.

'*Net liabilities*' meant the amount by which the aggregate of the company's liabilities (including any amount retained as reasonably necessary to provide for any liability or loss which was either likely to be incurred or certain to be incurred but uncertain as to amount and date) exceeded the aggregate amount of its assets, taking the amount of the assets and liabilities to be as stated in the company's accounting records immediately before the financial assistance was given.

[*CA 1985, s 274*].

(7) **Treatment of assets in the relevant accounts**

Provisions to be treated as realised losses. For purposes of (4) above,

(a) in the case of Companies Act individual accounts, provisions for depreciation or diminution in value of assets plus any provisions for liabilities which were reasonably necessary to provide for any liability the nature of which was clearly defined and which was either likely to be incurred, or certain to be incurred but uncertain as to amount or as date on which it would arise; and

(b) in the case of IAS individual accounts, provisions of any kind

other than 'revaluation provisions' were treated as realised losses.

A '*revaluation provision*' meant a provision in respect of a diminution in value of a fixed asset appearing on a revaluation of all the fixed assets of the company, or of all of its fixed assets other than goodwill.

[*CA 1985, s 275(1)(1A); SI 2004 No 2947, Sch 1 para 28*].

Subject to below, for the purpose of (*b*) above, any consideration by the directors of the value of any fixed assets was treated as a revaluation but where such assets had not actually been revalued, the directors had to be satisfied that their aggregate value at the time in question was not less than the aggregate amount at which they were for the time being stated in the company's accounts. Where, however, proper accounts were required under (7)(*a*)(i), (*b*)(i) or (*c*)(i) above, this did not apply in determining whether a revaluation affecting the relevant items in (7)(i)–(iii) above had taken place unless it was stated in a note to the accounts

- that the directors had considered the value at any time of any fixed assets without actually revaluing those assets;
- that they were satisfied that the aggregate value of those assets at the time in question was or was not less than the aggregate amount at which they were for the time being stated in the company's accounts; and
- that the relevant items in question were stated in the relevant accounts on the basis that a revaluation of the company's fixed assets, which by virtue of (*b*) above included the assets in question, took place at that time.

[*CA 1985, s 275(4)–(6)*].

Depreciation following revaluation of fixed asset. If an unrealised profit was made on the revaluation of a fixed asset and subsequently a sum was written off or retained for depreciation of that asset, then a *realised* profit was treated as made for the purposes of (4) above of the amount by which that depreciation was greater than it would have been but for the revaluation.

[*CA 1985, s 275(2)*].

Cost of asset unknown. Where there was no record of the original cost of an asset, or no record could be obtained without unreasonable expense or delay, then in determining whether the company had made a profit or loss on the asset, its cost was taken to be the value given to it in the earliest available record made on or after its acquisition by the company.

[*CA 1985, s 275(3)*].

(8) **Distribution in kind**

Where a company made a distribution of (or including) a non-cash asset, and any part of the amount at which that asset was stated in the accounts relevant for the purposes of the distribution under (5)–(7) above represented an *unrealised profit*, this profit was to be treated as *realised* for the purposes of

(a) determining the lawfulness of the distribution in accordance with the provisions of this chapter (whether before or after the distribution takes place); and

(b) the application of *CA 1985, Sch 4 paras 12(a), 34(3)(a) or Sch 8 paras 12(a), 34(3)(a)* (only realised profits are to be included in or transferred to the profit and loss account).

[*CA 1985, s 276; CA 1989, Sch 10 para 7; SI 1997 No 220, Reg 7*].

(9) **Consequences of unlawful distributions**

Where a distribution, or part of one, made by a company to one of its members was unlawful under the provisions of this chapter and at the time of the distribution the member knew, or has reasonable grounds for believing, it to be unlawful, he had to repay it to the company. In the case of a non-cash distribution, he had to repay an amount equal to the value of the distribution at the time it was made. [*CA 1985, s 277(1)*]. See *Precision Dippings Ltd v Precision Dippings Marketing Ltd and Others CA* [1985] 3 WLR 812.

The above was without prejudice to any obligation otherwise imposed on a member to repay an unlawful distribution, but did not apply to

- financial assistance given by a company in contravention of *CA 1985, s 151*; or
- any payment made by a company in respect of the redemption or purchase of shares in itself.

[*CA 1985, s 277(2)(3)*].

Directors who were parties to the payment of an unlawful dividend were jointly and severally liable to repay the amount. This applied even if the dividend was approved by a general meeting or the company's articles. See *Exchange Banking Co, Re, Flitcroft's Case* (1882) 21 Ch D 519, CA and also *Wallersteiner v Moir* [1974] 3 All ER 217, [1974] 1 WLR 991, CA; *Selangor United Rubber Estates Ltd v Cradock (a bankrupt) (No 3)* [1968] 2 All ER 1073, [1968] 1 WLR 1555 and *Belmont Finance Corpn Ltd v Williams Furniture Ltd (No 2)* [1980] 1 All ER 393, CA.

In *Bairstow v Queens Moat Houses plc* [2000] 1 BCLC 549, [2000] BCC 1025 it was held that a director who authorised the payment of an unlawful dividend in breach of his duty as a quasi trustee was liable to repay such a dividend if

- he knew the dividends were unlawful, whether or not that actual knowledge amounted to a fraud;
- he knew the facts that established the impropriety of the payments, even though he was unaware that such impropriety rendered the payment unlawful;
- he had to be taken in all the circumstances to have known all the facts which rendered the payments unlawful; or
- he ought to have known, as a reasonably competent and diligent director, that the payments were unlawful.

The decision was upheld in the Court of Appeal ([2001] 2 BCLC 531) which also held that the liability to repay applied whether the company was solvent or insolvent and that the amount to be repaid was the full amount of the unlawful dividend, not just the excess over the dividend which could lawfully have been paid.

(10) **Procedures, etc for payment of dividends**

Similar provisions applied as in **22.10** above.

(11) **Listed company requirements**

Similar provisions applied as in **22.11** above.

23 Insider Dealing and Market Abuse

23.1	**Introduction**	23.8	Market abuse: improper disclosure
23.2	**The offence of insider dealing**	23.9	Market abuse: manipulating transactions
23.3	Definitions		
23.4	Penalties	23.10	Market abuse: manipulating devices
23.5	Defences	23.11	Market abuse: dissemination
23.6	**Market abuse**	23.12	Exceptions
23.7	Market abuse: insider dealing	23.13	Penalties

Cross-references. See 33 Appendix Public and Listed Companies for the Model Code for listed companies.

23.1 INTRODUCTION

This chapter deals with two pieces of legislation which regulate the manipulation of the market and market abuse. The first is the *Criminal Justice Act 1993 (CJA)* which makes it a criminal offence for an individual to (a) deal with the benefit of inside information (b) encourage another person to deal on the basis of inside information and (c) disclose inside information (see **23.2** below). The second is the *Financial Services and Markets Act 2000 (FMSA 2000)*. This does not strictly provide criminal prosecution for breach of the market abuse provisions. Instead the FCA can impose penalties (see **23.13** below).

23.2 THE OFFENCE OF INSIDER DEALING

Subject to the defences in **23.5**, an individual who has 'information as an insider' is guilty of the offence of insider dealing in the following circumstances.

(a) He 'deals in securities' that are price-affected in relation to the 'inside information' in either of the following circumstances, namely

(i) the acquisition or disposal in question occurs on a regulated market; or

(ii) the person dealing relies on, or is himself acting as, a 'professional intermediary'.

A *'professional intermediary'* is a person who carries on a business, holds himself out as willing to engage in a business or is employed in a business which (other than on an incidental or occasional basis)

(1) acquires and disposes of securities (as principal or agent); or

(2) acts as an intermediary between other persons dealing in securities.

The person dealing in securities relies on a professional intermediary if (and only if) the person acting as a professional intermediary carries out an activity within (1) or (2) above.

(b) He encourages another person to 'deal in securities' that are (whether or not he knows it) price-affected securities in relation to the inside information and he knows (or has reasonable cause to believe) that dealing will take place in the securities under one of the circumstances as in (*a*)(i) or (ii) above.

(c) He discloses the information (otherwise than in the proper performance of the functions of his employment, office or profession) to another person.

[*CJA 1993, ss 52, 59*].

Territorial scope. An individual is not guilty of an offence under (a) above unless

- he was in the UK when he is alleged to have done any act forming part of the alleged deal;
- the regulated market on which the dealing in alleged to have occurred is identified (by order) as being regulated in the UK; or
- the professional intermediary was in the UK at the time when he is alleged to have done anything by means of which the offence is alleged to have been committed.

An individual is not guilty of an offence under (*b*) or (*c*) above unless

- he was in the UK at the time when he is alleged to have encouraged the dealing or disclosed the information; or
- the alleged recipient of the information or encouragement was in the UK at the time of the alleged receipt.

[*CJA 1993, s 62*].

23.3 Definitions

The following definitions apply for the purposes of the insider dealing provisions in **23.2** (above) and **23.5** below.

Acquire, in relation to a security, includes agreeing to acquire the security and entering into a contract which creates the security.

[*CJA 1993, s 55(2)*].

Company means any body (whether or not incorporated and wherever incorporated or constituted) which is not a 'public sector body'.

[*CJA 1993, s 60(3)*].

Dealing in securities. A person deals in securities if he

- 'acquires' or 'disposes' of the securities (as principal or agent); or
- procures (directly or indirectly) an acquisition or disposal of the securities by any other person (including his agent, his nominee or a person acting at his direction).

[*CJA 1993, s 55(1)(4)(5)*].

Dispose, in relation to a security, includes agreeing to disposal of the security and bringing to an end a contract which created the security.

[*CJA 1993, s 55(3)*].

Information as an insider. A person has information as an insider if (and only if)

- it is, and he knows that it is, 'inside information'; and

- he has it, and knows that he has it, from an inside source, ie

  (i) through being a director, employee or shareholder of an issuer of securities or through having access to the information by virtue of his employment, office or profession; or

  (ii) the direct or indirect source of his information is a person within (i) above.

[*CJA 1993, s 57*].

Inside information means information which

(a) relates to particular securities or issuer(s) and not to securities or issuers generally (but information is treated as relating to an issuer which is a company not only where it is about the company but also where it may affect the company's business prospects);

(b) is specific or precise;

(c) has not been 'made public'; and

(d) if it were made public would be likely to have a significant effect on the price of any securities.

Information is '*made public*' if

- it is published under the rules of a regulated market to inform investors and professional advisers;
- it is contained in public records;
- it can readily be obtained by those likely to 'deal in any securities'

  (i) to which the information relates; or

  (ii) of an the issuer to which the information relates;

- or it is derived from information which has been made public.

Information may be treated as made public even though

- it can be acquired only by persons exercising diligence or expertise;
- it is communicated only to a section of the public and not to the public at large;
- it can be acquired only by observation;
- it is communicated only on payment of a fee; or
- it is only published outside the UK.

[*CJA 1993, ss 56(1), 58, 60(4)*].

As regards (*b*) above, information such as 'our results will be much better than the market expects or knows' is not precise (as the actual results are not disclosed) but it is specific because it gives information about the results which has obviously not been made available to the public. A statement such as 'our profit will be at a certain level and the market does not know that', without stating whether they would be better or worse than the market expected, is precise information. It would be up to the recipient to judge whether the information is likely to be price-sensitive. (Hansard, Standing Committee B, col 175, 10 June 1993).

Market information is information consisting of one or more of the following facts.

(a) That securities of a particular kind have been, or are to be, acquired or disposed of (or such acquisition or disposal is under consideration or the subject of negotiation).

(b) That securities of a particular kind have not been, or are to be, acquired or disposed of.

(c) The number or price (or range of prices) of securities involved in a transaction within (*a*).

(d) The identity of the persons involved or likely to be involved in any capacity in an acquisition or disposal.

[*CJA 1993, Sch 1 para 4*].

Price-affected securities are securities in relation to which the 'inside information' would, if made public, be likely to have a significant effect on the price of the securities.

[*CJA 1993, s 56(2)*].

Price-sensitive information in relation to securities means 'inside information' which would, if made public, be likely to have a significant effect on the price of the securities.

[*CJA 1993, s 56(2)*].

Public sector body means the government of any country or territory; any local authority (in the UK or elsewhere); any international organisation of which any Member State is a member; and the Bank of England and the central bank of any sovereign state.

[*CJA 1993, s 60(3)*].

Securities. The insider dealing provisions apply to any of the following securities which satisfy the conditions set out below.

(a) Shares and stock in the share capital of a 'company'.

(b) Debt securities (ie any instrument creating or acknowledging indebtedness which is issued by a 'company' or 'public sector body' and including, in particular, debentures, loan stock, bonds and certificates of deposit).

(c) Warrants (ie any right to subscribe for shares or debt securities).

(d) Depositary receipts (ie a certificate or other record which is issued by, or on behalf of, a person who holds securities within (*a*)–(*c*) above of a particular issuer and which acknowledges that another person is entitled to rights in relation to those securities or such securities of the same kind).

(e) Options to acquire or dispose of any security within (*a*)–(*d*) above or (*f*) or (*g*) below.

(f) Futures (ie rights under a contract for the acquisition or disposal of any securities within (*a*)–(*e*) above or (*g*) below under which delivery is to be made at a future date and at a price agreed when the contract is made).

(g) Contracts for differences (ie rights under a contract which does not provide for the delivery of securities but whose purpose or pretended purpose is to secure a profit (or avoid a loss) by reference to fluctuations in a share index (or other similar factor) connected with securities within (*a*)–(*f*) above or the price of such securities or the interest rate offered on money placed on deposit).

The conditions are

(i) for any security within (*a*) or (*b*) above, that it is officially listed in a State within the European Economic Area (ie any Member State of the EC or Iceland, Norway or Liechtenstein) or is admitted to dealing on, or has its price quoted on or under the rules of, a 'regulated market';

(ii) for a warrant within (*c*) above, that *either* it satisfies the condition in (i) above *or* the right under it is a right to subscribe for any share or debt security of the same class as the share or debt security which satisfies the conditions in (i) above;

(iii) for a depositary receipt within (*d*) above, that *either* it satisfies the condition in (i) above *or* the rights under it are in respect of any share or debt security which satisfies the condition in (i) above;

(iv) for an option within (*e*) above or a future within (*f*) above, that *either* it satisfied the condition in (i) above *or* the option/rights under the future are in respect of any share or debt security which satisfies the condition in (i) above or any depositary receipt which satisfies that condition or the alternative condition in (iii) above); and

(v) for a contract for differences within (*g*) above, that *either* it satisfies the condition in (i) above *or* that the purpose (or pretended purpose) of the contract is to secure a profit or avoid a loss by reference to the fluctuations in the price (or an index of the price) of any shares or debt securities which satisfy the condition in (i) above.

A '*regulated market*' is any market established under the rules of

- The London Stock Exchange Ltd
- LIFFE Administration & Management
- OMLX, the London Securities and Derivatives Exchange Ltd
- Virt-x Exchange Ltd
- The exchange known as COREDEALMTS, together with the market known as OFEX
- The Irish Stock Exchange Ltd
- The exchange known as EASDAG
- The exchange known as NASDAQ
- The exchange known as the Nouveau Marché
- The exchange known as SWX Swiss Exchange
- The stock exchanges of Amsterdam, Antwerp, Athens, Barcelona, Bavaria, Berlin, Bilbao, Bologna, Bremen, Brussels, Copenhagen, Dusseldorf, Florence, Frankfurt, Genoa, Hamburg, Hanover, Helsinki, Iceland, Lisbon, Luxembourg, Lyon, Madrid, Milan, Naples, Oporto, Oslo, Palermo, Paris, Rome, Stockholm, Stuttgart, Trieste, Turin, Valencia, Venice or Vienna

[*CJA 1993, s 54, Sch 2; SI 1994 No 187; SI 1996 No 1561; SI 2000 No 1923, Art 2; SI 2002 No 1874, Art 2*].

23.4 Penalties

Penalties. A person guilty of the offence of insider dealing is liable (i) on conviction on indictment, to imprisonment for up to seven years or a fine or both, or (ii) on summary conviction, to imprisonment for up to six months or a fine not exceeding the statutory maximum or both. See **29.1 Offences and Legal Proceedings** for the statutory maximum. The consent of the Secretary of State or the Director of Public Prosecutions (in Northern Ireland, the Director of Public Prosecutions for Northern Ireland) must be obtained for proceedings to be instituted.

[*CJA 1993, s 61*].

Time limit for proceedings. In England and Wales, an information relating to an offence of insider dealing that is triable by a magistrates' court may be so tried if it is laid

- at any time within three years after the commission of the offence; and
- within twelve months after the date on which evidence sufficient in the opinion of the Director of Public Prosecutions or the Secretary of State (as the case may be) to justify the proceedings comes to that person's knowledge.

In Scotland, summary proceedings for an offence of insider dealing

- must not be commenced after the expiration of three years from the commission of the offence;
- subject to that, may be commenced at any time
  - (i) within twelve months after the date on which evidence sufficient in the Lord Advocate's opinion to justify the proceedings came to that person's knowledge; or
  - (ii) where such evidence was reported to the Lord Advocate by the Secretary of State, within twelve months after the date on which it came to the knowledge of the latter.

In Northern Ireland, a magistrates' court has jurisdiction to hear and determine a complaint charging the commission of a summary offence of insider dealing provided that the complaint is made

- within three years from the time when the offence was committed; and
- within twelve months from the date on which evidence sufficient in the opinion of the Director of Public Prosecutions for Northern Ireland or the Secretary of State (as the case may be) to justify the proceedings comes to that person's knowledge.

[*CJA 1993, s 61A*]

Effect on contracts. The fact that a person has been found guilty of the offence of insider dealing does not, in itself, make any contract void or unenforceable.

[*CJA 1993, s 63(2)*].

23.5 Defences

An individual is not guilty of dealing in securities or encouraging others to deal (see 23.2(*a*) or (*b*)) if he can show any of the following.

- He did not at the time expect the dealing to result in a profit (or avoidance or loss) attributable to the fact that the information in question was 'price-sensitive information' in relation to the securities.
- At the time he believed on reasonable grounds that the information had been (or, where the offence of encouraging others to deal applies, would be) disclosed widely enough to ensure that none of those taking part in the dealing would be prejudiced by not having the information.
- He would have done what he did even if he had not had the information.
- He acted in good faith in the course of his business as a 'market maker' or his employment in the business of a market maker. A '*market maker*' is a person who holds himself out at all normal times (in compliance with the rules of a regulated market or an approved international securities self-regulating organisation) as willing to acquire or dispose of securities and who is recognised as doing so under those rules.
- The information which he had as an insider was 'market information' and it was reasonable for an individual in his position to have acted as he did despite having the information as an insider at that time. In determining whether his actions were reasonable (despite having market information) there is, in particular, to be taken into account
  - (i) the contents of the information;
  - (ii) the circumstances in which he first had the information and in what capacity; and
  - (iii) the capacity in which he now acts.
- He acted in connection with, and with a view to facilitating, an acquisition or disposal which was under consideration or the subject of negotiation (or a series of such acquisitions or disposals). The information which he had as an insider must have been 'market information' arising directly out of his involvement in that acquisition, etc.
- He acted in conformity with the price stabilisation rules made under *FSMA 2000, s 144(1)* or the relevant provisions of *EC Regulation 2273/2003* implementing *Directive 2003/6/EC* (exemption for buy-back programmes and stabilisation of financial instruments).

[*CJA 1993, s 53(1)(2)(6), Sch 1 paras 1–3, 5; SI 2001 No 3649, Art 341; SI 2005 No 381, Reg 3*].

An individual is not guilty of disclosing inside information (see 23.2(*c*) above) if he can show that

- he did not at the time expect any person, because of the disclosure, to 'deal in securities'; or
- although he had such an expectation at that time, he did not expect the dealing to result in a profit (or avoidance of loss) attributable to the fact that the information was 'price-sensitive information' in relation to the securities.

[*CJA 1993, s 53(3)(6)*].

23.6 MARKET ABUSE

The market abuse regime in *FSMA 2000* was brought into force on 1 December 2001, providing a framework to regulate, amongst other things, dealing or attempted dealing by an 'insider', The regulatory framework comprises:

- *FSMA 2000, Pt VIII (ss 118–131A)* which implemented the 2003 EC Market Abuse Directive
- the *Financial Services and Markets Act 2000 (Market Abuse Regulations) 2005 (SI 2005 No 381)* which implemented EU Directive 2003/6/EC (the Market Abuse Directive). The Directive defines market abuse more narrowly than *FSMA 2000, section 118* and as a consequence the offences of misuse of information and misleading behaviour and distortion were only in force for a limited period. *Section 118(4)* ceased to have effect on 15 December 2014.

  [*FSMA 2000 (Market Abuse) Regulations 2009 (SI 2009 No 3128), (SI 2011 No 2928), (SI 2014 No 3081)*].
- FCA Business Standard MAR 1 The Code of Market Conduct, and
- the *Recognised Auction Platform Regulations 2011 (SI 2011 No 2699)*. These regulations amend *FSMA* in relation to recognised auction platforms which conduct auctions in EU emission allowances and are recognised and supervised by the FCA. For the purposes of this chapter 23, the amended *FSMA* provisions are not included as they have a very narrow application..

It runs alongside the criminal insider dealing legislation (see **23.2** above) and market manipulation offences in *FSMA 2000, s 397.*

FSMA 2000, s 118 defines market abuse as behaviour which can amount to market abuse, namely

- insider dealing (see **23.7**);
- improper disclosure (see **23.8**);
- manipulating transactions (see **23.9**);
- manipulating devices (see **23.10**); and
- dissemination (see **23.12**).

These headings contain descriptions of behaviour that, in the opinion of the FCA, do or do not amount to market abuse. The FCA Code of Market Conduct (MAR1) referred to above

- gives guidance on the market abuse regime
- provides assistance in determining whether or not behaviour amounts to market abuse and some useful practical example
- refers to a readers' guide which assists in the interpretation of MAR1
- considers the general concepts relevant to market abuse, then each type of behaviour in turn and then describes exceptions to market abuse.

It is referred to, where relevant, in each section of this chapter dealing with market abuse by indicating MAR and the paragraph number of MAR.

In addition, certain exceptions which are of general application are considered in **23.12**.

23.7 Market abuse: insider dealing

The first type of market abuse is where an 'insider' (see definition below) deals or attempts to deal in qualifying investments. It is defined subject to 23.12 EXCEPTIONS, as 'behaviour' (whether by one person alone or by two or more persons jointly or in concert)

- which occurs in the UK in relation to
  - (i) qualifying investments admitted to trading on a prescribed market situated in, or operating in, the UK,
  - (ii) qualifying investments in respect of which a request for admission to trading on such a market has been made, or
  - (iii) investments which are 'related investments' in relation to such qualifying investments, and
- where an 'insider' deals, or attempts to deal, in a qualifying investment or related investment 'on the basis of' 'inside information' relating to the investment in question.

'*Behaviour*' includes action or inaction.

'*Related investments*' are investments whose price or value depends on the price or value of the qualifying investments.

[*FSMA 2000, ss 118(1)(2), 118A(1), 130A(3); SI 2005 No 381*].

'Prescribed markets' and 'qualifying investments' are defined in the *Financial Services and Markets Act 2000 (Prescribed Markets and Qualifying Investments) Order 2001 (SI 2001 No 996)*.

An insider is any person who has inside information

(a) as a result of his membership of an administrative, management or supervisory body of an issuer of qualifying investments,

(b) as a result of his holding in the capital of an issuer of qualifying investments,

(c) as a result of having access to the information through the exercise of his employment, profession or duties,

(d) as a result of his criminal activities, or

(e) which he has obtained by other means and which he knows, or could reasonably be expected to know, is inside information.

[*FSMA 2000, s 118B; SI 2005 No 381*].

Inside information in defined as

(1) In relation to qualifying investments, or related investments, which are not commodity derivatives, information of a 'precise' nature which

- (i) is not 'generally available' (see below for FCA MAR 1 on what is 'generally available' information),
- (ii) relates, directly or indirectly, to one or more issuers of the qualifying investments or to one or more of the qualifying investments, and
- (iii) would, if generally available, be likely to have a 'significant effect on the price' of the qualifying investments or on the price of related investments.

(2) In relation to qualifying investments or related investments which are commodity derivatives, information of a 'precise' nature which

(i) is not 'generally available',

(ii) relates, directly or indirectly, to one or more such derivatives, and

(iii) users of markets on which the derivatives are traded would expect to receive in accordance with any 'accepted market practices' on those markets.

For the purposes of (iii) above, users of markets on which investments in commodity derivatives are traded are to be treated as expecting to receive information relating directly or indirectly to one or more such derivatives in accordance with any accepted market practices, which is

(a) routinely made available to the users of those markets, or

(b) required to be disclosed in accordance with any statutory provision, market rules, or contracts or customs on the relevant underlying commodity market or commodity derivatives market.

'*Accepted market practices*' means practices that are reasonably expected in the financial market or markets in question and are accepted by the FCA or, in the case of a market situated in another EEA State, the competent authority of that EEA State. See FCA Business Standard MAR 1, Annex 2 for factors which the FSA will take into account when assessing whether to accept a particular market practice.

(3) In relation to a person charged with the execution of orders concerning any qualifying investments or related investments, inside information includes information conveyed by a client and related to the client's 'pending orders' which

(i) is of a 'precise' nature,

(ii) is not generally available,

(iii) relates, directly or indirectly, to one or more issuers of qualifying investments or to one or more qualifying investments, and

(iv) would, if generally available, be likely to have a 'significant effect on the price' of those qualifying investments or the price of related investments.

Information is '*precise*' if it

- indicates circumstances that exist (or may reasonably be expected to come into existence) or an event that has occurred (or may reasonably be expected to occur), and
- is specific enough to enable a conclusion to be drawn as to the possible effect of those circumstances or that event on the price of qualifying investments or related investments.

Information would be likely to have a '*significant effect on the price*' if and only if it is information of a kind which a reasonable investor would be likely to use as part of the basis of his investment decisions.

Information which can be obtained by research or analysis conducted by, or on behalf of, users of a market is to be regarded as being generally available to them.

Dealing, in relation to an investment, means acquiring or disposing of the investment whether as principal or agent or directly or indirectly, and includes agreeing to acquire or dispose of the investment, and entering into and bringing to an end a contract creating it.

[*FSMA 2000, ss 118C, 130A(3); SI 2005 No 381*].

MAR 1.2.3: *section 118(1)(a)* of the *FSMA 2000* does not require the person engaging in the behaviour in question to have intended to commit market abuse.

Insiders. In the opinion of the FCA the following factors are to be taken into account in determining whether or not a person could reasonably be expected to know that information in his possession is inside information and therefore whether he is an insider under (e) above, and indicate that the person is an insider.

- If a normal and reasonable person in the position of the person who has inside information would know or should have known that the person from whom he received it is an insider, and
- If a normal and reasonable person in the position of the person who has inside information would know or should have known that it is inside information.

For the purposes of (*a*) to (*d*) above, the person concerned does not need to know that the information concerned is inside information.

(MAR: 1.2.8 and 1.2.9)

Inside information.

- What is '*generally available*'. In the opinion of the FCA following factors are to be taken into account in determining whether or not information is 'generally available' and are indications that it is (and therefore not inside information).

  (i) Whether the information has been disclosed to a prescribed market or a prescribed auction platform through a RIS or otherwise in accordance with the rules of that market.

  (ii) Whether the information is contained in records which are open to inspection by the public.

  (iii) Whether the information is otherwise generally available, including through the Internet, or some other publication (including if it is only available on payment of a fee), or is derived from information which has been made public.

  (iv) Whether the information can be obtained by observation by members of the public without infringing rights or obligations of privacy, property or confidentiality.

  (v) The extent to which the information can be obtained by analysing or developing other information which is generally available.

  It is not relevant that the information is only generally available outside the UK. In relation to (i), (iii), (iv) and (v), it is not relevant that the observation or analysis is only achievable by a person with above average financial resources, expertise or competence.

  (MAR 1.2.12 and 1.2.13)

- '*Pending order*'. In the opinion of the FCA a factor which indicates that there is a pending order or bid for a client is if a person is approached by another in relation to a transaction, and

(i) the transaction is not immediately executed on an arm's length basis in response to a price quoted by that person; and

(ii) the person concerned has taken on a legal or regulatory obligation relating to the manner or timing of the execution of the transaction.

(MAR 1.2.16)

On the basis of. The following factors are to be taken into account in determining whether or not a person's behaviour is 'on the basis of' inside information, and are each indications that it is not.

- If the decision to deal, or attempt to deal, was made before the person possessed the relevant inside information.
- If the person concerned is dealing to satisfy a legal or regulatory obligation which came into being before he possessed the relevant inside information.
- If a person is an organisation, if none of the individuals in possession of the inside information
  - (i) had any involvement in the decision to deal;
  - (ii) behaved in such a way as to influence, directly or indirectly, the decision to engage in the dealing; or
  - (iii) had any contact with those who were involved in the decision to engage in the dealing whereby the information could have been transmitted.

If the inside information is held behind an effective Chinese wall (or similarly effective arrangements) from the individuals who are involved in or who influence the decision to deal, that indicates that the decision to deal by an organisation is not 'on the basis of' inside information.

(MAR 1.3.3)

Behaviours which are market abuse within these provisions. The following behaviours are, in the opinion of the FCA, market abuse.

- Dealing on the basis of inside information which is not trading information.
- 'Front running/pre-positioning' ie a transaction for a person's own benefit, on the basis of and ahead of an order(including an order relating to a bid) which he is to carry out with or for another (in respect of which information concerning the order is inside information), which takes advantage of the anticipated impact of the order on the market or auction clearing price.
- In the context of a takeover, an offeror or potential offeror entering into a transaction in a qualifying investment, on the basis of inside information concerning the proposed bid, that provides merely an economic exposure to movements in the price of the target company's shares (eg a spread bet on the target company's share price).
- In the context of a takeover, a person who acts for the offeror or potential offeror dealing for his own benefit in a qualifying investment or related investments on the basis of information concerning the proposed bid which is inside information. (MAR 1.3.2)

Descriptions of behaviours which do not amount to market abuse (insider dealing) and relevant factors: legitimate business of market makers etc.

- A person will form an intention to buy or sell or submit or withdraw a bid for a qualifying investment or a related investment before doing so. His carrying out of his own intention is not in itself market abuse (insider dealing).

  (MAR 1.3.6)

- For market makers and persons that may lawfully deal in qualifying investments or related investments on their own account, pursuing their legitimate business of such dealing (including entering into an agreement for the underwriting of an issue of financial instruments) will not in itself amount to market abuse (insider dealing). This applies even if the person concerned in fact possesses trading information which is inside information.

  If the inside information is not limited to trading information (except in relation to an agreement for the underwriting of an issue of financial instruments), that indicates that the behaviour is not in pursuit of legitimate business.

  (MAR 1.3.7, 1.3.8 and 1.3.9)

- The dutiful carrying out (or arranging for the dutiful carrying out) of an order (including an order relating to a bid) on behalf of another (including as portfolio manager) will not in itself amount to market abuse (insider dealing) by the person carrying out that order. This applies whether or not the person carrying out the order (including an order relating to a bid), or the person for whom he is acting, in fact possesses inside information. Also, a person that carries out an order on behalf of another will not, merely as a result of that action, be considered to have any inside information held by that other person.

  If the inside information is not limited to trading information, that indicates that the behaviour is not dutiful carrying out of an order on behalf of a client.

  (MAR 1.3.12, 1.3.13 and 1.3.14)

- Behaviour, based on inside information relating to another company, in the context of a public takeover bid or merger for the purpose of gaining control of that company or proposing a merger with that company, does not of itself amount to market abuse (insider dealing). This includes

  (i) seeking from holders of securities, issued by the target, irrevocable undertakings or expressions of support to accept an offer to acquire those securities (or not to accept such an offer);

  (ii) making arrangements in connection with an issue of securities that are to be offered as consideration for the takeover or merger offer or to be issued in order to fund the takeover or merger offer, including making arrangements for the underwriting or placing of those securities and any associated hedging arrangements by underwriters or places which are proportionate to the risks assumed; and

  (iii) making arrangements to offer cash as consideration for the takeover or merger offer as an alternative to securities consideration.

  (MAR 1.3.17)

23.8 Market abuse: improper disclosure

Subject to **23.12**, market abuse includes 'behaviour' (whether by one person alone or by two or more persons jointly or in concert)

- which occurs in the UK in relation to
  - (i) qualifying investments admitted to trading on a prescribed market situated in, or operating in, the UK,
  - (ii) qualifying investments in respect of which a request for admission to trading on such a market has been made, or
  - (iii) investments which are 'related investments' in relation to such qualifying investments, and
- where an 'insider' discloses 'inside information' to another person otherwise than in the proper course of the exercise of his employment, profession or duties.

'*Behaviour*' includes action or inaction.

'*Related investment*', in relation to a qualifying investment, means an investment whose price or value depends on the price or value of the qualifying investment.

[*FSMA 2000, ss 118(1)(3), 118A(1), 130A(3); SI 2005 No 381*].

See **23.7** for '*behaviour*', '*related investments*', '*insider*' and '*inside information*' and provisions of FCA MAR 1 on those definitions.

Behaviours which are market abuse within these provisions. Behaviour falls within these provisions if it comprises

- disclosure of inside information by the director of an issuer to another in a social context; or
- selective briefing of analysts by directors of issuers or others who are 'persons discharging managerial responsibilities' (see **33.47** PUBLIC AND LISTED COMPANIES);

Behaviours that do not amount to market abuse (improper disclosure)

- disclosures made to a government department, the Bank of England, the Competition Commission, the Takeover Panel or any other regulatory body or authority for the purposes of fulfilling a legal or regulatory obligation;
- disclosures made otherwise to such a body in connection with the performance of the functions of that body; or
- disclosures required or permitted by listing rules, prospectus rules or disclosure rules made by the FCA; or
- disclosure of inside information by a broker to a potential buyer regarding the fact that the seller of qualifying investments is a person discharging managerial responsibilities or the identity of the person discharging managerial responsibilities or the purpose of the sale by the person discharging managerial responsibilities where the disclosure is made only to the extent necessary and solely in order to dispose of the investment, the liquidity of the stock is such that the transaction could not otherwise be completed and the transaction could not otherwise be completed without creating a disorderly market will not, of itself, amount to market abuse (improper disclosure)

The following factors should be taken into account in determining whether or not the disclosure was made by a person in the proper course of the exercise of his employment, profession or duties and are indications that it was.

(1) Whether the disclosure is permitted by the rules of a prescribed market, a prescribed auction platform of the FCA or the Takeover Code.

(2) Whether the disclosure is accompanied by the imposition of confidentiality requirements upon the person to whom the disclosure is made and is

- reasonable and is to enable a person to perform the proper functions of his employment, profession or duties;
- reasonable and is (eg to a professional adviser) for the purposes of facilitating or seeking or giving advice about a transaction or takeover bid;
- reasonable and is for the purpose of facilitating any commercial, financial or investment transaction (including prospective underwriters or placees of securities);
- reasonable and is for the purpose of obtaining a commitment or expression of support in relation to an offer which is subject to the Takeover Code; or
- in fulfilment of a legal obligation, including to employee representatives or trade unions acting on their behalf.

(3) Whether

- the information disclosed is trading information;
- the disclosure is made by a person ('A') only to the extent necessary, and solely in order, to offer to dispose of the investment to, or acquire the investment from, the person receiving the information; and
- it is reasonable for A to make the disclosure to enable him to perform the proper functions of his employment, profession or duties.

This is intended only to apply to an actual offer of the investment (and not to a disclosure of trading information to gauge potential interest in the investments to be offered or to help establish the likely price that will be obtained).

(MAR 1.4.2–1.4.5A).

23.9 Market abuse: manipulating transactions

Subject to **23.12**, market abuse includes 'behaviour' (whether by one person alone or by two or more persons jointly or in concert)

- which occurs in the UK in relation to
  - (i) qualifying investments admitted to trading on a prescribed market situated in, or operating in, the UK, or
  - (ii) qualifying investments in respect of which a request for admission to trading on such a market has been made, and
- where the behaviour consists of effecting transactions or orders to trade (otherwise than for 'legitimate reasons' and in conformity with 'accepted market practices' on the relevant market) which
  - (i) give, or are likely to give, a false or misleading impression as to the supply of, or demand for, or as to the price of, one or more qualifying investments, or

(ii) secure the price of one or more such investments at an abnormal or artificial level.

'*Accepted market practices*' means practices that are reasonably expected in the financial market or markets in question and are accepted by the FCA or, in the case of a market situated in another EEA State, the competent authority of that EEA State.

'*Behaviour*' includes action or inaction.

[*FSMA 2000, ss 118(1)(5), 118A(1), 130A(3); SI 2005 No 381*].

Behaviours which are market abuse within these provisions. The following behaviours are in the opinion of the FCA market abuse (manipulating transactions):

(a) *False or misleading impressions.*

- Buying or selling qualifying investments at the close of the market with the effect of misleading investors who act on the basis of closing prices (other than for legitimate reasons).
- 'Wash trades' (ie a sale or purchase of a qualifying investment where there is no change in beneficial interest or market risk, or where the transfer of beneficial interest or market risk is only between parties acting in concert or collusion, other than for legitimate reasons). For the avoidance of doubt a stock lending/borrowing or repo/reverse transaction, or another transaction involving the provision of collateral, do not constitute a wash trade.
- 'Painting the tape' (ie entering into a series of transactions that are shown on a public display for the purpose of giving the impression of activity or price movement in a qualifying investment).
- Entering orders into an electronic trading system at prices which are higher than the previous bid or lower than the previous offer, and withdrawing them before they are executed, in order to give a misleading impression that there is demand for or supply of the qualifying investment at that price, and
- Buying or selling on the secondary market of qualifying investments or related derivatives prior to the auction with the effect of fixing the auction clearing price for the auctioned products at an abnormal or artificial level or misleading bidders in the auctions other than for legitimate reasons.

(MAR 1.6.2 and 1.6.3)

(b) *Securing the price of a qualifying investment (price positioning).*

- Transactions or orders to trade by a person (or persons acting in collusion) that secure a dominant position over the supply of, or demand for, a qualifying investment and which have the effect of fixing directly or indirectly, purchase or sale prices or creating other unfair trading conditions (other than for legitimate reasons).
- Transactions where both buy and sell orders are entered at, or nearly at, the same time, with the same price and quantity by the same party (or different but colluding parties) other than for legitimate reasons, unless the transactions are legitimate trades carried out in accordance with the rules of the relevant trading platform (eg crossing trades).

- Entering small orders into an electronic trading system at prices which are higher than the previous bid or lower than the previous offer, in order to move the price of the qualifying investment (other than for legitimate reasons).
- An abusive squeeze (as defined).
- Parties, who have been allocated qualifying investments in a primary offering, colluding to purchase further tranches of those investments when trading begins in order to force the price of the investments to an artificial level and generate interest from other investors, and then sell the investments.
- Transactions or orders to trade employed so as to create obstacles to the price falling below a certain level, in order to avoid negative consequences for the issuer (eg a downgrading of its credit rating).
- Trading on one market or trading platform with a view to improperly influencing the price of the same or a related qualifying investment that is traded on another prescribed market, and
- Conduct by a person or persons acting in collusion, that secure a dominant position over the demand for a qualifying investment which has the effect of fixing, directly or indirectly, auction clearing prices or creating other unfair trading conditions, other than for legitimate reasons.

(MAR 1.6.4)

'*Legitimate reasons*'. The following factors are to be taken into account when considering whether behaviour is for legitimate reasons (and are indications that it is not).

- If the person has an actuating purpose behind the transaction to induce others to trade in, bid for, or to position or move the price of, a qualifying investment.
- If the person has another, illegitimate, reason behind the transactions, bid or order to trade.
- If the transaction was executed in a particular way with the purpose of creating a false or misleading impression.

The following factors are to be taken into account when considering whether behaviour is for legitimate reasons (and are indications that it is).

- If the transaction is pursuant to a prior legal or regulatory obligation owed to a third party.
- If the transaction is executed in a way which takes into account the need for the market or auction platform as a whole to operate fairly and efficiently.
- The extent to which the transaction generally opens a new position, so creating an exposure to market risk, rather than closes out a position and so removes market risk.
- If the transaction complied with the rules of the relevant prescribed markets or prescribed auction platform about how transactions are to be executed in a proper way (eg rules on reporting and executing cross-transactions).

(MAR 1.6.5 and 1.6.6)

Behaviour giving a false or misleading impression. The following factors are to be taken into account in determining whether or not a person's behaviour is likely to give a false or misleading impression.

- The extent to which orders to trade given, bids submitted or transactions undertaken

  (i) represent a significant proportion of the daily volume of transactions in the relevant qualifying investment on the regulated market or prescribed auction platform concerned, in particular when these activities lead to a significant change in the price of the qualifying investment;

  (ii) by persons with a significant buying or selling position in a qualifying investment lead to significant changes in the price of the qualifying investment or related derivative or underlying asset admitted to trading on a regulated market;

  (iii) whether transactions undertaken lead to no change in beneficial ownership of a qualifying investment admitted to trading on a regulated market.

- The extent to which orders to trade given or transactions undertaken

  (i) include position reversals in a short period and represent a significant proportion of the daily volume of transactions in the relevant qualifying investment on the regulated market concerned, and might be associated with significant changes in the price of a qualifying investment admitted to trading on a regulated market;

  (ii) are concentrated within a short time span in the trading session and lead to a price change which is subsequently reversed;

- The extent to which orders to trade given change the representation of the best bid or offer prices in a financial instrument admitted to trading on a regulated market, or more generally the representation of the order book available to market participants, and are removed before they are executed.

- The extent to which orders to trade given or transactions are undertaken at or around a specific time when reference prices, settlement prices and valuations are calculated and lead to price changes which have an effect on such prices and valuations.

  (MAR 1.6.9)

Behaviour securing an abnormal or artificial price level. In the opinion of the FCA the following factors are to be taken into account in determining whether or not a person's behaviour secures an abnormal or artificial price level.

- The extent to which the person had a direct or indirect interest in the price or value of the qualifying investment or related investment (ie an investment whose price or value depends on the price or value of the qualifying investment).

- The extent to which price, rate or option volatility movements, and the volatility of these factors for the investment in question, are outside their normal intra-day, daily, weekly or monthly range.

- Whether a person has successively and consistently increased or decreased his bid, offer or the price he has paid for a qualifying investment or related investment.

  (MAR 1.6.10)

Abusive squeezes. In the opinion of the FCA, the following factors are to be taken into account when determining whether a person has engaged in an abusive squeeze:

(1) the extent to which a person is willing to relax his control or other influence in order to help maintain an orderly market, and the price at which he is willing to do so; for example, behaviour is less likely to amount to an abusive squeeze if a person is willing to lend the investment in question;

(2) the extent to which the person's activity causes, or risks causing, settlement default by other market users on a multilateral basis and not just a bilateral basis. The more widespread the risk of multilateral settlement default, the more likely that an abusive squeeze has been effected;

(3) the extent to which prices under the delivery mechanisms of the market diverge from the prices for delivery of the investment or its equivalent outside those mechanisms. The greater the divergence beyond that to be reasonably expected, the more likely that an abusive squeeze has been effected; and

(4) the extent to which the spot or immediate market compared to the forward market is unusually expensive or inexpensive or the extent to which borrowing rates are unusually expensive or inexpensive.

Squeezes occur relatively frequently when the proper interaction of supply and demand leads to market tightness, but this is not of itself abusive. In addition, having a significant influence over the supply of, or demand for, or delivery mechanisms for an investment, for example, through ownership, borrowing or reserving the investment in question, is not of itself abusive.

The effects of an abusive squeeze are likely to be influenced by the extent to which other market users have failed to protect their own interests or fulfil their obligations in a manner consistent with the standards of behaviour to be expected of them in that market. Market users can be expected to settle their obligations and not to put themselves in a position where, to do so, they have to rely on holders of long positions lending when they may not be inclined to do so and may be under no obligation to do so. (MAR 1.6.11–1.6.13)

23.10 Market abuse: manipulating devices

Subject to **23.12**, market abuse includes 'behaviour' (whether by one person alone or by two or more persons jointly or in concert)

- which occurs in the UK in relation to
  - (i) qualifying investments admitted to trading on a prescribed market situated in, or operating in, the UK, or
  - (ii) qualifying investments in respect of which a request for admission to trading on such a market has been made, and
- where the behaviour consists of effecting transactions or orders to trade which employ fictitious devices or any other form of deception or contrivance.

'*Behaviour*' includes action or inaction.

[*FSMA 2000, ss 118(1)(6), 118A(1), 130A(3); SI 2005 No 381*]

Behaviours which are market abuse within these provisions. The following behaviours fall within these provisions.

- Taking advantage of occasional or regular access to the traditional or electronic media by voicing an opinion about a qualifying investment (or indirectly about its issuer) while having previously taken positions on, or submitted bids in relation to, that qualifying investment and profiting subsequently from the impact of the opinions voiced on the price of that instrument, without having simultaneously disclosed that conflict of interest to the public in a proper and effective way.
- A transaction or series of transactions that are designed to conceal the ownership of a qualifying investment, so that disclosure requirements are circumvented by the holding of the qualifying investment in the name of a colluding party, such that disclosures are misleading in respect of the true underlying holding. These transactions are often structured so that market risk remains with the seller. This does not include nominee holdings.
- 'Pump and dump' (ie taking a long position in a qualifying investment and then disseminating misleading positive information about the qualifying investment, with a view to increasing its price).
- 'Trash and cash' (ie taking a short position in a qualifying investment and then disseminating misleading negative information about the qualifying investment, with a view to driving down its price).

Factors to be taken into account in determining whether or not behaviour falls within these provisions are

- if orders to trade are given, bids submitted or transactions undertaken in qualifying investments by persons are preceded or followed by dissemination of false or misleading information by the same persons or persons linked to them; and
- if orders to trade are given, bids submitted or transactions are undertaken in qualifying investments by persons before or after the same persons or persons linked to them produce or disseminate research or investment recommendations which are erroneous or biased or demonstrably influenced by material interest.

  (MAR 1.7.2, 1.7.3).

23.11 Market abuse: dissemination

Subject to **23.12**, market abuse includes 'behaviour' (whether by one person alone or by two or more persons jointly or in concert)

- which occurs in the UK in relation to
  - (i) qualifying investments admitted to trading on a prescribed market situated in, or operating in, the UK, or
  - (ii) qualifying investments in respect of which a request for admission to trading on such a market has been made, and
- where the behaviour consists of the dissemination of information by any means which gives, or is likely to give, a false or misleading impression as to a qualifying investment by a person who knew, or could reasonably be expected to have known, that the information was false or misleading.

For these purposes, the dissemination of information by a person acting in the capacity of a journalist is to be assessed taking into account the codes governing his profession unless he derives, directly or indirectly, any advantage or profits from the dissemination of the information.

'*Behaviour*' includes action or inaction.

[*FSMA 2000, ss 118(1)(7), 118A(1)(4), 130A(3); SI 2005 No 381*].

Behaviours which are, in the opinion of the FCA, market abuse within these provisions. The following behaviours fall within these provisions.

- Knowingly or recklessly spreading false or misleading information about a qualifying investment through the media, including in particular through an RIS or similar information channel.
- Undertaking a course of conduct in order to give a false or misleading impression about a qualifying investment.

Factors to be taken into account in determining whether or not behaviour falls within these provisions are as follows.

- In the opinion of the FCA if a normal and reasonable person would know (or should have known) in all the circumstances that the information was false or misleading, that indicates that the person disseminating the information knew or could reasonably be expected to have known that it was false or misleading.
- If the individuals responsible for dissemination of information within an organisation could only know that the information was false or misleading if they had access to other information that was being held behind a Chinese wall or similarly effective arrangements, that indicates that the person disseminating did not know and could not reasonably be expected to have known that the information was false or misleading.

(MAR 1.8.3–1.8.5).

23.12 Exceptions

Behaviour does not amount to market abuse in the following circumstances.

(a) It conforms with a rule which includes a provision to the effect that behaviour conforming with the rule does not amount to market abuse. [*FSMA 2000, s 118A(5)(a); SI 2005 No 381*]. See, for example, FCA Listing Rules, LR1, para 1.4.7 and Annex 1 and FCA Disclosure Rules, DR1, para 1.5.2.

(b) It conforms with the relevant provisions of *EC Commission Regulation No 2273/2003* of 22 December 2003 as regards exemptions for buy-back programmes and stabilisation of financial instruments [*FSMA 2000, s 118A(5)(b); SI 2005 No 381*].

(c) It is done by a person acting on behalf of a public authority in pursuit of monetary policies or policies with respect to exchange rates or the management of public debt or foreign exchange reserves. [*FSMA 2000, s 118A(5)(c); SI 2005 No 381*].

(d) Behaviour conforming with certain of the rules of the Takeover Code does not, of itself, amount to market abuse if the rule of the Takeover Code is one of those set out in MAR 1.10.5C

(i) the behaviour is expressly required or expressly permitted by the rule in question (the notes for the time being associated with the rules identified in the Takeover Code are treated as part of the relevant rule for these purposes); and

(ii) it conforms to any General Principle set out at Section B of the Takeover Code relevant to that rule.

(FCA Business Standard MAR 1, paras 1.10.3–1.10.6).

(e) A disclosure which satisfies the following three conditions is not to be taken to breach any restriction on the disclosure of information (however imposed).

(i) The information or other matter causes the person making the disclosure to know or suspect (or gives him reasonable grounds for knowing or suspecting) that another person has engaged in market abuse.

(ii) The information or other matter disclosed came to the discloser in the course of his trade, profession, business or employment.

(iii) The disclosure is made to the FCA or to a nominated officer as soon as is practicable after the information or other matter comes to the discloser.

A disclosure to a nominated officer is a disclosure which is made to a person nominated by the discloser's employer to receive disclosures under these provisions, and is made in the course of the discloser's employment and in accordance with the procedure established by the employer for the purpose.

References to a person's employer include any body, association or organisation (including a voluntary organisation) in connection with whose activities the person exercises a function (whether or not for gain or reward) and references to employment must be construed accordingly.

[*FSMA 2000, s 131A; SI 2005 No 381*].

23.13 Penalties

If the FCA is satisfied that a person ('A')

(a) is or has engaged in market abuse, or

(b) by taking or refraining from taking any action has required or encouraged another person or persons to engage in behaviour which, if engaged in by A, would amount to market abuse,

it may impose on him a penalty of such amount as it considers appropriate.

The FCA must first issue a warning notice stating the amount of the proposed penalty. If, having considered any representations made to it in response to the warning notice, there are reasonable grounds for the FCA to be satisfied that the person

- believed, on reasonable grounds, that his behaviour did not fall within (*a*) or (*b*) above, or
- took all reasonable precautions and exercised all due diligence to avoid behaving in a way which fell within (*a*) or (*b*) above

the FCA cannot impose a penalty. But if, following any responses, the FCA decides to take action against a person under these provisions, it must give him a decision notice stating the amount of the penalty. The person may refer the matter to the Tribunal.

The imposition of a penalty does not make any transaction void or unenforceable.

Public statement. As an alternative to imposing a penalty on a person under the above provisions, the FCA may instead publish a statement to the effect that he has engaged in market abuse. If it decides to take this course of action, it must follow the same procedure of issuing a warning notice and, if it decides to proceed following any representations, a decision notice. Each must set out the terms of the statement.

[*FSMA 2000, ss 123, 126, 127, 131*].

The FCA can also apply to the court under *FSMA 2000, s 381* for an injunction restraining market abuse and under *FSMA 2000, s 381* for an order for restitution in market abuse cases. In these cases, under *FSMA 200, s 122*, it may ask the court to consider whether the circumstances are such that a penalty should be imposed on the person concerned.

FCA policy with regard to penalties and public statements. The FCA must issue a statement of its policy under the above provisions. [*FSMA 2000, s 124*]. It has issued this as FCA Decision, Procedure and Penalties Manual as amended by the FCA Decision Procedure and Penalties Manual and Enforcement Guide (Review) (March 2011.).

24 Interests in Public Company Shares

24.1	**Information about interests in a public company's shares**	24.7	Penalty for attempted evasion of restrictions
24.2	Power to investigate ownership of shares	24.8	Relaxation and removal of restrictions
24.4	Power of members to require company to act	24.9	Order for sale of shares
24.6	**Orders imposing restrictions on shares**		

24.1 INFORMATION ABOUT INTERESTS IN A PUBLIC COMPANY'S SHARES

There are two requirements which affect the obligation to disclose interests in the shares of a company. The first is *CA 2006, ss 793–828* which re-enact (with certain modifications) the disclosure obligations previously found in *CA 1985, ss 212–220.* These provisions give public companies the right to investigate who has an "interest" in its shares. The second requirements are the disclosure obligations in the Disclosure and Transparency Rules ("the DTRs") made by the FCA (see **33 Public and Listed Companies**).

The DTRs:

- Implement the provisions of the *EU Transparency Obligations Directive (Directive 2004/109/EC)*
- Apply only to companies with securities traded on a regulated or prescribed market and
- Replace *CA 1985, ss 198-220* which required the holder of shares in a public company to notify the company when that person's shareholding reached certain thresholds and also gave public companies the right to require shareholders or persons suspected of being interested in shares to disclose those interests. Those provisions were repealed in January 2007.
- can be found in the FCA handbook (www.fca.org.uk).

The distinction between the above requirements is that the *CA 2006* provisions apply to all public companies whereas the DTRs apply only to companies with securities traded on a regulated or prescribed market.

This chapter deals only with the *CA 2006* requirements.

Companies and shares to which the *CA 2006* provisions apply. The *CA 2006* provisions apply to a public company's issued shares carrying rights to vote at general meetings of the company (including any shares held as treasury shares). If voting rights are temporarily suspended (in respect of any shares) that does not affect the application of the disclosure obligations.

[*CA 2006, ss 791, 792*].

24.2 Power to investigate ownership of shares

Subject to the exemptions below, a public company may give notice to any person (including a person who is not a shareholder) whom it knows or has reasonable cause to believe is or, within the three years immediately preceding the date of the notice has been, 'interested' in the company's shares to confirm

(a) whether the person does or did in fact have such an interest [*s 792(2)(a)*]; and

(b) if that person does or did hold such an interest, to provide further information of that interest "as may be required" [*s 793(2)(b)*].

Note the permissive words of *s 793(2)(b)* ie "as may be required" so it is open to the company to decide how much information they ask for. If further information is asked for it must be 'in accordance' with *ss 793(3)–(7)* and so can

- Require the person to give particulars of his own past or present interests [*s 793(3)*]
- (Whether other interests in the shares subsist or subsisted during the three year period referred to above) require the person to give particulars about the other interests 'so far as lies within his knowledge' [*s 793(4)*].
- (Where the interest is a past interest) require the person to give details of the identity of the person who held the interest immediately after him "so far as lies within his knowledge" [*s 793(b)*]

The particulars referred to above include

- the identity of persons interested in the shares and
- whether persons interested in the same shares were parties to a *CA 2006, s 824* agreement (share acquisition agreements) or any agreement or arrangement relating to the exercise of rights conferred by the holding of the shares [*s 793(5)*].

Meaning of 'interest' in shares. The following rules apply to determine for these purposes whether a person has an interest in shares.

(1) A reference to an interest in shares includes an interest of any kind whatsoever in the shares.

[*CA 2006, s 820(2)*].

(2) Any restraints or restrictions to which the exercise of any right attached to the interest is or may be subject must be disregarded.

[*CA 2006, s 820(2)*].

(3) Where an interest in shares is comprised in property held on trust, every beneficiary of the trust is treated as having an interest in the shares.

[*CA 2006, s 820(3)*].

(4) A person is treated as having an interest in shares if

(i) he enters into a contract to acquire them;

(ii) not being the registered holder, he is entitled to exercise any right conferred by the holding of the shares or to control the exercise of any such right. For these purposes, a person is entitled to exercise or control the exercise of a right conferred by the holding of shares if he either has a right (whether subject to conditions or not) the exercise of which would make him so entitled or is under an obligation (whether subject to conditions or not) the fulfilment of which would make him so entitled;

(iii) he has a right to call for delivery of the shares to himself or to his order (whether the right is conditional or absolute); or

(iv) he has a right to acquire an interest in shares or is under an obligation to take an interest in shares (whether the right or obligation is conditional or absolute).

[*CA 2006, s 820(4)–(6)*].

(5) Persons having a joint interest are treated as each having that interest.

[*CA 2006, s 820(7)*].

(6) It is immaterial that shares in which a person has an interest are unidentifiable.

[*CA 2006, s 820(8)*].

(7) The requirement to provide information applies in relation to a person who has, or previously had, or is or was entitled to acquire, a right to subscribe for shares in the company as it applies in relation to a person who is or was interested in shares in that company.

[*CA 2006, s 821*].

(8) A person is taken to be interested in shares in which

(i) his spouse or civil partner, or

(ii) any infant child or step-child of his,

is interested.

In relation to Scotland 'infant' means a person under the age of 18 years.

[*CA 2006, s 822*].

(9) A person is taken to be interested in shares if a body corporate is interested in them and

(i) the body or its directors are accustomed to act in accordance with his directions or instructions; or

(ii) he is entitled to exercise or control the exercise of one-third or more of the voting power at general meetings of the body. A person is treated as entitled to exercise or control the exercise of voting power if

- another body corporate is entitled to exercise or control the exercise of that voting power and he is entitled to exercise or control the exercise of one-third or more of the voting power at general meetings of that body corporate;
- he has a right (whether or not subject to conditions) the exercise of which would make him so entitled; or
- he is under an obligation (whether or not subject to conditions) the fulfilment of which would make him so entitled.

[*CA 2006, s 823*].

(10) Subject to the exceptions below, special provisions apply in relation to an agreement between two or more persons that

(a) includes provision for the acquisition by any one or more of them of interests in shares of a particular public company (the '*target company*' for that agreement); and

(b) imposes obligations or restrictions on any one or more of the parties to it with respect to their 'use', retention or disposal of their interests in the shares of the target company acquired in pursuance of the agreement (whether or not together with any other interests of theirs in the company's shares to which the agreement relates).

Where an interest in the target company's shares is acquired by any of the parties in pursuance of the agreement, each party to the agreement is treated as interested in all shares in the target company in which any other party to the agreement is interested 'apart from the agreement' (whether or not the interest of the other party was acquired, or includes any interest that was acquired, in pursuance of the agreement).

An interest of a party to such an agreement in shares in the target company is an interest '*apart from the agreement*' if he is interested in those shares otherwise than by virtue of the application of these provisions in relation to the agreement. Accordingly, any such interest of the person (apart from the agreement) includes any interest treated as his under (8) or (9) above or by the application of these provisions in relation to any other agreement with respect to shares in the target company to which he is a party.

Once an interest in shares in the target company has been acquired in pursuance of the agreement, the agreement (and any substituted agreement) continue to be within these provisions so long as it continues to include provisions of any description mentioned (*b*) above. This applies irrespective of

- whether or not any further acquisitions of interests in the company's shares take place in pursuance of the agreement;
- any change in the persons who are for the time being parties to it; and
- any variation of the agreement.

'*Agreement*' for these purposes includes any arrangement, and the provisions of an agreement include undertakings, expectations or understandings operative under an arrangement, and may be express or implied and absolute or not.

Exceptions. These provisions do not apply

(i) to an agreement that is not legally binding unless it involves mutuality in the undertakings, expectations or understandings of the parties to it; or

(ii) to an agreement to underwrite or sub-underwrite an offer of shares in a company, provided the agreement is confined to that purpose and any matters incidental to it.

[*CA 2006, ss 824, 825*].

For the register entries required to be made by the company following receipt of information under these provisions, see **38.8 Registers**. For the removal of entries, see **38.10 Registers**.

Exemptions. A person is not obliged to comply with a notice if he is for the time being exempted by the Secretary of State. But the Secretary of State must not grant any such exemption unless

- he has consulted the Governor of the Bank of England; and

- he (the Secretary of State) is satisfied that, having regard to any undertaking given by the person in question with respect to any interest held or to be held by him in any shares, there are special reasons why that person should not be subject to those obligations.

[*CA 2006, s 796*].

24.3 *Consequences of failure to comply with notice*

(1) *Court order imposing restrictions on shares*

Where, within the time specified, a person fails to give a company the information required by a notice to under **24.2**, the company may apply to the court for an order directing that the shares in question be subject to restrictions. For the consequences of such an order, see **24.6** to **24.9**.

If the court is satisfied that such an order could unfairly affect the rights of third parties in respect of shares, the court may direct that such acts by specified persons as are set out in the order do not constitute a breach of the restrictions.

On application, the court may also make an interim order (either unconditionally or on such terms as it thinks fit).

[*CA 2006, s 794*].

(2) *Offences*

A person who

(a) fails to comply with a notice requiring disclosure of interests under **24.2**, or

(b) in purported compliance with such a notice

  (i) makes a statement that he knows to be false in a material particular, or

  (ii) recklessly makes a statement that is false in a material particular,

commits an offence except that a person does not commit an offence under (*a*) above if he proves that the requirement to give information was frivolous or vexatious.

A person guilty of such an offence is liable (i) on conviction on indictment, to imprisonment for a term not exceeding two years or a fine (or both); and (ii) on summary conviction, to imprisonment for a term not exceeding twelve months (six months in Scotland or Northern Ireland) or to a fine not exceeding the statutory maximum (or both). See **29.1 Offences and Legal Proceedings** for the statutory maximum.

[*CA 2006, s 795*].

24.4 Power of members to require company to act

The members of a company may require it to exercise its powers to investigate the ownership of shares . The company is required to do so once it has received requests from members holding at least 10% of such of the paid-up capital of the company as carries a right to vote at general meetings of the company (excluding any voting rights attached to any shares in the company held as treasury shares).

A request from members may be in hard copy form or in electronic form. It must

- state that the company is requested to exercise its powers to investigate the ownership of shares;

- specify the manner in which the company is requested to act;
- give reasonable grounds for requiring the company to exercise those powers in the manner specified; and
- be authenticated by the person or persons making it.

[*CA 2006, s 803*].

A company that is required under the above provisions to exercise its powers must exercise those powers in the manner specified in the requests. If it defaults, an offence is committed by every officer of the company who is in default. A person guilty of such an offence is liable (i) on conviction on indictment, to a fine; and (ii) on summary conviction, to a fine not exceeding the statutory maximum. See **29.1 Offences and Legal Proceedings** for the statutory maximum.

[*CA 2006, s 804*].

24.5 *Report to members on outcome of investigation*

On the conclusion of an investigation carried out by a company following a members' request, the company must prepare a report of the information received. The report must be made available for inspection within a reasonable period (not more than 15 working days) after the conclusion of the investigation.

Where a company undertakes such an investigation and it is not concluded within three months from the date on which the requirement to do so arose, it must prepare an interim report of the information received in that three-month period. It must similarly prepare a report for any succeeding three-month period until the conclusion of the investigation. Each such report must be made available for inspection within a reasonable period (not more than 15 working days) after the end of the period to which it relates. The report must not contain any information which does not have to be disclosed under regulations made under *CA 2006, s 409(3)*. These *Regulations* (the *Large and Medium-sized Companies and Groups (Accounts and Reports) Regulations 2008 (SI 2008 No 410)*) provide that information about related undertakings which must be disclosed in the accounts does not apply to companies that either are established under a law outside the UK or carry on business outside the UK provided that in the opinion of the directors disclosure would be seriously prejudicial to the business of the overseas undertaking or the company or any of its subsidiaries or any other undertaking included in the consolidated accounts or if the Secretary of State agrees that the information need not be disclosed. If the information is omitted from the members' report that fact must be stated in the report.

All the reports required above must be retained by the company for at least six years from the date on which they are first made available for inspection. They must be kept available for inspection during that time at the company's registered office or at a place specified in Regulations (see **36.2 Records**).

See also **36.2 Records** for provisions as to time available for inspection and copying.

The company must, within three working days of making any report (ie interim or final) prepared under these provisions available for inspection, notify the members who made the requests under **24.4** where the report is so available.

An investigation carried out by a company is concluded when

- the company has made all such inquiries as are necessary or expedient for the purposes of the requirement; and
- in the case of each such inquiry, either a response has been received by the company or the time allowed for a response has elapsed.

Offences. If default is made in complying with any of the above provisions, an offence is committed by every officer of the company who is in default. A person guilty of such an offence is liable (i) on conviction on indictment, to a fine; and (ii) on summary conviction, to a fine not exceeding the statutory maximum. See **29.1** Offences and Legal Proceedings for the statutory maximum.

Notice to the Registrar of Companies. The company must give notice to the Registrar of Companies of the place at which the reports are kept available for inspection and of any change in that place (unless they have at all times been kept at the company's registered office. If default is made for 14 days in complying with this requirement, an offence is committed by the company and every officer of the company who is in default. A person guilty of such an offence is liable, on summary conviction, to a fine not exceeding level 3 on the standard scale and, for continued contravention, a daily default fine not exceeding one-tenth of level 3 on the standard scale. See **29.1** Offences and Legal Proceedings for the statutory maximum.

[*CA 2006, ss 805, 806, 827*].

Right to inspect and request copy of reports. Any report prepared must be open to inspection by any person without charge. In addition, any person is entitled, on request and on payment of such fee as may be prescribed, to be provided with a copy of any such report or any part of it. The copy must be provided within ten working days after the request is received by the company.

If an inspection is refused, or a copy not provided, an offence is committed by the company and every officer of the company who is in default. A person guilty of such an offence is liable, on summary conviction, to a fine not exceeding level 3 on the standard scale and, for continued contravention, a daily default fine not exceeding one-tenth of level 3 on the standard scale. See **29.1** Offences and Legal Proceedings for the standard scale.

In the case of any such refusal or default, the court may compel an immediate inspection or, as the case may be, direct that the copy required be sent to the person requiring it.

[*CA 2006, ss 807, 827*].

24.6 ORDERS IMPOSING RESTRICTIONS ON SHARES

The provisions below and **24.7** to **24.9** restate, without substantive change, the provisions in *CA 1985, ss 454–457*. They set out the effect of a court order under imposing restrictions on shares and the penalties for attempted evasion of the restrictions. They also make provision for the relaxation or removal of restrictions or for an order for the sale of shares.

Subject to any directions by the court for protection of third parties or the terms of any interim order (see **24.3**) and subject to any relaxation of restrictions under **24.8**, the effect of a court order under *CA 2006, s 794* (see **24.3**) that shares are subject to restrictions is as follows.

(a) Any transfer of the shares is void.

(b) No voting rights are exercisable in respect of the shares.

(c) No further shares may be issued in right of the shares or in pursuance of an offer made to their holder.

(d) Except in a liquidation, no payment may be made of sums due from the company on the shares, whether in respect of capital or otherwise.

Agreements to transfer. Where shares are subject to the restriction

- in (*a*) above, an agreement to transfer the shares is also void (except for such an agreement on the making of an order for the removal of restrictions under **24.8**); and
- in (*c*) or (*d*) above, an agreement to transfer any right to be issued with other shares in right of those shares, or to receive any payment on them (otherwise than in a liquidation), is also void (except for an agreement to transfer any such right on the making of an order for the removal of restrictions under **24.8**).

[*CA 2006, s 797*].

24.7 Penalty for attempted evasion of restrictions

Subject to any directions by the court for protection of third parties or the terms of any interim order (see **24.3**) and subject to any relaxation or removal of restrictions under **24.8**, where shares are subject to restrictions, a person commits an offence if he

- exercises or purports to exercise any right
  - (i) to dispose of shares that to his knowledge, are for the time being subject to restrictions; or
  - (ii) to dispose of any right to be issued with any such shares;
- votes in respect of any such shares (whether as holder or proxy) or appoints a proxy to vote in respect of them;
- being the holder of any such shares, fails to notify the existence of the restrictions to any person whom he does not know to be aware of that fact but does know to be entitled (apart from the restrictions) to vote in respect of those shares (whether as holder or as proxy); or
- being the holder of any such shares, or being entitled to a right to be issued with other shares in right of them, or to receive any payment on them (otherwise than in a liquidation), enters into an agreement to transfer which is void under **24.6**.

If shares in a company are issued in contravention of the restrictions, an offence is committed by the company and every officer of the company who is in default. A person guilty of such an offence is liable (i) on conviction on indictment, to a fine; and (ii) on summary conviction, to a fine not exceeding the statutory maximum. See **29.1 Offences and Legal Proceedings** for the statutory maximum.

[*CA 2006, s 798*].

24.8 Relaxation and removal of restrictions

Relaxation of restrictions. An application may be made to the court, by the company or by any person aggrieved, on the ground that an order directing that shares are to be subject to restrictions unfairly affects the rights of third parties in respect of the shares. If the court is satisfied that the application is well-founded, it may, subject to such terms as it thinks fit, direct that specified acts by persons as set out in the order do not constitute a breach of the restrictions. [*CA 2006, s 799*].

Removal of restrictions. An application may be made to the court, by the company or by any person aggrieved, for an order directing that the shares cease to be subject to restrictions. The court must not make such an order unless

(a) it is satisfied that the relevant facts about the shares have been disclosed to the company and no unfair advantage has accrued to any person as a result of the earlier failure to make that disclosure; or

(b) the shares are to be transferred for valuable consideration and the court approves the transfer.

An order made under (*b*) above may continue, in whole or in part, the restrictions in **24.6**(*c*) or (*d*) so far as they relate to a right acquired or offer made before the transfer. Where any restrictions continue in force, an application may be made under these provisions for an order directing that the shares cease to be subject to those restrictions.

[*CA 2006, s 800*].

24.9 Order for sale of shares

The court may

(a) on an application by the company, order that the shares subject to restrictions be sold, subject to the court's approval as to the sale; and

(b) where it has made an order under (*a*) above, make such further order relating to the sale or transfer of the shares as it thinks fit on application by

  (i) the company;

  (ii) the person appointed to carry out the sale; or

  (iii) any person interested in the shares.

On making any such order, the court may also order that the applicant's costs (in Scotland, expenses) be paid out of the proceeds of sale.

Application of proceeds of sale. Where shares are sold in pursuance of an order as above, the proceeds of the sale, less the costs of the sale, must be paid into court for the benefit of the person or persons who are beneficially interested in the shares. On application by any person so interested, the court must order the payment to the applicant of the whole of the proceeds of sale together with any interest on them (or a proportionate part where more than one person has a beneficial interest). But where the court has ordered that the costs (in Scotland, expenses) of an applicant are to be paid out of the proceeds of sale (see above), the applicant is entitled to payment of his costs (or expenses) out of those proceeds before any person interested in the shares receives any part of those proceeds.

[*CA 2006, ss 801, 802*].

25 Investigations

25.1	**Introduction**
25.2	**Power of the Secretary of State to investigate companies**
25.3	Production of documents and evidence
25.4	Inspectors' reports
25.5	Investigation expenses
25.6	**Other powers of investigation**
25.7	Power to investigate company ownership
25.8	Power to obtain information as to those interested in shares etc
25.9	Powers of the Secretary of State relating to Inspectors
25.10	Resignation, removal and replacement of inspectors
25.11	**Requisition and seizure of books and papers**
25.12	Power to require production of documents
25.13	Entry and search of premises
25.14	Protection in relation to information provided to Secretary of State
25.15	Security of information obtained
25.16	Punishment for destroying, mutilating etc company documents
25.17	Punishment for furnishing false information
25.18	Disclosure of information by Secretary of State or inspector
25.19	**Power to enter and remain on premises**
25.20	Procedural matters
25.21	**Privileged information**
25.22	**Investigation of overseas companies**
25.23	**Orders imposing restrictions on shares**
25.24	Punishment for attempted evasion of restrictions
25.25	Relaxation and removal of restrictions

25.1 INTRODUCTION

One of the few parts of the *CA 1985* which has not been subject to repeal and revision by *CA 2006* is the part relating to investigations into companies and the powers to obtain information. The references therefore in this chapter to *CA 1985, Part XIV* and *CA 1989, Part III* are still relevant. *CA 2006* also confers powers on the Secretary of State to remove inspectors, to issue directions about the scope, direction and duration of an inspection and to terminate an inspection when it is no longer in the public interest for it to continue (see **25.8** and **25.9**).

25.2 POWER OF THE SECRETARY OF STATE TO INVESTIGATE COMPANIES

The Secretary of State *may* appoint one or more inspectors to investigate and report the results of their investigation to him either

(a) on the application of

  (i) in the case of a company having a share capital, *either* at least 200 members *or* members holding at least 10% of the shares issued (excluding any shares held as treasury shares);

  (ii) in the case of a company not having a share capital, at least 20% in number of the persons on the company's register of members; or

  (iii) the company itself; or

(b) (whether or not the company is in the course of being voluntarily wound up) if it appears to the Secretary of State that

  (i) the company's affairs are being or have been conducted

- with intent to defraud its creditors or the creditors of any other person;
- for a fraudulent or unlawful purpose; or
- in a manner unfairly prejudicial to some members (or to persons who are not members but to whom shares have been transferred or transmitted by operation of law);

(ii) any actual or proposed act or omission of the company or on its behalf is or would be so prejudicial;

(iii) the company was formed for any fraudulent or unlawful purpose;

(iv) persons concerned with the company's formation or management have in that connection been guilty of fraud, misfeasance or other misconduct towards the company or its members; or

(v) the company's members have not been given all the information with respect to its affairs which they might reasonably expect.

The Secretary of State is *required* to appoint one or more inspectors if a court having jurisdiction to wind up the company by order declares that the company's affairs ought to be so investigated.

[*CA 1985, ss 431(1), (2), 432(1), (2), (2A), (3), (4)*].

Any application either by members of the company or by the company itself under (*a*) above must be supported by such evidence as the Secretary of State requires in order to show good reason for requiring the investigation and the Secretary of State may require security (not exceeding £5,000) from the applicant(s) for payment of the costs of the investigation.

[*CA 1985, s 424(3)(4)*].

As regards (*b*) above, the appointment may be on terms that any report is not for publication, notwithstanding *CA 1985, s 437(3)* (see **25.4**).

[*CA 1985, s 432(2A)*].

Extension of powers to subsidiaries. Inspectors appointed as above have power, if they consider it necessary, to extend their investigation to the affairs of certain companies with a holding or subsidiary relationship to the company under investigation. Their report will then include a report on the affairs of such companies, so far as relevant to their main investigation.

[*CA 1985, s 433*].

25.3 Production of documents and evidence

Officers and 'agents' (past and present) of any company under investigation are under a duty to

- produce to the inspectors all 'documents' in their custody or power of or relating to the company;
- attend before the inspectors as required; and
- otherwise give them all reasonable assistance in connection with the investigation; and

- are also under the same duty if the inspectors consider they possess such information.

They are under the same duty if the inspectors consider that they possess such information.

An inspector may examine any person on oath, and an answer given by a person to a question put under any of the above powers may be used in evidence against him. However, in criminal proceedings in which that person is charged with an offence (other than an offence of making false statements under *Perjury Act 1911, ss 2* or *5*, *Criminal Law (Consolidation) (Scotland) Act 1995, s 44(1)* or *(2)* or *Perjury (Northern Ireland) Order 1979, Art 7* or *10*) no evidence relating to the answer may be adduced and no question relating to it may be asked by or on behalf of the prosecution unless evidence relating to it is adduced, or a question relating to it is asked, in the proceedings by or on behalf of that person. See *Saunders v United Kingdom* (Application 19187/91) (1996) 23 EHRR 313, [1998] 1 BCLC 362 where the European Court of Human Rights accepted that the use made of certain statements to inspectors was unfair and in violation of the European Convention on Human Rights and stated that the existing provisions of the *Companies Acts* could not properly override an individual's right not to be required to incriminate himself.

'*Agents*' in relation to a company includes its bankers, solicitors and auditor, whether or not they are officers but see **25.21** for privileged information.

'*Documents*' includes information recorded in any form.

The power to require production of a document includes power, in the case of a document not in hard copy form, to require the production of a copy of the document in hard copy form or in a form from which a hard copy form can readily be obtained.

Inspectors may take copies of, or extracts from, a document produced under these provisions.

[*CA 1985, s 434*].

Failure or refusal by any person to comply with any of the above requirements, or to answer any of the inspectors' questions, may be certified in writing by the inspector to the court, and may be treated as contempt of court.

[*CA 1985, s 436*].

25.4 Inspectors' reports

Final (and, if required, interim) reports are made by the inspectors to the Secretary of State, who is kept informed of any matters coming to the inspectors' knowledge as a result of their investigations.

[*CA 1985, s 437(1), (1A)*].

Where the inspectors were appointed following a declaration by order of the court (see **25.2**), a copy of any report must be furnished to the court. If the company is registered under *CA 2006* in Northern Ireland, the Secretary of State must send a copy of any interim or final report by the inspectors to the Department of Enterprise, Trade and Investment in Northern Ireland. In any case, if he thinks fit, the Secretary of State may forward a copy of any report to the company's registered office and, on request and on payment of a fee prescribed by him by statutory instrument, he may furnish a copy to

- any member of the company or other body corporate which is the subject of the report;

- the auditor of that company or body corporate;
- any person whose conduct is referred to in the report;
- the applicants for the investigation (see **25.2**); and
- any other person whose financial interests appear to the Secretary of State to be affected by the matters dealt with in the report.

He may also cause any report to be printed and published (but see **25.2** for certain reports excluded from publication under the terms of appointment of the inspectors).

[*CA 1985, ss 437(2), (2A), (3)*].

See, however, **25.7** as regards omission of certain parts of inspectors' reports from disclosure under these provisions.

A copy of the report is admissible in any legal proceedings as evidence of the inspectors' opinion in relation to any matter in the report, and in proceedings on an application under the *CDDA 1986, s 8* (see **18.15 Directors**) as evidence of any fact stated therein. The copy must be certified a true copy by the Secretary of State, and a document purporting to be such a certificate will be received in evidence as such unless the contrary is proved.

[*CA 1985, s 441*].

25.5 Investigation expenses

The expenses of an investigation under **25.2** (including reasonable general staff costs and overheads as determined by the Secretary of State) are defrayed, in the first place, by the Secretary of State. But he may, however, recover them as follows.

(a) A person convicted on a prosecution instituted as a result of the investigation may in those proceedings be ordered to pay investigation expenses to a specified extent.

(b) A company dealt with by an inspectors' report, where the inspectors were appointed otherwise than of the Secretary of State's own motion, is liable for investigation expenses, unless it was the applicant for the investigation, and except so far as the Secretary of State otherwise directs.

(c) Where inspectors were appointed by members of the company or by the company itself (see **25.2** (*a*)) or where the investigation relates to the ownership of the company (see **25.7**), the applicant or applicants for the investigation is or are liable for investigation expenses to such extent as the Secretary of State may direct.

Except where the inspectors were appointed of the Secretary of State's own motion, their report may (and must if so required by the Secretary of State) include a recommendation as to any appropriate direction(s) under (*b*) and (*c*) above in the light of their investigations.

A liability to repay the Secretary of State under (*a*) above is, subject to satisfaction of his right to repayment, also a liability to indemnify all persons against liability under (*b*) and (*c*) above. A person liable under any of (*a*) to (*c*) above is entitled to contribution from any other person liable under the same provision, according to the amount of their respective liabilities under that provision.

[*CA 1985, s 439*].

25.6 OTHER POWERS OF INVESTIGATION

Various powers of investigation are available to the Secretary of State, in addition to those described at **25.2** to **25.5**, under *CA 1985, ss 442–446E*.

25.7 Power to investigate company ownership

If there appears to be good reason to do so, the Secretary of State may appoint inspector(s) to investigate and report on the membership of any company, and otherwise with respect to the company, to determine the true persons financially interested in the success or failure (real or apparent) of the company, or able to control or materially to influence its policy. Subject to the terms of their appointment, the inspectors' powers extend to the investigation of any circumstances suggesting the existence of a relevant arrangement or understanding which, though not legally binding, is or was observed or likely to be observed in practice.

If an application is made to the Secretary of State by members of a company for such a limited investigation, and the applicants would meet the requirements in **25.2**(*a*)(i) or (ii) as regards numbers or shares, the Secretary of State must (except as below) appoint inspectors to conduct the investigation, unless he is satisfied that the application is vexatious. The terms of appointment will, however, exclude any matter in so far as he is satisfied that it is unreasonable for it to be investigated. He may, before appointing inspectors, require security (not exceeding £5,000) from the applicant(s) for payment of the costs of the investigation.

Where it appears to the Secretary of State that his powers under *CA 1985, s 444* (see **25.8**) are sufficient for the investigation of matters which inspectors would otherwise be appointed to investigate on an application as above, he may instead conduct the investigation under *section 444*.

[*CA 1985, s 442; CA 1989, s 62; CA 2006, s 1035(5)*].

The provisions of *CA 1985, ss 433* (power to investigate subsidiaries), *434* (officers and agents duty to produce documents and evidence), *436* (obstruction of inspectors treated as contempt of court) and *437* (production of reports) apply to an investigation under *section 442* above with appropriate modifications of references to the affairs of the company to those of any other body corporate. But, in addition, they apply to

- all persons who are or have been (or whom the inspector has reasonable cause to believe to be or have been)
  - (i) financially interested in the success or failure (real or apparent) of the company or any other body corporate whose membership is investigated with that of the company, or
  - (ii) able to control or materially influence its policy (including persons concerned only on behalf of others), and
- any other person whom the inspector has reasonable cause to believe possesses relevant information,

as they apply in relation to officers or agents of the company or other body corporate.

The Secretary of State may by order impose restrictions on shares and debentures under *CA 1985, ss 454–457* (see **25.23**) where there is difficulty in finding out the relevant facts about them in connection with an investigation under these provisions. But where he is satisfied that such on order may unfairly affect the rights of third parties in respect of shares, he may direct that specified acts by such persons do not constitute a breach of the restrictions.

If the Secretary of State considers there is good reason for not divulging any part of a report under these provisions, he may omit that part from the disclosure of the report under *CA 1985, s 437* (see **25.4**). He may cause a copy of any report to be kept by the Registrar of Companies, again with the omission of any part not disclosed under *CA 1985, s 437*. [*CA 1985, ss 443, 445*].

25.8 Power to obtain information as to those interested in shares, etc

The Secretary of State may act without the appointment of inspectors if there appears to be good reason to investigate the ownership of any shares or debentures of a company, and he considers their appointment unnecessary. He may require any person whom he has reasonable cause to believe to have, or to be able to obtain,

- any information as to the present and past interests in those shares, etc, and
- the names and addresses of the persons interested and of any persons who act or have acted on their behalf in relation to those shares etc,

to deliver such information to him.

A person has an interest for this purpose if

- he has any right to acquire or dispose of the shares, etc (or of an interest in them);
- he has any right to vote in respect of them;
- his consent is necessary for the exercise of any rights of other persons interested in them; or
- other persons interested in them can be required to, or are accustomed to, exercise their rights in accordance with his instructions.

Any person who

- fails to give information required as above,
- in giving such information makes any statement which he knows to be false in a material particular, or
- recklessly makes any statement which is false in a material particular,

commits an offence. A person guilty of such an offence is liable (i) on conviction on indictment, to imprisonment for a term not exceeding two years or a fine (or both); and (ii) on summary conviction to imprisonment for a term not exceeding twelve months (six months in Scotland or, with effect from 1 October 2009, Northern Ireland) or to a fine not exceeding the statutory maximum (or both) and, for continued contravention, a daily default fine not exceeding one-fiftieth of the greater of £5,000 or the amount corresponding to level 4 on the standard scale for summary offences. See **29.1 Offences and Legal Proceedings** for the statutory maximum.

See, however, **25.21** for privileged information.

[*CA 1985, s 444; SI 2015 No 664, Sch 3*].

The Secretary of State may by order impose restrictions on shares and debentures under *CA 1985, ss 454–457* (see **25.23**) where there is difficulty in ascertaining the relevant facts about them in connection with an investigation under these provisions. But where he is satisfied that such on order may unfairly affect the rights of third parties in respect of shares, he may direct that specified acts by such persons do not constitute a breach of the restrictions.

[*CA 1985, s 445*].

25.9 Powers of the Secretary of State relating to inspectors

The following provisions apply where an inspector is appointed after 30 September 2007.

General powers to give directions. In exercising his functions an inspector must comply with any direction given to him by the Secretary of State as follows.

- The Secretary of State may give an inspector appointed under **25.2**(*a*) or (*b*) or **25.7** a direction
  - (i) as to the subject matter of his investigation (whether by reference to a specified area of a company's operation, a specified transaction, a period of time or otherwise), or
  - (ii) which requires the inspector to take (or not to take) a specified step in his investigation.
- The Secretary of State may give an inspector appointed under any provision of this chapter a direction requiring him to secure that a specified report under **25.4**
  - (i) includes the inspector's views on a specified matter;
  - (ii) does not include any reference to a specified matter;
  - (iii) is made in a specified form or manner; or
  - (iv) is made by a specified date.

Any direction under the above provisions may be given on an inspector's appointment, may vary or revoke a direction previously given, and may be given at the request of an inspector.

For the above purposes, reference to an inspector's investigation includes any investigation he undertakes, or could undertake, under *CA 1985, s 433* into the affairs of a holding company or subsidiary (see **25.2**).

[*CA 1985, s 446A*].

Direction to terminate investigation. Subject to below, the Secretary of State may direct an inspector to take no further steps in his investigation and, if he does so, any direction already given to the inspector in connection with the preparation of an interim report ceases to have effect and the inspector must not make a final report to the Secretary of State.

But where the inspector was appointed at the instigation of the court under *CA 1985, s 432(1)* (see **25.2**) or following an application by the members of the company under *CA 1985, s 442(3)* (see **25.7**), the Secretary of State can give a direction under these provisions only on the grounds that

- matters have come to light in the course of the inspector's investigation which suggest that a criminal offence has been committed; and
- those matters have been referred to the appropriate prosecuting authority.

Where the Secretary of State gives a direction under those circumstances, the inspector must not make a final report to the Secretary of State unless either the inspector was appointed under *CA 1985, s 432(1)* or the Secretary of State directs the inspector to make a final report to him.

For the above purposes, reference to an inspector's investigation includes any investigation he undertakes, or could undertake, under *CA 1985, s 433* into the affairs of a holding company or subsidiary (see **25.2**).

[*CA 1985, s 446B*].

Obtaining information from former inspectors, etc. Where

- a person has been appointed as an inspector under the provisions in this chapter but has resigned or had his appointment revoked, or
- an inspector has been given a direction by the Secretary of State under *CA 1985, s 446B* (see above)

the Secretary of State may direct that person or inspector to produce documents (including information recorded in any form) obtained or generated by him during the course of his investigation to either the Secretary of State himself or a subsequent inspector appointed. Where any document is not in hard copy form, a copy of the document must be produced either in hard copy form or in a form from which a hard copy can be readily obtained.

The Secretary of State may take copies of, or extracts from, a document produced to him under these provisions. He may also direct a person to whom these provisions apply to inform him of any matters that came to that person's knowledge as a result of his investigation.

For the above purposes, reference to the investigation of a former inspector or inspector include any investigation he conducted under *CA 1985, s 433* into the affairs of a holding company or subsidiary (see **25.2**).

[*CA 1985, s 446E*].

25.10 Resignation, removal and replacement of inspectors

The following provisions apply where an inspector is appointed after 30 September 2007.

Resignation and revocation of appointment. An inspector may resign by notice in writing to the Secretary of State and the Secretary of State may revoke the appointment of an inspector by notice in writing to the inspector.

[*CA 1985, s 446C*].

Appointment of replacement inspectors. Where an inspector resigns or dies, or an inspector's appointment is revoked, the Secretary of State

- may appoint one or more inspectors to continue the investigation; and
- must secure that at least one inspector continues the investigation unless
  - (i) he could give any replacement inspector a direction to terminate the inspection under *CA 1985, s 446B* (see **25.9**); and
  - (ii) such a direction would under those provisions result in a final report not being made.

Any such appointment is treated as an appointment under the same provision of this chapter under which the former inspector was appointed.

For the above purposes, reference to an investigation include any investigation the former inspector conducted under *CA 1985, s 433* into the affairs of a holding company or subsidiary (see **25.2**). [*CA 1985, s 446D; CA 2006, s 1036*].

25.11 REQUISITION AND SEIZURE OF BOOKS AND PAPERS

Various powers set out below are available to the Secretary of State under *CA 1985, ss 447–451A* to require the production of documents, etc and to enter premises and seize books and papers.

25.12 Power to require production of documents

The Secretary of State may

(a) give directions to a company requiring it to

- produce such 'documents' (or documents of such description) as may be specified in the directions; and
- provide such information (or information of such description) as may be so specified; and

(b) authorise a person (an investigator) to require the company or any other person to

- produce such documents (or documents of such description) as the investigator may specify;
- provide such information (or information of such description) as the investigator may specify.

Any such requirement must be complied with at such time and place as may be specified in the directions or by the investigator (as the case may be). The Secretary of State or the investigator (as the case may be) may take copies of, or extracts from, a document so produced.

The production of a document under the above provisions does not affect any lien which a person has on the document.

'*Documents*' include information recorded in any form. The power to require production of a document includes power, in the case of a document not in hard copy form, to require production of a copy of it in hard copy form or in a form from which a hard copy can be readily obtained.

[*CA 1985, s 447*].

Penalties. If a person fails to comply with a requirement imposed under the above provisions, the inspector, the Secretary of State or an investigator (as the case may be) may certify the fact in writing to the court. If, after hearing any witnesses who may be produced against or on behalf of the alleged offender and any statement which may be offered in defence, the court is satisfied that the offender failed without reasonable excuse to comply with the requirement, it may deal with him as if he had been guilty of contempt of the court.

[*CA 1985, s 453C*].

Use of information provided in evidence. A statement made by a person in compliance with a requirement under *CA 1985, s 447* above may be used in evidence against him. But in criminal proceedings in which the person is charged with an offence (other than an offence under *CA 1985, s 451* (see **25.17**) or *Perjury Act 1911, s 5*, *Criminal Law (Consolidation) (Scotland) Act 1995, s 44(2)* or *Perjury (Northern Ireland) Order 1979, Art 10* (false statements made otherwise than on oath)

- no evidence relating to the statement may be adduced by or on behalf of the prosecution, and
- no question relating to it may be asked by or on behalf of the prosecution

unless evidence relating to it is adduced or a question relating to it is asked in the proceedings by or on behalf of that person.

[*CA 1985, s 447A*].

25.13 Entry and search of premises

A justice of the peace (in Scotland, a justice of the peace or a sheriff) may issue a warrant if satisfied, on information on oath (in Scotland, on evidence on oath) given by the Secretary of State or an inspector or investigator that there are reasonable grounds for believing that

(a) there are, on any premises, 'documents' whose production has been required under any of the provisions dealt with in this chapter but which have not been produced in compliance therewith; or

(b) an offence has been committed for which the penalty on conviction on indictment is imprisonment for a term of not less than two years, and that there are on any premises documents relating to whether the offence has been committed, provided

- the Secretary of State, inspector or investigator has power under the provisions in this chapter to require their production; and
- there are reasonable grounds for believing that if production was so required the documents would not be produced but would be removed from the premises, hidden, tampered with or destroyed.

'*Document*' for these purposes includes information recorded in any form.

The warrant continues in force for one month beginning with the day on which it is issued. It authorises a constable, together with any other person named on it and any other constables, to

- enter the specified premises (using reasonable force if necessary);
- search the premises and take possession of any documents appearing to be those referred to in (*a*) or (*b*) above (or take steps necessary to protect or prevent interference with those documents);
- take copies; and
- require any person named in the warrant to provide an explanation of them or state where they may be found.

See, however, **25.21** for privileged information.

A warrant issued under (*b*) above may also authorise such action in respect of other documents relevant to the investigation.

Documents taken possession of under these provisions may be retained for three months or, if within that period any proceedings to which the documents are relevant are commenced against any person for a criminal offence, until the conclusion of those proceedings.

Any person intentionally obstructing the exercise of rights under these provisions, or failing (without reasonable excuse) to provide an explanation of a document or state where it may be found when required to do so, is guilty of an offence. A person guilty of such an offence is liable (i) on conviction on indictment, to a fine; and (ii) on summary conviction, to a fine not exceeding the statutory maximum. See **29.1 Offences and Legal Proceedings** for the statutory maximum.

[*CA 1985, s 448*].

With effect from 6 April 2008, where an offence under the above provisions is committed by a body corporate, every officer of the body who is in default also commits the offence. For this purpose, any person who purports to act as a director, manager or secretary of the body is treated as an officer of the company and, if the body is a company, any shadow director is treated as an officer of the company (see **18.2(2) Directors**).

[*CA 1985, s 453D*].

25.14 Protection in relation to information provided to Secretary of State

A person who makes a 'relevant' disclosure is not liable, by reason only of that disclosure, in any proceedings relating to a breach of an obligation of confidence. A '*relevant disclosure*' is a disclosure which satisfies each of the following conditions.

(1) It is made to the Secretary of State otherwise than in compliance with a requirement under the provisions of this chapter relating to investigations (ie it relates to information which is volunteered rather than provided in response to the exercise of an investigation power).

(2) It is of a kind that the person making the disclosure *could* be required to make under the provisions of this chapter (ie it is relevant to a matter which could be investigated and is not covered by the provisions in **25.21** relating to privileged information).

(3) The person who makes the disclosure does so in good faith and in the reasonable belief that the disclosure is capable of assisting the Secretary of State for the purposes of carrying out an investigation. The 'good faith' requirement means, for example, that disclosure motivated by a desire to cause harm to a business competitor is not protected.

(4) The information disclosed is not more than is reasonably necessary for the purpose of assisting the Secretary of State in carrying out an investigation.

(5) The disclosure is not

- prohibited by virtue of any enactment (as defined in *CA 2006, s 1293*) whenever passed or made; or
- made by a person carrying on the business of banking or by a lawyer and involves the disclosure of information in respect of which he owes an obligation of confidence in that capacity.

[*CA 1985, s 448A*].

25.15 Security of information obtained

Where information (in whatever form) is obtained

- in pursuance of a requirement imposed under **25.12**,
- by means of a relevant disclosure within **25.14**, or

- by an investigator in consequence of the exercise of his powers under *CA 1985, s 453A* (see **25.19**),

it must not be disclosed unless the disclosure is

- made to a '*specified person*' (ie the Secretary of State, the Department of Enterprise, Trade and Investment for Northern Ireland, the Treasury, the Lord Advocate, the Director of Public Prosecutions, the Director of Public Prosecutions for Northern Ireland, the Financial Services Authority, a constable, a procurator fiscal, or the Scottish Ministers) or any officer or employee of that person; or
- of a 'specified description'. See *CA 1985, Sch 15D* for a large number of disclosures allowed, most of which are for the purpose of enabling or assisting a specified person to exercise a specific function.

Nothing in the above provisions

- prohibits the disclosure of information if it is, or has been, available to the public from any other source; or
- authorises the making of a disclosure in contravention of the *Data Protection Act 1998.*

A person who discloses any information in contravention of the above provisions is guilty of an offence. A person guilty of such an offence is liable (i) on conviction on indictment, to imprisonment for a term not exceeding two years or a fine (or both); and (ii) on summary conviction, to imprisonment for a term not exceeding twelve months (six months in Scotland or, with effect from 1 October 2009, Northern Ireland) or to a fine not exceeding the statutory maximum (or both). See **9.1 Offences and Legal Proceedings** for the statutory maximum.

[*CA 1985, s 449, Schs 15C, 15D*].

With effect from 6 April 2008, where an offence under the above provisions is committed by a body corporate, every officer of the body who is in default also commits the offence. For this purpose, any person who purports to act as a director, manager or secretary of the body is treated as an officer of the company and, if the body is a company, any shadow director is treated as an officer of the company (see **18.1(2) Directors**).

[*CA 1985, s 453D*].

25.16 Punishment for destroying, mutilating etc company documents

An officer of a company (or an officer of an authorised insurance company which is not a body corporate) who

(a) destroys, mutilates or falsifies a 'document' affecting or relating to the company's property or affairs (or is privy to such destruction, etc),

(b) makes a false entry in such a document (or is privy to any such act), or

(c) fraudulently either parts with, alters or makes an omission in any such document (or is privy to any such fraudulent act or omission)

is guilty of an offence unless, in the case of acts within (*a*) or (*b*) above, he proves that he had no intention to conceal the state of affairs of the company or to defeat the law. A person guilty of such an offence is liable (i) on conviction on indictment, to imprisonment for a term not exceeding seven years or a fine (or both); and (ii) on summary conviction, to imprisonment for a term not exceeding twelve months (six months in Scotland or, with effect from 1 October 2009, Northern Ireland) or to a fine not exceeding the statutory maximum (or both). See **29.1 Offences and Legal Proceedings** for the statutory maximum.

'*Document*' includes information recorded in any form.

[*CA 1985, s 450*].

With effect from 6 April 2008, where an offence under the above provisions is committed by a body corporate, every officer of the body who is in default also commits the offence. For this purpose, any person who purports to act as a director, manager or secretary of the body is treated as an officer of the company and is, if the body is a company, any shadow director.

[*CA 1985, s 453D*].

25.17 Punishment for furnishing false information

A person commits an offence if, in purporting to comply with a requirement under *CA 1985, s 447* (see **25.12**) to provide information, he

- provides information which he knows to be false in a material particular, or
- recklessly provides information which is false in a material particular.

A person guilty of such an offence is liable (i) on conviction on indictment, to imprisonment for a term not exceeding two years or a fine (or both); and (ii) on summary conviction, to imprisonment for a term not exceeding twelve months (six months in Scotland and, with effect from 1 October 2009, Northern Ireland) or to a fine not exceeding the statutory maximum (or both). See **29.1 Offences and Legal Proceedings** for the statutory maximum.

[*CA 1985, s 451*].

Where an offence under the above provisions is committed by a body corporate, every officer of the body who is in default also commits the offence. For this purpose, any person who purports to act as a director, manager or secretary of the body is treated as an officer of the company and is, if the body is a company, any shadow director.
[*CA 1985, s 453D*].

25.18 Disclosure of information by Secretary of State or inspector

Information obtained under *CA 1985, ss 434–446E* (see **25.3** to **25.10**) or by an inspector using his powers under *CA 1985, s 453A* (see **25.19**) may be disclosed as follows.

(a) The Secretary of State may

- disclose any such information to any person to whom, or for any purpose for which, disclosure is permitted under *CA 1985, s 449* (see **25.15**); or
- authorise or require an inspector to disclose such information to any such person or for any such purpose.

(b) Any such information may be disclosed by an inspector to

- another inspector;
- a person appointed under

(i) *FSMA 2000, s 167* (general investigations),

(ii) *FSMA 2000, s 168* (investigations in particular cases),

(iii) *FSMA 2000, s 169(1)(b)* (investigation in support of overseas regulator);

(iv) *FSMA 2000, s 284* (investigations into affairs of certain collective investment schemes), or

(v) regulations made under *FSMA 2000, s 262(2)(k)* (investigations into open-ended investment companies),

to conduct an investigation; or

- a person authorised to exercise powers under

(i) *CA 1985, s 447* (see **25.12**); or

(ii) *CA 1989, s 84* (exercise of powers to assist overseas regulatory authority).

Any information which may be so disclosed may also be disclosed to any officer or servant of that person.

The Secretary of State may also disclose any information obtained under *CA 1985, s 444* (see **25.8**) to

- the company whose ownership was the subject of the investigation,
- any member of the company,
- any person whose conduct was investigated in the course of the investigation,
- the auditor of the company, or
- any person whose financial interests appear to the Secretary of State to be affected by matters covered by the investigation.

[*CA 1985, s 451A*].

25.19 POWER TO ENTER AND REMAIN ON PREMISES

If an inspector appointed under **25.2** or **25.7** or an investigator authorised under **25.12** is

(a) authorised by the Secretary of State, and

(b) thinks that to do so will materially assist him in the exercise of his functions,

he may at all reasonable times

(i) require entry to any of a company's premises which he believes are used (wholly or partly) for the purposes of the company's business; and

(ii) remain there for such period as he thinks necessary for the purposes of (*b*) above.

In exercising these powers, an inspector or investigator may be accompanied by such other persons as he thinks appropriate.

Anyone who intentionally obstructs a person lawfully acting under these provisions is guilty of an offence and liable (i) on conviction on indictment, to a fine; and (ii) on summary conviction, to a fine not exceeding the statutory maximum. See **29.1 Offences and Legal Proceedings** for the statutory maximum.

[*CA 1985, s 453A*].

With effect from 6 April 2008, where an offence under the above provisions is committed by a body corporate, every officer of the body who is in default also commits the offence. For this purpose, any person who purports to act as a director, manager or secretary of the body is treated as an officer of the company and is, if the body is a company, any shadow director.

[*CA 1985, s 453D*].

25.20 Procedural matters

At the time an inspector or investigator seeks to enter the premises, he must produce evidence of his identity and evidence of his appointment or authorisation (as the case may be). Any person accompanying the inspector or investigator must also produce evidence of his identity.

Written statement. As soon as is practicable after obtaining entry, the inspector or investigator must give a written statement with details of his powers and the rights and obligations of the company, occupier and the persons present on the premises. The written statement must contain the list of matters contained in the regulations made under *CA 1985, s 435B* ie the *Companies Act 1985 (Power to Enter and Remain on Premises: Procedural) Regulations 2005 (SI 2005 No 684)* as follows:

- A statement that the inspector/investigator has been appointed/authorised by the Secretary of State to carry out an investigation and a reference to the enactment under which that appointment/authorisation was made.
- A statement that the inspector/investigator has been authorised by the Secretary of State under *CA 1985, s 453A* to exercise the powers in that section.
- A description of the conditions which are required by *CA 1985, s 453A(1)* to be satisfied (see **25.19**(*a*) and (*b*)) before an inspector/investigator can act.
- A description of the powers in *CA 1985, s 453A(2)* (see **25.19**(i) and (ii)).
- A statement that the inspector/investigator must, at the time he seeks to enter premises, produce evidence of his identity and evidence of his appointment/authorisation.
- A statement that any person accompanying the inspector/investigator when that person seeks to enter the premises must, at that time, produce evidence of his identity.
- A statement that entry to premises may be refused to an inspector, investigator or other person fails to produce the required evidence.
- A statement that the company, occupier and the persons present on the premises may be required by the inspector/investigator, while he is on the premises, to comply with any powers the inspector/investigator may have by virtue of his appointment/authorisation to require documents or information.
- A statement that the inspector/investigator is not permitted to use any force in exercising his powers under *CA 1985, s 453A* and is not permitted during the course of his visit to search the premises or to seize any document or other thing on the premises.
- A description of the effect of the penalty provisions in *CA 1985, s 453C* (see below) as it relates to a requirement imposed by an inspector/investigator under *CA 1985, s 453A*.

- A statement that it is an offence intentionally to obstruct an inspector, investigator or other person lawfully acting under these provisions.
- A description of the inspector's/investigator's obligations to prepare a written record of the visit and to give a copy of the record, when requested, to the company and any other occupier of the premises.
- Information about how any person entitled to receive a copy of that record can request it.

The written statement must be given to an '*appropriate recipient*', ie

(a) where the inspector/investigator thinks that the company is the sole occupier of the premises, a person who is present on the premises and who appears to the inspector/investigator to be

(i) an officer of the company; or

(ii) a person otherwise engaged in the business of the company if the inspector/investigator thinks that no officer of the company is present on the premises; and

(b) if the inspector/investigator thinks that the company is not the occupier or sole occupier of the premises, a person within (*a*) above or (if different) a person who is present on the premises and who appears to the inspector/investigator to be an occupier of the premises or otherwise in charge of them.

If, during the time the inspector/investigator is on the premises, there is no person present who appears to him to be an appropriate recipient, he must as soon as reasonably practicable send to the company a notice of the fact and time that the visit took place, together with the written statement.

Written record. As soon as reasonably practicable after exercising his powers under these provisions, the inspector/investigator must prepare a written record of the visit. He must give a copy of the record, if requested, to the company or, in a case where the company is not the sole occupier of the premises, an occupier.

The written record must contain the following information.

- The name by which the company in relation to which the powers were exercised was registered at the time of the authorisation.
- The company's registered number at that time.
- The postal address of the premises visited.
- The name of the inspector/investigator who visited the premises and the name of any person accompanying him.
- The date and time when the inspector/investigator entered the premises and the duration of his visit.
- The name (if known) of the person to whom the inspector/investigator and any person accompanying him produced evidence of their identity. (If the name is not known, an account of how he produced that evidence.)
- The name (if known) of the person to whom the inspector/investigator produced evidence of his appointment/authorisation (as the case may be). (If the name is not known, an account of how he produced that evidence.)
- The name (if known) of the person who admitted the inspector/investigator to the premises. (If the name is not known, an account of how he was admitted to the premises.)

- The name (if known) of every appropriate recipient to whom the inspector/investigator, while on the premises, gave a written statement. (If any name is not known, an account of how the written statement was given to that person.)

- The name (if known) of any person physically present on the premises (to the inspector's/investigator's knowledge) at any time during his visit (other than another inspector/investigator, a person accompanying the inspector/investigator or a person to whom a copy of the written statement was given) and with whom the inspector/investigator communicated in relation to that person's presence on the premises.

- A record of any apparent failure by any person during the course of the visit to the premises to comply with any requirement imposed by the inspector/investigator.

- A record of any conduct by any person during the course of the visit to the premises which the inspector/investigator believes amounted to the intentional obstruction of him, or anyone accompanying him, in the lawful exercise of the power to enter and remain on the premises.

[*CA 1985, s 453B*].

Penalties. If a person fails to comply with a requirement imposed under the above provisions, the inspector, the Secretary of State or an investigator (as the case may be) may certify the fact in writing to the court. If, after hearing any witnesses who may be produced against or on behalf of the alleged offender and any statement which may be offered in defence, the court is satisfied that the offender failed without reasonable excuse to comply with the requirement, it may deal with him as if he had been guilty of contempt of the court.

[*CA 1985, s 453C*].

25.21 PRIVILEGED INFORMATION

There are two categories of privileged information under the provisions described at **25.2** to **25.17**.

Legal professional privilege. Nothing in *CA 1985, ss 431–446E* (see **25.2** to **25.10**) compels the disclosure by any person to the Secretary of State or to an inspector appointed by him of information in respect of which

(a) in an action in the High Court, a claim to legal professional privilege, or

(b) in an action in the Court of Session a claim to confidentiality of communications

could be maintained.

Similarly, nothing in *CA 1985, ss 447–451* (**25.12** to **25.17**)

- compels the production by any person of a document or the disclosure by any person of information in respect of which a claim under (*a*) or (*b*) above could be maintained; or

- authorises the taking of possession of any such document which is in the person's possession.

Despite the above, a lawyer may be compelled to disclose the name and address of his client.

Obligation of confidence. Unless the making of the requirement is authorised by the Secretary of State, nothing in *CA 1985, ss 434* or *443* (see **25.3** and **25.7**) requires a person to disclose information or produce documents in respect of which he owes an obligation of confidence by virtue of carrying on a banking business, unless either

- that person, or the person to whom the obligation is owed, is the company or other body corporate under investigation, or
- the person to whom the obligation is owed consents to the disclosure or production.

Similarly, under *CA 1985, s 447* (see **25.12**), the Secretary of State must not require (or authorise a person to require)

- the production by a person carrying on a banking business of a document relating to a customer's affairs, or
- the disclosure by him of information relating to those affairs,

unless

- it is necessary to do so for the purpose of investigating the affairs of the person carrying on the banking business;
- the customer is a person on whom a requirement has been imposed under *CA 1985, s 447*; or
- the customer is a person on whom a requirement to produce information or documents has been imposed by an investigator appointed by the Secretary of State under *FSMA 2000, s 171* or *s 173*. [*CA 1985, s 452*].

25.22 INVESTIGATION OF OVERSEAS COMPANIES

The provisions of this chapter (apart from **25.2**(*a*), **25.7** and **25.8**) apply to bodies corporate incorporated outside the UK which carry on, or have carried on, business in the UK subject to such modifications and adaptations as the Secretary of State may specify by Regulations made by statutory instrument.

[*CA 1985, s 453*].

25.23 ORDERS IMPOSING RESTRICTIONS ON SHARES

The Secretary of State may, by order, impose restrictions on shares under *CA 1985, s 445* (see **25.7** and **25.8**). So long as shares are directed to be subject to such restrictions

(a) any transfer or issue of those shares, or of the right to be issued with them, is void;

(b) no voting rights are exercisable in respect of the shares;

(c) no further shares may be issued in right of them or in pursuance of any offer made to their holder; and

(d) (except in a liquidation) no payment may be made of any sums due from the company on them (whether in respect of capital or otherwise).

[*CA 1985, s 454(1)*].

As regards (*a*) above, any agreement to transfer the shares (or, in the case of unissued shares, any agreement to transfer the right to be issued with them) is also void (except as under **25.25**).

[*CA 1985, s 454(2)*].

As regards (*c*) and (*d*) above, an agreement to transfer any right to be issued with other shares in right of those shares (except as under **25.25**), or to receive any payment on them (other than in a liquidation), is void.

[*CA 1985, s 454(3)*].

25.24 Punishment for attempted evasion of restrictions

Subject to the terms of any direction by the Secretary of State and the provisions in **25.24**, a person commits an offence if he

- exercises (or purports to exercise) any right to dispose of any shares which, to his knowledge, are for the time being subject to restrictions under **25.23**, or of any right to be issued with such shares;
- votes in respect of any such shares (whether as holder or proxy), or appoints a proxy to vote in respect of them;
- being the holder of any such shares, fails to notify the existence of the restrictions to any person whom he knows is entitled (apart from the restrictions) to vote in respect of the shares (whether as holder or proxy) but whom he does not know to be aware of the restrictions; or
- being the holder of any such shares, or entitled to any right to be issued with other shares in right of them, or to receive any payment on them (other than in a liquidation), enters into any agreement which is void under *CA 1985, s 454(2)* or *(3)* (see **25.23**).

If shares in a company are issued in contravention of the restrictions, an offence is committed by the company and every officer of the company who is in default.

A person guilty of an offence under the above provisions is liable (i) on conviction on indictment, to a fine; and (ii) on summary conviction, to a fine not exceeding the statutory maximum. See **29.1 Offences and Legal Proceedings** for the statutory maximum.

[*CA 1985, s 455*].

25.25 Relaxation and removal of restrictions

Where shares in a company are subject to restrictions because of an order under **25.23**, any aggrieved person may apply to the court for an order directing that the shares should be no longer subject to the restrictions.

[*CA 1985, s 456(1)(2*].

Subject to below, an order lifting the restrictions may be made only if

- the relevant facts about the shares have been disclosed to the company and no unfair advantage has accrued to any person as a result of the earlier failure to make that disclosure; or
- the shares are to be transferred for valuable consideration and the court or the Secretary of State approves the transfer. [*CA 1985, s 456(3)*].

Where the court is satisfied that an order unfairly affects the rights of third parties, it may direct that specified acts by such persons do not constitute a breach of the restrictions and such an order is not subject to *CA 1985, s 456(3)* above.

[*CA 1985, s 456(1A)*].

Where shares in a company are subject to restrictions, the company or the Secretary of State may make an application to the court for the shares to be sold. The court may then order the shares to be sold, subject to its approval as to the sale, and may also direct that the restrictions be lifted. [*CA 1985, s 456(4)*]. Following such an order, the court may (on application by the Secretary of State, the company, the person appointed to effect the sale or by any person interested in the shares) make such further order relating to the sale or transfer of the shares as it thinks fit.

[*CA 1985, s 456(5)*].

The proceeds of sale (less costs) of shares sold in pursuance of a court order under *CA 1985, s 456(4)* above must be paid into court for the benefit of those beneficially interested in the shares. Any of these persons may apply to the court for payment of the whole or part of the proceeds which the court must pay together with any interest (but subject to retaining an appropriate proportion of the proceeds for other persons with a beneficial interest in the shares). Costs of a successful application under *CA 1985, s 456(4)* or *(5)* above may, if the court so orders, be a prior charge on the sale proceeds before any person interested in the shares receives any part of the proceeds. [*CA 1985, s 457*].

An order lifting any restrictions under **25.23**, if it is made under *CA 1985, s 456(4)* or expressed to be made with a view to permitting the transfer of the shares, may continue the restrictions not to issue further shares or pay any sums due on those shares (see **25.23**(*c*) and (*d*)), in whole or part, so far as they relate to any right acquired or offer made before the transfer. *CA 1985, s 456(3)* above does not apply to an order directing that such restrictions cease to apply.

[*CA 1985, s 456(6)(7)*].

26 Members

26.1	**The members of a company**
26.2	**Exercise of members' rights**
26.3	Effect of provision of articles as to enjoyment or exercise of members' rights
26.4	Traded companies: nomination of persons to enjoy information rights
26.5	Exercise of rights where shares held on behalf of others: exercise in different ways
26.6	Exercise of rights where shares held on behalf of others: members' requests
26.7	Prohibition on subsidiary being member of its holding company
26.8	**Minimum and maximum membership**
26.9	**Members' powers, rights and liabilities**
26.10	**Protection of members against unfair prejudice**
26.11	**Derivative claims and proceedings by members**
26.12	Derivative claims in England and Wales or Northern Ireland
26.13	Derivative proceedings in Scotland

Cross-references. See **9** **CLASS RIGHTS**; **44** **SECURITIES: CERTIFICATION AND TRANSFER**; **45** **SHARES**.

26.1 THE MEMBERS OF A COMPANY

There is no definition of 'shareholder' in *CA 2006* instead the more general term 'members' is used. The 'members' of a company are defined in *CA 2006* as

- the subscribers of a company's memorandum who are deemed to have agreed to become members of the company and, on its registration, become members and must be entered as such in its register of members (see **38.4** **REGISTERS**); and
- every other person who agrees to become a member of a company, and whose name is entered in its register of members (see **38.4** **REGISTERS**).

[*CA 2006, s 112*].

The bearer of a share warrant may, if the articles so provide, be deemed a member of the company, either to the full extent or for any purposes defined in the articles.

[*CA 2006, s 122(3)*].

Who may be members.

- A *company* may normally hold shares in *another* company. But see **34** **PURCHASE OF OWN SHARES** for restrictions on a company subscribing for or purchasing its own shares and **26.7** for prohibition on a subsidiary being a member of its own holding company.
- In England and Wales, *minors* (ie persons under the age of 18) may become shareholders unless the articles forbid this. On reaching majority, the minor may repudiate the contract and avoid liability for future calls but cannot recover money paid for the allotment of the shares as there has not been a total failure of consideration (*Steinberg v Scala (Leeds) Ltd* [1923] 2 Ch 452, 92 LJKB 944, CA). In Scotland, under *Age of Legal Capacity (Scotland) Act 1991*, a person has full legal capacity from the age of 16 subject to the right, while under the age of 21,

to apply to the court for the setting aside of a 'prejudicial transaction' which was entered into between the ages of 16 and 18. Prior to the age of 16, contracts made will be void subject to an exception where the terms of the contract are not unreasonable and the subject matter is of a kind commonly entered into by someone of his or her age and circumstances.

- A *bankrupt* may continue to be a shareholder even after his beneficial interest has vested in the trustee in bankruptcy, unless the articles provide otherwise. He must, however vote as directed by the trustee.
- *Personal representatives and trustees in bankruptcy*. See **44.9** SECURITIES: CERTIFICATION AND TRANSFERS.
- *Partnerships*, even though not legal persons in England and Wales, may be registered as members under the partnership name (*Land Credit Co of Ireland, Re, Weikersheim's Case* (1873) 8 Ch App 831).

Trustees and nominees as members. Members are defined as legal owners, that is they are the person whose names appear on the register of members. Legal and beneficial ownerships may however be separate and if that is the case the basic provision in *CA 2006* is that company only need to be concerned with the rights of the legal owner. *Section 126* of *CA 2006* provides that no notice of any trust, express or implied or constructive, must be entered on the register of members in the case of companies incorporated in England and Wales or Northern Ireland.

The company's articles also usually regulate legal and beneficial ownership of shares and the rights of beneficial owners

Where standard articles have been adopted, see

- *Table A, Reg 5*
- *Model Articles, Art 23* (private companies)
- *Model Articles, Art 45* (public companies)

Set out in APPENDIX 4 STANDARD ARTICLES OF ASSOCIATION.

The company is not therefore required to enquire as to whether any transfer is within the powers of the trustees and is not liable for registering a transfer which is in breach of trust (*Simpson v Molson's Bank* [1895] AC 270, PC). Equally, as the company cannot recognise any interest of a beneficiary in the shares, it has no lien on shares held by trustees for a debt due to it by a beneficiary (*Perkins, Re, ex p Mexican Santa Barbara Mining Co* (1890) 24 QBD 613, CA).

The law has however developed in response to the Final Report of the Company Law Review Steering Group who said (Vol 1 at para 7.1) that it is important that the law should provide "convenient mechanisms by which the beneficial owners or their representatives can participate in governance, and that any unnecessary obstacle to their participation should be removed" but that 'it is equally essential that any changes in the law should call into question the legal title of the registered holder'.

To that end *CA 2006, Pt 9* provides the following

- the right for members to nominate others to enjoy or exercise the rights of members (*CA 2006, s 145* see **26.2**)
- the right for the members of traded companies to nominate others to enjoy information rights (*CA 2006, s 146* see **26.4**)

- the right of the legal owner of shares to exercise rights in different ways (*CA 2006, s 152* see **26.5**) and
- the right for beneficial owners to make certain requests (*CA 2006, s 153* see **26.6**).

26.2 EXERCISE OF MEMBERS' RIGHTS

A member can nominate another person or persons to enjoy rights of the member in relation to the company. These fall into two categories.

(a) Where the articles permit such nomination, anything which can be done by or in relation to the member can be done instead by, or in relation to, the nominated person. See **26.3**, **THIS APPLIES TO ALL COMPANIES**.

(b) In the case of a company whose shares are admitted to trading on a regulated market, a member who holds shares on behalf of another person can nominate that person to enjoy information rights (whether or not the articles specifically permit nomination). See **26.4**, **THIS APPLIES TO TRADED COMPANIES ONLY**.

26.3 Effect of provision of articles as to enjoyment or exercise of members' rights

CA 2006, s 145 enables a member to nominate another person or persons to enjoy or exercise the rights of the member but only if provision is made in the company's articles. If the articles do, include such a provision then so far as is necessary to give effect to that provision, anything required/authorised by the *Companies Acts* to be done by or in relation to the member must/may instead be done by or in relation to the nominated person (or each of them) as if he were a member of the company.

This applies, in particular, to the rights conferred by

- *CA 2006, ss 291 and 293* (right to be sent proposed written resolution, see **42.7** and **42.8** RESOLUTIONS AND MEETINGS);
- *CA 2006, s 292* (right to require circulation of written resolution, see **42.8** RESOLUTIONS AND MEETINGS);
- *CA 2006, s 303* (right to require directors to call general meeting, see **42.13** RESOLUTIONS AND MEETINGS);
- *CA 2006, s 310* (right to notice of general meetings, see **42.16** RESOLUTIONS AND MEETINGS);
- *CA 2006, s 314* (right to require circulation of a statement, see **42.20** RESOLUTIONS AND MEETINGS);
- In relation to meetings notice of which is given on or after 3 August 2009, *CA 2006, s 319A* (right to ask question at a meeting of a traded company, see **42.23A** RESOLUTIONS AND MEETINGS);
- *CA 2006, s 324* (right to appoint a proxy to act at a meeting, see **42.26** RESOLUTIONS AND MEETINGS);
- *CA 2006, s 338* (right to require circulation of resolution for AGM of a public company, see **42.31** RESOLUTIONS AND MEETINGS);
- In relation to meetings notice of which is given on or after 3 August 2009, *CA 2006, s 338A* (traded companies: members power to include matters in business dealt with at AGM, see **42.31** RESOLUTIONS AND MEETINGS); and

- *CA 2006, s 423* (right to be sent a copy of annual accounts and reports, see **2.6 Accounts: General**).

The above provisions do not

- confer rights enforceable against the company by anyone other than the member; and
- affect the requirements for an effective transfer or other disposition of the whole or part of a member's interest in the company.

[*CA 2006, s 145*].

26.4 Traded companies: nomination of persons to enjoy information rights

Where the shares of a company are admitted to trading on a regulated market, a member of the company who holds shares on behalf of another person may nominate that person to enjoy 'information rights'.

'*Information rights*' means

- the right to receive a copy of all communications that the company sends to its members generally (including annual accounts and reports and summary financial statements (after 1 October 2013 a strategic report will replace the summary financial statement see **chapter 6**)), or to any class of its members that includes the person making the nomination; and
- the rights conferred by

  (i) *CA 2006, ss 431 or 432* (right to require copies of accounts and reports, see **2.7 Accounts: General**) or, before 6 April 2008, *CA 1985, s 239*; and

  (ii) *CA 2006, s 1145* (right to require hard copy version of document or information provided in another form, see **16.33 Dealings with Third Parties**).

A company need not act on a nomination purporting to relate to certain information rights only.

[*CA 2006, s 146*]

Form in which copies to be provided. If the person to be nominated wishes to receive hard copy communications, he must, before the nomination is made, request the person making the nomination to notify the company of that fact and provide an address to which such copies may be sent. If, having received such a request, the person making the nomination so notifies the company and provides the company with that address, the right of the nominated person is to receive hard copy communications. (This is subject to *CA 2006, Sch 5, paras 5–14* under which the company may take steps to enable it to communicate in electronic form or by means of a website. See **16.29** and **16.30 Dealings with Third Parties**.)

If no such notification is given (or no address is provided), the nominated person is taken to have agreed that documents or information may be sent or supplied to him by the company by means of a website. That agreement may be revoked by the nominated person and does not affect his right under *CA 2006, s 1145* to require a hard copy version of a document or information provided in any other form.

[*CA 2006, s 147*].

Termination or suspension of nomination. The nomination is terminated in the following circumstances.

- At any time at the request of the member or of the nominated person.
- If the member or the nominated person
  - (i) in the case of an individual, dies or becomes bankrupt; and
  - (ii) in the case of a body corporate, is dissolved or is the subject of a winding-up order otherwise than for the purposes of reconstruction.
- Where the company
  - (i) enquires of a nominated person whether he wishes to retain information rights; and
  - (ii) does not receive a response within the period of 28 days beginning with the date on which the company's enquiry was sent.

  In such a case, the nomination ceases to have effect at the end of that period. Such an enquiry is not to be made of a person more than once in any 12-month period.

The effect of any nominations made by a member is suspended

- at any time when there are more nominated persons than the member has shares in the company; and
- where
  - (i) the member holds different classes of shares with different information rights, and
  - (ii) there are more nominated persons than he has shares conferring a particular right,

  to the extent that they confer that right.

The termination or suspension of a nomination means that the company is not required to act on it. But it does not prevent the company from continuing to do so, to such extent or for such period as it thinks fit.

[*CA 2006, s 148*].

Information as to possible rights in relation to voting. Where a company sends a copy of a notice of a meeting to a nominated person, the copy of the notice must be accompanied by a statement that

- he may have a right under an agreement between him and the member by whom he was nominated to be appointed, or to have someone else appointed, as a proxy for the meeting; and
- if he has no such right or does not wish to exercise it, he may have a right under such an agreement to give instructions to the member as to the exercise of voting rights.

CA 2006, s 325 (notice of meeting to contain statement of member's rights in relation to appointment of proxy, see **42.26 Resolutions and Meetings**) does not apply to the copy, and the company must either omit the notice required by that section or include it but state that it does not apply to the nominated person. [*CA 2006, s 149*].

Status of rights. Enjoyment by the nominated person of

- information rights (as defined above), and
- where applicable, the right to hard copy communications and the information as to possible voting rights

is enforceable against the company by the member as if they were rights conferred by the company's articles.

Any enactment, and any provision of the company's articles, having effect in relation to communications with members has a corresponding effect (subject to any necessary adaptations) in relation to communications with the nominated person. In particular

- where the members of a company entitled to receive a document or information are determined as at a date or time before it is sent or supplied, the company need not send or supply it to a nominated person
  - (i) whose nomination was received by the company after that date or time; or
  - (ii) if that date or time falls in a period of suspension of his nomination; and
- where the right of a member to receive a document or information depends on the company having a current address for him, the same applies to any person nominated by him.

The rights conferred by the nomination are in addition to the rights of the member himself and do not affect any rights exercisable by virtue of any of the provisions mentioned in **26.3**.

A failure to give effect to the rights conferred by the nomination does not affect the validity of anything done by or on behalf of the company.

[*CA 2006, s 150*].

26.5 Exercise of rights where shares held on behalf of others: exercise in different ways

Where a member holds shares in a company on behalf of more than one person

- rights attached to the shares, and
- rights under any enactment exercisable by virtue of holding the shares,

need not all be exercised, and if exercised, need not all be exercised in the same way.

Where a member

- does not exercise all his rights, he must inform the company to what extent he is exercising the rights; and
- exercises his rights in different ways, he must inform the company of the ways in which he is exercising them and to what extent they are exercised in each way.

If a member exercises his rights but fails to give such information, the company is entitled to assume that he is exercising all his rights and is exercising them in the same way.

[*CA 2006, s 152*].

26.6 Exercise of rights where shares held on behalf of others: members' requests

Where a company receives a request for the purposes of

- *CA 2006, s 314* (power to require circulation of statement, see **42.20 Resolutions and Meetings**),
- *CA 2006, s 338* (public companies: power to require circulation of resolution for AGM, see **42.31 Resolutions and Meetings**),
- in relation to meetings notice of which is given on or after 3 August 2009, *CA 2006, s 338A* (traded companies: members power to include matters in business dealt with at AGM, see **42.31 Resolutions and Meetings**),
- *CA 2006, s 342* (power to require independent report on poll, see **42.34 Resolutions and Meetings**), or
- *CA 2006, s 527* (power to require website publication of audit concerns, see **8.45 Audit**)

it must act under any of those provisions if it receives a request in relation to which the following conditions are met.

(a) It is made by at least 100 persons.

(b) It is authenticated by all the persons making it.

(c) In the case of any of those persons who is not a member of the company, it is accompanied by a statement

  (i) of the full name and address of a person ('the member') who is a member of the company and holds shares on behalf of that person;

  (ii) that the member is holding those shares on behalf of that person in the course of a business;

  (iii) of the number of shares in the company that the member holds on behalf of that person;

  (iv) of the total amount paid up on those shares;

  (v) that those shares are not held on behalf of anyone else or, if they are, that the other person or persons are not among the other persons making the request;

  (vi) that some or all of those shares confer voting rights that are relevant for the purposes of making a request under the provision in question; and

  (vii) that the person has the right to instruct the member how to exercise those rights.

(d) In the case of any of those persons who is a member of the company, it is accompanied by a statement

  (i) that he holds shares otherwise than on behalf of another person; or

  (ii) that he holds shares on behalf of one or more other persons but those persons are not among the other persons making the request.

(e) It is accompanied by such evidence as the company may reasonably require of the matters mentioned in (*c*) and (*d*) above.

(f) The total amount of the sums paid up on

(i) shares held under (*c*) above, and

(ii) shares held (*d*) above,

divided by the number of persons making the request, is not less than £100.

(g) The request complies with any other requirements of the provision in question as to contents, timing and otherwise.

[*CA 2006, s 153*].

26.7 Prohibition on subsidiary being member of its holding company

Prohibition. Subject to the exceptions below, a body corporate cannot be a member of a company that is its holding company and any allotment or transfer of shares in a company to its subsidiary is void. [*CA 2006, s 136*]. The provisions apply

- in relation to a company other than a company limited by shares, but substituting references to the interest of its members as such (in whatever form) for the references to shares [*CA 2006, s 143*]; and
- to a nominee acting on behalf of a subsidiary as to the subsidiary itself. [*CA 2006, s 144*].

Shares acquired before prohibition became applicable. Where a body corporate became a holder of shares in a company

(a) before 1 July 1948 (1 April 1961 in the case of a company registered in Northern Ireland), or

(b) on or after the relevant date in (*a*) and before 1 October 2009 in circumstances in which the similar prohibition in *CA 1985, s 23(1)* or *Companies (Northern Ireland) Order 1986, Art 33(1)* (or any corresponding earlier enactment), as it then had effect, did not apply, or

(c) on or after 1 October 2009 in circumstances in which the prohibition above does not apply,

it may continue to be a member of its holding company. So long as it is permitted to continue as a member, an allotment to it of fully paid shares in the company may be validly made by way of capitalisation of reserves of the company. But, so long as the prohibition would otherwise apply, it has no right to vote in respect of the shares falling within (*a*)–(*c*) above (or any shares allotted to it in respect of those shares by way of capitalisation) on a written resolution or at meetings of the company or of any class of its members.

[*CA 2006, s 137*].

Exceptions.

(1) **Subsidiary acting as personal representative or trustee**

The prohibition on a subsidiary being a member of its holding company does not apply where the subsidiary is concerned only as a personal representative or trustee unless, in the latter case, the holding company, or a subsidiary of it, is beneficially interested under the trust. In determining whether the holding company or a subsidiary is so interested, there must be disregarded:

(a) Any interest held only by way of security for the purposes of a transaction entered into by the holding company or subsidiary in the ordinary course of a business that includes the lending or money.

(b) Where shares in a company are held on trust for the purposes of a pension scheme or employees' share scheme, any 'residual interest' that has not vested in possession.

A '*residual interest*' means a 'right' of the company or subsidiary ('the residual beneficiary') to receive any of the trust property in the event of

- all the 'liabilities arising under the scheme' having been satisfied or provided for;
- the residual beneficiary ceasing to participate in the scheme; or
- the trust property at any time exceeding what is necessary for satisfying the liabilities arising, or expected to arise, under the scheme.

'*Right*' includes a right dependent on the exercise of a discretion vested by the scheme in the trustee or another person, and '*liabilities arising under a scheme*' include liabilities that have resulted, or may result, from the exercise of any such discretion.

(c) Where shares in a company are held on trust for the purposes of a pension scheme or employees' share scheme, any charge or lien on, or set-off against, any benefit or other right or interest under the scheme for the purpose of enabling the employer or former employer of a member of the scheme to obtain the discharge or a monetary obligation due to him from the member.

(d) Where shares in a company are held on trust for the purposes of a pension scheme, any right to receive from the trustee of the scheme, or as trustee of the scheme to retain, an amount that can be recovered or retained under *Pension Schemes Act 1993, s 61* or *Pension Schemes (Northern Ireland) Act 1993, s 57* (deduction of contributions equivalent premium from refund of scheme contributions) or otherwise, as reimbursement or partial reimbursement for any contributions equivalent premium paid in connection with the scheme under *Part 3* of that *Act*.

(e) Any rights that the company or subsidiary has in its capacity as trustee, including in particular

- any right to recover its expenses or be remunerated out of the trust property; and
- any right to be indemnified out of the trust property for any liability incurred by reason of any act or omission in the performance of its duties as trustee.

[*CA 2006, ss 138–140*].

(2) **Subsidiary acting as dealer in securities**

The prohibition on a subsidiary being a member of its holding company does not apply where the shares are held by the subsidiary in the ordinary course of its business as an 'intermediary'.

An '*intermediary*' is a person who

- carries on a *bona fide* business of dealing in securities;
- is a member of or has access to a regulated market; and
- does not carry on an '*excluded business*', ie a business that consists
  - (i) wholly or mainly of making or managing investments;
  - (ii) wholly or mainly in providing services to connected persons (as determined in accordance with *Corporation Taxes Act 2010, s 1122*);
  - (iii) in insurance business;
  - (iv) in managing or acting as trustee in relation to a pension scheme or that is carried on by the manager or trustee of such a scheme in connection with or for the purposes of such a scheme; or
  - (v) in operating, or acting as trustee in relation to, a collective investment scheme or that is carried on by the operator or trustee of such a scheme in connection with or for the purposes of such a scheme.

Where

(a) a subsidiary that is a dealer in securities has purportedly acquired shares in its holding company in contravention of the prohibition above, and

(b) a person acting in good faith has agreed, for value and without notice of the contravention, to acquire shares in the holding company from

  (i) the subsidiary, or

  (ii) someone who has purportedly acquired the shares after their disposal by the subsidiary,

a transfer to that person of the shares in (*a*) above has the same effect as it would have had if their original acquisition by the subsidiary had not been in contravention of the prohibition.

[*CA 2006, ss 141, 142*].

26.8 MINIMUM AND MAXIMUM MEMBERSHIP

Minimum membership. *In relation to applications for registration received by the Registrar of Companies on or after 1 October 2009*, any company can be formed with one member.

[*CA 2006, s 7*].

For applications received before that date (and where the requirements for registration were met), a private company limited by shares or by guarantee could have one member but any other company had to be formed with at least two members. [*CA 1985, s 1(1)(3A)* (as amended)]. If the company carries on business without having at least two members for more than six months, a person who is a member of the company and knows that it is carrying on a business with only one member is liable (jointly and severally with the company) for the payment of the company's debts contracted after that period and whilst a member of the company. For these purposes, reference to a member does not include the company itself where it is a member by virtue of its

holding shares as treasury shares. [*CA 1985, s 24* (as amended; *SI 2008 No 2860, Sch 1*]. The repeal of *CA 1985, s 24* does not affect any liability under that section for debts of the company contracted before 1 October 2009.
[*SI 2008 No 2860, Sch 2 para 24*].

Maximum membership. There is no maximum number of members unless the company was incorporated between 1 July 1948 and 21 December 1980 and adopted *Table A, 1948* and has not since changed its articles. In such a case, there is an upper limit of 50 members (excluding employees and past employees who held when employed, and have continued to hold, shares in the company). For these purposes, joint holders are treated as a single member. There is no equivalent article in subsequent standard articles.

26.9 MEMBERS' POWERS, RIGHTS AND LIABILITIES

Reserve power. Power to manage the company is vested in the directors under the articles of association which (in the case of the Model Articles) provide that the directors are responsible for the management of the company's business. The members are however given reserve power. They may, in a case where a company has adopted the Model Articles, decide by special resolution to direct the directors to take, or refrain from taking, specified action (see *Art 4* of the *Model Articles* – **APPENDIX 4**).

Rights in general. No member has any right to any item of property owned by the company for he has no legal or equitable interest in it. The company's assets are its own property not the property of its members. See *Re George Newman & Co*, CA [1895] 1 Ch 674 and *Short v Treasury Comrs* [1948] 1 KB 116, [1947] 2 All ER 298, HL, where it was held that shareholders are not, in the eyes of the law, part owners of the undertaking which is something different from the totality of the shareholding. Neither does a member have an insurable interest in any particular assets which the company holds (*Macaura v Northern Assurance Co Ltd* [1925] AC 619, 94 LJPC 154, HL). A member is merely entitled to a *share* in the company and shares are merely a right of participation in the company on the terms of the articles of association (*Prudential Assurance Co Ltd v Newman Industries Ltd (No 2)* [1982] Ch 204, [1982] 1 All ER 354, CA). In that case it was held that a shareholder had no personal claim against a person whose actions had reduced the company's profits because the shares themselves were not directly affected and the right of participation remained intact. The correct action is one in the name of the company in respect of the loss or damage caused to it.

See also **14.12 CONSTITUTION – MEMORANDUM AND ARTICLES** for the contractual effect of the articles between members and between the company and its members.

Rights under ***CA 2006***. Members are given many rights under *CA 2006* including the right to

- receive and demand copies of the annual accounts (see **2.6** and **2.7 ACCOUNTS: GENERAL**);
- receive notice of, attend, vote at, and in certain circumstances requisition, meetings of the company (see **42 RESOLUTIONS AND MEETINGS**);
- inspect the statutory registers (see **38 REGISTERS**), minute books (see **42.43 RESOLUTIONS AND MEETINGS**), and directors' service contracts (see **18.56 DIRECTORS**);
- require the company to circulate statements and resolutions (see **42.20** and **42.31 RESOLUTIONS AND MEETINGS**);
- receive dividends if declared (see **22.10 DISTRIBUTIONS**);

- object to the payment for the redemption or purchase of the company's shares out of capital (see **34.13 Purchase of Own Shares**);
- apply to the court for a meeting following a proposed compromise with members and/or creditors (see **35.2 Reconstructions and Mergers**);
- apply to the court following the re-registration of a public company as a private company (see **41.9 Re-Registration**);
- be bought out following a takeover offer where the offeror holds at least 90% of the shares (see **48.15 Takeovers**);
- petition the court for the winding up of the company under the *IA 1986, s 124*; and
- apply to the Secretary of State to appoint an inspector to investigate the company's affairs (see **25 Investigations**).

Rights of members to damages, etc. A person is not debarred from obtaining damages or other compensation from a company by reason only that he holds, or has held,

- shares in the company; or
- any right to apply or subscribe for shares or to be included in the company's register in respect of shares.

[*CA 2006, s 655*].

Liabilities. The principal liabilities of a member are:

- To pay any outstanding amounts or calls on his shares as required by the company (see **47.23 Shares**). If the articles of the company provide, a member's shares may be forfeited for non-payment of calls (see **47.25 Shares**).
- In the event of a winding up, to contribute to the assets of the company in respect of any amounts unpaid on his shares.

  [*IA 1986, s 74*].

If the company adopts the Model Articles, Article 2 (of both private and public company articles) provides that the liability of members is limited to the amount, if any, unpaid on the shares held by them. For companies incorporated before 1 October 2009 the limitation of liability clause was contained in the company's memorandum. See **14 Constitution – Memorandum and Articles** for the effect of *CA 2006, s 28* as from 1 October 2009.

26.10 Protection of members against unfair prejudice

Petitions to the court. An application may be made to the court by petition by

(a) a member of a company (including a statutory water company),

(b) the Secretary of State where he has

  (i) received a report under *CA 1985, s 437* (inspector's report, see **25.3 Investigations**),

  (ii) exercised his powers under *CA 1985, s 447* or *448* (powers to require documents and information or to enter and search premises, see **25.12** and **25.13 Investigations**),

(iii) exercised his powers under *FSMA 2000, Pt 11* (information gathering and investigations), or

(iv) received a report from an investigator appointed by him or the FCA under that *Part*,

(c) the FCA where it has exercised its powers under *FSMA 2000, Pt 11*

on either of the following grounds.

- The company's affairs are being, or have been, conducted in a manner that is unfairly prejudicial to the interests of members generally or of some part of its members (including, where (*a*) above applies, at least the member bringing the petition).

  This includes, the removal from office of the company's auditor appointed for a financial year beginning on or after 5 April 2008 on the grounds of divergence of opinion on accounting treatment or audit procedures or any other improper grounds.

- Any actual or proposed act or omission of the company (including an act or omission on its behalf) is, or would be, so prejudicial.

Included under (*a*) above is a person who is not a member of a company but to whom shares in the company have been transferred or transmitted by operation of the law.

The powers of the Secretary of State to make an application under (*b*) above may be used in addition to, or instead of, the presenting of a winding-up petition against the company.

[*CA 2006, ss 994, 995; SI 2007 No 2194, Sch 1 para 19; SI 2007 No 3494, Reg 42*].

Before 1 October 2007, similar provisions applied under *CA 1985, ss 459, 460*.

See also *Meyer v Scottish Textile and Manufacturing Co Ltd (or Scottish Co-operative Wholesale Society)* 1954 SC 381, 1954 SLT 273 and *Scottish Co-operative Wholesale Society Ltd v Meyer* [1959] AC 324, [1958] 3 All ER 66, HL; *HR Harmer Ltd, Re* [1958] 3 All ER 689, [1959] 1 WLR 62, CA; *Company, a (No 004475 of 1982), Re* [1983] Ch 178, [1983] BCLC 126; *Company, a (No 002567 of 1982), Re* [1983] 2 All ER 854, [1983] BCLC 151; and *Re Bird Precision Bellows Ltd* [1986] Ch 658, [1985] BCLC 493, CA.

The above procedures are not available to a company's majority shareholders, having the power to procure the passing of any resolution of the company, in order to force the minority shareholder to give up his investment (*Morris v Hateley* [1999] 13 LS Gaz R 31, (1999) Times, 10 March, CA).

Provisions relating to petitions. The petition must be in the form set out in the Schedule to the *Companies (Unfair Prejudice Applications) Proceedings Rules 2009* (*SI 2009 No 2469*) with such variations, if any, as circumstances require. It must specify the grounds on which it is presented and the nature of the relief sought and be delivered to the court for filing with sufficient copies for service. The court must fix a hearing for a day (the 'return day') on which the petitioner and any respondent (including the company) must attend before the registrar or District Judge for directions to be given in relation to the procedure on the petition. On fixing the return day, the court must return to the petitioner sealed copies of the petition, each endorsed with the return day and the time of the hearing. At least 14 days before the return day the petitioner must serve a sealed copy of the petition on the company . If the petition is based on *CA 2006, s 994*, a sealed copy of the petition must be served on every respondent named in the petition at least 14 days before the return date.

On the return date or at any time after it, the court must give such directions as it thinks appropriate with respect to (i) service and advertisement of the petition; (ii) whether points of claim and defence are to be delivered; the manner in which evidence is to be given at the hearing; (iii) generally as to the procedure on the petition and the hearing and disposal of the petition and (iv) any orders, including a stay, with a view to mediation or other alternative dispute resolutions.

[*SI 2009 No 2469 Rules 1–6*].

Powers of the court. If the court is satisfied that a petition is well founded, it may make such order as it thinks fit for giving relief in respect of matters complained of, including

- regulating the conduct of the company's future affairs;
- requiring a company to
  - (i) refrain from doing or continuing an act complained of; or
  - (ii) do an act that the petitioner has complained it has omitted to do;
- authorising civil proceedings to be brought in the name and on behalf of the company by such persons and on such terms as it directs;
- requiring the company not to make any, or any specified, alterations in its articles without the leave of the court; and
- providing for the purchase of the shares of any members of the company by other members or by the company itself and, in the latter case, the reduction of the company's share capital accordingly.

[*CA 2006, s 996*].

Action following a court order.

(1) If the court considers that the order should be advertised, it may give directions as to the manner and time the order should be advertised [*SI 2009 No 2469, Rule 6*]

(2) Where an order of the court

- alters the company's constitution, or
- gives leave for the company to make any, or any specified, alterations to its constitution,

the company must deliver a copy of the order to the Registrar of Companies within 14 days from the making of the order or such longer period as the court may allow.

If a company makes default in complying with this provision, an offence is committed by the company and every officer of the company who is in default. A person guilty of such an offence is liable, on summary conviction, to a fine not exceeding level 3 on the standard scale and, for continued contravention, a daily default fine not exceeding one-tenth of level 3 on the standard scale. See **29.1 Offences and Legal Proceedings** for the standard scale.

[*CA 2006, s 998*].

(3) If the court order alters a company's constitution ie if the order amends

- a company's articles, or
- any resolution or agreement to which *CA 2006, ss 29, 30* apply (see **14 Constitution – Memorandum and Articles**),

the copy of the order delivered to the Registrar of Companies must be accompanied by a copy of the company's articles, or the resolution or agreement in question, as amended.

Every copy of a company's articles issued by the company after the order is made must be accompanied by a copy of the order, unless the effect of the order has been incorporated into the articles by amendment.

If a company makes default in complying with these requirements, an offence is committed by the company and every officer of the company who is in default. A person guilty of such an offence is liable, on summary conviction, to a fine not exceeding level 3 on the standard scale. See **29.1** Offences and Legal Proceedings for the standard scale.

[*CA 2006, s 999; SI 2007 No 2194, Sch 3 para 47*].

26.11 DERIVATIVE CLAIMS AND PROCEEDINGS BY MEMBERS

CA 2006, s 170(1) provides that a directors' general duties are owed to the company rather than to individual members. It follows that only the company can enforce them. There are three main ways in which a company can take legal action against a director (or former director) for breach of duty.

- If the board of directors decides to commence proceedings.
- If a liquidator or administrator decides to commence proceedings following the commencement of a formal insolvency procedure.
- Through a derivative claim or action brought by one or more members to enforce a right which is vested not in himself/ their selves but in the company.

The third of these procedures is considered below and in **26.12** and **26.13**.

Overview of old and new positions.

(1) *England and Wales and Northern Ireland*

Before 1 October 2007, the law relating to the ability of a member to bring proceedings on behalf of the company (a 'derivative claim') was not written down in statute but applied by common law. *Foss v Harbottle* (1843) 2 Hare 461 established the fundamental rule that to redress a wrong done to a company or to recover moneys or damages due to it, action must *prima facie* be brought by the company itself. But subsequent case law established exceptions to the rule. These were summarised in *Burland v Earle* [1902] AC 83, 71 LJPC 1, PC as applying where the persons against whom the relief was sought themselves control the majority of shares in the company and would not permit an action to be brought in the company's name. In such a case, the courts would permit the complaining shareholder to bring an action in the company's name. However, if a wrong had been effectively ratified by the company, there was a complete bar to a derivative claim and if a wrong was capable of being ratified, it might not have been possible for a minority shareholder to bring a derivative action (even if there had been no formal ratification). The cases in which the minority could maintain such an action were, therefore, largely confined to the following.

- Where the acts complained of were of a fraudulent character or *ultra vires*. See *Simpson v Westminster Palace Hotel Co* (1860) 8 HL Cas 712 and *Russell v Wakefield Waterworks Co* (1875) LR 20 Eq 474.

- Where the matter was one which could only validly be done or sanctioned, not by a simple majority, but only by a special majority. See *Cotter v National Union of Seamen* [1929] 2 Ch 58, 98 LJ Ch 323, CA and *Edwards v Halliwell* [1950] 2 All ER 1064, 94 Sol Jo 803, CA.
- Where the rights of an individual member had been infringed. See *Pender v Lushington* (1877) 6 Ch D 70.
- Where the majority were endeavouring to appropriate to themselves money, property or advantage which belonged to the company or in which the other shareholders were entitled to participate, ie a fraud on the minority. See *Atwool v Merryweather* (1867) LR 5 Eq 464n and *Burland v Earle* above.

With effect from 1 October 2007, the provisions in **26.12** do not form a substantive rule to replace the rule in *Foss v Harbottle* but reflect the recommendation of the Law Commission that there should be a derivative procedure with a more modern, flexible and accessible criteria for determining whether a shareholder can pursue an action. Derivative claims are expressly available for breach of the duty to exercise reasonable care, skill and diligence, even if the director has not benefited personally, and it is not necessary for the applicant to show that the directors in the wrong control the majority of the company's shares.

(2) *Scotland*

Before 1 October 2007, a member's right to raise on action was conferred by substantive law. Therefore, a member had title to raise proceedings in respect of a director's breach of duty to obtain a remedy for the company. The action was raised in the name of the member but the remedy was obtained for the company and the rights which the member could enforce against a director were those of the company. The member's right arose where the action complained of was fraudulent or *ultra vires* and so could not be validated by a majority of members of the company. The remedy was not available if the majority of members acting in good faith had validated or could validate the act complained of. Two rules of substantive law applied to actions bought by members to protect the company's interests. First, the directors of the company owed a duty to the company and not to the members. Secondly, the court would not interfere in matters of internal management which could be sanctioned by a majority of the members.

With effect from 1 October 2007, the provisions in **26.13** seek to ensure maximum consistency between the position in England and Wales and Northern Ireland and the position in Scotland (although reflecting the different procedural requirements). In view of this they also put the rights of a member to raise actions on behalf of the company on a statutory footing.

26.12 Derivative claims in England and Wales or Northern Ireland

The following provisions apply to a '*derivative claim*', ie proceedings by a member of a company

- in respect of a cause of action vested in the company; and
- seeking relief on behalf of the company.

A derivative claim may only be brought under these provisions or in pursuance of an order of the court in unfair prejudice proceedings (see **26.10** above). A derivative claim under these provisions may be brought only in respect of a cause of action arising from an actual or proposed act or omission involving negligence, default, breach of duty or breach of trust by a director of the company. The cause of action may be against the director or another person (or both). It is immaterial whether the cause of action arose before or after the person seeking to bring or continue the derivative claim became a member of the company. For these purposes

- 'director' includes a former director;
- a 'shadow director' is treated as a director; and
- references to a member of a company include a person who is not a member but to whom shares in the company have been transferred or transmitted by operation of law.

Applications to the court. Application to the court for permission (in Northern Ireland, leave) to continue a derivative claim is required in the following instances.

(a) Where a member of a company brings a derivative claim.

(b) Where

   (i) a member of the company wishes to continue a claim brought by a company as a derivative claim on the ground that

   - the manner in which the company commenced or continued the claim amounts to an abuse of the process of the court;
   - the company has failed to prosecute the claim diligently; and
   - it is appropriate for the member to continue the claim as a derivative claim; and

   (ii) the cause of action on which the claim is based could be pursued as a derivative claim under these provisions.

(c) Where a member of the company ('the applicant') wishes to continue a derivative claim which another member ('the claimant') has

- brought under (*a*) above,
- continued under (*b*) above, or
- continued under this provision

on the ground that

- the manner in which the proceedings have been commenced or continued by the claimant amounts to an abuse of the process of the court;
- the claimant has failed to prosecute the claim diligently; and
- it is appropriate for the applicant to continue the claim as a derivative claim.

If it appears to the court that the application and the evidence filed by the applicant in support of it do not disclose a *prima facie* case for giving permission (or leave), the court must dismiss the application and may make any consequential order it considers appropriate. If the application is not dismissed, the court may give directions as to the evidence to be provided by the company and may adjourn the proceedings to enable the evidence to be obtained.

On hearing the application, the court may (i) give permission (or leave) to continue the claim on such terms as it thinks fit; (ii) refuse permission (or leave) and dismiss the claim; or (iii) adjourn the proceedings on the application and give such directions as it thinks fit.

Matters to be taken into account by the court. In deciding whether to give permission (or leave) for an application under (*a*) or (*b*) above to be heard or, as the case may be, continued, as a derivative claim, the court must:

- Refuse permission (or leave) if it is satisfied
  - (i) that a person acting in accordance with *CA 2006, s 172* (duty to promote the success of the company, see **18.24 Directors**) would not seek to continue the claim;
  - (ii) where the cause of action arises from an act or omission that is yet to occur, that the act or omission has been authorised by the company; or
  - (iii) where the cause of action arises from an act or omission that has already occurred, that the act or omission was authorised by the company before it occurred or has been ratified by the company since it occurred.
- Take into account (in particular)
  - (i) whether the member is acting in good faith in seeking to continue the claim;
  - (ii) the importance that a person acting in accordance with *CA 2006, s 172* (duty to promote the success of the company) would attach to continuing it;
  - (iii) where the cause of action results from an act or omission that is yet to occur, whether the act or omission could be, and in the circumstances would be likely to be, authorised by the company before it occurs or ratified by the company after it occurs;
  - (iv) where the cause of action arises from an act or omission that has already occurred, whether the act or omission could be, and in the circumstances would be likely to be, ratified by the company;
  - (v) whether the company has decided not to pursue the claim; and
  - (vi) whether the act or omission in respect of which the claim is brought gives rise to a cause of action that the member could pursue in his own right rather than on behalf of the company.

The court must have particular regard to any evidence before it as to the views of members of the company who have no personal interest, direct or indirect, in the matter.

[*CA 2006, ss 260–264*].

26.13 Derivative proceedings in Scotland

A member of a company may, in order to protect the interests of the company and obtain a remedy on its behalf, raise proceedings ('*derivative proceedings*') in respect of any actual or proposed act or omission involving negligence, default, breach of duty or breach of trust by a director of the company (the '*cause of action*'). Proceedings may be raised against the director or another person (or both). It is immaterial whether the act or omission in question arose before or after the person seeking to raise them (or continue them as below) became a member of the company.

These provisions do not affect

- any right of a member of a company to raise proceedings in respect of such an act or omission as specified above in order to protect his own interests and obtain a remedy on his own behalf; or
- the court's power to authorise civil proceedings to be brought in the name and on behalf of the company by such persons and on such terms as it directs or anything done under such an order.

For the above purposes

- 'director' includes a former director;
- a 'shadow director' (see **18.1 Directors**) is treated as a director; and
- references to a member of a company include a person who is not a member but to whom shares in the company have been transferred or transmitted by operation of law.

Requirement for leave and notice. Derivative proceedings may be raised by a member of a company only with the leave of the court. An application for leave must specify the cause of action and summarise the facts on which the derivative proceedings are to be based.

If it appears to the court that the application and the evidence produced by the applicant in support of it do not disclose a *prima facie* case for granting it, the court must refuse the application. It may then make any consequential order it considers appropriate.

If the application is not refused, the applicant must serve the application on the company. The court may make an order requiring evidence to be produced by the company and may adjourn the proceedings on the application to enable the evidence to be obtained. The company is entitled to take part in the further proceedings on the application.

On hearing the application, the court may (i) grant the application on such terms as it thinks fit; (ii) refuse the application; or (iii) adjourn the proceedings on the application and make such order as to further procedure as it thinks fit.

Application to continue proceedings as derivative proceedings. Where a company has raised proceedings in respect of an act or omission which could be the basis for derivative proceedings, a member of the company may apply to the court to be substituted for the company in the proceedings, and for the proceedings to continue in consequence as derivative proceedings, on the ground that

- the manner in which the company commenced or continued the proceedings amounts to an abuse of the process of the court;
- the company has failed to prosecute the proceedings diligently; and
- it is appropriate for the member to be substituted for the company in the proceedings.

Matters then proceed as above depending upon whether or not the court accept that there is a *prima facie* case for granting the application.

Granting of leave. The court must refuse leave to raise derivative proceedings, or an application to continue proceedings as derivative proceedings, if it is satisfied

- that a person acting in accordance with *CA 2006, s 172* (duty to promote the success of the company, see **18.24 Directors**) would not seek to continue the proceedings;

- where the cause of action is an act or omission that is yet to occur, that the act or omission has been authorised by the company; or
- where the cause of action is an act or omission that has already occurred, that the act or omission was authorised by the company before it occurred or has been ratified by the company since it occurred.

It must also, in particular, take into account

- whether the member is acting in good faith in seeking to raise or continue the proceedings;
- the importance that a person acting in accordance with *CA 2006, s 172* (duty to promote the success of the company) would attach to raising or continuing them;
- where the cause of action is an act or omission that is yet to occur, whether the act or omission could be, and in the circumstances would be likely to be, authorised by the company before it occurs or ratified by the company after it occurs;
- where the cause of action is an act or omission that has already occurred, whether the act or omission could be, and in the circumstances would be likely to be, ratified by the company;
- whether the company has decided not to raise proceedings in respect of the same cause of action or to persist with the proceedings; and
- whether the cause of action is one which the member could pursue in his own right rather than on behalf of the company.

The court must have particular regard to any evidence before it as to the views of members of the company who have no personal interest, direct or indirect, in the matter.

Application by member to be substituted for member pursuing derivative proceedings. Where a member of a company (*'the claimant'*) has

- raised derivative proceedings,
- continued as derivative proceedings raised by the company, or
- continued derivative proceedings under this provision,

another member of the company (*'the applicant'*) may apply to the court to be substituted for the claimant in the action on the ground that

- the manner in which the proceedings have been commenced or continued by the claimant amounts to an abuse of the process of the court;
- the claimant has failed to prosecute the proceedings diligently; and
- it is appropriate for the applicant to be substituted for the claimant in the proceedings.

Matters then proceed as above depending upon whether or not the court accept that there is a *prima facie* case for granting the application.

[*CA 2006, ss 265–269*].

Transitional provisions. Where an application is made under the above provisions, if the cause of action arises (wholly or to any extent) from an act or omission that occurred before 1 October 2007, the court must exercise its powers under those provisions so as to secure that the proceedings in respect of that act or omission are allowed to proceed as derivative proceedings only to the extent that they could have been pursued by the applicant under the law in force immediately before that date.

[*SI 2007 No 2194, Sch 3 para 21*].

27 Names and Business Names

27.1	Names	27.18	Business names
27.2	Indication of type of company in name	27.19	Restricted and prohibited names
27.3	Prohibited names	27.23	Application for a business name
27.7	Sensitive words and expressions	27.24	Disclosure required by individuals and partnerships
27.8	Permitted characters	27.25	Disclosure required in business documents, etc
27.9	Length of name		
27.10	How to register a company name	27.26	Disclosure required at business premises
27.11	Compulsory change of name		
27.17	Voluntary change of name	27.27	Consequence of failure to disclose

Cross-references. See **16.13 Dealings With Third Parties** for display of name at business premises; **16.14 Dealings With Third Parties** for inclusion of name in documents and communications; **18.40 Directors** for re-use of company name following insolvent liquidation.

Background. The provisions in *CA 2006, Pts 6* and *41* which are considered in this chapter apply, unless otherwise stated, with effect from 1 October 2009. They replace the provisions in *CA 1985, Pt 1, Ch 2* relating to names and *BNA 1985* relating to business names.

27.1 NAMES

The provisions in **27.2** to **27.17** relate to the name which a company may, or may not, use and changes made in its name (whether compulsory or voluntary).

27.2 Indication of type of company in name

The name of a company must end

(a) in the case of a limited company that is a public company, with 'public limited company' or 'plc'; and

(b) subject to the exemptions below, in the case of a company that is a private company, with 'limited' or 'ltd'.

In the case of a Welsh company, its name may instead end with 'cwmni cyfyngedig cyhoeddus' or 'ccc' under (*a*) or 'cyfyngedig' or 'cyf' under (*b*).

The above provisions do not apply to community interest companies (for which see **10 Community Interest Companies**).

[*CA 2006, ss 58, 59*].

Exemptions. A private company is exempt from the requirements to have 'limited' or 'ltd' at the end of its name in the following circumstances.

(1) It is a charity.

[*CA 2006, s 60(1)(a)*].

(2) It is exempted from the requirement by Regulations made by the Secretary of State. [*CA 2006, s 60(1)(b)*]. These are the *Company, Limited Liability and Business (Names and Trading Disclosures) Regulations 2015 (the 2015 Regulations)* which are referred to where relevant throughout this chapter

(3) It is a private company limited by shares which has an existing exemption and can continue with that exemption if it meets the conditions set out in *section 61* of *CA 2006*.

[*CA 2006, ss 60(1)(c), 61*].

(4) It is a private company limited by guarantee which has an existing exemption and can continue with that exemption if it meets the conditions set out in *CA 2006, s 62*.

[*CA 2006, ss 60(1)(c), 62*].

The Registrar of Companies may refuse to register a private limited company by a name that does not include the word 'limited' (or a permitted alternative) unless a statement has been delivered to him that the company meets the conditions for exemption. The Registrar may accept the statement as sufficient evidence of the matters stated in it.

[*CA 2006, s 60(2), (3)*].

Restriction on amendment of articles. A private company that is exempt by virtue of continuing an existing exemption (see (3) and (4) above), and whose name does not include 'limited' or any of the permitted alternatives, must not amend its articles so that it ceases to comply with the conditions for exemption. In contravention, an offence is committed by the company and every officer of the company who is in default. For this purpose a shadow director is treated as an officer of the company. A person guilty of such an offence is liable, on summary conviction, to a fine not exceeding level 5 on the standard scale and, for continued contravention, to a daily default fine not exceeding one-tenth of the greater of £5,000 or level 4 on the standard scale. See **29.1 Offences and Legal Proceedings** for the standard scale.

If, immediately before 1 October 2009, a company was exempt (by virtue of *CA 1985, s 30* (or *Companies (Northern Ireland) Order 1986, Art 40*)) from the requirement to have a name including the word limited (or a permitted alternative), and the company's memorandum or articles could not be altered without the approval of

- the Board of Trade or a Northern Ireland department (or any other department or Minister), or
- the Charity Commission,

that provision, in the memorandum or articles and any condition of any such licence referred to in *sections 61(1)(a)(ii)* or *(b)(ii)* which required that provision in the memorandum or articles, ceased to have effect on 1 October 2009 (unless the provision is required by or under any other enactment). [*CA 2006, s 63; SI 2015 No 664, Sch 3*].

27.3 Prohibited names

A company cannot be registered with a proposed name in any of the circumstances set out in **27.4** to **27.6**.

27.4 *Offensive name*

A company cannot be registered by a name if, in the opinion of the Secretary of State,

- its use by the company would constitute an offence; or
- it is offensive.

[*CA 2006, s 53*].

27.5 *Inappropriate indication of company type or legal form. Name same as an existing name*

The Secretary of State can, by Regulations, prohibit the use in a company name of specified words, expressions or other indications that are

- associated with, or
- similar to words, expressions or other indications associated with,

a particular type of company or form of organisation. The making of regulations does not affect the continued registration of a company by a name by which it was duly registered immediately before 1 October 2009; and in the case of a 'transitional company', on its registration or re-registration.

A '*transitional company*' is one that applied for registration (or re-registration) before 1 October 2009 (and met all the necessary requirements before that date) but which was not registered (or re-registered) until on or after that date.

[*CA 2006, s 65; SI 2008 No 2860, Sch 2 para 17*].

The Regulations referred to above made under *s 65* are the *2015 Regulations referred to above.*

Under these Regulations, the following restrictions apply.

(1) *Generally applicable provisions*

Subject to (2)(*b*) and (3)(*b*) below, a company must not be registered under *CA 2006* by a name that includes

(a) otherwise than at the end of the name

any of the expressions or abbreviations 'PUBLIC LIMITED COMPANY', (or with or without full stops the abbreviation) 'PLC', 'CWMNI CYFYNGEDIG CYHOEDDUS', (or with or without full stops the abbreviation) 'CCC', 'COMMUNITY INTEREST COMPANY', (or with or without full stops the abbreviation) 'CIC', 'CWMNI BUDDIANT CYMUNEDOL', (or with or without full stops the abbreviation) 'CBC', 'COMMUNITY INTEREST PUBLIC LIMITED COMPANY', (or with or without full stops the abbreviation) 'COMMUNITY INTEREST PLC', 'CWMNI BUDDIANT CYMUNEDOL CYHOEDDUS CYFYNGEDIG', (or with or without full stops the abbreviation) 'CWMNI BUDDIANT CYMUNEDOL CCC';

(b) in any part of the name

'RIGHT TO ENFRANCHISEMENT', (or with or without full stops the abbreviation) 'RTE', 'HAWL I RYDDFREINIAD'; unless that company is a RTE company within the meaning of *Leasehold Reform, Housing and Urban Development Act 1993, s 4A*;

unless that company is a RTE company within the meaning of *Leasehold Reform, Housing and Urban Development Act 1993, s 4A*;

(c) in any part of the name

'RIGHT TO MANAGE', (or with or without full stops the abbreviation) 'RTM', 'CWMNI RTM CYFYNGEDIG'; unless that company is a RTM company within the meaning of *Commonhold and Leasehold Reform Act 2002, s 73*;

unless that company is a RTM company within the meaning of *Commonhold and Leasehold Reform Act 2002, s 73*;

(d) in any part of the name

'EUROPEAN ECONOMIC INTEREST GROUPING' (or with or without full stops the abbreviation) 'EEIG', 'INVESTMENT COMPANY WITH VARIABLE CAPITAL', 'CWMNI BUDDSODDI A CHYFALAF NEWIDIOL', 'LIMITED PARTNERSHIP' (or with or without full stops the abbreviation) LP, 'PARTNERIAETH CYFYNGEDIG' (or with or without full stops the abbreviation) PC, 'LIMITED LIABILITY PARTNERSHIP' (or with or without full stops the abbreviation) LLP, 'PARTNERIAETH ATEBOLRWYDD CYFYNGEDIG', (or with or without full stops the abbreviation) PAC, 'OPEN-ENDED INVESTMENT COMPANY', 'CWMNI BUDDSODDIANT PENAGORED', 'CHARITABLE INCORPORATED ORGANISATION', (or with or without full stops the abbreviation) CIC, or 'SEFDYDLIAD ELUSENNOL CORFFOREDIG', (or with or without full stops the abbreviation) SEC;

An '*expressions or abbreviations specified as similar*' to the above are any in which

- one or more permitted characters has been omitted;
- one or more permitted characters has been added; or
- each of one or more permitted characters has been substituted by one or more other permitted characters

in such a way as to be likely to mislead the public as to the legal form of a company or business if included in the registered name of the company or in a business name.

[*SI 2015 No 17, Reg 4, Sch 2*].

(2) *Companies exempt from requirement to have name ending in 'limited'*

A company which is exempt under *CA 2006, s 60* from the requirement to have a name ending with 'limited' or a permitted alternative (see **27.2** above) must not be registered by a name that ends with

(a) 'UNLIMITED' or 'ANGHYFYNGEDIG' (or any 'word specified as similar'); or

(b) 'PUBLIC LIMITED COMPANY', (or with or without full stops the abbreviation), 'PLC', 'CWMNI CYFYNGEDIG CYHOEDDUS' (or with or without full stops the abbreviation) 'CCC', 'COMMUNITY INTEREST COMPANY' (or with or without full stops the abbreviation) 'CIC', 'CWMNI BUDDIANT CYMUNEDOL' (or with or without full stops the abbreviation) 'CBC', 'COMMUNITY INTEREST PUBLIC LIMITED COMPANY' (or with or without full stops the abbreviation) 'COMMUNITY INTEREST PLC', 'CWMNI BUDDIANT CYMUNEDOL CYHOEDDUS CYFYNGEDIG' (or with or without full stops the abbreviation) 'CWMNI BUDDIANT CYMUNEDOL CCC', 'LP', 'PC', 'LLP', 'PAC', 'CIO' or 'SEC' (or any 'expression or abbreviation specified as similar').

See (1) above for '*expression or abbreviation specified as similar*' which also applies to '*word specified as similar*'.

[*SI 2015 No 17, Reg 4, 5,Sch 2*].

(3) *Unlimited companies*

An unlimited company must not be registered under *CA 2006, s 60* by a name that ends with

(a) 'LIMITED', (with or without full stops the abbreviation) 'LTD', 'CYFYNGEDIG', (with or without full stops the abbreviation) 'CYF' (or any 'word or abbreviation specified as similar'); or

(b) 'PUBLIC LIMITED COMPANY', (or with or without full stops the abbreviation), 'PLC', 'CWMNI CYFYNGEDIG CYHOEDDUS', (or with or without full stops the abbreviation) 'CCC', 'COMMUNITY INTEREST COMPANY', (or with or without full stops the abbreviation), 'CIC', 'CWMNI BUDDIANT CYMUNEDOL', (or with or without full stops the abbreviation) 'CBC', 'COMMUNITY INTEREST PUBLIC LIMITED COMPANY', (or with or without full stops the abbreviation) 'COMMUNITY INTEREST PLC', 'CWMNI BUDDIANT CYMUNEDOL CYHOEDDUS CYFYNGEDIG', (or with or without full stops the abbreviation) 'CWMNI BUDDIANT CYMUNEDOL CCC', 'LP', 'PC', 'LLP', 'PAC', 'CIO' or 'SEC' (or any 'expression or abbreviation specified as similar').

See (1) above for '*expression or abbreviation specified as similar*' which also applies to '*word specified as similar*'.

[*SI 2015 No 17, Reg 12, 13, Sch 2*].

(4) *Overseas companies*

An overseas company must not be registered under *CA 2006* by a name that

(a) ends with 'LIMITED', 'LTD', 'CYFYNGEDIG' or 'CYF' (or any 'word or abbreviation specified as similar') unless the liability of the members of the company is limited by its constitution;

(b) ends with 'UNLIMITED' or 'ANGHYFYNGEDIG' (or any word specified as similar) unless the liability of the members of the company is not limited by its constitution; or

(c) includes in any part of the name 'PUBLIC LIMITED COMPANY', (or with or without full stops the abbreviation) 'PLC, 'CWMNI CYFYNGEDIG CYHOEDDUS', (or with or without full stops the abbreviation) 'CCC, 'COMMUNITY INTEREST COMPANY', (or with or without full stops the abbreviation) 'CIC', 'CWMNI BUDDIANT CYMUNEDOL', (or with or without full stops the abbreviation) 'CBC, 'COMMUNITY INTEREST PUBLIC LIMITED COMPANY', (or with or without full stops the abbreviation) 'COMMUNITY INTEREST PLC' 'CWMNI BUDDIANT CYMUNEDOL CYHOEDDUS CYFYNGEDIG', (or with or without full stops the abbreviation) 'CWMNI BUDDIANT CYMUNEDOL CCC', 'RIGHT TO ENFRANCHISEMENT', (or with or without full stops the abbreviation) 'RTE', 'HAWL I RYDDFREINIAD', 'RIGHT TO MANAGE', (or with or without full stops the abbreviation) 'RTM', 'CWMNI RTM CYFYNGEDIG', 'EUROPEAN ECONOMIC INTEREST GROUPING', (or with or without full stops the abbreviation) 'EEIG', 'INVESTMENT COMPANY WITH VARIABLE CAPITAL', 'CWMNI BUDDSODDI A CHYFALAF

NEWIDIOL', 'LIMITED PARTNERSHIP', 'PARTNERIAETH CYFYNGEDIG', 'LIMITED LIABILITY PARTNERSHIP', 'PARTNERIAETH ATEBOLRWYDD CYFYNGEDIG', 'OPEN-ENDED INVESTMENT COMPANY', 'CWMNI BUDDSODDIANT PENAGORED', 'CHARITABLE INCORPORATED ORGANISATION', 'SEFDYDLIAD ELUSENNOL CORFFOREDIG', 'Industrian and Provident Society', Co-operative Society, Community Benefit Society 'LP', 'PC', 'LLP', 'PAC', 'CIO' or 'SEC' (or an expression or abbreviation specified as similar)

See (1) above for '*expression or abbreviation specified as similar*' which also applies to '*word specified as similar*'.

[*SI 2009 No 1085, Reg 10, Sch 2*].

27.6 *Name same as an existing name*

CA 2006, s 66 provides that a company must not be registered by a name that is 'the same as' another name appearing in the Registrar of Companies' index of company names. Regulations made under *s 66* (see above **27.5** for the relevant regulations) do not affect the continued registration of a company by a name by which it was duly registered immediately before 1 October 2009 and in the case of a 'transitional company', on its registration or re-registration.

See **27.5** for '*transitional company*'.

[*CA 2006, s 66; SI 2008 No 2860, Sch 2 para 17*].

In determining whether a name is the same as another appearing in the index of company names the provisions set out in *Sch 3* to the *2015 regulations* must be followed. First there are sets of permitted characters set out in columns 1 and 2 of *para 2* of the *schedule*. Take the name remaining after the application of *para 2* then disregard any word, expression or abbreviation set out below where it appears at the end of a name.

(1) The following words, expressions and abbreviations are to be disregarded where appearing at the end of the name.

- 'LIMITED' or (with or without full stops) the abbreviation 'LTD'
- 'CYFYNGEDIG' or (with or without full stops) the abbreviation 'CYF'
- 'UNLIMITED'
- 'ANGHYFYNGEDIG'
- 'PUBLIC LIMITED COMPANY' or (with or without full stops) the abbreviation 'PLC'
- 'CWMNI CYFYNGEDIG CYHOEDDUS' or (with or without full stops) the abbreviation 'CCC'
- 'COMMUNITY INTEREST COMPANY' or (with or without full stops) the abbreviation 'CIC'
- 'CWMNI BUDDIANT CYMUNEDOL' or (with or without full stops) the abbreviation 'CBC'
- 'COMMUNITY INTEREST PUBLIC LIMITED COMPANY' or (with or without full stops) the abbreviation 'COMMUNITY INTEREST PLC'

- 'CWMNI BUDDIANT CYMUNEDOL CYHOEDDUS CYFYNGEDIG' or (with or without full stops) the abbreviation 'CWMNI BUDDIANT CYMUNEDOL CCC'
- 'RIGHT TO ENFRANCHISEMENT' or (with or without full stops) the abbreviation 'RTE'
- 'HAWL I RYDDFREINIAD'
- 'RIGHT TO MANAGE' or (with or without full stops) the abbreviation 'RTM'
- 'CWMNI RTM CYFYNGEDIG'
- 'EUROPEAN ECONOMIC INTEREST GROUPING' or (with or without full stops) the abbreviation 'EEIG'
- 'INVESTMENT COMPANY WITH VARIABLE CAPITAL'
- 'CWMNI BUDDSODDI A CHYFALAF NEWIDIOL'
- 'LIMITED PARTNERSHIP' or (with or without full stops) the abbreviation 'LP'
- 'PARTNERIAETH CYFYNGEDIG' or (with or without full stops) the abbreviation 'PC'
- 'LIMITED LIABILITY PARTNERSHIP' or (with or without full stops) the abbreviation 'LLP'
- 'PARTNERIAETH ATEBOLRWYDD CYFYNGEDIG' or (with or without full stops) the abbreviation 'PAC'
- 'OPEN-ENDED INVESTMENT COMPANY'
- 'CWMNI BUDDSODDIANT PENAGORED'
- CHARITABLE INCORPORATED ORGANISATION' or (with or without full stops) the abbreviation 'CIO'
- 'SEFDYDLIAD ELUSENNOL CORFFOREDIG' or (with or without full stops) the abbreviation 'SEC'
- Industrial and Provident Society
- Co-operative Society
- Community Benefit Society

(2) Taking the name remaining after the application of (1) above, the following words, expressions, signs and symbols are regarded as the same as the other relevant matters set out below where each relevant matter:

(i) is preceded by and followed by a blank space; or

(ii) is at the beginning of the name where it is followed by a blank space.

The words, expressions, signs and symbols are

- 'AND' and '&'
- 'PLUS' and '+'
- '0', 'ZERO' and 'O'

- '1' and 'ONE'
- '2', 'TWO', 'TO' and 'TOO'
- '3' and 'THREE'
- '4', 'FOUR' and 'FOR'
- '5' and 'FIVE'
- '6' and 'SIX'
- '7' and 'SEVEN'
- '8' and 'EIGHT'
- '9' and 'NINE'
- '£' and 'POUND'
- '€' and 'EURO'
- '$' and 'DOLLAR'
- '¥' and 'YEN'
- '%', 'PER CENT', 'PERCENT', 'PER CENTUM' and 'PERCENTUM'
- '@' and 'AT'.

(3) Taking the name remaining after the application of (1) and (2) above, disregard at the end of the name the matters set out below (or any combination of such matters) where the matter (or combination) is preceded by

(i) a blank space;

(ii) a full stop; or

(iii) '@'.

The matters are

- '& Co'
- '& Company'
- 'AND CO'
- 'AND COMPANY'
- 'BIZ'
- 'CO'
- 'CO UK'
- 'CO.UK'
- 'COM'
- 'COMPANY'
- 'EU'
- 'GB'
- 'GREAT BRITAIN'

- 'NET'
- 'NI'
- 'NORTHERN IRELAND'
- 'ORG'
- 'ORG UK'
- 'ORG.UK'
- 'UK'
- 'UNITED KINGDOM'
- 'WALES'
- 'ALLFORION'
- '& CWMNI'
- 'A'R CWMNI'
- 'CWMNI'
- 'CYM'
- 'CYMRU'
- 'DU'
- 'MEWNFORION'
- 'PF'
- 'PRYDAIN FAWR'
- 'Y DEYRNAS UNEDIG'.

(4) Taking the name remaining after the application of (1)–(3) above, disregard the following matters in any part of the name.

- Any full stop, comma, colon, semi-colon or hyphen.
- Any of the following types of punctuation but only in the forms indicated:

  (i) Apostrophe: ‘ ’ ’

  (ii) Bracket: ( ) [ ] { } < >

  (iii) Exclamation mark: !

  (iv) Guillemet: « »

  (v) Inverted comma: “ ” ″

  (vi) Question mark: ?

  (vii) Solidus: \ /

- *, = and #.

(5) Taking the name remaining after the application of (1)–(4) above, disregard the letter 'S' at the end of the name.

(6) Taking the name remaining after the application of (1)–(5) above, disregard any '*permitted character*' (see **27.8**) after the first 60 permitted characters of the name (and for this purpose, any blank space between one permitted character and another is to be counted as a permitted character).

(7) Taking the name remaining after the application of (1)–(6) above, disregard the following matters or any combination of the following matters where they appear at the beginning of the name.

- '@'
- 'THE' (but only where followed by a blank space)
- 'WWW

(8) Taking the name remaining after the application of (1)–(7) above, disregard blank spaces.

[*SI 2015 No 17, Reg, 7, Sch 3*].

Example of names 'the same as'

Real Coffee Café Ltd is the same as

- Real Coffee Cafe Ltd

Plum Technology Ltd is the same as Plum Technology and Company Ltd.

(Companies House Guidance Booklet GP1 Incorporation and Names, Chr 6, para 6).

Exceptions. There is an exception to the rule that a company cannot be registered with the same name.

This is where the following conditions are met

- the company (company X) whose name already appears on the index of company names consents to the proposed name being the name of another company (company Y)
- company Y forms, or is to form, part of the same group as company X and
- company Y provides a statement to the Registrar of Companies made by company X indicating X's consent to the use of the name.

If the proposed same name is to be taken by a company which has not been incorporated, the copy consent must be delivered to the Registrar of Companies by the person who delivers the application for registration.

[*SI 2015 No 17, Reg 8*]

27.7 Sensitive words and expression

Certain names and expressions may suggest that a company has a particular status or function. If such words and expressions are included in a company's name then approval of the Secretary of State is required before a company can either be incorporated or change its name. Companies House administers this process.

The following provisions do not affect the continued registration of a company by a name by which it was duly registered immediately before 1 October 2009 and in the case of a 'transitional company', on its registration or re-registration.

See **27.5** for '*transitional company*'.

The approval of the Secretary of State is required for a company to be registered under *CA 2006* by a name that

- would be likely to give the impression that the company is connected with
  - (i) Her Majesty's Government, any part of the Scottish administration, the Welsh Assembly Government or Her Majesty's Government in Northern Ireland;
  - (ii) a local authority; or
  - (iii) any public authority specified for these purposes by Regulations; or
- includes a word or expression 'other sensitive words or expressions' specified in the *Company, Limited liability, Partnership and Business Names (Sensitive Words and Expressions) Regulations 2014 (SI 2014 No 3140)*.

[*CA 2006, ss 54, 55, 56(1)*].

A list of all the sensitive words and expressions together with details of any necessary consents (other than the Secretary of State) is set out in the Companies House Guidance Booklet GP1 'Incorporation and Names' at Annexes A, B and C.

Annex A contains a list of sensitive words and expressions specified in regulations (referred to above) that cannot be used in a company name or business name without the prior approval of the Secretary of State.

Annex B contains a list of sensitive words and expressions that could imply a connection with a government department, a devolved administration, a local or specified public authority or a relevant body.

Annex C contains a list of words and expressions controlled by other legislation. The use of any of these words and expressions in a chosen name could be a criminal offence. This list is not exhaustive and applicants should make their own checks.

27.8 Permitted characters

The Regulations referred to in **27.5** above contain a list of the letters or other characters, signs or symbols (including accents and other diacritical marks) and punctuation that may be used in the name of a company registered under *CA 2006*. The Regulations do not affect the continued registration of a company by a name by which it was duly registered immediately before 1 October 2009 and in the case of a 'transitional company', on its registration or re-registration.

See **27.5** for '*transitional company*'.

[*CA 2006, s 57*].

Under these Regulations, the following permitted characters may be used in any part of the name.

- A, B, C, D, etc to X, Y, Z
- &, @, £, $, €, and ¥
- 0, 1, 2, 3, 4, 5, 6, 7, 8 or 9
- Full stop, comma, colon, semi-colon or hyphen
- Any of the following types of punctuation but only in the forms indicated:

- (i) Apostrophe: ‘ ’ ’
- (ii) Bracket: ( ) [ ] { } < >
- (iii) Exclamation mark: !
- (iv) Guillemet: « »
- (v) Inverted comma: “ ” ″
- (vi) Question mark: ?
- (vii) Solidus: \ /

In addition, the following signs and symbols are permitted characters that may be used but *not* as one of the first three characters of the name.

*, =, #, %, and +

[*SI 2015 No 17, Reg 2, Sch 1*].

27.9 Length of name

The name of a company registered under *CA 2006* must not consist of more than 160 permitted characters (see **27.8**). For the purposes of computing the number of permitted characters in the name, any blank space between one permitted character and another in the name is to be counted as though it was a permitted character. [*SI 2009 No 1085, Regs 1(3), 2(4)*].

This does affect the continued registration of a company by a name by which it was duly registered immediately before 1 October 2009; and in the case of a ‘transitional company’, on its registration or re-registration.

See **27.5** for ‘*transitional company*’.

[*CA 2006, s 57*].

27.10 How to register a company name

Before applying to set up a company, or do anything to change its name, it is advisable to search the index at Companies House to see if there are already any companies with names similar to the one proposed. You can do this by using Companies House free ‘WebCheck’ service. If in doubt, contact Companies House (tel: 0303 123 4500) or search the company names index at:

www.companieshouse.gov.uk

An applicant should also consider whether it is ‘too like’ another name so that, although it may be accepted by the Registrar of Companies, another company complains and a direction to change the name is made (see**27.6**).

The Registrar of Companies does not consult the Trade Marks Register when considering applications for new company names. Applicants are advised to make appropriate enquiries of the Trade Mark Register and to consider consulting a solicitor. For further advice, including how to search the Trade Mark Register, contact the Trade Marks Registry of the UK Intellectual Property Office at:

e-mail: enquiries@ipo.gov.uk

website: www.ipo.gov.uk

Registration of a company name should not be assumed to imply any subsequent acceptance of the same name for the purpose of the *Consumer Credit Act 1974*. From 1 April 2014, responsibility for consumer credit regulation has passed from the Office of Fair Trading to the Financial Conduct Authority.

If the name is not the same as one in the Index, and does not require prior approval of the Secretary of State, the incorporation documents (or, in the case of a change of name, the special resolution) should be submitted to the appropriate Registrar of Companies. If the name is acceptable and the documents correctly completed, the company name will be registered and a certificate of incorporation issued.

For all names requiring the approval of the Secretary of State applicants should seek the advice of New Companies Section at Companies House in Cardiff (companies intending to have their registered office in England or Wales) or Edinburgh (companies intending to have their registered office in Scotland). Details about the requirements on the use of the name will then be sent to the applicant.

If the name includes any other words or expressions refer to Companies House Guidance Booklet GP1 (see **27.7**).

27.11 Compulsory change of name

A company may be directed to change its name in any of the circumstances in **27.12** to **27.16**.

27.12 *Company ceasing to be entitled to exemption*

If it appears to the Secretary of State that a company whose name does not include 'limited' (or any of the permitted alternatives) has ceased to be entitled to exemption under 27.2(1)–(4), he may direct the company to change its name within a specified period so that it ends with 'limited' (or one of the permitted alternatives).

A change of name in order to comply with such a direction can be made by resolution of the directors (without prejudice to any other method of changing the company's name). On the resolution being passed, the company must give notice to the Registrar of Companies of the change. *CA 2006, ss 80, 81* apply as regards the registration and effect of the change. See **27.17**.

If the company fails to comply with a direction an offence is committed by the company and every officer of the company who is in default. A person guilty of such an offence is liable, on summary conviction, to a fine not exceeding level 5 on the standard scale and, for continued contravention, to a daily default fine not exceeding one-tenth of the greater of £5,000 or level 4 on the standard scale. See **29.1** Offences and Legal Proceedings for the standard scale.

A company that has been directed to change its name may not, without the approval of the Secretary of State, subsequently change its name so that it does not include 'limited' (or one of the permitted alternatives). This does not apply to a change of name on re-registration or on conversion to a community interest company.

[*CA 2006, s 64; SI 2015 No 664, Sch 3*].

Before 1 October 2009, similar provisions applied under *CA 1985, s 31*. Where a direction was given under those provisions, it continues to apply on or after 1 October 2009 so that the company remains unable to be registered with a name that does not include 'limited' without the agreement of the Secretary of State. [*SI 2008 No 2860, Sch 2 para 20*].

27.13 *Similarity to existing name*

The Secretary of State may direct a company to change its name if it has been registered in a name that is 'the same as' or, in the opinion of the Secretary of State, 'too like' a name appearing at the time of the registration in the Registrar of Companies' index of company names (or a name that should have appeared in that index at that time). [*CA 2006, s 67*].

Any such direction must be in writing and be given within 12 months of the registration of the name in question and must specify the period within which the company is to change its name. This period may be extended by a further direction in writing (but only before the end of the period for the time being specified). If a company fails to comply with the direction, an offence is committed by the company and every officer of the company who is in default. For this purpose a shadow director is treated as an officer of the company. A person guilty of such an offence is liable, on summary conviction, to a fine not exceeding level 3 on the standard scale and, for continued contravention, a daily default fine not exceeding one-tenth of level 3 on the standard scale. See **29.1** OFFENCES AND LEGAL PROCEEDINGS for the standard scale.

[*CA 2006, s 68*].

See **27.6** for '*the same as*'.

A direction may be issued, for example, as a result of an objection being lodged by an interested party because one name is 'too like' another. A company wishing to object to another company name because of similarity to its own name should write to:

For companies incorporated in England and Wales:

The Secretary of State
New Companies Section
Companies House
Crown Way
Cardiff
CF14 3UZ

For companies incorporated in Scotland:

The Secretary of State
New Companies Section
Companies House
4th Floor Edinburgh Quay 2
139 Fountainbridge
Edinburgh
EH3 9FF

Companies House takes the view that a name is 'too like' an existing name if

- it differs from another name on the index by only a few characters, signs, symbols or punctuation; or
- the names look and sound the same.

When deciding whether names are 'too like' Companies House will not consider factors such as:

- alleged trademark/patents infringement
- geographic locations

- similarity of activities
- possible passing off
- implied associations

(Companies House Guidance Booklet GP1 Incorporation and Names, Chapter 8)

In considering whether names are similar, it is material to ascertain (i) what business has been or is intended to be carried on by the existing company and what is intended to be carried on by the new company; and (ii) what sort of name has been adopted by the existing company. See *Aerators Ltd v Tollitt* [1902] 2 Ch 319, 71 LJ Ch 727. The use of a name will not be allowed if it is intended to deceive or induce belief that the business is an extension of, or otherwise connected with, another company (*Ewing v Buttercup Margarine Co Ltd* [1917] 2 Ch 1, 86 LJ Ch 441, CA).

27.14 *Similarity to other name in which a person has goodwill ("Opportunistic registration")*

Any person ('the applicant') may object to a company's registered name on the ground that it is

(a) the same as a name associated with the applicant in which he has goodwill; or

(b) sufficiently similar to such a name that its use in the UK would be likely to mislead by suggesting a connection between the company and the applicant.

The objection must be made by application to the Company Names Tribunal. The company concerned is the primary respondent to the application but any of its members or directors may be joined as respondents. Companies House does not deal with this kind of application.

If the ground in (*a*) or (*b*) above is established, it is for the respondents to show that

(i) the name was registered before the commencement of the activities on which the applicant relies to show it has goodwill;

(ii) the company

- is operating under the name;
- is proposing to do so and has incurred substantial start-up costs in preparation; or
- was formerly operating under the name and is now dormant;

(iii) the name was registered in the ordinary course of a company formation business and the company is available for sale to the applicant on the standard terms of that business;

(iv) the name was adopted in good faith; or

(v) the interests of the applicant are not adversely affected to any significant extent.

If none of those is shown, the objection must be upheld. If the facts mentioned in (i), (ii) or (iii) above are established, the objection must nevertheless be upheld if the applicant shows that the main purpose of the respondents (or any of them) in registering the name was to obtain money (or other consideration) from the applicant or prevent him from registering the name.

'*Goodwill*' includes reputation of any description.

[*CA 2006, s 69*].

Full details of the application process and procedure can be found on the Company Names Tribunal website – www.ipo.gov.uk.

27.15 *Provision of misleading information*

Where it appears to the Secretary of State that

- misleading information has been given for the purposes of the company's registration by a particular name, or
- an undertaking or assurance has been given for that purpose and has not been fulfilled

he may direct the company in writing to change its name.

Such a direction must be given within five years of the company's registration by that name. It must be complied with in the period specified in the direction (or such longer period as is allowed by further direction in writing).

If a company fails to comply with the direction, an offence is committed by the company and every officer of the company who is in default. For this purpose a shadow director is treated as an officer of the company. A person guilty of such an offence is liable, on summary conviction, to a fine not exceeding level 3 on the standard scale and, for continued contravention, a daily default fine not exceeding one-tenth of level 3 on the standard scale. See **29.1 Offences and Legal Proceedings** for the standard scale.

[*CA 2006, s 75*].

27.16 *Misleading indication of activities*

If, in the opinion of the Secretary of State, the name by which a company is registered is so misleading an indication of the nature of its activities as to be likely to cause harm to the public, he may direct the company to change its name. The direction must be in writing and be complied with within six weeks of the direction or such longer period as is allowed. The company may, however, within three weeks of the direction, apply to the court for the direction to be set aside. If the direction is confirmed by the court, it must specify the period within which the direction must be complied with.

If a company fails to comply with the direction, an offence is committed by the company and every officer of the company who is in default. For this purpose a shadow director is treated as an officer of the company. A person guilty of such an offence is liable, on summary conviction, to a fine not exceeding level 3 on the standard scale and, for continued contravention, a daily default fine not exceeding one-tenth of level 3 on the standard scale. See **29.1 Offences and Legal Proceedings** for the standard scale.

[*CA 2006, s 76*].

Before 1 October 2009, similar provisions applied under *CA 1985, s 32*. Where such a direction was given, *CA 1985, s 32* continues to apply on or after 1 October 2009 in relation to the direction.

[*SI 2008 No 2860, Sch 2 para 21*].

27.17 Voluntary change of name

Transitional provisions. The provisions in this paragraph, to the extent that they relate to a change of name by special resolution, apply where

- the resolution was passed on or after 1 October 2009; or

- the resolution was passed before that date but no copy of the resolution was received by the Registrar of Companies under *CA 2006, s 30* (copies of resolutions affecting a company's constitution to be forwarded to the Registrar of Companies) before that date.

CA 1985, s 28(1)(6)(7) continues to apply to resolutions of which a copy is received by the Registrar of Companies before 1 October 2009.

[*SI 2008 No 2860, Sch 2 para 19*].

A company may change its name in the following ways.

(a) **By special resolution**. Where a change of name has been agreed to by a company by special resolution, the company must give notice to the Registrar of Companies. This is in addition to the obligation to forward a copy of the resolution to the Registrar.

Where a change of name by special resolution is conditional on the occurrence of an event, the notice given to the Registrar of Companies of the change must specify that the change is conditional and state whether the event has occurred. If the notice states that the event has not occurred,

- the Registrar of Companies is not required to act under *CA 2006, s 80* (see below) until further notice;
- when the event occurs, the company must give notice to the Registrar of Companies stating that it has occurred; and
- the Registrar of Companies may rely on the statement as sufficient evidence of the matters stated in it.

(b) **By other means provided for by the company's articles**. In such a case,

- the company must give notice to the Registrar of Companies; and
- the notice must be accompanied by a statement that the change of name has been made by means provided for by the company's articles.

The Registrar of Companies may rely on the statement as sufficient evidence of the matters stated in it.

(c) **By resolution of the directors to comply with a direction where the company ceases to be entitled to an exemption to use the word 'limited' in its name** (see **27.12**).

(d) **On the determination of a new name by the Company Names Adjudicator under** (see **27.14**).

(e) **On the determination of a new name by the court** following an appeal against a decision of the Company Names Adjudicator (see **27.14**).

(f) **On restoration of a company to the register** under *CA 2006, s 1033* (see **21.11** DISSOLUTION AND RESTORATION).

[*CA 2006, ss 77–79*].

Application to change a name

Application must be made to Companies House. If the name is not the same as an existing name on the index (see **27.6**), does not include any sensitive words (see **27.7**) and is a change of name by special resolution (without conditions) the application can be sent either by Companies House software filing or by using their webfiling system. Paper applications can also be made but only if the change is made by special resolution (which may be conditional) or by other means set out in the company's articles. Each requires specific notices and/or additional documents. If the change is by means provided for in the company's articles, the application can be sent using Companies House software filing service.

Registration and issue of new certificate of incorporation. If the Registrar of Companies is satisfied that

- the new name complies with the provisions of this chapter,
- the requirements of the *Companies Acts* and any relevant requirements of the company's articles have been complied with,

he must enter the new name on the register in place of the former name. On the registration of the new name, the Registrar of Companies must issue a certificate of incorporation altered to meet the circumstances of the case. [*CA 2006, s 80*].

Timing. Electronic applications for change of name are usually processed within 24 hours. The fee is £8. Same day service is also available for a fee of £30. Paper applications are normally processed within 5 working days. The fee is £10. Same day service is also available for a fee of £50 provided the documents are received before 3pm Monday- Friday.

Effect of change. The change of a company's name has effect from the date on which the new certificate of incorporation is issued. The change does not affect any rights or obligations of the company or render defective any legal proceedings by or against it. Any legal proceedings that might have been continued or commenced against it by its former name may be continued or commenced against it by its new name. [*CA 2006, s 81*].

Listed companies. Any change in name must be notified to a RIS and the FCA. See **33.26(4) Public and Listed Companies**.

27.18 BUSINESS NAMES

The provisions in **27.19–27.26** relate to business names and are all contained in *CA 2006*. They replace the provisions formerly found in the *Business Names Act 1985*.

27.19 Restricted and prohibited names

The provisions in **27.20–27.22** apply to any person carrying on business (including a profession) in the UK. But they do not prevent

- an individual carrying on business under a name consisting of his 'surname' without any addition other than a 'permitted addition'; or
- individuals carrying on business in 'partnership' under a name consisting of the surnames of all the partners without any addition other than a permitted addition.

'*Surname*', in relation to a peer or person usually known by a British title different from his surname, means the title by which he is known.

'*Partnership*' means

- a partnership within the *Partnership Act 1890*; or

- a limited partnership registered under the *Limited Partnerships Act 1907*; or
- a firm or entity of a similar character formed under the law of a country or territory outside the UK.

The '*permitted additions*' are

- in the case of an individual, his forename or 'initial';
- in the case of a partnership
  - (i) the forenames of individual partners or the initials of those forenames; or
  - (ii) where two or more individual partners have the same surname, the addition of 's' at the end of that surname; and
- in either case, an addition merely indicating that the business is carried on in succession to a former owner of the business.

'*Initial*' includes any recognised abbreviation of a name.
[*CA 2006, ss 1192, 1208*].

27.20 *Sensitive words and expressions*

Subject to the exceptions for existing names set out in **27.21**, the approval of the Secretary of State is required for a person to carry on a business in the UK by a name that

- would be likely to give the impression that the business is connected with
  - (i) Her Majesty's Government, any part of the Scottish administration, the Welsh Assembly Government or Her Majesty's Government in Northern Ireland;
  - (ii) a local authority; or
  - (iii) any public authority specified for these purposes by Regulations; or
- includes a word or expression 'other sensitive words or expressions' specified in the *Company, Limited Liability Partnership and Business Names (Sensitive Words and Expressions) Regulations 2014* (see **27.7** for details).

The Regulations may require that, in connection with an application for approval, the applicant must seek the view of a specified Government department or other body.

Offences. A person who contravenes these provisions commits an offence. Where such an offence is committed by a body corporate, an offence is also committed by every officer of the body who is in default. A person guilty of such an offence is liable, on summary conviction, to a fine not exceeding level 3 on the standard scale and, for continued contravention, a daily default fine not exceeding one-tenth of level 3 on the standard scale. See **29.1** OFFENCES AND LEGAL PROCEEDINGS for the statutory maximum. The provisions of *CA 2006, ss 1121–1123* and *1125–1131* (see **29.1–29.6** OFFENCES AND LEGAL PROCEEDINGS) apply in relation to this offence.

[*CA 2006, ss 1193, 1194, 1195(1), 1207*].

Withdrawal of approval. If it appears to the Secretary of State that there are overriding considerations of public policy that require any approval given to be withdrawn, the approval may be withdrawn by notice in writing to the person concerned. The notice must state the date as from which approval is withdrawn. [*CA 2006, s 1196*].

27.21 *Exception for existing lawful business names*

The provisions for approval of sensitive words and expressions (see **27.20**) do not apply in the following circumstances.

- To the carrying on of a business by a person who
  - (i) carried on the business immediately before 1 October 2009; and
  - (ii) continues to carry it on under the name that immediately before that date was its 'lawful business name'.
- Where
  - (i) a business is transferred to a person on or after 1 October 2009, and
  - (ii) that person carries on the business under the name that was its lawful business name immediately before the transfer,

  in relation to the carrying on of the business under that name during the period of twelve months beginning with the date of the transfer.

'*Lawful business name*', in relation to a business, means a name under which the business was carried on without contravening

- *Business Names Act 1985, s 2(1)* or *Business Names (Northern Ireland) Order 1986 (SI 1986 No 1033), Art 4(1)*, or
- after 1 October 2009, the provisions set out in **27.19–27.20**.

[*CA 2006, s 1199*].

27.22 *Misleading indication of activities*

A person must not carry on business in the UK under a name that gives so misleading an indication of the nature of the activities of the business as to be likely to cause harm to the public. A person who uses a name in contravention of this requirement commits an offence. Where such an offence is committed by a body corporate, an offence is also committed by every officer of the body who is in default. A person guilty of such an offence is liable, on summary conviction, to a fine not exceeding level 3 on the standard scale and, for continued contravention, a daily default fine not exceeding one-tenth of level 3 on the standard scale. See **29.1 Offences and Legal Proceedings** for the standard scale. The provisions of *CA 2006, ss 1121–1123* and *1125–1131* (see **29.1–29.6 Offences and Legal Proceedings**) apply in relation to this offence.

[*CA 2006, ss 1198, 1207*].

27.23 Application for a business name

For all names requiring the approval of the Secretary of State, applicants should seek the advice of Companies Registration Office in Cardiff (businesses in England or Wales) or Edinburgh (businesses in Scotland). Details about the requirements on the use of the name will then be sent to the applicant.

The application, together with any supporting information, should be submitted to the Secretary of State at the appropriate Companies Registration Office. If the name includes any word or expression which requires the consent of a relevant body (see **27.7**), the applicant must request (in writing) the relevant body to indicate whether (and if so why) it has any objection to the proposed name. A statement that such a request has been made, and a copy of any response received, must be submitted with the application to the Secretary of State, otherwise the he may refuse to consider it. [*CA 2006, s 1195(2)–(5)*].

Note that although the words in Appendix C of Companies House Guidance GP1 (see 27.7) do not require the permission of the Secretary of State, their use may constitute a criminal offence. Owners of businesses wishing to use any of these words in a name should seek legal advice and confirmation from the body concerned that the use of the word does not contravene the legislation (although such confirmation should not be regarded as conclusive).

27.24 DISCLOSURE REQUIRED BY INDIVIDUALS AND PARTNERSHIPS

The provisions in **27.25–27.27** apply to an individual or 'partnership' carrying on business (including a profession) in the UK under a 'business name'. References to '*a person to whom these provisions apply*' are to such individuals or partnerships. For the provisions relating to companies trading under a business name, see **16.12 DEALINGS WITH THIRD PARTIES**.

'*Partnership*' means

- a partnership within the *Partnership Act 1890*; or
- a limited partnership registered under the *Limited Partnerships Act 1907*; or
- a firm or entity of a similar character formed under the law of a country or territory outside the UK.

'*Business name*' means a name other than

- in the case of an individual, his surname without any addition other than a 'permitted addition'; and
- in the case of a partnership
  - (i) the 'surnames' of all partners who are individuals, and
  - (ii) the corporate names of all partners who are bodies corporate,

  without any addition other than a 'permitted addition'.

'*Permitted additions*' are

- in the case of an individual, his forename or 'initial'; and
- in the case of a partnership
  - (i) the forenames of individual partners or the initials of those forenames; or
  - (ii) where two or more individual partners have the same surname, the addition of 's' at the end of that surname; and
- in either case, an addition merely indicating that the business is carried on in succession to a former owner of the business.

'*Surname*', in relation to a peer or person usually known by a British title different from his surname, means the title by which he is known.

'*Initial*' includes any recognised abbreviation of a name.

[*CA 2006, ss 1200, 1208, 1287*].

27.25 Disclosure required in business documents, etc

A person to whom these provisions apply (see **27.24**) must

(a) subject to the exemption for large partnerships below, state the 'information required' in legible characters, on all

  (i) business letters;

  (ii) written orders for goods or services to be supplied to the business;

  (iii) invoices and receipts issued in the course of the business; and

  (iv) written demands for payment of debts arising in the course of the business; and

(b) secure that the information required is immediately given, by written notice, to any person with whom anything is done or discussed in the course of the business and who asks for that information.

The Secretary of State may by Regulations require that such notices be given in a specified form.

[*CA 2006, s 1202*].

'*Information required*' is

- in the case of an individual, his name; and
- in the case of a partnership, the name of each member of the partnership

and in relation to each person so named, an address in the UK at which service of any document relating in any way to the business will be effective. If the individual or partnership has a place of business in the United Kingdom, the address must be in the United Kingdom and if the individual or partnership does not have a place of business in the United Kingdom, the address must be an address at which service of documents can be effected by physical delivery and the delivery of documents is capable of being recorded by the obtaining of an acknowledgement of delivery.

[*CA 2006, s 1201*].

Exemption for large partnerships. The requirements in (*a*) above do not apply in relation to a document issued by a partnership of more than 20 persons if the following conditions are met.

- The partnership must maintain at its principal place of business a list of the names of all the partners.
- No partner's name must appear in the document, except in the text or as a signatory.
- The document must state in legible characters the address of the partnership's principal place of business and that the list of the partners' names is open to inspection there.

Where a partnership maintains a list of the partners' names for these purposes, any person may inspect the list during office hours. If an inspection is refused, an offence is committed by any member of the partnership concerned who, without reasonable excuse, refused the inspection or permitted it to be refused. A person guilty of such an offence is liable, on summary conviction, to a fine not exceeding level 3 on the standard scale and, for continued contravention, a daily default fine not exceeding one-tenth of level 3 on the standard scale. See **29.1 Offences and Legal Proceedings** for the standard scale. The provisions of *CA 2006, ss 1121–1123* and *1125–1131* (see **29.1–29.6 Offences and Legal Proceedings** apply in relation to this offence.

[*CA 2006, s 1203, 1207*].

27.26 Disclosure required at business premises

A person to whom these provisions apply (see **27.24**) must, in any premises

- where the business is carried on, and
- to which customers of the business or suppliers of goods or services to the business have access,

display in a prominent position, so that it may easily be read by such customers or suppliers, a notice containing the 'information required'.

The Secretary of State may by Regulations require that such notices be displayed in a specified form. [*CA 2006, s 1204*].

'*Information required*' is the same as in **27.25**.

27.27 Consequence of failure to disclose

Criminal consequences. A person who, without reasonable excuse, fails to comply with the requirements of **27.25** or **27.26** commits an offence. Where any such offence is committed by a body corporate, an offence is also committed by every officer of the body who is in default.

A person guilty of an offence under these provisions is liable, on summary conviction, to a fine not exceeding level 3 on the standard scale and, for continued contravention, a daily default fine not exceeding one-tenth of level 3 on the standard scale. See **29.1 Offences and Legal Proceedings** for the standard scale.

[*CA 2006, s 1205*].

Civil consequences. The following provisions apply to any legal proceedings, brought by an individual or partnership carrying on business in the UK under a business name, to enforce a right arising out of a contract made in the course of a business in respect of which that person was, at the time the contract was made, in breach of **27.25**(*a*) or (*b*) or **27.26**.

Such proceedings must be dismissed if the defendant (in Scotland, the defender) to the proceedings shows that

- he has a claim against the claimant (pursuer) arising out of the contract that he has been unable to pursue by reason of the latter's breach of those requirements, or
- he has suffered some financial loss in connection with the contract by reason of the claimant's (pursuer's) breach of those requirements,

unless the court before which the proceedings are brought is satisfied that it is just and equitable to permit the proceedings to continue.

This does not affect the right of any person to enforce such rights as he may have against another person in any proceedings brought by that person.

[*CA 2006, s 1206*].

General provisions about offences. The provisions of *CA 2006, ss 1121–1123* and *1125–1131* (see **29.1–29.6 Offences and Legal Proceedings**) apply in relation to the above offences. [*CA 2006, s 1207*].

28 Northern Ireland

28.1 EXTENSION OF LEGISLATION TO NORTHERN IRELAND

CA 2006 creates a single company law regime which applies to the whole of the UK. Previously, provisions of GB company law were broadly replicated in separate Northern Ireland legislation. In particular the following legislation applies to Northern Ireland.

- The provisions of the *Companies Acts* (unless the context requires otherwise), ie

  (i) the company law provisions of *CA 2006*, namely *CA 2006, Pts 1–39* together with *CA 2006, Pts 45–47* in so far as they apply for the purposes of those *Parts*;

  (ii) *C(AICE)A 2004, Pt 2* (community interest companies); and

  (iii) the provisions of *CA 1985* and *CC(CP)A 1985* that remain in force.

  As a result, *Companies (Northern Ireland) Order 1986 (SI 1986 No 1032), Companies Consolidation (Consequential Provisions) (Northern Ireland) Order 1986 (SI 1986 No 1035)* and *Companies (Audit, Investigations and Community Enterprise) Order 2005 (SI 2005 No 1967), Part 3* cease to have effect.

- The enactments in force in GB relating to SEs extend to Northern Ireland.

  As a result, *European Public Limited-Liability Company Regulations (Northern Ireland) 2004 (SR 2004 No 417)* and *European Public Limited-Liability Company (Fees) Regulations (Northern Ireland) 2004 (SR 2004 No 418)* cease to have effect.

- The enactments in force in GB relating to

  (i) limited liability partnerships;

  (ii) limited partnerships;

  (iii) open-ended investment companies; and

  (iv) European Economic Interest Groupings

  As a result, *Limited Liability Partnerships Act (Northern Ireland) 2002, Limited Partnerships Act 1907* as it formerly had effect in Northern Ireland, *Open-Ended Investment Companies Act (Northern Ireland) 2002* and *European Economic Interest Groupings Regulations (Northern Ireland) 1989 (SR 1989 No 216)* cease to have effect.

- The provisions of *CA 2006, Pt 41* (business names).

  As a result, *Business Names (Northern Ireland) Order 1986 (SI 1986 No 1033)* ceases to have effect.

[*CA 2006, ss 2, 1284–1287*].

29 Offences and Legal Proceedings

29.1 **Offences under the Companies Acts**
29.2 Liability of officer in default
29.3 Legal professional privilege
29.4 **Summary proceedings**
29.5 **Consent required in certain prosecutions**
29.6 **Proceedings against unincorporated bodies**
29.7 **Production and inspection of documents where offence suspected**
29.8 **Meaning of 'the court'**
29.9 **Power of court to grant relief**
29.10 **Security for costs (Scotland)**
APPENDIX **Offences under the Companies Acts (*CA 1985* provisions)**

General note. The provisions of *CA 2006* relating to offences and legal proceedings as detailed in this chapter were, unless otherwise stated, fully implemented with effect from 1 October 2009. But the provisions in this chapter do not apply to offences committed before the commencement of the relevant provision.

[*CA 2006, s 1133*].

For the provisions in *CA 1985* applying to offences committed before 1 October, see the Appendix at the end of the chapter.

29.1 OFFENCES UNDER THE COMPANIES ACTS

There are a large number of offences for failure to comply with the requirements of the *Companies Acts*. These are dealt with in the appropriate part of the text. For example it is an offence for a company to fail to deliver a fully completed annual return to the Registrar of Companies (see **7.4**) Punishment, depending on the offence, may be by way of imprisonment or a fine (or both).

On conviction on indictment, any fine imposed is unlimited.

On summary conviction fines in magistrates' courts are fixed up to a maximum level (the statutory maximum see below).Certain offences provide that a person guilty of the offence is liable to a fine not exceeding a specified amount (for example level 4 on the standard scale) and 'for continued contravention, a daily default fine' not exceeding a specified amount.

[*CA 2006, s 1125*].

Statutory maximum means, in England and Wales, the sum prescribed under the *Magistrates' Courts Act 1980, s 32* and, in Scotland, the sum prescribed under the *Criminal Procedure (Scotland) Act 1975, s 289B*. The statutory maximum is currently £5,000.

Standard scale. Certain penalties are determined by reference to the 'standard scale' (level 5 on which is equivalent to the statutory maximum).

'*Standard scale*' means the scale laid down by the *Criminal Justice Act 1991, s 17* (in Scotland the *Criminal Procedure (Scotland) Act 1975, s 289G*) and is as follows.

Level on the scale	*Amount of fine*
1	£200
2	£500
3	£1,000
4	£2,500
5	£5,000

Removal of upper limit for fines imposed on summary conviction in magistrates' courts

The *Legal Aid, Sentencing and Punishment of Offenders Act 2012* was given Royal Assent on 1 May 2012. *Sections 85–87* of this *Act* provide (in summary) that offences currently punishable on summary conviction with the statutory maximum (see above) will be punishable by an unlimited fine. This means that the same sentencing principles will apply whether the offence is tried summarily or on indictment and may potentially lead to greater fines being imposed on companies and their officers.

Various provisions of this Act came into force in May 2014. They are *s 85(3), (5)–(13)* and *(15)–(17)*. They provide in summary that where an offence is relevant for the purposes of *s 85*, the Secretary of State can disapply *s 85(1)* and *(2)* (removal of upper limits) and instead substitute new maximum fines or proportionate fines.

Section 85(1), (2) and *(4)* came into force in March 2015. At the same time regulations made under the Act (*The Legal Aid, Sentencing and Punishment of Offenders Act 2012 (Fines on Summary Conviction) Regulations 2015 (SI 2015 No 664)*) came into force and provide at *Sch 3* for certain offences currently punishable by a fine of a proportion of level 5 on the standard scale to be punishable by a fine of a proportion of the greater of £5,000 or level 4 on the standard scale. These mainly affect daily default fines imposed under *CA 2006* and are referred to where relevant throughout the text.

29.2 Liability of officer in default

Where an offence is committed by a company under any provision of the *Companies Acts*, an offence is committed by every 'officer' of the company who is 'in default'. For this purpose '*officer*' includes

- any director, manager or secretary; and
- any person who is to be treated as an officer of the company for the purposes of the provision in question.

Many offences provide that a shadow director is to be treated, for the purposes of the relevant offence as a director of the company. In other words, liability can extend to those who are not, or may not necessarily be, involved in the day to day decision making of the company.

An officer is '*in default*' for the purposes of the provision if he authorises or permits, participates in, or fails to take all reasonable steps to prevent, the contravention.

[*CA 2006, s 1121*].

Liability of company as officer in default. Where a company is an officer of another company, it does not commit an offence as an officer in default unless one of its officers is in default. But where an offence is committed by such a company, the officer in question also commits the offence and is liable to be proceeded against and punished accordingly.

The purpose of this provision is to ensure that where a company (company B) is an officer of another company (company A) (for example a company may be the company secretary of another company in the same group of companies) liability for an offence can only be fixed on company B as an "officer in default" if one of its own officers is in default. So for example if company A fails to submit an annual return within the time limit, company B can only be liable if one of its officers is also in default in failing to submit the annual return.

[*CA 2006, s 1122*].

Application to bodies other than companies. *CA 2006, s 1121* above applies to a body other than a company as it applies to a company and for these purposes

(a) in relation to a body corporate other than a company

- the reference to a director of the company must be read as referring
  - (i) where the body's affairs are managed by its members, to a member of the body; and
  - (ii) in any other case, to any corresponding officer of the body; and
- the reference to a manager or secretary of the company must be read as referring to any manager, secretary or similar officer of the body;

(b) in relation to a partnership

- the reference to a director of the company must be read as referring to a member of the partnership; and
- the reference to a manager or secretary of the company must be read as referring to any manager, secretary or similar officer of the partnership; and

(c) in relation to an unincorporated body other than a partnership

- the reference to a director of the company must be read as referring
  - (i) where the body's affairs are managed by its members, to a member of the body; and
  - (ii) in any other case, to a member of the governing body; and
- the reference to a manager or secretary of the company must be read as referring to any manager, secretary or similar officer of the body.

[*CA 2006, s 1123*].

29.3 Legal professional privilege

In proceedings against a person for an offence under the *Companies Acts*, nothing in those *Acts* is to be taken to require any person to disclose any information that he is entitled to refuse to disclose on grounds of legal professional privilege (in Scotland, confidentiality of communications).

Legal professional privilege protects all communications between a professional legal advisor and his client from being disclosed without the permission of the client. *CA 2006, s 1123* therefore protects the company and/ or its officers from having to disclose something in the course of proceedings which would otherwise be protected by client confidentiality (privilege). "Communications" between a client and advisor could for example be letters written from / to a company and its solicitors provided they are confidential and are written for the purposes of giving or seeking legal advice. It would not apply if the advice was purely commercial in nature and had no legal content. If legal advice is given to a subsidiary company which then reports it to its parent company, the advice may still be protected by privilege.

[*CA 2006, s 1129*].

29.4 SUMMARY PROCEEDINGS

Venue. Summary proceedings for an offence under the *Companies Acts* may be taken

- against a body company at any place at which the body has a place of business; and
- against any other person at any place at which he is for the time being.

This is without prejudice to any jurisdiction exercisable apart from the above.

[*CA 2006, s 1127*].

Time limit for proceedings.

(a) *In England and Wales*, an information relating to an offence under the *Companies Acts* that is triable by a magistrates' court may be so tried if it is laid

- at any time within three years after the commission of the offence; and
- within 12 months after the date on which evidence sufficient in the opinion of the Director of Public Prosecutions or the Secretary of State (as the case may be) to justify the proceedings comes to his knowledge.

(b) *In Scotland*, summary proceedings for an offence under the *Companies Acts*

- must not be commenced after the expiration of three years from the commission of the offence; and
- subject to that, may be commenced at any time

  (i) within 12 months after the date on which evidence sufficient in the Lord Advocate's opinion to justify the proceedings came to his knowledge; or

  (ii) where such evidence was reported to him by the Secretary of State, within 12 months after the date on which it came to the knowledge of the latter.

  Criminal Procedure (Scotland) Act 1995, s 136(3) (date when proceedings deemed to be commenced) applies for these purposes.

(c) *In Northern Ireland*, a magistrates' court has jurisdiction to hear and determine a complaint charging the commission of a summary offence under the *Companies Acts* provided that the complaint is made

- within three years from the time when the offence was committed; and
- within 12 months from the date on which evidence sufficient in the opinion of the Director of Public Prosecutions for Northern Ireland or the Secretary of State (as the case may be) to justify the proceedings comes to his knowledge.

For the above purposes, a certificate of the Director of Public Prosecutions, the Lord Advocate, the Director of Public Prosecutions for Northern Ireland or the Secretary of State (as the case may be) as to the date on which such evidence as is referred to above came to his notice is conclusive evidence.

[*CA 2006, s 1128*].

29.5 CONSENT REQUIRED IN CERTAIN PROSECUTIONS

With effect from 6 April 2008, proceedings for offences under the following provisions can only be instituted in England and Wales and Northern Ireland by, or with the consent of, the appropriate authority indicated.

(a) *CA 2006, ss 458, 460* (unauthorised disclosure of information, see **2.14 Accounts: General**) and *CA 2006, s 949* (unauthorised disclosure of information, see **48.2 Takeovers**) — the Secretary of State or the Director of Public Prosecutions (in Northern Ireland, the Secretary of State or the Director of Public Prosecutions for Northern Ireland).

(b) *CA 2006, s 953* (failure to comply with rules about takeover bid documents, see **48.3 Takeovers**) — the Secretary of State or the Director of Public Prosecutions (in Northern Ireland, the Secretary of State or the Director of Public Prosecutions for Northern Ireland).

(c) *CA 2006, s 798* (offence of attempting to evade restrictions on shares, see **24.7 Interests in Public Company Shares**) — the Secretary of State.

(d) *CA 1985, ss 448, 449–451, 453A* (offences in connection with company investigations, see **25.12, 25.14–25.16** and **25.18 Investigations**) — the Secretary of State or the Director of Public Prosecutions (in Northern Ireland, the Secretary of State or the Director of Public Prosecutions for Northern Ireland).

(e) *CA 1985, s 455* (offence of attempting to evade restrictions on shares, see **25.24 Investigations**) — the Secretary of State.

[*CA 2006, s 1126*].

29.6 PROCEEDINGS AGAINST UNINCORPORATED BODIES

CA 2006 provides for proceedings against unincorporated bodies to be brought against them as if they were corporate bodies. Proceedings for an offence under the *Companies Acts* alleged to have been committed by an unincorporated body must be brought in the name of the body (and not in that of any of its members).

For the purposes of such proceedings

- any rules of court relating to the service of documents have effect as if the body were a body corporate; and
- the provisions of
  - (i) in England and Wales, *Criminal Justice Act 1925, s 33* and *Magistrates' Courts Act 1980, Sch 3*,
  - (ii) in Scotland, *Criminal Procedure (Scotland) Act 1995, ss 70, 143*, and
  - (iii) in Northern Ireland, *Criminal Justice Act (Northern Ireland) 1945, s 18* and *Magistrates' Courts (Northern Ireland) Order 1981 (SI 1981 No 1675), Art 166, Sch 4*

  apply as they apply in relation to a body corporate.

A fine imposed on an unincorporated body on its conviction of an offence under the *Companies Acts* must be paid out of the funds of the body.

[*CA 2006, s 1130*].

29.7 PRODUCTION AND INSPECTION OF DOCUMENTS WHERE OFFENCE SUSPECTED

Where there is a reasonable cause to believe

- that any person has, while an officer of a company, committed an offence in connection with the management of the company's affairs, and
- that evidence of this is to be found in any 'documents' in the possession or control of the company,

on application, a court order may be made

- authorising any person named in it to inspect the documents in question, or any of them, for the purposes of investigating and obtaining evidence of the offence; and
- (except in the case of a banking company) requiring the secretary of the company, or such other officer as is named in the order, to produce the documents (or any of them) to a person named in the order at a place so named.

'*Document*' includes information recorded in any form. This could include documents in hard copy form or in electronic form such as e-mails or faxes.

There is no appeal against such an order.

An application for such an order may be made

- in England and Wales, to a judge of the High Court by the Director of Public Prosecutions, the Secretary of State or a chief officer of police;
- in Scotland, to one of the Lords Commissioners of Justiciary by the Lord Advocate; and
- in Northern Ireland, to the High Court by the Director of Public Prosecutions for Northern Ireland, the Department of Enterprise, Trade and Investment or a chief superintendent of the Police Service of Northern Ireland.

[*CA 2006, s 1132*].

29.8 MEANING OF 'THE COURT'

Unless it is otherwise provided, in the *Companies Acts* '*the court*' means

- in England and Wales, the High Court or a county court;
- in Scotland, the Court of Session or the sheriff court; and
- in Northern Ireland, the High Court.

The provisions of the *Companies Acts* that confer jurisdiction on 'the court' as defined above have effect subject to any enactment or rule of law relating to the allocation of jurisdiction or distribution of business between courts in any part of the UK.

This section of *CA 2006* defines the term "court" for the purposes of the Companies Acts. The effect of this definition is that except where "otherwise provided" (for example in other legislation) proceedings brought under the Companies Acts can only be heard in the courts provided for in *s 1156*.

[*CA 2006, s 1156*].

29.9 POWER OF COURT TO GRANT RELIEF

With effect from 1 October 2008, if in any proceedings for negligence, default, breach of duty or breach of trust against

- an officer of a company, or
- a person employed by a company as auditor (whether or not an officer of the company)

it appears to the court hearing the case that the officer or person is or may be liable but that he has acted honestly and reasonably, and that having regard to all the circumstances of the case (including those connected with his employment) he ought fairly to be excused, the court may relieve him, wholly or partly, from his liability on such terms as it thinks fit. If the case is being tried by a judge with a jury, the judge, after hearing the evidence, may, if satisfied that the defendant (in Scotland, the defender) ought to be relieved in whole or part from liability, withdraw the case from the jury and direct judgment to be entered for the defendant (in Scotland, grant decree of absolvitor) on such terms and costs (in Scotland, expenses) as he thinks proper.

Where such an officer or person has reason to apprehend that a claim will or might be made against him for negligence etc, he may apply to the court for relief. The court then has the same power to relieve him as it would have had in actual proceedings for negligence, etc as above.

[*CA 2006, s 1157*].

29.10 SECURITY FOR COSTS (SCOTLAND)

CA 1985, s 726(1) and *726(2)* provided that all companies, whether in England, Wales or Scotland, could be ordered. to provide (for example) assets of the company as security for costs in specific circumstances when making a claim. *Section 726(1)* was repealed on 1 October 2009 but section *726(2)* was specifically preserved. This section provides as follows:

where, in Scotland, a limited company is pursuer in legal proceedings, the court having jurisdiction may, if it appears by credible testimony that there is reason to believe that the company will be unable to pay the defender's expenses if successful in his defence, order the company to find caution and sist the proceedings until caution is found.

In *section 726(2)* the following words have the following (equivalent) meaning in English law:

"pursuer" means plaintiff or claimant

"defender" means defendant

"caution" means security and

"sist" means to stay proceedings

[*CA 1985, s 726(2); SI 2008 No 2860, Sch 1; SI 2009 No 1941, Art 13*].

Note that the effect of *SI 2009 No 1941* is to preserve *CA 1985, s 726(2)*.

OFFENCES UNDER THE COMPANIES ACTS (*CA 1985* PROVISIONS)

The provisions of *CA 2006* relating to offences and legal proceedings as detailed in the above chapter are fully implemented with effect from 1 October 2009. But

- those provisions do not apply to offences committed before the commencement of the relevant provision.

  [*CA 2006, s 1133*]; and

- the repeal of any provision in *CA 1985* creating an offence does not affect the continued operation of that provision in relation to an offence committed before 1 October 2009.

  [*SI 2008 No 2860, Sch 2 para 116*].

(1) Punishment of offences

The penalties for conviction of offences under the *CA 1985* (other than those relating to investigations and orders imposing restrictions on shares, see INVESTIGATIONS) are listed in *CA 1985, Sch 24*. The levels of penalties in order of seriousness are as follows.

		Punishment	*Daily default fine*
(a)	On indictment	7 years or a fine; or both	
	Summary	6 months or statutory maximum; or both	
(b)	On indictment	2 years or a fine; or both	
	Summary	6 months or statutory maximum; or both	
(c)	On indictment	A fine	
	Summary	Statutory maximum	One-tenth of statutory maximum
(d)	On indictment	A fine	
	Summary	Statutory maximum	
(e)	Summary	Statutory maximum	One-tenth of statutory maximum
(f)	Summary	One-fifth of statutory maximum	One-fiftieth of statutory maximum
(g)	Summary	One-fifth of statutory maximum	

		Punishment	Daily default fine
(h)	On indictment	A fine	
	Summary	Statutory maximum	£100

Punishment is the maximum fine or imprisonment which can be imposed on a person convicted of the offence in the way specified, a reference to a period of years or months being to a term of imprisonment of that duration. The fine on conviction on indictment is unlimited.

Daily default fine. Where a person is convicted of an offence (and incurs a penalty as under the *Punishment* column) but continues in contravention of the relevant provision, then, on a second or subsequent summary conviction of the offence, he is liable to a default fine for each day on which the contravention is continued (instead of the penalty under the *Punishment* column).

Statutory maximum means, in England and Wales, the sum prescribed under the *Magistrates' Courts Act 1980, s 32* and, in Scotland, the sum prescribed under the *Criminal Procedure (Scotland) Act 1975, s 289B*. The statutory maximum is currently £5,000.

[*CA 1985, s 730, Sch 24; CA 1989, Sch 19 para 17; SI 2007 No 2194, Sch 4 para 12*].

Standard scale. Certain new penalties under *CA 1985* are determined by reference to the 'standard scale' (level 5 on which is equivalent to the statutory maximum).

'*Standard scale*' means the scale laid down by the *Criminal Justice Act 1982, s 37* (in Scotland the *Criminal Procedure (Scotland) Act 1975, s 289G*) and is as follows.

Level on the scale	*Amount of fine*
1	£200
2	£500
3	£1,000
4	£2,500
5	£5,000

(2) **Summary proceedings**

Summary proceedings for an offence under the *CA 1985* (other than *Pt 14* or *Pt 15*), the insider dealing legislation, *Companies Consolidation (Consequential Provisions) Act 1985* or *BNA 1985* may be taken

- against a company at any place at which it has a place of business; and
- against any other person at any place at which he is for the time being.

In England and Wales, proceedings which are triable by a magistrates' court must be brought within three years of the commission of the offence and within twelve months of the date on which evidence sufficient, in the opinion of the Director of Public Prosecutions or the Secretary of State (as the case may be), to justify the proceedings comes to his knowledge.

In Scotland, summary proceedings must be commenced within three years of the commission of the offence. Subject to this, proceedings may be commenced within twelve months of the date on which evidence sufficient, in the Lord Advocate's opinion, to justify the proceedings came to his knowledge or, where the evidence was reported to him by the Secretary of State, within twelve months of the date on which it came to the notice of the latter.

[*CA 1985, s 731; BNA 1985, s 7(6); Criminal Procedure (Consequential Provisions) (Scotland) Act 1995, Sch 4 para 56; SI 2007 No 2194, Sch 4 para 14*].

(3) Prosecution by public authorities

Before 6 April 2008, proceedings in England and Wales for an offence under *CA 1985, ss 245E* or *245G* (restriction on further use/disclosure of information disclosed to HMRC or certain authorised persons) could only be brought with the consent of the Secretary of State or the Director of Public Prosecutions.

In any proceedings instituted under the *Companies Acts* (including *BNA 1985*) by the Director of Public Prosecutions, the Secretary of State or the Lord Advocate, nothing in those Acts was to be taken as requiring any person to disclose any information which he was entitled to refuse to disclose on the grounds of legal professional privilege or, in Scotland, confidentiality of communications.

[*CA 1985, s 732; BNA 1985, s 7(6); C(AICE)A 2004, Sch 2 paras 5, 7, 16, 22; SI 1995/710, Reg 5; SI 2007 No 2194, Sch 4 para 15*].

Transitional provisions. The repeal of the above provisions does not affect their operation in relation to offence committed before 6 April 2008.

[*SI 2007 No 3495, Sch 4 para 44*].

(4) Offences by bodies corporate

Before 6 April 2008, where a body corporate was guilty of an offence under the provisions listed below and it was proved that the offence occurred with the consent or connivance of, or was attributable to any neglect on the part of, any director, manager, secretary or other similar officer (or any person purporting to act in such a capacity) he, as well as the body corporate, was guilty of that offence and was liable to be proceeded against and punished accordingly. If the affairs of the company were managed by the members, this also applied in relation to any act or default of a member in connection with his functions of management as if he were a director.

The relevant provisions were as follows.

(a) *CA 1985, ss 245E(3)* and *245G(7)* (disclosure of information by HM Revenue and Customs or an authorised person).

(b) *CA 1985, s 394A(1)* (statement by person ceasing to hold office as auditor, see **8.21 Audit**).

[*CA 1985, s 733; CA 1989, s 123, Sch 24; IA 1985, Sch 6 para 7; IA 1986, Sch 13 Pt I; C(AICE)A 2004, Sch 2 paras 5, 8, 16, 23; SI 2007 No 2194, Sch 4 para 16*].

Transitional provisions. The repeal of the above provisions does not affect their operation in relation to offence committed before 6 April 2008.

[*SI 2007 No 3495, Sch 4 para 44*].

(5) **Criminal proceedings against unincorporated bodies**

Before 6 April 2008, proceedings for an offence alleged to have been committed by an unincorporated body under

(a) *CA 1985, ss 245E(3)* and *245G(7)* (disclosure of information by HM Revenue and Customs or an authorised person), or

(b) *CA 1985, s 394A(1)* (statement by person ceasing to hold office as auditor, see **8.21 Audit**)

had to be brought in the name of that body (and not any of its members). For the purposes of such proceedings, any rules of court relating to the service of documents applied as if that body were a corporation.

Any fine imposed on an unincorporated body on conviction of such an offence had to be paid out of the funds of the body.

Where an offence within (*a*) or (*b*) above was proved to have been committed with the consent or connivance of, or to be attributable to any neglect on the part of,

- in the case of a partnership, a partner, or
- in the case of any other unincorporated body, an officer of the body or a member of its governing body,

that person, as well as the body, was guilty of the offence and liable to be proceeded against and punished accordingly.

[*CA 1985, s 734; CA 1989, ss 120, 123, Sch 19 para 18; Criminal Procedures (Scotland) Act 1995, Sch 4 para 56; C(AICE)A 2004, Sch 2 paras 5, 9, 16, 24; SI 2007 No 2194, Sch 2, Sch 4 para 16; SI 2007 No 3495, Sch 5 para 2*].

Transitional provisions. The repeal of the above provisions does not affect their operation in relation to offence committed before 6 April 2008.

[*SI 2007 No 3495, Sch 4 para 44*].

(6) **Service of documents**

A document may be served on a company by leaving it at, or sending it by post to, the company's registered office. [*CA 1985, s 725(1)*]. See also *JC Houghton & Co v Nothard, Lowe and Wills Ltd* [1928] AC 1, 97 LJKB 76, HL.

Where a company registered in Scotland carries on business in England and Wales, the process of any court in England and Wales may be served on the company by leaving it at, or sending it by post to, the company's principal place of business in England and Wales. It should be addressed to the manager or other head officer of the company in England and Wales. The person issuing out the process must send a copy by post to the company's registered office.

[*CA 1985, s 725(2)(3)*].

(7) **Power of court to grant relief**

Before 1 October 2008, if in any proceedings for negligence, default, breach of duty or breach of trust against an officer of a company or auditor it appears to the court that that person, although liable, acted honestly and reasonably and ought fairly to be excused, the court may relieve him, wholly or partly, from liability on such terms as it thinks fit. If the case is being tried by a judge with a jury, the judge may, after hearing the evidence, withdraw the case in whole or part from the jury and direct judgment to be entered for the defendant.

[*CA 1985, s 727(1)(3)*].

Where an officer of a company or auditor has reason to believe that a claim will or might be made against him for negligence etc, he may apply to the court for relief. The court has the same powers of relief on such an application as it does above in actual proceedings for negligence etc.

[*CA 1985, s 727(2)*].

(8) **Security for costs and expenses in certain actions**

Where a limited company is plaintiff (in Scotland, pursuer) in legal proceedings and there is reason to believe that the company will be unable to pay the defendant's costs (in Scotland, the defender's expenses) if defence is successful, the court may require security to be given for those costs (in Scotland, order the company to find caution) and may determine not to proceed until such condition is satisfied. [*CA 1985, s 726*].

(9) **Production and inspection of books where offence suspected**

Where there is a reasonable cause to believe that any person has, while an officer of a company, committed an offence in connection with the management of the company's affairs and that evidence of this is to be found in any 'books or papers' of, or under the control of, the company, the Director of Public Prosecutions, the Secretary of State or a chief officer of police (in Scotland, the Lord Advocate) may obtain a court order

- authorising any person to inspect the books and papers in question in order to investigate the offence; and
- (except in the case of a banking company) requiring an officer to produce the books etc named in the order at a place so named.

There is no appeal against such an order.

'*Books or papers*' include accounts, deeds, writings and documents.

[*CA 1985, ss 721, 744*].

30 Overseas Companies – establishing a place of business in the UK

30.1	**Definition**
30.2	**Registration of particulars**
30.3	Initial registration
30.7	Alterations in registered particulars
30.11	**Registered name of overseas company**
30.12	**Usual residential addresses: protection from disclosure**
30.13	Restriction on use or disclosure of protected information
30.14	Permitted use or disclosure by the Registrar of Companies
30.16	Disclosure under a court order
30.17	Circumstances in which the Registrar of Companies can put a usual residential address on the public record
30.18	**Delivery of accounting documents: general requirements**
30.19	Companies required to prepare and disclose accounts under parent law
30.24	Companies not required to prepare and disclose accounts under parent law
30.35	**Delivery of accounting documents: credit or financial institutions**
30.36	Institutions required to prepare accounts under parent law
30.40	Institutions not required to prepare accounts under parent law
30.51	**Trading disclosures**
30.52	Display of name, etc at business location
30.53	Inclusion of names and other specified information in documents and communications
30.54	Disclosures relating to address for service
30.55	Civil consequences of failure to make a required disclosure
30.56	**Service of documents**
30.57	**Duty to give notice of closure of UK establishment**
30.58	**Registrar to whom returns, notices, etc to be delivered**
30.59	**Company contracts and execution of documents**
30.60	Company contracts
30.61	Deeds and documents: provisions applying in England and Wales and Northern Ireland
30.62	Execution of documents: provisions applying in Scotland
30.63	Pre-incorporation contracts, deeds and obligations
30.64	**Registration of charges**
30.65	Charges requiring registration
30.66	Duty to deliver particulars of charge etc for registration
30.67	Charge by way of ex facie absolute disposition (Scotland)
30.67A	Charges created on or after 1 October 2011
30.68	Special rules about debentures: charge in series of debentures
30.69	Endorsement of certificate on debentures
30.70	Register of charges to be kept by the Registrar of Companies
30.71	Rectification of register of charges by the court
30.72	Appointment/cessation of receiver, etc
30.73	Register of charges and copies of instruments creating charges
Appendix	**Provisions applying before 1 October 2009**

Background. The provisions in this chapter apply, unless otherwise stated, with effect from 1 October 2009. For the provisions applying before that date, see the Appendix at the end of the chapter. This chapter does not deal with the any of Listing Rules which apply to overseas companies. The *Companies Act 2006 (Strategic Report and Directors' Report) Regulations 2013* ('the *2013 Regulations*') which are referred to in various parts of this chapter, brought into force the requirement for a company to produce a strategic report for financial years ending on or after 30 September 2013.

30.1 DEFINITION

An '*overseas company*' means a company incorporated outside the UK.

[*CA 2006, s 1044*].

30.2 REGISTRATION OF PARTICULARS

If an overseas company wants to establish a business in the UK it can do so either by creating a subsidiary company or by opening a branch or place of business. This chapter deals only with the latter. When opening a business in the UK an overseas company is required by regulations made under *CA 2006* to register certain particulars and documents with the Registrar of Companies.

[*CA 2006, ss 1046, 1047, 1055, 1056, 1058*].

Those regulations are the *Overseas Companies Regulations 2009 (SI 2009 No 1801)*.

30.3 Initial registration

The provisions in this paragraph and in **30.4** to **30.6** apply to an overseas company that opens a UK establishment. '*Establishment*' means a branch within the meaning of the *EC Eleventh Company Law Directive* (*89/666/EEC*) or a place of business that is not such a branch, ie is a place where the company regularly conducts its business in the UK.

The company must, within one month of having opened a UK establishment,

- deliver to the Registrar of Companies a return containing the particulars in (1) and (2) below and, where appropriate, the statement of compliance with accounting requirements (see **30.5** below); and
- deliver with the return the documents required under **30.4**.

These requirements apply each time a company opens an establishment in the UK. It should be noted that the relocation of a UK establishment from one part of the UK to another counts as the closing of one UK establishment and the opening of another (although the relocation of a UK establishment within the same part of the UK does not).

[*CA 2006, s 1059*].

The particulars required are as follows. If the company has another UK establishment for which it has already delivered a return and has no obligation to alter the particulars in that return (see **30.7–30.9** re Alterations to Particulars) then the company may instead state in the return that the particulars are included in the return delivered for the other UK establishment and give the registered number of that other establishment. Also see Companies House Guidance Booklet GP01 'Overseas Companies registered in the UK' for details of which forms must be completed and relevant fees,

(1) **Particulars of the company**

- The company's name.
- The company's legal form.
- If it is registered in the country of its incorporation, the identity of the register in which it is registered and the number with which it is so registered.

- A list of its directors giving particulars of:

(a) *In the case of an individual*, (i) his name; (ii) any former name; (iii) a service address; (iv) usual residential address; (v) the country or state in which the individual is usually resident; (vi) nationality; (vii) business occupation (if any); and (viii) his date of birth.

(b) *In the case of a body corporate, or a firm that is a legal person under the law by which it is governed* (i) corporate or firm name; (ii) registered or principal office; (iii) in the case of an EEA company to which the *EC First Company Law Directive* applies, particulars of the register in which the company file mentioned in *Article 3* of that Directive is kept (including details of the relevant state) and the registration number in that register; and (iv) in any other case, particulars of the legal form of the company or firm and the law by which it is governed and, if applicable, the register in which it is entered (including details of the state) and its registration number in that register.

For the purposes of (*a*)(ii) above, where a person is (or was) formerly known by more than one former name, each of them must be stated. But it is not necessary to include particulars of a former name (i) in the case of a peer or an individual normally known by a title, where the name is one by which the person was known previous to the adoption of or succession to the title; or (ii) in the case of any person, where the former name was changed or disused before the person attained the age of sixteen years or has been changed or disused for twenty years or more.

For the purposes of (*a*)(iv) above, if the person's usual residential address is the same as his service address the return need only contain a statement to that effect.

- The secretary giving particulars of (where there are joint secretaries, with respect to each of them)

(a) *in the case of an individual*, (i) name; (ii) any former name; and (iii) a service address; and

(b) *in the case of a body corporate, or a firm that is a legal person under the law by which it is governed*, (i) corporate or firm name; (ii) registered or principal office; (iii) in the case of an EEA company to which the *EC First Company Law Directive* applies, particulars of the register in which the company file mentioned in *Article 3* of that Directive is kept (including details of the relevant state) and the registration number in that register; and (iv) in any other case, particulars of the legal form of the company or firm and the law by which it is governed and, if applicable, the register in which it is entered (including details of the state) and its registration number in that register.

But if all the partners in a firm are joint secretaries of the company it is sufficient to state the particulars that would be required if the firm were a legal person and the firm had been appointed secretary.

For the purposes of (*a*)(ii) above, where a person is (or was) formerly known by more than one former name, each of them must be stated. But it is not necessary to include particulars of a former name (i) in the case of a peer or an individual normally known by a title, where the name is one by which the person was known previous to the adoption of or succession to the title; or (ii) in the case of any person, where the former name was changed or disused before the person attained the age of 16 years or has been changed or disused for 20 years or more.

- The extent of the powers of the directors or secretary to represent the company in dealings with third parties and in legal proceedings, together with a statement as to whether they may act alone or must act jointly and, if jointly, the name of any other person concerned.
- Whether the company is a credit or financial institution.
- In the case of a company which is not incorporated in an EEA State,
  - (a) the law under which the company is incorporated;
  - (b) in the case of a company to which either **30.19** to **30.23** or **30.36** to **30.39** applies (companies required to prepare or disclose accounts under parent law), the period for which the company is required by its parent law to prepare accounts, together with the period allowed for the preparation and public disclosure (if any) of accounts for such a period,
  - (c) unless disclosed by company's constitution (see **30.4**(1)), the address of its principal place of business in its country of incorporation (or, if applicable, its registered office), its objects, and the amount of its issued share capital.

(2) **Particulars of the establishment**

(a) Address of the establishment.

(b) Date on which it was opened.

(c) Business carried on at it.

(d) Name of the establishment if different from the name of the company.

(e) Name and service address of every person resident in the UK authorised to accept service of documents on behalf of the company in respect of the establishment, or a statement that there is no such person.

(f) A list of every person authorised to represent the company as a permanent representative of the company in respect of the establishment, containing with respect to such person

- (i) name;
- (ii) any former name;
- (iii) service address; and
- (iv) usual residential address.

(g) Extent of the authority of any person falling within (*f*) above, including whether that person is authorised to act alone or jointly.

(h) if a person falling within (*f*) is not authorised to act alone, the name of any person with whom they are authorised to act.

For the purpose of paragraph (*f*)(iv) if the person's usual residential address is the same as the person's service address the return need only contain a statement to that effect. [*SI 2009 No 1801, Regs 3–7*].

Transitional provisions.

(a) An overseas company that immediately before 1 October 2009

(i) has a branch in the UK, and

(ii) has complied in respect of that branch with the registration requirements in **30.App (6)–(10)**

is treated as having complied in respect of that branch with the above requirements relating to particulars of the company and establishment

Certain particulars, as specified in *SI 2009 No 1801, Sch 8 paras 4, 5* are treated as if delivered and registered under (1) and (2) above. For those requirements which are not treated as registered, the company must deliver a transitional return in respect of the establishment to the Registrar of Companies by no later than 31 March 2010.

(b) An overseas company that immediately before 1 October 2009

(i) has a place of business (other than a branch) in the UK, and

(ii) has delivered to the Registrar of Companies in respect of that place of business the documents required in **30.App** (3)(*a*) and (*b*),

is treated as having complied in respect of that place of business with the requirements relating to particulars of the company and establishment.

Certain particulars, as specified in *SI 2009 No 1801, Sch 8 paras 10, 11* are treated as if delivered and registered under (1) and (2) above. For those requirements which are not treated as registered, the company must deliver a transitional return in respect of the establishment to the Registrar of Companies by no later than 31 March 2010.

A company which falls within (*a*)(i) or (*b*)(i) above but which has not complied with the requirements in (*a*)(ii) or, as the case may be, (*b*)(ii) above, is treated as if it had opened that establishment on 1 October 2009.

[*SI 2009 No 1801, Sch 8 paras 3–5, 9–11, 13(1)–(3), 14*].

30.4 *Documents to be delivered with the return*

The following documents must be delivered to the Registrar of Companies with the return required under **30.3**.

(1) *Copy of company's constitution*

A certified copy of the company's 'constitution' must be delivered to the Registrar of Companies with the return. But if, at the time the return is delivered, the company

- has another UK establishment,
- has delivered a certified copy of the company's constitution with a return relating to that establishment, and
- has no outstanding obligation under **30.7** to **30.9** in respect of an alteration to its constitution,

the company may instead state in the return that a certified copy of the company's constitution has been delivered in respect of another UK establishment (giving the registered number of that establishment).

Companies House requires that a certified translation of the constitution in English must also be sent if the original is in another language (see Companies House Guidance Booklet GP01 Chapter 1 para 1).

'*Constitution*', in relation to an overseas company, means the charter, statutes, memorandum and articles of association or other instrument constituting or defining the company's constitution.

[*SI 2009 No 1801, Regs 2, 8*].

(2) *Copies of accounting documents*

If the company is one to which **30.19** to **30.23** applies (companies required to prepare and disclose accounts under parent law), copies of the company's 'latest accounting documents' must be delivered to the Registrar of Companies with the return.

'*Latest accounting documents*' means the accounting documents, prepared for a financial period of the company, last disclosed in accordance with its parent law before the end of the period allowed for delivery of the return or, if earlier, the date on which the company delivers the return.

But if, at the time the return is delivered, the company

- has another UK establishment, and
- has delivered the latest accounting documents in connection with a return relating to that establishment,

the company may instead state in the return that the documents are included in the material delivered in respect of another UK establishment (giving the registered number of that establishment).

[*SI 2009 No 1801, Reg 9*].

The certified translations provisions (above) apply to the accounts as they do to the constitution delivered to Companies House.

Transitional provisions.

(a) An overseas company that immediately before 1 October 2009

(i) has a branch in the UK, and

(ii) has complied in respect of that branch with the registration requirements in **30.App (6)–(10)**

is treated as having complied in respect of that branch with the above requirements relating to delivering a certified copy of the company's constitution and accounting documents.

(b) An overseas company that immediately before 1 October 2009

(i) has a place of business (other than a branch) in the UK, and

(ii) has delivered to the Registrar of Companies in respect of that place of business the documents required in **30.App** (3)(*a*) and (*b*),

(c) is treated as having complied in respect of that place of business with the requirements relating to delivering a certified copy of the company's constitution.

A company which falls within (*a*)(i) or (*b*)(i) above but which has not complied with the requirements in (*a*)(ii) or, as the case may be, (*b*)(ii) above, is treated as if it had opened that establishment on 1 October 2009.

[*SI 2009 No 1801, Sch 8 paras 3, 6, 7, 9, 12, 14*].

30.5 *Statement of future manner of compliance with accounting requirements*

If the company is one to which the provisions in **30.18** to **30.34** apply (delivery of accounting documents: general), the return required under **30.3** must state

- in the case of a company to which **30.19** to **30.23** applies (companies required to file copies of accounting documents disclosed under parent law), whether it is intended to file copies of accounting documents in accordance with those provisions in respect of the establishment to which the return relates or in respect of another UK establishment; and
- in the case of a company to which **30.24** to **30.34** applies (companies required to file accounts under UK law), whether it is intended to file accounts in accordance with the provisions in respect of the establishment to which the return relates or in respect of another UK establishment.

If the return states that it is intended to file copies of accounting documents, or accounts, in respect of another UK establishment, it must give the registered number of that establishment.

[*SI 2009 No 1801, Reg 10*].

Transitional provisions. An overseas company that immediately before 1 October 2009

(i) has a branch in the UK, and

(ii) has complied in respect of that branch with the registration requirements in **30.App (6)–(10)**

is treated as having complied in respect of that branch with the above requirements.

If the company is one to which **30.19** to **30.23** applies (companies required to prepare and disclose accounts under parent law), then the following, as they appear on the register immediately before 1 October 2009, are treated as if delivered and registered under *Reg 10*, namely

- the statement in the return in respect of a branch whether it is intended to file copies of accounting documents in respect of that branch or in respect of another branch; and
- if the return states that it is intended to file copies of accounting documents in respect of another branch, the registered number of that branch.

But the company must have delivered any other information required under *Reg 10* to the Registrar of Companies in a transitional return in respect of the establishment by no later than 31 March 2010.

A company which falls within (i) above but which has not complied with the requirements in (ii) above is treated as if it had opened that establishment on 1 October 2009.

[*SI 2009 No 1801, Sch 8 paras 3, 8, 13, 14*].

30.6 *Penalty for non-compliance*

If a company fails to comply with any of the requirements in **30.3** to **30.5**, an offence is committed by the company and every officer or agent of the company who knowingly and wilfully authorises or permits the default. A person guilty of such an offence is liable, on summary conviction, to a fine not exceeding level 3 on the standard scale, and, for continued contravention, a daily default fine not exceeding one-tenth of level 3 on the standard scale. See **29.1** Offences and Legal Proceedings for the standard scale.

[*SI 2009 No 1801, Reg 11*].

30.7 Alterations in registered particulars

The provisions in this paragraph and in **30.8** to **30.10** apply to an overseas company that

- has complied with the initial registration requirements in **30.3** to **30.6** in respect of one or more UK establishments; and
- has not subsequently given notice under **30.57** (notice of closure of UK establishment) in respect of all those establishments.

[*SI 2009 No 1801, Reg 12*].

(1) **Return of alteration in registered particulars**

If an alteration is made in any of the particulars delivered under **30.3**(1) or (2), the company must deliver to the Registrar of Companies a return containing details of the alteration.

Where a company has more than one UK establishment, a return is required in respect of each UK establishment to which the alteration relates; but a return giving the registered numbers of more than one UK establishment is treated as a return in respect of each of them.

An alteration in any of the particulars specified in **30.3**(1) (particulars of the company) is treated as relating to every UK establishment of the company.

The details required of the alteration are

- the particular that has been altered;
- details of the particular as altered; and
- the date on which the alteration was made.

The return must also state the company's name and registered number and the name (if different from the company's name) and registered number of each UK establishment to which the return relates.

The period allowed for delivery of the return is

- in the case of an alteration of any of the particulars specified in **30.3**(1) (particulars of the company), 21 days after the date on which notice of the alteration in question could have been received in the UK in due course of post (if despatched with due diligence);
- in the case of an alteration of any of the particulars specified in **30.3**(2) (particulars of the establishment), 21 days after the alteration is made.

[*SI 2009 No 1801, Reg 13*].

Transitional provisions. The provisions in **30.**App**(4)** and **(11)** continue to apply in relation to an alteration made before 1 October 2009. The above provisions apply to alterations made on or after 1 October 2009.

[*SI 2009 No 1801, Sch 8 para 15*].

(2) **Return of alteration in company's constitution**

If any alteration is made in the company's 'constitution', the company must deliver to the Registrar of Companies a return stating

- that an alteration has been made to the company's constitution;
- the date on which the alteration was made;
- the company's name;
- the company's registered number; and
- the name (if different from the company's name) and registered number of each UK establishment to which the return relates.

The return must be accompanied by a certified copy of the constitution as altered.

'*Constitution*', in relation to an overseas company, means the charter, statutes, memorandum and articles of association or other instrument constituting or defining the company's constitution.

Where a company has more than one UK establishment, a return is required in respect of each UK establishment to which the alteration relates but a return giving the registered numbers of more than one UK establishment is treated as a return in respect of each of them.

An alteration in the company's constitution is treated as relating to a UK establishment only if a copy of the constitution is included in the material registered in respect of that establishment.

The period allowed for delivery of the return is 21 days after the date on which notice of the alteration in question could have been received in the UK in due course of post (if despatched with due diligence).

[*SI 2009 No 1801, Regs 2, 14*].

Transitional provisions. The provisions in **30.App(4)** and **(11)** continue to apply in relation to an alteration made before 1 October 2009. The above provisions apply to alterations made on or after 1 October 2009.

[*SI 2009 No 1801, Sch 8 para 16*].

30.8 *Return of alteration regarding filing of certified copy of constitution*

Where

- the company's initial return in respect of an establishment states that a certified copy of the company's 'constitution' has been delivered in respect of another UK establishment, and
- that statement ceases to be true

the company must deliver to the Registrar of Companies a further return in respect of the first-mentioned establishment

(a) stating that the previous statement has ceased to be true

(b) either

(i) accompanied by a certified copy of the company's constitution; or

(ii) stating that a copy of the company's constitution is included in the material delivered in respect of another UK establishment (giving the registered number of that establishment); and

(c) stating

(i) the company's name;

(ii) the company's registered number; and

(iii) the name (if different from the company's name) and registered number of each UK establishment to which the return relates.

'*Constitution*', in relation to an overseas company, means the charter, statutes, memorandum and articles of association or other instrument constituting or defining the company's constitution.

Where the company has more than one UK establishment a return giving the registered numbers of more than one UK establishment is treated as a return in respect of each of them.

The period allowed for delivery of the return is 21 days after the date on which notice of the fact that the statement in the earlier return has ceased to be true could have been received in the UK in due course of post (if despatched with due diligence).

Where, after a company has made a return under this provision, the statement mentioned in (*b*)(ii) ceases to be true, the above requirements apply again.

[*SI 2009 No 1801, Regs 2, 15*].

Transitional provisions. The provisions of *CA 1985, Sch 21A para 8* (see **30.App(11)**) continue to apply where the statement ceases to be true before 1 October 2009. The above provisions apply where that statement ceases to be true on or after 1 October 2009. [*SI 2009 No 1801, Sch 8 para 17*].

30.9 *Return of alteration of manner of compliance with accounting requirements*

Where

- a company's initial return in respect of a UK establishment states an intention as to whether accounting documents, or accounts, are to be filed in accordance in respect of that establishment or in respect of another UK establishment (see **30.5**), and
- that intention changes

the company must deliver to the Registrar of Companies a further return in respect of the first-mentioned establishment stating

(a) that the intention has changed;

(b) either

(i) that it is intended to file accounting documents, or accounts, in respect of the establishment to which the return relates; or

(ii) that it is intended to file accounting documents, or accounts, in respect of another UK establishment (giving the registered number of that establishment);

(c) the company's name;

(d) the company's registered number; and

(e) the name (if different from the company's name) and registered number of each UK establishment to which the return relates.

Where the company has more than one UK establishment, a return giving the registered numbers of more than one UK establishment is treated as a return in respect of each of them.

The period allowed for delivery of the return is 21 days after the date on which notice of the fact that the intention stated in the earlier return has changed could have been received in the UK in due course of post (if despatched with due diligence).

Where, after a company has made a return under the above provisions, the intention stated in accordance with (*b*)(i) or (*b*)(ii) changes again, the above requirements apply again.

[*SI 2009 No 1801, Reg 16*].

30.10 *Penalty for non-compliance*

If a company fails to comply with any of the requirements of **30.7** to **30.9**, an offence is committed by the company and every officer or agent of the company who knowingly and wilfully authorises or permits the default. A person guilty of such an offence is liable, on summary conviction, to a fine not exceeding level 3 on the standard scale and, for continued contravention, a daily default fine not exceeding one-tenth of level 3 on the standard scale. See **29.1 Offences and Legal Proceedings** for the standard scale.

[*SI 2009 No 1801, Reg 17*].

30.11 REGISTERED NAME OF OVERSEAS COMPANY

An overseas company that is required to register particulars must register its name (see **30.3**). This may be

- the company's corporate name (ie its name under the law of the country or territory in which it is incorporated); or
- an alternative name (see below).

Where the overseas company is incorporated in an EEA state, it may always register its corporate name (even if it does not comply with the requirement imposed on the names of companies formed under *CA 2006*) provided that it complies with the requirements in *CA 2006, s 57* (permitted characters, etc, see **27.8 Names and Business Names**).

In any other case, the corporate name of an overseas company can only be registered if it complies with the requirements imposed on the names of companies formed and registered under *CA 2006* (apart from the requirements for the names of certain types of company to end with certain words which are not appropriate for overseas companies). See **27.3–27.10 Names and Business Names**. [*CA 2006, s 1047; SI 2015 No 17, Regs 12–15*].

Registration under an alternative name. An overseas company that is required to register particulars with the Registrar of Companies may at any time deliver to the Registrar for registration a statement specifying a name, other than its corporate name, under which it proposes to carry on business in the UK. An overseas company that has registered an alternative name may then subsequently deliver to the Registrar of Companies for registration a statement specifying a different name under which it proposes to carry on business in the UK (which may be its corporate name or a further alternative) in substitution for the name previously registered.

But (wherever the overseas company is incorporated) any name other than its corporate name can be registered only if it complies with the requirements imposed on the names of companies formed and registered under *CA 2006* (apart from the requirements for the names of certain types of company to end with certain words which are not appropriate for overseas companies). See **27.3–27.10 Names and Business Names**.

The alternative name for the time being registered under this provision is treated for all purposes of the law applying in the UK as the company's corporate name. But this does not

- affect the references in this provision or *CA 2006, s 1047* above to the company's corporate name;
- affect any rights or obligation of the company; or
- render defective any legal proceedings by or against the company.

Any legal proceedings that might have been continued or commenced against the company by its corporate name, or any name previously registered under this provision, may be continued or commenced against it by its name for the time being so registered.

[*CA 2006, s 1048*].

30.12 USUAL RESIDENTIAL ADDRESSES: PROTECTION FROM DISCLOSURE

The provisions in **30.13** to **30.17** apply to an overseas company that has one or more UK establishments in respect of which it has registered particulars under **30.3**. They protect, in respect of

- a company director who is an individual and whose particulars have been delivered to the Registrar of Companies under **30.3**(1), and
- a permanent representative of the company whose particulars have been delivered under **30.3**(2)(*f*)

information as to his usual residential address and the information that his service address is his usual residential address.

That information is referred to as '*protected information*'.

Information does not cease to be protected information on the person ceasing to be a director or permanent representative and, to that extent, references to a director or permanent representative include a former director or permanent representative.

[*SI 2009 No 1801, Regs 18, 19*].

30.13 Restriction on use or disclosure of protected information

(1) *By the company*

A company must not use or disclose 'protected information' (see **30.12**) about a director or permanent representative, except

- for communicating with the individual concerned;
- in order to comply with any requirement of the *Overseas Companies Regulations 2009 (SI 2009 No 1801)* as to particulars to be sent to the Registrar of Companies; or
- in accordance with **30.16** (disclosure under a court order).

But this does not prohibit any use or disclosure of protected information with the consent of the director or permanent representative concerned.

[*SI 2009 No 1801, Reg 20*].

(2) *By the Registrar of Companies*

The Registrar of Companies

(a) must omit 'protected information' (see **30.12**) from the material on the register that is available for inspection where

 (i) it is contained in a document delivered to him in which such information is required to be stated, and

 (ii) in the case of a document having more than one part, it is contained in a part of the document in which such information is required to be stated;

(b) is not obliged

 (i) to check other documents or (as the case may be) other parts of the document to ensure the absence of protected information; or

 (ii) to omit from the material that is available for public inspection anything registered before 1 October 2009; and

(c) must not use or disclose protected information except as permitted under **30.14** or in accordance with **30.16**.

[*SI 2009 No 1801, Reg 21*].

Transitional provisions – where the protected information provisions do not apply.

- The provisions above do not apply to

 (i) material delivered to the Registrar of Companies before 1 October 2009; or

 (ii) material delivered to him on or after 1 October 2009 being a return of an alteration in particulars which occurred before that date.

- In (*b*)(ii) above, the reference to things being registered before 1 October 2009 is treated as including anything registered as a result of a return made on or after 1 October 2009 of an alteration occurring before that date.

But these transitional provisions have effect subject to the continued protection of information formerly protected by a confidentiality order.

[*SI 2009 No 1801, Sch 8 para 19*].

30.14 Permitted use or disclosure by the Registrar of Companies

The Registrar of Companies may use 'protected information' (see **30.12**) in the following ways.

(1) **Communication**

For communicating with the director or permanent representative.

[*SI 2009 No 1801, Reg 22*].

(2) **Disclosure to specified public authorities**

To disclose the protected information to a specified public authority where the following conditions are satisfied.

(a) The specified public authority has delivered to the Registrar of Companies a statement that it intends to use the protected information only for the purpose of facilitating the carrying out by it of a 'public function' ('*the permitted purpose*').

(b) Subject to below, the specified public authority has delivered to the Registrar of Companies a statement that it will, where it supplies a copy of the protected information to a 'processor' for the purpose of processing the information for use in respect of the permitted purpose

(i) ensure that the processor is one who carries on business in the EEA;

(ii) require that the information is not transmitted outside the EEA by the processor; and

(iii) require that the processor does not disclose the information except to the authority or an employee of the authority.

But this condition does not apply where the specified public authority is the Secret Intelligence Service, Security Service or Government Communications Headquarters.

'*Processor*' means any person who provides a service which consists of putting information into data form or processing information in data form, and reference to a processor includes a reference to the processor's employees.

An employee of a person who has access to protected information is deemed to include any person working or providing services for the purposes of that person or employed by or on behalf of, or working for, any person who is so working or who is supplying such a service.

'*Public function*' includes

- any function conferred by or in accordance with any provision contained in any enactment;
- any function conferred by or in accordance with any provision contained in the Community Treaties or any Community instrument;
- any similar function conferred on persons by or under provisions having effect as part of the law of a country or territory outside the UK; and
- any function exercisable in relation to the investigation of any criminal offence or for the purpose of any criminal proceedings.

The disclosure for the purpose of facilitating the carrying out of a public function includes disclosure in relation to, and for the purpose of, any proceedings whether civil, criminal or disciplinary in which the specified public authority engages while carrying out its public functions.

The specified public authorities for these purposes are

- the Secretary of State;
- any Northern Ireland Department;
- the Scottish Ministers;

- the Welsh Ministers;
- the Treasury;
- the Commissioners for Her Majesty's Revenue and Customs;
- the Bank of England;
- the Director of Public Prosecutions;
- the Director of Public Prosecutions for Northern Ireland;
- the Serious Fraud Office;
- the Secret Intelligence Service;
- the Security Service;
- the Government Communications Headquarters;
- the Financial Services Authority;
- the Competition Commission;
- the Pensions Regulator;
- the Panel on Takeovers and Mergers;
- the Regulator of Community Interest Companies;
- the Registrar of Credit Unions for Northern Ireland;
- the Office of the Information Commissioner;
- the Charity Commission;
- the Charity Commission for Northern Ireland;
- the Office of the Scottish Charity Regulator;
- the Postal Services Commission;
- the Gas and Electricity Markets Authority;
- the Northern Ireland Authority for Utility Regulation;
- the Gambling Commission;
- the Serious Organised Crime Agency;
- the Health and Safety Executive;
- the Health and Safety Executive for Northern Ireland;
- the Food Standards Agency;
- the Gangmasters Licensing Authority;
- the Security Industry Authority;
- a local authority (within the meaning of *CA 2006, s 54(2)*);
- an official receiver appointed under *IA 1986, s 399*;
- the Official Receiver for Northern Ireland;
- the Crown Office and Procurator Fiscal Services;

- a person acting as an insolvency practitioner within the meaning of *IA 1986, s 388* or *Insolvency (Northern Ireland) Order 1989, Art 3*;
- an inspector appointed under *CA 1985, Pt 14* or *Companies (Northern Ireland) Order 1986, Pt 15* (investigation of companies and their affairs: requisition of documents) or a person appointed under *Open-Ended Investment Companies Regulations 2001, Reg 30* or *Open-Ended Investment Companies Regulations (Northern Ireland) 2004, Reg 22* (power to investigate);
- any person authorised to exercise powers under *CA 1985, s 447* (power to require documents and information), or *CA 1989, s 84* (exercise of powers by officers, etc) or *Companies (Northern Ireland) Order 1986, Art 440*;
- any person exercising functions conferred by *FSMA 2000, Pt 6* (official listing) or the competent authority under that Part;
- a person appointed to make a report under *FSMA 2000, s 166* (reports by skilled persons);
- a person appointed to conduct an investigation under *FSMA 2000, s 167* (appointment of persons to carry out general investigations) or *FSMA 2000, s 168(3)* or *(5)* (appointment of persons to carry out investigations in particular cases);
- an inspector appointed under *FSMA 2000, s 284* (power to investigate);
- an overseas regulatory authority within the meaning of *CA 1989, s 82* (request for assistance by overseas regulatory authority); and
- a police force.

A specified public authority must deliver to the Registrar of Companies such information or evidence as he may direct to enable him to determine whether to disclose protected information. The Registrar may require such information or evidence to be verified in such manner as he may direct.

The specified public authority must inform the Registrar of Companies immediately of any change in respect of any statement delivered to him under (*a*) or (*b*) above or information or evidence provided to enabling him to determine whether to disclose protected information.

[*SI 2009 No 1801, Reg 23, Sch 1, Sch 2 paras 1–4, 11*].

(3) **Disclosure to credit agencies**

Subject to **30.15**, to disclose the protected information to a '*credit reference agency*' (ie a person carrying on a business comprising the furnishing of information relevant to the financial standing of individuals, being information collected by the agency for that purpose) where the following conditions are satisfied.

(a) The credit reference agency is carrying on in the UK or in another EEA State a business comprising the furnishing of information relevant to the financial standing of individuals, being information collected by the agency for that purpose.

(b) The credit reference agency maintains appropriate procedures

(i) to ensure that an independent person can investigate and audit the measures maintained by the agency for the purposes of ensuring the security of any protected information disclosed to that agency; and

(ii) for the purposes of ensuring that it complies with its obligations under the *Data Protection Act 1998* or, where the agency carries on business in a EEA State other than the UK, with its obligations under legislation implementing *EC Directive 95/46/EC* on the protection of individuals with regard to the processing of personal data and on the free movement of such data.

(c) The credit reference agency has not been found guilty of an offence under

(i) *CA 2006, s 1112* (general false statement offence) or *Fraud Act 2006, s 2* (fraud by false representation); or

(ii) *Data Protection Act 1998, s 47* (failure to comply with enforcement notice) in circumstances where it has used the protected information for purposes other than those in (*d*)(i)–(vi) below.

(d) The credit reference agency has delivered to the Registrar of Companies a statement that it intends to use the protected information only for the purposes of

(i) providing an assessment of the financial standing of a person;

(ii) meeting any obligations contained in the *Money Laundering Regulations 2007* or any rules made pursuant to *FSMA 2000, s 146* (money laundering rules), or in any legislation of another EEA State implementing *EC Directive 2005/60/EC* on the prevention of the use of the financial system for the purpose of money laundering and terrorist financing;

(iii) conducting conflict of interest checks required or made necessary by any enactment;

(iv) the provision of protected information to a public authority within (2) above which has satisfied the requirements of (2)(*a*) and (*b*) above;

(v) the provision of protected information to another credit reference agency which has itself satisfied necessary requirements for permitted disclosure to a credit reference agency; or

(vi) conducting checks for the prevention and detection of crime and fraud.

(e) The credit reference agency has delivered to the Registrar of Companies a statement that it intends to take delivery of and to use the protected information only in the UK or in another EEA State.

(f) The credit reference agency has delivered to the Registrar of Companies a statement that it will, where it supplies a copy of the protected information to a 'processor' for the purpose of processing the information for use in respect of the purposes referred to in (*d*) above

(i) ensure that the processor is one who carries on business in the EEA;

(ii) require that the information is not transmitted outside the EEA by the processor; and

(iii) require that the processor does not disclose the information except to the credit reference agency or an employee of the credit reference agency.

'*Processor*' means any person who provides a service which consists of putting information into data form or processing information in data form, and reference to a processor includes a reference to the processor's employees.

An employee of a person who has access to protected information is deemed to include any person working or providing services for the purposes of that person or employed by or on behalf of, or working for, any person who is so working or who is supplying such a service.

(g) The credit reference agency has delivered to the Registrar of Companies a statement that it meets the conditions in (*a*)–(*c*) above.

The Registrar of Companies may rely on the statement under (*g*) above as sufficient evidence of the matters stated in it. Notwithstanding this, a credit reference agency must deliver to the Registrar such information or evidence in addition to that statement as he may direct to enable him to determine whether to disclose protected information. The Registrar may require such information or evidence to be verified in such manner as he may direct.

The credit reference agency must inform the Registrar of Companies immediately of any change in respect of any statement delivered to him under (*a*)–(*g*) above or information or evidence provided to enable him to determine whether to disclose protected information.

[*SI 2009 No 1801, Reg 24, Sch 2 paras 5–11*].

30.15 *Application to prevent disclosure to a credit reference agency*

An application can be made to the Registrar of Companies to prevent the disclosure to a credit reference agency of protected information relating to a director or permanent representative (an '*application for higher protection*').

The Registrar of Companies must not disclose to a credit reference agency protected information relating to

- an individual in respect of whom a successful application for higher protection has been made;
- an individual in respect of whom an application for higher protection has been made where
  - (i) the Registrar of Companies has not made a determination; or
  - (ii) he has made a determination rejecting the application and an appeal against that determination has been brought but has not been determined; or
- an individual in relation to whom a confidentiality order was in force under *CA 1985, s 735B* immediately before 1 October 2009 and who, by virtue of the transitional provisions below is to be treated as having made a successful application for higher protection.

[*SI 2009 No 1801, Reg 25*].

The application must be made and determined in accordance with the following provisions.

(1) *Application by the individual concerned*

An application for higher protection may be made to the Registrar of Companies by an individual who is, or proposes to become, a director or permanent representative of a company on the grounds that the applicant considers that there is a serious risk that the applicant, or a person who lives with the applicant, will be subjected to violence or intimidation as a result of the activities of at least one of

(i) the overseas companies of which the applicant is, or proposes to become, a director or permanent representative;

(ii) the overseas companies of which the applicant was a director or permanent representative;

(iii) the companies of which the applicant is or has been a director; or

(iv) the limited liability partnerships of which the applicant is or has been a member.

The application must contain

- a statement of the grounds on which the application is made;
- the name and any former name of the applicant;
- the date of birth of the applicant;
- the usual residential address of the applicant;
- where the Registrar of Companies has allocated a unique identifier to the applicant, that unique identifier;
- the name and registered number of each overseas company of which the applicant is, or proposes to become, a director or permanent representative; and
- where the grounds of the application are those described in (ii), (iii) or (iv) above, the name and registered number of the overseas company, company or limited liability partnership.

The application must be accompanied by evidence which supports the applicant's statement of the grounds of the application. The Registrar of Companies may request additional information or evidence and may also refer to a 'relevant body' any question relating to an assessment of the nature and extent of any risk of violence or intimidation.

The Registrar of Companies may accept any answer from a relevant body as sufficient evidence of the matter referred to it.

A '*relevant body*' means any police force and any other person whom the Registrar of Companies considers may be able to assist in answering a question referred to that person by him.

The Registrar of Companies must determine the application and send the applicant notice of his determination to his usual residential address, as stated in his application, within five working days of the determination being made.

(2) *Application by a company*

An application for higher protection may be made to the Registrar of Companies by a company on behalf of its directors or permanent representatives on the grounds that the company considers that there is a serious risk that the director or permanent representative on behalf of whom the application is made, or a person who lives with that director or permanent representative, will be subjected to violence or intimidation as a result of the company's activities.

The application must contain

- a statement of the grounds on which the application is made;
- the name and registered number of the applicant;
- the name and any former name of each director or permanent representative on behalf of whom the application is made;
- the date of birth of each such director or permanent representative;
- the usual residential address of each such director or permanent representative;
- where the Registrar of Companies has allocated a unique identifier to any such director or permanent representative, that unique identifier; and
- the name and registered number of each UK-registered company or overseas company of which each such director or permanent representative is a director.

The application must be accompanied by evidence which supports the applicant's statement of the grounds of the application.

The Registrar of Companies may request additional information or evidence. He may also refer to a 'relevant body' (see (1) above) any question relating to an assessment of the nature and extent of any risk of violence or intimidation and may accept any answer as sufficient evidence of that risk.

The Registrar of Companies must then determine the application and send the applicant (to its registered office or, if it not registered, to the address of its principal place of business in its country of incorporation) and each director or permanent representative concerned (to their usual residential address as stated in the application) notice of his determination within five working days of the determination being made.

The Registrar of Companies must not make available for public inspection any application for higher protection, any documents provided in support of that application, or any representations received in connection with the revocation of a decision (see below).

Appeals. Unsuccessful applicants may, with leave of the court, appeal to the High Court (in Scotland, the Court of Session) on the grounds that the decision is unlawful, irrational or unreasonable, or has been made on the basis of a procedural impropriety or otherwise contravenes the rules of natural justice. Any appeal must be brought within 35 days of the date of the Registrar's notice (or later with the court's permission). The court may dismiss the appeal or quash the decision. In the later case, it may refer the matter to the Registrar of Companies with a direction to reconsider it and make a determination in accordance with the findings of the court.

Duration of favourable decision. Any decision of the Registrar of Companies in favour of the applicant on an application for higher protection continues to have effect until either

- the Registrar is notified by the individual in respect of whom the application was made (or their personal representative) of the wish that the decision should cease to apply; or
- the Registrar of Companies revokes the decision (see below).

Revocation. The Registrar of Companies may revoke a decision in favour of the applicant on an application for higher protection if the individual in respect of whom the application was made, or any other person, is found guilty of an offence under *CA 2006, s 1112* (general false statement offence) committed in purporting to comply with any of the above provisions.

If the Registrar of Companies proposes to make a revocation decision, he must send the individual notice of his intention

- informing the individual that he may, within 28 days of the notice, deliver representations in writing to the Registrar; and
- stating that if representations are not received by the Registrar within that period, the revocation decision will be made at the expiry of that period.

If the beneficiary delivers representations in the time allowed, the Registrar of Companies must consider them and, within five working days of making his decision, send notice of it to the beneficiary.

[*SI 2009 No 1801, Sch 3*].

Transitional provisions – protection of confidentiality orders

(1) A director or permanent representative of an overseas company in relation to whom a confidentiality order under *CA 1985, s 723B* was in force immediately before 1 October 2009 is treated on and after that date as if they had made an application under the above provisions and that application had been determined by the Registrar of Companies in their favour. The provisions of *SI 2009 No 1801, Sch 3* above relating to decisions of the Registrar in favour of an applicant (in particular, as to the duration and revocation of such a decision) apply accordingly. The reference to an offence under *CA 2006, s 1112* (general false statement offence) is to be read for this purpose as a reference to an offence in relation to the application for the confidentiality order.

(2) *CA 1985, s 723B(3)–(8)* (application for confidentiality order) continues to apply in relation to an application for a confidentiality order made before 1 October 2009 and (1) above applies to an individual in respect of whom such an application has been made, and has not been determined or withdrawn, as to an individual in relation to whom a confidentiality order was in force immediately before that date.

If the application is dismissed or withdrawn, (1) above ceases to apply but if the application is successful it continues to apply as in the case of an individual in relation to whom a confidentiality order was in force immediately before 1 October 2009.

[*SI 2009 No 1801, Sch 8 paras 21, 22*].

30.16 Disclosure under a court order

The court may make an order for the disclosure of protected information by the company or by the Registrar of Companies if

- there is evidence that service of documents at a service address other than the director or permanent representative's usual residential address is not effective to bring them to the notice of that individual; or
- it is necessary or expedient for the information to be provided in connection with the enforcement of an order or decree of the court,

and the court is otherwise satisfied that it is appropriate to make the order. The order must specify the persons to whom, and the purposes for which, disclosure is authorised.

An order for disclosure by the Registrar of Companies can only be made if the company

- does not have the director or permanent representative's usual residential address;
- no longer has a UK establishment and has given notice of that fact under **30.57**; or
- has been dissolved.

A court order can be made on the application of a liquidator, creditor or member of the company, or any other person appearing to the court to have a sufficient interest.

[*SI 2009 No 1801, Reg 26*].

30.17 Circumstances in which the Registrar of Companies can put a usual residential address on the public record

The Registrar of Companies can put a director or permanent representative's usual residential address on the public record if

- communications sent by the Registrar on or after 1 October 2009 to that individual and requiring a response within a specified period remain unanswered; or
- evidence comes to the Registrar's attention on or after 1 October 2009 that service of documents at a service address provided in place of their usual residential address is not effective to bring them to the notice of the director or permanent representative.

Before doing so, the Registrar must give notice of the proposed course of action to the director or permanent representative and to the company. The notice must state the grounds for doing so and specify a period within which representations may be made. It must be sent to the director or permanent representative at his usual residential address, unless it appears to the Registrar that service at that address may be ineffective to bring it to their notice, in which case it may be sent to any service address provided in place of that address.

On deciding that a director or permanent representative's usual residential address is to be put on the public record, the Register of Companies must proceed as if a return containing altered particulars had been made stating

- the usual residential address as the director or permanent representative's service address; and
- that their usual residential address is the same as their service address.

The Registrar must give notice of having done so to the director or permanent representative and to the company.

If the company has been notified by the director or permanent representative of a more recent address as their usual residential address, it must notify the Registrar of Companies in accordance with **30.7**(1) above. If a company fails to comply with this requirement, an offence is committed by the company and every officer of the company who is in default. A person guilty of such an offence is liable, on summary conviction, to a fine not exceeding level 5 on the standard scale and, for continued contravention, a daily default fine not exceeding one-tenth of level 5 on the standard scale. See **29.1** OFFENCES AND LEGAL PROCEEDINGS for the standard scale.

A director or permanent representative whose usual residential address has been put on the public record by the Registrar of Companies under the above provisions cannot register a service address other than his usual residential address for a period of five years from the date of the Registrar's decision.

[*SI 2009 No 1801, Regs 27–29, Sch 8 para 20*].

30.18 DELIVERY OF ACCOUNTING DOCUMENTS: GENERAL REQUIREMENTS

The Secretary of State has power to make provision by Regulations requiring an overseas company that is required to register particulars with the Registrar of Companies

- to prepare the like accounts and strategic report and directors' report, and
- cause to be prepared such an auditor's report,

as would be required if the company were formed and registered under *CA 2006*. The overseas company may also be required to deliver to the Registrar of Companies copies of those accounts or the accounts and reports that it is required to prepare and have audited under the law of the country in which it is incorporated.

[*CA 2006, s 1049*; *SI 2013 No 1970, Schedule, para 24*].

30.19 Companies required to prepare and disclose accounts under parent law

The provisions in **30.20** to **30.23** apply to every overseas company that has an establishment in the UK and is not

- a credit or financial institution (as to which, see **30.35** to **30.50**); or
- a company whose constitution does not limit the liability of its members;

and is either

- required by its parent law to prepare, have audited and disclose accounts; or
- incorporated in an EEA State, is required by its parent law to prepare and disclose accounts, but is not required by its parent law to have its accounts audited or deliver its accounts.

Definitions. For these purposes, the following definitions apply.

'*Accounting documents*' in relation to a financial period of a company, mean

(a) the accounts of the company for the period, including if it has one or more subsidiaries, any consolidated accounts of the group;

(b) any annual report of the directors for the period;

(c) any report of the auditors on the accounts within (*a*) above; and

(d) any report of the auditors on the report in (*b*) above

and for this purpose 'subsidiaries' and 'consolidated group accounts' have the meaning given to them by the company's parent law.

'*Disclosure*' means public disclosure.

'*Financial period*' means a period for which the company is required or permitted by its parent law to prepare accounts.

'*Parent law*', in relation to a company, means the law of the country in which the company is incorporated. [*SI 2009 No 1801, Regs 30, 31*].

Transitional provisions.

(i) The provisions in **30.20** to **30.23** apply in relation to accounting documents first disclosed in accordance with the company's parent law on or after 1 October 2009.

(ii) In the case of a company to which *CA 1985, s 699AA* applied before 1 October 2009, (company to which *EC 11th Company Law Directive* applies), the provisions in **30.App(41)** continue to apply in relation to accounting documents first disclosed in accordance with the company's parent law before 1 October 2009.

(iii) In the case of a company to which *CA 1985, s 700* applied before 1 October 2009 (company with place of business but not branch in UK), the provisions in **30.App(23)–(38)** continue to apply in relation to the period between

- the end of the last financial year of the company beginning before 1 October 2009, and
- the beginning of the first financial period of the company in respect of which accounting documents are first disclosed in accordance with the company's parent law on or after that date,

and that period is treated as a financial year of the company (if it would otherwise not be) for the purposes of those provisions.

[*SI 2009 No 1801, Sch 8 para 23*].

30.20 *Duty to file copies of accounting documents disclosed under parent law*

The directors of a company to which these provisions apply must deliver to the Registrar of Companies a copy of all the accounting documents prepared in relation to a financial period of the company that are disclosed in accordance with its parent law. But

(a) where the company's parent law permits it to discharge its obligation in this respect by disclosing documents in a modified form, the directors can similarly discharge their obligation to the Registrar of Companies by delivering a copy of documents modified as permitted by that parent law;

(b) where the company is incorporated in an EEA State

(1) the directors are not required to deliver copies of accounting documents to the Registrar of Companies if the company's parent law does not require it to deliver accounting documents; and

(2) the directors may discharge their obligation under this provision by delivering the accounting documents without an auditor's report if the company's parent law does not require it to have its accounts audited; and

(c) this provision does not apply in relation to copies of accounting documents disclosed under the company's parent law before

(i) the date on which the company first complied with the requirements of initial registration under **30.3** in respect of a UK establishment; or

(ii) if earlier, the last day of the period allowed for delivery of a return under **30.3** in respect of its first UK establishment.

Companies with more than one UK establishment. A company required by the above provisions to deliver copies of accounting documents must deliver them in respect of each UK establishment that it has at the end of the financial period to which the documents relate, except that this does not apply to an establishment if

- a return in respect of that establishment has stated the intention to file copies of accounting documents in respect of another UK establishment (giving the registered number of that establishment); and
- copies of the accounting documents are delivered in respect of that establishment before the end of the period allowed for doing so.

[*SI 2009 No 1801, Reg 32*].

30.21 *Statement of details of parent law and other information*

The accounting documents delivered to the Registrar of Companies under **30.20** must be accompanied by a statement containing the following information.

- The legislation under which the accounts have been prepared and, if applicable, audited.
- Whether those accounts have been prepared in accordance with a set of generally accepted accounting principles and, if so, the name of the organisation or other body which issued those principles.
- Whether the accounts have been audited.
- If they have been audited
  (i) whether they have been audited in accordance with a set of generally accepted auditing standards; and
  (ii) if so, the name of the organisation or other body which issued those standards.
- If they have not been audited, whether the company is not required to have its accounts audited.

[*SI 2009 No 1801, Reg 33*].

30.22 *Period allowed for filing copies of accounting documents*

The period allowed for delivering copies of documents required to be delivered under **30.20** is three months from the date on which the document is required to be disclosed in accordance with the company's parent law. [*SI 2009 No 1801, Reg 34*].

30.23 *Penalty for non-compliance*

If any of the requirements of **30.20** or **30.22** are not complied with in relation to a company's accounting documents before the end of the period allowed for delivering copies of those documents, every person who immediately before the end of that period was a director of the company commits an offence. A person guilty of such an offence is liable, on summary conviction, to a fine not exceeding level 5 on the standard scale and, for continued contravention, a daily default fine not exceeding one-tenth of level 5 on the standard scale. See **29.1 Offences and Legal Proceedings** for the standard scales.

It is a defence for a person charged with such an offence to prove that they took all reasonable steps for securing that those requirements would be complied with before the end of that period.

[*SI 2009 No 1801, Reg 35*].

30.24 Companies not required to prepare and disclose accounts under parent law

The provisions in **30.25** to **30.34** apply to an overseas company that has an establishment in the UK and is not

- a credit or financial institution (as to which, see **30.35 to 30.50**);
- a company whose constitution does not limit the liability of its members; or
- a company which is required to prepare and disclose accounts under parent law (see **30.19** to **30.23**).

[*SI 2009 No 1801, Regs 30, 36*].

Transitional provisions.

(a) The provisions in **30.25** to **30.34** apply in relation to accounting documents for financial years of the company beginning on or after 1 October 2009.

(b) The provisions of

(i) **30.App(44), (45)** (companies to which the *EC 11th Company Law Directive* applies), or

(ii) **30.App(23)–(38)** (companies with place of business but not branch in the UK)

continue to apply in relation to accounting documents for financial years beginning before that date.

[*SI 2009 No 1801, Sch 8 para 24*].

References to provisions of *CA 2006* "as modified" are to those provisions modified for overseas companies by the *Overseas Companies Regulations 2009 (SI 2009 No 1801).*

30.25 *Financial year, accounting reference dates and periods*

(1) *Financial year*

A company's first financial year

- begins with the first day of its first accounting reference period; and
- ends with the last day of that period or such other date, not more than seven days before or after the end of that period, as the directors may determine.

Subsequent financial years

- begin with the day immediately following the end of the company's previous financial year; and

- end with the last day of its next accounting reference period or such other date, not more than seven days before or after the end of that period, as the directors may determine.

[*CA 2006, s 390* (as modified); *SI 2009 No 1801, Reg 37*].

(2) *Accounting reference periods*

A company's accounting reference periods are determined according to its accounting reference date in each calendar year.

A company's first accounting reference period is the period of more than six months, but not more than eighteen months, beginning with the date of its becoming a relevant overseas company and ending with its accounting reference date. Its subsequent accounting reference periods are successive periods of twelve months beginning immediately after the end of the previous accounting reference period and ending with its accounting reference date.

[*CA 2006, s 391* (as modified); *SI 2009 No 1801, Reg 37*].

(3) *Accounting reference date*

Subject to (4) below, the accounting reference date of a company is the last day of the month in which the anniversary of its becoming a relevant overseas company falls.

[*CA 2006, s 391* (as modified); *SI 2009 No 1801, Reg 37*].

(4) *Alteration of accounting reference date*

A company may by notice given to the Registrar of Companies specify a new accounting reference date having effect in relation to either

- its current accounting reference period and subsequent periods; or
- its immediately preceding accounting reference period and subsequent periods. This option is not available if the period for filing accounts for the financial year determined by reference to the immediately preceding accounting reference period has already expired.

The notice must state whether the current or immediately preceding accounting reference period is to be shortened or extended (ie whether it is to end on the first or second occasion on which the new accounting reference date falls or fell after the beginning of the period).

An accounting reference period may not be extended so as to exceed 18 months (and any notice attempting to do this is ineffective) except where the company is in administration under *IA 1986, Pt II* or *Insolvency (Northern Ireland) Order 1989, Pt III*. [*CA 2006, s 392* (as modified); *SI 2009 No 1801, Reg 37*].].

30.26 *Individual accounts: duty to prepare*

Subject to **30.30** (duty to prepare group accounts), the directors of a company must prepare accounts for the company for each of its financial years. Those accounts are referred to as the company's 'individual accounts'.

A company's annual accounts may be prepared in accordance with one of the following.

(a) Its parent law ('*parent law individual accounts*') (but only if the content of those accounts includes that required under (*c*) below). Where the directors of a company prepare parent law individual accounts they must state in the notes

- that the accounts have been prepared in accordance with the company's parent law;
- the legislation under which the accounts have been prepared;
- whether the accounts have been prepared in accordance with a set of generally accepted accounting principles, and if so the name of the organisation or other body which issued those principles;
- whether the accounts have been audited; and
- if they have been audited
  - (i) whether they have been audited in accordance with a set of generally accepted auditing standards; and
  - (ii) if so, the name of the organisation or other body which issued those standards.

(b) International accounting standards ('*IAS individual accounts*'). Where the directors of a company prepare IAS individual accounts they must state in the notes

- that the accounts have been prepared in accordance with international accounting standards;
- whether the accounts have been audited; and
- if they have been audited
  - (i) whether they have been audited in accordance with a set of generally accepted auditing standards; and
  - (ii) if so, the name of the organisation or other body which issued those standards.

(c) *CA 2006, s 396* (as modified) ('*overseas companies individual accounts*'). This requires the individual accounts to

- comprise a balance sheet as at the last day of the financial year and a profit and loss account; and;
- comply with the provisions in **30.27** to **30.29** as to the content of the balance sheet and the profit and loss account and as to additional information to be provided by way of notes to the accounts.

Where the directors of a company prepare overseas companies individual accounts, they must state in the notes

- that the accounts have been prepared in accordance with *CA 2006, s 396*;
- whether the accounts have been prepared in accordance with a set of generally accepted accounting principles, and if so the name of the organisation or other body which issued those principles;
- whether the accounts have been audited; and
- if they have been audited
  - (i) whether they have been audited in accordance with a set of generally accepted auditing standards; and
  - (ii) if so, the name of the organisation or other body which issued those standards.

[*CA 2006, ss 394–397* (as modified); *SI 2009 No 1801, Reg 38*].

Information required to be given in notes to a company's annual accounts may be contained in the accounts or in a separate document annexed to the accounts.

[*CA 2006, s 472* (as modified); *SI 2009 No 1801, Reg 42*].

30.27 *Individual accounts: general rules*

Every balance sheet and profit and loss account must

- show each of the line items required to be included in a balance sheet or profit and loss account in accordance with international accounting standards, and
- clearly indicate in what currency it is prepared

but subject to the following.

(1) The company's directors must use the same line items in preparing overseas companies individual accounts for each financial year, unless in their opinion there are special reasons for a change. Particulars of any such change must be given in a note to the accounts in which the new line item is first used, and the reasons for the change must be explained.

(2) Where the company's directors consider it appropriate, the balance sheet or the profit and loss account may show a combination of line items where they are of a similar nature.

(3) Items that are not of a similar nature or function must be presented separately unless they are not material. For this purpose, an item is 'material' if it either supplements the information given with respect to any particular item shown in the balance sheet and profit and loss account or is otherwise relevant to assessing the company's state of affairs. Amounts which in the particular context of any provision in this paragraph or **30.28** or **30.29** are not material may be disregarded for the purposes of that provision.

(4) Where the nature of the company's business requires it, the company's directors must adapt the line items in the balance sheet or profit and loss account. They may combine items if

(a) their individual amounts are not material to assessing the state of affairs or profit or loss of the company for the financial year in question, or

(b) the combination facilitates that assessment

and where (*b*) above applies, the individual amounts of any items which have been combined must be disclosed in a note to the accounts.

(5) The directors may exclude an item in the balance sheet or profit and loss account if there is no amount to be shown for that item for the financial year to which the balance sheet or the profit and loss account relates. But where an amount can be shown for the item in question for the immediately preceding financial year, that amount must be shown under the line item for that item.

(6) For every item shown in the balance sheet or profit and loss account the corresponding amount for the immediately preceding financial year must also be shown. Where that corresponding amount is not comparable with the figure for the current year, the former amount may be adjusted, in which case particulars of the non-comparability and of any adjustment must be disclosed in a note to the accounts.

(7) Amounts in respect of items representing assets or income may not be set off against amounts in respect of items representing liabilities or expenditure (as the case may be), or *vice versa*.

(8) The company's directors must, in determining how amounts are presented within items in the profit and loss account and balance sheet, have regard to the substance of the reported transaction or arrangement, in accordance with generally accepted accounting principles or practice.

'*Line items*' for the above purposes has the same meaning as in International Accounting Standard 1 on the Presentation of Financial Statements.

[*SI 2009 No 1801, Sch 4 paras 1–9, 20*].

30.28 *Individual accounts: accounting principles and rules*

The amounts to be included in respect of all items shown in a company's accounts must be determined in accordance with the principles set out in (*a*)–(*e*) below. But if it appears to the company's directors that there are special reasons for departing from any of those principles in preparing the company's accounts in respect of any financial year, they may do so, in which case particulars of the departure, the reasons for it and its effect must be given in a note to the accounts.

(a) The company is presumed to be carrying on business as a going concern.

(b) If the accounts are not prepared on a going concern basis, that fact must be disclosed, together with the basis on which the accounts are prepared and the reason why the company is not a going concern.

(c) Accounting policies must be applied consistently within the same accounts and from one financial year to the next.

(d) All income and charges relating to the financial year to which the accounts relate must be taken into account, without regard to the date of receipt or payment.

(e) In determining the aggregate amount of any item, the amount of each individual asset or liability that falls to be taken into account must be determined separately.

[*SI 2009 No 1801, Sch 4 paras 10–14*].

30.29 *Individual accounts: notes to the accounts*

Any information required in the case of any company by the following provisions must (if not given in the company's accounts) be given by way of a note to the accounts.

(1) *Disclosure of accounting policies*

The accounting policies adopted by the company in determining the amounts to be included in respect of items shown in the balance sheet and in determining the profit or loss of the company must be stated (including such policies with respect to the depreciation and diminution in value of assets).

The company must include in the statement of accounting policies

- the measurement basis (or bases) used in preparing the accounts; and
- any other accounting policies used that are relevant to an understanding of the accounts.

(2) *Accounting standards*

It must be stated whether the accounts have been prepared in accordance with the applied accounting standards and particulars of any material departure from those standards and the reasons for it must be given.

(3) *Assessment of the company's state of affairs*

The company must provide information which is relevant to assessing the company's state of affairs. As a minimum that information must relate, where applicable, to

- property, plant and equipment;
- investment property;
- intangible assets;
- financial assets;
- biological assets;
- inventories;
- trade and other receivables (and the amount falling due after more than one year must be shown separately for each item included under receivables);
- trade and other payables (and the amount falling due after more than one year must be shown separately for each item included under payables);
- provisions;
- financial liabilities;
- issued capital and reserves;
- finance costs;
- finance income;
- expenses and interest paid to group undertakings (this must be shown separately from expenses and interest paid to other entities);
- income and interest derived from group undertakings (this must be shown separately from income and interest derived from other sources);
- transactions with related parties;
- dividends;
- items described as other, sundry, miscellaneous or equivalent;
- guarantees;
- contingent liabilities;
- commitments;
- other off-balance sheet arrangements; and
- financial instruments.

[*SI 2009 No 1801, Sch 1 paras 15–19*].

Information required to be given in notes to a company's annual accounts may be contained in the accounts or in a separate document annexed to the accounts.

[*CA 2006, s 472* (as modified); *SI 2009 No 1801, Reg 42*].

30.30 *Group accounts: duty to prepare*

If at the end of a financial year a company is a parent company (see **Appendix 1 Definitions**) the directors must, instead of preparing individual accounts for the year, prepare group accounts for the year. But a parent company is exempt from the requirement to prepare group accounts where

- it has prepared parent law individual accounts under **30.26**(*a*) and that parent law does not require consolidated accounts;
- it has prepared IAS individual accounts under **30.26**(*b*) and in accordance with the international accounting standards it is not required to prepare consolidated accounts; or
- it has prepared overseas companies individual accounts under **30.26**(*c*) and all of the company's subsidiary undertakings satisfy the requirement in **30.31**.

[*CA 2006, ss 399, 402* (as modified); *SI 2009 No 1801, Reg 38*].

Where a company, being a parent company, is required under the above provisions to prepare group accounts, and that company is itself the subsidiary of another company ('the holding company'), the group accounts of the holding company are deemed to satisfy the requirements of those provisions to prepare group accounts.

[*CA 2006, s 402A* (as modified); *SI 2009 No 1801, Reg 38*.

The group accounts may be prepared in accordance with one of the following.

(a) Its parent law ('*parent law group accounts*') but only if the content of those accounts includes that required under (*c*) below. Where the directors of a company prepare parent law group accounts they must state in the notes

- that the accounts have been prepared in accordance with the company's parent law;
- the name of the legislation under which the accounts have been prepared;
- whether the accounts have been prepared in accordance with a set of generally accepted accounting principles, and if so the name of the organisation or other body which issued those principles;
- whether the accounts have been audited; and
- if they have been audited
  - (i) whether they have been audited in accordance with a set of generally accepted auditing standards; and
  - (ii) if so, the name of the organisation or other body which issued those standards.

(b) International accounting standards ('*IAS group accounts*'). Where the directors of a company prepare IAS group accounts they must state in the notes

- that the accounts have been prepared in accordance with international accounting standards;

- whether the accounts have been audited; and
- if they have been audited

  (i) whether they have been audited in accordance with a set of generally accepted auditing standards; and

  (ii) if so the name of the organisation or other body which issued those standards.

(c) *CA 2006, s 404* as modified for overseas companies ('*overseas companies group accounts*'). This requires the individual accounts to

(i) comprise a consolidated balance sheet dealing with the state of affairs of the parent company and its subsidiary undertakings and a consolidated profit and loss account dealing with the profit or loss of the parent company and its subsidiary undertakings; and

(ii) comply with the provisions in **30.32** as to the content of the consolidated balance sheet and consolidated profit and loss account and additional information to be provided by way of notes to the accounts.

Where the directors of a company prepare overseas company group accounts, they must state in the notes

- that the accounts have been prepared in accordance with *CA 2006, s 404*;
- whether the accounts have been prepared in accordance with a set of generally accepted accounting principles, and if so the name of the organisation or other body which issued those principles;
- whether the accounts have been audited; and
- if they have been audited

  (i) whether they have been audited in accordance with a set of generally accepted auditing standards; and

  (ii) if so, the name of the organisation or other body which issued those standards.

[*CA 2006, ss 403, 404, 406* (as modified); *SI 2009 No 1801, Reg 38*].

Information required to be given in notes to a company's annual accounts may be contained in the accounts or in a separate document annexed to the accounts.

[*CA 2006, s 472* (as modified); *SI 2009 No 1801, Reg 42*].

30.31 *Group accounts: exclusion of subsidiary undertakings from consolidation*

Where a parent company prepares overseas companies group accounts, all the subsidiary undertakings of the company must normally be included in the consolidation, subject to the following exceptions.

(a) A subsidiary undertaking may be excluded from the consolidation if its inclusion is not material. Two or more undertakings may be excluded only if they are not material taken together.

(b) A subsidiary undertaking may be excluded from consolidation where

(i) severe long-term restrictions substantially hinder the exercise of the rights of the parent company over the assets or management of that undertaking;

(ii) the information necessary for the preparation of group accounts cannot be obtained without disproportionate expense or undue delay; or

(iii) the interest of the parent company is held exclusively with a view to subsequent resale.

The references in (i) and (iii) above to, respectively, the rights and the interest of the parent company are references to the right and interests held by or attributed to the company for the purposes of the definition of 'parent undertaking' (see **Appendix 1 Definitions**) in the absence of which it would not be the parent company.

[*CA 2006, s 405* (as modified); *SI 2009 No 1801, Reg 38*].

30.32 *Group accounts: form and content*

(1) *General rules*

- Overseas companies group accounts must comply so far as practicable with the provisions of **30.27** to **30.29** as if the undertakings included in the consolidation (*'the group'*) were a single company and, in the case of overseas companies group accounts, the minimum information listed **30.29**(3) must also relate to

  (i) investments accounted for using the equity method; and

  (ii) minority interest, presented within equity.

- The consolidated balance sheet and profit and loss account must incorporate, in full, the information contained in the individual accounts of the undertakings included in the consolidation, subject to the adjustments authorised or required by the following provisions of this paragraph and to such other adjustments (if any) as may be appropriate in accordance with generally accepted accounting principles or practice.

- Where assets and liabilities to be included in the group accounts have been valued or otherwise determined by undertakings according to accounting rules differing from those used for the group accounts, the values or amounts must be adjusted so as to accord with the rules used for the group accounts. But

  (i) if it appears to the directors of the parent company that there are special reasons for departing from this requirement, they may do so, in which case particulars of any such departure, the reasons for it and its effect must be given in a note to the accounts; and

  (ii) adjustments need not be made if they are not material.

- Amounts that in the particular context of any provision in this paragraph are not material may be disregarded for the purposes of that provision.

(2) *Elimination of group transactions*

- Unless the amounts concerned are not material, debts and claims between undertakings included in the consolidation, and income and expenditure relating to transactions between such undertakings, must be eliminated in preparing the group accounts.

- Unless the amounts concerned are not material, where profits and losses resulting from transactions between undertakings included in the consolidation are included in the book value of assets, they must be eliminated in preparing the group accounts. This may be effected in proportion to the group's interest in the shares of the undertakings.

- Where an undertaking becomes a subsidiary undertaking of the parent company, that acquisition must be accounted for by the acquisition method of accounting. If the generally accepted accounting principles under which the accounts have been prepared allow it to be accounted for by another method, that method may be used, but, if so, the method used must be disclosed in the notes to the accounts.

(3) *Minority interests*

- In the balance sheet there must be shown, as a separate item and under an appropriate line item, the amount of capital and reserves attributable to shares in subsidiary undertakings included in the consolidation held by or on behalf of persons other than the parent company and its subsidiary undertakings.
- In the profit and loss account formats there must be shown, as a separate item and under an appropriate line item

  (i) the amount of any profit or loss on ordinary activities; and

  (ii) the amount of any profit or loss on extraordinary activities,

  attributable to shares in subsidiary undertakings included in the consolidation held by or on behalf of persons other than the parent company and its subsidiary undertakings.

(4) *Joint ventures*

Where an undertaking included in the consolidation manages another undertaking jointly with one or more undertakings not included in the consolidation, that other undertaking ('the joint venture') may, if it is not

- a body corporate, or
- a subsidiary undertaking of the parent company,

be dealt with in the group accounts by the method of proportional consolidation. The provisions of this paragraph relating to the preparation of consolidated accounts apply, with any necessary modifications, to the proportional consolidation.

(5) *Associated undertakings*

An '*associated undertaking*' means an undertaking in which an undertaking included in the consolidation has a participating interest and over whose operating and financial policy it exercises a significant influence, and which is not

- a subsidiary undertaking of the parent company; or
- a joint venture dealt with in accordance with (4) above.

The interest of an undertaking in an associated undertaking, and the amount of profit or loss attributable to such an interest, must be shown by the equity method of accounting. If the generally accepted accounting principles under which the accounts have been prepared allow it to be accounted for by another method, that method may be used, but, if so, the method used must be disclosed in the notes to the accounts.

Where the associated undertaking is itself a parent undertaking, the net assets and profits or losses to be taken into account are those of the parent and its subsidiary undertakings (after making any consolidation adjustments).

[*SI 2009 No 1801, Sch 5*].

Information required to be given in notes to a company's annual accounts may be contained in the accounts or in a separate document annexed to the accounts.

[*CA 2006, s 472* (as modified); *SI 2009 No 1801, Reg 42*].

30.33 *Approval and signing of accounts*

A company's annual accounts must be approved by the board of directors and signed on behalf of the board by a director of the company. The signature must be on the company's balance sheet.

If annual accounts are approved that do not comply with the requirements of *CA 2006, Pt 15* as applied to an overseas company (with modifications) under **30.18** to **30.26**, every director of the company who

- knew that they did not comply, or was reckless as to whether they complied, and
- failed to take reasonable steps to secure compliance with those requirements or, as the case may be, to prevent the accounts from being approved,

commits an offence. A person guilty of such an offence is liable (i) on conviction on indictment, to a fine; and (ii) on summary conviction, to a fine not exceeding the statutory maximum. See **29.1 Offences and Legal Proceedings** for the statutory maximum.

[*CA 2006, s 414* (as modified); *SI 2009 No 1801, Reg 39*].

30.34 *Duty to file accounts and period allowed for filing*

(1) *Duty to file accounts with the Registrar of Companies*

The directors of a company must deliver to the Registrar of Companies for each financial year a copy of the company's annual accounts and such other reports as it is required to prepare. The copy of the balance sheet must state the name of the person who signed it on behalf of the board.

Accounts must be delivered in respect of each UK establishment that a company has at the end of the financial year, except that delivery of accounts is not required in respect of an establishment if

- a return under the *SI 2009 No 1801* in respect of that establishment has stated the intention to file accounts in respect of another UK establishment (giving the registered number of that establishment); and
- accounts are delivered in respect of that establishment before the end of the period allowed for doing so.

[*CA 2006, s 441* (as modified); *SI 2009 No 1801, Reg 40*].

(2) *Period allowed for filing accounts*

Subject to below, the period allowed for directors of a company to comply with their obligation under (1) above is 13 months after the end of the relevant accounting reference period.

The '*relevant accounting reference period*' is the accounting reference period by reference to which the financial year for the accounts in question was determined (see **30.25**).

Exceptions.

(a) If the relevant accounting reference period is the company's first and is a period of more than 12 months, the period allowed is 13 months from the first anniversary of the company becoming a relevant overseas company.

(b) If the relevant accounting reference period is treated as shortened by virtue of a notice given under **30.25**(4), the period is

(i) that applicable in accordance with the above provisions; or

(ii) three months from the date of the notice;

whichever expires last.

If for any special reason the Secretary of State thinks fit, he may, on an application made before the expiry of the period otherwise allowed, give notice in writing to a company extending that period by such further period as may be specified in the notice.

[*CA 2006, s 442* (as modified); *SI 2009 No 1801, Reg 40*].

Offences for default in filing accounts

If the requirements of (1) above are not complied with in relation to a company's accounts for a financial year before the end of the period for filing those accounts, every person who immediately before the end of that period was a director of the company commits an offence. A person guilty of such an offence is liable, on summary conviction, to a fine not exceeding level 5 on the standard scale and, for continued contravention, a daily default fine not exceeding one-tenth of the greater of £5,000 or level 4 on the standard scale. See **29.1 Offences and Legal Proceedings** for the standard scale.

It is a defence for a person charged with such an offence to prove that he took all reasonable steps for securing that those requirements would be complied with before the end of that period. It is not a defence to prove that the documents in question were not in fact prepared as required.

[*CA 2006, s 451* (as modified); *SI 2009 No 1801, Reg 41; SI 2015 No 664, Sch 3*].

30.35 DELIVERY OF ACCOUNTING DOCUMENTS: CREDIT OR FINANCIAL INSTITUTIONS

The Secretary of State has power to make provision by Regulations requiring a credit or financial institution

- that is incorporated or otherwise formed outside the UK and Gibraltar;
- whose head office is outside the UK and Gibraltar; and
- that has a 'branch' in the UK

to prepare the like accounts and *strategic report* and directors' report, and cause to be prepared such an auditor's report, as would be required if the institution were a company formed and registered under *CA 2006*. The overseas company may also be required to deliver to the Registrar of Companies copies of those accounts or the accounts and reports that it is required to prepare and have audited under the law of the country in which it has its head office.

'*Branch*' means a place of business that forms a legally dependent part of the institution and conducts directly all or some of the operations inherent in its business.

[*CA 2006, s 1050*; the *2013 Regulations, Schedule, para 25*].

30.36 Institutions required to prepare accounts under parent law

The provisions in **30.37** to **30.39** apply to a credit or financial institution within **30.35** that

- is required by its parent law to prepare and have audited accounts; or
- is incorporated in an EEA State, is required by its parent law to prepare and disclose accounts, but is not required by its parent law to have its accounts audited or deliver its accounts.

Definitions. For these purposes, the following definitions apply.

'*Accounting documents*' in relation to a financial period of an institution are

(a) the accounts of the institution for the period, including, if it has one or more subsidiaries, any consolidated accounts of its group,

(b) any annual report of the directors for the period,

(c) any report of the auditors on the accounts mentioned in (*a*) above,

(d) any report of the auditors on the report mentioned in (*b*) above,

and for this purpose 'subsidiaries' and 'consolidated group accounts' have the meaning given to them by the institution's parent law.

'*Director*', in the case of an institution which does not have directors, means persons occupying equivalent offices.

'*Disclosure*' means public disclosure, except where an institution is not required under its parent law, any enactment having effect for the UK or its constitution to publicly disclose its accounts, in which case it means disclosure of the accounts to the persons for whose information they have been prepared.

'*Financial period*' means a period for which the institution is required or permitted by its parent law to prepare accounts.

'*Parent law*' means the law of the country in which the institution has its head office.

[*SI 2009 No 1801, Regs 43, 44*].

30.37 *Duty to file copies of accounting documents*

Initial filing of copies of accounting documents. Subject to below, a credit or financial institution must within one month of becoming an institution to which these provisions apply deliver to the Registrar of Companies copies of the latest accounting documents of the institution prepared in accordance with its parent law to have been disclosed before the end of the period allowed for compliance with this provision, or, if earlier, the date of compliance with it.

[*SI 2009 No 1801, Reg 45*].

An institution that immediately before 1 October 2009

(i) has a branch in the UK, and

(ii) has complied with the requirements *CA 1985, Sch 21C para 2* (see **30.App(49)**),

is treated as having complied with the requirements of *Reg 45*.

[*SI 2009 No 1801, Sch 8 para 25*].

Filing of copies of subsequent accounting documents. Subject to below, a credit or financial institution must deliver to the Registrar of Companies copies of all the accounting documents of the institution prepared in accordance with its parent law that are disclosed

- on or after 1 October 2009; and
- on or after the end of the period allowed for compliance with *Reg 45* above, or, if earlier, the date on which it complies with that provision.

The period allowed for delivery is three months from the date on which the document is required to be disclosed in accordance with the institution's parent law.

Transitional provisions. CA 1985, Sch 21C para 3 (see **30.App(49)**) continues to apply in relation to accounting documents first disclosed in accordance with the company's parent law before 1 October 2009.

[*SI 2009 No 1801, Reg 46, Sch 8 para 25*].

Exceptions.

(1) Where an institution is incorporated or otherwise formed in an EEA State

- it is not required to deliver copies of accounting documents if its parent law does not require it to deliver accounting documents;
- it may discharge its obligation by delivering accounting documents without an auditor's report if its parent law does not require it to have its accounts audited; and
- if the institution's parent law permits it to discharge an obligation with respect to the disclosure of accounting documents by disclosing documents in a modified form, it may discharge its obligation by delivering copies of documents modified as permitted by that law.

(2) An institution is not required to deliver documents to the Registrar of Companies if, at the end of the period allowed for compliance,

(i) it is not required by its parent law to register them;

(ii) they are made available for inspection at each branch of the institution in the UK; and

(iii) copies of them are available on request at a cost not exceeding the cost of supplying them.

Where by virtue of this provision an institution is not required to deliver documents under *Reg 45* or *Reg 46* above and any of the conditions specified in (i)–(iii) above ceases to be met, the institution must deliver the documents to the Registrar of Companies for registration within seven days of the condition ceasing to be met.

[*SI 2009 No 1801, Regs 48, 49*].

30.38 *Statement of details of parent law and other information*

The copies of accounting documents delivered to the Registrar of Companies under **30.37** must be accompanied by a statement containing the following information.

- The legislation under which the accounts have been prepared and, if applicable, audited.
- Whether those accounts have been prepared in accordance with a set of generally accepted accounting principles, and if so the name of the organisation or other body which issued those principles.
- Whether the accounts have been audited.

- If they have been audited
  - (i) whether they have been audited in accordance with a set of generally accepted auditing standards; and
  - (ii) if so, the name of the organisation or other body which issued those standards.
- If they have not been audited, whether the institution is not required to have its accounts audited.

[*SI 2009 No 1801, Reg 47*].

30.39 *Penalty for non-compliance*

If any of the requirements of **30.37** or **30.38** are not complied with before the end of the period allowed for delivery of copies of accounting documents, an offence is committed by every person who immediately before the end of that period was a director of the institution. A person guilty of such an offence is liable, on summary conviction, to a fine not exceeding level 5 on the standard scale and, for continued contravention, a daily default fine not exceeding one-tenth of level 5 on the standard scale. See **29.1 Offences and Legal Proceedings** for the standard scale.

It is a defence for a person charged with such an offence to prove that he took all reasonable steps for securing that those requirements would be complied with before the end of that period.

[*SI 2009 No 1801, Reg 50*].

30.40 Institutions not required to prepare accounts under parent law

In relation to accounting documents for financial years of an institution beginning on or after 1 October 2009, the provisions in **30.41** to **30.50** apply to a credit or financial institution within **30.35** that is not an institution to which **30.36** to **30.39** applies.

In relation to accounting documents for financial years beginning before 1 October 2009, the provisions of *CA 1985, Sch 21C paras 9–15* (see **30.App(51)**) continue to apply.

[*SI 2009 No 1801, Reg 51, Sch 8 para 26*].

30.41 *Financial year, accounting reference dates and periods*

(1) *Financial year*

An institution's first financial year

- begins with the first day of its first accounting reference period; and
- ends with the last day of that period or such other date, not more than seven days before or after the end of that period, as the directors may determine.

Subsequent financial years

- begin with the day immediately following the end of the institution's previous financial year; and
- end with the last day of its next accounting reference period or such other date, not more than seven days before or after the end of that period, as the directors may determine.

[*CA 2006, s 390* (as modified); *SI 2009 No 1801, Reg 52*].

(2) *Accounting reference periods*

An institution's accounting reference periods are determined according to its accounting reference date in each calendar year.

An institution's first accounting reference period is the period of more than six months, but not more than eighteen months, beginning with the date of its becoming a relevant overseas institution and ending with its accounting reference date. Its subsequent accounting reference periods are successive periods of twelve months beginning immediately after the end of the previous accounting reference period and ending with its accounting reference date.

[*CA 2006, s 391* (as modified); *SI 2009 No 1801, Reg 52*].

(3) *Accounting reference date*

Subject to (4) below, the accounting reference date of an institution is the last day of the month in which the anniversary of its becoming a relevant overseas institution falls.

[*CA 2006, s 391* (as modified); *SI 2009 No 1801, Reg 52*].

(4) *Alteration of accounting reference date*

An institution may by notice given to the Registrar of Companies specify a new accounting reference date having effect in relation to either

- its current accounting reference period and subsequent periods; or
- its immediately preceding accounting reference period and subsequent periods. This option is not available if the period for filing accounts for the financial year determined by reference to the immediately preceding accounting reference period has already expired.

The notice must state whether the current or immediately preceding accounting reference period is to be shortened or extended (ie whether it is to end on the first or second occasion on which the new accounting reference date falls or fell after the beginning of the period).

An accounting reference period may not be extended so as to exceed 18 months (and any notice attempting to do this is ineffective) except where the institution is in administration under *IA 1986, Pt II* or *Insolvency (Northern Ireland) Order 1989, Pt III*.

[*CA 2006, s 392* (as modified); *SI 2009 No 1801, Reg 52*].

30.42 *Individual accounts: duty to prepare*

Subject to **30.46** (duty to prepare group accounts), the directors of an institution must prepare accounts for the institution for each of its financial years. Those accounts are referred to as the institution's 'individual accounts'.

An institution's annual accounts may be prepared in accordance with one of the following.

(a) Its parent law ('*parent law individual accounts*') (but only if the content of those accounts includes that required under (*c*) below). Where the directors of an institution prepare parent law individual accounts they must state in the notes

- that the accounts have been prepared in accordance with the institution's parent law;

- the name of the legislation under which the accounts have been prepared;
- whether the accounts have been prepared in accordance with a set of generally accepted accounting principles; and if so the name of the organisation or other body which issued those principles;
- whether the accounts have been audited; and
- if they have been audited
  - (i) whether they have been audited in accordance with a set of generally accepted auditing standards; and
  - (ii) if so, the name of the organisation or other body which issued those standards.

(b) International accounting standards (*'IAS individual accounts'*). Where the directors of an institution prepare IAS individual accounts they must state in the notes

- that the accounts have been prepared in accordance with international accounting standards;
- whether the accounts have been audited; and
- if they have been audited
  - (i) whether they have been audited in accordance with a set of generally accepted auditing standards; and
  - (ii) if so, the name of the organisation or other body which issued those standards.

(c) *CA 2006, s 396* as modified for overseas institutions (*'overseas institutions individual accounts'*). This requires the individual accounts to

- comprise a balance sheet as at the last day of the financial year and a profit and loss account; and;
- comply with the provisions in **30.43** to **30.45** as to the content of the balance sheet and the profit and loss account and as to additional information to be provided by way of notes to the accounts.

Where the directors of an institution prepare overseas institutions individual accounts, they must state in the notes

- that the accounts have been prepared in accordance with *CA 2006, s 396*;
- whether the accounts have been prepared in accordance with a set of generally accepted accounting principles, and if so the name of the organisation or other body which issued those principles;
- whether the accounts have been audited; and
- if they have been audited
  - (i) whether they have been audited in accordance with a set of generally accepted auditing standards; and
  - (ii) if so, the name of the organisation or other body which issued those standards.

[*CA 2006, ss 394–397* (as modified); *SI 2009 No 1801, Reg 53*.

Information required to be given in notes to an institution's annual accounts may be contained in the accounts or in a separate document annexed to the accounts.

[*CA 2006, s 472* (as modified); *SI 2009 No 1801, Reg 57*].

30.43 *Individual accounts: general rules*

Every balance sheet and profit and loss account must

- show each of the line items required to be included in a balance sheet or profit and loss account in accordance with international accounting standards, and
- clearly indicate in what currency it is prepared

but subject to the following.

(1) The institution's directors must use the same line items in preparing overseas institutions accounts for each financial year, unless in their opinion there are special reasons for a change. Particulars of any such change must be given in a note to the accounts in which the new line item is first used, and the reasons for the change must be explained.

(2) Where the institution's directors consider it appropriate, the balance sheet or the profit and loss account may show a combination of line items where they are of a similar nature.

(3) Items that are not of a similar nature or function must be presented separately unless they are not material. For this purpose, an item is '*material*' if it either supplements the information given with respect to any particular item shown in the balance sheet and profit and loss account or is otherwise relevant to assessing the institution's state of affairs. Amounts which in the particular context of any provision in this paragraph or **30.44** or **30.45** are not material may be disregarded for the purposes of that provision.

(4) Where the nature of the institution's business requires it, the directors must adapt the line items in the balance sheet or profit and loss account. They may combine items if

(a) their individual amounts are not material to assessing the state of affairs or profit or loss of the institution for the financial year in question, or

(b) the combination facilitates that assessment

and where (*b*) above applies, the individual amounts of any items which have been combined must be disclosed in a note to the accounts.

(5) The directors may exclude an item in the balance sheet or profit and loss account if there is no amount to be shown for that item for the financial year to which the balance sheet or the profit and loss account relates. But where an amount can be shown for the item in question for the immediately preceding financial year, that amount must be shown under the line item for that item.

(6) For every item shown in the balance sheet or profit and loss account the corresponding amount for the immediately preceding financial year must also be shown. Where that corresponding amount is not comparable with the figure for the current year, the former amount may be adjusted, in which case particulars of the non-comparability and of any adjustment must be disclosed in a note to the accounts.

(7) Amounts in respect of items representing assets or income may not be set off against amounts in respect of items representing liabilities or expenditure (as the case may be), or *vice versa*.

(8) The institution's directors must, in determining how amounts are presented within items in the profit and loss account and balance sheet, have regard to the substance of the reported transaction or arrangement, in accordance with generally accepted accounting principles or practice.

'*Line items*' for the above purposes has the same meaning as in International Accounting Standard 1 on the Presentation of Financial Statements.
[*SI 2009 No 1801, Sch 6 paras 1–9, 20*].

30.44 *Individual accounts: accounting principles and rules*

The amounts to be included in respect of all items shown in a institution's accounts must be determined in accordance with the principles set out in *(a)*–*(e)* below. But if it appears to the directors that there are special reasons for departing from any of those principles in preparing the accounts in respect of any financial year, they may do so, in which case particulars of the departure, the reasons for it and its effect must be given in a note to the accounts.

(a) The institution is presumed to be carrying on business as a going concern.

(b) If the accounts are not prepared on a going concern basis, that fact must be disclosed, together with the basis on which the accounts are prepared and the reason why the institution is not a going concern.

(c) Accounting policies must be applied consistently within the same accounts and from one financial year to the next.

(d) All income and charges relating to the financial year to which the accounts relate must be taken into account, without regard to the date of receipt or payment.

(e) In determining the aggregate amount of any item, the amount of each individual asset or liability that falls to be taken into account must be determined separately.

[*SI 2009 No 1801, Sch 6 paras 10–14*].

30.45 *Individual accounts: notes to the accounts*

Any information required in the case of any institution by the following provisions must (if not given in the accounts) be given by way of a note to the accounts.

(1) *Disclosure of accounting policies*

The accounting policies adopted by the institution in determining the amounts to be included in respect of items shown in the balance sheet and in determining the profit or loss of the institution must be stated (including such policies with respect to the depreciation and diminution in value of assets).

The institution must include in the statement of accounting policies

- the measurement basis (or bases) used in preparing the accounts; and
- any other accounting policies used that are relevant to an understanding of the accounts.

(2) *Accounting standards*

It must be stated whether the accounts have been prepared in accordance with the applied accounting standards and particulars of any material departure from those standards and the reasons for it must be given.

(3) *Assessment of the institution's state of affairs*

The institution must provide information which is relevant to assessing the institution's state of affairs. As a minimum that information must relate, where applicable, to

- property, plant and equipment;
- investment property;
- intangible assets;
- financial assets;
- biological assets;
- inventories;
- trade and other receivables (and the amount falling due after more than one year must be shown separately for each item included under receivables);
- trade and other payables (and the amount falling due after more than one year must be shown separately for each item included under payables);
- provisions;
- financial liabilities;
- issued capital and reserves;
- finance costs;
- finance income;
- expenses and interest paid to group undertakings (this must be shown separately from expenses and interest paid to other entities);
- income and interest derived from group undertakings (this must be shown separately from income and interest derived from other sources);
- transactions with related parties;
- dividends;
- items described as other, sundry, miscellaneous or equivalent;
- guarantees;
- contingent liabilities;
- commitments;
- other off-balance sheet arrangements; and
- financial instruments.

[*SI 2009 No 1801, Sch 6 paras 15–19*].

Information required to be given in notes to an institution's annual accounts may be contained in the accounts or in a separate document annexed to the accounts.

[*CA 2006, s 472* (as modified); *SI 2009 No 1801, Reg 57*].

30.46 *Group accounts: duty to prepare*

If at the end of a financial year an institution is a parent institution (see APPENDIX 1 DEFINITIONS) the directors must, instead of preparing individual accounts for the year, prepare group accounts for the year. But a parent institution is exempt from the requirement to prepare group accounts where

- it has prepared parent law individual accounts under **30.42**(*a*) and that parent law does not require consolidated accounts;
- it has prepared IAS individual accounts under **30.42**(*b*) and in accordance with the international accounting standards it is not required to prepare consolidated accounts; or
- it has prepared overseas institutions individual accounts under **30.42**(*c*) and all of the institution's subsidiary undertakings satisfy the requirement in **30.47**.

[*CA 2006, ss 399, 402* (as modified); *SI 2009 No 1801, Reg 53*].

Where an institution, being a parent institution, is required under the above provisions to prepare group accounts, and that institution is itself the subsidiary of another institution ('the holding institution'), the group accounts of the holding institution may be deemed to satisfy the requirements of those provisions to prepare group accounts.

[*CA 2006, s 402A* (as modified); *SI 2009 No 1801, Reg 53*].

The group accounts may be prepared in accordance with one of the following.

(a) Its parent law ('*parent law group accounts*') but only if the content of those accounts includes that required under (*c*) below. Where the directors of an institution prepare parent law group accounts they must state in the notes

  - that the accounts have been prepared in accordance with the institution's parent law;
  - the name of the legislation under which the accounts have been prepared;
  - whether the accounts have been prepared in accordance with a set of generally accepted accounting principles, and if so the name of the organisation or other body which issued those principles;
  - whether the accounts have been audited; and
  - if they have been audited

    (i) whether they have been audited in accordance with a set of generally accepted auditing standards; and

    (ii) if so, the name of the organisation or other body which issued those standards.

(b) International accounting standards ('*IAS group accounts*'). Where the directors of an institution prepare IAS group accounts they must state in the notes

  - that the accounts have been prepared in accordance with international accounting standards;
  - whether the accounts have been audited; and
  - if they have been audited

    (i) whether they have been audited in accordance with a set of generally accepted auditing standards; and

(ii) if so the name of the organisation or other body which issued those standards.

(c) *CA 2006, s 404* as modified for overseas institutions (‘*overseas institutions group accounts*’). This requires the individual accounts to

(i) comprise a consolidated balance sheet dealing with the state of affairs of the parent institution and its subsidiary undertakings and a consolidated profit and loss account dealing with the profit or loss of the parent institution and its subsidiary undertakings; and

(ii) comply with the provisions in **30.48** as to the content of the consolidated balance sheet and consolidated profit and loss account and additional information to be provided by way of notes to the accounts.

Where the directors of an institution prepare accounts in accordance with *CA 2006, s 404*, they must state in the notes

- that the accounts have been prepared in accordance with *CA 2006, s 404*;
- whether the accounts have been prepared in accordance with a set of generally accepted accounting principles, and if so the name of the organisation or other body which issued those principles;
- whether the accounts have been audited; and
- if they have been audited

(i) whether they have been audited in accordance with a set of generally accepted auditing standards; and

(ii) if so, the name of the organisation or other body which issued those standards.

[*CA 2006, ss 403, 404, 406* (as modified); *SI 2009 No 1801, Reg 53*].

Information required to be given in notes to an institution's annual accounts may be contained in the accounts or in a separate document annexed to the accounts.

[*CA 2006, s 472* (as modified); *SI 2009 No 1801, Reg 57*].

30.47 *Group accounts: exclusion of subsidiary undertakings from consolidation*

Where a parent institution prepares overseas institutions group accounts, all the subsidiary undertakings of the institution must normally be included in the consolidation, subject to the following exceptions.

(a) A subsidiary undertaking may be excluded from the consolidation if its inclusion is not material. Two or more undertakings may be excluded only if they are not material taken together.

(b) A subsidiary undertaking may be excluded from consolidation where

(i) severe long-term restrictions substantially hinder the exercise of the rights of the parent institution over the assets or management of that undertaking;

(ii) the information necessary for the preparation of group accounts cannot be obtained without disproportionate expense or undue delay; or

(iii) the interest of the parent institution is held exclusively with a view to subsequent resale.

The references in (i) and (iii) above to, respectively, the rights and the interest of the parent institution are references to the right and interests held by or attributed to the institution for the purposes of the definition of 'parent undertaking' (see APPENDIX 1 DEFINITIONS) in the absence of which it would not be the parent institution.

[*CA 2006, s 405* (as modified); *SI 2009 No 1801, Reg 53*].

30.48 *Group accounts: form and content*

(1) *General rules*

- Overseas institutions group accounts must comply so far as practicable with the provisions of **30.43** to **30.45** as if the undertakings included in the consolidation ('*the group*') were a single institution and, in the case of group accounts, the minimum information listed **30.45**(3) must also relate to

  (i) investments accounted for using the equity method; and

  (ii) minority interest, presented within equity.

- The consolidated balance sheet and profit and loss account must incorporate, in full, the information contained in the individual accounts of the undertakings included in the consolidation, subject to the adjustments authorised or required by the following provisions of this paragraph and to such other adjustments (if any) as may be appropriate in accordance with generally accepted accounting principles or practice.

- Where assets and liabilities to be included in the group accounts have been valued or otherwise determined by undertakings according to accounting rules differing from those used for the group accounts, the values or amounts must be adjusted so as to accord with the rules used for the group accounts. But

  (i) if it appears to the directors of the parent institution that there are special reasons for departing from this requirement, they may do so, in which case particulars of any such departure, the reasons for it and its effect must be given in a note to the accounts; and

  (ii) adjustments need not be made if they are not material.

- Amounts that in the particular context of any provision of this paragraph are not material may be disregarded for the purposes of that provision.

(2) *Elimination of group transactions*

- Unless the amounts concerned are not material, debts and claims between undertakings included in the consolidation, and income and expenditure relating to transactions between such undertakings, must be eliminated in preparing the group accounts.

- Unless the amounts concerned are not material, where profits and losses resulting from transactions between undertakings included in the consolidation are included in the book value of assets, they must be eliminated in preparing the group accounts. This may be effected in proportion to the group's interest in the shares of the undertakings.

- Where an undertaking becomes a subsidiary undertaking of the parent institution, that acquisition must be accounted for by the acquisition method of accounting. If the generally accepted accounting principles under which the accounts have been prepared allow it to be accounted for by another method, that method may be used, but, if so, the method used must be disclosed in the notes to the accounts.

(3) *Minority interests*

- In the balance sheet there must be shown, as a separate item and under an appropriate line item, the amount of capital and reserves attributable to shares in subsidiary undertakings included in the consolidation held by or on behalf of persons other than the parent institution and its subsidiary undertakings.
- In the profit and loss account formats there must be shown, as a separate item and under an appropriate line item

  (i) the amount of any profit or loss on ordinary activities, and

  (ii) the amount of any profit or loss on extraordinary activities,

  attributable to shares in subsidiary undertakings included in the consolidation held by or on behalf of persons other than the parent institution and its subsidiary undertakings.

(4) *Joint ventures*

Where an undertaking included in the consolidation manages another undertaking jointly with one or more undertakings not included in the consolidation, that other undertaking ('the joint venture') may, if it is not

- a body corporate, or
- a subsidiary undertaking of the parent institution,

be dealt with in the group accounts by the method of proportional consolidation. The provisions of this paragraph relating to the preparation of consolidated accounts apply, with any necessary modifications, to the proportional consolidation.

(5) *Associated undertakings*

An '*associated undertaking*' means an undertaking in which an undertaking included in the consolidation has a participating interest and over whose operating and financial policy it exercises a significant influence, and which is not

- a subsidiary undertaking of the parent institution; or
- a joint venture dealt with in accordance with (4) above.

The interest of an undertaking in an associated undertaking, and the amount of profit or loss attributable to such an interest, must be shown by the equity method of accounting. If the generally accepted accounting principles under which the accounts have been prepared allow it to be accounted for by another method, that method may be used, but, if so, the method used must be disclosed in the notes to the accounts.

Where the associated undertaking is itself a parent undertaking, the net assets and profits or losses to be taken into account are those of the parent and its subsidiary undertakings (after making any consolidation adjustments).

[*SI 2009 No 1801, Sch 7*].

Information required to be given in notes to an institution's annual accounts may be contained in the accounts or in a separate document annexed to the accounts.

[*CA 2006, s 472* (as modified); *SI 2009 No 1801, Reg 57*].

30.49 *Approval and signing of accounts*

An institution's annual accounts must be approved by the board of directors and signed on behalf of the board by a director of the institution. The signature must be on the institution's balance sheet.

If annual accounts are approved that do not comply with the requirements of *CA 2006, Pt 15* as applied to an overseas institution (with modifications) under **30.40** to **30.48**, every director of the institution who

- knew that they did not comply, or was reckless as to whether they complied, and
- failed to take reasonable steps to secure compliance with those requirements or, as the case may be, to prevent the accounts from being approved,

commits an offence. A person guilty of such an offence is liable (i) on conviction on indictment, to a fine; and (ii) on summary conviction, to a fine not exceeding the statutory maximum. See **29.1** OFFENCES AND LEGAL PROCEEDINGS for the statutory maximum.

[*CA 2006, s 414* (as modified); *SI 2009 No 1801, Reg 54*].

30.50 *Duty to file accounts and period allowed for filing*

(1) *Duty to file accounts with the Registrar of Companies*

The directors of an institution must deliver to the Registrar of Companies for each financial year a copy of the institution's annual accounts and such other reports as it is required to prepare. The copy of the balance sheet must state the name of the person who signed it on behalf of the board.

[*CA 2006, s 441* (as modified); *SI 2009 No 1801, Reg 55*].

(2) *Period allowed for filing accounts*

Subject to below, the period allowed for directors of an institution to comply with their obligation under (1) above is 13 months after the end of the relevant accounting reference period.

The '*relevant accounting reference period*' is the accounting reference period by reference to which the financial year for the accounts in question was determined (see **30.41**).

Exceptions.

(a) If the relevant accounting reference period is the institution's first and is a period of more than 12 months, the period allowed is 13 months from the first anniversary of the institution becoming a relevant overseas institution.

(b) If the relevant accounting reference period is treated as shortened by virtue of a notice given under **30.41**(4), the period is

(i) that applicable in accordance with the above provisions; or

(ii) three months from the date of the notice;

whichever expires last.

If for any special reason the Secretary of State thinks fit, he may, on an application made before the expiry of the period otherwise allowed, give notice in writing to an institution extending that period by such further period as may be specified in the notice.

[*CA 2006, s 442* (as modified); *SI 2009 No 1801, Reg 55*].

(3) *Offences for default in filing accounts*

If the requirements of (1) above are not complied with in relation to an institution's accounts for a financial year before the end of the period for filing those accounts, every person who immediately before the end of that period was a director of the institution commits an offence. A person guilty of such an offence is liable, on summary conviction, to a fine not exceeding level 5 on the standard scale and, for continued contravention, a daily default fine not exceeding one-tenth of the greater of £5,000 or level 4 on the standard scale. See **29.1 Offences and Legal Proceedings** for the standard scale.

It is a defence for a person charged with such an offence to prove that he took all reasonable steps for securing that those requirements would be complied with before the end of that period. It is not a defence to prove that the documents in question were not in fact prepared as required.

[*CA 2006, s 451* (as modified); *SI 2009 No 1801, Reg 56; SI 2015 No 664, Sch 3*].

30.51 TRADING DISCLOSURES

The Secretary of State may by Regulations make provision requiring overseas companies carrying on business in the UK to

- display specified information in specified locations;
- state specified information in specified descriptions of document or communication; and
- provide specified information on request to those they deal with in the course of their business.

[*CA 2006, s 1051*].

The provisions in **30.52** to **30.55** have been made by the *Overseas Companies Regulations 2009* and in those provisions

- a reference to any type of document is a reference to a document of that type in hard copy, electronic or any other form; and
- in relation to a company, a reference to 'its websites' includes a reference to any part of a website relating to that company which that company has caused or authorised to appear.

[*SI 2009 No 1801, Reg 58*].

30.52 Display of name, etc at business location

An overseas company must display the company's name and country of incorporation

(a) at every location in the UK at which it carries on business; and

(b) at the service address of every person resident in the UK authorised to accept service of documents on behalf of the company.

But (*a*) above does not apply to a location

- that is primarily used for living accommodation;

- at which business is carried on by a company of which every director or permanent representative who is an individual is entitled to higher protection from disclosure of their residential address (see **30.15**); or
- at which business is carried on by a company in respect of which a liquidator, administrator or administrative receiver has been appointed if the location is also a place of business of the liquidator, administrator or administrative receiver.

The company's name and country of incorporation must be displayed continuously. But if the place of business is shared by six or more companies, this requirement is treated as met if the company's name and country of incorporation are displayed for at least fifteen continuous seconds at least once in every three minutes.

The name and country of incorporation must be displayed in such a way so that they may be easily seen by any visitor to the location and must be in characters that can be read with the naked eye.

Penalties. Where a company fails, without reasonable excuse, to comply with any of the above requirements, an offence is committed by the company and every officer of the company who is in default. A person guilty of such an offence is liable, on summary conviction, to a fine not exceeding level 3 on the standard scale and, for continued contravention, a daily default fine not exceeding one-tenth of level 3 on the standard scale. See **29.1 Offences and Legal Proceedings** for the standard scale. For these purposes, a shadow director is to be treated as an officer of the company. [*SI 2009 No 1801, Regs 59–61, 67*].

30.53 Inclusion of names and other specified information in documents and communications

(a) An overseas company must state the company's name on all

(i) its business letters, notices and other official publications,

(ii) its bills of exchange, promissory notes, endorsements and order forms,

(iii) cheques purporting to be signed by or on behalf of the company,

(iv) orders for money, goods or services purporting to be signed by or on behalf of the company,

(v) its bills of parcels, invoices and other demands for payments, receipts, and letters of credit,

(vi) its applications for licences to carry on a trade or activity,

(vii) other forms of its business correspondence and documentation, and

(viii) its websites,

that are used in carrying on the activities of its business in the UK.

(b) An overseas company that has a UK establishment in respect of which it has registered particulars under **30.3** to **30.5** must state on all its business letters, order forms and websites that are used in carrying on the activities of a UK establishment of the company

(i) where the establishment is registered; and

(ii) its registered number.

(c) An overseas company which is not incorporated in an EEA State must state on its business letters, order forms and its websites that are used in carrying on business in the UK

(i) the company's country of incorporation;

(ii) the identity of the registry, if any, in which the company is registered in its country of incorporation;

(iii) if applicable, the number with which the company is registered in that registry;

(iv) the location of its head office;

(v) the legal form of the company;

(vi) if the liability of the members of the company is limited, the fact that it is a limited company; and

(vii) if applicable, the fact that the company is being wound up, or is subject to other insolvency proceedings or an arrangement or composition or any analogous proceedings (this does not apply where the company is required to make similar disclosures under various provisions of *IA 1986* or *Insolvency (NI) Order 1989*).

If, in the case of company having a share capital, there is reference to the amount of share capital on its business letters, order forms or websites, the reference must be to paid up share capital.

(d) Where a business letter of a company includes the name of any director of the company, other than in the text or as a signatory, the letter must disclose the name of every director of the company. In the case of a body corporate, or a firm that is a legal person under the law by which it is governed, its corporate or firm name must be given.

Any display or disclosure must be in characters that can be read with the naked eye.

Penalties. Where a company fails, without reasonable excuse, to comply with any of the above requirements, an offence is committed by the company and every officer of the company who is in default. A person guilty of such an offence is liable, on summary conviction, to a fine not exceeding level 3 on the standard scale and, for continued contravention, a daily default fine not exceeding one-tenth of level 3 on the standard scale. See **29.1 Offences and Legal Proceedings** for the standard scale. For these purposes, a shadow director is to be treated as an officer of the company.

[*SI 2009 No 1801, Regs 59, 62–64, 67*].

30.54 Disclosures relating to address for service

A company must disclose the address of any person resident in the UK authorised to accept service of documents on behalf of the company to any person it deals with in the course of business who makes a written request to the company for that information. The company must send a written response to that person within five working days of the receipt of the request.

Penalties. Where a company fails, without reasonable excuse, to comply with any of the above requirements, an offence is committed by the company and every officer of the company who is in default. A person guilty of such an offence is liable, on summary conviction, to a fine not exceeding level 3 on the standard scale and, for continued contravention, a daily default fine not exceeding one-tenth of level 3 on the standard scale. See **29.1 Offences and Legal Proceedings** for the standard scale. For these purposes, a shadow director is to be treated as an officer of the company.

[*SI 2009 No 1801, Regs 65, 67*].

30.55 Civil consequences of failure to make a required disclosure

Where

- any legal proceedings are brought by a company to enforce a right arising out of a contract made in the course of a business, and
- at the time the contract was made, the company was in breach of any of the requirements in **30.52** to **30.54**,

the proceedings must be dismissed if it is shown that the defendant (in Scotland, the defender)

- has a claim against the claimant (pursuer) arising out of the contract and has been unable to pursue that claim by reason of the latter's failure to comply with those requirements, or
- has suffered some financial loss in connection with the contract by reason of the claimant's (pursuer's) failure to comply with those requirements.

This does not apply if the court before which the proceedings are brought is satisfied that it is just and equitable to permit the proceedings to continue and does not affect the right of any person to enforce such rights as the person may have against another in any proceedings brought by the other. [*SI 2009 No 1801, Reg 66*].

30.56 SERVICE OF DOCUMENTS

(1) *Service of documents on the company*

A document may be served on an overseas company whose particulars are registered in the UK

- by leaving it at, or sending it by post to, the registered address of any person resident in the UK who is authorised to accept service of documents on the company's behalf; or
- if there is no such person, or if any such person refuses service or service cannot for any other reason be effected, by leaving it at or sending by post to any place of business of the company in the UK.

[*CA 2006, s 1139(2)*].

The place of business must exist at the time of the service and cannot merely be a former place of business (*Deverall v Grant Advertising Inc* [1955] Ch 111, [1954] 3 All ER 389, CA).

(2) *Service of documents on directors, secretaries and others*

In the case of an overseas company whose particulars are registered under the provisions in **30.3** *et* seq, a document may be served on a director, secretary or permanent representative by leaving it at, or sending it by post to, the person's registered address, ie any address for the time being shown as a current address in relation to that person in the part of the register available for public inspection.

This applies whatever the purpose of the document in question and is not restricted to service for purposes arising out of, or in connection with, the appointment or position mentioned or in connection with the company concerned.

Change of address. If notice of a change of that address is given to the Registrar of Companies, a person may validly serve a document at the address previously registered until the end of the period of 14 days beginning with the date on which notice of the change is registered.

Service cannot be effected under these provisions at an address

- if notice has been registered of the termination of the appointment in relation to which the address was registered and the address is not a registered address of the person concerned in relation to any other appointment; and
- if the overseas company has ceased to have any connection with the UK by virtue of which it is required to register particulars under *CA 2006, s 1046*.

[*CA 2006, s 1140; SI 2009 No 1801, Reg 75*].

30.57 DUTY TO GIVE NOTICE OF CLOSURE OF UK ESTABLISHMENT

If an overseas company closes a UK establishment in respect of which it has registered particulars under **30.3** *et seq*, it must forthwith give notice of that fact to the Registrar of Companies.

From the date on which such notice is given, the company is no longer obliged to deliver documents to the Registrar of Companies in respect of that establishment.

If a company fails to comply with this provision, an offence is committed by the company and every officer or agent of the company who knowingly and willingly authorises or permits the default. A person guilty of such an offence is liable, on summary conviction, to a fine not exceeding level 3 on the standard scale and, for continued contravention, a daily default fine not exceeding one-tenth of level 3 on the standard scale. See **29.1 Offences and Legal Proceedings** for the standard scale. [*SI 2009 No 1801, Reg 77*].

30.58 REGISTRAR TO WHOM RETURNS, NOTICES, ETC TO BE DELIVERED

Where an overseas company is required to register or has registered particulars in more than one part of the UK, the Secretary of State may provide by Regulations that, in the case of such a company, anything authorised or required to be delivered to the Registrar is to be delivered

- to the Registrar for each part of the UK in which the company is required to register or has registered particulars; or
- to the Registrar for such part or parts of the UK as may be specified in or determined in accordance with the Regulations.

[*CA 2006, s 1057*].

30.59 COMPANY CONTRACTS AND EXECUTION OF DOCUMENTS

The *Overseas Companies (Execution of Documents and Registration of Charges) Regulations 2009 (SI 2009 No 1917)* provide that with effect from 1 October 2009 parts of *sections 43–51* of *CA 2006* (as modified by the regulations) apply to overseas companies (see **30.60–30.63**).

30.60 Company contracts

Under the law of England and Wales or Northern Ireland, a contract may be made

- by an overseas company, by writing under its common seal or in any manner permitted by the laws of the territory in which the company is incorporated for the execution of documents by such a company; and
- on behalf of an overseas company, by any person who, in accordance with the laws of the territory in which the company is incorporated, is acting under the authority (express or implied) of that company.

Unless a contrary intention appears, any formalities required by law in the case of a contract made by an individual also apply to one made by or on behalf of an overseas company.

[*CA 2006, s 43* (as modified); *SI 2009 No 1917, Reg 4*].

30.61 Deeds and documents: Provisions applying in England and Wales and Northern Ireland

(1) *Execution of documents*

Under the law of England and Wales or Northern Ireland a document is executed by an overseas company in either of the following ways.

(a) By the affixing of its common seal.

(b) if it is executed in any manner permitted by the laws of the territory in which the company is incorporated for the execution of documents by such a company.

(c) If it is signed by a person who, in accordance with the laws of the territory in which an overseas company is incorporated, is acting under the authority (express or implied) of the company.

A document so signed and expressed, in whatever words, to be executed by the company has the same effect in relation to that company as it would have in relation to a company incorporated in England and Wales or Northern Ireland if executed under the common seal of a company so incorporated.

In favour of a 'purchaser', a document is deemed to have been duly executed by an overseas company if it purports to be signed in accordance with (*c*) above. A '*purchaser*' means a purchaser in good faith for valuable consideration and includes a lessee, mortgagee or other person who, for valuable consideration, acquires an interest in property.

Where a document is to be signed by a person on behalf of more than one overseas company, it is not duly signed by that person for the purposes of these provisions unless he signs it separately in each capacity.

References above to a document being (or purporting to be) signed by a person who, in accordance with the laws of the territory in which an overseas company is incorporated, is acting under the authority (express or implied) of the company are to be read, in a case where that person is a firm, as references to its being (or purporting to be) signed by an individual authorised by the firm to sign on its behalf.

The above provisions apply to a document that is (or purports to be) executed by an overseas company in the name of or on behalf of another person whether or not that person is also an overseas company.

[*CA 2006, s 44* (as modified); *SI 2009 No 1917, Reg 4*].

(2) *Execution of deeds*

A document is validly executed by an overseas company as a deed for the purposes of *Law of Property (Miscellaneous Provisions) Act 1989, s 1(2)(b)* and the law of Northern Ireland if, and only if, it is

- duly executed by the company; and
- delivered as a deed.

A document is presumed to be delivered for these purposes upon its being executed, unless a contrary intention is proved.

[*CA 2006, s 46* (as modified); *SI 2009 No 1917, Reg 4*].

30.62 Execution of documents: Provisions applying in Scotland

For the purposes of any enactment

- providing for a document to be executed by a company by affixing its common seal, or
- referring (in whatever terms) to a document so executed,

a document signed or subscribed by or on behalf of an overseas company in accordance with the provisions of the *Requirements of Writing (Scotland) Act 1995* has effect as if so executed. [[*CA 2006, s 48* (as modified); *SI 2009 No 1917, Reg 5*].].

30.63 Pre-incorporation contracts, deeds and obligations

A contract that purports to be made by or on behalf of an overseas company at a time when the company has not been formed has effect, subject to any agreement to the contrary, as one made with the person purporting to act for the company or as agent for it, and he is personally liable on the contract.

This also applies to

- the making of a deed under the law of England and Wales or Northern Ireland, and
- the undertaking of an obligation under the law of Scotland

as it applies to the making of a contract.

[*CA 2006, s 51* (as modified); *SI 2009 No 1917, Reg 6*].

30.64 REGISTRATION OF CHARGES

The regulations referred to in **30.59** (above) (as amended by the *Overseas Companies (Execution of documents and Registration of charges) Amendment Regulations* as from 1 October 2011) [*SI 2011 No 2194*] also regulate the registration of charges over property in the UK of a registered overseas company.

In relation to charges created on or after 1 October 2009 but before 1 October 2011, the provisions in **30.65** to **30.73** apply to an overseas company that is registered and for these purposes an overseas company

- becomes registered when it has complied with the provisions in **30.3** to **30.6** (initial registration of particulars) in respect of one or more UK establishments and those particulars have been registered; and
- ceases to be registered when it gives notice under **30.57** (notice of closure of UK establishment) in respect of *all* of its UK establishments and that notice has been registered.

For the above purposes, the particulars and notice referred to are not treated as registered unless and until they are on the register and therefore available for public inspection.

'*Establishment*' means a branch within the meaning of the *EC 11th Company Law Directive (89/666/EEC)* or a place of business that is not such a branch; and '*UK establishment*' means an establishment in the UK.

'*Charge*', in these provisions includes, in England and Wales and Northern Ireland, a mortgage and, in Scotland, any right in security.

In relation to a charge created under the law of Scotland, references to the date of creation of the charge are to

- in the case of a floating charge, the date on which the instrument creating the floating charge was executed by the company creating the charge; and
- in any other case, the date on which the right of the person entitled to the benefit of the charge was constituted as a real right.

[*SI 2009 No 1917, Regs 2, 8*].

Transitional provisions. The provisions in *CA 1985, Pt 12* relating to

- charges created by companies incorporated outside Great Britain continue to apply in relation to charges created before 1 October 2009; and
- charges existing on property acquired by a company incorporated outside Great Britain continue to apply to property acquired before 1 October 2009.

[*SI 2009 No 1917, Sch paras 2, 4*].

30.65 Charges requiring registration

A charge requires registration under these provisions if

(a) it is created by a company to which the provisions apply (see **30.64**);

(b) the property subject to the charge is situated in the UK; and

(c) the charge is of a type requiring registration.

Whether the conditions in (*a*) and (*b*) above are met is determined when the charge is created.

The types of charge requiring registration are as follows.

- A charge on land or any interest in land, other than a charge for rent or any other periodical sum issuing out of (in Scotland, payable in respect of) land. For this purpose,

(i) a charge on land includes a charge created by a heritable security within the meaning of *Conveyancing and Feudal Reform (Scotland) Act 1970, s 9(8)*; and

(ii) the holding of debentures entitling the holder to a charge on land is not an interest in the land.

- A charge created or evidenced by an instrument that, if executed by an individual, would require registration as a bill of sale.
- A charge for the purposes of securing any issue of debentures.
- A charge on uncalled share capital of the company.
- A charge on calls made but not paid.
- A charge on book debts of the company. For this purpose, the deposit by way of security of a negotiable instrument given to secure the payment of book debts is not a charge on those book debts.
- A floating charge on the company's property or undertaking.
- A charge on a ship or aircraft, or any share in a ship.
- A charge on goodwill or on any '*intellectual property*', ie any

(i) patent, trade mark, registered design, copyright or design right; or

(ii) any licence under or in respect of any such right.

Consequences of failure to register such a charge. If a company creates a charge requiring registration under these provisions, the charge is void (so far as any security on the company's property or undertaking is conferred by it) against a liquidator, administrator or creditor of the company if the charge is not registered in compliance with **30.66**. This is without prejudice to any contract or obligation for repayment of the money secured by the charge; and when a charge becomes void in these circumstances, the money secured by it immediately becomes payable.

[*SI 2009 No 1917, Regs 9, 19(1)(3)*].

30.66 Duty to deliver particulars of charge etc for registration

A company to which these provisions apply (see **30.64**) that creates a charge requiring registration must deliver the required particulars of the charge, together with a certified copy of the instrument (if any) by which the charge is created or evidenced, to the Registrar of Companies before the end of the period allowed for registration, ie

- 21 days, beginning with the day after the day on which the charge is created; or
- if the charge is created outside the UK, 21 days beginning with the day after the day on which the instrument by which the charge is created or evidenced (or a copy of it) could, in due course of post (and if despatched with due diligence) have been received in the UK.

But there is no requirement to deliver particulars if the property subject to the charge is, at the end of the period allowed for registration, no longer situated in the UK.

The required particulars are

- the date of the creation of the charge;
- a description of the instrument (if any) creating or evidencing the charge;

- the amount secured by the charge;
- the name and address of the person entitled to the charge;
- short particulars of the property charged; and
- in the case of a floating charge created under the law of Scotland, a statement as to any provisions of the charge and of any instrument relating to it
  - (i) which prohibit or restrict or regulate the power of the company to grant further securities ranking in priority to, or *pari passu* with, the floating charge; or
  - (ii) which vary or otherwise regulate the order of ranking of the floating charge in relation to subsisting securities.

Alternatively, registration of a charge may be effected on the application of a person interested in it, in which case that person is entitled to recover from the company any fees he has properly paid to the Registrar of Companies on registration.

[*SI 2009 No 1917, Regs 10–12)*].

30.67 Charge by way of ex facie absolute disposition (Scotland)

For the avoidance of doubt, in the case of a charge created under the law of Scotland by way of

- an *ex facie* absolute disposition or assignation qualified by a back letter or other agreement, or
- a standard security qualified by an agreement

compliance with **30.66** does not of itself render the charge unavailable as security for indebtedness incurred after the date of compliance.

Where the amount secured by a charge so created is purported to be increased by a further back letter or agreement, a further charge is held to have been created by the *ex facie* absolute disposition or assignation or (as the case may be) by the standard security, as qualified by the further back letter or agreement. In that case, the provisions relating to the registration of charges apply to the further charge as if

- references to the charge were references to the further charge; and
- references to the date of creation of a charge were references to the date on which the further back letter or agreement was executed. [*SI 2009 No 1917, Reg 13*].

30.67A Charges created on or after 1 October 2011

Charges created on or after 1 October 2011 over property in the UK of a registered overseas company are regulated by *SI 2009 No 1917* (see above) as amended by *SI 2011 No 2194*. The *2011 Regulations* provide in summary that the requirement for the registration of a charge set out in the *2009 Regulations* is removed. The effect of the *2011 Regulations* is:

(i) to remove references to the date a charge is created under the law of Scotland

[*SI 2011 No 2194, Reg 2(1)*]

(ii) to omit *Regulations 9–22* of the *2009 Regulations* so that a charge created on or after 1 October 2011 is no longer registrable with the Registrar of Companies

[*SI 2011 No 2194, Reg 2(3)*]

(iii) to require that overseas companies need to keep available for inspection copies of instruments creating charges referred to in *Regulation 24* of the 2009 regulations (as amended). *Regulation 24* now requires every overseas company to keep available for inspection a register of charges and to (as soon as practicable and in any event within 21 days of the creation of the charge) enter in the register any charge on land in the UK or any interest in such land, any charge on ships, aircraft or intellectual property registered in the UK, any floating charge on the whole or part of the company's property or undertaking situated in the UK with the exceptions set out in *Regulation 24(2A)*.

[*SI 2011 No 2194, Reg 2(4)* and *2(5)*].

(iv) to amend the time copies of instruments and the register of charges have to be available for inspection from 14 to 21 days [*SI 2011 No 2194, Reg 2(6)*] and to provide that the right to inspect the documents and register can be carried out by electronic means

[*SI 2011 No 2194, Reg 2(8)*]

Transitional provisions – the provision in *Reg 2(6)* amending the time limit does not apply where the company has given notice to the Registrar of Companies of the place where documents etc are kept available for inspection in respect of a charge created before 1 October 2011.

30.68 Special rules about debentures: charge in series of debentures

In circumstances where the first debenture in a series of debentures is executed on or after 1 October 2009, where a company creates a series of debentures containing, or giving by reference to another instrument, any charge which benefits the debenture holders of that series *pari passu*, it is sufficient for the purposes **30.66** if the following are delivered to the Registrar of Companies before the end of the period of 21 days beginning with the day after the date on which that instrument is executed. If there is no such instrument, they must be delivered within 21 days beginning with the day after the day on which the first debenture of the series is executed.

(a) Particulars of

- the total amount secured by the whole series;
- the dates of the resolutions authorising the issue of the series and the date of the covering instrument (if any) by which the series is created or defined;
- a general description of the property charged;
- the names of the trustees (if any) for the debenture holders; and
- In the case of a floating charge created under the law of Scotland, a statement as to any provisions of the charge and of any instrument relating to it

  (i) which prohibit or restrict or regulate the power of the company to grant further securities ranking in priority to, or *pari passu* with, the floating charge; or

  (ii) which vary or otherwise regulate the order of ranking of the floating charge in relation to subsisting securities.

(b) A certified copy of the instrument containing the charge or, if there is no such instrument, a certified copy of one of the debentures of the series.

Particulars must also be sent for registration of

(i) where more than one issue is made of debentures in the series, the date and amount of each issue of debentures of the series; and

(ii) where appropriate, the amount or rate per cent of any commission, discount or allowance which has been paid or made either directly or indirectly by a company to a person in consideration of their

- subscribing or agreeing to subscribe (whether absolutely or conditionally) for debentures in the company; or
- procuring or agreeing to procure subscriptions (whether absolute or conditional) for such debentures.

The deposit of debentures as security for a debt of the company is not treated as the issue of debentures at a discount for this purpose.

But failure to comply with (i) or (ii) above does not affect the validity of the debentures issued.

[*SI 2009 No 1917, Regs 14–16, 19(2), Sch para 3*].

Transitional provisions. The provisions of *CA 1985, Pt 12* relating to the registration of a series of debentures of a company incorporated outside Great Britain continue to apply where the first debenture of the series was executed before 1 October 2009.

[*SI 2009 No 1917, Sch para 3*].

The *2011 Regulations* (see **30.67A** above) also amend the provisions in *SI 2009 No 1917* relating to debentures for those debentures created on or after 1 October 2011. *Regulations 14–16* and *19(2)* of the *2009 Regulations* are removed and no longer apply so that particulars of any charge which benefits debenture holders no longer need to be registered. [*SI 2011 No 2194, Reg 2(3)*].

30.69 Endorsement of certificate on debentures

A company must cause a copy of every certificate of registration given by the Registrar of Companies under **30.70** to be endorsed on every debenture or certificate of debenture stock which is issued by the company, and the payment of which is secured by the charge so registered. But this does not require a company to cause a certificate of registration of any charge so given to be endorsed on any debenture or certificate of debenture stock issued by the company before the charge was created.

If a person knowingly and wilfully authorises or permits the delivery of a debenture or certificate of debenture stock in default of this requirement, he commits an offence. A person guilty of such an offence is liable, on summary conviction, to a fine not exceeding level 3 on the standard scale (see **29.1** Offences and Legal Proceedings).

[*SI 2009 No 1917, Reg 17*].

See above that these provisions do not apply to debentures created on or after 1 October 2011.

[*SI 2011, No 2194, Reg 2(3)*].

30.70 Register of charges to be kept by the Registrar of Companies

For each company to which these provisions apply (see **30.64**), the Registrar of Companies must keep, and make available for inspection by any person, a register of all the charges requiring registration under these provisions. The register must show

- the particulars required to be delivered to the Registrar of Companies under these provisions; and
- in the case of a charge imposed by the Enforcement of Judgments Office under *Judgments Enforcement (Northern Ireland) Order 1981, Art 46*, the date on which the charge became effective.

The Registrar must give a signed and authenticated certificate of registration of any charge so registered, stating the name of the company and the amount secured by the charge. Such a certificate is conclusive evidence that the registration requirements have been satisfied.

Entries of satisfaction and release. In relation to statements delivered to the Registrar of Companies on or after 1 October 2009, if a statement is delivered to the Registrar of Companies verifying with respect to a registered charge that

- the debt for which the charge was given has been paid or satisfied in whole or in part, or
- part of the property or undertaking charged has been released from the charge or has ceased to form part of the company's property or undertaking

the Registrar may enter on the register a memorandum of satisfaction of that fact.

In Scotland, if the charge is a floating charge created under the law of Scotland, the statement must be accompanied by either

- a statement by the creditor entitled to the benefit of the charge (or a person authorised by him) verifying that the statement is correct; or
- a direction obtained from the court, on the ground that such a statement could not be readily obtained, dispensing with the need for that statement,

but nothing in these provisions requires the company to submit particulars with respect to the entry in the register of a memorandum of satisfaction where the company, having created a floating charge under the law of Scotland over all or any part of its property, disposes of *part* of the property subject to the floating charge.

Where the Registrar enters a memorandum of satisfaction in whole, he must, if required, send the company a copy of it.

Transitional provisions. CA 1985, s 403 or *419* continues to apply where the relevant statement was received by the Registrar of Companies before 1 October 2009.

[*SI 2009 No 1917, Regs 18, 21, Sch para 7*].

See above that these provisions do not apply to debentures created on or after 1 October 2011.

[*SI 2011, No 2194, Reg 2(3)*].

30.71 Rectification of register of charges by the court

Where there has been

- a failure to register a charge within the time required, or

- an omission or mis-statement of any particular with respect to any such charge or in a memorandum of satisfaction

the court may, on the application of the company or a person interested, order the period allowed for registration to be extended or, as the case may be, the omission or mis-statement to be rectified where it is satisfied that

- the failure or omission
  - (i) was accidental or due to inadvertence or to some other sufficient cause; or
  - (ii) is not of a nature to prejudice the position of creditors or shareholders of the company; or
- it is just and equitable to grant relief on other grounds.

[*SI 2009 No 1917, Reg 22*].

See above that these provisions do not apply to debentures created on or after 1 October 2011

[*SI 2011, No 2194, Reg 2(3)*]

30.72 Appointment/cessation of receiver, etc

Subject to below, in relation to orders and appointments made on or after 1 October 2009, if a person

- obtains an order for the appointment of a receiver or manager of property of a company to which these provisions apply (see **30.64**), or
- appoints such a receiver or manager under powers contained in an instrument,

he must give notice of the fact to the Registrar of Companies within seven days of the order or of the appointment. The Registrar must then enter that fact in the register of charges.

Where a receiver or manager of a company's property appointed under powers contained in an instrument ceases to act he must give notice to that effect to the Registrar of Companies. The Registrar must then enter that fact in the register of charges.

A person who defaults in complying with the above requirements commits an offence. A person guilty of such an offence is liable, on summary conviction, to a fine not exceeding level 3 on the standard scale and, for continued contravention, a daily default fine not exceeding one-tenth of level 3 on the standard scale. See **29.1 Offences and Legal Proceedings** for the standard scale.

The above provisions do not apply in relation to the appointment of a receiver under *IA 1986, s 51(1)* or *(2)* (appointment under law of Scotland by holder of floating charge or by court on application of holder) as respects which *IA 1986, s 53(1)* or *54(3)* requires the delivery to the Registrar of Companies of a copy of the instrument or interlocutor making the appointment.

[*SI 2009 No 1917, Reg 20, Sch para 6*].

Transitional provisions. CA 1985, s 405 continues to apply where the order or appointment was made, or the receiver or manager ceased to act before 1 October 2009.

[*SI 2009 No 1917, Sch para 6*].

See above that these provisions do not apply to debentures created on or after 1 October 2011

[*SI 2011, No 2194, Reg 2(3)*]

30.73 Register of charges and copies of instruments creating charges

As from 1 October 2011 a company to which these provisions apply (see **30.64**) must keep available for inspection

(a) a copy of every instrument creating a charge requiring registration under these provisions (although in the case of a series of uniform debentures a copy of one of the debentures of the series is sufficient); and

(b) a register of charges and enter in it as soon as practicable and in any event within 21 days of the date of creation of the charge

   (i) any charge on land or any interest in such land of the company situated in the UK; and

   (ii) any floating charge on the whole or part of the company's property or undertaking situated in the UK.

   (iii) any charge on ships, aircraft or intellectual property registered in the UK.

The entry in the register under (*b*) above must in each case give

- a short description of the property and/or undertaking charged;
- the amount of the charge; and
- except in the cases of securities to bearer, the names of the persons entitled to it.

30.73(a)(ii) does not apply to a floating charge which expressly excludes all property or undertaking of the company situated in the UK or which purports to be a fixed charge.

If an officer of the company knowingly and wilfully authorises or permits the omission of an entry required to be made in the register, he commits an offence. A person guilty of such an offence is liable (i) on conviction on indictment, to a fine; and (ii) on summary conviction, to a fine not exceeding the statutory maximum. See **29.1 Offences and Legal Proceedings** for the statutory minimum.

[*SI 2009 No 1917, Regs 23, 24*; *SI 2011 No 2194, Reg 2(4)* and *2(5)*].

Inspection. The documents under (*a*) above and the company's register of charges under (*b*) above must be kept available for inspection at a location in the UK at which it carries on business. The company must give notice to the Registrar of Companies, within 14 days, of the place at which the documents and register are kept available for inspection and of any change in that place, within 21 days of any such change.

The documents and register must be open to the inspection of any creditor or member of the company without charge and any other person on payment of £3.50 for each hour or part thereof during which the right of inspection is exercised. Where the company and the person (making the inspection) agree, the inspection may be carried out by electronic means.

[*SI 2011 No 2194, Reg 26A*]

If default is made in notifying the Registrar of Companies or an inspection is refused, an offence is committed by the company and every officer of the company who is in default. A person guilty of such an offence is liable, on summary conviction, to a fine not exceeding level 3 on the standard scale and, for continued contravention, a daily default fine not exceeding one-tenth of level 3 on the standard scale. See **29.1** Offences and Legal Proceedings for the standard scale. In the case of refusal of inspection of the register, the court may by order compel an immediate inspection of it.

Availability for inspection. A company to which these provisions apply (see **30.64**) must make the documents and register referred to above available for inspection by a person on a day which has been specified by that person ('the specified day') provided that

- the specified day is a working day; and
- that person gives the company the required notice of the specified day.

  The required notice is at least 10 working days' notice of the specified day.

When a person gives notice of the specified day, he must also give notice of the time on that day at which he wishes to start the inspection (which must be any time between 9 am and 3 pm) and the company must make its company records available for inspection by that person for a period of at least two hours beginning with that time. If a company that fails to comply with this provision, it is treated as having refused inspection.

[*SI 2009 No 1917, Regs 25, 26*; *SI 2011 No 2194, Regs 2(6), 2(7) 2(8)*].

PROVISIONS APPLYING BEFORE 1 OCTOBER 2009

(1) Definition
(2) Registration and filing requirements, etc – place of business registration regime
(3) Documents to be delivered to the Registrar of Companies on establishing a place of business in Great Britain
(4) Registration of change in particulars
(5) Registration and filing requirements etc – branch registration regime
(6) Duty to register and documents to be delivered
(7) Particulars required about the company
(8) Particulars required about the branch
(9) Particulars in relation to registration of documents
(10) Documents required
(11) Registration of alteration in particulars
(12) Change in registration regime
(13) Change from place of business regime to branch regime
(14) Change from branch regime to place of business regime
(15) Miscellaneous matters
(16) Letter paper, notices etc
(17) Duty to state name etc – branches
(18) Company name
(19) Service of documents on an overseas company
(20) Penalties
(21) Channel Island and Isle of Man companies
(22) Accounts and reports
(23) Exceptions
(24) Oversea credit or financial institution with branch in Great Britain
(25) Duty to prepare annual accounts
(26) Individual accounts: form and content
(27) Group undertakings
(28) Group accounts of holding company
(29) Form and content of group accounts
(30) Small and medium-sized companies
(31) Directors' report
(32) Auditors' report
(33) Signing of the balance sheet
(34) Dormant companies
(35) Unlimited overseas companies
(36) Accounting reference dates
(37) Delivery of accounts to the Registrar of Companies
(38) Accounts and reports – companies with branches in Great Britain
(39) Companies required to make disclosure under parent law
(40) Duty to deliver accounting documents
(41) Companies not required to make disclosure under parent law
(42) Preparation of accounts and reports
(43) Duty to deliver accounts and reports
(44) Accounts and reports – credit and financial institutions with branches in Great Britain
(45) Institutions required to prepare accounts under parent law
(46) Duty to deliver accounting documents
(47) Institutions not required to prepare accounts under parent law
(48) Appropriate registrar of companies
(49) Companies within branch registration regime

Overseas Companies

Background. The provisions in this Appendix apply, unless otherwise stated, before 1 October 2009. Under transitional provisions, the provisions in *CA 1985, Chapter 1* (see (2)–(22), (48) and (49)) continue to have effect on and after 1 October 2009 so far as necessary for the purposes of the registration of returns or other documents delivered to the Registrar of Companies before that date.

[*SI 2009 No 1801, Sch 8 para 2*].

(1) Definition

An '*overseas company*' is a company incorporated elsewhere than in Great Britain which

- after 30 June 1985 'establishes a place of business' in Great Britain; or
- before 1 July 1985 established a place of business and continues to have an established place of business in Great Britain after that date.

[*CA 1985, s 744*].

There is no precise statutory definition of the meaning of 'establishes a place of business'. In *Act Dampskib Hercules v Grand Trunk Pacific Rly Co* [1912] 1 KB 222, Buckley LJ said on this point: 'We have only to see whether the corporation is "here" . . . the best test is to ascertain whether the business is carried on here and at a defined place.' It was held that a company, whose main object was to establish and maintain a railway company in Canada and which raised capital in London to do so, had established a place of business in England.

In *South India Shipping Corpn Ltd v Export-Import Bank of Korea* [1985] 2 All ER 219, [1985] BCLC 163, CA, it was held that a bank, which had premises and staff in England and carried on there the preliminary work necessary for granting and obtaining loans and giving publicity to the bank's activities, had established a place of business there. In *Oriel Ltd, Re* [1985] 3 All ER 216, [1985] BCLC 343, CA, Oliver LJ said that the meaning of the phrase 'established place of business' connotes not only the setting up of a place of business at a specific location, but also a degree of permanence as the location of the company's business. It need not necessarily be owned, or even leased, by the company but at least must be associated with it and business must be conducted from it habitually or with some degree of regularity.

(2) Registration and filing requirements, etc – place of business registration regime

As the general provisions of *CA 1985* apply only to companies formed and registered under the Act, special provisions apply regarding registration and filing requirements of overseas companies.

The provisions in (3) and (4) below do not apply to any limited company which is incorporated outside the UK and Gibraltar and which has a *branch* in Great Britain. [*CA 1985, s 690B; SI 1992 No 3179, Sch 2 para 2*]. A special branch registration regime applies to such companies (see (5) to (14) below). Where a company so incorporated has a place of business in Great Britain that is not a branch, and has no other branch in the UK, it remains subject to the provisions in (3) and (4) below.

'*Branch*' means a branch within the meaning of the *EC 11th Company Law Directive* (*89/666/EEC*), and where a branch comprises places of business in more than one part of the UK, it is treated as being situated in that part of the UK where its principal place of business is situated. [*CA 1985, s 698(2); SI 1992 No 3179, Sch 2 para 13(3)*]. In fact, the *11th Directive* does not specifically define a branch; its meaning ultimately depends on the views of the European Court of Justice when called upon to interpret the *11th Directive*. A Department of Trade and Industry Consultative Document published in July 1992 (Implementation of EC 11th Company Law Directive and Bank Branches Directive) gives useful guidance. It states that, in principle, a branch is a place of business which a company establishes in another State through which the company conducts its business such that persons resident in that State can deal with the branch instead of dealing directly with the representatives of the company in the company's home state. Places of business which perform operations ancillary or incidental to the company's business are, in general terms, not branches within the meaning of the *11th Directive*. Thus, 'branch' is a narrower concept than place of business, every company with a branch has a place of business, but not every place of business is a branch, and one branch can cover many places of business where there is a unified management structure.

(3) **Documents to be delivered to the Registrar of Companies on establishing a place of business in Great Britain**

When a company incorporated outside Great Britain establishes a place of business in Great Britain, it must within one month deliver the following to the appropriate Registrar of Companies for registration. See (48) below for the appropriate Registrar.

(a) A certified copy of the charter, statutes or memorandum and articles of the company or other instrument constituting or defining its constitution, together with a certified translation (if the original is not in English). The copy of the instrument constituting or defining the company's constitution must be certified, in the place of incorporation of the company, to be a true copy by

(i) an official of the government to whose custody the original is committed;

(ii) a notary public; or

(iii) an officer of the company on oath taken before a person authorised to administer oaths in that place or any of the British Officials mentioned in the *Commissioners for Oaths Act 1889, s 6*.

(b) A return in the prescribed form (Form 691) with details of the following.

(i) Directors (including any person in accordance with whose instructions the directors of the company are accustomed to act) and secretary (or any person occupying the position of secretary by whatever name called) as in **12 Company Formation and Types or Companies**, except that it is only necessary to give details of other directorships if the director has no business occupation in which case details of all other current directorships must be given.

(ii) Names and addresses of one or more persons resident in Great Britain authorised to accept on the company's behalf service of process and any notices required to be served on it.

(iii) Documents delivered under (*a*) above.

(iv) A statutory declaration by a director, secretary or person within (ii) above stating the date on which the company's place of business in Great Britain was established. Alternatively, in place of the statutory declaration there may be delivered to the Registrar of Companies using electronic communications a statement made by any person by whom the declaration could have been made stating the date on which the company's place of business in Great Britain was established. Any person who makes a false statement which he knows to be false or does not believe to be true is liable to a penalty.

(c) Where a confidentiality order is in force in respect of a director or secretary, in addition to the return under (*b*) above there must be also be delivered a separate return in the prescribed form containing particulars of the usual residential address of the director or secretary concerned.

[*CA 1985, ss 691, 698; CA 1989, Sch 19 para 6; SI 2000 No 3373, Art 26; SI 2002 No 912, Sch 2 para 5*].

See (20) below for penalties for non-compliance.

(4) **Registration of change in particulars**

If any alteration is made in

(a) any of the documents within (3)(*a*) above, or

(b) the directors or secretary or the particulars contained in the list of directors under (3)(*b*)(i) above, or

(c) the names and addresses of the persons authorised to accept service on behalf of the company under (3)(*b*)(ii) above, or

(d) the corporate name of the overseas company,

the company must, within the specified time, deliver to the appropriate Registrar of Companies a return in the prescribed form (Forms 692(1)(a), 692(1)(b), 692(1)(c) and 692(2) respectively) containing particulars of the alteration or change. See (48) below for the appropriate Registrar.

In the case of an alteration within (3)(*b*)(ii) above the specified time is 21 days after the date of alteration. Otherwise it is 21 days from the date on which notice of the alteration could have been received in Great Britain by post (assuming despatched with due diligence).

Confidentiality orders. The following provisions apply where the rules relating to confidentiality orders are relevant.

- If an individual in respect of whom a confidentiality order is in force becomes a director or secretary of an overseas company

  (i) the return required to be delivered to the Registrar under the above provisions must contain the address for the time being notified by the director or secretary to the company as his service address and must not contain his usual residential address; and

  (ii) with that return the company must deliver to the Registrar a return in the prescribed form containing the usual residential address of that director or secretary.

- If a confidentiality order is made in respect of an existing director or secretary of an overseas company, the company must within the time specified above deliver to the Registrar for registration a return in the prescribed form containing the address for the time being notified to it by the director or secretary as his service address.

- If while a confidentiality order is in force in respect of a director or secretary of an overseas company there is an alteration in his usual residential address, the company must within the time specified above deliver to the Registrar for registration a return in the prescribed form containing the new address.

[*CA 1985, s 692; SI 2002 No 912, Sch 2 para 6*].

See (21) below for penalties for non-compliance.

(5) **Registration and filing requirements etc – branch registration regime**

The provisions described in (6)–(14) below apply to any limited company which is incorporated outside the UK and Gibraltar and which has a 'branch' (see (2) above) in Great Britain.

[*CA 1985, s 690A; SI 1992 No 3179, Sch 2 para 2*].

(6) **Duty to register and documents to be delivered**

A company within (5) above must, within one month of having opened a branch in a part of Great Britain (or within one month of a branch having become situated in a part of Great Britain on ceasing to be situated elsewhere), deliver to the appropriate Registrar of Companies (see (548) below), for registration, a return in the prescribed form containing the particulars set out at (7) and (8) below. Further particulars and documents are required as set out in (9) and (10) below, subject to the exceptions noted in those paragraphs.

[*CA 1985, Sch 21A para 1(1)(4); SI 1992 No 3179, Sch 2 para 3*].

CA 1985, s 705A governs the duties and functions of the Registrar of Companies as regards branches of overseas companies. In particular, he must keep, for each company within (5) above, a register of branches registered by it under the above provisions, and must allocate a number to each such branch (to be known as the branch's registered number).

[*CA 1985, s 705A; SI 1992 No 3179, Reg 3*].

Further returns are required, under *CA 1985, ss 703P* or *703Q* (as inserted by *SI 1992 No 3179, Sch 2 para 19*) if on the date the Great Britain branch is opened, the company is subject to winding up or insolvency proceedings or if, on or before that date, a liquidator has been appointed and he continues in office at that date.

[*CA 1985, Sch 21A para 1(5); SI 1992 No 3179, Sch 2 para 3*].

See (20) below for penalties for non-compliance.

(7) **Particulars required about the company**

The return referred to at (6) above must contain the following particulars about the company.

(a) Its corporate name.

(b) Its legal form.

(c) If it is registered in the country of its incorporation, the identity of the register in which, and the number with which, it is registered.

(d) A list of its directors and secretary, containing (subject to the provisions below relating to confidentiality orders)

(i) with respect to each director (if an individual): his name (meaning usually his forename and surname), any former name (but excluding certain former names, eg a married woman's maiden name), his usual residential address, his nationality, his business occupation (if any), particulars of any other directorships held by him, and his date of birth;

(ii) with respect to the secretary (or each of joint secretaries) (if an individual): his name (meaning usually his forename and surname), any former name (but excluding certain former names, eg a married woman's maiden name) and his usual residential address (except that where all the partners in a firm are joint secretaries, the name and principal office of the firm may be stated instead); and

(iii) with respect to each director and secretary (if a corporation or Scottish firm), its corporate or firm name and registered or principal office.

(e) The extent of the powers of the directors to represent the company in dealings with third parties and in legal proceedings, together with a statement as to whether they may act alone or must act jointly and, if jointly, the name of any other person concerned.

(f) Whether the company is a credit or financial institution within *CA 1985, s 699A* (see (44) below) (or equivalent NI provision).

The following additional particulars are required if the company is not incorporated in an EC Member State.

- The law under which the company is incorporated.
- In the case of a company within the 'delivery of accounts' requirements of either *CA 1985, Sch 21C paras 2, 3* (see (46) below) or *Sch 21D* (see (39) to (43) below), the period for which it is required, by the law under which it is incorporated, to prepare accounts, and the period allowed for the preparation and public disclosure of accounts for such an accounting period.
- Unless otherwise disclosed by the documents referred to at (10) above (where relevant)

  (i) the address of its principal place of business in its country of incorporation;

  (ii) its objects; and

  (iii) the amount of its issued share capital.

Where

- at the time the return referred to in (6) above is delivered, the company has another branch in the same part of Great Britain as the branch covered by the return;
- the company has delivered the above particulars with respect to that other branch (or has done so to the extent required under the transitional provisions described in (13) below); and
- the company has no outstanding obligation to make a return in relation to any alteration of those particulars (see (11) below),

then instead of providing the particulars again, the company may simply refer in the current return to the fact that the particulars have been filed in respect of the other branch, giving the number with which the other branch is registered.

Confidentiality orders. Where a confidentiality order is in force in respect of a director or secretary required to be specified in the list under (*d*) above

- the requirement to give particulars of his usual residential address has effect in respect of that director or secretary as if the reference to his usual residential address were a reference to his services address for the time being notified by him to the company; and
- the company must deliver to the Registrar, in addition to the return required under the above provisions, a return in the prescribed form containing particulars of the usual residential address of the director or secretary to whom the confidentiality order relates, and any such return must be delivered to the Registrar within one month of the company having opened a branch in a part of Great Britain.

[*CA 1985, Sch 21A para 2; SI 1992 No 3179, Sch 2 para 3; SI 2002 No 912, Sch 2 para 8*].

(8) **Particulars required about the branch**

The return referred to in (6) above must also contain the following particulars about the branch.

(a) Its address.

(b) The date on which it was opened.

(c) The business carried on at it.

(d) If different from the name of the company, the name in which that business is carried on.

(e) A list of the names and addresses of all persons resident in Great Britain authorised to accept on the company's behalf service of process in respect of the business of the branch and of any notices required to be served on the company in respect of that business.

(f) A list of the names and, subject to the provisions below relating to confidentiality orders, usual residential addresses of all persons authorised to represent the company as its permanent representatives for the branch business.

(g) The extent of the authority of any person within (*f*) above, including whether that person is authorised to act alone or jointly.

(h) If a person within (*f*) above is not authorised to act alone, the name of any person with whom he is authorised to act.

Confidentiality orders. Where a confidentiality order is in force in respect of a permanent representative required to be specified in the list under (*f*) above

- that list has effect in respect of that permanent representative as if the reference to his usual residential address were a reference to his services address for the time being notified by him to the company; and
- the company must deliver to the Registrar, in addition to the return required under the above provisions, a return in the prescribed form containing particulars of the usual residential address of the director or

secretary to whom the confidentiality order relates, and any such return must be delivered to the Registrar within one month of the company having opened a branch in a part of Great Britain.

[*CA 1985, Sch 21A para 3; SI 1992 No 3179, Sch 2 para 3; SI 2002 No 912, Sch 2 para 8*].

(9) **Particulars in relation to registration of documents**

Unless the company is a credit or financial institution to which *CA 1985, s 699A* applies (see (44) below), the return referred to at (6) above must state whether it is intended to register documents under *CA 1985, Sch 21D para 2(2)* or, as the case may be, *Sch 21D para 10(1)* (duty to deliver accounts and reports – see (38) and (42) below respectively) in respect of the branch in question or in respect of some other branch in the UK. If the latter, the place of registration of the other branch and its registered number must also be stated.

[*CA 1985, Sch 21A paras 1(1)(c), 4; SI 1992 No 3179, Sch 2 para 3*].

(10) **Documents required**

The return referred to at (6) above must be accompanied by certain documents unless

(a) at the time of delivery of the return, the company has another branch in the UK;

(b) the return contains a statement to the effect that the documents otherwise required are included in the material registered in respect of the other branch; and

(c) the return states where the other branch is registered and gives its registered number.

The documents required in respect of all companies to which the above exception does not apply are a certified copy of the company's charter, statutes or memorandum and articles (or other instrument constituting or defining the company's constitution), together with an English translation (if the document is not written in English) certified in the prescribed manner to be a correct translation.

In the case of a company which is not a credit or financial institution within *CA 1985, s 699A* (see (44) below) and which is required by its parent law (ie the law of the country in which the company is incorporated) to prepare, have audited and disclose accounts, certain accounting documents are also required (unless the above exception applies). These accounting documents (ie accounts, consolidated accounts (if any), directors' report (if any) and auditors' report) in relation to a financial period of the company (ie a period for which it is required or permitted by its parent law to prepare accounts), being the latest documents to have been publicly disclosed in accordance with the company's parent law before the earlier of the expiry of the one-month period allowed for complying with (6) above and the actual date of compliance. If any of the accounting documents is not written in English, an English translation, certified in the prescribed manner to be a correct translation, must also be provided.

[*CA 1985, Sch 21A paras 1(2)(3), 5, 6; SI 1992 No 3179, Sch 2 para 3*].

(11) **Registration of alterations in particulars**

If, after a company has delivered a return under (6) above, any alteration is made in

(a) its charter, statutes or memorandum and articles (or other instrument constituting or defining its constitution), or

(b) any of the particulars referred to in (7) to (9) above,

the company must deliver to the appropriate Registrar of Companies (see (48) below), for registration, a return in the prescribed form containing the prescribed particulars of the alteration. If the alteration is one within (*a*) above, the return must be accompanied by a certified copy of the document as altered, together with, if the document is not written in English, an English translation certified in the prescribed manner to be a correct translation.

The return must be delivered within 21 days after the making of any alteration of the particulars in (8) above (particulars about the branch) or, as regards any other alteration, within 21 days after the date on which notice of the alteration could have been received by post in Great Britain (if despatched with due diligence).

Where a company has more than one branch in Great Britain and an alteration relates to more than one such branch, a return must be delivered in respect of each branch affected. For this purpose, an alteration in any of the particulars in (7) above (particulars about the company) is to be treated as relating to every branch. However, if there is more than one branch in a part of Great Britain, one return giving the branch numbers of two or more such branches counts as a return for each branch so specified. An alteration within (*a*) above is only treated as relating to a branch if the document altered is included in the material registered in respect of that branch.

[*CA 1985, Sch 21A para 7; SI 1992 No 3179, Sch 2 para 3*].

Action is also needed if the return under (6) above included a statement under (10)(*b*) above and that statement ceases to be true so far as concerns the documents, other than accounting documents, mentioned in (10) above. The company must then deliver for registration either the said documents or, if applicable, a return in the prescribed form containing a further statement to the effect that those documents are included in material registered in respect of another branch of the company in the UK, and stating the place of registration and registered number of that other branch. These provisions apply in respect of any such further statement as they apply in respect of the original statement. Where there is more than one branch affected, a single return under these provisions will cover more than one branch in a part of Great Britain to the extent that the relevant branch numbers are given in the return.

The above delivery requirements must be complied with within 21 days after the date on which notice of the fact that the statement in the earlier return has ceased to be true could have been received in Great Britain by post (if despatched with due diligence).

[*CA 1985, Sch 21A para 8; SI 1992 No 3179, Sch 2 para 3*].

See (20) below for penalties for non-compliance.

Confidentiality orders. The following additional provisions apply where a confidentiality order is in force.

- If an individual in respect of whom a confidentiality order is in force becomes a director, secretary or permanent representative of a company which has delivered a return under (6) above,

  (i) the return required to be delivered to the Registrar of Companies under *CA 1985, Sch 21A para 7* above must contain the address for the time being notified to the company by the director, secretary or permanent representative as his service address, but must not contain his usual residential address; and

  (ii) with that return the company must deliver to the Registrar a separate return in the prescribed form containing the usual residential address of that director, secretary or permanent representative.

- If, after a company has delivered a return under (6) above, a confidentiality order is made in respect of an existing director, secretary or permanent representative of the company, the company must deliver to the Registrar of Companies for registration a return in the prescribed form containing the address for the time being notified to it by the director, secretary or permanent representative as his service address. The return must be delivered within 21 days after the date on which notice of the revised address could have been received in Great Britain in due course of post (if despatched with due diligence).

- If, at any time after a company has delivered a return under (6) above, there is an alteration in the usual residential address of a director, secretary or permanent representative of the company in respect of whom a confidentiality order is in force, The company must deliver to the Registrar of Companies for registration a return in the prescribed form containing the new address. The return must be delivered within 21 days after the date on which notice of the alteration in question could have been received in Great Britain in due course of post (if despatched with due diligence).

Where a company has more than one branch in Great Britain and any provision of the above provisions requires a return to be made to the Registrar of Companies, that provision requires the company to deliver a return in respect of each of the branches; but a return which gives the branch numbers of two or more such branches is treated as a return in respect of each branch whose number is given.

[*CA 1985, Sch 21A para 9; SI 1992 No 3179, Sch 2 para 3; SI 2002 No 912, Sch 2 para 8*].

(12) **Change in registration regime**

The provisions described in (13) and (14) below cover the situation where a company makes a transition from being within the place of business registration regime to being within the branch registration regime, or vice versa. Separate transitional provisions apply in consequence of the introduction of the branch registration regime in Great Britain on 1 January 1993.

(13) **Change from place of business regime to branch regime**

The following provisions apply where a company becomes a company to which *CA 1985, s 690A* applies (branch registration regime) (see (5) above), having immediately beforehand been within *section 691* (place of business registration regime) (see (3) above).

The company need not include the particulars at (7)(*d*) above (list of directors and secretary) in its first return to be delivered under (6) above to the Registrar for a part of Great Britain (see (48) below) if, at the time of transition,

- it had an established place of business in that part;
- it had complied with (3)(*b*)(i) above (details of directors and secretary); and
- it had no outstanding obligation to make a return under *CA 1985, s 692(1)* in respect of an alteration of the kind mentioned at (4)(*b*) above (concerning directors and secretary).

To take advantage of this exemption, the company must state in the return under (6) above that the particulars have been previously filed in respect of a place of business in that part of Great Britain, giving the company's registered number.

A similar exemption applies with regard to the delivery of documents, other than accounting documents, referred to in (10) above, which broadly corresponds with the requirement at (3)(*a*) above under the place of business registration regime.

[*CA 1985, Sch 21B para 1; SI 1992 No 3179, Sch 2 para 5*].

Where a company

- becomes a company to which *CA 1985, s 690A* applies (see (5) above),
- immediately afterwards has in a part of Great Britain an established place of business but no branch, and
- immediately beforehand had an established place of business in that part of Great Britain,

then, in relation to that part of Great Britain, *CA 1985, ss 691, 692* (place of business registration regime) (see (3) and (4) above) continue to apply to the company (notwithstanding *section 690B* – see (2) above) until such time as it gives notice to the Registrar for that part of Great Britain (see (48) below) that it is a company within *section 690A* (branch registration regime).

[*CA 1985, s 692A(3); SI 1992 No 3179, Sch 2 para 4*].

(14) **Change from branch regime to place of business regime**

The following provisions apply where a company becomes a company to which *CA 1985, s 691* applies (place of business registration regime) (see (3) above), having immediately beforehand been within *section 690A* (branch registration regime) (see (5) above).

The company need not deliver the documents referred to at (3)(*a*) above to the Registrar for a part of Great Britain (see (48) below) if, at the time of transition,

- it had a branch in that part;
- the documents, other than accounting documents, referred to in (10) above were included in the material registered in respect of the branch; and
- the company had no outstanding obligation to make a return to the Registrar for that part of Great Britain under *CA 1985, Sch 21A para 7* (return of alterations – see (11) above) as regards any alteration in the said documents.

To take advantage of this exemption, the company must state in its return under *CA 1985, s 691* (see (3)(*b*)) above that the documents have been previously filed in respect of a branch of the company, giving the branch's registered number.

A similar exemption applies with regard to the information required by *CA 1985, s 691(1)(b)(i)* (details of directors and secretary – see (3)(*b*)(i) above) which broadly corresponds with the requirement at (7)(*d*) above under the branch registration scheme.

[*CA 1985, Sch 21B para 2; SI 1992 No 3179, Sch 2 para 5*].

Where a company ceases to be a company to which *CA 1985, s 690A* applies (branch registration regime) (see (5) above) and, immediately afterwards,

- continues to have in Great Britain a place of business which it had immediately beforehand, and
- does not have a branch in Northern Ireland,

it is treated for *section 691* purposes (place of business registration regime) (see (3) above) as having established the place of business on the date when it ceased to be a company to which *section 690A* applies.

[*CA 1985, s 692A(1); SI 1992 No 3179, Sch 2 para 4*].

Where a limited company incorporated outside the UK and Gibraltar

- ceases to have a branch in Northern Ireland, and
- both immediately beforehand and immediately afterwards, has a place of business, but not a branch, in Great Britain,

it is treated for *CA 1985, s 691* purposes as having established the place of business on the date when it ceased to have a branch in Northern Ireland. [*CA 1985, s 692A(2); SI 1992 No 3179, Sch 2 para 4*].

(15) **Miscellaneous matters**

Places of business. An overseas company must conspicuously exhibit in every place where it carries on business in Great Britain

- its name;
- its country of incorporation; and
- if applicable, the fact that its members have limited liability.

[*CA 1985, s 693(1)(b), (d); SI 1992 No 3179, Sch 2 para 6*].

See (20) below for penalties for non-compliance.

(16) **Letter paper, notices etc**

An overseas company must state in legible characters in all bill-heads, letter paper, notices and official publications

- its name and the country of incorporation; and
- if applicable, the fact that the liability of members is limited.

[*CA 1985, s 693(1)(c), (d); SI 1992 No 3179, Sch 2 para 6*].

See (21) below for penalties for non-compliance.

(17) **Duty to state name etc – branches**

The following provisions apply only to companies within *CA 1985, s 690A* (branch registration regime – see (5) above), and apply in addition to those relating to overseas companies generally at (13) and (14) above.

In the case of each company branch registered under *CA 1985, Sch 21A para 1* (see (6) above), the following particulars must be stated in legible characters in all letter paper and order forms used in carrying on the business of the branch.

(a) As regards such branches of all companies within *CA 1985, s 690A* (see (5) above)

(i) the place of registration of the branch; and

(ii) the registered number of the branch.

(b) As regards such branches of every company within *CA 1985, s 690A* which is not incorporated in an EC Member State and which is required by the law of the country in which it is incorporated to be registered

(i) the identity of the registry in which the company is registered in its country of incorporation; and

(ii) the number with which it is registered.

(c) As regards such branches of every company within *CA 1985, s 690A* which is not incorporated in an EC Member State

(i) the legal form of the company;

(ii) the location of its head office; and

(iii) if applicable, the fact that it is being wound up.

[*CA 1985, s 693(2)–(4); SI 1992 No 3179, Sch 2 para 6*].

Where a company is notified by the Registrar of a change of a branch's registered number, it may continue to use the old number for three years beginning with the date of notification without contravening (a)(ii) above.

[*CA 1985, s 705A(5); SI 1992 No 3179, Reg 3*].

(18) **Company name**

See (4) above for notification of change of name to Registrar of Companies and (16) and (17) above for disclosure of name on letter paper etc.

Notice may be served on an overseas company within twelve months of the 'relevant date' to the effect that

(a) its name would have been prohibited under *CA 1985, s 26* if it had been formed under *CA 1985*; or

(b) its name is too like a name already appearing in the Index of names kept by the Registrar of Companies.

The 'relevant date' is the date on which the company complied with the provisions of (3) above or those of (6) above, or the first such date, if more than one, since it became an overseas company. However, if on a later date the company's corporate name has been changed, the 'relevant date' is the date on which the company complied with the provisions of (4)(*b*) above or those of *CA 1985, Sch 21A para 7* (see (11) above) in respect of the change or, if more than one, the latest change.

The notice, which may be withdrawn within two months of service, must state the reason under (*a*) or the similar name under (*b*). The overseas company must not then, at any time after the expiration of two months from the date of notice, carry on business in Great Britain using the corporate name (although doing so does not invalidate any transaction entered into by the company). If it does, the company and every officer or agent who knowingly and wilfully authorises or permits the contravention is guilty of an offence and liable to a fine.

The company may, however, deliver to the appropriate Registrar of Companies (see (48) below) a statement in the prescribed form (Form 694(a)) specifying a name, other than its corporate name, under which it proposes to carry on business in Great Britain. This name may also be subsequently changed using Form 694(b). The new registered name is then deemed to be the company's corporate name but without affecting any rights or obligations of the company or any legal proceedings against the company under its corporate name or any previously registered name.

[*CA 1985, ss 694, 697(2), Sch 24; SI 1992 No 3179, Sch 2 para 7*].

(19) **Service of documents on an overseas company**

Any process or notice required to be served on an overseas company within *CA 1985, s 691* (place of business regime, see (3) above) is sufficiently served if addressed to any person whose name has been delivered to the Registrar of Companies under (3) or (4) above and left at, or sent by post to, his address. Where this is not possible (because no such names have been delivered or the persons named are dead, have moved or refuse to accept service) a document may be served on the company by leaving it at, or sending it by post to, any place of business established by the company in Great Britain. [*CA 1985, s 695; SI 1992 No 3179, Sch 2 para 9*]. The place of business must exist at the time of the service and cannot merely be a former place of business (*Deverall v Grant Advertising Inc* [1955] Ch 111, [1954] 3 All ER 389, CA).

Any process or notice required to be served on a company within *CA 1985, s 690A* (branch registration regime) (see (5) above) in respect of the carrying on of the business of a registered branch is sufficiently served if addressed to any person whose name has, in respect of the branch, been delivered to the Registrar as a person falling within (8)(*e*) above and left at, or sent by post to, the address of that person which has been so delivered. Where this is not possible, the same provisions apply as under *CA 1985, s 695* (see above). Where such a company has more than one branch in Great Britain, any process or notice which does not relate to the business of any one branch is treated for these purposes as being required to be served in respect of the business of each branch.

[*CA 1985, s 694A; SI 1992 No 3179, Sch 2 para 8*].

(20) **Penalties**

If an overseas company fails to comply with any of the provisions of (3), (4), (16), (17) above or (48) below, the company and every officer or agent of the company who knowingly and wilfully authorises or permits the default is liable to a fine. [*CA 1985, s 697(1), Sch 24*].

If an overseas company fails to comply with any of the provisions of (6) to (11) above or (49) below, the company and every officer or agent who knowingly and wilfully authorises or permits the default is liable on summary conviction to a maximum fine of one-fifth of level 5 on the standard scale and, in the case of a continuing offence, a daily default fine £100.

[*CA 1985, s 697(3), Sch 24; SI 1992 No 3179, Sch 2 para 12*].

(21) **Channel Islands and Isle of Man companies**

Subject to the exceptions below, the provisions of *CA 1985* and *CA 2006* requiring documents to be delivered or filed with the Registrar of Companies apply to an overseas company which is within *CA 1985, s 691* (place of business regime, see (3) above) and which is incorporated in the Channel Islands and the Isle of Man

- as if it were formed under *CA 1985*;
- if it has an established place of business in England and Wales, as if it were registered in England and Wales;
- if it has an established place of business in Scotland, as if it were registered there;
- if it has an established place of business in both England and Wales and Scotland, as if it were registered in both England and Wales and Scotland; and
- in a similar way to documents relating to things done outside Great Britain, as if they had been done in Great Britain.

The exceptions are as follows (for which the normal rules for overseas companies apply).

- *CA 1985, s 6(1)* (resolution altering the company's objects).
- *CA 1985, s 18* (alteration of memorandum and articles by statute or statutory instrument).
- *CA 1985, s 288(2)* (notice to Registrar of Companies of change of directors or secretary).
- *CA 2006, ss 29, 30* (resolutions and agreements affecting a company's constitution, so far as applicable to a resolution altering a company's memorandum or articles.
- *CA 2006, s 441* (directors' duty to file accounts).

[*CA 1985, s 699; CA 1989, Sch 10 para 12; SI 1992 No 3179, Sch 2 para 14; SI 2007 No 2194, Sch 4 para 1; SI 2008 No 948, Sch 1 para 84*].

(22) **Accounts and reports**

Every overseas company, other than those within (23) and (24) below, must, in respect of each financial year of the company, prepare like accounts and directors' report, and cause to be prepared such an auditors' report, as would be required if the company were formed and registered under *CA 1985*. [*CA 1985, s 700(1); CA 1989, Sch 10 para 13*]. The Secretary of State may, however, modify or exempt an overseas company from these requirements [*CA 1985, s 700(2)–(4); CA 1989, Sch 10 para 13*] and this has been done by the *Overseas Companies (Accounts) (Modifications and Exemptions) Order 1990* (*SI 1990 No 440*). The effect of the order is that, for accounts purposes, overseas companies are subject to certain of the provisions of *CA 1985, Pt VII* (accounts and audit) as if that part had not been amended by *CA 1989*.

This is considered more fully in (26) to (36) below. Note that if the company is listed, it must comply with certain necessary requirements, including circulating audited financial statements to members. Such a company may not therefore be able to take advantage of the exemptions available.

(23) **Exceptions**

Overseas company with UK branch. The provisions of (22) above and (26) to (38) below do not apply to any limited company which is incorporated outside the UK and Gibraltar and has a branch (as defined in (2) above) in the UK.

[*CA 1985, s 699B; SI 1992 No 3179, Sch 2 para 17*].

See also (39) to (46) below.

(24) **Oversea credit or financial institution with branch in Great Britain**

The provisions of (23) and (26) to (38) below do not apply to any credit or financial institution which

- is incorporated or otherwise formed outside the UK and Gibraltar,
- whose head office is outside the UK and Gibraltar, and
- which has a branch in Great Britain.

[*CA 1985, s 699B; SI 1992 No 3179, Reg 2*].

See (44) to (47) for the provisions applying to such institutions. See (44) below for the meaning of 'credit institution', 'financial institution' and, for these purposes, 'branch'.

(25) **Duty to prepare annual accounts**

For every oversea company, the directors must prepare a profit and loss account (or, if not trading for profit, an income and expenditure account) for each financial year and a balance sheet as at the last day of that year. In the case of a holding company, the directors must ensure that, except where there are good reasons, the financial year of its subsidiaries coincides with the company's own financial year.

[*CA 1985, s 227* as originally enacted].

(26) **Individual accounts: form and content**

The balance sheet and profit and loss account must give a true and fair view of the state of affairs of the company as at the end of the financial year and its profit or loss for that year.

The following information must be given as appropriate on the balance sheet, profit and loss account or in the notes. The Secretary of State may, on application or with the consent of the company's directors, modify any of the requirements in relation to the company in order to adapt them to the circumstances of the company.

(i) **Assets and liabilities generally**. Liabilities and assets must be summarised with such particulars as may be necessary to disclose their general nature. They must be classified under headings appropriate to the company's business unless a particular class is immaterial or, in the case of a class of assets, inseparable from another.

Fixed assets, current assets, and those neither fixed nor current, must be separately identified.

If the directors are of the opinion that any current assets would not realise their balance sheet value if realised in the ordinary course of business, they must state that fact in a note.

(ii) **Fixed assets.**

(a) The method or methods used to arrive at the amount of fixed assets under each heading must be stated.

(b) Subject to the exceptions below, the method of arriving at the amount of any fixed asset is to be taken as the difference between its cost (or, if standing in the company's books at valuation, its valuation) and the aggregate amount provided or written off since the date of acquisition (or valuation) for depreciation or diminution in value. Such totals must be given for each heading. Where the assets are included at valuation, the year of valuation (if known) must be stated in the notes. If valued during the financial year, the names and qualifications of the valuers, and basis of valuation, must also be given.

The provisions in (*b*) above does not apply to the following assets.

- Assets the replacement of which is provided either by making provision for renewals and charging the cost of replacement against that provision or by charging the cost of replacement direct to revenue. For such assets there must be stated the means by which their replacement is provided for and the aggregate amount of the provision (if any) made for renewals and not used.
- Listed or unlisted investments (see (6) and (7) below) of which the directors' valuation is shown either as a balance sheet figure or by way of note.
- Goodwill, patents or trademarks (see (4) below).

The aggregate amounts of assets acquired, and assets disposed of or destroyed, during the financial year must be stated by way of note for fixed assets under each heading.

(iii) **Preliminary expenses**. The amount of preliminary expenses (so far as not written off) must be shown in the balance sheet under a separate heading.

(iv) **Goodwill, patents etc**. The amount of goodwill, and of any patents or trademarks, so far as not written off, must be disclosed as a single item under a separate heading provided the amount is ascertainable from the company's books or from any contract or document relating to the sale or purchase.

(v) **Land**. In relation to any fixed asset shown in the balance sheet consisting of land there must be stated how much is ascribable to freehold land (or Scottish equivalent) and how much to leasehold land (or Scottish equivalent) and, of the latter, how much is ascribable to '*long leases*' (ie 'leases' with an unexpired term at the end of the financial year of at least 50 years) and how much to '*short leases*' (ie any other lease). '*Lease*' includes an agreement for a lease.

(vi) **Listed investments**.

(a) The aggregate amount of the company's 'listed investments' must be shown under a separate heading, subdivided where necessary to distinguish (i) those listed on a recognised investment exchange other than an overseas investment exchange within the meaning of the *FSMA 2000*; and (ii) those not so listed.

(b) There must be shown by way of note (i) the aggregate market value of the listed investments where it differs from the amount as stated in the balance sheet; and (ii) the stock exchange value of any investments of which the market value is shown as a higher figure.

'*Listed investments*' are those which have been granted a listing either on a recognised investment exchange (other than an overseas investment exchange within the meaning of *FSMA 2000*) or on any stock exchange of repute outside Great Britain.

(vii) **Unlisted investments**.

(a) The aggregate amount of the company's 'unlisted investments' must be shown under a separate heading.

(b) In the case of such investments in equity shares of other companies, unless the directors' estimated valuation is either included as the balance sheet figure or disclosed in a note, the following information must be stated by way of note: (i) the aggregate amount of the company's income for the financial year ascribable to the investment; (ii) the amount of the company's share in the net aggregate pre-tax profits of the companies in which the investments are held, and the amount of that share after taxation; (iii) the amount of the company's share in the net aggregate undistributed profits (less losses) accumulated by those companies since the time the investments were acquired; and (iv) the manner in which any losses incurred by those companies have been dealt with in the company's accounts.

'*Unlisted investments*' are any investments other than listed investments (see (6) above).

(viii) **Group undertakings**. Where the company is a parent company, there must be disclosed separately on the balance sheet

- the aggregate amount of assets consisting of shares in, or amounts owing from, the company's subsidiary undertakings (distinguishing shares from indebtedness); and
- the aggregate amount in indebtedness to the company's subsidiary undertakings.

Where the company is a subsidiary undertaking, the balance sheet must show the aggregate amount of

- indebtedness to undertakings of which it is a subsidiary undertaking or which are fellow subsidiary undertakings;
- indebtedness of all such undertakings to it, distinguishing in each case between indebtedness in respect of debentures and otherwise; and
- assets consisting of shares in fellow subsidiary undertakings.

(ix) **Current assets.**

(a) *Stocks.* The manner in which stock and work in progress has been computed must be stated by way of note if the amount is material to the company's state of affairs or its profit or loss for the financial year.

(b) *Foreign currencies.* The basis on which foreign currencies have been converted into sterling must be stated by way of note, if material.

(c) *Loans to purchase own shares.* There must be stated the aggregate amount of outstanding loans: (i) to employees' share schemes under *CA 1985, s 153(4)(b)* or employees and their families under *CA 1985, s 153(4)(c)*; or (ii) by private companies under *CA 1985, s 155*, in each case for the purpose of giving financial assistance to purchase shares in the company.

(x) **Loans.** There must be shown under separate headings

(a) the aggregate of bank loans and overdrafts; and

(b) the aggregate amount of other loans made to the company which are repayable (i) otherwise than by instalments and which fall due for repayment after the end of a five-year period beginning with the day after the end of the financial year; or (ii) by instalments any of which fall due after the end of that period.

For loans under (*b*) above, the terms of repayment and rate of interest for each loan must be disclosed by way of note unless, because of the number of such loans, the directors are of the opinion that compliance would result in a statement of excessive length. In such a case, a general indication of the terms and interest rates is sufficient.

A loan, or an instalment of a loan, is deemed to be due for repayment on the earliest date on which the lender could require repayment if he exercised all options and rights available to him.

(xi) **Taxation.** There must be stated

(a) the amount, if any, set aside to prevent undue fluctuations in charges to tax and, if during the financial year such a fund has been used for any other purpose, the amount used and the fact that it has been so used; and

(b) particulars of any special circumstances affecting liability in respect of taxation of profits, income or capital gains for the financial year in question and/or succeeding financial years.

(xii) **Secured liabilities**. Where any liability of the company is secured otherwise than by operation of the law on any asset of the company, that fact must be stated (although it is not necessary to specify the asset in question).

(xiii) **Guarantees and other financial commitments**. The following information must be stated.

(a) Particulars of any charge on the company's assets to secure the liabilities of any other person, including, where practicable, the amount secured.

(b) The general nature of any contingent liabilities not provided for and, where practicable, the aggregate amount or estimated amount if material.

(c) Where practicable, the aggregate amount or estimated amount, if material, of (i) contracts for capital expenditure, so far as not provided for; and (ii) capital expenditure authorised by the directors which has not been contracted for.

(xiv) **Distributions**. The aggregate amount of recommended dividends must be disclosed under a separate heading. In addition, there must be shown by way of note

(a) the amount of any arrears of fixed cumulative dividends on the company's shares and the period for which they are in arrears (detailing each class separately if more than one); and

(b) any distribution by an 'investment company' which reduces the amount of its net assets to less than the aggregate of called-up share capital and 'undistributable reserves'. See **22.1** DISTRIBUTIONS for *'investment company'* and *'undistributable reserves'*.

(xv) **Debentures**. There must be stated

(a) particulars of any redeemed debentures which the company has power to reissue;

(b) to the extent that they are not written off, and, if not, under separate headings (i) any expenses incurred in connection with any issue of debentures; (ii) any sums paid by way of commission in respect of any debentures; and (iii) any sums allowed by way of discount in respect of any debentures; and

(c) the nominal amount of any of the company's debentures which are held by a nominee of, or a trustee for, the company, together with the amount at which that are stated in the books of the company.

(xvi) **Reserves and provisions**.

(a) 'Reserves' and 'provisions' must be classified under headings appropriate to the company's business; provided that where the amount of any class is not material, it may be included under the same heading as some other class.

(b) There must be stated (if material) (i) the aggregate amount respectively of reserves and provisions (other than provisions for depreciation, renewals or diminution in value of assets) under separate headings; and (ii) (unless shown in the profit and loss account or by way of note) the source of any increase as compared with the amount at the end of the previous financial year and the application of any decrease.

If the reserves or provisions are divided into sub-headings, this information must be given for each sub-heading.

'*Provision*' means any amount written off or retained by way of providing for depreciation, renewals or diminution in value of assets or retained by way of providing for any known liability the amount of which cannot be determined with substantial accuracy. Where, however, such amount is in excess of that which in the opinion of the directors is reasonably necessary for the purpose, the excess is to be treated as a reserve and not as a provision.

'*Reserve*' does not include any provision (other than any excess provision as above) or any sum set aside to prevent undue fluctuations in charges for taxation.

The Secretary of State may direct that a separate statement of provisions is not required if satisfied that it would not be in the public interest and would prejudice the company.

(xvii) **Share premium**. The amount of the share premium account must be specified on the balance sheet.

(xviii) **Share capital**. There must be stated

(a) the authorised and issued share capital;

(b) any part of the issued share capital that consists of redeemable shares together with (i) the earliest and latest dates on which the company has power to redeem those shares; (ii) whether the shares must be redeemed in any event or are liable to be redeemed at the option of the company or the shareholder; and (iii) whether any (and, if so, what) premium is payable on redemption;

(c) (if not stated in the profit and loss account) any share capital on which interest has been paid out of capital during the financial year; and the rate at which interest has been so paid;

(d) to the extent that they are not written off, and if not under separate headings (i) any expenses incurred in connection with any issue of share capital; (ii) any sums paid by way of commission in respect of any shares; and (iii) the amount of the discount allowed on any issue of shares;

(e) the number, description and amount of any shares in the company which any person has the option to subscribe for, together with details of (i) the period during which the option is exercisable; and (ii) the price to be paid for the shares subscribed for under the option; and

(f) where shares in a public company are purchased or acquired by the company (by forfeiture or surrender in lieu) or by another person on the company's behalf, details must be given of the (i) number and nominal value of the shares involved; (ii) consideration paid, if any, and reason for the purchase; (iii) maximum number and nominal value of shares held during the year; (iv) number and nominal value of shares so acquired which are disposed of or cancelled in the year and the consideration; and (v) percentage of the called-up share capital involved for each of the above items.

(xix) **Separate statement of certain items of income and expenditure**. The following must be stated.

(a) The amount of interest on (i) bank loans and overdrafts and other loans made to the company which are repayable *either* otherwise than by instalments and fall due before the end of a five-year period beginning with the day after the end of the financial year *or* by instalments the last of which falls due for payment before the end of that period; and (ii) loans of any other kind made to the company. A loan or an instalment of a loan, is deemed to be due for repayment on the earliest date on which the lender could require repayment if he exercised all options and rights available to him.

(b) The amounts respectively set aside for redemption of share capital and for redemption of loans.

(c) The amount of income from listed investments and unlisted investments (see (6) and (7) above).

(d) The amount of rents from land (net of ground rents, rates and other outgoings including, in Scotland, feu-duty and ground annual) but only if a substantial part of the company's revenue for the financial year consists of such rents.

(e) The amount, if material, charged to revenue for the hire of plant and machinery.

(xx) **Depreciation**. The amount charged to revenue by way of provision for depreciation, renewals or diminution in value of fixed assets must be shown. In the case of assets for which an amount is charged to revenue by way of provision for depreciation or diminution in value

(a) if an amount is also charged by way of provision for renewal, that amount must be shown separately; and

(b) if the amount charged to revenue has been determined otherwise than by reference to the amount of those assets as determined for balance sheet purposes, that fact must be stated. This does not apply to provisions for diminution in investments.

If depreciation or replacement of fixed assets is provided for by some method other than a depreciation charge or provision for renewals (or is not provided for), the method by which it is provided (or that fact) must be stated by way of note.

(xxi) **Directors' emoluments**. Details must be disclosed of directors' emoluments, pensions of directors and past directors and compensation to directors for loss of office. See **3.44**, **3.46** and **3.47** ACCOUNTS: LARGE COMPANIES which apply ignoring

(a) amounts paid to or receivable by a connected person or a body corporate controlled by the director; and

(b) in relation to pensions and compensation for loss of office, the nature and estimated money value of any benefits paid otherwise than in cash.

Comparative figures for the immediately preceding financial year must also be given.

(xxii) **Dividends and transfers to and from reserves**. There must be disclosed

(a) the aggregate amount of dividends paid and proposed;

(b) the amount, if material, set aside to, or withdrawn from, provisions other than those within (xx) above. The Secretary of State may, however, direct that the company is not obliged to show such amount if it is not in the public interest and would prejudice the company.

See (xvi) above for 'provisions' and 'reserves'.

(xxiii) **Auditors' remuneration**. The amount of auditors' remuneration (if any) including expenses must be stated.

(xxiv) **Miscellaneous**.

(a) The amount of any charge arising in consequence of the occurrence of an event in the preceding financial year and of any credit so arising must, if not included in a heading related to other matters, be stated under a separate heading.

(b) Where any items in the profit and loss account are materially affected by (i) transactions of a sort not usually undertaken by the company or by circumstances of an exceptional or non-recurrent nature, or (ii) any change in the basis of accounting, this fact must be stated by way of note.

(xxv) **Comparative figures**. Comparative figures for all items in the balance sheet and profit and loss account at the end of, or for, the immediately preceding financial year must be shown.

[*CA 1985, s 258(1)(4), Sch 9, Pt I* as originally enacted; *SI 1990 No 440*].

(27) **Group undertakings**

Where the company is a holding company (whether or not it is itself a subsidiary) the following must be disclosed separately as indicated.

(a) The aggregate amount of assets consisting of shares in, or the amount owing from, the company's subsidiaries (distinguishing shares from indebtedness) must be shown in the balance sheet.

(b) The aggregate amount of indebtedness to the company's subsidiaries must be shown in the balance sheet.

(c) The number, description and amount of the shares in, and debentures of, the company held by its subsidiaries or their nominees must be shown as a note. Excluded are any shares held as personal representative or as trustee where neither the company nor any subsidiary is beneficially interested under the trust.

(d) Where group accounts are not submitted, there must be annexed to the balance sheet a statement showing

(i) the reasons why subsidiaries are not dealt with in group accounts;

(ii) the net aggregate amount, so far as it concerns members of the holding company and is not dealt with in the company's accounts, of the subsidiaries' profits after deducting losses (or vice versa) for the financial years of the subsidiaries ending with, or during, the financial year of the company. Comparative figures must also be given if they were then subsidiaries;

(iii) the net aggregate amount of the subsidiaries' profits after deducting losses (or vice versa) for the financial years of the subsidiaries ending with or during the financial year of the company so far as those profits are dealt with, or provision is made for those losses, in the company's accounts. Comparative figures must also be given if they were then subsidiaries;

(iv) any qualifications contained in the audit reports of the subsidiaries (or notes to the accounts which would have properly been referred to in such a qualification if not so disclosed) which is not covered in the company's own accounts and is material to the members;

(v) if any of the information required under (i) to (iv) above is not obtainable, a statement to that effect; and

(vi) in relation to any subsidiaries whose financial years do not end with that of the company, the directors' reasons for this and the dates on which the subsidiaries' financial years ended last before the end of the company's financial year (or the earliest and latest of those dates).

The provisions of (ii) and (iii) above only apply to profits properly treated as revenue profits (with certain exceptions). They do not apply where the company is a wholly-owned subsidiary of another company incorporated in Great Britain provided a statement is attached to the balance sheet that, in the directors' opinion, the aggregate values of the shares in, and amounts owing, from the company's subsidiaries is not less than the aggregate amounts at which those assets are stated or included in the balance sheet.

Where a company is a subsidiary (whether or not it is itself a holding company) the balance sheet must show the aggregate amount of

- indebtedness to companies of which it is a subsidiary or a fellow subsidiary;
- indebtedness of all such companies to it, distinguishing in each case between indebtedness in respect of debentures and otherwise; and
- assets consisting of shares in fellow subsidiaries.

[*CA 1985, Sch 9 paras 19, 20* as originally enacted; *SI 1990 No 440*].

(28) **Group accounts of holding company**

Subject to below, if an oversea company has subsidiaries at the end of its financial year, the directors must, in addition to the individual accounts, prepare a *consolidated* profit and loss account and balance sheet dealing with the state of affairs and profit or loss of the company and its subsidiaries. This does not apply if

(a) the company is, at the end of the financial year, a wholly-owned subsidiary of another body corporate incorporated in Great Britain; or

(b) the directors are of the opinion that

- it would be impracticable, disproportionately expensive or misleading;
- (provided the Secretary of State agrees) the result would be harmful or the businesses are so different that they cannot reasonably be treated as a single undertaking; or
- instead of consolidating figures for the whole group, either more than one set of consolidated accounts are prepared *or* separate accounts are prepared for each subsidiary *or* statements expanding on the information about the subsidiaries are given in the company's individual accounts *or* any combination of those forms.

[*CA 1985, s 229* as originally enacted].

(29) **Form and content of group accounts**

The group accounts must give a true and fair view of the state of affairs and profit or loss of the company and the subsidiaries dealt with by those accounts as a whole, so far as concerns members of the company.

Where the financial year of a subsidiary does not coincide with that of the holding company, the group accounts must deal with the subsidiary's state of affairs as at the end of its 'relevant financial year' and its profit or loss for that year. The '*relevant financial year*' is the financial year ending with that of the holding company or, if the subsidiary has no financial year so ending, its financial year ending last before that date.

The consolidated balance sheet and profit and loss account must combine the information contained in the separate balance sheets and profit and loss accounts of the holding company and subsidiaries dealt with by the consolidated accounts but with such adjustments as the directors of the holding company think necessary. Subject to that, the group accounts must comply, so far as practicable, with the provisions listed in (27) above as if the 'group' (meaning, for these purposes, all the companies included in the consolidation) were an individual company.

Where any subsidiaries of the holding company are not dealt with by the consolidated accounts

- the provisions of (28)(*a*)–(*c*) above apply as if such subsidiaries were subsidiaries of the 'group'; and
- there must be annexed to the accounts the like statement as is required by (28)(*d*)(i)–(iv) above but as if references to the holding company's accounts were references to the consolidated accounts.

In relation to any subsidiary (whether or not dealt with in the consolidated accounts) whose financial year did not end with that of the company, there must be annexed the like statement as is required under (28)(*d*)(vi) above where there are no group accounts.

[*CA 1985, s 259, Sch 9 paras 21–26, 31* as originally enacted; *SI 1990 No 440*].

(30) **Small and medium-sized companies**

The provisions for small and medium-sized companies do not apply to oversea companies. [SI *1990 No 440, Art 2(c)*].

(31) **Directors' report**

An oversea company need not prepare a directors' report or disclose any of the information required in such a report under *CA 1985, Sch 7* or *Sch 10*.

[*SI 1990 No 440, Sch 1 para 3*].

(32) **Auditors' report**

An oversea company is not required to have an auditors' report attached to its accounts.

[*SI 1990 No 440, Sch 1 para 4*].

(33) **Signing of the balance sheet**

An oversea company's accounts must be approved by the board and signed on its behalf by two directors (if there is only one director, by that one). Every copy laid before the company in general meeting or delivered to the Registrar of Companies (see (38) below) must be signed. If not, or if a copy is otherwise issued, circulated or published without being signed or bearing a copy of the signature(s), the company and every officer in default is liable to a fine.

[*CA 1985, s 238* as originally enacted; *SI 1990 No 440, Sch 1, para 4*].

(34) **Dormant companies**

The provisions of *CA 1985, ss 252, 253* as originally enacted (resolution of dormant company not to appoint auditors and laying and delivery of unaudited accounts) do not apply to oversea companies.

[*SI 1990 No 440, Reg 2(c)*].

(35) **Unlimited oversea companies**

An unlimited oversea company which at no time during the accounting reference period

- has been, to its knowledge, the subsidiary of a limited company, or
- has had, to its knowledge, shares owned or power exercised by two or more companies which if exercised by one would have made the company its subsidiary, or
- has been a promoter of a trading stamp scheme

is not required to prepare accounts or deliver them to the Registrar of Companies.

[*CA 1985, ss 241(4), 700(3)* as originally enacted; *SI 1990 No 440, Reg 2(3)*].

(36) **Accounting reference dates**

The provisions in 2 Accounting Reference Dates and Periods apply to oversea companies subject to the modification in **2.5**.

(37) **Delivery of accounts to the Registrar of Companies**

Subject to the following exceptions, the accounts and reports must be delivered to the appropriate Registrar of Companies (see (48) below), together with a certified translation if in a language other than English, within 13 months (or such longer period as the Secretary of State allows) after the end of the relevant accounting reference period. The exceptions are as follows.

- If the relevant accounting reference period is the company's first and is for a period of more than twelve months, the period allowed is 25 months from the company's establishing a place of business in Great Britain.
- If the relevant accounting period is shortened by notice under *CA 2006, s 392* (see **2.4 Accounting Reference Dates and Periods**), the period allowed is 13 months after the end of the relevant accounting reference period or three months from the date of notice, whichever last expires.

[*CA 1985, s 702; CA 1989, Sch 10 para 13; SI 2008 No 948, Sch 1 para 86*].

Penalties. Where the accounts are not filed in the period allowed or do not comply with the requirements of CA 1985, the company and every person who immediately before the end of that period was a director of the company is guilty of an offence and liable to a fine. It is a defence for a person charged with such an offence to prove that he took all reasonable steps to secure that the requirements in question were complied with but it is not a defence in relation to failure to deliver copies to the Registrar to prove that the documents were not in fact prepared as required by CA 1985.

[*CA 1985, s 703, Sch 24; CA 1989, Sch 10, para 10*].

(38) **Accounts and reports – companies with branches in Great Britain**

The provisions at (40) to (46) below apply to any company within *CA 1985, s 699AA*, ie any limited company which

- is incorporated outside the UK and Gibraltar,
- has a branch in Great Britain, and
- is not a credit or financial institution within *CA 1985, s 699A* (see (47) below).

[*CA 1985, s 699AA; SI 1992 No 3179, Sch 2 para 16*].

(39) **Companies required to make disclosure under parent law**

The provisions at (41) and (42) below apply to any company within (39) above which is required by its parent law (ie the law of the country in which it is incorporated) to prepare, have audited and publicly disclose accounts.

(40) **Duty to deliver accounting documents**

The following provisions apply in respect of each branch which a company within (40) above has in Great Britain.

The company must deliver to the Registrar of Companies, for registration in respect of the branch, copies of all the 'accounting documents' prepared in relation to a 'financial period' of the company which are disclosed in accordance with its parent law (ie the law of the country in which it is incorporated), where such disclosure occurs

- after the end of the period allowed for compliance with *CA 1985, Sch 21A para 1* in respect of the branch (see (6) above), or, if earlier,
- on or after the date on which such compliance occurs.

For these purposes, the following are '*accounting documents*' in relation to a 'financial period' of a company.

(i) The accounts of the company for the period, including, if it has one or more subsidiaries, any consolidated accounts of the group.

(ii) Any annual report of the directors for the period.

(iii) The auditors' report on the accounts in (i) above.

(iv) Any auditors' report on the report in (ii) above.

A '*financial period*' of a company means a period for which it is required or permitted by its parent law to prepare accounts.

Where the company's parent law permits it to publicly disclose accounting documents in a modified form only, the company will satisfy these provisions if it delivers copies of documents as so modified.

If any document is in a language other than English, there must be annexed to the copy delivered an English translation, certified in the prescribed manner to be a correct translation.

Documents are not required to be delivered for a particular branch if

- they are delivered in respect of another UK branch within the time limit allowed; and
- the particulars registered under *CA 1985, Sch 21A* in respect of the branch indicate an intention that the documents are to be registered in respect of that other branch and include the required details of that other branch. See (9) above.

Time limit. The period allowed for delivery, in relation to any document within these provisions, is three months from the date on which the document is first publicly disclosed in accordance with the company's parent law.

Penalties. On the failure of the company to comply with these provisions within the time limit, the company and every person who was a director immediately before expiry of the time limit is guilty of an offence and liable to a fine. It is a defence for a person charged with such an offence to prove that he took all reasonable steps to secure compliance.

[*CA 1985, Sch 21D paras 2–6, Sch 24; SI 1992 No 3179, Sch 2 para 18*].

(41) Companies not required to make disclosure under parent law

The provisions in (44) to (46) below apply to any company within (39) above which is *not* required by its parent law (ie the law of the country in which it is incorporated) to prepare, have audited and publicly disclose accounts.

(42) Preparation of accounts and reports

A company within (39) above must prepare the like accounts and directors' report, and cause to be prepared such an auditors' report, as would be required if the company were within *CA 1985, s 700* (see (23) above).

The provisions in to 2 ACCOUNTS (GENERAL) AND ACCOUNTING REFERENCE DATES AND PERIODS and the definition of 'financial year' in APPENDIX 1 DEFINITIONS apply with the following modifications.

(a) For the references to the incorporation of a company, there should be substituted references to its becoming a company within (39) above; and

(b) The restrictions in 2 on the frequency with which the current accounting reference period may be extended do not apply.

[*CA 1985, Sch 21D paras 8, 9; SI 1992 No 3179, Sch 2 para 18; SI 2008 No 948, Sch 1 para 94*].

(43) **Duty to deliver accounts and reports**

In respect of each financial year and in respect of each branch which it has in Great Britain at the end of that financial year, a company within (39) above must deliver to the Registrar of Companies copies of the accounts and reports prepared in accordance with (40) above. If any document comprised in those accounts or reports is in a language other than English, there must be annexed to the copy delivered an English translation, certified in the prescribed manner to be a correct translation.

Documents are not required to be delivered for a particular branch if

- they are delivered in respect of another UK branch within the time limit allowed; and
- the particulars registered under *CA 1985, Sch 21A* in respect of the branch indicate an intention that the documents are to be registered in respect of that other branch and include the required details of that other branch. See (9) above.

Time limits. The period allowed for delivering accounts and reports under these provisions is 13 months after the end of the relevant accounting reference period (ie the accounting reference period by reference to which the financial year for the accounts in question was determined), subject to the following exceptions.

(i) If the relevant accounting reference period is the company's first and it exceeds 12 months, the period allowed is 13 months from the first anniversary of the company's becoming a company within (39) above.

(ii) If the relevant accounting reference period is treated as shortened by virtue of a notice given by the company under *CA 2006, s 392* (see 2 ACCOUNTS (GENERAL) AND ACCOUNTING REFERENCE DATES AND PERIODS), the period allowed is that normally applicable or three months from the date of the said notice, whichever last expires.

(iii) The Secretary of State has the power, on an application made within the period otherwise allowed, to extend that period by such further period as he specifies in a written notice to the company.

Penalties. On the failure of the company to comply with these provisions within the time limit applicable, or if the accounts and reports delivered do not comply with the statutory requirements, the company and every person who was a director immediately before expiry of the time limit is guilty of an offence and liable to a fine. It is a defence for a person charged with such an offence to prove that he took all reasonable steps to secure compliance. It is not a defence, in relation to a failure to deliver copies, to prove that the documents in question were not in fact prepared as statutorily required.

[*CA 1985, Sch 21D paras 10–13, Sch 24; SI 1992 No 3179, Sch 2 para 18*].

(44) **Accounts and reports – credit and financial institutions with branches in Great Britain**

The provisions at (45) to (46) below apply to any 'credit institution' or 'financial institution' (see below) within *CA 1985, s 699A*, ie any such institution

- which is incorporated or otherwise formed outside the UK and Gibraltar,
- whose head office is outside the UK and Gibraltar, and
- which has a 'branch' (see below) in Great Britain.

'*Credit institution*' means a credit institution as defined in *EC Council Directive 2002/12/EC, Art 1(1)(a)*, ie an undertaking whose business is to receive deposits or other repayable funds from the public and to grant credits for its own account.

'*Financial institution*' means a financial institution within the meaning of *Article 1* of the EC Council Directive on the obligations of branches, established in a Member State, of credit and financial institutions having their head offices outside that Member State regarding the publication of annual accounting documents (the 'Bank Branches Directive') (*89/117/EEC*).

'*Branch*', in relation to a credit or financial institution, means a place of business which forms a legally dependent part of the institution and which conducts directly all or some of the operations inherent in its business.

[*CA 1985, s 699A; SI 1992 No 3179, Reg 2; SI 2000 No 2952; SI 2002 No 765, Reg 2*].

(45) **Institutions required to prepare accounts under parent law**

The provisions in (49) and (50) below apply to any institution within (47) above which is required by its parent law (ie the law of the country in which it has its head office) to prepare and have audited accounts for its 'financial periods' (see (49) below) and whose only or principal 'branch' (see (47) above) within the UK is in Great Britain.

(46) **Duty to deliver accounting documents**

Initial requirement. An institution within (44) above must, within one month of its becoming such an institution, deliver to the appropriate Registrar of Companies (see below), for registration, copies of the latest 'accounting documents' (see below) of the institution prepared in accordance with its parent law (ie the law of the country in which it has its head office) to have been 'disclosed' (see below) *before* the earlier of the end of the said one-month period allowed for compliance and the actual date of compliance. If any of the said documents is not written in English, there must also be delivered an English translation certified in the prescribed manner to be a correct translation.

Where an institution within (44) above had, immediately prior to becoming such an institution, a branch in Northern Ireland which was its only or principal branch within the UK, it need not deliver the said documents if they have been delivered to the Registrar for Northern Ireland pursuant to the *Companies (Northern Ireland) Order 1986 (SI 1986 No 1032)*. Instead, it may deliver a notice that it has become an institution within (44) above.

[*CA 1985, Sch 21C para 2; SI 1992 No 3179, Sch 1*].

Subsequent requirements. An institution within (44) above must deliver to the appropriate Registrar of Companies (see below), for registration, copies of all the 'accounting documents' (see below) of the institution prepared in accordance with its parent law which are 'disclosed' (see below) *after* the earlier of the end of the one-month period allowed for compliance with the above initial requirement and the actual date of such compliance. The same provision applies as above as regards English translations where appropriate.

The period allowed for delivery, in relation to any such document, is three months from the date on which the document is first 'disclosed'.

[*CA 1985, Sch 21C para 3; SI 1992 No 3179, Sch 1*].

Exceptions. An institution is excepted from both the initial and subsequent requirements above if, at the end of the period allowed for compliance with the relevant requirement,

- the institution is not required by its parent law to register the documents;
- the documents are made available for inspection at each branch of the institution in Great Britain; and
- copies of the documents are available on request at a cost not exceeding the cost of supplying them.

If any of the above conditions cease to be met, the institution must deliver copies of the documents to the Registrar, for registration, within seven days of the condition ceasing to be met.

[*CA 1985, Sch 21C para 5; SI 1992 No 3179, Sch 1*].

General. Where the company's parent law permits it to disclose accounting documents in a modified form only, the company will satisfy the above provisions if it delivers copies of documents as so modified.

For the purposes of these provisions, a 'financial period', in relation to an institution, means a period for which it is required or permitted by its parent law to prepare accounts. 'Accounting documents' has the same meaning as in (41) above, substituting 'institution' for 'company' and, in the case of an institution which does not have directors, substituting for 'directors' the persons occupying equivalent offices.

References in these provisions to disclosure are normally to public disclosure, except for an institution which is not required either by its parent law or by statute having effect in Great Britain or by its own constitution to publicly disclose accounts, in which case references to disclosure are to the disclosure of the accounts to the persons for whose information they have been prepared.

[*CA 1985, Sch 21C paras 4, 8; SI 1992 No 3179, Sch 1*].

Appropriate Registrar of Companies. The documents required to be delivered under these provisions are to be delivered to

- the Registrar for England and Wales if the institution's only branch, or its principal branch within the UK, is in England and Wales; and
- the Registrar for Scotland if the institution's only branch, or its principal branch within the UK, is in Scotland.

[*CA 1985, Sch 21C para 6; SI 1992 No 3179, Sch 1*].

Penalties. On the failure of the institution to comply with any of the above provisions (including the delivery requirement under 'Exceptions') within the time limit applicable, the institution and every person who was a director immediately before expiry of the time limit is guilty of an offence and liable to a fine. In the case of an institution not having directors, a person occupying an equivalent office is so liable. It is a defence for a director or other person charged with such an offence to prove that he took all reasonable steps to secure compliance.

[*CA 1985, Sch 21C para 7, Sch 24*].

(47) **Institutions not required to prepare accounts under parent law**

As regards an institution within (45) above which is incorporated and which is *not* required by its parent law (ie the law of the country in which it has its head office) to prepare, and have audited, accounts provisions almost identical to those (44) to (46) above (substituting 'institution' for 'company') apply as regards its duty both to prepare and to deliver accounts and reports. The only differences of substance are as follows.

- The requirement to deliver accounts and reports does not apply separately in respect of each branch in Great Britain.
- There are additional provisions as to the appropriate Registrar of Companies to whom documents are to be delivered – these are similar to those in (49) above, substituting 'Great Britain' for 'the UK'.
- Penalties for non-compliance apply, as they would to directors, to persons occupying an equivalent office in the case of an institution which does not have directors.

Thus, under the transitional provisions, the new provisions first apply in respect of financial years ending after 31 December 1992.

[*CA 1985, Sch 21C paras 9–15; SI 1992 No 3179, Sch 1, Sch 4 para 5; SI 2008 No 948, Sch 1 para 93*].

(48) **Appropriate registrar of companies**

Companies within place of business registration regime. The documents which an oversea company within *CA 1985, s 691* (see (3) above) is required to deliver to the Registrar of Companies must be delivered to

- the Registrar for England and Wales if the company has established a place of business in England and/or Wales; and
- the Registrar for Scotland if the company has established a place of business in Scotland.

If the company has an established place of business in both parts of Great Britain, documents must be delivered to both Registrars although if it subsequently ceases to have an establishment in one part, it must give notice of that fact to the Registrar for that part and is then only obliged to deliver documents to the other Registrar.

[*CA 1985, s 696; CA 1989, Sch 19 para 13; SI 1992 No 3179, Sch 2 para 11; Sch 3 para 17*].

See (20) above for penalties for non-compliance.

(49) **Companies within branch registration regime**

The documents which a company within *CA 1985, s 690A* (see (5) above) is required to deliver to the Registrar of Companies must be delivered to

- the Registrar for England and Wales, if required to be delivered in respect of a branch in England and Wales; and
- the Registrar for Scotland, if required to be delivered in respect of a branch in Scotland.

If the company closes a branch in a part of Great Britain, or a branch ceases to be situated in that part on becoming situated elsewhere, it must give notice of that fact to the Registrar for that part and is then no longer obliged to deliver documents to that Registrar in respect of that branch.

[*CA 1985, s 695A; SI 1992 No 3179, Sch 2 para 10*].

See (20) above for penalties for non-compliance.

31 Political Donations

31.1 **Introduction**
31.2 **Definitions**
31.3 **Authorisation required for donations or expenditure**
31.4 **Remedies in cases of unauthorised donations and expenditure**
31.5 Enforcement of directors' liabilities by shareholder action
31.6 Costs of shareholder action
31.7 Information for purposes of shareholder action
31.8 **Exemptions**

Background. The provisions in this chapter came into force, unless otherwise stated, on 1 October 2007 (1 November 2007 in Northern Ireland). [*SI 2007 No 2194, Regs 2, 3*]. They replaced earlier provisions in *CA 1985, ss 347A–347K*.

31.1 INTRODUCTION

The provisions in **31.2** to **31.8** apply to control

- political donations made by companies to political parties, to other political organisations and (with effect from 1 October 2008) to independent election candidates; and
- political expenditure incurred by companies.

They apply to

- a *political party* if
  - (i) it is registered under *Political Parties, Elections and Referendums Act 2000* (*PPERA 2000*), *Pt II*; or
  - (ii) it carries on (or proposes to carry on) activities for the purposes of, or in connection with, the participation of the party in any election or elections to public office held in a Member State other than the UK;
- a *political organisation* if it carries on (or proposes to carry on) activities that are capable of being reasonably regarded as intended to
  - (i) affect public support for a political party to which, or an independent election candidate to whom, the provisions apply, or
  - (ii) influence voters in relation to any national or regional referendum held under the law of the UK or another Member State; and
- an *independent election candidate* at any election to public office held in the UK or another Member State.

Any reference in **31.2** to **31.8** to a political party, political organisation, (with effect from 1 October 2008) independent election candidate or political expenditure is to a party, organisation, independent candidate or expenditure to which these provisions apply.

[*CA 2006, ss 362, 363*].

31.2 DEFINITIONS

Director includes shadow director. [*CA 2006, s 379(1)*].

Organisation includes any body corporate or unincorporated association and any combination of persons. [*CA 2006, s 379(1)*].

Political donation. Subject to below, a political donation means

- *in relation to a political party or other political organisation*, anything that in accordance with *PPERA 2000, ss 50–52* (meaning of donation) and *53* (value of donation)

  (i) constitutes a donation to a registered party for the purposes of *PPERA 2000, Pt 4, Ch 1* (control of donations to registered parties); or

  (ii) would constitute such a donation reading references in those *sections* to a registered party as references to any political party or other political organisation; and

- *in relation to an independent election* candidate, anything that in accordance with *PPERA 2000, ss 50–52* (meaning of donation) and *53* (value of donation) would constitute a donation for the purposes of *PPERA 2000, Pt 4, Ch 1* (control of donations to registered parties) reading references in those *sections* to a registered party as references to the independent election candidate.

Political donations broadly include (subject to certain specified exemptions)

- any gift to the party, organisation or candidate of money or other property;
- any 'sponsorship' provided in relation to the party, organisation or candidate;
- any subscription or other fee paid for affiliation to, or membership of, the party or organisation;
- any money spent in paying any expenses incurred directly or indirectly by the party, organisation or candidate;
- any money lent to the party, organisation or candidate otherwise than on commercial terms; and
- the provision, otherwise than commercial terms, of any property, services or facilities for use or benefit by the party, organisation or candidate (including the services of any person).

'*Sponsorship*' is provided if any money or other property is transferred to the party, organisation or candidate or to any person for their benefit, and the purpose (or one of the purposes) of the transfer is (or must, having regard to all the circumstances, reasonably be assumed to be) to help the party, etc to meet expenses incurred (or to be incurred) by or on their behalf (or to secure that to any extent any such expenses are not so incurred) in connection with

- any conference, meeting or other event organised by or on their behalf;
- the preparation, production or dissemination of any publication by or on their behalf; or
- any study or research organised by or on their behalf.

[*CA 2006, s 364; SI 2007 No 2194, art 5*].

Political expenditure, in relation to a company, means expenditure incurred by the company on

(a) the preparation, publication or dissemination of advertising or other promotional or publicity material

(i) of whatever nature, and

(ii) however published or otherwise disseminated,

that, at the time of publication or dissemination, is capable of being reasonably regarded as intended to affect public support for a political party or other political organisation or an independent election candidate; or

(b) activities on the part of the company that are capable of being reasonably regarded as intended

(i) to affect public support for a political party or other political organisation or an independent election candidate; or

(ii) to influence voters in relation to any national or regional referendum held under the law of a Member State.

For the purposes of these provisions a political donation does not count as political expenditure.

[*CA 2006, s 365*].

Time a donation is made or expenditure is incurred. Except as otherwise provided, any reference to the time a donation is made or expenditure is incurred is, in a case where the donation is made or expenditure incurred in pursuance of a contract, any earlier time at which that contract is entered into by the company. [*CA 2006, s 379(2)*].

31.3 AUTHORISATION REQUIRED FOR DONATIONS OR EXPENDITURE

Subject to the exemptions in **31.8**, a company must not

- make a political donation to a political party, other political organisation, or an independent election candidate, or
- incur any political expenditure,

unless the donation or expenditure is authorised

- in the case of a company that is not a subsidiary of another company, by a resolution of the members of the company; or
- in the case of a company that is a subsidiary of another company, by

  (i) a resolution of the members of the company; *and*

  (ii) a resolution of the members of any 'relevant holding company'.

  But no resolution is required on the part of a company that is a wholly-owned subsidiary of a UK-registered company.

A '*relevant holding company*' means a company that, at the time the donation was made or the expenditure was incurred

- was a holding company of the company by which the donation was made or the expenditure was incurred;

- was a UK-registered company; and
- was not a subsidiary of another UK-registered company.

Any required resolution must comply with the requirements as to form (see below) and must be passed before the donation is made or the expenditure incurred.

[*CA 2006, s 366*].

Form of authorising resolution. A resolution conferring authorisation for these purposes may relate to

- the company passing the resolution;
- one or more subsidiaries of that company; or
- the company passing the resolution and one or more subsidiaries of that company.

A resolution may be expressed to relate to all companies that are subsidiaries of the company passing the resolution

- at the time the resolution is passed, or
- at any time during the period for which the resolution has effect

without identifying them individually.

The resolution may authorise donations or expenditure under one or more of the following heads, ie

(a) donations to political parties or independent election candidates,

(b) donations to political organisations other than political parties, and

(c) political expenditure

and must specify a head or heads

- in the case of a resolution relating to all companies that are subsidiaries of the company passing the resolution, for all of the companies to which it relates taken together; and
- in the case of any other resolution, for each company to which it relates.

The resolution must be expressed in general terms conforming with (a)–(c) above and must not purport to authorise particular donations or expenditure.

For each of the specified heads in (*a*)–(*c*) above, the resolution must authorise donations or expenditure (as the case may be) up to a specified amount in the period for which the resolution has effect (see below). It must also specify such amounts

- in the case of a resolution relating to all companies that are subsidiaries of the company passing the resolution, for all of the companies to which it relates taken together; and
- in the case of any other resolution, for each company to which it relates.

[*CA 2006, s 367*].

Period for which resolution has effect. A resolution conferring authorisation for these purposes has effect for a period of four years beginning with the date on which it is passed (unless the directors determine, or the articles require, that it is to have effect for a shorter period beginning with that date). The power of the directors to make such a determination is subject to any provision of the articles preventing them from doing so. [*CA 2006, s 368*].

31.4 REMEDIES IN CASES OF UNAUTHORISED DONATIONS AND EXPENDITURE

Liability of directors. Where a company has made a political donation or incurred political expenditure without the necessary authorisation under 31.3, the 'directors in default' are jointly and severally liable

- to make good to the company the amount of the unauthorised donation or expenditure, with interest from the date when the expenditure was incurred at the prescribed rate (currently 8%); and
- to compensate the company for any loss or damage sustained by it as a result of the unauthorised donation or expenditure having been made.

The '*directors in default*' are

- those who, at the time the unauthorised donation was made or the unauthorised expenditure was incurred, were directors of the company by which the donation was made or the expenditure was incurred; and
- where
  - (i) that company was a subsidiary of a 'relevant holding company' (see 31.3), and
  - (ii) the directors of the relevant holding company failed to take all reasonable steps to prevent the donation being made or the expenditure being incurred,

  the directors of the relevant holding company.

Where only part of a donation or expenditure was unauthorised, the above provisions apply only to so much of it was unauthorised.
[*CA 2006, s 369*; *SI 2009 No 2242, Reg 2*].

31.5 Enforcement of directors' liabilities by shareholder action

Subject to below, any liability of a director under 31.4 is (in addition to the right of the company to which the liability is owed to bring proceedings itself to enforce the liability) enforceable

- in the case of a liability of a director of a company to that company, by proceedings brought in the name of the company by an 'authorised group' of its members; and
- in the case of a liability of a director of a holding company to a subsidiary, by proceedings brought in the name of the subsidiary by
  - (i) an authorised group of members of the subsidiary; or
  - (ii) an authorised group of members of the holding company.

31.5 Political Donations

An '*authorised group*' of members of a company means

- the holders of not less than 5% in nominal value of the company's issued share capital;
- if the company is not limited by shares, not less than 5% of its members; or
- not less than 50 of the company's members.

A group of members may not bring proceedings under these provisions in the name of a company unless

- the group has given written notice to the company stating
  - (i) the cause of action and a summary of the facts on which the proceedings are to be based;
  - (ii) the names and addresses of the members comprising the group; and
  - (iii) the grounds on which it is alleged that those members constitute an authorised group; and
- not less than 28 days have elapsed between the date of the giving of the notice to the company and the bringing of the proceedings.

Where such a notice is given to a company, any director of the company may apply to the court within 28 days of the giving of the notice for an order directing that the proposed proceedings are not to be brought. An application may be made on one or more of the following grounds, namely that

(a) the unauthorised amount has been made good to the company;

(b) proceedings to enforce the liability have been brought, and are being pursued with due diligence, by the company; or

(c) the members proposing to bring proceedings do not constitute an authorised group.

Where such an application is made on the ground in (*b*) above, the court has wide powers to direct that the proposed proceedings under these provisions are not brought or are brought on such terms and conditions as it thinks fit and that the proceedings brought by the company are to be discontinued or continued on such terms and conditions as it thinks fit.

The members by whom proceedings are brought under these provisions owe the same duties to the company in whose name they are brought as would be owed by the company's directors if the proceedings were being brought by the company itself. But proceedings to enforce any such duty may be brought by the company only with the permission of the court.

Proceedings cannot be discontinued or settled by the group except with the permission of the court, which may be given on such terms as the court thinks fit.

Nothing in the above provisions affects any right of a member of a company to bring or continue proceedings under *CA 2006, Pt 11* (derivative claims and proceedings by members, see **26.6 Members**).

[*CA 2006, ss 370, 371*].

31.6 Costs of shareholder action

In any proceedings brought under **31.5** in the name of the company by an authorised group, the group may apply to the court for an order directing the company to indemnify the group in respect of costs incurred, or to be incurred, by the group in connection with the proceedings. The court may then make such an order on such terms as it thinks fit. The group is not entitled to be paid any such costs out of the assets of the company except by virtue of such an order.

If no such order has been made with respect to the proceedings, then if

- the company is awarded costs in connection with the proceedings, or it is agreed that costs incurred by the company in connection with the proceedings should be paid by any defendant, or
- any defendant is awarded costs in connection with the proceedings, or it is agreed that any defendant should be paid costs incurred by him in connection with the proceedings,

the costs must be paid by the group.

In relation to Scotland, references to 'costs' are to 'expenses' and references to any 'defendant' are to any 'defender'.

[*CA 2006, s 372*].

31.7 Information for purposes of shareholder action

Where proceedings have been brought under **31.5** in the name of the company by an authorised group, the group is entitled to require the company to provide it with all information relating to the subject matter of the proceedings that is in the company's possession or under its control or which is reasonably obtainable by it.

If the company, having been required by the group to do so, refuses to provide the group with all or any of that information, the court may, on an application made by the group, make an order directing the company, and any of its officers or employees specified in the application, to provide the group with the information in question in such form and by such means as the court may direct.

[*CA 2006, s 373*].

31.8 EXEMPTIONS

The following exemptions apply for the purposes of **31.3**.

(1) Trade unions

A donation to a 'trade union', other than a contribution to the union's political fund, is not a political donation for the purposes of this chapter and a trade union is not a political organisation for the purposes of the definition of '*political expenditure*' (see **31.2**).

For these purposes,

- '*trade union*' has the meaning given by *Trade Union and Labour Relations (Consolidation) Act 1992, s 1* or *Industrial Relations (Northern Ireland) Order 1992 (SI 1992 No 807), Art 3*; and

- '*political fund*' means the fund from which payments by a trade union in the furtherance of political objects are required to be made by virtue of *Trade Union and Labour Relations (Consolidation) Act 1992, s 82(1)(a)* or *Industrial Relations (Northern Ireland) Order 1992 (SI 1992 No 807), Art 57(2)(a)*.

[*CA 2006, s 374*].

(2) **Subscription for membership of trade association**

A 'subscription' paid to a 'trade association' for membership of the association is not a political donation for the purposes of 31.3.

'*Trade association*' means an organisation formed for the purpose of furthering the trade interests of its members, or of persons represented by its members.

'*Subscription*' does not include a payment to the association to the extent that it is made for the purpose of financing any particular activity of the association.

[*CA 2006, s 375*].

(3) **All-party parliamentary groups**

An '*all-party parliamentary group*' (ie an all-party group composed of members of one or both of the Houses of Parliament (or of such members and other persons) is not a political organisation for the purposes of 31.3.

[*CA 2006, s 376*].

(4) **Donations not amounting to more than £5,000 in any twelve month period**

Authorisation under 31.3 is not needed for a donation to a political party, other political organisation or an independent election candidate except to the extent that the total amount of

- that donation, and
- 'other relevant donations' made in the period of 12 months ending with the date on which that donation is made,

exceeds £5,000.

'*Other relevant donations*' means

(i) in relation to a donation made by a company that is not a subsidiary, any other donations made by that company or by any of its subsidiaries; and

(ii) in relation to a donation made by a company that is a subsidiary, any other donations made by that company, by any holding company of that company or by any other subsidiary of any such holding company.

If or to the extent that a donation is so exempt from the requirement of authorisation, it is disregarded in determining what donations are authorised by any resolution passed for the purposes of this chapter.

[*CA 2006, s 378*].

(5) **Political expenditure exempted by order**

The Secretary of State may also, by statutory instrument, provide that any description of company or political expenditure is exempt from the requirement of authorisation. [*CA 2006, s 377*].

The *Companies (Political Expenditure Exemption) Order 2007* provides that a company whose ordinary course of business includes, or is proposed to include,

- the publication or dissemination to the public (or any part of the public) of material relating to
  - (i) news,
  - (ii) public and political affairs and events, and
  - (iii) views, opinion and comment on the news and on public and political affairs and events, or
- the preparation of such material for publication or dissemination to the public (or any part of the public)

is exempt in respect of political expenditure incurred in respect of the preparation, publication or dissemination of such material where that material contains matter which would render its preparation, etc on the part of the company an activity within (*b*) in the definition of '*political expenditure*' in **31.2**.

For these purposes, it is irrelevant

- by which means or modes the material is prepared, etc; or
- where the public (or any part of the public) to which such material is published or disseminated is located or the identity or description of the public (or any part of it).

[*SI 2007 No 2081*].

32 Prospectuses

32.1 **Introduction**
32.2 **Persons responsible for a prospectus**
32.3 **The need for a prospectus**
32.4 Exempt offers to the public
32.5 Exempt securities: offers to the public
32.6 Exempt securities: admission to trading
32.7 **Election to have a prospectus**
32.8 **Drawing up a prospectus**
32.9 Format
32.10 Minimum information
32.11 Incorporation of terms by reference
32.12 Omission of information
32.13 **Application for, and approval of, a prospectus**
32.14 Approval by FCA
32.15 Overseas matters
32.16 Powers of the FCA: infringement of rules
32.17 **Filing and publication of a prospectus**
32.18 **Advertisements**
32.19 **Supplementary prospectus**
32.20 **Annual information update**
32.21 **Remedies for investors**
32.22 Compensation for statements in prospectuses
32.23 **Penalties**
32.24 **Appointment of investigators by the FCA**
32.25 **FCA: exemption from liability in damages**

32.1 INTRODUCTION

The *Prospectus Directive 2003/71/EC* seeks to harmonise requirements for the drawing up, approval and distribution of the prospectus to be published when securities are offered to the public or admitted to trading on a regulated market situated or operating within a Member State.

The provisions of the *Directive* are implemented by

- *Financial Services and Markets Act 2000 (FSMA 2000), Pt VI*;
- the Prospectus Directive Regulation (*EC Commission Regulation 809/2004 of 29 April 2004*); and
- the Prospectus Rules made by the FCA (the UK Listing Authority) as the competent authority to make rules ('Part VI rules') under *FSMA 2000, s 73A(1)*.

In determining whether these provisions have been complied with, the FCA will take into account whether a person has complied with the recommendations for the consistent implementation of the Prospectus Directive *Regulation* published by the Committee of European Securities Regulators ('CESR recommendations'). (FCA Prospectus Rules, para 1.1.8).

Note that EU Regulations are binding and have effect in all member states ie they are directly applicable and do not have to be implemented by national legislation.

Application of the Prospectus Rules. Unless otherwise stated, the Prospectus Rules only apply to an offer or a request for admission to trading of transferable securities

(a) in respect of which *FSMA 2000, s 85* applies (see **32.3**) applies and in relation to which the UK is the 'Home State';

(b) where a person has elected to have a prospectus in relation to the transferable securities (see **32.7**);

(c) where (*a*) or (*b*) above does not apply and in relation to which the UK is the Home State; or

(d) where the competent authority of an EEA State has transferred the function of approving the prospectus to the FCA (see **32.15**).

(FCA Prospectus Rules, para 1.1.1).

'Transferable securities' means anything which is a transferable security for the purposes of Directive 2004/39/EC in markets in financial instruments, other than money-market instruments for the purposes of that Directive which have a maturity of less than 12 months.

Meaning of 'Home State'. In relation to an issuer of transferable securities, the Home State is the EEA State which is the 'Home Member State' for the purposes of the *Prospectus Directive*, namely:

(i) For all EC issuers of securities which are not mentioned in (ii), the Member State where the issuer has its registered office.

(ii) For any issues of non-equity securities

- whose denomination per unit amounts to at least 1,000 euros, and
- giving the right to acquire any transferable securities or to receive a cash amount, as a consequence of their being converted or the rights conferred by them being exercised,

provided that the issuer of the non-equity securities is not the issuer of the underlying securities or an entity belonging to the group of the latter issuer,

- the Member State where the issuer has its registered office, or
- where the securities were or are to be admitted to trading on a regulated market or where the securities are offered to the public, at the choice of the issuer, the Member State of the offeror or the person asking for admission, as the case may be.

The same regime is also applicable to non-equity securities in a currency other than euros, provided that the value of such minimum denomination is nearly equivalent to 1,000 euro.

(iii) For all issuers of securities incorporated in a third country, which are not mentioned in (ii) above, the Member State where

- the securities are intended to be offered to the public for the first time after 1 July 2005, or
- the first application for admission to trading on a regulated market is made,

at the choice of the issuer, the offeror or the person asking for admission, as the case may be, subject to a subsequent election by issuers incorporated in a third country if the home Member State was not determined by their choice.

[*Prospectus Directive, Art 2.1(m); FSMA 2000, ss 102A(3), 102C; SI 2005 No 1433*].

For the meaning of **EEA States** see APPENDIX 1 DEFINITIONS.

Persons responsible for complying with rules. A person must comply with all rules that are specified as being applicable to them. If a rule does not specify who is responsible for complying with it, then the following persons must comply with it.

- In relation to an offer, the issuer and the offeror (if this is a person other than the issuer).
- In relation to a request for the admission to trading of transferable securities, the issuer; and the person requesting admission to trading (if this is a person other than the issuer).

But an issuer is not responsible under either of these categories if it has not authorised or made the offer or the request for the admission to trading.

(FCA Prospectus Rules, paras 1.1.3, 1.1.4).

32.2 PERSONS RESPONSIBLE FOR A PROSPECTUS

The following rules only apply if the UK is the Home State (see 32.1) for the issuer in relation to the transferable securities to which the prospectus relates.

Equity shares. Where a prospectus relates to

- equity shares,
- warrants or options to subscribe for equity shares that are issued by the issuer of the equity shares, or
- other transferable securities that have similar characteristics

each of the following persons are, subject to below, responsible for the prospectus.

(a) The issuer of the transferable securities.

(b) If the issuer is a body corporate

(i) each person who is a director of that body corporate when the prospectus is published; and

(ii) each person who has authorised himself to be named, and is named, in the prospectus as a director or as having agreed to become a director of that body corporate either immediately or at a future time; and

(iii) each person who is a senior executive of any external management company of the issuer.

(c) Each person who accepts, and is stated in the prospectus as accepting, responsibility for the prospectus.

"External management company" means in relation to an issuer that is a company which is not a collective investment undertaking, a person who is appointed by the issuer (whether under contract for services or any other commercial arrangement) to perform functions that would ordinarily be performed by officers of the issuer and to make recommendations in relation to strategic matters. In considering whether the functions the person performs would ordinarily be performed by officers of the issuer, the FCA will consider, amongst other things:

(i) the nature of the board of the issuer to which the person provides services, and whether the board has the capability to act itself on strategic matters in the absence of that person's services;

(ii) whether the appointment relates to a one-off transaction or is a longer term relationship; and

(iii) the proportion of the functions ordinarily performed by officers of the issuer that is covered by the arrangements.

(d) In relation to an offer

(i) the offeror, if this is not the issuer; and

(ii) if the offeror is a body corporate and is not the issuer, each person who is a director of the body corporate when the prospectus is published.

(e) In relation to a request for the admission to trading of transferable securities

(i) the person requesting admission, if this is not the issuer; and

(ii) if the person requesting admission is a body corporate and is not the issuer, each person who is a director of the body corporate when the prospectus is published.

(f) Each person not falling within (*a*)–(*e*) above who has authorised the contents of the prospectus.

All other securities. Where a prospectus relates to any other transferable securities, each of the following persons is, subject to below, responsible for the prospectus.

(i) The issuer of the transferable securities.

(ii) Each person who accepts, and is stated in the prospectus as accepting, responsibility for the prospectus.

(iii) In relation to an offer, the offeror of the transferable securities, if this is not the issuer.

(iv) In relation to a request for an admission to trading of transferable securities, the person requesting admission, if this is not the issuer.

(v) If there is a guarantor for the issue, the guarantor in relation to information in the prospectus that relates to the guarantor and the guarantee.

(vi) Each person not falling within (i)–(v) above who has authorised the contents of the prospectus.

Exclusions.

(1) A person is not responsible for a prospectus under (*a*), (*b*) or (i) above if the issuer has not made or authorised the offer or the request for admission to trading in relation to which the prospectus was published.

(2) A person is not responsible for a prospectus under (*b*)(i) above if it is published without his knowledge or consent and, on becoming aware of its publication, he gives reasonable public notice as soon as practicable that it was published without his knowledge or consent.

(3) A person is not responsible for a prospectus under (*d*) or (iii) above if

- the issuer is responsible for the prospectus under these rules;
- the prospectus was drawn up primarily by the issuer, or by one or more persons acting on behalf of the issuer; and
- the offeror is making the offer in association with the issuer.

(4) A person who accepts responsibility for a prospectus under (*c*) or (ii) above or authorises the contents of a prospectus under (*f*) or (vi) above, may state that they do so only in relation to specified parts of the prospectus, or only in specified respects, and in that case the person is responsible

- only to the extent specified; and
- only if the material in question is included in (or substantially in) the form and context to which the person has agreed.

Nothing in the above rules is to be construed as making a person responsible for any prospectus by reason only of the person giving advice about its contents in a professional capacity.

(FCA Prospectus Rules, paras 5.5.1–5.5.9).

32.3 THE NEED FOR A PROSPECTUS

If the Listing Rules require a prospectus to be published then subject to the exemptions listed below, it is unlawful

(a) for 'transferable securities' to be offered to the public in the UK, or

(b) to request the admission of transferable securities to trading on a regulated market situated or operating in the UK

unless an 'approved prospectus' has been made available to the public before the offer or request is made.

A person who contravenes either of the above is guilty of an offence and liable

- on summary conviction, to imprisonment for a term not exceeding three months or a fine not exceeding the statutory maximum (see **29.1 Offences and Legal Proceedings**) or both; or
- on conviction on indictment, to imprisonment for a term not exceeding two years or a fine or both.

A contravention of (*a*) or (*b*) above is actionable, at the suit of a person who suffers loss as a result of the contravention, subject to the defences and other incidents applying to actions for breach of statutory duty.

Offer of transferable securities to the public. There is an offer of transferable securities to the public if there is a communication to any person which presents sufficient information on

- the transferable securities to be offered, and
- the terms on which they are offered,

to enable an investor to decide to buy or subscribe for the securities in question. This includes the placing of securities through a financial intermediary but does not include a communication in connection with trading on a regulated market, a multilateral trading facility, or any other market prescribed by an *Order*.

To the extent that an offer of transferable securities is made to a *person* in the UK, it is an offer of transferable securities to the *public* in the UK.

The communication may be made in any form and by any means.

'*Approved prospectus*' for these purposes means a prospectus approved by the competent authority of the 'Home State' (see **32.1**) in relation to the issuer of the securities.

For the meaning of "transferable securities" see **32.1**.

[*FSMA 2000, ss 85, 102B; CA 2006, Sch 15 para 10; SI 2005 No 1433*].

Exemptions. These fall into two categories, namely exempt offers and exempt securities.

- Certain offers to the public are exempt from the requirements of (*a*) above. See **32.4**.
- Certain securities are exempt from the requirements of (*a*) and (*b*) above under *FSMA 2000* and the FCA Prospectus Rules. See **32.5** and **32.6**.

Information to be disclosed to all investors to whom offer addressed. Where, in relation to an offer in the UK, no prospectus is required under *FSMA 2000*, the issuer and offeror must ensure that material information they provide to qualified investors (see **32.4**) or special categories of investors, including information disclosed in the context of meetings relating to offers, is disclosed to all qualified investors or special categories of investors to whom the offer is exclusively addressed. (FCA Prospectus Rules, para 5.6.1.)

32.4 Exempt offers to the public

A person does not contravene *FSMA 2000, s 85(1)* in the following circumstances.

(i) The offer is made to or directed at 'qualified investors' only.

(ii) The offer is made to or directed at fewer than 150 persons, other than qualified investors, per EEA State. For this purpose, the making of an offer of transferable securities to

- trustees of a trust,
- members of a partnership in their capacity as such, or
- two or more persons jointly,

is to be treated as the making of an offer to a single person.

(iii) The minimum consideration which may be paid by any person for transferable securities acquired by him pursuant to the offer is at least 100,000 euros (or an 'equivalent amount').

(iv) The transferable securities being offered are denominated in amounts of at least 100,000 euros (or equivalent amounts).

(v) The total consideration for the transferable securities being offered in the EEA states cannot exceed 100,000 euros (or an equivalent amount). In determining whether this is satisfied in relation to an offer ('offer A'), offer A is to be taken together with any other offer of transferable securities of the same class made by the same person which

- was open at any time within the period of 12 months ending with the date on which offer A is first made; and
- had previously satisfied the 100,000 euros requirement.

(vi) The offer falls within *FSMA 2000. s 86(1A)* if the transferable securities are being sold or placed through a financial intermediary where

(a) the transferable securities have previously been the subject of one or more offers to the public;

(b) in respect of one or more of those previous offers any of the paragraphs (a)–(e) of *s 86(1)* applies;

(c) a prospectus is available for the securities which has been approved by the FCA or the competent authority of another EEA state and meets either of the conditions in FSMA, s 86(1B); and

(d) the issuer or other person who was responsible for drawing up the prospectus has given written consent for the purpose of the current offer.

The conditions referred to in (c) are that the prospectus was approved by the FCA or the competent authority of another EEA state earlier than 12 months before the date the current offer is made and is supplemented by every supplementary prospectus which was required to be submitted under *FSMA 2000, s 87G(2)* or, in the case of non-equity transferable securities falling within *art 5(4)(b)* of the Prospectus Directive, that the securities concerned have not ceased to be issued in a continuous or repeated manner.

Where

- a person who is not a qualified investor ('the client') has engaged a qualified investor falling within (*a*)(i) below to act as his agent, and
- the terms on which the qualified investor is engaged enable him to make decisions concerning the acceptance of offers of transferable securities on the client's behalf without reference to the client,

an offer made to or directed at the qualified investor is not to be regarded for the above purposes as also having been made to or directed at the client.

'*Qualified investor*' in relation to an offer of transferable securities means

(a) A person described in points (1) to (4) of Section 1 of Annex 11 to the Markets in Financial Instruments Directive ("the Directive"), other than a person who, before the making of the offer, has agreed in writing with the relevant firm (or each of the relevant firms) to be treated as a non- professional client in accordance with the final paragraph of Section 1 of Annex 11 of the Directive.

(b) A person who has made a request to one or more relevant firms to be treated as a professional client in accordance with Section 11 of Annex 11 to the Directive and has not subsequently but before the making of the offer, agreed in writing with that relevant firm (or each of the relevant firms) to be treated as a non-professional client in accordance with the final paragraph of Section 1 of Annex 11 of the Directive.

(c) A person .who is an eligible counter party in accordance with Article 24 of the Directive and has not before the making of the offer agreed in writing with the relevant firm (or each of the relevant firms) to be treated as a non- professional client in accordance with the final paragraph of Section 1of Annex 11 to the Directive.

(d) A person whom any relevant firm is authorised to continue to treat as a professional client in accordance with Article 71 (6) of the Directive.

"Relevant firm" means:

an investment firm or credit institution acting in connection with the offer and "credit institution" means a credit institution authorised under the Capital Requirements Directive or an institution which would satisfy the requirements for authorisation as a credit institution under that Directive if it had its registered office (or if it does not have one its head office) in an EEE state.

Any '*equivalent amount*' not in euros is to be calculated at the latest practicable date before (but in any event not more than three working days before) the date on which the offer is first made.

[*FSMA 2000, s 86; SI 2005 No 1433*; *SI 2011 No 1668*; *SI 2012 No 1538, Reg 2, 3; SI 2013 No 3115, Sch 2 para 9; SI 2013 No 1125, Reg 2; SI 2014 No 3293, Reg 2(1)*].

32.5 Exempt securities: offers to the public

The following transferable securities are exempt from the requirements of *FSMA 2000, s 85(1)*.

(a) Units in an open-ended collective investment scheme.

(b) Non-equity transferable securities issued by

- the government of an EEA State;
- a local or regional authority of an EEA State;
- a public international body of which an EEA State is a member;
- the European Central Bank;
- the central bank of an EEA State.

(c) Shares in the share capital of the central bank of an EEA State.

(d) Transferable securities unconditionally and irrevocably guaranteed by the government, or a local or regional authority, of an EEA State.

(e) Non-equity transferable securities, issued in a continuous or repeated manner by a credit institution, where the securities

- are not subordinated, convertible or exchangeable;
- do not give a right to subscribe to or acquire other types of securities and are not linked to a derivative instrument;
- materialise reception of repayable deposits; and
- are covered by a deposit guarantee under *Directive 94/19/EC* of the European Parliament and of the Council on deposit-guarantee schemes.

(f) Non-fungible shares of capital

- the main purpose of which is to provide the holder with a right to occupy any immoveable property; and
- which cannot be sold without that right being given up.

(g) Transferable securities issued by one of the following bodies if, and only if, the proceeds of the offer of the transferable securities to the public will be used solely for the purposes of the issuer's objectives.

(i) A charity.

(ii) A housing association.

(iii) A registered industrial and provident society.

(iv) A non-profit making association or body recognised by an EEA State with objectives similar to those of a body falling within (i)–(iii) above.

(h) Non-equity transferable securities, issued in a continuous or repeated manner by a credit institution, which satisfy the conditions that

- the total consideration for the transferable securities being offered in the EEA states is less than 75 million euros (or an equivalent amount); and
- the securities
  - (i) are not subordinated, convertible or exchangeable; and
  - (ii) do not give a right to subscribe to or acquire other types of securities and are not linked to a derivative instrument.

In determining whether the total consideration requirement is satisfied in relation to an offer ('offer A'), offer A is to be taken together with any other offer of transferable securities of the same class made by the same person which

- was open at any time within the period of 12 months ending with the date on which offer A is first made; and
- had previously satisfied the total consideration requirement.

Any '*equivalent amount*' not in euros is to be calculated at the latest practicable date before (but in any event not more than three working days before) the date on which the offer is first made.

(i) Transferable securities included in an offer where the total consideration for the transferable securities being offered in the EEA states is less than 5 million euros (or an equivalent amount). Similar provisions as to the total consideration requirement and 'equivalent amount' apply as in (*h*) above.

[*FSMA 2000, s 85(5), Sch 11A; SI 2005 No 1433*; *SI 2011 No 1668*].

(j) Shares issued in substitution for shares of the same class already issued, if the issue of the new shares does not involve any increase in the issued capital.

(k) Transferable securities

- offered in connection with a takeover by means of an exchange offer, or
- offered, allotted or to be allotted in connection with a merger,

if a document is available containing information which is regarded by the FCA as being equivalent to that of the prospectus, taking into account the requirements of EU legislation.

(l) Shares offered, allotted or to be allotted free of charge to existing shareholders, and dividends paid out in the form of shares of the same class as the shares in respect of which the dividends are paid, if a document is made available containing information on the number and nature of the shares and the reasons for and details of the offer.

(m) Transferable securities offered, allotted or to be allotted to existing or former directors or employees by their employer which has transferable securities already admitted to trading or by an affiliated undertaking, if a document is made available containing information on the number and nature of the transferable securities and the reasons for and details of the offer.

(*FSMA, Sch 11A* and FCA Prospectus Rules, para 1.2.2).

32.6 Exempt securities: admission to trading

The following transferable securities are exempt from the requirements of *FSMA 2000, s 85(2)*.

(a) Transferable securities as in **32.5**(*a*)–(*f*).

[*FSMA 2000, s 85(6), Sch 11A Pt 1; SI 2005 No 1433*].

(b) Shares representing, over a period of 12 months, less than 10% of the number of shares of the same class already admitted to trading on the same regulated market.

(c) Shares issued in substitution for shares of the same class already admitted to trading on the same regulated market, if the issue of the shares does not involve any increase in the issued capital.

(d) Transferable securities

- offered in connection with a takeover by means of an exchange offer, and
- offered, allotted or to be allotted in connection with a merger,

if a document is available containing information which is regarded by the FCA as being equivalent to that of the prospectus, taking into account the requirements of EC legislation.

(e) Shares offered, allotted or to be allotted free of charge to existing shareholders, and dividends paid out in the form of shares of the same class as the shares in respect of which the dividends are paid, if the shares are of the same class as the shares already admitted to trading on the same regulated market and if a document is made available containing information on the number and nature of the shares and the reasons for and details of the offer.

(f) Transferable securities offered, allotted or to be allotted to existing or former directors or employees by their employer or an affiliated undertaking, if the transferable securities are of the same class as the transferable securities already admitted to trading on the same regulated market and if a document is made available containing information on the number and nature of the transferable securities and the reasons for and detail of the offer.

(g) Shares resulting from the conversion or exchange of other transferable securities or from the exercise of the rights conferred by other transferable securities, if the shares are of the same class as the shares already admitted to trading on the same regulated market.

(h) Transferable securities already admitted to trading on another regulated market on the following conditions

(i) these transferable securities, or transferable securities of the same class, have been admitted to trading on that other regulated market for more than 18 months;

(ii) for transferable securities first admitted to trading after 31 December 2003, the admission to trading on that other regulated market was associated with an approved prospectus made available to the public in accordance *EC Prospectus Directive, Art 14*;

(iii) except where (ii) applies, for transferable securities first admitted to listing after 30 June 1983, listing particulars were approved in accordance with the requirements of *Directive 80/390/EEC* or *Directive 2001/34/EC*;

(iv) the ongoing obligations for trading on that other regulated market have been fulfilled;

(v) the person requesting the admission to trading under this exemption makes a summary document available to the public in a language accepted by the competent authority of the EEA State of the regulated market where admission is sought;

(vi) the summary document referred to in (v) above is made available to the public in the EEA State of the regulated market where admission to trading is sought in the manner set out in *EC Prospectus Directive, Art 14*; and

(vii) the contents of the summary document comply with *EC Prospectus Directive, Art 5(2)*. The document must also state where the most recent prospectus can be obtained and where the financial information published by the issuer pursuant to its ongoing disclosure obligations is available.

(FCA Prospectus Rules, para 1.2.3).

32.7 ELECTION TO HAVE A PROSPECTUS

A person who proposes to

- issue,
- offer to the public, or
- request the admission to a regulated market of

certain transferable securities which would otherwise be exempt securities may elect to have a prospectus in relation to the securities. The transferable securities in question are those falling within **32.4**(*b*), (*d*), (*h*) or (*i*) where the UK is the Home State (see **32.1**) in relation to the issuer of the securities.

On such an election, the provisions of *FSMA 2000, Pt VI* and the FCA Prospectus Rules apply as if those securities were transferable securities for which an approved prospectus would be required under **32.3**. But FCA Listing Rules do not apply to securities which are the subject of an election.

[*FSMA 2000, s 87; SI 2005 No 1433*].

32.8 DRAWING UP A PROSPECTUS

A prospectus must contain the information necessary to enable investors to make an informed assessment of

- the assets and liabilities, financial position, profits and losses, and prospects of the issuer of the transferable securities and of any guarantor; and
- the rights attaching to the transferable securities.

If, in the case of transferable securities to which FSMA 2000, s 87 applies, the prospectus states that the guarantor is a specified EEA state, the prospectus is not required to include other information about the guarantor.

The necessary information must be presented in a form which is comprehensible and easy to analyse and must be prepared having regard to the particular nature of the transferable securities and their issuer.

[*FSMA 2000, s 87A(2)–(4); SI 2005 No 1433; SI 2013 No 1538, Reg 2*].

Summary. Unless the FCA Prospectus Rules provide otherwise, a prospectus must include a summary which conveys concisely in non-technical language, and in an appropriate structure, the key information relevant to the securities which are the subject of the prospectus and, when read with the rest of the prospectus, must be an aid to investors considering whether to invest in the securities.

The "key information" means the information which is essential to enable investors to understand the transferable securities to which the prospectus relates and to decide whether to consider the offer further. The key information must include:

(a) the essential characteristics of, and risks associated with, the issuer and any guarantor, including their assets, liabilities and financial positions;

(b) the essential characteristics of, and risks associated with investment in the transferable securities including any rights attaching to those securities;

(c) the general terms of the offer, including an estimate of the expenses charged to an investor by the issuer and the person offering the securities to the public, if not the issuer;

(d) details of the admission to trading; and

(e) the reasons for the offer and proposed use of the proceeds.

[*FSMA 2000, s 87A(5), (6); SI 2005 No 1433; SI 2012 No 1538, Reg 4*].

A summary is not required for a prospectus relating to non-equity transferable securities that have a denomination of at least 100,000 euros (or an equivalent amount) if the prospectus relates to an admission to trading. (FCA Prospectus Rules, para 2.1.3).

The summary should generally not exceed 2,500 words. The issuer, the offeror or the person seeking admission to trading decides on the detailed content of the summary but it must contain a warning to the effect that

- it should be read as an introduction to the prospectus;
- any decision to invest in the transferable securities should be based on consideration of the prospectus as a whole by the investor;
- where a claim relating to the information contained in a prospectus is brought before a court, the plaintiff might, under the national legislation of the EEA States, have to bear the costs of translating the prospectus before the legal proceedings are initiated; and
- civil liability attaches to those persons who are responsible for the summary (including any translation) but only if the summary is misleading, inaccurate or inconsistent when read together with the other parts of the prospectus.

(FCA Prospectus Rules, paras 2.1.4, 2.1.5, 2.1.7).

32.9 Format

A prospectus may be drawn up as a single document or separate documents. Where it is composed of separate documents, it must divide the required information into the following.

- *A summary*. See **32.8**.
- *A registration document* containing the information relating to the issuer.
- *A securities note* containing the information concerning the transferable securities to be offered or to be admitted to trading.

An issuer, offeror or person requesting admission who already has a registration document approved by the FCA is required to draw up only the securities note and the summary when transferable securities are offered or a request is made for admission to trading. Where there has been a material change which could affect investor's assessments since the latest updated registration document (or any supplementary prospectus) was approved, the securities note must provide that information.

(FCA Prospectus Rules, paras 2.2.1–2.2.5).

Base prospectuses. Where the transferable securities are

- non-equity transferable securities (including warrants in any form) issued under an offering programme, or
- certain non-equity transferable securities issued in a continuous or repeated manner by credit institutions

the prospectus can, at the choice of the issuer, offeror or person requesting admission, consist of a base prospectus containing all relevant information concerning the issuer and the transferable securities to be offered or to be admitted to trading. For further information see FCA Prospectus Rules, paras 2.2.7–2.2.9 and *EC Commission Regulation 809/2004, Art 26*.

32.10 Minimum information

A prospectus must be drawn up by using one, or a combination of, the schedules and building blocks as set out in *EC Commission Regulation 809/2004, Arts 3–23* and *Annexes I–XVII*, according to the combinations for various types of securities provided for in *Art 21* and *Annex XVIII*. These depend on the type of issuer and securities involved (see below). The provisions provide for the minimum information to be included in a prospectus. More information can be included but the FCA cannot request that a prospectus contains information items which are not included in those *Annexes* (except where *Art 4a* applies). [*EC Commission Regulation 809/2004, Art 3 and FCA Prospectus Rules, para 2.3.1 and Appendix 3*].

Final offer price and amount of securities not included in prospectus. If a prospectus for which approval is sought does not include the final offer price or the amount of transferable securities to be offered the applicant must, as soon as that element is finalised inform, in writing, the competent authority and any competent authority of any EEA state which the applicant has requested be supplied with a certificate of approval under *FSMA 2000, s 87I* and make that information available, in writing, to prospective investors.

[*FSMA 2000, s 87A(7); SI 2005 No 1433*]. (FCA Prospectus Rules, para 2.3.2).

32.11 Incorporation of terms by reference

Information may be incorporated in a prospectus by reference to one or more previously or simultaneously published documents that have been approved by the competent authority of the Home State (see **32.1**) or filed with or notified to it in accordance with the *Prospectus Directive* or the *Consolidated Admissions and Reporting Directive (CARD), Titles IV and V*.

Information that may be incorporated by reference includes

- information filed under the annual information update (see 32.20);
- annual and interim financial information (eg annual and half-yearly accounts and reports);
- documents prepared on the occasion of a specific transaction such as a merger or demerger;
- audit reports and financial statements;
- memorandum and articles of association;
- earlier approved and published prospectuses, listing particulars and supplementary listing particulars;
- regulated information; and
- circulars to security holders.

A cross-reference list must be provided in the prospectus specifying where the information can be accessed by investors.

Any information incorporated by reference must be the latest available to the issuer, offeror or person requesting admission. Where a document which may be incorporated by reference contains information which has undergone material changes, the prospectus must clearly state this and give the updated information.

Information may be incorporated by making reference only to certain parts of a document, provided that it states that the non-incorporated parts are either not relevant or covered elsewhere in the prospectus.

The summary (see 32.8) must not incorporate information by reference.

(FCA Prospectus Rules, paras 2.4.1–2.4.6).

32.12 Omission of information

The FCA may authorise the omission from a prospectus of any information, the inclusion of which would otherwise be required, on the grounds that

- its disclosure would be contrary to the public interest;
- its disclosure would be seriously detrimental to the issuer and the omission would be unlikely to mislead the public on any facts or circumstances which are essential for an informed assessment; or
- the information is only of minor importance and unlikely to influence an informed assessment.

The Secretary of State or the Treasury may issue a certificate to the effect that the disclosure of any information would be contrary to the public interest. If so, the FCA is entitled to act on any such certificate in exercising its powers under these provisions.

[*FCA 2000, s 87B; SI 2005 No 1433*].

A request to the FCA to authorise the omission of specific information must be in writing from the applicant, identify the specific information concerned and the specific reasons for its omission. It must state why, in the applicant's opinion, one or more of the above grounds apply. (FCA Prospectus Rules, para 2.5.3).

Equivalent information. In exceptional cases, if certain information required to be included in a prospectus is inappropriate to the issuer's activity, the legal form of the issuer or to the transferable securities in question, the prospectus must contain information equivalent to the required information (unless there is no such information). (FCA Prospectus Rules, para 2.5.1).

32.13 APPLICATION FOR, AND APPROVAL OF, A PROSPECTUS

An applicant must submit the following information to the FCA.

- A completed Form A.
- The prospectus.
- If the order of items in the prospectus does not coincide with the order in the schedules and building blocks in the *EC Commission Regulation* (see **32.10**), a cross-reference list identifying the pages where each item can be found in the prospectus.
- A letter identifying any items from the schedules and building blocks that have not been included because they are not applicable.
- If information is incorporated in the prospectus by reference to another document (see **32.11**), a copy of the document (annotated to indicate which item of the schedules and building blocks in the *EC Commission Regulation* it relates to).
- If the applicant is requesting the FCA to authorise the omission of information from the prospectus, the information required by FCA Prospectus Rules, paras 2.5.3 (see **32.12**).
- Contact details of individuals who are
  - (i) sufficiently knowledgeable about the documentation to be able to answer queries from the FCA; and
  - (ii) available to answer queries between the hours of 7am and 6pm.
- Any other information that the FCA may require.

The applicant must submit to the FCA the completed Form A (in final form), the relevant fee, and the other information listed above (in draft form)

(i) if the applicant does not have transferable securities admitted to trading and has not previously made an offer, at least 20 working days before the intended approval date of the prospectus; or

(ii) in other cases, at least 10 working days before the intended approval date of the prospectus.

All drafts must be submitted in a substantially complete form and either in duplicate in hard copy or an agreed electronic format. They should be annotated in the margin to show compliance with *FSMA 2000, Pt VI* and the FCA Prospectus Rules. If further drafts are required, they must also be marked to show all changes made since the last draft and all changes made as a consequence of the FCA's comments (in a distinguishable way from other changes).

The draft information must be submitted in final form before midday on the day on which approval is required to be granted.

An applicant must keep a copy of the board resolution allotting or issuing the transferable securities for six years after the application for approval of the prospectus for those securities.

Prospectus comprising separate documents. In such a case, an application for approval may relate to one or more of those separate documents; if so, references above to a prospectus are, unless the context otherwise requires, to be taken to be references to the document or documents to which the application relates.

Vetting of equivalent documents. A person who wishes the FCA to vet an equivalent document referred **32.5**(*k*) or **32.6**(*d*) must submit to the FCA (together with any relevant fee)

- a copy of the document;
- a cross-reference list identifying the pages in the document where each item that is equivalent to the disclosure requirements for a prospectus may be found;
- contact details of individuals who are
  - (i) sufficiently knowledgeable about the documentation to be able to answer queries from the FCA; and
  - (ii) available to answer queries between the hours of 7am and 6pm; and
- any other information that the FCA may require.

The documents must be submitted at least ten working days before the date on which the vetting is required to be completed (20 working days if the person does not have transferable securities admitted to trading and has not previously made an offer). (FCA Prospectus Rules, paras 3.1.1–3.1.5A, 3.1.11, 3.1.14–3.1.16).

32.14 Approval by FCA

The FCA may not approve a prospectus unless it is satisfied that

- the UK is the Home State (see **32.1**) in relation to the issuer of the transferable securities to which it relates;
- the prospectus contains the necessary information; and
- all of the other relevant requirements under the legislation or FCA Prospectus Rules have been complied with.

[*FSMA 2000, s 87A(1); SI 2005 No 1433*].

The "necessary information" for the above is the information necessary to enable investors to make an informed assessment of:

(a) the assets and liabilities, financial position, profits and losses, and prospects of the issuer of the transferable securities and of any guarantor; and

(b) the rights attaching to the transferable securities.

If, in the case of transferable securities to which *FSMA 2000, s 87* applies, the prospectus states that the guarantor is a specified EEA state, the prospectus is not required to include other information about the guarantor. Further requirements are set out in *FSMA 2000, s 87A(3)–(10)*.

[*FSMA 2000, s 87A(2); SI 2012 No 1538, Regs 2, 4*]

The FCA must notify the applicant of its decision on an application for approval of a prospectus before the end of the period for consideration. This period

- begins on the first working day after the date on which the application is received (or, where the FCA reasonably requires further documents or information and gives notice to that effect, on the first working day after the date on which the notice is complied with); and
- ends 10 working days (in the case of a new issuer, 20 working days) thereafter.

But no notice requesting further information can be given more than 10 working days (in that case of a new issuer, 20 working days) after the date on which the application is received.

Supplementary prospectuses. In the case of a supplementary prospectus (see **32.19**), the FCA must notify the applicant of its decision on an application for approval before the end of the period of seven working days beginning with the date on which the application is received. It may request further documents or information if these are reasonably required.

Failure by the FCA to notify its decision on a prospectus or supplementary prospectus within the time limit does not constitute approval of the application in question.

[*FSMA 2000, s 87C; SI 2005 No 1433*].

Notifying the applicant. The FCA must notify the applicant in writing whether it decides to approve or refuse to approve a prospectus. In the latter case, it must state the reasons for refusing the application; and inform the applicant of his right to refer the matter to the Tribunal.

[*FSMA 2000, s 87D; SI 2005 No 1433*].

Requirements imposed as condition of approval. As a condition of approving a prospectus, the FCA may by notice in writing

- require the inclusion in the prospectus of such supplementary information necessary for investor protection it specifies;
- require a person controlling, or controlled by, the applicant to provide specified information or documents;
- require an auditor or manager of the applicant to provide specified information or documents; and
- require a financial intermediary, commissioned to assist either in carrying out the offer to the public or in requesting their admission to trading, to provide specified information or documents. [*FSMA 2000, s 87J; SI 2005 No 1433*].

32.15 Overseas matters

(1) *Transfer of application for approval by FCA to another EEA State*

A person seeking to have the function of approving a prospectus transferred to the competent authority of another EEA State (see **32.1**) must make a written request to the FCA at least ten working days before the date the transfer is sought. The request must

- set out the reasons for the proposed transfer;
- state the name of the competent authority to whom the transfer is sought; and
- include a copy of the draft prospectus.

The FCA will consider transferring the function of approving a prospectus to the competent authority of another EEA State

- if requested to do so by the issuer, offeror or person requesting admission or by another competent authority; or
- in other cases if the FCA considers it would be more appropriate for another competent authority to perform that function.

The FCA may then transfer the function to the competent authority of another EEA State provided that it first obtains the agreement of the transferee authority. The FCA must inform the applicant of the transfer within three working days beginning with the first working day after the date of the transfer.

[*FSMA 2000, s 87E; SI 2005 No 1433*]. (FCA Prospectus Rules, paras 3.1.12, 3.1.13).

(2) *Transfer of application for approval to FCA by another EEA State*

Where the FCA agrees to the transfer to it of an application for the approval of a prospectus made to the competent authority of another EEA State (see **32.1**)

- the UK is to be treated as the Home State (see **32.1**) in relation to the issuer of the transferable securities to which the prospectus relates; and
- *FSMA 2000, Part VI* applies to the application as if it had been made to the FCA except that for the purposes of notification in *FSMA 2000, s 87C* (see **32.14**) the date of the transfer is taken to be the date on which the application was received by the FCA.

[*FSMA 2000, s 87F; SI 2005 No 1433*].

Final terms issued in relation to a prospectus must only contain information that relates to the securities note and must not be used to supplement the prospectus.

Where the FCA in its capacity as the competent authority of the home state receives final terms issued in relation to a prospectus it must communicate those final terms as follows

- where an offer of transferable securities to the public is to be made in another EEA state, to the competent authority of that EEA state, where possible before that offer begins or as soon as practicable following the making of that offer
- where transferable securities are to be admitted to trading on a regulated market in another EEA state, to the competent authority of that EEA state, where possible before the admission occurs or as soon as practicable following the admission of those transferable securities to trading on a regulated market.

The FCA must communicate all final terms in relation to a prospectus it receives in its capacity as the competent authority of the home state to ESMA.

[*FSMA 2000, s 87FA, B; SI 2014 No 3293, Reg 3*].

(3) *Prospectus approved in another EEA State*

A prospectus approved by the competent authority of another EEA State (see **32.1**) is not an approved prospectus for the purposes of *FSMA 2000, s 85* (see **32.3**) unless that authority has provided the FCA with

- a certificate of approval;
- a copy of the prospectus as approved; and
- if requested by the FCA, a translation of the summary of the prospectus.

A document is not a certificate of approval unless it states

- that the prospectus has been drawn up in accordance with the *Prospectus Directive* and approved, in accordance with that *Directive*, by the competent authority providing the certificate; and
- whether (and, if so, why) the competent authority providing it authorised, in accordance with the *Prospectus Directive*, the omission from the prospectus of information which would otherwise have been required to be included.

[*FSMA 2000, s 87H; SI 2005 No 1433*].

(4) *Prospectus approved in a third country*

If a prospectus relating to an issuer that has its registered office in a country that is not an EEA State (see **32.1**) is drawn up in accordance with the legislation of that country, the FCA may, if the UK is the Home State (see **32.1**) in relation to the issuer, approve the prospectus if it is satisfied that

- the prospectus has been drawn up in accordance with international standards set by international securities commission organisations, including the IOSCO disclosure standards; and
- the information requirements, including information of a financial nature, are equivalent to the requirements under *FSMA 2000, Pt VI*, the *EC Commission Regulation* and the FCA Prospectus Rules.

  (FCA Prospectus Rules, paras 4.2.1.)

(5) *Provision of information to host Member State*

The FCA must, if requested to do so, supply the competent authority of a specified Host State (ie an EEA State where an offer to the public is made or admission to trading is sought, when different from the Home State, see **32.1**) with

- a certificate of approval;
- a copy of the specified prospectus (as approved by the FCA); and
- a translation of the summary of the specified prospectus (if the request states that one has been requested by the other competent authority).

The only persons who can make such a request are

- the issuer of the transferable securities in question;
- a person who wishes to offer the transferable securities in question to the public in an EEA State other than (or as well as) the UK;
- a person requesting the admission of the transferable securities in question to a regulated market situated or operating in an EEA State other than (or as well as) the UK.

Similar provisions as to the requirements of a certificate of approval apply as in (3) above.

The FCA must comply with a request under these provisions

- if the prospectus has been approved before the request is made, within three working days beginning with the date the request is received; or

- if the request is submitted with an application for the approval of a prospectus, on the first working day after the date on which it approves the prospectus.

[FSMA 2000, s 87I; SI 2005 No 1433; SI 2012 No 1538, Reg 6].

(6) *Exercise of powers at request of competent authority of another EEA State*

If

(i) the competent authority of another EEA State (see **32.1**) has approved a prospectus,

(ii) the transferable securities to which the prospectus relates have been offered to the public in the UK or their admission to trading on a regulated market has been requested, and

(iii) that competent authority makes a request that the FCA assist it in the performance of its functions under the law of that State in connection with the *Prospectus Directive*

for the purpose of complying with the request in (iii) above, the powers conferred by *FSMA 2000, ss 87K, 87L* (see **32.16**) may be exercised as if the prospectus were one which had been approved by the FCA. [*FSMA 2000, s 87P; SI 2005 No 1433*].

(7) *Use of languages*

If an offer is made, or admission to trading is sought

- only in the UK and the UK is the Home State (see **32.1**), the prospectus must be drawn up in English;
- in more than one EEA State (see **32.1**) including the UK and the UK is the Home State, the prospectus must be drawn up in English and must also be made available either in a language accepted by the competent authorities of each Host State or in a language 'customary in the sphere of international finance', at the choice of the issuer, offeror or person requesting admission (as the case may be);
- in one or more EEA States excluding the UK and the UK is the Home State, the prospectus must be drawn up in a language accepted by the competent authorities of those EEA States or in a language customary in the sphere of international finance, at the choice of the issuer, offeror or person requesting admission (as the case may be).

The FCA consider language to be '*customary in the sphere of international finance*' if documents in that language are accepted in at least three international capital markets in each of Europe, Asia and the Americas.

For the purpose of the scrutiny by the FCA where the UK is the Home State, the prospectus must be drawn up either in English or in another language customary in the sphere of international finance, at the choice of the issuer, offeror or person requesting admission (as the case may be).

Translation of summary into English. If

- an offer is made in the UK,
- a prospectus relating to the transferable securities has been approved by the competent authority of another EEA State and the prospectus contains a summary, and

- the prospectus is drawn up in a language other than English that is customary in the sphere of international finance (see above),

the offeror must ensure that the summary is translated into English.

(FCA Prospectus Rules, paras 4.1.1–4.1.3, 4.1.5A, 4.1.6).

32.16 Powers of the FCA: infringement of rules

The FCA has the following powers where it believes the rules relating to prospectuses have been infringed.

(1) **Power to suspend or prohibit offer to the public**

Where a person has made an offer of transferable securities to the public in the UK,

- if the FCA finds that any provision of *FSMA 2000, Pt VI* or the FCA Prospectus Rules or any other provision made in accordance with the *Prospective Directive* has been infringed, it may require the offeror to withdraw the offer;
- if the FCA has reasonable grounds for suspecting that any such provision made in accordance with the *Prospective Directive* has been infringed, it may
  - (i) require the offeror to suspend the offer for a period not exceeding ten working days; and
  - (ii) require a person not to advertise the offer, or to take such steps as the FCA may specify to suspend any existing advertisement of the offer, for a period not exceeding ten working days; and
- if the FCA has reasonable grounds for suspecting that it is likely that any such provision will be infringed, it may require the offeror to withdraw the offer.

[*FSMA 2000, s 87K; SI 2005 No 1433*].

(2) **Power to suspend or prohibit admission to trading on a regulated market**

Where a person has requested the admission of transferable securities to trading on a regulated market situated or operating in the UK,

- if the FCA finds that any provision of *FSMA 2000, Pt VI* or the FCA Prospectus Rules or any other relevant provision made in accordance with the *Prospective Directive* has been infringed, it may require the market operator to prohibit trading in the securities on the regulated market in question;
- if the FCA has reasonable grounds for suspecting that any such provision has been infringed and the securities have not yet been admitted to trading on the regulated market in question, it may
  - (i) require the person requesting admission to suspend the request for a period not exceeding ten working days; and
  - (ii) require a person not to advertise the securities to which it relates, or to take such steps as the authority may specify to suspend any existing advertisement in connection with those securities, for a period not exceeding ten working days; and

- if the FCA has reasonable grounds for suspecting that any such provision has been infringed and the securities have been admitted to trading on the regulated market in question, it may
  - (i) require the market operator to suspend trading in the securities for a period not exceeding ten working days; and
  - (ii) require a person not to advertise the securities, or to take such steps as the authority may specify to suspend any existing advertisement in connection with those securities, for a period not exceeding ten working days.

[*FSMA 2000, s 87L; SI 2005 No 1433*].

(3) **Public censure of issuer**

If the FCA finds that

- an issuer of transferable securities,
- a person offering transferable securities to the public, or
- a person requesting the admission of transferable securities to trading on a regulated market,

is failing or has failed to comply with his obligations under any provision of *FSMA 2000, Pt VI* or the FCA Prospectus Rules or any other provision made in accordance with the *Prospective Directive*, it may publish a statement to that effect.

If it proposes to do so, the FCA must give the person a warning notice setting out the terms of the proposed statement. If, after considering any representations made in response to the warning notice, the FCA decides to make the proposed statement, it must give the person a decision notice setting out the terms of the statement.

A person to whom a decision notice is given can appeal to the Tribunal.

[*FSMA 2000, ss 87M, 87N; SI 2005 No 1433*].

32.17 FILING AND PUBLICATION OF A PROSPECTUS

A prospectus must not be published until approved by the FCA. Once it is approved, it must be filed with the FCA at the same time as it is made available to the public. A prospectus must be filed with the FCA by uploading it to the system identified by the FCA on its website. The prospectus must be made available to the public as soon as practicable and at a reasonable time in advance of, or at the latest at the beginning of, the offer or the admission to trading of the transferable securities involved. The exception is in the case of an initial public offer of a class of shares not already admitted to trading that is to be admitted to trading for the first time, in which case the prospectus must be made available to the public at least six working days before the end of the offer.

A prospectus is deemed to be made available to the public for these purposes when published in either of the following ways.

- By insertion in one or more newspapers circulated throughout, or widely circulated in, the EEA States in which the offer is made or the admission to trading is sought.

- In a printed form to be made available, free of charge, to the public at the offices of the regulated market on which the transferable securities are being admitted to trading, or at the registered office of the issuer and at the offices of the financial intermediaries placing or selling the transferable securities, including paying agents.
- In an electronic form on

  (i) the issuer's website or, if applicable, on the website of the financial intermediaries placing or selling the transferable securities, including paying agents, or

  (ii) in an electronic form on the website of the regulated market where the admission to trading is sought

  but in either case a paper copy must be delivered to the investor, upon his request and free of charge, by the issuer, the offeror, the person requesting admission or the financial intermediaries placing or selling the transferable securities.

  The prospectus must be easily accessible when entering the website and must not contain hyper-links (apart from links to the electronic addresses where information incorporated by reference is available (see **32.11**)). The investors must have the possibility of downloading and printing the prospectus.

  The websites must avoid targeting residents in Members States or third countries where the offer of securities to the public does not take place (eg by the insertion of a disclaimer as to who are the addressees of the offer).

The text and format of the prospectus made available to the public must at all times be identical to the original version approved by the FCA.

If a prospectus consists of several documents or incorporates information by reference (see **32.11**), the documents and information making up the prospectus may be published and circulated separately if the documents are made available, free of charge, to the public, as above. Each document must indicate where the other constituent documents of the full prospectus may be obtained.

[*EC Commission Regulation, Arts 29, 30*]. (FCA Prospectus Rules, paras 3.1.10, 3.2.1–3.2.6, 3.2.8.)

32.18 ADVERTISEMENTS

In the case of an offer, or an admission to trading of transferable securities, for which

- a prospectus is required to be made available (see **32.3**), or
- a person elects to have a prospectus (see **32.7**),

an 'advertisement' relating to the offer or to the admission to trading must not be issued unless

- it states that a prospectus has been or will be published and indicates where investors are, or will be, able to obtain it;
- it is clearly recognisable as an advertisement;
- information in the advertisement is not inaccurate, or misleading; and
- information in the advertisement is consistent with the information contained in the prospectus (if already published) or with the information required to be in the prospectus (if the prospectus is published afterwards).

Any written advertisement must also contain a bold and prominent statement to the effect that it is not a prospectus but an advertisement and investors should not subscribe for any securities referred to in the advertisement except on the basis of information in the prospectus.

'*Advertisement*' means an announcement relating to a specific offer to the public of securities or to an admission to trading on a regulated market and aiming to specifically promote the potential subscription or acquisition of securities.

Advertisements covered by these provisions include (but are not restricted to) those communicated by any of the following means: addressed or unaddressed printed matter; electronic message or advertisement received via a mobile telephone or pager; standard letter; press advertising with or without order form; catalogue; telephone with or without human intervention; seminars and presentations; radio; videophone; videotext; electronic mail; facsimile machine (fax); television; notice; bill; poster; brochure; web posting including internet banners.

[*EC Commission Regulation, Art 34*]. (FCA Prospectus Rules, paras 3.3.1–3.3.3, Appendix 1).

32.19 SUPPLEMENTARY PROSPECTUS

If, during the period ("the relevant period")

- beginning with the time that the prospectus is approved, and
- ending with the closure of the offer to which the prospectus relates or when trading in the securities on a regulated market begins

there is a significant new factor, material mistake or inaccuracy relating to the information included in the prospectus, then the person on whose application the prospectus was approved must, as soon as practicable after the new factor, etc arises, submit to the FCA for its approval a supplementary prospectus containing details.

Where a prospectus relates both to an offer of transferable securities to the public and the admission of those securities to trading on a regulated market, the relevant period referred to above does not apply and the relevant period begins when the prospectus is approved and ends with the later of the closure of the offer to the public to which the prospectus relates or the time when trading in those securities on a regulated market begins.

'*Significant*' means significant for the purposes of making an informed assessment of assets and liabilities, financial position, profits and losses and prospects of the issuer (and any guarantor) and the rights attaching to the securities.

Any person responsible for the prospectus (see **32.2**) who is aware of any new factor, etc which may require the submission of a supplementary prospectus must give notice of it to

- the issuer of the transferable securities to which the prospectus relates; and
- the person on whose application the prospectus was approved.

A supplementary prospectus must provide sufficient information to correct any mistake or inaccuracy which gave rise to the need for it. It must also, if necessary, include an amendment or supplement to the summary (and any translations of the summary) to take into account the new information.

Unless the context otherwise requires, provisions in this chapter relating to prospectuses also apply to supplementary prospectuses and the provisions above also apply to any required changes for further significant factors, etc following the publication of a supplementary prospectus.

See also **32.21** for the rights of investors to withdraw their acceptances after a supplementary prospectus is published.

[*FSMA 2000, s 87G; SI 2005 No 1433; SI 2012 No 1538, Reg 5*]. (FCA Prospectus Rules, paras 3.4.2, 3.4.3).

32.20 ANNUAL INFORMATION UPDATE

Subject to below, an issuer whose securities are admitted to trading and in relation to whom the UK is the Home State (see **32.1**) must prepare an annual information update (AIU) that refers to or contains all information that has been published or made available to the public over the previous 12 months in one or more EEA States and in third countries in compliance with its obligations under EU and national laws and rules dealing with the regulation of securities, issuers of securities and securities markets.

This does not apply in relation to non-equity transferable securities whose denomination per unit amounts to at least 50,000 euros (or an equivalent amount) unless the issuer has elected by notice in writing to the FCA to comply with the requirements. If an issuer so elects, it must comply with the requirements on an ongoing basis until it withdraws the election (which cannot be done within three years from the date of the initial election).

The FCA expect the AIU to refer to or contain information that is published or made available under

- *FSMA 2000, Pt VI*;
- FCA Rules made under *FSMA 2000, Pt VI*;
- *EC Regulation No 1606/2002* on the application of international accounting standards;
- *CA 2006* (or, for an overseas company, the relevant companies legislation of the place where it is incorporated, relating to the regulation of securities, issuers and securities markets); and
- laws and rules of other EEA States and third countries that relate to the regulation of securities, issuers of securities and securities markets.

The AIU must include a statement indicating that some information may be out-of-date, if such is the case.

If the AIU refers to information rather than including that information, it must

- state where the information can be obtained;
- give a short description of the nature of the information; and
- specify the date and place of filing (if applicable), and the date of publication, of the information.

Filing and publication. The issuer must file the AIU with the FCA, and make it available to the public, at the latest 20 working days after the publication of the annual financial statements. The AIU can be made available to the public by any of the means permitted under **32.17**.

[*EC Commission Regulation 809/2004, Art 27*].

32.21 REMEDIES FOR INVESTORS

Right of investor to withdraw. Subject to below, where a person agrees to buy or subscribe for transferable securities in circumstances where

- the final offer price, or
- the amount of transferable securities to be offered to the public

is not included in the prospectus, he may withdraw his acceptance before the end of the withdrawal period. The withdrawal period

- begins with the investor's acceptance; and
- ends at the end of the second working day after the date on which the FCA is informed of the outstanding information.

The above does not apply if the prospectus contains the criteria or conditions (or both) according to which the final offer price or amount of transferable securities will be determined, or, in the case of the offer price, the maximum price.

A person "P" may withdraw his acceptance .of an offer of transferable securities to the public before the end of the second working day after the day on which the supplementary prospectus was published or such later time as may be specified in the supplementary prospectus if the following conditions are satisfied:

- a prospectus which relates to an offer of transferable securities to the public has been published
- a supplementary prospectus has been published prior to the publication of the supplementary prospectus P agreed to buy or subscribe for transferable securities to which the offer relates and
- the significant new factor, material mistake or inaccuracy referred to in *FSMA 2000, s 87G(1)* which caused the supplementary prospectus to be published arose before delivery of the securities.

[*FSMA 2000, s 87Q; SI 2005 No 1433; SI 2012 No 1538, Reg 5*].

32.22 Compensation for statements in prospectuses

A remedy may be available to a person who acquires transferable securities and suffers loss in respect of them. Subject to below, there are two heads of liability.

(a) Any person responsible for a prospectus (see **32.2**) or supplementary prospectus is liable to pay compensation to a person who has acquired securities to which the prospectus applies and suffered loss in respect of them as a result of any untrue or misleading statement in the prospectus or the omission of any matter required to be included by *FSMA 2000, ss 80* or *81*. If a prospectus is required to include information about the absence of a particular matter, the omission of that information is treated as a statement that there is no such matter.

(b) Any person who fails to comply with the requirements relating to supplementary prospectuses is liable to pay compensation to anyone who has acquired securities and suffered loss as a result of that failure.

References to acquiring securities include contracting to acquire them or any interest in them.

Exemption from liability.

A person does not incur liability under the above provisions in the following circumstances.

(i) Under (*a*) above, a person does not incur liability if he satisfies the court that, having made reasonable enquiries, he reasonably believed at the time when the prospectus was submitted to the FCA, that the statement was true and not misleading or that the matter omitted was properly omitted. He must also show that one or more of the following conditions are satisfied.

- He continued in that belief until the securities were acquired.
- They were acquired before it was reasonably practicable to bring a correction to the attention of potential investors.
- He had, before the securities were acquired, taken all reasonable steps to bring a correction to the attention of potential investors.
- he continued in that belief until after the commencement of dealings in the securities following their admission to trading and that the securities were acquired after such a lapse of time that he ought to be excused.

(ii) Under (*a*) above, a person does not incur any liability if the statement was made (or purports to be made) by another person as an 'expert' and was stated to be included with the consent of that other person, and the person satisfies the court that, at the time the prospectus was submitted to the FCA for approval, he reasonably believed that the other person

- was competent to make or authorise the statement; and
- had consented to its inclusion.

He must in addition satisfy the court that one or more of the following conditions are satisfied.

- He continued in that belief until the securities were acquired.
- They were acquired before it was reasonably practicable to bring the fact that the expert was not competent or had not consented to the attention of potential investors.
- He had, before the securities were acquired, taken all reasonable steps to bring those facts to the attention of potential investors.
- He continued in that belief until after the commencement of dealings in the securities following their admission to trading and the securities were acquired after such a lapse of time that he ought to be excused.

'*Expert*' includes any engineer, valuer, accountant or other person whose profession, qualifications or experience give authority to a statement made by him.

(iii) Under (*a*) above, a person does not incur any liability if he satisfies the court that

- before the securities were acquired

  (i) a correction, or

  (ii) the fact that the expert was not competent or had not consented had been published in a manner calculated to bring it to the attention of potential investors; or

- he has taken all reasonable steps to secure such publication and reasonably believed that publication had taken place before the securities were acquired.

(iv) Under (*a*) above, a person does not incur any liability if the statement was made by an official person or contained in a public official document and he satisfies the court that it is accurately and fairly reproduced.

(v) Under (*a*) and (*b*) above, a person does not incur any liability if he satisfies the court that the person suffering the loss acquired the securities with knowledge that the statement was false or misleading or, as the case may be, knowledge of the omitted matter or the change or new matter.

(vi) Under (*b*) above, a person does not incur any liability if he satisfies the court that the change or new matter in question was not such as to call for a supplementary prospectus.

A person is not to be subject to civil liability solely on the basis of a summary (or any translation of it) in a prospectus unless the summary, when read with the rest of the prospectus, is misleading, inaccurate or inconsistent or does not provide key information as defined in *FSMA 2000, s 87A(9)* and *(10)*.

[*FSMA 2000, s 90, Sch 10; SI 2005 No 1433; SI 2012 No 1538, Reg 7*].

32.23 PENALTIES

The FCA may impose a penalty of such amount as it considers appropriate if it considers that

(a) an issuer of transferable securities,

(b) a person offering transferable securities to the public or requesting their admission to trading on a regulated market,

(c) an applicant for the approval of a prospectus in relation to transferable securities,

(d) a person on whom a requirement has been imposed under *FSMA 2000, ss 87K* or *87L* (see **32.16**), or

(e) any other person to whom a provision of the *Prospectus Directive* applies,

has contravened a provision of *FSMA 2000, Pt VI*, the FCA Prospectus Rules, or a provision otherwise made in accordance with the *Prospectus Directive* or a requirement imposed on him under such a provision.

Where the person in (*a*)–(*e*) above is a company, if the FCA considers that a person who was at the material time a director of the company was knowingly concerned in the contravention, it may impose upon him a penalty of such amount as it considers appropriate.

As an alternative to a penalty, the FCA may instead publish a statement censuring the person concerned.

Any action (whether penalty or censure) taken by the FCA under these provisions must be within two years beginning with the first day on which it knew of the contravention unless proceedings against that person, in respect of the contravention, were begun before the end of that period.

Procedure. If the FCA proposes to take action against a person under these provisions, it must give him a warning notice which must state the amount of the proposed penalty or, as the case may be, set out the terms of the proposed statement.

If, after considering any representations made in response to the warning notice, the FCA decides to take action, it must issue a decision notice which must state the amount of the penalty or, as the case may be, set out the terms of the statement.

Where the FCA decides to take action against a person, that person may refer the matter to the Tribunal.

[*FSMA 2000, ss 91, 92; CA 2006, Sch 15 para 6; SI 2005 No 1433*].

32.24 APPOINTMENT OF INVESTIGATORS BY THE FCA

If it appears to the FCA that there are circumstances suggesting that

- there may have been a contravention of a provision of *FSMA 2000, Pt VI*, the FCA Prospectus Rules or a provision otherwise made in accordance with the *Prospectus Directive*, or
- a person, who was at the material time a director of a company falling within **32.23**, has been knowingly concerned in a contravention of any such provision,

the FCA may appoint one or more competent persons to conduct an investigation on its behalf.

[*FSMA 2000, s 97; CA 2006, Sch 15 para 8; SI 2005 No 433*].

32.25 FCA: EXEMPTION FROM LIABILITY IN DAMAGES

Neither the FCA nor any person who is a member, officer or member of staff of the FCA is to be liable in damages for anything done or omitted in the discharge of the authority's functions unless the act or omission is shown to have been in bad faith. But this exemption does not prevent an award of damages made in respect of an act or omission on the ground that it was unlawful as a result of *Human Rights Act 1998, s 6(1)*. [*FSMA 2000, s 102*].

33 Public and Listed Companies

33.1 **Public companies**
33.2 Comparison with private companies
33.3 Trading certificate and minimum share capital
33.4 **Listed companies – the Listing Rules**
33.5 Enforcement of the Listing Rules
33.6 Requirements for listing
33.8 Application for listing
33.9 Listing particulars where prospectus not required
33.14 Suspending, cancelling and restoring listing
33.15 The Listing Principles: Premium listing
33.16 Sponsors: Premium listing
33.21 Continuing obligations
33.31 Significant transactions: Premium listing
33.33 Related party transactions: Premium listing
33.36 Dealing in own securities and treasury shares: Premium listing
33.37 Circulars
33.39 **Listed companies – Disclosure Rules**
33.40 Disclosure Rules – general provisions
33.41 Disclosure and control of inside information by issuers
33.47 Transactions by persons discharging managerial responsibilities and their connected persons
33.48 **Listed companies – the Transparency Rules**
33.49 Transparency Rules – general provisions
33.50 Periodic financial reporting
33.54 Vote holder and issuer notification rules
33.65 Information requirements for issuers of shares and debt securities
33.66 Filing information and use of language
33.67 Dissemination of information
33.68 Disclosure of information in a non-EEA State
33.69 Compensation for statements in certain publications
33.70 **Penalties**
33.71 **Appointment of investigators by the FCA**
33.72 **FCA: exemption from liability in damages**
APPENDIX **The Model Code**

33.1 PUBLIC COMPANIES

A public company is defined as a company limited by shares or limited by guarantee and having a share capital

- whose certificate of incorporation states that it is a public company; and
- in relation to which the requirements of the *Companies Acts* or the '*former Companies Acts*' (see APPENDIX 1 DEFINITIONS) as to registration or re-registration as a public company have been complied with
  - (i) in relation to registration or re-registration in Great Britain, on or after 22 December 1980; and
  - (ii) in relation to registration or re-registration in Northern Ireland, on or after 1 July 1983.

[*CA 2006, s 4*].

33.2 Comparison with private companies

The main differences between private and public companies are:

33.2 Public and Listed Companies

- **Prohibition of public offers by private companies**. A private company limited by shares or limited by guarantee and having a share capital must not

  (i) offer to the public any securities of the company; or

  (ii) allot or agree to allot any securities of the company with a view to their being offered to the public.

  [*CA 2006, s 755*]. See **47.21 Shares** for full details.

- **Minimum share capital requirement for a public company**. A public company (other than a company re-registered as a public company) must not do business or exercise any borrowing rights unless the Registrar of Companies has issued it with a trading certificate. A trading certificate will only be issued if the company's allotted share capital is not less than the "authorised minimum". See **33.3**. (For the requirements when a private company is re-registered as a public company, see **41.2 Re-Registration**.)

- **Directors**. A private company must have at least one director and a public company must have at least two (see **18.2 Directors**).

- **Company secretaries**. A private company is not required to have a company secretary (although it may choose to do so). A public company must have a company secretary. See **13.1 Company Secretaries**).

- **Name**. The name of a limited private company must normally end in 'limited' or 'Ltd' (or the Welsh equivalent). The name of a limited public company must normally end with 'public limited company' or 'plc' (or Welsh equivalent). See **27.2 Names and Business Names**.

- **Distributions**. A public company may only make a distribution if, after that distribution, the net assets of that company are not less than the aggregate of its called-up share capital and undistributed reserves (see **22.5 Distributions**).

- **Accounts**. A private company, or a group of companies all of which are private companies, may take advantage of the exemptions for small and medium-sized companies (see **4 Accounts: Medium-Sized Companies** and **5 Accounts: Small Companies**).

- The period allowed after the end of the relevant accounting reference period for delivering a copy of the accounts and reports to the Registrar of Companies is shorter for a public company than for a private company. See **2.11 Accounts: General**.

- **Regulatory provisions and corporate governance**. Public companies whose securities are admitted to trading on a regulated or prescribed market are subject to substantial regulatory control by virtue of

  - the Listing Rules (for companies whose securities are admitted to the Official List) – see **33.4**
  - the Prospectus Rules (see **32 Prospectuses**)
  - the Disclosure and Transparency Rules (see **33.39** and **33.48**)
  - the UK Corporate Governance Code issued by the Financial Reporting Council and associated Turnbull, Smith and Higgs best practice guidance
  - the Model Code on dealing in securities (see **Appendix** to this chapter) and

- the Aim Rules for companies admitted to the Alternative Investment Market.

33.3 Trading certificate and minimum share capital

Issue of trading certificate. See above that a public company (other than a company re-registered as a public company) must not do business or exercise any borrowing powers unless the Registrar of Companies has issued it with a trading certificate. (For the requirements when a private company is re-registered as a public company, see **41.2 RE-REGISTRATION**.)

The Registrar of Companies must issue such a certificate if, on an application made in accordance with the provisions described below, he is satisfied that the nominal value of the company's allotted share capital is not less than the authorised minimum (see below). For this purpose, a share allotted in pursuance of an employees' share scheme must not be taken into account unless paid up as to

- at least one-quarter of the nominal value of the share; and
- the whole of any premium on the share.

A trading certificate has effect from the date on which it is issued and is conclusive evidence that the company is entitled to do business and exercise any borrowing powers.

[*CA 2006, s 761*].

Procedure for obtaining a trading certificate. An application (Form SH50) for a certificate must

(a) state that the nominal value of the company's allotted share capital is not less than the authorised minimum;

(b) specify the amount, or estimated amount, of the company's preliminary expenses;

(c) specify any amount or benefit paid or given, or intended to be paid or given, to any promoter of the company, and the consideration for the payment or benefit; and

(d) be accompanied by a statement of compliance, ie a statement that the company meets the requirements for the issue of a certificate.

The Registrar of Companies may accept the statement of compliance as sufficient evidence of the matters stated in it.

[*CA 2006, s 762*].

The authorised minimum. The '*authorised minimum*', in relation to the nominal value of a public company's allotted share capital is

- £50,000; or
- the euro equivalent as prescribed by the Secretary of State, currently 57,100 euros. The euro equivalent is changed from time to time. It is currently 57,100 euros.

[*CA 2006, s 763; SI 2008 No 729, Reg 2; SI 2009 No 2425, Reg 2*].

The Secretary of State may, by order, alter the sterling amount of the authorised minimum, and make a corresponding alteration of the prescribed euro equivalent. Where any such order increases the authorised minimum, it may also require a public company that has an allotted share capital of which the nominal value is less than the increased amount to

- increase the nominal value of its allotted share capital to not less than that amount; or
- re-register as a private company. [*CA 2006, s 764*].

Application of initial requirement. The initial requirement for a public company to have allotted share capital of a nominal value not less than the authorised minimum, must be met either by reference to allotted share capital denominated in sterling or allotted share capital denominated in euros (but not partly in one and partly in the other). Whether the requirement is met is determined, in the first case, by reference to the sterling amount and, in the second case, by reference to the prescribed euro equivalent. No account is to be taken of any allotted share capital of the company denominated in a currency other than sterling or, as the case may be, euros.

If the company could meet the requirement either by reference to share capital denominated in sterling or by reference to share capital denominated in euros, it must elect in its application for a trading certificate or, as the case may be, for re-registration as a public company which is to be the currency by reference to which the matter is determined.

[*CA 2006, s 765*].

Application where shares denominated in different currencies etc. The Secretary of State may make provision by Regulations as to the application of the authorised minimum in relation to a public company that

- has shares denominated in more than one currency or in a currency other than sterling or euros;
- redenominates the whole or part of its allotted share capital; or
- allots new shares.

[*CA 2006, s 766; SI 2011 No 1265, Reg 28(2)*].

Penalties. If a company does business or exercises any borrowing powers without having a trading certificate issued to it, an offence is committed by the company and every officer of the company who is in default. A person guilty of such an offence is liable (i) on conviction on indictment, to a fine; and (ii) on summary conviction, to a fine not exceeding the statutory maximum. See **29.1** Offences and Legal Proceedings for the statutory maximum.

Any breach of the above provisions does not affect the validity of a transaction entered into by the company, but if a company

- enters into a transaction in contravention of the provisions, and
- fails to comply with its obligations in connection with the transaction within 21 days from being called on to do so

the directors of the company are jointly and severally liable to indemnify any other party to the transaction in respect of any loss or damage suffered by him by reason of the company's failure to comply with its obligations. The directors who are so liable are those who were directors at the time the company entered into the transaction.

[*CA 2006, s 767*].

33.4 LISTED COMPANIES – THE LISTING RULES

The Financial Conduct Authority (FCA), (which from 1 April 2013 replaced the FSA as the UK Listing Authority under *FSMA 2000*) must maintain the Official List and may admit such securities as it considers appropriate but

- nothing may be admitted to the Official List except in accordance with the provisions of *FSMA 2000, Pt VI*; and
- the Treasury may, by order, provide that anything which falls within a specified description or category may not be admitted. They have so provided in respect of securities issued by
  - (i) a private company where the securities in question are securities within the meaning of *Financial Services and Markets Act 2000 (Regulated Activities) Order 2001* (*SI 2001 No 544*); and
  - (ii) an old public company (see APPENDIX 1 DEFINITIONS).

The FCA is authorised to make rules for these purposes and those that relate to the Official List are referred to as the Listing Rules. Listing rules may provide that securities cannot be admitted to the Official List unless listing particulars have been submitted to, and approved by, the FCA and published. The Listing Rules may also specify other documents that have to be published.

Admission to the Official List can be granted only if an application is made to the FCA by (or with the consent of) the issuer and the FCA is satisfied that the requirements of the Listing Rules (and any other requirements it imposes in relation to the application) have been complied with.

[*FSMA 2000, ss 73A(1), (2), 74(1)–(3), 75(1)–(4), 79(1)*].

Review of the Listing regime and rules The whole of the listing regime (the Prospectus Rules, the Listing Rules and the Disclosure and Transparency Rules) was reviewed in 2009 to clarify the structure so that investors can make more informed investment decisions and issuers have more flexibility when raising capital. As a consequence of this review the revised Listing regime and rule changes came into effect on 6 April 2010. The important changes made from 6 April 2010 were to:

- restructure the listing regime for existing and potential issuers, into two segments, premium and standard. 'Premium' indicates standards which are more stringent ,super equivalent standards and 'Standard' indicates EU minimum standards;
- strengthen the corporate governance standards for overseas companies (this chapter does not specifically deal with overseas companies)
- require overseas companies with a Standard listing of shares or global depository receipts to comply with the EU Company Reporting Directive; and
- make the Standard listing segment available to UK companies as well as overseas companies.

Further major consultation took place in 2013 and the Listing Rules were amended in May 2014 with the changes coming into effect on 16 May 2014.

The Listing Rules are divided into 20 sections and 2 appendices as follows.

LR 1	Preliminary: All securities (see **33.5**)
LR 2	Requirements for listing: All securities (see **33.6**)
LR 3	Listing applications: All securities (see **33.8**)
LR 4	Listing particulars for professional securities market and certain other securities: All securities (see **33.9–33.12**)

LR 5	Suspending, cancelling and restoring listing: All securities (see **33.14**)
LR 6	Additional requirements for premium listing (commercial company) (see **33.7**)
LR 7	Listing principles: Premium listing (see **33.15**)
LR 8	Sponsors: Premium listing (see **33.16–33.20**)
LR 9	Continuing obligations (see **33.21–33.30**)
LR 10	Significant transactions: Premium listing (see **33.31–33.32**)
LR 11	Related party transactions: Premium listing (see **33.33–33.35**)
LR 12	Dealing in own securities and treasury shares: Premium listing (see **33.36**)
LR 13	Contents of circulars: Premium listing (see **33.37–33.38**)
LR 14	Standard listing (shares) (see **33.7A**)
LR 15	Closed-Ended Investment Funds: Premium listing
LR 16	Open-Ended Investment Companies: Premium listing
LR 17	Debt and debt-like securities: Standard listing
LR 18	Certificates representing certain securities: Standard listing
LR 19	Securitised derivatives: Standard listing
LR 20	Miscellaneous securities: Standard listing
App 1	Relevant definitions
App 2	Annual financial report for certain listed companies

Compliance with the Listing Rules falls into three categories:

(1) all securities have to comply with LR1, 2, 3, 4 and 5

(2) Premium listing – issuers who are commercial companies seeking a Premium listing for equity shares also need to comply with Chapters 6, 7, 8, 9, 10, 11, 12 and 13 (these are the so called 'super equivalent' provisions). Closed-ended investment funds and open-ended investment companies that have Premium listed equity shares must also comply with Chapters 15 and 16 respectively.

A 'Premium listing' is only open to equity shares that are issued by commercial companies and investment entities. An 'equity share' is a share that conveys an unlimited right to the dividends of the company and/or unlimited rights to distribution if the company is liquidated.

(3) Standard listing – in addition to compliance with LR1, 2, 3, 4 and 5 a standard listing is available for securities where EU requirements (that is the Prospectus Directive, Prospectus Rules, Market Abuse Directive, DTRs, Transparency Directive) are met. An issuer with a Standard listing is not required to comply with the 'super equivalent' provisions (see above).

The FCA may dispense with or modify the Listing Rules in such cases and by reference to such circumstances as it considers appropriate in individual cases (subject to the terms of *EU Directives* and *FSMA 2000*). An application to dispense with or modify a Listing Rule should ordinarily be made,

- in the case of a continuing obligation, at least five business days before, and
- for any other Listing Rule, at least ten business days before

the proposed dispensation or modification is to take effect. A dispensation or modification may be either unconditional or subject to specified conditions.

Where an issuer or sponsor has applied for or been granted a dispensation or modification, it must notify the FCA immediately it becomes aware of any matter which is material to the relevance or appropriateness of the dispensation or modification.

(FCA Listing Rules, paras 1.2.1, 1.2.3).

33.5 Enforcement of the Listing Rules

Issuers must provide the FCA as soon as possible with

(a) any information and explanations that the FCA may reasonably require to decide whether to grant an application for admission;

(b) any information the FCA considers appropriate to protect investors or ensure the smooth operation of the market; and

(c) any other information or explanation that the FCA may reasonably require to verify whether the Listing Rules are being and have been complied with.

The FCA may, at any time, require an issuer to publish such information (in such form and within such time limits) as it considers appropriate for the purposes of (b) above and, if the issuer fails to do so, the FCA may publish the information itself (after giving the issuer an opportunity to explain why the information should not be published). .

(FCA Listing Rules, paras 1.3.1, 1.3.2).

33.6 Requirements for listing

The provisions of this paragraph apply to all applicants for admission to listing (unless specified otherwise). See **33.7** for additional requirements for premium listings and **33.7** for additional requirements for standard listings. The FCA may not grant an application for admission unless it is satisfied that the Listing Rules and any special requirements are complied with.

- The applicant (other than a public sector issuer) must be
  - (i) duly incorporated or otherwise validly established according to the relevant laws of its place of incorporation or establishment; and
  - (ii) operating in conformity with its constitution.
- The securities must
  - (i) conform with the law of the applicant's place of incorporation;
  - (ii) be duly authorised according to the requirements of the applicant's constitution; and
  - (iii) have any necessary statutory or other consents.
- Other than securities to which LR4 applies (ie professional securities market and certain other securities), equity shares must be admitted to trading on a regulated market for listed securities operated by a recognised investment exchange' (RIE). All other securities must be admitted to trading on a RIE's market for listed securities. For the meaning of 'equity securities' see **33.4** above.
- The securities must be freely transferable.
- Shares must be fully paid and free from all liens and from any restriction on the right of transfer (except any restriction imposed for failure to comply with a notice under *Companies Act 2006 (CA 2006), s 793* (notice by company requiring information about interests in its shares)).

- Unless the FCA agrees otherwise, the expected aggregate market value of all securities (excluding treasury shares) to be listed must be at least

  (i) £700,000 for shares, and

  (ii) £200,000 for debt securities

  unless either relating to a tap issue where the amount of the debt securities is not fixed or securities of the same class are already listed.

- An application for listing of securities of any class must

  (i) if no securities of that class are already listed, relate to all securities of that class, issued or proposed to be issued; or

  (ii) if securities of that class are already listed, relate to all further securities of that class, issued or proposed to be issued.

- If, under *FSMA 2000* or the law of another EEA State, a prospectus must be approved and published for the securities or the applicant is permitted and elects to have a prospectus (see **32.3** and **32.7 Prospectuses** respectively), in order to be listed

  (i) a prospectus must have been approved by the FCA and published in relation to the securities; or

  (ii) if another EEA State is the Home State for the securities (see **32.1 Prospectuses**), the relevant competent authority must have supplied the FCA with a certificate of approval, a copy of the prospectus as approved, and (if applicable) a translation of the summary of the prospectus.

- If, under LR 4 (see **33.9**), listing particulars must be approved and published for the securities, those listing particulars must have been approved and published by the FCA.

- Unless the FCA dispenses with LR 2.2.12, convertible securities and miscellaneous securities giving the holder the right to buy or subscribe for other securities may be admitted to listing only if the securities into which they are convertible or over which they give a right to buy or subscribe are already, or will become at the same time, listed securities or securities listed on a regulated, regularly operating, recognised open market.

(FCA Listing Rules, paras 2.2.1–2.2.13).

EEA States – see **Appendix 1 Definitions**.

33.7 *Additional requirements for listing for equity securities*

Premium listings

The provisions below apply to a new applicant for the admission of equity shares to premium listing but do not apply where a company with an existing premium listing of equity shares introduces a new holding company to its existing group and no transaction as defined in LR 10.1.3 is being undertaken that would otherwise increase the assets or liabilities of the group. See **33.31** and **33.32** for transactions covered by LR 10.

An applicant to Premium listing (commercial company) for the admission of equity shares must satisfy the requirements in Chapter 6 Listing Rules as well as those in LR 2 (see **33.6**) (unless the FCA modify or dispense with the requirements).

(1) *Historical financial information*

A new applicant for the admission of equity shares to a Premium listing must have published or filed historical financial information that

- covers at least three years;
- has a latest balance sheet date that is not more than six months before the date of the prospectus or listing particulars for the relevant shares and not more than nine months before the date the shares are admitted to listing unless LR 5.6.21 applies;
- includes the consolidated accounts for the applicant and all its subsidiary undertakings;
- has been audited or reported on in accordance with the standards acceptable under item 20.1 of Annex 1 of the Prospectus Directive Regulation; and
- is not subject to a modified report, except as set out in LR 6.1.3 AG or LR 5.6.21

A new applicant must

- take all reasonable steps to ensure that the person providing the opinion pursuant to LR 6.1.3(1) (e) and LR 6.1.3D(3) is independent of it; and
- obtain written confirmation from that person that it complies with guidelines on independence issued or approved by its national accountancy or auditing bodies.

The FCA may accept that LR 6.1.3(1)(e) and LR 6.1.3D(3) (above) have been satisfied where a modified report is present only as a result of

(i) the presence of an emphasis – of matter paragraph which arises in any of the earlier periods required by LR 6.1.3 and the opinion on the final period is unmodified or

(ii) the opinion on the historical financial information for the final period under LR 6.1.3 includes an emphasis – of matter paragraph with regard to going concern and LR 6.1.16 is complied with.

The historical information required by LR 6.1.3(1) must represent at least 75% of the new applicant's business for the full period referred to in LR6.1.3(1)(a) and put prospective investors in a position to make an informed assessment of the business for which admission is sought.

In determining what amounts to 75% of the new applicant's business the FCA will consider the size, in aggregate, of all the acquisitions that the new applicant has entered into during the period required by LR6.1.3(1)(a) and up to the date of the prospectus, relative to the size of the new applicant as enlarged by the acquisitions.

In ascertaining the size of the acquisitions relative to the new applicant the FCA will take into account factors such as the assets, profitability and market capitalisation of the businesses. The figures should be the latest available for the acquired entity and the new applicant as enlarged by the acquisition or acquisitions.

Where the new applicant has made an acquisition or series of acquisitions such that its own consolidated financial information is insufficient to meet the 75% requirement (referred to above) there must be historical financial information relating to the acquired entity or entities which has been published or filed and that

- covers the period from at least three years prior to the date under LR 6.1.3(1)(b) up to the earlier of the date in LR 6.1.3(1)(b) or the date of acquisition by the new applicant,
- is presented in a form that is consistent with the accounting policies adopted in the financial information required by LR6.1.3,
- is not subject to a modified report except as set out in LR6.1.3A and in aggregate with its own historical financial information represents at least 75% of the enlarged new applicant's business for the full period referred to in LR 6.1.3(1)(a).

The purpose of LR6.1.3B is to ensure that the issuer has representative financial information throughout the period required by LR6.1.3(1)(a) and to assist prospective investors to make a reasonable assessment of what the future prospects of the new applicant's business might be. Investors are then able to consider the new applicant's historic revenue earning record in light of its particular competitive advantages, the outlook for the sector in which it operates and the general macro economic climate. The FCA may consider that a new applicant does not have representative historical financial information and that its equity shares are not eligible for a premium listing if a significant part or all of its business has one or more of the following characteristics:

- a business strategy that places significant emphasis on the development or marketing of products or services which have not formed a significant part of the new applicant's historical financial information
- the value of the business on admission will be determined, to a significant degree, by reference to future developments rather than past performance
- the relationship between the value of the business and its revenue or profit earning record is significantly different from those of similar companies in the same sector
- there is no record of consistent revenue, cash flow or profit growth throughout the period of the historical financial information
- the new applicant's business has undergone a significant change in its scale of operations during the period of the historical financial information or is due to do so before or after admission
- it has significant levels of research and development expenditure or significant levels of capital expenditure.

(2) *Control of assets and independence*

A new applicant for the admission of equity shares to a Premium listing must demonstrate that

it will be carrying on an independent business as its main activity.

(1) Notwithstanding any agreement entered into under 2(a) factors that may indicate that a new applicant does not satisfy (4) include situations where

(a) a majority of the revenue generated by the new applicant's business is attributable to business conducted directly or indirectly with a controlling shareholder (or any associate thereof) of the new applicant; or

(b) a new applicant does not have

- strategic control over the commercialisation of its products;

- strategic control over its ability to earn revenue;
- freedom to implement its business strategy;

(c) a new applicant cannot demonstrate that it has access to financing other than from a controlling shareholder (or any associate thereof);

(d) a new applicant has granted or may be required to grant security over its business in connection with the funding of a controlling shareholder or a member of a controlling shareholder's group;

(e) except in relation to a mineral company, a new applicant's business consists principally of holdings of shares in entities that it does not control, including entities where

- the new applicant is only able to exercise negative control; and/or
- the new applicant's control is subject to contractual arrangements which could be altered without its agreement or could result in a temporary or permanent loss of control; or

(f) a controlling shareholder (or any associate thereof) appears to be able to influence the operations of the new applicant outside its normal governance structures or via material shareholdings in one or more significant subsidiary undertakings.

(2) Where a new applicant for the admission of equity shares to a premium listing will have a controlling shareholder upon admission, it must have in place

(a) a written and legally binding agreement which is intended to ensure that the controlling shareholder complies with the independence provisions set out in (4); and

(b) a constitution that allows the election and re-election of independent directors to be conducted in accordance with the election provisions set out in LR 9.2.2E and LR 9.2.2F.

(3) In order to comply with (2)(a), where a new applicant will have more than one controlling shareholder, the new applicant will not be required to enter into a separate agreement with each controlling shareholder if

(a) the new applicant reasonably considers, in light of its understanding of the relationship between the relevant controlling shareholders, that a controlling shareholder can procure the compliance of another controlling shareholder and that controlling shareholder's associates with the independence provisions contained in the relevant agreement; and

(b) the agreement, which contains the independence provisions set out in (4), entered into with the relevant controlling shareholder also contains

- a provision in which the controlling shareholder agrees to procure the compliance of a non-signing controlling shareholder and its associates with the independence provisions contained within the agreement; and
- the names of any such non-signing controlling shareholder.

(4) The independence provisions referred to in (1) are undertakings that

(1) transactions and arrangements with the controlling shareholder (and/or any of its associates) will be conducted at arm's length and on normal commercial terms;

(2) neither the controlling shareholder nor any of its associates will take any action that would have the effect of preventing the new applicant or listed company from complying with its obligations under the listing rules; and

(3) neither the controlling shareholder nor any of its associates will propose or procure the proposal of a shareholder resolution which is intended or appears to be intended to circumvent the proper application of the listing rules.

The FCA can modify or dispense with the requirement to provide historical financial information (but only the requirements that the accounts cover at least three years or to show that the historical financial information represents at least 75% of the new applicant's business for that period and puts prospective investors in a position to make an informed assessment of the business for which admission is sought) if it is satisfied that it is desirable in the interests of investors and that investors have the necessary information available to arrive at an informed judgment about the applicant and the equity shares for which a premium listing is sought. Before modifying or dispensing with the second requirement the FCA must also be satisfied that there is an overriding reason for the applicant seeking listing (rather than seeking admission to the market more suited to a company without sufficient historical financial information to be eligible for a premium listing and will take into account whether the applicant is attracting significant funds from sophisticated investors, is undertaking a significant marketing of equity shares in connection with the admission and has demonstrated that having listed shares is a significant factor in the ability to raise funds and that it will have a significant market capitalisation on admission.

(3) *Working capital*

An applicant must satisfy the FCA that it and its subsidiary undertakings (if any) have sufficient working capital available for the group's requirements for at least the next 12 months from the date of publication of the prospectus or listing particulars (as the case may be) for the shares that are being admitted.

(4) *Shares in public hands*

If an application is made for the admission of a class of shares, 25% of shares of that class must, no later than the time of admission, be distributed to the public in one or more EEA States (see APPENDIX 1 DEFINITIONS). Account may also be taken of holders in non-EEA States if the shares are listed in the relevant State.

For these purposes, shares are not held in public hands if they are held, directly or indirectly, by

- a director of the applicant or of any of its subsidiaries (or a person connected with that person);
- the trustees of any employees' share scheme or pension fund established for the benefit of any directors and employees of the applicant and its subsidiaries;
- any person who has a right to nominate a person to the board of directors of the applicant; or
- any person or persons in the same group, or persons acting in concert, who have an interest in 5% or more of the shares of the relevant class or
- if the shares are subject to a lock-up period of more than 180 calendar days.

Treasury shares are not to be taken into consideration when calculating the number of shares of the class.

The FCA may modify LR 6.1.19 to accept a percentage lower than 25% if it considers that the market will operate properly with a lower percentage in view of the large number of shares of the same class and the extent of their distributions to the public. Specific factors set out in LR 6.1.20A (2) must be taken into account by the FCA in considering whether to grant such a modification.

(5) *Shares of a non-EEA company*

The FCA will not admit shares of a company incorporated in a non-EEA State (see **33.6**) that are not listed either in its country of incorporation or in the country in which a majority of its shares are held, unless it is satisfied that the absence of the listing is not due to the need to protect investors.

(6) *Warrants or options to subscribe*

The total of all issued warrants to subscribe or options to subscribe for equity shares must not exceed 20% of the issued equity share capital (excluding treasury shares) of the applicant as at the time of issue of the warrants or options. Rights under employees' share schemes are not included for the purpose of the 20%.

(7) *Settlement*

To be listed the constitution of the company and the terms of its equity shares must be compatible with electronic settlement. This is intended to ensure that there is nothing inherent in a company's constitution which prevents electronic settlement of its equity securities. The FCA does recognise that there may be external factors which affect the eligibility of an equity share for electronic settlement.

(FCA Listing Rules, paras 6.1.3, 6.1.4, 6.1.13, 6.1.16, 6.1.19, 6.1.20A, 6.1.21–6.1.23). See also FCA Listing Rules, paras 6.1.8–6.1.12 for special requirements for mineral companies and scientific research based companies.

33.7A *Standard listings*

A company applying for a standard listing of shares (other than equity shares issued by an investment entity and preference shares that are specialist securities), must comply with the following requirements of Chapter 14 Listing Rules as well as the requirements set out in **33.6** (above).

(1) Shares in public hands

If an application is made for the admission of a class of shares, 25% of shares of that class must, no later than the time of admission, be distributed to the public in one or more EEA States (see APPENDIX 1 DEFINITIONS). Account may also be taken of holders in non-EEA States if the shares are listed in the state or states.

For these purposes, shares are not held in public hands if they are held, directly or indirectly, by

- a director of the applicant or of any of its subsidiaries (or a person connected with that person);
- the trustees of any employees' share scheme or pension fund established for the benefit of any directors and employees of the applicant and its subsidiaries;
- any person who has a right to nominate a person to the board of directors of the applicant; or
- any person or persons in the same group, or persons acting in concert, who have an interest in 5% or more of the shares of the relevant class or

- if the shares are subject to a lock-up period of more than 180 days.

Treasury shares are not to be taken into consideration when calculating the number of shares of the class.

The FCA can modify Listing Rule 14 and accept a lower percentage than 25% if it considers that the market will operate properly with a lower percentage in view of the large numbers of shares of the same class and the extent of their distribution to the public. For that purpose the FCA can take account of shares of the same class held in non EEA sates even though they are not listed in those non EEA states.

(2) Shares of a non EEA company

The FCA will not admit shares of a company incorporated in a non-EEA State (see **33.6**) that are not listed either in its country of incorporation or in the country in which a majority of its shares are held, unless it is satisfied that the absence of the listing is not due to the need to protect investors.

(FCA Listing Rules paras 14.1 and 14.2)

33.8 Application for listing

All applicants for admission must apply to the FCA by submitting

(a) certain documents in final form by midday two business days before the FCA is to consider the application;

(b) certain documents in final form on the day the FCA is to consider application;

(c) all additional documents, explanations and information as required by the FCA; and

(d) verification of any information in such manner as the FCA may specify.

The applicant must also pay the appropriate fee.

The documents to be submitted under *(a)* and *(b)* above depend upon the type of security involved and, in the case of shares, whether or not a prospectus has been produced.

For full details, see FCA Listing Rules, paras 3.3 and 3.4.

If the process of applying for admission of securities is likely to be very onerous due to the frequent or irregular nature of allotments and if no prospectus or listing particulars are required for the securities, an applicant may apply for a block listing of a specific number of securities. See FCA Listing Rules, para 3.5.

33.9 Listing particulars where prospectus not required

Where an issuer has applied for the admission of

(a) securities specified in **32.5**(*a*)(*c*)(*e*)–(*h*) **Prospectuses**, or

(b) any other specialist securities for which a prospectus is not required under the *Prospectus Directive*

as no prospectus is required, listing particulars must instead be prepared, approved and published.

(FCA Listing Rules, paras 4.1.1, 4.1.2).

General duty of disclosure. In addition to any information required by the Listing Rules or otherwise by the FCA, listing particulars submitted to the FCA must contain all such information as investors and their professional advisers would reasonably require, and reasonably expect to find there, for the purpose of making an informed assessment of

- the assets and liabilities, financial position, profits and losses, and prospects of the issuer of the securities; and
- the rights attaching to the securities.

The information to be included is that which is within the knowledge of the persons responsible for the listing particulars or which it would be reasonable for them to obtain by making enquiries. In determining this, regard must be had to

- the nature of the securities and the issuer;
- the nature of the potential investors;
- the fact that certain matters may reasonably be expected to be within the knowledge of professional advisers of a kind which potential investors may reasonably be expected to consult; and
- any information available to investors or their professional advisers as a result of requirements imposed on the issuer by a recognised investment exchange, by Listing Rules or by or under any other *Act*.

[*FSMA 2000, s 80*].

Exemptions from disclosure. The FCA may authorise the omission from listing particulars of any information which would otherwise be required on the following grounds.

(i) Its disclosure would be contrary to the public interest. The Secretary of State or the Treasury may issue a certificate to the effect that the disclosure of any information would be contrary to the public interest. In such a case, the FCA is entitled to act on any such certificate in exercising its powers under this provision.

(ii) Its disclosure would be seriously detrimental to the issuer. But no authorisation can be granted, and any authorisation granted does not extend to, '*essential information*', ie information which a person considering acquiring securities of the kind in question would be likely to need in order not to be misled about any facts which it is essential for him to know in order to make an informed assessment.

(iii) In the case of specified securities, its disclosure is unnecessary for persons of the kind who may be expected normally to buy or deal in securities of that kind.

[*FSMA 2000, s 82*].

Contents and format.

(1) *Summary*

The listing particulars of securities within (*a*) above must contain a summary as required for a prospectus under the Prospectus Rules (see 32.8 **Prospectuses**).

(2) *Format*

The listing particulars must be in a format that complies with the relevant requirements in the Prospectus Rules and *EC Commission Regulation 809/2004* (as if those requirements applied to the listing particulars).

(3) *Minimum information to be included*

The following minimum information must be included in listing particulars (see **32.10 Prospectuses**).

- For an issue of bonds (including bonds convertible into the issuer's shares or exchangeable into a third party issuer's shares or derivative securities), irrespective of the denomination of the issue, the information required by *Annex IX*.
- The additional information required by the underlying share building block where relevant.
- For an issue of asset-backed securities, irrespective of the denomination per unit of the issue, the information required by *Annexes VII* and *VIII*.
- For an issue of certificates representing shares, irrespective of the denomination per unit of the issue, the information required by *Annex X* (except for item 13.2 relating to profit forecasts).
- For an issue of securities by the government of a non-EEA State (see **33.6**) or a local or regional authority of a non-EEA State, the information required by *Annex XVI*.
- For all issues that are guaranteed, the information in *Annex VI*.

For all other issues, the FCA would expect issuers to follow the most appropriate schedules and building blocks to determine the minimum information to be included in listing particulars.

(4) *Incorporation by reference*

An issuer may incorporate information by reference in the listing particulars as in **32.11 Prospectuses**.

(5) *Equivalent information*

An issuer may include equivalent information in listing particulars as in **32.12 Prospectuses**.

(6) *English language*

Listing particulars must be in English.

(7) *Omission of information*

A request to the FCA to authorise the omission of specific information in a particular case must be in writing from the issuer and identify the specific information concerned and the specific reasons for the omission. It must state why, in the issuer's opinion, one or more of the grounds for exemption from disclosure in *FSMA 2000, s 82* above applies.

(FCA Listing Rules, paras 4.2.2–4.2.10).

Final terms. If final terms of the offer are not included in the listing particulars,

- the final terms must be provided to investors, filed with the FCA, and made available to the public (as if the relevant requirements in 32.17 PROSPECTUSES relating to filing and making available applied to the final terms of the offer); and
- the listing particulars must disclose the criteria and/or the conditions in accordance with which the above elements will be determined or, in the case of price, the maximum price.

(FCA Listing Rules, para 4.4.3).

33.10 *Responsibility for listing particulars*

Subject to below, the persons responsible for listing particulars (including supplementary listing particulars) are as follows.

(a) The issuer of the securities.

(b) Where the issuer is a body corporate, each person who is a director of that body at the time when the particulars are submitted to the FCA. But a person is not to be treated as responsible in these circumstances if the particulars are published without his knowledge or consent and, on becoming aware of their publication, he forthwith gives reasonable public notice that they were published without his knowledge or consent.

(c) Where the issuer is a body corporate, each person who has authorised himself to be named, and is named, in the particulars as a director or as having agreed to become a director of that body either immediately or at a future time.

(d) Each person who accepts, and is stated in the particulars as accepting, responsibility for the particulars.

(e) Each person not falling within (*a*)–(*d*) above who has authorised the contents of the particulars.

When accepting responsibility for particulars under (*d*) above or authorising their contents under (*e*) above, a person may state that he does so only in relation to certain specified parts of the particulars, or only in certain specified respects. In such a case he is responsible only to the extent specified and only if the material in question is included in (or substantially in) the form and context to which he has agreed.

Nothing in the above rules is to be construed as making a person responsible for any particulars by reason of giving advice as to their contents in a professional capacity.

[*SI 2001 No 2956, Reg 6*].

Specialist securities. Where listing particulars relate to securities of a kind specified by the Listing Rules for the purposes of 33.9(iii) (disclosure of information unnecessary for persons of the kind who may be expected normally to buy or deal in securities of that kind) no person is to be treated as responsible for the particulars under (*a*)–(*c*) above but without prejudice to his being responsible under (*d*) above. [*SI 2001 No 2956, Reg 9*].

In the case of listing particulars for specialist securities

- the issuer must state in the listing particulars that it accepts responsibility for the listing particulars;
- the directors may state that they accept responsibility for the listing particulars; and
- other persons may state that they accept responsibility for all or part of the listing particulars, in which case the statement by the issuer or directors may be appropriately modified.

An issuer that is the government of a non-EEA State (see **33.6**) or a local or regional authority of a non-EEA State is not required to state that it accepts responsibility for the listing particulars.

(FCA Listing Rules, para 4.2.13).

33.11 *Supplementary listing particulars*

An issuer must submit supplementary listing particulars if at any time

- after the preparation of listing particulars which have been submitted to the FCA, and
- before the commencement of dealings in the securities concerned following their admission to the official list

there is a 'significant' change affecting any matter contained in those particulars or a significant new matter arises, the inclusion of information in respect of which would have been required.

'*Significant*' means significant for the purposes of making an informed assessment of assets and liabilities, financial position, profits and losses and prospects of the issuer and any rights attaching to the securities.

If the issuer is not aware of the change or new matter in question, he is not under a duty to comply unless he is notified of the change or new matter by a person responsible for the listing particulars. But it is the duty of any person responsible for those particulars who is aware of such a change or new matter to give notice of it to the issuer.

The provisions also apply to matter contained in any supplementary listing particulars previously published under these provisions in respect of the securities in question.

[*FSMA 2000, s 81*].

33.12 *Approval and publication of listing particulars*

An application for approval of listing particulars or supplementary listing particulars must comply with the procedures in **32.13 Prospectuses** (as if those procedures applied to the application), except that the applicant does not need to submit a completed Form A.

The FCA cannot grant an application for admission unless it is satisfied that the requirements of *FSMA 2000* and the Listing Rules are complied with.

Notifying decision. The FCA must notify the applicant in writing of its decision within six months of the date on which the application is received (or, where the applicant is asked to provide further information, within six months of the date on which that information is provided). [*FSMA 2000, s 76(1)–(3)*]. However, in practice, the FCA will try to notify the applicant of its decision within the same time limits as are specified in *FSMA 2000, s 87C* for approval of a prospectus or supplementary prospectus (see **32.14 Prospectuses**). (FCA Listing Rules, para 4.3.3).

Refusal of application. The FCA may refuse an application for listing

- if it considers that, for a reason relating to the issuer, granting it would be detrimental to the interests of the investor; or
- in the case of securities already officially listed in another EEA State (see **33.6**), if the issuer has failed to comply with any obligations to which he is subject as a result of that listing.

If it decides to do so, the FCA must give the applicant a warning notice. If, following comments from the applicant (if any), it still decides to refuse the application, it must give the applicant a decision notice. The applicant may then refer the matter to the Tribunal.

[*FSMA 2000, ss 75(5)(6), 76(3)–(6)*].

Publication of listing particulars. An issuer must ensure that listing particulars or supplementary listing particulars are not published until they have been approved by the FCA. Once approved, the issuer must ensure that they are filed and published as if the relevant requirements in **32.17** Prospectuses applied to them.

33.13 *Compensation for statements in listing particulars*

A remedy may be available to a person who acquires securities and suffers loss in respect of them. Subject to below, there are two heads of liability.

(a) Any person responsible for listing particulars (see **33.10**) or supplementary listing particulars is liable to pay compensation to a person who has acquired securities to which the particulars apply and suffered loss in respect of them as a result of any untrue or misleading statement in the particulars or the omission of any matter required to be included. If listing particulars are required to include information about the absence of a particular matter, the omission of that information is treated as a statement that there is no such matter.

(b) Any person who fails to comply with the requirements relating to supplementary listing particulars is liable to pay compensation to anyone who has acquired securities and suffered loss as a result of the failure.

References to acquiring securities include contracting to acquire them or any interest in them.

Exemption from liability. A person does not incur liability under the above provisions in the following circumstances.

(i) Under (*a*) above, a person does not incur liability if he satisfies the court that, having made reasonable enquiries, he reasonably believed at the time when the listing particulars were submitted to the FCA, that the statement was true and not misleading or that the matter omitted was properly omitted. He must also show that one or more of the following conditions are satisfied.

- He continued in that belief until the securities were acquired.
- They were acquired before it was reasonably practicable to bring a correction to the attention of potential investors.
- He had, before the securities were acquired, taken all reasonable steps to bring a correction to the attention of potential investors.
- He continued in that belief until after the commencement of dealings in the securities following their admission to trading and that the securities were acquired after such a lapse of time that he ought to be excused.

(ii) Under (*a*) above, a person does not incur any liability if the statement was made (or purports to be made) by another person as an 'expert' and was stated to be included with the consent of that other person, and the person satisfies the court that, at the time the listing particulars were submitted to the FCA for approval, he reasonably believed that the other person

- was competent to make or authorise the statement; and

- had consented to its inclusion.

He must in addition satisfy the court that one or more of the following conditions are satisfied.

- He continued in that belief until the securities were acquired.
- They were acquired before it was reasonably practicable to bring the fact that the expert was not competent, or had not consented, to the attention of potential investors.
- He had, before the securities were acquired, taken all reasonable steps to bring those facts to the attention of potential investors.
- He continued in that belief until after the commencement of dealings in the securities following their admission to trading and the securities were acquired after such a lapse of time that he ought to be excused.

'*Expert*' includes any engineer, valuer, accountant or other person whose profession, qualifications or experience give authority to a statement made by him.

(iii) Under (*a*) above, a person does not incur any liability if he satisfies the court that

- before the securities were acquired

  (i) a correction, or

  (ii) the fact that the expert was not competent or had not consented

  had been published in a manner calculated to bring it to the attention of potential investors; or

- he has taken all reasonable steps to secure such publication and reasonably believed that publication had taken place before the securities were acquired.

(iv) Under (*a*) above, a person does not incur any liability if the statement was made by an official person or contained in a public official document and he satisfies the court that it is accurately and fairly reproduced.

(v) Under (*a*) and (*b*) above, a person does not incur any liability if he satisfies the court that the person suffering the loss acquired the securities with knowledge that the statement was false or misleading or, as the case may be, knowledge of the omitted matter or the change or new matter.

(vi) Under (*b*) above, a person does not incur any liability if he satisfies the court that the change or new matter in question was not such as to call for supplementary listing particulars.

A person is not to be subject to civil liability solely on the basis of a summary (or any translation of it) in listing particulars unless the summary, when read with the rest of the listing particulars is misleading, inaccurate or inconsistent or does not provide key information as defined in *FSMA 2000*.

[*FSMA 2000, s 90, Sch 1; SI 2012 No 1538 Reg 7*].

Suspending, cancelling and restoring listing

Suspending of listing by FCA. The FCA may, in accordance with the Listing Rules

- discontinue the listing of any securities if satisfied that there are special circumstances which preclude normal dealings in the securities; and

- suspend the listing of any securities.

It may do so on its own initiative or on the application of the issuer. In the former case, the issuer may refer the matter to the Tribunal.

[*FSMA 2000, s 77; SI 2007 No 1973*].

See *FSMA 2000, ss 78, 78A* for the procedures which the FCA must follow if it proposes to discontinue or suspend a listing of securities (or does so with immediate effect) on its own initiative or at the request of the issuer respectively.

The FCA may take such action if the smooth operation of the market is, or may be, temporarily jeopardised or it is necessary to protect investors. (FCA Listing Rules, para 5.1.1).

Cancelling of listing by FCA. The FCA may cancel the listing of securities if satisfied that there are special circumstances that preclude normal regular dealings in them. It will generally seek to cancel the listing of an issuer's equity shares or certificates representing equity securities when the issuer completes a reverse takeover. (FCA Listing Rules, paras 5.2.1, 5.2.3).

Cancellation of listing of equity shares at issuer's request. Subject to below, an issuer that wishes the FCA to cancel the listing of any of its equity shares with a *premium* listing must (even if the listing of the shares is suspended)

(a) send a circular to the holders of the securities which must
- comply with the requirements of **33.38** applying to all circulars;
- be submitted to the FCA for approval prior to publication; and
- include the anticipated date of cancellation (not less than 20 business days following the passing of the resolution referred to in (*b*) below);

(b) obtain, at a general meeting, the prior approval of a resolution for the cancellation from a majority of not less than 75% of the votes attaching to the shares voted on the resolution and where an issuer has a controlling shareholder (see definition in **33.7**) , a majority of the votes attaching to the shares of independent shareholders voted on the resolution.

(c) notify a RIS, at the same time as the circular is despatched to the relevant holders of the shares, of the intended cancellation and of the notice period and meeting; and

(d) notify a RIS of the passing of the resolution.

An issuer is not required to seek the prior approval of security holders under (*b*) above if

- it notifies a RIS
  - (i) that the financial position of the issuer or its group is so precarious that, but for the proposal in (*b*) above there is no reasonable prospect that the issuer will avoid going into formal insolvency proceedings;
  - (ii) that there is a proposal for a transaction, arrangement or other form of reconstruction of the issuer or its group which is necessary to ensure the survival of the issuer or its group and the continued listing would jeopardise the successful completion of the proposal; and

(iii) explaining why the cancellation is in the best interests of those to whom the issuer or its directors have responsibilities (including the bodies of securities holders and creditors, taken as a whole) and why the approval of shareholders will not be sought prior to the cancellation of listing and giving at least 20 business days' notice of the intended cancellation

Cancellation of listing of other securities (other than equity shares with a premium listing) at the issuer's request. The issuer must notify a RIS, giving at least 20 business days' notice of the intended cancellation, but is not required to obtain the approval of the holders of those securities as under (*b*) above. Where the securities are debt securities, the issuer must also notify the holders or a representative of the holders, in accordance with the terms and conditions of the issue of those securities, of intended cancellation but the prior approval of holders in general meeting does not need to be obtained.

Cancellation in relation to takeover offers: offeror interested in 50% or less of the voting rights. The requirements in (*a*)–(*d*) above do not apply to the cancellation of equity shares with a premium listing when, in the case of a takeover offer

- the offeror or any controlling shareholder who is an offeror is interested in 50% or less off the voting rights of an issuer before announcing its firm intention to make its takeover offer;
- the offeror has by virtue of its shareholdings and acceptances of the offer, acquired or agreed to acquire issued share capital carrying 75% of the voting rights of the issuer; and
- the offeror has stated in the offer document or any subsequent circular sent to shareholders that a notice period of not less than 20 business days prior to cancellation will commence either on the offeror attaining the required 75% or on the first date of issue of compulsory acquisition notices under *CA 2006, s 979* (right of offeror to buy out minority shareholder). For these purposes the offer document or circular must make clear that the notice period begins only when the offeror has announced that it has acquired or agreed to acquire shares representing 75% of the voting rights.

In such circumstances, the issuer must notify shareholders that the required 75% has been obtained and that the notice period has commenced and of the anticipated date of cancellation. Alternatively, the explanatory letter or the material accompanying the compulsory acquisition notice must state that the notice period has commenced and the anticipated date of cancellation.

Cancellation in relation to takeover offers: offeror interested in more than 50% of voting rights.

The requirements in (a)–(d) above do not apply to the cancellation of equity shares with a premium listing in the case of a takeover offer if

- the offeror or any controlling shareholder who is an offeror is interested in more than 50% of the voting rights of an issuer before announcing its firm intention to make its takeover offer;
- the offeror has by virtue of its shareholdings and acceptances of its takeover offer, acquired or agreed to acquire issued share capital carrying 75% of the voting rights of the issuer;
- unless LR 5.2.11D applies, the offeror has obtained acceptances of its takeover offer or acquired or agreed to acquire shares from independent shareholders that represent a majority of the voting rights held by the independent shareholders on the date its firm intention to make its takeover offer was announced; and

- the offeror has stated in the offer document or any subsequent circular sent to the holders of the shares that a notice period of not less than 20 business days prior to cancellation will commence either on the offeror obtaining the relevant shareholding and acceptances as described in LR 5.2.11A(2)–(3) or as described in LR 5.2.11D or on the first date of issue of compulsory acquisition notices under CA 2006, s 979.

For the purposes of LR 5.2.11A(4), the offer document or circular must make clear that the notice period begins only when the offeror has announced that it has acquired or agreed to acquire shares representing 75% of the voting rights and, if relevant, has obtained acceptances of its takeover offer or acquired or agreed to acquire shares from independent shareholders that represent a majority of the voting rights held by the independent shareholders.

The issuer must notify shareholders that the relevant thresholds described in LR 5.2.11A(2)–(3) or LR 5.2.11D have been obtained and that the notice period has commenced and of the anticipated date of cancellation, or the explanatory letter or other material accompanying the s 979 notice must state that the notice period has commenced and the anticipated date of cancellation.

LR 5.2.11A(3) does not apply where the offeror has by virtue of its shareholdings and acceptances of its takeover offer acquired or agreed to acquire issued share capital carrying more than 80% of the voting rights of the issuer.

Cancellation as a result of schemes of arrangement, etc. The requirements in *(a)*–*(d)* above do not apply to the cancellation of equity shares with a premium listing as a result of the matters set out in LR 5.2.12.

(FCA Listing Rules, paras 5.2.4–5.2.12).

Information to be supplied to the FCA. See FCA Listing Rules, paras 5.3.1 and 5.3.2 for information to be included in, and supplied with, a request to suspend or cancel a listing.

Timing of requests. A written request by an issuer to have the listing of its securities

- suspended should be made as soon as practicable (suspension requests received for the opening of the market should allow sufficient time for the FCA to deal with the request before trading starts); and
- cancelled must be made not less than 24 hours before the cancellation is expected to take effect.

(FCA Listing Rules, paras 5.3.4, 5.3.5).

Withdrawing request. An issuer may withdraw its request at any time before the suspension or cancellation takes effect. (FCA Listing Rules, para 5.3.7).

Restoring listing. If an issuer has the listing of its securities cancelled, it may only have them re-admitted to the official list by re-applying for their listing.

The FCA may restore the listing of any securities that have been suspended if it considers that the smooth operation of the market is no longer jeopardised or if the suspension is no longer required to protect investors. The FCA may restore the listing even though the issuer does not request it.

An issuer that has the listing of any of its securities suspended may request the FCA to have them restored. The FCA will refuse such a request if it is not satisfied that the smooth operation of the market is no longer jeopardised or if the suspension is still required to protect investors.

(FCA Listing Rules, paras 5.4.1–5.4.4).

Suspension, cancellation or restoration by overseas exchange or authority. An issuer must inform the FCA if its listing has been suspended, cancelled or restored by an overseas exchange or overseas authority. (FCA Listing Rules, para 5.5.2).

33.15 The Listing Principles: Premium listing

The Listing Principles apply to every listed company with a premium listing of equity shares.

The purpose of the Listing Principles below is to ensure that listed companies pay due regard to the fundamental role they play in maintaining market confidence and ensuring fair and orderly markets They are designed to assist listed companies in identifying their obligations and responsibilities under the Listing Rules, Disclosure Rules Transparency Rules and corporate governance rules.

(1) A listed company must take reasonable steps to enable its directors to understand their responsibilities and obligations as directors.

(2) A listed company must take reasonable steps to establish and maintain adequate procedures, systems and controls to enable it to comply with its obligations.

(3) A listed company must act with integrity towards holders and potential holders of its premium listed shares.

(4) A listed company must communicate information to holders and potential holders of its listed equity shares in such a way as to avoid the creation or continuation of a false market in those listed equity shares.

(5) A listed company must ensure that it treats all holders of the same class of its listed equity shares that are in the same position equally in respect of the rights attaching to such listed equity shares.

(6) A listed company must deal with the FCA in an open and co-operative manner.

(7) All equity shares in a class that have been admitted to premium listing must carry an equal number of votes on any shareholder vote.

(8) Where a listed company has more than one class of equity shares admitted to premium listing, the aggregate voting rights of the shares in each class should be broadly proportionate to the relative interests of those classes in the equity of the listed company.

(FCA Listing Rules, paras 7.1.2, 7.1.3, 7.2.1, 7.2.1A, 7.2.2, 7.2.3).

Guidance on the listing and premium listing principles

Listing Principle 1 is intended to ensure that listed companies have adequate procedures, systems and controls to enable them to comply with their obligations under the listing rules, disclosure rules, transparency rules and corporate governance rules. In particular, the FCA considers that listed companies should place particular emphasis on ensuring that they have adequate procedures, systems and controls in relation to, where applicable

- identifying whether any obligations arise under LR 10 (Significant transactions) and LR 11 (Related party transactions); and
- the timely and accurate disclosure of information to the market.

Timely and accurate disclosure of information to the market is a key obligation of listed companies. For the purposes of Listing Principle 1 a listed company should have adequate systems and controls to be able to

- ensure that it can properly identify information which requires disclosure under the listing rules, disclosure rules, transparency rules or corporate governance rules in a timely manner; and
- ensure that any information identified under the above is properly considered by the directors and that such a consideration encompasses whether the information should be disclosed.

In assessing whether the voting rights attaching to different classes of premium listed shares are proportionate for the purposes of Premium Listing Principle 4, the FCA will have regard to the following non-exhaustive list of factors

- the extent to which the rights of the classes differ other than their voting rights, for example with regard to dividend rights or entitlement to any surplus capital on winding up;
- the extent of dispersion and relative liquidity of the classes; and/or
- the commercial rationale for the difference in the rights.

(FCA Listing Rules, paras 7.2.2–7.2.4).

33.16 Sponsors: Premium listing

A company with, or applying for, a premium listing of its equity shares must appoint a sponsor on each occasion that it

(a) is required to submit any of the following documents to the FCA in connection with an application for admission of equity shares to premium listing

(i) a prospectus, supplementary prospectus or equivalent document;

(ii) a certificate of approval from another competent authority;

(iii) a summary document as required by **32.6**(*h*) PROSPECTUSES; or

(iv) listing particulars referred to in FCA Listing Rules 15.3.3 (closed-ended investment funds) or 16.3.4 (open-ended investment companies) or supplementary listing particulars.

(b) is required to submit to the FCA a class 1 circular for approval; or

(c) is required to submit to the FCA a circular that proposes a reconstruction or a refinancing which is required by LR 9.5.12 to include a working capital statement; or

(d) is required to submit to the FCA a circular for the proposed purchase of own shares which is required by LR 13.7.1 to include a working capital statement; or

(e) is required to do so by the FCA because it appears to the FCA that there is, or there may be, a breach of the Listing Rules, Disclosure Rules or Transparency Rules by the listed company; or

(f) is required by LR 11.1.10(2) to provide the listed company with a confirmation that the terms of the proposed related party transaction are fair and reasonable; or

(g) is required to submit to the FCA a related party circular which is required by LR 13.6.1(5) to include a statement by the board that the transaction or arrangement is fair and reasonable; or

(h) is required by LR 8.4.3(4) to submit to the FCA a letter from a sponsor in relation to the applicant's eligibility; or

(i) is required to make an announcement or request a suspension in connection with a reverse takeover under LR 5.6.6; or

(j) provides to the FCA a disclosure regime confirmation in connection with a reverse takeover under LR 5.6.12G(1); or

(k) makes a disclosure announcement in connection with a reverse takeover under LR 5.6.15G that contains a declaration described in LR 5.6.15G(3) or (4); or

(l) submits to the FCA a letter in relation to the issuer's eligibility in connection with a reverse takeover under LR 5.6.23G(2); or

(m) provides confirmation to the FCA of its severe financial difficulty for the purposes of LR 10.8.3G(2); or

(n) is required to provide an assessment of the appropriateness of an investment exchange or multilateral trading facility under LR 13.5.27B; or

(o) is required to provide a written opinion to the FCA under LR11 Annex 1(8) (joint investment arrangements).

A company must appoint a sponsor where it applies to transfer its category of equity shares listing from

- a standard listing (shares) to a premium listing (commercial company);
- a standard listing (shares) to a premium listing (investment company);
- a premium listing (investment company) to a premium listing (commercial company); or
- a premium listing (commercial company) to a premium listing (investment company).

A listed company with a premium listing must also obtain a sponsor's guidance if it is proposing to enter into a transaction which due to its size or nature could amount to a Class 1 transaction or a reverse takeover in order to assess the application of the Listing Rules, Disclosure Rules and the Transparency Rules (see 33.31); or enter into a transaction which is, or may be, a related party transaction in order to assess the application of the Listing Rules, the Disclosure Rules and the Transparency Rules (see 33.33).

(FCA Listing Rules, paras 8.2.1–8.2.3).

For details of the specific duties of a sponsor in relation to applications for admission of equity shares to listing and Class 1 circulars, see FCA Listing Rules, paras 8.4.1–8.4.13.

33.17 *Approval, appointment and dismissal*

Approval. Sponsors must be approved by the FCA which maintains a list of approved sponsors on its website.

The FCA will approve a person as a sponsor only if it is satisfied that the person

- is an authorised person or a member of a designated professional body;
- is competent to perform sponsor services in accordance with LR8; and
- has appropriate systems and controls in place to ensure that it can carry out its role as a sponsor in accordance with LR 8.

A sponsor, or a person applying for approval as a sponsor, will not satisfy LR 8.6.5R(2) unless it has:

(1) submitted a sponsor declaration to the FCA

- for a person applying for approval as a sponsor, within three years of the date of its application; and
- for a sponsor, within the previous three years; and

(2) a sufficient number of employees with the skills, knowledge and expertise necessary for it to

- provide sponsor services in accordance with LR 8.3;
- understand

(i) the rules, guidance and ESMA publications directly relevant to sponsor services;

(ii) the procedural requirements and processes of the FCA;

(iii) the due diligence process required in order to provide sponsor services in accordance with LR 8.3 and LR 8.4;

(iv) the responsibilities and obligations of a sponsor in LR 8;

(v) specialist industry sectors, if relevant to the sponsor services it provides or intends to provide; and

(vi) be able to comply with the key contact requirements in LR 8.6.19 R.

To determine whether a sponsor or a person applying for approval as a sponsor is able to satisfy LR 8.6.7R(1)(a), the FCA may consider whether any of the person's employees have had material involvement in the provision of sponsor services that have required the submission of a sponsor declaration within the previous three years.

In exceptional circumstances, the FCA may consider dispensing with, or modifying, the requirement in LR 8.6.7R(1) in accordance with LR 1.2.1R.

In assessing whether a sponsor or a person applying for approval as a sponsor satisfies LR 8.6.7R (2), the FCA will consider a variety of factors including

(1) the nature, scale and complexity of its business;

(2) the diversity of its operations;

(3) the volume and size of transactions it undertakes;

(4) the volume and size of transactions it anticipates undertaking in the following year; and

(5) the degree of risk associated with the transactions it undertakes or anticipates undertaking in the following year.

Notwithstanding LR 8.6.7CG, when considering whether a sponsor satisfies LR 8.6.7R(2)(c) the FCA expects a sponsor to have no less than two employees who are able to satisfy the key contact requirements in LR 8.6.19R(2).

(FCA Listing Rules, paras 8.6.1, 8.6.5, 8.6.7).

Appointment. A listed company or applicant must ensure that the FCA is informed promptly of the name and contact details of any sponsor appointed (by the listed company, applicant or sponsor).

Where more than one sponsor is appointed, the company must

(a) ensure that one of the sponsors takes primary responsibility for contact with the FCA in respect of the entire application or transaction; and

(b) inform the FCA, in writing, of the name and contact details of the sponsor taking responsibility under (*a*) above.

(FCA Listing Rules, paras 8.5.1–8.5.3).

33.18 *Responsibilities of a sponsor*

A listed company must appoint a sponsor where it applies to transfer its category of equity shares listing from

- a standard listing (shares) to a premium listing (commercial company) ;or
- a standard listing (shares) to a premium listing (investment company) ;or
- a premium listing (investment company) to a premium listing (commercial company) ;or
- a premium listing (commercial company) to a premium listing (investment company).

A sponsor must in relation to a sponsor service

- referred to in **33.16**(*a*)–(*d*), (*k*) and where relevant (*e*) provide assurance to the FCA when required that the responsibilities of the company with or applying for a premium listing of its equity shares under the Listing Rules have been met; and
- provide to the FCA any explanation or confirmation in such form and within such time limit as the FCA reasonably requires for the purposes of ensuring that the listing rules are being complied with by a company with or applying for a premium listing of its equity shares; and
- guide the company with or applying for a premium listing of its equity shares in understanding and meeting its responsibilities under the Listing Rules the Disclosure Rules and the Transparency Rules.

A sponsor must, for so long as it provides a sponsor service, take such reasonable steps as are sufficient to ensure that any communication or information it provides to the FCA in carrying out the sponsor service is, to the best of its knowledge and belief, accurate and complete in all material respects and as soon as possible provide to the FCA any information of which it becomes aware that materially affects the accuracy or completeness of information it has previously provided.

Where a sponsor provides information to the FCA which is or is based on information it has received from a third party, in assessing whether a sponsor has complied with its obligations in LR 8.3.1A(1) the FCA will have regard, amongst other things, to whether a sponsor has appropriately used its own knowledge, judgment and expertise to review and challenge the information provided by the third party.

The sponsor will be the main point of contact with the FCA for any matter referred to in LR8.2. The FCA expects to discuss all issues relating to a transaction and any draft or final document directly with the sponsor. However in appropriate circumstances the FCA will communicate directly with the company with or applying for a premium listing of its equity shares.

A sponsor remains responsible for complying with LR 8.3 even where a sponsor relies on the company with or applying for a premium listing of its equity shares or a third party when providing an assurance or confirmation to the FCA.

(FCA Listing Rules, paras 8.3.1, 8.3.1A, 8.3.1B, 8.3.2, 8.3.2A).

33.19 *Principles for sponsors*

A sponsor must keep to the following principles.

(a) A sponsor must act with due care and skill in relation to a sponsor service.

(b) Where, in relation to a sponsor service, a sponsor gives any guidance or advice to a listed company or applicant on the application or interpretation of the Listing Rules or Disclosure Rules and Transparency Rules, the sponsor must take reasonable steps to satisfy itself that the director or directors of the listed company understand their responsibilities and obligations under those Rules.

(c) A sponsor must at all times (whether in relation to a sponsor service or otherwise)

  (i) deal with the FCA in an open and co-operative way, and

  (ii) deal with all enquiries raised by the FCA promptly.

(d) If in connection with the provision of a sponsor service a sponsor becomes aware that it, or the company with or applying for a premium listing of its equity shares is failing or has failed to comply with its obligations under FCA the Listing Rules the Disclosure Rules or the Transparency Rules the sponsor must promptly notify the FCA.

(e) A sponsor must, in relation to a sponsor service, act with honesty and integrity.

The purpose of LR 8.3.7 to 8.3.13 is to ensure that conflicts of interest do not adversely affect the ability of a sponsor to perform its functions properly under the Listing Rules or market confidence in sponsors.

(f) A sponsor must take all reasonable steps to identify conflicts of interest that could adversely affect its ability to perform its functions properly

(g) In identifying conflicts of interest sponsors should also take into account circumstances that could create a perception in the market that a sponsor may not be able to perform its functions properly or compromise the ability of a sponsor to fulfil its obligations to the FCA in relation to the provision of sponsor services.

(h) A sponsor must take all reasonable steps to put in place and maintain effective organisational and administrative arrangements that ensure conflicts of interest do not adversely affect its ability to perform its functions. Disclosure of a conflict of interest will not usually be considered to be an effective organisational or administrative arrangement. If a sponsor is not sure of this in relation to a sponsor service, it must decline or cease to provide the sponsor services. In case of doubt, it should discuss the issue with the FCA before it decides if it can provide a sponsor service. Listing Rules 8.3.7, 8.3.9 and 8.3.11 apply for so long as the sponsor provides a sponsor service.

(i) If a listed company or applicant appoints more than one sponsor to provide sponsor services in relation to a transaction,

  (i) the appointment does not relieve either of the appointed sponsors of their obligations under Listing Rules, Chapter 8; and

  (ii) the sponsors are each responsible for complying with the obligations under those provisions in relation to the transaction.

(FCA Listing Rules, paras 8.3.3–8.3.14).

33.20 *Supervision of sponsors*

A sponsor must:

(a) Pay the annual fee in order to remain on the list of sponsors.

(b) Provide to the FCA on or after the first business day in January in each year but no later than the last business day of January in each year

(i) written confirmation that it continues in **33.17** to satisfy the criteria for approval as a sponsor;

(ii) for each of those criteria, evidence of the basis upon which it considers it meets that criterion.

(c) Notify the FCA in writing as soon as possible if

(i) it ceases to satisfy the criteria for approval as a sponsor set out in LR 8.6.5. or becomes aware of any matter which in its reasonable opinion would be relevant to the FCA in considering whether the sponsor continues to comply with LR 8.6.6 or the sponsor becomes aware of any fact or circumstance relating to the sponsor or any of its employees engaged in the provision of sponsor services by the sponsor which, in its reasonable opinion, would be likely to adversely affect market confidence in the sponsors; or

(ii) the sponsor, or any of its employees engaged in the provision of sponsor services by the sponsor, are convicted of any offence involving fraud, theft or other dishonesty or the subject of a bankruptcy proceeding, a receiving order or an administration order;

(iii) any of its employees engaged in the provision of sponsor services by the sponsor are disqualified by a court from acting as a director of a company or from acting in a management capacity or conducting the affairs of any company;

(iv) the sponsor, or any of its employees engaged in the provision of sponsor services by the sponsor, are subject to any public criticism, regulatory intervention or disciplinary action by the FCA or any designated professional body (or any comparable body inside or outside the UK) or under any comparable legislation in any jurisdiction outside the UK;

(v) the sponsor resigns or is dismissed by a listed company or applicant giving details of any relevant facts or circumstances;

(vi) the sponsor changes its name;

(vii) a listed company or applicant denies the sponsor access to documents or information that have been the subject of a reasonable request by the sponsor;

(viii) it identifies or otherwise becomes aware of any material deficiency in the sponsor's systems and controls; or

(ix) there is intended to be a change of control of the sponsor, any restructuring of the sponsor's group or a reorganisation of, or a substantial change to the directors, partners or employees engaged in the provision of sponsor services by the sponsor;

(x) there is expected to be a change in the financial position of the sponsor or any of its group companies that would be likely to adversely affect the sponsor's ability to perform the sponsor services or otherwise comply with LR8.

Where a sponsor is of the opinion that notwithstanding the circumstances giving rise to a notification obligation under (*c*) above it continues to satisfy the ongoing criteria for approval as a sponsor it must include in its notification to the FCA a statement to that effect and the basis for its opinion.

(d) Not delegate any of its functions as such, or permit another person to perform those functions

(e) Inform the FCA in writing if it wishes to have its approval as a sponsor cancelled and must give

(i) the sponsor's name and a clear explanation of the background and reasons for the request;

(ii) the date on which the sponsor requests the cancellation should take effect (bearing in mind that under the statutory notice procedure a request for cancellation of approval will take a minimum of eight weeks to take effect);

(iii) a signed confirmation that the sponsor will not provide any sponsor services as of the date the request is submitted to the FCA; and

(iv) the name and contact details of the person at the sponsor with whom the FCA should liaise with in relation to the request.

Examples of when a sponsor should submit a cancellation request include, but are not limited to, situations where the sponsor ceases to satisfy the ongoing criteria for approval as a sponsor in accordance with LR 8.6.6 and following notification made under LR 8.7.8 there are no ongoing discussions with the FCA which could lead to the conclusion that the sponsor remains eligible or where there is a change of control of the sponsor or any restructuring of the sponsor's group that will result in sponsor services being provided by a different person, in which case the person that is intended to provide the sponsor services should apply for approval as a sponsor under LR 8.6 before it provides any sponsor services. A sponsor may withdraw its cancellation request at any time before the cancellation takes effect. The withdrawal request should initially be made by telephone and then confirmed in writing as soon as possible, with an explanation of the reasons for the withdrawal.

(FCA Listing Rules, paras 8.7.6–8.7.8, 8.7.8A, 8.7.16, 8.7.21, 8.7.21A, 8.7.22, 8.7.23).

33.21 Continuing obligations

Once its securities have been admitted to listing, there are still continuing obligations which a listed company must observe in order to maintain an orderly market in securities and to ensure that all users of the market have simultaneous access to the same information. The provisions of Chapter 9 of the Listing Rules only apply to a company that has a Premium listing of equity securities. Companies with a Standard listing are bound by the continuing obligations of Chapter 14 para 3 of the Listing Rules.

The continuing obligations are considered in **33.22** to **33.30**.

33.22 *Requirements with continuing application*

(1) *Admission to trading*

A listed company's securities must at all times be admitted to trading on an RIE's market for listed securities. The company must inform the FCA in writing as soon as possible if it has

- requested an RIE to admit or re-admit any of its listed equity shares to trading;
- requested an RIE to cancel or suspend trading of any of its listed equity shares; or
- been informed by an RIE that trading of any of its listed equity shares will be cancelled or suspended.

(2) *Independent business*

A listed company must carry on an independent business as its main activity at all times. Where a listed company has a controlling shareholder, it must have in place at all times

- a written and legally binding agreement which is intended to ensure that the controlling shareholder complies with the independence provisions set out in LR 6.1.4D; and
- a constitution that allows the election and re-election of independent directors to be conducted in accordance with the election provisions set out in LR 9.2.2E R and LR 9.2.2F.

In order to comply with LR 9.2.2A(2)(a), where a listed company will have more than one controlling shareholder, the listed company will not be required to enter into a separate agreement with each controlling shareholder if

- the listed company reasonably considers, in light of its understanding of the relationship between the relevant controlling shareholders, that a controlling shareholder can procure the compliance of another controlling shareholder and that controlling shareholder's associates with the independence provisions contained in the relevant agreement; and
- the agreement, which contains the independence provisions set out in LR 6.1.4D, entered into with the relevant controlling shareholder also contains

(a) a provision in which the controlling shareholder agrees to procure the compliance of a non-signing controlling shareholder and its associates with the independence provisions contained within the agreement; and
(b) the names of any such non-signing controlling shareholder.
Where as a result of changes in ownership or control of a listed company, a person becomes a controlling shareholder of the listed company, the listed company will be allowed

- a period of not more than six months from the event that resulted in that person becoming a controlling shareholder to comply with LR 9.2.2A(2)(a); and
- in the case of a listed company which did not previously have a controlling shareholder, until the date of the next annual general meeting of the listed company, other than an annual general meeting for which notice has already been given or is given within a period of three months from the event that resulted in that person becoming a controlling shareholder to comply with LR 9.2.2A(2)(b).

In complying with LR 9.2.2A(2)(b), a listed company may allow an existing independent director who is being proposed for re-election (including any such director who was appointed by the board of the listed company until the next annual general meeting) to remain in office until any resolution required by LR 9.2.2F has been voted on.

Where LR 9.2.2A(2) applies, the election or re-election of any independent director by shareholders must be approved by

- the shareholders of the listed company; and
- the independent shareholders of the listed company.

Where LR 9.2.2E applies, if the election or re-election of an independent director is not approved by both the shareholders and the independent shareholders of the listed company, but the listed company wishes to propose that person for election or re-election as an independent director, the listed company must propose a further resolution to elect or re-elect the proposed independent director which

- must not be voted on within a period of 90 days from the date of the original vote;
- must be voted on within a period of 30 days from the end of the 90 day-period set out above and
- must be approved by the shareholders of the listed company.

A listed company must comply with the independence provisions contained in any agreement entered into under LR 6.1.4B(1) or LR 9.2.2A(2)(a) at all times.

In addition to the annual confirmation required to be included in a listed company's annual financial report under LR 9.8.4(14), the FCA may request information from a listed company under LR 1.3.1(3) to confirm or verify that an independence provision contained in any agreement entered into under LR 6.1.4B(1) or LR 9.2.2A(2)(a) or a procurement obligation (as set out in LR 6.1.4C(2)(a) or LR 9.2.2B(2)(a)) contained in an agreement entered into under LR 6.1.4B(1) or LR 9.2.2A(2)(a) is being or has been complied with.

(3) *Settlement arrangements*

A listed company's securities must comply with LR 6.1.2.3 (electronic settlement) at all times.

(4) *Compliance with the Disclosure and Transparency Rules*

A listed company whose equity shares are admitted to trading on a Part 2 regulated market in the UK should consider its obligations under DTR 2 (Disclosure and control of inside information by issuers) and under DTR Parts 4, 5 and 6.

A listed company that is not already required to comply with Disclosure and Transparency Rules, Part 2 (disclosure and control of inside information by issuers) or with the Transparency Rules) (or with corresponding requirements imposed by another EEA Member State), must comply with those provisions as if it were an issuer for those purposes. See **33.32–33.46** and **33.50–33.68** respectively.

(5) *Compliance with the Model Code*

The Model Code (see Appendix 1 at the end of this chapter) imposes restrictions on dealing in the securities of a listed company beyond those imposed by law. Its purpose is to ensure that persons discharging managerial responsibilities and employee insiders do not abuse, and do not place themselves under suspicion of abusing, inside information that they may be thought to have, especially in periods leading up to an announcement of the company's results.

The Listing Rules require that:

- No dealings in any securities may be effected by or on behalf of a listed company (or any other member in its group) at a time when, under the provisions of the Model Code, a director of the company would be prohibited from dealing in its securities. The only exceptions are where such dealings are entered into

  (i) in the ordinary course of business by a securities dealing business; or

  (ii) on behalf of third parties by the company or any other member of its group.

- A listed company must require every person discharging managerial responsibilities (see **33.47**), including directors to comply with the Model Code and take all proper and reasonable steps to secure their compliance, although it may impose more rigorous dealing obligations than those required by the Model Code. *FSMA 2000* provides that an individual who is not a director can still be a person discharging managerial responsibilities in relation to an issuer if they are a "senior executive of such an issuer" and they meet the criteria set out in *FSMA 2000*. An individual may be a "senior executive of such an issuer" irrespective of the nature of any contractual arrangements between the individual and the issuer and notwithstanding the absence of a contractual arrangement between the individual and the issuer, provided the individual has regular access to inside information relating directly or indirectly to the issuer and has power to make managerial decisions affecting the future development and business prospects of the issuer.

Where clearance is given to a person to deal in exceptional circumstances in a close period (see paragraph 9 of the Model Code), the notification to a RIS required by FCA Disclosure and Transparency Rules, para 3.1.4 (see **33.47**) must also include a statement of the exceptional circumstances.

(6) *Contact details*

A listed company must ensure that the FCA is provided with up-to-date contact details of at least one appropriate person nominated by it to act as the first point of contact with the FCA in relation to the company's compliance with the Listing Rules and the Disclosure and Transparency Rules. The contact person will be expected to be

(i) knowledgeable about the listed company and the Listing Rules applicable to it;

(ii) capable of ensuring that appropriate action is taken on a timely basis; and

(iii) contactable on business days between the hours of 7am to 7pm.

(7) *Sponsors*

A listed company should consider its notification obligations on the appointment of sponsors (see **33.17**).

In relation to the provision of a sponsor service, a company with a premium listing of its equity shares must cooperate with its sponsor by providing the sponsor with all information reasonably requested by the sponsor for the purpose of carrying out the sponsor service in accordance with LR 8.

(8) *Shares in public hands*

A listed company must comply the requirements in **33.7**(4) at all times.

(9) *Publication of unaudited financial information*

Where a listed company has published

- any unaudited financial information in a Class 1 circular or a prospectus, or
- any profit forecast or profit estimate

the first time it publishes financial information as required by disclosure and transparency rule 4.1 after the publication of unaudited financial information, it must

(a) reproduce that material in its next annual report and accounts;

(b) produce and disclose in the annual report and accounts the actual figures for the same period covered by that material; and

(c) provide an explanation of the difference, if there is a difference of 10% or more between the figures required by (*b*) and those reproduced under (*a*) above.

This does not apply to pro-forma financial information prepared in accordance with Annex 1 and 2 of the Prospectus Directive Regulation or to any preliminary statements of annual results or half-yearly or quarterly reports that are reproduced with the unaudited financial information.

(FCA Listing Rules, paras 9.2.1–9.2.16, 9.2.2A–H, 9.2.18, 9.2.19).

33.23 *Continuing obligations – holders*

(1) *Proxy forms*

A listed company must ensure that, in addition to its obligation under *CA 2006*, a proxy form

- provides for at least three-way voting on all resolutions to be proposed (except procedural resolutions); and
- states that, if it is returned without an indication as to how the proxy shall vote on any particular matter, the proxy will exercise his discretion as to whether, and if so how, he votes.

If the proposed resolutions include the re-election of more than five retiring directors, the proxy form may give shareholders the opportunity to vote for or against (or abstain from voting on) the re-election of the retiring directors as a whole but must also allow votes to be cast for or against (or for shareholders to abstain from voting on) the re-election of the retiring directors individually.

(2) *Sanctions*

Where a listed company has taken a power in its constitution to impose sanctions on a shareholder who is in default in complying with a notice served under *CA 2006, s 793* (notice by company requiring information about interests in its shares, see **24.2 Interests in Public Company Shares**)

(i) sanctions may not take effect earlier than 14 days after service of the notice;

(ii) for a shareholding of less than 0.25% of the shares of a particular class (exclusive of treasury shares), the only sanction the constitution may provide for is a prohibition against attending meetings and voting;

(iii) for a shareholding of 0.25% or more of the shares of a particular class (exclusive of treasury shares), the constitution may additionally provide for

  - the withholding of dividends (including shares issued in lieu of dividend) on the shares concerned; and

- the placing of restrictions on the transfer of shares (other than the sale to a genuine unconnected third party such as through a RIE or an overseas exchange or by the acceptance of a takeover offer); and

(iv) any sanctions imposed under (i) or (iii) above must cease to apply after a specified period of not more than seven days after the earlier of

- receipt by the issuer of notice that the shareholding has been sold to an unconnected third party through a RIE or an overseas exchange or by the acceptance of a takeover offer; and
- due compliance, to the satisfaction of the issuer, with the notice under *CA 2006, s 793.*

(3) *Pre-emption rights*

Subject to below, a listed company proposing to issue equity shares for cash or sell treasury shares that are equity shares for cash, must first offer them *pro rata* to

- existing holders of that class of equity shares (other than the listed company itself by virtue of its holding treasury shares); and
- holders of other equity shares of the listed company who are entitled to be offered them.

The above does not apply if

- a general disapplication of statutory pre-emption rights has been authorised by shareholders in accordance with *CA 2006, ss 570* or *571* and the issue of equity securities or sale of treasury shares that are equity shares is within the terms of the authority; or
- the listed company is undertaking a rights issue or open offer and the disapplication of pre-emption rights is with respect to
  (i) equity securities representing fractional entitlements; or
  (ii) equity securities which the company considers necessary or expedient to exclude from the offer on account of the laws or regulatory requirements of a territory other than its country of incorporation unless that territory is the UK.
- the listing company is selling treasury shares for cash to an employee share scheme, or
- an overseas company with a premium listing has obtained the consent of its shareholders to issue equity shares either within the terms of an authority equivalent to that required by *ss 570* or *571* of *CA 2006* or in accordance with the law of its country of incorporation provided that the country had implemented *Article 29* of *EU Directive 77/91.*

(FCA Listing Rules, paras 9.3.6, 9.3.7, 9.3.9, 9.3.11, 9.3.12).

Use of electronic communications. If the Listing Rules require an issuer to send documents to its security holders, the issuer may use electronic means to do so in accordance with the FCA Disclosure and Transparency Rules. See **33.65**(6). (FCA Listing Rules, para 1.4.9).

33.24 *Share schemes, options, etc requiring prior approval*

(1) *Employees' share schemes and long-term incentive plans*

Subject to below, a listed company incorporated in the UK must ensure that any

- employees' share scheme (if the scheme involves or may involve the issue of new shares or the transfer of treasury shares), or
- long-term incentive scheme in which one or more directors of the listed company is eligible to participate

of the company or any of its 'major subsidiary undertakings' (even if incorporated or operates overseas) is approved by an ordinary resolution of the shareholders of the listed company in general meeting before it is adopted.

'*Major subsidiary undertaking*' is a subsidiary undertaking that represents 25% or more of the aggregate of the gross assets or profits (after deducting all charges except taxation) of the group.

The above does not apply to any long-term incentive scheme which is an arrangement where

(a) participation is offered on similar terms to all (or substantially all) employees of the listed company or any of its subsidiaries whose employees are eligible to participate in the arrangement (provided that all, or substantially all, employees are not directors of the listed company); or

(b) where the only participant is a director of the listed company (or an individual whose appointment as a director of the listed company is being contemplated) and the arrangement is established specifically to facilitate, in unusual circumstances, the recruitment or retention of the relevant individual. Instead, the information in FCA Listing Rules, paras 9.4.3 and 13.8.11 must be disclosed in the first annual report published after the date on which the relevant individual becomes eligible to participate in the arrangement.

(2) *Discounted option arrangements*

Subject to below, a listed company must not, without the prior approval by an ordinary resolution of its members in a general meeting, grant to a director or employee of the company (or any of its subsidiary companies)

- an option to subscribe,
- warrant to subscribe, or
- other similar right to subscribe

for shares in the capital of the company (or any of its subsidiary companies) if the price per share payable on the exercise of the option, etc is less than whichever of the following is used to calculate the exercise price:

- The market value of the share on the date when the exercise price is determined.
- The market value of the share on the business day before that date.
- The average of the market values for a number of dealing days within a period not exceeding 30 days immediately before that date.

The above does not apply to the grant of an option, etc

- under an employees' share scheme if participation is offered on similar terms to all (or substantially all) employees of the company or any of its subsidiary undertakings whose employees are entitled to participate in the scheme; or
- following a take-over or reconstruction, in replacement for and on comparable terms with options, etc held immediately before the take-over or reconstruction for shares in either a company of which the listed company thereby obtains control or in any of that company's subsidiary undertakings.

(FCA Listing Rules, paras 9.4.1–9.4.5).

33.25 *Transactions*

(1) *Rights issues*

See **47.65 Shares**.

(2) *Open offers*

A listed company must ensure that the timetable for an open offer is approved by the RIE on which its equity securities are traded and that the open offer remains open for acceptance for at least 10 business days (for the purposes of calculating the 10 business days, the first business day is the date on which the offer is first open for acceptance).

When communicating information on an open offer, a listed company must ensure that

- if the offer is subject to approval in general meeting, the announcement must state that this is the case; and
- the circular dealing with the offer must not contain any statement that might be taken to imply that the offer gives the same entitlements as a rights issue unless it is an offer with a compensatory element. If existing shareholders do not take up their rights to subscribe in an open offer with a compensatory element, the listed company must ensure that the equity securities to which the offer relates are offered for subscription or purchase on terms that any premium obtained over the subscription or purchase price (net of expenses) is to be for the account of the holders, except that if the proceeds for an existing holder do not exceed £5, the proceeds may be retained for the company's benefit and the equity securities may be allotted or sold to underwriters, if on the expiry of the subscription period no premium (net of expenses) has been obtained.

A listed company must ensure that for a subscription in an open offer with a compensatory element the following are notified to a RIS as soon as possible

(i) the offer price and principal terms of the offer, and

(ii) the results of the offer and, if any securities not taken up are sold, details of the sale, including the date and price per share.

(3) *Vendor consideration placing*

A listed company must ensure that in a vendor consideration placing all vendors have an equal opportunity to participate in the placing.

A '*vendor consideration placing*' is a marketing, by or on behalf of vendors, of securities that have been allotted as consideration for an acquisition.

(4) *Discounts not to exceed 10%*

Subject to below, if a listed company makes an open offer, placing, vendor consideration placing, offer for subscription of equity shares or an issue out of treasury (other than in respect of an employees' share scheme) of a class already listed, the price must not be at a discount of more than 10% to the middle market price of those shares at the time of announcing the terms of the offer for an open offer or offer for subscription of equity shares or, at the time of agreeing the placing for a placing or vendor consideration placing.

The above provisions do not apply if

- the terms of the offer or placing at a higher discount have been specifically approved by the issuer's shareholders; or
- it is an issue of shares for cash or the sale of treasury shares for cash under a pre-existing general authority to disapply *CA 2006, s 561* (before 1 October 2009, *CA 1985, s 89*) (existing shareholders' right of pre-emption).

If a listed company makes an open offer, placing, vendor consideration placing or offer for subscription of equity shares during the trading day it may use an appropriate on-screen intra-day price derived from another market.

On each occasion that the listed company plans to use an on-screen intra-day price it should discuss the source of the price in advance with the FCA. The FCA may be satisfied that there is sufficient justification for its use if the alternative market has an appropriate level of liquidity and the source is one that is widely accepted by the market.

The listed company must notify a RIS as soon as possible after it has agreed the terms of the offer or placing.

(5) *Offer for sale or subscription*

A listed company must ensure that for an offer for sale or an offer for subscription of equity securities

- letters of allotment or acceptance are all issued simultaneously and numbered serially (and where appropriate split and certified by the company's registrars);
- if the equity securities may be held in uncertificated form, there is equal treatment with those who elect to hold the equity securities in certificated form and those who elect to hold them in uncertificated form;
- letters of regret are posted not later than three business days after the letters of allotment or acceptance. If not posted at the same time as those letters, a notice to that effect must be inserted in a national newspaper, to appear on the morning after the letters of allotment or acceptance are posted.

(6) *Reconstruction or refinancing*

If a listed company produces a circular containing proposals to be put to shareholders in a general meeting relating to a reconstruction or a re-financing, the circular must be produced in accordance with **33.38** and must include a working capital statement (except for a closed-end investment fund).

(7) *Fractional entitlements*

If, for an issue of equity securities (other than an issue in lieu of dividend), a shareholder's entitlement includes a fraction of a security, a listed company must ensure that the fraction is sold for the benefit of the holder except that if its value (net of expenses) does not exceed £5 it may be sold for the company's benefit. Sales of fractions may be made before listing is granted.

(8) *Further issues*

When shares of the same class as shares that are listed are allotted, an application for admission to listing of such shares must be made as soon as possible and in any event within one month of the allotment.

(9) *Temporary documents of title (including renounceable documents)*

A listed company must ensure that any temporary document of title (other than one issued in global form) for an equity security is serially numbered and states where applicable

- the name and address of the first holder and names of joint holders (if any);
- for a fixed income security, the amount of the next payment of interest or dividend;
- the pro rata entitlement;
- the last date on which transfers were or will be accepted for registration for participation in the issue;
- how the securities rank for dividend or interest;
- the nature of the document of title and proposed date of issue;
- how fractions (if any) are to be treated; and
- for a rights issue, the time (not less than 10 business days) in which the offer may be accepted, and how equity securities not taken up will be dealt with.

If renounceable, the temporary document of title must also

- state in a heading that the document is of value and negotiable;
- advise holders of equity securities who are in any doubt as to what action to take to consult appropriate independent advisers immediately;
- state that where all of the securities have been sold by the addressee (other than 'ex rights' or 'ex capitalisation'), the document should be passed to the person through whom the sale was effected for transmission to the purchaser;
- have the form of renunciation and the registration instructions printed on the back of, or attached to, the document;
- include provision for splitting (without fee) and for split documents to be certified by an official of the company or authorised agent;
- provide for the last day for renunciation to be the second business day after the last day for splitting; and
- if, at the same time as an allotment is made of shares issued for cash, shares of the same class are also allotted credited as fully paid to vendors or others, provide for the period for renunciation to be the same as but no longer than that provided for in the case of shares issued for cash.

(10) *Definitive documents of title*

A listed company must ensure that any definitive document of title for an equity share (other than a bearer security) includes the following matters on its face (or on the reverse in the case of (v) and (vi)).

(i) The authority under which the company is constituted and the country of incorporation and registered number (if any).

(ii) The number or amount of securities the certificate represents and, if applicable, the number and denomination of units (in the top right-hand corner).

(iii) A footnote stating that no transfer of the security or any portion of it represented by the certificate can be registered without production of the certificate.

(iv) If applicable, the minimum amount and multiples thereof in which the security is transferable.

(v) The date of the certificate.

(vi) For equity shares with preferential rights, on the face (or, if not practicable, on the reverse), a statement of the conditions thereof as to capital, dividends and (where applicable) conversion.

(FCA Listing Rules, paras 9.5.7–9.5.16).

33.26 *Notifications*

(1) *Copies of documents*

A company must send to the FCA

- two copies of all circulars, notices, reports and other documents to which the Listing Rules apply at the same time as they are issued; and
- two copies of all resolutions passed by the company (other than ordinary business at an AGM) as soon as possible after the relevant general meeting.

The company must notify a RIS as soon as possible when a document has been forwarded to the FCA as above (unless the full text of the document is provided to the RIS). The notification must set out where copies of the relevant document can be obtained.

(2) *Notifications relating to capital*

A listed company must notify a RIS as soon as possible (unless otherwise indicated) of the following information relating to its capital.

- Any proposed change in the capital structure including listed debt securities (except that an announcement of a new issue may be delayed while marketing or underwriting is in progress).
- Any redemption of listed shares including details of the number of shares redeemed and the number of shares of that class outstanding following the redemption.
- Any extension of time granted for the currency of temporary documents of title.
- (Except in relation to a block listing of securities) the results of any new issue of equity securities or a public offering of existing equity securities.

(3) *Notification of board changes and directors' details*

A listed company must notify a RIS of any change to the board as soon as possible and in any event by the end of the business day following the decision or receipt of notice about the change by the company. This includes

- the appointment of a new director stating the appointee's name and whether the position is executive, non-executive or chairman and the nature of any specific function or responsibility of the position;
- the resignation, removal or retirement of a director (unless the director retires by rotation and is re-appointed at a general meeting of the company's shareholders);
- important changes to the role, functions or responsibilities of a director; and

- the effective date of the change if it is not with immediate effect.

Where the effective date of the board change is not yet known, the notification should state this fact and the company should notify a RIS as soon as the effective date has been decided.

In respect of any new director, a listed company must notify a RIS as soon as possible following the decision to appoint the director (and in any event within five business days of the decision) of the following (including a nil notification where appropriate).

(a) All directorships held in any other publicly quoted company at any time in the previous five years, indicating whether or not he is still a director.

(b) Any unspent convictions in relation to indictable offences.

(c) Any insolvency arrangements of any

(i) company where the director was an executive director, or

(ii) partnership where he was a partner

at the time of, or within the 12 months preceding, such arrangements.

(d) Receiverships of any asset of such person or of a partnership of which the director was a partner at the time of, or within the 12 months preceding, such event.

(e) Details of any public criticisms of the director by statutory or regulatory authorities (including designated professional bodies) and whether the director has ever been disqualified by a court from acting as a director of a company or from acting in the management or conduct of the affairs of any company.

A listed company must, in respect of any current director, notify a RIS as soon as possible of

- any change in the information in (*b*) to (*e*) above; and
- any new directorships held by the director in any other publicly quoted company

(4) *Change of name*

A listed company which changes its name must, as soon as possible

- notify a RIS of the change, stating the date on which it has taken effect;
- inform the FCA in writing of the change; and
- where the company is incorporated in the UK, send the FCA a copy of the revised certificate of incorporation issued by the Registrar of Companies.

(5) *Change of accounting date*

A listed company must notify a RIS as soon as possible of any change in its accounting reference date (see **2.17 Accounting Reference Dates and Periods**) and the new date. It must prepare and publish a second interim report in accordance with **33.52** if the effect of the change is to extend the accounting period to more than 14 months. The second interim report must be prepared and published in respect of either

- the period up to the old accounting reference date; or
- the period up to a date not more than six months prior to the new accounting reference date.

(FCA Listing Rules, paras 9.6.1–9.6.4, 9.6.11–9.6.15, 9.6.19–9.6.22).

33.27 *Preliminary statement of annual results, statement of dividends and half-yearly reports*

Preliminary statement of annual results. If a listed company prepares a preliminary statement of annual results, the statement must

- be published as soon as possible after it has been approved by the board;
- be agreed with the company's auditors prior to publication;
- show the figures in the form of a table, including the items required for a half-yearly report, consistent with the presentation to be adopted in the annual accounts for that financial year;
- give details of the nature of any likely modification or emphasis –of-matter paragraphs that may be contained in the auditors' report required to be included with the annual financial report; and
- include any significant additional information necessary for the purpose of assessing the results being announced.

Statement of dividends. A listed company must notify a RIS as soon as possible after the board has approved any decision to pay or make any dividend or other distribution on listed equity or to withhold any dividend or interest payment on listed securities giving details of

- the exact net amount payable per share;
- the payment date;
- the record date (where applicable); and
- any foreign income dividend election, together with any income tax treated as paid at the lower rate and not repayable.

Omission of information. The FCA may authorise the omission of information required by either of the above requirements if it considers that disclosure of such information would be contrary to the public interest or seriously detrimental to the listed company, provided that such omission would not be likely to mislead the public with regard to facts and circumstances, knowledge of which is essential for the assessment of the shares.

(FCA Listing Rules, paras 9.7A.1–9.7A.3).

33.28 *Annual financial report*

In addition to the requirements set out in **33.51**, a listed company must include, where applicable, the following information in its annual financial report.

(a) *Interest capitalised.* The amount of interest capitalised by the group during the period under review, with an indication of the amount and treatment of any related tax relief.

(b) *Unaudited financial information.* Any information required under **33.22**(9).

(c) *Long-term incentive schemes.* Details of any long-term incentive scheme as required by LR 9.4.3.

(d) *Waiver of emoluments.* Particulars of any arrangement under which a director has waived, or agreed to waive, emoluments from the company or any subsidiary. Where a director has agreed to waive future emoluments, details of such waiver together with those relating to emoluments which were waived during the period under review.

(e) *Allotments for cash*. Where there has been an allotment of equity securities for cash in the period under review (otherwise than to the holders of the company's equity shares in proportion to their holdings of such shares) and has not been specifically authorised by the shareholders

- the classes of shares allotted and for each class of shares, the number allotted, their aggregate nominal value, and the consideration received by the company for the allotment;
- the names of the allottees (if less than six) or otherwise a brief generic description of each new class of equity holder (eg holder of loan stock);
- the market price of the securities on the date the terms of the issue were fixed; and
- the date on which the terms of the issue were fixed.

The above information must be given for any unlisted '*major subsidiary undertaking*' of the company, ie any subsidiary undertaking that represents 25% or more of the aggregate of the gross assets or profits (after deducting all charges except taxation) of the group.

(f) *Parent undertaking participation in a placing*. Where a company has listed shares in issue and is a subsidiary of another company, details of the participation by the parent company in any placing made during the period under review.

(g) *Contracts of significance*. Details of any 'contract of significance' existing during the period under review

- to which the listed company (or one of its subsidiaries) is a party and in which a director of the listed company is or was materially interested; and
- between the listed company (or one of its subsidiaries) and a controlling shareholder.

A '*contract of significance*' is one which represents, in the case of a capital transaction, 1% or more of the group's share capital and reserves and, in the case of other transactions, 1% of annual purchases, sales, payments or receipts.

(h) *Contracts for services*. Details of any contract for the provision of services to the listed company (or any subsidiary) by a controlling shareholder subsisting during the period under review (unless it is a contract for the provision of services which it is the principal business of the shareholder to provide and it is not a contract of significance).

(i) *Waiver of dividends*. Details of any arrangement under which a shareholder has waived, or agreed to waive, dividends. Where a shareholder has agreed to waive future dividends, details of such waiver together with those relating to dividends which are payable during the period under review.

(j) *Statement made by the board*. Statements by the board that

- the listed company has entered into any agreement required under LR 9.2.2A(2)(a) or where the listed company has not entered into an agreement required under LR 9.2.2A(2)(a) a statement that the FCA has been notified of that non-compliance in accordance with LR 9.2.23; and a brief description of the background to and reasons for failing to enter into the agreement that enables shareholders to evaluate the impact of non-compliance on the listed company.

- the listed company has complied with the independence provisions included in any agreement entered into under LR 6.1.4B(1) or LR 9.2.2A(2)(a) during the period under review;
- so far as the listed company is aware, the independence provisions included in any agreement entered into under LR 6.1.4B(1) or LR 9.2.2A(2)(a) have been complied with during the period under review by the controlling shareholder or any of its associates; and
- so far as the listed company is aware, the procurement obligation (as set out in LR 6.1.4C(2)(a) or LR 9.2.2B(2)(a)) included in any agreement entered into under LR 6.1.4B(1) or LR 9.2.2A(2)(a) has been complied with during the period under review by a controlling shareholder.

Where an independence provision included in any agreement entered into under LR 6.1.4B(1) or LR 9.2.2A(2)(a) or a procurement obligation (as set out in LR 6.1.4C(2)(a) or LR 9.2.2B(2)(a)) included in any agreement entered into under LR 6.1.4B(1) or LR 9.2.2A(2)(a) has not been complied with during the period under review a statement that the FCA has been notified of that non-compliance in accordance with LR 9.2.24 and a brief description of the background to and reasons for failing to comply with the relevant independence provision or procurement obligation that enables shareholders to evaluate the impact of non-compliance on the listed company.

In the case of listed companies incorporated in the UK, the following additional items must be included:

(k) *Directors' interests in shares.* A statement setting out all the interests (in respect of which transactions are notifiable to the company under FCA Disclosure and Transparency Rules, para 3.1.2, see **33.47**(1)) of each person who is a director of the listed company as at the end of the period under review. All changes in the interests of each director that have occurred between the end of the period under review and a date not more than one month prior to the date of the notice of the AGM must be included (or if there have been no such changes, a statement that there have been no changes). Interests of each director include the interests of connected persons of which the listed company is, or ought upon reasonable enquiry to become, aware. The effect of this requirement is that the company is required to set out a snapshot of the total interests of a director and his or her connected persons, as at the end of the period under review (including certain information to update it as at a date not more than a month before the date of the notice of AGM). Persons who are directors during, but not at the end of the period under review, need not be included.

(l) *Major interests in shares.* A statement showing the interests disclosed to the listed company in accordance with DTR 5 as at the end of the period under review and all interests disclosed in accordance with that rule that have occurred between the end of the period under review and a date not more than one month prior to the date of the notice of the AGM. If no interests have been disclosed, a statement that no interests have been disclosed.

(m) *Going concern.* A statement by the directors that the business is a going concern (with supporting assumptions and qualifications as necessary) that has been prepared in accordance with "Going Concern and Liquidity Risk Guidance for Directors of UK Companies 2009" published October 2009 by the FRC. The company must ensure that the auditors review this statement before the annual report is published.

(n) *Purchase by company of its own shares and sales for cash of treasury shares.*

- Details of any shareholders' authority for the purchase by the company of its own shares still valid at the end of the period under review;
- in the case of purchases made otherwise than through the market or by tender to all shareholders, the names of sellers of such shares purchased (or proposed to be purchased) by the listed company in the period under review;
- in the case of any purchases made otherwise than through the market or by tender or partial offer to all shareholders, or options or contracts to make such purchases entered into since the beginning of the period covered by the report, information equivalent to that required under *SI 2008 No 410, Part 2, Schedule 7* (Disclosure required by company acquiring its own shares): and
- in the case of sales of treasury shares for cash made otherwise than through the market, or in connection with an employees' share scheme, or otherwise than pursuant to an opportunity which (so far as was practicable) was made to all holders of the listed company's securities (or to all holders of a relevant class of its securities) on the same terms, particulars of the names of the purchasers of such shares sold (or proposed to be sold) by the company during the period under review.

(o) *Application of the UK Corporate Governance Code.* A statement of how the listed company has applied the Main Principles set out in the UK Corporate Governance Code, in a manner that would enable shareholders to evaluate how the principles have been applied.

(p) *Statement on compliance with the UK Corporate Governance Code.* A statement to whether the company has complied throughout the accounting period with all relevant provisions set out in the UK Corporate Governance Code or has not complied. A company which has not done so must specify

- those provisions, if any, it has not complied with;
- in the case of provisions whose requirements are of a continuing nature, the period within which, if any, it did not comply with some or all of those provisions; and
- the company's reasons for non-compliance and a report to the shareholders by the board (see (*q*) below).

The company must ensure that the auditors review the parts of the statement which relate to the Combined Code, paras C1.1, C.2.1 and C3.1 to C3.7 before the annual report is published.

(q) *Report to shareholders.* The report to the shareholders must contain details of the unexpired term of any directors' service contract of a director proposed for election or re-election at the forthcoming annual general meeting and, if any director proposed for election or re-election does not have a directors' service contract, a statement to that effect.

(FCA Listing Rules, paras 9.8.4–9.8.6, 9.8.6A, 9.8.8, 9.8.10).

33.29 *Strategic report with supplementary information*

Any strategic report with supplementary information provided to shareholders (see **6 Accounts: Strategic Reports**) must disclose earnings per share and the information for a strategic report set out in or under *CA 2006* and the supplementary material required under *CA 2006, s 426A*.

(FCA Listing Rules, para 9.8.13)

33.30 *Half-yearly report*

The requirements relating to half-yearly reports are included in the FCA Disclosure and Transparency Rules. See 33.52.

33.31 Significant transactions: Premium listing

The following provisions apply to a company that has a premium listing of equity shares. The purpose of the provisions is to ensure that shareholders of such a company are notified of certain transactions entered into by the company and have the opportunity to vote on larger proposed transactions.

Transactions. For these purposes, a '*transaction*' includes

- all agreements (including amendments to agreements) entered into by the company or its subsidiaries; and
- the grant or acquisition of an option as if the option had been exercised (except that, if exercise is solely at the discretion of the company or a subsidiary, the transaction will be classified on exercise and only the consideration (if any) for the option will be classified on the grant or acquisition;

but excludes

- a transaction of a revenue nature in the ordinary course of business;
- an issue of securities, or a transaction to raise finance, which does not involve the acquisition or disposal of any fixed asset of the company or its subsidiaries; and
- any transaction between the company and a wholly-owned subsidiary or between its wholly-owned subsidiaries.

Classification of transactions. A transaction is classified (by assessing its size relative to that of the company proposing to make it) as follows.

- *Class 2 transaction* (where any percentage ratio is 5% or more but each is less than 25%).
- *Class 1 transaction* (where any percentage ratio is 25% or more).

  If an issuer is proposing to enter into a transaction classed as a reverse takeover it should consider LR 5.6.

The percentage ratios are:

- The *gross assets ratio* calculated by dividing the gross assets the subject of the transaction by the gross assets of the listed company.
- The *profits ratio* calculated by dividing the profits attributable to the assets the subject of the transaction by the profits of the listed company.
- *consideration ratio* calculated by dividing the consideration for the transaction by the aggregate market value of all the ordinary shares (except treasury shares) of the listed company.
- The *gross capital ratio* calculated by dividing the gross capital of the company or business being acquired by the gross capital of the listed company.

Transaction treated as Class 1 transaction. The following transactions are to be treated as Class 1 transaction even if not satisfying the percentage ratio test.

(1) *Indemnities and similar arrangements*

Any exceptional agreement or arrangement with a party (other than a wholly-owned subsidiary) under which

(i) a listed company agrees to discharge any liabilities for costs, expenses, commissions or losses incurred by or on behalf of that party, whether or not on a contingent basis; and

(ii) the maximum liability is either unlimited, or is equal to or exceeds an amount equal to 25% of the average of the listed company's profits for the last three financial years (losses should be taken as 'nil' profit and included in this average).

(2) *Break fees*

An arrangement is a break fee arrangement if the purpose of the arrangement is that a compensatory sum will become payable by a listed company to another party (or parties) to a proposed transaction if the proposed transaction fails or is materially impeded and there is no independent substantive commercial rationale for the arrangement. Sums payable pursuant to break fee arrangements in respect of a transaction are to be treated as a Class 1 transaction if the total value of those sums exceeds

(i) if the listed company is being acquired, 1% of the value of the listed company calculated by reference to the offer price; and

(ii) in any other case, 1% of the market capitalisation of the listed company.

The total value of sums payable pursuant to break fee arrangements for the above purposes is the sum of

(i) any amounts paid or payable pursuant to break fee arrangements in relation to the same transaction or in relation to the same target assets or business in the 12 months prior to the date the most recent arrangements were agreed unless those arrangements were approved by shareholders ;and

(ii) the aggregate of the maximum amounts payable pursuant to break fee arrangements in relation to the transaction

save that if the arrangements are such that a particular sum will only become payable in circumstances in which another sum does not, the lower sum may be left out of the calculation of the total value.

(3) *Issues by major subsidiary undertakings*

If

(i) a major subsidiary undertaking of a listed company issues equity shares for cash or in exchange for other securities or to reduce indebtedness;

(ii) the issue would dilute the listed company's percentage interest in the major subsidiary undertaking; and

(iii) the economic effect of the dilution is equivalent to a disposal of 25% or more of the aggregate of the gross assets or profits (after the deduction of all charges except taxation) of the group.

then the issue is to be treated as a Class 1 transaction.

This does not apply if the major subsidiary undertaking is itself a listed company.

'*Major subsidiary undertaking*' is a subsidiary undertaking that represents 25% or more of the aggregate of the gross assets or profits (after deducting all charges except taxation) of the group.

Aggregating transactions. Except in relation to a break fee arrangement (see above), transactions completed during the 12 months before the date of the latest transaction must be aggregated with that transaction for the purposes of classification if

- they are entered into by the company with the same person or with persons connected with one another;
- they involve the acquisition or disposal of securities or an interest in one particular company; or
- together they lead to substantial involvement in a business activity which did not previously form a significant part of the company's principal activities.

If, under this rule, aggregation of transactions results in a requirement for shareholder approval, then that approval is required only for the latest transaction.

(FCA Listing Rules, paras 10.1.1–10.1.3, 10.2.1–10.2.4, 10.2.6A, 10.2.7–10.2.10).

33.31A*Reverse takeovers*

LR 5.6 applies to an issuer with:

(1) a premium listing;

(2) a standard listing (shares); or

(3) a standard listing of certificates representing equity securities.

Categories of reverse takeover to which LR 5.6 does not apply

LR 5.6 does not apply where an issuer acquires the shares or certificates representing equity securities of a target with the same category of listing as the issuer.

Class 1 requirements

Notwithstanding the effect of LR 5.6.2 R, an issuer with a premium listing must in relation to a reverse takeover comply with the requirements of LR 10.5 (Class 1 requirements) for that transaction.

Definition

A reverse takeover is a transaction, whether effected by way of a direct acquisition by the issuer or a subsidiary, an acquisition by a new holding company of the issuer or otherwise, of a business, a company or assets:

(1) where any percentage ratio is 100% or more; or

(2) here any percentage ratio is 100% or more; or (2) which in substance results in a fundamental change in the business or in a change in board or voting control of the issuer.

When calculating the percentage ratio, the issuer should apply the class tests.

For the purpose of LR 5.6.4R (2), the FCA considers that the following factors are indicators of a fundamental change:

(1) the extent to which the transaction will change the strategic direction or nature of its business; or

(2) whether its business will be part of a different industry sector following the completion of the transaction; or

(3) whether its business will deal with fundamentally different suppliers and end users.

Requirement for a suspension

An issuer, or in the case of an issuer with a premium listing, its sponsor, must contact the FCA as early as possible:

(1) before announcing a reverse takeover which has been agreed or is in contemplation, to discuss whether a suspension of listing is appropriate; or

(2) where details of the reverse takeover have leaked, to request a suspension.

Examples of where the FCA will consider that a reverse takeover is in contemplation include situations where:

(1) the issuer has approached the target's board;

(2) the issuer has entered into an exclusivity period with a target; or

(3) the issuer has been given access to begin due diligence work (whether or not on a limited basis).

Generally, when a reverse takeover is announced or leaked, there will be insufficient publicly available information about the proposed transaction and the issuer will be unable to assess accurately its financial position and inform the market accordingly. In this case, the FCA will often consider that suspension will be appropriate, as set out in LR 5.1.2G (3) and (4). However, if the FCA is satisfied that there is sufficient publicly available information about the proposed transaction it may agree with the issuer that a suspension is not required.

LR 5.6.10 G to LR 5.6.18 R set out circumstances in which the FCA will generally be satisfied that a suspension is not required.

Target admitted to a regulated market

The FCA will generally be satisfied that there is sufficient information in the market about the proposed transaction if:

(1) the target has shares or certificates representing equity securities admitted to a regulated market; and

(2) the issuer makes an announcement stating that the target has complied with the disclosure requirements applicable on that regulated market and providing details of where information disclosed pursuant to those requirements can be obtained.

An announcement made for the purpose of LR 5.6.10G (2) must be published by means of an RIS.

Target subject to the disclosure regime of another market

The FCA will generally be satisfied that there is sufficient publicly available information in the market about the proposed transaction if the target has securities admitted to an investment exchange or trading platform that is not a regulated market and the issuer:

(1) confirms, in a form acceptable to the FCA, that the disclosure requirements in relation to financial information and inside information of the investment exchange or trading platform on which the target's securities are admitted are not materially different from the disclosure requirements under DTR; and

(2) makes an announcement to the effect that:

(a) the target has complied with the disclosure requirements applicable on the investment exchange or trading platform to which its securities are admitted and provides details of where information disclosed pursuant to those requirements can be obtained; and

(b) there are no material differences between those disclosure requirements and the disclosure requirements under DTR.

Where an issuer has a premium listing, a written confirmation provided for the purpose of LR 5.6.12G (1) must be given by the issuer's sponsor.

An announcement made for the purpose of LR 5.6.12G (2) must be published by means of an RIS.

Target not subject to a public disclosure regime

Where the target in a reverse takeover is not subject to a public disclosure regime, or if the target has securities admitted on an investment exchange or trading platform that is not a regulated market but the issuer is not able to give the confirmation and make the announcement contemplated by LR 5.6.12 G, the FCA will generally be satisfied that there is sufficient publicly available information in the market about the proposed transaction such that a suspension is not required where the issuer makes an announcement containing:

(1) financial information on the target covering the last three years. Generally, the FCA would consider the following information to be sufficient:

(a) profit and loss information to at least operating profit level;

(b) balance sheet information, highlighting at least net assets and liabilities;

(c) relevant cash flow information; and

(d) a description of the key differences between the issuer's accounting policies and the policies used to present the financial information on the target;

(2) a description of the target to include key non-financial operating or performance measures appropriate to the target's business operations and the information as required under PR Appendix 3 Annex 1 item 12 (Trend information) for the target;

(3) a declaration that the directors of the issuer consider that the announcement contains sufficient information about the business to be acquired to provide a properly informed basis for assessing its financial position; and

(4) a declaration confirming that the issuer has made the necessary arrangements with the target vendors to enable it to keep the market informed without delay of any developments concerning the target that would be required to be released were the target part of the issuer.

An announcement made for the purpose of LR 5.6.15 must be published by means of an RIS.

Where an issuer has a premium listing, a sponsor must provide written confirmation to the FCA that in its opinion, it is reasonable for the issuer to provide the declarations described in LR 5.6.15G (3) and (4).

Where the FCA has agreed that a suspension is not necessary as a result of an announcement made for the purpose of LR 5.6.15 G the issuer must comply with DTR 2.2.1 R on the basis that the target already forms part of the enlarged group.

Cancellation of listing

The FCA will generally seek to cancel the listing of an issuer's equity shares or certificates representing equity securities when the issuer completes a reverse takeover.

LR 5.6.23 G to LR 5.6.29 G set out circumstances in which the FCA will generally be satisfied that a cancellation is not required.

Where the issuer's listing is cancelled following completion of a reverse takeover, the issuer must re-apply for the listing of the shares or certificates representing equity securities and satisfy the relevant requirements for listing, except that for an issuer with a premium listing, LR 6.1.3 R (1)(b) and LR 6.1.3 R (1)(e) will not apply in relation to the issuer's accounts.

Notwithstanding LR 5.6.21 R, financial information provided in relation to the target will need to satisfy LR 6.1.3 R (1)(b) and LR 6.1.3 R (1)(e).

Acquisitions of targets from different listing categories: issuer maintaining its listing category

Where an issuer acquires the shares or certificates representing equity securities of a target with a different listing category from its own and the issuer wishes to maintain its existing listing category, the FCA will generally be satisfied that a cancellation is not required on completion of a reverse takeover if:

(1) the issuer will continue to be eligible for its existing listing category following completion of the transaction;

(2) the issuer provides an eligibility letter setting out how the issuer as enlarged by the acquisition satisfies each listing rule requirement that is relevant to it being eligible for its existing listing category; and

(3) the issuer makes an announcement or publishes a circular explaining:

   (a) the background and reasons for the acquisition;

   (b) any changes to the acquiring issuer's business that have been made or are proposed to be made in connection with the acquisition;

   (c) the effect of the transaction on the acquiring issuer's obligations under the listing rules;

   (d) (where appropriate) how the acquiring issuer will continue to meet the eligibility requirements referred to in LR 5.6.21 R; and

   (e) any other matter that the FCA may reasonably require.

An announcement or circular published for the purpose of LR 5.6.23 G must be published by means of an RIS.

An eligibility letter prepared for the purposes of LR 5.6.23 G must be provided to the FCA not less than 20 business days prior to the announcement of the transaction referred to in LR 5.6.24 R.

Where an issuer has a premium listing, the eligibility letter provided for the purposes of LR 5.6.23 G must be provided by a sponsor.

Acquisitions of targets from different listing categories: issuer changing listing category

The FCA will generally be satisfied that a cancellation is not required on completion of a reverse takeover if the target is listed with a different listing category from that of the issuer and the issuer wishes to transfer its listing to a different listing category in conjunction with the acquisition and the issuer as enlarged by the relevant acquisition complies with the relevant requirements of LR 5.4A to transfer to a different listing category.

An issuer wishing to transfer a listing of its equity shares from a premium listing (investment company) to a standard listing (shares) should note LR 5.4A.2 G which sets out limitations resulting from the application of LR 14.1.1 R (application of the listing rules to a company with or applying for a standard listing of shares).

Where an issuer is applying LR 5.4A in order to avoid a cancellation as contemplated by LR 5.6.27 G, the FCA will normally waive the requirement for shareholder approval under LR 5.4A.4R (2)(c) where the issuer is obtaining separate shareholder approval for the acquisition.

(FCA Listing Rules, para 5.6.1- to 5.6.29)

33.32 *Notifying significant transactions*

The notification requirements of the various classifications of transaction are as follows.

(1) *Class 2 requirements*

A listed company must notify a RIS as soon as possible after the terms of a Class 2 transaction are agreed. Notification must include

- details of the transaction, including the name of the other party to the transaction;
- a description of the business carried on by, or using, the net assets the subject of the transaction;
- the consideration and how it is being satisfied (including the terms of any arrangement for deferred consideration);
- the value of the gross assets the subject of the transaction;
- the profit attributable to those assets;
- the effect of the transaction on the listed company including any benefits which are expected to accrue;
- details of any service contracts of proposed directors of the listed company;
- for a disposal, the application of the sales proceeds;
- for a disposal, if securities are to form part of the consideration received, a statement whether such securities are to be sold or retained; and
- details of any key individuals important to the business or company the subject of the transaction.

Supplementary notification. A RIS must also be notified as soon as possible if, at any time after the notification as above has been made, the company becomes aware that there has been a 'significant' change in any matter contained in the earlier notification or there is any significant new matter which requires notification. The supplementary notification must give details of the change or new matter and also contain a statement that, except as disclosed, there has been no other significant change or new matter which would have been required to be mentioned in that earlier notification if known at the time. '*Significant*' means significant for the purpose of making an informed assessment of the assets and liabilities, financial position, profits and losses and prospects of the listed company and the rights attaching to any securities forming part of the consideration. It includes a change in the terms of the transaction that affects the percentage ratios and requires the transaction to be reclassified into a higher category.

(2) *Class 1 requirements*

In the case of a Class 1 transaction, a listed company must

- comply with the Class 2 requirements under (2) above;
- send an explanatory circular to the shareholders and obtain their prior approval in a general meeting for the transaction; and
- ensure that any agreement effecting the transaction is conditional on such approval being obtained.

If, after the production of a circular and before the completion of a Class 1 transaction or a reverse takeover, there is a material change to the terms of the transaction, the listed company must comply again separately with the above requirements in relation to the transaction. The FCA would (amongst other things) consider an increase of 10% or more in the consideration payable to be a material change.

A listed company in severe financial difficulty may find itself with no alternative but to dispose of a substantial part of its business within a short time frame to meet its ongoing working capital requirements or to reduce its liabilities. Due to time constraints, it may not be able to prepare a circular and convene an extraordinary general meeting to obtain prior shareholder approval. In such circumstances, the FCA may modify the above requirements if the company can demonstrate that it is in severe financial difficulty and satisfies the requirements set out in FCA Listing Rules, paras 10.8.2–10.8.6.

An application to modify LR 10.5 should be brought to the FCA's attention at the earliest available opportunity and at least five clear business days before the terms of the disposal are agreed.

(FCA Listing Rules, paras, 10.4.1, 10.4.2, 10.5.1, 10.5.2, 10.8.1).

33.33 Related party transactions: Premium listing

The following provisions apply to a company that has a premium listing. The purpose of the provisions is to set out safeguards that apply to transactions arrangements between a listed company and a related party or any other person that may benefit a related party.

Where a company has a premium listing:

(1) it is not in compliance with:

(a) the provisions in LR 9.2.2AR (2)(a) ; or

(b) LR 9.2.2G R; or

(2) it becomes aware that a controlling shareholder or any of its associates is not in compliance with an independence provision contained in an agreement entered into under LR 6.1.4BR (1) or LR 9.2.2AR (2)(a);

(3) it becomes aware that a procurement obligation (as set out in LR 6.1.4CR (2)(a) or LR 9.2.2BR (2)(a) contained in an agreement entered into under LR 6.1.4BR (1) or LR 9.2.2AR (2)(a) has not been complied with by a controlling shareholder; or

(4) an independent director declines to support a statement made under LR 9.8.4R (14)(a) or LR 9.8.4R (14)(c).

LR 11.1.1C R applies.

In exceptional circumstances, the FCA may consider dispensing with or modifying the application of LR 11.1.1A R, in accordance with LR 1.2.1 R.

The company cannot rely on any of the following provisions in relation to a transaction or arrangement with or for the benefit of the relevant controlling shareholder or any associate of that controlling shareholder:

(1) the concessions specified in LR 11.1.5R (1), LR 11.1.5R (2) and LR 11.1.5R (3) in relation to transactions or arrangements in the ordinary course of business;

(2) LR 11.1.6 R; and

(3) LR 11.1.10 R.

If the FCA considers that it would be appropriate to do so, the FCA may dispense with or modify the application of LR 11.1.1CR (1), in accordance with LR 1.2.1 R.

Where a company that has a premium listing has been subject to the provisions of LR 11.1.1A R, LR 11.1.1C R will continue to apply to the company until the publication of an annual financial report which:

(1) contains the statements required under LR 9.8.4R (14)(a) and LR 9.8.4R (14)(c); and

(2) does not contain a statement made under LR 9.8.4A R.

(FCA Listing Rules, paras 11.1.1A–E).

Transactions. For these purposes, a reference to a transaction or arrangement by a listed company includes a transaction or arrangement by one of its subsidiaries and, unless the contrary intention appears, a transaction or arrangement includes the entering into of the agreement for the transaction or the entering into of the arrangement.

Related party. Related party is broadly defined to cover

- any person who is (or was in the 12 months before the date of the transaction)
  - (i) a substantial shareholder (ie a person who controls 10% or more of the voting rights at general meeting of the company (or any subsidiary, fellow subsidiary or parent company); or
  - (ii) a director or shadow director of the company (or any subsidiary, fellow subsidiary or parent company);
- a person exercising significant influence; or

- an associate of any of the above.

Related party transaction. A related party transaction is

- a transaction (other than a transaction in the ordinary course of business) between a listed company and a related party;
- an arrangement(other than an arrangement in the ordinary course of business) pursuant to which a listed company and a related party each invests in, or provides finance to, another undertaking or asset; or
- any other similar transaction or arrangement (other than a transaction in the ordinary course of business) between a listed company and any other person the purpose and effect of which is to benefit a related party.

In assessing whether a transaction is in the ordinary course of business, the FCA will have regard to the size and incidence of the transaction and also whether the terms and conditions are unusual. See LRs 11.1.3, 11.1.4 and 11.1.4A for the definitions of 'transaction', 'related party' and 'substantial shareholder'.

(FCA Listing Rules, paras 11.1.1–11.1.5).

33.34 *Requirements for related party transactions*

Subject to the exemptions in 33.35, if a listed company enters into a related party transaction, it must

(a) make a notification in accordance with 33.32(2) (notification of a Class 2 transaction) and in addition give details of the name of the related party and the nature and extent of the related party's interest in the transaction;

(b) send a circular to its shareholders containing both the information required by all circulars (see 33.38) and the specific information required of circulars for related party transactions in FCA Listing Rules, paras 13.6.1–13.6.3;

(c) obtain approval of its shareholders for the transaction either before it is entered into or, if the transaction is expressed to be conditional on such approval, before it is completed; and

(d) ensure that the related party does not vote on the relevant resolution and takes all reasonable steps to ensure that the related party's associates do not vote on the relevant resolution.

If after obtaining shareholder approval but before the completion of a related party transaction, there is a material change to the terms of the transaction, the listed company must comply again separately with LR11.1.7 ((a)-(e) above) in relation to the transaction. The FCA would (amongst other things) generally consider an increase of 10% or more in the consideration payable to be a material change to the terms of the transaction.

A listed company must comply with LR10.5.4 in relation to a related party transaction.

This applies to the variation or novation of an existing agreement between the listed company and a related party whether or not, at the time the original agreement was entered into, that party was a related party.

Modified requirements for smaller related party transactions. Where each of the percentage ratios in 33.31 is less than 5%, but one or more exceeds 0.25%, instead of having to comply with *(a)*–*(d)* above, the listed company must, before entering into the transaction

(i) before entering into the transaction or arrangement obtain written confirmation from a sponsor that the terms of the proposed transaction or arrangement with the related party are fair and reasonable as far as the shareholders of the listed company are concerned; and

(ii) as soon as possible upon entering into the transaction or arrangement make a RIS announcement which sets out the identity of the related party, the value of the consideration for the transaction or arrangement, a brief description of the transaction or arrangement, the fact that the transaction or arrangement fell within LR 11.1.10 and any other relevant circumstances.

Aggregation of transactions. If a listed company enters into transactions with the same related party (and any of its associates) in any 12-month period and the transactions have not been approved by shareholders, the transactions or arrangements, including transactions or arrangements falling under LR 11.1.10 or small related party transactions under LR 11 Annex 1.1.1 must be aggregated. If any percentage ratio in **33.31** is 5% or more for the aggregated transactions, the company must comply with *(a)*–*(d)* above in respect of the latest transaction.

If transactions that are small transactions under **33.35**(1) are aggregated as above and for the aggregated small transactions each of the percentage ratios is less than 5% but one or more exceeds 0.25%, the listed company must comply with (ii) above in respect of the latest small transaction and (i) and (iii) above in respect of the aggregated small transactions.

(FCA Listing Rules, paras 11.1.7, 11.1.9–11.1.11).

33.35 *Exempt transactions*

The requirements in **33.34** do not apply to a transaction within (1) below or a transaction within (2)–(9) below provided it does not have any unusual features.

(1) *Small transactions.* A small transaction, ie a transaction where each of the applicable percentage ratios in **33.31** is equal to or less than 0.25%.

(2) *Transactions agreed before person became a related party.* A transaction the terms of which

(i) were agreed at a time when no party to the transaction (or person who was to receive the benefit of the transaction) was a related party, and

(ii) have not been amended, or required the exercise of discretion by the listed company under those terms, since the party or person became a related party.

(3) *Issue of new securities and sale of treasury shares.* A transaction that consists of

(i) the take up by a related party of new securities or treasury shares under its entitlement in a pre-emptive offering; or

(ii) an issue of new securities made under the exercise of conversion or subscription rights attaching to a listed class of securities.

(4) *Employees' share schemes or long-term incentive schemes.* In accordance with the terms of an employees' share scheme or a long-term incentive scheme, the transaction

(i) involves the receipt of any asset (including cash or securities of the company or any of its subsidiaries) by a director of the company, its parent or any of its subsidiaries;

(ii) is the grant of an option or other right to such a director to acquire (whether or not for consideration) any asset (including cash or new or existing securities of the company or any of its subsidiaries); or

(iii) is a gift or loan to the trustees of an employee benefit trust to finance the provisions of assets under (i) or (ii) above.

(5) *Credit.* The transaction is a grant of credit (including the lending of money or the guaranteeing of a loan)

(i) to the related party on normal commercial terms;

(ii) to a director for an amount and on terms no more favourable than those offered to employees of the group generally; or

(iii) by the related party on normal commercial terms and on an unsecured basis.

(6) *Directors' indemnities and loans.* The transaction is

(i) the grant of an indemnity to, or the maintenance of a contract of insurance for, a director of the listed company (or any of its subsidiaries) which is specifically permitted under *CA 2006*; or

(ii) a loan or assistance to a director by a listed company (or any of its subsidiaries) if the terms of the loan or assistance are in accordance with those specifically permitted under *CA 2006, s 204, 205* or *206*.

(7) *Underwriting.* The transaction is the underwriting by a related party of all or part of an issue of securities by the listed company (or any of its subsidiaries) provided the consideration is no more than commercial consideration and is the same as that paid to other underwriters (if any).

(8) *Joint investment arrangements.* An arrangement where a listed company (or any of its subsidiaries) and a related party each invests in, or provides finance to, another undertaking or asset if the following conditions are satisfied.

(i) The amount invested by the related party is not more than 25% of the amount invested by the listed company (or any of its subsidiaries) and the listed company has advised the FCA in writing that this condition has been met.

(ii) An independent adviser acceptable to the FCA has provided a written opinion to the FCA that the terms of the investment by the listed company (or any of its subsidiaries) are no less favourable than those applying to the investment by the related party.

(iii) The advice in (i) and the opinion in (ii) are provided before the investment is made.

(9) *Insignificant subsidiary undertakings.* A transaction where the following conditions are satisfied.

(i) The party to the transaction is only a related party because

- it is (or was within the 12 months before the date of the transaction) a substantial shareholder or its associate, or
- it is a person who is (or was within the 12 months before the date of the transaction) a director or shadow director or his associate

of a subsidiary or subsidiaries of the listed company that has contributed less than 10% (10% in aggregate if more than one subsidiary) of the profits of, and represented less than 10% of the assets of, the listed company for the 'relevant period'.

'*Relevant period*' means each of the three financial years before the date of the transaction for which accounts have been published (where the subsidiary or subsidiaries have only been part of the listed company's group for more than one but less than three years, each of the financial years before the date of the transaction for which accounts have been published).

(ii) The subsidiary (or each of the subsidiaries as the case may be) have been in the listed company's group for one year or more.

(iii) If the subsidiary (or subsidiaries) are themselves party to the transaction or if securities in them or their assets are the subject of the transaction, the consideration ratio must be less than 10%.

(FCA Listing Rules, para 11.1.6, LR 11 Annex).

33.36 Dealing in own securities and treasury shares: Premium listing

The provisions in this paragraph apply to a company that has a premium listing of equity shares except that the provisions in (1)–(4) below do not apply to a transaction entered into

- in the ordinary course of business by a securities dealing business, or
- on behalf of third parties either by the company or any member of its group

if the listed company has established and maintains effective Chinese walls between those responsible for any decision relating to the transaction and those in possession of inside information relating to the listed company.

(1) *Prohibition on purchase of own securities*

A listed company must not purchase or redeem (or make any early redemptions of) its own securities, and must ensure that no purchases in its securities are effected on its behalf or by any member of its group, during a 'prohibited period' (as defined in the Model Code, see Appendix 1 at the end of this chapter) unless the company

- has put in place a buy-back programme prior to the commencement of the prohibited period in which the dates and quantities of securities to be traded during the relevant period are fixed and have been disclosed in a notification prior to purchase made in accordance with (3) below;
- has put in place a buy-back programme managed by an independent third party which makes its trading decisions in relation to the company's securities independently of, and uninfluenced by, the company;
- is purchasing or redeeming securities other than shares and securities whose price or value would be likely to be substantially affected by the publication of the information giving rise to the prohibited period; or
- is redeeming securities (other than equity shares) which, at the time of issue, set out

(i) the date of redemption;

(ii) the number of securities to be redeemed or the formula used to determine that number; and

(iii) the redemption price or the formula used to determine the price.

(2) *Purchases from a related party*

Where a purchase by a listed company of its own equity securities or preference shares is to be made from a related party (whether directly or through intermediaries), the related party transactions (see **33.33–33.35**) must be complied with unless

- a tender is made to all holders of the class of securities; or
- in the case of a market purchase authorised under a general authority granted by shareholders, it is made without prior understanding, arrangement or agreement between the company and any related party.

(3) *Purchases of own equity shares*

Purchases by a listed company of less than 15% of any class of its equity shares (excluding treasury shares) under a general authority granted by shareholders can only be made if

- a tender offer is made to all holders of the class; or
- the price to be paid is not more than the higher of 5% above the average market values of those shares for the five business days before the purchase is made and the price stipulated by the *Buy-back and Stabilisation Regulation, Art 5(1)*.

Purchases by a listed company of 15% or more of any class of equity shares (excluding treasury shares) pursuant to a general authority by the shareholders must be by way of a tender offer to all shareholders of that class. Purchases of 15% or more of any class of its own equity shares may be made by a listed company, other than by way of a tender offer, provided that the full terms of the share buyback have been specifically approved by shareholders. Where a series of purchases in aggregate amount to 15% or more, a tender offer need only be made in respect of any purchase that takes the aggregate to or above that level. Purchases that have been specifically approved by shareholders are not to be taken into account in determining whether the 15% level has been reached.

Notification prior to purchase. Any decision by the board to submit to shareholders a proposal for the listed company to be authorised to purchase its own equity shares (other than a renewal of an existing authority) must be notified to a RIS as soon as possible. Notification must indicate whether the proposal relates to specific purchases (in which case the names of the persons from whom the purchases are made must be given) or a general authorisation to make purchases. The outcome of the shareholders' meeting must also be notified.

Notification of purchases. Purchases must be notified to a RIS as soon as possible and in any event no later than 7.30am on the next business day. The notification must include

- the date of purchase;
- the number of equity shares purchased;

- the purchase price for each of the highest and lowest prices paid (where relevant);
- the number of the equity shares purchased for cancellation and purchased to be held as treasury shares; and
- where equity shares were purchased to be held as treasury shares, a statement of
  - (i) the total number of treasury shares of each class held by the company following the purchase and non-cancellation as such equity shares; and
  - (ii) the number of equity shares of each class that the company has in issue less the total number of treasury shares of each class held by the company following the purchase and non-cancellation of such equity shares.

Consent of other classes. Where there are in issue listed convertible securities which are convertible into the equity shares in question,

- a separate meeting of the holders of those convertible securities must be held, and
- their approval for the proposed purchase of equity shares obtained by a special resolution,

before the company enters into any agreement to purchase the shares. This does not apply if the trust deed or terms of issue of the relevant securities authorise the listed company to purchase its own equity shares.

(4) *Purchase of own securities other than equity shares*

Except where the purchase will consist of individual transactions made in accordance with the terms of issue of the relevant securities, where a listed company intends to purchase any of its securities convertible into its equity shares with a premium listing, it must

- ensure that no dealings in the relevant securities are carried out by or on behalf of the company (or another group member) until the proposal has either been notified to a RIS or abandoned; and
- notify a RIS of its decision to purchase.

Notification of purchases, early redemptions and cancellations. Any purchases, early redemptions or cancellations of a company's own securities by or on behalf of the company or any other group member must be notified to a RIS when an aggregate of 10% of the initial amount of the relevant class of securities has been purchased, redeemed or cancelled and for each 5% in aggregate of the initial amount of that class acquired thereafter. This must be done as soon as possible and in any event no later than 7.30am on the next business day. Notification must include

- the amount of securities acquired, redeemed or cancelled since the last notification; and
- whether or not the securities acquired are to be cancelled and the number of that class of securities that remain outstanding.

Warrants and options. Where, within a period of 12 months, a listed company purchases warrants or options over its own equity shares which, on exercise, give the entitlement to equity shares representing 15% or more of the company's existing issued shares (excluding treasury shares), the company must send to its shareholders a circular containing the following information.

- A statement of the directors' intentions regarding future purchases of the company's warrants and options.
- The number and terms of the warrants or options acquired and to be acquired and the method of acquisition.
- Where warrants or options have been, or are to be, acquired from specific parties, a statement of the names of those parties and all material terms of the acquisition.
- Details of the prices to be paid.

(5) *Treasury shares*

Sales for cash (or transfers in connection with an employees' share scheme) of treasury shares (see **34.14** for the meaning of 'treasury shares') must not be made during a 'prohibited period' (as defined in the Model Code, see Appendix 1 at the end of this chapter) subject to the following exemptions.

- Transfers of treasury shares in connection with the operation of an employee's share scheme where the transfer facilitates dealings that do not fall within the provisions of the Model Code.
- Sales or transfers by the company of treasury shares (other than equity shares) of a class whose price or value would not be likely to be significantly affected by the publication of the information giving rise to the prohibited period.

Capitalisation issues and sales, transfers and cancellations of treasury shares. Where, by virtue of it holding treasury shares, a company is allotted shares as part of a capitalisation issue, it must notify a RIS as soon as possible and in any event no later than 7.30 am on the next business day. The notification must state

- the date of the allotment;
- the number of shares allotted;
- a statement as to what number of the shares allotted have been cancelled and what number is being held as treasury shares; and
- where shares allotted are being held as treasury shares, a statement of
  - (i) the total number of treasury shares of each class held by the company following the allotment; and
  - (ii) the number of shares of each class that the company has in issue less the total number of treasury shares of each class held by the company following the allotment.

Any sale for cash, transfer for the purposes of or pursuant to an employees' share scheme or cancellation of treasury shares that represents over 0.5% of the listed company's share capital must be notified to a RIS as soon as possible and in any event by no later than 7.30am on the next business day. The notification must include

- the date of the sale, transfer or cancellation;

- the number of the shares sold, transferred or cancelled;
- the sale or transfer price for each of the highest and lowest prices paid, where relevant; and
- a statement of
  - (i) the total number of treasury shares of each class held by the company following the sale, transfer or cancellation; and
  - (ii) the number of shares of each class that the company has in issue less the total number of treasury shares of each class held by the company following the sale, transfer or cancellation.

(FCA Listing Rules, paras 12.1.1, 12.1.3, 12.2.1, 12.3.1, 12.4.1, 12.4.2, 12.4.2A, 12.4.3, 12.4.4–12.4.8, 12.5.1–12.5.3, 12.5.7, 12.6.1–12.6.4).

33.37 Circulars: Premium listing

Chapter 13 of the Listing Rules applies only to a company that has a premium listing. A listed company that has a premium listing must ensure that circulars it issues to holders of listed equity shares comply with the provisions of Chapter 13.

Incorporation by reference. With the exception of the information in 33.38, information may be incorporated in a circular issued by a listed company by reference to relevant information contained in an approved prospectus or listing particulars of that listed company or any other published document of that listed company that has been filed with the FCA. Such information must be the latest available to the company. When information is incorporated by reference, a cross-reference list must be provided in the circular so that security holders can easily identify specific items of information.

Approval of circulars. Apart from the exceptions below, a listed company must not circulate or publish a circular unless it has been approved by the FCA. The following documents (to the extent applicable) must be lodged with the FCA in final form before it will approve a circular.

(a) A Sponsors Declaration for the Production of a Circular completed by the sponsor.

(b) For a Class 1 circular or related party circular, a letter setting out any items of information required by the Listing Rules that are not applicable in that particular case.

(c) Any other document that the FCA has asked for in advance from the listed company or its sponsor.

At least 10 clear business days before the date on which it is intended to publish the circular, two copies of the draft circular, draft copies of the letters and documents in (*a*) and (*b*) above in final form must be submitted to the FCA.

Where a circular submitted for approval is amended, two copies of amended drafts must be resubmitted, marked to show changes made to conform with FCA comments and to indicate other changes.

A listed company must send a circular to holders of its listed equity shares as soon as practicable after it has been approved.

Exceptions. A circular does not need to be approved if the following conditions are satisfied.

- It is any of the types listed below or only relates to a proposed change of name or is an information only circular which does not relate to a shareholder vote other than of a type referred to in LR 13.4.3(3).
- It complies with the general requirements for all circulars in 33.38 and, if it is a circular listed below, it complies with the requirements of the Listing Rules indicated.
- Neither the circular nor the transaction or matter to which it relates has unusual features.

The FCA may agree to waive the requirement for approval in circumstances other than those set out above.

Circulars not needing approval	*FCA Listing Rules*
Authority to allot shares	Para 13.8.1
Disapplying pre-emption rights	Para 13.8.2
Reduction of capital	Para 13.8.4
Capitalisation or bonus issue	Para 13.8.5
Scrip dividend alternative	Para 13.8.6
Scrip dividend mandate schemes/dividend reinvestment plans	Para 13.8.7
Notices of meetings	Para 13.8.8
Amendments to constitution	Para 13.8.10
Employees' share schemes, etc	Para 13.8.11–13.8.13
Amendment to employees' share schemes, etc	Para 13.8.14
Discounted option arrangements	Para 13.8.15
Reminders of conversion rights	Para 13.8.16

Purchase of own equity shares. A circular relating to a resolution to give a listed company authority to purchase its own equity shares must be approved by the FCA if

- the purchase is to be made from a related party (whether directly or through intermediaries) unless
  - (i) a tender is made to all holders of the class of securities on the same terms; or
  - (ii) for a market purchase under a general authority granted by shareholders, it is made without prior understanding, arrangement or agreement between the company and any related party; or
- the exercise in full of the authority sought would result in the purchase of 25% or more of the company's issued equity shares (excluding treasury shares).

(FCA Listing Rules, paras 13.1.1–13.1.6, 13.2.1–13.2.7, 13.2.10).

33.38 *Contents of circulars*

Contents of all circulars. Every circular sent by a listed company to holders of its listed securities must

- provide a clear and adequate explanation of its subject matter giving due prominence to its essential characteristics, benefits and risks;

- state why the security holder is being asked to vote or, if no vote is required, why the circular is being sent;
- if voting or other action is required
  - (i) contain all information necessary to allow the security holders to make a properly informed decision;
  - (ii) contain a heading drawing attention to the document's importance and advising security holders who are in any doubt as to what action to take to consult appropriate independent advisers; and
  - (iii) contain a recommendation from the Board as to the voting action security holders should take for all resolutions proposed, indicating whether or not the proposal described in the circular is, in the Board's opinion, in the best interests of security holders as a whole;
- state that if all the securities have been sold or transferred by the addressee the circular and any other relevant documents should be passed to the person through whom the sale or transfer was effected for transmission to the purchaser or transferee;
- if new securities are being issued in substitution for existing securities, explain what will happen to existing documents of title;
- not include any reference to a specific date on which listed securities will be marked 'ex' any benefit or entitlement which has not been agreed in advance with the RIE on which the company's securities are or are to be traded;
- if it relates to a transaction in connection with which securities are proposed to be listed, include a statement that application has been or will be made for the securities to be admitted and, if known, a statement of
  - (i) the dates on which the securities are expected to be admitted and on which dealings are expected to commence;
  - (ii) how the new securities rank for dividend or interest;
  - (iii) whether the new securities rank equally with any existing listed securities;
  - (iv) the nature of the document of title;
  - (v) the proposed date of issue;
  - (vi) the treatment of any fractions;
  - (vii) whether or not the security may be held in uncertificated form; and
  - (viii) the names of the RIEs on which securities are to be traded;
- if a person is named in the circular as having advised the listed company or its directors, a statement that the adviser has given and has not withdrawn its written consent to the inclusion of the reference to the adviser's name in the form and context in which it is included; and
- if the circular relates to cancelling listing, state whether it is the company's intention to apply to cancel the securities' listing.

If another part of the Listing Rules provides that a circular of a particular type must include specified information, then that information is (unless the contrary intention appears) in addition to the information required above.

(FCA Listing Rules, paras 13.3.1, 13.3.2).

Specified information. The Listing Rules also contain specified information to be included in certain types of circulars as follows.

Circular	*FCA Listing Rules*
Class 1 circulars	Paras 13.4.1–13.4.8 and 13.5.1–13.5.34
Related party circulars	Paras 13.6.1–13.6.4
Circulars about purchase of own equity securities	Paras 13.7.1–13.7.2

33.39 LISTED COMPANIES – DISCLOSURE RULES

The FCA is authorised to make rules under *FSMA 2000, Pt VI* and those rules relating to disclosure of information in respect of financial instruments which have been admitted to trading on a regulated market (or for which a request for admission to trading on such a market has been made) are known as Disclosure Rules. [*FSMA 2000, s 73A(3)*]. The Rules implement *EC Market Abuse Directive, Art 6*, *EC Commission Directive 2003/124/EC, Arts 2, 3* and *EC Commission Directive 2004/72/EC, Arts 5, 6*.

Modifying or dispensing with Rules. The FCA can dispense with, or modify, the Disclosure Rules as it thinks fit. It can subsequently revoke or modify a dispensation or modification.

An application to the FCA to dispense with or modify, a Disclosure Rule must be in writing and

- contain a clear explanation of why the dispensation or modification is requested;
- include details of any special requirements;
- contain all relevant information that should reasonably be brought to the FCA's attention;
- contain any statement or information that is required by the Disclosure Rule to be included for a specific type of dispensation or modification; and
- include copies of all documents relevant to the application.

Any application should ordinarily be made at least five business days before the proposed dispensation or modification is to take effect.

Where a dispensation or modification has been granted, the FCA must be notified immediately of any matter which is material to the relevance or appropriateness of the dispensation or modification.

(FCA Disclosure and Transparency Rules, paras 1.2.1–1.2.3).

33.40 Disclosure Rules – general provisions

(1) *Supply of information to the FCA*

An issuer, 'person discharging managerial responsibilities' or a 'connected person' must provide to the FCA as soon as possible following a request

- any information that the FCA considers appropriate to protect investors or ensure the smooth operation of the market; and

- any other information or explanation that the FCA may require to verify whether the Disclosure Rules are being and have been complied with.

See **33.47** for '*person discharging managerial responsibilities*' and '*connected person*'.

(2) *Requirements of FCA for publication of information*

The FCA may, at any time, require an issuer to publish information, in such form and within such time limits as it considers appropriate, to protect investors or to ensure the smooth operation of the market. If an issuer fails to comply, the FCA may itself publish the information (after giving the issuer an opportunity to make representations as to why it should not be published).

(3) *Misleading information not to be published*

An issuer must take all reasonable care to ensure that any information it notifies to a RIS is not misleading, false or deceptive and does not omit anything likely to affect the import of the information. Behaviour conforming with this Rule does not amount to market abuse under *FSMA 2000, s 118(1)*.

An issuer must also not combine, in a manner likely to be misleading, a RIS announcement with the marketing of its activities.

(4) *Notification when a RIS is not open for business*

If an issuer is required to notify information to a RIS at a time when a RIS is not open for business, it must distribute the information as soon as possible to

- not less than two national newspapers in the UK;
- two newswire services operating in the UK; and
- a RIS for release as soon as it opens.

Behaviour conforming with this Rule does not amount to market abuse under *FSMA 2000, s 118(1)*.

The fact that a RIS is not open for business is not, in itself, sufficient grounds for delaying the disclosure or distribution of inside information.

(5) *English language*

A notification to a RIS that is required under the Disclosure Rules must be in English.

(FCA Disclosure and Transparency Rules, paras 1.3.1, 1.3.3–1.3.6, 1.3.8).

Suspension of trading. The FCA may, in accordance with Disclosure Rules, suspend trading in a financial instrument. If it does so, the issuer may refer the matter to the Tribunal. [*FSMA 2000, s 96C; SI 2005 No 381*]. The FCA may take this action if there are reasonable grounds to suspect non-compliance with the Disclosure Rules. Examples of when it may require the suspension of trading include

- if an issuer fails to make a required RIS announcement within the time allowed and the FCA considers this could affect the interests of investors or affect the smooth operation of the market; or
- if there is or may be a leak of inside information and the issuer is unwilling or unable to issue an appropriate RIS announcement within a reasonable period of time.

If trading of an issuer's financial instruments is suspended, the issuer, any persons discharging managerial responsibilities and any connected person must continue to comply with all applicable Disclosure Rules.

(FCA Disclosure and Transparency Rules, paras 1.4.1, 1.4.2, 1.4.4).

33.41 Disclosure and control of inside information by issuers

The purpose of these provisions is to

- promote prompt and fair disclosure of relevant information to the market; and
- set out specific circumstances when an issuer can delay public disclosure of inside information and requirements to ensure that such information is kept confidential in order to protect investors and prevent insider dealing.

If an issuer is involved in a matter which also falls within the scope of the Takeover Code, it must still comply with its obligations under these provisions.

Requirement to disclose inside information. Unless **33.44** applies, an issuer must notify a RIS as soon as possible of any 'inside information' which directly concerns the issuer. Information is '*inside information*' if each of the criteria in the definition of inside information is met. See **23.2 Insider Dealing and Market Abuse**. Behaviour conforming with this Rule does not amount to market abuse under *FSMA 2000, s 118(1)*.

(FCA Disclosure and Transparency Rules, paras 1.5.2, 2.1.2, 2.1.3, 2.2.1, 2.2.3).

33.42 *Publication of information on the internet*

Where an issuer has a website,

- inside information announced via a RIS must be available on the issuer's internet site by the close of the next business day at the latest and must be notified to a RIS before, or simultaneously with, publication on its internet;
- it should not publish inside information on its website as an alternative to its disclosure via a RIS; and
- it must ,for a period of one year following publication, post on its website all inside information that it is required to disclose via a RIS.

(FCA Disclosure and Transparency Rules, paras 2.3.1–2.3.5).

33.43 *Synchronised release of information*

Without prejudice to its obligations to disclose inside information under **33.41**, an issuer must take reasonable care to ensure that the disclosure of inside information to the public is synchronised as closely as possible in all jurisdictions in which it has

- financial instruments admitted to trading on a regulated market;
- requested admission to trading of its financial instruments on a regulated market; or
- financial instruments listed on any other overseas stock exchange.

If the rules of another regulated market or overseas stock exchange require an issuer to disclose inside information at a time when a RIS is not open for business, it should disclose the information in accordance with **33.40**(4) at the same time as it is released to the public in the other jurisdiction.

(FCA Disclosure and Transparency Rules, paras 2.4.1, 2.4.2).

33.44 *Delaying disclosure of inside information*

An issuer may, under its own responsibility, delay the public disclosure of inside information so as not to prejudice its legitimate interests provided that

- the omission would not be likely to mislead the public;
- any person receiving the information owes the issuer a duty of confidentiality, regardless of whether such duty is based on law, regulations, articles of association or contract; and
- the issuer is able to ensure the confidentiality of that information.

Behaviour conforming with this Rule does not amount to market abuse under *FSMA 2000, s 118(1)*.

Legitimate interests may, in particular, relate to the following circumstances.

- Negotiations in course which would be likely to be affected by public disclosure. In particular, where the financial viability of the issuer is in imminent danger, although not within the scope of the insolvency laws, public disclosure of information may be delayed for a limited period where disclosure would seriously jeopardise the interest of existing and potential shareholders by undermining specific negotiations designed to ensure the long-term financial recovery of the issuer. This does not allow an issuer to delay public disclosure of the fact that it is in financial difficulty or of its worsening financial condition and is limited to the fact or substance of the negotiations to deal with such a situation and an issuer cannot delay disclosure of inside information on the basis that its position in subsequent negotiations to deal with the situation will be jeopardised by the disclosure of its financial condition.
- Decisions taken or contracts made by the management of an issuer which need the approval of another body of the issuer in order to become effective, where the organisation of such an issuer requires separation between these bodies (eg a management board and a supervisory board), provided that a public disclosure of the information before such approval together with the simultaneous announcement that this approval is still pending would jeopardise the correct assessment of the information by the public. This legitimate interest described refers to an issuer with a dual board structure. An issuer with a unitary board structure would be unable to take advantage of this provision and therefore it should only be available to a very limited number of issuers in the United Kingdom.

An issuer should not be obliged to disclose impending developments that could be jeopardised by premature disclosure. Whether or not an issuer has a legitimate interest which would be prejudiced by the disclosure of certain inside information is an assessment which must be made by the issuer in the first instance. However the FCA considers that other than in relation to impending developments or matters described in DTR 2.5.3 or DTR 2.5.5A, there are unlikely to be other circumstances where delay would be justified.

An issuer may have a legitimate interest to delay disclosing inside information concerning the provision of liquidity support by the Bank of England or by another central bank to it or to a member of the same group as the issuer.

Selective disclosure. Unless the above Rule applies, whenever an issuer (or a person acting on his behalf or for his account) discloses any inside information to any third party in the normal exercise of his employment, profession or duties, the issuer must make complete and effective public disclosure of that information via a RIS. This must be done simultaneously in the case of an intentional disclosure and as soon as possible in the case of a non-intentional disclosure.

(FCA Disclosure and Transparency Rules, paras 1.5.2, 2.5.1, 2.5.3, 2.5.4, 2.5.5A, 2.5.6).

33.45 *Control of inside information*

An issuer must establish effective arrangements to

- deny access to inside information to persons other than those who require it for the exercise of their functions within the issuer; and
- enable public disclosure to be made via a RIS as soon as possible in case the issuer is not able to ensure the confidentiality of the relevant inside information.

(FCA Disclosure and Transparency Rules, paras 2.6.1, 2.6.2).

33.46 *Insider lists*

An issuer must ensure that it, and persons acting on its behalf or on its account, draw up a list of those persons working for them, under a contract of employment or otherwise, who have access to inside information relating directly or indirectly to the issuer, whether on a regular or occasional basis. On request, this list must be supplied to the FCA as soon as possible.

The insider list must include the

- identity of each person having access to inside information;
- reason why such person is on the insider list; and
- date on which the insider list was created and updated

and must be promptly updated

- when there is a change in the reason why a person is already on the list;
- when any new person is provided with access to inside information; and
- to indicate the date on which a person on the list ceases to have access to inside information.

Every insider list prepared by the issuer (or by persons acting on its account or on its behalf) must be kept for at least five years from the date on which it was drawn up or updated, whichever is the latest.

Acknowledgement of legal and regulatory duties. An issuer must ensure that

- its employees with access to inside information acknowledge the legal and regulatory duties entailed (including dealing restrictions in relation to the issuer's financial instruments) and are aware of the sanctions attaching to the misuse or improper circulation of such information; and
- any person that is acting on its behalf or on its account and has drawn up an insider list has taken the necessary measures to ensure that every person whose name is on that list acknowledges the legal and regulatory duties entailed and is aware of the sanctions attaching to the misuse or improper circulation of such information.

(FCA Disclosure and Transparency Rules, paras 2.8.1–2.8.5, 2.8.9, 2.8.10).

33.47 Transactions by persons discharging managerial responsibilities and their connected persons

These provisions set out the notification obligations of issuers, 'persons discharging managerial responsibilities' and their 'connected persons' in respect of transactions conducted on their own account in shares of the issuer, or derivatives or any other financial instrument relating to those shares. The provisions apply to

(a) an issuer incorporated in the UK whose financial instruments are admitted to trading on a regulated market or for whose financial instruments a request for admission to trading on a regulated market in the UK has been made; and

(b) a non-EEA State issuer which is required to file with the FCA annual information in relation to shares in accordance with *EC Prospectus Directive, Art 10*.

(FCA Disclosure and Transparency Rules, paras 1.1.1, 3.1.1).

'*Person discharging managerial responsibilities within an issuer*' means

- a director of an issuer falling within (*a*) or (*b*) above); or
- a senior executive of such an issuer who
  - (i) has regular access to inside information relating, directly or indirectly, to the issuer; and
  - (ii) has power to make managerial decisions affecting the future development and business prospects of the issuer.

A person '*connected*' with a person discharging managerial responsibilities within an issuer means

- a 'connected person' within the meaning in *CA 2006, s 252*, see **18.1 Directors** (but reading those provisions as if any reference to a director of a company were a reference to a person discharging managerial responsibilities within an issuer);
- a relative of a person discharging managerial responsibilities within an issuer, who, on the date of the transaction in question, has shared the same household as that person for at least 12 months; and
- a body corporate in which
  - (i) a person discharging managerial responsibilities within an issuer, or
  - (ii) any person connected with him by virtue of the above

  is a director or a senior executive who has the power to make management decisions affecting the future development and business prospects of that body corporate.

  [*FSMA 2000, s 96B; CA 2006, Sch 15 para 7*].

(1) *Notification of transactions by persons discharging managerial responsibilities*

'Persons discharging managerial responsibilities' and their 'connected persons', must notify the issuer in writing of the occurrence of all transactions conducted on their own account in the shares of the issuer, or derivatives or any other financial instruments relating to those shares within four business days of the day on which the transaction occurred.

Notification must contain the following information.

- The name of the person discharging managerial responsibilities within the issuer, or, where applicable, the name of the person connected with such a person.
- The reason for responsibility to notify.
- The name of the relevant issuer.
- A description of the financial instrument.
- The nature of the transaction.
- The date and place of the transaction.
- The price and volume of the transaction.

FSMA provides that an individual who is not a director can still be a person discharging managerial responsibilities in relation to an issuer if they are a "senior executive of such an issuer" and they meet the criteria set out in FSMA. An individual may be a "senior executive of such an issuer" irrespective of the nature of any contractual arrangement between the individual and the issuer and notwithstanding the absence of a contractual arrangement between the individual and the issuer, provided the individual has regular access to inside information relating directly or indirectly to the issuer and has power to make managerial decisions affecting the future development and business of the issuer.

(2) *Notification of transactions by issuers to a RIS*

An issuer must notify a RIS of any information notified to it in accordance with

(i) (1) above,

(ii) *CA 2006, s 793* (notice requiring information about interests in shares, see **24.2 Interests in Public Company Shares**) to the extent that it relates to the interests of a director or, as far as the issuer is aware, any connected person, and

(iii) the Model Code, para 26 (see **33 Appendix**).

but if it makes the appropriate notification under (i) it is not required to make a further notification under (ii) in the event of receiving information regarding the same dealing in a notification under *CA 2006, s 793*.

The notification must be made as soon as possible and in any event by no later than the end of the next business day following the receipt of the information by the issuer. It must contain the same information as required under (1) above, together with the date on which the notification was made to the issuer.

An issuer with financial instruments admitted to trading on a regulated market in the UK that does not fall within (*a*) or (*b*) above must notify equivalent information to a RIS as soon as possible after the issuer becomes aware of the information.

(FCA Disclosure and Transparency Rules, paras 3.1.2–3.1.6, 3.1.8).

33.48 LISTED COMPANIES – THE TRANSPARENCY RULES

CA 2006, ss 1265–1268, 1270–1272 implement the provisions of the *Transparency Obligations Directive* (*Directive 2004/109/EC*) which imposes minimum harmonisation requirements on the information to be provided to the public about 'issuers' and the control of votes attached to shares in those issuers. Under *FSMA 2000, ss 89A–89L* (as inserted by *CA 2006, ss 1266–1268*), the Financial Conduct Authority (FCA) as the competent authority are given powers to make Transparency Rules and call for information from specified persons. The FCA is also given powers in case of infringement of the rules, including public censure of the issuer and power to suspend or prohibit trading of securities.

In relation to the Transparency Rules, '*issuer*' means a legal person whose securities are admitted to trading on a regulated market or whose voting shares are admitted to trading on a UK market other than a regulated market, and in the case of depository receipts representing securities, the issuer is the issuer of the securities represented. [*FSMA 2000, s 102A(6); CA 2006, Sch 15 para 10*].

There are three main categories of obligation that are imposed and that the Transparency Rules implement in respect of UK markets and issuers.

- Requirements for issuers to make public, at regular intervals, information about their financial position and the progress and management of the business of the issuer. See **33.50–33.53**.
- Requirements for holders of votes attached to shares of issuers to notify the issuers when the number of votes they control reach a proportion of the total votes available that is specified. See **33.54–33.64**.
- Requirements for issuers to treat holders of the same securities equally. See **33.65–33.68**.

Transparency Rules are not Listing Rules, Disclosure Rules or Prospectus Rules but are Part 6 Rules. [*FSMA 2000, s 73A(6); CA 2006, Sch 15 para 3*].

Units trusts, etc. The provisions do not apply to an undertaking if it is a unit trust or investment company

- the object of which is the collective investment of capital provided by the public and which operates on the principle of risk spreading; and
- the units of which are, at the request of the holder of such units, repurchased or redeemed, directly or indirectly, out of the assets of that undertaking.

(FCA Disclosure and Transparency Rules, para 1A.1).

Modifying or dispensing with rules. The FCA can dispense with, or modify, the Transparency Rules as it thinks fit (subject to the terms of *CA 2006* and the *Directive*). Any dispensation or modification may be either unconditional or subject to specified conditions. The FCA can subsequently revoke or modify a dispensation or modification.

An application to the FCA to dispense with or modify, a Transparency Rule must be in writing and

- contain a clear explanation of why the dispensation or modification is requested;
- include details of any special requirements;
- contain all relevant information that should reasonably be brought to the FCA's attention;
- contain any statement or information that is required by the Transparency Rules to be included for a specific type of dispensation or modification; and
- include copies of all documents relevant to the application.

An application should ordinarily be made at least five business days before the proposed dispensation or modification is to take effect.

Where a dispensation or modification has been applied for or granted, the FCA must be notified immediately of any matter which is material to the relevance or appropriateness of the dispensation or modification.

(FCA Disclosure and Transparency Rules, para 1A.2).

33.49 Transparency Rules – general provisions

The purpose of the Transparency Rules is to implement the *Transparency Directive* and to make other rules to ensure there is adequate transparency of, and access to, information in the UK financial markets.

(1) *Early consultation with FCA*

An issuer or other person should consult with the FCA at the earliest possible stage if they are in doubt about how the Transparency Rules apply in a particular situation or consider that it may be necessary for the FCA to dispense with or modify a rule. The address for any such correspondence is

Company Monitoring Team

Markets Division

The Financial Services Authority

25 The North Colonnade

Canary Wharf

London

E14 5HS

Fax: 020 7066 8368

(2) *Requirements of FCA for publication of information*

The FCA may, at any time, require an issuer to publish such information in such form and within such time limits as it considers appropriate to protect investors or to ensure the smooth operation of the market. If an issuer fails to comply, the FCA may itself publish the information (after giving the issuer an opportunity to make representations as to why it should not be published).

(3) *Misleading information not to be published*

An issuer must take all reasonable care to ensure that any information it notifies to a RIS is not misleading, false or deceptive and does not omit anything likely to affect the import of the information.

(4) *Notification when a RIS is not open for business*

If an issuer is required to notify information to a RIS at a time when a RIS is not open for business, it must distribute the information as soon as possible to

- not less than two national newspapers in the UK;
- two newswire services operating in the UK; and
- a RIS for release as soon as it opens.

(5) *Meaning of 'Home State'*

The '*Home State*' of an issuer is

(a) in the case of an issuer of debt securities the denomination per unit of which is less than 1,000 euros or an issuer of shares

(i) if the issuer is incorporated in the EC, the Member State in which it has its registered office; and

(ii) if the issuer is incorporated in a third country, the Member State in which it is required to file annual information with the competent authority; and

(b) for an issuer not covered by (i) above, the Member State chosen by the issuer from among the Member States in which the issuer has its registered office and those Member States which have admitted its securities to trading on a regulated market on their territory. The issuer may choose only one Member State as its home Member State. Its choice remains valid for at least three years unless its securities are no longer admitted to trading on any regulated market in the EC.

The same rules apply to debt securities in a currency other than euros, provided that the value of such minimum denomination is nearly equivalent to 1,000 euros.

(FCA Disclosure and Transparency Rules, paras 1A.2, 1A.3, Glossary of definitions).

33.50 Periodic financial reporting

The requirements for periodic financial reporting cover the requirements for

- annual financial reports (see **33.51**);
- half-yearly financial reports (see **33.52**). In addition to the general exemption from the Transparency Rules for unit trusts, etc (see **33.48**), there are specific exemptions from the requirements for periodic financial reporting in **33.53** below.

33.51 *Annual financial reports*

Subject to the exemptions under **33.53** below, these provisions apply to an issuer whose transferable securities are admitted to trading and whose Home State (see **33.49**(5)) is the UK. (An issuer that is also admitted to the official list should also consider its obligations under the Listing Rules in addition to these requirements.)

An issuer must make public its annual financial report at the latest four months after the end of each financial year. It must also ensure that its annual financial report remains publicly available for at least five years.

The annual financial report must include the following.

(a) *Audited financial statements*

If an issuer is required to prepare consolidated accounts, the audited financial statements must comprise

- consolidated accounts prepared in accordance with International Financial Reporting Standards; and
- accounts of the parent company prepared in accordance with the national law of the EEA State in which the parent company is incorporated.

If an issuer is not required to prepare consolidated accounts, the audited financial statements must comprise accounts prepared in accordance with the national law of the EEA State in which the issuer is incorporated.

The audit report, signed by the person or persons responsible for auditing the financial statements, must be disclosed in full to the public together with the annual financial report.

An issuer which is a UK-traded non-EEA company must ensure that the person who provides the audit report is

- on the register of third country auditors (see **8.14 Audit**);
- eligible for appointment as statutory auditor (see **8.8 Audit**); or
- an EEA auditor (see **8.8 Audit**).

(b) *Management report*

The management report must

- contain a fair review of the issuer's business and a description of the principal risks and uncertainties facing the issuer;
- be a balanced and comprehensive analysis of the development and performance of the issuer's business during the financial year and the position of the issuer's business at the end of that year, consistent with the size and complexity of the business;
- include (to the extent necessary for an understanding of the development, performance or position of the issuer's business) analysis using financial key performance indicators and, where appropriate, analysis using other key performance indicators including information relating to environmental matters and employee matters; and
- include references to, and additional explanations of, amounts included in the issuer's annual financial statements, where appropriate.

The management report must also give an indication of

- any important events that have occurred since the end of the financial year;
- the issuer's likely future development;
- activities in the field of research and development;
- information concerning acquisitions of own shares;
- the existence of branches of the issuer; and
- in relation to the issuer's use of financial instruments and where material for the assessment of its assets, liabilities, financial position and profit or loss, the issuer's financial risk management objectives and policies (including its policy for hedging each major type of forecasted transaction for which hedge accounting is used) and the issuer's exposure to price risk, credit risk, liquidity risk and cash flow risk.

(c) *Responsibility statements*

Responsibility statements must be made by the persons responsible within the issuer. The name and function of any person who makes a responsibility statement must be clearly indicated in that statement.

For each person making a responsibility statement, the statement must set out that to the best of his or her knowledge

- the financial statements, prepared in accordance with the applicable set of accounting standards, give a true and fair view of the assets, liabilities, financial position and profit or loss of the issuer and the undertakings included in the consolidation taken as a whole; and
- the management report includes a fair review of the development and performance of the business and the position of the issuer and the undertakings included in the consolidation taken as a whole, together with a description of the principal risks and uncertainties that they face.

(FCA Disclosure and Transparency Rules, para 4.1).

33.52 *Half-yearly financial reports*

Subject to the exemptions in **33.53** below, these provisions apply to an issuer whose

- shares or debt securities are admitted to trading; and
- Home State (see **33.49**(5)) is the UK

But as a transitional provision, in the case of an issuer of debt securities where the securities were admitted to the official list before 1 January 2005, there is no requirement to disclose half-yearly financial reports until 1 January 2015.

An issuer must make public a half-yearly financial report covering the first six months of the financial year. It must be made public as soon as possible, but no later than two months, after the end of the period to which the report relates. An issuer must also ensure that the half-yearly financial report remains available to the public for at least five years.

A half-yearly financial report must include the following information.

(a) *A condensed set of financial statements*

If an issuer is required to prepare consolidated accounts, the condensed set of financial statements must be prepared in accordance with IAS 34.

If an issuer is not required to prepare consolidated accounts, the condensed set of financial statements must contain, as a minimum, a condensed balance sheet and profit and loss account and explanatory notes on these accounts. In preparing the condensed balance sheet and profit and loss account, an issuer must follow the same principles for recognising and measuring as when preparing annual financial reports. Each must show the same headings and subtotals as were included in the most recent annual financial statements of the issuer. Additional line items must be included if, as a result of their omission, the half-yearly financial statements would give a misleading view. A comparative balance sheet as at the end of the immediate preceding financial year and a comparative profit and loss account for the first six months of the preceding financial year must be included. The explanatory notes must include sufficient information to ensure the comparability of the condensed half-yearly financial statements with the annual financial statements; and to ensure a user's proper understanding of any material changes in amounts and of any developments in the half-year period concerned.

The accounting policies and presentation applied to half-yearly figures must be consistent with those applied in the latest published annual accounts except where

- the accounting policies and presentation are to be changed in the subsequent annual financial statements (in which case the new accounting policies and presentation should be followed and the changes and the reasons for the changes should be disclosed in the half-yearly report); or
- the FCA otherwise agrees.

(b) *An interim management report*

The interim management report must include *as a minimum*

- an indication of important events that have occurred during the first six months of the financial year, and their impact on the condensed set of financial statements, together with a description of the principal risks and uncertainties for the remaining six months of the financial year;
- in the case of an issuer of shares,
  (i) related parties' transactions that have taken place in the first six months of the current financial year and that have materially affected the financial position or the performance of the enterprise during that period;
  (ii) any changes in the related parties transactions described in the last annual report that could have a material effect on the financial position or performance of the enterprise in the first six months of the current financial year; and
  (iii) if it is not required to prepare consolidated accounts, any transactions which have been entered into with related parties by the issuer, including the amount of such transactions, the nature of the related party relationship and other information about the transactions necessary for an understanding of the financial position of the issuer (but only where such transactions are material and have not been concluded under normal market conditions). Any such information may be aggregated according to their nature except where separate information is necessary for an understanding of the effects of related party transactions on the financial position of the issuer.

If the half-yearly financial report has been audited or reviewed by auditors pursuant to the Auditing Practices Board guidance on Review of Interim Financial Information, the audit report or review report must be reproduced in full. If the half-yearly financial report has not been audited or so reviewed, an issuer must make a statement to this effect in its report.

(c) *Responsibility statements*

Responsibility statements must be made by the persons responsible within the issuer. The name and function of any person who makes a responsibility statement must be clearly indicated in that statement.

For each person making a responsibility statement, the statement must confirm that to the best of his or her knowledge

(i) the condensed set of financial statements, prepared in accordance with the applicable set of accounting standards, gives a true and fair view of the assets, liabilities, financial position and profit or loss of the issuer, or the undertakings included in the consolidation as a whole; and

(ii) the interim management report includes a fair review of the information required under (*b*) above.

A person making a responsibility statement satisfies the requirement in (i) above by including a statement that the condensed set of financial statements have been prepared in accordance with

- IAS 34;
- for UK issuers not using International Financial Reporting Standards, pronouncements on interim reporting issued by the Accounting Standards Board; or
- for all other issuers not using International Financial Reporting Standards, a national accounting standard relating to interim reporting,

provided always that a person making such a statement has reasonable grounds to be satisfied that the condensed set of financial statements prepared in accordance with such a standard is not misleading.

(FCA Disclosure and Transparency Rules, para 4.2).

33.53 *Exemptions*

The following exemptions apply to the requirements in **33.51–33.52**.

(a) *Public sector issuers*

The rules on annual financial reporting and half yearly financial reporting and interim management statements in **33.51–33.52** above do not apply to a state, a regional or local authority of a state, a public international body of which are least one EEA State is a member, the ECB and EEA States' national central banks.

(b) *Debt issuers*

The rules in **33.51–33.52** above do not apply to an issuer that issues exclusively debt securities admitted to trading, the denomination per unit of which is at least 100,000 euros (or an equivalent amount).

The rules in **33.52** above do not apply to a credit institution whose shares are not admitted to trading and which has, in a continuous or repeated manner, only issued debt securities provided that

- the total nominal amount of all such debt securities remains below 100 million euros; and
- the credit institution has not published a prospectus in accordance with the *Prospectus Directive*.

The rules in **33.52** above do not apply to an issuer already existing on 31 December 2003 which exclusively issue debt securities unconditionally and irrevocably guaranteed by the issuer's Home Member State or by a regional or local authority of that state, on a regulated market.

(c) *Issuers of convertible securities*

The rules in **33.52** above do not apply to an issuer of transferable securities convertible into shares.

(d) *Issuers of depository receipts*

The rules in **33.52** above do not apply to an issuer of depository receipts.

(e) *Non-EEA States with equivalent laws*

An issuer whose registered office is in a non-EEA State, and whose relevant laws are considered equivalent by the FCA, is exempted from the rules in **33.51–33.52**. The FCA maintains a published list of non-EEA States which are judged to have laws which lay down requirements equivalent to those imposed upon issuers by this paragraph.

(FCA Disclosure and Transparency Rules, para 4.4).

33.54 Vote holder and issuer notification rules

The Transparency Rules require holders of votes attached to shares of issuers to notify the issuers when the number of votes they control reach a specified proportion of the total votes. These provisions are considered in **33.56–33.64**.

For these purposes:

- '*Issuer*', in relation to shares admitted to trading on a regulated market, is an issuer whose Home State (see **33.49(5)**) is the UK;
- '*Non-UK issuer*' is an issuer whose shares are admitted to trading on a regulated market and whose Home State is the UK other than
  - (i) a public company within the meaning of s 4(2) of CA 2006; and
  - (ii) a company which is otherwise incorporated in, and whose principal place of business is in, the UK;
- '*Shares*' means shares which are
  - (i) already issued and carry rights to vote which are exercisable in all circumstances at general meetings of the issuer including shares (eg preference shares) which, following the exercise of an option for their conversion, event of default or otherwise, have become fully enfranchised for voting purposes; and
  - (ii) admitted to trading on a regulated or prescribed market;
- *An acquisition or disposal of shares* is to be regarded as effective when the relevant transaction is executed (unless the transaction provides for settlement to be subject to conditions which are beyond the control of the parties, in which case the acquisition or disposal is to be regarded as effective on the settlement of the transaction).
- A *stock-lending agreement* which provides for the outright transfer of securities and which provides the lender with a right to call for re-delivery of the lent stock (or its equivalent) is not (as respects the lender) to be taken as involving a disposal of any shares which may be the subject of the stock loan.

Calculating percentages. For the purposes of calculating whether any percentage threshold is reached, exceeded or fallen below and in any resulting notification, the proportion of voting rights held must, if necessary, be rounded down to the next whole number.

(FCA Disclosure and Transparency Rules, para 5.1.1).

33.55 *Notification of the acquisition or disposal of major shareholdings*

Subject to the exemption for certain third country issuers, a person must notify the issuer of the percentage of its voting rights he holds as shareholder or is deemed to hold through his direct or indirect holding of financial instruments (see **33.57**) falling within Rules 5.3.1 (R) 1 (subject to exceptions in 5.3.1R(2) (or a combination of such holdings) if the percentage of those voting rights.

(a) reaches, exceeds or falls below 3%, 4%, 5%, 6%, 7%, 8%, 9%, 10% and each 1% threshold thereafter up to 100% (or in the case of a non-UK issuer on the basis of thresholds at 5%, 10%, 15%, 20%, 25%, 30%, 50% and 75%) as a result of an acquisition or disposal of shares or financial instruments falls within DTR 5.3R; or

(b) reaches, exceeds or falls below an applicable threshold in (*a*) above as a result of events changing the breakdown of voting rights and on the basis of information disclosed by the issuer in accordance with **33.60**;

and in the case of an issuer which is not incorporated in an EEA state a notification under (*b*) above must be made on the basis of equivalent events and disclosed information.

See **33.64** for an exemption for certain third country issuers.

Voting rights that can be disregarded. Voting rights attaching to the following shares are to be disregarded for the purposes of determining whether a person has a notification obligation under the above provisions.

- Shares acquired for the sole purpose of clearing and settlement within a settlement cycle not exceeding the period beginning with the transaction and ending at the close of the third trading day following the day of the execution of the transaction (irrespective of whether the transaction is conducted on-exchange).
- Shares held by a custodian (or nominee) in its custodian (or nominee) capacity (whether operating from an establishment in the UK or elsewhere) provided such a person can only exercise the voting rights attached to such shares under instructions given in writing or by electronic means.
- Shares held by a market maker acting in that capacity subject to the percentage of such shares not being equal to or in excess of 10% and subject to the market maker satisfying the criteria and complying with the conditions and operating requirements set out in the Transparency Rules.
- Shares or shares underlying financial instruments within DTR 5.3.1 held by a credit institution or investment firm provided that

  (i) the shares or financial instruments are held within its trading book;

  (ii) the voting rights attached to such shares do not exceed 5%; and

  (iii) it ensures that the voting rights attached to shares in or related to financial instruments the trading book are not exercised or otherwise used to intervene in the management of the issuer.
- Shares held by a collateral taker under a collateral transaction which involves the outright transfer of securities provided the collateral taker does not declare any intention of exercising (and does not exercise) the voting rights attaching to such shares.
- Shares acquired by a borrower under a stock lending agreement provided

(i) such shares (or equivalent stock) are on-lent or otherwise disposed of by the borrower by not later than close of business on the next trading day; and

(ii) the borrower does not declare any intention of exercising (and does not exercise) the voting rights attaching to the shares.

Voting rights that can be disregarded except at 5%, 10% and higher thresholds. The following can be disregarded in determining whether a person has a notification obligation under the above provisions except at the thresholds of 5% and 10% and above.

- Voting rights attaching to shares forming part of property belonging to another which that person lawfully manages under an agreement in, or evidenced in, writing. For these purposes, a person ('A') may lawfully manage investments belonging to another if

  (i) A can manage those investments in accordance with a permission under *FSMA 200, Part IV*;

  (ii) A is an EEA firm other than one mentioned in *FSMA 2000, Sch 3 para 5(c) or (e)* and can manage those investments in accordance with its EEA authorisation;

  (iii) A can, in accordance with *FSMA 2000, s 327*, manage those investments without contravening the prohibition contained in *FSMA 2000, s 19*;

  (iv) A can lawfully manage those investments in another EEA State and would, if he were to manage those investments in the UK, require a permission under *FSMA 200, Part IV*; or

  (v) A is a category of investment manager prescribed for this purpose by the FCA.

- Voting rights attaching to shares which may be exercisable by a person in his capacity as the operator of an authorised unit trust scheme, an authorised contractual scheme, a recognised scheme, or a UCITS scheme.

- Voting rights attaching to shares which may be exercisable by an Investment Company with Variable Capital.

- Voting rights attaching to shares which may be exercised by a category of investment entity which for this purpose is prescribed by the FCA.

(FCA Disclosure and Transparency Rules, paras 5.1.2–5.1.5).

33.56 *Direct and indirect holders of shares (acquisition or disposal of major proportions of voting rights)*

A person is an indirect holder of shares for the purpose of the applicable definition of shareholder to the extent that he is entitled to acquire, to dispose of, or to exercise voting rights in any of the following cases or a combination of them.

(a) Voting rights held by a third party with whom that person has concluded an agreement, which obliges them to adopt, by concerted exercise of the voting rights they hold, a lasting common policy towards the management of the issuer in question.

(b) Voting rights held by a third party under an agreement concluded with that person providing for the temporary transfer for consideration of the voting rights in question.

(c) Voting rights attaching to shares which are lodged as collateral with that person provided that person controls the voting rights and declares its intention of exercising them.

(d) Voting rights attaching to shares in which that person has the life interest.

(e) Voting rights which are held, or may be exercised within the meaning of points (*a*) to (*d*) above or, in cases (*f*) and (*h*) below, by a person undertaking investment management, or by a management company, by an undertaking controlled by that person.

In the FCA's view, this produces the result that it is always necessary for the parent undertaking of a controlled undertaking to aggregate its holding with any holding of the controlled undertaking (subject to the exemptions implicit in the wording and in 33.58).

(f) Voting rights attaching to shares deposited with that person which the person can exercise at its discretion in the absence of specific instructions from the shareholders.

In the FCA's view, this includes a person carrying on investment management and which is also the custodian of shares to which voting rights are attached.

(g) Voting rights held by a third party in his own name on behalf of that person.

In the FCA's view this does not result in a unit holder in a collective investment scheme or other investment entity being treated as the holder of voting rights in the scheme property (provided always such persons do not have any entitlement to exercise, or control the exercise of, such voting rights). Neither are such persons to be regarded as holding shares 'indirectly'.

(h) Voting rights which that person may exercise as a proxy where that person can exercise the voting rights at his discretion in the absence of specific instructions from the shareholders.

In the FCA's view, although this refers to proxies, it also describes and applies to a person undertaking investment management, and to a management company, and which is able effectively to determine the manner in which voting rights attached to shares under its control are exercised (eg through instructions given directly or indirectly to a nominee or independent custodian). Case (*e*) above provides for the voting rights which are under the control of such a person to be aggregated with those of its parent undertaking.

The indirect holdings within Cases (*a*) to (*h*) have to be aggregated, but also separately identified, in a notification to the issuer. Apart from those identified in the Cases (*a*) to (*h*) above, the FCA does not expect any other significant category 'indirect shareholder' to be identified.

Cases (*a*) to (*h*) above are also relevant in determining whether a person is an indirect holder of qualifying financial instruments which result in an entitlement to acquire shares (see 33.57).

(FCA Disclosure and Transparency Rules, para *5.2*).

33.57 *Notification of voting rights arising from the holding of certain financial instruments*

A person must make a notification in accordance with the applicable thresholds in 33.55 in respect of any financial instruments which they hold (directly or indirectly) which are qualifying financial instruments within DTR 5.3.2 or (unless the exemptions in DTR

5.3.1.(2) or(2A) apply) are referenced to the shares of an issuer, other than a non-UK issuer and have similar economic effects to (but which are not) qualifying financial instruments. Detailed provisions and definitions are set out in DTR 5.3.1, 5.3.1A, 5.3.2, 5.3.3. and 5.3.4.

(FCA Disclosure and Transparency Rules, para 5.3).

33.58 *Aggregation of managed holdings*

Aggregation is not required in the following cases.

(a) *The parent undertaking of a management company* is not required to aggregate its holdings with the holdings managed by the management company under the conditions laid down in the *Undertakings for Collective Investment in Transferable Securities (UCITS) Directive (No 85/611/EEC)*, provided such management company exercises its voting rights independently from the parent undertaking. But the requirements for the aggregation of holdings applies if the parent undertaking, or another controlled undertaking of the parent undertaking, has invested in holdings managed by such management company and the management company has no discretion to exercise the voting rights attached to such holdings and may only exercise such voting rights under direct or indirect instructions from the parent or another controlled undertaking of the parent undertaking.

(b) *The parent undertaking of an investment firm* authorised under the *Markets in Financial Instruments Directive (MiFID) (No 2004/39/EC)* is not required to aggregate its holdings with the holdings which such investment firm manages on a client-by-client basis within the meaning of *MiFID, Art 4(1), point 9* provided that

   (i) the investment firm is authorised to provide such portfolio management;

   (ii) it may only exercise the voting rights attached to such shares under instructions given in writing or by electronic means or it ensures that individual portfolio management services are conducted independently of any other services under conditions equivalent to those provided for under the *UCITS Directive* by putting into place appropriate mechanisms; and

   (iii) the investment firm exercises its voting rights independently from the parent undertaking.

   But the requirements for the aggregation of holdings applies if the parent undertaking, or another controlled undertaking of the parent undertaking, has invested in holdings managed by such investment firm and the investment firm has no discretion to exercise the voting rights attached to such holdings and may only exercise such voting rights under direct or indirect instructions from the parent or another controlled undertaking of the parent undertaking.

Conditions for exemption. For the purposes of the exemption to the aggregation of holdings provided in (*a*) and (*b*) above, a parent undertaking of a management company or of an investment firm must comply with the following conditions.

- It must not interfere by giving direct or indirect instructions (as defined) or in any other way in the exercise of the voting rights held by the management company or investment firm.
- The management company or investment firm must be free to exercise, independently of the parent undertaking, the voting rights attached to the assets it manages.

FCA requirements. A parent undertaking which wishes to make use of the exemption in relation to issuers subject to these provisions must, without delay, notify the following to the FCA.

(i) A list of the names of the management companies, investment firms or other entities, indicating the competent authorities that supervise them, but with no reference to the issuers concerned; and

(ii) a statement that, in the case of each such management company or investment firm, the parent undertaking complies with the conditions for exemption set out above.

The list must be updated on an ongoing basis.

Where the parent undertaking intends to benefit from the exemptions only in relation to the financial instruments referred to in the *Transparency Directive Art 13*, it must (in relation to financial instruments giving an entitlement to acquire shares which are admitted to trading on a regulated market) notify to the FCA only the list referred to in (i) above.

A parent undertaking of a management company or of an investment firm must be able to demonstrate to the FCA on request that

- the organisational structures of the parent undertaking and the management company or investment firm are such that the voting rights are exercised independently of the parent undertaking (which requirement implies, as a minimum, that the parent undertaking and the management company or investment firm have established written policies and procedures reasonably designed to prevent the distribution of information between the parent undertaking and the management company or investment firm in relation to the exercise of voting rights);
- the persons who decide how the voting rights are exercised act independently; and
- if the parent undertaking is a client of its management company or investment firm or has a holding in the assets managed by the management company or investment firm, there is a clear written mandate for an arm's-length customer relationship between the parent undertaking and the management company or investment firm.

(FCA Disclosure and Transparency Rules, paras 5.4.1 to 5.4.8). See paras 5.4.9 to 5.4.11 for the position where an undertaking is involved whose registered office is in a third country.

33.59 *Acquisition or disposal by issuer of own shares*

An issuer of shares must, if it acquires or disposes of its own shares (either itself or through a person acting in his own name but on the issuer's behalf), make public the percentage of voting rights attributable to those shares it holds as a result of the transaction as a whole, as soon as possible, but not later than four trading days following the acquisition or disposal, where that percentage reaches, exceeds or falls below the thresholds of 5% or 10% of the voting rights.

The percentage must be calculated on the basis of the total number of shares to which voting rights are attached.

For additional requirements in relation to a listed company which purchases its own equity shares, see **33.36**.

(FCA Disclosure and Transparency Rules, para 5.5).

33.60 *Disclosures by issuers*

An issuer must, at the end of each calendar month during which an increase or decrease has occurred, disclose to the public

- the total number of voting rights and capital in respect of each class of share which it issues; and
- the total number of voting rights attaching to shares of the issuer which are held by it in treasury.

Notwithstanding the above, if a relevant increase or decrease in the total number of voting rights occurs, an issuer must disclose the information (above) to the public as soon as possible and in any event no later than the end of the business day following the day on which the increase or decrease occurs. "Relevant increase or decrease" is any increase or decrease in the total number of voting rights produced when an issuer completes a transaction unless its effect on the total number of voting rights is immaterial when compared with the position before completion. It is for the issuer to assess whether the effect is immaterial. In the view of the FCA an increase or decrease of 1% or more is likely to be material both to the issuer and to the public.

The disclosure of the total number of voting rights should be in respect of each class of shares which is admitted to trading on a regulated or prescribed market.

Responsibility for all information drawn up and made public lies with the issuer.

(FCA Disclosure and Transparency Rules, para 5.6).

33.61 *Notification of combined holdings*

A person making a notification in accordance with **33.55** must do so by reference to each of the following.

- The aggregate of all voting rights which the person holds as shareholder and as the direct or indirect holder of financial instruments and financial instruments with similar economic effects.
- The aggregate of all voting rights held as direct or indirect shareholder (disregarding for this purpose holdings of financial instruments).
- The aggregate of all voting rights held as a result of direct and indirect holdings of and qualifying financial instruments. The aggregate of all voting rights deemed to be held as a result of direct and indirect holdings of financial instruments having similar economic effects to (but not including) qualifying financial instruments.

The effect of this is that a person may have to make a notification if the overall percentage level of his voting rights remains the same but there is notifiable change in the percentage level of one or more of the categories of voting rights held.

(FCA Disclosure and Transparency Rules, para 5.7).

33.62 *Procedures for the notification and disclosure of major holdings*

(1) *Information to be included*

(a) A notification in accordance with **33.55** must include the following information.

- The resulting situation in terms of voting rights.

- The chain of controlled undertakings through which voting rights are effectively held, if applicable.
- The date on which the threshold was reached or crossed.
- The identity of the shareholder, even if that shareholder is not entitled to exercise voting rights under the conditions laid down in **33.55**, and of the person entitled to exercise voting rights on behalf of that shareholder.

(b) A notification required of voting rights arising from the holding of financial instruments must include the following information.

- The resulting situation in terms of voting rights.
- If applicable, the chain of controlled undertakings through which financial instruments are effectively held.
- The date on which the threshold was reached or crossed.
- For instruments with an exercise period, an indication of the date or time period where shares will or can be acquired, if applicable.
- The date of maturity or expiration of the instrument.
- The identity of the holder.
- The name of the underlying issuer.

The notification must be made to the issuer of each of the underlying shares to which the financial instrument relates and, in the case of shares admitted to trading on a regulated market, to each competent authority of the Home States of such issuers.

If a financial instrument relates to more than one underlying share, a separate notification must be made to each issuer of the underlying shares.

(2) *Time of notification*

The notification to the issuer must be effected as soon as possible, but not later than four trading days in the case of a non-UK issuer and two trading days in all other cases, the first of which is the day after the date on which the relevant person

(a) learns of the acquisition or disposal or of the possibility of exercising voting rights, or on which, having regard to the circumstances, should have learned of it, regardless of the date on which the acquisition, disposal or possibility of exercising voting rights takes effect; or

(b) is informed about the event mentioned in **33.55**(*b*).

For the purposes of (*a*) above a person must, in relation to a transaction to which he is a party or which he has instructed, be deemed to have knowledge of the acquisition, disposal or possibility to exercise voting rights no later than two trading days following the transaction in question and where a transaction is conditional upon the approval by public authorities of the transaction or on a future uncertain event the occurrence of which is outside the control of the parties to the agreement, the parties are deemed to have knowledge of the acquisition, disposal or possibility of exercising voting rights only when the relevant approvals are obtained or when the event happens.

(3) *Obligation to notify*

The notification obligation following transactions of a kind mentioned in 33.56 are individual obligations of each direct shareholder or indirect shareholder there mentioned or both if the proportion of voting rights held by each party reaches, exceeds or falls below an applicable threshold.

In the circumstances in 33.56(*h*),

- if a shareholder gives the proxy in relation to one shareholder meeting, notification may be made by means of a single notification when the proxy is given, provided it is made clear in the notification what the resulting situation in terms of voting rights will be when the proxy may no longer exercise the voting rights discretion; and
- If the proxy holder receives one or more proxies in relation to one shareholder meeting, notification may be made by means of a single notification on or after the deadline for receiving proxies, provided that it is made clear in the notification what the resulting situation in terms of voting rights will be when the proxy may no longer exercise the voting rights at its discretion.

When the duty to make notification lies with more than one person, notification may be made by means of a single common notification but this does not release any of those persons from their responsibilities in relation to the notification.

(4) *Notification by parent undertaking, etc*

An undertaking is not required to make a notification if instead it is made by its parent undertaking or, where the parent undertaking is itself a controlled undertaking, by its own parent undertaking.

(5) *Calculation of voting rights*

Voting rights must be calculated on the basis of all the shares to which voting rights are attached even if the exercise of such rights is suspended and must be given in respect of all shares to which voting rights are attached.

The number of voting rights to be considered when calculating whether a threshold is reached, exceeded or fallen below is the number of voting rights in existence according to the issuer's most recent disclosure made in accordance with 33.60 but disregarding voting rights attached to any treasury shares held by the issuer (in accordance with the issuer's most recent disclosure of such holdings).

(6) *Notification to public by issuer*

An issuer must, on receipt of a notification, make public all of the information contained in it

(i) where the issuer does not fall within (ii) below and the shares in question are admitted to trading on a regulated market, as soon as possible and in any event by not later than the end of the trading day following receipt of the notification; and

(ii) where the issuer is a non-UK issuer or any other issuer whose shares are admitted to trading on a prescribed (but not a regulated) market, as soon as possible and in any event by not later than the end of the third trading day following receipt of the notification.

(FCA Disclosure and Transparency Rules, para 5.8).

33.63 *Filing of information with the FCA*

A person making a notification to an issuer to which these provisions apply must, if the notification relates to shares admitted to trading on a regulated market, at the same time file a copy of such notification with the FCA.

The information to be filed with the FCA must include a contact address of the person making the notification (but such details must be in a separate annex and not included on the form which is sent to the issuer).

Information filed with the FCA for these purposes must be filed using electronic means.

(FCA Disclosure and Transparency Rules, paras 5.9, 5.10).

33.64 *Non-EEA state issuers*

An issuer whose registered office is in a non-EEA State will be treated as meeting equivalent requirements to those set out in:

- **33.62**(6)(ii) (public notifications) provided that the period of time within which the notification of the major holdings is to be effected to the issuer and is to be made public by the issuer is in total equal to or shorter than seven trading days.
- **33.59** (treasury shares) provided that

  (i) if the issuer is only allowed to hold up to a maximum of 5% of its own shares to which voting rights are attached, a notification requirement is triggered under the law of the third country whenever this maximum threshold of 5% of the voting rights is reached or crossed;

  (ii) if the issuer is allowed to hold up to a maximum of between 5% and 10% of its own shares to which voting rights are attached, a notification requirement is triggered under the law of the non-EEA state whenever this maximum threshold and/or the 5% threshold of the voting rights are reached or crossed; and

  (iii) if the issuer is allowed to hold more than 10% of its own shares to which voting rights are attached, a notification requirement is triggered under the law of the non-EEA state whenever the 5% or 10% thresholds of the voting rights are reached or crossed.

  Notification above the 10% threshold is not required for this purpose.
- **33.60** (disclosure by issuers of total voting rights) provided that the issuer is required under the law of the non-EEA State to disclose to the public the total number of voting rights and capital within 30 calendar days after an increase or decrease of such total number has occurred.

An issuer whose registered office is in a non-EEA State whose relevant laws are considered equivalent by the FCA is exempted from the corresponding obligation in **33.55–33.63**.

The FCA maintains a published list of non-EEA States which, for the purposes of *Transparency Directive, Art 23.1*, are judged to have laws which lay down requirements equivalent to those imposed upon issuers under these provisions.

The notification requirements in **33.55** do not apply to a person in respect of the shares of an issuer which has its registered office in a non-EEA State whose laws have been considered equivalent for the purposes of *Transparency Directive, Art 23.1*.

(FCA Disclosure and Transparency Rules, para 5.11).

33.65 Information requirements for issuers of shares and debt securities

Unless otherwise stated, and subject to the exemptions listed at the end of the paragraph, the following provisions apply in relation to an issuer whose Home State (see **33.49**(5)) is the UK and references to transferable securities, shares and debt securities are to such instruments as are admitted to trading.

(1) **Amendments to constitution**

If an issuer of transferable securities proposes to amend its constitution, it must communicate the draft amendment to the FCA and the regulated market on which its securities have been admitted to trading. This must be done without delay but at the latest on the date of calling the general meeting which is to vote on, or be informed of, the amendment.

(2) **Equality of treatment**

An issuer of shares must ensure equal treatment for all holders of shares who are in the same position.

An issuer of debt securities must ensure that all holders of debt securities ranking pari passu are given equal treatment in respect of all the rights attaching to those debt securities.

(3) **Exercise of rights by holders**

An issuer of shares or debt securities must ensure that all the facilities and information necessary to enable holders of shares or debt securities to exercise their rights are available in the Home State and that the integrity of data is preserved.

(4) **Exercise of rights by proxy**

Shareholders and debt securities holders must not be prevented from exercising their rights by proxy, subject to the law of the country in which the issuer is incorporated.

An issuer of shares or debt securities must make available a proxy form, on paper or, where applicable, by electronic means to each person entitled to vote at a meeting of shareholders or a meeting of debt securities holders. The proxy form must be made available either together with the notice concerning the meeting or after the announcement of the meeting.

(5) **Appointment of a financial agent**

An issuer of shares or debt securities must designate, as its agent, a financial institution through which shareholders or debt securities holders may exercise their financial rights.

(6) **Electronic communications**

An issuer of shares or debt securities may use electronic means to convey information to shareholders or debt securities holders. To do so, it must comply with the following.

- A decision to use electronic means must be taken in a general meeting. But where the issuer is a company within the meaning of *CA 2006*, this does not prevent it from using other means to make the decision if it could have used such means before 20 January 2007.
- The use of electronic means must not depend upon the location of the seat or residence of
  - (i) the shareholder;
  - (ii) the persons referred to **33.56**(*a*)–(*h*); or
  - (iii) a proxy representing a debt security holder.

- Identification arrangements must be put in place so that the shareholders, debt security holders or other persons entitled to exercise or to direct the exercise of voting rights are effectively informed.

- Shareholders, debt security holders or persons referred to **33.56**(*a*)–(*e*) who are entitled to acquire, dispose of or exercise voting rights must be

  (i) contacted in writing to request their consent for the use of electronic means for conveying information and if they do not object within a reasonable period of time, their consent can be considered to have been given; and

  (ii) able to request at any time in the future that information be conveyed in writing.

  But this does not apply in any case where *CA 2006, Sch 5* applies. See **16.28 Dealings With Third Parties**.

- Any apportionment of the costs entailed in the conveyance of information by electronic means must be determined by the issuer in compliance with the principle of equal treatment in (2) above.

(7) **Information about changes in rights attaching to securities**

An issuer of shares must without delay disclose to the public any change in the rights attaching to its various classes of shares, including changes in the rights attaching to derivative securities issued by the issuer giving access to the shares of that issuer.

An issuer of securities other than shares admitted to trading on a regulated market must disclose to the public without delay any changes in the rights of holders of securities other than shares, including changes in the terms and conditions of such securities which could indirectly affect those rights, resulting in particular from a change in loan terms or in interest rates.

An issuer of securities admitted to trading on a regulated market (other than an issuer which is a public international body of which at least one EEA State is a member) must disclose to the public without delay any new loan issues and in particular any guarantee or security in respect of such issues.

(8) **Information about meetings, issue of new shares and payment of dividends – share issuers**

An issuer of shares must

- provide information to holders on

  (i) the place, time and agenda of meetings;

  (ii) the total number of shares and voting rights; and

  (iii) the rights of holders to participate in meetings; and

- publish notices or distribute circulars concerning the allocation and payment of dividends and the issue of new shares, including information on any arrangements for allotment, subscription, cancellation or conversion.

(9) **Information about meetings, and payment of interest – debt security issuers**

An issuer of debt securities must publish notices or distribute circulars concerning

- the place, time and agenda of meetings of debt securities holders;
- the payment of interest;
- the exercise of any conversion, exchange, subscription or cancellation rights and repayment; and
- the rights of holders to exercise their rights in relation to the above.

If only holders of debt securities whose denomination per unit amounts to at least 50,000 euros (or an equivalent amount) are to be invited to a meeting, the issuer may choose as a venue any EEA State, provided that all the facilities and information necessary to enable such holders to exercise their rights are made available in that EEA State.

Exemptions.

(a) *Non-EEA State exemption*

An issuer whose registered office is in a non-EEA State whose relevant laws are considered equivalent by the FCA is exempted from (2)–(9) above. The FCA maintains a published list of non-EEA States which, for the purposes of *Transparency Directive, Art 23.1*, are judged to have laws which lay down requirements equivalent to those imposed upon issuers under these provisions.

(b) *Regional or local authorities*

A regional or local authority with securities admitted to trading is not required to comply with (3)–(6) and (9) above.

(c) *Issuers of convertible securities, preference shares and depository receipts*

The provisions in (2)–(6), (8) and (9) above do not apply to

- an issuer of transferable securities convertible into shares;
- an issuer of preference shares; or
- an issuer of depository receipts.

(FCA Disclosure and Transparency Rules, para 6.1).

33.66 Filing information and use of language

The provisions in this paragraph apply to

- an issuer whose transferable securities are admitted to trading and whose Home State (see **33.49**(5)) is the UK; and
- a person who has requested, without the issuer's consent, the admission of its transferable securities to trading on a regulated market.

(1) **Filing of information with the FCA**

An issuer or person that discloses regulated information must, at the same time, file that information with the FCA. The requirement can be complied with by using a primary information provider to disseminate the information in accordance with **33.67**.

(2) **Language**

If transferable securities are admitted to trading

(a) only in the UK and the UK is the Home State, regulated information must be disclosed in English;

(b) in more than one EEA State including the UK and the UK is the Home State, regulated information must be disclosed

  (i) in English; and

  (ii) either in a language accepted by the competent authorities of each Host State or in a language customary in the sphere of international finance, at the choice of the issuer;

(c) in one or more EEA States excluding the UK and the UK is the Home State, regulated information must be disclosed either

  (i) in a language accepted by the competent authorities of those Host States; or

  (ii) in a language customary in the sphere of international finance, at the choice of the issuer; and

(d) without the issuer's consent, *(a)*–*(c)* above apply to the person who has requested such admission (and do not apply to the issuer).

If transferable securities whose denomination per unit amounts to at least 50,000 euros (or an equivalent amount) are admitted to trading in the UK or in one or more EEA States, regulated information must be disclosed to the public in either a language accepted by the competent authorities of the Home State and Host States or in a language customary in the sphere of international finance, at the choice of the issuer or of the person who, without the issuer's consent, has requested such admission.

(FCA Disclosure and Transparency Rules, para 6.2).

33.67 Dissemination of information

This paragraph applies to

- an issuer whose transferable securities are admitted to trading and whose Home State (see **33.49**(5)) is the UK;
- a person who has applied, without the issuer's consent, for the admission of its transferable securities to trading on a regulated market; and
- transferable securities that are admitted to trading only in the UK which is the Host State and not in the Home State.

An issuer or person must disclose 'regulated information' in the manner set out in (1)–(8) below. When disseminating such information, an issuer or other person must ensure that the minimum standards described below are met and must entrust a RIS with the disclosure of the information to the public, ensuring that the RIS complies with those minimum standards.

Where an issuer uses a RIS (other than a RIS which is a primary information provider or an EEA approved incoming society service or a person to whom DTR TP 1.22 applies), the issuer must provide an annual written confirmation to the FCA that all regulated information disseminated by a RIS in the previous financial year was disseminated in accordance with the minimum standards set out in DTR 6.3.4 to DTR 6.3.8.

The confirmation must

(a) be provided by, in the case of an issuer the audit committee or the body referred to in DTR7.1.1 or in the case of a person which is not an issuer but is a body corporate, the audit committee or the board of directors or in the case of a person which is not an issuer or a body corporate, a person with corresponding powers to a director;

(b) set out the basis for making the confirmation, including the steps taken to determine its accuracy; and

(c) be supported by records which are sufficient to reasonably demonstrate the basis for making the confirmation and capable of timely retrieval.

The FCA may also request information from an issuer or person under *FSMA 2000, s 89H* on an *ad hoc* basis to verify that the regulated information disseminated by a RIS (as above) has been disseminated in accordance with DTR 6.3.4 to DTR6.3.8.

'*Regulated information*' means all information which that person must disclose under the *Transparency Directive*, the *Market Abuse Directive, Art 6*, the Listing Rules or the Disclosure and Transparency Rules.

(1) Regulated information must be disseminated in a manner ensuring that it is capable of being disseminated to as wide a public as possible, and as close to simultaneously as possible in the Home Member State and in other EEA States.

(2) Regulated information, other than regulated information within (3) below) must be communicated to the media in unedited full text.

(3) An annual financial report that is required by **33.51** to be made public is not required to be communicated to the media in unedited full text unless the information is of a type that would be required to be disseminated in a half-yearly financial report.

(4) The announcement relating to the publication of the following regulated information must include an indication of the website on which the relevant documents are available.

- An annual financial report that is required by **33.51** to be made public.
- A half-yearly financial report that is required by **33.52** to be made public.

(5) Regulated information must be communicated to the media in a manner which ensures the security of the communication, minimises the risk of data corruption and unauthorised access, and provides certainty as to the source of the regulated information. Security of receipt must be ensured by remedying as soon as possible any failure or disruption in the communication of regulated information. An issuer or person is not responsible for systemic errors or shortcomings at the media to which the regulated information has been communicated.

(6) Regulated information must be communicated to a RIS in a way which

- makes clear that the information is regulated information;
- identifies clearly
  - (i) the issuer concerned;
  - (ii) the subject matter of the regulated information; and
  - (iii) the time and date of the communication of the regulated information by the issuer or the person.

(7) Upon request, an issuer or other person must be able to communicate to the FCA, in relation to any disclosure of regulated information

- the name of the person who communicated the regulated information to the RIS;
- the security validation details;
- the time and date on which the regulated information was communicated to the RIS;
- the medium in which the regulated information was communicated; and
- details of any embargo placed by the issuer on the regulated information, if applicable.

(8) An issuer or person must not charge investors any specific cost for providing regulated information.

(FCA Disclosure and Transparency Rules, para 6.3).

33.68 Disclosure of information in a non-EEA State

Information that is disclosed in a non-EEA State which may be of importance to the public in the EEA must be disclosed in accordance with the provisions in **33.66** and **33.67**. This also applies to information that is not regulated information.

(FCA Disclosure and Transparency Rules, para 6.3.10).

33.69 Compensation for statements in certain publications

FSMA 2000, s 90A provides that *Schedule 10A* (*FSMA*) makes provision for the liability of issuers of securities to pay compensation to persons who have suffered loss as a result of

(i) a misleading statement or dishonest omission in certain published information relating to the securities or

(ii) a dishonest delay in publishing such information.

Schedule 10A applies to securities that are with the consent of the issuer

- admitted to trading on a securities market situated or operating in the UK; or
- traded on a regulated market situated or operating outside the UK but issued by an issuer where the UK is the issuer's home state

The issuer of securities to which these provisions apply is liable to pay compensation to a person who

(a) acquires, continues to hold or disposes of such securities issued by it in reliance on published information to which *FSMA 2000, Schedule 10A* applies and

(b) suffers loss in respect of the securities as a result of

  (i) any untrue or misleading statement in that published information; or

  (ii) the omission from that published information of any matter required to be included in it or

  (iii) the delay by the issuer in publishing information to which FSMA 2000 Schedule 10A relates

FSMA 2000, Schedule 10A only applies to information published by the issuer of securities by recognised means or by other means where the availability of the information has been announced by the issuer by recognised means. It is immaterial whether the information is required to be published (by recognised means or otherwise).

"Recognised means" are either a recognised information service as defined in *FSMA 2000, Schedule 10A, para 2(4)* or other means required or authorised to be used to communicate information to the market in question, or to the public, when a recognised information service is available.

The issuer is liable

- only if a 'person discharging managerial responsibilities' within the issuer
  - (i) knew the statement to be untrue or misleading or was reckless as to whether it was untrue or misleading; or
  - (ii) knew the omission to be a dishonest concealment of a material fact; or
  - (iii) acted dishonestly in delaying the publication of the information.
- a loss is not regarded as suffered as a result of the statement or omission unless the person suffering it acquired, continued to hold or disposed of the relevant securities
  - (i) in reliance on the information in question; and
  - (ii) at a time when, and in circumstances in which, it was reasonable for him to rely on it

An issuer is also not liable to pay compensation if the published information is contained in listing particulars or a prospectus (or supplementary listing particulars or a supplementary prospectus) and the issuer is liable under *FSMA 2000, s 90* to pay compensation.

The issuer is not subject to any liability other than provided for in respect of such loss suffered and a person other than the issuer is not subject to any liability other than to the issuer in respect of any such loss. This does not affect

- civil liability under *FSMA 2000, s 90* or *CA 2006, s 954* or for breach of contract or under the *Misrepresentation Act 1967* or arising from a person's having assumed responsibility to a particular person, for a particular purpose, for the accuracy or completeness of the information concerned
- liability to a civil penalty
- criminal liability
- the powers conferred by *FSMA 2000, ss 382* and *384*.

'*Relevant publications*' are

- any reports and statements published in response to a requirement imposed by a provision of the Transparency Rules; and
- any preliminary statement made in advance of such a report or statement to the extent that it contains information that is intended will appear in the report or statement and will be presented there is substantially the same form.

A '*person discharging managerial responsibilities*' within an issuer is

(i) any director of the issuer (or person occupying the position of director, by whatever name called);

(ii) in the case of an issuer whose affairs are managed by its members, any member of the issuer; and

(iii) in the case of an issuer that has no persons within (i) or (ii) above, any senior executive of the issuer having responsibilities in relation to the information in question or its publication.

"Securities" means transferable securities within the meaning of Article 4.1.18 of the Markets in Financial Instruments Directive (the Directive) other than money-market instruments as defined in Article 4.1.19 of the Directive that have a maturity of less than 12 months.

"Securities market" means a regulated market as defined in Article 4.1.14 of the Directive, a mutilateral trading facility as defined in Article 4.1. 15 of the Directive or a market or facility of a corresponding description outside the EEA.

[*FSMA 2000, s 90A; CA 2006, s 1270*].

33.70 PENALTIES

The FCA may impose a penalty of such amount as it considers appropriate in the following circumstances.

(a) If it considers that an issuer of listed securities or an applicant for listing has contravened any provision of the Listing Rules.

(b) If it considers that

(i) an issuer who has requested or approved the admission of a financial instrument to trading on a regulated market,

(ii) a 'person discharging managerial responsibilities within such an issuer' (see 33.47), or

(iii) a person connected to such a person discharging managerial responsibilities (see 33.47),

has contravened any provision of the Disclosure Rules.

(c) If it considers that

(i) a person has contravened a provision of the Transparency Rules or a provision otherwise made in accordance with the *Transparency Obligations Directive*,

(ii) a person on whom a requirement has been imposed under *FSMA 2000, s 89L* (power to suspend or prohibit trading of securities in a case of infringement of an applicable transparency obligation) has contravened that requirement.

(d) If it considers that any person has contravened a provision of the Corporate Governance Rules.

Where the person in (*a*), (*b*)(i), (*c*) or (*d*) above is a company, if the FCA considers that a person who was at the material time a director of the company was knowingly concerned in the contravention, it may impose upon him a penalty of such amount as it considers appropriate.

As an alternative to a penalty, the FCA may instead publish a statement censuring the person concerned.

Any action (whether penalty or censure) taken by the FCA under these provisions must be within two years beginning with the first day on which it knew of the contravention unless proceedings against that person, in respect of the contravention, were begun before the end of that period.

Procedure. If the FCA proposes to take action against a person under these provisions, it must give him a warning notice which must state the amount of the proposed penalty or, as the case may be, set out the terms of the proposed statement.

If, after considering any representations made in response to the warning notice, the FCA decides to take action, it must issue a decision notice which must state the amount of the penalty or, as the case may be, set out the terms of the statement.

Where the FCA decides to take action against a person, he may refer the matter to the Tribunal.

[*FSMA 2000, ss 91, 92; CA 2006, Sch 15 para 6*].

33.71 APPOINTMENT OF INVESTIGATORS BY THE FCA

If it appears to the FCA that there are circumstances suggesting that

- there may have been a contravention of a
  - (i) a provision of *FSMA 2000, Pt VI*,
  - (ii) a provision of the Listing Rules, Disclosure Rules, Transparency Rules or Corporate Governance Rules, or
  - (iii) a provision otherwise made in accordance with the *Prospective Directive* or the *Transparency Obligations Directive*, or
- a person, who was at the material time a director of a company falling within **33.70** (*a*), (*b*)(i), (*c*) or (*d*) and has been knowingly concerned in a contravention of any such provision,

the FCA may appoint one or more competent persons to conduct an investigation on its behalf.

[*FSMA 2000, s 97; CA 2006, Sch 15 para 8*].

33.72 FCA: EXEMPTION FROM LIABILITY IN DAMAGES

Neither the FCA nor any person who is a member, officer or member of staff of the FCA is to be liable in damages for anything done or omitted in the discharge of the authority's functions unless the act or omission is shown to have been in bad faith. But this exemption does not prevent an award of damages made in respect of an act or omission on the ground that it was unlawful as a result of *Human Rights Act 1998, s 6(1)*.

[*FSMA 2000, s 102*].

33: APPENDIX: THE MODEL CODE

Introduction

This Code imposes restrictions on dealing in the securities of a listed company beyond those imposed by law. Its purpose is to ensure that persons discharging managerial responsibilities do not abuse, and do not place themselves under suspicion of abusing, inside information that they may be thought to have, especially in periods leading up to an announcement of the company's results.

Nothing in this Code sanctions a breach of [*FSMA 2000, s 118*] (market abuse), the insider dealing provisions of the *Criminal Justice Act 1993* or any other relevant legal or regulatory requirements.

Definitions

1 In this Code the following definitions, in addition to those contained in the Listing Rules, apply unless the context requires otherwise:

(a) '*close period*' means:
- (i) the period of 60 days immediately preceding a preliminary announcement of the listed company's annual results or, if shorter, the period from the end of the relevant financial year up to and including the time of announcement; or
- (ii) the period of 60 days immediately preceding the publication of its annual financial report or if shorter the period from the end of the relevant financial year up to and including the time of such publication; and
- (iii) if the listed company reports on a half-yearly basis, the period from the end of the relevant financial period up to and including the time of such publication; and
- (iv) if the listed company reports on a quarterly basis, the period of 30 days immediately preceding the announcement of the quarterly results or, if shorter, the period from the end of the relevant financial period up to and including the time of the announcement;

(b) '*connected person*' has the meaning given in [*FSMA 2000, s 96B(2)*] (persons discharging managerial responsibilities and connected persons [see **33.47**]);

(c) '*dealing*' includes:
- (i) any acquisition or disposal of, or agreement to acquire or dispose of any of the securities of the company;
- (ii) entering into a contract (including a contract for difference) the purpose of which is to secure a profit or avoid a loss by reference to fluctuations in the price of any of the securities of the company;
- (iii) the grant, acceptance, acquisition, disposal, exercise or discharge of any option (whether for the call, or put or both) to acquire or dispose of any of the securities of the company;
- (iv) entering into, or terminating, assigning or novating any stock lending agreement in respect of the securities of the company;
- (v) using as security, or otherwise granting a charge, lien or other encumbrance over the securities of the company;
- (vi) any transaction, including a transfer for nil consideration, or the exercise of any power or discretion effecting a change of ownership of a beneficial interest in the securities of the company; or

(vii) any other right or obligation, present or future, conditional or unconditional, to acquire or dispose of any securities of the company;

(d) . . .

(e) '*prohibited period*' means:

(i) any close period; or

(ii) any period when there exists any matter which constitutes inside information in relation to the company;

(f) '*restricted person*' means a person discharging managerial responsibilities; and

(g) '*securities of the company*' means any publicly traded or quoted securities of the company or any member of its group or any securities that are convertible into such securities.

Dealings not subject to the provisions of this Code

2 The following dealings are not subject to the provisions of this Code:

(a) undertakings or elections to take up entitlements under a rights issue or other offer (including an offer of securities of the company in lieu of a cash dividend);

(b) the take up of entitlements under a rights issue or other offer (including an offer of securities of the company in lieu of a cash dividend);

(c) allowing entitlements to lapse under a rights issue or other offer (including an offer of securities of the company in lieu of a cash dividend);

(d) the sale of sufficient entitlements nil-paid to take up the balance of the entitlements under a rights issue;

(e) undertakings to accept, or the acceptance of, a takeover offer;

(f) dealing where the beneficial interest in the relevant security of the company does not change;

(g) transactions conducted between a person discharging managerial responsibilities and their spouse, civil partner, child or step-child (within the meaning of *FSMA 2000, s 96B(2)*);

(h) transfers of shares arising out of the operation of an employees' share scheme into a savings scheme investing in securities of the company following:

(i) exercise of an option under an approved SAYE option scheme; or

(ii) release of shares from a HM Revenue and Customs approved share incentive plan;

(i) with the exception of a disposal of securities of the company received by a restricted person as a participant, dealings in connection with the following employees' share schemes

- an HM Revenue and Customs approved SAYE option scheme or share incentive plan, under which participation is extended on similar terms to all or most employees of the participating companies in that scheme; or
- a scheme on similar terms to a HM Revenue and Customs approved SAYE option scheme or share incentive plan, under which participation is extended on similar terms to all or most employees of the participating companies in that scheme;

(j) the cancellation or surrender of an option under an employees' share scheme;

(k) transfers of the securities of the company by an independent trustee of an employees' share scheme to a beneficiary who is not a restricted person;

(l) transfers of securities of the company already held by means of a matched sale and purchase into a saving scheme or into a pension scheme in which the restricted person is a participant or beneficiary;

(m) an investment by a restricted person in a scheme or arrangement where the assets of the scheme (other than a scheme investing only in the securities of the company) or arrangement are invested at the discretion of a third party;

(n) a dealing by a restricted person in the units of an authorised unit trust or in shares in an open-ended investment company; and
(o) *bona fide* gifts to a restricted person by a third party.

Dealing by restricted persons

3 A restricted person must not deal in any securities of the company without obtaining clearance to deal in advance in accordance with paragraph 4 of this Code.

Clearance to deal

4 (a) A director (other than the chairman or chief executive) or company secretary must not deal in any securities of the company without first notifying the chairman (or a director designated by the board for this purpose) and receiving clearance to deal from him.

(b) The chairman must not deal in any securities of the company without first notifying the chief executive and receiving clearance to deal from him or, if the chief executive is not present, without first notifying the senior independent director, or a committee of the board or other officer of the company nominated for that purpose by the chief executive, and receiving clearance to deal from that director, committee or officer.

(c) The chief executive must not deal in any securities of the company without first notifying the chairman and receiving clearance to deal from him or, if the chairman is not present, without first notifying the senior independent director, or a committee of the board or other officer of the company nominated for that purpose by the chairman, and receiving clearance to deal from that director, committee or officer.

(d) If the role of chairman and chief executive are combined, that person must not deal in any securities of the company without first notifying the board and receiving clearance to deal from the board.

(e) Persons discharging managerial responsibilities (who are not directors) must not deal in any securities of the company without first notifying the company secretary or a designated director and receiving clearance to deal from him.

5 A response to a request for clearance to deal must be given to the relevant restricted person within five business days of the request being made.

6 The company must maintain a record of the response to any dealing request made by a restricted person and of any clearance given. A copy of the response and clearance (if any) must be given to the restricted person concerned.

7 A restricted person who is given clearance to deal in accordance with paragraph 4 must deal as soon as possible and in any event within two business days of clearance being received.

Circumstances for refusal

8 A restricted person must not be given clearance to deal in any securities of the company:

(a) during a prohibited period; or
(b) on considerations of a short term nature. An investment with a maturity of one year or less will always be considered to be of a short term nature.

Dealings permitted during a prohibited period: Dealing in exceptional circumstances

9 A restricted person, who is not in possession of inside information in relation to the company, may be given clearance to deal if he is in severe financial

difficulty or there are other exceptional circumstances. Clearance may be given for such a person to sell (but not purchase) securities of the company when he would otherwise be prohibited by this Code from doing so. The determination of whether the person in question is in severe financial difficulty or whether there are other exceptional circumstances can only be made by the director designated for this purpose.

10 A person may be in severe financial difficulty if he has a pressing financial commitment that cannot be satisfied otherwise than by selling the relevant securities of the company. A liability of such a person to pay tax would not normally constitute severe financial difficulty unless the person has no other means of satisfying the liability. A circumstance will be considered exceptional if the person in question is required by a court order to transfer or sell the securities of the company or there is some other overriding legal requirement for him to do so.

11 The FCA should be consulted at an early stage regarding any application by a restricted person to deal in exceptional circumstances.

Awards of securities and options

12 The grant of options by the board of directors under an employees' share scheme to individuals who are not restricted persons may be permitted during a prohibited period if such grant could not reasonably be made at another time and failure to make the grant would be likely to indicate that the company was in a prohibited period.

13 The award by the company of securities, the grant of options and the grant of rights (or other interests) to acquire securities of the company to restricted persons is permitted in a prohibited period if:

(a) the award or grant is made under the terms of an employees' share scheme and the scheme was not introduced or amended during the relevant prohibited period; and
(b) either:
  (i) the terms of such employees' share scheme set out the timing of the award or grant and such terms have either previously been approved by shareholders or summarised or described in a document sent to shareholders, or
  (ii) the timing of the award or grant is in accordance with the timing of previous awards or grants under the scheme; and
(c) the terms of the employees' share scheme set out the amount or value of the award or grant or the basis on which the amount or value of the award or grant is calculated and do not allow the exercise of discretion; and
(d) the failure to make the award or grant would be likely to indicate that the company is in a prohibited period.

Exercise of options

14 Where a company has been in an exceptionally long prohibited period or the company has had a number of consecutive prohibited periods, clearance may be given to allow the exercise of an option or right under an employees' share scheme, or the conversion of a convertible security, where the final date for the exercise of such option or right, or conversion of such security, falls during a prohibited period and the restricted person could not reasonably have been expected to exercise it at a time when he was free to deal.

15 Where the exercise or conversion is permitted pursuant to paragraph 14, clearance may not be given for the sale of the securities of the company acquired pursuant to such exercise or conversion including the sale of sufficient securities of the company to fund the costs of the exercise or conversion and/or any tax liability arising from the exercise or conversion unless a binding undertaking to do so was entered into when the company was not in a prohibited period.

Qualification shares

16 Clearance may be given to allow a director to acquire qualification shares where, under the company's constitution, the final date for acquiring such shares falls during a prohibited period and the director could not reasonably have been expected to acquire those shares at another time.

Saving schemes

17 A restricted person may enter into a scheme under which only the securities of the company are purchased pursuant to a regular standing order or direct debit or by regular deduction from the person's salary, or where such securities are acquired by way of a standing election to re-invest dividends or other distributions received, or are acquired as part payment of the person's remuneration without regard to the provisions of this Code, if the following provisions are complied with:

(a) the restricted person does not enter into the scheme during a prohibited period, unless the scheme involves the part payment of remuneration in the form of securities of the company and is entered into upon the commencement of the person's employment or in the case of a non-executive director his appointment to the board;
(b) the restricted person does not carry out the purchase of the securities of the company under the scheme during a prohibited period, unless the restricted person entered into the scheme at a time when the company was not in a prohibited period and that person is irrevocably bound under the terms of the scheme to carry out a purchase of securities of the company (which may include the first purchase under the scheme) at a fixed point in time which falls in a prohibited period;
(c) the restricted person does not cancel or vary the terms of his participation, or carry out sales of securities of the company within the scheme during a prohibited period; and
(d) before entering into the scheme, cancelling the scheme or varying the terms of his participation or carrying out sales of the securities of the company within the scheme, the restricted person obtains clearance in accordance with paragraph 4.

Acting as a trustee

18 Where a restricted person is acting as a trustee, dealing in the securities of the company by that trust is permitted during a prohibited period where:

(a) the restricted person is not a beneficiary of the trust; and
(b) the decision to deal is taken by the other trustees or by investment managers on behalf of the trustees independently of the restricted person.

19 The other trustees or investment managers acting on behalf of the trustees can be assumed to have acted independently where the decision to deal:

(a) was taken without consultation with, or other involvement of, the restricted person; or
(b) was delegated to a committee of which the restricted person is not a member.

Dealing by connected persons and investment managers

20 A person discharging managerial responsibilities must take reasonable steps to prevent any dealings by or on behalf of any connected person of his in any securities of the company on considerations of a short term nature.

21 A person discharging managerial responsibilities must seek to prohibit any dealings in the securities of the company during a close period:

(a) by or on behalf of any connected person of his; or

(b) by an investment manager on his behalf or on behalf of any person connected with him where either he or any person connected has funds under management with that investment fund manager, whether or not discretionary (save as provided by paragraphs 17 and 18).

22 A person discharging managerial responsibilities must advise all of his connected persons and investment managers acting on his behalf:

(a) of the name of the listed company within which he is a person discharging managerial responsibilities;
(b) of the close periods during which they cannot deal in the securities of the company; and
(c) that they must advise the listed company immediately after they have dealt in securities of the company.

Dealing under a trading plan

23 A restricted person may deal in securities of a company pursuant to a trading plan if clearance has first been given in accordance with paragraph 4 of this Code to the person entering into the plan and to any amendment to the plan. A restricted person must not cancel a trading plan unless clearance has first been given in accordance with paragraph 4 of this Code for its cancellation.

24 A restricted person must not enter into a trading plan or amend a trading plan during a prohibited period and clearance under paragraph 4 of this Code must not be given during a prohibited period to the entering into, or amendment of, a trading plan. Clearance under paragraph 4 of this Code may be given during a prohibited period to the cancellation of a trading plan but only in the exceptional circumstances referred to in paragraphs 9 and 10 of this Code.

25 A restricted person may deal in securities of a company during a prohibited period pursuant to a trading plan if:

(a) the trading plan was entered into before the prohibited period;
(b) clearance under paragraph 4 of this Code has been given to the person entering into the trading plan and to any amendment to the trading plan before the prohibited period; and
(c) the trading plan does not permit the restricted person to exercise any influence or discretion over how, when, or whether to effect dealings.

26 Where a transaction occurs in accordance with a trading plan, the restricted person must notify the issuer at the same time as he makes the notification required by DTR 3.1.2 R [see 33.47] of:

(a) the fact that the transaction occurred in accordance with a trading plan; and
(b) the date on which the relevant trading plan was entered into.

(FCA Listing Rules, Chapter 9, Annex).

34 Purchase of Own Shares

34.1 **General rule against company acquiring its own shares**
34.2 **Redeemable shares**
34.3 Provisions relating to the redemption
34.4 **Purchase of own shares**
34.5 Provisions relating to the purchase
34.6 Authority for off-market purchase
34.7 Authority for market purchase
34.8 Payments apart from purchase price to be made out of distributable profits
34.9 Disclosure requirements
34.10 **Redemption or purchase by private company out of capital**
34.11 Available profits
34.12 Requirements for payment out of capital
34.12A Reduced requirements for payments out of capital for purchase of own shares: employees' share schemes
34.13 Objections by members or creditors
34.14 **Treasury shares**
34.15 Disposal of treasury shares
34.16 Cancellation of treasury shares
34.17 Offences relating to treasury shares
34.18 **The capital redemption reserve**
34.19 **Effect of company's failure to purchase or redeem shares**
34.20 **Financial assistance for purchase of own shares**
34.21 Exceptions from prohibition
34.22 **Shares held by company's nominee**
34.23 **Duty to cancel shares in public company held by or for the company**
34.24 Notice of cancellation of shares
34.25 Re-registration as a private company in consequence of cancellation
34.26 Offences for failure to cancel or re-register
34.27 Application of the provisions to company re-registering as a public company
34.28 Accounting treatment of shares held by public company or nominee
34.29 **Beneficial interest**
34.30 **Charges of public company on own shares**

Cross-references. See **33.28** and **33.36 Public and Listed Companies** for additional requirements of listed companies in connection with own share purchase under the Listing Rules.

34.1 GENERAL RULE AGAINST COMPANY ACQUIRING ITS OWN SHARES

Subject to the exceptions below, a limited company must not acquire its own shares, whether by purchase, subscription or otherwise, except in accordance with the provisions in this chapter. [*CA 2006, s 658(1)*]. See *Trevor v Whitworth* (1887) 12 App Cas 409, HL.

If a company purports to act in contravention of this,

- the purported acquisition is void; and
- an offence is committed by the company and every officer of the company who is default. A person guilty of such an offence is liable (i) on conviction on indictment, to imprisonment for a term not exceeding two years or a fine (or both); and (ii) on summary conviction, to imprisonment for a term not exceeding twelve months (six months in Scotland and Northern Ireland) or to a fine not exceeding the statutory maximum (or both). See **29.1 Offences and Legal Proceedings** for the statutory maximum.

[*CA 2006, s 658(2)(3)*].

Exceptions.

(a) A limited company may acquire any of its own fully paid shares otherwise than for valuable consideration. See *Kirby v Wilkins* [1929] 2 Ch 444, [1929] All ER Rep 356 and *Castiglione's Will Trusts, Re, Hunter v Mackenzie* [1958] Ch 549, [1958] 1 All ER 480 for shares acquired by way of gift and bequeathed by will respectively.

(b) The general provisions in *CA 2006, s 658* above do not prohibit

- the acquisition of shares in a reduction of share capital duly made (see **47.51 Shares**);
- the purchase of shares in pursuance of a court order under
  - (i) *CA 2006, s 98* (application to court to cancel resolution for re-registration as a private company, see **41.9 Re-Registration**);
  - (ii) *CA 2006, s 721(6)* (powers of court on objection to redemption or purchase of shares out of capital, see **34.13**(*d*));
  - (iii) *CA 2006, s 759* (remedial order in case of breach of prohibition of public offers by private company, see **47.22 Shares**); or
  - (iv) *CA 2006, ss 994–999* (protection of members against unfair prejudice, see **26.10 Members**); and
- the forfeiture of shares, or the acceptance of shares surrendered in lieu, in pursuance of the articles, for failure to pay any sum payable in respect of the shares (see **47.25 Shares**).

[*CA 2006, s 659*].

The above provisions do not preclude a company from acquiring the shares of another company even in circumstances where the sole asset of the acquired company is shares in the acquiring company (*Acatos & Hutcheson plc v Watson* [1995] 1 BCLC 218, [1995] BCC 446).

34.2 REDEEMABLE SHARES

A limited company having a share capital may issue shares that are to be redeemed or are liable to be redeemed at the option of the company or the shareholder ('*redeemable shares*'), subject to the following provisions.

- The articles of a private limited company may exclude or restrict the issue of redeemable shares.
- A public limited company may only issue redeemable shares if it is authorised to do so by its articles.
- No redeemable shares must be issued at a time when there are no issued shares of the company that are not redeemable.

[*CA 2006, s 684*].

See **34.10–34.13** for provisions applying where a private company makes a payment for the redemption out of capital and **34.18** for the requirement to create a capital redemption reserve.

34.3 Provisions relating to the redemption

Terms and manner of the redemption. The directors of a limited company may determine the terms, conditions and manner of the redemption of shares if authorised to do so by

- the articles; or
- a resolution of the company (which may be an ordinary resolution even though it amends the articles).

Where the directors are so authorised, they must determine the terms, etc before the shares are allotted. Any obligation of the company to state in a statement of capital (see below) the rights attached to shares extends to the terms, conditions and manner of redemption.

Where the directors are not so authorised, the terms, conditions and manner of redemption of any redeemable shares must be stated in the company's articles.

[*CA 2006, s 685*].

Payment for redeemable shares. Redeemable shares in a limited company

(a) may not be redeemed unless they are fully paid; and

(b) must be paid for on the redemption date unless the terms of redemption provide that, by agreement between the company and the shareholders, the amount payable may be paid on a later date.

[*CA 2006, s 686*].

Transitional provisions. The provisions in (*b*) above apply to

(i) shares issued on or after 1 October 2009; and

(ii) shares issued before that date where the terms of redemption have been amended on or after that date to allow for payment on a date later than the redemption date.

[*SI 2008 No 2860, Sch 2 para 73*].

Financing of the redemption. Subject to the power of *private* companies to redeem shares out of capital (see **34.10**) and the enforcement of redemption against a company when shares have not been redeemed at the commencement of winding up (see **34.19**)

- redeemable shares in a limited company may only be redeemed out of
  - (i) 'distributable profits' of the company; or
  - (ii) the proceeds of a fresh issue of shares made for the purpose of the redemption; and
- any premium payable on redemption of shares in a limited company must be paid out of distributable profits of the company except that if the redeemable shares were issued at a premium, any premium payable on redemption may be paid out of the proceeds of a fresh issue of shares made for the purpose of the redemption, up to an amount equal to
  - (i) the aggregate of the premiums received by the company on the issue of the shares redeemed, or

(ii) the current amount of the company's share premium account (including any amount transferred to that account in respect of premiums on the new shares),

whichever is the less. The amount of the company's share premium account is reduced by a sum corresponding (or by sums in aggregate corresponding) to the amount of any premium payable on redemption.

'*Distributable profits*' are those profits out of which the company could lawfully make a distribution (see **22.1 Distributions**) equal in value to the payment. [*CA 2006, ss 687, 736*].

Cancellation of shares. When shares in a limited company are redeemed, the shares are treated as cancelled and the company's issued share capital is diminished by the nominal value of those shares. [*CA 2006, s 688*].

Notice to Registrar of Companies of redemption. If a limited company redeems any redeemable shares, it must within one month give notice to the Registrar of Companies, specifying the shares redeemed. The notice must be accompanied by a statement of capital. This must state, with respect to the company's share capital immediately following the redemption, the following particulars.

- The total number of shares of the company.
- The aggregate nominal value of those shares.
- For each class of shares
  - (i) particulars of any voting rights attached to the shares, including rights that arise only in certain circumstances;
  - (ii) particulars of any rights attached to the shares, as respects dividends, to participate in a distribution;
  - (iii) particulars of any rights attached to the shares, as respects capital, to participate in a distribution (including on a winding up);
  - (iv) whether the shares are to be redeemed or are liable to be redeemed at the option of the company or the shareholder;
  - (v) the total number of shares of that class; and
  - (vi) the aggregate nominal value of shares of that class.
- The amount paid up and the amount (if any) unpaid on each share (whether on account of the nominal value of the share or by way of premium).

If default is made in complying with this provision, an offence is committed by the company and every officer of the company who is in default. A person guilty of such an offence is liable, on summary conviction, to a fine not exceeding level 3 on the standard scale and, for continued contravention, a daily default fine not exceeding one-tenth of level 3 on the standard scale. See **29.1 Offences and Legal Proceedings** for the standard scale.

[*CA 2006, s 689*].

Listed companies. See **33.36 Public and Listed Companies** for provisions in the FCA Listing Rules.

34.4 PURCHASE OF OWN SHARES

A limited company having a share capital may purchase its own shares (including any redeemable shares) subject to the provisions in **34.5–34.9** and any restriction or prohibition in the company's articles.

A limited company may not, however, purchase its own shares

- if, as a result of the purchase, there would no longer be any issued shares of the company other than redeemable shares or shares held as treasury shares; and
- unless they are fully paid.

[*CA 2006, ss 690, 691(1)*].

34.5 Provisions relating to purchase

Payment for purchase. Where a limited company purchases its own shares, the shares must be paid for on purchase. This does not apply where a private limited company is purchasing shares for the purposes of or pursuant to an employees' share scheme. [*CA 2006, s 691(2); SI 2013 No 999, Reg 3*].

Financing of purchase. Subject to the power of *private* companies to redeem shares out of capital or with cash (see **34.10**) and the enforcement of redemption against a company when shares have not been redeemed at the commencement of winding up (see **34.19**)

- a limited company may only purchase its own shares out of
  (i) 'distributable profits' of the company; or
  (ii) the proceeds of a fresh issue of shares made for the purpose of financing the purchase; and
- any premium payable on the purchase by a limited company of its own shares must be paid out of distributable profits of the company except that if the shares to be purchased were issued at a premium, any premium payable on their purchase by the company may be paid out of the proceeds of a fresh issue of shares made for the purpose of financing the purchase, up to an amount equal to
  (i) the aggregate of the premiums received by the company on the issue of the shares purchased, or
  (ii) the current amount of the company's share premium account (including any amount transferred to that account in respect of premiums on the new shares),

  whichever is the less. The amount of the company's share premium account is reduced by a sum corresponding (or by sums in aggregate corresponding) to the amount of any premium payable on their purchase.

'*Distributable profits*' are those profits out of which the company could lawfully make a distribution (see **22.1 Distributions**) equal in value to the payment.

[*CA 2006, ss 692, 736; SI 2013 No 999 Reg 4*].

Treatment of shares purchased. Where a limited company makes a purchase of its own shares

- if *Companies Act 2006 (CA 2006), s 724* (treasury shares) applies, the shares may be held and dealt with in accordance with **34.14–34.17**; and

- in any other case, the shares are treated as cancelled and the amount of the company's issued share capital is diminished by the nominal value of the shares cancelled.

[*CA 2006, s 706*].

34.6 Authority for off-market purchase

Authority. A company may only make an 'off-market purchase' of its own shares authorised in accordance with *CA 2006, s 693A* or in pursuance of a contract approved prior to the purchase if

- the terms of the contract have been authorised by resolution of the company before the contract is entered into; or
- the contract provides that no shares may be purchased in pursuance of the contract until its terms have been authorised by a resolution of the company.

An '*off-market purchase*' is one where the shares are either

- purchased otherwise than on a 'recognised investment exchange'; or
- purchased on a recognised investment exchange but
  - (i) the shares are not listed under *FSMA 2000, Pt 6;* and
  - (ii) the company has not been afforded facilities for dealings in those shares to take place on the exchange without prior permission for individual transactions from the governing authority and without limit as to the time during which those facilities are to be available.

For these purposes '*recognised investment exchange*' means a recognised investment exchange within the meaning of *FSMA 2000, Pt 18* other than an overseas exchange (within the meaning of that *Part*).

The contract may be a contract, entered into by the company and relating to shares in the company, that does not amount to a contract to purchase the shares but under which the company may (subject to any conditions) become entitled or obliged to purchase the shares.

[*CA 2006, ss 693(1)(a)(2)(3)(5), 694(1)–(3); SI 2013 No 999, Reg 5*].

Resolutions. The authority conferred by a resolution under the above provisions may be varied, revoked or (from time to time) renewed by a resolution of the company. In the case of a public company, a resolution conferring, varying or renewing authority must specify a date on which the authority is to expire, which must not be later than five years after the date on which the resolution is passed.

[*CA 2006, s 694(4), (5); SI 2013 No 999, Reg 5*].

A resolution conferring, varying, revoking or renewing authority as above is subject to following.

(a) *Exercise of voting rights.*

- Where the resolution is proposed as a written resolution, a member who holds shares to which the resolution relates is not an eligible member (and therefore not entitled to receive or vote on the resolution).

- Where the resolution is proposed at a meeting of the company, it is not effective if
  - (i) any member of the company holding shares to which the resolution relates exercises the voting rights carried by any of those shares in voting on the resolution; and
  - (ii) the resolution would not have been passed if he had not done so.

  For these purposes
  - (1) a member who holds shares to which the resolution relates is regarded as exercising the voting rights carried by those shares not only if he votes in respect of them on a poll on the question whether the resolution should be passed, but also if he votes on the resolution otherwise than on a poll;
  - (2) any member of the company may demand a poll on that question; and
  - (3) a vote and a demand for a poll by a person as proxy for a member are the same respectively as a vote and a demand by the member.

(b) A copy of the contract (if it is in writing) or of a memorandum setting out its terms (if it is not) must be made available to members

- in the case of a written resolution, by being sent or submitted to every eligible member at or before the time at which the proposed resolution is sent or submitted to him; and
- in the case of a resolution at a meeting, by being made available for inspection by members of the company both at the company's registered office for not less than 15 days ending with the date of the meeting and at the meeting itself.

A memorandum of contract terms so made available must include the names of the members holding shares to which the contract relates. A copy of the contract so made available must have annexed to it a written memorandum specifying such of those names as do not appear in the contract itself.

[*CA 2006, ss 694(6), 695, 696*].

Variation of contract. A company may only agree to a variation of a contract authorised under the above provisions if the terms of the variation are authorised by a resolution of the company before it is agreed to. [*CA 2006, s 697(1)(2); SI 2013 No 999, Reg 5*]. The conditions set out in (a) and (b) (above) under the heading *Resolutions* apply to the authority for a proposed variation (with the terminology amended for variations) as they apply to the authority for a proposed contract. In addition, there must also be made available to members under (*b*) above a copy of the original contract or, as the case may be, a memorandum of its terms, together with any variations previously made.

[*CA 2006, ss 697(3)–(5), 698, 699*].

Release of company's rights. An agreement by a company to release its rights under a contract approved as above is void unless the terms of the release agreement are authorised by a resolution of the company before the agreement is entered into. That authority may be varied, revoked or from time to time renewed by a resolution of the company. In the case of a public company such a resolution must specify a date on which the authority is to expire which must be no later than five years after the date on which the resolution is passed.

[*CA 2006, s 700(1)(2)(3)(4) SI 2009 No 1917, Reg 4; SI 2013 No 999, Reg 5*].

The conditions set out in (a) and (b) (above) under the heading *Resolutions* apply to a resolution authorising a proposed release agreement as they apply to the authority for a proposed contract. In addition, there must also be made available to members under (*b*) above a copy of the original contract or, as the case may be, a memorandum of its terms, together with any variations previously made.
[*CA 2006, ss 698, 699, 700(5)*].

Assignment of rights. The rights of a company under a contract authorised under *CA 2006, s 693A* (authority for an off-market purchase for the purposes of or pursuant to an employees' share scheme) or *CA 2006, s 694* (authority for an off-market purchase) are not capable of being assigned.
[*CA 2006, s 704; SI 2013 No 999, Reg 9*].

Transitional provisions.

(1) The above provisions for off-market purchase apply to

- contracts entered into on or after 1 October 2009; and
- contracts entered into before that date that
  - (i) provide that no shares may be purchased in pursuance of a contract until its terms have been authorised by a special resolution of the company; and
  - (ii) are authorised by special resolution passed on or after that date.

[*SI 2008 No 2860, Sch 2 para 76*].

(2) Where, immediately before 1 October 2009, a resolution is in force having been passed under the corresponding provisions of *CA 1985*, the resolution has effect on or after that date as if passed under the *CA 2006* provisions above.

[*SI 2008 No 2860, Sch 2 para 75*].

Authority for off-market purchase for an employees' share scheme. A company may make an off-market purchase of its own shares for the purposes of or pursuant to an employees' share scheme if the purchase has first been authorised by a resolution of the company. That authority

- may be general or limited to the purchase of shares of a particular class or description
- may be unconditional or subject to conditions
- must specify the maximum number of shares authorised to be acquired and determine both the maximum and minimum prices that may be paid for the shares
- may be varied ,revoked or from time to time renewed by a resolution of the company.

A resolution to confer, vary or renew authority must specify a date on which it is to expire, which must be not later than five years after the date on which the resolution is passed but a company may make a purchase of its own shares after the expiry of the time limit specified if the contract of purchase was concluded before the authority expired and the terms of the authority permitted the company to make a contract of purchase that would or might be executed wholly or partly after its execution.

A resolution to confer or vary authority may determine the maximum or minimum price for the purchase by specifying a particular sum or by providing a basis or formula for calculating the amount of the price (but without reference to a person's discretion or opinion). *CA 2006 Chapter 3, Part 3* (Resolutions affecting a company's constitution) applies to a resolution under these provisions.

[*CA 2006 s 693A; SI 2013 No 999 Reg 7*]

34.7 Authority for market purchase

A limited company may only make a 'market purchase' of its own shares if the purchase has first been authorised by a resolution of the company.

A '*market purchase*' is a purchase made on a 'recognised investment exchange' other than one where

- the shares are not listed under *FSMA 2000, Pt 6;* and
- the company has not been afforded facilities for dealings in those shares to take place on the exchange without prior permission for individual transactions from the governing authority and without limit as to the time during which those facilities are to be available.

For these purposes, '*recognised investment exchange*' means a recognised investment exchange (within the meaning of *FSMA 2000, Pt 18*) other than an overseas exchange (within the meaning of that *Part*). [*CA 2006, ss 693(1)(b), (4), (5), 701(1)*].

The authority for the purchase may be

- general or limited to the purchase of shares of a particular class or description;
- unconditional or subject to conditions; and
- varied, revoked or from time to time renewed by a resolution of the company.

In addition, the authority must

- specify the maximum number of shares authorised to be acquired; and
- determine the maximum and minimum prices that may be paid for the shares. This may be done by specifying a particular sum, or by providing a formula or basis for calculating the price (but without reference to any person's discretion or opinion).

A resolution conferring, varying or renewing authority must specify a date on which it is to expire, which must not be later than five years after the date on which the resolution is passed. A company may make a purchase of its own shares after the expiry of the time limit specified if

- the contract of purchase was concluded before the authority expired; and
- the terms of the authority permitted the company to make a contract of purchase that would or might be executed wholly or partly after its expiration.

CA 2006, ss 29, 30 (resolutions affecting a company's constitution) apply to a resolution under these provisions. See **14.10 Constitution – Memorandum and Articles**. [*CA 2006, s 701(2)–(8))*].

Assignment of rights. The rights of a company under a contract for a market purchase are not capable of being assigned.

34.7 Purchase of Own Shares

[*CA 2006, s 704*].

Transitional provisions. Where, immediately before 1 October 2009, a resolution is in force having been passed under the corresponding provisions of *CA 1985*, the resolution has effect on or after that date as if passed under the *CA 2006* provisions above.

[*SI 2008 No 2860, Sch 2 para 75*].

34.8 Payments apart from purchase price to be made out of distributable profits

Apart from the purchase price itself (for which see **34.5**) a payment made by a company in consideration of

(a) acquiring any right with respect to the purchase of its own shares in pursuance of a contingent purchase contract approved under **34.6**,

(b) the variation of any contract approved under **34.6**, or

(c) the release of any of the company's obligations with respect to the purchase of any of its own shares under a contract approved under **34.6** or authorised under **34.7**

must be made out of the company's '*distributable profits*', ie those profits out of which it could lawfully make a distribution (see **22.1 Distributions**) equal in value to the payment.

If this requirement is not met in relation to a contract,

- in a case within (*a*) above, no purchase by the company of its own shares in pursuance of that contract may be made;
- in a case within (*b*) above, no such purchase following the variation may be made; and
- in a case within (*c*) above, the purported release is void.

[*CA 2006, ss 705, 736*].

34.9 Disclosure requirements

Copy of contract or memorandum of terms to be available for inspection. Where a company has entered into a contract approved under **34.6** or authorised under **34.7**, it must keep available for inspection at the company's registered office or a place specified in Regulations (see **36.2 Records**)

- a copy of the contract; or
- if the contract is not in writing, a written memorandum setting out its terms.

The contract or memorandum must be kept available for inspection from the conclusion of the contract until ten years from the date on which the purchase of all shares under the contract is completed or (as the case may be) the date on which the contract otherwise determines. This applies to any variation of the contract as it applies to the original contract.

The company must give notice to the Registrar of Companies within 14 days of the place at which the copy or memorandum is kept available for inspection and of any change in that place (unless it has at all times been kept at the company's registered office).

Every copy or memorandum required to be kept must be open to inspection without charge by any member of the company and, in the case of a public company, any other person.

In default of complying with any of the above requirements, or if an inspection is refused, an offence is committed by the company and every officer of the company who is in default. A person guilty of such an offence is liable, on summary conviction, to a fine not exceeding level 3 on the standard scale and, for continued contravention, a daily default fine not exceeding one-tenth of level 3 on the standard scale. See **29.1** Offences and Legal Proceedings for the standard scale. In the case of a refusal of an inspection, the court may compel an immediate inspection.

[*CA 2006, ss 702, 703*].

Availability for inspection and copying. See **36.2** Records.

Return to Registrar of Companies of purchase of own shares. Where a company purchases shares under **34.4** above, it must deliver a return to the Registrar of Companies within 28 days from the date on which the shares are delivered to it.

The return must

(a) distinguish treasury shares (see **34.14**) and shares which are not treasury shares;

(b) in the case of treasury shares, distinguish those that are cancelled forthwith (see **34.16**) and those are not so cancelled;

(c) state, with respect to shares of each class purchased

  (i) the number and nominal value of the shares; and

  (ii) the date on which they were delivered to the company; and

(d) in the case of a public company, state

  (i) the aggregate amount paid by the company for the shares; and

  (ii) the maximum and minimum prices paid in respect of shares of each class purchased.

Particulars of shares delivered to the company on different dates and under different contracts may be included in a single return. In such a case, the amount required to be stated under (*d*)(i) above is the aggregate amount paid by the company for all the shares to which the return relates.

Penalties. If default is made in delivering to the Registrar of Companies any return or statement required above, an offence is committed by every officer of the company who is in default. A person guilty of such an offence is liable (i) on conviction on indictment, to a fine; and (ii) on summary conviction, to a fine not exceeding the statutory maximum and, for continued contravention, a daily default fine not exceeding one-tenth of the greater of £5,000 or the amount corresponding to level 4 on the standard scale for summary offences. See **29.1** Offences and Legal Proceedings for the statutory maximum.

[*CA 2006, s 707; SI 2015 No 664, Sch 3*].

Notice to Registrar of Companies of cancellation of shares. If, on the purchase by a company of any of its own shares,

- *CA 2006, s 724* (treasury shares, see **34.14**) does not apply (so that the shares are treated as cancelled), or

- *CA 2006, s 724* applies but the shares are cancelled forthwith under *CA 2006, s 729* (see **34.16**),

the company must give notice of cancellation to the Registrar of Companies within 28 days from the date on which the shares are delivered to it, specifying the shares cancelled.

The notice must be accompanied by a statement of capital (except where the statement of capital would be the same as a statement of capital that is required to be delivered to the Registrar of Companies under *CA 2006, s 720B(1)* (see **34.12**(4)) which must state the following information with respect to the company's share capital immediately following the cancellation.

(a) The total number of shares of the company.

(b) The aggregate nominal value of those shares.

The *Small Business, Enterprise and Employment Act 2015 (SBEE 2015)* introduces a requirement to also include in the statement of capital the aggregate amount (if any) unpaid on those shares (whether on account of their nominal value or by way of premium). As at May 2015 this provision is not in force.

(c) For each class of shares

(i) particulars of any voting rights attached to the shares, including rights that arise only in certain circumstances;

(ii) particulars of any rights attached to the shares, as respects dividends, to participate in a distribution;

(iii) particulars of any rights attached to the shares, as respects capital, to participate in a distribution (including on a winding up);

(iv) whether the shares are to be redeemed or are liable to be redeemed at the option of the company or the shareholder;

(v) the total number of shares of that class; and

(vi) the aggregate nominal value of shares of that class.

(d) The amount paid up and the amount (if any) unpaid on each share (whether on account of the nominal value of the share or by way of premium).

Penalties. If default is made in complying with the above provisions, an offence is committed by the company and every officer of the company who is in default. A person guilty of such an offence is liable, on summary conviction, to a fine not exceeding level 3 on the standard scale and, for continued contravention, a daily default fine not exceeding one-tenth of level three on the standard scale. See **29.1** OFFENCES AND LEGAL PROCEEDINGS for the standard scale.

[*CA 2006, s 708; SI 2009 No 388, Art 2; SI 2015 No 532, Art 4*].

34.10 REDEMPTION OR PURCHASE BY PRIVATE COMPANY OUT OF CAPITAL OR WITH CASH

A private limited company may purchase of its own shares (a) out of capital in accordance with *CA 2006, Ch 5* (and *Ch 5* is subject to *CA 2006, s 692(1ZA)* (purchase of own shares up toannual limit) or (b) if authorised to do so by its articles, out of capital otherwise than in accordance with *CA 2006*, Ch 5, up to an aggregate purchase price in a financial year of the lower of £15,000 or the nominal value of 5% of its fully paid share capital as at the beginning of the financial year.

If the share capital of the company is not denominated in sterling, the value of sterling shall be calculated for the purposes of (b) at an appropriate spot rate of exchange.

Provided it is made in accordance with the provisions in **34.11–34.13**, the payment that may be made out of capital (the '*permissible capital payment*') is such an amount as, after applying for that purposes

- any available profits of the company (see **34.11**), and
- the proceeds of any fresh issue of shares made for the purpose of the redemption or purchase

is required to meet the price of redemption or purchase.

[*CA 2006, ss 692 (1)(1A), (1ZA), 709, 710, 736; SI 2013 No 999 Reg 4; SI 2015 No 532, Reg 3, 5*].

Accounting consequences. Subject to below, if the permissible capital payment for shares redeemed or purchased

(a) is less than the nominal amount of those shares, the amount of the difference must be transferred to the company's capital redemption reserve (see **34.18**); and

(b) is greater than the nominal amount of those shares, then

- the amount of any capital redemption reserve, share premium account (see **46 Share Premium**) or fully paid share capital of the company, and
- any amount representing unrealised profits of the company standing to the credit of any revaluation reserve maintained by the company

may be reduced by a sum not exceeding (or by sums not in total exceeding) the amount by which the permissible capital payment exceeds the nominal amount of the shares.

Where the proceeds of a fresh issue are applied by the company in making a redemption or purchase of its own shares in addition to a payment out of capital under these provisions, the permissible capital payment for the purposes of (*a*) and (*b*) above is to be read as referring to the aggregate of that payment and those proceeds.

In relation to a payment made under *CA 2006, s 692 (1ZA)*, references to the permissible capital payment are to the purchase price of the shares or (if less) the part of it met out of the payment under *CA 2006, s 692 (1ZA)* and any proceeds of a fresh issue used to make the payment.

[*CA 2006, s 734; SI 2015 No 532, Reg 9*].

34.11 Available profits

The reference in **34.12** to available profits of a company is to the company's profits which are available for distribution (see generally **22 Distributions**) but the question whether a company has any profits so available, and the amount of any such profits, is not determined as in **22.2–22.4 Distributions** but as follows.

(1) Determine the profits of the company by reference to the following items as stated in the 'relevant accounts'.

(a) Profits, losses, assets and liabilities.

(b) Provisions of the following kinds:

- Where the relevant accounts are Companies Act accounts, (i) provisions for depreciation or diminution in value of assets; and (ii) any provision for liabilities (or, in the case of insurance companies, provisions for other risks), ie any amount retained as reasonably necessary for the purpose of providing for any liability the nature of which is clearly defined and which is either likely to be incurred, or certain to be incurred but uncertain as to the amount or as to the date on which it will arise; and
- Where the relevant accounts are IAS accounts, provisions of any kind.

(c) Share capital and reserves (including undistributable reserves, see **22.1 Distributions**).

(2) Determine the amount of

(a) any distribution lawfully made by the company; and

(b) any 'other relevant payment lawfully made' by the company out of distributable profits,

after the date of the relevant accounts and before the end of the 'relevant period'.

'*Other relevant payment lawfully made*' include

- financial assistance lawfully given out of distributable profits in accordance with *CA 2006, ss 677–683* (see **34.19** and **34.20**);
- payments lawfully made out of distributable profits in respect of the purchase by the company of any shares in the company; and
- payments of any description specified in **34.8**(*a*)–(*c*) lawfully made by the company.

(3) Available profits are (1) minus (2).

The '*relevant accounts*' are any accounts that are

- prepared as at a date within the relevant period; and
- such as to enable a reasonable judgment to be made as to the amounts of the items mentioned in (1) above.

The '*relevant period*' means the period of three months ending with the date on which the solvency statement is made in accordance with *CA 2006, s 720A* or the directors' statement is made (see **34.12**).

[*CA 2006, ss 711, 712; SI 2008 No 409, Sch 7 paras 2, 4; SI 2008 No 410, Sch 9 paras 1, 2, 4 ;SI 2013 No 999, Reg 10*].

34.12 Requirements for payments out of capital

Subject to *CA 2006, s 720A* and any court order made under **34.13**, a payment out of capital by a private company for the redemption or purchase of its own shares is not lawful unless the following conditions are satisfied.

[*CA 2006, s 713; SI 2013 No 999, Reg 11*].

(1) **Directors' statement and auditor's report**

The directors must make a statement specifying the amount of the permissible capital payment for the shares and stating that, having made full inquiry into the affairs and prospects of the company, they have formed the opinion that

(a) as regards its initial situation immediately after the date on which the payment out of capital is proposed to be made, there will be no grounds on which the company could then be found to be unable to pay its debts (taking into account all of the company's liabilities, including any contingent or prospective liabilities); and

(b) as regards its prospects for the year following that date (having regard to their intentions with regard to the management of the company's business, and the amount and character of the financial resources that will in their view be available, during that year), the company will be able to carry on business as a going concern (and will accordingly be able to pay its debts as they fall due) throughout that year.

It must have annexed to it a report addressed to the directors by the company's auditor stating that

- he has inquired into the company's state of affairs;
- the amount specified in the statement as the permissible capital payment for the shares in question is, in his view, properly determined in accordance with **34.10** and **34.11**; and
- he is not aware of anything to indicate that the opinion expressed by the directors in the statement under (*a*) and (*b*) above is unreasonable in all the circumstances. [*CA 2006, s 714*].

The statement must be in writing, indicate that it is a directors' statement under *CA 2006, s 714* and be signed by each of the company's directors. It must also state whether the company's business includes that of a banking company or of an insurance company.

[*SI 2009 No 388, Art 5*].

Penalties. If the directors make a statement as above without having reasonable grounds for the opinion expressed in it, an offence is committed by every director who is in default. A person guilty of such an offence is liable (i) on conviction on indictment, to imprisonment for a term not exceeding two years or a fine (or both); and (ii) on summary conviction, to imprisonment for a term not exceeding twelve months (six months in Scotland or Northern Ireland) or to a fine not exceeding the statutory maximum (or both). See **29.1** OFFENCES AND LEGAL PROCEEDINGS for the statutory maximum.

[*CA 2006, s 715*].

(2) **Special resolution**

The payment out of capital must be approved by a special resolution passed on, or within the week immediately following, the date on which the directors make the statement under (1) above. [*CA 2006, s 716*]. The special resolution is subject to following.

Exercise of voting rights

Where the resolution is proposed as a written resolution, a member who holds shares to which the resolution relates is not an eligible member (and therefore not entitled to receive or vote on the resolution).

Where the resolution is proposed at a meeting of the company, it is not effective if

(i) any member of the company holding shares to which the resolution relates exercises the voting rights carried by any of those shares in voting on the resolution; and

(ii) the resolution would not have been passed if he had not done so.

For these purposes

- a member who holds shares to which the resolution relates is regarded as exercising the voting rights carried by those shares not only if he votes in respect of them on a poll on the question whether the resolution should be passed, but also if he votes on the resolution otherwise than on a poll;
- any member of the company may demand a poll on that question; and
- a vote and a demand for a poll by a person as proxy for a member are the same respectively as a vote and a demand by the member.

[*CA 2006, s 717*].

Disclosure of directors' statement and auditor's report

A copy of the directors' statement and auditor's report under (1) above must be made available to members

- in the case of a written resolution, by being sent or submitted to every eligible member at or before the time at which the proposed resolution is sent or submitted to him; and
- in the case of a resolution at a meeting, by being made available for inspection by members of the company at the meeting.

The resolution is ineffective if this requirement is not complied with.

[*CA 2006, s 718*].

(3) **Public notice of proposed payment**

Within the week immediately following the date of the special resolution, the company must

(a) cause to be published in the Gazette, and

(b) *either* send to each of its creditors *or* cause to be published in a newspaper circulating throughout the part of the UK in which the company is registered

a notice

- stating that the company has approved a payment out of capital for the purpose of acquiring its own shares by redemption or purchase or both (as the case may be);
- specifying the amount of the permissible capital payment for the shares (see **34.10**) and the date of the resolution;

- stating where the directors' statement and auditor's report required under (1) above are available for inspection; and
- stating that any creditor of the company may, at any time within the five weeks immediately following the date of the special resolution, apply to the court under *CA 2006, s 721* (see **34.13**) for an order prohibiting the payment.

Not later than the day on which the company first publishes or gives notice under (*a*) or (*b*) above, it must deliver to the Registrar of Companies a copy of the directors' statement and auditor's report required under (1) above.

[*CA 2006, s 719*].

(4) **Inspection of directors' statement and auditor's report**

The directors' statement and auditor's report under (1) above must be kept available for inspection at the company's registered office or a place specified in Regulations (see **36.2 Records**) throughout the period beginning with the day on which the company first publishes or gives notice under (3)(*a*) or (*b*) above and ending five weeks after the date of the resolution for payment out of capital.

The statement and report must be open to the inspection of any member or creditor of the company without charge.

The company must give notice to the Registrar of Companies within 14 days of the place at which the statement and report are kept available for inspection and of any change in that place (unless they have at all times been kept at the company's registered office).

If the company fails to notify the Registrar of Companies or if an inspection is refused, an offence is committed by the company and every officer of the company who is in default. A person guilty of such an offence is liable, on summary conviction, to a fine not exceeding level 3 on the standard scale and, for continued contravention, a daily default fine not exceeding one-tenth of level 3 on the standard scale. See **29.1 Offences and Legal Proceedings** for the standard scale. In the case of a refusal of an inspection, the court may by order compel an immediate inspection.

[*CA 2006, s 720*].

Time available for inspection and copying. See **36.2 Records**.

(5) **Timing when payment out of capital to be made or shares to be surrendered**

Subject to the exercise of the courts powers under **34.13**, the payment out of capital if made in accordance with a resolution under *CA 2006, s 716* must be surrendered no earlier than five weeks, but no more than seven weeks, after the date on which the special resolution under (2) above is passed. Shares to be purchased in accordance with a resolution under *CA 2006, s 720A* must be surrendered no earlier than five weeks after the date on which the resolution under *s 720A* is passed and no later than seven weeks after that date.

[*CA 2006, s 723; SI 2013 No 999, Reg 13*].

For cases on whether the directors and auditor owe a duty of responsibility to individual shareholders who suffer loss, see *Prudential Assurance Co Ltd v Newman Industries Ltd (No 2)* [1982] Ch 204, [1982] 1 All ER 354, CA; *Hedley Byrne & Co Ltd v Heller &*

Partners Ltd [1964] AC 465, [1963] 2 All ER 575, HL; *Caparo Industries plc v Dickman* [1990] 2 AC 605, [1990] BCLC 273, HL; and *JEB Fasteners Ltd v Marks, Bloom & Co (a firm)* [1983] 1 All ER 583, [1982] Com LR 226, CA.

Reduced requirements for payments out of capital for purchase of own shares: employees' share schemes

34.12A *CA 2006, s 713* (see **34.12**) does not apply to the purchase out of capital by a private company of its own shares for the purposes of or pursuant to an employees' share scheme when approved by special resolution supported by a solvency statement. A resolution is supported by a solvency statement if

- the directors of the company make a solvency statement not more than 15 days before the date on which the resolution is passed, and
- the resolution and solvency statement are registered in accordance with *CA 2006, s 720B*.

Where the resolution is proposed as a written resolution, a copy of the solvency statement must be sent or submitted to every eligible member at or before the time at which the proposed resolution is sent or submitted to the member. Where the resolution is proposed at a general meeting, a copy of the solvency statement must be made available for members of the company throughout that meeting. The validity of a resolution is not affected by a failure to comply with either of these requirements.

[*CA 2006, s 720A; SI 2013 No 999, Reg 12*]

Registration of resolution and supporting documents

Within 15 days after the passing of the resolution for a payment out of capital by a private company for the purchase of its own shares for the purposes of or pursuant to an employees' share scheme, the company must deliver to the Registrar of Companies

(a) a copy of the solvency statement (see above)

(b) a copy of the resolution

(c) a statement of capital. The statement of capital must state with respect to the company's share capital as reduced by the resolution the total number of shares of the company; the aggregate nominal value of those shares; for each class of shares prescribed particulars of the rights attached to the shares, the total number of shares of that class and the aggregate nominal value of shares of that class; the amount paid up and the amount (if any) unpaid on each share (whether on account of the nominal value of the share or by way of premium).

    The *SBEE 2015* introduces a requirement to also include in the statement of capital the aggregate amount (if any) unpaid on those shares (whether on account of their nominal value or by way of premium). As at May 2015 this provision is not in force.

(d) a statement by the directors of the company confirming that the solvency statement was made not more than 15 days before the date on which the resolution was passed and was provided to the members in accordance with *CA 2006, s 720A(3)* or *(4)*.

[*CA 2006 ,s 720B (1), (2), (5); SI 2013 No 999, Reg 12*]

Effect of delivering documents

The Registrar of Companies must register the documents delivered to him as above. The resolution does not take effect until those documents are registered and the validity of a resolution is not affected by a failure to deliver the documents required to be delivered to the Registrar of Companies within the 15 day time specified or by a failure to comply with (d) above.

[*CA 2006 s 720B (3), (4), (6); SI 2013 No 999, Reg 12*]

Default

If the company delivers to the Registrar of Companies a solvency statement that was not provided to members in accordance with *CA 2006, s 720A(3)* or *(4)*, an offence is committed by every officer of the company who is in default. If default is made in complying with *CA 2006, s 720B*, an offence is committed by the company and every officer of the company who is in default. A person guilty of an offence under these provisions is liable on conviction on indictment to a fine or on summary conviction to a fine not exceeding the statutory maximum (see **29 Offences and Legal Proceedings**).

[*CA 2006 s 720B (7)(8)(9); SI 2013 No 999, Reg 12*]

34.13 Objections by members or creditors

Where a private company passes a special resolution approving a payment out of capital for the redemption or purchase of any of its shares, any creditor and any member (other than one who consented to or voted in favour of the resolution) may, within five weeks of it being passed, apply to the court for the resolution to be cancelled. The application may be made on behalf of the persons entitled to make it by one or more of their number as they may appoint in writing.

The court must make an order on such terms and conditions as it thinks fit either confirming or cancelling the special resolution. It may

(a) adjourn the proceedings in order that an arrangement may be made to purchase the interests of dissentient members or for the protection of dissentient creditors;

(b) give such directions as it thinks expedient for putting the arrangements into effect;

(c) if it confirms the resolution, alter or extend any date or period of time applying to the redemption or purchase of the shares;

(d) provide for the purchase by the company of the shares of any of its members and for the reduction accordingly of the company's capital;

(e) make any alterations in the company's articles that may be required in consequence of any such purchase or reduction; and

(f) require the company not to make any, or any specified, alteration in its articles without leave of the court.

[*CA 2006, s 721*].

Notice to Registrar of Companies. On making an application as above, the applicants, or the person making the application on their behalf, must immediately give notice to the Registrar of Companies.

On being served with notice of any such application, the company must also immediately give notice to the Registrar of Companies. Subsequently, within 15 days of the making of the court's order on the application (or such longer period as the court may at any time direct), the company must deliver to the Registrar a copy of the order. If a company fails to comply with either of these requirements, an offence is committed by the company and every officer of the company who is in default. A person guilty of such an offence is liable, on summary conviction, to a fine not exceeding level 3 on the standard scale and, for continued contravention, a daily default fine not exceeding one-tenth of level 3 on the standard scale. See **29.1 OFFENCES AND LEGAL PROCEEDINGS** for the standard scale.

[*CA 2006, s 722*].

34.14 TREASURY SHARES

Where a limited company makes a purchase of its own shares in accordance with the provisions in *CA 2006, Ch 4* and the purchase is made out of 'distributable profits' the company may

- hold the shares (or any of them),
- dispose of them under the provision in **34.15**, or
- cancel them under the provisions in **34.16**.

and in *Companies Acts* references to a company holding shares as '*treasury shares*' are to the company holding shares that

- were (or are treated as having been) purchased by it in circumstances in which the above provisions apply; and
- have been held by the company continuously since they were so purchased (or treated as purchased).

'*Distributable profits*' are those profits out of which the company could lawfully make a distribution (see **22.1 DISTRIBUTIONS**) equal in value to the payment.

Register of members. Where shares are held by the company, the company must be entered in its register of members as the member holding the shares.

[*CA 2006, ss 724, 736, SI 2013 No 999, Reg 14; SI 2015 No 532, Reg 7*].

Any outstanding obligation to dispose of or cancel excess shares arising under *CA 2006, s725(3)* ceased to exist on 1 October 2009 whether or not the 12 month period in that *section 725(3)* has expired. But this does not affect the liability for offences under *CA 2006, s 732* where the 12 month period expired before 1 October 2009.

[*CA 2006, s 725* (repealed on 1 October 2009); *SI 2009 No 2022, Reg 5*].

Exercise of rights. The company must not exercise any right in respect of the treasury shares, and any purported exercise of such a right is void. This includes rights to attend or vote at meetings.

No dividend may be paid, and no other distribution (whether in cash or otherwise) of the company's assets (including any distribution of assets to members on a winding up) may be made, to the company in respect of the treasury shares.

The company is, however, entitled to

- any allotment of shares as fully paid bonus shares in respect of the treasury shares (in which case the shares allotted are treated as if purchased by the company at the time they were allotted); and

- the payment of any amount payable on the redemption of the treasury shares (if they are redeemable shares).

[*CA 2006, s 726*].

34.15 Disposal of treasury shares

Where shares are held as treasury shares, a company may at any time

(a) sell the shares (or any of them) for a 'cash consideration'; or

(b) transfer the shares (or any of them) for the purposes of, or pursuant to, an employees' share scheme.

'*Cash consideration*' means

- cash (including foreign currency) received by the company;
- a cheque received by the company in good faith that the directors have no reason for suspecting will not be paid;
- a release of a liability of the company for a liquidated sum;
- an undertaking to pay cash (including foreign currency) to the company on or before a date not more than 90 days after the date on which the company agrees to sell the shares; or
- payment by any other means giving rise to a present or future entitlement (of the company or a person acting on the company's behalf) to a payment, or credit equivalent to a payment, in cash. Included is a settlement bank's obligation to make a payment in respect of treasury shares under the CREST system.

But if the company receives a notice under *CA 2006, s 979* (right of offeror to buy out minority shareholders, see **48.12 Takeovers**) that a person desires to acquire shares held by the company as treasury shares, the company must not sell or transfer the shares to which the notice relates except to that person.

[*CA 2006, s 727; SI 2009 No 388, Art 4*].

Notice of disposal. Where shares held by a company as treasury shares are sold or transferred for the purposes of an employees' share scheme, the company must deliver a return to the Registrar of Companies not later than 28 days after the shares are disposed of. The return must state with respect to shares of each class disposed of

- the number and nominal value of the shares; and
- the date on which they were disposed of.

Particulars of shares disposed of on different dates may be included in a single return.

If default is made in complying with this requirement, an offence is committed by every officer of the company who is in default. A person guilty of such an offence is liable (i) on conviction on indictment, to a fine; and (ii) on summary conviction, to a fine not exceeding the statutory maximum and, for continued contravention, a daily default fine not exceeding one-tenth of the greater of £5000 or level 4 on the standard scale for summary offences. See **29.1 Offences and Legal Proceedings** for the statutory maximum.

[*CA 2006, s 728; SI 2015 No 664, Sch 3*].

Proceeds of sale. Where shares held as treasury shares are sold, the proceeds of sale must be dealt with as follows.

- If the proceeds of sale are equal to or less than the purchase price paid by the company for the shares, the proceeds must be treated for the purposes of distributions as a realised profit of the company.
- If the proceeds of sale exceed the purchase price paid by the company
  - (i) an amount equal to the purchase price paid is treated as a realised profit of the company for the purposes of distributions; and
  - (ii) the excess must be transferred to the company's share premium account.

For these purposes

- the purchase price paid by the company must be determined by the application of a weighted average price method; and
- if the shares were allotted to the company as fully paid bonus shares, the purchase price paid for them is to be treated as being nil.

[*CA 2006, s 731*].

34.16 Cancellation of treasury shares

Where shares are held as treasury shares, the company may at any time cancel the shares (or any of them).

If the company cancels shares held as treasury shares, the amount of the company's share capital is reduced accordingly by the nominal value of the shares cancelled.

The directors may take any steps required to enable the company to cancel its shares without complying with *CA 2006, ss 641–653* (reduction of share capital, see **47.51–47.58 SHARES**).

[*CA 2006, s 729, SI 2013 No 999, Reg 15*].

Notice of cancellation. In relation to shares cancelled on or after 1 October 2009, where shares held by a company as treasury shares are cancelled, the company must deliver a return to the Registrar of Companies within 28 days from the date the shares are cancelled. (This does not apply to shares that are cancelled forthwith on their acquisition by the company, see **34.9**.) The return must state with respect to shares of each class cancelled

- the number and nominal value of the shares; and
- the date on which they were cancelled.

Particulars of shares cancelled on different dates may be included in a single return.

The notice must be accompanied by a statement of capital which must state the following with respect to the company's share capital immediately following the cancellation.

(a) The total number of shares of the company.

(b) The aggregate nominal value of those shares.

> The *SBEE 2015* introduces a requirement to also include in the statement of capital the aggregate amount (if any) unpaid on those shares (whether on account of their nominal value or by way of premium). As at May 2015 this provision is not in force.

(c) For each class of shares

- (i) particulars of any voting rights attached to the shares, including rights that arise only in certain circumstances;
- (ii) particulars of any rights attached to the shares, as respects dividends, to participate in a distribution;
- (iii) particulars of any rights attached to the shares, as respects capital, to participate in a distribution (including on a winding up);
- (iv) whether the shares are to be redeemed or are liable to be redeemed at the option of the company or the shareholder;
- (v) the total number of shares of that class; and
- (vi) the aggregate nominal value of shares of that class.

(d) The amount paid up and the amount (if any) unpaid on each share (whether on account of the nominal value of the share or by way of premium).

Penalties. If default is made in complying with the above requirements, an offence is committed by the company and every officer of the company who is in default. A person guilty of such an offence is liable, on summary conviction, to a fine not exceeding level 3 on the standard scale and, for continued contravention, a daily default fine not exceeding one-tenth of level 3 on the standard scale. See **29.1 Offences and Legal Proceedings** for the standard scale.

[*CA 2006, s 730; SI 2009 No 388, Art 2*].

34.17 Offences relating to treasury shares

If a company contravenes any of the provisions of **34.14–34.16** (except notice of cancellation under **34.16**), an offence is committed by the company and every officer of the company who is in default. A person guilty of such an offence is liable (i) on conviction on indictment, to a fine; and (ii) on summary conviction, to a fine not exceeding the statutory maximum. See **29.1 Offences and Legal Proceedings** for the statutory maximum.

[*CA 2006, s 732*].

34.18 THE CAPITAL REDEMPTION RESERVE

Where shares of a limited company are redeemed or purchased wholly out of the company's profits, the amount by which the company's issued share capital is diminished in accordance with

- *CA 2006, s 688(b)* (ie the nominal value of the redeemed shares treated as cancelled, see **34.3**); or
- *CA 2006, s 706(b)(ii)* (ie the nominal value of the shares purchased treated as cancelled, see **34.5**),

must be transferred to the capital redemption reserve.

[*CA 2006, s 733(2)*].

Where the shares are redeemed or purchased wholly or partly out of the proceeds of a fresh issue, and the aggregate amount of the proceeds is less than the aggregate nominal value of the shares redeemed or purchased, the amount of the difference must be transferred to the capital redemption reserve. But this does not apply in the case of a private company if, in addition to the proceeds of the fresh issue, the company applies a payment out of capital under **34.10–34.13** in making the redemption or purchase.

[*CA 2006, s 733(3)*].

Where shares are held as treasury shares, the amount by which a company's share capital is diminished in accordance with *CA 2006, s 729(4)* on the cancellation of any such shares (see **34.16**) must be transferred to the capital redemption reserve.

[*CA 2006, s 733(4)*].

Use of the capital redemption reserve. The company may use the capital redemption reserve to pay up new shares to be allotted to members as fully paid bonus shares. Subject to that, the provisions of the *Companies Acts* relating to the reduction of a company's share capital apply as if the capital redemption reserve were part of its paid up share capital.

[*CA 2006, s 733(5)(6)*].

34.19 EFFECT OF COMPANY'S FAILURE TO PURCHASE OR REDEEM SHARES

The following consequences apply where a company has issued shares on terms that they are (or are liable to be) redeemed or agreed to purchase any of its own shares.

(a) The company is not liable in damages in respect of any failure on its part to redeem or purchase any of the shares. This is, however, without prejudice to any right of the holder of the shares (eg to present a petition for the company to be wound up, see *Re Holders Investment Trust Ltd* [1971] 2 All ER 289, [1971] 1 WLR 583) other than his right to sue the company for damages in respect of its failure. The court will not grant an order for specific performance of the terms of redemption or purchase if the company shows that it is unable to meet the costs of redeeming or purchasing the shares out of distributable profits.

(b) If the company is wound up and at the commencement of the winding up any of the shares have not been redeemed or purchased, subject to below, the terms of redemption or purchase may be enforced against the company with the shares being treated as cancelled.

This does not apply if

- the terms provide for the redemption or purchase to take place at a date later than the commencement of the winding up; or
- during the period from the date on which the redemption or purchase was to have taken place to the commencement of the winding up, the company could not at any time have lawfully made a distribution equal in value to the price at which the shares were to have been redeemed or purchased.

There must be paid, in priority to any amount that the company is liable to pay in respect of any shares at the commencement of winding up

- all other debts and liabilities of the company (other than any due to members in their character as such); and
- if other shares carry rights (whether as to capital or as to income) that are preferred to the rights as to capital attaching to the first-mentioned shares, any amount due in satisfaction of those preferred rights.

Subject to that, any such amount must be paid in priority to any amounts due to members in satisfaction of their rights (whether as to capital or income) as members.

[*CA 2006, s 735*].

34.20 FINANCIAL ASSISTANCE FOR PURCHASE OF OWN SHARES

The prohibitions in *CA 1985* on a private company giving financial assistance for the purchase of own shares were abolished on 1 October 2008. The following paragraphs therefore only apply to

- Public companies
- Private companies which are subsidiaries of public companies
- Private companies with public company subsidiaries (where financial assistance is being given by the public company (see (b)).

Subject to 34.21, 'financial assistance' is prohibited in the following circumstances.

(a) *Assistance for acquisition of shares in a public company*

(i) Where a person is acquiring or proposing to acquire shares in a public company, it is not lawful for that company, or a company that is a subsidiary of that company, to give financial assistance directly or indirectly for the purpose of the acquisition before or at the same time as the acquisition takes place.

(ii) Where a person has acquired shares in a company ('the company') and a liability has been incurred (by that or another person) for the purpose of the acquisition, it is not lawful for that company, or a company that is a subsidiary of that company, to give financial assistance directly or indirectly for the purpose of reducing or discharging the liability if, at the time the assistance is given, the company in which the shares were acquired is a public company.

(b) *Assistance by public company for acquisition shares in its private holding company*

(i) Where a person is acquiring or proposing to acquire shares in a private company, it is not lawful for a public company that is a subsidiary of that company to give financial assistance directly or indirectly for the purpose of the acquisition before or at the same time as the acquisition takes place.

(ii) Where a person has acquired shares in a private company and a liability has been incurred (by that or another person) for the purpose of the acquisition, it is not lawful for a public company that is a subsidiary of that company to give financial assistance directly or indirectly for the purpose of reducing or discharging the liability.

For the above purposes:

- A reference to a person incurring a liability includes his changing his financial position by making an agreement or arrangement (whether enforceable or unenforceable, and whether made on his own account or with any other person) or by any other means.

- A reference to a company giving financial assistance for the purposes of reducing or discharging a liability incurred by a person for the purpose of the acquisition of shares includes its giving such assistance for the purpose of wholly or partly restoring his financial position to what it was before the acquisition took place.

Offences. If a company contravenes the above provisions, an offence is committed by the company and every officer of the company who is in default. A person guilty of such an offence is liable (i) on conviction on indictment, to imprisonment for a term not exceeding two years or a fine (or both); and (ii) on summary conviction, to imprisonment for a term not exceeding twelve months (six months in Scotland or Northern Ireland) or to a fine not exceeding the statutory maximum (or both).

[*CA 2006, ss 678(1)(3)(5), 679(1)(3)(5), 680*].

Financial assistance. '*Financial assistance*' means any of the following.

- Financial assistance by way of gift. This may include a sale or transfer at an undervalue (see *Letts v IRC* [1956] 3 All ER 588, [1957] 1 WLR 201; *A-G v Kitchin* [1941] 2 All ER 374) but possibly only to the extent of the undervalue (*Plant v Steiner* (1989) 5 BCC 352).
- Financial assistance by way of guarantee, security or indemnity (other than an indemnity in respect of the indemnifier's own neglect or default).
- Financial assistance given by way of release or waiver.
- Financial assistance given
  - (i) by way of a loan or any other agreement under which any of the obligations of the person giving the assistance are to be fulfilled at a time when, in accordance with the agreement, any obligation of another party to the agreement remains unfulfilled; or
  - (ii) by way of the novation of, or the assignment (in Scotland, assignation) of rights arising under, a loan or such other agreement.
- Any other financial assistance given by a company where
  - (i) the 'net assets' of the company are thereby reduced to a material extent by the giving of the assistance; or
  - (ii) the company has no net assets.

  '*Net assets*' means the aggregate of the company's assets less the aggregate of its liabilities. For this purpose, liabilities include

  - (a) where the company draws up Companies Act accounts, any provisions for liabilities (or, in the case of insurance companies, provisions for other risks), ie any amount retained as reasonably necessary for the purpose of providing for any liability the nature of which is clearly defined and which is either likely to be incurred, or certain to be incurred but uncertain as to amount or as to the date on which it will arise; and
  - (b) where the company draws up IAS individual accounts, any provision that is made in those accounts.

[*CA 2006, s 677; SI 2008 No 409, Sch 7 paras 2, 3; SI 2008 No 410, Sch 9 paras 2, 3*].

For a consideration of the meaning of financial assistance, see *Charterhouse Investment Trust Ltd v Tempest Diesels Ltd* [1986] BCLC 1, 1 BCC 544 and *Wallersteiner v Moir* [1974] 3 All ER 217, [1974] 1 WLR 991, CA. Once assistance has been established, the fact that money is involved in some form will make the assistance financial assistance (*Armour Hick Northern Ltd v Whitehouse* [1980] 1 WLR 1520, 124 Sol Jo 864). It is not necessary that the assistance costs the provider anything. For example, in *Belmont Finance Corpn Ltd v Williams Furniture Ltd (No 2)* [1980] 1 All ER 393, CA the purchase of an asset for cash at full value from a potential purchaser was held to be financial assistance as it provided the purchaser with cash to buy the shares.

34.21 Exceptions from prohibition

The following transactions are not prohibited under **34.20**.

(a) A distribution of the company's assets by way of dividend lawfully made.

(b) A distribution of the company's assets made by way of distribution in the course of the company's winding up.

(c) An allotment of bonus shares (see **47.62 Shares**).

(d) A reduction of capital under *CA 2006, ss 641–653* (see **47.51–47.58 Shares**).

(e) A redemption of shares under **34.2** and **34.3** or a purchase of shares under **34.4 to 34.9**.

(f) Anything done in pursuance of a court order under *CA 2006, Pt 26* (order sanctioning compromise or arrangement with members or creditors, see **35.1–35.5 Reconstructions and Mergers**).

(g) Anything done under an arrangement made

- in pursuance of *IA 1986, s 110* or *Insolvency (NI) Order 1989 (SI 1989 No 2405), Art 96* (acceptance of shares by a liquidator as consideration for sale of property); or
- between a company and its creditors which is binding on the creditors under *IA 1986, Pt I* or *Insolvency (NI) Order 1989 (SI 1989 No 2405), Pt 2*.

(h) Where the lending of money is part of the ordinary business of the company, the lending of money in the ordinary course of the company's business. This exception does not apply to a company merely because it has the power to lend money (*Steen v Law* [1964] AC 287, [1963] 3 All ER 770, PC).

(i) The provision by the company, in good faith in the interests of the company or its holding company, of financial assistance for the purposes of an employees' share scheme.

(j) The provision of financial assistance by the company for the purposes of, or in connection with, anything done by the company (or another company in the same group) to enable or facilitate transactions in shares in the first-mentioned company or its holding company between, and involving the acquisition of beneficial ownership of those shares by

(i) *bona fide* employees or former employees of that company (or another company in the same group); or

(ii) spouses or civil partners, widows, widowers or surviving civil partners, or minor children or step-children of any such employees or former employees.

For these purposes, a company is in the same '*group*' as another company if it is a holding company or a subsidiary of that company, or a subsidiary of a holding company of that company.

(k) The making by a company of loans to persons (other than directors) employed in good faith by the company with a view to enabling those persons to acquire fully paid shares in the company or its holding company to be held by them by way of beneficial ownership.

(l) Under 34.20(*a*)(i), the giving of financial assistance by a company for the acquisition of shares in it or its holding company if

- the company's principal purpose in giving the assistance is not to give it for the purpose of any such acquisition,
- or the giving of the assistance for that purpose is only an incidental part of some larger purpose of the company,

and the assistance is given in good faith in the interests of the company.

(m) Under 34.20(*a*)(ii), the giving of financial assistance by a company if

- the company's principal purpose in giving the assistance is not to reduce or discharge any liability incurred by a person for the purpose of the acquisition of shares in the company or its holding company, or
- the reduction or discharge of any such liability is only an incidental part of some larger purpose of the company

and the assistance is given in good faith in the company's interests (see *Brady v Brady* [1989] AC 755, [1988] BCLC 579, HL).

(n) Under 34.20(*b*)(i) the giving of financial assistance by a company for the acquisition of shares in its holding company if

- the company's principal purpose in giving the assistance is not to give it for the purpose of any such acquisition, or
- the giving of the assistance for that purpose is only an incidental part of some larger purpose of the company

and the assistance is given in good faith in the interests of the company.

(o) Under 34.20(*b*)(ii), the giving of financial assistance by a company if

(a) the company's principal purpose in giving the assistance is not to reduce or discharge any liability incurred by a person for the purpose of the acquisition of the shares in its holding company, or

(b) the reduction or discharge of any such liability is only an incidental part of some larger purpose of the company

and the assistance is given in good faith in the interests of the company.

Public companies. If the company giving the assistance is a public company, the exceptions in (*h*)–(*k*) above only apply if

- the company has 'net assets' that are nor reduced by the giving or assistance; or
- to the extent that those assets are so reduced, the assistance is provided out of 'distributable profits'.

'*Net* assets' are the amount by which the aggregate of the company's assets exceeds the aggregate of its liabilities, in each case as stated in the company's accounting records immediately before the financial assistance is given. Liabilities include any amount retained as reasonably necessary for the purpose of providing for any liability the nature of which is clearly defined and that is either likely to be incurred, or certain to be incurred but uncertain as to amount or as to the date on which it will arise.

'*Distributable profits*' means those profits out of which the company could lawfully make a distribution equal in value to that assistance. It includes, in a case where the financial assistance consists of or includes, or is treated as arising in consequence of, the sale, transfer or other disposition of a non-cash asset, any profit that, if the company were to make a distribution of that character, would be available for that purpose. See **22 Distributions** generally and particularly **22.1** for the meaning of '*distribution*'.

[*CA 2006, ss 678(2)(4), 679(2)(4), 681–683*].

34.22 SHARES HELD BY COMPANY'S NOMINEE

The provisions in (1) and (2) below apply where shares in a limited company are

(a) taken by a subscriber to the memorandum as nominee of the company;

(b) issued to a nominee of the company; or

(c) acquired by a nominee of the company, partly paid up, from a third person.

(1) **Treatment of shares**

For all purposes

- the shares are to be treated as held by the nominee on his own account; and
- the company is to be regarded as having no 'beneficial interest' in them.

This does not apply to shares acquired

- otherwise than by subscription by a nominee of a public company, where
  - (i) a person acquires shares in the company with financial assistance given to him, directly or indirectly, by the company for the purpose of or in connection with the acquisition; and
  - (ii) the company has a beneficial interest in the shares; and
- by a nominee of the company when the company has no beneficial interest in the shares.

[*CA 2006, s 660*].

(2) **Liability of others where nominee fails to make payment in respect of shares**

If the nominee, having been called on to pay any amount for the purposes of paying up, or paying any premium on, the shares, fails to pay that amount within 21 days from being called on to do so, then

- in the case of shares that he agreed to take as subscriber to the memorandum, the other subscribers to the memorandum, and
- in any other case, the directors of the company when the shares were issued to or acquired by him,

are jointly and severally liable with him to pay that amount.

If, in proceedings for the recovery of an amount due as above, it appears to the court that the subscriber or director has acted honestly and reasonably and, having regard to all the circumstances of the case, ought fairly to be relieved from liability, the court may relieve him, either wholly or in part, from his liability on such terms as the court thinks fit.

If a subscriber to a company's memorandum or a director of a company has reason to apprehend that a claim will or might be made for the recovery of any such amount from him, he may apply to the court for relief. The court then has the same power to relieve him as it would have had in proceedings for recovery of that amount.

The above provisions do not apply to shares acquired by a nominee of the company when the company has no beneficial interest in the shares.

[*CA 2006, s 661*].

See **34.29** for '*beneficial interests*' in this context.

34.23 DUTY TO CANCEL SHARES IN PUBLIC COMPANY HELD BY OR FOR THE COMPANY

The following provisions apply in the case of a public company where

(a) shares in the company are forfeited, or surrendered to the company in lieu of forfeiture, in pursuance of the articles, for failure to pay any sum payable in respect of the shares;

(b) shares in the company are surrendered to the company in pursuance of *Building Societies Act 1986, s 102C(1)(b)*;

(c) shares in the company are acquired by it (otherwise than in accordance with this chapter or the provisions in *CA 2006, ss 994–999*, see **26.10 MEMBERS**) and the company has a 'beneficial interest' in the shares;

(d) a nominee of the company acquires shares in the company from a third party without financial assistance being given directly or indirectly by the company and the company has a beneficial interest in the shares; or

(e) a person acquires shares in the company, with financial assistance given to him, directly or indirectly, by the company for the purpose of or in connection with the acquisition, and the company has a beneficial interest in the shares.

Where any of the situations in (*a*)–(*e*) above apply, then, unless the shares or any interest of the company in them are previously disposed of, the company must

- cancel the shares and diminish the amount of the company's share capital by the nominal value of the shares cancelled; and
- where the effect is that the nominal value of the company's allotted share capital is brought below the authorised minimum (see **33.3 PUBLIC AND LISTED COMPANIES**), apply for re-registration as a private company (see **34.25**), stating the effect of the cancellation.

It must do so no later than

(i) in a case within (*a*) or (*b*) above, three years from the date of the forfeiture or surrender;

(ii) in a case within (*c*) or (*d*) above, three years from the date of the acquisition; and

(iii) in a case within (*e*) above, one year from the date of the acquisition.

The directors of the company may take any steps necessary to enable the company to comply with these requirements, and may do so without complying with the provisions of *CA 2006, ss 641–653* (reduction of capital, see **47.51–47.58** SHARES).

Neither the company nor, in a case within (*d*) or (*e*) above, the nominee or other shareholder may exercise any voting rights in respect of the shares. Any purported exercise of those rights is void.

[*CA 2006, s 662*].

See **34.29** for '*beneficial interests*' in this context.

The above provisions apply where

- the event in (*a*)–(*e*) above, or
- the event in **34.27**(*a*)–(*d*)

occurs on or after 1 October 2009. They also apply where a similar event in *CA 1985, s 146(1)* occurred before 1 October 2009 unless, before that date, the company complied with *CA 1985, s 146(2)* or the period for compliance specified in *CA 1985, s 146(3)* has expired.

Old public companies. In the provisions above and in **34.24–34.28** references to a public company do not include an 'old public company' (see APPENDIX 1 DEFINITIONS). [*SI 2009 No 1917, Schedule para 7*].

34.24 Notice of cancellation of shares

Where a company cancels shares in order to comply with **34.23**, it must within one month after the shares are cancelled give notice to the Registrar of Companies, specifying the shares cancelled. The notice must be accompanied by a statement of capital, stating the following particulars with respect to the company's share capital immediately following the cancellation.

(a) The total number of shares of the company.

(b) The aggregate nominal value of those shares.

(c) For each class of shares

  (i) particulars of any voting rights attached to the shares, including rights that arise only in certain circumstances;

  (ii) particulars of any rights attached to the shares, as respects dividends, to participate in a distribution;

  (iii) particulars of any rights attached to the shares, as respects capital, to participate in a distribution (including on a winding up);

  (iv) whether the shares are to be redeemed or are liable to be redeemed at the option of the company or the shareholder;

  (v) the total number of shares of that class; and

  (vi) the aggregate nominal value of shares of that class.

(d) The amount paid up and the amount (if any) unpaid on each share (whether on account of the nominal value of the share or by way of premium).

If default is made in complying with this provision, an offence is committed by the company and every officer of the company who is in default. A person guilty of such an offence is liable, on summary conviction, to a fine not exceeding level 3 on the standard scale and, for continued contravention, a daily default fine not exceeding one-tenth of level 3 on the standard scale. See **29.1 Offences and Legal Proceedings** for the standard scale.

[*CA 2006, s 663; SI 2009 No 388, Art 2*].

34.25 Re-registration as a private company in consequence of cancellation

Where a company is obliged to re-register as a private company to comply with *CA 2006, s 662* (see **34.23**), the directors may resolve that the company should be so re-registered.

CA 2006, ss 29, 30 (resolutions affecting company's constitution, see **14.10 Constitution – Memorandum and Articles**) apply to any such resolution. The resolution may make such changes in the company's name and in the company's articles as are necessary in connection with its becoming a private company.

The application for re-registration must contain a statement of the company's proposed name on re-registration and must be accompanied by

- a copy of the resolution (unless a copy has already been forwarded);
- a copy of the company's articles as amended by the resolution; and
- a statement of compliance confirming that the requirements of these provisions as to re-registration as a private company have been complied with. The Registrar of Companies may accept the statement of compliance as sufficient evidence that the company is entitled to be re-registered as a private company.

[*CA 2006, s 664*].

Issue of certificate of incorporation on re-registration. If, on an application under the above provisions, the Registrar of Companies is satisfied that the company is entitled to be re-registered as a private company, the company must be re-registered accordingly. The Registrar must issue a certificate of incorporation altered to meet the circumstances of the case. It must state that it is issued on re-registration and the date on which it is issued.

On the issue of the certificate, the company becomes a private company and the changes in the company's name and articles take effect. The certificate is conclusive evidence that the requirements of *CA 2006* as to re-registration have been complied with.

[*CA 2006, s 665*].

Effect of failure to re-register. If a public company that is required by **34.23** to apply to be re-registered as a private company fails to do so within the specified time, *CA 2006, ss 755–760* (prohibition of public offers by private company, see **47.21** and **47.22 Shares**) apply to it as if it were a private company. Subject to that, the company continues to be treated as a public company until it is so re-registered.

[*CA 2006, s 666*].

Transitional provisions. The above provisions apply in any case where *CA 2006, s 662* applies (see **34.23**).

34.26 Offences for failure to cancel or re-register

Where a company, when required to do by under **34.23**, fails within the specified time to

- cancel any shares,
- make an application for re-registration as a private company,

an offence is committed by the company and every officer of the company who is in default. A person guilty of such an offence is liable, on summary conviction, to a fine not exceeding level 3 on the standard scale and, for continued contravention, a daily default fine not exceeding one-tenth of level 3 on the standard scale. See **29.1 Offences and Legal Proceedings** for the standard scale.

[*CA 2006, s 667*].

34.27 Application of the provisions to company re-registering as a public company

Where, after shares in a private company have been

(a) forfeited in pursuance of the company's articles or are surrendered to the company in lieu of forfeiture,

(b) acquired by the company (otherwise than by any of the methods permitted in this chapter or under the provisions in *CA 2006, ss 994–999*, see **26.10 Members**), the company having a 'beneficial interest' in the shares,

(c) acquired by a nominee of the company from a third party without financial assistance being given directly or indirectly by the company, the company having a beneficial interest in the shares, or

(d) acquired by a person with financial assistance given to him, directly or indirectly, by the company for the purpose of or in connection with the acquisition, the company having a beneficial interest in the shares,

the company is re-registered as a public company, the provisions of **34.23–34.26** apply to the company as if it had been a public company at the time of the forfeiture, surrender or acquisition, subject to the following modification. The modification is that the period specified in **34.23**(i)–(iii) runs from the date of the re-registration of the company as a public company.

[*CA 2006, s 668*].

See **34.29** for '*beneficial interests*' in this context.

Transitional provisions. See **34.23** for transitional provisions affecting the above.

Old public companies. The above provisions apply to an 'old public company' (see **Appendix 1 Definitions**) as to a private company.

[*SI 2009 No 1917, Schedule para 7*].

34.28 Accounting treatment of shares held by public company or nominee

Where

- a public company, or a nominee of a public company, acquires shares in the company, and
- those shares are shown in a balance sheet of the company as an asset,

an amount equal to the value of the shares must be transferred out of profits available for dividend to a reserve fund and is not then available for distribution.

This applies to an interest in shares as it applies to shares, in which case the reference to the value of the shares must be read as a reference to the value to the company of its interest in the shares. [*CA 2006, s 669*].

34.29 BENEFICIAL INTEREST

In determining for the purposes of **34.22**, **34.23** and **34.27** whether a company has a beneficial interest in shares, the following interests are to be disregarded. [*CA 2006, s 671*].

(1) **Residual interests under pension and share schemes**

Where the shares are held on trust for the purposes of a 'pension scheme' or employees' share scheme, any 'residual interest' of the company that has not vested in possession. A '*residual interest*' means a right of the company to receive any of the trust property in the event of

(i) all the liabilities arising under the scheme having been satisfied or provided for;

(ii) the company ceasing to participate in the scheme; or

(iii) the trust property at any time exceeding what is necessary for satisfying the liabilities arising or expected to arise under the scheme.

A residual interest vests in possession under (i) above on the occurrence of the event mentioned there and under (ii) and (iii) above when the company becomes entitled to require the trustee to transfer to it any of the property receivable pursuant to that right.

Where by virtue of these provisions shares are

- exempt from **34.22**(1) or (2) at the time they are taken, issued or acquired but the residual interest in question vests in possession before they are disposed of or fully paid up, **34.22**(1) and (2) apply to the shares as if they had been taken, issued or acquired on the date on which that interest vests in possession; and
- exempt from **34.23**–**34.27** at the time they are acquired but the residual interest in question vests in possession before they are disposed of, those provisions apply to the shares as if they had been acquired on the date on which the interest vests in possession.

[*CA 2006, s 672*].

(2) **Employer's charges and other rights of recovery**

Where the shares are held on trust for the purposes of a 'pension scheme' there must be disregarded

- any charge or lien on, or set-off against, any benefit or other right or interest under the scheme for the purpose of enabling the employer or former employer of a member of the scheme to obtain the discharge of a monetary obligation due to him from the member; and
- any right to receive from the trustee of the scheme, or as trustee of the scheme to retain, an amount that can be recovered or retained under

  (i) *Pension Schemes Act 1993, s 61* or otherwise, as reimbursement or partial reimbursement for any contributions equivalent premium paid in connection with the scheme under *Part 3* of that *Act*; or

(ii) *Pension Schemes (Northern Ireland) Act 1993, s 57* or otherwise, as reimbursement or partial reimbursement for any contributions equivalent premium paid in connection with the scheme under *Part 3* of that *Act*.

Where the shares are held on trust for the purposes of an employees' share scheme, there must be disregarded any charge or lien on, or set-off against, any benefit or other right or interest under the scheme for the purpose of enabling the employer or former employer of a member of the scheme to obtain the discharge of a monetary obligation due to him from the member. [*CA 2006, s 673*].

(3) **Rights as personal representative or trustee**

Where the company is a personal representative or trustee, there must be disregarded any rights that the company has in that capacity including, in particular

- any right to recover its expenses or be remunerated out of the estate or trust property; and
- any right to be indemnified out of that property for any liability incurred by reason of any act or omission of the company in the performance of its duties as personal representative or trustee.

[*CA 2006, s 674*].

'*Pension scheme*' means a scheme for the provision of benefits consisting of, or including, 'relevant benefits' for, or in respect of, employees or former employees and for this purposes, employee is read as if a director of a company were employed by it. '*Relevant benefits*' means any pension, lump sum, gratuity or other like benefit given or to be given on retirement or on death or in anticipation of retirement or, in connection with past service, after retirement or death. [*CA 2006, ss 675, 676*].

34.30 CHARGES OF PUBLIC COMPANY ON OWN SHARES

A lien or other charge of a public company on its own shares (whether taken expressly or otherwise) is void with the following exceptions.

(a) In the case of any description of company, a charge is permitted if the shares are not fully paid up and the charge is for an amount payable in respect of the shares.

(b) In the case of a company whose ordinary business

(i) includes the lending of money, or

(ii) consists of the provision of credit or the bailment (in Scotland, hiring) of goods under a hire purchase agreement, or both,

a charge is permitted (whether the shares are fully paid or not) if it arises in connection with a transaction entered into by the company in the ordinary course of that business.

(c) In the case of a company that has been re-registered as a public company, a charge is permitted if it was in existence immediately before the application for re-registration.

(d) In the case of a company that

(i) after 22 March 1982 (if registered in Great Britain) or after 30 September 1984 (if registered in Northern Ireland) remained an 'old public company' (see **Appendix 1 Definitions**), and

(ii) did not apply before that date to be re-registered as a public company

any charge on its own shares which was in existence on or immediately before that date. [*CA 2006, s 670; SI 2009 No 1917, Schedule para 7*].

35 Reconstructions and Mergers

35.1	**Arrangements and reconstructions**
35.2	Meeting of creditors or members
35.3	Court sanction for compromise or arrangement
35.4	Power of court to facilitate reconstruction or amalgamation
35.5	Obligations with respect to articles, etc
35.6	**Mergers and divisions of public companies**
35.7	Mergers
35.18	Divisions
35.30A	Disregard of website failures beyond control of company
35.31	Expert's report: supplementary provisions
35.32	Powers of the court
35.33	**Merger references**
35.34	**EC Merger Control Regulations**
35.35	**Cross-border mergers**
35.36	Meaning of cross-border merger
35.37	Pre-merger requirements
35.46	Power of court to summon meetings of members or creditors
35.47	Court approval of cross-border merger
35.48	Consequences of a cross-border merger
35.49	Copies of order to be provided to members and delivered to the Registrar of Companies
35.50	Amendment of transferee company's articles, etc
35.51	Notification of registration by Registrar of Companies
35.52	Employee participation
35.60	Unregistered companies
35.61	Application of certain provisions of *CA 2006*

Cross-references. See **47.51** SHARES for reduction of share capital.

35.1 ARRANGEMENTS AND RECONSTRUCTIONS

The provisions in **35.2** to **35.5** enable companies to apply to the court for an order sanctioning an arrangement or reconstruction. They have effect where a compromise or 'arrangement' is proposed between a 'company' and

- its creditors (or any class of them); or
- its members (or any class of them).

'*Arrangement*' for these purposes includes a reorganisation of the company's share capital by the consolidation of shares of different classes or by the division of shares into shares of different classes or both.

'*Company*' means any company liable to be wound up under *IA 1986* or *Insolvency (Northern Ireland) Order 1989* except in **35.4** where it means any company within the meaning of *CA 2006* (see **12.1** COMPANY FORMATION AND TYPES OF COMPANIES).

The provisions have effect subject to **35.6** to **35.32** (mergers and divisions of public companies) where those provisions apply (see **35.6**).

[*CA 2006, s 895*].

A '*class*' must be confined to those persons whose rights are not so dissimilar as to make it impossible for them to consult together with a view to their common interest (*Sovereign Life Assurance Co v Dodd* [1892] 2 QB 573, CA). See, for example, *Re Hellenic*

& General Trust Ltd [1975] 3 All ER 382, [1976] 1 WLR 123 where 53% of the ordinary shares were held by a company interested in the proposed arrangement. It was held that the remaining 47% of shareholders formed a separate class of whom the necessary three-quarters majority approval was required.

35.2 Meeting of creditors or members

Where an application is made to the court by

- a company liable to be wound up,
- any creditor or member of the company,
- if the company is being wound up, the liquidator, or
- if the company is in administration, the administrator

the court may order a meeting of the creditors (or any class of them) or the members (or any class of them) of the company, as the case may be, to be summoned in such manner as the court directs. At any such meeting, *CA 2006, s 323* (representation of corporations at meetings (see **42.25 Resolutions and Meetings**) applies to a meeting of the creditors summoned under these provisions as to a meeting of the company (the references to a member of the company being read as references to the creditor).

[*CA 2006, s 896*].

Statement to be circulated. Where such a meeting is summoned, every notice summoning the meeting that is sent to a creditor or member must be accompanied by a statement

- explaining the effect of the compromise or arrangement;
- in particular, stating
  - (i) any material interests of the company's directors (whether as directors or as members or as creditors of the company or otherwise); and
  - (ii) the effect on those interests of the proposed compromise or arrangement, insofar as it is different from the effect on like interests of other persons; and
- where the compromise or arrangement affects the rights of debenture-holders, giving the like explanation as respects the trustees of any deed for securing the issue of the debentures as it is required to give as respects the company's directors.

Where any notice summoning the meeting is given by advertisement, it must either include such a statement as required above or state where and how creditors or members entitled to attend the meeting may obtain copies of such a statement (which must be supplied free of charge on application in the manner indicated by the notice).

[*CA 2006, s 897(1)–(4)*].

It is essential that the explanatory circulars sent out by the company are perfectly fair and, as far as possible, give all the information reasonably necessary to enable the recipients to determine how to vote (*Re Dorman, Long & Co Ltd, Re South Durham Steel and Iron Co Ltd* [1934] Ch 635, 103 LJ Ch 316).

If a company defaults in complying with any requirements set out above, an offence is committed by the company and every officer of the company who is in default. (For this purpose, a liquidator or administrator of the company and a trustee of a deed for securing the issue of debentures of the company is treated as an officer of the company.) A person guilty of such an offence is liable (i) on conviction on indictment, to a fine; and (ii) on summary conviction, to a fine not exceeding the statutory maximum. See **29.1 OFFENCES AND LEGAL PROCEEDINGS** for the statutory maximum. A person is not guilty of an offence if he shows that the default was due to the refusal of a director or trustee for debenture holders to supply the necessary particulars of his interests. [*CA 2006, s 897(5)–(8)*].

Duty of directors and trustees to provide information. A director or trustee for debenture holders must give notice to the company of such matters relating to himself as may be necessary for the statement to be circulated. Any person in default of this requirement commits an offence and is liable, on summary conviction, to a fine not exceeding level 3 on the standard scale (see **29.1 OFFENCES AND LEGAL PROCEEDINGS**).

[*CA 2006, s 898*].

35.3 Court sanction for compromise or arrangement

If a majority in number representing 75% in value of the creditors (or class of creditors) or members (or class of members), as the case may be, present and voting either in person or by proxy at the meeting summoned under **35.2** agree a compromise or arrangement, the court may sanction the compromise or arrangement on an application by

- the company;
- any creditor or member of the company;
- if the company is being wound up, the liquidator; or
- if the company is in administration, the administrator.

A compromise or arrangement sanctioned by the court is binding on

- all creditors/members (or class thereof) concerned; and
- the company or, where the company is being wound up, the liquidator and contributories of the company.

The court's order has no effect until a copy of it has been delivered to the Registrar of Companies.

[*CA 2006, s 899*].

In deciding whether to sanction the compromise or arrangement, the court must ensure not only that the statutory provisions are complied with but also that the majority has acted *bona fide*. It must see that the minority is not being overridden by a majority with adverse interests and that the scheme overall is reasonable. A scheme cannot be reasonable where a party gets nothing and gives up everything (*Re Alabama, New Orleans, Texas and Pacific Junction Rly Co* [1891] 1 Ch 213, CA). See also *NFU (or National Farmers' Union) Development Trust Ltd, Re* [1973] 1 All ER 135, [1972] 1 WLR 1548.

35.4 Powers of court to facilitate reconstruction or amalgamation

Where

- a compromise or arrangement is proposed between a company and its creditors (or any class of them) or its members (or any class of them),

- an application is made to the court to sanction that compromise or arrangement under 35.3, and
- it is shown that the compromise or arrangement is proposed for the purposes of, or connected with,

  (i) a scheme for the reconstruction of any two or more companies, or

  (ii) the amalgamation of any two or more companies

  under which the whole or a part of the undertaking or the 'property' of any company concerned in the scheme (a 'transferor company') is to be transferred to another (the 'transferee company'),

the court may provide, either by order sanctioning the compromise or arrangement or by any subsequent order, for all or any of the following.

- The transfer to the transferee company of the whole or any part of the undertaking, and of the property or 'liabilities', of any transferor company.
- The allotting or appropriation by the transferee company of any shares, debentures, policies, etc under the compromise or arrangement to or for any person.
- The continuation by or against the transferee company of any legal proceedings pending by or against any transferor company.
- The dissolution, without winding up, of any transferor company.
- Provision to be made for dissenters.
- Any such incidental, consequential and supplemental matters as are necessary to ensure that the reconstruction or amalgamation is fully and effectively carried out.

If the order provides for the transfer of property or liabilities, that property is thereby transferred to, and vests in, the transferee company and those liabilities are transferred to, and become liabilities of, that company.

The property (if the order so directs) vests freed from any charge that is by virtue of the compromise or arrangement to cease to have effect.

'*Property*' for these purposes includes property, rights and powers of every description.

'*Liabilities*' includes duties.

Where an order as above is made, every company in relation to which the order is made must cause a copy of the order to be delivered to the Registrar of Companies for registration within seven days after its making. In default in complying with this requirement, an offence is committed by the company and every officer of the company who is in default. A person guilty of such an offence is liable, on summary conviction, to a fine not exceeding level 3 on the standard scale and, for continued contravention, a daily default fine not exceeding one-tenth of level 3 on the standard scale. See **29.1** Offences and Legal Proceedings for the standard scale.

[*CA 2006, s 900*].

35.5 Obligations with respect to articles, etc

Where an order under the provisions in 35.3, or an order under the provisions in 35.4 altering a company's constitution, amends

- the company's articles, or
- any resolution or agreement to which *CA 2006, ss 29, 30* apply (resolution or agreement affecting a company's constitution, see **14.10** CONSTITUTION – MEMORANDUM AND ARTICLES),

the copy of the order required to delivered to the Registrar of Companies by the company under those provisions must be accompanied by a copy of the company's articles' or the resolution or agreement in question, as amended.

Every copy of the company's articles issued by the company after the order is made must be accompanied by a copy of the order (unless the effect of the order has been incorporated into the articles by amendment).

In the case of a company not having articles, references above to its articles must be read as references to the instrument constituting the company or defining its constitution.

If a company makes default in complying with these requirements, an offence is committed by the company, and every officer of the company who is in default. A person guilty of such an offence is liable, on summary conviction, to a fine not exceeding level 3 on the standard scale. See **29.1** OFFENCES AND LEGAL PROCEEDINGS for the standard scale. [*CA 2006, s 901*].

35.6 MERGERS AND DIVISIONS OF PUBLIC COMPANIES

The provisions in **35.7** to **35.32** apply where

- a compromise or arrangement is proposed between a public company and
  - (i) its creditors (or any class of them), or
  - (ii) its members (or any class of them)

  for the purposes of, or in connection with, a scheme for the reconstruction of any company or companies or the amalgamation of any two or more companies;
- the scheme involves
  - (i) a merger (see **35.7**); or
  - (ii) a division (see **35.18**); and
- the consideration for the transfer (or each of the transfers) envisaged is to be shares in the transferee company (or one or more of the transferee companies) receivable by members of the transferor company (or transferor companies), with or without any cash payment to members.

For these purposes

- a '*new company*' means a company formed for the purposes of, or in connection with, the scheme; and
- an '*existing company*' means a company other than one formed for the purposes of, or in connection with, the scheme.

The provisions do not apply where the company in respect of which the compromise or arrangement is proposed is being wound up. [*CA 2006, s 902*].

Relationship to the provisions in 35.1 to 35.5 above. The court must not sanction a compromise or arrangement unless the relevant requirements of the provisions in 35.7 to 35.32 have been complied with. For this purpose,

(1) the requirements applicable to a merger of public companies are detailed in 35.7 to 35.16, although certain of those requirements, and certain general requirements of 35.1 to 35.5, are modified or excluded by the provisions in 35.17; and

(2) the requirements applicable to a division of public companies are detailed in 35.18 to 35.28, although certain of those requirements, and certain general requirements of 35.1 to 35.5, are modified or excluded by the provisions of 35.29.

[*CA 2006, s 903*].

35.7 Mergers

A scheme involves a merger where under the scheme the undertaking, 'property' and 'liabilities' of

- one or more public companies, including the company in respect of which the compromise or arrangement is proposed, are to be transferred to another existing public company (a '*merger by absorption*'); or
- two or more public companies, including the company in respect of which the compromise or arrangement is proposed, are to be transferred to a new company, whether or not a public company, (a '*merger by formation of a new company*').

The '*merging companies*' are

- in relation to a merger by absorption, to the transferor and transferee companies; and
- in relation to a merger by formation of a new company, to the transferor companies.

'*Property*' includes property, rights and powers of every description.

'*Liabilities*' include duties.

[*CA 2006, ss 904, 941*].

35.8 *Draft terms of scheme*

The directors of the merging companies must draw up, and adopt, a draft of the proposed terms of the scheme. These draft terms must give particulars of *at least* the following matters.

(a) In respect of each transferor company and the transferee company

   (i) its name;

   (ii) the address of its registered office; and

   (iii) whether it is a company limited by shares or a company limited by guarantee and having a share capital.

(b) The number of shares in the transferee company to be allotted to members of a transferor company for a given number of their shares (the '*share exchange ratio*') and the amount of any cash payment.

(c) The terms relating to the allotment of shares in the transferee company.

(d) The date from which the holding of shares in the transferee company will entitle the holders to participate in profits, and any special conditions affecting that entitlement.

(e) The date from which the transactions of a transferor company are to be treated for accounting purposes as being those of the transferee company.

(f) Any rights or restrictions attaching to shares or other securities in the transferee company to be allotted under the scheme to the holders of shares or other securities in a transferor company to which any special rights or restrictions attach, or the measures proposed concerning them.

(g) Any amount of benefit paid or given or intended to be paid or given

(i) to any of the experts referred to in **35.11** (expert's report); or

(ii) to any director of a merging company,

and the consideration for the payment of benefit.

But see **35.17**(1) for circumstances in which the information in (*b*), (*c*) and (*d*) is not required.

[*CA 2006, s 905*].

Publication of draft terms. The directors of each of the merging companies must deliver a copy of the draft terms to the Registrar of Companies. The Registrar must then publish in the Gazette notice of receipt from that company of a copy of the draft terms. That notice must be published at least one month before the date of any meeting of that company summoned for the purpose of approving the scheme. [*CA 2006, s 906*].

The requirements of *s 906* (above) do not apply if:

- the draft terms of the merger are made available on a website which is maintained by or on behalf of the company and identifies the company;
- and neither access to the draft terms on the website nor the supply of a hard copy of them is conditional on payment of a fee or otherwise restricted;
- and the directors of the company deliver a notice giving details of the website to the Registrar of Companies;
- and the Registrar publishes the notice in the Gazette at least one month before the date of any meeting summoned for the purpose of approving the scheme;
- and the draft terms remain available on the website throughout the period beginning one month before and ending on the date of any such meeting.

See **35.30A** for disregard of website failures

[*CA 2006, s 906A*]

35.9 *Approval of members of merging companies*

The scheme must be approved by a majority in number, representing 75% in value, of each class of members of each of the merging companies, present and voting either in person or by proxy at a meeting. But see **35.17**(2)–(4) for circumstances in which meetings of members are not required. [*CA 2006, s 907*].

35.10 *Directors' explanatory report*

The directors of each of the merging companies must draw up and adopt a report consisting of

- the statement required to be circulated under **35.2** (statement explaining effect of compromise or arrangement); and
- insofar as that statement does not deal with the following matters, a further statement
  - (i) setting out the legal and economic grounds for the draft terms, and in particular for the share exchange ratio; and
  - (ii) specifying any special valuation difficulties.

But see **35.17(1)**; **35.17(1A)** and **35.17(5)** for circumstances in which this report is not required.

[*CA 2006, s 908*].

35.11 *Expert's report*

An expert's written report to the members on the draft terms must be drawn up on behalf of each of the merging companies. On the joint application of all the merging companies, the court may approve the appointment of a joint expert to draw up a single report on behalf of all those companies but, if no such appointment is made, there must be a separate expert's report to the members of each merging company drawn up by a separate expert appointed on behalf of that company.

The expert must be a person who is eligible for appointment as a statutory auditor (see **8.8 Audit**) and who meets the independence requirement in **35.31(2)**.

The expert's report must

- indicate the method or methods used to arrive at the share exchange ratio;
- give an opinion as to whether the method or methods used are reasonable in all the circumstances of the case, indicate the values arrived at using each such method and (if there is more than one method) give an opinion on the relative importance attributed to such methods in arriving at the value decided on;
- describe any special valuation difficulties that have arisen;
- state whether, in the expert's opinion, the share exchange ratio is reasonable; and
- in the case of a valuation made by a person other than himself (see **35.31(1)**), state that it appeared to him reasonable to arrange for and accept the valuation.

For the purposes of making his report, the expert (or each of them) has

- the right of access to all such documents of all the merging companies, and
- the right to require from the companies' officers all such information,

as he thinks necessary.

But see **35.17(1)** and **35.17(1A)** for circumstances in which this report is not required and **35.17(5)** for agreement to dispense with an expert's report.

[*CA 2006, s 909*].

35.12 *Supplementary accounting statement*

If the last annual accounts of any of the merging companies relate to a financial year ending before the date seven months before the first meeting of the company summoned for the purposes of approving the scheme (or, if no meeting is required (by virtue of any of *CA 2006 ss 916–918*), the date six months before the directors of the company adopt the draft terms of the scheme, and if the company has not made public a half-yearly financial report relating to a period ending on or after the relevant date, the directors of that company must prepare a supplementary accounting statement. This must consist of

- a balance sheet dealing with the state of affairs of the company as at a date not more than three months before the draft terms were adopted by the directors; and
- where the company would be required to prepare group accounts if that date were the last day of a financial year, a consolidated balance sheet dealing with the state of affairs of the company and the undertakings that would be included in such a consolidation.

The requirements of *CA 2006* (and where relevant *IAS Regulation, Art 4*) as to matters to be included in a balance sheet and the notes to it apply to a balance sheet required under these provisions but with such modifications as are necessary by reason of its being prepared otherwise than as at the last day of a financial year. Similarly, the normal provisions as to the approval and signing of accounts (see **2.2 Accounts: General**) apply to the balance sheet required for an accounting statement under these provisions.

See **35.17(1A)** for circumstances in which reports and inspection are not required and **37.17(5)** for agreement to dispense with reports etc.

[*CA 2006, s 910; SI 2011 No 1606, Reg 9.2* and *9.3*].

35.13 *Inspection of documents*

The members of each of the merging companies must be able (i) to inspect, at the registered office of that company, copies of the following documents relating to that company and every other merging company (this is however subject to the provisions in **35.13A** (below)); and (ii) to obtain copies of those documents, or any part of them, on request and free of charge. The right to a hard copy of the document under *CA 2006, s 1145* does not apply here to a member who has consented to information being sent or supplied by the company by electronic means and who has not revoked that consent.

(a) The draft terms.

(b) The directors' explanatory report (subject to the exceptions in **35.17(1)** and **35.17(5)**).

(c) The expert's report (subject to the exceptions in **35.17(1)** and **35.17(5)**).

(d) The company's annual accounts and reports for the last three financial years ending on or before the first meeting of the members (or any class of members) of the company summoned for the purposes of approving the scheme.

(e) Any supplementary accounting statement required under **35.12**; and

(f) If no supplementary accounting statement is required under **35.12** because the company has made public a recent half-yearly financial report that report.

The period of for inspection or obtaining copies begins one month before, and ends on the date of, the first meeting of the members (or any class of members) of the company for the purposes of approving the scheme.

CA 2006, s 1145 (right to hard copy) does not apply to a document sent or supplied in accordance with (b) (above) to a member who has consented to information being sent or supplied by the company by electronic means and has not revoked that consent and *CA 2006, Schedule 5, Part 4* (communications by means of a website) also does not apply for the purposes of (b).

All of the requirements of *s 911* are subject to **35.17**(1A).

[*CA 2006, s 911; SI 2011 No 1606, Reg 10*].

35.13A *Publication of documents on company website*

The right in **35.13** for members to inspect documents does not apply if

- the document is made available on a website which is maintained on or behalf of the company and identifies the company; and
- access to the document on the website is not conditional on payment of a fee or otherwise restricted; and
- the document remains available on the website throughout the period beginning one month before, and ending on the date of any meeting of the company summoned for the purpose of approving the scheme.

A person is able to obtain a copy of a document free of charge (see **35.13** (above)) if the document is made available on the website and the person is able throughout the period beginning one month before and ending on the date set out above to retain a copy of the document made available on the website and to produce a hard copy of it. Where members are only able to obtain copies of a document in this way, the requirement to make the documents available for inspection set out in **35.13** still applies even if the conditions set out in this paragraph are met.

See **35.30A** for disregard of website failures.

[*CA 2006, s 911A; SI 2011 No 1606, Reg 11*]

Report on material changes of assets of merging companies

35.13B The directors of each of the merging companies must report to every meeting of members, or any class of members, of that company summoned for the purpose of agreeing to the scheme and to the directors of every other merging company, any material changes in the property and liabilities of that company between the date when the draft terms were adopted and the date of the meeting in question. The directors of each of the merging companies must in turn report those matters to every meeting of the members or any class of members of the company summoned for the purpose of agreeing to the scheme or must send a report of those matters to every member entitled to receive notice of the meeting. This requirement is subject to the exceptions in **35.17**(1)A and **35.17**(5).

[*CA 2006, s 911B; SI 2011 No 1606, Reg 12*]

35.14 *Approval of articles of new transferee company*

In the case of a merger by formation of a new company, the articles of the transferee company, or a draft of them, must be approved by ordinary resolution each of the transferor companies. [*CA 2006, s 912*].

35.15 *Protection of holders of securities with special rights*

The scheme must provide that where any securities of a transferor company (other than shares) to which special rights are attached are held by a person otherwise than as a member or creditor of the company, that person is to receive rights in the transferee company of equivalent value unless

- the holder has agreed otherwise; or
- the holder is, or under the scheme is to be, entitled to have the securities purchased by the transferee company on terms that the court considers reasonable.

[*CA 2006, s 913*].

35.16 *No allotment of shares to transferor company or transferee company*

The scheme must not provide for any shares in the transferee company to be allotted to

- a transferor company (or its nominee) in respect of shares in the transferor company held by the transferor company itself (or its nominee); or
- the transferee company (or its nominee) in respect of shares in a transferor company held by the transferee company (or its nominee).

[*CA 2006, s 914*].

35.17 *Exceptions*

(1) *Circumstances in which certain particulars and reports not required*

In the case of a merger by absorption (see **35.7**), if all of the 'relevant securities' of the transferor company (or, if there is more than one transferor company, of each of them) are held by or on behalf of the transferee company

(a) the draft terms of the scheme need not give the particulars mentioned in **35.8**(*b*), (*c*) or (*d*) (particulars relating to allotment of shares to members of transferor company);

(b) the requirement for an explanatory statement to be circulated or made available (see **35.2**) does not apply;

(c) the provisions in **35.10** (directors' explanatory report) and **35.11** (expert's report) do not apply;

(d) the requirements for inspection of documents under **35.13** do not apply so far as relating to any document required to be drawn up under the provisions mentioned in (*c*) above.

[*CA 2006, s 915*].

(1A) *Other circumstances in which reports and inspection not required*

In the case of a merger by absorption (see **35.7**) ,where 90% or more (but not all) of the relevant securities of the transferor company (or, if there is more than one transferor company, each of them) are held by or on behalf of the transferee company then if the scheme provides that every other holder of relevant securities has the right to require the transferee company to acquire those securities, if a holder of securities exercises that right and the consideration to be given for those securities is fair and reasonable then the following do not apply

(a) *CA 2006, s 908* (directors' explanatory report)

(b) *CA 2006, s 909* (expert's report)

(c) *CA 2006, s 910* (supplementary accounting statement)

(d) *CA 2006, s 911* (inspection of documents) and

(e) *CA 2006, s 911B* (report on material changes of assets of merging company).

[*CA 2006, s 915A ; SI 2011 No 1606, Reg 14*]

(2) *Circumstances in which meeting of members of transferee company not required*

In the case of a merger by absorption (see **35.7**), if 90% or more (but not all) of the relevant securities of the transferor company (or, if there is more than one transferor company, of each of them) are held by or on behalf of the transferee company, it is not necessary for the scheme to be approved at a meeting of the members (or any class of members) of the transferee company if the court is satisfied that the following conditions have been complied with.

(a) Publication of notice of receipt of the draft terms by the Registrar of Companies took place in respect of the transferee company at least one month before the date of the first meeting of members (or any class of members) of the transferor company summoned for the purpose of agreeing to the scheme or the draft terms are made available on a website which is maintained by the company and identifies the company and access to the draft terms on the website is not conditional on the payment of a fee or otherwise restricted and the directors of the company deliver a notice to the Registrar giving details of the website and the Registrar published that notice in the *Gazette* at least one month before the date of the first meeting of members (or any class of members) of the transferor company summoned for the purpose of agreeing to the scheme and the draft terms remained available on the website throughout the period beginning one month before, and ending on, that date.

(b) The members of the transferee company were able during the period beginning one month before, and ending on, the date mentioned in **35.2**(a) to

(i) inspect copies of the documents listed in the applicable paragraphs of **35.13**(a)–(f) relating to the transferee company and the transferor company (or, if there is more than one transferor company, each of them) at the registered office of that company or the document is made available on a website which is maintained by the company and identifies the company and access to the. document on the website is not conditional on the payment of a fee or otherwise restricted and the document remains available on the website throughout the period beginning one month before and ending on the date mentioned in **35.15**(2)(a); and

(ii) obtain copies of those documents, or any part of them, on request and free of charge throughout the period beginning one month before, and ending on, the date mentioned in **35.15**(2)(a)

(c) One or more members of the transferee company, who together held not less than 5% of the paid-up capital of the company which carried the right to vote at general meetings of the company (excluding any shares in the company held as treasury shares) would have been able, during that period, to require a meeting of each class of members to be called for the purpose of deciding whether or not to agree to the scheme and no such requirement was made.

For these purposes, '*relevant securities*', in relation to a company, means shares or other securities carrying the right to vote at general meetings of the company.

See **35.30A** for disregard of website failures. [*CA 2006, s 916, SI 2011 No 1606, Reg 15.2–15.4*].

(3) *Circumstances in which no meetings required*

In the case of a merger by absorption (see **35.7**) if all of the relevant securities of the transferor company (or, if there is more than one transferor company, of each of them) are held by or on behalf of the transferee company, it is not necessary for the scheme to be approved at a meeting of the members (or any class of members) of any of the merging companies (see 35.7) if the court is satisfied that the following conditions have been complied with.

(a) Publication of notice of receipt of the draft terms by the Registrar of Companies took place in respect of all the merging companies at least one month before the date of the court's order or the draft terms are made available on a website which is maintained by or on behalf of the company and identifies the company and access to those draft terms or the supply of a hard copy of them is not conditional on the payment of a fee or otherwise restricted and the directors deliver a notice giving details of the website to the Registrar and in each case the Registrar published the notice in the Gazette at least one month before the date of the court's order and the draft terms remain available on the website throughout the period beginning one month before and ending on that date.

(b) The members of the transferee company were able during the period beginning one month before, and ending on, that date to

   (i) inspect at the registered office of that company copies of the applicable documents listed in 35.13(a)–(f) relating to the transferee company and the transferor company (or, if there is more than one transferor company, each of them) or the document is made available on a website which is maintained by or on behalf of the transferee company and identifies the company and access to the document is not conditional on the payment of a fee or otherwise restricted and the document remains available on the website throughout the period beginning one month before and ending on the date mentioned in (a) above; and

   (ii) obtain copies of those documents, or any part of them, on request and free of charge throughout the period beginning one month before, and ending on, the date mentioned in (a) above.

(c) One or more members of the transferee company, who together held not less than 5% of the paid-up capital of the company which carried the right to vote at general meetings of the company (excluding any shares in the company held as treasury shares) would have been able, during that period, to require a meeting of each class of members to be called for the purpose of deciding whether or not to agree to the scheme and no such requirement was made.

For these purposes, '*relevant securities*', in relation to a company, means shares or other securities carrying the right to vote at general meetings of the company.

[*CA 2006, s 917; SI 2011 No 1606, Reg 16.2–16.4*].

(4) *Other circumstances in which meeting of members of transferee company are not required*

In the case of any merger by absorption (see 35.7), it is not necessary for the scheme to be approved by the members of the transferee company if the court is satisfied that the following conditions have been complied with.

(a) Publication of notice of receipt of the draft terms by the Registrar of Companies took place in respect of the transferee company at least one month before the date of the first meeting of members (or any class of members) of the transferor company (or, if there is more than one transferor company, any of them) summoned for the purposes of agreeing to the scheme or the draft terms are made available on a website which is maintained by the company and identifies the company and access to the draft terms on the website is not conditional on the payment of a fee or otherwise restricted and the directors of the company deliver a notice to the Registrar giving details of the website and the Registrar published that notice in the Gazette at least one month before the date of the first meeting of members (or any class of members) of the transferor company (or, if there is more than one transferor company, any of them) summoned for the purpose of agreeing to the scheme and the draft terms remained available on the website throughout the period beginning one month before, and ending on, that date.

(b) The members of that company were able during the period beginning one month before, and ending on, the date of any such meeting to

(i) inspect at the registered office of that company copies of the documents specified in the applicable paragraphs of **35.13**(a)–(f) relating to the transferee company and the transferor company (or, if there is more than one transferor company, each of them) or the document is made available on a website which is maintained by or on behalf of the transferee company and identifies the company and access to the document is not conditional on the payment of a fee or otherwise restricted and the document remains available on the website throughout the period beginning one month before and ending on the date mentioned in (a) above; and

(ii) obtain copies of those documents or any part of them on request and free of charge throughout the period beginning one month before and ending on the date of any such meeting mentioned in (a) above.

(c) One or more members of that company, who together held not less than 5% of the paid-up capital of the company which carried the right to vote at general meetings of the company (excluding any shares in the company held as treasury shares) would have been able, during that period, to require a meeting of each class of members to be called for the purpose of deciding whether or not to agree to the scheme and no such requirement was made.

[*CA 2006, s 918; SI 2011 No 1606, Reg 17.2–17.4*].

(5) *Agreement to dispense with reports etc*

If all members holding shares in, and all persons holding other securities of, the merging companies, being shares or securities that carry a right to vote in general meetings of the company in question, so agree, the following requirements do not apply

- *CA 2006, s 908* (directors' explanatory report)
- *CA 2006, s 909* (expert's reports)
- *CA 2006, s 911B* (report on material changes of company assets of merging company) and
- *CA 2006, s 911* (inspection of documents) so far as relating to any documents required to be drawn up under *CA 2006, ss 908, 909* or *910*.

For these purposes

- the members, or holders of other securities, of a company, and
- whether shares or other securities carry a right to vote in general meetings of the company,

are determined as at the date of the application to the court under *CA 2006, s 896* (see **35.2**).

[*CA 2006, s 918A*].

35.18 Divisions

A scheme involves a division where under the scheme the undertaking, 'property' and 'liabilities' of the company in respect of which the compromise or arrangement is proposed are to be divided among and transferred to two or more companies each of which is either

- an existing public company; or
- a new company (whether or not a public company).

References to the companies involved in the division are to the transferor company and any existing transferee companies.

'*Property*' includes property, rights and powers of every description.

'*Liabilities*' include duties.

[*CA 2006, ss 919, 941*].

35.19 *Draft terms of scheme*

A draft of the proposed terms of the scheme must be drawn up and adopted by the directors of each of the companies involved in the division. The draft terms must cover at least the following.

(a) In respect of the transferor company and each transferee company,

  (i) its name;

  (ii) the address of its registered office; and

  (iii) whether it is a company limited by shares or a company limited by guarantee and having a share capital.

(b) The number of shares in a transferee company to be allotted to members of the transferor company for a given number of their shares (the '*share exchange ratio*') and the amount of any cash payment.

(c) The terms relating to the allotment of shares in a transferee company.

(d) The date from which the holding of shares in a transferee company will entitle the holders to participate in profits, and any special conditions affecting that entitlement.

(e) The date from which the transactions of the transferor company are to be treated for accounting purposes as being those of a transferee company.

(f) Any rights or restrictions attaching to shares or other securities in a transferee company to be allotted under the scheme to the holders of shares or other securities in the transferor company to which any special rights or restrictions attach, or the measures proposed concerning them.

(g) Any amount of benefit paid or given or intended to be paid or given

  (i) to any of the experts referred to in **35.22**, or

  (ii) to any director of a company involved in the division,

  and the consideration for the payment of benefit.

(h) Particulars of the 'property' and 'liabilities' to be transferred (to the extent that these are known to the transferor company) and their allocation among the transferee companies.

(i) Provision for the allocation among, and transfer to, the transferee companies of any other property and liabilities that the transferor company has acquired or may subsequently acquire.

(j) Specify the allocation to members of the transferor company of shares in the transferee companies and the criteria upon which that allocation is based.

'*Property*' includes property, rights and powers of every description.

'*Liabilities*' include duties. [*CA 1006, s 920*].

Publication of draft terms by Registrar. The directors of each company involved in a division must deliver a copy of the draft terms to the Registrar of Companies. The Registrar must then publish in the Gazette notice of receipt from that company of a copy of the draft terms. That notice must be published at least one month before the date of any meeting of that company summoned for the purpose of approving the scheme. But these requirements are subject to **35.19A** (publication of draft terms on company website) and **35.29**(4) (power of court to exclude certain requirements).

[*CA 2006, s 921; SI 2011 No 1606, Reg 19(1)* and *19(2)*]

35.19A *Publication of draft terms on company website*

The provisions set out in **35.19** do not apply if

- the draft terms are available on a website which is maintained by or on behalf of the company and identifies the company
- access to the draft terms on the website or the supply of a hard copy of them is not conditional on payment of a fee or otherwise restricted
- directors of the company deliver a notice to the Registrar giving details of the website
- the Registrar publishes the notice in the Gazette at least one month before the date of any meeting of the company summoned for the purpose of approving the scheme and
- the draft terms remain available on the website throughout the period beginning one month before, and ending on, the date of any such meeting.

[*CA 2006, s 921A; SI 2011, No 1606 Reg 20*]

35.20 *Approval of members of companies involved in the division*

The compromise or arrangement must be approved by a majority in number, representing 75% in value, of each class of members of each of the companies involved in the division, present and voting either in person or by proxy at a meeting. But see **35.29**(1) and (2) for circumstances in which meetings of members are not required. [*CA 2006, s 922*].

35.21 *Directors' explanatory report*

The directors of the transferor and each existing transferee company must draw up and adopt a report consisting of

- the statement required to be circulated under **35.2** (statement explaining effect of compromise or arrangement); and

- insofar as that statement does not deal with the following matters, a further statement
  - (i) setting out the legal and economic grounds for the draft terms, and in particular for the share exchange ratio and for the criteria on which the allocation to the members of the transferor company of shares in the transferee companies was based; and
  - (ii) specifying any special valuation difficulties.

The report must also state

- whether a report has been made to any transferee company under *CA 2006, s 593* (valuation of non-cash consideration for shares, see **47.31** SHARES); and
- if so, whether that report has been delivered to the Registrar of Companies.

But see **35.29**(3) and **35.29**(3A) for circumstances in which this report is not required.

[*CA 2006, s 923*].

35.22 *Expert's report*

An expert's written report to the members on the draft terms must be drawn up on behalf of each company involved in the division. On the joint application of the companies involved in the division, the court may approve the appointment of a joint expert to draw up a single report on behalf of all those companies but, if no such appointment is made, there must be a separate expert's report to the members of each company involved in the division drawn up by a separate expert appointed on behalf of that company.

The expert must be a person who is eligible for appointment as a statutory auditor (see **8.8** AUDIT) and who meets the independence requirement in **35.31**(2).

The expert's report must

- indicate the method or methods used to arrive at the share exchange ratio;
- give an opinion as to whether the method or methods used are reasonable in all the circumstances of the case, indicate the values arrived at using each such method and (if there is more than one method) give an opinion on the relative importance attributed to such methods in arriving at the value decided on;
- describe any special valuation difficulties that have arisen;
- state whether, in the expert's opinion, the share exchange ratio is reasonable; and
- in the case of a valuation made by a person other than himself (see **35.31**(1)), state that it appeared to him reasonable to arrange for and accept the valuation.

For the purposes of making his report, the expert (or each of them) has

- the right of access to all such documents of the companies involved in the division, and
- the right to require from the companies' officers all such information,

as he thinks necessary.

But see **35.29**(3) and **35.29**(3A) for circumstances in which this report is not required.

[*CA 2006, s 924*].

35.23 *Supplementary accounting statement*

If the last annual accounts of a company involved in the division relate to a financial year ending before the date seven months before the first meeting of the company summoned for the purposes of approving the scheme (or if no meeting of the company is required (by virtue of *CA 2006, ss 931* or *932*) the date six months before the directors of the company adopt the draft terms of the scheme) and if the company has not made public a half-yearly financial report relating to a period ending on or after the relevant date, the directors of that company must prepare a supplementary accounting statement. This must consist of

- a balance sheet dealing with the state of affairs of the company as at a date not more than three months before the draft terms were adopted by the directors; and
- where the company would be required to prepare group accounts if that date were the last day of a financial year, a consolidated balance sheet dealing with the state of affairs of the company and the undertakings that would be included in such a consolidation.

The requirements of *CA 2006* (and where relevant *IAS Regulation, Art 4*) as to matters to be included in a balance sheet and the notes to it apply to a balance sheet required under these provisions but with such modifications as are necessary by reason of its being prepared otherwise than as at the last day of a financial year. Similarly, the normal provisions as to the approval and signing of accounts (see **2.2 Accounts: General**) apply to the balance sheet required for an accounting statement under these provisions.

But see **35.29**(3) and **35.29**(3A) for circumstances in which a supplementary accounting statement is not required.

[*CA 2006, s 925; SI 2011 No 1606, Reg 23.2*].

35.24 *Inspection of documents*

The members of each company involved in the division must be able (i) to inspect, at the registered office of that company, copies of the following documents relating to that company and every other company involved in the division; and (ii) to obtain copies of those documents, or any part of them, on request free of charge.

(a) The draft terms.

(b) The directors' explanatory report.

(c) The expert's report.

(d) The company's annual accounts and reports for the last three financial years ending on or before the first meeting of the members (or any class of members) of the company summoned for the purposes of approving the scheme.

(e) Any supplementary accounting statement required under **35.23**.

(f) If no statement is required under **35.23** because the company has not made public a recent half-yearly financial report, that report.

The period of for inspection or obtaining copies begins one month before, and ends on the date of, the first meeting of the members (or any class of members) of the company for the purposes of approving the scheme.

The right to inspect documents is subject to the provisions set out in **35.24A** and the requirements in (b), (c) and (e) above are subject to **35.29**(3) (Agreement to dispense with reports), **35.29**(3A) (Certain requirements excluded where shareholders given proportional rights) and **35.29**(4) (Power of court to exclude certain requirements).

CA 2006, s 1145 (right to hard copy) does not apply to a document sent or supplied in accordance with (b) (above) to a member who has consented to information being sent or supplied by the company by electronic means and has not revoked that consent and *CA 2006, Sch 5, Pt 4* (communications by means of a website) also does not apply for the purposes of (b) .

[*CA 2006, s 926*].

35.24A *Publication of documents on company website*

The rights in **35.24** for members to inspect documents do not apply if

- the document is made available on a website which is maintained on or behalf of the company and identifies the company; and
- access to the document on the website is not conditional on payment of a fee or otherwise restricted; and
- the document remains available on the website throughout the period beginning one month before, and ending on the date of any meeting of the company summoned for the purpose of approving the scheme.

A person is able to obtain a copy of a document free of charge if the document is made available on the website and the person is able throughout the period beginning one month before and ending on the date set out above to retain a copy of the document made available on the website and to produce a hard copy of it. Where members are only able to obtain copies of a document in this way, the requirement to make the documents available for inspection set out in **35.24** still applies even if the conditions set out in this paragraph are met. [*CA 2006, s 926A; SI 2011 No 1606, Reg 25*].

35.25 *Report on material changes of assets of transferor company*

The directors of the transferor company must report to

- every meeting of the members (or any class of members) of that company summoned for the purpose of agreeing to the scheme, and
- the directors of each existing transferee company,

any material changes in the 'property' and 'liabilities' of the transferor company between the date when the draft terms were adopted and the date of the meeting in question.

The directors of each existing transferee company must in turn

- report those matters to every meeting of the members (or any class of members) of that company summoned for the purpose of agreeing to the scheme, or
- send a report of those matters to every member entitled to receive notice of such a meeting.

'*Property*' includes property, rights and powers of every description.

'*Liabilities*' include duties.

But see **35.29**(3) and **35.29**(3A) for circumstances in which such a report is not required.

[*CA 2006, ss 927, 941, SI 2011 No 1606, Reg 26*].

35.26 *Approval of articles of new transferee company*

The articles of every new transferee company, or a draft of them, must be approved by ordinary resolution of the transferor company. [*CA 2006, s 928*].

35.27 *Protection of holders of securities with special rights*

The scheme must provide that where any securities of a transferor company (other than shares) to which special rights are attached are held by a person otherwise than as a member or creditor of the company, that person is to receive rights in the transferee company of equivalent value unless

- the holder has agreed otherwise; or
- the holder is, or under the scheme is to be, entitled to have the securities purchased by a transferee company on terms that the court considers reasonable.

[*CA 2006, s 929*].

35.28 *No allotment of shares to transferor company or to transferee company*

The scheme must not provide for any shares in a transferee company to be allotted to

- the transferor company (or its nominee) in respect of shares in the transferor company held by the transferor company itself (or its nominee); or
- a transferee company (or its nominee) in respect of shares in the transferor company held by the transferee company (or its nominee).

[*CA 2006, s 930*].

35.29 *Exceptions*

(1) *Circumstances in which meeting of members of transferor company not required (division)*

In the case of a division where all of the shares or other securities of the transferor company carrying the right to vote at general meetings of the company are held by or on behalf of one or more existing transferee companies, it is not necessary for the scheme to be approved by a meeting of the members (or any class of members) of the transferor company if the court is satisfied that the following conditions have been complied with.

(a) Publication of notice of receipt of the draft terms by the Registrar of Companies took place in respect of all the companies involved in the division at least one month before the date of the court's order or the draft terms are made available on a website which is maintained by or on behalf of the company and identifies the company and access to the draft terms on the website or the supply of a hard copy of them from the website is not conditional on payment of a fee or otherwise restricted and the directors of the company deliver a notice giving details of the website to the Registrar of Companies.

This must be satisfied in respect of each of the companies involved in the division. In each case the Registrar must have published the notice in the *Gazette* at least one month before the date of the court's order and the draft terms must have remained available on the website throughout the period beginning one month before, and ending on, that date.

(b) The members of every company involved in the division were able, during the period beginning one month before, and ending on, the date of the court's order, to

(i) inspect at the registered office of their company copies of the documents listed in the applicable paragraphs of **35.24**(*a*)–(*f*) relating to every company involved in the division or the document is made available on a website which is maintained by or on behalf of the company to which it relates and identifies the company, access to the document on the website is not conditional on payment of a fee or otherwise restricted and the document remains available on the website throughout the period beginning one month before, and ending on, the date of the court's order.

(ii) obtain copies of those documents, or any part of them, on request and free of charge throughout the period beginning one month before, and ending on, the date of the court's order.

(c) One or more members of the transferor company, who together held not less than 5% of the paid-up capital of the company (excluding any shares in the company held as treasury shares) would have been able, during that period, to require a meeting of each class of members to be called for the purpose of deciding whether or not to agree to the scheme.

(d) No such requirement as under (*c*) above was made.

(e) The directors of the transferor company have sent to

(i) every member who would have been entitled to receive notice of a meeting to agree to the scheme (had any such meeting been called), and

(ii) the directors of every existing transferee company,

a report of any material change in the 'property' and 'liabilities' of the transferor company between the date when the terms were adopted by the directors and the date one month before the date of the court's order.

'*Property*' includes property, rights and powers of every description.

'*Liabilities*' include duties. [*CA 2006, ss 931, 941, SI 2011 No 1606, Reg 27(2)–27(4)*].

(2) *Circumstances in which meeting of members of transferee company not required (division)*

In the case of a division, it is not necessary for the scheme to be approved by the members of a transferee company if the court is satisfied that the following conditions have been complied with in relation to that company.

(a) Publication of notice of receipt of the draft terms by the Registrar of Companies took place in respect of the transferee company at least one month before the date of the first meeting of members of the transferor company summoned for the purposes of agreeing to the scheme or the draft terms are made available on a website which is maintained by or on behalf of the company and identifies the company and access to the draft terms on the website or the supply of a hard copy of them from the website is not conditional on payment of a fee or otherwise restricted and the directors of the company deliver a notice giving details of the website to the Registrar of Companies.

In each case the Registrar must have published the notice in the Gazette at least one month before the date of first meeting of the transferor company summoned for the purpose of agreeing to the scheme and the draft terms must have remained available on the website throughout the period beginning one month before, and ending on, that date.

(b) The members of the transferee company were able, during the period beginning one month before and ending on that date, to

(i) inspect at the registered office of that company copies of the documents listed in the applicable paragraphs of **35.24**(*a*)–(*f*) relating to that company and every other company involved in the division or the document is made available on a website which is maintained by or on behalf of the transferee company and identifies the company, access to the document on the website is not conditional on payment of a fee or otherwise restricted and the document remains available on the website throughout the period beginning one month before, and ending on, the date in **35.29**(2)(a); and

(ii) obtain copies of those documents or any part of them on request and free of charge throughout the period beginning one month before and ending on the date in **35.29**(2)(a).

(c) One or more members of that company, who together held not less than 5% of the paid-up capital of the company which carried the right to vote at general meetings of the company (excluding any shares in the company held as treasury shares) would have been able, during that period, to require a meeting of each class of members to be called for the purpose of deciding whether or not to agree to the scheme and no such requirement was made.

But the conditions in (*a*) and (*b*) above are subject to (4) below.

[*CA 2006, s 932, SI 2011 No 1606, Reg 28(2)–(5)*].

(3) *Agreement to dispense with reports, etc*

If all members holding shares in, and all persons holding other securities of, the companies involved in the division (being shares or securities that carry a right to vote in general meetings of the company in question) so agree, the following requirements may be dispensed with.

- The requirement for a
  - (i) directors' explanatory report (see **35.21**);
  - (ii) expert's report (see **35.22**);
  - (iii) supplementary accounting statement (see **35.23**); and
  - (iv) report on material changes in the assets of the transferor company (see **35.25**).
- The requirements for inspection of documents under **35.24** do not apply so far as relating to any document required to be drawn up under the provisions mentioned in (i)–(iii) above.

For these purposes, the members, or holders of other securities, of a company, and whether shares or other securities carry a right to vote in general meetings of the company, are determined as at the date of the application to the court under **35.2**.

[*CA 2006, s 933*].

(3A) *Certain requirements excluded where shareholders given proportional rights*

In the case of a division where each of the transferee companies is a new company, if all the shares in each of the transferee companies are to be allotted to the members of the transferor company in proportion to their rights in the allotted share capital of the transferor company, the following requirements do not apply

- *CA 2006, s 923* (directors' explanatory report)
- *CA 2006, s 924* (expert's report)
- *CA 2006, s 925* (supplementary accounting statement)

- *CA 2006, s 927* (report on material changes in assets of the transferor company) and
- *CA 2006, s 926* (inspection of documents)

so far as they relate to any documents required to be drawn up under *CA 2006 ss 923, 924* and *925*.

[*CA 2006, s 933A, SI 2011 No 1606, Reg 29*]

(4) *Power of court to exclude certain requirements*

In the case of a division, the court may by order direct that

- in relation to any company involved in the division, the requirements for publication of the draft terms under **35.19** and inspection of documents under **35.24** do not apply, and
- in relation to an existing transferee company, (2) above has effect with the omission of conditions (2)(*a*) and (*b*)

if it is satisfied that the following conditions will be fulfilled in relation to that company.

(a) The members of that company will have received, or will have been able to obtain free of charge, copies of the documents listed in **35.24**

  (i) in time to examine them before the date of the first meeting of the members (or any class of members) of that company summoned for the purposes of agreeing to the scheme; or

  (ii) in the case of an existing transferee company where in the circumstances described in (2) above no meeting is held, in time to require a meeting as mentioned in (2)(*d*) above.

(b) The creditors of that company will have received, or will have been able to obtain free of charge, copies of the draft terms in time to examine them

  (i) before the date of the first meeting of the members (or any class of members) of the company summoned for the purposes of agreeing to the scheme; or

  (ii) in the circumstances mentioned in (*a*)(ii) above, at the same time as the members of the company.

(c) No prejudice would be caused to the members or creditors of the transferor company or any transferee company by making the order in question. [*CA 2006, s 934*].

35.30 *Liability of transferee companies for each other's defaults*

Subject to below, in the case of a division, each transferee company is jointly and severally liable for any liability transferred to any other transferee company under the scheme to the extent that the other company defaults in satisfying that liability.

But

- this does not apply to liabilities owed to the creditors (or a class of creditors) of the transferor company if a majority in number representing 75% in value of the creditors (or class of creditors), present and voting either in person or by proxy at a meeting summoned for the purposes of agreeing to the scheme, so agree in relation to the liabilities owed to them; and

- a transferee company is not liable under this provision for an amount greater than the 'net value transferred' to it under the scheme. '*Net value transferred*' is the value (at the time of the transfer) of the property transferred to it under the scheme less the amount at that date of the liabilities so transferred.

'*Liabilities*' include duties. [*CA 2006, s 940, 941*].

35.30A Disregard of website failures beyond control of company

A failure to make information or a document available on the website throughout the period specified in the following provisions is to be disregarded if it is made available on the website for any part of that period and the failure to make it available is wholly attributable to circumstances that it would not be reasonable to have expected the company to prevent or avoid. The provisions are

- *CA 2006, s 906A(6)*
- *CA 2006, s 911A(4)*
- *CA 2006, s 916(3B)* and *(4B)*
- *CA 2006, s 917(3B)* and *(4B)*
- *CA 2006, s 918(2B)* and *(3B)*
- *CA 2006, s 921A(6)*
- *CA 2006, s 926A(4)*
- *CA 2006, s 931(3B)* and *(4B)*
- *CA 2006, s 932(2B)* and *(3B)*; and
- [*CA 2006, s 940A*]

35.31 Expert's report: supplementary provisions

(1) *Valuation by another person*

Where an expert thinks that it is reasonably necessary for a valuation to be made to enable him to draw up his report, he can arrange for another person, who appears to him to have the requisite knowledge and experience, to make the valuation. The person must meet the independence requirement in (2) below.

In such a case, the expert's report must state that fact and must also

- state the valuer's name and what knowledge and experience he has to carry out the valuation; and
- describe so much of the undertaking, 'property' and 'liabilities' as was valued by the other person, and the method used to value them, and specify the date of the valuation.

'*Property*' includes property, rights and powers of every description.

'*Liabilities*' include duties.

[*CA 2006, ss 935, 941*].

(2) *Experts and valuers: independence requirement*

A person meets the independence requirement for the purposes of 35.11, 35.22 and (1) above only if

- he is not
  - (i) an officer or employee of any of the 'companies concerned in the scheme'; or
  - (ii) a partner or employee of such a person, or a partnership of which such a person is a partner;
- he is not
  - (i) an officer or employee of an 'associated undertaking' of any of the companies concerned in the scheme; or
  - (ii) a partner or employee of such a person, or a partnership of which such a person is a partner; and
- there does not exist between
  - (i) the person or an associate of his, and
  - (ii) any of the companies concerned in the scheme or an associated undertaking of such a company,

  a connection of any such description as may be specified by Regulations.

For these purposes, an auditor of a company is not regarded as an officer or employee of the company.

The '*companies concerned in the scheme*' are every transferor and existing transferee company.

An '*associated undertaking*', in relation to a company, means *either* a parent undertaking or subsidiary undertaking of the company *or* a subsidiary undertaking of a parent undertaking of the company.

'*Associate*' means

(a) in relation to an individual,
   - (i) that individual's spouse or civil partner or minor child or step-child;
   - (ii) any body corporate of which that individual is a director (or, in the case of a LLP, member); and
   - (iii) any employee or partner of that individual.

(b) in relation to a body corporate,
   - (i) any body corporate of which that body is a director (or, in the case of a LLP, member);
   - (ii) any body corporate in the same group as that body; and
   - (iii) any employee or partner of that body or of any body corporate in the same group;

(c) in relation to a partnership that is a legal person under the law by which it is governed,
   - (i) any body corporate of which that partnership is a director (or, in the case of a LLP, member);

(ii) any employee of or partner in that partnership; and

(iii) any person who is an associate of a partner in that partnership; and

(d) in relation to a partnership that is not a legal person under the law by which it is governed, any person who is an associate of any of the partners.

[*CA 2006, ss 936, 937*].

35.32 Powers of the court

Power of court to summon meeting of members or creditors of existing transferee company. The court may order a meeting of the members or creditors of an existing transferee company (or any class of them), to be summoned on an application by

- the company concerned;
- a member or creditor of the company;
- if the company is being wound up, the liquidator; or
- if the company is in administration, the administrator.

CA 2006, s 323 (representation of corporations at meetings, see **42.25 Resolutions and Meetings**) applies to a meeting of creditors summoned under these provisions as to a meeting of the company (the references to a member of the company being read as references to a creditor).

Court to fix date for transfer of undertaking, etc of transferor company. Where the court sanctions a compromise or arrangement, it must fix a date on which the transfer (or transfers) to the transferee company (or transferee companies) of the undertaking, 'property' and 'liabilities' of the transferor company is (or are) to take place. This may be done in the order sanctioning the compromise or arrangement or in a subsequent order under **35.4**. Any such order that provides for the dissolution of the transferor company must fix the same date for the dissolution.

If it is necessary for the transferor company to take steps to ensure that the undertaking, property and liabilities are fully transferred, the court must fix a subsequent date, not later than six months after the date fixed above, by which such steps must be taken. In such a case, the court may postpone the dissolution of the transferor company until that subsequent date. The court may postpone (or further postpone) that subsequent date if it is satisfied that the necessary steps cannot be completed by the date (or latest date) fixed.

'*Property*' includes property, rights and powers of every description.

'*Liabilities*' include duties.

[*CA 2006, ss 938, 939, 941*].

35.33 MERGER REFERENCES

A merger control regime applies under *Enterprise Act 2002, Part 3*. The Office of Fair Trading (OFT) has power to make references of most merger situations to the Competition Commission (CC). Final decisions on mergers are taken by the independent competition authorities, except in the small minority of mergers and markets cases which raise national security issues. The CC is able to impose the full range of competition remedies, including divestment remedies.

A statutory maximum timetable is set for market inquiries. To ensure that it can meet these deadlines, the CC can impose sanctions on parties who do not provide information on time.

Parties aggrieved by decisions of the independent competition authorities have a right of appeal.

In assessing mergers, both the OFT and CC must apply a 'substantial lessening of competition' test.

The OFT has a duty so to refer a merger to the CC if it believes that

- a relevant merger situation has been created; and
- it is, or may be, the case that the merger has resulted, or may be expected to result, in a substantial lessening of competition within any market for goods and services in the UK.

Detailed coverage of the provisions are beyond the scope of this book.

35.34 EC MERGER CONTROL REGULATIONS

The *EC Council Regulation of 20 January 2004* [*139/2004*] (replacing the earlier *EC Council Regulation* of 21 December 1989 [*89/4064*]) is designed to deal specifically with cross-border mergers. The provisions have direct effect in the UK in relation to concentrations with a '*community dimension*', ie where

- the combined aggregate worldwide turnover of all the undertakings concerned is more than €5,000 million; and
- the aggregate Community-wide turnover of each of at least two of the undertakings concerned is more than €250 million,

unless each of the undertakings concerned achieves more than two-thirds of its aggregate Community-wide turnover within the same Member State.

A concentration that does not meet the above thresholds still has a community dimension where

- the combined aggregate worldwide turnover of all the undertakings concerned is more than €2,500 million;
- in each of at least three Member States, the combined aggregate turnover of all the undertakings concerned is more than €100 million and the aggregate turnover of each of at least two of those undertakings is more than €25 million; and
- the aggregate Community-wide turnover of each of at least two of the undertakings concerned is more than €100 million,

unless each of the undertakings concerned achieves more than two-thirds of its aggregate Community-wide turnover within the same Member State.

Any concentration having a community dimension is dealt with by the European Commission unless remitted to a Member State. Conversely, a concentration falling short of having a community dimension is dealt with by the Member State applying its own national law (see **35.33** for the UK provisions) although the Member State can chose to refer the matter to the Commission.

35.35 CROSS-BORDER MERGERS

The provisions of *The Companies (Cross-border Mergers) Regulations 2007 (SI 2007 No 2974)* in **35.36** to **35.61** implement *EC Directive 2005/56/EC* (the Cross-border Mergers Directive) and provide a framework for limited liability companies to engage in cross-border mergers.

35.36 Meaning of 'cross-border merger'

Cross-border merger means a merger by one of the following three methods.

(1) **Merger by absorption**, ie an operation in which

- there are one or more transferor companies;
- there is an existing transferee company. The meaning of "existing transferee "was at issue in the case *Re Itau BBA International Ltd* [2012] ALL ER (D) 206. The merger was between a company registered in Portugal and a UK company, purchased as a shelf company for the purposes of the merger. The issue for the court was whether the shelf company could be an "existing" company as this is defined in the *Companies (Cross-border) Regulations* (see above) as a "transferee company other than one formed for the purposes of or in connection with a cross-border merger". The court concluded that a literal interpretation of the definition would put an entirely pointless and unexplained restriction in the *Regulations* and it was therefore open to the court to correct the drafting error in the *Regulations.*
- at least one of those companies is a UK company;
- at least one of those companies is an '*EEA company*' (ie a body corporate governed by the law of an EEA State other than the UK);
- every transferor company is dissolved without going into liquidation, and on its dissolution transfers all its assets and liabilities to the transferee company; and
- the consideration for the transfer is
  - (i) shares or other securities representing the capital of the transferee company, and
  - (ii) if so agreed, a cash payment,

  receivable by members of the transferor company.

(2) **Merger by absorption of a wholly-owned subsidiary**, ie an operation in which

- there is one transferor company, of which all the shares or other securities representing its capital are held by an existing transferee company;
- either the transferor company or the transferee company is a UK company;
- either the transferor company or the transferee company is an EEA company (see above); and
- the transferor company is dissolved without going into liquidation, and on its dissolution transfers all its assets and liabilities to the transferee company.

(3) **Merger by formation of a new company**, ie an operation in which

- there are two or more transferor companies, at least two of which are each governed by the law of a different EEA State;
- every transferor company is dissolved without going into liquidation, and on its dissolution transfers all its assets and liabilities to a transferee company formed for the purposes of, or in connection with, the operation;
- the consideration for the transfer is

  (i) shares or other securities representing the capital of the transferee company, and

  (ii) if so agreed, a cash payment,

  receivable by members of the transferor company; and
- at least one of the transferor companies or the transferee company is a UK company.

[*SI 2007 No 2974, Reg 2*].

35.37 Pre-merger requirements

A UK merging company may apply to the court for an order certifying for the purposes of *EC Directive 2005/56/EC, Art 10.2* (issue of pre-merger certificate) that the company has completed properly the pre-merger acts and formalities for the cross-border merger. The court must not make such an order unless the requirements of **35.38** to **35.45** (pre-merger requirements) have been complied with.

[*SI 2007 No 2974, Reg 6*].

35.38 *Draft terms of merger*

The directors of the UK merging company must draw up and adopt a draft of the proposed terms of the cross-border merger. Subject to below, the draft must give particulars of at least the following matters.

(a) In relation to each transferor company and transferee company

  (i) its name,

  (ii) its registered office, and

  (iii) its legal form and the law by which it is governed.

(b) The share exchange ratio and the amount of any cash payment.

(c) The terms relating to the allotment of shares or other securities in the transferee company.

(d) The likely effects of the cross-border merger for employees of each merging company.

(e) The date from which the holding of shares or other securities in the transferee company will entitle the holders to participate in profits, and any special conditions affecting that entitlement.

(f) The date from which the transactions of the transferor companies are to be treated for accounting purposes as being those of the transferee company.

(g) Any rights or restrictions attaching to shares or other securities in the transferee company to be allotted under the cross-border merger to the holders of shares or other securities in a transferor company to which any special rights or restrictions attach, or the measures proposed concerning them.

(h) Any amount or benefit paid or given (or intended to be paid or given) to the independent expert (see **35.40**) or to any director of a merging company, and the consideration for the payment of benefit.

(i) The transferee company's articles of association, or if it does not have articles, the instrument constituting the company or defining its constitution. (Before 1 October 2008, 'articles' include the company's memorandum of association.)

(j) Information on the procedures by which any employee participation rights are to be determined in accordance with **35.52** *et seq.*

(k) Information on the evaluation of the assets and liabilities to be transferred to the transferee company.

(l) The dates of the accounts of every merging company which were used for the purpose of preparing the draft terms of merger.

But particulars of the matters referred to in (*b*), (*c*) and (*e*) may be omitted in the case of a merger by absorption of a wholly-owned subsidiary.

The draft must

- *not* provide for any shares in the transferee company to be allotted to
  (i) a transferor company (or its nominee) in respect of shares in the transferor company held by the transferor company itself (or its nominee); or
  (ii) the transferee company (or its nominee) in respect of shares in the transferor company held by the transferee company (or its nominee); and
- provide that where any securities of a UK transferor company (other than shares) to which special rights are attached are held by a person other than as a member or creditor of the company, that person is to receive rights in the transferee company of equivalent value, unless
  (i) the holder has agreed otherwise; or
  (ii) the holder is (or under the draft will be) entitled to have the securities purchased by the transferee company on terms which the court considers reasonable.

[*SI 2007 No 2974, Reg 7, Sch 1 para 3*].

35.39 *Directors' report*

The directors of the UK merging company must draw up and adopt a report which must

- explain the effect of the cross-border merger for members, creditors and employees of the company;
- state
  (i) the legal and economic grounds for the draft terms;
  (ii) any material interests of the directors (whether as directors or as members or as creditors or otherwise); and

- (iii) the effect on those interests of the cross-border merger, in so far as it is different from the effect on the like interests of other persons; where information to be provided explains the effect of the cross-border merger for employees (see above), it must include suitable information relating to the use of agency workers (this provision came into force on 1 October 2011 – see *Reg 8 para (2A)* inserted by the *Agency Workers Regulations 2010 (SI 2010 No 93)*; and

- (where the cross-border merger affects the rights of debenture holders of the company), state
  - (i) any material interests of the trustees of any deed for securing the issue of the debentures (whether as trustees or as members or as creditors or otherwise); and
  - (ii) the effect on those interests of the cross-border merger, in so far as it is different from the effect on the like interests of other persons.

  Any trustee for the company's debenture holders must give notice to the company's directors of such matters relating to himself as may be necessary for these purposes. Any person in default commits an offence. A person guilty of such an offence is liable, on summary conviction, to a fine not exceeding level 3 on the standard scale. See **29.1** Offences and Legal Proceedings.

The directors must deliver copies of the report to its employee representatives (or if there are no such representatives, the employees) not less than two months before the date of the first meeting of the members (or any class of members) of the company (see **35.43**). If the employee representatives deliver an opinion on the report to the company's registered office not less than one month before the date of the first meeting of the members (or any class of members) of the company, every copy of the report issued after the date on which the opinion was delivered must be accompanied by the opinion.

[*SI 2007 No 2974, Reg 8*].

35.40 *Independent expert's report*

Apart from the exceptions below, a report must be drawn up by

- an 'independent expert' who has been appointed for the UK merging company by its directors;
- an independent expert who has been appointed for all the merging companies by the court on the joint application of all the merging companies; or
- a person who has been appointed for all the merging companies by a competent authority of another EEA State.

An '*independent expert*' is a person who is eligible for appointment as a statutory auditor (see **8.8** Audit) and is independent. A person is not independent unless he satisfies the independence test for a statutory auditor in respect of all the merging companies (on the assumption that all these companies were required to appoint an auditor). See **8.9** Audit.

Where he thinks it is necessary to enable him to draw up the report, an independent expert may arrange for a valuation (or accept one which has already been made) by another person, together with a report which will enable him to prepare his own report. That other person must be someone who appears to him to have the requisite knowledge and experience to make the valuation and who is independent (applying the same test as above).

In the report the independent expert must

- indicate

  (i) the methods used to arrive at the share exchange ratio; and

  (ii) the values arrived at using each such method;

- describe any special valuation difficulties which have arisen;

- give an opinion

  (i) as to whether the methods used are reasonable in all the circumstances of the case;

  (ii) if there is more than one method, on the relative importance attributed to each method in arriving at the value decided on; and

  (iii) as to whether the share exchange ratio is reasonable;

- in the case of a valuation made by another person

  (i) state that fact and the date of the valuation;

  (ii) state the person's name and what knowledge and experience he has to carry out the valuation;

  (iii) describe so much of the assets and liabilities as was valued by the other person, and the method used to value them; and

  (iv) state that it appeared to him reasonable to arrange for the valuation to be so made or to accept a valuation so made.

In making his report, the independent expert has the right of access to all such documents, and information from officers, of every merging company as he thinks necessary for the purpose of making his report.

Exceptions. A report need not be drawn up where

- the cross-border merger is a merger by absorption of a wholly-owned subsidiary;
- the cross-border merger is a merger by absorption where 90% or more (but not all) of the 'relevant securities' of the transferor company (or, if there is more than one transferor company, of each of them) are held by or on behalf of the transferee company; or
- every member of every merging company agrees that such a report is not required.

'*Relevant securities*', in relation to a transferor company, means shares or other securities carrying the right to vote at general meetings of the company. [*SI 2007 No 2974, Reg 9*].

35.41 *Inspection of documents*

The members of the UK merging company and its employee representatives (or if there are no such representatives, the employees) must be able

- to inspect at the registered office of the company copies of

  (i) the draft terms of merger;

  (ii) the directors' report;

  (iii) the independent expert's report, if such a report is required; and

- to obtain copies of those documents or any part of them on request free of charge during the period beginning one month before, and ending on the date of, the first meeting of the members (or any class of members) of the company. [*SI 2007 No 2974, Reg 10*].

35.42 *Public notice of receipt of registered documents*

The directors of the UK merging company must deliver to the Registrar of Companies particulars of the date, time and place of every meeting summoned by the court under **35.46**, together with

(a) a copy of the court order;

(b) a copy of the draft terms of merger; and

(c) documents giving particulars in relation to each merging company of

  (i) its name;

  (ii) its registered office;

  (iii) its legal form and the law by which it is governed;

  (iv) in the case of a UK company, its registered number;

  (v) in the case of an EEA company (ie a body corporate governed by the law of an EEA State other than the UK) to which the *First Company Law Directive* applies, particulars of the register in which the company file mentioned in *Article 3* of that *Directive* (file for each registered company to be kept in national register) is kept (including details of the relevant State) and its registration number in that register; and

  (vi) in the case of any other EEA company, particulars, if any, of the register in which it is entered (including details of the relevant State) and its registration number in that register.

The documents must be delivered to the Registrar of Companies not less than two months before the date of the first meeting of the members (or any class of members) of the company (see **35.43**).

The Registrar of Companies must publish notice of his receipt of the documents at least one month before the date of the first meeting of the members (or any class of members) of the company. His notice must state

- the date of receipt of the documents;
- the particulars referred to in (*c*) above;
- in relation to each UK merging company, a statement that information related to the company is kept in the UK register;
- a statement that the *Regulations* require copies of the draft terms of merger, the directors' report and (if there is one) the independent expert's report to be kept available for inspection; and
- the date, time and place of every meeting summoned under **35.46**.

[*SI 2007 No 2974, Reg 12*].

35.43 *Approval of members in meeting*

Subject to below, the draft terms of merger must be approved by a majority in number, representing 75% in value, of each class of members of the UK merging company, present and voting either in person or by proxy at a meeting summoned under **35.46**. The approval of the members may be made subject to

- ratification of any arrangements adopted for employee participation in the transferee company; or
- an order of a competent authority of another EEA State which amends the share exchange ratio in accordance with *EC Directive 2005/56/EC, Art 10.3* (national procedure allowing for amendment of share exchange ratio).

The approval of the members is not required

- in the case of a transferor company concerned in a merger by absorption of a wholly-owned subsidiary; and
- in the case of an existing transferee company if
  - (i) the publication of the notice required under **35.42** took place in respect of the company at least one month before the date of the first meeting of members of the transferor companies;
  - (ii) the members of the transferee company were able during a period beginning one month before, and ending on, the date of the first such meeting to inspect at the registered office of the transferee company copies of the documents listed in **35.41** in relation to all the merging companies, and to obtain copies of those documents or any part of them on request; and
  - (iii) one or more members of the transferee company, who together held not less than 5% of the paid-up capital of the company which carried the right to vote at general meetings of the company (excluding any shares held as treasury shares), would have been able, during that period, to require a meeting of each class of members to be called for the purpose of deciding whether or not to agree to the scheme, and no such requirement was made.

[*SI 2007 No 2974, Reg 13*].

35.44 *Approval of creditors in meeting*

If a meeting of creditors or a class of creditors is summoned under **35.46**, the draft terms of merger must be approved by a majority in number, representing 75% in value, of the creditors or class of creditors (as the case may be), present and voting either in person or by proxy at the meeting. [*SI 2007 No 2974, Reg 14*].

35.45 *Documents to be circulated or made available*

Where a meeting is summoned under **35.46**,

- every notice summoning the meeting that is sent to a member or creditor must include copies of the documents referred to **35.41**; and
- every notice summoning the meeting that is given by advertisement must
  - (i) include copies of those documents, or
  - (ii) state where and how members or creditors may obtain copies of those documents free of charge.

[*SI 2007 No 2974, Reg 15*].

35.46 Power of court to summon meeting of members or creditors

The court may, on an application by

- the UK merging company,

- any member of the UK merging company in the case of a meeting of members or a class of members,
- any creditor of the UK merging company in the case of a meeting of creditors or a class of creditors, or
- in the case of a UK merging company in administration, the administrator

order a meeting of members (or a class of members) for the purposes of **35.43** or creditors (or a class of creditors) for the purposes of **35.44** to be summoned in such manner as the court directs.

CA 2006, s 323 (representation of corporations at meetings, see **42.25** RESOLUTIONS AND MEETINGS) applies to a meeting of the creditors summoned under these provisions as to a meeting of the company (the references to a member of the company being read as references to a creditor).

[*SI 2007 No 2974, Reg 11*].

35.47 Court approval of cross-border merger

The court may, on the joint application of all the merging companies, make an order approving the completion of the cross-border merger for the purposes of *EC Directive 2005/56/EC, Art 11* (scrutiny of completion of merger) if

(a) the transferee company is a UK company;

(b) a court order has been made under **35.37** in relation to each UK merging company;

(c) an order has been made by a competent authority of another EEA State for the purposes of *EC Directive 2005/56/EC, Art 10.2* (issue of pre-merger certificate) in relation to each merging company which is an EEA company (ie a body corporate governed by the law of an EEA State other than the UK);

(d) the application is made to the court on a date not more than six months after the making of any order under (*b*) or (*c*) above;

(e) the draft terms of merger approved by every order referred under (*b*) or (*c*) above are the same; and

(f) where appropriate, any arrangements for employee participation in the transferee company have been determined in accordance with **35.52** *et seq.*

Where the court makes such an order, it must in the order fix a date on which the consequences of the cross-border merger (see **35.48**) are to have effect That date must be not less than 21 days after the date on which the order is made. After the consequences of the cross-border merger have taken effect (see **35.48**), an order made under these provisions is conclusive evidence that the conditions set out above have been satisfied and the requirements in **35.38–35.45** have been complied with and the cross-border merger may not be declared null and void.

[*SI 2007 No 2974, Reg 16; SI 2015 No 180 , Reg 2*].

35.48 Consequences of a cross-border merger

The consequences of a cross-border merger are that

- the assets and liabilities of the transferor companies are transferred to the transferee company;

- the rights and obligations arising from the contracts of employment of the transferor companies are transferred to the transferee company;
- the transferor companies are dissolved; and
- in the case of a merger by absorption or a merger by formation of a new company, the members of the transferor companies except the transferee company (if it is a member of a transferor company) become members of the transferee company.

The consequences take effect

- where a court order has been made **35.47**, on the date fixed in that order; or
- where an order has been made by a competent authority of another EEA State for the purposes of *EC Directive 2005/56/EC, Art 11* (scrutiny of completion of merger), on the date fixed in accordance with the law of that State.

The transferee company must take such steps as are required by law (including by the law of another EEA State) for the transfer of the assets and liabilities of the transferor companies to be effective in relation to other persons.

[*SI 2007 No 2974, Reg 17*].

35.49 Copies of order to be provided to members and delivered to the Registrar of Companies

Where an order is made under **35.48** approving the completion of a cross-border merger,

(a) the UK transferee company must, on request by any member, send him a copy of the order; and

(b) the UK transferee company and every UK transferor company must deliver the following documents and particulars to the Registrar of Companies for registration not more than seven days after the date on which it was made.

- A copy of the court order made **35.47**. See also **35.50**.
- In the case of a transferor company which is an EEA company (ie a body corporate governed by the law of an EEA State other than the UK) to which the *First Company Law Directive* applies, particulars of the register in which the company file mentioned in *Article 3* of that *Directive* (file for each registered company to be kept in national register) is kept (including details of the relevant State) and its registration number in that register.
- In the case of any other transferor company which is a EEA company, particulars, if any, of the register in which it is entered (including details of the relevant State) and its registration number in that register.

(c) Where an order is made by a competent authority of another EEA State approving the completion of a cross-border merger for the purposes of *EC Directive 2005/56/EC, Art 11* (scrutiny of completion of merger), every transferor company which is a UK company must deliver a copy of the order to the Registrar of Companies for registration not more than 14 days after the date on which it was made.

If a company defaults in complying with (*a*) above, an offence is committed by every officer of the company who is in default. If a UK merging company defaults in complying with (*b*) or (*c*) above, an offence is committed by the company and every officer of the company who is in default. A person guilty of either offence is liable, on summary conviction, to a fine not exceeding level 3 on the standard scale and for continued contravention, in the case of (*b*) above to a daily default fine not exceeding one-tenth of level 3 on the standard scale. See **29.1 Offences and Legal Proceedings** for the standard scale.

[*SI 2007 No 2974, Regs 18, 19*].

35.50 Amendment of transferee company's articles, etc

If an order made under **35.47** amends

- the articles of association of the UK transferee company, or
- any resolution or agreement in relation to the UK transferee company to which *CA 2006, ss 29, 30* apply (resolutions and agreements affecting a company's constitution, see **14.10 Company Constitution**),

the copy of the court order delivered to the Registrar of Companies by the UK transferee company under **35.49** must be accompanied by a copy of the company's articles, or the resolution or agreement in question, as amended.

Every copy of the company's articles issued by the company after the order is made must be accompanied by a copy of the order, unless the effect of the order has been incorporated into the articles by amendment.

In the case of a company not having articles, references above to its articles are to be read as references to the instrument constituting the company or defining its constitution.

If a UK transferee company defaults in complying with the above provisions, an offence is committed by the company and every officer of the company who is in default. A person guilty of such an offence is liable, on summary conviction, to a fine not exceeding level 3 on the standard scale. See **29.1 Offences and Legal Proceedings** for the standard scale.

[*SI 2007 No 2974, Reg 20*].

35.51 Notification of registration by Registrar of Companies

Where the Registrar of Companies receives a copy of a court order made under **35.47** approving the completion of a cross-border merger, he must without undue delay

(a) in relation to each transferor company which is an EEA company (ie a body corporate governed by the law of an EEA State other than the UK) to which the *First Company Law Directive* applies, give notice of that order to the register in which the company file mentioned in *Article 3* of that *Directive* (file for each registered company to be kept in national register) is kept;

(b) in relation to any other transferor company which is a EEA company, give notice of the order to the register, if any, in which it is entered; and

(c) on or after the date fixed in the order as the date on which the consequences of the cross-border merger are to have effect,

  (i) strike the name of the UK transferor company from the UK register; and

  (ii) place a note in the register stating that, as from that date, the assets and liabilities of the UK transferor company were transferred to the transferee company.

Where the Registrar of Companies receives from the registry of another EEA State notice for the purposes of *EC Directive 2005/56/EC, Art 13* (notification of registries in other Member States) of an order approving the completion of a cross-border merger, he must on, or without undue delay after, the date fixed for the purposes of *EC Directive 2005/56/EC, Art 12* (entry into effect of the cross-border merger) take the steps specified in (*c*)(i) and (ii) above in relation to every UK transferor company.

[*SI 2007 No 2974, Reg 21*].

35.52 Employee participation

The provisions in **35.53** to **35.59** apply where the transferee company is a UK company and where

- a merging company has, in the six months before the publication of the draft terms of merger, an average number of employees that exceeds 500 and has a system of 'employee participation',
- For the purposes of calculating the average number of employees, agency workers whose contract was not a contract of employment with one or more temporary work agencies which were merging companies at the relevant time, are treated as having been employed by such a temporary work agency or agencies for the duration of their assignment with a hirer (see *Reg, para 22(1A)* inserted by the *Agency Worker Regulations 2010 (SI 2010 No 93)* and *reg 3(1)(b)* of those regulations for the meaning of 'contract). *Reg 22(1A)* came into force on 1 October 2011.
- a UK merging company has a proportion of employee representatives amongst the directors, or
- a merging company has 'employee representatives' amongst members of the administrative or supervisory organ or their committees or of the management group which covers the profit units of the company

except that the provisions for ballot arrangements (see **35.55**) and the provisions for confidential information and protection for employees (see **35.57** to **35.59**) apply to a UK merging company, its employees or their representatives, regardless of whether the transferee company is a UK company.

'*Employee participation*' means the influence of the employees and/or the employee representatives in the transferee company or a merging company by way of the right to

- elect or appoint some of the members of the transferee company's or the merging company's supervisory or administrative organ; or
- recommend and/or oppose the appointment of some or all of the members of the transferee's or the merging company's supervisory or administrative organ.

'*Employee representatives*' mean

- if the employees are of a description in respect of which an independent trade union is recognised by their employer for the purpose of collective bargaining, representatives of the trade union who normally take part as negotiators in the collective bargaining process; and
- any other employees of their employer who are elected or appointed as employee representatives to positions in which they are expected to receive, on behalf of the employees, information

(i) which is relevant to the terms and conditions of employment of the employees; or

(ii) about the activities of the undertaking which may significantly affect the interests of the employees,

but excluding representatives who are expected to receive information relevant only to a specific aspect of the terms and conditions or interests of the employees (eg health and safety, collective redundancies or pension schemes).

[*SI 2007 No 2974, Regs 3, 22*].

35.53 *Merging companies and the special negotiating body*

(1) *Duty on merging company to provide information*

As soon as possible after adopting the draft terms of merger, each merging company must provide information to the employee representatives of that company or, if no such representatives exist, the employees themselves. This information must include, as a minimum, information

- identifying the merging companies;
- of any decision of the merging companies to select standard rules of employee participation, see **35.56**(1)); and
- giving the number of employees employed by each merging company.

When a special negotiating body has been formed in accordance with (2) below, each merging company must provide that body with such information as is necessary to keep it informed of the plan and progress of establishing the UK transferee company until the date upon which the consequences of the cross-border merger take effect.

[*SI 2007 No 2974, Reg 23*].

The information to be provided under *reg 23* must include suitable information relating to the use of agency workers (if any) in that company (see *reg 23(4)* inserted by the *Agency Workers Regulations 2010* which came into force on 1 October 2011).

See *SI 2007 No 2974, Reg 24, Sch 2 para 1* for the complaints procedure where an employee representative or, where no such representative exists, any employee believes that a merging company has failed to provide the required information or that the information provided is false or incomplete in a material particular.

(2) *The special negotiating body*

Subject to the merging companies selecting standard rules of employee participation (see **35.56**(1)), each merging company must make arrangements for the establishment of a special negotiating body. The task of this body is to reach an employee participation agreement with the merging companies (see **35.54**).

[*SI 2007 No 2974, Reg 25*].

Employees of merging companies registered in each EEA State (including the UK) must be given an entitlement to elect one member of the special negotiating body for each 10% (or fraction thereof) which employees of merging companies registered in that State represent of the total workforce of the merging companies (the '*constituent members*'). [*SI 2007 No 2974, Reg 26(1)*]. But if, following that election, the members elected to the special negotiating body do not include at least one constituent member in respect of each merging company, the employees of any merging company in respect of which there is no constituent member are given the entitlement (subject to limitations) to elect an additional member to the special negotiating body.

[*SI 2007 No 2974, Reg 26(2)(3)*].

Each merging company must, as soon as reasonably practicable and in any event no later than one month after the establishment of the special negotiating body, inform their employees of the outcome of any elections held under these provisions.

[*SI 2007 No 2974, Reg 26(4)*].

There are also special rules for re-elections if changes to the merging bodies result in the number of members which employees would be entitled to elect either increasing or decreasing, and for the election of a substitute member if a member is no longer willing or able to continue serving.

[*SI 2007 No 2974, Reg 26(5)*].

See *SI 2007 No 2974, Reg 27, Sch 2 para 2* for the complaints procedure about the establishment of a special negotiating body (that is a complaint that a special negotiating body has not been established).

35.54 *Negotiation of the employee participation agreement*

(1) *Negotiations*

Subject to below the merging companies selecting standard rules of employee participation (see **35.56**(1)), the parties are under a duty to negotiate in a spirit of cooperation with a view to reaching an employee participation agreement. The duty commences one month after the election of the members of the special negotiating body (or the last member if there is more than one election) and lasts for a period of six months (or until the completion of the negotiations, if earlier). The period can be extended by a further six months.

[*SI 2007 No 2974, Reg 28*].

(2) *The employee participation agreement*

The agreement must be in writing and must specify

- the scope of the agreement;
- if, during negotiations, the parties decide to establish arrangements for employee participation, the substance of those arrangements including (if applicable) the number of directors of the UK transferee company which the employees will be entitled to elect, appoint, recommend or oppose, the procedures as to how these directors may be elected, appointed, recommended or opposed by the employees, and their rights; and
- the date of entry into force of the agreement, its duration, the circumstances, if any, in which the agreement is required to be re-negotiated and the procedure for its re-negotiation.

If the transferee company is to provide information on the employment situation in the transferee company under the employee participation agreement, the information must include suitable information relating to the use of agency workers (if any) in that company (see *reg 29(2A)*) inserted by the *Agency Workers Regulations 2010 (SI 2010 No 93)* which came into force on 1 October 2011.

The employee participation agreement must not be subject to the standard rules of employee participation (see **35.56**), unless it contains a provision to the contrary.

[*SI 2007 No 2974, Reg 29*].

(3) *Decisions of the special negotiating body*

Each member of the special negotiating body has one vote. Subject to (4) below the special negotiating body must take decisions by an absolute majority vote, although where at least 25% of the employees of the merging companies have participation rights, any decision which would result in a 'reduction of participation rights' must be taken by a two-thirds majority vote.

A '*reduction of participation rights*' means that the proportion of directors of the UK transferee company who may be elected or appointed (or whose appointment may be recommended or opposed) by virtue of employee participation is lower than the proportion of such directors or members in the merging company which had the highest proportion of such directors or members.

The special negotiating body must publish the details of any decision taken (including under (4) below) in such a manner as to bring the decision, so far as reasonably practicable, to the attention of the employees whom they represent. Publication must take place as soon as reasonably practicable and, in any event, no later than 14 days after the decision has been taken.

For the purpose of negotiations, the special negotiating body may be assisted by experts of its choice.

The merging companies must pay for any reasonable expenses of the functioning of the special negotiating body and any reasonable expenses relating to the negotiations that are necessary to enable the special negotiating body to carry out its functions in an appropriate manner. But where the special negotiating body is assisted by more than one expert, the merging companies are not required to pay such expenses in respect of more than one of them. [*SI 2007 No 2974, Reg 30*].

(4) *Decision not to open or to terminate negotiations*

The special negotiating body may decide, by a majority vote of two-thirds of its members, representing at least two-thirds of the employees of the merging companies, including the votes of members representing employees in at least two different EEA States, not to open negotiations under (1) above or to terminate negotiations already opened.

Following any such decision, the duty of the parties under (1) above to negotiate with a view to establishing an employee participation agreement cease as from the date of the decision. [*SI 2007 No 2974, Reg 31*].

(5) *Complaints about decisions of special negotiating body. SI 2007 No 2974, Reg 32, Sch 2, para 3.*

A member of the special negotiating body, an employee representative, or where there is no such representative in respect of an employee, that employee may present a complaint to the CAC if he believes that the special negotiating body has taken a decision referred to in *SI 2007 No 2974*, *Reg 30* or *31* and—

(a) that the decision was not taken by the majority required by *SI 2007 No 2974*, *Reg 30 or 31*; or

(b) (b) that the special negotiating body failed to publish the decision in accordance with *SI 2007 No 2974*, *Reg 30(5)*.

The complaint must be presented to the CAC—

(a) in the case of a complaint under (a) within 21 days of publication of the decision of the special negotiating body;

(b) in the case of a complaint under (b) within 21 days of the date by which the decision should have been published.

(3) Where the CAC finds the complaint well-founded it shall make a declaration that the decision was not taken properly and that it shall have no effect.

[*SI 2007 No 2974, Reg 32*].

35.55 *Election of UK members of the special negotiating body*

(1) *Ballot arrangements*

SI 2007 No 2974, Reg 33, Sch 2, para 1 contain detailed provisions for the holding of ballots for the UK members of the special negotiating body. This includes the appointment of one or more independent ballot supervisors and a complaints procedure if the requirements are not followed.

(2) *Conduct of the ballot*

There are detailed provisions relating to the conduct of ballots. As soon as reasonably practicable after the holding of the ballot, the ballot supervisor must publish the results of the ballot in such manner as to make them available to the directors and, so far as reasonably practicable, the UK employees entitled to vote in the ballot and the persons who stood as candidates. He must also publish a report where he considers that

- any of the requirements as to the conduct of the ballot was not satisfied with the result that the outcome of the ballot would have been different; or
- there was interference with the carrying out of his functions or a failure by the directors to comply with all reasonable requests made by him with the result that he was unable to form a proper judgement as to whether each of the requirements as to the conduct of the ballot was satisfied.

A fresh ballot or ballots must then be held.

All costs relating to the holding of a ballot of UK employees, including payments made to a ballot supervisor for supervising the conduct of the ballot, must be borne by the UK merging company (whether or not an ineffective ballot report has been published).

[*SI 2007 No 2974, Reg 34*].

(3) *Representation of employees*

A constituent member elected to the special negotiating body in accordance with *Regulation 26(1)* (see **35.53**(2)) is to be treated as representing the employees for the time being of the merging company whose employees were entitled to vote in the ballot in which he was elected. But if an additional member is elected in accordance with *Regulation 26(2)(3)* (see **35.53**(2)) he, and not any member elected in accordance with *Regulation 26(1)*, is to be treated as representing those employees.

[*SI 2007 No 2974, Reg 35*].

35.56 *Standard rules of employee participation in a UK transferee company*

(1) *Selection of standard rules of employee participation*

The merging companies may choose, without negotiating with the special negotiating body, the employee representatives or the employees, that a UK transferee company is to be subject to the standard rules of employee participation (see (3) below) from the date upon which the consequences of the cross-border merger take effect.

[*SI 2007 No 2974, Reg 36*].

(2) *Application of the standard rules*

The standard rules of employee participation also apply to a UK transferee company where the circumstances in (*a*) and (*b*) apply.

(a) Before registration of the UK transferee company, one or more forms of employee participation existed in at least one of the merging companies and either

  (i) that participation applied to at least one-third of the total number of employees of the merging companies; or

  (ii) that participation applied to less than one third of the total number of employees of the merging companies but the special negotiating body has decided that the standard rules of employee participation should apply.

  (iii) For the purposes of calculating the number of employees in (a) agency workers are treated as having been employed by a temporary work agency or agencies (see **35.52** (above)) and *reg 37(2A)* inserted by the *Agency Workers Regulations 2010 (SI 2010 No 93)* which came into force on 1 October 2011.

(b) Either

  (i) the merging companies and the special negotiating body agree that the standard rules should apply; or

  (ii) the period specified in **35.54**(1) for them to negotiate an employee participation agreement has expired without the parties reaching an agreement, the merging companies agree that the standard rules should apply, and the special negotiating body has *not* taken any decision under **35.54**(4) either not to open or to terminate the negotiations.

Where the standard rules of employee participation apply and more than one form of employee participation existed in the merging companies, the special negotiating body must decide which of the existing forms of participation apply in the UK transferee company. If it fails to do so (or where one or more form of employee participation existed in the merging companies and the merging companies have chosen, without any prior negotiation, to be directly subject to the standard rules of employee participation), the merging companies are responsible for determining the form of employee participation in the UK transferee company.

[*SI 2007 No 2974, Reg 37*].

(3) *The standard rules*

Under the standard rules, the employee representatives of the UK transferee company (or if there are no such representatives, the employees)

- subject to (4) below, have the right to elect, appoint, recommend or oppose the appointment of a number of directors of the transferee company, such number being equal to the number in the merging company which had the highest proportion of directors (or their EEA equivalent) so elected or appointed; and
- taking into account the proportion of employees of the transferee company formerly employed in each merging company, must decide on the allocation of directorships, or on the means by which the transferee's employees may recommend or oppose the appointment of directors. In making this decision, if the employees of one or more merging company are not covered by the proportional criterion, they must appoint a member from one of those merging companies including one from the UK, if appropriate.

Every director of the transferee company so elected, appointed or recommended must be a full director with the same rights and obligations as the directors representing shareholders, including the right to vote.

If under the standard rules of employee participation the transferee company has to provide information on the employment situation in that company, that must include suitable information relating to the use of agency workers (if any) in that company (see *reg 38(5)*) inserted by the *Agency Workers Regulations 2010 (SI 2010 No 93)* which came into force on 1 October 2011.

[*SI 2007 No 2974, Reg 38*].

(4) *Limit on level of employee participation*

Where, following prior negotiation, the standard rules of employee participation apply, the UK transferee company may limit the proportion of directors elected, appointed, recommended or opposed through employee participation to a level which is the lesser of

- the highest proportion in force in the merging companies prior to registration; and
- one third of the directors.

[*SI 2007 No 2974, Reg 39*].

(5) *Subsequent domestic mergers*

A transferee company resulting from a cross-border merger that operates under an employee participation system must ensure that employees' rights to employee participation are not affected, before the end of the period of three years beginning with the date on which the consequences of the cross-border merger have effect (see **35.48**) by any court order under *CA 2006, s 899* for the purposes of

- a reconstruction of the company or the amalgamation of the company with another company; or
- a merger involving a public company.

[*SI 2007 No 2974, Reg 40*].

35.57 *Confidential information*

Duty of confidentiality. Where a transferee company or merging company entrusts a person, pursuant to any provision relating to employee participation in **35.52** to **35.59**, with any information or document on terms requiring it to be held in confidence, the person must not disclose it except in accordance with the terms on which it was disclosed to him. Procedures are laid down for the recipient to apply to the Central Arbitration Committee (in Northern Ireland, the Industrial Court) for a declaration as to whether it was reasonable for the company to require him to hold the information or document in confidence.

[*SI 2007 No 2974, Reg 41, Sch 2 para 4*].

Withholding of information by the transferee or merging company. Neither a transferee company nor a merging company is required to disclose any information or document to a person for the purposes of **35.52** to **35.59** where the nature of the information or document is such that, according to objective criteria, the disclosure would seriously harm or be prejudicial to the transferee company or merging company. Where there is any dispute, application may be made to the Central Arbitration Committee (in Northern Ireland, the Industrial Court) for a declaration as to whether the information or document is of such a nature.

[*SI 2007 No 2974, Reg 42, Sch 2 para 5*].

35.58 *Protection for employees and members of special negotiating body, etc*

(1) *Right to time off for members of special negotiating body, etc*

An employee who is

- a member of a special negotiating body,
- a director of a transferee company, or
- a candidate in an election in which any person elected will, on being elected, be such a director or member,

is entitled to be permitted by his employer to take reasonable time off during the employee's working hours in order to perform his functions as such a member, director or candidate.

[*SI 2007 No 2974, Reg 34*].

(2) *Right to remuneration for time off under (1) above*

An employee who is permitted to take time off under (1) above is entitled to be paid remuneration by his employer for the time taken off at the '*appropriate hourly rate*', ie the amount of one week's pay divided by the number of normal working hours in a week for that employee when employed under the contract of employment in force on the day when the time is taken. There are special provisions where the number of normal working hours differs from week to week or over a longer period.

[*SI 2007 No 2974, Reg 44*].

(3) *Complaints to employment tribunals*

An employee may present a complaint to an employment tribunal (in Northern Ireland, an industrial tribunal) that his employer has

- unreasonably refused to permit him to take time off as required under (1) above; or
- failed to pay the whole or any part of any amount to which the employee is entitled under (2) above.

The complaint must be made within three months of the date on which the time off was taken or on which it is alleged the time off should have been permitted (or such longer period as the tribunal allows).

[*SI 2007 No 2974, Reg 45; Sch 2 para 6*].

(4) *Unfair dismissal of employee*

An employee who is dismissed is regarded as unfairly dismissed for the purposes of *Employment Rights Act 1996, Pt 10* if the reason (or, if more than one, the principal reason) for the dismissal is that he

(i) took, or proposed to take, any proceedings before an employment tribunal (in Northern Ireland, an industrial tribunal) to enforce any right conferred on him by *SI 2007 No 2974* (and for these purposes it is immaterial whether or not the employee has the right or entitlement and whether or not the right has been infringed provided the employee has acted in good faith);

(ii) exercised, or proposed to exercise, any entitlement to apply or complain to the Central Arbitration Committee or the Employment Appeal Tribunal (in Northern Ireland, the Industrial Court and the High Court in Northern Ireland) conferred by *SI 2007 No 2974* or exercised or proposed to exercise the right to appeal in connection with any rights conferred by those Regulations;

(iii) acted with a view to securing that a special negotiating body did or did not come into existence;

(iv) indicated that he did or did not support the coming into existence of a special negotiating body;

(v) stood as a candidate in an election in which any person elected would, on being elected, be a member of a special negotiating body or a director of a UK transferee company;

(vi) influenced or sought to influence by lawful means the way in which votes were to be cast by other employees in a ballot arranged under *SI 2007 No 2974*;

(vii) voted in such a ballot;

(viii) expressed doubts, whether to a ballot supervisor or otherwise, as to whether such a ballot had been properly conducted; or

(ix) proposed to do, failed to do, or proposed to decline to do, any of the things mentioned in (v) to (viii) above.

[*SI 2007 No 2974, Reg 46, Sch 2 para 7*].

(5) *Unfair dismissal of member of special negotiating body, etc*

An employee who is

- a member of a special negotiating body,
- a director of a transferee company, or
- a candidate in an election in which any person elected will, on being elected, be such a director or member,

who is dismissed is regarded as unfairly dismissed for the purposes of *Employment Rights Act 1996, Pt 10* if the reason (or, if more than one, the principal reason) for the dismissal is that

(i) the employee performed or proposed to perform any functions or activities as such a member, director or candidate; or

(ii) the employee or a person acting on his behalf made or proposed to make a request to exercise an entitlement conferred on the employee under (1) or (2) above.

[*SI 2007 No 2974, Reg 47*].

(6) *Detriment*

An employee has the right not to be subjected to any detriment by any act, or deliberate failure to act, by his employer, done on a ground specified in (4)(i)–(ix) above, unless the detriment in question amounts to dismissal.

[*SI 2007 No 2974, Reg 49, Sch 2 para 9*].

(7) *Detriment for member of special negotiating body, etc*

An employee who is

- a member of a special negotiating body,
- a director of a transferee company, or
- a candidate in an election in which any person elected will, on being elected, be such a director or member,

has the right not to be subjected to any detriment by any act, or deliberate failure to act, by his employer, done on a ground specified in (5)(i) or (ii) above, unless the detriment in question amounts to dismissal. [*SI 2007 No 2974, Reg 50*].

(8) *Detriment: enforcement*

An employee may present a complaint to an employment tribunal (in Northern Ireland, an industrial tribunal) that he has been subjected to a detriment in contravention of (6) or (7) above.

[*SI 2007 No 2974, Reg 51, Sch 2 para 10*].

35.59 *Compliance and enforcement*

(1) *Disputes about the operation of an employee participation agreement or the standard rules of employee participation*

Where

- an employee participation agreement has been agreed, or
- the standard rules of employee participation apply,

a complaint may be presented to the CAC (in Northern Ireland, the Industrial Court) by

- a special negotiating body, or
- in a case where no special negotiating body has been elected or appointed, or has been dissolved, an employee representative or employee of the transferee company

who considers that the transferee company has failed to comply with the terms of the employee participation agreement or, where applicable, the standard rules of employee participation.

Such a complaint must be brought within the three months beginning with the date of the alleged failure (or where the failure takes place over a period, the last day of that period).

Where the CAC (in Northern Ireland, the Industrial Court) finds the complaint well founded, it must make a declaration to that effect and may make an order requiring the transferee company, by a specified date, to take such steps as are necessary to comply with the terms of the employee participation agreement or, where applicable, the standard rules of employee participation. The applicant may then, within three months of the decision, make an application to the Employment Appeal Tribunal (in Northern Ireland, the High Court in Northern Ireland) for a penalty notice to be issued. On such an application, that body must issue a written penalty notice to the transferee company requiring it to pay a penalty to the Secretary of State in respect of the failure (up to a maximum of £75,000) unless satisfied, on hearing representations from the transferee company, that the failure resulted from a reason beyond its control or that it has some other reasonable excuse for its failure.

No order of the CAC (in Northern Ireland, the Industrial Court) has the effect of suspending or altering the effect of any act done or of any agreement made by the transferee company or merging company.

[*SI 2007 No 2974, Regs 53, 55, Sch 2 para 12*].

(2) *Misuse of procedures*

If an employee representative (or where there is no such representative in relation to an employee, an employee) believes that a transferee company or merging company is misusing or intending to misuse the transferee company or the powers in *SI 2007 No 2974* for the purpose of

- depriving the employees of that merging company or the transferee company of their rights to employee participation, or
- withholding such rights from any of those people,

he may make a complaint to the CAC (in Northern Ireland, the Industrial Court).

Such a complaint must be made before the date upon which the consequences of the cross-border merger take effect (see **35.48**) or within a period of 12 months after that date.

The CAC (in Northern Ireland, the Industrial Court) must uphold the complaint unless the respondent proves the contrary. Where it finds the complaint to be well-founded, it must make a declaration to that effect and may make an order requiring the transferee company or merging company to take action to ensure that the employees involved are not deprived of their rights to employee participation or that such rights are not withheld from them. The complainant may then, within three months of the decision, make an application to the Employment Appeal Tribunal (in Northern Ireland, the High Court in Northern Ireland) for a penalty notice to be issued. On such an application, that body must issue a written penalty notice to the transferee company or merging company requiring it to pay a penalty to the Secretary of State in respect of the failure (up to a maximum of £75,000) unless satisfied, on hearing representations from the transferee company or merging company, that the failure resulted from a reason beyond its control or that it has some other reasonable excuse for its failure.

No order of the CAC (in Northern Ireland, the Industrial Court) has the effect of suspending or altering the effect of any act done or of any agreement made by the transferee company or merging company.

[*SI 2007 No 2974, Regs 54, 55, Sch 2 para 13*].

35.60 Unregistered companies

The provisions in **35.35** to **35.59** apply to an unregistered company as they apply to a company formed and registered under *CA 2006* (or earlier provisions). In the application of the provisions to an unregistered company

- any reference to a UK company's registered office is to be read as a reference to the unregistered company's principal office in the UK;
- any reference to a part of the UK in which a UK company is registered is to be read as a reference to the part of the UK in which the unregistered company's principal office is situated; and
- **35.42**(*c*) applies with the omission of (iv) (duty to state company's registered number).

[*SI 2007 No 2974, Reg 5*].

35.61 Application of certain provisions of CA 2006

The following provisions apply for the purposes of **35.35** to **35.59** as they apply for the purposes of the Companies Acts.

- *CA 2006, s 1081* (annotation of the register, see **39.10 Registrar of Companies**).
- *CA 2006, ss 1102–1104, 1107* (language requirements for documents delivered to Registrar, see **39.13 Registrar of Companies**).
- *CA 2006, s 1105* (documents that may be drawn up and delivered in other languages, see **39.13 Registrar of Companies**) applies to the documents required to be delivered to the Registrar of Companies under **35.42**(*b*) (draft terms of merger) and **35.49**(*c*) (order of competent authority of another EEA State).
- *CA 2006, s 1106* (voluntary filing of translations, see **39.13 Registrar of Companies**) applies in relation to
  - (i) all official languages of EEA States; and
  - (ii) all documents required to be delivered to the Registrar of Companies under *SI 2007 No 2974*.
- *CA 2006, s 1112* (offence of false statement to Registrar, see **39.18 Registrar of Companies**) with effect from 1 October 2008.
- *CA 2006, s 1113* (enforcement of company's filing obligations, see **39.16 Registrar of Companies**).
- *CA 2006, ss 1121–1123* (liability of officer in default, see **29.2 Offences and Legal Proceedings**).
- *CA 2006, s 1125* (meaning of 'daily default fine', see **29.1 Offences and Legal Proceedings**).
- *CA 2006, ss 1127, 1128* (summary proceedings, see **29.4 Offences and Legal Proceedings**).
- *CA 2006, s 1129* (legal professional privilege, see **29.3 Offences and Legal Proceedings**).
- *CA 2006, s 1130* (proceedings against unincorporated bodies, see **29.6 Offences and Legal Proceedings**).

[*SI 2007 No 2974, Reg 4, Sch 1 para 2*].

36 Records

36.1 **Form of records generally**
36.2 Inspection of records and provision of copies
36.3 Duty to take precautions against falsification
36.4 Preservation of records
36.5 **Duty to keep accounting records**
36.6 Location and inspection of accounting records
36.7 Preservation of accounting records
36.8 Criminal destruction, etc of accounting records

Cross-references. See **38 Registers; 42.40, 42.41 Resolutions and Meetings** for minutes of directors' meetings and general meetings respectively.

36.1 FORM OF RECORDS GENERALLY

'Company records' may be

- kept in 'hard copy' or 'electronic form', and
- arranged in such manner as the directors of the company think fit,

provided the information in question is adequately recorded for future reference.

Any provision of an instrument made by a company before 12 February 1979 that requires a register of holders of the company's debentures to be kept in hard copy form is to be read as requiring it to be kept in hard copy or electronic form.

Where the records are kept in electronic form, they must be capable of being reproduced in hard copy form.

'*Company records*' means

(a) any register, index, accounting records, agreement, memorandum, minutes or other document required by the *Companies Acts* to be kept by a company; and

(b) any register kept by the company of its debenture holders

See **Appendix 1 Definitions** for the meaning of '*hard copy*' and '*electronic form*'.

Offences. If a company fails to comply with these requirements, an offence is committed by every officer of the company who is in default. A person guilty of such an offence is liable, on summary conviction, to a fine not exceeding level 3 on the standard scale and, for continued contravention, a daily default fine not exceeding one-tenth of level 3 on the standard scale. See **29.1 Offences and Legal Proceedings** for the standard scale.

[*CA 2006, ss 1134, 1135*].

36.2 Inspection of records and provision of copies

(1) Inspection location

Certain specified records (see below) may be kept available for inspection at

- the company's registered office; or
- at one location other than the registered office provided that
  - (i) it is situated in the same part of the UK in which the company is registered;
  - (ii) all the specified records are kept at that same place; and
  - (iii) the place has been notified to the Registrar of Companies as being the company's alternative inspection location.

See **7.2** and **7.3** for details to be included in a company's annual return of the company's registered office address and alternative inspection location (SAIL) and how changes must be notified to Companies House.

[*CA 2006, s 1136(1); SI 2008 No 3006, Reg 3*].

The specified records are

- the register of members (see **38.5 Registers**);
- the register of directors (see **38.2 Registers**);
- directors' service contracts (see **18.52 Directors**);
- directors' indemnities (see **18.44 Directors**);
- the register of secretaries (see **38.4 Registers**);
- records of resolution (see **42.41 Resolutions**);
- contracts relating to purchase of own shares (see **34.9 Purchase of Own Shares**);
- documents relating to redemption or purchase of own shares out of capital by private company (see **34.12 Purchase of Own Shares**);
- the register of debenture holders (see **38.12 Registers**);
- report to members of outcome of investigation by public company into interests in its shares (see **24.5 Interests in Public Company Shares**);
- the register of interests in shares disclosed to public company (see **38.8 Registers**); and
- the register of charges and copies of instruments creating charges (see **38.11 Registers**).

[*CA 2006, s 1136(2)*].

(2) **Availability for inspection – private companies**

A private company must make its company records available for inspection by a person on a day which has been specified by that person ('the specified day') provided that

- the specified day is a working day; and
- the person gives the company the required notice of the specified day.

The required notice is:

- At least two working days' notice if

(i) the notice is given during the period of notice for a general meeting or a class meeting; or

(ii) where the company circulates a written resolution, the notice is given during the period provided for in *CA 2006, s 297(1)*, ie the period specified for the purpose in the company's articles or, if none is specified, the period of 28 days beginning with the circulation date

provided that the notice given both begins and ends during the period referred to in (i) or (ii) above (as the case may be).

- In all other cases, at least 10 working days' notice of the specified day.

When the person gives notice of the specified day, he must also give notice of the time on that day at which he wishes to start the inspection (which must be any time between 9am and 3pm) and the company must make its company records available for inspection by that person for a period of at least two hours beginning with that time.

[*SI 2008 No 3006, Reg 4*].

(3) **Availability for inspection – public companies**

A public company must make its company records available for inspection for at least two hours between 9am and 5pm on each working day.

[*SI 2008 No 3006, Reg 5*].

(4) **Inspection: general**

A company is not required for the purposes of inspection of any its records to present information in that record in a different order, structure or form from that set out in that record.

[*SI 2008 No 3006, Reg 6(1)*].

See APPENDIX 3 (FEES PAYABLE TO COMPANIES) for details of fees payable for inspection of certain documents.

(5) **Copying of information**

A company must permit a person to make a copy of the whole or any part of a company record in the course of inspection at the location at which the record is made available for inspection and at any time during which the record is made available for inspection, but a company is not required to assist that person in making his copy of that record.

Where a person requests a company to provide a copy of a company record

- in hard copy form, the company must provide that copy in hard copy form; and
- in electronic form, the company must provide that copy in such electronic form as the company decides except that where the company keeps a company record in hard copy form only, it is not required to provide a copy of that record in electronic form.

Where a company provides a copy of a company record in electronic form to a member of the company or to a holder of the company's debentures, the company is not also required to provide a hard copy of that record in accordance with *CA 2006, s 1145*.

A company is not required to present information in a copy of a company record that it provides in a different order, structure or form from that set out in the record.

[*SI 2008 No 3006, Regs 6(2), 7–9*].

See **Appendix 3 (Fees payable to companies)** for details of fees payable for inspection of certain documents.

(6) **Inspection of accounting records**

Subject to (1)–(5) above no right is given to inspect the accounting records or other books and documents of the company unless that right is given by the articles. Where a company has adopted standard articles, see

- *Table A 1985, Reg 109* (which provides in summary that no member has the right to inspect accounting records or "other book or document of the company" unless the right is conferred by law or authorised by the directors or by an ordinary resolution of members)"
- *Model Articles, Art 50* (private companies)
- *Model Articles, Art 83* (public companies)

  (which both provide in summary that no person is entitled to inspect any of the company's accounting records or "other records or documents" except as provided by law or authorised by the directors or by an ordinary resolution of members.)

set out in **Appendix 4 Standard Articles of Association.**

See also *McCusker v McRae* 1966 SC 253 and *Conway v Petronius Clothing Co Ltd* [1978] 1 All ER 185, [1978] 1 WLR 72.

36.3 Duty to take precautions against falsification

Where company records are kept otherwise than in bound books, adequate precautions must be taken to guard against falsification and to facilitate the discovery of falsification. This does not apply to documents required to be kept under

(a) *CA 2006, s 228* (copies of director's service contract or memoranda of their terms); or

(b) *CA 2006, s 237* (qualifying indemnity provisions made for directors).

If a company fails to comply with this requirement, an offence is committed by every officer of the company who is in default. A person guilty of such an offence is liable, on summary conviction, to a fine not exceeding level 3 on the standard scale and, for continued contravention, a daily default fine not exceeding one-tenth of level 3 on the standard scale. See **29.1 Offences and Legal Proceedings** for the standard scale.

[*CA 2006, s 1138*].

36.4 Preservation of records

Where there are specific provisions in the legislation relating to the preservation of records (eg accounting records as under **36.7**), these are covered in the relevant part of this book. Otherwise, companies' legislation does not set out any general provisions as to the period for preservation of a company's records. It is recommended practice to keep

- memorandum of association, articles of association, certificate of incorporation, statutory registers and copies of published accounts for the life of the company;
- invoices, receipts, returned cheques, paying-in books, bank statements, etc for six years;
- title deeds and related correspondence for twelve years after disposal; and
- contracts and agreements for six years after expiry (twelve years if under seal).

Where standard articles have been adopted, see

- *Model Articles, Art 82* (public companies) which provides which documents may be destroyed and when. The Model Articles for private companies do not contain the same or similar provisions.

The Model Articles are set out in **APPENDIX 4 STANDARD ARTICLES OF ASSOCIATION**.

36.5 DUTY TO KEEP ACCOUNTING RECORDS

Every company must keep adequate accounting records sufficient to show and explain the company's transactions and to

- disclose with reasonable accuracy, at any time, the financial position of the company at that time; and
- enable the directors to ensure that any accounts required to be prepared comply with the requirements of *CA 2006* and, where applicable, *International Accounting Standards Regulation, Art 4*.

The accounting records must, in particular, contain

- entries from day-to-day of all sums of money received and expended by the company and the matters in respect of which the receipt and expenditure takes place; and
- a record of the assets and liabilities of the company.

If the company's business involves dealing in goods, the accounting records must also contain

(i) statements of stock held by the company at the end of each financial year;

(ii) all statements of stock-taking from which any statement of stock in (i) above has been or is to be prepared; and

(iii) (except in the case of goods sold by way of ordinary retail trade) statements of all goods sold and purchased, showing sufficient detail of the goods, buyers and sellers to enable all these to be identified.

A parent company with a subsidiary undertaking in relation to which the above requirements do not apply must take reasonable steps to ensure that the undertaking keeps such accounting records as to enable the directors of the parent company to ensure that any accounts required to be prepared comply with the requirements of *CA 2006* and, where applicable, *IAS Regulation, Art 4*.

[*CA 2006, s 386*].

Offences. If a company fails to comply with the above provisions, an offence is committed by every officer of the company who is in default. A person guilty of such an offence is liable (i) on conviction on indictment, to imprisonment for a term not exceeding two years or a fine (or both); and (ii) on summary conviction, to imprisonment for a term not exceeding twelve months (six months in Scotland or Northern Ireland) or to a fine not exceeding the statutory maximum (or both). See **29.1** OFFENCES AND LEGAL PROCEEDINGS for the statutory maximum. It is a defence for a person charged with such an offence to show that he acted honestly and that in the circumstances in which the company's business was carried on the default was excusable.

[*CA 2006, s 387*].

Interpretation of the above provisions. See the ICAEW technical release (TECH 01/11) "Guidance for directors on accounting records under the Companies Act 2006"

Lien over accounting records. As *CA 2006, s 386* above imposes mandatory duties on a company in connection with the keeping of accounting records and criminal penalties for breach of those duties. An accountant (or solicitor) cannot claim a lien over books and documents for unpaid fees. See *DTC (CNC) Ltd v Gary Sargeant & Co (a firm)* [1996] 2 All ER 369, [1996] 1 BCLC 529 where an accountant asserted a lien over sales and purchase invoices, cheque books, paying-in books and bank statements.

See also ICAEW guidance "Documents and records : ownership, lien and rights of access".

36.6 Location and inspection of accounting records

The accounting records must be kept at the company's registered office or such other place as the directors think fit and must at all times be open to inspection by the company's officers.

If the accounting records are kept outside the UK, accounts and returns which

- disclose with reasonable accuracy the financial position of the business at intervals of not more than six months, and
- enable the directors to ensure that the accounts required to be prepared comply with the requirements of *CA 2006* (and, where applicable, the requirements of *IAS Regulation, Art 4*)

must be sent to, and kept in, a place in the UK, and must at all times be open to inspection by the company's officers.

[*CA 2006, s 388(1)–(3)*].

Offences. If a company fails to comply with the above provisions, an offence is committed by every officer of the company who is in default. A person guilty of such an offence is liable (i) on conviction on indictment, to imprisonment for a term not exceeding two years or a fine (or both); and (ii) on summary conviction, to imprisonment for a term not exceeding twelve months (six months in Scotland and Northern Ireland) or to a fine not exceeding the statutory maximum (or both). See **29.1** OFFENCES AND LEGAL PROCEEDINGS for the statutory maximum. It is a defence for a person charged with such an offence to show that he acted honestly and that in the circumstances in which the company's business was carried on the default was excusable.

[*CA 2006, s 389(1)(2)(4)*].

36.7 Preservation of accounting records

The accounting records that a company is required to keep under **36.5** must be preserved

- in the case of a private company, for three years from the date on which they are made; and
- in the case of a public company, for six years from the date on which they are made.

This is subject to any provision contained in rules made under *IA 1986, s 411* or *Insolvency (Northern Ireland) Order 1989 (SI 1989 No 2405), Art 359*.

[*CA 2006, s 388(4)(5)*].

It should also be noted that records may be required to be preserved longer for other purposes. HM Revenue and Customs require VAT records to be preserved for six years (or such lesser period as they allow) and direct tax assessments may be raised for up to six years after the chargeable accounting period (20 years in the case of fraud or negligent conduct).

Offences. An officer of a company commits an offence if he

- fails to take all reasonable steps for securing compliance by the company with *CA 2006, s 388(4)*; or
- intentionally causes any default by the company under that provision.

A person guilty of such an offence is liable (i) on conviction on indictment, to imprisonment for a term not exceeding two years or a fine (or both); and (ii) on summary conviction, to imprisonment for a term not exceeding twelve months (six months in Scotland and Northern Ireland) or to a fine not exceeding the statutory maximum (or both). See **29.1** Offences and Legal Proceedings for the statutory maximum. It is a defence for a person charged with such an offence to show that he acted honestly and that in the circumstances in which the company's business was carried on the default was excusable.

[*CA 2006, s 389(3)(4)*].

36.8 Criminal destruction etc of accounting records

Where a person dishonestly, with a view to gain for himself or another or intent to cause loss to another,

- destroys, defaces, conceals or falsifies any account or any other record or document made or required for any accounting purpose, or
- makes use of any such account, etc which he knows to be materially misleading, false or deceptive

he is, on conviction, liable to imprisonment for a term not exceeding seven years.

[*Theft Act 1968, s 17*].

37 Registered Office

37.1 Requirement to have a registered office
37.2 Change of address
37.3 Welsh companies

Cross-references. See **16.13–16.16 Dealings With Third Parties** for various disclosure requirements concerning the registered office.

Background. The provisions in this chapter apply, unless otherwise stated, with effect from 1 October 2009.

37.1 REQUIREMENT TO HAVE A REGISTERED OFFICE

A company must at all times have a registered office to which all communications and notices may be addressed. [*CA 2006, s 86*]. On formation, the address is that specified in the registration documents sent to the Registrar of Companies under *CA 2006, s 9* (see **12.3 Company Formation and Types of Companies**).

37.2 CHANGE OF ADDRESS

A company may change the address of its registered office by giving notice to the Registrar of Companies. The change takes effect upon the notice being registered by the Registrar of Companies but for the next 14 days any document can still be validly served at the address previously registered.

Where a company has given notice, for the purposes of any duty

(a) to keep available for inspection at its registered office any register, index or other document, or

(b) to mention the address of its registered office in any document,

the company may act on the change as from such date, not more than 14 days after the notice is given, as it may determine.

Where a company unavoidably ceases to perform at its registered office any duty within (*a*) above in circumstances in which it was not practicable to give prior notice to the Registrar of Companies of a change in the address of its registered office (eg in the case of fire), it is not to be treated as having failed to comply with that duty provided it

- resumes performance of that duty at other premises as soon as practicable; and
- gives notice accordingly to the Registrar of Companies of a change in the situation of its registered office within 14 days of doing so.

[*CA 2006, s 87*].

37.3 WELSH COMPANIES

A '*Welsh company*' means a company as to which it is stated in the register that its registered office is to be situated in Wales (as opposed to England and Wales). A company can be set up as a Welsh company by delivering to the Registrar of Companies a statement to this effect on formation (see **12.3 Company Formation and Types of Companies**).

(a) **Becoming a Welsh company.** A company

- whose registered office is in Wales, and
- as to which it is stated in the register that its registered office is to be situated in England and Wales,

may by special resolution require the register to be amended so that it states that the company's registered office is to be situated in Wales.

(b) **Ceasing to be a Welsh company.** A company

- whose registered office is in Wales, and
- as to which it is stated in the register that its registered office is to be situated in Wales,

may by special resolution require the register to be amended so that it states that the company's registered office is to be situated in England and Wales.

Where a company passes a resolution under (*a*) or (*b*) above it must give notice to the Registrar of Companies who must amend the register accordingly and issue a new certificate of incorporation altered to meet the circumstances of the case.

[*CA 2006, s 88*]

38 Registers

38.1 **Form in which register kept**
38.2 **Register of directors**
38.3 **Register of directors' residential addresses**
38.4 **Register of secretaries**
38.5 **Register of members**
38.6 Location and inspection of register
38.7 Overseas branch registers
38.8 **Register of disclosed interests in public company shares**
38.9 Location and inspection of register
38.10 Removal of entries from the register
38.11 **Register of charges and copies of instruments creating charges**
38.12 **Register of debenture holders**
38.13 **Register of directors' interests**
38.14 **Reforms – Register of people with significant interests; option to keep information on Companies House Register**

38.1 FORM IN WHICH REGISTER KEPT

Any register or index which a company is required to keep under the *Companies Acts* may be kept in hard copy or electronic form and may be arranged in such manner as the directors of the company think fit, provided the information in question is adequately recorded for future reference. This is subject to the requirements that where the records are kept

- in electronic form, they must be capable of being reproduced in hard copy form; and
- otherwise than in bound books, adequate precautions must be taken to guard against falsification and to facilitate its discovery.

If a company fails to comply with the above provisions, an offence is committed by every officer of the company who is in default. A person guilty of such an offence is liable, on summary conviction, to a fine not exceeding level 3 on the standard scale and, for continued contravention, a daily default fine not exceeding one-tenth of level 3 on the standard scale. See **29.1 Offences and Legal Proceedings** for the standard scale.

[*CA 2006, ss 1135(1)–(4), 1138(1)–(3)*].

38.2 REGISTER OF DIRECTORS

Every company must

- keep a register of its directors containing the required particulars of each person who is a director;
- keep the register available for inspection at the company's registered office or at a place specified in Regulations. The regulations are the *Companies (Company Records) Regulations 2008 (SI 2008 No 3006)* (see **36.2** Records). It must be open to the inspection of any member of the company without charge and any other person on payment of such fee as may be prescribed. The fee is £3.50 for each hour or part of an hour during which the right of inspection of exercised (see **Appendix 3 Fees**);
- give notice to the Registrar of Companies of the place at which the register is kept available for inspection and any change in that place (unless it has at all times been kept at the company's registered office); and

- give notice to the Registrar of Companies, within 14 days, of any change in the particulars contained on the register and the date on which the change occurred. Where

  (i) a company gives notice of a change of a director's service address as stated in the company's register of directors, and

  (ii) the notice is not accompanied by notice of any resulting change in the particulars contained in the company's register of directors' residential addresses (see 38.3),

  the notice must be accompanied by a statement that no such change is required.

Offences. If

- default is made in complying with the requirements to

  (i) keep a register with the required particulars,

  (ii) keep the register available for inspection at the correct location,

  (iii) notify the Registrar of Companies of the place, or any change in the place, where the register is available for inspection, or

  (iv) notify the Registrar of Companies of any changes in the particulars contained on the register, or

- an inspection is refused,

an offence is committed by the company and every officer of the company who is in default. For these purposes, a shadow director is treated as an officer of the company. A person guilty of such an offence is liable, on summary conviction, to a fine not exceeding level 5 on the standard scale and, for continued contravention, a daily default fine not exceeding one-tenth of the greater of £5,000 or level 4 on the standard scale. See **29.1 Offences and Legal Proceedings** for the standard scale. In the case of a refusal of inspection of the register, the court may by order compel an immediate inspection of it.

Particulars of directors to be disclosed. A company's register of directors must contain the following particulars.

(a) In the case of an individual

  (i) 'name' and any 'former name';

  (ii) a service address (which may be stated to be 'the company's registered office');

  (iii) the country or state (or part of the UK) in which he is usually resident;

  (iv) nationality;

  (v) business occupation (if any); and

  (vi) date of birth.

  '*Name*' means a Christian name (or other forename) and surname. But in the case of a peer or an individual usually known by a title, the title may be stated instead of his Christian name (or other forename) and surname or in addition to either or both of them.

'*Former name*' means a name by which the individual was formerly known for business purposes. Where a person is (or was) formerly known by more than one such name, each of them must be stated. It is not necessary for the register to contain particulars of a former name

- in the case of a peer or an individual normally known by a British title, where the name is one by which the person was known previous to the adoption of or succession to the title; and
- in the case of any person, where the former name *either* was changed or disused before the person attained the age of 16 *or* has been changed or disused for 20 years or more.

(b) In the case of a body corporate, or a firm that is a legal person under the law by which it is governed

(i) corporate or firm name;

(ii) registered or principal office;

(iii) in the case of an EEA company to which the *First Company Law Directive* applies, particulars of

(i) the register in which the company file mentioned in *Article 3* of that *Directive* is kept (including details of the relevant state); and

(ii) the registration number in that register; and

(iv) in any other case, particulars of

- the legal form of the company or firm and the law by which it is governed; and
- if applicable, the register in which it is entered (including details of the state) and its registration number in that register.

The Secretary of State may, by Regulations, add to or remove items from the above requirements.

[*CA 2006, ss 162–164, 166, 167*].

Directors' residential addresses. See **18.72 Directors** for entries required to be made in the register following action by the Registrar of Companies under *Companies Act 2006 (CA 2006), ss 245, 246* (putting usual residential address on public record).

Time available for inspection and copying. See **36.2 Records**.

Obligation to keep separate registers

(1) On or after 1 October 2009, the register of directors and secretaries kept by a company under *CA 1985, s 288(1)* is treated as two separate registers, ie a register of directors under *CA 2006, s 162* (see above) and a register of secretaries under *CA 2006, s 275* (see **38.4**).

[*SI 2008 No 2860, Sch 2 para 25*].

(2) A company incorporated before 1 October 2009 does not need to comply with the any provision of *CA 2006* requiring the company's register of directors or secretaries to contain particulars additional to those required by *CA 1985* until the earlier of

- the date to which the company makes up its first annual return made up to a date on or after 1 October 2009; and

- the last date to which the company should have made up that return

except that this provision

(i) does not apply in relation to a director of whom particulars are first registered on or after 1 October 2009 (whether the director was appointed before or on or after that date); and

(ii) ceases to apply in relation to a director whose registered particulars fall to be altered on or after 1 October 2009 because they have changed (whether the change occurred before, on or after that date).

None of the above provisions affect the particulars required to be included in the company's annual return.

[*SI 2008 No 2860, Sch 2 para 26*].

(3) In the case of a company incorporated before 1 October 2009,

- the 'relevant existing address' of a director is deemed, on or after 1 October 2009, to be a service address; and
- any entry in the company's register of directors stating that address is treated, on or after that date, as complying with the obligation under (*a*)(ii) (particulars of director above) to state a service address.

The 'relevant service address' is

(i) the address that immediately before 1 October 2009 appears in the company's register of directors and secretaries as having been notified to the company as the service address notified by an individual applying for a confidentiality order in respect of a usual residential address; or

(ii) if no such address appeared, the address that immediately before 1 October 2009 appears in the company's register of directors and secretaries as the director's usual residential address.

Any notification of a change of a relevant existing address before 1 October 2009 that is received by the company on or after that date is treated as being or, as the case may be, including notification of a change of service address.

The operation of this provision does not give rise to any duty to notify the Registrar of Companies under *CA 2006, s 167* (duty to notify the Registrar of Companies of change of particulars in the register).

[*SI 2008 No 2860, Sch 2 para 27*].

(4) A company incorporated before 1 October 2009, must have removed from its register of directors on 1 October 2009 any entry relating to a 'shadow director'. *CA 2006, s 167* (duty to notify the Registrar of Companies of changes in particulars in the register) applies as if the shadow director had ceased to be a director on that date.

[*SI 2008 No 2860, Sch 2 para 28*].

(5) The removal by a company incorporated before 1 October 2009, from its register of directors on or after 1 October 2009 of particulars required by *CA 1985* but not required by *CA 2006* does not give rise to any duty to notify the Registrar of Companies under *CA 2006, s 167* (duty to notify Registrar of Companies of changes of particulars in the register).

[*SI 2008 No 2860, Sch 2 para 29*].

(6) *CA 2006, s 167* (duty to notify Registrar of Companies of changes of particulars in the register) applies in relation to

- a change among a company's directors, or
- a change in the particulars contained in the register

occurring on or after 1 October 2009.

38.3 REGISTER OF DIRECTORS' RESIDENTIAL ADDRESSES

Every company must comply with the requirement on or after 1 October 2009 to

- keep a register of directors' residential addresses stating the usual residential address of each of the company's directors; and
- give notice to the Registrar of Companies, within 14 days, of any change in the particulars contained on the register and the date on which the change occurred. If a director's usual residential address is the same as his service address (as stated in the company's register of directors under **38.2**), the register of directors' residential addresses need only contain an entry to that effect. But this does not apply if his service address is stated to be 'The company's registered office'.

If default is made in complying with the above provisions, an offence is committed by the company and every officer of the company who is in default. For this purpose, a 'shadow director' is treated as an officer of the company. A person guilty of such an offence is liable, on summary conviction, to a fine not exceeding the greater of £5000 or level 4 on the standard scale and, for continued contravention, a daily default fine not exceeding one-tenth of the greater of £5,000 or level 4 on the standard scale. See **29.1 Offences and Legal Proceedings** for the standard scale.

The above provisions apply only to directors who are individuals, not where the director is a body corporate or a firm that is a legal person under the law by which it is governed.

[*CA 2006, ss 165, 167; SI 2015 No 664, Sch 3*].

The entry on that register of information which immediately before 1 October 2009 was contained in the company's register of directors and secretaries does not give rise to any duty to notify the Registrar of Companies under *CA 2006, s 167* (duty to notify Registrar of Companies of changes of particulars in the register).

[*SI 2008 No 2860, Sch 2 para 30*].

38.4 REGISTER OF SECRETARIES

Every company must

- keep a register of its secretaries containing the required particulars of the person who is, or persons who are, the secretary or joint secretaries of the company;
- keep the register available for inspection at the company's registered office or at a place specified in Regulations (see **36.2 Records**). It must be open to the inspection of any member of the company without charge and any other person on payment of such fee as may be prescribed (see **Appendix 3 Fees**);
- give notice to the Registrar of Companies, within 14 days, of the place at which the register is kept available for inspection and any change in that place (unless it has at all times been kept at the company's registered office); and

- give notice to the Registrar of Companies, within 14 days, of any change in the particulars contained on the register.

Offences. If

- default is made in complying with the requirements to
  - (i) keep a register with the required particulars,
  - (ii) keep the register available for inspection at the correct location,
  - (iii) notify the Registrar of Companies of the place, or any change in the place, where the register is available for inspection, or
  - (iv) notify the Registrar of Companies of any changes in the particulars contained on the register, or
- an inspection is refused,

an offence is committed by the company and every officer of the company who is in default. For these purposes, a 'shadow director' is treated as an officer of the company. A person guilty of such an offence is liable, on summary conviction, to a fine not exceeding the greater of £5000 or level 4 on the standard scale and, for continued contravention, a daily default fine not exceeding one-tenth of the greater of £5,000 or level 4 on the standard scale. See **29.1** OFFENCES AND LEGAL PROCEEDINGS for the standard scale. In the case of a refusal of inspection of the register, the court may by order compel an immediate inspection of it.

Particulars of secretaries to be disclosed. A company's register of secretaries must contain the following particulars.

(a) In the case of an individual:

- (i) Name, ie Christian name (or other forename) and surname. In the case of a peer or an individual usually known by a title, the title may be stated instead of his Christian name (or other forename) and surname or in addition to either or both of them.
- (ii) Any former name, ie any name by which the individual was formerly known for business purposes. Where a person is (or was) formerly known by more than one such name, each of them must be stated. It is not necessary for the register to contain particulars of a former name
  - in the case of a peer or an individual normally known by a British title, where the name is one by which the person was known previous to the adoption of or succession to the title; and
  - in the case of any person, where the former name *either* was changed or disused before the person attained the age of 16 *or* has been changed or disused for 20 years or more.
- (iii) A service address. This may be stated to be 'The company's registered office'.

(b) In the case of a body corporate, or a firm that is a legal person under the law by which it is governed

- (i) corporate or firm name;
- (ii) registered or principal office;
- (iii) in the case of an EEA company to which the *First Company Law Directive* applies, particulars of

- the register in which the company file mentioned in *Article 3* of that *Directive* is kept (including details of the relevant state); and
- the registration number in that register; and

(iv) in any other case, particulars of

- the legal form of the company or firm and the law by which it is governed; and
- if applicable, the register in which it is entered (including details of the state) and its registration number in that register.

If all the partners in a firm are joint secretaries it is sufficient to state the particulars that would be required if the firm were a legal person and the firm had been appointed secretary.

The Secretary of State may, by Regulations, add to or remove items from the above requirements.

[*CA 2006, ss 275, 276(1), 277–279*].

Time available for inspection and copying. See 36.2 RECORDS.

For companies incorporated before 1 October 2009 see **38.2** (above) *Obligation to keep separate registers* which also apply to the keeping of the register of secretaries.

38.5 REGISTER OF MEMBERS

Particulars to be disclosed. Every company must keep a register of its members containing the following information.

(a) The names and addresses of the members.

(b) The date on which each person was registered as a member.

(c) The date at which any person ceased to be a member.

(d) In the case of a company having a share capital, with the names and addresses of the members, a statement of

- the shares held by each member, distinguishing each share by its number (where applicable) and, where the company has more than one class of issued shares, by its class; and
- the amount paid (or agreed to be considered as paid) on the shares of each member.

If the company has converted any of its shares into stock, and given notice of the conversion to the Registrar of Companies, the amount and class of stock held by each member must be shown instead of the amount of shares and the particulars relating to shares specified above.

In the case of joint holders of shares or stock in a company, the names of each joint holder must be stated but, in other respects, joint holders are regarded as a single member (so that the register must show a single address).

(e) In the case of a company that does not have a share capital but has more than one class of members, the class to which each member belongs.

[*CA 2006, s 113(1)–(6)*].

Treasury shares. Where a company purchases its own shares as treasury shares (see **34.14 PURCHASE OF OWN SHARES**),

- the requirements of (*a*)–(*d*) above need not be complied with if the company cancels all of the shares forthwith after the purchase; and
- if the company does not cancel all of the shares forthwith after the purchase, any share that is so cancelled can be disregarded for those purposes.

Subject to this, where a company holds shares as treasury shares, it must be entered in the register as the member holding those shares.

[*CA 2006, s 124*].

Index of members. Every company with more than 50 members must keep an index of the names of the members of the company, unless the register of members is in such a form as to constitute an index. The index must enable the account of each member in the register to be readily found. Any necessary alteration in the index must be made within 14 days of any alteration to the register of members.

[*CA 2006, s 115(1)–(3)*].

Single member companies. If a limited company is formed under *CA 2006* with only one member, a statement that the company has only one member must be entered in the company's register of members, together with the name and address of that sole member.

If

- the number of members of a limited company falls to one (or, as the case may be, increases from one to two or more), or
- an unlimited company with only one member becomes a limited company or re-registration

a statement that the company has (or, as the case may be, has ceased to have) one member, and the date on which the event occurred, must at that time be entered in the register of members, together with the name and address of the sole member (or, as the case may be, the former sole member).

[*CA 2006, s 123(1)–(3)*].

Offences by the company. If a company makes default in complying with the above provisions relating to particulars to be disclosed, index of members or single member companies, an offence is committed by the company and every officer of the company who is in default. A person guilty of such an offence is liable, on summary conviction, to a fine not exceeding level 3 on the standard scale and, for continued contravention, to a daily default fine not exceeding one-tenth of level 3 on the standard scale. See **29.1 OFFENCES AND LEGAL PROCEEDINGS** for the standard scale.

[*CA 2006, ss 113(7)(8), 115(5)(6), s 123(4)(5)*].

Share warrants. Until a share warrant issued by a company is surrendered, the following are deemed to be the particulars required to be entered in the register of members:

- the fact of the issue of the warrant;
- a statement of the shares included in the warrant, distinguishing each share by its number (if it has one); and

- the date of the issue of the warrant.

The bearer of a share warrant may, if the articles of the company so provide, be deemed a member of the company within the meaning of *CA 2006*, either to the full extent or for any purposes defined in the articles.

The company is responsible for any loss incurred by any person by reason of the name of a bearer of a share warrant being entered in the register in respect of the shares specified in it without the warrant being surrendered and cancelled.

See 44.12 hat as from May 2015 share warrants to bearer have been abolished.

[*CA 2006, s 122; SBEE 2015, Sch 4 para 23*].

Removal of entries relating to former members. An entry relating to a former member of the company may be removed from the register 10 years after the date on which he ceased to be a member (whenever the period of 10 years expired). A copy of any details that were included in the register immediately 6 April 2008 and that are removed from the register must be retained by the company until 6 April 2018 or, if earlier, 20 years after the member concerned ceased to be a member.

[*CA 2006, s 121; SI 2007 No 3495, Art 3, Sch 4 para 2*].

Shares held in trust. No notice of any trust (expressed, implied or constructive) must be entered on the register of members of a company registered in England and Wales or Northern Ireland, or be receivable by the Registrar of Companies. [*CA 2006, s 126*]. A company is not, therefore, required to enquire as to whether a transfer is within the powers of the trustees.

Power of court to rectify register. If

- any person's name is, without sufficient cause, entered in or omitted from the register of members, or
- there is default or unnecessary delay in entering on the register the fact of any person having ceased to be a member,

that person, the company or any member of the company can apply to the court for rectification of the register. The court may decide any question relating to the title of a person who is a party to the application to have his name entered in or omitted from the register. It may either refuse the application or may order rectification of the register. It may also order payment by the company of any damages sustained by any party aggrieved. Where the company is required to send a list of its members to the Registrar of Companies, the court must, when making an order for rectification of the register, direct such notice to be given to the Registrar of Companies. [*CA 2006, s 125*]. See also *Re Sussex Brick Co* [1904] 1 Ch 598.

Register to be evidence. The register of members is *prima facie* evidence of any matters which are directed or authorised by *CA 2006* to be inserted in it.

[*CA 2006, s 127*].

Time limit for claims arising from entry in register. *In relation to causes of action arising on or after 6 April 2008*, liability incurred by a company from the making or deletion of an entry in the register of members (or a failure to do so) is not enforceable more than 10 years after the date of the error or failure. This is without prejudice to any lesser period of limitation and, in Scotland, to any rule that the obligation giving rise to the liability prescribes before the expiry of that period. [*CA 2006, s 128*].

In relation to causes of action arising before 6 April 2008, the time limit is either 6 April 2018 or 20 years from when the cause of action arose (as provided by *CA 1985, s 52(7)*) whichever expires first. This is similarly without prejudice to any lesser period of limitation and, in Scotland, to any rule that the obligation giving rise to the liability prescribes before the expiry of that period.

[*SI 2007 No 3495, Art 3, Sch 4 para 3*].

Changes in particulars. It is the responsibility of members to keep the company informed of any changes in address or name. Any change of address should be signed by the member. In practice, companies frequently send out a standard form for the member to sign and return. On a change of name, more formal documentary proof is required to avoid fraud (eg production of the marriage certificate). On the change of name of a corporate member, a copy of the new certificate of incorporation should be produced. All such amendments have to be approved by the directors.

Reform – see 38.14 for reforms relating to the register of members.

38.6 Location and inspection of register

Location of register. A company's register of members must be kept available for inspection at its registered office or a place specified in the *Companies (Company Records) Regulations 2008 (SI 2008 No 3006)* which provide that the specified place is a place that is situated in a part of the UK in which the company is registered. It must be the same specified place for all relevant provisions of *CA 2006* dealing with inspection and must be notified to the Registrar of Companies as the alternative inspection location.

[*CA 2006, s 114(1)*].

Notice to Registrar of Companies. A company must give notice to the Registrar of Companies of the place where its register of members is kept available for inspection and of any change in that place. No such notice is required if the register has, at all times since it came into existence (or, in the case of a register in existence on 1 July 1948 (1 April 1961 in Northern Ireland), at all times since then) been kept available for inspection at the company's registered office.

[*CA 2006, s 114(2)–(4)*].

Location of index. The index must be at all times kept available for inspection at the same place as the register of members.

[*CA 2006, s 115(4)*].

Right to inspect and request copies. The register and index of members' names must be open to inspection by any member without charge and any other person on payment of a fee The fee is £3.50 per hour or part of an hour during which the right of inspection is exercised. See APPENDIX 3 FEES PAYABLE TO COMPANIES.

Any person may require a copy of a company's register of members, or of any part of it, on payment of such fee as may be prescribed. These are prescribed at a set rate per number of copies and the 'reasonable costs' incurred by the company (see APPENDIX 3 FEES PAYABLE TO COMPANIES)

A person seeking to exercise either of the above rights (ie inspection or copy) must make a request to the company to that effect. The request must contain the following information.

- In the case of an individual, his name and address.

- In the case of an organisation, the name and address of an individual responsible for making the request on behalf of the organisation.
- The purpose for which the information is to be used.
- Whether the information will be disclosed to any other person, and if so
  - (i) where that person is an individual, his name and address;
  - (ii) where that person is an organisation, the name and address of an individual responsible for receiving the information on its behalf; and
  - (iii) the purpose for which the information is to be used by that person.

On receipt of such a request, the company must, within five working days, either comply with the request or apply to the court (and notify the person making the request that it has done so). If, on an application, the court is satisfied that the inspection or copy is not sought for a proper purpose, it must direct the company not to comply with the request. It may also further order that the company's costs (in Scotland, expenses) on the application be paid in whole or in part by the person who made the request (even if he is not a party to the application). Where the court makes such a direction and it appears to the court that the company is (or may be) subject to other requests made for a similar purpose (whether made by the same person or different persons), it may direct that the company is not to comply with any such request. If, on an application, the court does not direct the company not to comply with the request, the company must comply with the request immediately upon the court giving its decision or, as the case may be, the proceedings being discontinued.

[*CA 2006, ss 116, 117*].

Offences in connection with request for or disclosure of information. It is an offence for a person, when requesting an inspection or copy of a register of members, knowingly or recklessly to make a statement that is misleading, false or deceptive in a material particular. It is also an offence for a person in possession of information obtained in such a way to

- do anything that results in the information being disclosed to another person, or
- fail to do anything with the result that the information is disclosed to another person,

knowing or having reason to suspect that person may use the information for a purpose that is not a proper purpose.

A person guilty of such an offence is liable (i) on conviction on indictment, to imprisonment for a term not exceeding two years or a fine (or both); and (ii) on summary conviction, to imprisonment for a term not exceeding twelve months (six months in Scotland or Northern Ireland) or to a fine not exceeding the statutory maximum (or both). See **29.1 Offences and Legal Proceedings** for the statutory maximum. [*CA 2006, s 119*].

Time available for inspection and copying. See **36.2 Records**.

Information as to the state of the register and index. When a person

- inspects the register, or the company provides him with a copy of the register or any part of it, the company must inform him of the most recent date (if any) on which alterations were made to the register and there were no further alterations to be made; and

- inspects the index of members' names, the company must inform him whether there is any alteration to the register that is not reflected in the index.

[*CA 2006, s 120(1)(2)*].

Offences by company. If a company

(a) fails to give notice to the Registrar of Companies of where the register of members is kept available for inspection within 14 days of any change,

(b) refuses to allow an inspection of the register, or fails to provide a copy, as required above (otherwise than in accordance with a court order), or

(c) fails to provide the necessary information as to the state of the register or index

an offence is committed by the company and every officer of the company who is in default. A person guilty of such an offence is liable, on summary conviction, to a fine not exceeding level 3 on the standard scale and, for continued contravention under (*a*) or (*b*) above, a daily default fine not exceeding one-tenth of level 3 on the standard scale. See **29.1 Offences and Legal Proceedings** for the standard scale.

In the case of any refusal or failure under (*b*) above, the court may by order compel an immediate inspection or, as the case may be, direct that the copy required be sent to the person requesting it.

[*CA 2006, ss 114(5)(6), 118, 120(3)(4)*].

38.7 Overseas branch registers

A company having a share capital which transacts business in any of the countries or territories listed below may cause to be kept a branch register of members resident there. Such a branch register is known as an '*overseas branch register*' and a reference in any Act or the articles of a company to a 'dominion register' or 'colonial register' are to be read as referring to such an overseas branch register (unless the context requires otherwise).

The countries and territories referred to above are any part of the dominions outside the UK, Channel Islands or Isle of Man, together with

Bangladesh	Cyprus	Dominica
The Gambia	Ghana	Guyana
The Hong Kong Special Administrative Region of the People's Republic of China	India	Ireland
Kenya	Kiribati	Lesotho
Malawi	Malaysia	Malta
Nigeria	Pakistan	Seychelles
Sierra Leone	Singapore	South Africa
Sri Lanka	Swaziland	Trinidad and Tobago
Uganda	Zimbabwe	

[*CA 2006, s 129*].

Notice of opening of overseas branch register. A company that begins to keep an overseas branch register must give notice to the Registrar of Companies within 14 days of doing so, stating the country or territory in which the register is kept.

[*CA 2006, s 130(1)*].

Keeping of overseas branch register. An overseas branch register is regarded as part of the company's register of members ('the main register') and must therefore be kept in the same manner (see **38.5**) unless the Secretary of State provides otherwise by Regulations. Subject to this, a company may by its articles make such provision as it thinks fit as to the keeping of overseas branch registers. [*CA 2006, s 131*].

Register or duplicate to be kept available for inspection in UK. A company that keeps an overseas branch register must keep the register, or a duplicate of the register duly entered up from time to time, available for inspection at the place in the UK where the company's main register is kept available for inspection. Any such duplicate is treated for all purposes of *CA 2006* as part of the main register.

[*CA 2006, s 132(1)(2)*].

Transactions in shares registered in overseas branch register. Shares registered in an overseas branch register must be distinguished from those registered in the main register and no transaction with respect to such shares may be registered in any other register. An instrument of transfer of a share registered in an overseas branch register

- is regarded as a transfer of property situated outside the UK; and
- unless executed in a part of the UK, is exempt from stamp duty.

[*CA 2006, s 133*].

Discontinuance of overseas branch register. A company may discontinue an overseas branch register. If it does so, all the entries in that register must be transferred to some other overseas branch register kept in the same country or territory or to the main register. The company must give notice to the Registrar of Companies of the discontinuance within 14 days.

[*CA 2006, s 135(1)–(3)*].

Offences. If default is made in complying with the provisions above relating to

- notice of opening,
- keeping the register or a duplicate available for inspection in the UK, or
- discontinuance

an offence is committed by the company and every officer of the company who is in default. A person guilty of such an offence is liable, on summary conviction, to a fine not exceeding level 3 on the standard scale and, for continued contravention, a daily default fine not exceeding one-tenth of level 3 on the standard scale. See **29.1** Offences and Legal Proceedings for the standard scale.

[*CA 2006, ss 130(2)(3), 132(3)(4), 135(4)(5)*].

Jurisdiction of local courts. A competent court in a country or territory where an overseas branch register is kept may exercise the same jurisdiction as is exercisable by a court in the UK to rectify the register (see **38.5**) or in relation to a request for inspection or a copy of the register (see **38.6**). The offences of refusing inspection, failing to provide a copy of the register and making a false, misleading or deceptive statement in a request for inspection or a copy (see **38.6**) may be prosecuted summarily before any tribunal having summary criminal jurisdiction in the country or territory where the register is kept.

These provisions on jurisdiction extend only to those countries and territories to which *CA 1985, Sch 14 para 3* (which made similar provision) extended immediately before 1 October 2009. [*CA 2006, s 134*].

38.8 REGISTER OF DISCLOSED INTERESTS IN PUBLIC COMPANY SHARES

Automatic disclosure rules are set out in the Transparency Rules made by the FCA (under power given to them by *FSMA 2000*) and notification is to the FCA rather than the company. A company is only therefore required to maintain a register covering disclosures following its own investigations into shareholdings. Any separate part of the register kept by the company before 20 January 2007 relating to investigations must continue to be kept and is treated as part of the register kept for these purposes.

[*SI 2006 No 3428, Sch 5 para 2*].

Updating the register. A company which receives information in pursuance of a requirement imposed by it under *CA 2006, s 793* (see **24.2** INTERESTS IN PUBLIC COMPANY SHARES) must, within three days (see below) of receipt of the information, enter in the register

- the fact that the requirement was imposed and the date on which it was imposed; and
- the information received in pursuance of the requirement.

The information must be entered against the name of the present holder of the shares in question or, if there is no present holder or the present holder is not known, against the name of the person holding the interest. Entries against each name entered must appear in chronological order.

The company is not, by virtue of anything done for these purposes, affected with notice of, or put upon inquiry as to, the rights of any person in relation to any shares (eg it is not concerned with the existence of any trust over the shares).

[*CA 2006, s 808(1)–(4)(7)*].

Associated index. Unless the register kept as above is kept in such a form as itself to constitute an index, the company must keep an index of the names entered in it. It must make any necessary entry or alteration in the index within 10 days (see below) after the date on which any entry or alteration is made in the register. The index must contain, in respect of each name, a sufficient indication to enable the information entered against it to be readily found.

[*CA 2006, s 810(1)–(3)*].

Reckoning of number of days. Where the period allowed above for fulfilling an obligation is expressed as a number of days, any day that is a Saturday, Sunday or a bank holiday in the part of the UK in which the company is registered is to be disregarded.

[*CA 2006, s 827*].

Duty of company ceasing to be public company. If a company ceases to be a public company, it must continue to keep any register and any associated index until the end of the period of six years after it ceased to be such a company.

[*CA 2006, s 819(1)*].

Penalties. If a company fails to

(a) keep and update the register as required,

(b) keep and properly update any associated index required, or

(c) continue to keep any register and any associated index for the required period after ceasing to be a public company

an offence is committed by the company and every officer of the company who is in default. A person guilty of such an offence is liable, on summary conviction, to a fine not exceeding level 3 on the standard scale and, for continued contravention, a daily default fine not exceeding one-tenth of level 3 on the standard scale. See **29.1 Offences and Legal Proceedings** for the standard scale. [*CA 2006, ss 808(5)(6), 810(5)(6), 819(2)(3)*].

Adjustment of entry relating to share acquisition agreement. If a person who is identified in the register as being a party to an agreement to which *CA 2006, s 824* applies (certain share acquisition agreements, see **24.1 Interests in Public Company Shares**) ceases to be a party to the agreement, he may apply to the company for the inclusion of that information in the register. If the company is satisfied that he has ceased to be a party to the agreement, it must record that information (if not already recorded) in every place where his name appears in the register as a party to the agreement. If an application to the company is refused (otherwise than on the ground that the information has already been recorded), the applicant may apply to the court for an order directing the company to include the information in question in the register. The court may then make such an order if it thinks fit.

[*CA 2006, s 818*].

38.9 Location and inspection of register

Location of register. The register must be kept available for inspection at the company's registered office or a place specified in Regulations (see **36.2 Records**).

[*CA 2006, s 809(1)*].

Notice to Registrar of Companies. A company must give notice to the Registrar of Companies within 14 days of the place where the register is kept available for inspection and of any change in that place. No such notice is required if the register has at all times been kept available for inspection at the company's registered office. [*CA 2006, s 809(2)(3)*]. In calculating the 14 days allowed, any day that is not a working day is to be disregarded.

[*CA 2006, s 827*].

Location of index. The index must be at all times kept available for inspection at the same place as the register.

[*CA 2006, s 810(4)*].

Right to inspect and request copies of entries. The register (and any associated index) must be open to inspection by any person without charge. Any person is also entitled, on request and on payment of such fee as may be prescribed (see **38.2** above for details of prescribed fees and **Appendix 3 Fees**), to be provided with a copy of any entry in the register.

A person seeking to exercise either of the rights conferred by these provisions (ie inspection or copy) must make a request to the company to that effect. The request must contain the following information.

- In the case of an individual, his name and address.

- In the case of an organisation, the name and address of an individual responsible for making the request on behalf of the organisation.
- The purpose for which the information is to be used.
- Whether the information will be disclosed to any other person, and if so
  - (i) where that person is an individual, his name and address;
  - (ii) where that person is an organisation, the name and address of an individual responsible for receiving the information on its behalf; and
  - (iii) the purpose for which the information is to be used by that person.

Where a company receives such a request, it must

- comply with the request if satisfied that it is made for a proper purpose; or
- refuse the request if not so satisfied and inform the person making the request, stating the reason why it is not satisfied.

A person whose request is refused may then apply to the court. If he does so, he must notify the company which in turn must use its best endeavours to notify any persons whose details would be disclosed if the company were required to comply with the request. If the court is not satisfied that the inspection or copy is sought for a proper purpose, it must direct the company not to comply with the request. Where the court makes such a direction and it appears to the court that the company is (or may be) subject to other requests made for a similar purpose (whether made by the same person or different persons), it may direct that the company is not to comply with any such request. If the court does not direct the company not to comply with the request, the company must comply with the request immediately upon the court giving its decision or, as the case may be, the proceedings being discontinued.

[*CA 2006, ss 811, 812*].

Offences in connection with request for or disclosure of information. It is an offence for a person, when requesting an inspection or copy of the register, knowingly or recklessly to make a statement that is misleading, false or deceptive in a material particular. It is also an offence for a person in possession of information obtained in such a way to

- do anything that results in the information being disclosed to another person, or
- fail to do anything with the result that the information is disclosed to another person,

knowing, or having reason to suspect, that person may use the information for a purpose that is not a proper purpose.

A person guilty of such an offence is liable (i) on conviction on indictment, to imprisonment for a term not exceeding two years or a fine (or both); and (ii) on summary conviction, to imprisonment for a term not exceeding twelve months (six months in Scotland or Northern Ireland) or to a fine not exceeding the statutory maximum (or both). See **29.1** Offences and Legal Proceedings for the statutory maximum.

[*CA 2006, s 814*].

Information protected from wider disclosure. Information about related undertakings must not be made available for inspection if the company is for the time being entitled to any exemption from disclosing the information in the notes to its accounts because to do so would be harmful to the company's business.

[*CA 2006, s 826*].

Time available for inspection and copying. See **36.2** **Records**.

Penalties. If a company fails to

(a) keep a register or any index available for inspection as required,

(b) notify the Registrar of Companies of the place where the register is kept within the time allowed, or

(c) allow inspection of the register or provide copies of entries when required to do so (otherwise than in accordance *CA 2006, s 812*)

an offence is committed by the company and every officer of the company who is in default. A person guilty of such an offence is liable, on summary conviction, to a fine not exceeding level 3 on the standard scale and, for continued contravention, a daily default fine not exceeding one-tenth of level 3 on the standard scale. See **29.1** **Offences and Legal Proceedings** for the standard scale.

Where (*c*) above applies, the court may by order compel an immediate inspection or, as the case may be, direct that the copy required be sent to the person requiring it.

[*CA 2006, ss 809(4)(5), 810(5)(6), 813; SBEE 2015, s 83*].

38.10 Removal of entries from the register

Entries in the register of interests disclosed in shares must not be deleted except in the following circumstances.

- A company may remove an entry from the register if more than six years have elapsed since the date the entry was made.
- Where, in pursuance of an obligation imposed by a notice under *CA 2006, s 793* (see **24.2** **Interests in Public Company Shares**) a person gives to a company the name and address of another person as being interested in shares in the company, that other person may apply to the company for the removal of the entry from the register. If the company is satisfied that the information is incorrect, it must remove the entry. If such an application is refused, the applicant may apply to the court for an order directing the company to remove the entry in question from the register.

If an entry is deleted for any other reason, the company must restore it as soon as reasonably practicable.

Penalties. If the company defaults in complying with any of the above requirements, an offence is committed by the company and every officer of the company who is in default. A person guilty of such an offence is liable, on summary conviction, to a fine not exceeding level 3 on the standard scale and, for continued contravention of failure to restore an entry, a daily default fine not exceeding one-tenth of level 3 on the standard scale. See **29.1** **Offences and Legal Proceedings** for the standard scale.

[*CA 2006, ss 815–817*].

38.11 REGISTER OF CHARGES AND COPIES OF INSTRUMENTS CREATING CHARGES

As from 6 April 2013, *CA 2006, Pt 25, Chs 1* and *2* were repealed and replaced by provisions in the *Companies Act 2006 (Amendment of Part 25) Regulations 2013 (SI 2013 No 600)* which apply to charges created on or after 6 April 2013. The provisions of *CA 2006, Part 25* as they stood immediately before 6 April 2013 continue to apply to charges created before that date. This chapter covers both pre and post 6 April 2013 regulatory provisions

Charges created before 6 April 2013 — documents available for inspection

Every company must keep available for inspection

(a) a copy of every instrument creating a charge requiring registration (see **40** REGISTRATION OF CHARGES) (although in the case of a series of uniform debentures a copy of one debenture in the series is sufficient); and

(b) a register of charges and enter in it

  (i) all charges specifically affecting property of the company; and

  (ii) all floating charges on the whole or part of the company's property or undertaking.

The entry in the register under (*b*) above must give

- a short description of the property charged;
- the amount of the charge; and
- except in the case of securities to bearer, the names of the persons entitled to it.

If an officer of the company knowingly and wilfully authorises or permits the omission of an entry required to be made in the register, he commits an offence. A person guilty of such an offence is liable (i) on conviction on indictment, to a fine; and (ii) on summary conviction, to a fine not exceeding the statutory maximum. See **29.1** OFFENCES AND LEGAL PROCEEDINGS for the statutory maximum.

[*CA 2006, ss 875, 876, 890, 891*].

The documents under (*a*) above and the register under (*b*) above must be kept available for inspection at the company's registered office or a place specified in *Regulations* (see **36.2** RECORDS). They must be open to the inspection of any creditor or member of the company without charge and any other person on payment of such fee as may be prescribed (see APPENDIX 3 FEES).

The company must give notice to the Registrar of Companies, within 14 days, of the place at which the documents and register are kept available for inspection and of any change in that place (unless they have at all times been kept at the company's registered office).

If default is made in notifying the Registrar of Companies or an inspection required is refused, an offence is committed by the company and every officer of the company who is in default. A person guilty of such an offence is liable, on summary conviction, to a fine not exceeding level 3 on the standard scale and, for continued contravention, to a daily default fine not exceeding one-tenth of level 3 on the standard scale. See **29.1** OFFENCES AND LEGAL PROCEEDINGS for the standard scale. In the case of refusal of inspection of the register, the court may by order compel an immediate inspection of it.

[*CA 2006, ss 877, 892*].

Time available for inspection and copying. See **36.2** Records.

Charges created on or after 6 April 2013

Every company must keep available for inspection

(a) a copy of every instrument creating a charge capable of registration (see **40** Registration of Charges) (although in the case of a charge contained in a series of uniform debentures a copy of one of the debentures of the series is sufficient);

(b) a copy of every instrument effecting any variation or amendment of such a charge; and

(c) a copy of any other documents which contain the particulars referred to in *CA 2006, s 859D(1)* or the particulars of the property or undertaking charged which are not contained in the instrument creating the charge but are instead contained in those other documents which are referred to or otherwise incorporated into the instrument.

It is sufficient for the purposes of the inspection requirements above if the company keeps a copy of the instrument in the form delivered to the Registrar of Companies under *CA 2006, s 859A(3), 859B(3), 859B(4)* or *859C(3)*.

Where a translation has been delivered to the Registrar of Companies in accordance with *CA 2006, s 1105*, the company must keep a copy of the translation available for inspection.

[*CA 2006, s 859P; SI 2013 No 600, Schedule 1*]

The documents under the above provisions must be kept available for inspection at the company's registered office or a place specified in *Regulations* (see **36.2** Records). They must be open to the inspection of any creditor or member of the company without charge and any other person on payment of such fee as may be prescribed (see Appendix **3** Fees).

The company must give notice to the Registrar of Companies, within 14 days, of the place at which the documents are kept available for inspection and of any change in that place (unless they have at all times been kept at the company's registered office).

If default is made in notifying the Registrar of Companies or an inspection required is refused, an offence is committed by the company and every officer of the company who is in default. A person guilty of such an offence is liable, on summary conviction, to a fine not exceeding level 3 on the standard scale and, for continued contravention, to a daily default fine not exceeding one-tenth of level 3 on the standard scale. See **29.1** Offences and Legal Proceedings for the standard scale. In the case of refusal of inspection of the register, the court may by order compel an immediate inspection of it.

Where the company and a person wishing to carry out an inspection agree, the inspection may be carried out by electronic means.

[*CA 2006, s 859Q; SI 2013 No 600, Schedule 1*]

38.12 REGISTER OF DEBENTURE HOLDERS

A company is not obliged to keep a register of debenture holders but, where it does, the following provisions apply with effect from 6 April 2008 (unless otherwise stated).

Location of register. Any register of debenture holders of a company must be kept available for inspection at the company's registered office or a place specified in *Regulations*. The regulations are the *Companies (Company Records) Regulations 2008 (SI 2008 No 3006)*. See **38.6** above and **36.2** Records).

[*CA 2006, s 743(1); SI 2007 No 3495, Art 3*].

Notice to Registrar of Companies. A company must give notice to the Registrar of Companies within 14 days of the place where the register is kept available for inspection and of any change in that place. No such notice is required if the register has, at all times since it came into existence, been kept available for inspection at the company's registered office. If a company defaults in complying with these requirements, an offence is committed by the company and every officer of the company who is in default. A person guilty of such an offence is liable, on summary conviction, to a fine not exceeding level 3 on the standard scale and, for continued contravention, to a daily default fine not exceeding one-tenth of level 3 on the standard scale. See **29.1 OFFENCES AND LEGAL PROCEEDINGS** for the standard scale.

[*CA 2006, s 743(2)–(5); SI 2007 No 3495, Art 3*].

Rights to inspect and request copies. The register, except when 'duly closed', must be open to the inspection of

- a registered debenture holder or any shareholder in the company, without charge; and
- any other person on payment of such fee as may be prescribed (see **APPENDIX 3 FEES**).

A register is '*duly closed*' if it is closed in accordance with provision contained in the articles, debentures, stock certificates (in the case of debenture stock), trust deed or other document securing the debentures or debenture stock. The total period for which a register is closed in any year must not exceed 30 days.

Any person may require a copy of the register, or of any part of it, on payment of such fee as may be prescribed (see **APPENDIX 3 FEES**).

A person seeking to exercise either of the above rights (ie inspection or copy) must make a request to the company to that effect. The request must contain the following information.

- In the case of an individual, his name and address.
- In the case of an organisation, the name and address of an individual responsible for making the request on behalf of the organisation.
- The purpose for which the information is to be used.
- Whether the information will be disclosed to any other person, and if so
  - (i) where that person is an individual, his name and address;
  - (ii) where that person is an organisation, the name and address of an individual responsible for receiving the information on its behalf; and
  - (iii) the purpose for which the information is to be used by that person.

On receipt of such a request, the company must, within five working days, either comply with the request or apply to the court (and notify the person making the request that it has done so). If, on an application the court is satisfied that the inspection or copy is not sought for a proper purpose, it must direct the company not to comply with the request. It may also further order that the company's costs (in Scotland, expenses) on the application be paid in whole or in part by the person who made the request (even if he is not a party to the application). Where the court makes such a direction and it appears to the court that the company is (or may be) subject to other requests made for a similar purpose (whether made by the same person or different persons), it may direct that the company is not to comply with any such request. If, on an application, the court does not direct the company not to comply with the request, the company must comply with the request immediately upon the court giving its decision or, as the case may be, the proceedings being discontinued.

[*CA 2006, s 744, 745*].

Offences in connection with request for or disclosure of information. It is an offence for a person, when requesting an inspection or copy of a register of members, knowingly or recklessly to make a statement that is misleading, false or deceptive in a material particular. It is also an offence for a person in possession of information obtained in such a way to

- do anything that results in the information being disclosed to another person, or
- fail to do anything with the result that the information is disclosed to another person,

knowing or having reason to suspect that person may use the information for a purpose that is not a proper purpose.

A person guilty of such an offence is liable (i) on conviction on indictment, to imprisonment for a term not exceeding two years or a fine (or both); and (ii) on summary conviction, to imprisonment for a term not exceeding twelve months (six months in Scotland or Northern Ireland) or to a fine not exceeding the statutory maximum (or both). See **29.1 Offences and Legal Proceedings** for the statutory maximum.

[*CA 2006, s 747*].

Time available for inspection and copying. See **36.2 Records**.

Offences by company. If a company refuses to allow an inspection of the register, or fails to provide a copy as required above (otherwise than in accordance with a court order), an offence is committed by every officer of the company who is in default and, in addition in the case of (*a*) above, by the company. A person guilty of such an offence is liable, on summary conviction, to a fine not exceeding level 3 on the standard scale and, for continued contravention, a daily default fine not exceeding one-tenth of level 3 on the standard scale. See **29.1 Offences and Legal Proceedings** for the standard scale. The court may also compel an immediate inspection or, as the case may be, direct that the copy required be sent to the person requiring it.

[*CA 2006, s 746*].

Duplicate register. References above to a register of debenture holders include a duplicate of a register of debenture holders that is kept outside the UK or any part of such a register.

[*CA 2006, ss 743(6), 744(6)*].

Time limit for claims arising from entry in register. In respect of causes of action arising on or after 6 April 2008, liability incurred by a company from the making or deletion of an entry in the register (or from a failure to do so) is not enforceable more than 10 years after the date on which the entry was made or deleted or, as the case may be, the failure first occurred. This is without prejudice to any lesser period of limitation (and, in Scotland, to any rule that the obligation giving rise to the liability prescribes before the expiry of that period). [*CA 2006, s 748; SI 2007 No 3495, Art 3*]. The time limit for causes of action arising before 6 April 2008 is

- 10 years after 6 April 2008, or
- 20 years from the date when the cause of action arose,

whichever expires first. This is without prejudice to any lesser period of limitation (and, in Scotland, to any rule that the obligation giving rise to the liability prescribes before the expiry of that period).

[*SI 2007 No 3495, Sch 4 para 23*].

Form in which register to be kept. The register can be kept in hard copy or electronic form. With effect from 1 October 2009, any provision of an instrument made by a company before 12 February 1979 that requires a register of holders of the company's debentures to be kept in hard copy form is to be read as requiring it to be kept in hard copy or electronic form.

[*CA 2006, s 1135(5)*].

38.13 REGISTER OF DIRECTORS' INTERESTS

With effect from 6 April 2007, a company is no longer required to keep a register of directors' interests. [*CA 2006, s 1177*].

38.14 REFORMS – REGISTER OF PEOPLE WITH SIGNIFICANT INTERESTS; OPTION TO KEEP MEMBERS' INFORMATION ON COMPANIES HOUSE REGISTER

Provisions contained in the *Small Business, Enterprise and Employment Act 2015 (SBEE 2015)* require companies to keep a new register of people who have significant control over the company ('a PSC register'). A person who has 'significant control' over a company is an individual who holds more than 25% of a company's shares or voting rights or who otherwise exercises control over a company or its management. Individuals are either 'registrable' or' non-registrable'. The main requirements of SBEE 2015 are

- the provisions apply to all companies other than DTR 5 issuers (ie an issuer to which *Ch 5* of the FCA Disclosure Rules and Transparency Rules apply) and to any other companies specified in regulations which will be made under *SBEE 2015*;
- companies are under a duty to investigate whether there is anyone who is a registrable person or registrable relevant legal entity in relation to the company and, if so, to identify them;
- an initial statement of PSCs is to be provided on incorporation and an update given to the Registrar of Companies every 12 months;
- companies are under a duty to keep the information up to date;
- failure to comply with information duties is an offence;
- registrable persons or registrable legal entities must supply certain information to the company and keep that information up to date;
- required particulars relating to those who are registrable must be entered in the PSC register;
- the PSC register must be kept available for inspection at the company's registered office or at a place specified in regulations and the company must notify the Registrar of Companies where its PSC register is kept. The register must be open for inspection free of charge. There are detailed provisions relating to rights to inspect and obtain copies of the register;

- a PSCs' usual residential address is not disclosable; and
- private companies can elect to keep the information on Companies House register rather than keep it on a PSC register.

The above is a summary of the provisions which are not, as at May 2015, yet in force but it is anticipated they will be brought into force before the end of 2016.

[*CA 2006, Pt 21A; SBEE 2015, Sch 3*].

The *SBEE 2015* also sets out rules allowing private companies only to elect to keep information relating to members on Companies House Register rather than in the company's own register of members. As with the provisions for PSC registers there is substantial detail in the provisions for election and they are also, as at May 2015, not in force.

[*SBEE 2015, ss 94, 95, Sch 5*].

39 Registrar of Companies

39.1	**Registrars and their contact details**
39.2	**Guidance booklets**
39.3	**Duties and powers of the Registrar of Companies**
39.4	Certificates of incorporation
39.5	Registered numbers
39.6	Delivery of documents to the Registrar of Companies
39.8	Public notice of receipt of certain documents
39.9	Maintaining company records on the register
39.10	Inspection and copying of the register
39.11	Correction or removal of material on the register
39.12	Index of company names
39.13	Language requirements: translation
39.14	Language requirements: transliteration
39.15	Requirements as to certification or verification
39.16	Enforcement of company's filing obligations
39.17	**Alternative to publication in the Gazette**
39.18	**Offence of general false statement**
39.19	**Application to make address unavailable for public inspection**
39.20	**Companies House WebFiling**

39.1 REGISTRARS AND THEIR CONTACT DETAILS

There must be a Registrar of Companies for England and Wales, Scotland and Northern Ireland, each appointed by the Secretary of State. [*CA 2006, s 1060*].

Company information can be obtained by post, fax, courier or through a personal visit to any one of the Information Centres at the offices in Cardiff, London and Edinburgh.

Contact centre—this is the main route for all general enquiries	
Telephone	+44 (0)303 1234 500
Please see Companies House website (companieshouse.gov.uk) for the latest contact details including opening hours.	
Companies House Information Centres	
For England and Wales: *Cardiff*: Crown Way, Maindy, Cardiff CF14 3UZ	
London: 4 Abbey Orchard Street, London SW1P 2HT	
Office hours	Monday to Friday 9.00am – 5.00pm
For Scotland: *Edinburgh*: 4th Floor, Edinburgh Quay 2, 139 Fountainbridge, Edinburgh, EH3 9FF	
For Northern Ireland: 2nd Floor, The Linenhall, 32–38 Linenhall Street, Belfast BT28BG	Monday to Friday 9.00am – 5.00pm

39.2 GUIDANCE BOOKLETS

The following *CA 2006* guidance booklets are available from Companies House. They can also be freely downloaded from the internet on: www.companieshouse.gov.uk.

39.2 Registrar of Companies

GP1	Incorporation and Names
GP2	Life of a Company - Part 1 Annual Requirements
GP3	Life of a Company - Part 2 Event Driven Filings
GP4	Strike off, Dissolution and Restoration
GP5	Late filing penalties
GP6	Registrar's Rules and Powers
GP7	Restricting the disclosure of your address
Limited liability partnerships	
GPLLP1	Limited Liability Partnerships Incorporation and names
GPLLP2	Life of a Limited Liability Partnership
GPLLP3	Limited Liability Partnerships Strike off, Dissolution and Restoration
GPLLP4	LLP late filing penalty
GPLLP5	Limited Liability Partnerships Liquidation and Insolvency
GPLLP5s	Limited Liability Partnerships Liquidation and Insolvency (Scotland)
GPLLP5n	Limited Liability Partnerships Liquidation and Insolvency (Northern Ireland)
Other legislation	
GP01	Overseas companies registered in the UK
GP02	Limited Partnership Act
GP03	Newspaper Libel and Registration Act
GP04	European Economic Interest Groupings
GP05	Conducting Business in Welsh
GP06	The European company: Societas Europaea (SE)
GP07	Cross border mergers
GP08	Liquidation and Insolvency
GP08s	Liquidation and Insolvency (Scotland)
GP08n	Liquidation and Insolvency (Northern Ireland)

39.3 DUTIES AND POWERS OF THE REGISTRAR OF COMPANIES

The Registrar of Companies must perform a wide range of duties conferred on him by and under the *Companies Acts* and other legislation, together with other functions in relation to the registration of companies and other matters which the Secretary of State may from time to time direct him to perform. [*CA 2006, s 1061*]. Some of these duties and related powers are considered in **39.4** to **39.19** below. Unless the context requires otherwise, the provisions apply to an overseas company. [*CA 2006, s 1059A(5)*].

39.4 Certificates of incorporation

Public notice of issue. The Registrar of Companies must cause to be published, in the Gazette or in accordance with **39.17**, notice of the issue of any certificate of incorporation of a company on formation, change of name or re-registration. He must also publish notice on a company becoming, or ceasing to become, a Welsh company under **37.3** REGISTERED OFFICE. The notice must state the name and registered number of the company and the date of issue of the certificate.

[*CA 2006, s 1064*].

Any person may require the Registrar of Companies to provide him with a copy of any certificate of incorporation of a company (whenever issued), signed by the Registrar or authenticated by the registrar's seal.

[*CA 2006, s 1065*].

39.5 Registered numbers

The Registrar of Companies must allocate a number (the company's 'registered number') to every company. This includes an overseas company whose particulars have been registered under *CA 2006, s 1046* unless the Registrar is of the opinion that the company is not required to register particulars under that section.

The Registrar may determine what form registered numbers take (eg one or more sequences of figures or letters) and may adopt a new form of registered number, making such changes to existing registered numbers as appear necessary. Any such change has effect from the date on which the company is notified by the Registrar of the change. For a period of three years beginning with that date, any requirement to disclose the company's registered number imposed by the provisions relating to trading disclosures (see **16.12 Dealings With Third Parties**) is satisfied by the use of either the old number or the new.

[*CA 2006, s 1066*].

Similar provisions apply to the allocation to every UK establishment of an overseas company whose particulars are registered under *CA 2006, s 1046* of a number to be known as the UK establishment's registered number.

[*CA 2006, s 1067*].

39.6 Delivery of documents to the Registrar of Companies

Under the *Companies Acts* and other legislation, a wide variety of documents must be delivered to the Registrar of Companies for filing. The Registrar of Companies may impose requirements as to the form, authentication and manner of delivery of these documents. [*CA 2006, s 1068(1)*].

The requirements in (1)–(3) below apply to documents delivered to the Registrar of Companies on or after 1 October 2013.

[*SI 2009 No 1802, Schedule; SI 2013 No 1947, Reg 2*].

(1) **Form**

The Registrar of Companies may

- require the contents of a document to be in a standard form; and
- impose requirements for the purpose of enabling the document to be scanned or copied.

[*CA 2006, s 1068(2)*].

Documents delivered to the Registrar of Companies are scanned to produce an electronic image. The original documents are stored away and the electronic image is used as the working document. If documents are filed electronically, the Registrar automatically creates an electronic image from the data provided. Documents delivered to the Registrar must, therefore, comply with requirements set out below as specified by the Registrar. If they do not, the Registrar can reject them.

Documents filed electronically must comply with the Registrar's specifications in the rules on electronic filing (the formats are in the rules published on Companies House website).

Paper documents. Every document sent to the Registrar of Companies must state in a prominent position the registered name and number of the company and must comply with any requirements specified by the Registrar relating to the legibility of that document.

Briefly, documents should be on A4 size, plain white paper with a matt finish. Text should be black, clear, legible, and of uniform density. Letters and numbers must be clear and legible so that Companies House can make an acceptable copy.

There are guidelines for completing forms and documents and a warning that failure to follow the guidelines is likely to result in the document being rejected.

GP2 Life of a Company – Part 1 Chapter 14.

(2) **Authentication**

The Registrar of Companies may

- require the document to be authenticated by a particular person or a person of a particular description;
- specify the means of authentication; and
- require the document to contain, or be accompanied by, the name or registered number (or both) of the company (or other body) to which it relates.

[*CA 2006, s 1068(3)*].

(3) **Manner of delivery**

The Registrar of Companies may specify requirements as to

- the physical form of the document (eg hard copy or electronic form);
- the means to be used for delivering the document (eg by post or electronic means);
- the address to which the document is to be sent; and
- in the case of a document to be delivered by electronic means, the hardware and software to be used, and technical specifications (eg matters relating to protocol, security, anti-virus protection or encryption).

All documents subject to the Directive disclosure requirements (see **39.8**) *may* be delivered to the Registrar by 'electronic means' (see **Appendix 1 Definitions**). But nothing in these provisions authorises the Registrar to require documents to be delivered by electronic means unless the Secretary of State has made the appropriate Regulations and the Registrar's rules covering the detailed requirements for electronic delivery have been published.

[*CA 2006, ss 1068(4)–(6), 1069*].

Any requirements imposed by the Registrar under (1)–(3) above must not be inconsistent with requirements imposed by any enactment.

[*CA 2006, s 1068(7)*].

Agreement for delivery by electronic means. In relation to all documents delivered to the Registrar of Companies, the Registrar may agree with a company (or other body) that documents relating to the company (or other body) that are required or authorised to be delivered to the Registrar will be delivered by electronic means, except as provided for in the agreement. Documents in relation to which an agreement is in force must then be delivered in accordance with the agreement.

[*CA 2006, s 1070*].

Documents not delivered until received. In relation to documents delivered on or after 1 October 2009 (other than those delivered in pursuance of an obligation arising before that date, in which case the provisions which would have applied if the document had been delivered before that date continue to apply), a document is not delivered to the Registrar of Companies until it is received by him.

[*CA 2006, s 1071; SI 2008 No 2860, Sch 2 para 99; SI 2009 No 1802, Sch*].

39.7 *Requirements for proper delivery*

The provisions in this paragraph apply to documents delivered to the Registrar of Companies (other than those delivered in pursuance of an obligation arising before 1 October 2009, in which case the provisions which would have applied if the document had been delivered before that date and the Registrar of Companies former practice continue to apply).

[*SI 2008 No 2860, Sch 2 paras 100–102; SI 2009 No 1802, Sch*].

A document delivered to the Registrar of Companies is not properly delivered unless all the following requirements are met.

- The requirements of the appropriate provision as regards the contents of the document and form, authentication and manner of delivery.
- Any applicable requirements under **39.6**.
- Any requirements as to the language in which the document is drawn up and delivered or as to its being accompanied on delivery by a certified translation into English.
- In so far as it consists of or includes names and addresses, any requirements as to permitted characters, letters or symbols or as to its being accompanied on delivery by a certificate as to the transliteration of any element.
- Any applicable requirement as to certification or verification (see **39.15**).
- Any requirement as to the use of unique identifiers (see **39.9**).
- Any requirements as regards payment of a fee in respect of its receipt by the Registrar.

A document that is not properly delivered is treated for the purposes of the provision requiring it or authorising it to be delivered as not having been delivered (subject to below).

[*CA 2006, s 1072*].

Power to accept documents not meeting requirements for proper delivery. The Registrar of Companies can accept (and register) a document that does not comply with the above requirements. If he does so, the document is treated as received for the purposes **39.8**. No objection may be taken to the legal consequences of a document being so accepted (or registered) by the Registrar of Companies on the ground that the requirements for proper delivery were not met.

39.7 Registrar of Companies

The acceptance of a document by the Registrar of Companies under this provision does not affect

- the continuing obligation to comply with the requirements for proper delivery; or
- subject to what follows, any liability for failure to comply with those requirements.

For the purposes of *CA 2006, s 453* (civil penalty for failure to file accounts and reports, see **2.10** ACCOUNTS: GENERAL) and any enactment imposing a daily default fine for failure to deliver the document, the period after the document is accepted does not count as a period during which there is default in complying with the requirements for proper delivery. But if, subsequently,

- the Registrar of Companies issues a notice under **39.11**(1) in respect of the document (notice of administrative removal from the register), and
- the requirements for proper delivery are not complied with before the end of the period of 14 days after the issue of that notice,

any subsequent period of default does count for the purposes of those provisions.

[*CA 2006, s 1073*].

Documents containing unnecessary material. Where a document delivered to the Registrar of Companies contains 'unnecessary material',

- if the unnecessary material cannot readily be separated from the rest of the document, the document is treated as not meeting the requirements for proper delivery; and
- if the unnecessary material can readily be separated from the rest of the document, the Registrar of Companies may register the document either
  - (i) with the omission of the unnecessary material; or
  - (ii) as delivered.

'*Unnecessary material*' means material that is not necessary in order to comply with an obligation under any Act and is not specifically authorised to be delivered to the Registrar of Companies. [*CA 2006, s 1074*].

Informal correction of document. Where a document has not been registered under *CA 2006, s 1073* above, the Registrar of Companies may corrected a document delivered to him if it appears to him to be incomplete or internally inconsistent but only on instructions and with the consent of the company (or other body) concerned. Any document that is so corrected is treated as having been delivered when the correction is made. This provision applies in relation to documents delivered in connection with registration of charges by a person other than the company (or other body) as if the references to the company (or other body) were to the company (or other body) or the person by whom the document was delivered.

[*CA 2006, s 1075*].

Replacement of a document not meeting requirements for delivery. The Registrar of Companies may accept a replacement for a document previously delivered that did not comply with the requirements for proper delivery or contained unnecessary material. The replacement document must be delivered by the same person who delivered the original document or the company (or other body) to which the original document relates. This provision for voluntary replacement does not apply where the original document related to company charges (for which see *CA 2006, s 859M* at **39.9** and **39.17** **Registration of Charges**.

[*CA 2006, s 1076; SI 2013 No 600, Schedule 2, para 3*].

39.8 Public notice of receipt of certain documents

The Registrar of Companies must cause to be published, in the *Gazette* or in accordance with **39.17**, notice of the receipt of any document that, on receipt, is subject to the requirements of *First Company Law Directive (68/151/EEC), Art 3* (the '*Directive disclosure requirements*'). The notice must state the name and registered number of the company, the description of document and the date of receipt. The Registrar is not required to cause notice of the receipt of a document to be published before the date of incorporation of the company to which the document relates.
[*CA 2006, s 1077*].

The documents subject to the *Directive* disclosure requirements are as follows.

All companies

(A) *Constitutional documents*

- (1) The company's memorandum and articles.
- (2) Any amendment of the company's articles (including every resolution or agreement required to be embodied in or annexed to copies of the company's articles issued by the company) and, before 1 October 2009, any amendment of the company's memorandum.
- (3) After any amendment of the company's articles (or, before 1 October 2009, memorandum), the text of the document as amended.
- (4) With effect from 1 October 2009, any notice of a change of the company's name.

(B) *Directors*

- (1) The statement of proposed officers required on formation of the company.
- (2) Notification of any change among the company's directors.
- (3) Notification of any change in the particulars of directors required to be delivered to the Registrar.

(C) *Accounts, reports and returns*

- (1) All documents required to be delivered to the Registrar under *CA 2006, s 441* (annual accounts and reports).
- (2) All documents delivered to the Registrar under *CA 2006, ss 394A(2)(e), 448A(2)(e)* and *479A(2)(e)* (qualifying subsidiary companies: conditions for exemption from the audit, preparation and filing of individual accounts)
- (3) The company's annual return.

(D) *Registered office*

Notification of any change of the company's registered office.

(E) *Winding up*

(1) Copy of any winding-up order in respect of the company.

(2) Notice of the appointment of liquidators.

(3) Order for the dissolution of a company on a winding up.

(4) Return by a liquidator of the final meeting of a company on a winding up.

Public companies

(A) *Share capital*

(1) Any statement of capital and initial shareholdings.

(2) Any return of allotment and, with effect from 1 October 2009, the statement of capital accompanying it.

(3) Copy of any resolution under *CA 2006, ss 570, 571* (disapplication of pre-emption rights).

(4) Copy of any report under *CA 2006, ss 593* as to the value of a non-cash asset.

(5) A statement of capital accompanying notice given under *CA 2006, s 625* (notice by company of redenomination of shares).

(6) A statement of capital accompanying notice given under *CA 2006, s 627* (notice by company of reduction of capital in connection with redenomination of shares).

(7) Notice delivered under *CA 2006, s 636* (notice of new name of class of shares) or *CA 2006, s 637* (notice of variation of rights attached to shares) (registration of particulars of specified rights)).

(8) A statement of capital accompanying order delivered under *CA 2006, s 649* (order of court confirming reduction of capital).

(9) Notification (under *CA 2006, s 689*) of the redemption of shares and the statement of capital accompanying it.

(10) A statement of capital accompanying return delivered under *CA 2006, s 708* (notice of cancellation of shares on purchase of own shares or *CA 2006, s 730* (notice of cancellation of shares held as treasury shares).

(11) Any statement of compliance delivered under *CA 2006, s 762* (statement that company meets conditions for issue of trading certificate) (public company share capital requirements)).

The *Small Business, Enterprise and Employment Act 2015 (SBEE 2015)* introduces a requirement to also include in the statement of capital the aggregate amount (if any) unpaid on those shares (whether on account of their nominal value or by way of premium). As at May 2015 this provision is not in force.

(B) *Mergers and divisions*

(1) Copy of any draft of the terms of a scheme required to be delivered to the Registrar under *CA 2006, s 906* or *CA 2006, s 921*.

(2) Copy of any order under *CA 2006, s 899* or *CA 2006, s 900* in respect of a compromise or arrangement to which *CA 2006, Pt 27* (mergers and divisions of public companies) applies.

Private company re-registering as a public company

(1) The last statement of capital relating to the company received by the Registrar of Companies under any provision of the *Companies Acts* becomes subject to the Directive disclosure requirements. *CA 2006, s 1077* above applies as if the statement had been received by the Registrar of Companies when the re-registration takes effect.

Overseas companies

(1) Any return or document delivered under *Overseas Companies Regulations 2009, Part 2* (initial registration of particulars, see **30.3–30.5 Overseas Companies**).

(2) Any return or document delivered under *Overseas Companies Regulations 2009, Part 3* (alterations in registered particulars, see **30.8** and **30.9 Overseas Companies**).

(3) Any document delivered under *Overseas Companies Regulations 2009, Part 5* (delivery of accounting documents: general, see **30.18** *et seq* **Overseas Companies**).

(4) Any document delivered under *Overseas Companies Regulations 2009, Part 6* (delivery of accounting documents: credit or financial institutions, see **30.35** *et seq* **Overseas Companies**).

(5) Any notice under *Overseas Companies Regulations 2009, Reg 77* (duty to give notice of closure of UK establishment, see **30.57 Overseas Companies**).

[*CA 2006, s 1078; SI 2009 No 1801, Reg 76; SI 2009 No 1801 Overseas Companies Regulations 2009, Reg 76; SI 2012 No 2301, Reg 19*].

39.9 Maintaining company records on the register

The Registrar of Companies must keep records of

- the information contained in documents delivered to the Registrar under any enactment; and
- certificates issued by the Registrar under any enactment.

The records relating to companies are referred to collectively as '*the register*'.

Information deriving from documents subject to the *Directive* disclosure requirements (see **39.8**) must be kept by the Registrar in electronic form. Otherwise, information contained in documents delivered to the Registrar may be recorded and kept in any form the Registrar thinks fit, provided it is possible to inspect it and produce a copy of it and provided the records enable all the information relating to a particular company or other registered body to be retrieved.

[*CA 2006, s 1080*].

Annotation of the register. *In relation to documents delivered to the Registrar of Companies on or after 1 October 2009* (other than those delivered in pursuance of an obligation arising before that date to which the provisions applying before 1 October 2009 continue to apply), the Registrar of Companies

(a) *must* place a note in the register recording

- the date on which a document is delivered to the Registrar;
- if a document is corrected (see **39.7**), the nature and date of the correction;
- if a document is replaced (whether or not material derived from it is removed), the fact that it has been replaced and the date of delivery of the replacement; and
- if material is removed
  - (i) what was removed (giving a general description of its contents);
  - (ii) under what power; and
  - (iii) the date on which that was done;
    - if a document is rectified under *CA 2006, s 859M*, the nature and date of rectification; and
    - if a document is replaced under *CA 2006, s 859N*, the fact that it has been replaced and the date of delivery of the replacement.

(b) *may* place a note in the register containing such information as appears to the Registrar to be necessary to remedy, as far as possible, any material on the register that is misleading or confusing.

A note may be removed if it no longer serves any useful purpose. Any duty or power of the Registrar with respect to annotation of the register is subject to the court's power under *CA 2006, s 1097* (see **39.11**(4)) to direct that a note be removed from the register or that no note should made of the removal of material that is the subject of the court's order.

[*CA 2006, s 1081; SI 2009 No 1802, Sch; SI 2009 No 1803, Reg 3; SI 2013 No 600, Schedule 2, para 3*].

Allocation of unique identifiers. The Secretary of State may make provision for the use, in connection with the register, of reference numbers ('unique identifiers') to identify each person who

- is a director of a company;
- is secretary (or a joint secretary) of a company; or
- in the case of an overseas company whose particulars are registered under *CA 2006, s 1046*, holds any such position as may be specified for the purposes of these provisions.

[*CA 2006, s 1082*].

Preservation of original documents. The originals of documents delivered to the Registrar of Companies in hard copy form must be kept for three years after they are received by the Registrar, after which they may be destroyed provided the information contained in them has been recorded. But material not available for public inspection (see **39.10**) need only be kept as long as appears necessary to the Registrar for the purposes for which the material was delivered to him.

The Registrar is under no obligation to keep the originals of documents delivered in electronic form, provided the information contained in them has been recorded.

[*CA 2006, s 1083*].

Records relating to companies that have been dissolved, etc. Where a company is dissolved, at any time after two years from the date of dissolution the Registrar of Companies may direct that records relating to the company may be removed to the Public Record Office or, as the case may be, the Public Records Office for Northern Ireland. The records must then be disposed of under the rules relating to that Office.

Similar rules apply to records where an overseas company ceases to have any connection with the UK by virtue of which it is required to register particulars.

The above provisions do not extend to Scotland.

[*CA 2006, s 1084*].

39.10 Inspection and copying of the register

Any person may inspect the register or require a copy of any material on the register (subject to a fee). The right of inspection extends to the originals of documents delivered to the Registrar of Companies in hard copy form if, and only if, the record kept by the Registrar of the contents of the document is illegible or unavailable (but note that the period for which hard copy originals are kept is limited under **39.9**). Certain material as specified in *CA 2006, s 1087* is not, however, available for public inspection or copying. This includes (see *s 1087* for a full list of materials not available for inspection)

- protected information under *CA 2006, s 242(1)* (directors' residential addresses, see **18.70 Directors**) or corresponding provisions relating to overseas companies;
- any address in respect of which a successful application under **39.19** is made to make as address on the public register unavailable for public inspection;
- the contents of any instrument creating or evidencing a charge, or the certified or verified copy of such an instrument, and delivered to the Registrar in Companies for filing.

Section 96 of the *SBEE 2015* inserts *CA 2006, s 1087A* and *1087B*. These detailed provisions provide for protection of the date of birth of people entered onto the company's PSC register (see 38.14). As at May 2015 these provisions are not yet in force.

Application for inspection or copy. The Registrar of Companies can specify the form and manner in which an application for inspection or copies should be made except that applications in respect of documents subject to the Directive disclosure requirements (see **39.8**) may be submitted to the Registrar in hard copy or electronic form, as the applicant chooses.

Form and manner in which copies to be provided. Copies of documents subject to the Directive disclosure requirements (see **39.8**) must be provided in hard copy or electronic form, as the applicant chooses except that the Registrar is not obliged to provide copies in electronic form of a document that was delivered to the Registrar in hard copy form if

- the document was delivered on or before 31 December 1996; or
- the document was delivered on or before 31 December 2006 and ten years or more elapsed between the date of delivery and the date of receipt of the first application for a copy on or after 1 January 2007.

Subject to this, the Registrar may determine the form and manner in which copies are to be provided.

39.10 Registrar of Companies

Certification of copies as accurate. Copies provided in hard copy form must be certified as true copies (unless the applicant dispenses with such certification).

Copies provided in electronic form must not be certified as true copies unless the applicant expressly requests such certification. Where he does so request, the Registrar's certificate must be authenticated by means of an electronic signature that

- is uniquely linked to the Registrar;
- indicates that the Registrar has caused it to be applied;
- is created using means that the Registrar can maintain under his sole control; and
- is linked to the certificate and to the copy provided in such a manner that any subsequent change of the data comprised in either is detectable.

Any copy certified by the Registrar of Companies to be an accurate record of the contents of the original document is in all legal proceedings admissible in evidence as

- of equal validity with the original document; and
- evidence (in Scotland, sufficient evidence) of any fact stated in the original document of which direct oral evidence would be admissible.

[*CA 2006, ss 1085–1087, 1089–1091; SI 2006 No 3429, Reg 2*].

Application to Registrar to make address unavailable for public inspection. See **39.19**.

See APPENDIX 1 DEFINITIONS for the meaning of 'hard copy' and 'electronic form'.

39.11 Correction or removal of material on the register

In relation to documents delivered to, and certificates issued by, the Registrar of Companies (otherwise than in pursuance of an obligation arising before 1 October 2009, in which case the provisions applicable before that date continue to apply), the Registrar has various powers and duties to rectify the register.

(1) **Inconsistencies**

Where it appears that the information contained in a document delivered to the Registrar of Companies is inconsistent with other information on the register, the Registrar may give notice to the company requiring it to take steps to resolve the inconsistency within 14 days. If the necessary documents are not delivered within that period, an offence is committed by the company and every officer of the company who is in default. A person guilty of such an offence is liable, on summary conviction, to a fine not exceeding level 5 on the standard scale and, for continued contravention, a daily default fine not exceeding one-tenth of the greater of £5000 or level 4 on the standard scale. See **29.1** OFFENCES AND LEGAL PROCEEDINGS for the standard scale. [*CA 2006, s 1093; SI 2015 No 664, Sch 3*].

(2) **Administrative removal of material**

The Registrar of Companies may remove from the register anything that there was power, but no duty, to include. This covers, in particular, unnecessary material (see **39.7**) and material derived from a document that has been replaced by voluntary replacement under **39.7** or because of inconsistencies under (*a*) above.

On or before removing any material under this provision (otherwise than at the request of the company) the Registrar must give notice

(i) to the person by whom the material was delivered (if the identity, and name and address of that person are known); or

(ii) to the company to which the material relates (if notice cannot be given under (i) above and the identity of that company is known).

[*CA 2006, s 1094*].

(3) **Rectification of register on application to Registrar of Companies**

On application (but not if there is a valid objection to the application, see below) the Registrar of Companies must remove from the register any 'relevant material' that

- derives from anything invalid or ineffective or that was done without the authority of the company or overseas company to which the material relates; or
- is factually inaccurate, or is derived from something that is factually inaccurate or forged.

'*Relevant material*', in the case of a company, is material concerning its officers or registered office and that was included in, or is derived from material that was included in, a company form delivered to the Registrar of Companies by any person. In the case of an overseas company, it is material concerning its officers, permanent representatives, persons authorised to accept service of documents and addresses of UK establishments.

An application relating to the address of a registered office or UK establishment can only be made by the company or overseas company concerned. Any other application can only be made by the person who delivered the form in question, the company or overseas company to which it relates, or any other person to whom the material relates.

The application must

- specify what is to be removed from the register and indicate where on the register it is;
- be accompanied by a statement that the material specified in the application complies with these provisions;
- state the applicant's name and address;
- where the application relates to the address of a registered office or UK establishment, confirm that the applicant is the company or overseas company to which the relevant material relates;
- in any other case, state whether the applicant is
  (i) the person who delivered the form in question;
  (ii) the company or overseas company to which it relates; or
  (iii) another person to whom the material relates; and
- state whether the relevant material which is the subject of the application
  (i) derives from anything invalid or ineffective;
  (ii) derives from anything that was done without the authority of the company or overseas company to which the material relates;

(iii) is factually inaccurate or is derived from something that is factually inaccurate; or

(iv) is derived from something that is forged.

The Registrar is obliged to give notice of the application to specified person including the company, every person who (to the Registrar's knowledge) was a director or secretary of the company and, in the case of an overseas company, every person who, at the time the application was delivered to the Registrar, was authorised to accept documents on behalf of the overseas company or was the permanent representative of one of its UK establishments. The notice must, amongst other things,

- specify what is to be removed from the register and indicate where on the register it is;
- give particulars of the recipient's right to object to the application and the requirements applying to that right; and
- explain the effect of a valid objection.

An objection to an application may be made to the Registrar of Companies in writing by any person, stating the name and address of the person making the objection and identify the application to which the objection relates, within 28 days of the Registrar's notice.

If no valid objection is made to an application, the Registrar of Companies may accept the statement as sufficient evidence that the material specified in the application should be removed from the register and must notify the applicant of that fact. But if a valid objection is made to the application, the Registrar of Companies must reject the application and

- send an acknowledgment of receipt to the person who made the objection;
- notify the applicant of the fact that an objection has been made; and
- notify every other person to whom he gave notice of the application.

[*CA 2006, s 1095; SI 2009 No 1802, Schedule; SI 2009 No 1803, Regs 4, 5*].

(4) **Rectification of the register under court order**

The Registrar of Companies must remove from the register any material that

- derives from anything that the court has declared to be invalid or ineffective, or to have been done without the authority of the company, or
- a court declares to be factually inaccurate, or to be derived from something that is factually inaccurate, or forged,

and that the court directs should be removed from the register.

A copy of the court's order must be sent to the Registrar of Companies for registration.

[*CA 2006, ss 1096, 1097*].

(5) **Rectification of the register relating to a company's registered office**

Section 99 of the *SBEE 2015* (see **39.10**) inserts *CA 2006, s 1097A*. This enables the Registrar of Companies, on application, to change the address of a company's registered office. Enabling regulations will need to be made to allow the new powers to be used. As at May 2015 the new provisions are not in force and regulations have not been published.

Public notice of removal of certain material from the register. *With effect from 1 October 2009*, the Registrar of Companies must cause to be published, in the *Gazette* or in accordance with **39.17**, notice of the removal from the register of any document subject to the Directive disclosure requirements (see **39.8**) or of any material derived from such a document. The notice must state the name and registered number of the company, the description of document and the date of receipt.

[*CA 2006, s 1098*].

39.12 Index of company names

The Registrar of Companies must keep an index of the names of the following companies and other bodies (the '*Registrar's index of company names*').

- UK-registered companies.
- Any body to which any provision of the *Companies Acts* applies by virtue of regulations under *CA 2006, s 1043* (unregistered companies).
- Overseas companies that have registered particulars with the Registrar under *CA 2006, s 1046*, other than companies that appear to the Registrar not to be required to do so.
- Limited partnerships registered in the UK.
- Limited liability partnerships incorporated in the UK.
- European Economic Interest Groupings registered in the UK.
- Open-ended investment companies authorised in the UK.
- Societies registered under the *Industrial and Provident Societies Act 1965* or the *Industrial and Provident Societies Act (Northern Ireland) 1969*.

[*CA 2006, s 1099*].

Any person may inspect the registrar's index of company names.

[*CA 2006, s 1100*].

39.13 Language requirements: translation

The provisions in (1) to (4) below apply to all documents required to be delivered to the Registrar of Companies under any provision of the *Companies Acts* or the *Insolvency Act 1986* or the *Insolvency (Northern Ireland) Order 1989 (SI 1989 No 2405)*.

[*CA 2006, s 1102*].

(1) **Documents to be drawn up and delivered in English**

Subject to (2) and (3) below, the general rule is that all documents required to be delivered to the Registrar of Companies must be drawn up and delivered in English.

[*CA 2006, s 1103*].

(2) **Documents relating to Welsh companies**

Documents relating to a Welsh company may be drawn up and delivered to the Registrar of Companies in Welsh. Any such document must be accompanied by a certified translation into English with the following exceptions.

- A non-traded company's memorandum of association.
- A non-traded company's articles.
- A community interest company report prepared for a non-traded company under *C(AICE)A 2004, s 34* (see **10.18** COMMUNITY INTEREST COMPANIES).
- A resolution or agreement which was agreed to by members of a non-traded company and to which *CA 2006, ss 29, 39* apply (see **14.10** COMPANY CONSTITUTION) apart from

  (a) a special resolution that (i) a private company should be re-registered as a public company; (ii) a public company should be re-registered as a private limited company; (iii) a private limited company should be re-registered as an unlimited company; or (iv) an unlimited company should be re-registered as a limited company;

  (b) a special resolution agreeing to the change of a company's name;

  (c) a special resolution required by *C(AICE)A 2004, s 37* (requirements for an existing company to become a community interest company, see **10.5** COMMUNITY INTEREST COMPANIES);

  (d) a resolution or agreement as altered by an enactment other than an enactment amending the general law, required to be delivered to the Registrar of Companies under *CA 2006, s 34* (see **14.13** CONSTITUTION – MEMORANDUM AND ARTICLES);

  (e) a resolution or agreement as altered by an order of a court or other authority, required to be delivered to the Registrar of Companies under *CA 2006, s 35* (see **14.13** CONSTITUTION – MEMORANDUM AND ARTICLES) or *CA 2006, s 999* (see **26.5** MEMBERS);

  (f) a special resolution under *CA 2008, s 88(2)* requiring the register to be amended so that it states that a company's registered office is to be situated in Wales;

  (g) a special resolution under *CA 2006, s 626* (reduction of capital in connection with redenomination);

  (h) a special resolution under *CA 2006, s 641(1)(a)* (resolution for reducing the share capital of a private limited company supported by a solvency statement); or

  (i) a resolution under *CA 2006, s 664(1)* that a public company should be re-registered as a private company to comply with *CA 2006, s 662*.

- Annual accounts and reports of a non-traded company required to be delivered to the Registrar of Companies.

- A declaration referred to in *C(AICE)A 2004, s 11(1)(b)* (see **10.4**(*b*) COMMUNITY INTEREST COMPANIES) or *C(AICE)A 2004, s 12(1)(b)* or *(c)* (see **10.5**(*b*)(*c*) COMMUNITY INTEREST COMPANIES) which relates to a non-traded company.
- Revised accounts and any revised report of a non-traded company, and any auditor's report on such revised accounts and reports, required to be delivered to the Registrar of Companies.
- A document required to be appended to the group accounts of a non-traded company by *SI 2008 No 410, Sch 6 para 30(2)* (banking groups: information as to undertaking in which shares held as a result of financial assistance operation).
- All documents to be delivered to the Registrar by a non-traded company under *CA 2006, ss 394A(2)(e), 448A(2)(e)* and *479(2)(e)* (qualifying subsidiaries: conditions for exemption from the audit, preparation and filing of individual accounts).
- A document in a form prescribed in Welsh (or partly in Welsh and partly in English) by virtue of *Welsh Language Act 1993, s 26*.

Where a document is properly delivered to the Registrar of Companies in Welsh without a certified translation into English, the Registrar must obtain such a translation if the document is to be available for public inspection. The translation is treated as if delivered to the Registrar in accordance with the same provision as the original.

A Welsh company may deliver to the Registrar of Companies a certified translation into Welsh of any document in English that relates to the company and is, or has been, delivered to the Registrar.

The provisions of *CA 2006, s 1105* in (3) below do not apply to a document relating to a Welsh company that is drawn up and delivered in Welsh.

[*CA 2006, s 1104; SI 2009 No 1803, Reg 6; SI 2012 No 2301, Reg 21*].

(3) **Documents that may be drawn up and delivered in other languages**

The documents listed below may be drawn up and delivered to the Registrar of Companies in a language other than English, but when delivered they must be accompanied by a certified translation into English. The documents in question are

- agreements required to be forwarded to the Registrar of Companies under *CA 2006, ss 29, 30* (agreements affecting the company's constitution, see **14.10** CONSTITUTION – MEMORANDUM AND ARTICLES)
- documents required to be delivered under *CA 2006, s 400(2)(e)* or *s 401(2)(f)* (company included in accounts of larger group);
- certified copies required to be delivered relating to registration of charges; and
- a memorandum of association;
- a company's articles;
- a valuation report required to be delivered to the Registrar of Companies under *CA 2006, s 94(2)(d)* (application for a private company to be re-registered as a public company, see **41.6** RE-REGISTRATION);

- any order made by a competent court in the UK or elsewhere;
- copies of the consolidated accounts, the auditor's report and the consolidated annual report to be delivered to the Registrar under *CA 2006, ss 394A(2)(e), 448A(2)(e)* or *479A(2)(e)* (qualifying subsidiaries: conditions for exemption from the audit, preparation and filing of individual accounts).
- in the case of an overseas company,

  (i) a certified copy of the constitution required to be delivered to the Registrar of Companies under *Overseas Companies Regulations 2009, Reg 8, 14* or *15* (see **30.4, 30.7** and **30.8 Overseas Companies** respectively);

  (ii) copies of accounting documents required to be delivered under *Overseas Companies Regulations 2009, Reg 9, 32, 45* or *46* (see **30.4, 29.20,** and **30.37 Overseas Companies** respectively);

  (iii) copies of accounts required to be delivered under *CA 2006, s 441* as modified by *Overseas Companies Regulations 2009, Regs 40* and *55* (see **30.44** and **30.50 Overseas Companies** respectively); and

  (iv) a certified copy of a debenture or other instrument creating or evidencing a charge over the property of the company to which *Overseas Companies (Execution of Documents and Registration of Charges) Regulations 2009, Pt 3* applies.

[*CA 2006, s 1105; SI 2006 No 3429, Reg 4; SI 2007 No 2974; SI 2009 No 1801, Reg 78; SI 2009 No 1803, Reg 7; SI 2009 No 1917, Reg 27; SI 2012 No 2301, Reg 21; SI 2013 No.600, Schedule 2, para 3*].

(4) **Certified translations**

In the case of any discrepancy between the original language version of a document and a 'certified translation'

- the company may not rely on the translation as against a 'third party'; but
- a third party may rely on the translation unless the company shows that the third party had knowledge of the original.

A '*certified translation*' means a translation certified to be a correct translation.

A '*third party*' means a person other than the company or the Registrar of Companies.

[*CA 2006, s 1107*]

Voluntary filing of translations. A company may deliver to the Registrar of Companies one or more certified translations of any document relating to the company that is, or has been, delivered to the Registrar.

The Secretary of State may by *Regulations* specify the languages and descriptions of document in relation to which this facility is available. The facility must be available in relation to all the official languages of the EU and all documents subject to the *Directive* disclosure requirements (see **39.8**).

These provisions do not apply where the original document was delivered to the Registrar of Companies before 8 November 2006.

[*CA 2006, s 1106; SI 2006 No 3429, Reg 5; SI 2007 No 2974*].

39.14 Language requirements: transliteration

The following provisions apply in relation to all documents delivered to the Registrar of Companies.

Permitted characters. Subject to the exceptions below, names and addresses in a document delivered to the Registrar of Companies must contain only letters, characters and symbols (including accents and other diacritical marks) that are permitted. Those permitted are:

- Letters A to Z (in upper and lower case)
- Numerals 0, 1, 2, 3, 4, 5, 6, 7, 8 and 9
- &, @, £, $, €, ¥, *, =, #, %, and +
- Any of the following types of punctuation but only in the forms indicated:
  - (i) Apostrophe: ‘ ’ ‘
  - (ii) Bracket: ( ) [ ] { } < >
  - (iii) Exclamation mark: !
  - (iv) Guillemet: « »
  - (v) Inverted comma: “ ” ″
  - (vi) Question mark: ?
  - (vii) Solidus: \ /
- Full stop, comma, colon, semi-colon or hyphen

The above requirement does not apply to the following documents.

(a) A memorandum of association.

(b) A company's articles.

(c) An order made by a competent court in the UK or elsewhere.

(d) An agreement required to be forwarded to the Registrar of Companies under *CA 2006, ss 29, 30* (agreements affecting a company's constitution see **14.10** CONSTITUTION – MEMORANDUM AND ARTICLES).

(e) A valuation report required to be delivered to the Registrar of Companies under *CA 2006, s 94(2)(d)* (application for a private company to be re-registered as a public company).

(f) A document required to be delivered to the Registrar of Companies under *CA 2006, s 400(2)(e)* or *s 401(2)(f)* (company included in accounts of larger group: requirement to deliver copy of group accounts).

(g) An instrument or copy instrument required to be delivered to the Registrar of Companies under *CA 2006, Pt 25* (company charges).

(h) A certified copy of the constitution of an overseas company required to be delivered to the Registrar of Companies under *Overseas Companies Regulations 2009, Reg 8, 14* or *15*.

(i) A copy of accounting documents of an overseas company required to be delivered to the Registrar of Companies under *Overseas Companies Regulations 2009, Reg 9, 32, 45* or *46*.

(j) A copy of the annual accounts of an overseas company, or of a credit or financial institution to which *Overseas Companies Regulations 2009, Pt 6 Chapter 2* applies, required to be delivered to the Registrar of Companies under *CA 2006, s 441*.

(k) copies of the consolidated accounts, the auditor's report and the consolidated annual report to be delivered to the Registrar under *CA 2006, ss 394A(2)(e), 448A(2)(e)* or *479A(2)(e)* (qualifying subsidiaries: conditions for exemption from the audit, preparation and filing of individual accounts).

[*CA 2006, s 1108; SI 2009 No 1803, Reg 8, Sch; SI 2012 No 2301, Reg 21*].

Voluntary transliteration into Roman characters. Where a name or address is, or has been, delivered to the Registrar of Companies in a permitted form using other than Roman characters, the company (or other body) to which the document relates may deliver to the Registrar a transliteration into Roman characters.

[*CA 2006, s 1109*].

Certification. The Secretary of State may make provision by Regulations requiring the certification of transliterations and prescribing the form of certification.

[*CA 2006, s 1110*].

39.15 Requirements as to certification or verification

Where a document required or authorised to be delivered to the Registrar of Companies under any enactment is required

- to be certified as an accurate translation or transliteration, or
- to be certified as a correct copy or verified,

the Registrar may impose requirements as to the person, or description of person, by whom the certificate or verification is to be given provided such requirements are not inconsistent with requirements imposed by any enactment with respect to the certification or verification of the document concerned.

The power conferred on the Registrar of Companies under *CA 2006, s 1068* (see **39.6**) is exercisable in relation to the certificate or verification as if it were a separate document.

[*CA 2006, s 1111*].

39.16 Enforcement of company's filing obligations

Where a company has made default in complying with any obligation under the *Companies Acts* to

- deliver a document to the Registrar of Companies, or
- give notice to the Registrar of Companies of any matter

the Registrar, or any member or creditor of the company, may give notice to the company requiring it to comply with the obligation.

If the company fails to make good the default within 14 days after service of the notice, the Registrar, or any member or creditor of the company, may apply to the court for an order directing the company, and any specified officer of it, to make good the default within a specified time. The court's order may provide that all costs (in Scotland, expenses) of, or incidental to, the application are to be borne by the company or by any officers of it responsible for the default.

These provisions do not affect the operation of any enactment making it an offence, or imposing a civil penalty, for the default.

[*CA 2006, s 1113*].

39.17 ALTERNATIVE TO PUBLICATION IN THE GAZETTE

Notices that would otherwise need to be published by the Registrar in the Gazette may instead be published by such means as may from time to time be approved by the Registrar in accordance with Regulations made by the Secretary of State.

Nothing in these provisions prevents the Registrar from giving public notice both in the Gazette and by means approved under these provisions. In such a case, the requirement of public notice is met when notice is first given by either means.

[*CA 2006, s 1116*].

39.18 OFFENCE OF GENERAL FALSE STATEMENT

It is an offence for a person knowingly or recklessly to

- deliver or cause to be delivered to the Registrar of Companies, for any purpose of the *Companies Acts*, a document, or
- to make to the Registrar, for any such purpose, a statement

that is misleading, false or deceptive in a material particular.

A person guilty of such an offence is liable (i) on conviction on indictment, to imprisonment for a term not exceeding two years or a fine (or both); and (ii) on summary conviction, to imprisonment for a term not exceeding twelve months (six months in Scotland and Northern Ireland) or to a fine not exceeding the statutory maximum (or both). See **29.1 Offences and Legal Proceedings** for the statutory maximum.

[*CA 2006, s 1112*].

39.19 APPLICATION TO MAKE AN ADDRESS UNAVAILABLE FOR PUBLIC INSPECTION

An application may be made to the Registrar of Companies requiring him to make an address on the register unavailable for public inspection. The application can be made as follows.

(1) **By an individual**

An application may be made by an individual whose usual residential address was placed on the register after 31 December 2002

- under *CA 1985, s 10* (documents to be sent to Registrar of Companies), *CA 1985, s 288* (register of directors and secretaries), *CA 2006, s 363* (duty to deliver annual returns), *CA 1985, s 691* (documents to be delivered to Registrar of Companies), *CA 1985, s 692* (registration of altered particulars), or *CA 1985, Sch 21A, para 2* (registration of UK branch by overseas company);
- under the equivalent NI legislation; or

- as a service address under *CA 2006, s 12* (statement of proposed officers), *CA 2006, s 167* (duty to notify Registrar of Companies of changes of director's particulars) or *CA 2006, s 855* (contents of annual return) or under regulations made under *CA 2006, s 1046*.

The grounds on which an application may be made are that the individual concerned

- considers that there is a serious risk that he, or a person who lives with him, will be subjected to violence or intimidation as a result of the activities of at least one of the companies of which
  - (i) he is, or proposes to become, a director; or
  - (ii) he is not a director but of which he has been at any time a director, secretary or permanent representative;
- he is or has been employed by a 'relevant organisation';
- he has made, or has had made on his behalf, a successful application requiring the Registrar of Companies not to disclose protected information about him to credit reference agencies under *CA 2006, s 243* (see **18.72 Directors**); or
- had a confidentiality order in force in relation to him immediately before 1 October 2009.

A '*relevant organisation*' means the Government Communications Headquarters, the Secret Intelligence Service, the Security Service or a police force.

The application must contain

- a statement of the grounds on which the application is made;
- the name and any former name of the applicant;
- the usual residential address of the applicant that is to be made unavailable for public inspection;
- an address for correspondence in respect of the application;
- the name and registered number of each company of which the applicant is or has been at any time since 1 January 2003 a director, secretary or permanent representative;
- the service address which is to replace that usual residential address on the register;
- Subject to below
  - (i) the date of birth of the applicant;
  - (ii) the name of each company of which the applicant proposes to become a director; and
  - (iii) where the Registrar of Companies has allotted a unique identifier to the applicant, that unique identifier.

  except that the application need not contain this information where the application is delivered to the Registrar of Companies on the same day as the applicant delivers an application under *CA 2006, s 243* (application not to disclose protected information to credit reference agencies, see **18.72 Directors**).

The application must be accompanied by evidence that the relevant grounds apply.

The Registrar of Companies may request additional information and evidence and may refer to a 'relevant body' any question relating to an assessment of the nature and extent of any risk of violence or intimidation or, as the case may be, as to whether the applicant is or has been employed by a relevant organisation. He may accept any answer from the relevant body as sufficient evidence of the matter referred to it.

A '*relevant body*' means any police force and any other person whom the Registrar of Companies considers may be able to assist in answering a question referred to that person by him.

The Registrar of Companies must determine the application and send the applicant, to the address for correspondence stated in his application, notice of his determination within five working days of that determination being made.

(2) **Application by a company**

An application may be made by a company in respect of the addresses of

- all of its members and former members whose addresses were contained in an annual return or a return of allotment of shares, or
- the subscribers to its memorandum of association.

where the relevant document was delivered to the Registrar of Companies after 31 December 2002.

The grounds on which an application may be made are that the company making the application considers that, as a result of its activities, the availability to members of the public of those addresses creates a serious risk that its members or former members or subscribers, or persons who live at those addresses, will be subjected to violence or intimidation.

The application must contain

- the name of the applicant and its registered number; and
- a statement of the grounds on which the application is made.

It must be accompanied by evidence which supports the applicant's assertion that its application falls within the grounds stated. Alternatively, where the court has made an order under *CA 2006, s 117(3)* (register of members: response to request for inspection or copy) directing the applicant not to comply with a request under *CA 2006, s 116* (rights to inspect and require copies), a copy of that order can be submitted.

The Registrar of Companies may direct that additional information or evidence be delivered to him and he may also refer to a 'relevant body' (see (1) above) any question relating to the assessment of the nature and extent of any risk of violence or intimidation. He may accept any answer from the relevant body as sufficient evidence of the matter referred to it.

The Registrar of Companies must determine the application and send the applicant, to its registered office, notice of his determination within five working days of that determination being made.

(3) **Application by a person who registers a charge**

An application may be made to the Registrar of Companies by a person who

- registered a charge under *CA 1985, Pt 12* (or NI equivalent) after 31 December 2002 or has registered a charge under *CA 2006, Pt 25* or regulations made under *CA 2006, s 1052*, and
- is not the company which created the charge or acquired the property subject to a charge,

in respect of his address delivered to the Registrar of Companies for the purposes of that registration.

The grounds on which an application may be made are that the person making the application considers that there is a serious risk that he, or if applicable his employees, or persons who live with him or his employees, will be subjected to violence or intimidation as a result of the activities of the company which is, or was, subject to the charge.

The application must contain

- a statement of the grounds on which the application is made;
- the name of the applicant, and where the applicant is a company, its registered number;
- the address of the applicant that is to be made unavailable for public inspection;
- the name and registered number of the company which is or was subject to the charge;
- an address for correspondence with the Registrar of Companies in respect of the application;
- where the applicant is the chargee, the service address which is to replace the address of the applicant on the register.

It must be accompanied by evidence which supports the applicant's assertion that there is a serious risk that he or, if applicable, his employees, or persons who live with him or his employees, will be subjected to violence or intimidation as a result of the activities of the company which is or was subject to the charge.

The Registrar of Companies may direct that additional information or evidence should be delivered to him and he may also refer to a 'relevant body' (see (1) above) any question relating to the assessment of the nature and extent of any risk of violence or intimidation. He may accept any answer from the relevant body as sufficient evidence of the matter referred to it.

The Registrar of Companies must determine the application and send the applicant, to the address stated in the application, notice of his determination within five working days of that determination being made.

Effect of a successful application. Where an application has been determined in favour of the applicant, the Registrar of Companies must

- in the case of an application made under (1) or (3) above, make the specified address unavailable for public inspection; and
- in the case of an application under (2) above, make all of the members', former members' or subscribers' addresses unavailable for public inspection.

A person in relation to whom a confidentiality order was in force immediately before 1 October 2009 is treated, on or after that date, as if they had made a successful application to make their usual residential address unavailable for inspection under these provisions. [*SI 2008 No 2860, Sch 2 para 36*]. The Registrar of Companies must therefore continue to make that address unavailable for public inspection.

Appeals. Unsuccessful applicants may, with leave of the court, appeal to the High Court (in Scotland, the Court of Session) on the grounds that the decision is unlawful, irrational or unreasonable, or has been made on the basis of a procedural impropriety or otherwise contravenes the rules of natural justice. Any appeal must be brought within 21 days of the date of the Registrar's notice (or later with the court's permission). The court may dismiss the appeal or quash the decision. In the later case, it may refer the matter to the Registrar of Companies with a direction to reconsider it and make a determination in accordance with the findings of the court.

Duration of decision. A decision continues to have effect until the Registrar of Companies revokes the decision.

Revocation. The Registrar of Companies may revoke a decision at any time if he is satisfied that the 'beneficiary' of that decision or any other person, in purported compliance with any of the above provisions, is found guilty of an offence under *CA 2006, s 1112* (general false statement offence).

If the Registrar of Companies proposes to make a revocation decision, he must send the beneficiary notice of his intention

- informing the beneficiary that he may, within 28 days of the notice, deliver representations in writing to the Registrar; and
- stating that if representations are not received by the Registrar within that period, the revocation decision will be made at the expiry of that period.

If the beneficiary delivers representations in the time allowed, the Registrar of Companies must consider them and, within five working days of making his decision, send notice of it to the beneficiary.

[*CA 2006, s 1088; SI 2009 No 214, Regs 9–16; SI 2009 No 1917, Reg 27*].

39.20 COMPANIES HOUSE WEBFILING

Instead of filling and updating certain company details in paper form, it is possible to use the Companies House WebFiling service on its website. Nearly 90% of companies are already filing some or all of their information electronically.

Newcomers to WebFiling must first register (free of charge) for the following two codes.

- *Security code* — this identifies the company as a user. It is sent by email when a company registers and is linked to its email address.
- *Company authentication code* — this is posted to the company's registered office address and is the electronic equivalent of a company director's signature. Companies must keep it safe and only share it with someone they trust to file information for the company.

For most companies, WebFiling covers all the information they will need to file in a typical year. It covers all of the most commonly filed document types, including

- the annual return;

- change of accounting reference date;
- change of name;
- appointment of a director or secretary;
- terminating appointment as director or secretary;
- change of particulars for director or secretary;
- change in situation or address of registered office;
- return of allotments of shares – excluding non-cash;
- audit-exempt abbreviated accounts;
- location of register of members;
- location of register of debenture holders; and
- dormant company accounts.

Companies House aims to expand WebFiling further over the next few years to provide a 100% electronic filing capability. It is available 24 hours seven days a week.

Currently, all information filing options on the service are free, except for the annual return and change of name (see APPENDIX 3: COMPANIES HOUSE FEES). Annual return fees can be paid online by credit or debit card. Alternatively, companies filing ten or more annual returns each year can apply for a Companies House e-filing credit account. The main advantages of Webfiling are:

- time saving- information can be filed directly from a PC
- security of information
- cost–annual returns are filed at half the cost of a paper filing
- benefit from PROOF (Protected online filing scheme)
- less chance of forms and returns being rejected

40 Registration of Charges

40.1	**Introduction**
40.2	**England and Wales and Northern Ireland: Charges created before 6 April 2013**
40.2A	UK registered companies. Charges created on or after 6 April 2013
40.3	Charges existing on property acquired
40.4	Special rules about debentures
40.5	Endorsement of certificate on debentures
40.6	Charges in other jurisdictions
40.7	Northern Ireland: registration of certain charges affecting land
40.8	Register of charges to be kept by the Registrar of Companies: Charges created before 6 April 2013
40.9	Rectification of register of charges by court
40.9A	Notification of, addition to, or amendment of charge. Charges created before, on or after 6 April 2013
40.10	Registration of enforcement of security
40.11	**Scotland**
40.12	Charges existing on property acquired
40.13	Charges by way of *ex facie* absolute disposition, etc
40.14	Special rules about debentures
40.15	Charges on property outside the UK
40.16	Register of charges to be kept by the Registrar of Companies
40.17	Rectification of register of charges by court
40.18	**Registration in special register**
40.19	**Companies' records and registers**

Cross-references. See **38.11** Registers for the requirement for a company to keep a register of charges and copies of instruments creating charges; **45** for security taken when a charge is given; **30.64** for registration of charges over UK property of an overseas company

40.1 INTRODUCTION

Companies are able to use all or any of their assets as security for loans. This usually involves the creation of a charge over its assets. Certain charges on a company's property must be registered with the Registrar of Companies. The provisions for companies registered in England and Wales and Northern Ireland are covered in **40.2** and those for companies registered in Scotland are covered in **40.11–40.17**. As from 6 April 2013, *Companies Act 2006 (CA 2006), Pt 25, Chs 1* and *2* were repealed and *SI 2008 No 2296* referred to in this chapter is revoked. Both are replaced by provisions in the *Companies Act 2006 (Amendment of Part 25) Regulations 2013 (SI 2013 No 600)* which came into force on 6 April 2013 and which apply to charges created on or after that date. The provisions of *CA 2006, Pt 25* as they stood immediately before 6 April 2013 continue to apply to charges created before that date together with new provisions (*CA 2006, s 859K, 859L* and *859O*) which also apply to charges created before 6 April 2013. This chapter includes covers both pre and post 6 April 2013 regulatory provisions.

40.1 Registration of Charges

ENGLAND AND WALES AND NORTHERN IRELAND

40.2 Charges created before 6 April 2013

Charges created by a company. A company registered in England and Wales or in Northern Ireland that creates a charge (which includes a mortgage see definition below) must deliver the prescribed particulars of the charge, together with the instrument (if any) by which the charge is created or evidenced, to the Registrar of Companies for registration before the end of the period allowed for registration, ie

- 21 days beginning with the day after the day on which the charge is created; or
- if the charge is created outside the UK (see **40.6**), 21 days beginning with the day after the day on which the instrument by which the charge is created or evidenced (or a copy of it) could, in due course of post (and if despatched with due diligence) have been received in the UK.

The prescribed particulars for these purposes are

- the date of the creation of the charge;
- a description of the instrument (if any) creating or evidencing the charge;
- the amount secured by the charge;
- the name and address of the person entitled to the charge; and
- short particulars of the property charged.

Alternatively, registration of a charge may be effected on the application of a person interested in it, in which case that person is entitled to recover from the company any fees he has properly paid to the Registrar of Companies on the registration.

If the company fails to comply with these provisions then, unless the registration of charge has been effected by another person, an offence is committed by the company and every officer of the company who is in default. A person guilty of such an offence is liable (i) on conviction on indictment, to a fine; or (ii) on summary conviction, to a fine not exceeding the statutory maximum. See **29.1 Offences and Legal Proceedings** for the statutory maximum.

The charges to which these provisions apply are as follows.

- A charge on land (wherever situated) or any interest in land, other than a charge for any rent or other periodical sum issuing out of land. The holding of debentures entitling the holder to a charge on land is not, for this purpose, an interest in the land.
- A charge created or evidenced by an instrument which, if executed by an individual, would require registration as a bill of sale.
- A charge for the purposes of securing any issue of debentures.
- A charge on uncalled share capital of the company.
- A charge on calls made but not paid.
- A charge on book debts of the company. The deposit by way of security of a negotiable instrument given to secure the payment of book debts is not, for this purpose, a charge on those book debts.
- A floating charge on the company's property or undertaking.

- A charge on a ship or aircraft, or any share in a ship.
- A charge on goodwill or on any 'intellectual property'. For this purpose, '*intellectual property*' means
  - (i) any patent, trade mark, registered design, copyright or design right; and
  - (ii) any licence under or in respect of any such right.

[*CA 2006, ss 860, 861, 870(1); SI 2008 No 2996, Reg 2*].

40.2A UK registered companies: Charges created on or after 6 April 2013

A UK registered company (irrespective of the place of incorporation of the company within the UK) that creates a charge (see below for definition) must (or a person interested in such a charge must) deliver a "*section 859D* statement of particulars" and, where the charge is created or evidenced by an instrument, a certified copy of the instrument, to the Registrar of Companies for registration before the "period allowed for delivery".

The period allowed for delivery is a period of 21 days beginning with the day after the date of creation of the charge unless a court order allowing an extended period is made under *CA 2006, s 859F(3)* (see below). If such an order is made, a copy of the order must be delivered to the Registrar of Companies with the *section 859D* statement of particulars. If these provisions are complied with the Registrar of Companies must register the charge.

Extension of the period allowed for delivery may be granted under *CA 2006, s 859F* where the court is satisfied that neither the company nor any other person interested in the charge has delivered to the Registrar of Companies the documents required under *s 859A* or *859B* before the end of the period allowed for delivery and that the failure to deliver those documents was accidental or due to inadvertence or to some other sufficient cause or is not of a nature to prejudice the position of creditors or shareholders of the company or that on other grounds it is just and equitable to grant relief. The court may, on the application of the company or a person interested, and on such terms and conditions as seem to the court just and expedient, order that the period allowed for delivery be extended.

For the purposes of the provisions in *CA 2006, Part 25* a charge includes a mortgage, a standard security, assignation in security and any other right in security constituted under the law of Scotland including any heritable security, but not including a pledge. A charge does not include a charge in favour of a landlord on a cash deposit given as security in connection with the lease of land or a charge created by a member of Lloyd's (within the meaning of the *Lloyd's Act 1982*) to secure its obligations in connection with its underwriting business at Lloyd's and "cash" includes foreign currency.

Where a certified copy of an instrument is delivered to the Registrar of Companies the following information is not required to be included:

- personal information relating to an individual (other than the name of the individual);
- the number or other identifier of a bank or securities account of a company or individual;
- a signature.

But the Registrar of Companies is entitled, without further enquiry, to accept the certified copy of an instrument whether or not any of the above information is contained within the instrument.

40.2A Registration of Charges

The "date of creation of a charge" is defined in the Table set out in *CA 2006, s 859E.*

For the purposes of (*CA 2006, Pt 25*) a charge of a type described in column 1 of the Table is taken to be created on the date given in relation to it in column 2.

1. Type of charge	*2. When charge created*
Standard security	The date of its recording in the Register of Sasines or its registration in the Land Register of Scotland
Charge other than a standard security, where created or evidenced by an instrument	Where the instrument is a deed that has been executed and has immediate effect on execution and delivery, the date of delivery
	Where the instrument is a deed that has been executed and held in escrow, the date of delivery into escrow
	Where the instrument is a deed that has been executed and held as undelivered, the date of delivery
	Where the instrument is not a deed and has immediate effect on execution, the date of execution
	Where the instrument is not a deed and does not have immediate effect on execution, the date on which the instrument takes effect
Charge other than a standard security, where not created or evidenced by instrument	The date on which the charge comes into effect

Where a charge is created or evidenced by an instrument made between two or more parties, references in the above Table to "execution" are to execution by all the parties to the instrument whose execution is essential for the instrument to take effect as a charge.

CA 2006, s 859E applies for the purposes of *CA 2006, Part 25, Chapter 1* even if further forms, notices, registrations or other actions or proceedings are necessary to make the charge valid or effectual for any other purposes.

For the purposes of *CA 2006, Part 25, Chapter 1*, the Registrar of Companies is entitled without further enquiry to accept a charge as created on the date given as the date of creation of the charge in a *section 859D* statement of particulars (see below).

In *CA 2006, s 859E*, "deed" means a deed governed by the law of England and Wales and Northern Ireland or an instrument governed by a law other than the law of England or Wales or Northern Ireland which requires delivery under that law in order to take effect and references to "delivery", in relation to a deed includes delivery as a deed where required.

[*CA 2006, s 859A, s 859E, s 859F, s 859G; SI 2013 No 600, Schedule 1.*]

A statement of particulars relating to a charge created by a company is a *section 859D* statement of particulars if it contains the following particulars:

- the registered name and number of the company;
- the date of the creation of the charge and (if the charge is one to which *CA 2006, s 859C* applies) the date of acquisition of the property or undertaking concerned;
- where the charge is created or evidenced by an instrument the following particulars;

(a) any of the following: the name of each of the persons in whose favour the charge has been created or of the security agents or trustees holding the charge for the benefit of one or more persons or where there are more than four such persons; security agents or trustees; the names of any four such persons; security agents or trustees listed in the charge instrument and a statement that there are other such persons, security agents or trustees;

(b) whether the instrument is expressed to contain a floating charge and, if so, whether it is expressed to cover all the property and undertaking of the company;

(c) whether any of the terms of the charge prohibit or restrict the company from creating further security that will rank equally with or ahead of the charge;

(d) whether (and if so a short description of) any land, ship, aircraft or intellectual property that is registered or required to be registered in the United Kingdom, is subject to a charge (which is not a floating charge) or fixed security included in the instrument;

(e) whether the instrument includes a charge (which is not a floating charge) or fixed security over any tangible or corporeal property or any intangible or incorporeal property not described in (d);

- where the charge is not created or evidenced by an instrument the following particulars:

  (a) a statement that there is no instrument creating or evidencing the charge;

  (b) the names of each of the persons in whose favour the charge has been created or the names of any security agents or trustees holding the charge for the benefit of one or more persons;

  (c) the nature of the charge;

  (d) a short description of the property or undertaking charged;

  (e) the obligations secured by the charge.

"Fixed security" has the meaning given in *CA 1985, s 486(1)* and "intellectual property" includes any patent, trade mark, registered design, copyright or design right and any licence under or in respect of any such right.

[*CA 2006, s 859D; SI 2013 No 600, Schedule 1*]

Consequence of failure to register such a charge. Charges created before 6 April 2013. If a company creates a charge within the above provisions, the charge is void (so far as any security on the company's property or undertaking is conferred by it) against a liquidator, administrator or creditor of the company unless it is registered as required above. This is without prejudice to any contract or obligation for repayment of the money secured by the charge; and when a charge becomes void in these circumstances, the money secured by it immediately becomes payable.
[*CA 2006, s 874*].

The charge is void even if the liquidator or creditor has notice of the unregistered charge (*Monolithic Building Co, Re, Tacon v Monolithic Building Co* [1915] 1 Ch 643, 84 LJ Ch 441, CA).

Consequence of failure to register such a charge. Charges created on or after 6 April 2013. If a company creates a charge to which *CA 2006, s 859A* (charges created by a company) or *s 859B* (charge in a series of debentures) applies and the documents required by the relevant section are not delivered to the Registrar of Companies by the company or by another person interested in the charge before the end of the relevant period allowed for delivery (see above for definition), the charge is void (so far as any security on the company's property or undertaking is conferred by it) against a liquidator, administrator or creditor of the company. This is without prejudice to any contract or obligation for repayment of the money secured by the charge; and when a charge becomes void in these circumstances, the money secured by it immediately becomes payable.

[*CA 2006, s 859H; SI 2013 No 600, Schedule 1*]

40.3 Charges existing on property acquired

Charges created before 6 April 2013

Where a company registered in England and Wales or in Northern Ireland acquires property which is subject to a charge which would, if it had been created by the company after the acquisition of the property, require registration under the provisions in **40.2** to **40.10**, the company must deliver

- particulars of the charge, and
- a certified copy of the instrument (if any) by which the charge was created or evidenced

to the Registrar of Companies for registration before the end of the period allowed for registration, ie

- 21 days beginning with the day after the day on which the acquisition is completed; or
- if the property is situated and the charge was created outside the UK (see **40.6**), 21 days beginning with the day after the day on which the instrument by which the charge is created or evidenced (or a copy of it) could, in due course of post (and if despatched with due diligence) have been received in the UK.

The prescribed particulars for these purposes are

- the date of the creation of the charge;
- a description of the instrument (if any) creating or evidencing the charge;
- the amount secured by the charge;
- the name and address of the person entitled to the charge;
- short particulars of the property charged; and
- the date of the acquisition of the property which is subject to the charge.

If default is made in complying with these provisions, an offence is committed by the company and every officer of the company in default. A person guilty of such an offence is liable (i) on conviction on indictment, to a fine; or (ii) on summary conviction, to a fine not exceeding the statutory maximum. See **29.1 Offences and Legal Proceedings** for the statutory maximum.

[*CA 2006, ss 862, 870(2); SI 2008 No 2996, Reg 4*].

Charges created on or after 6 April 2013

Where a company acquires property which is subject to a charge which would have been capable of being registered under **40.2A** if it had been created by the company after the acquisition of the property or undertaking, the company or any person interested in the charge must deliver a *section 859D* statement of particulars (see **40.2A**) to the Registrar of Companies for registration together with, where the charge is created or evidenced by an instrument, a certified copy of the instrument.

[*CA 2006, s 859C; SI 2013 No 600, Schedule 1*]

40.4 Special rules about debentures

Debentures created before 6 April 2013

Where a company registered in England and Wales or in Northern Ireland creates a series of debentures containing, or giving by reference to another instrument, a charge which benefits the debenture holders of the series *passu*, it is sufficient for the purposes of **40.2** if the following are delivered to the Registrar of Companies within 21 days after the day on which the deed containing the charge is executed. If there is no such deed, they must be delivered within 21 days after the day on which the first debenture of the series is executed.

(a) Particulars of

- the total amount secured by the whole series;
- the dates of the resolutions authorising the issue of the series and the date of the covering deed (if any) by which the security is created or defined;
- a general description of the property charged; and
- the names of the trustees for the debenture-holders (if any).

(b) The deed containing the charge or, if there is no deed, one of the debentures of the series.

Particulars must also be sent for registration of

(i) the date and amount of each issue of debentures of a series; and

(ii) where appropriate, the amount or rate per cent of any commission, discount or allowance which has been paid or made directly or indirectly by a company to a person in consideration of his

- subscribing or agreeing to subscribe (whether absolutely or conditionally) for debentures of the company; or
- procuring or agreeing to procure subscriptions (whether absolute or conditional) for such debentures.

The deposit of debentures as security for a debt of the company is not to be treated as the issue of debentures at a discount for these purposes.

But failure to register particulars under (i) or (ii) above does not affect the validity of the debentures issued.

Registration of a series of debentures may be effected by the company or on the application of a person interested in them, in which case that person is entitled to recover from the company any fees he has properly paid to the Registrar of Companies on the registration.

If the company fails to comply with these provisions then, unless the registration of the series of debentures has been effected by another person, an offence is committed by the company and every officer of the company who is in default. A person guilty of such an offence is liable (i) on conviction on indictment, to a fine; or (ii) on summary conviction, to a fine not exceeding the statutory maximum. See **29.1 Offences and Legal Proceedings** for the statutory maximum.

[*CA 2006, ss 863, 864, 870(3)*].

Debentures created on or after 6 April 2013

Where a company creates a series of debentures containing, or giving by reference to another instrument, a charge which benefits the debenture holders of the series *pari passu*, the company must (or a person interested in such a charge must) deliver a "*section 859D* statement of particulars" and, where the charge is created or evidenced by an instrument, a certified copy of the instrument, to the Registrar of Companies for registration before the "period allowed for delivery". The period allowed for delivery is, if there is a deed containing the charge, 21 days beginning with the day after the date on which the deed is executed or, if there is no deed containing the charge, 21 days beginning with the day after the date on which the first debenture of the series is executed unless a court order allowing an extended period is made under *CA 2006, s 859F(3)* (see **40.2A** for details of when the court may make such an order). If such an order is made, a copy of the order must be delivered to the Registrar of Companies with the *section 859D* statement of particulars. If these provisions are complied with the Registrar of Companies must register the charge. Where the charge is not created or evidenced by an instrument, the Registrar of Companies is required to register it only if a certified copy of one of the debentures in the series is delivered to the Registrar of Companies with the *section 859D* statement of particulars.

Where the charge is contained in a series of debentures the *section 859D* statement of particulars must, in addition to the matters set out in **40.2A**, also contain the following:

- either the name of each of the trustees for the debenture holders or where there are more than four such persons, the names of any four persons listed in the charge instrument as trustees for the debenture holders ,and a statement that there are other such persons;
- the dates of the resolutions authorising the issue of the series;
- the date of the covering instrument (if any) by which the series is created or defined.

For the purposes of *CA 2006, s 859B*, a statement of particulars is taken to be a *section 859D* statement of particulars even if it does not contain the names of the debenture holders.

In *CA 2006, s 859B*, "deed" means a deed governed by the law of England and Wales and Northern Ireland or an instrument governed by a law other than the law of England or Wales or Northern Ireland which requires delivery under that law in order to take effect.

[*CA 2006, s 859B; SI 2013 No 600, Schedule 1*]

40.5 Endorsement of certificate on debentures

Charges created before 6 April 2013

A company must cause a copy of every certificate of registration given by the Registrar of Companies under **40.8** to be endorsed on every debenture or certificate of debenture stock which is issued by the company, and the payment of which is secured by the charge so registered. But this does not require a company to cause a certificate of registration of any charge so given to be endorsed on any debenture or certificate of debenture stock issued by the company before the charge was created.

If a person knowingly and wilfully authorises or permits the delivery of a debenture or certificate of debenture stock in default of this requirement, he commits of an offence. A person guilty of such an offence is liable, on summary conviction, to a fine not exceeding level 3 on the standard scale (see **29.1** OFFENCES AND LEGAL PROCEEDINGS).

[*CA 2006, s 865*].

There are no corresponding provisions for charges created on or after 6 April 2013.

40.6 Charges in other jurisdictions

Charges created before 6 April 2013

Charges created outside the UK comprising property situated outside the UK. The delivery to the Registrar of Companies of a verified copy of the instrument by which the charge is created or evidenced has the same effect for the purposes of **40.2** to **40.10** as the delivery of the instrument itself. [*CA 2006, s 866(1)*].

Charges created in the UK comprising property situated outside the UK. The instrument creating or purporting to create the charge may be sent for registration under **40.2** even though further proceedings may be necessary to make the charge valid or effectual according to the law of the country where the property is situated.

[*CA 2006, s 866(2)*].

Charges created in, or over property in, another UK jurisdiction. Where

- a charge comprises property situated in a part of the UK other than the part in which the company is registered, and
- registration in that other part is necessary to make the charge valid or effectual under the law of that part of the UK,

the delivery to the Registrar of Companies of a verified copy of the instrument by which the charge is created or evidenced, together with a certificate stating that the charge was presented for registration in that other part of the UK on the date on which it was so presented, has the same effect for the purposes of **40.2** to **40.10** as the delivery of the instrument itself.

[*CA 2006, s 867*].

There are no corresponding provisions for charges created on or after 6 April 2013.

40.7 Northern Ireland: registration of certain charges affecting land

Charges created before 6 April 2013

Where a charge imposed by an order under *Judgments Enforcement (Northern Ireland) Order 1981, Art 46* or notice of such a charge is registered in the Land Registry against registered land or any estate in registered land of a company, the Registrar of Titles must, as soon as may be, cause two copies of that order or notice to be delivered to the Registrar of Companies.

Where a charge imposed by an order under *Judgments Enforcement (Northern Ireland) Order 1981, Art 46* is registered in the Registry of Deeds against any unregistered land or estate in land of a company, the Registrar of Deeds must, as soon as may be, cause two copies of the order to be delivered to the Registrar of Companies.

40.7 Registration of Charges

On delivery of copies under either of the above provisions, the Registrar of Companies must

- register one of them in accordance with **40.8**; and
- not later than seven days from that date of delivery, cause the other copy, together with a certificate of registration, to be sent to the company against which judgment was given.

Where a charge to which the above provisions applies is vacated, the Registrar of Titles or, as the case may be, the Registrar of Deeds must cause a certified copy of the certificate of satisfaction lodged under *Judgments Enforcement (Northern Ireland) Order 1981, Art 132(1)* to be delivered to the Registrar of Companies for entry of a memorandum of satisfaction in accordance with **40.8**.

[*CA 2006, s 868*].

There are no corresponding provisions for charges created on or after 6 April 2013.

40.8 Register of charges to be kept by the Registrar of Companies

Charges created before 6 April 2013

For every company, the Registrar of Companies must keep, and make available for inspection by any person, a register of all the charges requiring registration under the provisions in **40.2** to **40.10**. The register must show

- in the case of a charge to the benefit of which the holders of a series of debentures are entitled, the particulars specified in **40.4**(*a*);
- in the case of a charge imposed by the Enforcement of Judgments Office under *Judgments Enforcement (Northern Ireland) 1981, Art 46*, the date on which the charge became effective; and
- in the case of any other charge
  (i) the date of creation (in the case of a charge created by the company) or the date of acquisition of the property (in the case of a charge which was existing on property acquired by the company);
  (ii) the amount secured by the charge;
  (iii) short particulars of the property charged; and
  (iv) the persons entitled to the charge.

The Registrar of Companies must give a signed or authenticated certificate of registration of any charge so registered, stating the amount secured by the charge. Such a certificate is conclusive evidence that the registration requirements have been complied with. See *Exeter Trust Ltd v Screenways Ltd* [1991] BCLC 888, [1991] BCC 477, CA.

[*CA 2006, s 869*].

Charges created on or after 6 April 2013

For every company, the Registrar of Companies must allocate to the charge a unique reference code and place a note in the register recording that reference code and include in the register any documents delivered under *CA 2006, s 859A(3)* (certified copy of an instrument where the charge is created or evidenced by an instrument), *s 859A(5)* (a court order made under *s 859F(3)* extending the period for delivering a charge), *s 859B(3)* (certified copy of an instrument where the charge is created or evidenced by an instrument), *s 859B(4)* (certified copy of one of the debentures in the series), *s 859B(7)* (a court order made under *s 859F(3)* extending the period for delivering a charge) or *s 859C(3)* (certified copy of an instrument where the charge is created or evidenced by an instrument).

The Registrar of Companies must give a signed or authenticated certificate of registration of the charge to the person who delivered the *section 859* statement of particulars to that Registrar. The certificate must state the registered name and number of the company in respect of which the charge was registered and the unique reference code allocated to the charge. In the case of registration under *s 859A* or *859B* the certificate is conclusive evidence that the documents required by the section concerned were delivered to the Registrar of Companies before the end of the relevant period allowed for delivery.

The relevant period allowed for delivery is the period allowed for delivery under the section in question (see **40.2A** and **40.4A**) or if a court order under *CA 2006, s 859F(3)* has been made, the period allowed by the order.

Where a company is acting as trustee of property or undertaking which is the subject of a charge delivered for registration, the company or any person interested in the charge may deliver to the Registrar of Companies a statement to that effect. A statement which is delivered after the delivery for registration of the charge must include the registered name and number of the company and the unique reference code allocated to the charge.

[*CA 2006, s 859L, s 859J; SI 2013 No 600, Schedule 1*]

***Entries of satisfaction and release.* Charges created before, on or after 6 April 2013**

If a statement is delivered to the Registrar of Companies with respect to a registered charge to the effect that:

- the debt for which the charge was given has been paid or satisfied in whole or in part, or
- all or part of the property or undertaking charged has been released from the charge or has ceased to form part of the company's property or undertaking (and where the statement relates to part only of the property or undertaking charged, the statement must include a short description of that part).

and also the following particulars with respect to the registered charge are delivered to the Registrar of Companies

- the name and address of the person delivering the statement and an indication of their interest in the charge;
- the registered name and number of the company that created the charge or acquired the property or undertaking subject to the charge;
- in respect of a charge created before 6 April 2013 the date of creation of the charge, a description of the instrument (if any) by which the charge is created or evidenced, short particulars of the property or undertaking charged; and
- in respect of a charge created on or after 6 April 2013, the unique reference code allocated to the charge.

the Registrar of Companies must include in the register a statement of satisfaction in whole or in part or a statement of the fact that all or part of the property or undertaking has been released from the charge or has ceased to form part of the company's property or undertaking (as the case may be).

[*CA 2006, s 859L; SI 2013 No 600, reg 3* and *Schedule 1*]

40.9 Rectification of register of charges by court

Charges created before 6 April 2013

Where there has been

- a failure to register a charge within the time required, or
- an omission or mis-statement of any particulars with respect to any such charge or in a memorandum of satisfaction.

the court may, on the application of the company or a person interested, order the period allowed for registration to be extended or, as the case may be, the omission or mis-statement to be rectified where it is satisfied that

- the failure or omission
  - (i) was accidental or due to inadvertence or to some other sufficient cause; or
  - (ii) is not of a nature to prejudice the position of creditors or shareholders of the company; or
- it is just and equitable to grant relief on other grounds.

[*CA 2006, s 873*].

Charges created on or after 6 April 2013

Where there has been an omission or mis-statement in any statement or notice delivered to the Registrar in accordance with *CA 2006, Chapter 1, Part 25* and the court is satisfied that:

- the omission or mis-statement
  - (i) was accidental or due to inadvertence or to some other sufficient cause; or
  - (ii) is not of a nature to prejudice the position of creditors or shareholders of the company; or
- that on other grounds it is just and equitable to grant relief,

the court may, on the application of the company or a person interested, and on such terms and conditions as seem to the court just and expedient, order that the omission or mis-statement be rectified.

A copy of the court order must be sent by the applicant to the Registrar of Companies for registration.

[*CA 2006, s 859M; SI 2013 No 600, Schedule 1*]

If the court is satisfied that a copy of an instrument or debenture delivered to the Registrar of Companies contains material which could have been omitted (see **40.2A**) or the wrong instrument or debenture was delivered to the Registrar of Companies or the copy was defective, the court may, on the application of the company or a person interested, and on such terms as seem to the court just and expedient, order that the copy of the instrument or debenture be removed from the register and replaced. A copy of the court order must be sent by the applicant to the Registrar of Companies for registration.

[*CA 2006, s 859N; SI 2013 No 600, Schedule 1*]

40.9A Notification of addition to or amendment of charge: charges created before, on or after 6 April 2013

Where after the creation of a charge, the charge is amended by adding or amending a term:

(a) that prohibits or restricts the creation of any fixed security or any other charge having priority over or ranking *pari passu* with the charge; or

(b) varies or otherwise regulates the order of the ranking of the charge in relation to any fixed security or any other charge,

either the company that created the charge or the person taking the benefit of the charge (or another charge referred to in (b)) may deliver the following to the Registrar of Companies for registration.

- a certified copy of the instrument effecting the amendment, variation or regulation and
- a statement of the following particulars
  - (i) the registered name and number of the company
  - (ii) in the case of a charge created before 6 April 2013 the date of creation of the charge, a description of the instrument (if any) by which the charge was created or evidenced and short particulars of the property or undertaking charged as set out when the charge was registered and in the case of a charge created on or s 6 April 2013, (where allocated) the unique reference code allocated to the charge.

"Fixed security" has the meaning given in *CA 1985, s 486(1)* and the provisions above do not affect the continued application of *CA 1985, s 466*.

[*CA 2006, s 859O; SI 2013 No 600, Schedule 1*]

40.10 Registration of enforcement of security

Charges created before, on or after 6 April 2013

If a person

- obtains an order for the appointment of a receiver or manager of a company's property or undertaking, or
- appoints such a person under powers contained in an instrument.

he must, within seven days of the order or appointment, give notice of the fact to the Registrar of Companies and also if the order was obtained, or the appointment made, by virtue of a registered charge held by the person give the Registrar of Companies a notice containing the following:

- in the case of a charge created before 6 April 2013, the date of the creation of the charge, a description of the instrument (if any) creating or evidencing the charge and short particulars of the property or undertaking charged;
- in the case of a charge created on or after 6 April 2013, the unique reference code allocated to the charge.

The Registrar of Companies must then enter that fact on the register of charges.

Where a receiver or manager of a company's property appointed under powers contained in an instrument ceases so to act the person must on so ceasing, give notice of that fact to the Registrar of Companies and give the Registrar of Companies a notice containing:

- in the case of a charge created before 6 April 2013, the date of the creation of the charge, a description of the instrument (if any) creating or evidencing the charge and short particulars of thee property or undertaking charged;
- in the case of a charge created on or after 6 April 2013, the unique reference code allocated to the charge.

The Registrar of Companies must then enter that fact on the register of charges.

A person who defaults in complying with the above provisions commits an offence. A person guilty of such an offence is liable, on summary conviction, to a fine not exceeding level 3 on the standard scale and, for continued contravention, a daily default fine not exceeding one-tenth of level 3 on the standard scale. See **29.1** OFFENCES AND LEGAL PROCEEDINGS for the standard scale.

CA 2006, s 859K applies only to a receiver or manager appointed by a court in England and Wales or Northern Ireland or under an instrument governed by the law of England and Wales or Northern Ireland but does not apply to a receiver appointed under *Chapter 2* of *Part 3* of the *Insolvency Act 1986* (Receivers (Scotland)).

[*CA 2006, s 859K; SI 2013 No 600, reg 3* and *Schedule 1*].

40.11 SCOTLAND

The provisions set out in **40.11–40.17** apply only to charges created before 6 April 2013. See above for provisions which apply to charges created on or after that date.

Charges created by a company. An incorporated company registered in Scotland that creates a charge listed below must deliver the prescribed particulars of the charge, together with a copy certified as a correct copy of the instrument (if any) by which the charge is created or evidenced, to the Registrar of Companies for registration before the end of the period allowed for registration, ie

- 21 days beginning with the day after the 'date of creation of the charge'; or
- if the charge is created outside the UK (see **40.15**), 21 days beginning with the day after the day on which a copy of the instrument by which the charge is created or evidenced could, in due course of post (and if despatched with due diligence) have been received in the UK.

The prescribed particulars for these purposes are

- the date of the creation of the charge;

- a description of the instrument (if any) creating or evidencing the charge;
- the amount secured by the charge;
- the name and address of the person entitled to the charge;
- short particulars of the property charged; and
- in the case of a floating charge, a statement as to any provisions of the charge and of any instrument relating to it which prohibit or restrict or regulate the power of the company to grant further securities ranking in priority to, or *pari passu* with, the floating charge, or which vary or otherwise regulate the order of ranking of the floating charge in relation to subsisting securities.

Alternatively, registration of a charge may be effected on the application of a person interested in it, in which case that person is entitled to recover from the company any fees he has properly paid to the Registrar of Companies on the registration.

If the company fails to comply with these provisions then, unless the registration of charge has been effected by another person, an offence is committed by the company and every officer of the company who is in default. A person guilty of such an offence is liable (i) on conviction on indictment, to a fine; or (ii) on summary conviction, to a fine not exceeding the statutory maximum. See **29.1 Offences and Legal Proceedings** for the statutory maximum.

The charges to which these provisions apply are as follows.

(a) A charge on land (wherever situated) or any interest in such land This does not include a charge for any rent or other periodical sum payable in respect of the land but does include a charge created by a heritable security within the meaning of *Conveyancing and Feudal Reform (Scotland) Act 1970, s 9(8)*. The holding of debentures entitling the holder to a charge on land is not for these purposes deemed to be an interest in land.

(b) A security over incorporeal moveable property comprising

 (i) goodwill;

 (ii) a patent or a licence under a patent;

 (iii) a trade mark;

 (iv) a copyright or a licence under a copyright;

 (v) a registered design or a licence in respect of such a design;

 (vi) a design right or a licence under a design right;

 (vii) book debts (whether book debts of the company or assigned to it);

 (viii) uncalled share capital of the company or calls made but not paid.

(c) A security over a ship or aircraft or any share in a ship.

(d) A floating charge.

For the purposes of (*b*)(vii) above, the deposit by way of security of a negotiable instrument given to secure the payment of book debts is not to be treated as a charge on those book debts.

The '*date of creation of the charge*' is

- in the case of a floating charge, the date when the instrument creating it was executed by the company; and

- in any other case, the date when the right of the person entitled to the benefit of the charge was constituted as a real right.

[*CA 2006, ss 878, 879, 886(1); SI 2008 No 2996, Reg 3*].

Consequence of failure to register such a charge. If a company creates a charge within the above provisions, the charge is void (so far as any security on the company's property or any part of it is conferred by the charge) against a liquidator, administrator or creditor of the company unless it is registered as required above. This is without prejudice to any contract or obligation for repayment of the money secured by the charge; and when a charge becomes void in these circumstances, the money secured by it immediately becomes payable. [*CA 2006, s 889*].

The charge is void even if the liquidator or creditor has notice of the unregistered charge (*Monolithic Building Co, Re, Tacon v Monolithic Building Co* [1915] 1 Ch 643, 84 LJ Ch 441, CA).

40.12 Charges existing on property acquired

Where a company registered in Scotland acquires property which is subject to a charge which would, if it had been created by the company after the acquisition of the property, have been required to be registered under the provisions in **40.11** to **40.17**, the company must deliver

- the prescribed particulars of the charge, and
- a copy (certified to be a correct copy) of the instrument (if any) by which the charge was created or is evidenced

to the Registrar of Companies for registration before the end of the period allowed for registration, ie

- 21 days beginning with the day after the day on which the transaction is settled; or
- if the property is situated and the charge was created outside the UK (see **40.15**), 21 days beginning with the day after the day on which a copy of the instrument by which the charge is created or evidenced could, in due course of post (and if despatched with due diligence) have been received in the UK.

The prescribed particulars for these purposes are

- the date of the creation of the charge;
- a description of the instrument (if any) creating or evidencing the charge;
- the amount secured by the charge;
- the name and address of the person entitled to the charge;
- short particulars of the property charged; and
- the date of the acquisition of the property which is subject to the charge.

If default is made in complying with these provisions, an offence is committed by the company and every officer of the company in default. A person guilty of such an offence is liable (i) on conviction on indictment, to a fine; or (ii) on summary conviction, to a fine not exceeding the statutory maximum. See **29.1** Offences and Legal Proceedings for the statutory maximum.

[*CA 2006, s 880, 888(2); SI 2008 No 2996, Reg 4*].

40.13 Charges by way of *ex facie* absolute disposition, etc

For the avoidance of doubt, in the case of a charge created by way of

- an *ex facie* absolute disposition or assignation qualified by a back letter or other agreement, or
- a standard security qualified by an agreement

compliance with **40.11** does not of itself render the charge unavailable as security for indebtedness incurred after the date of compliance.

Where the amount secured by a charge so created is purported to be increased by a further back letter or agreement, a further charge is held to have been created by the *ex facie* absolute disposition or assignation or (as the case may be) by the standard security, as qualified by the further back letter or agreement. In that case, the provisions in **40.11** to **40.17** apply to the further charge as if

- references to the charge were references to the further charge; and
- references to the date of creation of the charge were references to the date on which the further back letter or agreement was executed.

[*CA 2006, s 881*].

40.14 Special rules about debentures

Where a company registered in Scotland creates a series of debentures containing, or giving by reference to any other instrument, any charge to the benefit of which the debenture holders of that series are entitled *pari passu*, it is sufficient for the purposes of **40.11** if the following are delivered to the Registrar of Companies within 21 days after the day on which the deed containing the charge is executed. If there is no such deed, they must be delivered within 21 days after the day on which the first debenture of the series is executed.

(a) Particulars of

- the total amount secured by the whole series;
- the dates of the resolutions authorising the issue of the series and the date of the covering deed (if any) by which the security is created or defined;
- a general description of the property charged;
- the names of the trustees for the debenture-holders (if any); and
- in the case of a floating charge, a statement of any provision of the charge and of any instrument relating to it which *either* prohibit, restrict or regulate the company's power to grant further securities ranking in priority to, or *pari passu* with, the floating charge *or* otherwise regulate the order of ranking of the floating charge in relation to subsisting securities.

(b) A copy of the deed containing the charge or, if there is no deed, one of the debentures of the series.

Particulars must also be sent for registration of

(i) where more than one issue is made of debentures in a series, the date and amount of each issue of debentures of the series; and

(ii) where appropriate, the amount or rate per cent of any commission, discount or allowance which has been paid or made directly or indirectly by a company to a person in consideration of his

- subscribing or agreeing to subscribe (whether absolutely or conditionally) for debentures of the company; or
- procuring or agreeing to procure subscriptions (whether absolute or conditional) for such debentures.

(iii) The deposit of debentures as security for a debt of the company is not to be treated as the issue of debentures at a discount for these purposes.

But failure to register particulars under (i) or (ii) above does not affect the validity of the debentures issued.

Registration of a series of debentures may be effected by the company or on the application of a person interested in them, in which case that person is entitled to recover from the company any fees he has properly paid to the Registrar of Companies on the registration.

If the company fails to comply with these provisions then, unless the registration of series of debentures has been effected by another person, an offence is committed by the company and every officer of the company who is in default. A person guilty of such an offence is liable (i) on conviction on indictment, to a fine; or (ii) on summary conviction, to a fine not exceeding the statutory maximum. See **29.1 OFFENCES AND LEGAL PROCEEDINGS** for the statutory maximum.

[*CA 2006, ss 882, 883, 886(3)*].

40.15 Charges on property outside the UK

Charges created in the UK but comprising property outside the UK. The copy of the instrument creating or purporting to create the charge may be sent for registration under **40.10** even if further proceedings may be necessary to make the charge valid or effectual according to the law of the country where the property is situated.

[*CA 2006, s 884*].

40.16 Register of charges to be kept by the Registrar of Companies

For every company, the Registrar of Companies must keep, and make available for inspection by any person, a register of all charges requiring registration. The register must show

- in the case of a charge to the benefit of which the holders of a series of debentures are entitled; the particulars specified in **40.14**(*a*); and
- in the case of any other charge

  (i) the date of creation (if created by the company) or the date of acquisition of the property (if the charge was existing on property acquired by the company);

  (ii) the amount secured by the charge;

  (iii) short particulars of the property charged;

  (iv) the persons entitled to the charge; and

(v) in the case of a floating charge, a statement of any of the provisions of the charge and of any instrument relating to it which *either* prohibit, restrict or regulate the company's power to grant further securities ranking in priority to, or *pari passu* with, the floating charge *or* regulate the order of ranking of the floating charge in relation to subsisting securities.

The Registrar of Companies must give a signed or authenticated certificate of registration of any charge so registered, stating the name of the company, the person first-named in the charge among those entitled to the benefit of the charge (or, in the case of a series of debentures, the name of the holder of the first such debenture issued) and the amount secured by the charge. Such a certificate is conclusive evidence that the registration requirements have been complied with.

[*CA 2006, s 885*].

Entries of satisfaction and relief. If a statement is delivered to the Registrar of Companies verifying with respect to a registered charge that

- the debt for which the charge was given has been paid or satisfied in whole or in part, or
- part of the property charged has been released from the charge or has ceased to form part of the company's property

the Registrar of Companies may enter on the register a memorandum of satisfaction (in whole or in part) regarding that fact. If the charge is a floating charge, the statement must be accompanied by either

- a statement by the creditor entitled to the benefit of the charge (or a person authorised by him) verifying that the statement is correct; or
- a direction obtained from the court, on the ground that such a statement could not be readily obtained, dispensing with the need for that statement.

Where the Registrar of Companies enters a memorandum of satisfaction in whole, he must, if required, supply a copy of it to the company.

Nothing in any of the above provisions requires the company to submit particulars with respect to an entry in the register of a memorandum of satisfaction where, having created a floating charge over all or any part of its property, it disposes of part of the property subject to the floating charge.

[*CA 2006, s 887*].

40.17 Rectification of register of charges by court

Where there has been

- a failure to register a charge within the time required, or
- an omission or mis-statement of any particulars with respect to any such charge or in a memorandum of satisfaction,

the court may, on the application of the company or a person interested, order the period allowed for registration to be extended or, as the case may be, the omission or mis-statement to be rectified where it is satisfied that

- the failure or omission

(i) was accidental or due to inadvertence or to some other sufficient cause, or

(ii) is not of a nature to prejudice the position of creditors or shareholders of the company; or

- it is just and equitable to grant relief on other grounds.

[*CA 2006, s 888*].

40.18 REGISTRATION IN SPECIAL REGISTER

Charges created before 6 April 2013

The Secretary of State may provide, by order, that the Registrar of Companies need not register a charge of a specified description under the provisions in **40.2** to **40.17**, but that the charge is instead registered in a special register. Any charge that is properly registered in the special register is to be treated as if it had been registered (and certified by the Registrar of Companies as registered) in accordance with those provisions. The person responsible for maintaining the special register and the Registrar of Companies must have information-sharing arrangements in place which must ensure that persons inspecting the register are made aware of the existence of charges in the special register and are able to obtain information from the special register about any such charge. [*CA 2006, s 893; SI 2013 No 600, Schedule 2, para 3*].

There are no corresponding provisions for charges created on or after 6 April 2013.

40.19 COMPANIES' RECORDS AND REGISTERS

See **36** (**Records**) and **38.11** (**Register of charges**) for details of copies which must be kept for inspection.

41 Re-Registration

41.1 **Introduction**
41.2 **A private company becoming a public company**
41.3 Share capital requirements
41.4 Net assets requirements
41.5 Recent allotment of shares for non-cash consideration
41.6 Application and accompanying documents
41.7 Issue of certificate of incorporation on re-registration
41.8 **A public company becoming a private company**
41.9 Application to court to cancel resolution
41.10 Application and accompanying documents
41.11 Issue of certificate of incorporation on re-registration
41.12 **A private limited company becoming unlimited**
41.13 Application and accompanying documents
41.14 Issue of certificate of incorporation on re-registration
41.15 **An unlimited private company becoming a private limited company**
41.16 Application and accompanying documents
41.17 Issue of certificate of incorporation on re-registration
41.18 Statement of capital required where company already has share capital
41.19 **A public company becoming private and unlimited**
41.20 Application and accompanying documents
41.21 Issue of certificate of incorporation on re-registration
41.22 **Old public company re-registering as a public company**
41.23 **Old public company becoming a private company**

Cross-references. See **30.2** Overseas Companies for registration of overseas companies.

41.1 INTRODUCTION

A company may alter its status by re-registration. The following possibilities are allowed for under *CA 2006*.

- A private company becoming a public company (see **41.2** to **41.7**).
- A public company becoming a private company (see **41.8** to **41.11**).
- A private limited company becoming unlimited (see **41.12** to **41.14**).
- An unlimited private company becoming a limited (see **41.15** to **41.18**).
- A public company becoming a private and unlimited (see **41.19** to **41.21**).

[*CA 2006, s 89*].

41.2 A PRIVATE COMPANY BECOMING A PUBLIC COMPANY

A private company (whether limited or unlimited) may be re-registered as a public company limited by shares if the following conditions are met.

- A special/written resolution that it should be so re-registered is passed.

- The company has a share capital and the requirements in **41.3** are met as regards its share capital.
- The requirements of **41.4** are met as regards its net assets.
- If **41.5** applies (recent allotment of shares for non-cash consideration), the requirements of that paragraph are met.
- The company has not previously been re-registered as unlimited.
- An application for re-registration is delivered to the Registrar of Companies, together with the other documents required and a statement of compliance (see **41.6**).
- The company makes such changes in its name and in its articles as are necessary in connection with its becoming a public company.
- If the company is unlimited, it makes such changes in its articles as are necessary in connection with its becoming a company limited by shares.

[*CA 2006, s 90*].

41.3 Share capital requirements

The following requirements must be met at the time the special resolution is passed that the company should be re-registered as a public company.

(a) The nominal value of the company's allotted share capital must be not less than the authorised minimum. See **33.3 Public and Listed Companies**.

(b) Each of the company's allotted shares must be paid up at least as to one-quarter of the nominal value of that share and the whole of any premium on it.

(c) If any shares in the company or any premium on them have been fully or partly paid up by an undertaking given by any person that he or another should do work or perform services (whether for the company or any other person), the undertaking must have been performed or otherwise discharged.

(d) If shares have been allotted as fully or partly paid up as to their nominal value or any premium on them otherwise than in cash, and the consideration for the allotment consists of or includes an undertaking to the company (other than one to which (*c*) above applies), then either

  (i) the undertaking must have been performed or otherwise discharged; or

  (ii) there must be a contract between the company and some person pursuant to which the undertaking is to be performed within five years from the time the special resolution is passed.

Disregarded shares. For the purpose of determining whether the requirements in (*b*), (*c*) and (*d*) are met, the following may be disregarded.

(i) Shares allotted before

  - 22 June 1982 in the case of a company then registered in Great Britain; or
  - 31 December 1984 in the case of a company then registered in Northern Ireland.

But no more than one-tenth of the nominal value of the company's allotted share capital (excluding shares disregarded under (ii) below) is to be disregarded under this provision.

(ii) Shares allotted in pursuance of an employees' share scheme by reason of which the company would, but for this provision, be precluded under (*b*) above (but not otherwise) from being re-registered as a public company.

Any shares so disregarded are treated as not forming part of the allotted share capital for the purposes of (*a*) above.

Proposed reduction in share capital. A company must not be re-registered as a public company if it appears to the Registrar of Companies that

- the company has resolved to reduce its share capital;
- the reduction
  - (i) is made under *CA 2006, s 626* (reduction of capital in connection with redenomination of share capital, see **47.50** SHARES);
  - (ii) is supported by a solvency statement in accordance with *CA 2006, s 643* (see **47.53** SHARES); or
  - (iii) has been confirmed by an order of the court under *CA 2006, s 648* (see **47.55** SHARES); and
- the effect of the reduction is, or will be, that the nominal value of the company's allotted share capital is below the authorised minimum.

[*CA 2006, s 91*].

41.4 Net assets requirements

A company applying to re-register as a public company must obtain the following.

(a) A balance sheet prepared as at a date not more than seven months before the date on which the application is delivered to the Registrar of Companies.

(b) An 'unqualified report' by the company's auditor on that balance sheet.

An '*unqualified report*' means

(i) if the balance sheet was prepared for a financial year of the company, a report stating without material qualification the auditor's opinion that the balance sheet has been properly prepared in accordance with the requirements of *CA 2006*; or

(ii) if the balance sheet was not prepared for a financial year of the company, a report stating without material qualification the auditor's opinion that the balance sheet has been properly prepared in accordance with the provisions of *CA 2006* which would have applied if it had been prepared for a financial year of the company.

A qualification is 'material' unless the auditor states in his report that the matter giving rise to the qualification is not material for these purposes.

(c) A written statement by the company's auditor that, in his opinion, at the balance sheet date the amount of the company's 'net assets' was not less than the aggregate of its called-up share capital and 'undistributable reserves'. See **22.5** DISTRIBUTIONS for the meaning of '*net assets*' and **22.1** DISTRIBUTIONS for the meaning of '*undistributable reserves*'.

41.4 Re-Registration

Between the balance sheet date and the date on which the application for re-registration is delivered to the Registrar of Companies, there must be no change in the company's financial position that results in the amount of its net assets becoming less than the aggregate of its called-up share capital and undistributable reserves.

[*CA 2006, s 92*].

41.5 Recent allotment of shares for non-cash consideration

Where the company has, between the date as at which the balance sheet required under **41.4** is prepared and the passing of the special resolution, allotted shares as fully or partly paid up (as to their nominal value or any premium on them) otherwise than in cash, the Registrar of Companies cannot entertain an application by the company for re-registration as a public company unless *one* of the following conditions is satisfied.

(1) The requirements of *CA 2006, s 593(1)(a)* and *(b)* have been have been complied with (independent valuation of non-cash consideration; valuer's report to company not more than six months before allotment, see **47.32**(*a*)(*b*) **Shares**).

(2) The allotment is in connection with a share exchange, ie

- the shares are allotted in connection with an 'arrangement' under which the whole or part of the consideration for the shares allotted is provided by
  - (i) the transfer to the company allotting the shares of shares (or shares of a particular class) in another company; or
  - (ii) the cancellation of shares (or shares of a particular class) in another company; and
- the allotment is open to all the holders of the shares of the other company in question (or, where the arrangement applies only to shares of a particular class, to all the holders of the company's shares of that class) to take part in the arrangement in connection with which the shares are allotted.

In determining whether a person is a holder of shares for these purposes, there must be disregarded

- shares held by, or by a nominee of, the company allotting the shares; and
- shares held by, or by a nominee of
  - (i) the holding company of the company allotting the shares;
  - (ii) a subsidiary of the company allotting the shares; or
  - (iii) a subsidiary of the holding company of the company allotting the shares.

In deciding whether an allotment is in connection with a share exchange, it is immaterial whether or not the arrangement in connection with which the shares are allotted involves the issue to the company allotting the shares of shares (or shares of a particular class) in the other company.

'*Arrangement*' means any agreement, scheme or arrangement, including an arrangement sanctioned in accordance with *CA 2006, Pt 26* (company compromise with creditors and members, see **35 Reconstructions and Mergers**) or *IA 1986, s 110* or *Insolvency (Northern Ireland) Order 1989 (SI 1989 No 2405), Art 96* (liquidator in winding up accepting shares as consideration for sale of company's property).

(3) The allotment is in connection with a proposed merger with another company, ie where one of the companies concerned proposes to acquire all the assets and liabilities of the other in exchange for the issue of its shares or other securities to shareholders of the other (whether or not accompanied by a cash payment).

[*CA 2006, s 93*].

41.6 Application and accompanying documents

An application for re-registration as a public company on Form RR01 must contain/be accompanied by the following.

- A statement of the company's proposed name on re-registration.
- In the case of a company without a secretary, a statement of the company's proposed secretary. This must contain particulars that will be required to be stated in the company's register of secretaries (see **38.4 Registers**) of the person who is (or the persons who are) to be the secretary or joint secretaries of the company. The statement must also contain a consent by the person named as secretary (or each of the persons named as joint secretaries) to act in the relevant capacity. If all the partners in a firm are to be joint secretaries, consent may be given by one partner on behalf of all of them.
- A copy of the special/written resolution that the company should re-register as a public company (unless a copy has already been forwarded to the Registrar of Companies under *CA 2006, ss 29, 30*, see **14.10 Constitution – Memorandum and Articles**).
- A copy of the company's articles as proposed to be amended.
- A copy of the balance sheet and other documents referred to in **41.4**(*a*)–(*c*).
- If **41.5** applies, a copy of the valuation report (if any) under those provisions.
- A statement of compliance that the requirements as to re-registration as a public company have been complied with. The Registrar of Companies may accept this statement as sufficient evidence that the company is entitled to be re-registered as a public company.

Companies Act 2006, s 94 is amended by the *Small Business, Enterprise and Employment Act 2015 (SBEE 2015), s 98* which provides that a company's application will also have to be accompanied by a statement of the aggregate amount paid up on the shares of the company on account of their nominal value. As at May 2015 this provision is not yet in force.

[*CA 2006, ss 94, 95*].

41.7 Issue of certificate of incorporation on re-registration

If, on an application for re-registration as a public company, the Registrar of Companies is satisfied that the company is entitled to be so re-registered, the company must be re-registered accordingly. The Registrar must then issue a certificate of incorporation, altered to meet the circumstances of the case, stating that it is issued on re-registration and the date on which it is issued.

41.7 Re-Registration

On the issue of the certificate

- the company by virtue of the issue of the certificate becomes a public company;
- the changes in the company's name and articles take effect; and
- where the application contained a statement of the company's proposed secretary, that person is (or the persons named as joint secretaries are) deemed to have been appointed to that office.

The certificate is conclusive evidence that the requirements of *CA 2006* as to re-registration have been complied with.

[*CA 2006, s 96*].

41.8 A PUBLIC COMPANY BECOMING A PRIVATE COMPANY

A public company may be re-registered as a private limited company if the following conditions are met.

- A special resolution that it should be so re-registered is passed.
- Where no application under **41.9** for cancellation of the resolution has been made
  - (i) having regard to the number of members who consented to or voted in favour of the resolution, no such application may be made; or
  - (ii) the period within which such an application could be made has expired.
- Where an application under **41.9** for cancellation of the resolution has been made
  - (i) the application has been withdrawn; or
  - (ii) an order has been made confirming the resolution and a copy of that order has been delivered to the Registrar of Companies.
- An application for re-registration is delivered to the Registrar of Companies, together with the other documents required and a statement of compliance (see **41.10**).
- The company makes such changes in its name and in its articles as are necessary in connection with its becoming a private company limited by shares or, as the case may be, by guarantee.

[*CA 2006, s 97*].

41.9 Application to court to cancel resolution

Where a special resolution under **41.8** has been passed, an application may be made to the court for the cancellation of the resolution by

- the holders of not less in aggregate than 5% in nominal value of the company's issued share capital or any class of the company's issued share capital (disregarding any shares held by the company as treasury shares, see **34.14** PURCHASE OF OWN SHARES),
- if the company is not limited by shares, not less than 5% of its members, or
- not less than 50 of the company's members

but not by a person who has consented to or voted in favour of the resolution.

The application must be made within 28 days after the passing of the resolution and may be made on behalf of the persons entitled to make it by one or more of their number as they appoint for the purpose.

On making the application, the applicants, or the person making the application on their behalf, must immediately give notice to the Registrar of Companies. On being served with notice of any such application, the company must immediately give notice to the Registrar of Companies.

The court, on hearing the application, must make an order either cancelling or confirming the resolution. It may

- make that order on such terms and conditions as it thinks fit;
- adjourn the proceedings in order that an arrangement may be made to the satisfaction of the court for the purchase of the interests of dissentient members;
- provide for the purchase by the company of the shares of any of its members and for the reduction accordingly of the company's capital;
- make such alteration in the company's articles as may be required in consequence; and
- require the company *not* to make any, or any specified, amendments to its articles without the leave of the court.

Within 15 days of the making of the court's order on the application (or such longer period as the court may direct), the company must deliver to the Registrar a copy of the order.

Offences. If the company fails to

- notify the Registrar of Companies that it has been served with notice of an application, or
- send the Registrar a copy of the court order in the time allowed

an offence is committed by the company and every officer of the company who is in default. A person guilty of such an offence is liable, on summary conviction, to a fine not exceeding level 3 on the standard scale and, for continued contravention, a daily default fine not exceeding one-tenth of level 3 on the standard scale. See **29.1** Offences and Legal Proceedings for the standard scale.
[*CA 2006, ss 98, 99*].

41.10 Application and accompanying documents

An application for re-registration as a private limited company on Form RRO2 must contain/be accompanied by the following.

- A statement of the company's proposed name on re-registration.
- A copy of the resolution that the company should re-register as a private limited company (unless a copy has already been forwarded to the Registrar of Companies under *CA 2006, ss 29, 30*, see **14.10** Constitution – Memorandum and Articles).
- A copy of the company's articles as proposed to be amended.
- A statement of compliance that the requirements as to re-registration as a private limited company have been complied with. The Registrar of Companies may accept this statement as sufficient evidence that the company is entitled to be re-registered as a private limited company.

41.10 Re-Registration

[*CA 2006, s 100*].

41.11 Issue of certificate of incorporation on re-registration

If, on an application for re-registration as a private limited company, the Registrar of Companies is satisfied that the company is entitled to be so re-registered, the company must be re-registered accordingly. The Registrar must then issue a certificate of incorporation, altered to meet the circumstances of the case, stating that it is issued on re-registration and the date on which it is issued.

On the issue of the certificate

- the company by virtue of the issue of the certificate becomes a private limited company; and
- the changes in the company's name and articles take effect.

The certificate is conclusive evidence that the requirements of *CA 2006* as to re-registration have been complied with. [*CA 2006, s 101*].

41.12 A PRIVATE COMPANY BECOMING UNLIMITED

A private limited company may be re-registered as an unlimited company if the following conditions are met.

- All the members of the company have assented to its being so re-registered.
- The company has not previously been re-registered as limited.
- An application for re-registration is delivered to the Registrar of Companies, together with the other documents required and a statement of compliance (see **41.13**).
- The company makes such changes in its name and its articles
  - (i) as are necessary in connection with its becoming an unlimited company; and
  - (ii) if the company is to have a share capital, as are necessary in connection with its becoming an unlimited company having a share capital.

For the above purposes,

- a trustee in bankruptcy of a member of the company (including, in Scotland, a permanent trustee or an interim trustee on the sequestrated estate of a member of the company and a trustee under a protected trustee deed granted by a member of the company) is entitled, to the exclusion of the member, to assent to the company's becoming unlimited; and
- the personal representative of a deceased member of the company may assent on behalf of the deceased.

[*CA 2006, s 102*].

41.13 Application and accompanying documents

An application for re-registration as an unlimited company on Form RRO5 must contain/be accompanied by the following.

- A statement of the company's proposed name on re-registration.
- The form of assent to the company's being registered as an unlimited company (see *SI 2008 No 3014, Sch 3*), authenticated by or on behalf of all the members of the company.
- A copy of the company's articles as proposed to be amended.
- A statement of compliance that the requirements as to re-registration as an unlimited company have been complied with. The statement must contain a statement by the directors of the company that

  (i) the persons by whom or on whose behalf the form of assent is authenticated constitute the whole membership of the company; and

  (ii) if any of the members have not authenticated that form themselves, the directors have taken all reasonable steps to satisfy themselves that each person who authenticated it on behalf of a member was lawfully empowered to do so.

  The Registrar of Companies may accept the statement of compliance as sufficient evidence that the company is entitled to be re-registered as an unlimited company.

[*CA 2006, s 103; SI 2008 No 3014, Reg 5*].

41.14 Issue of certificate of incorporation on re-registration

If, on an application for re-registration of a private company as an unlimited company, the Registrar of Companies is satisfied that the company is entitled to be so re-registered, the company must be re-registered accordingly. The Registrar must then issue a certificate of incorporation, altered to meet the circumstances of the case, stating that it is issued on re-registration and the date on which it is issued.

On the issue of the certificate

- the company by virtue of the issue of the certificate becomes an unlimited company; and
- the changes in the company's name and articles take effect.

The certificate is conclusive evidence that the requirements of *CA 2006* as to re-registration have been complied with.

[*CA 2006, s 104*].

41.15 AN UNLIMITED PRIVATE COMPANY BECOMING A PRIVATE LIMITED COMPANY

An unlimited company may be re-registered as a private limited company if the following conditions are met.

- A special resolution that it should be so re-registered is passed. The resolution must state whether the company is to be limited by shares or by guarantee.
- The company has not previously been re-registered as unlimited.
- An application for re-registration is delivered to the Registrar of Companies, together with the other documents required and a statement of compliance (see **41.16**).

- The company makes such changes in its name and in its articles as are necessary in connection with its becoming a company limited by shares or, as the case may be, by guarantee.

[*CA 2006, s 105*].

41.16 Application and accompanying documents

An application for re-registration as a limited company on Form RRO6 must contain/be accompanied by the following.

- A statement of the company's proposed name on re-registration.
- A copy of the resolution that the company should re-register as a private limited company (unless a copy has already been forwarded to the Registrar of Companies under *CA 2006, ss 29, 30*, see **14.10 Constitution – Memorandum and Articles**).
- If the company is to be limited by guarantee, a statement of guarantee which must state that each member undertakes that, if the company is wound up while he is a member or within one year after he ceases to be a member, he will contribute to the assets of the company such amount as may be required for
  - (i) payment of the debts and liabilities of the company contracted before he ceases to be a member,
  - (ii) payment of the costs, charges and expenses of winding up, and
  - (iii) adjustment of the rights of the contributories among themselves
  - (iv) not exceeding a specified amount.
- A copy of the company's articles as proposed to be amended.
- A statement of compliance that the requirements as to re-registration as a limited company have been complied with. The Registrar of Companies may accept the statement of compliance as sufficient evidence that the company is entitled to be re-registered as a limited company.

[*CA 2006, s 106*].

41.17 Issue of certificate of incorporation on re-registration

If, on an application for re-registration of an unlimited company as a limited company, the Registrar of Companies is satisfied that the company is entitled to be so re-registered, the company must be re-registered accordingly. The Registrar must then issue a certificate of incorporation, altered to meet the circumstances of the case, stating that it is issued on re-registration and the date on which it is issued.

On the issue of the certificate

- the company by virtue of the issue of the certificate becomes a limited company; and
- the changes in the company's name and articles take effect.

The certificate is conclusive evidence that the requirements of *CA 2006* as to re-registration have been complied with.

[*CA 2006, s 107*].

41.18 Statement of capital required where company already has share capital

A company which on re-registration under **41.17** already has allotted share capital must, within 15 days after the re-registration, deliver a statement of capital to the Registrar of Companies. This does not apply if the information which would be included in the statement has already been sent to the Registrar in a statement of capital and initial shareholdings under *CA 2006, s 10* (see **12.3 Company Formation and Types of Companies**) or a statement of capital contained in an annual return under *CA 2006, s 856(2)* (see **7.2 Annual Returns**).

The statement of capital must state with respect to the company's share capital on re-registration:

(a) The total number of shares of the company.

(b) The aggregate nominal value of those shares. *Small Business, Enterprise and Employment Act 2015* (see **41.10**) introduces a requirement to also include in the statement of capital the aggregate amount (if any) unpaid on those shares (whether on account of their nominal value or by way of premium). As at May 2015 this provision is not in force.

(c) For each class of shares

  (i) particulars of any voting rights attached to the shares, including rights that arise only in certain circumstances;

  (ii) particulars of any rights attached to the shares, as respects dividends, to participate in a distribution;

  (iii) particulars of any rights attached to the shares, as respects capital, to participate in a distribution (including on a winding up);

  (iv) whether the shares are to be redeemed or are liable to be redeemed at the option of the company or the shareholder;

  (v) the total number of shares of that class; and

  (vi) the aggregate nominal value of shares of that class.

(d) The amount paid up and the amount (if any) unpaid on each share (whether on account of the nominal value of the share or by way of premium).

If default is made in complying with these provisions, an offence is committed by the company and every officer of the company who is in default. A person guilty of such an offence is liable, on summary conviction, to a fine not exceeding level 3 on the standard scale and, for continued contravention, a daily default fine not exceeding one-tenth of level 3 on the standard scale. See **29.1 Offences and Legal Proceedings** for the standard scale.

[*CA 2006, s 108; SI 2009 No 388, Art 2*].

41.19 A PUBLIC COMPANY BECOMING PRIVATE AND UNLIMITED

A public company limited by shares may be re-registered as an unlimited private company if the following conditions are met.

- All the members of the company have assented to its being so re-registered.
- The company has not previously been re-registered as limited or as unlimited.
- An application for re-registration is delivered to the Registrar of Companies, together with the other documents required and a statement of compliance (see **41.20**).

- The company makes such changes in its name and its articles as are necessary in connection with its becoming an unlimited private company.

For the above purposes,

- a trustee in bankruptcy of a member of the company (including, in Scotland, a permanent trustee or an interim trustee on the sequestrated estate of a member of the company and a trustee under a protected trustee deed granted by a member of the company) is entitled, to the exclusion of the member, to assent to the company's re-registration; and
- the personal representative of a deceased member of the company may assent on behalf of the deceased.

[*CA 2006, s 109*].

41.20 Application and accompanying documents

An application for re-registration of a public company as an unlimited private company on Form RRO7 must contain/be accompanied by the following.

- A statement of the company's proposed name on re-registration.
- The form of assent to the company's being registered as a private and unlimited company (see *SI 2008 No 3014, Sch 4*), authenticated by or on behalf of all the members of the company.
- A copy of the company's articles as proposed to be amended.
- A statement of compliance that the requirements as to re-registration as an unlimited private company have been complied with. The statement must contain a statement by the directors of the company that

  (i) the persons by whom or on whose behalf the form of assent is authenticated constitute the whole membership of the company; and

  (ii) if any of the members have not authenticated that form themselves, the directors have taken all reasonable steps to satisfy themselves that each person who authenticated it on behalf of a member was lawfully empowered to do so.

  The Registrar of Companies may accept the statement of compliance as sufficient evidence that the company is entitled to be re-registered as an unlimited private company.

[*CA 2006, s 110; SI 2008 No 3014, Reg 6*].

41.21 Issue of certificate of incorporation on re-registration

If, on an application for re-registration of a public company as an unlimited private company, the Registrar of Companies is satisfied that the company is entitled to be so re-registered, the company must be re-registered accordingly. The Registrar must then issue a certificate of incorporation, altered to meet the circumstances of the case, stating that it is issued on re-registration and the date on which it is issued.

On the issue of the certificate

- the company by virtue of the issue of the certificate becomes an unlimited private company; and

- the changes in the company's name and articles take effect.

The certificate is conclusive evidence that the requirements of *CA 2006* as to re-registration have been complied with.

[*CA 2006, s 111*].

41.22 OLD PUBLIC COMPANY RE-REGISTERING AS A PUBLIC COMPANY

The provisions in **41.2** to **41.7** also apply to an old public company (see **Appendix 1 Definitions**) but with

- references to a private company being read as references to an old public company; and
- references to a special resolution of the company being read as references to a resolution of the directors.

CA 2006, ss 29, 30 (resolutions affecting a company's constitution, see **14.10 Constitution – Memorandum and Articles**) apply to any such resolution.

[*SI 2009 No 1941, Sch 3 para 3*].

41.23 OLD PUBLIC COMPANY BECOMING A PRIVATE COMPANY

An old public company (see **Appendix 1 Definitions**) may pass a special resolution *not* to be re-registered as a public company. The provisions in **41.9** (application to the court to cancel the resolution) apply to such a resolution as they would apply to a special resolution by a public company to be re-registered as private.

The Registrar of Companies must issue the company with a certificate stating that it is a private company if

(a) a special resolution not to be re-registered as a public company has been passed and either

   (i) 28 days from the passing of the resolution elapse without an application being made under **41.9** (as applied); or

   (ii) such an application is made and proceedings are concluded on the application without the court making an order for the cancellation of the resolution; or

(b) an old public company delivers a statutory declaration by a director or secretary of the company that the company does not at the time of the declaration satisfy the conditions for the company to be re-registered as public.

For the purposes of (*a*)(ii) above, proceedings on the application are concluded

- at the expiration of the period of 15 days from the making of the court's order on the application (or such longer period as the court may direct); or
- when the company has been notified that the application has been withdrawn.

The company then becomes a private company by virtue of the issue of the certificate.

[*SI 2009 No 1941, Sch 3 paras 4, 5*].

Failure by old public company to obtain new classification. If, at any time, an old public company has not delivered to the Registrar of Companies a statutory declaration under (*b*) above, then unless at the time the company has

- applied to be re-registered as a public company (and the application has not been refused or withdrawn), or
- passed a special resolution under (*a*) above not to be re-registered as a public company (and the resolution has not been revoked and has not been cancelled by the court as above)

the company and any officer of it who is in default is guilty of an offence. A person guilty of such an offence is liable, on summary conviction, to a fine not exceeding level 3 on the standard scale and, for continued contravention, a daily default fine not exceeding one-tenth of level 3 on the standard scale. See **29.1 Offences and Legal Proceedings** for the standard scale.

[*SI 2009 No 1941, Sch 3 para 6*].

42 Resolutions and Meetings

42.1 **Resolutions: general provisions**
42.2 Ordinary resolutions
42.3 Special resolutions
42.4 Members' votes
42.5 **Written resolutions of private companies**
42.6 Eligible members and circulation date
42.7 Written resolutions proposed by directors
42.8 Written resolutions proposed by members
42.9 Agreeing to written resolutions
42.10 Sending relevant documents by electronic means
42.11 Publication on website
42.12 **Meetings and resolutions at meetings**
42.12A Electronic meetings and voting
42.13 Calling meetings
42.14 Notice of meetings
42.20 Members' statements
42.21 Procedure at meetings
42.26 Proxies
42.27 Adjourned meetings
42.28 Sending documents relating to meetings, etc in electronic form
42.29 Class meetings
42.30 **Public companies and traded companies: annual general meetings**
42.31 Circulation of members' resolutions
42.32 **Quoted companies and traded companies: additional requirements**
42.33 Website publication of poll results
42.34 Quoted companies: independent report on poll
42.38 Class meetings
42.38A **Traded companies: requirements for participating in and voting at general meetings**
42.39 **Directors' meetings**
42.40 Minutes of directors' meetings
42.41 **Records of resolutions and meetings**
42.42 Records of decisions of sole member
42.43 Inspection of records of resolutions and meetings
42.44 Resolutions and meetings of class of members
42.45 **Information as to exercise of voting rights by institutional investors**

Cross-references. See **2.9** Accounts: General for laying of accounts and reports before company in general meeting; **8.37** Audit for rights of an auditor to attend company general meetings.

42.1 RESOLUTIONS: GENERAL PROVISIONS

Extraordinary resolutions: The term "extraordinary resolution" does not appear in the *2006 Act*. Articles of association based on *Table A, 1985* may continue to refer to such resolutions (unless amended). If this is the case any reference to an extraordinary resolution in a provision of a contract or a company's memorandum or articles continues to have effect and continues to be construed in accordance with *CA 1985, s 378* as if that section had not been repealed.

[*SI 2007 No 2194, Sch 3 para 23*].

Resolutions. A resolution of the members (or of a class of members)

- of a private company must be passed

(i) as a written resolution in accordance with **42.5** to **42.11**; or

(ii) at a meeting of the members to which the provisions in **42.12** to **42.29** apply; and

- of a public company must be passed at a meeting of the members to which the provisions in **42.12** to **42.29** and, where relevant, **42.30** and **42.31** apply. If the company is also quoted, there are additional requirements in **42.32** to **42.38**.

Where a provision of *CA 2006* requires a resolution of a company (or of the members or a class of members of a company) and does not specify what kind of resolution is required, then an ordinary resolution is required unless the company's articles require a higher majority (or unanimity). [*CA 2006, s 281(1)–(3)*].

But none of the provisions in this chapter affect any enactment or rule of law as to

- things done otherwise than by passing a resolution;
- circumstances in which a resolution is or is not treated as having been passed; or
- cases in which a person is precluded from alleging that a resolution has not been duly passed.

[*CA 2006, s 281(4)*].

This preserves the common law unanimous consent rule. Unless *CA 2006* provides otherwise, a number of decided cases have held that a company is bound in a matter *intra vires* by the unanimous but informal agreement of its members. See, for example, *Re Express Engineering Works Ltd* [1920] 1 Ch 466, 89 LJ Ch 379, CA. This applies even if there is no actual meeting but only informal discussions (*Parker & Cooper Ltd v Reading* [1926] Ch 975, 96 LJ Ch 23). The agreement must, however, be unanimous; it is not enough that a majority sufficient to pass the appropriate resolution agrees to the proposal (*EBM Co Ltd v Dominion Bank* [1937] 3 All ER 555, 81 Sol Jo 814, PC). See also *Re Duomatic Ltd* [1969] 2 Ch 365, [1969] 1 All ER 161 where it was held that, where all shareholders who have a right to attend and *vote* at a general meeting of the company assent to some matter which a general meeting could carry into effect, that assent is as binding as a resolution in general meeting would be.

42.2 Ordinary resolutions

An ordinary resolution of the members (or of a class of members) of a company means a resolution that is passed by a simple majority.

- *A written resolution* is passed by a simple majority if it is passed by members representing a simple majority of the total voting rights of eligible members (see **42.6**).
- *A resolution passed at a meeting on a show of hands* is passed by a simple majority if it is passed by a simple majority of the votes cast by those entitled to vote.
- *A resolution passed at a meeting on a poll taken* is passed by a simple majority if it is passed by members representing a simple majority of the total voting rights of members who (being entitled to do so) vote

  (i) in person or by proxy, or

  (ii) (in relation to meetings notice of which is given on or after 3 August 2009) in advance (see **42.24**)

  on the resolution.

Anything that may be done by ordinary resolution may also be done by special resolution (see **42.3**). [*CA 2006, s 282*].

42.3 Special resolutions

A special resolution of the members (or of a class of members) of a company means a resolution passed by a majority of not less than 75%.

- *A written resolution* is passed by a majority of not less than 75% if it is passed by members representing not less than 75% of the total voting rights of eligible members (see **42.6**).

  Where a resolution of a private company is passed as a written resolution,

  (i) the resolution is not a special resolution unless it stated that it was proposed as a special resolution; and

  (ii) if the resolution so stated, it may only be passed as a special resolution.

- *A resolution passed at a meeting on a show of hands* is passed by a majority of not less than 75% if it is passed by not less than 75% of the votes cast by those entitled to vote.

- *A resolution passed at a meeting on a poll taken* is passed by a majority of not less than 75% if it is passed by members representing not less than 75% of the total voting rights of the members who (being entitled to do so) vote

  (i) in person or by proxy, or

  (ii) in advance (see **42.24**)

  on the resolution.

Where a resolution is passed at a meeting

(a) the resolution is not a special resolution unless the notice of the meeting included the text of the resolution and specified the intention to propose the resolution as a special resolution; and

(b) if the notice of the meeting so specified, the resolution may only be passed as a special resolution.

[*CA 2006, s 283*].

42.4 Members' votes

(1) *General rules*

The following provisions have effect subject to any provision of the company's articles.

- *On a vote on a written resolution*

  (i) in the case of a company having a share capital, every member has one vote in respect of each share or each £10 of stock held by him; and

  (ii) in any other case, every member has one vote.

- *On a vote on a resolution on a show of hands at a meeting*, every member present in person has one vote. See (2) below for proxies.

- *On a vote on a resolution on a poll taken at a meeting*

(i) in the case of a company having a share capital, every member has one vote in respect of each share or each £10 of stock held by him; and

(ii) in any other case, every member has one vote.

Nothing in the above provisions is to be read as restricting the effect of *CA 2006, s 152* (exercise of rights by nominees, see **26.5 Members**), voting by proxies (see (2) below), voting on a poll (see **42.24**(3)), votes cast in advance (see **42.24**(4)), or representation of corporations at meetings (see **42.25**).

[*CA 2006, s 284*].

(2) *Voting by proxies*

On a vote on a resolution on a show of hands at a meeting:

(a) Subject to (*b*) below, every proxy present who has been duly appointed by one or more members entitled to vote on the resolution has one vote.

(b) A proxy has one vote for and one vote against the resolution if

  (i) the proxy has been duly appointed by more than one member entitled to vote on the resolution; and

  (ii) the proxy has been instructed by one or more of those members to vote for the resolution and by one or more other of those members to vote against it.

But this has effect subject to any provision of the company's articles.

On a poll taken at a meeting of a company, all or any of the voting rights of a member may be exercised by one or more duly appointed proxies. But where a member appoints more than one proxy, this does not authorise the exercise by the proxies taken together of more extensive voting rights than could be exercised by the member in person.

[*CA 2006, s 285*].

(3) *Voting rights on a poll or written resolution*

In relation to a resolution required or authorised by an enactment, if a private company's articles provide that a member has a different number of votes in relation to a resolution when it is passed as a written resolution and when it is passed on a poll taken at a meeting

- the provision about how many votes a member has in relation to the resolution passed on a poll is void; and
- a member has the same number of votes in relation to the resolution when it is passed on a poll as the member has when it is passed as a written resolution.

[*CA 2006, s 285A*].

(4) *Votes of joint holders of shares*

Subject to any provision of the company's articles, in the case of joint holders of shares of a company, only the vote of the 'senior holder' who votes (and any proxies duly authorised by him) may be counted by the company. The '*senior holder*' for these purposes is determined by the order in which the names of the joint holders appear in the register of members. [*CA 2006, s 286*].

(5) *Provisions of articles as to determination of entitlement to vote*

Nothing in **42.1** to **42.3** or the provisions above affects

- any provision of a company's articles
  - (i) requiring an objection to a person's entitlement to vote on a resolution to be made in accordance with the articles; and
  - (ii) for the determination of any such objection to be final and conclusive; or
- the grounds on which such a determination may be questioned in legal proceedings.

[*CA 2006, s 287*].

See also *Wall v London and Northern Assets Corpn* [1899] 1 Ch 550, 68 LJ Ch 248 and *Wall v Exchange Investment Corpn* [1926] Ch 143, 95 LJ Ch 132, CA.

(6) *Exercise of members' rights*

A member may nominate another person or persons to enjoy rights of the member in relation to the company. See **26.3 MEMBERS**.

(7) *Standard articles*

Where the company has adopted standard articles, see:

- *Table A, 1985, Regs 54–59*,
- *Model Articles, Art 43* (private companies),
- *Model Articles, Art 35* (public companies),

set out in **APPENDIX 4 STANDARD ARTICLES OF ASSOCIATION**.

(8) *Bankruptcy*

Unless there is any contrary provision in the articles, a bankrupt still remains a member of the company as long as his name appears on the register and his trustee in bankruptcy has not secured registration in his own name (*Morgan v Gray* [1953] Ch 83, [1953] 1 All ER 213).

42.5 WRITTEN RESOLUTIONS OF PRIVATE COMPANIES

General provisions. In the *Companies Acts* a '*written resolution*' means a resolution of a private company proposed and passed in accordance with the provisions in this paragraph and **42.6** to **42.11**. It does not mean that there is a requirement for 'writing' in the sense of a hard copy.

With certain exceptions, a private company may pass any resolution using the written resolution procedure. Any provision of the articles of a private company is void in so far as it would have the effect that a resolution that is required by or otherwise provided for in an enactment could not be proposed and passed as a written resolution. The exceptions are a resolution under

- *CA 2006, s 168* (removing a director before the expiration of his period of office, see **18.9 DIRECTORS**); and
- *CA 2006, s 510* (removing an auditor before the expiration of his term of office, see **8.16 AUDIT**).

42.5 Resolutions and Meetings

A resolution may be proposed as a written resolution by the directors (see **42.7**) or by the members (see **42.8**).

From 1 October 2007 there has been no requirement to pass written resolutions unanimously. As a result

(a) references in enactments passed or made before 1 October 2007 to

(i) a resolution of a company in general meeting, or

(ii) a resolution of a meeting of a class of members of the company,

have effect as if they included references to a written resolution of the members, or of a class of members, of a private company (as appropriate); and

(b) a written resolution of a private company has effect as if passed (as the case may be)

(i) by the company in general meeting, or

(ii) by a meeting of a class of members of the company,

and references in enactments passed or made before 1 October 2007 to a meeting at which a resolution is passed or to members voting in favour of a resolution are construed accordingly.

[*CA 2006, ss 288, 300; SI 2007 No 2194, Art 1, Sch 1 para 13; SI 2007 No 3495, Art 10*].

42.6 Eligible members and circulation date

The '*eligible members*' in relation to a resolution proposed as a written resolution of a private company are the members who would have been entitled to vote on the resolution on the 'circulation date' of the resolution.

If the persons entitled to vote on a written resolution change during the course of the day that is the circulation date, the eligible members are the persons entitled to vote on the resolution at the time that the first copy of the resolution is sent or submitted to a member for his agreement.

[*CA 2006, s 289*].

The '*circulation date*' of a written resolution is the date on which copies of it are sent or submitted to members (or if copies are sent or submitted to members on different days, to the first of those days).

[*CA 2006, s 290*].

42.7 Written resolutions proposed by directors

Where a resolution is proposed as a written resolution by the directors of the company, the company must send or submit a copy of the resolution to every eligible member by

(a) sending copies at the same time (so far as reasonably practicable) to all eligible members in hard copy form, in electronic form or by means of a website;

(b) if it is possible to do so without undue delay, submitting the same copy to each eligible member in turn (or different copies to each of a number of eligible members in turn); or

(c) a combination of (*a*) and (*b*).

The copy of the resolution must be accompanied by a statement informing the member how to signify agreement to the resolution and as to the date by which the resolution must be passed if it is not to lapse. See **42.9**.

In the event of default in complying with these provisions, an offence is committed by every officer of the company who is in default. A person guilty of such an offence is liable (i) on conviction on indictment, to a fine; and (ii) on summary conviction, to a fine not exceeding the statutory maximum. See **29.1 Offences and Legal Proceedings** for the statutory maximum. The validity of the resolution, if passed, is not affected by a failure to comply with these provisions. [*CA 2006, s 291*].

42.8 Written resolutions proposed by members

The members of a private company may require the company to circulate a resolution that may properly be moved, and is proposed to be moved, as a written resolution. Any resolution may properly be moved as a written resolution unless

- it would, if passed, be ineffective (whether by reason of inconsistency with any enactment or the company's constitution or otherwise);
- it is defamatory of any person; or
- it is frivolous or vexatious.

Where the members require the company to circulate a resolution, they may also require the company to circulate with it a statement (of not more than 1,000 words) on the subject matter of the resolution.

The company is required to circulate the resolution, and any accompanying statement, once it has received requests from members representing not less than 5% (or such lower percentage as is specified for this purpose in the company's articles) of the total voting rights of all members entitled to vote on the resolution.

A request may be in hard copy form or in electronic form. It must identify the resolution and any accompanying statement and must be authenticated by the person or persons making it.

[*CA 2006, s 292*].

Circulation of resolution. Where a company is required under the above provisions to circulate a written resolution, it must send or submit to every eligible member a copy of the resolution and a copy of any accompanying statement (but see below for expenses of circulation and application to the court). The company must do so by

(a) sending copies at the same time (so far as reasonably practicable) to all eligible members in hard copy form, in electronic form or by means of a website;

(b) if it is possible to do so without undue delay, submitting the same copy to each eligible member in turn (or different copies to each of a number of eligible members in turn); or

(c) a combination of (*a*) and (*b*).

The company must send or submit the copies (or, if copies are sent or submitted to members on different days, the first of those copies) not more than 21 days after it becomes subject to the requirement to circulate the resolution. The copy of the resolution must be accompanied by guidance as to how to signify agreement to the resolution and the date by which the resolution must be passed if it is not to lapse. See **42.9**.

In the event of default in complying with these provisions, an offence is committed by every officer of the company who is in default. A person guilty of such an offence is liable (i) on conviction on indictment, to a fine; and (ii) on summary conviction, to a fine not exceeding the statutory maximum. See **29.1 Offences and Legal Proceedings** for the statutory maximum. The validity of the resolution, if passed, is not affected by a failure to comply with these provisions.

[*CA 2006, s 293*].

Expenses of circulation. The expenses of the company in circulating a written resolution of members must be paid by the members who requested it, unless the company resolves otherwise. Unless the company has previously resolved to pay the expenses, it is not bound to circulate the resolution unless a sum reasonably sufficient to meet its expenses is deposited with, or tendered to, it.

[*CA 2006, s 294*].

Application to court not to circulate members' statement. A company is not required to circulate a members' statement if, on an application by the company or another person who claims to be aggrieved, the court is satisfied that the rights conferred by the above provisions are being abused. The court may order the members who requested the circulation of the statement to pay the whole or part of the company's costs (in Scotland, expenses) on such an application, even if they are not parties to the application.

[*CA 2006, s 295*].

42.9 Agreeing to written resolutions

A written resolution is passed when the required majority of eligible members have signified their agreement to it. A member signifies his agreement to a proposed written resolution when the company receives from him (or from someone acting on his behalf) an authenticated document

- identifying the resolution to which it relates; and
- indicating his agreement to the resolution.

The document must be sent to the company in hard copy form or in electronic form.

A member's agreement to a written resolution, once signified, may not be revoked.

[*CA 2006, s 296*].

Period for agreeing to written resolution. A proposed written resolution lapses if it is not passed before the end of

- the period specified for this purpose in the company's articles; or
- if none is specified, the period of 28 days beginning with the circulation date.

The agreement of a member to a written resolution is ineffective if signified after the expiry of that period.

[*CA 2006, s 297*].

42.10 Sending relevant documents by electronic means

Where a company has given an 'electronic address' in any document containing or accompanying a proposed written resolution, it is deemed to have agreed that any document or information relating to that resolution may be sent by electronic means to that address (subject to any conditions or limitations specified in the document).

'*Electronic address*' means any address or number used for the purposes of sending or receiving documents or information by electronic means.

[*CA 2006, s 298*].

42.11 Publication on website

Where a company sends a written resolution, or a statement relating to a written resolution, to a person by means of a website, the resolution or statement is not validly sent for these purposes unless the resolution is available on the website throughout the period beginning with the circulation date and ending on the date on which the resolution lapses under **42.10**. [*CA 2006, s 299*].

42.12 MEETINGS AND RESOLUTIONS AT MEETINGS

A resolution of the members of a company is validly passed at a general meeting if

- notice of the meeting and of the resolution is given, and
- the meeting is held and conducted,

in accordance with the provisions in **42.13** to **42.29** (and, where relevant, **42.30** and **42.31**) and the company's articles.

[*CA 2006, s 301*].

Amendments to resolutions. Where standard articles have been adopted, see

- *Model Articles, Art 47* (private companies),
- *Model Articles, Art 40* (public companies),

set out in **Appendix 4 Standard Articles of Association**. Both these provisions allow for the amendment of both ordinary and special resolutions but only if certain conditions are met.

Electronic meetings and voting

42.12A

Nothing in *CA 2006, Part 13* (Resolutions and Meetings) precludes the holding and conducting of a meeting in such a way that persons who are not present together at the same place may, by electronic means, attend and speak and vote at it.

In the case of a traded company (see **Appendix 1 Definitions**) the use of electronic means for the purpose of enabling members to participate in a general meeting may be made subject only to such requirements and restrictions as are

- necessary to ensure the identification of those taking part and the security of the electronic communication; and
- proportionate to the achievement of those objectives,

but this does not affect any power of a company to require reasonable evidence of the entitlement of any person who is not a member to participate in the meeting.

[*CA 2006, s 360A; SI 2009 No 1632, Reg 8*].

42.13 Calling meetings

(1) *Directors' power to call general meetings*

The directors of a company may call a general meeting of the company. [*CA 2006, s 302*].

Where standard articles have been adopted, if there are not sufficient directors in the UK to call a meeting, see

- *Table A, 1985, Reg 37*

set out in **Appendix 4 Standard Articles of Association.**

(2) *Meetings called by members*

Directors' duty to call meetings required by members. The members of a company may require the directors to call a general meeting of the company. The directors must do so once the company has received requests to do so from

- members representing at least 5% of such of the paid-up capital of the company as carries the right of voting at general meetings of the company (excluding any paid-up capital held as treasury shares); or
- in the case of a company not having a share capital, members who represent at least 5% of the total voting rights of all the members having a right to vote at general meetings.

A request must state the general nature of the business to be dealt with at the meeting and may include the text of a resolution that may properly be moved, and is intended to be moved, at the meeting. A resolution may properly be moved at a meeting unless

- it would, if passed, be ineffective (whether by reason of inconsistency with any enactment or the company's constitution or otherwise);
- it is defamatory of any person; or
- it is frivolous or vexatious.

A request may be in hard copy form or in electronic form and must be authenticated by the person or persons making it.

[*CA 2006, s 303*].

Directors' duty to call meetings required by members. Where the directors are required to call a general meeting of the company, they must call it within 21 days from the date on which they become subject to the requirement. It must be held on a date not more than 28 days after the date of the notice convening the meeting.

If the members' requests for the meeting identify a resolution to be moved at the meeting, the notice of the meeting must include notice of the resolution. If the resolution is to be proposed as a special resolution, the directors are treated as not having duly called the meeting if they do not give the required notice of the resolution in accordance with **42.3**.

[*CA 2006, s 304*].

Power of members to call meeting at company's expense. If the directors are required as above to call a meeting and do not do so, the members who requested the meeting, or any of them representing more than one half of the total voting rights of all of them, may themselves call a general meeting. Where the requests received by the company included the text of a resolution intended to be moved at the meeting, the notice of the meeting must include notice of the resolution.

The meeting must be called for a date not more than three months after the date on which the directors become subject to the requirement to call a meeting. It must be called in the same manner, as nearly as possible, as that in which meetings are required to be called by directors of the company.

Any reasonable expenses incurred by the members requesting the meeting because of the failure of the directors must be reimbursed by the company. Any sum so reimbursed must then be retained by the company out of any sums due or becoming due from the company by way of fees or other remuneration in respect of the services of such of the directors as were in default.

[*CA 2006, s 305*].

(3) *Resigning auditor*

In certain circumstances, a resigning auditor may request the directors to call a general meeting. See **8.20** Audit.

(4) *Power of court to order meeting*

If, for any reason, it is impracticable to

- call a meeting of a company in any manner in which meetings of that company may be called, or
- to conduct the meeting in the manner prescribed by the company's articles or *CA 2006*,

the court may (either of its own motion, on the application of a director or on the application of a member of the company who would be entitled to vote at the meeting) order a meeting to be called, held and conducted in any manner the court thinks fit.

Where such an order is made, the court may give such ancillary or consequential directions as it thinks expedient (including that one member of the company present at the meeting be deemed to constitute a quorum).

A meeting called, held and conducted in accordance with an order under this provision is deemed, for all purposes, to be a meeting of the company duly called, held and conducted.

[*CA 2006, s 306; SI 2008 No 2860, Art 6*].

The power of the court, on application, to call a meeting cannot be used by one group of shareholders to defeat the class rights of another group. See *BML Group Ltd v Harman* (1994) Times, 8 April, CA.

For a case where the court exercised its discretion under these provisions, see *Re Sticky Fingers Restaurant Ltd* [1992] BCLC 84, [1991] BCC 754 where the only two directors and members of the company were in dispute and one was refusing to attend meetings so that the company was effectively deadlocked. The court stipulated that any director appointed at the meeting would not be allowed to act unless he gave specified undertakings designed to protect the existing directors (eg not to vote for their dismissal).

42.14 Notice of meetings

(1) Companies other than traded companies and opted in companies (see (*b*) below)

The following provisions apply to all general meetings where the company is

(a) not a traded company (see Appendix 1 Definitions); or

(b) a traded company that is an opted-in company (see **48.9 Takeovers**) where

(i) the meeting is held to decide whether to take any action that might result in the frustration of a takeover bid for the company; or

(ii) the meeting is held by virtue of *CA 2006, s 969* (power of offeror to require general meeting to be held).

Subject to below,

- a general meeting of a private company (other than an adjourned meeting) must be called by notice of at least 14 days; and
- a general meeting of a public company (other than an adjourned meeting) must be called by notice of

  (i) in the case of an annual general meeting (see **42.30**), at least 21 days, and

  (ii) in any other case, at least 14 days.

In calculating the periods of notice referred to above, the day on which notice is given and the day of the meeting are excluded.

The above requirements for notice are subject to the following.

- A company's articles may require a longer period of notice.
- A general meeting may be called by shorter notice if agreed to by the members. Apart from the AGM of a public company (for which see **42.30**) the shorter notice must be agreed to by a majority in number of the members having a right to attend and vote at the meeting, being a majority who

  (i) together hold not less than the 'requisite percentage' in nominal value of the shares giving a right to attend and vote at the meeting (excluding any shares in the company held as treasury shares); or

  (ii) in the case of a company not having a share capital, together represent not less than the requisite percentage of the total voting rights at that meeting of all the members.

The '*requisite percentage*' is, in the case of a private company, 90% (or such higher percentage not exceeding 95% as may be specified in the company's articles) and, in the case of a public company, 95%.

Elective resolutions of private companies

Before 1 October 2007, private companies (only) could pass an elective resolution authorising shorter notice of meeting than required by *CA 1985 s 369(4)*. If, immediately before 1 October 2007, there was such an elective resolution in force under *CA 1985, s 369(4)* which

- specified 90% as the requisite percentage (or under which resolution the company in general meeting had determined that the percentage should be 90%), or

- specified a percentage greater than 90% but less than 95% as the requisite percentage (or under which resolution the company in general meeting had determined a percentage greater than 90% but less than 95%),

any provision in the company's articles adopted before 1 October 2007 specifying a different percentage is to be disregarded.

[*CA 2006, ss 307, 360; SI 2007 No 2194, Sch 3 paras 26, 26A; SI 2008 No 674, Sch 3 para 2*].

(2) ***Traded companies*** *(other than an opted in company see (1)(b) above)*

Unless the company's articles require a longer period of notice, a general meeting of a traded company (see APPENDIX 1 DEFINITIONS) must be called by notice of

- in the case where conditions A to C below are met, at least 14 days; and
- in any other case, at least 21 days.

In calculating the periods of notice referred to above, the day on which notice is given and the day of the meeting are excluded.

Condition A is that the general meeting is not an AGM.

Condition B is that the company offers the facility for members to vote by electronic means accessible to all members who hold shares that carry rights to vote at general meetings. This condition is met if there is a facility, offered by the company and accessible to all such members, to appoint a proxy by means of a website.

Condition C is that a special resolution reducing the period of notice to not less than 14 days has been passed at the immediately preceding AGM or at a general meeting held since that AGM. In the case of a company which has not yet held an AGM, the condition is that a special resolution reducing the period of notice to not less than 14 days has been passed at a general meeting.

Where a general meeting is adjourned, the adjourned meeting may be called by shorter notice than required above except that, in the case of an adjournment for lack of a quorum, this applies only if

- no business is to be dealt with at the adjourned meeting the general nature of which was not stated in the notice of the original meeting; and
- the adjourned meeting is to be held at least 10 days after the original meeting.

[*CA 2006, ss 307A, 360*].

42.15 *Ways of giving notice*

Notice of a general meeting of a company must be given

- in hard copy form;
- in electronic form;
- by means of a website (see below); or
- by a combination of the above.

[*CA 2006, s 308*].

Publication of notice of meeting on website. Notice of a meeting is not validly given by a company by means of a website unless

- when the company notifies a member of the presence of the notice on the website, the notification
  - (i) states that it concerns a notice of a company meeting;
  - (ii) specifies the place, date and time of the meeting; and
  - (iii) in the case of a public company, states whether the meeting will be an annual general meeting; and
- the notice is available on the website throughout the period beginning with the date of that notification and ending with the conclusion of the meeting.

[*CA 2006, s 309*].

Where standard articles have been adopted, for general provisions relating to the giving of notice, see *Table A, 1985, Regs 111–116*, set out in APPENDIX 4 STANDARD ARTICLES OF ASSOCIATION.

42.16 *Persons entitled to receive notice*

Subject to any enactment and the provisions of the company's articles, notice of a general meeting of a company must be sent to

(a) every member (including any person who is entitled to a share in consequence of the death or bankruptcy of a member, if the company has been notified of their entitlement); and

(b) every director.

The reference in (*a*) above to the bankruptcy of a member includes the sequestration of the estate of a member and a member's estate being the subject of a protected trust deed (within the meaning of the *Bankruptcy (Scotland) Act 1985*).

[*CA 2006, s 310*].

42.17 *Contents of notice*

(1) *General requirements*

Notice of a general meeting of a company is given must state:

- The time and date of the meeting.
- The place of the meeting.
- The general nature of the business to be dealt with at the meeting. In relation to a company other than a traded company (in relation to meetings of which notice is given before 3 August 2009, in relation to any company) this has effect subject to any provision of the company's articles.

[*CA 2006, s 311(1)(2)*].

Where standard articles have been adopted, for general provisions relating to the giving of notice, see *Table A, 1985, Reg 38*, set out in APPENDIX 4 STANDARD ARTICLES OF ASSOCIATION.

See *Tiessen v Henderson* [1899] 1 Ch 861. The time and place of the meeting are at the discretion of the directors but this must be exercised in good faith. See *Cannon v Trask* (1875) LR 20 Eq 669 where the company was restrained from bringing forward the date of a meeting before share transfers were registered to persons opposed to the board.

(2) *Traded companies: additional disclosures in notice*

Notice of a general meeting of a 'traded company' (see **Appendix 1 Definitions**) must also include:

- A statement giving the address of the website on which the information required under (3) below is published.
- A statement
  - (i) that the right to vote at the meeting is determined by reference to the register of members; and
  - (ii) of the time when that right is determined in accordance with *CA 2006, s 360B(2)* (traded companies: share dealings before general meetings, see **42.38A**).
- A statement of the procedures with which members must comply in order to be able to attend and vote at the meeting (including the date by which they must comply).
- A statement giving details of any forms to be used for the appointment of a proxy.
- Where the company offers the facility for members to vote in advance (see **42.24**) or by electronic means (see **42.12A**), a statement of the procedure for doing so (including the date by which it must be done and details of any forms to be used).
- A statement of the right of members to ask questions in accordance with *CA 2006, s 319A* (traded companies: questions at meetings, see **42.23A**).

[*CA 2006, s 311(3)*].

(3) *Traded companies: publication of information in advance of general meeting*

A traded company (see **Appendix 1 Definitions**) must publish ensure that the information in (*a*)–(*d*) below relating to a general meeting is available on a website that identifies the company and is maintained by or on behalf of the company.

(a) The matters set out in the notice of the meeting (see (1) and (2) above).

(b) The total numbers of

- (i) shares in the company, and
- (ii) shares of each class,

in respect of which members are entitled to exercise voting rights at the meeting.

(c) The totals of the voting rights that members are entitled to exercise at the meeting in respect of the shares of each class.

(d) Members' statements, members' resolutions and members' matters of business received by the company after the first date on which notice of the meeting is given.

Access to the information on the website, and the ability to obtain a hard copy of the information from the website, must not be conditional on payment of a fee or otherwise restricted.

The information

- must be made available

(i) in the case of (*a*)–(*c*) above, on or before the first date on which notice of the meeting is given; and

(ii) in the case of (*d*) above, as soon as reasonably practicable; and

- must be kept available throughout the period of two years beginning with the date on which it is first made available on a website under these provisions, although a failure to do so is disregarded if

(i) the information is made available on the website for part of that period; and

(ii) the failure is wholly attributable to circumstances that it would not be reasonable to have expected the company to prevent or avoid.

The amounts in (*b*) and (*c*) above must be ascertained at the latest practicable time before the first date on which notice of the meeting is given.

If these provisions are not complied with in respect of any meeting, an offence is committed by every officer of the company who is in default. A person guilty of such an offence is liable, on summary conviction, to a fine not exceeding level 3 on the standard scale. See **29.1 Offences and Legal Proceedings** for the standard scale. Failure to comply does not, however, affect the validity of the meeting or of anything done at the meeting.

[*CA 2006, s 311A*].

42.18 *Resolutions requiring special notice*

Where by any provision of the *Companies Acts* special notice is required of a resolution, the resolution is not effective unless notice of the intention to move it has been given to the company at least 28 days before the meeting at which it is moved.

The company must, where practicable, give its members notice of any such resolution in the same manner and at the same time as it gives notice of the meeting. But where that is not practicable, the company must give its members notice at least 14 days before the meeting

- by advertisement in a newspaper having an appropriate circulation; or
- in any other manner allowed by the company's articles.

If, after notice of the intention to move such a resolution has been given to the company, a meeting is called for a date 28 days or less after the notice has been given, the notice is deemed to have been properly given, though not given within the time required.

[*CA 2006, s 312*].

In calculating the periods of notice referred to above, the day on which notice is given and the day of the meeting are excluded.

[*CA 2006, s 360*].

42.19 *Accidental failure to give notice of resolution or meeting*

Where a company gives notice of a general meeting or a resolution intended to be moved at a general meeting, any accidental failure to give notice to one or more persons is disregarded for the purpose of determining whether notice of the meeting or resolution (as the case may be) is duly given.

The above has effect subject to any provision of the companies articles, except in relation to notice given under

- *CA 2006, s 304* (directors' duty to call meetings required by members, see **42.13**);
- *CA 2006, s 305* (notice of meetings called by members following failure of directors, see **42.13**); and
- *CA 2006, s 339* (notice of resolutions at AGMs proposed by members, see **42.31**).

[*CA 2006, s 313; SI 2007 No 2194, Sch 3 para 28*].

Where standard articles have been adopted, for general provisions relating to the giving of notice, see *Table A, 1985, Reg 39*, set out in **Appendix 4 Standard Articles of Association**.

See also *Re West Canadian Collieries Ltd* [1962] Ch 370, [1962] 1 All ER 26. Failure to give notice under the mistaken belief that a person is not a shareholder for the purpose of a particular meeting is not an accidental omission (*Musselwhite v C H Musselwhite & Son Ltd* [1962] Ch 964, [1962] 1 All ER 201).

42.20 Members' statements

Members' power to require circulation of statement. The members of a company may require the company to circulate, to members of the company entitled to receive notice of a general meeting, a statement of not more than 1,000 words with respect to a matter referred to in a proposed resolution to be dealt with at that meeting or other business to be dealt with at that meeting.

A company is required to circulate a statement once it has received requests to do so from

- members representing at least 5% of the total voting rights of all the members who have a right to vote on the matter in question (excluding any voting rights attached to any shares in the company held as treasury shares); or
- at least 100 members who have a right to vote on the matter in question and hold shares in the company on which there has been paid up an average sum, per member, of at least £100.

A request may be in hard copy form or in electronic form. It must identify the statement to be circulated, be authenticated by the person or persons making it, and be received by the company at least one week (excluding the day the request is received and the day of the meeting) before the meeting to which it relates.

[*CA 2006, ss 314, 360*].

Company's duty to circulate members' statement. A company that is required under the above provisions to circulate a statement must send a copy of it to each member of the company entitled to receive notice of the meeting in the same manner as the notice of the meeting and at the same time as, or as soon as reasonably practicable after, it gives notice of the meeting (but see below for expenses of circulation and application to the court).

In the event of default in complying with this requirement, an offence is committed by every officer of the company who is in default. A person guilty of such an offence is liable (i) on conviction on indictment, to a fine; and (ii) on summary conviction, to a fine not exceeding the statutory maximum. See **29.1 Offences and Legal Proceedings** for the statutory maximum.

[*CA 2006, s 315*].

Expenses of circulating members' statement. The expenses of the company in circulating a members' statement need not be paid by the members who requested the circulation of the statement if

- the meeting to which the requests relate is an annual general meeting of a public company; and
- requests sufficient to require the company to circulate the statement are received before the end of the financial year preceding the meeting.

Apart from this exception, the expenses of the company must be paid by the members who requested the circulation of the statement unless the company resolves otherwise. Unless the company has previously resolved to pay the expenses, it is not bound to circulate the resolution unless a sum reasonably sufficient to meet its expenses is deposited with it, or tendered to it, not later than one week before the meeting. In calculating the period of one week, the day the sum is deposited or tendered and the day of the meeting are excluded.

[*CA 2006, ss 316, 360*].

Application to court not to circulate members' statement. A company is not required to circulate a members' statement if, on an application by the company or another person who claims to be aggrieved, the court is satisfied that the rights conferred by the above provisions are being abused. The court may order the members who requested the circulation of the statement to pay the whole or part of the company's costs (in Scotland, expenses) on such an application, even if they are not parties to the application.

[*CA 2006, s 317*].

42.21 Procedure at meetings

Where standard articles have been adopted, see

(a) for attendance and speaking at general meetings

- *Model Articles, Art 37* (private companies)
- *Model Articles, Art 29* (public companies)

(b) for no voting of shares on which money is owed to the company

- *Model Articles, Art 41* (public companies)

set out in **Appendix 4 Standard Articles of Association**.

42.22 *Quorum*

In the case of a company limited by shares or guarantee and having only one member, one 'qualifying person' present at a meeting is a quorum. In any other case, subject to the provisions of the company's articles, two qualifying persons present at a meeting are a quorum, unless each is a qualifying person only because he is

- authorised under **42.25** to act as the representative of a corporation in relation to the meeting, and they are representatives of the same corporation; or
- he is appointed as proxy of a member in relation to the meeting, and they are proxies of the same member.

A '*qualifying person*' means

- an individual who is a member of the company;
- a person authorised under **42.25** to act as the representative of a corporation in relation to the meeting; or
- a person appointed as proxy of a member in relation to the meeting.

[*CA 2006, s 318*].

Where standard articles have been adopted, see

- *Table A, 1985, Regs 40, 41*
- *Model Articles, Art 38* (private companies)
- *Model Articles, Art 38* (public companies)

set out in **Appendix 4 Standard Articles of Association.**

42.23 *Chairman and directors*

Subject to any provision of the company's articles that states who may or may not be chairman, a member may be elected to be the chairman of a general meeting by a resolution of the company passed at the meeting.

[*CA 2006, s 319*].

Where standard articles have been adopted, see

- *Table A 1985, Regs 42, 43*
- *Model Articles, Art 39* (private companies),
- *Model Articles, Art 31* (public companies),

set out in **Appendix 4 Standard Articles of Association.**

Directors. A director, even if not a member, will normally be entitled to attend and speak at any general meeting and any separate meeting of the holders of any class of shares. Where standard articles have been adopted, see

- *Table A 1985, Reg 44*
- *Model Articles, Art 40* (private companies),
- *Model Articles, Art 32* (public companies),

set out in **Appendix 4 Standard Articles of Association.**

Traded companies: questions at meetings

42.23A

At a general meeting of a traded company (see **Appendix 1 Definitions**), the company must answer any question relating to the business being dealt with at the meeting put by a member attending the meeting unless

- to do so would

  (i) interfere unduly with the preparation for the meeting; or

  (ii) involve the disclosure of confidential information;

- the answer has already been given on a website in the form of an answer to a question; or
- it is undesirable in the interests of the company or the good order of the meeting that the question be answered.

[*CA 2006, s 319A*].

42.24 *Voting procedure*

(1) *Declaration by chairman on a show of hands*

On a vote on a resolution at a meeting on a show of hands, a declaration by the chairman that the resolution has or has not been passed, or passed with a particular majority, is conclusive evidence of that fact without proof of the number or proportion of the votes recorded in favour of or against the resolution. An entry in respect of such a declaration in minutes of the meeting recorded in accordance with **42.41** is also conclusive evidence of that fact without such proof.

These provisions do not have effect if a poll is demanded in respect of the resolution (and the demand is not subsequently withdrawn).

[*CA 2006, s 320*].

Where standard articles have been adopted, see

- *Table A 1985, Regs 46, 47,*
- *Model Articles, Art 42* (private companies),
- *Model Articles, Art 34* (public companies),

set out in **Appendix 4 Standard Articles of Association**.

Where no poll is demanded, a resolution is passed on a show of hands even if, on a poll, a different result would have been obtained (*Re Horbury Bridge Coal, Iron and Waggon Co* (1879) 11 Ch D 109, CA).

(2) *Demanding a poll*

Where standard articles have been adopted, see

- *Table A 1985, Regs 46, 48, 51,*
- *Model Articles, Art 44* (private companies),
- *Model Articles, Arts 36, 37* (public companies),

set out in **Appendix 4 Standard Articles of Association**.

A provision of a company's articles is void in so far as it would have the effect of

- excluding the right to demand a poll at a general meeting on any question other than
  - (i) the election of the chairman of the meeting; or
  - (ii) the adjournment of the meeting; or
- making ineffective a demand for a poll on any such question which is made by
  - (i) not less than five members having the right to vote on the resolution;

(ii) a member or members representing not less than 10% of the total voting rights of all the members having the right to vote on the resolution (excluding any voting rights attached to any shares in the company held as treasury shares); or

(iii) a member or members holding shares in the company conferring a right to vote on the resolution, being shares on which an aggregate sum has been paid up equal to not less than 10% of the total sum paid up on all the shares conferring that right (excluding shares in the company conferring a right to vote on the resolution which are held as treasury shares).

[*CA 2006, s 321*].

For these purposes, where a member has appointed a proxy to vote on his behalf, the proxy is treated as the member.

[*CA 2006, s 329(2)*].

(3) *Voting on a poll*

Where standard articles have been adopted, for general provisions relating to the giving of notice, see *Table A, 1985, Regs 49–52*, set out in **Appendix 4 Standard Articles of Association**.

On a poll taken at a general meeting of a company, a member entitled to more than one vote need not, if he votes, use all his votes or cast all the votes he uses in the same way.

[*CA 2006, s 322*].

(4) *Votes cast in advance*

A company's articles may contain provision to the effect that on a vote on a resolution on a poll taken at a meeting, the votes may include votes cast in advance.

(a) Any provision of a company's articles is void in so far as it would have the effect of requiring any document casting a vote in advance to be received by the company or another person earlier than

- in the case of a poll taken more than 48 hours after it was demanded, 24 hours before the time appointed for the taking of the poll; and
- in the case of any other poll, 48 hours before the time for holding the meeting or adjourned meeting.

In calculating these periods, no account is to be taken of any part of a day that is not a working day.

(b) In the case of a traded company (see **Appendix 1 Definitions**), any provision in the articles in relation to advance voting at a general meeting may be made subject only to such requirements and restrictions as are

- necessary to ensure the identification of the person voting; and
- proportionate to the achievement of that objective.

But nothing in this provision affects any power of a company to require reasonable evidence of the entitlement of any person who is not a member to vote.

[*CA 2006, s 322A*].

(5) *Casting vote of chairman*

Where, immediately before 1 October 2007, the articles of a company provided that, in the event of equality of votes on an ordinary resolution (whether on a show of hands or on a poll), the chairman should have a casting vote in addition to any other vote that he might have

- if that provision has not been removed by a subsequent alteration of the articles, it continues to have effect notwithstanding *CA 2006, s 282* (see **42.2**); and
- if that provision has been removed by a subsequent alteration of the articles, the company may at any time restore the provision which has effect notwithstanding *CA 2006, s 282*.

In relation to meetings of which notice is given on or after 3 August 2009, nothing in the above applies in relation to a traded company (see **Appendix 1 Definitions**) (in other words traded companies cannot in any circumstances use the casting vote of a chairman on an ordinary resolution).

[*SI 2007 No 2194, Sch 3 para 23A; SI 2007 No 3495, Sch 5 para 2(5); SI 2009 No 1632, Reg 22*].

42.25 *Representation of corporations at meetings*

If a corporation (whether or not a company within the meaning of *CA 2006*) is a member of a company, it may, by resolution of its directors or other governing body, authorise a person or persons to act as its representative or representatives at any meeting of the company. Where it does so, the position is as follows.

(a) Subject to (*b*) below, a person authorised by a corporation is entitled to exercise (on behalf of the corporation) the same powers as the corporation could exercise if it were an individual member of the company.

(b) Where a company authorises more than one person,

(i) on a vote on a resolution on a show of hands at a meeting of the company, each authorised person has the same voting rights as the corporation would be entitled to; and

(ii) where (i) above does not apply and more than one authorised person purport to exercise a power under (*a*) above in respect of the same shares

- if they purport to exercise the power in the same way as each other, the power is treated as exercised in that way; and
- if they do not purport to exercise the power in the same way as each other, the power is treated as not exercised.

In relation to meeting of which notice is given before 3 August 2009, where the corporation authorises more than one person and more than one of them purport to exercise such power

- if they purport to exercise the power in the same way, the power is treated as exercised in that way; and
- if they do not purport to exercise the power in the same way, the power is treated as not exercised.

[*CA 2006, s 323*].

42.26 Proxies

Nothing in *CA 2006, ss 324–330* (below) prevents a company's articles from conferring more extensive rights on members or proxies.

[*CA 2006, s 331*].

(1) **Rights to appoint proxies**

A member of a company is entitled to appoint another person as his proxy to exercise all or any of his rights to attend and to speak and vote at a meeting of the company.

In the case of a company having a share capital, a member may appoint more than one proxy in relation to a meeting, provided that each proxy is appointed to exercise the rights attached to a different share or shares held by him, or (as the case may be) to a different £10, or multiple of £10, of stock held by him.

[*CA 2006, s 324*].

(2) **Obligation of proxy to vote in accordance with instructions**

A proxy must vote in accordance with any instructions given by the member by whom the proxy is appointed.

[*CA 2006, s 324A*].

(3) **Notice of meeting to contain statement of rights**

In every notice calling a meeting of a company there must appear, with reasonable prominence, a statement informing the member of his rights under (1) above and any more extensive rights conferred by the company's articles to appoint more than one proxy.

Failure to comply with this requirement does not affect the validity of the meeting or of anything done at the meeting but an offence is committed by every officer of the company who is in default. A person guilty of such an offence is liable, on summary conviction, to a fine not exceeding level 3 on the standard scale. See **29.1 Offences and Legal Proceedings** for the standard scale.

[*CA 2006, s 325*].

(4) **Company-sponsored invitations to appoint proxies**

If, for the purposes of a meeting, a company issues at its own expense invitations to members to appoint as proxy a specified person or a number of specified persons, the invitations must be issued to all members entitled to vote at the meeting. This is not contravened if

- there is issued to a member at his request a form of appointment naming the proxy or a list of persons willing to act as proxy; and
- the form or list is available on request to all members entitled to vote at the meeting.

If this provision is contravened as respects a meeting, an offence is committed by every officer of the company who is in default. A person guilty of such an offence is liable, on summary conviction, to a fine not exceeding level 3 on the standard scale. See **29.1 Offences and Legal Proceedings** for the standard scale.

[*CA 2006, s 326*].

(5) **Notice required of appointment of proxy, etc**

(a) *All companies*

Any provision of a company's articles is void if would have the effect of requiring

- the appointment of a proxy, or
- any document necessary to show the validity of, or otherwise relating to, the appointment of a proxy

to be received by the company or another person earlier than the following time.

- In the case of a meeting or adjourned meeting, 48 hours before the time for holding the meeting or adjourned meeting.
- In the case of a poll taken more than 48 hours after it was demanded, 24 hours before the time appointed for the taking of the poll.
- In the case of a poll taken not more than 48 hours after it was demanded, the time at which it was demanded.

In calculating these periods, no account must be taken of any part of a day that is not a working day.

[*CA 2006, s 327(1)–(3)*].

(b) *Traded companies*

In the case of a traded company (see APPENDIX 1 DEFINITIONS)

- the appointment of a person as proxy for a member must be notified to the company in writing; and
- where such an appointment is made, the company may require reasonable evidence of (i) the identity of the member and of the proxy; (ii) the member's instructions (if any) as to how the proxy is to vote; and (iii) where the proxy is appointed by a person acting on behalf of the member, authority of that person to make the appointment. The company may not require to be provided with anything else related to the appointment.

[*CA 2006, s 327(A1)*].

(6) **Chairing meetings**

Subject to any provision of the company's articles that states who may or who may not be chairman, a proxy may be elected to be the chairman of a general meeting by a resolution of the company passed at the meeting.

[*CA 2006, 328*].

(7) **Right of proxy to demand a poll**

The appointment of a proxy to vote on a matter at a meeting of a company authorises the proxy to demand, or join in demanding, a poll on that matter.

[*CA 2006, s 329(1)*].

(8) **Notice required of termination of proxy's authority**

In relation to meetings of a traded company (see APPENDIX 1 DEFINITIONS) the termination of the authority of a person to act as proxy must be notified to the company in writing.

[*CA 2006, s 330(A1)*].

In relation to meetings generally, the following provisions apply in the case of *any* company as regards notice that the authority of a person to act as proxy is terminated.

Any provision of the company's articles is void if it would have the effect of requiring notice of termination to be received by the company or another person earlier than the following time.

- In the case of a meeting or adjourned meeting, 48 hours before the time for holding the meeting or adjourned meeting.
- In the case of a poll taken more than 48 hours after it was demanded, 24 hours before the time appointed for the taking of the poll.
- In the case of a poll taken not more than 48 hours after it was demanded, the time at which it was demanded.

In calculating these periods, no account must be taken of any part of a day that is not a working day.

Subject to the above, and subject to any provision of the company's articles which has the effect of requiring notice of termination to be received by the company or another person at a time earlier than that specified below, the termination of the authority of a person to act as proxy

(a) does not affect

(i) whether he counts in deciding whether there is a quorum at a meeting;

(ii) the validity of anything he does as chairman of a meeting;

(iii) the validity of a poll demanded by him at a meeting;

unless the company receives notice of the termination before the commencement of the meeting; and

(b) does not affect the validity of a vote given by that person unless the company receives notice of the termination

(i) before the commencement of the meeting or adjourned meeting at which the vote is given; or

(ii) in the case of a poll taken more than 48 hours after it is demanded, before the time appointed for taking the poll. In calculating this period, no account must be taken of any part of a day that is not a working day.

If the company's articles require or permit members to give notice of termination to a person other than the company, the references above to the company receiving notice have effect as if they were or (as the case may be) included a reference to that person.

[*CA 2006, s 330(1)–(7)*].

Where a shareholder has given a proxy, in the absence of any special circumstances or any special contract expressly excluding the right to vote in person, his right to vote at a meeting is paramount to the right of the proxy to vote (*Cousins v International Brick Co Ltd* [1931] 2 Ch 90, 100 LJ Ch 404, CA).

(9) **Listed companies – special provisions**

A proxy form must be sent, to each person entitled to vote at the meeting, with the notice convening a meeting of holders of listed securities. The proxy form must provide for at least three way voting on all resolutions (except procedural resolutions) and must state that if it is returned without an indication as to how the proxy shall vote on any particular matter, the proxy will exercise his discretion as to whether, and if so how, he votes. Where the resolutions to be proposed include the re-election of retiring directors and the number of retiring directors standing for re-election exceeds five, the proxy must give each shareholder the opportunity to vote for or against (or abstain from voting on) the re-election of the retiring directors as a whole but must also allow votes to be cast for or against(or for shareholders to abstain from voting on) the re-election of them individually. (FCA Listing Rules, paras 9.3.6, 9.3.7).

(10) **Standard articles**

Where standard articles have been adopted, see

- *Table A, 1985, Regs 59–63*,
- *Model Articles, Arts 45, 46* (private companies),
- *Model Articles, Arts 38, 39* (public companies),

set out in APPENDIX 4 STANDARD ARTICLES OF ASSOCIATION.

42.27 Adjourned meetings

Adjournment of meeting. Where standard articles have been adopted, see

- *Table A, 1985, Reg 45*
- *Model Articles, Art 41* (private companies)
- *Model Articles, Art 33* (public companies)

set out in APPENDIX 4 STANDARD ARTICLES OF ASSOCIATION.

A chairman cannot adjourn a meeting at his own will and pleasure. If he no longer wishes to take part, the meeting itself can resolve to go on and appoint a new chairman (*National Dwellings Society v Sykes* [1894] 3 Ch 159).

Resolution passed at adjourned meeting. Where a resolution is passed at an adjourned meeting of a company, the resolution is for all purposes to be treated as having been passed on the date on which it was in fact passed, and is not to be deemed passed on any earlier date.

[*CA 2006, s 332*].

42.28 Sending documents relating to meetings, etc in electronic form

Where a company has given an 'electronic address' in

(a) a notice calling a meeting,

(b) an instrument of proxy sent out by the company in relation to the meeting, or

(c) an invitation to appoint a proxy issued by the company in relation to the meeting,

it is deemed to have agreed that any document or information relating to proceedings at the meeting or, as the case may be, proxies for that meeting may be sent by electronic means to that address (subject to any conditions or limitations specified in the notice).

'*Electronic address*' means any address or number used for the purposes of sending or receiving documents or information by electronic means.

For these purposes, documents relating to proxies include

- the appointment of a proxy in relation to a meeting;
- any document necessary to show the validity of, or otherwise relating to, the appointment of a proxy; and
- notice of the termination of the authority of a proxy.

[*CA 2006, s 333*].

Traded companies: duty to provide electronic address for receipt of proxies, etc. A traded company (see **Appendix 1 Definitions**) must provide an electronic address for the receipt of any document or information relating to proxies for a general meeting.

The company must provide the address either

- by giving it when sending out an instrument of proxy for the purposes of the meeting or issuing an invitation to appoint a proxy for those purposes; or
- by ensuring that it is made available, throughout the period beginning with the first date on which notice of the meeting is given and ending with the conclusion of the meeting, on the website on which the information required by **42.17**(3) above is made available.

The company is deemed to have agreed that any document or information relating to proxies for the meeting may be sent by electronic means to the address provided (subject to any limitations specified by the company when providing the address).

Documents relating to proxies include

- the appointment of a proxy for a meeting;
- any document necessary to show the validity of, or otherwise relating to, the appointment of a proxy; and
- notice of the termination of the authority of a proxy.

'*Electronic address*' has the same meaning as in *CA 2006, s 333* above.

[*CA 2006, s 333A*].

42.29 Class meetings

The provisions in **42.12** to **42.28** apply (with necessary modifications) in relation to a meeting of holders of a class of shares (or meeting of a class of members of a company without a share capital) as they apply in relation to a general meeting but with the following variations.

(a) The provisions in **42.13**(2) and (4).

(b) The additional requirements relating to traded companies (see Appendix 1 Definitions) in *CA 2006, ss 311(3), 311A, 319A, 327(A1), 330(A1)* and *333A* (see **42.17**(2), **42.17**(3), **42.23A**, **42.26**(5)(*b*), **42.26**(8) and **42.28** respectively) do not apply.

(c) The provisions in **42.14**(1) apply in relation to a meeting of holders of a class of shares in a traded company as they apply in relation to a meeting of holders of a class of shares in a company other than a traded company (and, accordingly the provisions in **42.14**(2) do not apply in relation to such a meeting).

(d) The provisions in *CA 2006, s 318* (quorum, see **42.22**) and *CA 2006, s 321* (right to demand a poll, see **42.24**(2)) do not apply in relation to a meeting in connection with the variation of rights attached to a class of shares (or class of members of a company without a share capital). Instead the following provisions apply.

Quorum. The quorum for such a meeting is:

- In the case of a meeting of holders of a class of shares
  - (i) for a meeting other than an adjourned meeting, two persons present holding at least one-third in nominal value of the issued shares of the class in question (excluding any shares of that class held as treasury shares); and
  - (ii) for an adjourned meeting, one person present holding shares of the class in question.

  Where a person is present by proxy or proxies, he is treated as holding only the shares in respect of which those proxies are authorised to exercise voting rights.
- In the case of a meeting of a class of members of a company without a share capital
  - (i) for a meeting other than an adjourned meeting, two members of the class present (in person or by proxy) who together represent at least one-third of the voting rights of the class; and
  - (ii) for an adjourned meeting, one member of the class present (in person or by proxy).

Right to demand a poll. At a variation of class rights meeting

- in the case of a meeting of holders of a class of shares, any holder of shares of the class in question present may demand a poll; and
- in the case of a meeting of a class of members of a company without a share capital, any member present (in person or by proxy) may demand a poll.

For the purposes of the above provisions,

- any amendment of a provision contained in a company's articles for the variation of the rights attached to a class of shares (class of members in the case of a company without a share capital), or the insertion of any such provision into the articles, is itself to be treated as a variation of those rights; and
- references to the variation of rights attached to a class of shares (class of members in the case of a company without a share capital) include references to their abrogation.

[*CA 2006, ss 334, 335*].

42.30 PUBLIC COMPANIES AND TRADED COMPANIES: ANNUAL GENERAL MEETINGS

(1) *Public companies: holding meetings*

Every public company must hold a general meeting as its annual general meeting (AGM)

(a) where it has given notice of the alteration of its accounting reference date under *CA 2006, s 392* (see **2.19** Accounting Reference Dates and Periods), specifying a new accounting reference date and stating that the current accounting reference period or the previous accounting reference period is to be shortened, within three months of giving that notice; and

(b) in all other circumstances, in each period of six months beginning with the day following its accounting reference date (see **2.18** Accounting Reference Dates and Periods).

Before 6 April 2008, the period was seven months. The reduction from seven to six months also does not have effect in relation to a company until

(i) the directors of the company have complied with *CA 1985, s 241* (laying of accounts and reports before the company in general meeting) in respect of its last financial year beginning before 6 April 2008; or

(ii) the first financial year of the company beginning on or after that date comes to an end.

This is in addition to any other meetings held during that period.

If a company fails to comply with this requirement, an offence is committed by every officer of the company who is in default. A person guilty of such an offence is liable (i) on conviction on indictment, to a fine; and (ii) on summary conviction, to a fine not exceeding the statutory maximum. See **29.1** Offences and Legal Proceedings for the statutory maximum.

[*CA 2006, s 336(1)(2)–(4)*].

In the case of a company formed and registered before 1 October 2007 that is a public company immediately before that date,

- *CA 1985, s 366* (duty to hold AGM) continues to apply to determine the date by which the company must hold its first AGM after 30 September 2007; and
- *CA 2006, s 336* (see above) applies in relation to subsequent AGMs.

Private companies are not required to hold an AGM after 1 October 2007 but the repeal of *CA 1985, s 366* (duty to hold AGM) does not affect any provision of a private company's memorandum or articles that expressly requires the company to hold an AGM. Any such provision continues to have such effect as it had immediately before 1 October 2007. But for this purpose, a provision specifying that one or more directors are to retire at an AGM is not provision expressly requiring the company to hold an AGM.

With effect from 31 December 2007, a company is not to be treated as one whose articles expressly require it to hold an AGM if, immediately before 1 October 2007, there was in force in relation to the company a resolution under *CA 1985, s 366A* (election to dispense with AGM).

(2) *Traded companies that are private companies: holding meetings*

Every private company that is a traded company (see **Appendix 1 Definitions**) must hold a general meeting as its annual general meeting (AGM)

- where it has given notice of the alteration of its accounting reference date under *CA 2006, s 392* (see **2.18 Accounting Reference Dates and Periods**), specifying a new accounting reference date and stating that the current accounting reference period or the previous accounting reference period is to be shortened, within 3 months of giving that notice; and
- in all other circumstances, in each period of nine months beginning with the day following its accounting reference date (in addition to any other meetings held during that period).

This is in addition to any other meetings held during that period.

If a company fails to comply with this requirement, an offence is committed by every officer of the company who is in default. A person guilty of such an offence is liable (i) on conviction on indictment, to a fine; and (ii) on summary conviction, to a fine not exceeding the statutory maximum. See **29.1 Offences and Legal Proceedings** for the statutory maximum.

[*CA 2006, s 336(1A)(2)–(4)*].

(3) *Public companies and traded companies: Notice of AGM*

A notice calling an AGM must state that the meeting is an AGM.

See **42.14** for notice of general meetings which also applies to AGMs. An AGM of a public company may be called by shorter notice than that required under **42.14** or by the company's articles (as the case may be), if *all* the members entitled to attend and vote at the meeting agree to the shorter notice.

Where a notice calling an AGM of a traded company is given more than six weeks before the meeting, the notice must include

- if the company is a public company, a statement of the right under *CA 2006, s 338* (see **42.31**) to require the company to give notice of a resolution to be moved at the meeting; and
- whether or not the company is a public company, a statement of the right under *CA 2006, s 338A* (see **42.31**) to require the company to include a matter in the business to be dealt with at the meeting.

In calculating the six-week period referred to above, the day on which the notice is given and the day of the meeting are excluded.

[*CA 2006, ss 337, 360*].

(4) *Business of the meeting*

There is no set business which must be held at the AGM but it is usual to consider the annual accounts, declare the final dividend (if any), deal with the election of directors, approve directors' remuneration and re-appoint the auditor, fixing the level of his remuneration.

42.31 Circulation of members' resolutions

(1) Public companies: power to require circulation of resolutions for AGM

The members of a public company may require the company to give, to members of the company entitled to receive notice of the next AGM, notice of a resolution which may properly be moved and is intended to be moved at that meeting. A resolution may properly be moved at an AGM unless

- it would, if passed, be ineffective (whether by reason of inconsistency with any enactment or the company's constitution or otherwise);
- it is defamatory of any person; or
- it is frivolous or vexatious.

A company must give notice of a resolution once it has received requests that it do so from

- members representing at least 5% of the total voting rights of all the members who have a right to vote on the resolution at the AGM to which the requests relate (excluding any voting rights attached to any shares in the company held as treasury shares); or
- at least 100 members who have a right to vote on the resolution at the AGM to which the requests relate and hold shares in the company on which there has been paid up an average sum, per member, of at least £100.

Under *CA 2006, s 153*, a company must also act under these provisions where it receives the necessary number of requests from persons nominated by members to enjoy their rights in relation to the company. See **26.6 Members** for full details

The request may be in hard copy form or in electronic form. It must identify the resolution of which notice is to be given and must be authenticated by the person or persons making it. It must be received by the company not later than six weeks (excluding the day the request is received and the day of the meeting) before the AGM to which the requests relate or, if later, the time at which notice is given of that meeting.

[*CA 2006, ss 338, 360*].

(2) Traded companies: members' power to include other matters in business dealt with at AGM

The members of a traded company (see **Appendix 1 Definitions**) may request the company to include in the business to be dealt with at an AGM any matter (other than a proposed resolution) unless it is defamatory of any person, frivolous or vexatious.

A company is required to include such a matter once it has received requests that it do so from

- members representing at least 5% of the total voting rights of all the members who have a right to vote at the meeting; or
- at least 100 members who have a right to vote at the meeting and hold shares in the company on which there has been paid up an average sum, per member, of at least £100.

See also *CA 2006, s 153* (exercise of rights where shares held on behalf of others, see **26.6 Members**).

A request

- may be in hard copy form or in electronic form;
- must identify the matter to be included in the business;
- must be accompanied by a statement setting out the grounds for the request;
- must be authenticated by the person or persons making it; and
- must be received by the company not later than
  - (i) six weeks (excluding the day the request is received and the day of the meeting) before the meeting; or
  - (ii) if later, the time at which notice is given of that meeting.

[*CA 2006, ss 338A, 360*].

(3) **Public companies: company's duty to circulate members' resolutions for AGMs**

A public company required under (1) above to give notice of a resolution must send a copy of it to each member of the company entitled to receive notice of the AGM in the same manner as notice of the meeting and at the same time as, or as soon as reasonably practicable after, it gives notice of the meeting. But see below for the requirement to deposit or tender a sum in respect of expenses of circulation.

In the event of default in complying with this requirement, an offence is committed by every officer of the company who is in default. A person guilty of such an offence is liable (i) on conviction on indictment, to a fine; and (ii) on summary conviction, to a fine not exceeding the statutory maximum. See **29.1** OFFENCES AND LEGAL PROCEEDINGS for the statutory maximum.

[*CA 2006, s 339*].

Expenses of circulating members' resolutions for AGM. The expenses of the company in complying with the above requirements need not be paid by the members who requested the circulation of the resolution if

- requests sufficient to require the company to circulate it are received before the end of the financial year preceding the meeting; or
- company resolves otherwise.

Otherwise, the expenses of the company must be paid by the members who requested the circulation of the resolution and the company is not bound to circulate the resolution unless there is deposited with it, or tendered to it, a sum reasonably sufficient to meet its expenses not later than

- six weeks before the AGM to which the requests relate; or
- if later, the time at which notice is given of that meeting.

In calculating the periods of six weeks, the day the sum is deposited or tendered and the day of the meeting are excluded.

[*CA 2006, ss 340, 360*].

(4) Traded companies: company's duty to circulate members' matters for AGM

A traded company that is required under (2) above to include any matter in the business to be dealt with at an AGM must give notice of it to each member of the company entitled to receive notice of the AGM in the same manner as notice of the meeting and at the same time as, or as soon as reasonably practicable after, it gives notice of the meeting. It must also publish it on the same website as that on which the company published the information required by *CA 2006, s 311A* (publication of information in advance of the AGM, see **42.17**). But see below where the members concerned need to deposit or tender a sum to cover the expenses of circulation.

In the event of default in complying with this requirement, an offence is committed by every officer of the company who is in default. A person guilty of such an offence is liable (i) on conviction on indictment, to a fine; and (ii) on summary conviction, to a fine not exceeding the statutory maximum. See **29.1 Offences and Legal Proceedings** for the statutory maximum. [*CA 2006, s 340A*].

Expenses of circulating members' matters to be dealt with at AGM. The expenses of the company in complying with the above requirements need not be paid by the members who requested the inclusion of the matter in the business to be dealt with at the AGM if

- requests sufficient to require the company to include the matter are received before the end of the financial year preceding the meeting; or
- company resolves otherwise.

Otherwise, the expenses of the company must be paid by the members who requested the inclusion of the matter and the company is not bound to comply with those provisions unless there is deposited with it, or tendered to it, a sum reasonably sufficient to meet its expenses not later than

- six weeks before the AGM to which the requests relate; or
- if later, the time at which notice is given of that meeting.

In calculating the six-week period, the day on which the sum is deposited or tendered and the day of the AGM are excluded.

[*CA 2006, s 340B*].

42.32 QUOTED COMPANIES AND TRADED COMPANIES: ADDITIONAL REQUIREMENTS

Quoted companies (**Appendix 1 Definitions**) must comply with the relevant requirements in **42.33–42.38** in relation to meetings.

Traded companies (see **Appendix 1 Definitions**) must comply with the relevant requirements in **42.33–42.38A** in relation to meetings.

42.33 Website publication of poll results

(1) *Quoted companies other than traded companies*

Where a poll is taken at a general meeting of a quoted company that is not a traded company, the company must ensure that the following information is made available on a website.

- The date of the meeting.
- The text of the resolution or, as the case may be, a description of the subject matter of the poll.
- The number of votes cast in favour and the number of votes cast against.

The information must be made available on a website that is maintained by or on behalf of the company and identifies the company in question. Access to the information on the website, and the ability to obtain a hard copy of the information from the website, must not be conditional on the payment of a fee or otherwise restricted. The information must be made available as soon as reasonably practicable and must be kept available throughout the period of two years beginning with the date on which it is first made available on a website in accordance with this requirement. A failure to make information available on a website throughout this period can, however, be disregarded if

- the information is made available on the website for part of that period; and
- the failure is wholly attributable to circumstances that it would not be reasonable to have expected the company to prevent or avoid.

In the event of default in complying with the above requirements, an offence is committed by every officer of the company who is in default. A person guilty of such an offence is liable, on summary conviction, to a fine not exceeding level 3 on the standard scale. See **29.1 Offences and Legal Proceedings** for the standard scale. But failure to comply does not affect the validity of the poll or the resolution or other business (if passed or agreed to) to which the poll relates.

[*CA 2006, ss 341(1)(2)–(6), 353*].

(2) *Traded companies*

Where a poll is taken at a general meeting of a traded company, the company must ensure that the following information is available on a website.

- The date of the meeting.
- The text of the resolution or, as the case may be, a description of the subject matter of the poll.
- The number of votes validly cast.
- The proportion of the company's issued share capital determined at the time at which the right to vote is determined under *CA 2006, s 360B(2)* (see **42.38A**) represented by those votes.
- The number of votes cast in favour.
- The number of votes cast against.
- The number of abstentions (if counted).

A traded company must comply with these requirements by

- the end of 16 days beginning with the date of the meeting; or
- if later, the end of the first working day after the day on which the result of the poll is declared.

The information must be made available on a website that is maintained by or on behalf of the company and identifies the company in question. Access to the information on the website, and the ability to obtain a hard copy of the information from the website, must not be conditional on the payment of a fee or otherwise restricted. The information must be made available as soon as reasonably practicable and must be kept available throughout the period of two years beginning with the date on which it is first made available on a website in accordance with this requirement. A failure to make information available on a website throughout this period can, however, be disregarded if

- the information is made available on the website for part of that period; and
- the failure is wholly attributable to circumstances that it would not be reasonable to have expected the company to prevent or avoid.

In the event of default in complying with the above requirements, an offence is committed by every officer of the company who is in default. A person guilty of such an offence is liable, on summary conviction, to a fine not exceeding level 3 on the standard scale. See **29.1 Offences and Legal Proceedings** for the standard scale. But failure to comply does not affect the validity of the poll or the resolution or other business (if passed or agreed to) to which the poll relates. [*CA 2006, ss 341(1A)(1B)(2)–(6), 353*].

42.34 Quoted companies: Independent report on poll

The members of a quoted company may require the directors to obtain an independent report on any poll taken, or to be taken, at a general meeting of the company. The directors must obtain an independent report if they receive requests to do so from

(a) members representing not less than 5% of the total voting rights of all the members who have a right to vote on the matter to which the poll relates (excluding any voting rights attached to any shares in the company held as treasury shares); or

(b) not less than 100 members who have a right to vote on the matter to which the poll relates and hold shares in the company on which there has been paid up an average sum, per member, of not less than £100.

Where the requests relate to more than one poll, the requirements of (*a*) or (*b*) above must be satisfied in relation to each of them.

Under *CA 2006, s 153*, a company must also act under these provisions where it receives the necessary number of requests from persons nominated by members to enjoy their rights in relation to the company. See **26.6 Members** for full details.

A request may be in hard copy form or in electronic form. It must identify the poll or polls to which it relates and be authenticated by the person or persons making it. It must be received by the company not later than one week after the date on which the poll is taken.

[*CA 2006, s 342*].

The report. The independent assessor's report must state his name and his opinion whether

- the procedures adopted in connection with the poll or polls were adequate;
- the votes cast (including proxy votes) were fairly and accurately recorded and counted;
- the validity of members' appointments of proxies was fairly assessed;
- the notice of the meeting contained the necessary statement of rights to appoint a proxy (see **42.26**(3); and

- the provisions relating to company-sponsored invitations to appoint proxies (see **42.26**(4)) were complied with in relation to the meeting.

The report must give the assessor's reasons for the opinions stated. If he is unable to form an opinion on any of those matters, the report must record that fact and state the reasons for it.

[*CA 2006, s 347*].

42.35 *Appointment of independent assessor*

Where the directors are required to obtain an independent report on a poll or polls, they must within one week appoint a person they consider to be appropriate to prepare the report. They must not appoint a person who does not meet the independence requirement (see below) or who has another role in relation to any poll on which he is to report (including, in particular, a role in connection with collecting or counting votes or with the appointment of proxies).

In the event of default in complying with this requirement, an offence is committed by every officer of the company who is in default. A person guilty of such an offence is liable, on summary conviction, to a fine not exceeding level 5 on the standard scale. See **29.1 Offences and Legal Proceedings** for the standard scale.

If, at the meeting, no poll on which a report is required is taken, the directors are not required to obtain a report from the independent assessor and his appointment ceases (but without prejudice to any right to be paid for work done before the appointment ceased).

[*CA 2006, s 343*].

Independence requirement. A person may not be appointed as an independent assessor if

- he is
  - (i) an officer or employee of the company; or
  - (ii) a partner or employee of such a person, or a partnership of which such a person is a partner;
- he is
  - (i) an officer or employee of an 'associated undertaking' of the company; or
  - (ii) a partner or employee of such a person, or a partnership of which such a person is a partner; or
- there exists between
  - (i) the person or an 'associate' of his, and
  - (ii) the company or an associated undertaking of the company,

  a connection of any such description as may be specified by Regulations made by the Secretary of State.

An auditor of the company is not regarded as an officer or employee of the company for this purpose.

'*Associated undertaking*' means a

- parent undertaking or subsidiary undertaking of the company; or
- subsidiary undertaking of a parent undertaking of the company.

'*Associate*' means

- in relation to an individual,
  - (i) that individual's spouse or civil partner or minor child or step-child;
  - (ii) any body corporate of which that individual is a director; and
  - (iii) any employee or partner of that individual;
- in relation to a body corporate,
  - (i) any body corporate of which that body is a director;
  - (ii) any body corporate in the same group as that body; and
  - (iii) any employee or partner of that body or of any body corporate in the same group; and
- in relation to a partnership that is a legal person under the law by which it is governed,
  - (i) any body corporate of which that partnership is a director;
  - (ii) any employee of or partner in that partnership; and
  - (iii) any person who is an associate of a partner in that partnership.

In relation to a partnership that is not a legal person under the law by which it is governed, 'associate' means any person who is an associate of any of the partners.

[*CA 2006, ss 344, 345*].

Effect of appointment of a partnership. Where a partnership that is not a legal person under the law by which it is governed is appointed as an independent assessor, unless a contrary intention appears, the appointment is of the partnership as such and not of the partners. Where the partnership ceases, the appointment is to be treated as extending to the following.

- Any partnership that succeeds to the practice of that partnership.
- Any other person who succeeds to that practice having previously carried it on in partnership.

For these purposes

- a partnership is regarded as succeeding to the practice of another partnership only if the members of the successor partnership are substantially the same as those of the former partnership; and
- a partnership or other person is regarded as succeeding to the practice of a partnership only if it or he succeeds to the whole or substantially the whole of the business of the former partnership.

Where the partnership ceases and the appointment is not so treated as extending to any partnership or other person, the appointment may, with the consent of the company, be treated as extending to a partnership, or other person, who succeeds to the business of the former partnership (or such part of it as is agreed by the company is to be treated as comprising the appointment).

[*CA 2006, s 346*].

42.36 *Rights of independent assessor*

Right to attend meeting, etc. Where an independent assessor has been appointed to report on a poll, he is entitled to attend the meeting at which the poll may be taken and any subsequent proceedings in connection with the poll. If the independent assessor is a firm, such rights are exercisable by an individual authorised by the firm in writing to act as its representative for that purpose.

The independent assessor is also entitled to be provided by the company with a copy of the notice of the meeting and any other communication provided by the company in connection with the meeting to persons who have a right to vote on the matter to which the poll relates.

These rights are only to be exercised to the extent that the independent assessor considers necessary for the preparation of his report.

[*CA 2006, s 348*].

Right to information. The independent assessor is entitled to access to the company's records relating to any poll on which he is to report and the meeting at which the poll or polls may be, or were, taken. He may require anyone who at any material time was a director, secretary, employee, member or agent (including banker, solicitor and auditor) of the company, or a person holding or accountable for any of the company's records, to provide him with information or explanations for the purpose of preparing his report.

Any statement made by a person in response to a requirement under this provision may not be used in evidence against him in criminal proceedings except proceedings for an offence under *CA 2006, s 350* (see below).

A person is not required to disclose information in respect of which a claim to legal professional privilege (in Scotland, to confidentiality of communications) could be maintained in legal proceedings.

[*CA 2006, s 349*].

Offences relating to provision of information. A person who fails to comply with a requirement under *CA 2006, s 349* above without delay commits an offence unless it was not reasonably practicable for him to provide the required information or explanation. A person guilty of such an offence is liable, on summary conviction, to a fine not exceeding level 3 on the standard scale. See **29.1 Offences and Legal Proceedings** for the standard scale.

A person also commits an offence who knowingly or recklessly makes to an independent assessor a statement (oral or written) that

- conveys, or purports to convey, any information or explanations which the independent assessor requires, or is entitled to require; and
- is misleading, false or deceptive in a material particular.

A person guilty of such an offence is liable (i) on conviction on indictment, to imprisonment for a term not exceeding two years or a fine (or both); and (ii) on summary conviction, to imprisonment for a term not exceeding twelve months (six months in Scotland and Northern Ireland) or to a fine not exceeding the statutory maximum (or both). See **29.1 Offences and Legal Proceedings** for the statutory maximum.

Nothing in these provisions relating to offences affects any right of an independent assessor to apply for an injunction (in Scotland, an interdict or an order for specific performance) to enforce his rights.

[*CA 2006, s 350*].

42.37 *Making information available on the website*

Where an independent assessor has been appointed to report on a poll, the company must ensure that the following information is made available on a website.

- The fact of his appointment.
- His identity.
- The text of the resolution or, as the case may be, a description of the subject matter of the poll to which his appointment relates.
- A copy of a report by him which complies with the requirements in **42.34**.

The information must be made available on a website that is maintained by or on behalf of the company and identifies the company in question. Access to the information on the website, and the ability to obtain a hard copy of the information from the website, must not be conditional on the payment of a fee or otherwise restricted. The information must be made available as soon as reasonably practicable and must be kept available throughout the period of two years beginning with the date on which it is first made available on a website in accordance with this requirement. A failure to make information available on a website throughout this period can, however, be disregarded if

- the information is made available on the website for part of that period; and
- the failure is wholly attributable to circumstances that it would not be reasonable to have expected the company to prevent or avoid.

In the event of default in complying with the above requirements, an offence is committed by every officer of the company who is in default. A person guilty of such an offence is liable, on summary conviction, to a fine not exceeding level 3 on the standard scale. See **29.1 Offences and Legal Proceedings** for the standard scale. But failure to comply does not affect the validity of the poll or the resolution or other business (if passed or agreed to) to which the poll relates.

[*CA 2006, ss 351, 353*].

42.38 Class meetings

The provisions of

- **42.33** apply (with any necessary modification) in relation to a meeting of holders of a class of shares of a quoted company or traded company in connection with the variation of the rights attached to such shares as they apply in relation to a general meeting of the company; and
- **42.34** to **42.37** apply (with any necessary modifications) in relation to a meeting of holders of a class of shares of a quoted company in connection with the variation of the rights attached to such shares as they apply in relation to a general meeting of the company.

For these purposes

- any amendment of a provision contained in a company's articles for the variation of the rights attached to a class of shares, or the insertion of any such provision into the articles, is itself to be treated as a variation of those rights; and

- references to the variation of rights attached to a class of shares include references to their abrogation.

[*CA 2006, s 352*].

TRADED COMPANIES: REQUIREMENTS FOR PARTICIPATING IN AND VOTING AT GENERAL MEETINGS

42.38A

The requirements are—

(a) Any provision of the articles of a traded company (see APPENDIX 1 DEFINITIONS) is void in so far as it would have the effect of

(i) imposing a restriction on a right of a member to participate in and vote at a general meeting of the company unless the member's shares have (after having been acquired by the member and before the meeting) been deposited with, or transferred to, or registered in the name of another person.

(ii) imposing a restriction on the right of a member to transfer shares in the company during the period of 48 hours before the time for the holding of a general meeting of the company if that right would not otherwise be subject to that restriction; and

(b) A Traded company must determine the right to vote at a general meeting of the company by reference to the register of members as at a time (determined by the company) that is not more than 48 hours before the time for the holding of the meeting.

In calculating the period mentioned in (*a*)(ii) and (*b*) above, no account is to be taken of any part of a day that is not a working day.

Nothing in the above provisions affects

- the operation of *CA 2006, Pt 22* or *CA 1985, Pt 15* (see **24** INTERESTS IN PUBLIC COMPANY SHARES) or any provision in a company's articles relating to the application of those provisions; or
- the validity of articles prescribed, or to the same effect as articles prescribed, under *CA 2006, s 19* (power of Secretary of State to prescribe model articles).

[*CA 2006, s 360A; SI 2009 No 1632, Reg 20*].

42.39 DIRECTORS' MEETINGS

Apart from the provisions relating to minutes in **42.40**, there are no provisions in *CA 2006* with regard to the holding of directors' meetings and, subject to the terms of the articles, the directors may regulate their proceedings as they think fit. Where the company has adopted standard articles, see

- *Table A 1985, Regs 88–98*,
- *Model Articles, Arts 7–14* (private companies),
- *Model Articles, Arts 7–17* (public companies),

set out in APPENDIX 4 STANDARD ARTICLES OF ASSOCIATION.

Standard articles may stipulate that written resolutions, signed by all directors entitled to receive notice of a directors' meeting, are as valid as if passed at a duly convened meeting (see, for example *Table A 1985, Reg 93* and Model Articles, *Art 18* (public companies)). This, however, does not override a requirement of the articles that a quorum exists for board meetings. For example, where the quorum to conduct business is two directors, a written resolution signed by one director is invalid even if the only other director is outside the UK and not entitled to receive notice of the meeting (see *Hood Sailmakers Ltd v Axford* [1996] 4 All ER 830, [1997] 1 BCLC 721).

42.40 Minutes of directors' meetings

Every company must cause minutes of all proceedings at meetings of its directors to be recorded. Such records must be then be kept for at least ten years from the date of the meeting.

If a company fails to comply with this requirement, an offence is committed by every officer of the company who is in default. A person guilty of such an offence is liable, on summary conviction, to a fine not exceeding level 3 on the standard scale and, for continued contravention, a daily default fine not exceeding one-tenth of level 3 on the standard scale. See **29.1** OFFENCES AND LEGAL PROCEEDINGS for the standard scale.

[*CA 2006, s 248*].

Where standard articles have been adopted, for general provisions relating to the giving of notice, see *Model Articles, Art 15*, set out in APPENDIX 4 STANDARD ARTICLES OF ASSOCIATION.

Minutes as evidence. Where minutes of a directors' meeting have been duly recorded as above, then

- if purporting to be authenticated by the chairman of the meeting or by the chairman of the next directors' meeting, they are evidence (in Scotland, sufficient evidence) of the proceedings at the meeting; and
- until the contrary is proved
  (i) the meeting is deemed duly held and convened;
  (ii) all proceedings at the meeting are deemed to have duly taken place; and
  (iii) all appointments at the meeting are deemed valid.

[*CA 2006, s 249*].

42.41 RECORDS OF RESOLUTIONS AND MEETINGS

Every company must keep records comprising the following.

(a) Copies of all resolutions of members passed otherwise than at general meetings.

Such a record, if purporting to be signed by a director of the company or by the company secretary, is evidence (in Scotland, sufficient evidence) of the passing of the resolution.

Where there is a record of a written resolution of a private company, the requirements of *CA 2006* with respect to the passing of the resolution are deemed to be complied with unless the contrary is proved.

(b) Minutes of all proceedings of general meetings.

Such minutes, if purporting to be signed by the chairman of that meeting or by the chairman of the next general meeting, are evidence (in Scotland, sufficient evidence) of the proceedings at the meeting.

Where there is a record of proceedings of a general meeting of a company, then, until the contrary is proved

- the meeting is deemed duly held and convened;
- all proceedings at the meeting are deemed to have duly taken place; and
- all appointments at the meeting are deemed valid.

(c) Details provided to the company in accordance with **42.42**.

The records must be kept for at least ten years from the date of the resolution, meeting or decision (as appropriate).

If a company fails to comply with these requirements, an offence is committed by every officer of the company who is in default. A person guilty of such an offence is liable, on summary conviction, to a fine not exceeding level 3 on the standard scale and, for continued contravention, a daily default fine not exceeding one-tenth of level 3 on the standard scale. See **29.1 Offences and Legal Proceedings** for the standard scale. [*CA 2006, ss 355, 356*].

Where standard articles have been adopted, see *Table A 1985, Reg 100*, set out in **Appendix 4 Standard Articles of Association**.

Form of minute book. See **36.1 Records** for the provisions relating to form of records generally.

42.42 Records of decisions of sole member

If a company limited by shares or by guarantee has only one member, where the member takes any decision that

- may be taken by the company in general meeting, and
- has effect as if agreed by the company in general meeting,

he must (unless that decision is taken by way of a written resolution) provide the company with details of that decision. If he fails to comply with this requirement, he commits an offence and is liable, on summary conviction, to a fine not exceeding level 2 on the standard scale. See **29.1 Offences and Legal Proceedings** for the standard scale.

Failure to comply with these requirements does not affect the validity of any decision referred to above.

[*CA 2006, s 357*].

42.43 Inspection of records of resolutions and meetings

The records referred to in **42.41** relating to the previous ten years must be kept available for inspection at the company's registered office or at a place specified in Regulations (see **36.2 Records**).

The company must give notice to the Registrar of Companies of

- the place at which the records are kept available for inspection, and
- any change in that place,

unless they have at all times been kept at the company's registered office.

The records must be open to the inspection of any member of the company without charge and a member may require a copy of any of the records on payment of such fee as may be prescribed.

Time available for inspection and copying. See **36.2 Records**.

Offences. If

- default is made for 14 days in notifying the Registrar of Companies as above,
- inspection is refused, or
- a copy requested is not sent,

an offence is committed by every officer of the company who is in default. A person guilty of such an offence is liable, on summary conviction, to a fine not exceeding level 3 on the standard scale and, for continued contravention, to a daily default fine not exceeding one-tenth of level 3 on the standard scale. See **29.1 Offences and Legal Proceedings** for the standard scale.

In a case in which an inspection is refused or a copy requested is not sent, the court may by order compel an immediate inspection of the records or direct that the copies required be sent to the persons who requested them.

[*CA 2006, s 358*].

42.44 Resolutions and meetings of class of members

The provisions in **42.41–42.43** apply (with necessary modifications) in relation to resolutions and meetings of

- holders of a class of shares, and
- in the case of a company without a share capital, a class of members,

as they apply in relation to resolutions of members generally and to general meetings.

[*CA 2006, s 359*].

42.45 INFORMATION AS TO EXERCISE OF VOTING RIGHTS BY INSTITUTIONAL INVESTORS

The Treasury or the Secretary of State may make provision by Regulations requiring certain institutions to provide information about the exercise of voting rights attached to specific shares.

The institutions to which the provisions apply are

- unit trust schemes;
- open-ended investment companies;

- investment trusts;
- pension schemes;
- undertakings authorised to carry on long-term insurance; and
- collective investment schemes.

Regulations may require the provision of specified information about, amongst other things,

- the exercise or non-exercise of voting rights by the institution or any person acting on its behalf;
- any instructions given by the institution or any person acting on its behalf as to the exercise or non-exercise of voting rights; and
- any delegation by the institution or any person acting on its behalf of any functions in relation to the exercise or non-exercise of voting rights or the giving of such instructions.

[*CA 2006, ss 1277–1280*].

Although Regulations have not been published which require voting information, the UK Stewardship Code (see **15 Corporate Governance**) requires institutional investors to have a clear policy on voting and to disclose their voting activity under the principles and guidance set out in the Code.

43 Scotland

43.1	**Introduction**	43.5	Alteration of a floating charge
43.2	**Floating charges**	43.6	**Charitable companies**
43.3	Effect of floating charge on winding up	43.7	Name of company not including 'charity', etc
43.4	Priority of floating charge		

Cross-references. See **16.21** Dealing With Third Parties for service of documents on a company registered in Scotland carrying on a business in England and Wales; **17.17** Debt Finance–Debentures and Other Borrowing for debentures to bearer; **29.4** Offences and Legal Proceedings for summary proceedings in Scotland; **39.1** Registrar of Companies for Companies Registration Office in Scotland; **44.12** Securities: Certification and Transfers for offences in connection with share warrants.

43.1 INTRODUCTION

The *Companies Acts* apply in Scotland as they do in the rest of the UK but subject to certain variations and modifications to allow for the different legal system applying there. Apart from the cross-references above, the main provisions which specifically refer to Scotland are as follows.

- Registration of charges (see **40** Registration of Charges).
- Floating charges (see **43.2** to **43.5**).
- Charitable companies (see **43.6** and **43.7**).
- Execution of documents (see **16.7** Dealing With Third Parties).

43.2 FLOATING CHARGES

Note. The provisions in this paragraph and in **43.3** to **43.5** are repealed by *Bankruptcy and Diligence etc (Scotland) Act 2007, s 46(1)* with effect from a date to be appointed. They will then be replaced by provisions in *Part 2* of that *Act*.

Under the law of Scotland, an incorporated company (whether within the meaning of *CA 1985* or not) may, for the purpose of securing any debt or other obligation incurred or binding upon the company or any other person, create in favour of the creditor a floating charge over all or any part of its property (including uncalled capital) or undertaking.

Subject to the provisions of *CA 1985*, a floating charge in relation to any heritable property in Scotland has effect in accordance with these provisions and *IA 1986, Pt III* notwithstanding that the instrument creating it is not recorded in the Register of Sasines or, as appropriate, registered in accordance with the *Land Registration (Scotland) Act 1979*.

[*CA 1985, s 462*].

Any floating charge which purported to subsist as a floating charge before 17 November 1972 and which, if created on or after that date, would have been validly created under *Companies (Floating Charges and Receivers) (Scotland) Act 1972* is deemed to have subsisted as a valid floating charge from the day of its creation. [*CA 1985, s 465(1)*].

43.3 Effect of floating charge on winding up

Where a company goes into liquidation, a floating charge created by the company attaches to the relevant property or undertaking but subject to the rights of any person who

- has executed diligence on the property (or part); or
- holds a fixed security or another floating charge over the property (or part) ranking in priority to that floating charge.

Subject to the above, the provisions of *IA 1986, Pt IV* (except *section 185*) apply in relation to the floating charge as if it were a fixed security over the property to which it has attached in respect of

- the principal amount of the debt or obligation; and
- any interest which accrues thereon until payment of the sum due under the charge.

[*CA 1985, ss 463, 486*].

43.4 Priority of floating charge

The order of ranking of floating charges and fixed securities is as follows.

(a) Where all or part of a company's property is subject to a floating charge *and* a fixed security arising by operation of the law, the fixed security has priority.

(b) Subject to (*a*) above the instrument creating a floating charge over all or any part of the company's property may

   (i) determine the order of ranking by prohibiting or restricting the creation, after the date of the instrument, of a fixed security or other floating charge having priority over it or ranking *pari passu* with it (and such a provision is effective to confer priority); or

   (ii) determine the order in which the floating charge is to rank over the same property (or part) with any other subsisting or future floating charges or fixed securities. The consent is required of the holders of any subsisting floating charge or fixed security which would be adversely affected.

(c) Subject to (*a*) and (*b*) above

   (i) a fixed security, the right to which has been constituted as a real right before a floating charge has attached to all or any part of the company's property, has priority over a floating charge;

   (ii) floating charges rank with one another according to the time of registration (see **40** REGISTRATION OF CHARGES); and

   (iii) floating charges received by the Registrar of Companies for registration by the same postal delivery rank equally with one another.

   Where the holder of a floating charge within (ii) or (iii) above has received notice in writing of the subsequent registration of another floating charge over the same property (or part), the preference in ranking of the first-mentioned floating charge is restricted to security for

   - the holder's present advances;

- any further advances he is required to make under the instrument creating the floating charge or any ancillary document;
- interest due or becoming due on all such advances;
- expenses etc reasonably incurred; and
- in the case of a floating charge to secure a contingent liability (other than a liability arising under any further advances made from time to time), the maximum sum to which that contingent liability is capable of amounting whether or not it is contractually limited. [*CA 1985, ss 464, 486*].

For the above purposes, any provision relating to ranking of charges contained in an instrument creating a floating charge (or any ancillary document) executed prior to 17 November 1972 and which, if made on or after that date would have been a valid provision under *Companies (Floating Charges and Receivers) (Scotland) Act 1972* is deemed to have been a valid provision from the date of its making. [*CA 1985, s 465(2)*].

43.5 Alteration of a floating charge

The instrument creating a floating charge (or any ancillary document) may be altered by the execution of an instrument of alteration by the company, the holder of the charge and the holder of any other charge (including a fixed security) which would be adversely affected by the alteration.

Without prejudice to any enactment or rule of law regarding the execution of documents, such an instrument of alteration is validly executed if it is executed

(a) where trustees for debenture-holders are acting in accordance with a trust deed, by those trustees; or

(b) where, in the case of a series of debentures, no such trustees are acting, by or on behalf of

- a majority in nominal value of those present (or represented by proxy) and voting at a meeting of debenture-holders at which holders of at least one-third in nominal value of the outstanding debentures of the series are present (or so represented); or
- where no such meeting is held, the holders of at least one-half in nominal value of the outstanding debentures of the series.

The provisions of **43.4** apply to the instrument of alteration as they apply to the instrument creating a floating charge. [*CA 1985, ss 466, 486*].

CA 1985, s 466(4A) applies to an alteration of a floating charge where the alteration is one which

- prohibits or restricts the creation of any fixed security or any other floating charge having priority over, or ranking *pari passu* with, the floating charge, or
- varies, or otherwise regulates, the ranking of the floating charge in relation to fixed securities or to other floating charges, or
- releases property from a floating charge, or
- increases the amount secured by a floating charge

[*CA 1985, s 466(4)*].

43.5 Scotland

Every alteration to a floating charge created by a company is, so far as any security on the company's property or any part of it is conferred by the alteration, void against the liquidator or administrator and any creditor of the company, unless the documents referred to in the following paragraph are delivered by the company or any person interested in the charge to the Registrar of Companies for registration before the end of the relevant period allowed for delivery.

This is without prejudice to any contract or obligation for repayment of the money secured by the alteration to the charge and when an alteration becomes void the money secured by it immediately becomes payable.

The "relevant period allowed for delivery" is the period of 21 days beginning with the day after the date of execution of the instrument of alteration or, if an order under *CA 2006, s 859F(3)* has been made (see **40.2A**) the period allowed by the order

The documents which must be delivered are

- a certified copy of the instrument of alteration, and
- a statement of particulars including the registered name and number of the company, the date of creation of the charge, a description of the instrument (if any) by which the charge was created or evidenced, shot particulars of the property or undertaking charged as set out when the charge was registered, date(s) of execution of the instrument of alteration and names and address(es) of the persons who have executed the instrument of alteration.

CA 2006, s 859F (Extension of period allowed for delivery), *s 859G*, (Personal information in certified copies), *s 859I* (Entries on the register), *s 859M* (rectification of register) and *s 859N* (Replacement of instrument or debenture) (see Chapter **40** for all details) apply to an alteration to a floating charge to which the above applies as they apply to a charge as if:

(a) references to the documents required or delivered under *CA 2006, s 859A* or *859B* were the documents referred to above;

(b) references to the period allowed for delivery under the section concerned were to the relevant period allowed for delivery period referred to above;

(c) references to delivery of a certified copy of an instrument to the Registrar of Companies for the purposes of *CA 2006, Chapter A1, Part 25* were to the delivery of a certified copy of an instrument of alteration to the Registrar of Companies;

(d) references to registration in accordance with a provision of *CA 2006, Chapter A1, Part 25*, were to registration in accordance with CA 1985, s 466

(e) references to registration under *CA 2006, s 859A* or *859B* were to registration under *CA 1985, s 466*; and

(f) references to a statement or notice delivered to the Registrar of Companies in accordance with *CA 2006, Chapter A1, Part 25* were to a statement delivered to the Registrar of Companies in accordance with this *CA 1985, s 466(4A)*.

[*CA 1985, s 466(4A), SI 2013 No.600, Schedule 2, para 1*]

43.6 CHARITABLE COMPANIES

In Scotland, where a charity is a company or other body corporate having power to alter the instruments establishing or regulating it, no exercise of that power which has the effect of the body ceasing to be a charity is valid so as to affect the application of

(a) any property acquired by virtue of any transfer, contract or obligation previously effected otherwise than for full consideration in money or money's worth;

(b) any property representing property acquired under (*a*);

(c) any property representing income which has accrued before the alteration is made; or

(d) the income from any property in (*a*) to (*c*) above.

[*CA 1989, s 112(2); SI 2006 No 242, Sch*].

See also **16.4 Dealings With Third Parties** for the restriction on the provisions of *CA 2006, s 39* (company's capacity) and *CA 2006, s 40* (power of directors to bind the company) in relation to such a charitable company.

43.7 Name of company not including 'charity', etc

Where a company is a charity and its name does not include the word 'charity' or 'charitable', the fact that the company is a charity must be stated in English in legible characters in all

(a) business letters;

(b) notices and other official publications;

(c) bills of exchange, promissory notes, endorsements, cheques and orders for money or goods purporting to be signed by or on behalf of the company;

(d) documents for the creation, transfer, variation or extinction of an interest in land purporting to be executed by the company; and

(e) bills of parcels, invoices, receipts and letters of credit.

If a company fails to comply with these requirements, it commits an offence. An officer of the company, or a person acting on its behalf, also commits an offence if he

(i) issues, or authorises the issue of, any document within (*a*), (*b*) or (*e*) above, or

(ii) signs, or authorises to be signed on behalf of the company, any document within (*c*) above

in which the required statement required does not appear. A person guilty of such an offence is liable, on summary conviction, to a fine not exceeding level 3 on the standard scale (see **29.1 Offences and Legal Proceedings**).

Additionally, a person in breach of (ii) above is personally liable to the holder of the bill of exchange, promissory note, endorsement, cheque or order for money or goods for the amount of it (unless it is duly paid by the company).

[*CA 1989, s 112(6)–(11); SI 2008 No 948, Sch 3 para 6*].

44 Securities: Certification and Transfers

44.1	**Share certificates**	44.9	**Transmission of shares**
44.2	**Issue of certificates, etc on allotment**	44.10	**Issue of certificates, etc on transfer**
44.3	**Transfers of securities**	44.11	Contents and replacement of share certificates
44.4	*Stock Transfer Act 1963*	44.12	**Share warrants**
44.5	Action by transferor/transferee of securities	44.13	**Issue of certificates: court order to make good default**
44.6	Registration of transfer	44.14	**Stock Exchange transfers**
44.7	Restrictions on transfers		
44.8	Certification of instrument of transfer		

Cross-references. See 17 Debt Finance–Debentures and Other Borrowings; 47 Shares.

44.1 SHARE CERTIFICATES

In the case of a company registered in England and Wales or Northern Ireland, a certificate under the common seal of the company specifying any shares held by a member is *prima facie* evidence of his title to the shares.

In the case of a company registered in Scotland,

- a certificate under the common seal of the company specifying any shares held by a member, or
- a certificate specifying any shares held by a member and subscribed by the company in accordance with the *Requirements of Writing (Scotland) Act 1995*,

is sufficient evidence, unless the contrary is shown, of his title to the shares.

[*CA 2006, s 768*].

Share certificates are issued for the benefit of the company in general; they are a declaration by the company to all the world that the person in whose name the certificate is made out, and to whom it is given, is a shareholder in the company. The company is therefore estopped from denying the accuracy of a vendor's certificate and the purchaser is entitled to damages (*Bahia and San Francisco Rly Co, Re* (1868) LR 3 QB 584).

Where a company issues an incorrect certificate, the company may also be estopped from denying the correctness of the certificate against the person to whom it is issued, in the absence of fraud or forgery, where he enters into a contract to sell the shares (*Dixon v Kennaway & Co* [1900] 1 Ch 833). See also *Bloomenthal v Ford* [1897] AC 156, HL.

44.2 ISSUE OF CERTIFICATES, ETC ON ALLOTMENT

Subject to below, a company must, within two months after the allotment of any of its shares, debentures or debenture stock, complete and have ready for delivery

- the certificates of the shares allotted;

- the debentures allotted; or
- the certificates of the debenture stock allotted.

This does not apply in the following circumstances.

- If the conditions of issue of the shares, debentures or debenture stock provide otherwise.
- Where shares, debentures or debenture stock are allotted to a 'financial institution' a company is not required, in consequence of that allotment, to comply with the above provisions. A '*financial institution*' means
  - (i) a recognised clearing house acting in relation to a recognised investment exchange; or
  - (ii) a nominee of a recognised clearing house acting in that way or a recognised investment exchange, in either case designated for these purposes in the rules of the recognised investment exchange in question.
- In the case of an allotment of shares if, following the allotment, the company has issued a share warrant in respect of the shares (see **44.12**).

If default is made in complying with these requirements, an offence is committed by every officer of the company who is in default. A person guilty of such an offence is liable, on summary conviction, to a fine not exceeding level 3 on the standard scale and, for continued contravention, a daily default fine not exceeding one-tenth of level 3 on the standard scale. See **29.1 Offences and Legal Proceedings** for the statutory maximum.

[*CA 2006, ss 769, 778*].

See **44.13** for the court's power to order a company to make good any default under these provisions.

44.3 TRANSFERS OF SECURITIES

The shares or other interest of any member in a company are transferable in accordance with the company's articles, subject to

- the *Stock Transfer Act 1963* or the *Stock Transfer Act (Northern Ireland) 1963* (which enable securities of certain descriptions to be transferred by a simplified process, see **44.4**); and
- regulations which enable title to securities to be evidenced and transferred without a written instrument (see **44.13**).

[*CA 2006, s 544*].

The procedure for transferring securities is outlined in **44.4** to **44.8**. Special provisions apply in relation to Stock Exchange transactions. These are outlined in **44.14**.

44.4 Stock Transfer Act 1963

STA 1963 provides a simplified procedure for the transfer of *fully paid-up* 'registered securities' of any description, being

(a) securities issued by any company as defined in *Companies Act 2006 (CA 2006), s 1(1)* (see **12.1 Company Formation and Types of Companies**) except a company limited by guarantee or an unlimited company;

(b) securities issued by any other body incorporated in Great Britain by or under any enactment or by Royal Charter, except a building society or industrial and provident society;

(c) UK Government securities, except stock or bonds in the National Savings Stock Register and national savings certificates;

(d) local authority securities;

(e) units of an authorised unit trust scheme, an authorised contractual scheme or a recognised scheme within the meaning of *FSMA 2000, Pt 17*; and

(f) shares issued by an open-ended investment company within the meaning of the *Open-Ended Investment Companies Regulations 2001* (*SI 2001 No 1228*).

[*STA 1963, s 1(4); SI 2013 No 1388, Reg 4*].

'*Registered securities*' means transferable securities the holders of which are entered in a register, whether or not maintained in Great Britain.

'*Securities*' means shares, stock, debentures, debenture stock, loan stock, bonds, units of a collective investment scheme within the meaning of *FSMA 2000*, and other securities of any description.

[*STA 1963, s 4(1)*].

Registered securities within (*a*) to (*d*) above may be transferred by means of an instrument in the form set out in *STA 1963, Sch 1* (a stock transfer), executed by the transferor only and specifying

- the full name and address of the transferee;
- the consideration;
- the description and number or amount of the securities; and
- the transferor.

The form need not be attested. Where the transfer has been executed for the purpose of a Stock Exchange transaction, the particulars of the consideration and of the transferee may either be inserted in that transfer or supplied by means of a broker's transfers.

[*STA 1963, s 1(1)(2)*].

Nothing in the above provisions affects the validity of what would otherwise be a valid instrument of transfer. [*STA 1963, s 1(3)*]. For example, where a company has adopted standard articles, see

- *Table A, 1985, Reg 23*
- *Model Articles, Art 26* (private companies)

set out in APPENDIX 4 STANDARD ARTICLES OF ASSOCIATION.

Note that *STA 1963* does not apply to transfers of partly-paid shares. Where such shares are being transferred, the instrument of transfer will require execution by the transferee and attestation. This is because the liability to pay up the sum outstanding on the shares is being transferred from the transferor to the transferee.

Similar provisions apply in Northern Ireland under *Stock Transfer Act (Northern Ireland) 1963*.

44.5 Action by transferor/transferee of securities

Stock Exchange transactions. See **44.14**.

Other transactions. The procedure required depends on the circumstances.

(a) *Transferor disposing of entire holding to one transferee*. The transferor executes a 'proper instrument of transfer' (normally a stock transfer form – see **44.4**) in favour of the transferee, which he hands to the transferee, together with the share certificate(s), in exchange for the agreed consideration. The transferee then pays the necessary stamp duty on the transfer and delivers the transfer, duly stamped, together with the share certificate(s), to the company for registration. If the company's directors approve the transfer (see **44.6**), the transferee's name is entered in the register of members, the previous share certificate is cancelled, and a new certificate issued to the transferee.

(b) *Transferor disposing of part only of holding to one transferee*. The transferor executes a 'proper instrument of transfer' (normally a stock transfer form – see **44.4**) and hands it, together with the share certificate(s), to the company (rather than the transferee). The form of transfer is then certificated by the company, ie it is endorsed with the words 'certificate lodged' or similar words (see **44.8**). The company returns the certificated transfer to the transferor, but retains the share certificate. The transferor then hands the certified transfer form to the transferee, in exchange for the agreed consideration. The transferee pays the necessary stamp duty on the transfer and delivers the stamped transfer to the company for registration. If the company's directors approve the transfer (see **44.6**), new share certificates are issued to the transferor (for the balance retained) and the transferee (for the shares acquired) and the transferee's name is also entered in the register of members.

(c) *Transferor disposing of shares to more than one transferee*. A similar procedure applies as in (*b*) above) but the transferor executes a separate form of transfer for each transferee.

44.6 Registration of transfer

A company may not register a transfer of shares in, or debentures of, the company unless

- a 'proper instrument of transfer' has been delivered to it; or
- the transfer is
  - (i) an exempt transfer within the *Stock Transfer Act 1982*; or
  - (ii) a Stock Exchange transaction in accordance with **44.14**.

But this does not affect any power of the company to register as shareholder or debenture holder a person to whom the right to any shares in, or debentures of, the company has been transmitted by operation of law. See **44.9**.

[*CA 2006, s 770*].

A conventional stock transfer form is a '*proper instrument of transfer*' even if it does not state the consideration money and is not stamped. The defects in the form are mere irregularities and the registration of the transfer is not invalid (*Nisbet v Shepherd* [1994] 1 BCLC 300, [1994] BCC 91, CA).

Procedure on transfer being lodged. Subject to below, when a transfer of shares in, or debentures of, a company has been lodged with the company on or after 6 April 2008, the company must either

- register the transfer, or
- give the transferee notice of refusal to register the transfer, together with its reasons for the refusal

as soon as practicable and in any event within two months after the date on which the transfer is lodged with it. If the company refuses to register the transfer (see **44.7**), it must provide the transferee with such further information about the reasons for the refusal as the transferee may reasonably request (but this does *not* include copies of minutes of meetings of directors).

If a company fails to comply with this requirement, an offence is committed by the company and every officer of the company who is in default. A person guilty of such an offence is liable, on summary conviction, to a fine not exceeding level 3 on the standard scale and, for continued contravention, a daily default fine not exceeding one-tenth of level 3 on the standard scale. See **29.1 Offences and Legal Proceedings** for the standard scale.

These provisions do not apply in relation to the transmission of shares or debentures by operation of law (see **44.9**) or a transfer of shares if the company has issued a share warrant in respect of the shares (see **44.12**).

[*CA 2006, s 771*].

Failure to notify within the time limit means that the power of refusal to register is lost and the court may grant an application for rectification of the register under *CA 2006, s 125*, see **38.5 Registers** (*Re Inverdeck Ltd* [1998] 2 BCLC 242, [1998] BCC 256).

Transfer of shares on application of transferor. On the application of the transferor of any share or interest in a company, the company must enter in its register of members the name of the transferee in the same manner and subject to the same conditions as if the application for the entry were made by the transferee.

[*CA 2006, s 772*].

Standard articles. Where a company has adopted standard articles, see

- *Table A, 1985, Regs 25–28*
- *Model Articles, Art 26* (private companies)
- *Model Articles, Arts 63, 64* (public companies)

set out in **Appendix 4 Standard Articles of Association**.

A company's articles may contain other provisions restricting the right of its members to transfer their shares (see **44.7**).

44.7 Restrictions on transfers

A public company which wishes to have its shares quoted on the Stock Exchange cannot impose restrictions on the transfer of its shares (other than in exceptional circumstances), since to do so would adversely affect their marketability. By contrast, the articles of a private company frequently contain such restrictions. Where restrictions are imposed, they are normally either refusal powers or pre-emption provisions.

Refusal powers. A company's articles may empower the directors to refuse to register a transfer, either at their complete discretion or on specified grounds. Such a power, as with any other power conferred on the directors, must be exercised in good faith for the benefit of the company (*Smith & Fawcett Ltd, Re* [1942] Ch 304, [1942] 1 All ER 542,

CA) and not for some personal motive of the directors (see *Tett v Phoenix Property and Investment Co Ltd* [1984] BCLC 599). Furthermore, the power must be exercised by the making of a positive decision at a board meeting (see *Moodie v W and J Shepherd (Bookbinders) Ltd* [1949] 2 All ER 1044, 94 Sol Jo 95, HL), failing which the transfer must be registered (*Re Hackney Pavilion Ltd* [1924] 1 Ch 276, 93 LJ Ch 193).

Where a company has adopted standard articles, see

- *Table A, 1985, Reg 24*
- *Model Articles, Art 26* (private companies)
- *Model Articles, Arts 63, 64* (public companies)

set out in APPENDIX **4** STANDARD ARTICLES OF ASSOCIATION.

The remedy for the refusal to register a transfer is for the person aggrieved to apply to the court for rectification of the register of members under *CA 2006, s 125*. See **38.5** REGISTERS.

Pre-emption provisions. A company's articles may contain pre-emption provisions, ie provisions requiring any member who wishes to sell his shares to offer them first to existing members, normally at a fair price to be determined by the articles. The effect of such a provision will depend on its precise wording, and there have been numerous decided cases on the subject. See, for example, *Lyle & Scott Ltd v Scott's Trustees; Lyle & Scott Ltd v British Investment Trust Ltd* [1959] AC 763, [1959] 2 All ER 661, HL.

44.8 Certification of instrument of transfer

An instrument of transfer (normally a stock transfer form – see **44.4**) is certificated if it bears the words 'certificate lodged' (or words to the like effect). The certification is made by a company if

- the person issuing the instrument is a person authorised to issue certificated instruments of transfer on the company's behalf; and
- the certification is signed by a person authorised to certificate transfers on the company's behalf or by an officer or employee either of the company or of a body corporate so authorised. A certification is treated as signed by a person if
  - (i) it purports to be authenticated by his signature or initials (whether handwritten or not); and
  - (ii) it is not shown that the signature or initials was or were placed there neither by himself nor by a person authorised to use the signature or initials for the purpose of certificating transfers on the company's behalf.

  [*CA 2006, s 775(4)*].

The certification by a company of an instrument of transfer of any shares in, or debentures of, the company is to be taken as a representation by the company, to any person acting on the faith of the certification, that documents have been produced to the company that on their face show a *prima facie* title to the shares or debentures in the transferor named in the instrument. However, the certification is not to be taken as a representation that the transferor has any title to the shares or debentures.

[*CA 2006, s 775(1)(2)*].

Where a person acts on the faith of a false certification by a company made negligently, the company is under the same liability to him as if the certification had been made fraudulently. [*CA 2006, s 775(3)*].

Where a company erroneously returned a share certificate to the transferor together with the certificated transfer, and the transferor purported to execute a second 'transfer' in favour of a third party, it was held that the company's duty in relation to the share certificate was owed only to the original transferees, and not to the third party (*Longman v Bath Electric Tramways Ltd* [1905] 1 Ch 646, 74 LJ Ch 424, CA).

44.9 TRANSMISSION OF SHARES

Transmission occurs most commonly on the death or bankruptcy of a shareholder but it can also arise on a person becoming of unsound mind and the subject of an order of the Court of Protection. Following the death of a shareholder, the legal title to his shares vests in his personal representatives or, where the shares were held jointly, in the surviving holder(s).

Execution of share transfer by personal representatives and trustees in bankruptcy. An instrument of transfer of the share or other interest of a deceased member of a company may be made by his personal representative, although the personal representative is not himself a member of the company, and is as effective as if the personal representative had been such a member at the time of the execution of the instrument. [*CA 2006, s 773*].

If the personal representative does have the shares transferred into his own name and becomes registered as a member, he is personally liable for calls on outstanding shares (with a right of indemnity against the deceased's estate); otherwise he will only be liable for outstanding calls to the extent of the deceased's assets in his hands (*Cheshire Banking Co, Re, Duff's Executors' Case* (1886) 32 Ch D 301, CA).

A trustee in bankruptcy may similarly transfer the bankrupt's shares without first becoming registered as a member.

[*Insolvency Act 1986, s 314, Sch 5*].

Evidence of grant of probate, etc. The production to a company of any document that is, by law, sufficient evidence of the grant of

- probate of the will of a deceased person,
- letters of administration of the estate of a deceased person, or
- confirmation as executor of a deceased person,

must be accepted by the company as sufficient evidence of the grant.
[*CA 2006, s 774*].

Standard articles. Where a company has adopted standard articles, see

- *Table A, 1985, Regs 29–31*
- *Model Articles, Arts 27, 28* (private companies)
- *Model Articles, Arts 65–68* (public companies)

set out in APPENDIX 4 STANDARD ARTICLES OF ASSOCIATION.

44.10 ISSUE OF CERTIFICATES, ETC ON TRANSFER

Duty of company as to issue of certificates, etc on transfer. Subject to below, a company must, within two months after the date on which a transfer of any of its shares, debentures or debenture stock is lodged with the company, complete and have ready for delivery

- the certificates of the shares transferred;
- the debentures transferred; or
- the certificates of the debenture stock transferred.

For this purpose a '*transfer*' means either a transfer duly stamped and otherwise valid or an exempt transfer within *Stock Transfer Act 1982* and does not include a transfer that the company is for any reason entitled to refuse to register and does not register.

The provisions above do not apply in the following circumstances.

(a) If the conditions of issue of the shares, debentures or debenture stock provide otherwise.

(b) If a transfer for transferring shares, debentures or debenture stock to a 'financial institution' is lodged with a company, the company is not required, in consequence of that transfer, to comply with the above provisions. A '*financial institution*' means

(i) a recognised clearing house acting in relation to a recognised investment exchange; or

(ii) a nominee of a recognised clearing house acting in that way or a recognised investment exchange, in either case designated for these purposes in the rules of the recognised investment exchange in question.

(c) In the case of a transfer of shares if, following the transfer, the company has issued a share warrant in respect of the shares (see **44.12**).

(d) In the case of a transfer to a person where, by virtue of Regulations under *Stock Transfer Act 1982, s 3* the transferee is not entitled to a certificate or other document evidencing title in respect of the securities transferred. But if, in such a case, the transferee subsequently becomes entitled to such a certificate, etc by virtue of any provision of those Regulations, and gives notice in writing of that fact to the company, the provisions then apply as if the reference to the date of the lodging of the transfer were a reference to the date of the notice.

If default is made in complying with the above requirements, an offence is committed by every officer of the company who is in default. A person guilty of such an offence is liable, on summary conviction, to a fine not exceeding level 3 on the standard scale and, for continued contravention, a daily default fine not exceeding one-tenth of level 3 on the standard scale. See **29.1 Offences and Legal Proceedings** for the standard scale.

[*CA 2006, s 776–778*].

Where a company has adopted standard articles, see, *Model Articles, Art 46* (public companies), set out in **Appendix 4 Standard Articles of Association**.

See **44.13** for the court's power to order a company to make good any default under these provisions.

44.11 Contents and replacement of share certificates

A company's articles frequently include provisions with respect to the contents of, and replacement of lost or destroyed, share certificates including that the shareholder is entitled to a replacement and that the directors may decide that an indemnity must be provided (see example indemnity below). Where a company has adopted standard articles, see

- *Table A, 1985, Regs, 6, 7,*
- *Model Articles, Arts 24, 25* (private companies),
- *Model Articles, Arts 47–49* (public companies),

set out in **Appendix 4 Standard Articles of Association.**

44.12 SHARE WARRANTS

A company limited by shares may, if authorised by its articles, issue with respect to any fully paid shares a warrant (known as a 'share warrant') stating that the bearer of the warrant is entitled to the shares specified in it. A share warrant issued under the company's common seal (or, in the case of a company registered in Scotland, subscribed in accordance with the *Requirements of Writing (Scotland) Act 1995*) entitles the bearer to the shares specified in it and the shares may be transferred by delivery of the warrant.

A company that issues a share warrant may also, if authorised by its articles, provide (by coupons or otherwise) for the payment of the future dividends on the shares included in the warrant.

As from May 2015 share warrants to bearer have been abolished by *Small Business, Enterprise and Employment Act 2015 (SBEE 2015), ss 84, 85, 86 and Sch 4*. The effect of these provisions is as follows:

- *CA 2006, s 779* is amended to include a new *s 779(4)* which provides that no share warrants may be issued by a company on or after the date *SBEE 2015, s 84* comes into force irrespective of whether the company's articles purport to authorise it to do so.
- *SBEE 2015, s 84* comes into force May 2015 (see *SBEE 2015, s 164*).
- share warrants issued before May 2015 have to be either converted into registered shares or cancelled in accordance with *SBEE 2015, Sch 4*.
- if the company's articles authorise the issue of share warrants the company must amend its articles to remove the provision and can so amend without the need for a special resolution or without complying with any provision for entrenchment relevant to that provision.

A copy of the articles as amended must be sent to the Registrar of Companies

[*CA 2006, s 779; SBEE 2015, ss 84, 85, 86, 164, Sch 4*].

See **38.4 Registers** regarding entries in a company's register of members in relation to share warrants.

Duty of company to issue certificate on surrender of share warrant. In relation to share warrants surrendered to a company unless the articles provide otherwise, the company must, within two months of the surrender of the share warrant for cancellation, complete and have ready for delivery the certificates of the shares specified in the warrant.

If default is made in complying with this requirement, an offence is committed by every officer of the company who is in default. A person guilty of such an offence is liable on summary conviction to a fine not exceeding level 3 on the standard scale and, for continued contravention, a daily default fine not exceeding one-tenth of level 3 on the standard scale. See **29.1 Offences and Legal Proceedings** for the standard scale.

[*CA 2006, s 780*].

See **44.13** for the court's power to order a company to make good any default under this provision.

Standard articles. Where a company has adopted standard articles, see *Model Articles, Art 51* (public companies), set out in APPENDIX 4 STANDARD ARTICLES OF ASSOCIATION.

Offences in connection with share warrants (Scotland). In Scotland, a person commits an offence if

(a) with intent to defraud, he forges or alters, or offers, utters, disposes of, or puts off, knowing the same to be forged or altered, any share warrant or coupon, or any document purporting to be a share warrant or coupon issued under *CA 2006*;

(b) by means of any such forged or altered share warrant, coupon or document, he demands or tries to obtain or receive

- any share or interest in a company under *CA 2006*, or
- any dividend or money payment in respect of any such share or interest,

knowing the warrant, coupon or document to be forged or altered;

(c) without lawful authority or excuse (of which proof lies on him), he

- engraves, or makes on any plate or other material, any share warrant or coupon purporting to be
  - (i) a share warrant or coupon issued or made by any particular company; or
  - (ii) a blank share warrant or coupon so issued or made; or
  - (iii) a part of such a share warrant or coupon; or
- uses any such plate or other material for the making or printing of any such share warrant or coupon, or of any such blank share warrant or coupon or of any part of such a share warrant or coupon; or
- he knowingly has in his custody or possession any such plate or other material.

A person guilty of an offence under (*a*) or (*b*) above is liable, on summary conviction, to imprisonment for a term not exceeding six months or to a fine not exceeding level 5 on the standard scale (or both). A person guilty of an offence under (*c*) above is liable (i) on conviction on indictment, to imprisonment for a term not exceeding seven years or a fine (or both); and (ii) on summary conviction, to imprisonment for a term not exceeding six months or a fine not exceeding the statutory maximum (or both). See **29.1** OFFENCES AND LEGAL PROCEEDINGS for the standard scale and statutory maximum.

[*CA 2006, s 781*].

44.13 ISSUE OF CERTIFICATES: COURT ORDER TO MAKE GOOD DEFAULT

If a company, on which a notice has been served requiring it to make good any default in complying with its duty as to the issue of certificates, etc under **44.2**, **44.10** or **44.12** above, fails to make good the default within ten days after service of the notice, the person entitled to have the certificates or the debentures delivered to him may apply to the court.

The court may make an order directing the company, and any officer of it, to make good the default within such time as is specified in the order. The order may also provide that all costs (in Scotland, expenses) of, and incidental to, the application are to be borne by the company or by an officer of it responsible for the default.

[*CA 2006, s 782*].

44.14 STOCK EXCHANGE TRANSFERS

A more complex system of transfers is required for dealings carried out on the Stock Exchange to provide an effective centralised method for the settlement of bargains.

The *Uncertificated Securities Regulations 2001* (*SI 2001 No 3755*) (as amended by the *Companies Act 2006 (Consequential Amendments) (Uncertificated Securities) Order 2009 (SI 2009 No 1889)* and the *Uncertificated Securities (Amendment) Regulations 2013 (SI 2013 No 632)*), contain the concept of a '*relevant system*' which is defined as a computer-based system and procedures which enable title to units of security to be evidenced and transferred without a written instrument.

The Bank of England has powers (which it has delegated to the FCA) to approve a person who wishes to be the 'Operator' of a relevant system. [*SI 2001 No 3755, Regs 4–13, Sch 1*]. Euroclear UK (formerly CRESTCo) has been approved as Operator of a relevant system in respect of CREST. Euroclear is responsible for establishing and running the central computer system and for specifying the technical requirements which must be met by networks through which messages are sent to and from the central computer system.

CREST enables 'participating securities' to be held without the need for a share certificate to be issued and to be transferred without the need for an executed stock transfer form to be submitted to the company. It is a voluntary system in two ways. First, an issuer may choose whether or not a particular class of securities issued by it is to be eligible for transfer through CREST. (There is no requirement that listed securities should be eligible for CREST although in practice most securities listed on the London Stock Exchange or dealt in on the Alternative Investment Market have joined CREST.) Secondly, even if a particular security is admitted to CREST, a shareholder may choose whether to hold the security in certificated or uncertificated form.

The CREST central computer system maintains records called 'stock accounts'. A stock account is maintained for each separate 'participating security' held by each 'system-member'. The account relates to the entries on the register maintained by the 'participating issuer'. When the central computer system receives an instruction from a system-member transferor and a system-member transferee in relation to a transfer, it checks that the transferor is able to transfer the relevant number of securities and that the transferee has a payment bank which is willing to make the payment for the transfer. The computer system then itself generates an 'operator instruction' to the company instructing it to register the transfer which it is required to do within two hours. All messages are sent to and from the central computer system and the participants in the system (eg companies and their shareholders) do not communicate directly with each other. At no point does Euroclear act as a principal either in holding securities itself or as obligor under the payment arrangements.

A '*participating security*' is a security title to units of which is permitted by an Operator to be transferred by means of a relevant system. [*SI 2001 No 3755, Reg 3(1)*]. The Regulations allow most securities issued by companies incorporated in the UK under the Companies Acts to be eligible for CREST (including debenture and loan stocks, preference shares and subscription warrants). In order for a security to be admitted to

CREST, an issuer must comply with the CREST procedures for admission of securities. Securities are admitted by class and so, for example, the ordinary shares of a particular company may be a participating security whilst its preference shares exist only in certificated form.

A company's articles normally contain provisions concerning the transfer of shares in the company. If the articles are in all respects consistent with

(i) holding shares of a class in uncertificated form,

(ii) transfer of title to shares of the class by means of a relevant system, and

(iii) the Regulations,

that class of shares may become a participating security. To the extent that a company's articles are inconsistent with (i)–(iii) above, the directors may pass a resolution that title to shares of that class may be transferred by means of a relevant system. Notice must be given to each member of the company either of the intention to pass such a resolution or that such a resolution has been passed. In the latter case, notice must be given within 60 days of the passing of the resolution. [*SI 2001 No 3755, Regs 14–19*]. In the case of convertible and redeemable shares, other changes to the articles may be necessary to disapply the provisions relating to the *means* by which convertible shares are converted or redeemable shares are redeemed. For example, articles may require amendment so that a system message can constitute a conversion notice.

A '*participating issuer*' is a person who has issued a security which is a participating security. Except where an issuer acts as its own registrar, CREST is unlikely to have any significant impact on the issuer. The company's registrar needs to participate in CREST and be in a position to send and receive messages (or have them sent and received on their behalf).

A '*system-member*' is a person who has been permitted by Euroclear to transfer through CREST title to uncertificated units of a participating security held by him. [*SI 2001 No 3755, Reg 3(1)*]. The system-member is the person whose name appears on the register of securities maintained by the participating issuer. The only requirements imposed by Euroclear on a person wishing to be a system-member are that

- a settlement bank has agreed to provide settlement bank facilities; and
- the system-member has the ability to send and receive messages through the system (either himself or through a 'sponsor').

A '*sponsored member*' is a system-member who has appointed a sponsor to send and receive messages on his behalf. Individuals are unlikely to have the necessary computer network to enable them to send and receive messages directly. The concept of a sponsored member enables a person to hold shares in uncertificated form, and therefore to be a registered shareholder, by appointing another person (eg a broker or bank) to send and receive electronic messages relating to those shares.

A '*system-participant*' or '*user*' is a person permitted by the Operator to send and receive messages. In practical terms this is the person with the computer and network connection. A '*sponsoring system-participant*' is a person who has been permitted to send and receive instructions on behalf of other persons. Thus a system member may, but need not be, a system-participant. A company which does not maintain its own register is not a system-participant – its registrar will be a system-participant and will be a sponsoring system-participant for the issuer.

Changes of form. There are special provisions to enable a unit of a security to be changed from certificated to uncertificated form and vice versa (whether at the time of a transfer of title or without there being a change of holder).

Registers of members. A company any of whose securities can be transferred through CREST must subdivide its register of those securities to show how many securities each person holds in uncertified form and certified form respectively. [*SI 2001 No 3755, Reg 20*]. For these purposes, any overseas branch register (see **38.7 REGISTERS**) maintained by a company is not regarded as forming part of the company's register of members. It is not therefore possible to hold shares in uncertificated form on an overseas branch register. A person who is recorded on such a register who wishes to hold shares in uncertificated form must first have his entry transferred to the principal register and then take the necessary steps to convert his holding from certificated to uncertificated form.

Rectification of a register. A participating issuer can only rectify a register of securities in relation to uncertificated units with the consent of the Operator or by order of the court. [*SI 2001 No 3755, Reg 25*].

Registration of transfers. A participating issuer

(a) must register a transfer of title to uncertificated units in accordance with an operator instruction unless the transfer is prohibited by court order or the issuer has actual notice that the transfer is prohibited or avoided by or under an enactment or a transfer to a deceased person; and

(b) must not register a transfer of title to uncertificated units unless required to do so

- by an operator instruction;
- by court order; or
- by or under any enactment.

An issuer who registers a transfer other than under (*b*) above is in breach of statutory duty and may incur liability in damages to anyone who suffers loss as a result of the default.

An issuer may refuse to register a transfer if, *inter alia*, the instruction requires a transfer of units to an entity which is not a natural or legal person or to a minor.

[*SI 2001 No 3755, Regs 28, 46*].

Standard articles. Where a company has adopted standard articles, see, *Model Articles, Art 50* (public companies), set out in **APPENDIX 4 STANDARD ARTICLES OF ASSOCIATION**.

45 Security for company borrowing

45.1 Introduction
45.2 Taking security and giving financial assistance
45.3 Charges
45.4 Fixed charges
45.5 Floating charges
45.6 Registration of charges
45.7 Validity and priority

Cross-references: See **17** DEBT FINANCE-DEBENTURES AND OTHER BORROWING, **40** REGISTRATION OF CHARGES.

45.1 INTRODUCTION

A company may need to borrow for a variety of reasons for example to expand the company through asset or share acquisitions. The purpose for which the money is being borrowed will usually determine the nature of the loan. Project finance for example is usually used for long term financing of building and industrial projects. The finance is usually a mixture of equity investment and syndicated bank loans, secured over the project assets. See **17.4** for types of company borrowing. This chapter is concerned only with the types of security a lender can take for company loans and the validity and priority of that secured lending in the event (usually) of company insolvency. It does not deal with details of insolvency law and procedures. For further information see *Tolley's Insolvency Law*.

45.2 TAKING SECURITY AND GIVING FINANCIAL ASSISTANCE

"Security" is defined in the *Insolvency Act 1986* as, in relation to England and Wales, any mortgage, charge, lien, or other security (*IA 1986, s 248 (1)(b)*) and "secured creditor" in relation to a company, means a creditor of the company who holds in respect of his/her debt a security over property of the company (*IA 1986, s 248(1)(a)*) Taking security for a loan to a company provides a degree of protection which an unsecured loan often does not. The main protection is that subject to the validity and priority of any security taken, a fixed charge secured creditor, when enforcing the security, ranks ahead of preferential and unsecured creditors. Generally also a secured charge holder is able (subject to the validity of the charge) to sell the assets secured by the charge in the event of the borrower's default in payment and is able to appoint a receiver to realise the property subject to the charge. The appointment and powers of receivers and administrators is outside the scope of this chapter. The lender may also take additional/other security from for example members of the same group of companies as the primary borrower and/or from the company's directors (by way of personal guarantees). The personal liabilities of directors under such guarantees are outside the scope of this chapter. Future assets of the company may also be secured by a charge. Historically only floating charges were created over future assets, but given the disadvantages of floating charges (see **45.5**) fixed charges also now are created over future as well as present assets of the company. There is a distinction in the priorities afforded to charges depending on whether the security is by way of fixed or floating charge. See **17.5** and **45.4** and **45.5** below for the meaning of fixed and floating charges, **45.5** below for the meaning of preferential creditors and **45.7** for priority of charges.

45.2 Security for company borrowing

Financial assistance

On 1 October 2008 the prohibition on a private company giving financial assistance for the purchase of its own shares was abolished. The prohibition was retained for public companies (*CA 2006, s 678*). When giving financial assistance (for example as part of an acquisition finance arrangement) pre 1 October 2008, private companies would have to go through what was called the "whitewash" procedure. Although strictly *CA 2006*, in abolishing the financial assistance provisions for private companies does not require the whitewash procedure to be followed, commercial practice still dictates that lenders need some comfort when what would have amounted to financial assistance is involved on a loan transaction. The Financial Law and Company Law committees of the City of London Law Society issued a joint memorandum in September 2008 recommending that certain general company law principles should continue to be taken into account when a private company is giving what would have amounted to financial assistance. These principles are:

- that the transaction must be in the best interests of the company ("likely to promote the success of the company for the benefit of its members");
- the transaction must not breach the rules on distributions or otherwise constitute an illegal reduction in the capital of the company;
- that the validity of the transaction may be called into question as a transaction at an undervalue for the purposes of the *Insolvency Act ("IA") 1986, s 238*. See the City of London Law Society website at www.citysolicitors.org.uk (go to Committees tab and then Company Law) for the full text of the paper "*The implications for leveraged transactions of the repeal of the statutory prohibition of financial assistance by private companies*": The paper further commented on the following practical issues involved.

Best interests of the company

The requirement to show that the transaction is in the best interests of the company may be considered in the same way as any other "upstream" commitment by a subsidiary for the benefit of other members of the group and the following may be considered as practical measures to give assurance that this requirement is met:

- board minutes that confirm the board has considered the matter and concluded that the transaction should be approved. It may be helpful to identify the "corporate benefit" in the minutes (whether tangible (guarantee fees) or intangible (the benefit of remaining part of the group)) and the board's assessment of the solvency of the company;
- approval by a shareholder resolution, which can reduce or eliminate the risk of a company/shareholder challenge based on breach of duty by the directors (the risk remains of a challenge if the company is insolvent, or is threatened by insolvency but as to this, see below).

No reduction of capital

If the transaction involves an outright transfer of assets to or for the benefit of the shareholders of the company it may amount to a distribution, in which case the statutory rules on distributions must be complied with:

- if it is gratuitous, or
- if it involves a transfer at less than the lower of fair market value and book value (if the company has distributable reserves) or less than fair market value (if the company does not have distributable reserves).

Any other transaction which involves (or may in future involve) the transfer of assets to or for the benefit of shareholders and involves:

- a gift (not amounting to a distribution),
- a loan, or
- a guarantee or indemnity, the grant of security or any other assumption of a liability by the company

may amount to an unlawful reduction of capital if, as a result of the transaction, there would be a reduction in the net assets recorded in the company's books and that reduction exceeds the amount of the distributable reserves of the company.

If a transaction is on arm's length terms, it may be lawful even if the transaction would result in accounting net assets being reduced by more than the distributable reserves of the company. However, such situations are likely to be relatively rare and will require case-by-case analysis.

The effect on net assets should be determined according to normal accounting principles, so that if the transaction does not require an immediate accounting loss to be recognised there will be no effect on net assets. Accordingly, none of the issue of an upstream guarantee, the creation of upstream security or the making of an upstream loan will offend the rules concerning the maintenance of capital unless in the books of the company concerned the loan receivable falls to be recorded at less than the amount advanced or the guarantee or security requires the immediate recognition of a liability (and then only to the extent that the amount of the loss exceeds the distributable reserves of the company).

The steps that should be taken to provide assurance that the validity of the transaction cannot be challenged effectively will depend on the circumstances, but may include:

- being able to demonstrate that the directors of the company entering into the transaction have considered whether it will lead to a reduction in net assets and, if so, the amount of profits available for distribution. This will involve an assessment of the likelihood of any guarantee being called or any loan not being repaid and, under some accounting standards, the market value of a guarantee given or of a loan made. The amount of detail considered appropriate in any such assessment may depend on the degree of uncertainty as to (a) the possibility of a payment having to be made and (b) the potential magnitude of the payment (taking into account any right of indemnity and any right of contribution);
- in some circumstances the directors may wish to arrange for an independent review of the cash flows and projections relied on for this purpose or of the processes used to develop them. However, we expect this to be an exception rather than the usual case;
- if the transaction will reduce the accounting net assets of the company and therefore requires distributable reserves in order to be lawful, it may be appropriate to arrange for a detailed review of the distributable reserves position to be carried out and for the auditors to be consulted on the conclusions of that review.

Insolvency/potential insolvency

If the company concerned is, or is at risk of becoming, insolvent (or if the transaction causes the company to become insolvent), the risk of challenge to the transaction is much increased. The usual assessment of the creditworthiness of the overall transaction should identify any solvency issues that may exist independent of the proposed transaction. It is likely that the steps outlined above will identify any threat to solvency created by the transaction itself.

Conclusion: impact on financing transactions

Although some more cautious views have been expressed, the City of London Law Society believe there is a significant consensus supporting the approach set out above. As a result, they consider that the abolition of the prohibition on financial assistance for private companies will not, by itself, throw up any problems additional to those which have always required consideration when dealing with cross guarantees, upstream loans and upstream security.

They expect, therefore, that procedures adopted to assure interested parties that financing and refinancing of share acquisitions are not vulnerable to legal challenge should now come into line with those familiar to practitioners in other financing transactions.

45.3 CHARGES

Charges are the most common form of security granted over a company's assets and can be fixed or floating (see **45.4** and **45.5**). Mortgages over the company's real property are an additional and other usual form of security. A "charge" is not defined in either *CA 2006* or *IA 1986* – see **17.5** and does not transfer legal or equitable title to the chargee. A mortgage by contrast transfers the title subject to the mortgage to the lender by way of security and can be by way of a legal or equitable mortgage. Creation of a mortgage over property prevents the borrower dealing with the asset in any way without the consent of the chargeholder.

45.4 Fixed charges

A fixed charge is a direct charge over a specific asset or category of assets and has the effect that the company is not free to deal with or dispose of the charged asset(s) even in the ordinary course of business without the consent of the chargee. With a view to improving the security of creditors, an increasing proportion of assets are being made the subject of fixed charges rather than floating charges: in particular, book debts have been targeted. The court, in deciding whether a charge is fixed or floating, will look not only at the intention of the parties when creating the charge but also at the effect of that charge. If the company can use the book debts as cash flow this is not consistent with a fixed charge. The debts must be put in a blocked account or otherwise controlled by the chargee for the fixed charge to be considered as such. There have been decisions in which it has been held that there can be a valid fixed charge over book debts (*Re Siebe Gorman & Co Ltd v Barclays Bank Ltd* [1979] 2 Lloyd's Rep 142, 10 LDAB 94), (*Re Keenan Bros* [1986] BCLC 242, 2 BCC 98, 970, Ir SC) and (*New Bullas Trading Ltd* [1994] 1 BCLC 485, [1994] BCC 36, CA). Where a charge lacks the relevant control provisions, a charge on book debts may be held to be only a floating charge (*Re Armagh Shoes Ltd* [1982] NI 59, [1984] BCLC 405 and *Brumark Investments Limited reported under the name of Richard Dale Agnew and Kevin James Bearsley v The Commissioner of Inland Revenue and Official Assignee for the estate in bankruptcy of Bruce William Birtwhistle and Mark Leslie Birtwhistle* [2001] 3 WLR 454 and [2001] BCC 259) with the consequence that the charged assets must be used to pay any preferential claims.

Following the decision in Brumark Investments Limited it is believed that the majority of fixed charges over book debts encountered by the official receiver will be floating charges as the elements of control over the collection and disposition of the debts will be absent.

45.5 Floating charges

A floating charge (by contrast to a fixed charge) constitutes a present security, on a class of assets. It leaves a company free to deal with its assets in the ordinary course of business until some further step by or on behalf of those interested in the charge causes the charge to crystallise. In addition, when the charge is enforced it can help to preserve the business as a going concern by enabling an appointed receiver to trade on and to sell the business to a purchaser without the need for court involvement. A floating charge has three elements:

- it is a charge on a class of assets of a company present and future;
- the class of assets may change from time to time; and
- the company may carry on business in the ordinary way until action is taken by the chargeholder.

Certain events cause crystallisation of a floating charge:

- the winding up of the company,
- the appointment of a receiver, and
- the cessation of the company's business.

(See In *Re Woodroffes (Musical Instruments) Ltd* [1986] Ch 366, [1985] 3 WLR 543, [1985] 2 All ER 908.) Crystallisation takes place on the occurrence of any of those events, even though nothing is stated in the debenture and even if it is contrary to what is stated in the debenture.

In addition, the parties to the charge can agree contractually that a floating charge, created by a debenture, may be crystallised into a fixed charge by intervention of the debenture holder. Most commonly this intervention will take the form of the appointment of a receiver out of court by the debenture holder but it may take other forms, eg the service of a notice converting the floating charge into a fixed charge in respect of specified assets.

Floating chargeholders are disadvantaged by the following:

- preferential creditors are paid in priority insofar as the company's assets available for payment of general creditors are insufficient to meet them. This includes a floating charge which has subsequently (ie after it is made) become a fixed charge (*IA 1986, s 175(2)(b)* and *(3)*). "Preferential creditors" are defined in *IA 1986, Schedule 6* and comprise in the main payments to occupational pension funds and payments to employees (*Schedule 6, paras 8–14*). The *Enterprise Act 2002* reduced the number of preferred creditors and abolished the right of Crown departments (such as HMRC) to be preferred creditors where the petition for winding up was presented on or after 15 September 2003;
- fixed charge holders may sell assets the subject of the charge (see above);
- payment of expenses of winding up, insofar as the company's assets available for general creditors are insufficient to meet those expenses, have priority over the claims of floating charge holders (*IA 1986, s 176ZA*). This applies to winding up

orders made after 6 April 2008 (see **45.7**). Before that date ie where a winding up order is made after 6 April 2008 following a resolution for a voluntary winding up passed before that date, payment is subject to the decision in *Buchler and another v Talbot and another and others* [2004] UKHL 9 (known as the *Leyland DAF Limited* case). The judgment substantially altered the way in which liquidators of companies, which had granted floating charges over their assets, could attempt to recover the payment of the liquidation expenses and pay the (liquidation) preferential creditors .In the *Leyland DAF Limited* case their Lordships concluded that the assets of a company that has gone into liquidation are comprised in two separate funds:

- charged assets (ie those which are subject to a floating or fixed charge), and
- free assets (ie those which are not subject to a floating or fixed charge but which are held in trust for the unsecured creditors).

Each fund should bear its own costs and there is no reason why either interested group (the debenture holder and the unsecured creditors) should contribute towards the costs of the other fund. A debenture holder has no liability for the general costs of the winding-up. See above that *IA 1986, s 176ZA* effectively reversed this decision for a winding up after 6 April 2008; and

- *ring fencing*: *IA 1986, s 176A* provides (in summary) that: where a floating charge relates to property of a company:

  (a) which has gone into liquidation,

  (b) which is in administration,

  (c) of which there is a provisional liquidator, or

  (d) of which there is a receiver.

then the liquidator, administrator or receiver must set aside a prescribed part of the company's net property which is available for the satisfaction of unsecured debts, and must not distribute that part to the floating charge holder except in so far as it exceeds the amount required for the satisfaction of unsecured debts. In other words the liquidator, administrator or receiver must ring fence a prescribed part of the assets for unsecured creditors.

The calculation of the prescribed part of the company's assets which must be set apart is set out in the *Insolvency Act 1986 (Prescribed Part) Order 2003 (SI 2003 No 2097)* which provides that where the company's net property does not exceed £10,000 in value the prescribed part is 50% of that property. Subject to *art 2* of the *Order*, where the company's net property exceeds £10,000 in value the prescribed part is the sum of—

(i) 50% of the first £10,000 in value; and

(ii) 20% of that part of the company's net property which exceeds £10,000 in value.

Article 2 of the *Order* says that the value of the prescribed part of the company's net property to be made available for the satisfaction of unsecured debts of the company pursuant to *IA 1986, s 176A* shall not exceed £600,000.

45.6 REGISTRATION OF CHARGES

In order to be valid a charge must be properly registered at Companies House within the time limits imposed by *CA 2006, s 860*. If the charge is not registered within the statutory time limits, the charge is void (so far as any security on the company's property or undertaking is conferred by it) against a liquidator, administrator or creditor of the company [*CA 2006, s 874*]. The charge is void even if the liquidator or creditor has notice of the unregistered charge (*Monolithic Building Co, Re Tacon v Monolithic Building Co* [1915] 1 Ch 643, 84 LJ Ch 441, CA). See **Chapter 40** of this book for full details of the registration of charges under *CA 2006* and **Appendix 2** for details of forms to be used when registering a charge. As mentioned above a company may also grant security by way of a mortgage over real property. Where this is the case the charge must be registered with the Land Registry.

45.7 VALIDITY AND PRIORITY

In order for a charge to be effective against the borrower or against a liquidator, administrator or receiver it must be valid. To be valid:

- the company must have the power to create the charge. This type of power would historically have been set out in the company's objects (in its memorandum.) As from 1 October 2009 a company's objects are unrestricted unless the company's articles provide otherwise [*CA 2006, s 31(1)*]. A company incorporated on or after 1 October 2009 may adopt restricted objects which have to be set out in the company's articles of association. A charge may still be valid even if the company has exceeded its powers in creating the charge.

- the document must be properly executed. An agreement to dispose of an interest in land must be in writing and signed by or on behalf of each party to the agreement and must incorporate all the agreed terms in one document [*Law of Property (Miscellaneous Provisions) Act 1989, s 2*]. A mortgage or charge of an equitable interest or trust must be made in writing and signed by the chargor [*Law of Property Act 1925, s 53(1)(c)*]. The person who signed it should have had the power to do so on behalf of the company. Where the document was signed by the director(s), or someone authorised by them to do so, and provided that the chargeholder acted in good faith, the charge will be valid even if the director(s) exceeded their powers [*CA 2006, s 40*].

The director(s) may be personally liable in an action for misfeasance or breach of duty if they caused the company to act outside the scope of its constitution [*CA 2006, s 40(5)*].

- the charge must be registered (see **45.6**) If the company does not register a charge within the time prescribed by *CA 2006, s 860*, the charge is void against a liquidator, administrator or creditor of the company and cannot be enforced in priority to a subsequent charge which is properly registered (see below for priority) but the charge remains enforceable against the company (provided the company is not in administration or liquidation) and the debt secured by the charge remains enforceable [*CA 2006, s 874(3)*]. Additionally the company and every officer of the company commit an offence [*CA 2006, s 860(4)* and *(5)*]. CA 2006 contains provisions to enable a company to register a charge out of time. This involves an application to the court by the company itself or by "a person interested" [*CA 2006, s 873(2)*]. The court has the discretion on hearing the application to order that the period allowed for registration shall be extended provided it is satisfied that the failure to register the charge before the end of the time period allowed was accidental or due to inadvertence or to some other sufficient cause or is not of a nature to prejudice the position of the company's creditors or shareholders [*CA 2006, s 873(1)*]. In making the order the court can impose such terms and conditions as seem to the court to be just and expedient.

  [*CA 2006, s 873(2)*].

Priority

In addition to ensuring that a charge is valid, the chargeholder will also want to ensure that they have priority over other creditors. "Priority" means the order in which creditors are paid in the event for example of company liquidation.

The basic rules of priority are:

- *unsecured creditors*: (apart from preferential creditors (see **45.5** above) who may take priority) all other unsecured creditors rank *pari passu*, that is equally amongst themselves.

  [*IA 1986, s 107*]

- *secured creditors*. As a general rule a fixed charge created first in time and duly registered (see **45.6**) takes priority over later fixed charges [*James v Boythorpe Colliery Co* [1890] 2 Meg 55]. A fixed charge takes priority over a floating charge even if created after the floating charge unless the fixed charge is made subject to the prior floating charge [*Re Robert Stephenson & Co Ltd* [1913] 2 Ch 201]. This can be done by a deed of priority which is made between the company and the chargeholders. A deed of priority is effective even if results in a floating charge taking priority over a fixed charge [*Re Portabase Clothing Ltd* [1993] BCC 96]. A floating charge created first in time takes priority over later floating charges even if the later chargeholder has notice that the earlier charge exists [*Re Benjamin Cope & Sons Ltd* [1914] 1 Ch 800].

- *debenture holders*. See **17.14** that where debentures are secured by a floating charge, if possession is taken of property subject to the charge and the company is not, at the time, being wound up, the preferential debts must be paid in priority to any claims under the debenture (either for the principal sum or interest).

  [*CA 2006, s 754*].

Expenses of liquidation – winding-up order made after 6 April 2008

IA 1986, s 176ZA provides that the liquidator's general expenses shall, where the unencumbered assets are insufficient to meet those expenses, be paid in priority to the claims of preferential creditors and floating charge-holders, therefore effectively reversing the decision in *Leyland DAF Ltd*. This section may not be applied retrospectively and therefore applies only to winding-up orders made after 6 April 2008. Where the winding-up order is made following a resolution for a voluntary winding up passed by the company before 6 April 2008 the provisions of *IA 1986, s 176ZA* will not apply.

46 Share Premium

46.1 Transfers to, and applications of, share premium account
46.2 Merger relief
46.3 Group reconstruction relief
46.4 Supplementary provisions

46.1 TRANSFERS TO, AND APPLICATIONS OF, SHARE PREMIUM ACCOUNT

A company issues shares at a premium if the consideration which it receives for them exceeds in value the nominal amount of the shares issued.

Subject to **46.2** and **46.3**, if a company issues shares at a premium, whether for cash or otherwise, a sum equal to the aggregate amount or value of the premiums on those shares must be transferred to an account called the 'share premium account'. See *Henry Head & Co Ltd v Ropner Holdings Ltd* [1952] Ch 124, [1951] 2 All ER 994 for a consideration of the words 'or otherwise' and also Viscount Simon's opinion in *Gold Coast Selection Trust Ltd v Humphrey (Inspector of Taxes)* [1948] AC 459, [1948] 2 All ER 379, HL where an asset is difficult to value.

The share premium account can be used as follows.

- To pay up new shares to be allotted to members as fully paid bonus shares.
- Where, on issuing shares, a company has transferred a sum to the share premium account, it may use that sum to write off
  - (i) the expenses of the issue of those shares; and
  - (ii) any commission paid on the issue of those shares.

Subject to this, the provisions of the *Companies Acts* relating to the reduction of a company's share capital apply as if the share premium account were part of its paid up share capital. See also **47.51 Shares** for the reduction of share capital.

[*CA 2006, s 610*].

The Secretary of State may make Regulations relieving companies from the above requirements in relation to premiums other than cash premiums or otherwise restricting or modifying any relief from the requirements above and in **46.2** to **46.4**.

[*CA 2006, s 614*].

46.2 MERGER RELIEF

Unless the issue falls within **46.3**, the provisions of **46.1** do not apply to the premiums on any 'equity shares' issued in pursuance of an 'arrangement' providing for the allotment of equity shares in the issuing company ('company A') on terms that the consideration for shares allotted is to be provided by

- the issue or transfer to company A of equity shares in the other company ('company B'), or
- the cancellation of any such shares not held by company A

on condition that Company A must have secured at least a 90% equity holding in company B.

In determining whether the 90% test is satisfied, Company A has secured at least a 90% equity holding in company B if, in consequence of an acquisition or cancellation of equity shares in company B (in pursuance of the arrangement) it holds equity shares in company B of an aggregate amount equal to 90% or more of the nominal value of that company's equity share capital. For this purposes

- it is immaterial whether any of those shares were acquired in pursuance of the arrangement; and
- shares in the company B held by the company as treasury shares (see **34.14** PURCHASE OF OWN SHARES) are excluded in determining the nominal value of company B's share capital.

Where the equity share capital of company B is divided into different classes of shares, company A is not regarded as having secured at least a 90% equity holding in company B unless the 90% test is met in relation to each of those classes taken separately.

For these purposes, shares held by

- a company that is company A's holding company or subsidiary,
- a subsidiary of company A's holding company, or
- its or their nominee

are treated as held by company A.

Non-equity shares. Where the arrangement also provides for the allotment of any shares in company A on terms that the consideration for those shares is to be provided by

- the issue or transfer to company A of *non-equity* shares in company B, or
- the cancellation of any such shares in that company not held by company A

relief extends to any shares in company A allotted on those terms in pursuance of the arrangement.

'*Equity shares*' means shares comprised in a company's '*equity share capital*' (see **APPENDIX 1 DEFINITIONS**) and '*non-equity shares*' means shares (of any class) that are not so comprised.

'*Arrangement*' means any agreement, scheme or arrangement (including an arrangement sanctioned under *CA 2006, Pt 26* (arrangements and reconstructions, see **35.1 RECONSTRUCTIONS AND MERGERS**) or *IA 1986, s 110* (liquidator accepting shares as consideration for sale of company property)).

[*CA 2006, ss 612, 613, 616(1)*].

Reflection of relief in the company's balance sheet. The amount corresponding to the amount representing the premiums (or part of the premiums) on shares issued by a company that, by virtue of any relief under these provisions, is not included in the company's share premium account may also be disregarded in determining the amount at which any shares, or other consideration provided for the shares issued, is to be included in the company's balance sheet. [*CA 2006, s 615*].

See also **46.4**.

46.3 GROUP RECONSTRUCTION RELIEF

Where the issuing company

- is a wholly-owned subsidiary of another company (the 'holding company'), and
- allots shares at a premium to

  (i) the holding company, or

  (ii) another wholly-owned subsidiary of the holding company

  in consideration for the transfer to the issuing company of non-cash assets of a company (the 'transferor company') that is a member of the group of companies that comprises the holding company and all its wholly-owned subsidiaries

it is not required by the provisions in **46.1** to transfer an amount in excess of the 'minimum premium value' to the share premium account.

'*Minimum premium value*' is given by the formula

$$(A - L) - N$$

where

A = the base value of the assets transferred, ie the lesser of

- the cost of those assets to the transferor company; or
- the amount at which those assets are stated in the transferor company's accounting records immediately before the transfer.

L = the base value of the liabilities of the transferor company assumed by the issuing company as part of the consideration for the assets transferred, taken as the amount at which they are stated in the transferor company's accounting records immediately before the transfer.

N = the aggregate nominal value of the shares issued.

[*CA 2006, s 611*].

Reflection of relief in the company's balance sheet. The amount corresponding to the amount representing the premiums (or part of the premiums) on shares issued by a company that, by virtue of any relief under these provisions, is not included in the company's share premium account may also be disregarded in determining the amount at which any shares, or other consideration provided for the shares issued, is to be included in the company's balance sheet. [*CA 2006, s 615*].

See also **46.4**.

46.4 SUPPLEMENTARY PROVISIONS

For the purposes of **46.2** and **46.3**

- references to

  (i) the acquisition by a company of shares in another company, and

  (ii) the issue or allotment of shares to, or the transfer of shares to or by, a company

  include (respectively) the acquisition of shares by, and the issue or allotment or transfer of shares to or by, a nominee of that company;

- references to the transfer of shares in a company include the transfer of a right to be included in the company's register of members in respect of those shares; and
- 'company', except in references to the issuing company, includes any body corporate.

[*CA 2006, s 616*].

47 Shares

47.1 **Shares**
47.2 Nominal value of shares
47.3 Numbering of shares
47.4 Transferability of shares
47.5 Classification of shares
47.6 **Share capital**
47.7 Minimum share capital requirements for public companies
47.8 **Allotment of shares**
47.9 Power of directors to allot shares
47.10 Commissions, discounts and allowances
47.11 Registration of allotment
47.12 Return of allotments
47.13 Existing shareholders' right of pre-emption
47.20 Public companies: allotment where issue not fully subscribed
47.21 Prohibition of public offers by private companies
47.23 **Payment for shares**
47.24 Allotment of shares at a discount not permitted
47.25 Calls
47.26 Additional rules for public companies
47.27 Liability of subsequent holder of shares
47.28 Power of court to grant relief
47.29 Penalty for contravention
47.30 Enforceability of undertakings to do work etc
47.31 **Public companies: independent valuation of non-cash consideration**
47.32 Non-cash consideration for shares
47.36 Transfer of non-cash assets to a public company in the initial period
47.41 Requirements as to independent valuation
47.42 Liability of subsequent holders of shares
47.43 Power of court to grant relief
47.44 Penalty for contravention
47.45 Enforceability of undertakings to do work, etc
47.46 **Alteration of share capital**
47.47 Sub-division or consolidation of shares
47.48 Reconversion of stock into shares
47.49 Redenomination of share capital
47.51 **Reduction of share capital**
47.52 Private companies: reduction of capital supported by a solvency statement
47.55 Reduction of capital confirmed by court
47.57 Public company reducing capital below the authorised minimum
47.58 Effect of reduction of capital
47.59 Treatment of reserve arising from reduction of capital
47.60 **Maintenance of capital**
47.61 Duty of directors to call meeting on serious loss of capital
47.62 **Bonus issues**
47.63 Funds available for making bonus issues
47.64 **Rights issues**
47.65 Listed companies

Cross-references. See 9 CLASS RIGHTS; 17 DEBT FINANCE–DEBENTURES AND OTHER BORROWING; 22 DISTRIBUTIONS; 23 INSIDER DEALING AND MARKET ABUSE; 24 INTERESTS IN PUBLIC COMPANY SHARES; 32 PROSPECTUSES; 34 PURCHASE OF OWN SHARES; 35 RECONSTRUCTIONS AND MERGERS; 44 SECURITIES: CERTIFICATION AND TRANSFERS; 46 SHARE PREMIUM; 48 TAKEOVERS.

47.1 SHARES

In the *Companies Acts*, '*share*', in relation to a company, means share in the company's share capital and references to:

- shares include stock (except where a distinction between share and stock is express or implied); and
- a number of shares include an amount of stock (where the context allows the reference to shares being read as including stock).

A company's shares may not be converted into stock. This does not affect any conversion of shares into stock carried out pursuant to a resolution of the company in general meeting passed, or a written resolution agreed to, before 1 October 2009. Stock created before 1 October 2009 (including stock created under a resolution of the company in general meeting) may be reconverted into shares (see **47.48**).

[*CA 2006, s 540*].

Nature of shares. The shares (or other interest of a member in a company) are personal property (in Scotland, moveable property) and are not in the nature of real estate (or heritage). [*CA 2006, s 541*]. See also the judicial definitions in *Borland's Trustee v Steel Bros & Co Ltd* [1901] 1 Ch 279, 70 LJ Ch 51 and *IRC v Crossman* [1937] AC 26, 66, [1936] 1 All ER 762, HL.

The assets of a company are owned by the company itself and the ownership of shares does not entitle the holder to any property rights to the company's assets; he is merely entitled to a *share* in the company and *not* to an interest in every asset the company owns. Shares may be of different classes (see **47.5**) and the rights and obligations of the holders of each class are normally set out in the company's constitution.

47.2 Nominal value of shares

Shares in a limited company having a share capital must each have a fixed nominal value and an allotment of a share that does not have a fixed nominal value is void. If a company purports to allot shares in contravention of this provision, an offence is committed by every officer of the company who is in default. A person guilty of such an offence is liable (i) on conviction on indictment, to a fine; and (ii) on summary conviction, to a fine not exceeding the statutory maximum. See **29.1 Offences and Legal Proceedings** for the statutory maximum.

[*CA 2006, s 542(1)(2)(4)(5)*].

Although shares must have a nominal value (ie no-par value shares are not permitted) this need not be paid at the time of issue. Shares may therefore be nil paid, partly paid or fully paid but where they are not fully paid the shareholder has a liability to pay up the nominal amount of his shares in the event of a call (see **47.25**) or on the winding up of the company. See, however, **47.26** for the minimum amount to be paid on shares allotted by a public company.

Currency. Shares in a limited company having a share capital may be denominated in any currency, and different classes of shares may be denominated in different currencies. But see **33.3 Public and Listed Companies** for the requirement that the initial authorised minimum share capital requirement for a public company must be denominated in sterling or euros. [*CA 2006, s 542*]. See **47.49** for the redenomination of shares into a different currency.

47.3 Numbering of shares

Each share in a company having a share capital must be distinguished by its appropriate number, unless, at any time:

- all the issued shares in a company are fully paid up and rank *pari passu* for all purposes, or
- all the issued shares of a particular class in a company are fully paid up and rank *pari passu* for all purposes,

in which case none of those shares need thereafter have a distinguishing number so long as it remains fully paid up and ranks *pari passu* for all purposes with all shares of the same class for the time being issued and fully paid up. [*CA 2006, s 543*].

47.4 Transferability of shares

The shares (or other interest of any member in a company) are transferable in accordance with the company's articles, but subject to the *Stock Transfer Act 1963* (or, in Northern Ireland, the *Stock Transfer Act (Northern Ireland) 1963*) and Regulations which enable title to securities to be evidenced and transferred without a written instrument. See **44 Securities: Certification and Transfer** generally.

[*CA 2006, s 544*].

47.5 Classification of shares

Where there are no different or separate rights attaching to a particular class of shares in a company then all shares rank equally (*Birch v Cropper, Re Bridgewater Navigation Co Ltd* (1889) 14 App Cas 525, HL). A company may, however, subject to the provisions of *CA 2006* and its constitution and without prejudice to any rights attaching to existing shares, issue any shares with such rights and restrictions as the company determines by ordinary resolution. Where a company has adopted standard articles, see:

- *Table A, 1985, Art 2*
- *Model Articles, Art 22* (private companies)
- *Model Articles, Art 43* (public companies)

set out in **Appendix 4 Standard Articles of Association** which all (in summary) enable a company to issue shares with different rights and restrictions provided the company in general meeting determine those rights etc.

Different classes of shares are most commonly distinguished by different rights and restrictions relating to dividends, voting, return of capital in a winding up and transferability. The more common classifications of shares are as follows.

(1) **Ordinary shares**

Ordinary shares, sometimes referred to as 'equity' or 'risk' capital, are the basic shares of a company and confer residual rights on their holders, ie after all other classes of shares have been satisfied. Generally, the ordinary shares carry voting rights and rights to dividends (if any after preferred holders are paid), and give a right to participate on a winding up in any excess assets. Some companies do, however, issue ordinary shares (sometimes referred to as 'A' ordinary shares) which do not carry voting rights.

(2) **Preference shares**

Generally, preference shares carry no voting rights but are are entitled to a dividend and to other rights, whether to income or capital, in preference to ordinary shareholders. Any rights expressed as attaching to the shares on their creation are, *prima facie*, a definition of the whole of their rights (see *Scottish Insurance Corpn Ltd v Wilsons & Clyde Coal Co Ltd* [1949] AC 462, [1949] 1 All ER 1068, HL) and negative any other rights to which, but for the specified rights, they would have been entitled (*Re National Telephone Co* [1914] 1 Ch 755, 83 LJ Ch 552). Preference shares include the following:

- *Cumulative preference shares* where the right to a dividend, if profits are insufficient in any year, accumulates until profits become sufficient. Unless otherwise stated, the right to receive a preference dividend is cumulative (*Webb v Earle* (1875) LR 20 Eq 556). Even where dividends are cumulative, there is no absolute right to the dividend unless and until the dividend is declared out of available profits (compare interest on debentures). See *Buenos Ayres Great Southern Rly Co Ltd, Re, Buenos Ayres Great Southern Rly Co Ltd v Preston* [1947] Ch 384, [1947] 1 All ER 729.
- Non-cumulative preference shares where there is no right to the accumulation of unpaid dividends because this has been rebutted by the terms of issue (see, for example, *Staples v Eastman Photographic Materials Co* [1896] 2 Ch 303, CA where dividends were to be paid 'out of the net profits each year').
- *Participating preference shares* where there is a right to a dividend and/or return of capital on winding up in preference to the ordinary shares, together with a right to participate in a further distribution of income or capital as the case may be if there remains a surplus after a dividend and/or return of capital to the ordinary shareholders. The right to participate in surplus profits must be expressly stated (*Will v United Lankat Plantations Co Ltd* [1914] AC 11, 83 LJ Ch 195, HL) as must the rights to participate in capital (*Scottish Insurance Corporation v Wilsons & Clyde Coal Co Ltd supra*; *Isle of Thanet Electric Supply Co Ltd, Re* [1950] Ch 161, [1949] 2 All ER 1060, CA).
- *Redeemable preference shares* which a company may redeem at a fixed time or at its option. See **34.2 Purchase of Own Shares** which applies to the redemption of any class of shares (not just preference shares) and **34.5** for the relaxation of rules relating to the payment by private companies for share buy backs from employees' share scheme.

(3) **Founders', management and deferred shares**

Such shares are normally subscribed for by the promoters and are usually deferred in priority to the ordinary shares, ie. the rights of the holders to receive a dividend are deferred until a dividend at a specific rate has been paid out on other shares.

(4) **Redeemable shares**

A company limited by shares may issue redeemable shares. See **34.2 Purchase of Own Shares**.

(5) **Employees' or workers' shares**

In recent years, many companies have issued shares to their employees under one of the many employees' share schemes (see **Appendix 1 Definitions**). As well as encouraging employee involvement in the company, they offer considerable tax incentives. In the early years of ownership there are normally restrictions on transfers. See **47.16** for the disapplication of the pre-emption rules to shares allotted to such schemes.

47.6 SHARE CAPITAL

Company having a share capital. References in the *Companies Acts* to a 'company having a share capital' are to a company that has power under its constitution to issue shares.

Allotted share capital means the shares of a company that have been allotted. It includes shares taken on the formation of the company by the subscribers to the company's memorandum.

Authorised share capital. Companies formed on or after 1 October 2009 are not required to have an authorised share capital. Companies formed before that date may continue to have an authorised share capital but, as such a provision is treated as a provision of the company's articles, it can be amended in the same way as any other change in the articles. See **14 CONSTITUTION – MEMORANDUM AND ARTICLES.**

If a company has an authorised share capital, it cannot issue shares beyond the amount of that authorised capital. If it does so, the issue is void and the allottee can recover any money paid (*Bank of Hindustan, China and Japan Ltd v Alison* (1871) LR 6 CP 222).

Companies incorporated before 1 October 2009 with an authorised share capital.

(1) Any provision of a company's memorandum as to the amount of the company's authorised share capital that was in force immediately before 1 October 2009 is treated, on or after that date, as a provision of the company's articles setting out the maximum amount of shares that may be allotted by the company. As such, it may be amended or revoked by the company by ordinary resolution in the same way as any other change in the articles. See **14 CONSTITUTION – MEMORANDUM AND ARTICLES.**

(2) The provisions in (1) above do not affect the power of a company, by special resolution, to adopt new articles (with effect from 1 October 2009 or any later date) that make no provision as to the maximum number of shares that may be allotted by the company.

(3) Any amendment of a company's articles on or after 1 October 2009 authorising the directors to allot shares in excess of the amount of the authorised share capital that was in force immediately before that date has effect although not expressed as amending or revoking that amount.

[*SI 2008 No 2860, Sch 2 para 42*]

Called-up share capital means so much of a company's share capital as equals the aggregate amount of the calls made on its shares (whether or not those calls have been paid), together with:

- any share capital paid up without being called; and
- any share capital to be paid on a specified future date under the articles, the terms of allotment of the relevant shares or any other arrangements for payment of those shares.

Equity share capital means a company's issued share capital excluding any part of that capital that, neither as respects dividends nor as respects capital, carries any right to participate beyond a specified amount in a distribution.

Issued share capital means the shares of a company that have been issued, ie the shares which have been taken up by shareholders who agree to pay for them either in cash or in kind, together with shares issued as fully paid bonus shares (see **47.62**). It includes shares taken on the formation of the company by the subscribers to the company's memorandum.

Uncalled share capital is construed from the definition of called-up share capital.

[*CA 2006, ss 545–548*].

Reserve liability. *Before 1 October 2009*, a limited company could, by special resolution, determine that any part of its share capital not already called up could only be called up in the event, and for the purposes of, winding up. [*CA 1985, s 120*]. This reserve liability was also known as the reserve capital. Any mortgage of reserve capital is void, see *Mayfair Property Co, Re, Bartlett v Mayfair Property Co* [1898] 2 Ch 28, CA. With effect from 1 October 2009, *CA 1985, s 120* was repealed.

[*CA 2006, Sch 16*].

47.7 Minimum share capital requirements for public companies

A public company must not do business or exercise any borrowing powers unless the Registrar of Companies has issued it with a trading certificate on being satisfied that the nominal value of the company's allotted share capital is not less than the 'authorised minimum'.

See **33.3** Public and Listed Companies for full details.

47.8 ALLOTMENT OF SHARES

The provisions in **47.9** to **47.22** deal with the general requirements of *CA 2006* relating to the allotment of shares. They have no application in relation to the taking of shares by the subscribers to the memorandum on the formation of the company.

For the purposes of the *Companies Acts*, shares in a company are taken to be allotted when a person acquires the unconditional right to be included in the company's register of members in respect of the shares. See also *Florence Land and Public Works Co, Re, Nicol's Case, Tufnell and Ponsonby's Case* (1885) 29 Ch D 421, CA.

[*CA 2006, ss 558, 559*].

47.9 Power of directors to allot shares

For cases involving the contractual aspects of application for, and allotment of, shares, see *Jackson v Turquand* (1869) LR 4 HL 305 (application for shares is normally the offer with acceptance being the notification of the allotment but a letter of rights from a company is an offer which may be accepted by the shareholder); *Brewery Assets Corpn, Re, Truman's Case* [1894] 3 Ch 272, *Byrne & Co v Leon Van Tienhoven & Co* (1880) 5 CPD 344, *London and Northern Bank, Re, ex p Jones* [1900] 1 Ch 220 (revocation of offer); *Household Fire and Carriage Accident Insurance Co v Grant* (1879) 4 Ex D 216, CA, *Holwell Securities Ltd v Hughes* [1974] 1 All ER 161, [1974] 1 WLR 155, CA (notification of allotment by post); and *Ramsgate Victoria Hotel Co v Montefiore* (1866) LR 1 Exch 109 (allotment must be made within a reasonable time of application).

The directors of a company must not exercise any power of the company:

(a) to allot shares in the company, or

(b) to grant rights to subscribe for, or to convert any security into, shares in the company,

except in accordance with the provisions in (1) or (2) below. But:

- this does not apply to the allotment of shares in pursuance of an employees' share scheme or to the grant of a right to subscribe for, or to convert any security into, shares so allotted;

- where (*b*) above applies, the requirement does not apply in relation to the allotment of shares pursuant to that right;
- nothing in these provisions affects the validity of an allotment or other transaction; and
- the directors' actions can be subsequently ratified by the company in general meeting (*Bamford v Bamford* [1970] Ch 212, [1969] 1 All ER 969, CA).

A director who knowingly contravenes, or permits or authorises a contravention of these provisions commits an offence. A person guilty of such an offence is liable (i) on conviction on indictment, to a fine; and (ii) on summary conviction, to a fine not exceeding the statutory maximum. See **29.1 Offences and Legal Proceedings** for the statutory maximum.

[*CA 2006, s 549*].

(1) **Private company with only one class of shares**

Where a private company has only one class of shares, the directors may allot shares or grant rights to subscribe for, or convert any security into, shares in the company except to the extent that they are prohibited from doing so by the company's articles ie the directors no longer need shareholder authority unless the articles provide otherwise. [*CA 2006, s 550*].

Transitional provisions: companies incorporated before 1 October 2009 and "transitional companies".

(i) The power of the directors of a private company to allot shares referred to above only applies to a company existing immediately before 1 October 2009 or a 'transitional company' if the members of the company have resolved that the directors should have such power. The resolution may be by ordinary resolution (even if taking the form of an alteration of the company's articles). Once the members of the company have passed such a resolution, the application of *CA 2006, s 550* in relation to the company is not affected by any subsequent resolution (except one altering the company's articles so as to prohibit, to any extent, exercise of the powers mentioned in that section).

A '*transitional company*' means a company that was formed and registered (or re-registered) under *CA 1985* on or after 1 October 2009 where an application for registration (or re-registration) was received by the Registrar of Companies and the requirements as to registration or re-registration (as the case may be) were met before 1 October 2009.

(ii) For the purposes of *CA 2006, s 550*, provisions of the articles of a company existing on 1 October 2009 or a transitional company (see (i) above):

- authorising the directors to allot shares in accordance with *CA 1985, s 80*, or
- added following an elective resolution under *CA 1985, s 80A* and authorising the directors to allot shares,

are not to be treated as provisions prohibiting the directors from exercising the powers conferred by *CA 2006, s 550* in cases to which the authority does not extend.

[*SI 2008 No 2860, Sch 2 paras 43, 44*].

(2) **Other companies not covered by (1) above ie private companies with more than one class of shares and public companies**

The directors of these companies may allot shares or grant rights to subscribe for, or convert any security into, shares in the company if they are authorised to do so by the company's articles or by resolution of the company.

Authorisation may be given for a particular exercise of the power or for its exercise generally, and may be unconditional or subject to conditions. The authorisation must:

- state the maximum amount of shares that may be allotted under it; and
- specify the date on which it will expire, which must be not more than five years from:

  (i) in the case of authorisation contained in the company's articles at the time of its original incorporation, the date of that incorporation;

  (ii) in any other case, the date on which the resolution is passed by virtue of which the authorisation is given.

Renewal of authorisation. Authorisation may be renewed or further renewed by resolution of the company for a further period not exceeding five years. It may also be revoked or varied at any time by resolution of the company. Any resolution renewing authorisation must:

- state (or restate) the maximum amount of shares that may be allotted under the authorisation or, as the case may be, the amount remaining to be allotted under it; and
- specify the date on which the renewed authorisation will expire.

Where (*b*) above applies, references above to the maximum amount of shares that may be allotted under the authorisation are to the maximum amount of shares that may be allotted pursuant to the rights.

Allotment after expiration of authority. The directors may allot shares (or grant rights to subscribe for or to convert any security into shares) after authorisation has expired if:

- the shares are allotted (or the rights are granted) in pursuance of an offer or agreement made by the company before the authorisation expired; and
- the authorisation allowed the company to make an offer or agreement which would or might require shares to be allotted (or rights to be granted) after the authorisation had expired.

Resolutions. A resolution of a company to give, vary, revoke or renew authorisation under these provisions may be an ordinary resolution, even though it amends the company's articles.

CA 2006, ss 29, 30 (resolutions affecting a company's constitution) apply to a resolution under these provisions. See **14.10 Constitution – Memorandum and Articles**. [*CA 2006, s 551*].

Pre 1 October 2009 authorisations. An authorisation in force immediately before 1 October 2009 under *CA 1985, ss 80* or *80A* has effect on or after that date as if given under *CA 2006, s 551*.

[*SI 2008 No 2860, Sch 2 para 45*].

See also **47.21** for prohibition of public offers by private companies.

47.10 Commissions, discounts and allowances

Permitted commission. A company may pay a commission to a person in consideration of his subscribing or agreeing to subscribe (whether absolutely or conditionally) for shares in the company, or procuring or agreeing to procure subscriptions (whether absolute or conditional) for shares in the company if the following conditions are satisfied:

- The payment of the commission is authorised by the company's articles.
- The commission paid or agreed to be paid does not exceed:

  (i) 10% of the price at which the shares are issued, or

  (ii) the amount or rate authorised by the articles,

  whichever is the less.

[*CA 2006, s 553(1)(2)*].

Where standard articles have been adopted, see:

- *Table A, 1985, Reg 4*
- *Model Articles, Art 44* (public companies)

set out in **Appendix 4** standard articles of association.

Commission paid by other persons. A vendor to, or promoter of, or other person who receives payment in money or shares from, a company may apply any part of the money or shares so received in payment of any commission the payment of which directly by the company would be permitted under the above provisions. [*CA 2006, s 553(3)*].

General prohibition of commissions, discounts and allowances. Except as permitted above, a company must not apply any of its shares or capital money, either directly or indirectly, in payment of any commission, discount or allowance to any person in consideration of his

- subscribing or agreeing to subscribe (whether absolutely or conditionally) for shares in the company; or
- procuring or agreeing to procure subscriptions (whether absolute or conditional) for shares in the company.

This applies whether the shares or money are so applied by being added to the purchase money of property acquired by the company or to the contract price of work to be executed for the company, or being paid out of the nominal purchase money or contract price, or otherwise.

But this does not affect the payment of such brokerage as has previously been lawful.

[*CA 2006, s 552*].

47.11 Registration of allotment

A company must register an allotment of shares as soon as practicable, and in any event within two months after the date of the allotment. This does not apply if the company has issued a share warrant in respect of the shares (see **44.12** Securities: Certification and Transfers).

If a company fails to comply with these requirement, an offence is committed by the company and every officer of the company who is in default. A person guilty of such an offence is liable, on summary conviction, to a fine not exceeding level 3 on the standard scale and, for continued contravention, a daily default fine not exceeding one-tenth of level 3 on the standard scale. See **29.1 Offences and Legal Proceedings** for the standard scale.

For the company's duties as to the issue of share certificates, see **44 Securities: Certification and Transfers**

[*CA 2006, s 554*].

47.12 Return of allotments

Limited companies. A company:

- limited by shares, or
- limited by guarantee and having a share capital

must, within one month of making an allotment of shares, deliver to the Registrar of Companies for registration a return of the allotment on form SSSHO1. The return must contain the following information.

(i) The class of shares and the number of shares allotted.

(ii) The currency (if this is not completed Companies House will assume currency is in pounds sterling).

(iii) The number of shares allotted.

(iv) The amount paid up and the amount (if any) unpaid on each allotted share (whether on account of the nominal value of the share of by way of premium).

(v) Where the shares are allotted as fully or partly paid (as to their nominal value or any premium on them) otherwise than in cash, the consideration for the allotment together, in the case of a public company, a valuation of the consideration.

The return must also be accompanied by a statement of capital that states the following information with respect to the company's share capital at the date to which the return is made up.

- The total number of shares of the company.
- The class of shares, the number of those shares and the aggregate nominal value of those shares. The *Small Business, Enterprise and Employment Act 2015 (SBEE 2015)* introduces a requirement to also include in the statement of capital the aggregate amount (if any) unpaid on those shares (whether on account of their nominal value or by way of premium). As at May 2015 this provision is not in force.
- For each class of shares:

  (i) particulars of any voting rights attached to the shares, including rights that arise only in certain circumstances;

  (ii) particulars of any rights attached to the shares, as respects dividends, to participate in a distribution;

  (iii) particulars of any rights attached to the shares, as respects capital, to participate in a distribution (including on a winding up);

(iv) whether the shares are to be redeemed or are liable to be redeemed at the option of the company or the shareholder;

- The amount paid up and the amount (if any) unpaid on each share (whether on account of the nominal value of the share or by way of premium).

[*CA 2006, s 555; SI 2009 No 388, Arts 2, 3*].

Unlimited companies allotting a new class of shares. An unlimited company that allots shares of a class with rights that are not in all respects uniform with shares previously allotted must, within one month of making such an allotment, deliver to the Registrar of Companies for registration a return of the allotment. The return must contain the following information of the rights attached to the shares.

(i) Particulars of any voting rights attached to the shares, including rights that arise only in certain circumstances.

(ii) Particulars of any rights attached to the shares, as respects dividends, to participate in a distribution.

(iii) Particulars of any rights attached to the shares, as respects capital, to participate in a distribution (including on a winding up).

(iv) Whether the shares are to be redeemed or are liable to be redeemed at the option of the company or the shareholder.

For these purposes, shares are not to be treated as different from shares previously allotted by reason only that the former do not carry the same rights to dividends as the latter during the twelve months immediately following the former's allotment.

[*CA 2006, s 556; SI 2009 No 388, Art 2*].

Failure to make return. If a company defaults in complying with any of the above provisions, an offence is committed by every officer of the company who is in default. A person guilty of such an offence liable (i) on conviction on indictment, to a fine; and (ii) on summary conviction, to a fine not exceeding the statutory maximum and, for continued contravention, a daily default fine not exceeding one-tenth of the greater of £5000 or the amount corresponding to level 4 on the standard scale for summary offences. See **29.1** Offences and Legal Proceedings for the statutory maximum.

In the case of default in delivering the required return to the Registrar of Companies within one month period allowed, any person liable for the default may apply to the court for relief. If the court is satisfied that:

- the omission to deliver the document was accidental or due to inadvertence, or
- it is just and equitable to grant relief,

it may make an order extending the time for delivery of the document for such period as it thinks proper.

[*CA 2006, s 557; SI 2015 No 664, Sch 3*].

47.13 Existing shareholders' right of pre-emption

In addition to the general restrictions on the powers of directors of a company to allot shares (see **47.9**) there are also restrictions on their power to allot shares to persons other than existing members of the company. These are considered in this paragraph and in **47.14–47.19**. The provisions have no application in relation to the taking of shares by the subscribers to the memorandum on the formation of the company.

[*CA 2006, s 577*].

For these purposes:

(a) '*equity securities*' means:

(i) ordinary shares in the company; or

(ii) rights to subscribe for, or to convert securities into, ordinary shares in the company;

(b) '*ordinary shares*' means shares other than shares that as respects dividends and capital carry a right to participate only up to a specified amount in a distribution; and

(c) the '*allotment of equity securities*' includes:

(i) the grant of a right to subscribe for, or to convert any securities into, ordinary shares in the company but does not include the allotment of shares pursuant to such a right; and

(ii) the sale of ordinary shares in the company that immediately before the sale are held by the company as treasury shares.

[*CA 2006, s 560*].

Subject to **47.16–47.19**, a company must not allot equity securities to a person on any terms unless:

(i) it has made an offer to each person who holds ordinary shares in the company to allot to him on the same or more favourable terms a proportion of those securities that is as nearly as practicable equal to the proportion in nominal value held by him of the ordinary share capital of the company, and

(ii) the period during which any such offer may be accepted has expired or the company has received notice of the acceptance or refusal of every offer so made.

Securities that a company has offered to allot to a holder of ordinary shares may be allotted to him, or anyone in whose favour he has renounced his right to their allotment, without contravening (ii) above.

Treasury shares. Shares held by the company as treasury shares are disregarded for the purposes of these provisions (so that the company is not treated as a person who holds ordinary shares and the shares are not treated as forming part of the ordinary share capital of the company).

[*CA 2006, s 561; SI 2008 No 2860, Sch 2 para 49*].

'*Holder of the shares*'. References above (however expressed) to the 'holder' of shares of any description is to whoever was the holder of shares of that description at the close of business on a date to be specified in the offer. That date must fall within the period of 28 days immediately before the date of the offer. [*CA 2006, s 574*].

47.14 *Communication of pre-emption offers*

Offers that are required to be made to holders of a company's shares under **47.13** may be made in hard copy or electronic form. See **Appendix 1 Definitions** for the meaning of these terms.

If the holder:

- has no registered address in an EEA State and has not given the company an address in an EEA State for the service of notices on him, or

- is the holder of a share warrant,

the offer may be made by either publishing it in the *Gazette* or publishing a notice in the *Gazette* specifying where a copy of it can be obtained or inspected.

The offer must state a period during which it may be accepted and cannot be withdrawn before the end of that period. The period must be one of at least 14 days beginning in the case of an offer made:

- in hard copy form, with the date on which the offer is sent or supplied;
- in electronic form, with the date on which the offer is sent; and
- by publication in the Gazette, with the date of publication.

[*CA 2006, s 562; SI 2009 No 2022, Reg 2*].

See also **16.22–16.34 Dealings With Third Parties** for the 'company communication provisions' relating to communications sent by companies, including the provisions in **16.32** relating to communications to joint holders and communications following the death or bankruptcy of the shareholder.

47.15 *Liability in case of contravention*

Where there is a contravention of **47.13** or **47.14**, the company, and every officer of it who knowingly authorised or permitted the contravention, are jointly and severally liable to compensate any person to whom an offer should have been made for any loss, damage, costs or expenses which the person has sustained or incurred by reason of the contravention. But no proceedings to recover any such loss, etc may be commenced after the expiration of two years:

- from the delivery to the Registrar of Companies of the return of allotment; or
- where equity securities other than shares are granted, from the date of the grant.

[*CA 2006, s 563*].

47.16 *Exceptions to right of pre-emption*

The provisions in **47.13** do not apply:

- in relation to the allotment of bonus shares;
- to a particular allotment of equity securities if these are, or are to be, wholly or partly paid up otherwise than in cash; and
- to the allotment of securities that would, apart from any renunciation or assignment of the right to their allotment, be held under an employees' share scheme (see **Appendix 1 Definitions**).

[*CA 2006, ss 564–566*].

47.17 *Exclusion of pre-emption rights*

(1) *Private companies*

All or any of the requirements of **47.13** and **47.14** may be excluded by provision contained in the articles of a private company. They can be excluded:

- generally in relation to the allotment by the company of equity securities; or
- in relation to allotments of a particular description.

Any requirement or authorisation contained in the articles of a private company that is inconsistent with the requirements of paragraph **47.13** or **47.14** (as the case may be) is treated for these purposes as a provision excluding that paragraph.

A provision to which (2) below applies is not to be treated as inconsistent with the provisions set out in **47.13**.

[*CA 2006, s 567*].

Exclusion of pre-emption rights in force pre 1 October 2009. Where provision was made under *CA 1985, s 91* excluding the pre-emption requirements of *CA 1985, ss 89 or 90* and was in force immediately before 1 October 2009, the provision has effect on or after that date as if it was, or included, provision made by *CA 2006, s 567* above excluding the corresponding requirements of **47.3** and **47.14**. [*SI 2008 No 2860, Sch 2 para 50*].

(2) *Articles conferring corresponding right*

The provisions of *CA 2006, s 568* apply where in a case in which *CA 2006, s 561* (see **47.13**) would otherwise apply:

- a company's articles contain provision ('pre-emption provision') prohibiting the company from allotting ordinary shares of a particular class unless it has complied with the condition that it makes a pre-emption offer as is described in **47.13** to each person who holds ordinary shares of that class, and
- in accordance with that provision:
  - (i) the company makes an offer to allot shares to such a holder, and
  - (ii) he or anyone in whose favour he has renounced his right to their allotment accepts the offer.

In that case *CA 2006, s 561* does not apply to the allotment of those shares and the company may allot them accordingly. The provisions of **47.14** regarding the communication of pre-emption offers to shareholders also apply in relation to offers made in pursuance of the pre-emption provision of the company's articles (but subject to (1) above).

If there is a contravention of the pre-emption provision of the company's articles, the company, and every officer of it who knowingly authorised or permitted the contravention, are jointly and severally liable to compensate any person to whom an offer should have been made under the provision for any loss, damage, costs or expenses which the person has sustained or incurred by reason of the contravention. But no proceedings to recover any such loss, etc may be commenced after the expiration of two years:

- from the delivery to the Registrar of Companies of the return of allotment; or
- where equity securities other than shares are granted, from the date of the grant.

[*CA 2006, s 568*]

'*Holder of the shares*'. See **47.13** for the meaning of.

47.18 *Disapplication of pre-emption rights*

(1) *Private company with only one class of shares*

The directors of a private company that has only one class of shares may be given power by the articles, or by a special resolution of the company, to allot equity securities of that class as if the provisions in **47.13**:

- did not apply to the allotment; or
- applied to the allotment with such modifications as the directors determine.

Where the directors make such an allotment, the provisions in **47.13–47.19** have effect accordingly.

[*CA 2006, s 569*].

(2) *Directors acting under general authorisation*

Where the directors of a company are generally authorised to allot shares under *CA 2006, s 551* (see **47.9**(2)), they may be given power by the articles, or by a special resolution of the company, to allot equity securities pursuant to that authorisation as if the provisions of **47.13**:

- did not apply to the allotment; or
- applied to the allotment with such modifications as the directors may determine.

Where the directors make such an allotment, the provisions in **47.13–47.19** have effect accordingly.

The power conferred by these provisions ceases to have effect when the authorisation to which it relates is revoked or would (if not renewed) expire. But if the authorisation is renewed, the power may also be renewed, for a period not longer than that for which the authorisation is renewed, by a special resolution of the company.

Despite the fact that the power conferred by these provisions has expired, the directors may allot equity securities in pursuance of an offer or agreement previously made by the company if the power enabled the company to make an offer or agreement that would or might require equity securities to be allotted after it expired.

[*CA 2006, s 570*].

Exclusion of pre-emption in force pre 1 October 2009. Where pre-emption provisions excluding or modifying *CA 1985, s 89(1)* were made by virtue of *CA 1985, s 95(1)* and were in force immediately before 1 October 2009, the provisions have effect on or after that date as if they had been made by virtue of *CA 2006, s 570* above and excluded or modified *CA 2006, s 561* (see **47.13**). The power conferred to allot equity securities may accordingly be renewed under *CA 2006, s 570(3)*. [*SI 2008 No 2860, Sch 2 para 52*].

(3) *Disapplication by special resolution*

Where the directors of a company are authorised to allot shares under **47.9**(2), whether generally or otherwise, the company may by special resolution resolve that the provisions in **47.13**:

- do not apply to a specified allotment of equity securities to be made pursuant to that authorisation; or
- apply to such an allotment with such modifications as may be specified in the resolution.

Where such a resolution is passed, the provisions in **47.13–47.19** have effect accordingly.

A special resolution under these provisions ceases to have effect when the authorisation to which it relates is revoked or would (if not renewed) expire. But if the authorisation is renewed, the resolution may also be renewed, for a period not longer than that for which the authorisation is renewed, by a special resolution of the company.

[*CA 2006, s 571(1)–(3)*].

Despite the fact that any such resolution has expired, the directors may allot equity securities in pursuance of an offer or agreement previously made by the company if the resolution enabled the company to make an offer or agreement that would or might require equity securities to be allotted after it expired.

A special resolution under these provisions, or a special resolution to renew such a resolution, must not be proposed unless:

- it is recommended by the directors; and
- the directors have made a written statement setting out:
  - (i) their reasons for making the recommendation;
  - (ii) the amount to be paid to the company in respect of the equity securities to be allotted; and
  - (iii) the directors' justification of that amount.

If the resolution is proposed at a general meeting, the directors' statement must be circulated to the members entitled to notice of the meeting with that notice. Alternatively, if the resolution is proposed as a written resolution, it must be sent or submitted to every eligible member at or before the time at which the proposed resolution is sent or submitted to him.

[*CA 2006, s 571(4)–(7)*].

Exclusion of pre-emption rights pre 1 October 2009.

(a) Where a special resolution excluding or modifying *CA 1985, s 89(1)* was passed by virtue of *CA 1985 s 95(2)* and was in force immediately before 1 October 2009, the resolution has effect on or after that date as if it had been passed by virtue of *CA 2006, s 571* above and excluded or modified *CA 2006, s 561*. The resolution may accordingly be renewed under *CA 2006, s 571(3)*.

(b) It is immaterial whether the directors' statement required before a resolution can be proposed under *CA 2006, s 571* above is made, or is sent, submitted or circulated as required by that section, before on or after 1 October 2009.

[*SI 2008 No 2860, Sch 2 paras 53, 54(1)*].

Liability for false statement in directors' statement. Where a directors' statement is sent, submitted or circulated to a member, a person who knowingly or recklessly authorises or permits the inclusion of any matter that is misleading, false or deceptive in a material particular in such a statement commits an offence. A person guilty of such an offence is liable (i) on conviction on indictment, to imprisonment for a term not exceeding two years or a fine (or both); and (ii) on summary conviction, to imprisonment for a term not exceeding 12 months (in Scotland or Northern Ireland, 6 months) or to a fine not exceeding the statutory maximum (or both). See **29.1 Offences and Legal Proceedings** for the statutory maximum.

[*CA 2006, s 572*].

(4) *Sale of treasury shares*

Where a sale of treasury shares is an allotment of equity securities by virtue of **47.13**(*c*)(ii), the directors of a company may be given power by the articles, or by a special resolution of the company, to allot equity securities as if **47.13**:

- did not apply to the allotment; or
- applied to the allotment with such modifications as the directors may determine.

Where the directors make such an allotment, the provisions in **47.13–47.19** have effect accordingly.

The power conferred by these provisions ceases to have effect when the authorisation to which it relates is revoked or would (if not renewed) expire. But if the authorisation is renewed, the power may also be renewed, for a period not longer than that for which the authorisation is renewed, by a special resolution of the company.

Despite the fact that the power conferred by these provisions has expired, the directors may allot equity securities in pursuance of an offer or agreement previously made by the company if the power enabled the company to make an offer or agreement that would or might require equity securities to be allotted after it expired.

The company may by special resolution resolve that the provisions of **47.13**:

- do not apply to a specified allotment of securities; or
- do apply to the allotment with such modifications as may be specified in the resolution.

In such a case, the provisions in **47.13–47.19** have effect accordingly and, in particular, the provisions of *CA 2006, s 571(4)–(7)* (see (3) above) apply.

[*CA 2006, s 573*].

Exclusion of pre-emption rights pre 1 October 2009.

Where provision excluding or modifying *CA 1985, s 89(1)* was made by virtue of *CA 1985, s 95(2A)* and was in force immediately before 1 October 2009, the provision has effect on or after that date as if it had been made by virtue of *CA 2006, s 573* above and excluded or modified *CA 2006, s 561* (see **47.13**). The power conferred to allot equity securities may accordingly be renewed under *CA 2006, s 570(3)* or *CA 2006, s 571(3)*.

[*SI 2008 No 2860, Sch 2 para 55*].

47.19 *Saving provisions*

Other restrictions on offer or allotment. The provisions in **47.13–47.18** are without prejudice to any other Act by virtue of which a company is prohibited (whether generally or in specified circumstances) from offering or allotting equity securities to any person. Where a company cannot by virtue of such an Act offer or allot equity securities to a holder of ordinary shares of the company, those shares are disregarded for the purposes of **47.13** so that:

- the person is not treated as a person who holds ordinary shares; and
- the shares are not treated as forming part of the ordinary share capital of the company.

[*CA 2006, s 575*].

Older pre-emption requirements.

(1) In the case of a public company, the provisions in **47.13–47.18** do not apply to an allotment of equity securities that are subject to a pre-emption requirement in relation to which *CA 1985, s 96(1)* or *Companies (Northern Ireland) Order 1986, Art 106(1)* applied before 1 October 2009 (ie allotments of equity securities

subject to a requirement imposed before 22 June 1982, whether by the company's memorandum or articles or otherwise, that the company must, when allotting securities, offer to allot them, or some of them, in a manner which is inconsistent with these provisions).

(2) In the case of a private company, a pre-emption requirement to which *CA 1985, s 96(3)* or *Companies (Northern Ireland) Order 1986, Art 106(3)* applied before 1 October 2009 has effect, so long as the company remains a private company, as if it were contained in the company's articles. Under those provisions, a requirement which was imposed on a private company before 22 June 1982, otherwise than by the company's memorandum or articles, and which would have had the effect of excluding the pre-emption provisions if contained in the memorandum or articles, has effect as if it were so contained.

(3) A pre-emption requirement to which *CA 1985, s 96(4)* or *Companies (Northern Ireland) Order 1986, Art 106(4)* applied before 1 October 2009 is treated for the purposes of the provisions in **47.13–47.18** as if it were contained in the company's articles.

[*CA 2006, s 576*].

47.20 Public companies: allotment where issue not fully subscribed

No allotment must be made of shares of a public company offered for subscription unless:

- the issue is subscribed for in full; or
- the offer is made on terms that the shares subscribed for may be allotted in any event or if specified conditions are met (and those conditions are met).

If shares are prohibited from being allotted by the above provisions and 40 days have elapsed after the first making of the offer, all money received from applicants for shares must be repaid forthwith, initially without interest. But if any of the money is not repaid within 48 days after the first making of the offer, the directors of the company are jointly and severally liable to repay it, with interest at the rate for the time being specified under *Judgments Act 1838, s 17* from the expiration of the 48th day. A director is not so liable if he proves that the default in the repayment of the money was not due to any misconduct or negligence on his part.

Any condition requiring or binding an applicant for shares to waive compliance with any requirement of this section is void. [*CA 2006, s 578(1)–(3), (6)*].

Shares offered as wholly or partly payable otherwise than in cash. The above provisions also apply to such shares, the word 'subscribed' being construed accordingly. References to repayment of money received from applicants include:

- the return of any other consideration received (including, if the case so requires, the release of the applicant from any undertaking); or
- if it is not reasonably practicable to return the consideration, the payment of money equal to its value at the time it was so received;

[*CA 2006, s 578(4)(5)*].

Effect of irregular allotment. Where an allotment is made in contravention of the *CA 2006, s 578*, it is voidable at the instance of the applicant within one month after the date of the allotment, and not later. This applies even if the company is in the course of being wound up. A director of the company who knowingly contravenes, or permits or authorises the contravention of, any of the provisions of *section 578* (above) with respect to allotment is liable to compensate the company and the allottee respectively for any loss, damages, costs or expenses that the company or allottee may have sustained or incurred by the contravention provided proceedings are brought within two years of the date of the allotment.

[*CA 2006, s 579*].

47.21 Prohibition of public offers by private companies

A private company limited by shares, or limited by guarantee and having a share capital, must not:

- 'offer to the public' any 'securities' of the company; or
- allot or agree to allot any securities of the company with a view to their being offered to the public.

Unless the contrary is proved, an allotment or agreement to allot securities is presumed to be made with a view to their being offered to the public if an offer of the securities (or any of them) to the public is made:

- within six months after the allotment or agreement to allot; or
- before the receipt by the company of the whole of the consideration to be received by it in respect of the securities.

But a company does not contravene these provisions if:

(a) it acts in good faith in pursuance of arrangements under which it is to re-register as a public company before the securities are allotted; or

(b) as part of the terms of the offer it undertakes to re-register as a public company within a period ending not later than six months after the day on which the offer is made (or, in the case of an offer made on different days, first made), and that undertaking is complied with.

[*CA 2006, s 755(1)–(4)*].

'Offer to the public'. An offer to the public includes an offer to any section of the public, however selected.

An offer is not regarded as an offer to the public if it can properly be regarded, in all the circumstances, as:

- not being calculated to result, directly or indirectly, in securities of the company becoming available to persons other than those receiving the offer; or
- otherwise being a '*private concern of the person receiving it and the person making it*'. Unless the contrary is proved, this means that:

  (a) it is made to a '*person already connected with the company*' and, where it is made on terms allowing that person to renounce his rights, the rights may only be renounced in favour of another person already connected with the company; or

  (b) it is an offer to subscribe for securities to be held under an employees' share scheme (see APPENDIX 1 DEFINITIONS) and, where it is made on terms allowing that person to renounce his rights, the rights may only be renounced in favour of:

(i) another person entitled to hold securities under the scheme; or

(ii) a person already connected with the company.

For these purposes, a '*person already connected with the company*' means

(i) an existing member or employee of the company;

(ii) a member of the family of a person who is or was a member or employee of the company (ie that person's spouse or civil partner and children, including step-children, and their descendants);

(iii) the widow or widower, or surviving civil partner, of a person who was a member or employee of the company;

(iv) an existing debenture holder of the company; or

(v) a trustee (acting in his capacity as such) of a trust of which the principal beneficiary is a person within any of (i)–(iv) above).

[*CA 2006, s 756*].

'Securities' means shares or debentures. [*CA 2006, s 755(5)*].

Validity of allotment, etc. Nothing in the above provisions or in **47.22** affects the validity of any allotment or sale of securities or of any agreement to allot or sell securities.

[*CA 2006, s 760*].

47.22 *Enforcement of prohibition*

Contravention of the provisions in **47.21** can be enforced in any of the following ways.

(1) *Court order restraining proposed contravention*

If it appears to the court:

- on an application under these provisions made by:
  - (i) a member or creditor of the company, or
  - (ii) the Secretary of State, or
- in proceedings under *CA 2006, Pt 30* (protection of members against unfair prejudice, see **26.5 Members**),

that a company is *proposing to act* in contravention of the provisions in **47.21**, the court must make an order restraining it from so doing.

[*CA 2006, s 757*].

(2) *Orders available to the court after contravention*

If it appears to the court:

- on an application under these provisions made by:
  - (i) a member of the company who *either* was a member at the time the offer was made (or, if the offer was made over a period, at any time during that period) *or* became a member as a result of the offer,
  - (ii) a creditor of the company who was a creditor at the time the offer was made (or, if the offer was made over a period, at any time during that period), or

(iii) the Secretary of State, or

- in proceedings under *CA 2006, Pt 30* (protection of members against unfair prejudice, see **26.10 Members**),

that a company *has acted* in contravention of the provisions in **47.21**, the court must make an order requiring the company to re-register as a public company unless it appears to the court that:

- the company does not meet the requirements for re-registration as a public company; and
- it is impractical or undesirable to require it to take steps to do so.

If the court does not make an order for re-registration, it may make a remedial order under (3) below and/or an order for the compulsory winding up of the company.

[*CA 2006, s 758*].

(3) *Remedial orders*

A '*remedial order*' is an order for the purpose of putting a person affected by anything done in contravention of the provisions in **47.21** in the position he would have been in if it had not been done. Without prejudice to the generality of the power of the court to make such an order:

- where a private company has:

  (i) allotted securities pursuant to an offer to the public, or

  (ii) allotted or agreed to allot securities with a view to their being offered to the public,

a remedial order may require any person knowingly concerned in the contravention to offer to purchase any of those securities at such price and on such other terms as the court thinks fit;

- a remedial order may be made:

  (i) against any person knowingly concerned in the contravention, whether or not an officer of the company;

  (ii) notwithstanding anything in the company's constitution (which includes, for this purpose, the terms on which any securities of the company are allotted or held); and

  (iii) whether or not the holder of the securities subject to the order is the person to whom the company allotted or agreed to allot them; and

- where a remedial order is made against the company itself, the court may provide for the reduction of the company's capital accordingly.

[*CA 2006, s 759*].

47.23 PAYMENT FOR SHARES

Where shares are issued in a company, a shareholder is liable to pay up the nominal value of each of his shares, together with any premium, and the amount owing to the company is a debt which can be 'called up' (see **47.25**). The company may not require him to pay the full amount when he first takes up the shares (but see **47.26** for the minimum value which must be paid up on allotment of public company shares).

Subject to **47.26**, shares allotted by a company, and any premium on them, may be paid up in money or money's worth (including goodwill and know-how). This does not prevent a company from:

- allotting bonus shares to its members; or
- paying up, with sums available for the purpose, any amounts for the time being unpaid on any of its shares (whether on account of the nominal value of the shares or by way of premium).

[*CA 2006, s 582*].

47.24 Allotment of shares at a discount not permitted

A company's shares must not be allotted at a discount. If shares are allotted in contravention of this, the allottee is liable to pay the company an amount equal to the amount of the discount, with interest at the 'appropriate rate'. [*CA 2006, s 580*]. The '*appropriate rate*' of interest is 5% a year or such other rate as specified by statutory instrument.

[*CA 2006, s 592*].

See *Ooregum Gold Mining Co of India v Roper* [1892] AC 125, HL. See also *Welton v Saffrey* [1897] AC 299 where, although a company being wound up could pay all its creditors, it was held that holders of shares issued at a discount were still liable to account to the company for the discount in order to adjust the rights of the shareholders *inter se*.

47.25 Calls

Generally, a company will call up the amount it is owed on its shares rateably for all shareholders. But, if so authorised by its articles, it may:

- make arrangements on the issue of shares for a difference between the shareholders in the amounts and times of payment of calls on their shares; and
- accept from any member the whole or part of the amount remaining unpaid on any shares held by him, although no part of that amount has been called up.

Where it does so, and where the articles permit, the company may subsequently pay any dividends in proportion to the amount paid up on each share where a larger amount is paid up on some shares than on others. [*CA 2006, s 581*].

Where a company has adopted standard articles, see:

- *Table A, 1985, Reg 17*
- *Model Articles, Art 55* (public companies)

set out in **Appendix 4 Standard Articles of Association**.

General provisions relating to calls in the articles. A company's articles will usually contain provisions relating to the procedure, timing and liability for calls on shares. Where a company has adopted standard articles, see:

- *Table A, 1985, Regs 12–16*
- *Model Articles, Art 21* (private companies)
- *Model Articles, Arts 54–57* (public companies)

set out in **Appendix 4 Standard Articles of Association**.

Lien on shares for unpaid calls. A company's articles will usually contain provisions relating to its lien on shares for outstanding calls, etc. Where a company has adopted standard articles, see:

- *Table A, 1985, Regs 8–11*
- *Model Articles, Arts 52, 53* (public companies)

set out in **Appendix 4 Standard Articles of Association**.

Where a shareholder has lodged his share certificate with a bank as security for a loan and the bank has given notice of this to the company, the company cannot, in respect of moneys due to it from the shareholder after notice of the bank's security, claim priority over advances made by the bank after such notice (*Bradford Banking Co v Briggs, Son & Co Ltd* (1886) 12 App Cas 29, HL).

Forfeiture for non-payment of calls. If the articles of a company provide, the company may forfeit shares for failure to pay calls. It may also accept surrender in lieu of forfeiture. [*CA 2006, s 659(2)(c)*]. Where a company has adopted standard articles, see:

- *Table A, 1985, Regs 18–22*
- *Model Articles, Arts 58–62* (public companies)

set out in **Appendix 4 Standard Articles of Association**.

See also *Ladies' Dress Association Ltd v Pulbrook* [1900] 2 QB 376, CA and *Bolton, Re, ex p North British Artificial Silk Ltd* [1930] 2 Ch 48, 99 LJ Ch 209.

See **34.23 Purchase of Own Shares** for cancellation of the shares forfeited in the case of a public company.

47.26 Additional rules for public companies

(1) *Shares taken by subscribers to the memorandum*

Shares taken by a subscriber to the memorandum of a public company, in pursuance of an undertaking of his in the memorandum, and any premium on the shares, must be paid up in cash. [*CA 2006, s 584*].

Meaning of payment in cash. For the purposes of *CA 2006*, a share in a company is deemed '*paid up in cash*' (as to its nominal value or any premium on it) or '*allotted for cash*', if the consideration received for the allotment or payment up is a 'cash consideration', ie:

- cash received by the company;
- a cheque received by the company in good faith that the directors have no reason for suspecting will not be paid;

- a release of a liability of the company for a liquidated sum;
- an undertaking to pay cash to the company at a future date; or
- in relation to consideration received in pursuance of an obligation entered into on or after 1 October 2009, payment by any other means giving rise to a present or future entitlement (of the company or a person acting on the company's behalf) to a payment, or credit equivalent to payment, in cash. Included is a settlement bank's obligation to make a payment in respect of the allotment or payment up of shares under the CREST system.

"Cash" includes foreign currency.

Except for the purpose of existing shareholders rights of pre-emption under **47.13–47.19**, the payment of cash, or an undertaking to pay cash, to a person *other than* the company counts as consideration other than cash.

[*CA 2006, s 583; SI 2009 No 388, Art 4*].

(2) *Prohibition on accepting undertaking to do work or perform services*

A public company must not accept at any time, in payment up of its shares or any premium on them, an undertaking given by any person that he or another will do work or perform services for the company or any other person.

If a public company accepts such an undertaking, when the shares or the premium are treated as paid up (in whole or in part) by the undertaking, the 'holder of the shares':

(a) remains liable to pay the company an amount equal to the nominal value of the shares, together with the whole of any premium (or, if the case so requires, such proportion of that amount as is treated as paid up by the undertaking); and

(b) is liable to pay interest at the 'appropriate rate' on the amount payable under (*a*) above. The '*appropriate rate*' of interest is 5% a year or such other rate as specified by statutory instrument.

The '*holder of the shares*' includes a person who has an unconditional right to:

- be included in the company's register of members in respect of those shares; or
- have an instrument of transfer of them executed in his favour.

[*CA 2006, ss 585, 592*].

(3) *Shares must be at least one-quarter paid up*

Apart from shares allotted under an employees' share scheme (see **Appendix 1 Definitions**), a public company must not allot a share unless it is paid up at least as to one-quarter of its nominal value and the whole of any premium on it.

If a company allots a share in contravention of this:

- the share is to be treated as if one-quarter of its nominal value, together with the whole of any premium on it, had been received; and
- the allottee is liable to pay the company the minimum amount which should have been received in respect of the share under this provision (less the value of any consideration actually applied in payment up, to any extent, of the share and any premium on it), with interest at the 'appropriate rate'. The '*appropriate rate*' of interest is 5%pa or such other rate as specified by statutory instrument.

This does not apply to the allotment of bonus shares, unless the allottee knew (or ought to have known) the shares were allotted in contravention of this provision.

[*CA 2006, s 586*].

(4) *Payment by long-term undertaking*

A public company must not allot shares as fully or partly paid up (as to their nominal value or any premium on them) otherwise than in cash if the consideration for the allotment is, or includes, an undertaking which is to be, or *may be*, performed more than five years after the date of the allotment.

[*CA 2006, s 587(1)*].

If:

(a) a company allots shares in contravention of this provision, or

(b) an undertaking which is to be performed within five years of the allotment is not performed within the period allowed by the contract for the allotment of the shares,

the allottee is liable to pay the company (where (*b*) applies, at the end of the period so allowed) an amount equal to the aggregate of the nominal value of the shares and the whole of any premium (or, if the case so requires, so much of that aggregate as is treated as paid up by the undertaking), with interest at the 'appropriate rate'. The '*appropriate rate*' of interest is 5% pa or such other rate as specified by statutory instrument.

[*CA 2006, s 587(2)(4)*].

Where a contract for the allotment of shares does not contravene this provision, any variation of the contract (which includes an ancillary contract relating to payment for the shares) is void if its effect is that the contract would have contravened this provision if the terms of the contract as varied had been its original terms. This also applies to the variation by a public company of the terms of a contract entered into before the company was re-registered as a public company.

[*CA 2006, s 587*(3)].

47.27 Liability of subsequent holder of shares

If a person (A) becomes a 'holder' of shares in respect of which:

- there has been a contravention of any provision relating to payment for shares in **47.23–47.30** (including a failure to carry out an undertaking under **47.26**(4)(*b*)), and
- by virtue of that contravention another is liable to pay any amount under the provision contravened,

then A is also liable to pay that amount (jointly and severally with any other person so liable) unless:

- he is a purchaser for value and, at the time of the purchase, he did not have actual notice of the contravention concerned; or
- he derived title to the shares (directly or indirectly) from a person who became a holder of them after the contravention and was not liable under the above provisions.

[*CA 2006, s 588*].

'*Holder*', see **47.13**.

47.28 Power of court to grant relief

Where, under **47.26**(2) or (4) or **47.27**, a person is liable to a company:

(a) in relation to payment in respect of shares in the company, or

(b) by virtue of an undertaking given to it in, or in connection with, payment for shares in the company,

that person may apply to the court to be exempted in whole or in part from the liability.

There are two overriding principles to which the court must have regard in determining whether it should exempt the applicant in whole or in part from any liability. First, a company that has allotted shares should receive money or money's worth at least equal in value to the aggregate of the nominal value of those shares and the whole of any premium or, if the case so requires, so much of that aggregate as is treated as paid up. Subject to that, secondly, where a company would, if the court did not grant the exemption, have more than one remedy against a particular person, it should be for the company to decide which remedy it should remain entitled to pursue. Because these are 'overriding principles', a court will need very good reasons to accept that it is just and equitable to exempt an applicant from liability where the company has not received sufficient value (*Bradford Investments plc (No 2), Re* [1991] BCLC 688, [1991] BCC 379).

Otherwise, the court may exempt the applicant from the liability only if and to the extent that it appears to the court just and equitable to do so. In reaching its decision, the court must have regard to the following (except in relation to a decision whether to grant relief in respect of a liability for interest arising before 1 October 2009).

Where (*a*) above applies,

- whether the applicant has paid, or is liable to pay, any amount in respect of:
  - (i) any other liability arising in relation to those shares under any provision relating to payment for shares in **47.23–47.27** or any provision relating to independent valuation of non-cash consideration in **47.32–47.42**; or
  - (ii) any liability arising by virtue of any undertaking given in or in connection with payment for those shares;
- whether any person other than the applicant has paid or is likely to pay, whether in pursuance of any order of the court or otherwise, any such amount; and
- whether the applicant or any other person:
  - (i) has performed in whole or in part, or is likely so to perform, any such undertaking; or
  - (ii) has done, or is likely to do, any other thing in payment or part payment for the shares.

Where (*b*) above applies,

- whether the applicant has paid or is liable to pay any amount in respect of liability arising in relation to the shares under any provision relating to payment for shares in **47.23–47.30** or any provision relating to independent valuation of non-cash consideration in **47.31–47.45**; or

- whether any person other than the applicant has paid or is likely to pay, whether in pursuance of any order of the court or otherwise, any such amount.

[*CA 2006, s 589(1)–(5)*].

Proceedings against a contributor. Certain powers are conferred on the court where a person brings proceedings against another (the '*contributor*') for a contribution in respect of liability to a company arising under any provision relating to payment for shares in **47.23–47.30** or any provision relating to independent valuation of non-cash consideration in **47.31–47.45** and it appears to the court that the contributor is liable to make such a contribution. The court may, if and to the extent that it appears to be just and equitable to do so, having regard to the respective culpability (in respect of the liability to the company) of the contributor and the person bringing the proceedings:

- exempt the contributor in whole or in part from his liability to make such a contribution; or
- order the contributor to make a larger contribution than, but for this provision, he would be liable to make.

[*CA 2006, s 589(6)*].

47.29 Penalty for contravention

If a company contravenes any of the provisions in **47.23–47.27**, an offence is committed by the company and every officer of the company who is in default. A person guilty of such an offence is liable (i) on conviction on indictment, to a fine; and (ii) on summary conviction, to a fine not exceeding the statutory maximum. See **29.1 Offences and Legal Proceedings** for the statutory maximum.

[*CA 2006, s 590*].

47.30 Enforceability of undertakings to do work, etc

Without prejudice to **47.28**, where:

- an undertaking to do work or perform services or to do any other thing is given by any person, in or in connection with payment for shares in a company, and
- that undertaking is enforceable by the company apart from any of the provisions in **47.23–47.27**

the undertaking is so enforceable notwithstanding that there has been a contravention in relation to it of any provision relating to payment for shares in **47.23–47.30** or any provision relating to independent valuation of non-cash consideration in **47.31–47.45**.

[*CA 2006, s 591*].

47.31 PUBLIC COMPANIES: INDEPENDENT VALUATION OF NON-CASH CONSIDERATION

There are two situations in which a public company may be required to obtain an independent valuer's report of non-cash consideration.

- Where a public company seeks to allot shares as fully or partly paid otherwise than in cash, the consideration for the allotment must be independently valued. See **47.32–47.35**.

- Where a public company formed as such enters unto an agreement with a subscriber to the memorandum for the transfer by him to the company, or another, of non-cash assets within two years of commencing to trade and the consideration for the transfer to be given by the company is one-tenth or more of the company's issued share capital. See **47.36–47.40**.

See also **47.41** for the requirements of independent valuations and **47.42–47.44** for supplementary provisions.

47.32 Non-cash consideration for shares

Subject to **47.33**, a public company must not allot shares as fully or partly paid up (as to their nominal value or any premium on them) otherwise than in cash unless:

(a) the consideration for the allotment has been independently valued;

(b) the valuer's report has been made to the company in the six months immediately preceding the allotment of the shares; and

(c) a copy of the report has been sent to the proposed allottee.

See **47.26**(1) above for the meaning of '*allotted for cash*'.

Effect of contravention. If a company allots shares in contravention of the above and either:

- the allottee has not received the valuer's report required to be sent to him, or
- there has been some other contravention of the requirements of this provision or the valuation and reporting requirements (see **47.34**) that the allottee knew, or ought to have known, amounted to a contravention,

the allottee is liable to pay the company an amount equal to the aggregate of the nominal value of the shares and the whole of any premium (or, if the case so requires, so much of that aggregate as is treated as paid up by the consideration), with interest at the 'appropriate rate'. The '*appropriate rate*' of interest is 5% pa or such other rate as specified by statutory instrument.

[*CA 2006, ss 593(1)(3)(4), 609*].

47.33 *Exceptions to the valuation requirement*

(1) *Application of reserves*

The application of an amount standing to the credit of any of a company's reserve accounts or its profit and loss account in paying up (to any extent) shares allotted to members of the company, or premiums on shares so allotted, does not count as consideration for the allotment. Accordingly, the requirement for a report does not apply in that case.

[*CA 2006, s 593(2)*].

(2) *Arrangements with another company*

The provisions in **47.32** do not apply to an 'arrangement' for the allotment of shares in a company (company A) on terms that the whole or part of the consideration for the shares allotted is to be provided by:

- the transfer to that company A, or
- the cancellation,

of all or some of the shares (or shares of a particular class) in another company (company B). It is immaterial whether the arrangement provides for the issue to company A of shares (or shares of any particular class) in company B. The arrangement must be open to all the holders of the shares in company B (or, where the arrangement applies only to shares of a particular class, to all the holders of shares of that class) but disregarding shares held:

- by, or by a nominee of, company A;
- by, or by a nominee of, a company which is:
  - (i) the holding company, or a subsidiary, of company A; or
  - (ii) a subsidiary of such a holding company;
- shares held as treasury shares by company B.

'*Arrangement*' means any agreement, scheme or arrangement, including an arrangement sanctioned in accordance with:

- *CA 2006, Pt 26* (see **35.1** to **35.5** **Reconstructions and Mergers**); or
- *IA 1986, s 110* or *Insolvency (Northern Ireland) Order 1989, Art 96* (liquidator in winding up accepting shares as consideration for sale of company property).

[*CA 2006, s 594*].

(3) *Mergers or divisions*

The provisions in **47.32** do not apply to the allotment of shares by a company as part of a scheme to which *CA 2006, Pt 27* (Mergers and Divisions of public companies) applies if, in the case of a scheme involving a merger, an expert's report is drawn up as required by *CA 2006, s 909* or, in the case of a scheme involving a division, an expert's report is drawn up as required by *CA 2006, s 924*.

[*CA 2006, s 595*].

47.34 *Valuation and reporting requirements*

The provisions in **47.41** (general provisions as to independent valuation and report) apply to the valuation and report required under **47.32**.

The valuer's report must state:

- the nominal value of the shares to be wholly or partly paid for by the consideration in question;
- the amount of any premium payable on the shares;
- the description of the consideration and, as respects so much of the consideration as he himself has valued, a description of that part of the consideration, the method used to value it and the date of the valuation;
- the extent to which the nominal value of the shares and any premium are to be treated as paid up:
  - (i) by the consideration;
  - (ii) in cash (see **47.26**(1) above for the meaning of '*allotted for cash*'); and
- either in the report itself or an accompanying note that:
  - (i) in the case of a valuation made by another person, it appeared to the valuer reasonable to arrange for it to be so made or to accept a valuation so made;

(ii) whoever made the valuation, that the method of valuation was reasonable in all the circumstances;

(iii) it appears to the valuer that there has been no material change in the value of the consideration in question since the valuation; and

(iv) on the basis of the valuation, the value of the consideration, together with any cash by which the nominal value of the shares or any premium payable on them is to be paid up, is not less than so much of the aggregate of the nominal value and the whole of any such premium as is treated as paid up by the consideration and any such cash.

Position where consideration accepted is only partly for shares. Where the consideration to be valued is accepted partly in payment up of the nominal value of the shares and any premium and partly for some other consideration given by the company, the provisions above and those in **47.32** apply as if references to the consideration accepted by the company included the proportion of that consideration that is properly attributable to the payment up of that value and any premium. In such a case:

(a) the valuer must carry out, or arrange for, such other valuations as will enable him to determine that proportion; and

(b) his report must state what valuations have been made under (*a*) above and also the reason for, and method and date of, any such valuation and any other matters which may be relevant to that determination.

[*CA 2006, s 596*].

47.35 *Copy report to be delivered to the Registrar of Companies*

A company to which a report is made as to the value of any consideration for which, or partly for which, it proposes to allot shares must deliver a copy of the report to the Registrar of Companies for registration. This must be done at the same time that the company files the return of the allotment of those shares under **47.12**.

If default is made in complying with these requirements, an offence is committed by every officer of the company who is in default. A person guilty of such an offence is liable (i) on conviction on indictment, to a fine; and (ii) on summary conviction, to a fine not exceeding the statutory maximum and, for continued contravention, a daily default fine not exceeding one-tenth of the greater of £5000 or the amount corresponding to level 4 on the standard scale for summary offences. See **29.1 Offences and Legal Proceedings** for the statutory maximum.

In the case of default in delivering to the Registrar of Companies any document as required by these provisions, any person liable for the default may apply to the court for relief. If the court is satisfied that:

- the omission to deliver the document was accidental or due to inadvertence, or
- it is just and equitable to grant relief,

it may extend the time for delivery of the document for such period as it thinks proper.

[*CA 2006, s 597; SI 2015 No 664, Sch 3*].

47.36 Transfer of non-cash assets to a public company in the initial period

Subject to the exceptions below, a public company formed as such must not enter into an agreement:

(a) with a subscriber to the company's memorandum,

(b) for the transfer by him to the company, or another, before the end of the company's 'initial period' of one or more 'non-cash assets',

(c) under which the consideration for the transfer to be given by the company is, at the time of the agreement, equal in value to one-tenth or more of the company's issued share capital

unless the conditions below have been complied with. The company's '*initial period*' means the period of two years beginning with the date of the company being issued with a trading certificate under *CA 2006, s 761* (see **33.3 Public and Listed Companies**). See **Appendix 1 Definitions** for '*non-cash assets*'.

[*CA 2006, s 598(1)–(3)*].

Conditions. The conditions are as follows.

(1) *Independent valuation*

The consideration to be received by the company (ie the asset to be transferred to it or, as the case may be, the advantage to the company of the asset's transfer to another person) and any non-cash consideration to be given by the company must have been independently valued.

The valuer's report must have been made to the company during the six months immediately preceding the date of the agreement.

A copy of the report must have been sent to the 'other party' to the proposed agreement not later than the date on which copies have to be circulated to members under (2) below. The '*other party*' is the person referred to in (*a*) above but if he has received a copy of the report under the provisions in (2) below in his capacity as a member of the company, it is not necessary to send another copy under this provision.

These provisions do not affect any requirement to value any consideration for purposes of **47.32** (non-cash consideration for shares).

[*CA 2006, s 599*].

(2) *Approval by members*

- The terms of the agreement must have been approved by an ordinary resolution of the company.
- Copies of the valuer's report must have been circulated to the members entitled to notice of the meeting at which the resolution is proposed, not later than the date on which notice of the meeting is given.
- A copy of the proposed resolution must have been sent to the other party to the proposed agreement (ie the person referred to (*a*) above).

[*CA 2006, s 601; SI 2009 No 1941, Sch 1 para 260*].

Exceptions. The above provisions do not apply (and no valuer's report is required):

- where it is part of the company's ordinary business to acquire, or arrange for other persons to acquire, assets of a particular description, and the agreement is entered into by the company in the ordinary course of that business; or
- to an agreement entered into by the company under the supervision of the court or of an officer authorised by the court for the purpose.

[*CA 2006, s 598(4), (5)*].

47.37 *Valuation and reporting requirements*

The provisions in **47.41** below (general provisions as to independent valuation and report) apply to the valuation and report required under **47.36** above.

The valuer's report must state:

- the consideration to be received by the company, describing the asset in question (specifying the amount to be received in cash) and the consideration to be given by the company (specifying the amount to be given in cash);
- the method and date of valuation; and
- either in the report itself or an accompanying note that:
  - (i) in the case of a valuation made by another person, it appeared to the valuer reasonable to arrange for it to be so made or to accept a valuation so made;
  - (ii) whoever made the valuation, the method of valuation was reasonable in all the circumstances;
  - (iii) it appears to the valuer that there has been no material change in the value of the consideration in question since the valuation; and
  - (iv) on the basis of the valuation, the value of the consideration to be received by the company is not less than the value of the consideration to be given by it.

Position where consideration given only partly for transfer of asset. Any reference above or in **47.36** to consideration given for the transfer of an asset includes consideration given partly for its transfer. In such a case:

- the value of any consideration partly so given is to be taken as the proportion of the consideration properly attributable to its transfer;
- the valuer must carry out or arrange for such valuations of anything else as will enable him to determine that proportion; and
- his report must state what valuations have been made for that purpose and also the reason for, and method and date of, any such valuation and any other matters which may be relevant to that determination.

[*CA 2006, s 600*].

47.38 *Copy report to be delivered to the Registrar of Companies*

A company that has passed a resolution under **47.36**(2) with respect to the transfer of an asset must, within 15 days of doing so, deliver to the Registrar of Companies a copy of the resolution together with the valuer's report.

If a company fails to comply to do so, an offence is committed by the company and every officer of the company who is in default. A person guilty of such an offence is liable, on summary conviction, to a fine not exceeding level 3 on the standard scale and, for continued contravention, to a daily default fine not exceeding one-tenth of level three on the standard scale. See **29.1 Offences and Legal Proceedings** for the standard scale. [*CA 2006, s 602*].

47.39 *Company re-registering as a public company*

The provisions in **47.36–47.38** apply with the following adaptations in relation to a company re-registered as a public company.

- The reference in **47.36**(*a*) to a person who is a subscriber to the company's memorandum should be read as a reference to a person who is a member of the company on the date of re-registration.
- The 'initial period' is the period of two years beginning with the date of re-registration.

[*CA 2006, s 603*].

47.40 *Effect of contravention*

Where a public company enters into an agreement in contravention of **47.36** above and either:

- the other party to the agreement has not received the valuer's report required to be sent to him, or
- there has been some other contravention of the requirements of these provisions that the other party to the agreement knew or ought to have known amounted to a contravention,

the company is entitled to recover from that person any consideration given by it under the agreement, or an amount equal to the value of the consideration at the time of the agreement. The agreement, so far as not carried out, is void.

But if the agreement is or includes an agreement for the allotment of shares in the company, then:

- whether or not the agreement also contravenes **47.32** (valuation of non-cash consideration for shares), this provision does not apply to it in so far as it is for the allotment of shares; and
- the allottee is liable to pay the company an amount equal to the aggregate of the nominal value of the shares and the whole of any premium (or, if the case so requires, so much of that aggregate as is treated as paid up by the consideration), with interest at the 'appropriate rate'. The '*appropriate rate*' of interest is 5% pa or such other rate as specified by statutory instrument.

[*CA 2006, ss 604, 609*].

47.41 Requirements as to independent valuation

The provisions in this paragraph apply to the valuation and report required under **47.32** and **47.36**. They also apply to the valuation and report required under *CA 2006, s 93* (see **41.5 Re-Registration**).

[*CA 2006, s 1149*].

Requirements for being a valuer. The valuation and report must be made by a person (the valuer) who is eligible for appointment as a statutory auditor under *CA 2006, s 1212* (see **8.8 Audit**) and who meets the independence requirement.

[*CA 2006, s 1150(1)*].

The independence requirement. A person meets the independence requirement only if:

- he is not:

  (i) an officer or employee of the company; or

(ii) a partner or employee of such a person, or a partnership of which such a person is a partner;

- he is not:

  (i) an officer or employee of an 'associated undertaking' of the company; or

  (ii) a partner or employee of such a person, or a partnership of which such a person is a partner; and

- there does not exist between:

  (i) the person or an 'associate' of his, and

  (ii) the company or an associated undertaking of the company,

  a connection of any such description as may be specified by regulations.

For this purposes, an auditor of the company is not regarded as an officer or employee of the company.

'*Associated undertaking*' means:

- a parent undertaking or subsidiary undertaking of the company; or
- a subsidiary undertaking of a parent undertaking of the company.

'*Associate*' means:

(a) in relation to an individual,

  (i) that individual's spouse or civil partner or minor child or step-child;

  (ii) any body corporate of which that individual is a director; and

  (iii) any employee or partner of that individual;

(b) in relation to a body corporate,

  (i) any body corporate of which that body is a director;

  (ii) any body corporate in the same group as that body; and

  (iii) any employee or partner of that body or of any body corporate in the same group;

(c) in relation to a partnership that is a legal person under the law by which it is governed,

  (i) any body corporate of which that partnership is a director;

  (ii) any employee of or partner in that partnership; and

  (iii) any person who is an associate of a partner in that partnership; and

(d) in relation to a partnership that is not a legal person under the law by which it is governed, any person who is an associate of any of the partners.

In relation to a limited liability partnership, in (*a*)–(*d*) above for 'director' read 'member'.

[*CA 2006*, *ss 1151, 1152*].

Use of other valuers. Where the valuer thinks that it is reasonable for the valuation of the consideration (or part of it) to be made by another person who:

- appears to him to have the requisite knowledge and experience to value the consideration or that part of it, and
- is not an officer or employee of:

  (i) the company, or

  (ii) any other body corporate that is that company's subsidiary or holding company or a subsidiary of that company's holding company,

  or a partner of or employed by any such officer or employee,

he may arrange for such a valuation, together with a report which will enable him to make his own report under this provision. For these purposes, however, an auditor is not regarded as an officer or employee.

Where the consideration (or part of it) is valued by a person other than the valuer himself, the latter's report must state that fact and must also:

- state the former's name and what knowledge and experience he has to carry out the valuation; and
- describe so much of the consideration as was valued by the other person, and the method used to value it, and specify the date of that valuation.

[*CA 2006, s 1150(2)-(4)*].

Valuer entitled to full disclosure. A person carrying out a valuation or making a report with respect to any consideration proposed to be accepted or given by a company, is entitled to require from the officers of the company such information and explanation as he thinks necessary to enable him to carry out the valuation or make the report and provide any note required where the valuation is carried out by another person.

Where a person knowingly or recklessly makes a statement (whether orally or in writing) to a person carrying out a valuation or making a report which conveys (or purports to convey) any information or explanation which that person requires and which is misleading, false or deceptive in a material particular, the person making the statement commits an offence. A person guilty of such an offence is liable (i) on conviction on indictment, to imprisonment for a term not exceeding two years or a fine (or both); and (ii) on summary conviction to imprisonment for a term not exceeding twelve months (in Scotland and Northern Ireland, six months) or to a fine not exceeding the statutory maximum (or both). See **29.1** **Offences and Legal Proceedings** for the statutory maximum.

[*CA 2006, s 1153*].

47.42 Liability of subsequent holders of shares

A person (A) who subsequently becomes a 'holder' of shares may incur liable in the following cases.

(a) Where:

- there has been a contravention of **47.32** (valuation of non-cash consideration for shares), and
- by virtue of that contravention another person is liable to pay any amount under the provision contravened,

then, subject to below, A is also liable to pay that amount (jointly and severally with any other person so liable).

(b) If a company enters into an agreement in contravention of **47.36** (agreement for transfer of non-cash asset in initial period) and:

- the agreement is or includes an agreement for the allotment of shares in the company,
- A becomes a holder of shares allotted under the agreement, and
- by virtue of the agreement and allotment under it another person is liable to pay an amount under **47.40**,

then, subject to below, A is also liable to pay that amount (jointly and severally with any other person so liable). This applies whether or not the agreement also contravenes **47.32**.

A is exempt from liability under (*a*) and (*b*) above if:

- he is a purchaser for value and, at the time of the purchase, he did not have actual notice of the contravention concerned; or
- he derived title to the shares (directly or indirectly) from a person who became a holder of them after the contravention and who was not liable under the above provision.

'*Holder*', in relation to shares in a company, include any person who has an unconditional right to be included in the company's register of members in respect of those shares or to have an instrument of transfer of the shares executed in his favour.

[*CA 2006, s 605*].

47.43 Power of court to grant relief

A person who is liable to a company:

- under any provision in **47.32–47.42** in relation to payment in respect of any shares in the company, or
- by virtue of an undertaking given to it in, or in connection with, payment for any shares in the company,

may apply to the court to be exempted in whole or in part from the liability.

There are two overriding principles to which the court must have regard in determining whether it should exempt the applicant in whole or in part from any liability. First, a company that has allotted shares should receive money or money's worth at least equal in value to the aggregate of the nominal value of those shares and the whole of any premium or, if the case so requires, so much of that aggregate as is treated as paid up. Subject to that, secondly, where a company would, if the court did not grant the exemption, have more than one remedy against a particular person, it should be for the company to decide which remedy it should remain entitled to pursue. Because these are 'overriding principles', a court will need very good reasons to accept that it is just and equitable to exempt an applicant from liability where the company has not received sufficient value (*Bradford Investments plc (No 2), Re* [1991] BCLC 688, [1991] BCC 379).

Otherwise, the court may exempt the applicant from the liability only if and to the extent that it appears to the court just and equitable to do so. In reaching its decision, the court must have regard to the following (except in relation to a decision whether to grant relief in respect of a liability for interest arising before 1 October 2009).

Where (*a*) above applies,

- whether the applicant has paid, or is liable to pay, any amount in respect of:
  - (i) any other liability arising in relation to those shares under any provision in **47.32–47.42** relating to independent valuation of non-cash consideration or **47.23–47.27** relating to payment for shares; or
  - (ii) any liability arising by virtue of any undertaking given in or in connection with payment for those shares;
- whether any person other than the applicant has paid or is likely to pay, whether in pursuance of any order of the court or otherwise, any such amount; and
- whether the applicant or any other person:
  - (i) has performed in whole or in part, or is likely so to perform, any such undertaking; or
  - (ii) has done, or is likely to do, any other thing in payment or part payment for the shares.

Where (*b*) above applies,

- whether the applicant has paid or is liable to pay any amount in respect of liability arising in relation to the shares under any provision in **47.32–47.42** relating to independent valuation of non-cash consideration or **47.23–47.27** relating to payment for shares; or
- whether any person other than the applicant has paid, or is likely to pay, whether in pursuance of any order of the court or otherwise, any such amount.

[*CA 2006, s 606(1)–(4)*].

Proceedings against a contributor. Certain powers are conferred on the court where a person brings proceedings against another (the '*contributor*') for a contribution in respect of liability to a company arising under any provision relating to payment for shares in **47.23–47.27** or any provision relating to independent valuation of non-cash consideration in **47.32–47.42** and it appears to the court that the contributor is liable to make such a contribution. The court may, if and to the extent that it appears to be just and equitable to do so, having regard to the respective culpability (in respect of the liability to the company) of the contributor and the person bringing the proceedings:

- exempt the contributor in whole or in part from his liability to make such a contribution; or
- order the contributor to make a larger contribution than, but for this provision, he would be liable to make.

[*CA 2006, s 606(5)*].

Where a person is liable to a company under **47.40**, the court may, on application, exempt him in whole or in part from that liability if and to the extent that it appears to the court to be just and equitable to do so having regard to any benefit accruing to the company by virtue of anything done by him towards the carrying out of the agreement.

[*CA 2006, s 606(6)*].

47.44 Penalty for contravention

In relation to consideration received in pursuance of an obligation entered into on or after 1 October 2009, where a company contravenes the requirements of **47.32** or **47.36**, an offence is committed by the company, and every officer of the company who is in default. A person guilty of such an offence is liable (i) on conviction on indictment, to a fine; and (ii) on summary conviction, to a fine not exceeding the statutory maximum. See **29.1 Offences and Legal Proceedings** for the statutory maximum.

[*CA 2006, s 607*].

47.45 Enforceability of undertakings to do work, etc

Without prejudice to **47.43**, where:

- an undertaking to do work or perform services or to do any other thing is given by any person, in or in connection with payment for shares in a company, and
- that undertaking is enforceable by the company apart from any of the provisions in **47.32–47.43**

the undertaking is so enforceable notwithstanding that there has been a contravention in relation to it of any provision relating to payment for shares in **47.23–47.30** or any provision relating to independent valuation of non-cash consideration in **47.32–47.43**.

[*CA 2006, s 608*].

47.46 ALTERATION OF SHARE CAPITAL

A limited company having a share capital can only alter its share capital by:

- increasing its share capital by allotting new shares (see **47.8**);
- reducing its share capital (see **47.51**);
- sub-dividing or consolidate all or any of its share capital (see **47.47**); or
- reconverting stock into shares (see **47.48**).

The company may redenominate all or any of its shares in accordance **47.49** and may reduce its share capital in connection with such a redenomination (see **47.50**).

[*CA 2006, s 617(1)–(4)*].

Nothing in the above provisions affects:

- the power of a company to purchase its own shares or to redeem shares (see **34 Purchase of Own Shares**);
- the power of a company to purchase its own shares in pursuance of an order of the court under:
  - (i) *CA 2006, s 98* (application to court to cancel resolution for re-registration as a private company, see **41.9 Re-Registration**);
  - (ii) *CA 2006, s 721(6)* (powers of court on objection to redemption or purchase of shares out of capital, **34.13 Purchase of Own Shares**);
  - (iii) *CA 2006, s 759* (remedial order in case of breach of prohibition of public offers by private company, see **47.22**), or

- (iv) *CA 2006, Pt 30* (protection of members against unfair prejudice, see **26.10 MEMBERS**);
- the forfeiture of shares, or the acceptance of shares surrendered in lieu, in pursuance of the company's articles, for failure to pay any sum payable in respect of the shares;
- the cancellation of shares under *CA 2006, s 662* (duty to cancel shares held by or for a public company, see **34.23 PURCHASE OF OWN SHARES**); or
- the power of a company to:
  - (i) to enter into a compromise or arrangement in accordance with *CA 2006, Pt 26* (arrangements and reconstructions, see **35.1** to **35.5 RECONSTRUCTIONS AND MERGERS**), or
  - (ii) to do anything required to comply with an order of the court on an application under that *Part*.

[*CA 2006, s 617(5)*].

47.47 Sub-division or consolidation of shares

A limited company having a share capital may:

- sub-divide its shares, or any of them, into shares of a smaller nominal amount than its existing shares; or
- consolidate and divide all or any of its share capital into shares of a larger nominal amount than its existing shares.

In any sub-division, consolidation or division of shares, the proportion between the amount paid and the amount (if any) unpaid on each resulting share must be the same as it was in the case of the share from which that share is derived.

[*CA 2006, s 618(1)(2)*].

Authorisation. A company may only exercise a power to sub-divide or consolidate if its members have passed a resolution authorising it to do so. The resolution may authorise the company to exercise:

- more than one of the powers;
- a power on more than one occasion; or
- a power at a specified time or in specified circumstances.

The articles may exclude or restrict the exercise of any power conferred by *CA 2006, s 618*.

[*CA 2006, s 618(3)–(5)*].

Where standard articles have been adopted, see:

- *Table A, 1985, Regs 32, 33*
- *Model Articles, Art 69* (public companies)

Set out in **APPENDIX 4 STANDARD ARTICLES OF ASSOCIATION**.

Notice to Registrar of Companies. If a company exercises the power conferred above, it must, within one month after doing so, give notice to the Registrar of Companies, specifying the shares affected. The notice must be accompanied by a statement of capital giving details of the following with respect to the company's share capital immediately following the exercise of the power.

- The total number of shares of the company.
- The aggregate nominal value of those shares.
- For each class of shares:

  (i) particulars of any voting rights attached to the shares, including rights that arise only in certain circumstances;

  (ii) particulars of any rights attached to the shares, as respects dividends, to participate in a distribution;

  (iii) particulars of any rights attached to the shares, as respects capital, to participate in a distribution (including on a winding up);

  (iv) whether the shares are to be redeemed or are liable to be redeemed at the option of the company or the shareholder;

  (v) the total number of shares of that class; and

  (vi) the aggregate nominal value of shares of that class. The *SBEE 2015* introduces a requirement to also include in the statement of capital the aggregate amount (if any) unpaid on those shares (whether on account of their nominal value or by way of premium). As at May 2015 this provision is not in force.

- The amount paid up and the amount (if any) unpaid on each share (whether on account of the nominal value of the share or by way of premium).

If default is made in complying with this requirement, an offence is committed by the company and every officer of the company who is in default. A person guilty of such an offence is liable, on summary conviction, to a fine not exceeding level 3 on the standard scale and, for continued contravention, a daily default fine not exceeding one-tenth of the standard scale. See **29.1 Offences and Legal Proceedings** for the standard scale. [*CA 2006, s 619; SI 2009 No 388, Art 2*].

47.48 Reconversion of stock into shares

A limited company that has converted paid-up shares into stock (before the repeal by *CA 2006* of the power to do so) may reconvert that stock into paid-up shares of any nominal value.

This power may only be exercised if its members have passed an ordinary resolution authorising it to do so. The resolution may authorise the company to exercise the power:

- on more than one occasion; or
- at a specified time or in specified circumstances.

[*CA 2006, s 620*].

Notice to Registrar of Companies. If a company exercises the power conferred above, it must, within one month after doing so, give notice to the Registrar of Companies, specifying the stock affected. The notice must be accompanied by a statement of capital giving details of the following with respect to the company's share capital immediately following the exercise of the power.

- The total number of shares of the company.
- The aggregate nominal value of those shares. The *SBEE 2015* introduces a requirement to also include in the statement of capital the aggregate amount (if any) unpaid on those shares (whether on account of their nominal value or by way of premium). As at May 2015 this provision is not in force.
- For each class of shares:
  - (i) particulars of any voting rights attached to the shares, including rights that arise only in certain circumstances;
  - (ii) particulars of any rights attached to the shares, as respects dividends, to participate in a distribution;
  - (iii) particulars of any rights attached to the shares, as respects capital, to participate in a distribution (including on a winding up);
  - (iv) whether the shares are to be redeemed or are liable to be redeemed at the option of the company or the shareholder;
  - (v) the total number of shares of that class; and
  - (vi) the aggregate nominal value of shares of that class.
- The amount paid up and the amount (if any) unpaid on each share (whether on account of the nominal value of the share or by way of premium).

If default is made in complying with this requirement, an offence is committed by the company and every officer of the company who is in default. A person guilty of such an offence is liable, on summary conviction, to a fine not exceeding level 3 on the standard scale and, for continued contravention, a daily default fine not exceeding one-tenth of the standard scale. See **29.1 Offences and Legal Proceedings** for the standard scale. [*CA 2006, s 621; SI 2009 No 388, Art 2*].

47.49 Redenomination of share capital

Subject to its articles (which may prohibit or restrict the exercise of the power), a limited company having a share capital may, by resolution, 'redenominate' its share capital or any class of its share capital, ie convert shares from having a fixed nominal value in one currency to having a fixed nominal value in another currency. The resolution may specify conditions which must be met before the redenomination takes effect.

The conversion must be made at a spot rate of exchange specified in the resolution. The rate must be either:

- a rate prevailing on a day specified in the resolution, or
- a rate determined by taking the average of rates prevailing on each consecutive day of a period specified in the resolution

and the day or period specified must be within the period of 28 days ending on the day before the resolution is passed.

Redenomination in accordance with a resolution under these provisions takes effect on the day on which the resolution is passed or on such later day as determined in accordance with the resolution.

A resolution under this provision lapses if the redenomination for which it provides has not taken effect at the end of the period of 28 days beginning on the date on which it is passed.

CA 2006, ss 29, 30 (resolutions affecting a company's constitution, see **14.10** CONSTITUTION – MEMORANDUM AND ARTICLES) apply to a resolution under this provision.

[*CA 2006, s 622*].

Calculation of new nominal values. For each class of share, the new nominal value of each share is calculated as follows.

(1) Take the aggregate of the old nominal values of all the shares of that class.

(2) Translate that amount into the new currency at the rate of exchange specified in the resolution.

(3) Divide that amount by the number of shares in the class.

[*CA 2006, s 623*].

Effect of redenomination. The redenomination of shares does not affect any rights or obligations of members under the company's constitution, or any restrictions affecting members under the company's constitution. In particular, it does not affect entitlement to dividends (including entitlement to dividends in a particular currency), voting rights or any liability in respect of amounts unpaid on shares. For this purpose, the company's constitution includes the terms on which any shares of the company are allotted or held.

Subject to this, references to the old nominal value of the shares in any agreement or statement, or in any deed, instrument or document, are (unless the context otherwise requires) be read after the resolution takes effect as references to the new nominal value of the shares.

[*CA 2006, s 624*].

Notice to Registrar of Companies. A company must, within one month after redenomination, give notice to the Registrar of Companies specifying the shares redenominated and stating the date on which the resolution was passed. The notice must be accompanied by a statement of capital giving details of the following with respect to the company's share capital as redenominated by the resolution.

- The total number of shares of the company
- The aggregate nominal value of those shares. The *SBEE 2015* introduces a requirement to also include in the statement of capital the aggregate amount (if any) unpaid on those shares (whether on account of their nominal value or by way of premium). As at May 2015 this provision is not in force.
- For each class of shares:

  (i) particulars of any voting rights attached to the shares, including rights that arise only in certain circumstances;

  (ii) particulars of any rights attached to the shares, as respects dividends, to participate in a distribution;

  (iii) particulars of any rights attached to the shares, as respects capital, to participate in a distribution (including on a winding up);

  (iv) whether the shares are to be redeemed or are liable to be redeemed at the option of the company or the shareholder;

  (v) the total number of shares of that class; and

  (vi) the aggregate nominal value of shares of that class.

- The amount paid up and the amount (if any) unpaid on each share (whether on account of the nominal value of the share or by way of premium).

If default is made in complying with this requirement, an offence is committed by the company and every officer of the company who is in default. A person guilty of such an offence is liable, on summary conviction, to a fine not exceeding level 3 on the standard scale and, for continued contravention, a daily default fine not exceeding one-tenth of level 3 on the standard scale. See **29.1** Offences and Legal Proceedings for the standard scale.

[*CA 2006, s 625; SI 2009 No 388, Art 2*].

47.50 *Reduction of capital in connection with redenomination*

A limited company that passes a resolution under **47.49** may, for the purpose of adjusting the nominal values of the redenominated shares to obtain values that are, in the opinion of the company, more suitable, reduce its share capital. The reduction of capital:

- requires a special resolution of the company (which must be passed within three months of the resolution effecting the redenomination); and
- does not extinguish or reduce any liability in respect of share capital not paid up.

The amount by which share capital is reduced must not exceed 10% of the nominal value of the company's allotted share capital immediately after the reduction.

The provisions in **47.51–47.58** (reduction of share capital) do not apply to a reduction of capital under this provision.

[*CA 2006, s 626*].

Notice to Registrar of Companies. Where such a resolution is passed, the company must, within 15 days after the resolution is passed, give notice to the Registrar of Companies stating the date of the resolution and the date of the resolution to redenominate share capital under **47.49** in connection with which it was passed. This is in addition to the copies of the resolutions themselves that are required to be delivered to the Registrar of Companies under **14.10** Constitution – Memorandum and Articles.

The notice must be accompanied by a statement of capital giving details of the following with respect to the company's share capital as reduced by the resolution.

- The total number of shares of the company.
- The aggregate nominal value of those shares. The *SBEE 2015* introduces a requirement to also include in the statement of capital the aggregate amount (if any) unpaid on those shares (whether on account of their nominal value or by way of premium). As at May 2015 this provision is not in force.
- For each class of shares:
  - (i) particulars of any voting rights attached to the shares, including rights that arise only in certain circumstances;
  - (ii) particulars of any rights attached to the shares, as respects dividends, to participate in a distribution;
  - (iii) particulars of any rights attached to the shares, as respects capital, to participate in a distribution (including on a winding up);
  - (iv) whether the shares are to be redeemed or are liable to be redeemed at the option of the company or the shareholder;

(v) the total number of shares of that class; and

(vi) the aggregate nominal value of shares of that class.

- The amount paid up and the amount (if any) unpaid on each share (whether on account of the nominal value of the share or by way of premium).

On receipt, the Registrar of Companies must register the notice and the statement. The reduction of capital is not effective until those documents are registered.

The company must also deliver to the Registrar of Companies, within 15 days after the resolution is passed, a statement by the directors confirming that the reduction in share capital does not exceed 10% of nominal value of allotted shares immediately after reduction.

If default is made in complying with any of these requirements, an offence is committed by the company and every officer of the company who is in default. A person guilty of such an offence is liable (i) on conviction on indictment to a fine; and (ii) on summary conviction, to a fine not exceeding the statutory maximum. See **29.1 Offences and Legal Proceedings** for the statutory maximum.

[*CA 2006, s 627; SI 2009 No 388, Art 2*].

Redenomination reserve. The amount by which a company's share capital is reduced must be transferred to a reserve, called the '*redenomination reserve*'. This reserve may be applied by the company in paying up shares to be allotted to members as fully paid bonus shares. But, subject to that, the provisions of the *Companies Acts* relating to the reduction of a company's share capital apply as if the redenomination reserve were paid-up share capital of the company.

[*CA 2006, s 628*].

47.51 REDUCTION OF SHARE CAPITAL

Subject to any provision of the company's articles (or, before 1 October 2009, the company's memorandum) restricting or prohibiting the reduction of the company's share capital, a limited company having a share capital may reduce its share capital:

(a) in the case of a private company limited by shares, by special resolution supported by a solvency statement (see **47.52–47.54**);

(b) in any case, by special resolution confirmed by the court (see **47.55–47.57**).

A company may not reduce its capital under (*a*) above if, as a result of the reduction, there would no longer be any member of the company holding shares other than redeemable shares.

But subject to that, a company may reduce its share capital under *CA 2006, s 641* in any way and, in particular, it may:

- extinguish or reduce the liability on any of its shares in respect of share capital not paid up (see *Doloswella Rubber and Tea Estates Ltd and Reduced, Re* [1917] 1 Ch 213, 86 LJ Ch 223); or
- either with or without extinguishing or reducing liability on any of its shares:

(i) cancel any paid-up share capital that is lost or unrepresented by available assets; or

(ii) repay any paid-up share capital in excess of the company's wants.

See *Westburn Sugar Refineries Ltd, ex p* [1951] AC 625, [1951] 1 All ER 881, HL; *Thomas De La Rue & Co Ltd and Reduced, Re* [1911] 2 Ch 361, 81 LJ Ch 59; and *Re Jupiter House Investments (Cambridge) Ltd* [1985] 1 WLR 975, [1985] BCLC 222.

The special resolution may not provide for a reduction of share capital to take effect later than the date on which the resolution has effect.

[*CA 2006, s 641*].

Where the company has adopted standard articles, see *Table A, 1985, Reg 34*, set out in APPENDIX 4 STANDARD ARTICLES OF ASSOCIATION.

47.52 Private companies: reduction of capital supported by a solvency statement

A resolution for reducing share capital of a private company under **47.51**(*a*) is supported by a solvency statement if:

- the directors of the company make a statement of the solvency of the company in accordance with **47.53** not more than 15 days before the date on which the resolution is passed; and
- the resolution and solvency statement are registered in accordance with **47.53**.

Where the resolution is proposed:

- as a written resolution, a copy of the solvency statement must be sent or submitted to every eligible member at or before the time at which the proposed resolution is sent or submitted to him; and
- at a general meeting, a copy of the solvency statement must be made available for inspection by members of the company throughout that meeting.

The validity of a resolution is not affected by a failure to comply with this requirement.

[*CA 2006, s 642*].

47.53 *Solvency statement*

A solvency statement is a statement that each of the directors:

- has formed the opinion, as regards the company's situation at the date of the statement, that there is no ground on which the company could then be found to be unable to pay (or otherwise discharge) its debts; and
- has also formed the opinion:
  - (i) if it is intended to commence the winding up of the company within twelve months of that date, that the company will be able to pay (or otherwise discharge) its debts in full within twelve months of the commencement of the winding up; or
  - (ii) in any other case, that the company will be able to pay (or otherwise discharge) its debts as they fall due during the year immediately following that date.

In forming those opinions, the directors must take into account all of the company's liabilities (including any contingent or prospective liabilities).

The solvency statement must be in writing in the prescribed form and must:

- state the date on which it is made;
- state the name of each director of the company;
- indicate that it is a solvency statement for the purposes of *CA 2006, s 642*; and
- be signed by each of the directors of the company.

Offence. If the directors make a solvency statement without having reasonable grounds for the opinions expressed in it, and the statement is delivered to the Registrar of Companies, an offence is committed by every director who is in default. A person guilty of such an offence is liable (i) on conviction on indictment, to imprisonment for a term not exceeding two years or a fine (or both); and (ii) on summary conviction, to imprisonment for a term not exceeding twelve months (in Scotland and Northern Ireland, six months) or to a fine not exceeding the statutory maximum (or both). See **29.1 Offences and Legal Proceedings** for the statutory maximum.

[*CA 2006, s 643; SI 2008 No 1915, Art 2*].

47.54 *Registration of resolution and supporting documents*

Within 15 days after the resolution for reducing share capital is passed, the company must deliver the following documents to the Registrar of Companies.

(a) A copy of the resolution (see **14.10 Constitution – Memorandum and Articles**).

(b) A copy of the solvency statement under **47.53**.

(c) A statement of capital which must state, with respect to the company's share capital as reduced by the resolution:

- The total number of shares of the company.
- The aggregate nominal value of those shares. The *SBEE 2015* introduces a requirement to also include in the statement of capital the aggregate amount (if any) unpaid on those shares (whether on account of their nominal value or by way of premium). As at May 2015 this provision is not in force.
- For each class of shares:

  (i) particulars of any voting rights attached to the shares, including rights that arise only in certain circumstances;

  (ii) particulars of any rights attached to the shares, as respects dividends, to participate in a distribution;

  (iii) particulars of any rights attached to the shares, as respects capital, to participate in a distribution (including on a winding up);

  (iv) whether the shares are to be redeemed or are liable to be redeemed at the option of the company or the shareholder;

  (v) the total number of shares of that class; and

  (vi) the aggregate nominal value of shares of that class.
- The amount paid up and the amount (if any) unpaid on each share (whether on account of the nominal value of the share or by way of premium).

(d) A statement by the directors confirming that the solvency statement was:

- made not more than 15 days before the date on which the resolution was passed; and
- provided to members in accordance with 47.52.

The Registrar of Companies must register the documents delivered to him under (*b*)–(*d*) above and the resolution does not take effect until those documents are registered.

The validity of a resolution is not affected by a failure to deliver the documents under (*b*)–(*e*) above within the time specified.

Offences. If the company delivers to the Registrar of Companies a solvency statement that was not provided to members in accordance with **47.52**, an offence is committed by every officer of the company who is in default. Additionally, if default is made in complying with the above requirements as to delivery of documents to the Registrar of Companies, an offence is committed by the company and every officer of the company who is in default. A person guilty of an offence under either of these provisions is liable (i) on conviction on indictment, to a fine; and (ii) on summary conviction, to a fine not exceeding the statutory maximum. See **29.1 Offences and Legal Proceedings** for the statutory maximum.

[*CA 2006, s 644; SI 2009 No 388, Art 2*].

47.55 Reduction of capital confirmed by the court

Where a company has passed a resolution for reducing share capital, it may apply to the court for an order confirming the reduction.

[*CA 2006, s 645(1)*].

Where such an application is made the provisions in this paragraph and in **47.56** and **47.57** apply.

Creditors entitled to object to reduction. If the proposed reduction of capital involves either:

- diminution of liability in respect of unpaid share capital, or
- the payment to a shareholder of any paid-up share capital,

and in any other case where the court directs, every creditor of the company who:

- at a date fixed by the court, is entitled to any debt or claim that would be admissible in a winding up of the company commencing on that date, and
- can show that there is a real likelihood that the reduction would result in the company being unable to discharge his debt or claim when it fell due

is entitled to object to the reduction of capital.

The court must settle a list of creditors entitled to object. For that purpose, it must ascertain, as far as possible without requiring an application from any creditor, the names of those creditors and the nature and amount of their debts or claims. It may then publish notices fixing a time within which creditors not entered on the list are to claim to be so entered or are to be excluded from the right of objecting to the reduction of capital.

If a creditor entered on the list whose debt or claim is not discharged (or has not determined) does not consent to the reduction, the court may, if it thinks fit, dispense with the consent of that creditor if the company secures payment of his debt or claim.

For this purpose, the debt or claim must be secured by appropriating (as the court may direct) the full amount of the debt or claim or, if the company does not admit the full amount (or the amount is contingent or not ascertained) an amount fixed by the court.

[*CA 2006, ss 645(2)(4), 646; SI 2009 No 2022, Reg 3*].

The court may, however,

- direct that this is not to apply; or
- if, having regard to any special circumstances it thinks proper to do so, direct that this is not to apply as regards any class or classes of creditors.

[*CA 2006, ss 645(2)(3), 646*].

(In most schemes for reduction of capital this power will be used because the company will either have agreed the capital reduction with creditors or secured its liabilities by means of a guarantee.)

See also *Re Lucania Temperance Billiard Halls (London) Ltd* [1966] Ch 98, [1965] 3 All ER 879 and *Re Antwerp Waterworks Co Ltd* [1931] WN 186, 172 LT Jo 75.

As well as the position of creditors the court must also consider present and future shareholders (see *Poole v National Bank of China Ltd* [1907] AC 229, 76 LJ Ch 458, HL). See also *Ratners Group plc, Re [1988] BCLC 685*, 4 BCC 293. It must carefully scrutinise any scheme which does not provide for uniform treatment of shareholders with similar rights and must be satisfied that it is not unjust or inequitable, although this does not mean that it cannot sanction such a scheme (*British and American Trustee and Finance Corpn v Couper* [1894] AC 399, HL).

Offences in connection with list of creditors. If an officer of the company:

- intentionally or recklessly:
  - (i) conceals the name of a creditor entitled to object to the reduction of capital, or
  - (ii) misrepresents the nature or amount of the debt or claim of a creditor, or
- is knowingly concerned in any such concealment or misrepresentation,

he commits an offence. A person guilty of such an offence is liable (i) on conviction on indictment, to a fine; and (ii) on summary conviction, to a fine not exceeding the statutory maximum. See **29.1 Offences and Legal Proceedings** for the statutory maximum.

[*CA 2006, s 647*].

Court order confirming reduction. The court may make an order confirming the reduction of capital on such terms and conditions as it thinks fit. But it must not confirm the reduction unless it is satisfied, with respect to every creditor of the company who is entitled to object to the reduction of capital that either:

- his consent to the reduction has been obtained; or
- his debt or claim has been discharged, or has determined or has been secured.

Where the court confirms the reduction, it may order the company to publish the reasons for reduction of capital or any other information in connection with the reduction where it thinks expedient to give proper information to the public. This can include the causes that led to the reduction.

The court may also, if for any special reason it thinks proper to do so, make an order directing that the company must, during a period commencing on or at any time after the date of the order, add to its name as its last words the words 'and reduced'. If such an order is made, those words are, until the end of the period specified, deemed to be part of the company's name.

[*CA 2006, s 648*].

47.56 *Registration of order and statement of capital*

The Registrar of Companies, on production of an order of the court confirming the reduction of a company's share capital and the delivery of a copy of the order and of a statement of capital (approved by the court), must register the order and statement. This is subject to the provisions set out in **47.57**. Notice of the registration must be published in such manner as the court may direct.

The statement of capital must give details of the following with respect to the company's share capital as altered by the order.

- The total number of shares of the company.
- The aggregate nominal value of those shares.
- For each class of shares:
  - (i) particulars of any voting rights attached to the shares, including rights that arise only in certain circumstances;
  - (ii) particulars of any rights attached to the shares, as respects dividends, to participate in a distribution;
  - (iii) particulars of any rights attached to the shares, as respects capital, to participate in a distribution (including on a winding up);
  - (iv) whether the shares are to be redeemed or are liable to be redeemed at the option of the company or the shareholder;
  - (v) the total number of shares of that class; and
  - (vi) the aggregate nominal value of shares of that class. The *SBEE 2015* introduces a requirement to also include in the statement of capital the aggregate amount (if any) unpaid on those shares (whether on account of their nominal value or by way of premium). As at May 2015 this provision is not in force.
- The amount paid up and the amount (if any) unpaid on each share (whether on account of the nominal value of the share or by way of premium).

The resolution for reducing share capital, as confirmed by the court's order, takes effect:

- in the case of a reduction of share capital that forms part of a compromise or arrangement sanctioned by the court under *CA 2006, Pt 26* (arrangements and reconstructions):
  - (i) on delivery of the order and statement of capital to the Registrar of Companies; or
  - (ii) if the court so orders, on the registration of the order and statement of capital; and
- in any other case, on the registration of the order and statement of capital.

Certification. The Registrar of Companies must also certify the registration of the order and statement of capital. The certificate must be signed by the Registrar (or authenticated by the Registrar's official seal) and is conclusive evidence that the requirements of *CA 2006* with respect to the reduction of share capital have been complied with and that the company's share capital is as stated in the statement of capital. [*CA 2006, s 649; SI 2009 No 388, Art 2*].

47.57 Public company reducing capital below the authorised minimum

Where the court makes an order confirming a reduction of a public company's capital that has the effect of bringing the nominal value of its allotted share capital below the authorised minimum (see **29.3 Offences and Legal Proceedings**), the Registrar of Companies must not register the order unless either:

- the court so directs; or
- the company is first re-registered as a private company.

[*CA 2006, s 650*].

In these circumstances, the court may authorise the company to be re-registered as a private company without its having passed the special resolution otherwise required by *CA 2006, s 97* (see **41.8 Re-Registration**). If it does so, the court must specify in the order the changes to the company's name and articles to be made in connection with the re-registration. The company may then be re-registered as a private company if an application to that effect is delivered to the Registrar of Companies together with:

- a copy of the court's order; and
- notice of the company's name, and a copy of the company's articles, as altered by the court's order.

The Registrar of Companies must issue a certificate of incorporation stating that it is issued on re-registration and the date on which it is issued. On the issue of the certificate:

- the company becomes a private company; and
- the changes in the company's name and articles take effect.

The certificate is conclusive evidence that the requirements of *CA 2006* as to re-registration have been complied with.

[*CA 2006, s 651*].

Where a public company reduces its share capital to less than the authorised minimum but immediately increases it again to more than authorised minimum by a resolution which takes effect before, or at the same time as, the reduction resolution, the company is not obliged to re-register as a private company (*Re MB Group Ltd* [1989] BCLC 672, 5 BCC 684).

47.58 Effect of reduction of capital

(1) *Liability of members generally*

Subject to (2) below, where a company's share capital is reduced, a member of the company (past or present) is not liable in respect of any share to any call or contribution exceeding in amount the difference (if any) between:

- the nominal amount of the share as notified to the Registrar of Companies in the statement of capital delivered under **47.54** or **47.56**; and
- the amount paid on the share or the reduced amount (if any) which is deemed to have been paid on it, as the case may be.

Nothing in the above affects the rights of the contributories among themselves. [*CA 2006, s 652*].

(2) *Liability of members to creditor in case of omission from list of creditors*

Where, in the case of a reduction of capital confirmed by the court under **47.55**,

- a creditor entitled to object to the reduction of share capital is, by reason of his ignorance of the proceedings for reduction of share capital or of their nature and effect with respect to his debt or claim, not entered on the list of creditors, and
- after the reduction of capital the company is unable (within the meaning of the *Insolvency Act 1986, s 123* or *Insolvency (Northern Ireland) Order 1989, Art 103*) to pay the amount of his debt or claim,

every member of the company at the date on which the resolution for reducing capital took effect (see **47.56**) is liable to contribute for the payment of the debt or claim an amount not exceeding that which he would have been liable to contribute if the company had commenced to be wound up on the day before that date.

If the company is wound up, the court may, on the application of the creditor in question and proof of his ignorance,

- settle a list of persons liable to contribute under this provision; and
- make and enforce calls and orders on them as if they were ordinary contributories in a winding up.

[*CA 2006, s 653*].

47.59 Treatment of reserve arising from reduction of capital

A reserve arising from the reduction of a company's share capital is not distributable with the following exceptions.

(a) Where an unlimited company reduces its share capital.

(b) If a private company limited by shares reduces its share capital and the reduction is supported by a solvency statement but has not been the subject of an application to the court for an order confirming it.

(c) If a limited company having a share capital reduces its share capital and the reduction is confirmed by order of the court.

In such cases, the reserve arising from the reduction is to be treated for the purposes of *CA 2006, Pt 23* (distributions) as a realised profit (unless, where (*c*) applies, the court orders otherwise). The exceptions do not, however, affect the operation of anything to the contrary in:

- an order of, or undertaking to, the court;
- the resolution for, or any other resolution relevant to, the reduction; or
- the company's memorandum or articles of association.

[*CA 2006, s 645; SI 2008 No 1915, Art 3*].

47.60 MAINTENANCE OF CAPITAL

There are a number of provisions in *CA 2006* which seek to ensure that a company's capital is maintained other than by being lost in the ordinary course of business. This is because the issued share capital is the ultimate fund for payment of the company's creditors. See *Exchange Banking Co, Re, Flitcroft's Case* (1882) 21 Ch D 519, CA.

(1) **Allotment of shares at a discount**

A company's shares must not be allotted at a discount. See **47.24**.

(2) **Company not to acquire own shares**

Subject to certain exceptions, a company must not acquire its own shares whether by purchase, subscription or otherwise. See **34.1 Purchase of Own Shares** for details and exceptions.

(3) **Acquisition of shares by company's nominee**

With certain exceptions, shares issued to or acquired by a nominee of the company are treated as held by the nominee on his own account. See **34.22 Purchase of Own Shares**.

47.61 Duty of directors to call meeting on serious loss of capital

Where the net assets of a public company are half or less of its called-up share capital, the directors must, within 28 days from the earliest date on which that fact is known to any director, call a general meeting of the company, for a date not later than 56 days from that date, to consider what (if any) steps should be taken to deal with the situation.

In default, each director who knowingly authorises or permits the failure, or after the 56-day period knowingly authorises or permits the failure to continue, commits an offence. A person guilty of such an offence is liable (i) on conviction on indictment, to a fine; and (ii) on summary conviction, to a fine not exceeding the statutory maximum. See **29.1 Offences and Legal Proceedings** for the statutory maximum.

Nothing in *CA 2006, s 656* authorises the consideration at a convened meeting of any matter that could not have been considered at that meeting apart from (this) *section 656*.

[*CA 2006, s 656*].

47.62 BONUS ISSUES

A company may 'capitalise' its profits by applying them in wholly or partly paying up unissued shares in the company to be allotted to members as fully or partly paid bonus shares. [*CA 2006, s 853(3)*]. The procedure is known as a 'bonus issue' or alternatively a 'scrip issue' or 'capitalisation issue'. To make a bonus issue, a company must be authorised by its articles to do so. Where standard articles have been adopted, see:

- *Table A, 1985, Reg 110*
- *Model Articles, Art 36* (private companies
- *Model Articles, Art 78* (public companies)

set out in Appendix 4 Standard Articles of Association.

In practice, the bonus shares will generally be fully paid. If this is a requirement under the articles, any alteration of the articles to allow for partly-paid bonus shares would require written agreement by a member before he became liable for any unpaid share capital. [*CA 2006, s 25*]. See **14.7** Constitution – Memorandum and Articles.

Effect of *CA 2006* provisions. The general rule that shares, and any premium payable on them, must be paid up in money or money's worth does not prevent a company from allotting bonus shares to its members. [*CA 2006 s 582(2)*]. However, like other shares, bonus shares must not be allotted at a discount (*Welton v Saffery* [1897] AC 299, HL). See **47.24**.

The provisions in **47.32** which require a public company allotting shares otherwise than in cash to have the consideration independently valued do not apply to bonus shares. See **47.33**(1).

Return of allotments. Where a company makes any allotment of shares (including a bonus issue), it must within one month thereafter deliver to the Registrar of Companies a return in the prescribed form. See **47.12**.

47.63 Funds available for making bonus issues

A company's profits available for distribution are the excess of its accumulated, realised profits over its accumulated, realised losses. [*CA 2006, s 830(2)*]. However, an issue of fully or partly paid bonus shares is not a distribution for this purpose [*CA 2006, s 829(2)(a)*] and *unrealised* profits may therefore be utilised for paying up bonus shares, although they cannot be applied in paying up bonus *debentures* [*CA 2006, s 849*]. In addition, the share premium account [*CA 2006, s 610(3)*] and the capital redemption reserve [*CA 2006, s 733(5)*] may also be utilised in paying up fully paid bonus shares (but not debentures).

Where standard articles have been adopted, see:

- *Table A, 1985, Reg 110*
- *Model Articles, Art 36* (private companies)
- *Model Articles, Art 78* (public companies)

set out in Appendix 4 Standard Articles of Association.

Where, immediately before 22 December 1980 (1 July 1983 in Northern Ireland) a company was authorised by a provision of its articles to apply unrealised profits in paying up in full or in part unissued shares to be allotted to members as fully or partly paid bonus shares, the provision continues (subject to any alteration in the articles) as authority for those profits to be applied after that date.

[*CA 2006, s 848*].

47.64 RIGHTS ISSUES

In order to raise new capital, a company may make a rights issue to existing members or debenture-holders by which they are given the right to subscribe for new securities in a fixed proportion to their existing holdings. The price at which the new securities are offered is normally below the market price. It should be noted that under *CA 2006, ss 560–577* there are pre-emption provisions restricting the allotment of shares to persons other than existing members of the company (see **47.13–47.19**).

Procedure for making rights issues. The directors must ensure that the company has authority to issue the securities (see **47.9**).

In the case of a private company, the procedure is relatively straightforward, an issue being made to existing members in accordance with the articles of association and the securities normally being paid for in cash at that time.

47.65 Listed companies

A rights offer is made by a renounceable letter (or other negotiable document) which may be traded (as 'nil paid' rights) for a period before payment for the securities is due. The offer must remain open for acceptance for at least 10 business days.

For a placing of rights arising from a rights issue before the official start of dealings, a listed company must ensure that:

- the placing relates to at least 25% of the maximum number of equity securities offered;
- the placees are committed to take up whatever is placed with them;
- the price paid by the placees does not exceed the price at which the equity securities which are the subject of the rights issue are offered by more than one half of the calculated premium over that offer price (that premium being the difference between the offer price and the theoretical ex-rights price); and
- the equity securities which are the subject of the rights issue are of the same class as the equity securities already listed.

The FCA may modify LR 9.5.1(1) to allow the placing to relate to less than 25% if it is satisfied that requiring at least 25% would be detrimental to the success off the issue and may list the equity securities at the same time as they are admitted to trading in 'nil paid' form. On the equity securities being paid up and the allotment becoming unconditional, the listing will continue without any need for a further application to list fully paid securities.

If the existing shareholders do not take up their rights to subscribe in a rights issue:

- the listed company must ensure that the equity securities to which the offer relates are offered for subscription or purchase on terms that any premium obtained over the subscription or purchase price (net of expenses) is to be for the account of the holders, except that if the proceeds for an existing holder do not exceed £5, the proceeds may be retained for the company's benefit; and
- the equity securities may be allotted or sold to underwriters, if on the expiry of the subscription period no premium (net of expenses) has been obtained.

A listed company must ensure that for a rights issue a Regulatory Information Service must be notified, as soon as possible, of the issue price and principal terms of the issue; the results of the issue; and details of the sale (including date and price per share) if any rights not taken up are sold.

A listed company must ensure that the offer relating to a rights issue remains open for acceptance for at least 10 business days. (FCA Listing Rules, paras 9.5.1–9.5.6).

48 Takeovers

48.1	**Background**
48.2	**The Panel on Takeovers and Mergers**
48.3	Failure to comply with rules about bid documentation
48.4	Enforcement by the court
48.5	Effect of non-compliance with rules
48.6	Exemption from liability in damages
48.7	**Impediments to takeovers**
48.8	Opting in and opting out
48.9	Consequences of opting in
48.10	**'Squeeze-out' and 'sell-out'**
48.11	Takeover offers and related terms
48.12	Squeeze-out: right of offeror to buy out minority shareholder
48.15	Sell-out: right of minority shareholder to be bought out by the offeror
48.18	Applications to the court
48.19	Joint offers
Appendix	**The City Code on Takeovers and Mergers**

Cross-references. See 35 Reconstructions and Mergers.

48.1 BACKGROUND

From 1968, takeover regulation in the UK has been overseen by the Panel on Takeovers and Mergers ('the Panel') which, prior to the *European Directive on Takeover Bids* (*EC Directive 2004/25/EC*) (the '*Takeovers Directive*'), administered non statutory rules and principles contained in the City Code on Takeovers and Mergers (the 'Code').

Companies Act 2006 (CA 2006), Pt 28 was brought into force on 6 April 2007. It put both the Takeover Panel and the Code on a statutory footing and also provided for full implementation of the Takeovers Directive (see 48.2).

48.2 THE PANEL ON TAKEOVERS AND MERGERS

The Panel may do anything that it considers necessary for the purposes of, and in connection with, its functions. [*CA 2006, s 942(2)*].

Rules. The Panel must make rules giving effect to the following *Articles* of the *Takeovers Directive*.

- *Art 3.1* (general principles);
- *Art 4.2* (jurisdictional rules);
- *Art 5* (matters related to the protection of minority shareholders, mandatory bid and equitable price);
- *Art 6.1–6.3* (contents of the bid documentation);
- *Arts 7, 8* (time allowed for the acceptance of a bid and publication of a bid);
- *Art 9* (obligations of the management of the target company); and
- *Art 13* (other rules applicable to the conduct of bids).

[*CA 2006, s 943(1)*].

The rules made may also make other provision

- for or in connection with the regulation of
  - (i) takeover bids;
  - (ii) merger transactions, and
  - (iii) other transactions that have or may have, directly or indirectly, an effect on the ownership or control of companies;
- for or in connection with the regulation of things done in consequence of, or otherwise in relation to, any such bid or transaction; and
- about cases where
  - (i) any such bid or transaction is, or has been, contemplated or apprehended; or
  - (ii) an announcement is made denying that any such bid or transaction is intended.

[*CA 2006, s 943(2)*].

All rules must be made by an instrument in writing. Immediately after an instrument containing rules is made, the text must be made available to the public, with or without payment, in whatever way the Panel thinks appropriate. A person is not to be taken to have contravened a rule if he shows that, at the time of the alleged contravention, the text of the rule had not been so made available.

[*CA 2006, s 944(2)–(4)*].

The City Code on Takeovers and Mergers. The rules made under the above are contained in the City Code on Takeovers and Mergers. See Appendix to this chapter for a summary of the provisions of the Code.

Rulings. The Panel may give rulings on the interpretation, application or effect of rules. To the extent and in the circumstances specified in rules, and subject to any review or appeal, a ruling has binding effect.

[*CA 2006, s 945*].

Directions. Rules may contain provisions conferring power on the Panel to give any direction that appears necessary to restrain a person from acting or potentially acting in breach of the rules.

[*CA 2006, s 946*].

Power to require documents and information. The Panel may, by notice in writing, require a person (at a place specified and within a reasonable time) to

- produce any documents that are specified in the notice; and
- provide such information as may be reasonably required in connection with the exercise of its functions.

It may require any document to be authenticated or any information to be verified in such manner as it may reasonably require. It may take copies of or extracts from a document produced.

The production of a document does not affect any lien that a person has on the document and a person is not required to disclose documents or information in respect of which a claim to legal professional privilege (in Scotland, to confidentiality of communications) could be maintained in legal proceedings.

[*CA 2006, s 947*].

Restrictions on disclosure of information. Information concerning the private affairs of an individual or a business provided to the Panel in connection with its functions may not be disclosed during the individual's lifetime or while the business is carried on without the consent of the individual or business in question except for

- the purposes of carrying out the Panel's functions; or
- disclosure to a person, or for a purpose, set out in *CA 2006, Sch 2*.

The provisions do not prohibit the disclosure of information if it is or has been available to the public from any other source.

A person who discloses information in contravention of these provisions is guilty of an offence unless *either* he did not know, and had no reason to suspect, that the information fell within the provisions *or* he took all reasonable steps and exercised all due diligence to avoid the commission of the offence.

[*CA 2006, ss 948, 949, Sch 2; SI 2009 No 1208*].

Duty of co-operation. The Panel must take such steps as it considers appropriate to co-operate with

- the FCA;
- an authority designated as a supervisory authority for the purposes of *Takeovers Directive, Art 4.1*; and
- any other person or body that exercises functions of a public nature, under legislation in any country or territory outside the UK, that appear to the Panel to be similar to its own functions or those of the FCA.

[*CA 2006, s 950*].

Hearings and appeals. Rules must provide for a decision of the Panel to be subject to review by a committee of the Panel (the 'Hearings Committee') and for there to be a right of appeal against a decision of the Hearings Committee to an independent tribunal (the 'Takeover Appeal Board').

[*CA 2006, s 951(1)(3)*].

Sanctions. Rules may contain provision conferring power on the Panel to impose sanctions on a person who has acted in breach of rules or failed to comply with a direction (see above). [*CA 2006, s 952*].

Compensation. Rules may confer power on the Panel to order a person to pay such compensation (with interest) as it thinks just and reasonable if he is in breach of a rule the effect of which is to require the payment of money.

[*CA 2006, s 954*].

Isle of Man. With effect from 1 March 2009, the provisions in *CA 2006, Pt 28 Chap 1* are extended to the Isle of Man, with certain modification to reflect the differences in the legal system and governmental and regulatory structures of the Isle of Man. Among other things, the modifications impose a duty on the Island's Financial Supervision Commission to co-operate with the Takeover Panel. The modifications also provide for the exchange of information about takeovers.[*SI 2008 No 3122*]. See *SI 2008 No 3122, Sch* for full details of the modifications.

48.3 Failure to comply with rules about bid documentation

Provisions relating to bid documentation are laid down in *Takeovers Directive, Arts 6.3, 9.5* which are implemented in the UK by rules which the Panel are obliged to make under *CA 2006, s 943* (see **48.2**). The offences detailed below apply in relation to bid documentation where a takeover bid is made for a company that has securities carrying voting rights admitted to trading on a regulated market in the UK.

(a) Where an offer document published in respect of the bid does not comply with offer document rules, an offence is committed by

(i) the person making the bid; and

(ii) where the person making the bid is a body of persons, any director, officer or member of that body who caused the document to be published.

A person commits an offence for these purposes only if

- he knew that the offer document did not comply, or was reckless as to whether it complied; and
- he failed to take all reasonable steps to secure that it did comply.

(b) Where a response document published in respect of the bid does not comply with response document rules, an offence is committed by any director or other officer of the company subject to the bid who

(i) knew that the response document did not comply, or was reckless as to whether it complied, and

(ii) failed to take all reasonable steps to secure that it did comply.

Where either offence is committed by a corporate body (eg a corporate director), it is also committed by the director, officers or members of that body.

A person guilty of an offence under the above provisions is liable (i) on conviction on indictment, to a fine; and (ii) on summary conviction, to a fine not exceeding the statutory maximum. See **29.1 Offences and Legal Proceedings** for the statutory maximum.

[*CA 2006, s 953*].

48.4 Enforcement by the court

If, on the application of the Panel, the High Court (in Scotland the Court of Session) is satisfied that

- there is a reasonable likelihood that a person will contravene a rule-based requirement, or
- a person has contravened a rule-based requirement or a disclosure requirement,

the court may make any order it thinks fit to secure compliance with the requirement. Apart from this, no person has a right to seek an injunction (in Scotland, has title or interest to seek an interdict or an order for specific performance) to prevent a person from contravening (or continuing to contravene) a rule-based requirement or a disclosure requirement. [*CA 2006, s 955*].

48.5 Effect of non-compliance with rules

Compliance with the rules made by the Panel is a matter solely for the Panel. It is therefore specifically provided that

- contravention of a rule-based requirement or a disclosure requirement does not give rise to any right of action for breach of statutory duty; and
- contravention of a rule-based requirement does not make any transaction void or unenforceable or (subject to any provision of the rules) affect the validity of any other thing (although transactions will be capable of being set aside or unravelled in cases of, for example, misrepresentation or fraud).

[*CA 2006, s 956*].

48.6 Exemption from liability in damages

Neither the Panel nor any person who is a member, officer or member of staff of the Panel is to be liable in damages for anything done or omitted in the discharge of the Panel's functions unless the act or omission is shown to have been in bad faith. But this exemption does not prevent an award of damages made in respect of an act or omission on the ground that it was unlawful as a result of *Human Rights Act 1998, s 6(1)* (acts of public authorities incompatible with Convention rights). [*CA 2006, s 962*].

48.7 IMPEDIMENTS TO TAKEOVERS

The *Takeovers Directive, Art 11* seeks to override, in certain circumstances, a number of defensive mechanisms that may be adopted by companies prior to a bid. These include

- differential share structures under which minority shareholders can exercise disproportionate voting rights;
- restrictions on transfers of shares in the company articles or in contractual agreements; and
- limitations on share ownership.

As permitted by *Takeovers Directive, Art 12*, the UK has decided not to apply the provisions of *Art 11* in all cases but instead to include in *CA 2006* provisions for companies with voting shares traded on regulated markets to opt in to its provisions should they choose to do so.

These provisions are outlined in **48.8** and **48.9**.

48.8 Opting in and opting in

A company may by special resolution (an '*opting-in resolution*') opt in for the purposes of these provisions if the following three conditions are met in relation to the company.

(1) The company has voting shares admitted to trading on a regulated market.

(2) The company's articles of association

 (i) do not contain any such restrictions as are mentioned in *Takeovers Directive, Art 11* or, if they do contain any such restrictions, provide for the restrictions not to apply at a time when (or in circumstances in which) they would be disapplied by that *Article*; and

 (ii) do not contain any other provision which would be incompatible with that *Art 11.*

Takeovers Directive, Art 11 relates to both the takeover bid period and the time following the bid when the bidder has acquired 75% or more of the company's capital carrying voting rights. It provides that restrictions both on the right to transfer shares and on voting rights that are contained in the articles of the company should not apply. It also provides that, in certain circumstances, shares carrying multiple voting rights will only have one vote and extraordinary rights of shareholders concerning the appointment or removal of board members should be disapplied.

(3) No shares conferring special rights in the company are held by

(a) a 'minister',

(b) a nominee of, or any other person acting on behalf of, a minister, or

(c) a company directly or indirectly controlled by a minister,

and no such rights are exercisable by or on behalf of a minister under any Act.

By order, this can be extended to include a specified person or body that exercises functions of a public nature as it applies in relation to a minister.

'*Minister*' means the holder of an office in Her Majesty's Government in the UK, the Scottish Ministers, a minister within the meaning given by *Northern Ireland Act 1998, s 7(3)* and the Welsh Ministers.

A company may revoke an opting-in resolution by a further special resolution (an '*opting-out resolution*').

[*CA 2006, s 966*].

An opting-in or an opting-out resolution must specify the date from which it is to have effect.

- The effective date of an opting-in resolution may not be earlier than the date on which the resolution is passed. Conditions (2) and (3) above must be met at the time when an opting-in resolution is passed but condition (1) does not need to be met until the effective date. An opting-in resolution passed before the time when voting shares of the company are admitted to trading on a regulated market complies with this requirement if, instead of specifying a particular date, it provides for the resolution to have effect from that time.
- The effective date of an opting-out resolution may not be earlier than the first anniversary of the date on which a copy of the opting-in resolution was forwarded to the Registrar of Companies.

Where a company has passed an opting-in resolution, any alteration of its articles of association that would prevent condition (2) above from being met is of no effect until the effective date of an opting-out resolution passed by the company.

[*CA 2006, s 967*].

Communication of decisions. A company that has passed an opting-in or an opting-out resolution must notify

(a) the Panel, and

(b) where the company has voting shares admitted to trading on a regulated market in an EEA State other than the UK (or has requested such admission), the takeover supervisory authority of that state.

Notification must be given within 15 days after the resolution is passed and, if any admission or request under (*b*) above occurs at a later time, within 15 days after that time.

If a company fails to comply with these provisions, an offence is committed by the company and every officer of it who is in default. A person guilty of such an offence is liable, on summary conviction, to a fine not exceeding level 3 on the standard scale and, for continued contravention, a daily default fine not exceeding one-tenth of level 3 on the standard scale. See **29.1** Offences and Legal Proceedings for the standard scale. [*CA 2006, s 970*].

48.9 Consequences of opting out

Effect on contractual restrictions. Where a takeover bid is made for an '*opted-in company*' (ie one to which an opting-in resolution has effect and to which the conditions in **48.8**(1) and (3) still apply), an agreement entered into

- between a person holding shares in the company and another such person on or after 21 April 2004, or
- at any time between such a person and the company,

is invalid in so far as it places any restriction on the following.

(a) On the transfer to the offeror, or at his direction to another person, of shares in the company during the offer period.

(b) On the transfer to any person of shares in the company at a time during the offer period when the offeror holds shares amounting to not less than 75% in value of all the 'voting shares' in the company.

(c) On rights to vote at a general meeting (including rights to vote on a written resolution) of the company that decides whether to take any '*action which might result in the frustration of the bid*' ie any action of that kind specified in rules under *CA 2006, s 943(1)* giving effect to *Takeovers Directive, Art 9* (see **48.2**).

(d) On rights to vote at a general meeting of the company that

   (i) is the first such meeting to be held after the end of the offer period; and

   (ii) is held at a time when the offeror holds shares amounting to not less than 75% in value of all the voting shares in the company.

The above applies to such an agreement even if the law applicable to the agreement (apart from these provisions) is not the law of a part of the UK.

If a person suffers loss as a result of any act or omission that would, but for these provisions, be a breach of an agreement to which the provisions apply (ie as a result of a contractual agreement being overridden), he is entitled to compensation, of such amount as the court considers just and equitable, from any person who would (but for these provisions) be liable to him for committing or inducing the breach.

For the above purposes, '*voting shares*' in the company do not include

- debentures; or
- shares that, under the company's articles of association, do not normally carry rights to vote at its general meetings (eg shares carrying rights to vote that, under those articles, arise only where specified pecuniary advantages are not provided).

[*CA 2006, ss 968, 971*].

Power of offeror to require general meeting to be called. Where a takeover bid is made for an opted-in company, the offeror may by making a request to the directors of the company require them to call a general meeting of the company if, at the date at which the request is made, he holds shares amounting to not less than 75% in value of all the 'voting shares' (see above) in the company.

CA 2006, ss 303–305 (members' power to require general meetings to be called, see **42.13**(2) Resolutions and Meetings) apply as if a request by the offeror for a meeting in the circumstances above was substituted for requests from members representing the required percentage under those provisions.

[*CA 2006, s 969, 972*].

48.10 'SQUEEZE-OUT' AND 'SELL-OUT'

The concepts of 'squeeze-out' and 'sell-out' are designed to address problems of, and for, residual minority shareholders following a successful takeover bid. Squeeze-out rights enable a successful bidder to compulsorily purchase the shares of remaining minority shareholders who have not accepted the bid. Sell-out rights enable minority shareholders, following a bid, to require the majority shareholder to purchase their shares. As they both involve the compulsory acquisition of shares against the will of one of the parties, high thresholds apply to the exercising of such rights and there are protective rules on the price that must be paid for the shares concerned.

The provisions of *CA 2006, ss 974–991* in **48.11–48.19** restate *CA 1985, Part 13A* in a clearer form but also make changes to comply with the *Takeovers Directive, Arts 15, 16*.

48.11 Takeover offers and related terms

The following definitions and related terms apply for the purposes of **48.12–48.19**.

(1) **Meaning of 'takeover offer'**

An offer to acquire 'shares' in a company is a '*takeover offer*' if the following two conditions are satisfied in relation to the offer.

(a) It is an offer to acquire

- all the shares in a company; or
- where there is more than one class of shares in a company, all the shares of one or more classes,

other than 'shares already held by the offeror' at the date of the offer.

This condition is treated as satisfied where the offer does not extend to shares that associates of the offeror hold or have contracted to acquire (whether unconditionally or subject to conditions being met) *and* the condition would be satisfied if the offer did extend to those shares.

'*Shares already held by the offeror*' includes a reference to shares that he has contracted to acquire (whether unconditionally or subject to conditions being met) but *excludes* a reference to shares that are the subject of a contract

- intended to secure that the holder of the shares will accept the offer when it is made; and

- entered into *either* by deed and for no consideration (in Scotland, for no consideration) *or* for consideration of negligible value *or* for consideration consisting of a promise by the offeror to make the offer.

(b) The terms of the offer are the same

- in relation to all the shares to which the offer relates; or
- where the shares to which the offer relates include shares of different classes, in relation to all the shares of each class.

This condition is treated as satisfied

- where
  - (i) shares carry an entitlement to a particular dividend which other shares of the same class, by reason of being allotted later, do not carry;
  - (ii) there is a difference in the value of consideration offered for the shares allotted earlier as against that offered for those allotted later;
  - (iii) that difference merely reflects the difference in entitlement to the dividend; and
  - (iv) the condition would be satisfied but for that difference; *or*
- where
  - (i) the law of a country or territory outside the UK precludes an offer of consideration in the form, or any of the forms, specified in the terms of the offer ('the specified form') or precludes it except after compliance by the offeror with conditions with which he is unable to comply or which he regards as unduly onerous;
  - (ii) the persons to whom an offer of consideration in the specified form is precluded are able to receive consideration in another form that is of substantially equivalent value; and
  - (iii) the condition would be satisfied but for the fact that an offer of consideration in the specified form to those persons is precluded.

For the above purposes, '*shares*' means shares, other than 'relevant treasury shares', that have been allotted on the date of the offer. But a takeover offer *may* include among the shares to which it relates

- all or any shares that are allotted after the date of the offer but before a specified date;
- all or any relevant treasury shares that cease to be held as treasury shares before a specified date; and
- all or any other relevant treasury shares.

'*Relevant treasury shares*' means shares that are held by the company as treasury shares on the date of the offer or become shares held by the company as treasury shares after that date but before a date specified in, or determined in accordance with, the terms of the offer.

Revised offers. Where the terms of an offer make provision for their revision and for acceptances on the previous terms to be treated as acceptances on the revised terms, then, if the terms of the offer are revised in accordance with that provision, the revision is not to be regarded for these purposes as the making of a fresh offer. References to the date of the offer are accordingly to be read as references to the date of the original offer.

Effect of impossibility, etc of communicating or accepting offer. Where there are holders of shares in a company to whom an offer to acquire shares in the company is not communicated, that does not prevent the offer from being a takeover offer for these purposes if

- those shareholders have no registered address in the UK;
- the offer was not communicated to those shareholders in order not to contravene the law of a country or territory outside the UK, and
- either
  - (i) the offer is published in the Gazette; or
  - (ii) the offer can be inspected, or a copy of it obtained, at a place in an EEA State or on a website, and a notice is published in the Gazette specifying the address of that place or website.

Where an offer is made to acquire shares in a company and there are persons for whom, by reason of the law of a country or territory outside the UK, it is impossible to accept the offer, or more difficult to do so, that does not prevent the offer from being a takeover offer for these purposes.

[*CA 2006, s 974–976, 978*].

(2) **Shares to which the offer relates**

Subject to *CA 2006, s 979(8)(9)* in **48.12** below, for these purposes

(a) where a takeover offer is made and, during the period beginning with the date of the offer and ending when the offer can no longer be accepted, the offeror

- acquires or unconditionally contracts to acquire any of the shares to which the offer relates, but
- does not do so by virtue of acceptances of the offer,

those shares are treated as excluded from those to which the offer relates; and

(b) shares that an associate of the offeror holds or has 'contracted' to acquire, whether at the date of the offer or subsequently, are not treated as shares to which the offer relates, even if the offer extends to such shares.

'*Contracted*' means contracted unconditionally or subject to conditions being met.

[*CA 2006, s 977*].

(3) **Associates**

'*Associate*', in relation to an offeror, means any of the following.

- A nominee of the offeror.
- A holding company, subsidiary or fellow subsidiary of the offeror or a nominee of such a holding company, subsidiary or fellow subsidiary.

  For these purposes, a company is a fellow subsidiary of another body corporate if both are subsidiaries of the same body corporate but neither is a subsidiary of the other.
- A body corporate in which the offeror is substantially interested

  For these purposes, an offeror has a substantial interest in a body corporate if

  (i) the body or its directors are accustomed to act in accordance with his directions or instructions; or

  (ii) he is entitled to exercise, or control the exercise of, one-third or more of the voting power at general meetings of the body. See 24.1 INTERESTS IN PUBLIC COMPANY SHARES for when a person is treated as entitled to exercise or control the exercise of voting power, which provisions also apply for these purposes.
- A person who is, or is a nominee of, a party to a 'share acquisition agreement' with the offeror.

  For these purposes, an agreement is a '*share acquisition agreement*' if

  (i) it is an agreement for the acquisition of, or of an interest in, shares to which the offer relates;

  (ii) it includes provisions imposing obligations or restrictions on any one or more of the parties to it with respect to their use, retention or disposal of such shares, or their interests in such shares, acquired in pursuance of the agreement (whether or not together with any other shares to which the offer relates or any other interests of theirs in such shares); and

  (iii) it is not an 'excluded agreement'. An agreement is an '*excluded agreement*' if it is not legally binding, unless it involves mutuality in the undertakings, expectations or understandings of the parties to it. It is also an excluded agreement if it is an agreement to underwrite or sub-underwrite an offer of shares in a company, provided the agreement is confined to that purpose and any matters incidental to it.

  The reference in (ii) above to the use of interests in shares is to the exercise of any rights or of any control or influence arising from those interests (including the right to enter into an agreement for the exercise, or for control of the exercise, of any of those rights by another person).
- Where the offeror is an individual, his spouse or civil partner and any minor child or step-child of his.

[*CA 2006, s 988*].

(4) **Convertible securities**

For these purposes, securities of a company are treated as shares in the company if they are convertible into, or entitle the holder to subscribe for, such shares. References to the 'holder of shares' or a 'shareholder' are to be read accordingly.

This is not to be read as requiring any securities to be treated as shares of the same class as

- those into which they are convertible or for which the holder is entitled to subscribe; or
- other securities by reason only that the shares into which they are convertible or for which the holder is entitled to subscribe are of the same class.

[*CA 2006, s 989*].

(5) **Debentures carrying voting rights**

For these purposes, debentures issued by a company that has voting shares, or debentures carrying voting rights, which are admitted to trading on a regulated market are treated as shares in the company if they carry voting rights.

In relation to debentures so treated as shares, references to

- the 'holder of shares' or a 'shareholder' are to be read accordingly; and
- shares being allotted are to be read as references to debentures being issued.

[*CA 2006, s 990*].

(6) **Date of the offer**

'Date of the offer' means

- where the offer is published, the date of publication; and
- where the offer is not published, or where any notices of the offer are given before the date of publication, the date when notices of the offer (or the first such notices) are given.

See (1) above where an offer is revised.

[*CA 2006, s 991(1)*].

(7) **Unconditional contracts**

For these purposes, a person contracts unconditionally to acquire shares if his entitlement under the contract to acquire them is not (or is no longer) subject to conditions or if all conditions to which it was subject have been met.

[*CA 2006, s 991(2)*].

(8) **When shares are allotted**

Shares in a company are taken to be allotted when a person acquires the unconditional right to be included in the company's register of members in respect of the shares.

[*CA 2006, s 468*].

48.12 Squeeze-out: right of offeror to buy out minority shareholder

Entitlement to give notice. If the offeror has, by virtue of acceptances of the offer, acquired or unconditionally contracted to acquire

- not less than 90% in value of the 'shares to which the offer relates' (see **48.11**(2)), and
- in a case where the shares to which the offer relates are voting shares, not less than 90% of the voting rights carried by those shares,

he may give notice to the holder of any shares to which the offer relates which the offeror has not acquired, or unconditionally contracted to acquire, that he desires to acquire those shares.

If the offer relates to shares of different classes, similar provisions apply but to each class separately.

[*CA 2006, s 979(1)–(4)*].

Treatment of options, etc and treasury shares. In the case of a takeover offer which includes among the shares to which it relates

- shares that are allotted after the date of the offer, or
- relevant treasury shares (see **48.11**(1)) that cease to be held as treasury shares after the date of the offer,

the offeror's entitlement to give a notice as above on any particular date is determined as if the shares to which the offer relates did not include any allotted, or ceasing to be held as treasury shares, on or after that date.

[*CA 2006, s 979(5)*].

The effect of this is that the offeror need only bring into the calculation shares which are actually in issue (ie allotted) at the relevant time. If more share are subsequently allotted which takes the percentage of acceptances then received below 90%, that will not invalidate squeeze-out notices already issued. But if the offeror wishes to serve further squeeze-out notices, he must have at least 90% of shares (or shares in a class) then in issue and subject to the offer at the time he sends the notices out.

Contracts to acquire shares which have not become unconditional. Where

(a) the requirements for giving notice as above are satisfied, and

(b) there are shares in the company which the offeror (or an associate of his) has contracted to acquire subject to conditions being met, and in relation to which the contract has not become unconditional,

the offeror's entitlement to give a notice is determined as if

- the shares to which the offer relates included shares falling within (*b*) above; and
- in relation to those shares, the words 'by virtue of acceptances of the offer' above were omitted.

[*CA 2006, s 979(6), (7)*].

Other shares acquired during the offer period. Where a takeover offer is made and during the period beginning with the date of the offer and ending when the offer can no longer be accepted, the offeror

- acquires, or unconditionally contracts to acquire, any of the shares to which the offer relates but otherwise than by acceptances of the offer, and
- the value of the consideration for which they are acquired or contracted to be acquired ('the acquisition consideration') does not exceed the value of the consideration specified in the terms of the offer (or as subsequently increased on a revised offer),

then for these purposes those shares are not excluded under **48.11**(2)(*a*) from those to which the offer relates, and the offeror is treated as having acquired or contracted to acquire them by virtue of acceptances of the offer.

Where, in similar circumstances, an associate (see **48.11**(3)) of the offeror acquires, or unconditionally contracts to acquire, any of the shares to which the offer relates, those shares are not excluded by **48.11**(2)(*b*) above from those to which the offer relates.

[*CA 2006, s 979(8)–(10)*].

Example

A Ltd makes an offer for the 1 million issued shares in B Ltd at £1 per share which is subsequently increased to £1.20 per share. It receives acceptances from holders of 800,000 shares. During the offer period, A Ltd also buys 110,000 shares on the open market at £1.10 per share.

A Ltd will be treated as having acquired the 110,000 shares under the terms of the offer. Although £1.10 is higher than the offer price at the time the shares are purchased, it is less than the subsequently increased offer price of £1.20. A Ltd has therefore acquired 910,000 (800,000 + 110,000) shares under the offer and as this represents 91% it can buy out the minority. If, on the other hand, A Ltd had bought the 110,000 shares at £1.30 per share, these shares would have been excluded from the shares subject to the offer. A Ltd would be treated as having acquired 800,000 out of 890,000 (1,000,000 – 110,000) shares under the offer (ie 89.89%) and would not therefore be able to buy out the minority.

48.13 *Provisions relating to the giving of notice*

Method of giving notice. The notice to shareholders by the offeror under **48.12** must be given

(a) personally; or

(b) by recorded delivery post to

  (i) his address in the UK registered in the company's books; or

  (ii) if no such address is registered, the address (if any) in the UK given by him to the company for the giving of notices; or

(c) if no address is registered under (*b*)(i) above or has been notified under (*b*)(ii) above, by air mail (if available) to the address outside the UK registered in the company's books.

Where notice cannot be given under (*a*) to (*c*) above because the holder of the shares is the holder of a share warrant to bearer, it must be given by advertisement as provided in the company's articles or, if no such provision is made, by advertisement in the *Gazette*.

[*SI 1987 No 752, Reg 4*].

Time limit. No notice may be given after the end of

- the period of three months beginning with the day after the last day on which the offer can be accepted; or

- the period of six months beginning with the date of the offer, where that period ends earlier and the offer is one under which the time allowed for acceptance of the offer is not governed by rules under *CA 2006, s 943(1)* that give effect to *Takeovers Directive, Art 7*. (This will apply to the takeover of most private companies.)

Notice to the company. At the time when the offeror first gives a notice in relation to an offer, he must send to the company a copy of the notice and a statutory declaration by him in the prescribed form, stating that the conditions for the giving of the notice are satisfied. Where the offeror is a company, the statutory declaration must be signed by a director.

A person commits an offence if he

- fails to send a copy of a notice or a statutory declaration as required; or
- makes such a declaration knowing it to be false or without having reasonable grounds for believing it to be true.

It is a defence for a person charged with an offence for failing to send a copy of a notice to prove that he took reasonable steps for securing compliance.

A person guilty of an offence under this section is liable (i) on conviction on indictment, to imprisonment for a term not exceeding two years or a fine (or both); and (ii) on summary conviction, to imprisonment for a term not exceeding twelve months (six months in Scotland and Northern Ireland) or to a fine not exceeding the statutory maximum (or both) and, for continued contravention, a daily default fine not exceeding one-fiftieth of the greater of £5000 or the amount corresponding to level 4 on the standard scale for summary offences. See **29.1 Offences and Legal Proceedings** for the statutory maximum.

[*CA 2006, s 980*; *SI 2015 No 664, Sch 3*].

48.14 *Effect of notice*

Subject to **48.18**, where notice is given, the offeror is *entitled and bound* to acquire the shares to which the notice relates on the terms of the offer. Where the terms of an offer give the shareholder a choice of consideration, the notice must give particulars of the choice and state

- that the shareholder may, within six weeks from the date of the notice, indicate his choice in writing to the offeror at an address specified in the notice; and
- which consideration specified in the offer will apply if he does not indicate a choice.

This applies whether or not any time-limit or other conditions applicable to the choice under the terms of the offer can still be complied with.

If the consideration offered to or (as the case may be) chosen by the shareholder

- is not cash and the offeror is no longer able to provide it, or
- was to have been provided by a third party who is no longer bound or able to provide it,

the consideration is to be taken to consist of an amount of cash, payable by the offeror, which at the date of the notice is equivalent to the consideration offered or (as the case may be) chosen.

At the end of six weeks from the date of the notice, the offeror must immediately

(a) send a copy of the notice to the company, together with

  (i) if the shares to which the notice relates are registered, an instrument of transfer executed on behalf of the holder of the shares by a person appointed by the offeror (on receipt of which the company must register the offeror as holder of those shares); or

  (ii) if the shares to which the notice relates are transferable by the delivery of warrants or other instruments, a statement to that effect (on receipt of which the company must issue the offeror with warrants or other instruments in respect of the shares, and those warrants, etc already in issue in respect of the shares become void).

(b) Pay or transfer to the company the consideration for the shares to which the notice relates (or where the consideration consists of shares or securities to be allotted by the offeror, allot the shares or securities to the company).

Consideration held on trust by the company. The company must hold any money or other consideration received by it on trust for the person who, before the offeror acquired them, was entitled to the shares in respect of which the money or other consideration was received. Any money that it receives, together with any dividends or other sum accruing, must be paid into a separate bank account bearing interest at an appropriate rate.

If the person entitled to the consideration held on trust

- cannot be found,
- reasonable enquiries have been made at reasonable intervals to find the person, and
- either 12 years have elapsed since the consideration was received or the company is wound up

then

- for companies registered in England and Wales or Northern Ireland, the consideration (together with any interest, dividend or other benefit that has accrued from it) must be paid into court; and
- for companies registered in Scotland,

  (i) the trust terminates;

  (ii) the company or (if the company is wound up) the liquidator must sell any consideration other than cash and any benefit other than cash that has accrued from the consideration; and

  (iii) a sum representing the consideration so far as it is cash, the proceeds of any sale under (ii) above, and any interest, dividend or other benefit that has accrued from the consideration,

  must be deposited in the name of the Accountant of Court in a separate bank account and the receipt for the deposit must be transmitted to the Accountant of Court.

  Bankruptcy (Scotland) Act 1985, s 58 (so far as consistent with *CA 2006*) applies (with any necessary modifications) to sums so deposited as it applies to sums deposited under *s 57(1)(a)* of that *Act*.

The expenses of any reasonable enquiry that is made may be paid out of the money or other property held on trust for the person to whom the enquiry relates.

[*CA 2006, ss 981, 982*].

48.15 Sell-out: right of minority shareholder to be bought out by offeror

Offers relating to all the shares in a company

(a) The holder of any *voting* shares to which the offer relates who has not accepted the offer may write to the offeror and require him to acquire those shares if, at any time before the end of the period within which the offer can be accepted

(i) the offeror (or an associate of his) has, by virtue of acceptances of the offer, acquired or unconditionally contracted to acquire some (but not all) of the shares to which the offer relates; and

(ii) those shares, with or without any other shares in the company which he has acquired or contracted to acquire (whether unconditionally or subject to conditions being met)

- amount to not less than 90% in value of all the voting shares in the company (or would do so but for **48.11**(5)); and

- carry not less than 90% of the voting rights in the company (or would do so but for **48.11**(5)).

(b) The holder of any *non-voting* shares to which the offer relates who has not accepted the offer may write to the offeror and require him to acquire those shares if, at any time before the end of the period within which the offer can be accepted

(i) the offeror (or an associate of his) has by virtue of acceptances of the offer acquired or unconditionally contracted to acquire some (but not all) of the shares to which the offer relates; and

(ii) those shares, with or without any other shares in the company which he has acquired or contracted to acquire (whether unconditionally or subject to conditions being met), amount to not less than 90% in value of all the shares in the company (or would do so but for **48.11**(5)).

Offers for shares of one or more classes only

(c) If a takeover offer relates to shares of one or more classes and at any time before the end of the period within which the offer can be accepted

(i) the offeror (or an associate of his) has by virtue of acceptances of the offer acquired or unconditionally contracted to acquire some (but not all) of the shares of any class to which the offer relates; and

(ii) those shares, with or without any other shares of that class which he has acquired or contracted to acquire (whether unconditionally or subject to conditions being met)

- amount to not less than 90% in value of all the shares of that class; and

- in a case where the shares of that class are voting shares, carry not less than 90% of the voting rights carried by the shares of that class, the holder of any shares of that class to which the offer relates who has not accepted the offer may write to the offeror and require him to acquire those shares.

For the purposes of (*a*) and (*b*) above, a takeover offer relates to all the shares in a company if it is an offer to acquire all the shares in the company within the meaning of *CA 2006, s 974* (see **48.11**(1)).

[*CA 2006, ss 983(1)–(4)(8), 984(1)*].

Treasury shares. For the above purposes, in calculating 90% of the value of any shares, shares held by the company as treasury shares are to be treated as having been acquired by the offeror.

[*CA 2006, s 983(5)*].

Contracts to acquire shares which have not become unconditional. Where

- a shareholder exercises rights conferred on him in (*a*)–(*c*) above,
- at the time when he does so, there are shares in the company which the offeror (or an associate of his) has contracted to acquire subject to conditions being met, and in relation to which the contract has not become unconditional, and
- the appropriate 90% test(s) in (*a*)(ii), (*b*)(ii) or (*c*)(ii) (as the case may be) would not be satisfied if those shares were not taken into account,

the shareholder is treated for the purposes of **48.17** as not having exercised his rights unless the 90% test(s) would be satisfied if

- the reference in (*a*)(ii), (*b*)(ii) or (*c*)(ii) (as the case may be) to other shares in the company which the offeror (or an associate of his) has contracted to acquire unconditionally or subject to conditions being met were a reference to such shares which he has unconditionally contracted to acquire; and
- the reference in (*a*), (*b*) or (*c*) above (as the case may be) to the period within which the offer can be accepted were a reference to the period referred to in **48.16** below.

[*CA 2006, s 983(6)(7)(8)*].

48.16 *Provisions relating to giving notice*

Time limit. Rights conferred on a shareholder under **48.15** are not exercisable after the end of the period of three months from

- the end of the period within which the offer can be accepted; or
- if later, the date of the notice that must be given below.

Within one month of the time specified in **48.15**(*a*), (*b*) or (*c*) (as the case may be), the offeror must give any shareholder who has not accepted the offer notice in the prescribed manner of the rights that are exercisable by the shareholder under that provision and the period within which the rights are exercisable. If the notice is given before the end of the period within which the offer can be accepted, it must state that the offer is still open for acceptance. This requirement to give notice does not apply if the offeror has given the shareholder a notice in respect of the shares in question under **48.12** (notice of intention to buy the shares).

An offeror who fails to comply with this requirement commits an offence. If the offeror is a company, every officer of that company who is in default, or to whose neglect the failure is attributable, also commits an offence. If an offeror other than a company is charged with such an offence, it is a defence for him to prove that he took all reasonable steps for securing compliance with the requirement.

A person guilty of such an offence is liable (i) on conviction on indictment, to a fine; and (ii) on summary conviction, to a fine not exceeding the statutory maximum and, for continued contravention, a daily default fine not exceeding one-fiftieth of the greater of £5000 or level 4 on the standard scale for summary offences. See **29.1 Offences and Legal Proceedings** for the statutory maximum.

[*CA 2006, s 984*; *SI 2015 No 664, Sch 3*].

Method of giving notice by the offeror. The notice to shareholders by the offeror must be given

(a) personally; or

(b) by recorded delivery post to

  (i) his address in the UK registered in the company's books; or

  (ii) if no such address is registered, the address (if any) in the UK given by him to the company for the giving of notices; or

(c) if no address is registered under (*b*)(i) above or has been notified under (*b*)(ii) above, by air mail (if available) to the address outside the UK registered in the company's books.

Where notice cannot be given under (*a*) to (*c*) above because the holder of the shares is the holder of a share warrant to bearer, it must be given by advertisement as provided in the company's articles or, if no such provision is made, by advertisement in the *Gazette*.

[*SI 1987 No 752, Reg 4*].

48.17 *Effect of notice*

Subject to **48.18**, where a shareholder exercises his rights under **48.16** in respect of any shares held by him, the offeror is entitled and bound to acquire those shares on the terms of the offer or on such other terms as may be agreed.

Where the terms of an offer are such as to give the shareholder a choice of consideration

- the shareholder may indicate his choice when requiring the offeror to acquire the shares; and
- the notice given to the shareholder under **48.16**
  - (i) must give particulars of the choice and of the shareholder's rights to chose; and
  - (ii) may state which consideration specified in the offer will apply if he does not indicate a choice.

This applies whether or not any time limit or other conditions applicable to the choice under the terms of the offer can still be complied with.

If the consideration offered to or (as the case may be) chosen by the shareholder

- is not cash and the offeror is no longer able to provide it, or
- was to have been provided by a third party who is no longer bound or able to provide it,

the consideration is to be taken to consist of an amount of cash, payable by the offeror, which at the date when the shareholder requires the offeror to acquire the shares is equivalent to the consideration offered or (as the case may be) chosen.

[*CA 2006, s 985*].

48.18 Applications to the court

Application may be made to the court in the following circumstances.

(a) Where a notice is given under **48.12** to a shareholder, the shareholder may apply to the court within six weeks from the date of notice. The court may order that

- the offeror is not entitled and bound to acquire the shares to which the notice relates; or
- the terms on which the offeror is entitled and bound to acquire the shares are such as the court thinks fit.

If such an application is pending at the end of that six-week period, the requirements of **48.14**(*a*) and (*b*) do not have to be complied with until the application has been disposed of.

In the ordinary case of such an offer where the 90% who accepted the offer are unconnected with the offeror, the court will pay the greatest attention to the views of the majority. Where, however, as a matter of substance the persons putting forward the offer are the majority shareholders, the onus must fall on the majority shareholders to satisfy the court that the scheme is one with which the minority shareholders ought reasonably to be compelled to fall in with (*Bugle Press Ltd, Re, Re Houses and Estates Ltd* [1961] Ch 270, [1960] 1 All ER 768).

(b) Where a shareholder exercises his rights under **48.15** (right of minority shareholder to be bought out) the court may, on an application made by him or the offeror, order that the terms on which the offeror is entitled and bound to acquire the shares are such as the court thinks fit.

(c) Where a takeover offer has not been accepted to the extent necessary for entitling the offeror to give notices under **48.12**, the court may, on an application made by him, make an order authorising him to give notices under those provisions if it is satisfied that

(i) the offeror has, after reasonable enquiry, been unable to trace one or more of the persons holding shares to which the offer relates;

(ii) the requirements would have been met if the person, or all the persons, in (i) above had accepted the offer;

(iii) the consideration offered is fair and reasonable; and

(iv) it is just and equitable to do so having regard, in particular, to the number of shareholders who have been traced but who have not accepted the offer.

On an application

- a shareholder who has made an application under (*a*) or (*b*) above must give notice of the application to the offeror;
- an offeror who is given notice of such an application under (*a*) or (*b*) above must then give a copy of the notice to

  (i) any person (other than the applicant) to whom a notice has been given under **48.12**; and

  (ii) any person who has exercised his rights under **48.15**;

- an offeror who makes an application under (*b*) above must give notice of the application to
  - (i) any person to whom a notice has been given under **48.12**; and
  - (ii) any person who has exercised his rights under **48.15**.
- the court may not require consideration of a
  - (i) higher value than that specified in the terms of the offer ('the offer value') to be given for the shares to which the application relates unless the holder of the shares shows that the offer value would be unfair; and
  - (ii) lower value than the offer value to be given for the shares; and
- no order for costs or expenses may be made against a shareholder unless the court considers that
  - (i) the application was unnecessary, improper or vexatious;
  - (ii) there has been unreasonable delay in making the application; or
  - (iii) there has been unreasonable conduct on the shareholder's part in conducting the proceedings on the application.

[*CA 2006, s 986*].

48.19 Joint offers

Where a takeover offer is made by two or more persons jointly, the conditions for the exercise of the rights conferred by **48.12** and **48.15** are satisfied

- in the case of acquisitions by virtue of acceptances of the offer, by the joint offerors acquiring or unconditionally contracting to acquire the necessary shares jointly; and
- in other cases, by the joint offerors
  - (i) (where **48.12** applies) acquiring or unconditionally contracting to acquire the necessary shares either jointly or separately; and
  - (ii) (where **48.15** applies) acquiring or contracting (whether unconditionally or subject to conditions being met) to acquire the necessary shares either jointly or separately.

The rights and obligations of the offeror under **48.12–48.17** are respectively joint rights and joint and several obligations of the joint offerors, subject to certain exceptions in *CA 2006, s 987(5)–(10)*.

[*CA 2006, s 987(1)–(4)*].

THE CITY CODE ON TAKEOVERS AND MERGERS

Introduction

The Panel on Takeovers and Mergers (the 'Panel') is an independent body whose main functions are to issue and administer the City Code on Takeovers and Mergers (the 'Code') and to supervise and regulate takeovers and other matters to which the Code applies. It has been designated as the supervisory authority to carry out certain regulatory functions in relation to takeovers pursuant to the *EC Directive 2004/25/EC* (the '*Directive*').

Nature and purpose of the Code. The Code is mainly designed to ensure that

- shareholders in an offeree company are treated fairly and are not denied an opportunity to decide on the merits of a takeover; and
- shareholders in the offeree company of the same class are afforded equivalent treatment by an offeror.

The Code also provides a framework within which takeovers are conducted. The Code is not concerned with the financial or commercial advantages or disadvantages of a takeover nor is it the purpose of the Code either to facilitate or impede takeovers.

General Principles and Rules. The Code is based upon:

- *General Principles.* These are expressed in broad terms which are essentially statements of standards of commercial behaviour as set out in *Directive, Art 3*.
- *Rules.* Although most of the *Rules* are expressed in less general terms, they are not framed in technical language and, like the *General Principles*, should be interpreted to achieve their underlying purpose and spirit as well as their letter.
  In most cases, a *Rule* in the Code is followed by notes which explain and expand on the basic *Rule*. These are generally not covered within this Appendix unless necessary in the context of the wording of a particular *Rule*. The reader should therefore refer to the full text of the Code if necessary.

Derogations and waivers. The Panel may derogate or grant a waiver to a person from the application of a *Rule* either in the circumstances set out in the *Rule* or where the Panel considers that the particular *Rule* would be unduly harsh, restrictive or burdensome (in which case a reasoned decision will be given).

Companies covered. The Code applies to the following offers.

(a) Offers (not falling within (*c*) below) for companies and Societas Europaea (and, where appropriate, statutory and chartered companies) which have their registered offices in the UK, the Channel Islands or the Isle of Man if any of their securities are admitted to trading on a regulated market or a multilateral trading facility in the UK or on any stock exchange in the Channel Islands or the Isle of Man.

(b) Offers (not falling within (*a*) above or (*c*) below) for public and private companies and Societas Europaea (and, where appropriate, statutory and chartered companies) which have their registered offices in the UK, the Channel Islands or the Isle of Man and which are considered by the Panel to have their place of central management and control in the UK, the Channel Islands or the Isle of Man. In relation to a private company this only applies when at any time during the 10 years before the date of an announcement of the proposed or possible offer for the company (or the date on which some other event occurs in relation to the company which has significance under the Code)

- any of its securities have been admitted to trading on a regulated market or a multilateral trading facility in the UK or on any stock exchange in the Channel Islands or the Isle of Man;
- dealings and/or prices at which persons were willing to deal in its securities have been published on a regular basis for a continuous period of at least six months, whether via a newspaper, electronic price quotation system or otherwise;
- any of its securities have been subject to a marketing arrangement as described in *CA 2006, s 693(3)(b)*; or
- it has filed a prospectus for the offer, admission to trading or issue of securities with the Registrar of Companies or any other relevant authority in the UK, the Channel Islands or the Isle of Man (but in the case of any such other authority only if the filing is on a public record).

(c) The Code also applies (to the extent described below) to offers for the following companies.

- A company which has its registered office in the UK whose securities are admitted to trading on a regulated market in one or more Member States of the EEA but not on a regulated market in the UK.
- A company which has its registered office in another Member State of the EEA whose securities are admitted to trading only on a regulated market in the UK and not on a regulated market in any other member state of the EEA.
- A company which has its registered office in another Member State of the EEA whose securities are admitted to trading on regulated markets in more than one Member State of the EEA including the UK (but not on a regulated market in the Member State of the EEA in which it has its registered office) if
  - (i) the securities of the company were first admitted to trading only in the UK;
  - (ii) the securities of the company are simultaneously admitted to trading on more than one regulated market on or after May 2006 if the company notifies the Panel and the relevant regulatory authorities on the first day of trading that it has chosen the Panel to regulate it; or
  - (iii) the Panel is the supervisory authority pursuant to *Directive, Art 4(2)(c)*.

The provisions of the Code which will apply to such offers is determined by the Panel on the basis set out in *Directive, Art 4(2)(e)*.

The Code does not apply to offers for open-ended investment companies.

Transactions covered. In cases falling within (*a*) or (*b*) above, the Code is concerned with regulating takeover bids and merger transactions of the relevant companies, however effected, including by means of statutory merger or scheme of arrangement. The Code is also concerned with regulating other transactions (including offers by a parent company for shares in its subsidiary, dual holding company transactions, new share issues, share capital reorganisations and offers to minority shareholders) which have the effect of obtaining or consolidating control of the relevant companies, as well as partial offers.

In cases falling within (*c*) above, 'offers' only means any public offer (other than by the company itself) made to the holders of the company's securities to acquire those securities which has as its objective the acquisition of control of the company concerned.

The Code applies to all the above transactions at whatever stage of their implementation, including possible transactions which have not yet been announced.

The Code does not apply to offers for non-voting, non-equity capital unless they are offers required by *Rule 15*.

Code responsibilities and obligations. The Code applies to a range of persons who participate in, or are connected with, or who in any way seek to influence, intervene in, or benefit from, takeovers or other matters to which the Code applies. The Code also applies to all advisers to such persons and all advisers in so far as they advise on takeovers or other matters to which the Code applies. The Code also applies to any directors, employees or representatives through whom any body corporate, partnership or other entity to which the Code applies acts.

General Principles

The six General Principles are as follows.

(1) All holders of the securities of an offeree company of the same class must be afforded equivalent treatment; moreover if a person acquires control of a company, the other holders of securities must be protected.

(2) The holders of the securities of an offeree company must have sufficient time and information to enable them to reach a properly informed decision on the bid. Where it advises the holders of securities, the board of the offeree company must give its views on the effects of implementation of the bid on employment, conditions of employment and the locations of the company's places of business.

(3) The board of an offeree company must act in the interests of the company as a whole and must not deny the holders of securities the opportunity to decide on the merits of the bid.

(4) False markets must not be created in the securities of the offeree company, offeror company or any other company concerned by the bid in such a way that the rise or fall of the prices of the securities becomes artificial and the normal functioning of the markets is distorted.

(5) An offeror must announce a bid only after ensuring that it can fulfil in full any cash consideration (if offered) and after taking all reasonable measures to secure the implementation of any other type of consideration.

(6) An offeree company must not be hindered in the conduct of its affairs for longer than is reasonable by a bid for its securities.

The approach, announcements and independent advice

Rule 1 The approach

An offeror (or its advisors) must notify a firm intention to make an offer in the first instance to the board of the offeree company or to its advisers. If the offer, or an approach with regard to a possible offer is not made by the offeror or potential offeror, the identity of that person must be disclosed to the board of the offeree company at the outset.

Rule 2 Secrecy before announcements; the timing and contents of announcements

Secrecy. Prior to the announcement of an offer or possible offer all persons privy to confidential information, and particularly price-sensitive information, concerning the offer or possible offer must treat that information as secret and can only pass it to another person if it is necessary to do so and if that person is made aware of the need for secrecy. All such persons must act so as to minimise the chances of any leak of information.

(*Rule 2.1*).

Financial advisers must at the very beginning of discussions warn clients of the importance of secrecy and security. Attention should be drawn to the Code, in particular to this *Rule 2.1* and to restrictions on dealings.

When an announcement is required. An announcement is required

- when a firm intention to make an offer is notified to the board of the offeree company by or on behalf of an offeree (irrespective of the attitude of the board to the offer);
- immediately upon an acquisition of any interest in shares which gives rise to an obligation to make an offer under *Rule 9.1*. The announcement that an obligation has been incurred should not be delayed while full information is being obtained; additional information can be the subject of a later supplementary announcement;
- when, following an approach by or on behalf of a potential offeror to the board of the offeree company, the offeree company is the subject of rumour and speculation or there is an untoward movement in its share price;
- when, after a potential offeror first actively considers an offer but before an approach has been made to the board of the offeree company, the offeree company is the subject of rumour and speculation or there is an untoward movement in its share price and there are reasonable grounds for concluding that it is the potential offeror's actions (whether through inadequate security or otherwise) which have led to the situation;
- when negotiations or discussions relating to a possible offer are about to be extended to include more than a very restricted number of people (outside those who need to know in the parties concerned and their immediate advisers) or
- when a purchaser is being sought for an interest or interests in shares carrying in aggregate 30% or more of the voting rights of a company or when the board of a company is seeking one or more potential offerors, and
  - (i) the company is the subject of rumour and speculation or there is an untoward movement in its share price; or
  - (ii) the number of potential purchasers or offerors approached is about to be increased to include more than a very restricted number of people.

(*Rule 2.2*).

Responsibilities of offerors and the offeree company. Before a potential offeror approaches the board of the offeree company the potential offeror is responsible for making any announcement required under *Rule 2.2*. When an obligation to make a mandatory offer under *Rule 9.1* is incurred, the offeror is responsible for making the announcement required under *Rule* 2.2(b).

Following an approach to the board of the offeree company the offeree company is responsible for making any announcement required under *Rule 2.2*, except for an announcement required under *Rule* 2.2(b) or, where a purchaser is being sought for an interest in shares carrying 30% or more of the voting rights of a company without the involvement of the board of the offeree company, *Rule* 2.2(f) (in which case responsibility will rest with the potential seller of the interest.) A potential offeror must not attempt to prevent the board of an offeree company from making an announcement relating to a possible offer, or publicly identifying the potential offeror at any time the board considers appropriate. (*Rule 2.3*).

An announcement by the offeree company which commences an offer period must identify any potential offeror with which the offeree company is in talks or from which an approach has been received (and not unequivocally rejected).

Any subsequent announcement by the offeree company which refers to the existence of a new potential offeror must identify that potential offeror, except where the announcement is made after an offeror has announced a firm intention to make an offer for the offeree company.

Any announcement which commences an offer period and any subsequent announcements which first identifies a potential offeror must specify the date on which the deadline (thereby set in accordance with *Rule 2.6*(a)) will expire and include a summary of the provisions of *Rule 8*.

(*Rule 2.4*)

The Panel must be consulted in advance if, prior to the announcement of a firm intention to make an offer, any person proposes to make a statement in relation to the terms on which an offer might be made for the offeree company. If a potential offeror, (or its directors, officials or advisers) makes such a statement and it is not withdrawn immediately if incorrect, the potential offeror will be bound by the statement if an offer for the offeree company is subsequently made except where it specifically reserved the right not to be so bound in certain circumstances at the time the statement was made and those circumstances subsequently arise or in wholly exceptional circumstances. In particular where the statement concerned relates to the price of a possible offer (or a particular exchange ratio in the case of a possible securities exchange offer:

(i) any offer made by the potential offeror for the offeree company will be required to be made on the same or better terms. Where all or part of the consideration is expressed in terms of monetary value, the offer or that element of the offer must be made at the same time or at a higher monetary value. Where all or part of the consideration has been expressed in terms of a securities exchange ratio, the offer or that element of the offer must be made on the same (or an improved) securities exchange ratio; and

(ii) where the statement concerned includes reference to the fact that the terms of the possible offer "will not be increased" or are "final" or uses a similar expression, the potential offeror will not be allowed subsequently to make the offer on better terms.

The consequences of a statement to which *Rule 2.5(a)* applies will normally apply also to any person acting in concert with the potential offeror and to any person who is subsequently acting in concert with the potential offeror or such person.

The Panel must be consulted in advance if, prior to announcing a firm intention to make an offer, a potential offeror proposes to announce any pre-conditions to the making of an offer. Any such pre-conditional possible offer announcement must clearly state whether or not the pre-conditions must be satisfied before an offer can be made or whether they are waivable and include a prominent warning to the effect that the announcement does not amount to a firm intention to make an offer and that, accordingly, there can be no certainty that any offer will be made even if the pre-conditions are satisfied or waived.

(*Rule 2.5*).

Timing following a possible offer announcement

Subject to *Rule 2.6*(b), by not later than 5.00 pm on the 28th day following the date of the announcement in which it is first identified, or by not later than any extended deadline, a potential offeror must either:

(i) announce a firm intention to make an offer in accordance with *Rule 2.7*; or

(ii) announce that it does not intend to make an offer, in which case the announcement will be treated as a statement to which *Rule 2.8* applies, unless the Panel has consented to an extension of the deadline. *Rule 2.6*(a) will not apply, or will cease to apply, to a potential offeror if another offeror has already announced, or subsequently announces (prior to the relevant deadline), a firm intention to make an offer for the offeree company. In such circumstances, the potential offeror will be required to clarify its intentions in accordance with *Rule 2.6*(d) below.

(c) The Panel will normally consent to an extension of a deadline set in accordance with *Rule 2.6(*a), or any previously extended deadline, at the request of the board of the offeree company and after taking into account all relevant factors, including:

(i) the status of negotiations between the offeree company and the potential offeror; and

(ii) the anticipated timetable for their completion. Where the Panel consents to an extension of a deadline, the offeree

company must promptly make an announcement setting out the new deadline and commenting on the matters referred to in paragraphs (i) and (ii) above.

(d) When an offeror has announced a firm intention to make an offer and it has been announced that a publicly identified potential offeror might make a competing offer (whether that announcement was made prior to or following the announcement of the first offer), the potential offeror must, by 5pm on the 53rd day following the publication of the first offeror's initial offer document, either:

(i) announce a firm intention to make an offer in accordance with *Rule 2.7*; or

(ii) announce that it does not intend to make an offer, in which case the announcement will be treated as a statement to which *Rule 2.8* applies.

(See Section 4 of Appendix 7 where the first offeror is proceeding by way of a scheme of arrangement).

When an offeror has announced a firm intention to make an offer and the offeree company subsequently refers to the existence of a potential competing offeror which has not been identified, the potential competing offeror so referred to must, by a date in the later stages of the offer period to be announced by the Panel, either:

(i) announce a firm intention to make an offer in accordance with *Rule 2.7*; or

(ii) confirm to the offeree company that it does not intend to make an offer, in which case the offeree company must promptly announce that fact and the potential competing offeror will then be treated as if it had made a statement to which *Rule 2.8* applies

(See Section 4 of Appendix 7 where the first offeror is proceeding by way of a scheme of arrangement).

(*Rule 2.6*)

An offeror should announce a firm intention to make an offer only after the most careful and responsible consideration and when the offeror has every reason to believe that it can and will continue to be able to implement the offer.

Following an announcement of a firm intention to make an offer, the offeror must proceed to make the offer unless, in accordance with *Rule 13*, it is permitted to invoke a pre-condition to the making of an offer or would be permitted to invoke a condition to the offer if the offer were made. However, with the consent of the Panel, an offeror need not make the offer if a competing offeror subsequently announces a firm intention to make a higher offer.

When a firm intention to make an offer is announced, the announcement must state

- the terms of the offer;
- the identity of the offeror;
- all conditions or pre-conditions to which the offer or the making of an offer is subject;
- details of any agreements or arrangements to which the offeror is party which relate to the circumstances in which it may or may not invoke or seek to invoke a pre-condition or a condition to its offer including the consequences of its doing so including details of any break fees payable as a result;
- details of any relevant securities of the offeree company in which the offeror or any person acting in concert with it has an interest or in respect of which it has a right to subscribe, in each case specifying the nature of the interests or rights concerned (see Note 5 on Rule 8). Similar details of any short positions (whether conditional or absolute and whether in the money or otherwise), including any short position under a derivative, any agreement to sell, any delivery obligation or right to require another person to purchase or take delivery, must also be stated;
    - details of any irrevocable commitment or letter of intent procured by the offeror or any person acting in concert with it (see Note 3 on Rule 2.11);
    - details of any relevant securities of the offeree company which the offeror or any person acting in concert with it has borrowed or lent, save for any borrowed relevant securities which have been either on-lent or sold and details of any financial collateral arrangements which the offeror or any person acting in concert with it has entered into (see Note 4 on Rule 4.6);
- details of any dealing arrangement of the kind referred to in Note 11 on the definition of acting in concert to which the offeror and any person acting in concert with it is a party;
- a summary of the provisions of *Rule 8*
    - a summary of any offer–related arrangement or other agreement, arrangement or commitment permitted under or excluded from *Rule 21.2*;
- a list of the documents published on a website in accordance with *Rule 26.1* and the address of the website on which the documents are published.

Where the offer is for cash or includes an element of cash the announcement must include confirmation by the financial adviser or by another appropriate third party that resources are available to the offeror sufficient to satisfy full acceptance of the offer. (The party confirming that resources are available will not be expected to produce the cash itself if, in giving the confirmation, it acted responsibly and took all reasonable steps to assure itself that the cash was available.)

(*Rule 2.7*).

Statements of intention not to make an offer.

A person making a statement that he does not intend to make an offer for a company should make the statement as clear and unambiguous as possible. Except in the circumstances described in Note 2 or otherwise with the consent of the Panel neither the person making the statement nor any person who acted in concert with that person nor any person who is subsequently acting in concert with either of them, may within six months from the date of the statement

- announce an offer or possible offer for the offeree company (including a partial offer which would result in the offeror and persons acting in concert with it being interested in shares carrying 30% or more of the voting rights of the offeree company);
- acquire any interest in shares of the offeree company if any such person would thereby become obliged under *Rule 9* to make an offer;
- acquire any interest in, or procure an irrevocable commitment in respect of, shares of the offeree company if the shares in which such person, together with any persons acting in concert with him, would be interested and the shares in respect of which he, or they, had acquired irrevocable commitments would in aggregate carry 30% or more of the voting rights of the offeree company;
- make any statement which raises or confirms the possibility that an offer might be made for the offeree company; or
- take any steps in connection with a possible offer for the offeree company where knowledge of the possible offer might be extended outside those who need to know in the potential offeror and its immediate advisers.

Failure to comply with these requirements may lead to the period of six months referred to above being extended.

(*Rule 2.8*).

Announcement of an offer or possible offer to be published via a RIS.

(a) When an offer or possible offer is announced, the announcement must be published in typed format and sent to a RIS by fax or electronic delivery.

(b) Where the announcement is published outside normal business hours, it must be submitted as required, for release as soon as the relevant service re-opens. It must also be distributed to not less than two national newspapers and two newswire services in the UK.

(c) These requirements are in addition to any other announcement obligations to which the offeror may be subject.

(*Rule 2.9*).

Announcement of numbers of relevant securities in issue.

When an offer period begins, the offeree company must announce, as soon as possible and in any case by 7.15am on the next business day, details of all classes of relevant securities issued by the company, together with the numbers of such securities in issue. An offeror or publicly identified potential offeror must also announce the same details relating to its relevant securities as soon as possible and in any case by 7.15am on the business day following any announcement identifying it as an offeror or potential offeror (unless it has stated that its offer is likely to be solely in cash).

Any such announcement should include, where relevant, the International Securities Identification Number ("ISIN") for each relevant security.

If the information included in an announcement made under this *Rule* changes during the offer period, a revised announcement must be made as soon as possible.

(*Rule 2.10*).

Irrevocable commitments and letters of intent

(a) During an offer period, if any party to the offer or any person acting in concert with it procures an irrevocable commitment or a letter of intent, the relevant party to the offer must publicly disclose the details in accordance with the Notes on this *Rule 2.11* by no later than 12 noon on the following business day.

(b) If any party to an offer or any person acting in concert with it has procured an irrevocable commitment or a letter of intent prior to the commencement of the offer period it must publicly disclose the details in accordance with the Notes on this Rule 2.11 by no later than 12 noon on the business day following either the commencement of the offer period or (in the case of an offeror) the date of the announcement that first identifies the offeror as such (as appropriate).

(c) If, during the offer period and prior to midnight on the day before an Opening Position Disclosure is made under *Rule 8.1*(a) or *8.2*(a), a party to the offer or any person acting in concert with it procures an irrevocable commitment or a letter of intent and the details are disclosed in accordance with *Rule 2.11*(a), that disclosure must also include details of any other commitments or letters which have been procured prior to the date of the disclosure and which have not previously been disclosed.

(d) If a person who has given an irrevocable commitment or a letter of intent either becomes aware that he will not be able to comply with the terms of that commitment or letter or no longer intends to do so, that person must:

(i) promptly announce an update of the position together with all relevant details; or

(ii) promptly notify the relevant party to the offer and the Panel of the up-to-date position. Upon receipt of such a notification, the relevant party to the offer must promptly make an appropriate announcement of the information notified to it together with all relevant details.

(*Rule 2.11*).

Obligation to send announcements to shareholders and make them available to employee representatives or employees

(a) Promptly after the commencement of an offer period (except where an offer period begins with an announcement under *Rule 2.7*), a copy of the relevant announcement must be sent by the offeree company to its shareholders, persons with information rights and the Panel, and must be made readily available to its employee representatives or, where there are no employee representatives, to the employees themselves.

(b) Promptly after the publication of an announcement made under *Rule 2 7*: (i) the offeree company must send a copy of that announcement, or a circular summarising the terms and conditions of the offer, to its shareholders, persons with information rights and the Panel; and (ii) both the offeror and the offeree company must make that announcement, or a circular summarising the terms and conditions of the offer, readily available to their employee representatives or, where there are no employee representatives, to the employees themselves.

(c) Where necessary, the offeror or the offeree company, as the case may be, should explain the implications of the announcement and, in the case of the offeree company, the fact that addresses, electronic addresses and certain other information provided by offeree company shareholders, persons with information rights and other relevant persons for the receipt of communications from the offeree company may be provided to an offeror during the offer period as required under Section 4 of Appendix 4. Any circular published under this Rule should also include a summary of the provisions of *Rule 8* (see the Panel's website at www.thetakeoverpanel.org.uk).

(d) When, under the above, the offeree company makes a copy of an announcement or a circular summarising the terms and conditions of the offer available to its employee representatives or employees, it must at the same time inform them of the right of employee representatives under *Rule 25.9* to have a separate opinion appended to the offeree board's circular, when published in accordance with *Rule 25.1*, and of the offeree company's responsibility for the costs reasonably incurred by the employee representatives in obtaining advice required for the verification of the information contained in that opinion.

(*Rule 2.12*).

Rule 3 Independent advice

Board of the offeree company. The board of the offeree company must obtain competent independent advice as to whether the financial terms of any offer (including alternative offers) are fair and reasonable and the substance of such advice must be made known to its shareholders.

(*Rule 3.1*).

Board of an offeror company. The board of an offeror must obtain competent independent advice on any offer when the offer being made is a reverse takeover or when the directors are faced with a conflict of interest. The substance of such advice must be made known to its shareholders.

(*Rule 3.2*).

Disqualified advisers. The Panel will not regard as an appropriate person to give independent advice a person who is in the same group as the financial or other professional adviser (including a corporate broker) to an offeror or who has a significant interest in, or financial connection, with either an offeror or the offeree company of such a kind as to create a conflict of interest.

(*Rule 3.3*).

Restrictions on dealings

Note. Apart from this rule, a person may be precluded from dealing or procuring others to deal by virtue of restrictions in *CJA 1993* regarding insider dealing and *FSMA 2000* regarding market abuse. See **23 Insider Dealing and Market Abuse**.

Rule 4

Prohibited dealings by persons other than the offeror. No dealings in securities of the offeree company by any person (other than the offeror) who is privy to confidential price-sensitive information concerning an offer can take place between the time when there is reason to suppose that an approach or an offer is contemplated and the announcement of the approach or offer (or of the termination of the discussions). No person who is privy to such information may make any recommendation to any other person as to dealing in the relevant securities.

In addition, no such dealings may take place in securities of the offeror unless the proposed offer is not price-sensitive in relation to such securities.

(*Rule 4.1*).

Restriction on dealings by the offeror and concert parties. During an offer period, the offeror and persons acting in concert with it must not sell any securities in the offeree company except

- with the prior consent of the Panel; and
- following 24 hours' public notice that such sales might be made.

Sales below the value of the offer will not be permitted.

After there has been an announcement that sales may be made, neither the offeror nor persons acting in concert with it may acquire an interest in any securities of the offeree company and only in exceptional circumstances will the Panel permit the offer to be revised.

During an offer period, the offeror and persons acting in concert with it must not acquire an interest in any securities of the offeree company through any anonymous order book system, or through any other means unless, in either case, it can be established that the seller (or other party to the transaction in question) is not an exempt principal trader connected with the offeror.

(*Rule 4.2*).

Gathering of irrevocable commitments. Any person proposing to contact a private individual or small corporate shareholder with a view to seeking an irrevocable commitment must consult the Panel in advance.

(*Rule 4.3*).

Dealings in offeree securities by certain offeree company associates. During the offer period, no financial adviser or corporate broker to an offeree company (or any of its parents, subsidiaries or fellow subsidiaries, or their associated companies or companies of which such companies are associated companies) must, except with the consent of the Panel

- acquire any interest in offeree company shares (either for its own account or on behalf of discretionary clients);
- make any loan to a person to assist him in acquiring any such interest (apart from lending in the ordinary course of business and on normal commercial terms to persons with which they have an established customer relationship); or

- enter into any indemnity, option arrangement, agreement or understanding which may be an inducement for a person to retain, deal or refrain from dealing in relevant securities of the offeree company.

This also applies to any person controlling, controlled by or under the same control as any such financial adviser or corporate broker. But it does not apply to exempt principal traders and exempt fund managers.

(*Rule 4.4*).

Treasury shares. An offeree company may not accept an offer in respect of treasury shares until after the offer is unconditional as to acceptances.

(*Rule 4.5*).

Restriction on securities borrowing and lending transactions. During the offer period, none of the following persons may, except with the consent of the Panel, enter into or take action to unwind a securities borrowing or lending transaction in respect of relevant securities.

- The offeror.
- The offeree company.
- A company which is an associate of the offeror or the offeree company.
- A connected adviser or persons controlling, controlled by or under the same control as any such adviser (except for an exempt principal trader or an exempt fund manager).
- A pension fund of the offeror or the offeree company or of a company which is an associate of the offeror or the offeree company.
- Any other person acting in concert with the offeror or with the offeree company.

(*Rule 4.6*).

Rule 5 Timing restrictions on acquisitions

Note. For the purposes of *Rule 5* only, the number of shares in which a person is treated as having an interest includes any shares in respect of which he has received an irrevocable commitment.

Restrictions. Except as permitted by *Rule 5.2*, when a person (including any persons acting in concert with him) is interested in shares which in the aggregate carry

- less than 30% of the voting rights of a company, he may not acquire an interest in any other shares carrying voting rights in that company which, when aggregated with the shares in which he is already interested, would carry 30% or more of the voting rights; and
- 30% or more of the voting rights of a company but does not hold shares which carry more than 50% of the voting rights, he may not acquire an interest in any other shares carrying voting rights in that company.

(*Rule 5.1*).

Exceptions to restrictions. The restrictions in *Rule 5.1* do not apply to an acquisition of an interest in shares carrying voting rights in a company by a person:

(a) At any time from a single shareholder if it is the only such acquisition within any period of 7 days (see also *Rules 5.3* and *5.4*). But this exception does not apply when the person has announced a firm intention to make an offer and the making of the offer is not subject to a pre-condition.

(b) Immediately before the person announces a firm intention to make an offer, provided that the offer will be publicly recommended by, or the acquisition is made with the agreement of, the board of the offeree company and the acquisition is conditional upon the announcement of the offer.

(c) After the person has announced a firm intention to make an offer provided that at the time of the acquisition, there is no pre- condition to which the making of an offer is subject and
- the acquisition is made with the agreement of the board of the offeree company;
- that offer or any competing offer has been publicly recommended by the board of the offeree company, even if such recommendation is subsequently withdrawn;
- the first closing date of that offer or any competing offer has passed or
- that offer is unconditional in all respects.

(d) If the acquisition is by way of acceptance of the offer.

(e) If the acquisition is permitted by Note 11 on *Rule 9.1* or Note 5 of the Notes on Dispensation from *Rule 9*.

(*Rule 5.2*).

Consequences of acquisitions from a single shareholder. A person who acquires an interest in shares from a single shareholder permitted by *Rule 5.2(a)* may not acquire an interest in any other shares carrying voting rights in a company, except in the circumstances set out in *Rule 5.2(b)*, *(c)*, *(d)* and *(e)*. If that person makes an offer for the company which subsequently lapses, this restriction will cease to apply.

(*Rule 5.3*).

Disclosure of acquisition from a single shareholder. A person who acquires an interest in shares carrying voting rights in a company from a single shareholder permitted by *Rule 5.2(a)* must notify the company, a RIS and the Panel, not later than 12 noon on the business day following the date of the acquisition, of

- that acquisition; and
- any shares of the company in which he has an interest or in respect of which he has a right to subscribe (in each case specifying the nature of the interests or rights concerned). Similar details of any short position (including any short position under a derivative), any agreement to sell or any delivery obligation or right to require another person to purchase or take delivery, must also be disclosed.

(*Rule 5.4*).

Rule 6 Acquisitions resulting in an obligation to offer a minimum level of consideration

(1) *Acquisitions before a firm offer announcement*
Except with the consent of the Panel in cases falling under *(a)* or *(b)* below, when an offeror (or any person acting in concert with it) has acquired an interest in shares in the offeree company

(a) within the three month period prior to the commencement of the offer period,

(b) during the period, if any, between the commencement of the offer period and an announcement made by the offeror in accordance with *Rule 2.7*, or

(c) prior to the three month period referred to in *(a)*, if in the view of the Panel there are circumstances which render such a course necessary in order to give effect to General Principle 1,

the offer to the holders of shares of the same class must not be on less favourable terms.

If an acquisition of an interest in shares in the offeree company has given rise to an obligation under *Rule 11*, compliance with that *Rule* will normally be regarded as satisfying any obligation under this *Rule* in respect of the acquisition.
(*Rule 6.1*).

(2) *Acquisitions after a firm offer announcement*

(a) If, after an announcement made in accordance with *Rule 2.7* and before the offer closes for acceptance, an offeror (or any person acting in concert with it) acquires any interest in shares at above the offer price (being the then current value of the offer), it must increase its offer to not less than the highest price paid for the interest in shares so acquired.

(b) Immediately after the acquisition, the offeror must announce that a revised offer will be made in accordance with this *Rule* (see also *Rule 32*). Whenever practicable, the announcement should also state the nature of the interest, the number of shares concerned and the price paid.

(c) Acquisitions of interests in shares in the offeree company may also give rise to an obligation under *Rule 11*, in which case compliance with that *Rule* will normally be regarded as satisfying any obligation under this *Rule* in respect of the acquisition.

(*Rule 6.2*).

Rule 7 Consequences of certain dealings

Immediate announcement required if the offer has to be amended. The acquisition of an interest in offeree company shares by an offeror (or any person acting in concert with it) may give rise to an obligation under *Rule 6*, *Rule 9* or *Rule 11*. Immediately after such an acquisition, an appropriate announcement must be made by the offeror. Whenever practicable, the announcement should also state the nature of the interest, the number of shares concerned and the price paid.

(*Rule 7.1*).

Dealings by connected discretionary fund managers and principal traders. The following provisions apply to discretionary fund managers and principal traders who do not have exempt status.

- If connected with an offeror or potential offeror, they will not normally be presumed to be acting in concert with that person until its identity as an offeror or potential offeror is publicly announced or, if prior to that, the time at which the connected party had actual knowledge of the possibility of an offer being made by a person with whom it is connected. *Rules 5*, *6*, *9*, *11* and *36* will then be relevant to acquisitions of interests in offeree company securities and *Rule 4.2* to sales of offeree company securities by such persons. *Rule 4.6* will be relevant to securities borrowing and lending transactions.
- If connected with the offeree company, they will not normally be presumed to be acting in concert with the offeree company until the commencement of the offer period or, if prior to that, the time at which the connected party had actual knowledge of the possibility of an offer being made for the offeree company and that it was connected with the offeree company. *Rules 4.4*, *5* and *9* may then be relevant to acquisitions of interests in offeree company securities. *Rule 4.6* will be relevant to securities borrowing and lending transactions.

An exempt fund manager or exempt principal trader which is connected for the sole reason that it is controlled by, controls or is under the same control as a connected adviser will not be presumed to be in concert even after the commencement of the offer period or the identity of the offeror being publicly announced (as the case may be).

(*Rule 7.2*).

Partial offers and 'whitewashes'. The acquisition of an interest in offeree company shares by an offeror (or any person acting in concert with it) may result in the Panel refusing to exercise its discretion to permit a partial offer or to grant a dispensation. (*Rule 7.3*).

Rule 8 Disclosure of dealings and positions

Disclosure by an offeror

An offeror must make a public Opening Position Disclosure:

(a) after the announcement that first identifies it as an offeror; and
(b) after the announcement that first identifies a competing securities exchange offeror.

An offeror must also make a public Dealing Disclosure if it deals in any relevant securities of the offeree company or any securities exchange offeror during an offer period for its own account or for the account of discretionary investment clients.

(*Rule 8.1*)

Disclosure by the offerree company

An offeree company must make a public Opening Position Disclosure:

(a) after the commencement of the offer period; and
(b) if later, after the announcement that first identifies any securities exchange offeror.

An offeree company must also make a public Dealing Disclosure if it deals in any relevant securities of the offeree company or any securities exchange offeror during an offer period for its own account or for the account of discretionary investment clients.

(*Rule 8.2*)

Disclosure by persons with interests in securities representing 1% or more

Any person who at the relevant time is interested (directly or indirectly) in 1% or more of any class of relevant securities of the offeree company or any securities exchange offeror must make a public Opening Position Disclosure:

(a) after the commencement of an offer period; and
(b) if later, after the announcement that first identifies any securities exchange offeror.

Any person who is (or as a result of any dealing becomes) interested (directly or indirectly) in 1% or more of any class of relevant securities of the offeree company or any securities exchange offeror must make a public Dealing Disclosure if he deals in any relevant securities of the offeree company or any securities exchange offeror during an offer period.

Where two or more persons act pursuant to an agreement or understanding, whether formal or informal, to acquire or control an interest in relevant securities, they will normally be deemed to be a single person for the purpose of Rule 8.3.

If a person manages investment accounts on a discretionary basis, he, and not the person on whose behalf the relevant securities (or interests in relevant securities) are managed, will be treated for the purpose of this Rule as interested in the relevant securities concerned.

Except with the consent of the Panel, where more than one discretionary investment management operation is conducted in the same group, the interests in relevant securities of all such operations will be treated for the purpose of this Rule as those of a single person and must be aggregated.

The above Rules do not apply to recognised intermediaries acting in a client-serving capacity.

A person making a disclosure in accordance with Rules 8.1, 8.2, 8.4 or 8.5 need not also disclose the same information pursuant to Rule 8.3.

(*Rule 8.3*)

Disclosure by concert parties

A person acting in concert with any party to an offer must make a public Dealing Disclosure if he deals in any relevant securities of the offeree company or any securities exchange offeror during an offer period for his own account or for the account of discretionary investment clients.

(*Rule 8.4*)

Disclosure by exempt principal traders

An exempt principal trader connected with an offeror which does not have recognised intermediary status or which does have recognised intermediary status but which holds any interest or short position in, or right to subscribe for, any relevant securities of the offeree company or any securities exchange offeror in a proprietary capacity must make a public Opening Position Disclosure:

(a) after the announcement that first identifies the offeror with which it is connected as an offeror; and
(b) after the announcement that first identifies a competing securities exchange offeror.

An exempt principal trader connected with the offeree company which does not have recognised intermediary status or which does have recognised intermediary status but which holds any interest or short position in, or right to subscribe for, any relevant securities of the offeree company or any securities exchange offeror in a proprietary capacity must make a public Opening Position Disclosure:

(a) after the commencement of the offer period; and
(b) if later, after the announcement that first identifies any securities exchange offeror.

An exempt principal trader connected with a party to the offer must make a public Dealing Disclosure if it deals in any relevant securities of the offeree company or any securities exchange offeror during an offer period, stating the following details:

(a) if the exempt principal trader does not have recognised intermediary status, or if it does but it is dealing in a proprietary capacity, the details required under Note 5(a) on Rule 8; and

(b) if the exempt principal trader has recognised intermediary status and is dealing in a client-serving capacity, the details required under Note 5(b) on Rule 8.

(*Rule 8.5*)

Disclosure by exempt fund managers with no interests in securities of any party to the offer representing 1% or more dealing for discretionary clients

An exempt fund manager connected with a party to the offer must make a private Dealing Disclosure if it deals in any relevant securities of the offeree company or any securities exchange offeror for the benefit of discretionary investment clients during an offer period.

The above rule does not apply if the exempt fund manager is also required to make a disclosure in accordance with Rule 8.3.

(*Rule 8.6*)

Disclosure of non-discretionary dealings by parties and concert parties

A party to the offer and any person acting in concert with it must make a private Dealing Disclosure if it deals in any relevant securities of the offeree company or any securities exchange offeror during an offer period for the account of non-discretionary investment clients (other than a non-discretionary client that is a party to the offer or any person acting in concert with it).

(*Rule 8.7*)

The mandatory offer and its terms

Rule 9 When a mandatory offer is required and who is primarily responsible for making it

Except with the consent of the Panel, when

- any person acquires (whether by a series of transactions over a period of time or not) an interest in shares which (taken together with shares in which persons acting in concert with him are interested) carry 30% or more of the voting rights of a company, or
- any person (together with persons acting in concert with him) is interested in shares which in the aggregate carry not less than 30% of the voting rights of a company but does not hold shares carrying more than 50% of such voting rights and such person (or any person acting in concert with him) acquires an interest in any other shares which increases the percentage of shares carrying voting rights in which he is interested,

such person must extend offers, on the basis set out in *Rules 9.3*, *9.4* and *9.5*, to the holders of any class of equity share capital whether voting or non-voting and also to the holders of any other class of transferable securities carrying voting rights. Offers for different classes of equity share capital must be comparable. The Panel should be consulted in advance in such cases.

An offer will not be required under this *Rule* where control of the offeree company is acquired as a result of a voluntary offer made in accordance with the Code to all the holders of voting equity share capital and other transferable securities carrying voting rights.

(*Rule 9.1*).

Obligations of other persons. In addition to the person specified in *Rule 9.1*, each of the principal members of a group of persons acting in concert with him may, according to the circumstances of the case, have the obligation to extend an offer.

(*Rule 9.2*).

Conditions and consents. Except with the consent of the Panel

- offers made under *Rule 9* must be conditional only upon the offeror having received acceptances in respect of shares which, together with shares acquired or agreed to be acquired before or during the offer, will result in the offeror and any person acting in concert with it holding shares carrying more than 50% of the voting rights; and
- no acquisition of any interest in shares which would give rise to a requirement for an offer under this *Rule* may be made if the making or implementation of such offer would or might be dependent on the passing of a resolution at any meeting of shareholders of the offeror or upon any other conditions, consents or arrangements.

(*Rule 9.3*).

The CMA and the European Commission. Offers under this *Rule* must, if appropriate, contain the terms required by *Rule 12.1*(*a*) and (*b*).

(*Rule 9.4*).

Consideration to be offered. An offer made under *Rule 9* must, in respect of each class of share capital involved, be in cash or be accompanied by a cash alternative at not less than the highest price paid by the offeror (or any person acting in concert with it) for any interest in shares of that class during the 12 months prior to the announcement of that offer. The Panel should be consulted where there is more than one class of share capital involved.

If, after an announcement of an offer made under *Rule 9* for a class of share capital and before the offer closes for acceptance, the offeror (or any person acting in concert with it) acquires any interest in shares of that class at above the offer price, it must increase its offer for that class to not less than the highest price paid for the interest in shares so acquired. Immediately after the acquisition, an appropriate announcement must be made in accordance with *Rule 7.1*.

The cash offer or the cash alternative must remain open after the offer has become unconditional as to acceptances for not less than 14 days after the date on which it would otherwise have expired.

(*Rule 9.5*).

Obligations of directors. When directors (and their close relatives and related trusts) sell shares to a person (or enter into options, derivatives or other transactions) as a result of which that person is required to make an offer under this *Rule*, the directors must ensure that as a condition of the sale (or other relevant transaction) the person undertakes to fulfil his obligations under the *Rule*. In addition, except with the consent of the Panel, such directors should not resign from the board until the first closing date of the offer or the date when the offer becomes wholly unconditional, whichever is the later.

(*Rule 9.6*).

Voting restrictions and disposals of interests. Where the Panel agrees to the disposal of interests in shares as an alternative to making an offer, the Panel must be consulted as to the interests being disposed of and any restrictions on the exercise of voting rights attaching to the shares. Similarly if an offer lapses for a reason other the acceptance condition not being satisfied, or where a new offer is required, the Panel must be consulted regarding the offeror's (and any person acting in concert with it) ability to exercise or procure the exercise of the voting rights attached to the shares.

(*Rule 9.7*).

Dispensations. There are a number of dispensations from *Rule 9* for which see the detailed notes to the *Rule*.

The Voluntary offer and its terms

Rule 10 The acceptance condition

Unless waived by the Panel, it must be a condition of any offer

- for voting equity share capital or for other transferable securities carrying voting rights
- which, if accepted in full, would result in the offeror holding shares carrying over 50% of the voting rights of the offeree company

that the offer will not become or be declared unconditional as to acceptances unless the offeror has acquired or agreed to acquire (either pursuant to the offer or otherwise) shares carrying over 50% of the voting rights.

Rule 11 Nature of consideration to be offered

When a cash offer is required. Except with the consent of the Panel in cases falling under (*a*) or (*b*) below, a cash offer is required where:

- The shares of any class under offer in the offeree company in which interests are acquired for cash by an offeror (and any person acting in concert with it) during the offer period and within 12 months prior to its commencement carry 10% or more of the voting rights currently exercisable at a class meeting of that class. In such a case, the offer for that class must be in cash or accompanied by a cash alternative at not less than the highest price paid by the offeror (or any person acting in concert with it) for any interest in shares of that class acquired during the offer period and within 12 months prior to its commencement.
- Subject to (*a*) above, any interest in shares of any class under offer in the offeree company is acquired for cash by an offeror (or any person acting in concert with it) during the offer period. In such case, the offer for that class must be in cash or accompanied by a cash alternative at not less than the highest price paid by the offeror (or any person acting in concert with it) for any interest in shares of that class acquired during the offer period.
- In the view of the Panel there are circumstances which render such a course necessary in order to give effect to General Principle 1.

(*Rule 11.1*).

When a securities offer is required. Where interests in shares of any class of the offeree company carrying 10% or more of the voting rights currently exercisable at a class meeting of that class have been acquired by an offeror (and any person acting in concert with it) in exchange for securities in the three months prior to the commencement of and during the offer period, such securities will normally be required to be offered to all other holders of shares of that class.

Unless the vendor or other party to the transaction giving rise to the interest is required to hold the securities received or receivable until either the offer has lapsed or the offer consideration has been sent to accepting shareholders, an obligation to make an offer in cash or to provide a cash alternative will also arise under *Rule 11.1*.

(*Rule 11.2*).

Dispensation from highest price. If the offeror considers that the highest price (for the purpose of *Rules 11.1* and *11.2*) should not apply in a particular case, the offeror should consult the Panel, which has discretion to agree an adjusted price.

(*Rule 11.3*).

Rule 12 The CMA and the European Commission

Requirement for appropriate term in offer.

(a) Where an offer comes within the statutory provisions for a possible Phase 2 CMA reference, it must be a term of the offer that
 (i) in the case of a contractual offer, it will lapse if there is a Phase 2 CMA reference before the first closing date or the date when the offer becomes or is declared unconditional as to acceptances (whichever is the later); or
 (ii) in the case of an offer being implemented by way of a scheme of arrangement, the offer will lapse and the scheme will not become effective if there is a Phase 2 CMA reference before the shareholder meetings.

(b) Where an offer would give rise to a concentration with an EU dimension within the scope of *Council Regulation 139/2004/EC*, it must be a term of the offer that if Phase 2 European Commission proceedings are initiated or there is a Phase 2 reference following a referral by the European Commission under *Art 9(1)* to a competent authority in the UK,
 (i) in the case of a contractual offer, the offer will lapse if this occurs before the first closing date or the date when the offer becomes or is declared unconditional as to acceptances (whichever is the later); or
 (ii) in the case of an offer being implemented by a scheme of arrangement, the offer will lapse and the scheme will not become effective if this occurs before the shareholder meetings.

(c) Except in the case of an offer under *Rule 9*, the offeror may, in addition, make the offer conditional on a decision being made that there will be no Phase 2 CMA reference, initiation of Phase 2 European Commission proceedings or referral by the European Commission under *Article 9(1)* of *Council Regulation 39/2004/EC*. In such a case, the condition may state, that the decision must be on terms satisfactory to the offeror. The offeror or potential offeror whose offer is prohibited, together with any person acting in concert with it, will, except with the consent of the Panel, be subject to the restrictions in *Rule 2.8* for six months from the date on which the relevant decision is issued.

(*Rule 12.1*).

Competition reference periods. When there is a Phase 2 CMA reference or Phase 2 European Commission proceedings are initiated, the offer period will end except where

- the offer was announced subject to a pre-condition as permitted under Rule 13.3(*b*); or
- in the case of an offer being implemented by way of a scheme of arrangement, where the Phase 2 reference or initiation of Phase 2 European Commission proceedings does not cause the offer to lapse as a result of a term included pursuant to Rule 12.1(*a*) or (*b*) or upon a condition included pursuant to Rule 12.1(c) being invoked.

If the offer period ends in accordance with the above,

(a) during the competition reference period, except with the consent of the Panel, neither the offeror, nor any person who acted in concert with the offeror in relation to the referred offer or possible offer, nor any person who is subsequently acting in concert with any of them may
 - announce an offer or possible offer for the offeree company (including a partial offer which could result in the offeror and persons acting in concert with it being interested in shares carrying 30% or more of the voting rights of the offeree company);
 - acquire any interest in shares of the offeree company if the offeror or any such person would thereby become obliged under Rule 9 to make an offer;

- acquire an interest in, or procure an irrevocable commitment in respect of, shares of the offeree company if the shares in which such person (together with any persons acting in concert with him) would be interested and the shares in respect of which he, or they, had acquired irrevocable commitments would in aggregate carry 30% or more of the voting rights of the offeree company;
- make any statement which raises or confirms the possibility that an offer might be made for the offeree company; or
- take any steps in connection with a possible offer for the offeree company where knowledge of the possible offer might be extended outside those who need to know in the offeror and its immediate advisers;

(b) at the end of the competition reference period, if the offer is allowed to proceed (whether conditionally or unconditionally)

- any cleared offeror or potential offeror must, normally within 21 days of the offer's being allowed to proceed, clarify its intentions with regard to the offeree company by making an announcement either of a firm intention to make an offer for the offeree company in accordance with *Rule 2.7* or that it does not intend to make an offer for the offeree company, in which latter case the announcement will be treated as a statement to which *Rule 2.8* applies; and
- a new offer period will begin and, if no announcement of a new offer is made within the 21 day period referred to above, will end when each cleared offeror or potential offeror has announced that it does not intend to make an offer; and

(c) where the competition reference period ends when either the CMA or the Secretary of State issues a prohibition decision or when the European Commission issues a decision under *Council Regulation 139/2004/EC, Art 8(3)*, no new offer period will begin. The offeror or potential offeror whose offer is prohibited, together with any person acting in concert with it will, except with the consent of the Panel, be subject to the restrictions in Rule 2.8 for six months from the date on which the relevant decision is issued.

(*Rule 12.2*).

Rule 13 Pre-conditions in firm offer announcements and offer conditions

Subjectivity. An offer must not normally be subject to conditions or pre-conditions which depend solely on subjective judgements by the offeror or the offeree company (as the case may be) or in either case its directors the fulfilment of which is in their hands. The Panel may accept an element of subjectivity in certain circumstances where it is not practicable to specify all the factors on which satisfaction of a particular condition or pre-condition may depend, especially in cases involving official authorisations or regulatory clearances, the granting of which may be subject to additional material obligations for the offeror or offeree company (as the case may be)

(*Rule 13.1*).

The CMA and the European Commission. Neither a condition included pursuant to *Rule 12.1(c)* nor a pre-condition included pursuant to *Rule 13.3(a)* or *(b)*) will be subject to the provisions of *Rules 13.1* or *13.5(a)*.

(*Rule 13.2*).

Acceptability of pre-conditions. The Panel must be consulted in advance if a person proposes to include in an announcement any pre-condition to which the making of the offer will be subject. Except with the consent of the Panel, an offer must not be announced subject to a pre-condition unless the pre-condition

(a) relates to a decision that there will be no Phase 2 CMA reference or initiation of Phase 2 European Commission proceedings;
(b) relates to a decision that there will be no Phase 2 CMA reference or initiation of Phase 2 European Commission proceedings or, if there is such a reference or initiation of proceedings, a decision by the relevant authority to allow the offer to proceed (the decision may, in each case, be stated to be on terms satisfactory to the offeror); or
(c) involves another material official authorisation or regulatory clearance relating to the offer and
  (i) the offer is publicly recommended by the board of the offeree company; or
  (ii) the Panel is satisfied that it is likely to prove impossible to obtain the authorisation or clearance within the Code timetable.

(*Rule 13.3*).

Financing conditions and pre-conditions.

(a) Subject to *Rules 13.4*(b) and (c), an offer must not be made subject to a condition or pre-condition relating to financing.
(b) Where the offer is for cash, or includes an element of cash, and the offeror proposes to finance the cash consideration by an issue of new securities, the offer must be made subject to any condition required, as a matter of law or regulatory requirement, in order validly to issue such securities or to have them listed or admitted to trading. Conditions which will normally be considered necessary for such purposes include:
  (i) the passing of any resolution necessary to create or allot the new securities and/or to allot the new securities on a non-pre-emptive basis (if relevant); and
  (ii) where the new securities are to be admitted to listing or to trading on any investment exchange or market, any necessary listing or admission to trading condition (see also *Rule 24.10*). Such conditions must not be waivable and the Panel must be consulted in advance.
(c) In exceptional cases, the Panel may be prepared to accept a pre-condition relating to financing either in addition to another precondition permitted by *Rule 13.3* or otherwise, for example where, due to the likely period required to obtain any necessary material official authorisation or regulatory clearance, it is not reasonable for the offeror to maintain committed financing throughout the offer period. In such a case:
  (i) the financing pre-condition must be satisfied (or waived), or the offer must be withdrawn, within 21 days after the satisfaction (or waiver) of any other pre-condition or pre-conditions permitted by *Rule 13.3*; and
  (ii) the offeror and its financial adviser must confirm in writing to the Panel before announcement of the offer that they are not aware of any reason why the offeror would be unable to satisfy the financing pre-condition within that 21 day period.
(d) If, at any time, the offeror or its financial adviser becomes aware, or considers it likely, that the offeror would be unable to satisfy a financing pre-condition, it must promptly notify the Panel.

(*Rule 13.4*)

Invoking conditions and pre-conditions.

(a) An offeror should not invoke any condition or pre-condition in order to cause the offer not to proceed, to lapse or to be withdrawn unless the circumstances which give rise to the right to invoke the condition or pre-condition are of material significance to the offeror in the context of the offer. The acceptance condition is not subject to this provision.

(b) Following the announcement of a firm intention to make an offer, an offeror should use all reasonable efforts to ensure the satisfaction of any conditions or pre-conditions to which the offer is subject.

(*Rule 13.5*).

Invoking offeree protection conditions. An offeree company should not invoke, or cause or permit the offeror to invoke, any condition to an offer unless the circumstances which give rise to the right to invoke the condition are of material significance to the shareholders in the offeree company in the context of the offer.

(*Rule 13.6*).

Provisions applicable to all offers

Rule 14 Where there is more than one class of share capital

Comparable offers. Where a company has more than one class of equity share capital, a comparable offer must be made for each class (whether or not carrying voting rights). An offer for non-voting equity should not be made conditional on any particular level of acceptances unless the offer for the voting equity is also conditional on the success of the offer for the non-voting equity. Classes of non-voting, non-equity share capital need not be the subject of an offer, except in the circumstances referred to in *Rule 15*.

(*Rule 14.1*).

Separate offers for each class. Where an offer is made for more than one class of share, separate offers must be made for each class.

(*Rule 14.2*).

Rule 15 Appropriate offer for convertibles, etc

When an offer is made for voting equity share capital or for other transferable securities carrying voting rights and the offeree company has convertible securities outstanding, the offeror must make an appropriate offer or proposal to the stockholders to ensure that their interests are safeguarded. The offeree company must obtain independent advice on the offer and make this known to its stockholders, together with the board's views.

Whenever practicable, the offer or proposal should be sent to stockholders at the same time as the offer document is published but, if this is not practicable, the Panel should be consulted. A copy of the offer or proposal should be sent to the Panel at the time of publication.

The offer or proposal to stockholders required by this *Rule* should not normally be made conditional on any particular level of acceptances. But it may be put by way of a scheme to be considered at a stockholders' meeting.

If an offeree company has options or subscription rights outstanding, the provisions of this *Rule* apply *mutatis mutandis*.

Rule 16 Special deals with favourable conditions

Except with the consent of the Panel, an offeror (or persons acting in concert with it) may not, either during an offer or when one is reasonably in contemplation,

- make any arrangements with shareholders,

- deal or enter into arrangements to deal in shares of the offeree company, or
- enter into arrangements which involve acceptance of an offer,

if there are favourable conditions attached which are not being extended to all shareholders.

An arrangement made with a person who, while not a shareholder, is interested in shares carrying voting rights in the offeree company is also be prohibited by this *Rule* (but there is no requirement to extend an offer or any arrangement which would otherwise be prohibited to any person who is interested in shares but is not a shareholder).

(*Rule 16.1*).

Management Incentivisation

(a) Except with the consent of the Panel, where an offeror has:
(i) entered into; or
(ii) reached an advanced stage of discussions on proposals to enter into any form of incentivisation arrangements with members of the offeree company's management who are interested in shares in the offeree company, relevant details of the arrangements or proposals must be disclosed and the independent adviser to the offeree company must state publicly that in its opinion the arrangements are fair and reasonable. If it is intended to put incentivisation arrangements in place following completion of the offer, but either no discussions or only limited discussions have taken place, this fact must be stated publicly and relevant details of the discussions disclosed. Where no incentivisation arrangements are proposed, this must be stated publicly.
(b) Where the value of arrangements entered into or proposed to be entered into is significant and/or the nature of the arrangements is unusual either in the context of the relevant industry or good practice, the Panel must be consulted and its consent to the arrangements obtained. The Panel may also require, as a condition of its consent, that the arrangements be approved at a general meeting of the offeree company's shareholders.
(c) Where the members of the management are shareholders in the offeree company and, as a result of the incentivisation arrangements, they will become shareholders in the offeror on a basis that is not being made available to all other offeree company shareholders, such arrangements must be approved at a general meeting of the offeree company's shareholders.
(d) Any approval as required by paragraph (*b*) or (*c*) above must be by a separate vote of independent shareholders, taken on a poll.

(*Rule 16.2*).

Rule 17 Announcement of acceptance levels

Timing and contents. An offeror must make an appropriate announcement by 8am at the latest on the business day following the day on which an offer is due to expire, becomes or is declared unconditional as to acceptances, or is revised or extended. The announcement must state:

- The number of shares for which acceptances have been received, specifying the extent to which acceptances have been received from persons acting in concert with the offeror or in respect of shares which were subject to an irrevocable commitment or a letter of intent procured by the offeror or any of its associates.
- Details of any relevant securities of the offeree company in which the offeror (or any person acting in concert with it) has an interest or in respect of which he has a right to subscribe.

- Details of any relevant securities of the offeree company in respect of which the offeror or any of its associates has an outstanding irrevocable commitment or letter of intent.
- Details of any relevant securities of the offeree company which the offeror (or any person acting in concert with it) has borrowed or lent, save for any borrowed shares which have been either on-lent or sold.

It must also specify the percentages of each class of relevant securities represented by these figures.

(*Rule 17.1*).

Consequences of failure to announce. If an offeror, having announced the offer to be unconditional as to acceptances, fails by 3.30pm on the relevant day to comply with any of the requirements of *Rule 17.1*, immediately thereafter any acceptor is entitled to withdraw his acceptance. Subject to *Rule 31.6*, this right of withdrawal may be terminated not less than eight days after the relevant day by the offeror confirming, if such is the case, that the offer is still unconditional as to acceptances and complying with *Rule 17.1*.

For the purpose of *Rule 31.4*, the offer must remain open for acceptance for not less than 14 days after the date of such confirmation and compliance.

(*Rule 17.2*).

Rule 18 The use of proxies and other authorities in relation to acceptances

An offeror may not require a shareholder, as a term of his acceptance of an offer, to appoint a proxy to vote in respect of his shares in the offeree company (or to exercise any other rights or take any other action in relation to those shares) unless the appointment is on the following terms, which must be set out in the offer document.

- The proxy may not vote (or the rights be exercised or other action taken) unless the offer is wholly unconditional or, in the case of voting by the proxy, the resolution in question concerns the last remaining condition of the offer and the offer will become wholly unconditional or lapse depending upon the outcome of that resolution.
- Where relevant, the votes are to be cast as far as possible to satisfy any outstanding condition of the offer.
- The appointment ceases to be valid if the acceptance is withdrawn.
- The appointment applies only to shares assented to the offer.

Conduct during the offer

Rule 19 Information

Standards of care. Each document, announcement or other information published, or statement made, during the course of an offer must be prepared with the highest standards of care and accuracy. The language used must clearly and concisely reflect the position being described and the information given must be adequately and fairly presented. These requirements apply whether the document, announcement or other information is published or the statement is made by the party concerned or by an adviser on its behalf.

(*Rule 19.1*).

Responsibility for information. Each document, or advertisement published, in connection with an offer by, or on behalf of, the offeror or the offeree company, must state that

- the directors of the offeror and/or, where appropriate, the offeree company accept responsibility for the information contained in the document or advertisement; and
- to the best of their knowledge and belief (having taken all reasonable care to ensure that such is the case), the information contained in the document or advertisement is in accordance with the facts and, where appropriate, that it does not omit anything likely to affect the import of such information.

This *Rule* does not apply to advertisements falling within *Rule 19.4*(i), (ii) or (viii) and advertisements which only contain information already published in a circular which included the statement required by this *Rule* and any separate opinion of the employee representatives of the offeree company on the effects of the offer on employment as referred to in Rule *25.9* or *32.6*.

The Panel's approval is required if it is proposed that any director should be excluded from such a statement. Such consent is given only in exceptional circumstances and in such cases the omission and the reasons for it must be stated in the document or advertisement.

(*Rule 19.2*).

Unacceptable statements. Parties to an offer or potential offer and their advisers must take care not to issue statements which, while not factually inaccurate, may be misleading or may create uncertainty. In particular, an offeror must not make a statement to the effect that it may improve its offer without committing itself to doing so and specifying the improvement.

(*Rule 19.3*).

Advertisements. The publication of advertisements connected with an offer or potential offer is prohibited unless the advertisement falls within one of the following categories. Except where the advertisement falls within (i) or (viii), it must be cleared with the Panel in advance.

(i) Product advertisements not bearing on an offer or potential offer.
(ii) Corporate image advertisements not bearing on an offer or potential offer.
(iii) Advertisements confined to non-controversial information about an offer (eg reminders as to closing times or the value of an offer). Such advertisements must avoid argument or invective.
(iv) Advertisements comprising preliminary or interim results and their accompanying statement (provided the latter is not used for argument or invective concerning an offer).
(v) Advertisements giving information, the publication of which by advertisement is required or specifically permitted by the Listing Rules.
(vi) Advertisements communicating information relevant to holders of bearer securities.
(vii) Advertisements comprising a tender offer.
(viii) Advertisements which are notices relating to a scheme of arrangement.
(ix) Advertisements published with the specific prior consent of the Panel.

(*Rule 19.4*).

Telephone campaigns. Except with the consent of the Panel, campaigns in which shareholders or other persons interested in shares are contacted by telephone may be conducted only by staff of the financial adviser who are fully conversant with the requirements of, and their responsibilities under, the Code. Only previously published information which remains accurate, and is not misleading at the time it is quoted, may be used. Shareholders and other persons interested in shares must not be put under pressure and must be encouraged to consult their professional advisers.

(*Rule 19.5*).

Interviews and debates. Parties to an offer should, if interviewed on radio, television or any other media, seek to ensure that the sequence of the interview is not broken by the insertion of comments or observations by others not made in the course of the interview. Further joint interviews or public confrontation between representatives of the offeror and the offeree company, or between competing offerors, should be avoided.

(*Rule 19.6*).

Post-offer undertakings. A party to an offer must consult the Panel in advance if it wishes to make a post-offer undertaking.

A post-offer undertaking must

- state that it is a post-offer undertaking;
- specify the period of time for which the undertaking is made or the date by which the course of action committed to will be completed; and
- prominently state any qualifications or conditions to which the undertaking is subject.

The terms of any post-offer undertaking made by a party to an offer, including the course of action committed to be taken, or not taken, and the qualifications or conditions to which it is subject, must

- be specific and precise;
- be readily understandable and capable of objective assessment; and
- not depend on subjective judgements of the party to the offer or its directors.

Any post-offer undertaking made by a party to an offer other than in a document published by that party in connection with the offer must be included in the next such document published by that party. The Panel may, in addition, require a document to be sent to the offeree company's shareholders and persons with information rights and made readily available to its and the offeror's employee representatives (or, where there are no employee representatives, to the employees themselves) and to the trustees of the offeree company's pension scheme(s).

Any subsequent reference by the party to the offer concerned to any post-offer undertaking which it has made must be accompanied by a reference to any qualifications or conditions to which the undertaking is subject or to the relevant sections of the document, announcement or other information in which they were included.

A party to an offer must comply with the terms of any post-offer undertaking for the period of time specified in the undertaking and must complete any course of action committed to by the date specified in the undertaking.

A party to an offer will be excused compliance with the terms of a post-offer undertaking only if a qualification or condition set out in the undertaking applies. If a party to an offer wishes to rely on a qualification or condition to a post-offer undertaking in order to take, or not take, a course of action otherwise than in compliance with the terms of that undertaking, that party must consult the Panel in advance and obtain the Panel's consent to rely on that qualification or condition.

Except with the consent of the Panel, if such a course of action is then taken or not taken (as appropriate) with the Panel's consent, the party must promptly make an announcement in accordance with the requirements of Rule 2.9 describing the course of action it has taken, or not taken, and explaining how and why the relevant qualification or condition applies.

A party to an offer which has made a post-offer undertaking must submit written reports to the Panel after the end of the offer period at such intervals and in such form as the Panel may require. Such reports must, as appropriate

- indicate whether any course of action that the party has committed to take has been implemented or completed within the specified period of time and, if not, the progress made to date and the steps being taken to implement or complete the course of action and the expected timetable for completion;
- confirm that any course of action that the party has committed not to take has not been taken;
- include such other documents or information as the Panel may require; and
- if so required by the Panel, be published, in whole or in part, in accordance with the requirements of Rule 2.9.

The Panel may require a party to an offer which has made a post offer undertaking to appoint a supervisor to

- monitor compliance by that party with that undertaking; and
- submit written reports to the Panel, at such intervals and in such form as the Panel may require, as to the compliance by that party with that undertaking, in accordance with arrangements made between the Panel and the supervisor. The party to the offer must comply with any obligations imposed on it in the supervisor's terms of appointment.

(*Rule 19.7*).

Post- offer intention statements. Any post-offer intention statement made by a party to an offer must be

- an accurate statement of that party's intention at the time that it is made; and
- made on reasonable grounds.

If a party to an offer has made a post-offer intention statement and,during the period of 12 months from the date on which the offer period ended, or such other period of time as was specified in the statement, that party decides either

- to take a course of action different from its stated intentions; or
- not to take a course of action which it had stated it intended to take, it must consult the Panel. Except with the consent of the Panel, if such a course of action is then taken or not taken (as appropriate), the party must promptly make an announcement in accordance with the requirements of Rule 2.9 describing the course of action it has taken, or not taken, and explaining its reasons for taking, or not taking, that course of action (as appropriate).

(*Rule 19.8*).

Information published following the ending of an offer period. The requirements of the Code relating to the publication of information do not normally apply once an offer period has ended pursuant to *Rule 12.2(a)*. However, if thereafter the merger is allowed and, as a result, the offeror announces a further offer, the Panel may require that statements (including valuations of assets) made during the competition reference period be substantiated or, if this is not possible, withdrawn. The parties must therefore take care to ensure that any statements made during the competition reference period are capable of substantiation.

(*Rule 19.9*).

Rule 20 Equality of information

Equality of information to shareholders. Information about parties to an offer must be made equally available to all offeree company shareholders and persons with information rights as nearly as possible at the same time and in the same manner.

(*Rule 20.1*).

Equality of information to competing offerors. Any information, given to one offeror or potential offeror, whether publicly identified or not must, on request, be given equally and promptly to another offeror or bona fide potential offeror (even if that other offeror is less welcome). This requirement will usually only apply when there has been a public announcement of the existence of the offeror or potential offeror to which information has been given or, if there has been no public announcement, when the offeror or bona fide potential offeror requesting information under this Rule has been informed authoritatively of the existence of another potential offeror.

(*Rule 20.2*).

Information to independent directors in management buy-outs. If the offer or potential offer is a management buy-out or similar transaction, the offeror or potential offeror must, on request, promptly furnish the independent directors of the offeree company or its advisers with all information which has been furnished by the offeror or potential offeror to external providers or potential providers of finance (whether equity or debt) for the buy-out.

(*Rule 20.3*).

Rule 21 Restrictions on frustrating action

During the course of an offer or even before the date of the offer if the board of the offeree company has reason to believe that a *bona fide* offer might be imminent, the board must not, without the approval of the shareholders in general meeting

- take any action which may result in any offer or *bona fide* possible offer being frustrated or in shareholders being denied the opportunity to decide on its merits; or
- issue any shares or transfer or sell, or agree to transfer or sell, any shares out of treasury or effect any redemption or purchase by the company of its own shares;
- issue or grant options in respect of any unissued shares;
- create or issue, or permit the creation or issue of, any securities carrying rights of conversion into or subscription for shares;
- sell, dispose of or acquire, or agree to sell, dispose of or acquire, assets of a material amount; or
- enter into contracts otherwise than in the ordinary course of business.

In cases of doubt, the Panel must be consulted and its consent to proceed without a shareholders' meeting obtained.

(*Rule 21.1*).

Inducement fees and other offer-related arrangements

(a) Except with the consent of the Panel, neither the offeree company nor any person acting in concert with it may enter into any offer-related arrangement with either the offeror or any person acting in concert with it during an offer period or when an offer is reasonably in contemplation.

(b) An offer-related arrangement means any agreement, arrangement or commitment in connection with an offer, including any inducement fee arrangement or other arrangement having a similar or comparable financial or economic effect, but excluding:
  (i) a commitment to maintain the confidentiality of information provided that it does not include any other provisions prohibited by *Rules 21.2*(a) or *2.3*(d) or otherwise under the Code;
  (ii) a commitment not to solicit employees, customers or suppliers;
  (iii) a commitment to provide information or assistance for the purposes of obtaining any official authorisation or regulatory clearance;
  (iv) irrevocable commitments and letters of intent;
  (v) any agreement, arrangement or commitment which imposes obligations only on an offeror or any person acting in concert with it, other than in the context of a reverse takeover; and
  (vi) any agreement relating to any existing employee incentive arrangement.

(c) If there is any doubt as to whether any proposed agreement, arrangement or commitment is subject to this Rule, the Panel should be consulted at the earliest opportunity.

(*Rule 21.2*).

Rule 22 Responsibilities of the offeree company and an offeror regarding registration procedures and persons with interests in securities representing 1% or more

The board of the offeree company should take action to ensure that its registrar complies fully with the procedures set out in Appendix 4 to the Code. The board should also ensure prompt registration of transfers during an offer.

Documents from the offeror and the offeree board

Rule 23 General obligations as to information

Sufficient information. Shareholders must be given sufficient information and advice to enable them to reach a properly informed decision as to the merits or demerits of an offer. Such information must be available to shareholders early enough to enable them to make a decision in good time. No relevant information should be withheld from them. The obligation of the offeror in these respects towards the shareholders of the offeree company is no less than an offeror's obligation towards its own shareholders.

(*Rule 23.1*).

Making documents, announcements and information available to shareholders, persons with information rights and employee representatives or employees

If a document, an announcement or any information is required to be sent, published or made available to:

(a) shareholders in the offeree company;
(b) persons with information rights; or
(c) employee representatives or employees of the offeror or the offeree company, pursuant to *Rule 2.12, 20.1, 23.1, 24.1, 24.15, 25.1, 26.1,*

30.2, 30.4, 32.1 or *32.6*(a), it must be sent, published or made available (as the case maybe) to all such persons, including those who are located outside the EEA, unless there is sufficient objective justification for not doing so

(*Rule 23.2*).

Financial advisers' opinion

If any document published in connection with an offer includes a recommendation or an opinion of a financial adviser for or against acceptance of the offer, the document must, unless published by the financial adviser in question, include a statement that the financial adviser has given and not withdrawn its consent to the publication of the document with the inclusion of its recommendation or opinion in the form and context in which it is included.

(*Rule 23.3*).

Rule 24 Offeror documents

The offer document

(a) The offeror must, normally within 28 days of the announcement of a firm intention to make an offer, send an offer document to shareholders of the offeree company and persons with information rights, in accordance with *Rule 30.1*. At the same time, both the offeror and the offeree company must make the offer document readily available to their employee representatives or, where there are no employee representatives, to the employees themselves. The Panel must be consulted if the offer document is not to be published within this period.

(b) On the day of publication, the offeror must:
  (i) publish the offer document on a website in accordance with *Rule 26.1*; and
  (ii) announce via a RIS that the offer document has been so published.

(*Rule 24.1*).

(1) *Intentions of the offeror with regard to the business, employees and pension scheme(s)*
In the offer document the offeror must explain the long-term commercial justification for the offer and must state
  (a) Its intentions with regard to the future business of the offeree company.
  (b) Its intentions with regard to the continued employment of employees and management of the offeree company and of its subsidiaries including any material change in the conditions of employment.
  (c) Its strategic plans for the offeree company, and their likely repercussions on employment and the locations of the offeree company's places of business.
  (d) Its intentions with regard to employer contributions into the offeree company's pension scheme (s) (including with regard to current arrangements for the funding of any scheme deficit), the accrual of benefits for existing members, and the admission of new members.
  (e) Its intentions with regard to any redeployment of the fixed assets of the offeree company.
  (f) Its intentions with regard to the maintenance of any existing trading facilities for the relevant securities of the offeree company.

If the offeror has no intention to make any changes in relation to the matters described under (b)–(e) above or if it considers that its strategic plans for the offeree company will have no repercussions on employment or the location of the offeree company's places of business, it must make a statement to that effect.

Where the offeror is a company and insofar as it is affected by the offer, the offeror must state its intentions with regard to its future business and comply with (b) and (c) above with regard to itself.
(*Rule 24.2*).

(2) *Financial and other information on the offeror, the offeree company and the offer*

Except with the consent of the Panel:

(a) where the offeror is a company incorporated under the *CA 2006* (or its predecessors) and its shares are admitted to trading on a UK regulated market or on AIM or ISDX Growth Market, the offer document must contain:

(i) the names of its directors;

(ii) the nature of its business and its financial and trading prospects;

(iii) details of the website address where its audited consolidated accounts for the last two financial years have been published and a statement that the accounts have been incorporated into the offer document by reference to that website in accordance with Rule 24.15;

(iv) details of the website address where any interim statement and/or preliminary announcement made since the date of its last published audited accounts have been published and a statement that any such statement or announcement has been incorporated into the offer document by reference to that website in accordance with Rule 24.15;

(v) in the case of a securities exchange offer, a description of any known significant change in its financial or trading position which has occurred since the end of the last financial period for which either audited financial information or interim financial information has been published, or provide an appropriate negative statement;

(vi) a statement of the effect of full acceptance of the offer upon its earnings and assets and liabilities; and

(vii) a summary of the principal contents of each material contract (not being a contract entered into in the ordinary course of business) entered into by the offeror or any of its subsidiaries during the period beginning two years before the commencement of the offer period, including particulars of dates, parties, terms and conditions and any consideration passing to or from the offeror or any of its subsidiaries;

(b) if the offeror is other than a company referred to in (a) above, the offer document must contain:

(i) in respect of the offeror, the information described in (a) above (so far as appropriate) and such further information as the Panel may require in the particular circumstances of the case

(ii) in respect of any person who has made (or proposes to make or increase) an investment in the offeror for the purposes of the offer such that he has or will have a potential direct or indirect interest in any part of the capital of the offeree company which the Panel regards as equity capital, details of his identity and of his interest in the offeror and such further information as the Panel may require in the particular circumstances of the case and

(iii) in respect of any person not included in (ii) above whose pre-existing interest in the offeror is such that he has a potential direct or indirect interest of 5% or more in any part of the capital of the offeree company which the Panel regards as equity capital, details of his identity and of his interest in the offeror and such further information as the Panel may require in the particular circumstances of the case

(c) the offer document must contain summary details of any current ratings and outlooks publicly accorded to the offeror and the offeree company by ratings agencies prior to the commencement of the offer period, any changes made to previous ratings or outlooks during the offer period, and a summary of the reasons given, if any, for any such changes;

(d) the offer document (including, where relevant, any revised offer document) must include:

(i) a heading stating "If you are in doubt about this offer you should consult an independent financial adviser authorised under the FSMA";

(ii) the date when the document is published, the name and address of the offeror (including, where the offeror is a company, the type of company and the address of its registered office);

(iii) the identity of any person acting in concert with the offeror and, to the extent that it is known, the offeree company, including, in the case of a company, its type, registered office and relationship with the offeror and, where possible, with the offeree company.

(iv) details of each class of security for which the offer is made, including whether those securities will be transferred "cum" or "ex" any dividend and the maximum and minimum percentages of those securities which the offeror undertakes to acquire;

(v) the terms of the offer, including the consideration offered for each class of security, the total consideration offered and particulars of the way in which the consideration is to be paid in accordance with *Rule 31.8* or, in the case of a scheme of arrangement, Section 10 of Appendix 7;

(vi) all conditions to which the offer is subject;

(vii) particulars of all documents required, and procedures to be followed, for acceptance of the offer or, in the case of a scheme of arrangement, for voting;

(viii) the middle market quotations for the securities to be acquired, and (in the case of a securities exchange offer) securities offered, for the first business day in each of the six months immediately before the date of the offer document, for the last business day before the commencement of the offer period and for the latest available date before the publication of the offer document, together with the source (or, if any of the securities are not admitted to trading, any information available as to the number and price of transactions which have taken place during the preceding six months, together with the source, or an appropriate negative statement);

(ix) details of any agreements or arrangements to which the offeror is party which relate to the circumstances in which it may or may not invoke or seek to invoke a condition to its offer and the consequences of its doing so, including details of any break fees payable as a result;

(x) details of any irrevocable commitment or letter of intent which the offeror or any person acting in concert with it has procured in relation to relevant securities of the offeree company (or, if appropriate, the offeror)

(xi) in the case of a securities exchange offer, full particulars of the securities being offered, including the rights attaching to them, the first dividend or interest payment in which the securities will participate and how the securities will rank for dividends or interest, capital and redemption; a statement indicating the effect of acceptance on the capital and income position of the offeree company's shareholders; and details of any applications for admission to listing or admission to trading that have been or will be made in any jurisdiction in respect of the securities;

(xii) a summary of the provisions of *Rule 8* (see the Panel's website at www.thetakeoverpanel.org.uk);

(xiii) the national law which will govern contracts concluded between the offeror and holders of the offeree company 's securities as a result of the offer and the competent courts;

(xiv) the compensation (if any) offered for the removal of rights pursuant to *Article 11* of the *Directive* together with particulars of the way in which the compensation is to be paid and the method employed in determining it;

(xv) any post-offer undertakings made by the offeror (see *Rule 19.7*);

(xvi) a summary of any offer-related arrangement or other agreement, arrangement or commitment permitted under, or excluded from, *Rule 21.2*;

(xvii) a list of the documents which the offeror has published on a website in accordance with *Rules 26.1* and *26.2* and the address of the website on which the documents are published ; and

(xviii) any profit forecast or quantified financial benefits statement and any related reports or confirmations required by *Rule 28*.

(e) the offer document must contain information on the offeree company on the same basis as set out in (a)(i) to (v) above;

(f) the offer document must contain a description of how the offer is to be financed and the source(s) of the finance. Details must be provided of the debt facilities or other instruments entered into in order to finance the offer and to refinance the existing debt or working capital facilities of the offeree company and, in particular:

(i) the amount of each facility or instrument;

(ii) the repayment terms;

(iii) interest rates, including any "step up" or other variation provided for;

(iv) any security provided;

(v) a summary of the key covenants;

(vi) the names of the principal financing banks; and

(vii) if applicable, details of the time by which the offeror will be required to refinance the acquisition facilities and of the consequences of its not doing so by that time; and

(g) if any document published by the offeror contains a comparison of the value of the offer with previous prices of the offeree company 's shares, a comparison between the current value of the offer and the price of the offeree company's shares on the last business day prior to the commencement of the offer period must be prominently included, no matter what other comparisons are made.

(*Rule 24.3*).

(3) *Interests and dealings*

The offer document must state

(a) details of any relevant securities of the offeree company in which the offeror has an interest or in respect of which he has a right to subscribe, specifying the nature of the interests or rights concerned. Similar details of any short positions (whether conditional or absolute and whether in the money or otherwise), including any short position under a derivative, any agreement to sell or any delivery obligation or right to require another person to purchase or take delivery, must also be stated;

(b) the same details as in (a) above in relation to each of
  (i) the directors of the offeror;
  (ii) any other person acting in concert with the offeror; and
  (iii) any person with whom the offeror (or any person acting in concert with the offeror) has any arrangement of the kind referred to in Note 11 on the definition of acting in concert.

(c) in the case of a securities exchange offer, the same details as in (*a*) above in respect of any relevant securities of the offeror in relation to each of the persons listed in (*b*) above; and

(d) details of any relevant securities of the offeree company and (in the case of a securities exchange offer only) the offeror which the offeror (or any person acting in concert with it) has borrowed or lent, save for any borrowed shares which have been either on-lent or sold.

If, in the case of any of the persons referred to in *Rule 24.4*(a) there are no interests or short positions to be disclosed, this fact should be stated. This will not apply to b(iii) (above) if there are no such arrangements.

If any person referred to above has dealt in any relevant securities of the offeree company (or, in the case of a securities exchange offer only, of the offeror) during the period beginning 12 months prior to the offer period and ending with the latest practicable date prior to the publication of the offer document, the details, including dates, must be stated. If no such dealings have taken place, this fact should be stated.

(*Rule 24.4*).

(4) *Directors' emoluments*

The offer document must state (in the case of a securities exchange offer only) whether and in what manner the emoluments of the offeror directors will be affected by the acquisition of the offeree company or by any other associated transaction. If there will be no effect, this must be stated.

(*Rule 24.5*).

(5) *Special arrangements*

Unless otherwise agreed with the Panel, the offer document must contain a statement as to whether or not any agreement, arrangement or understanding (including any compensation arrangement) exists between the offeror (or any person acting in concert with it) and any of the directors, recent directors, shareholders or recent shareholders of the offeree company, or any person interested or recently interested in shares of the offeree company, having any connection with or dependence upon the offer, and full particulars of any such agreement, arrangement or understanding. See also Rule 16.2.

(*Rule 24.6*).

(6) *Incorporation of obligations and rights*

The offer document must state the time allowed for acceptance of the offer and any alternative offer and must incorporate language which appropriately reflects Notes 4–8 on *Rule 10* and those parts of *Rules 13.5*(a) and *13*(b) (if applicable), *17* and *31–34* which impose timing obligations or confer rights or impose restrictions on offerors, offeree companies or shareholders of offeree companies.

(*Rule 24.7*).

(7) *Cash confirmation*

When the offer is for cash or includes an element of cash, the offer document must include confirmation by an appropriate third party (eg the offeror's bank or financial adviser) that resources are available to the offeror sufficient to satisfy full acceptance of the offer. (*Rule 24.8*).

(8) *Ultimate owner of securities acquired*

Unless otherwise agreed with the Panel, the offer document must contain a statement as to whether or not any securities acquired in pursuance of the offer will be transferred to any other persons, together with the names of the parties to any such agreement, arrangement or understanding and particulars of all interests in the securities of the offeree company held by such persons, or a statement that no such interests are held.

(Rule 24.9).

(9) *Admission to listing and admission to trading conditions*
Where securities are offered as consideration and it is intended that they should be admitted to listing on the Official List or to trading on AIM, the relevant admission to listing or admission to trading condition should, except with the consent of the Panel, be in terms which ensure that it is capable of being satisfied only when the decision to admit the securities to listing or trading has been announced by the Listing Authority or the Stock Exchange, as applicable. Where securities are offered as consideration and it is intended that they should be admitted to listing or to trading on any other investment exchange or market, the Panel should be consulted.
(Rule 24.10).

(10) *Estimated value of unquoted paper consideration*
When the offer involves the issue of securities of a class which is not admitted to trading, the offer document and any subsequent circular from the offeror must contain an estimate of the value of such securities by an appropriate adviser.
(Rule 24.11).

(11) *No set-off of consideration*
The offer document must contain a statement to the effect that, except with the consent of the Panel, settlement of the consideration to which any shareholder is entitled under the offer will be implemented in full in accordance with the terms of the offer without regard to any lien, right of set-off, counterclaim or other analogous right to which the offeror may otherwise be, or claim to be, entitled against such shareholder.
(Rule 24.12).

(12) *Arrangements in relation to dealings*
The offer document must disclose any arrangements of the kind referred to in Note 6(b) on *Rule 8* which exist between the offeror (or any person acting in concert with the offeror) and any other person; if there are no such arrangements, this should be stated. If the directors or their financial advisers are aware of any such arrangements between any other associate of the offeror and any other person, such arrangements must also be disclosed.
(Rule 24.13).

(13) *Cash underwritten alternatives which may be shut off*
The procedure for acceptance of a cash underwritten alternative which is capable of being shut off must be prominently stated in relevant documents and acceptance forms. In particular, it must be made clear (in the offer document, the acceptance form and any subsequent documents) whether shareholders must lodge their certificates by the closing date of the cash underwritten alternative, in addition to their completed acceptance forms, in order to receive cash. *(Rule 24.14).*

Incorporation of information by reference

(a) In addition to the requirements under *Rule 24.3(a)(iii)* and *(iv)* (and insofar as they refer to *Rules 24.3(a)(iii)* and *(iv)*, *Rules 24.3(b)* and *(e)*) for certain information to be incorporated into an offer document by reference to a website, information that is required to be included in a document under other Rules may be incorporated by reference to another source with the Panel's consent.

(b) Information that is incorporated into a document by reference to another source must be published on a website by no later than the date on which the document is published. The information published on a website must be published:

(i) in a form that may be printed, read and retained by the person to whom the document must be sent; and

(ii) in a "read-only" format so that it may not be amended or altered in any way.

(c) If a person is sent a document which incorporates information by reference to another source, that person may request a copy of the information so incorporated in hard copy form. If such a request is made, the party which published the document must ensure that a copy of the requested information is sent to the relevant person in hard copy form as soon as possible and in any event within two business days of the request being received by the relevant party.

(d) Any document which incorporates information by reference to another source (and any related website notification) must contain a statement that a shareholder, person with information rights or other person to whom it is sent may request a copy of any such information in hard copy form. Attention should be drawn to the fact that a hard copy of the information will not be sent to that person unless requested and details must be provided of how a hard copy may be obtained (including an address in the United Kingdom and a telephone number to which requests may be submitted).

(Rule 24.15).

Fees and expenses

(a) The offer document must contain an estimate of the aggregate fees and expenses expected to be incurred by the offeror in connection with the offer and, in addition, separate estimates of the fees and expenses expected to be incurred in relation to:
   (i) financing arrangements;
   (ii) financial and corporate broking advice;
   (iii) legal advice;
   (iv) accounting advice;
   (v) public relations advice;
   (vi) other professional services (including, for example, management consultants, actuaries and specialist valuers); and
   (vii) other costs and expenses.

(b) Where any fee is variable between defined limits, a range must be given in respect of the aggregate fees and expenses and of the fees and expenses of each relevant category, setting out the expected maximum and minimum amounts payable.

(c) Where the fees and expenses payable within a particular category are likely to exceed the estimated maximum previously disclosed by 10% or more, the offeror must promptly disclose to the Panel revised estimates of the aggregate fees and expenses expected to be incurred in relation to the offer and of the fees and expenses expected to be incurred within that category. The Panel may require the public disclosure of such revised estimates where it considers this to be appropriate.

(d) Where the final fees and expenses actually paid within a particular category exceed the amount publicly disclosed as the estimated maximum payable by 10% or more, the offeror must promptly disclose to the Panel the final amount paid in respect of that category. The Panel may require the public disclosure of such final amount where it considers this to be appropriate.

(*Rule 24.16*).

Rule 25 The Offeree board circular

(a) The board of the offeree company must, normally within 14 days of the publication of the offer document, send a circular to the offeree company's shareholders and persons with information rights, in accordance with *Rule 30.1* and must, at the same time, make it readily available to its employee representatives or, where there are no employee representatives, to the employees themselves.

(b) On the day of publication the offeree company must publish the circular on a website in accordance with *Rule 26.1* and announce via a RIS that it has been so published.

(*Rule 25.1*).

(1) *Views of the offeree board on the offer, including the offeror's plans for the company and its employees*

(a) The offeree board circular must set out the opinion of the board on the offer (including any alternative offers) and the board's reasons for forming its opinion and must include its views on

- the effects of implementation of the offer on all the company's interests, including, specifically, employment, and
- the offeror's strategic plans for the offeree company and their likely repercussions on employment and the locations of the offeree company's places of business, as set out in the offer document pursuant to *Rule 24.2*,

(b) In addition the circular must include the substance of the advice given to the board of the offeree company by the independent adviser appointed under *Rule 3.1*.

(*Rule 25.2*).

(2) *Financial and other information*

The offeree board circular must contain a description of any known material change in the financial or trading position of the offeree company which has occurred since the end of the last financial period for which either audited financial information or interim financial information has been published or provide an appropriate negative statement.

(*Rule 25.3*).

(3) *Interests and dealings*

The offeree board circular must state

(a) details of any relevant securities of the offeror in which the offeree company or any of the directors of the offeree company has an interest or in respect of which it or he has a right to subscribe, in each case specifying the nature of the interests or rights concerned. Similar details of any short positions (whether conditional or absolute and whether in the money or otherwise), including any short position under a derivative, any agreement to sell or any delivery obligation or right to require another person to purchase or take delivery, must also be stated;

(b) the same details as in (*a*) above in respect of any relevant securities of the offeree company in relation to each of

(i) the directors of the offeree company;

(ii) any other person acting in concert with the offeree company; and

(iii) any person with whom the offeree company or any person acting in concert with the offeree company has an arrangement of the kind referred to in Note 11 on the definition of acting in concert;

(c) in the case of a securities exchange offer, the same details as in (a) above in respect of any relevant securities of the offeror in relation to each of the persons listed in (b)(ii)and (iii) above;

(d) details of any relevant securities of the offeree company and (in the case of a securities exchange offer only) the offeror which the offeree company or any person acting in concert with the offeree company has borrowed or lent, (including for these purposes any financial collateral arrangements of the kind referred to in Note 4 on *Rule 4.6*) save for any borrowed shares which have been either on-lent or sold; and

(e) whether the directors of the offeree company intend, in respect of their own beneficial shareholdings, to accept the offer (and if there are alternative offers, and if so required by the Panel, which alternative they intend to elect for) or to reject the offer.

If, in the case of any of the persons referred to above, there are no interests or short positions to be disclosed, this fact should be stated. This will not apply to (*b*)(iii) if there are no such arrangements.
If any person referred to in (a) above has dealt in any relevant securities of the offeree company or the offeror between the start of the offer period and the latest practicable date prior to the publication of the circular, the details, including dates, must be stated. If any person referred to in (b)(ii)–(iii) has dealt in relevant securities of the offeree company (or, in the case of a securities exchange offer only, the offeror) during the same period, similar details must be stated. In all cases, if no such dealings have taken place this fact should be stated.
(*Rule 25.4*).

(4) *Directors' service contracts*
The offeree board circular must contain particulars of all service contracts of any director or proposed director of the offeree company with the company or any of its subsidiaries. If there are none, this should be stated. If any such contracts have been entered into or amended within six months of the date of the document, particulars must be given in respect of the earlier contracts (if any) which have been replaced or amended as well as in respect of the current contracts. If there have been none, this should be stated.
(*Rule 25.5*).

(5) *Arrangements in relation to dealings*
The offeree board circular must disclose any arrangements of the kind referred to in Note 11 on the definition of acting in concert which exist between the offeree company, or any person acting in concert with the offeree company, and any other person. If there are no such arrangements, this should be stated.
(*Rule 25.6*).

(6) *Other information*
The offeree board circular must contain
(a) a summary of the principal contents of each material contract (not being a contract entered into in the ordinary course of business) entered into by the offeree company or any of its subsidiaries during the period beginning two years before the commencement of the offer period, including particulars of dates, parties, terms and conditions and any consideration passing to or from the offeree company or any of its subsidiaries;
(b) details of any irrevocable commitment or letter of intent which the offeree company or any of its associates has procured in relation to relevant securities of the offeree company (or, if appropriate, the offeror);
(c) any post-offer undertaking or post-offer intention statement made by the offeree company (see *Rules 19.7 and 19.8*);
(d) a list of the documents which the offeree company has published on a website in accordance with *Rules 26.2* and *26.3* and the address of the website on which the documents are published; and
(e) any profit forecast or quantified financial benefits statement and any related reports or confirmations required by *Rule 28*.
(*Rule 25.7*).

Fees and expenses

The offeree board circular must contain an estimate of the aggregate fees and expenses expected to be incurred by the offeree company in connection with the offer and, in addition, separate estimates of the fees and expenses expected to be incurred in relation to the matters specified in paragraphs (ii) to (vii) of *Rule*

24.16(a). The other provisions of *Rule 24.16* and Note 2 on *Rule 24.16* also apply as if references to the offeror were references to the offeree company.

(*Rule 25.8*).

The employee representatives' opinion and the pension scheme trustees' opinion

Where the board of the offeree company receives in good time before publication of its circular on the offer, an opinion from employee representatives on the effects of the offer on employment or an opinion from the trustees of any of its pension scheme(s) on the effects of the offer on the pension scheme(s), any such opinion must be appended to the circular. Where any such opinion is received but not in good time before publication of the offeree board circular, the offeree company must promptly publish the opinion on a website and announce via a RIS that it has been so published, provided that it is received no later than 14 days after the date on which the offer becomes or is declared wholly unconditional.

(*Rule 25.9*).

Rule 26 Documents, announcements and information to be published on a website during an offer

The following documents, announcements and information must be published on a website by the offeror or offeree company, as relevant,by no later than 12 noon on the business day following the date of the relevant document, announcement or information:

(i) any document or information in relation to an offer sent to shareholders, persons with information rights or other relevant persons in accordance with Rule 30.1; or

(ii) any announcement (other than an announcement referred to in Note 8 below) published via a RIS (whether related to the offer or not).

Any such document, announcement or information must include the address of the website on which it will be published. This address must be for either the webpage on which the relevant document, announcement or information may be found or a webpage which includes a clear link to the relevant webpage.

(*Rule 26.1*).

Documents to be published on a website following the announcement of a firm offer

The following documents must be published on a website by no later than 12 noon on the business day following the announcement of a firm intention to make an offer or, if later, the date of the relevant document)

(a) memorandum and articles of association of the offeror or the offeree company or equivalent documents;

(b) any report, letter, valuation or other document any part of which is exhibited or referred to in any document published by or on behalf of the offeror or the offeree company (other than the service contracts of offeree company directors and any material contracts that are not entered into in connection with the offer);

(c) written consents of the financial advisers (Rule 23.3);

(d) any material contract entered into by an offeror or the offeree company, or any of their respective subsidiaries, in connection with the offer that is described in the offer document or offeree board circular (as appropriate) in compliance with Rule 24.3(a), Rule 24.3(b) or Rule 25.7(a);or entered into after the publication of the offer document or offerree board circular(as appropriate)

(e) where a profit forecast has been made:
  (i) the reports of the auditors or consultant accountants and of the financial advisers (Rule 28.3); and
  (ii) the letters giving the consent of the auditors or consultant accountants and of the financial advisers to the publication of the relevant document with the report in the form and context in which it is included or, if appropriate, to the continued use of the report in a subsequent document (Rules 28.4 and 28.5);

(f) where an asset valuation has been made:
  (i) the valuation certificate and associated report or schedule containing details of the aggregate valuation (Rule 29.5(c)); and
  (ii) a letter stating that the valuer has given and not withdrawn his consent to the publication of his name in the relevant document (Rule 29.5(b));

(g) where the Panel has given consent to aggregation of dealings, a full list of all dealings (Note 2 on Rule 24.4); and

(h) all derivative contracts which in whole or in part have been disclosed under Rules 24.4(a) and (c) and 25.4(a) and (c) or in accordance with Rules 8.1, 8.2 or 8.4. Documents in respect of the last mentioned must be published from the time the offer document or the offeree board circular is published or from the time of disclosure, whichever is the later.

(*Rule* 26.2).

Documents to be published on a website following the making of an offer

The following documents must be published on a website from the time the offer document or offeree board circular, as appropriate, is published (or, if later, the date of the relevant document):

(a) memorandum and articles of association of the offeror or the offeree company or equivalent documents;

(b) any report, letter, valuation or other document any part of which is exhibited or referred to in any document published by or on behalf of the offeror or the offeree company (other than the service contracts of offeree company directors and any material contracts that are not entered into in connection with the offer);

(c) any written consents of an independent financial adviser to the inclusion of its advice in the relevant document in the form and context in which it is included (*Rule 23.3(a)*);

(d) any material contract entered into by an offeror or the offeree company, or any of their respective subsidiaries, in connection with the offer that is:
  - described in the offer document or offeree board circular (as appropriate) in compliance with *Rule 24.3(a)*, *Rule 24.3(b)* or *Rule 25.7(a)*; or
  - entered into after the publication of the offer document or offeree board circular (as appropriate);

(e) where a profit forecast or quantified financial benefits statement has been published:
  - the reports of the reporting accountants and of the financial advisers *(Rules 28.1(a)* and *(b))*; and
  - the written consents of the reporting accountants and of the financial advisers to the inclusion of their reports in the relevant document in the form and context in which they are included (*Rule 23.3(b)*) and, if appropriate, the confirmations that their reports continue to apply (*Rule 27.2(d)*);

(f) where an asset valuation has been published:
  - the valuation certificate and associated report or schedule containing details of the aggregate valuation (*Rule 29.5(c)*); and
  - (ii) the written consent of the independent valuer to the inclusion of its opinion on value in the relevant document in the form and context in which it is included (*Rule 23.3(c)*) and, if appropriate, the confirmation that its report continues to apply (*Rule 27.2(d)*);

(g) where the Panel has given consent to aggregation of dealings, a full list of all dealings (Note 2 on *Rule 24.4*); and

(h) all derivative contracts which in whole or in part have been disclosed under *Rules 24.4(a)* and *(c)* and *25.4(a)* and *(c)* or in accordance with Rules 8.1, 8.2 or 8.4. Documents in respect of the last mentioned must be published from the time the offer document or the offeree board circular is published or from the time of disclosure, whichever is the later.

(*Rule 26.3*).

Rule 27 Material changes and subsequent documents

Material changes. Except with the consent of the Panel, following the publication of the initial offer document or offeree board circular (as appropriate) and until the end of the offer period, the offeror or the offeree company (as appropriate) must promptly announce: (a) any changes in information disclosed in any document or announcement published by it in connection with the offer which are material in the context of that document or announcement; and (b) any material new information which would have been required to have been disclosed in any previous document or announcement published during the offer period, had it been known at the time. Where an announcement is required to be made under Rule 27.1(a),the Panel may, in addition, require a document setting out the relevant information to be:

(a) sent to shareholders in the offeree company and persons with information rights; and

(b) made readily available to the offeree company's employee representatives (or, where there are no employee representatives to the employees themselves) and to the trustees of the offeree company's pension scheme(s).

(*Rule 27.1*).

Subsequent documents. If, following the publication of the initial offer document or offeree board circular (as appropriate) and before the end of the offer period, an offeror or the offeree company publishes any subsequent document in connection with the offer, that document must include:

(a) any changes in information disclosed in any previous document published by it in connection with the offer which are material in the context of that document (or a statement that there have been no such material changes); and

(b) details of any material changes to the matters listed in Rule 27.2(b) (in the case of an offeror) or in Rule 27.2(c) (in the case of the offeree company) which have occurred since the publication of any previous document published by it in connection with the offer (or a statement that there have been no such material changes).

In the case of an offeror, the matters referred to in (b) are as follows:

(i) its intentions with regard to the matters referred to in *Rule 24.2*;

(ii) any known significant change in its or the offeree company's financial or trading position (to the extent required under *Rule 24.3(a)(v)*) (see above *Rule 24.3*, para *(2)(v)*);

(iii) material contracts (*Rule 24.3(a)(vii)*) (see above *Rule 24.3*, para *(2)(vii)*);

(iv) ratings and outlooks (*Rule 24.3(c)*) (see above *Rule 24.3*), para *(2)(c)*);

(v) the terms of the offer (*Rule 24.3(d)(v)*) (see above *Rule 24.3*, para *(2)(d)(v)*);

(vi) any agreements or arrangements which relate to the invocation of the conditions to its offer (*Rule 24.3(d)(ix)*) (see above *Rule 24.3*, para *(2)(d)(ix)*);

(vii) irrevocable commitments and letters of intent (*Rule 24.3(d)(x)*) (see above *Rule 24.3*, para *(2)(d)(x)*);
(viii) post-offer undertakings (*Rule 24.3(d)(xv)*) (see above *Rule 24.3*, para *(2)(d)(xv)*);
(ix) any offer-related arrangements etc permitted under, or excluded from, *Rule 21.2 (Rule 24.3(d)(xvi))* (see above *Rule 24.3*, para *(2)(d)(xvi)*);
(x) profit forecasts and quantified financial benefits statements (*Rule 24.3(d)(xviii)*) (see above *Rule 24.3*, para *(2)(d)(xviii)*);
(xi) financing arrangements (*Rule 24.3(f)*);
(xii) interests and dealings in relevant securities (*Rule 24.4*);
(xiii) the effect of the offer on the emoluments of the offeror's directors (*Rule 24.5*);
(xiv) any special arrangements, including management incentivisation arrangements (*Rule 16.2* and *Rule 24.6*);
(xv) the ultimate owner of any securities acquired (*Rule 24.9*);
(xvi) any arrangements of the kind referred to in Note 11 on the definition of acting in concert (*Rule 24.13*); and
(xvii) fees and expenses (to the extent required under *Rule 24.16*).

(c) In the case of the offeree company, the matters referred to in *Rule 27.2(a)(ii)* are as follows:
(i) its opinion on the offer and the other matters referred to in *Rule 25.2(a)*;
(ii) the substance of the independent financial adviser's advice (*Rule 25.2(b)*);
(iii) any known significant changes in its financial or trading position (*Rule 25.3*);
(iv) interests and dealings in relevant securities (*Rule 25.4*);
(v) the service contracts of the offeree company's directors (*Rule 25.5*);
(vi) any arrangements of the kind referred to in Note 11 on the definition of acting in concert (*Rule 25.6*);
(vii) material contracts (*Rule 25.7(a)*);
(viii) irrevocable commitments and letters of intent (*Rule 25.7(b)*);
(ix) post-offer undertakings and post-offer intention statements (*Rule 25.7(c)*);
(x) profit forecasts and quantified financial benefits statements (*Rule 25.7(e)*); and
(xi) fees and expenses (to the extent required under *Rule 25.8*).

(d) If any document or announcement published by the offeror or the offeree company included a profit forecast, a quantified financial benefits statement or an asset valuation, any document subsequently published by that party in connection with the offer must, unless superseded by information included in the new document, include a statement by the directors of that party confirming: (i) that the profit forecast, quantified financial benefits statement or asset valuation (as appropriate) remains valid; (ii) where reports were obtained on a profit forecast or quantified financial benefits statement, that the reporting accountants and financial adviser(s) have confirmed that their reports continue to apply; and (iii) where an opinion on value was obtained on an asset valuation, that the independent valuer has confirmed that its opinion continues to apply.

(*Rule 27.2*).

Profit forecasts and quantified financial benefits statements

Rule 28 Standards of care

Except with the consent of the Panel, if, during an offer period (or in an announcement which commences an offer period), the offeree company or a securities exchange offeror publishes a profit forecast or a quantified financial benefits statement, the document or announcement in which the forecast or statement is first published must include:

(a) a report from its reporting accountants stating that, in their opinion, the forecast or statement has been properly compiled on the basis stated and (in the case of a profit forecast only) that the basis of accounting used is consistent with the company's accounting policies; and
(b) a report from its financial adviser(s) stating that, in its (or their) opinion, the forecast or statement has been prepared with due care and consideration.

Except with the consent of the Panel, if the offeree company or a securities exchange offeror published a profit forecast before the offer period commenced but after it received or made an approach with regard to a possible offer, the offer document or offeree board circular (as appropriate), or any earlier document or announcement published during the offer period in which the profit forecast is referred to, must repeat the profit forecast and include the reports from its reporting accountants and financial adviser(s) specified in Rule 28.1(a)(i) and (ii).

Except with the consent of the Panel, and subject to Note 3 (management buy-outs and offers by controllers), if the offeree company or a securities exchange offeror published a profit forecast before it received or made an approach with regard to a possible offer, the offer document or offeree board circular (as appropriate), or any earlier document or announcement published during the offer period in which the profit forecast is referred to, must:

(a) repeat the profit forecast and include a statement by the directors that it remains valid and confirmations by the directors that the profit forecast has been properly compiled on the basis of the assumptions stated and that the basis of accounting used is confirmations"); or
(b) include a statement by the directors that the profit forecast is no longer valid and an explanation of why that is the case; or
(c) include a new profit forecast for the relevant period and the reports from its reporting accountants and financial adviser(s) specified in Rule 28.1(a)(i) and (ii).

(*Rule 28.1*).

Profit forecasts for future financial periods.

The Panel will normally grant a dispensation from the requirement to include reports from reporting accountants and the financial adviser(s) in the case of a profit forecast for a financial period ending more than 15 months from the date on which it is, or was, first published. Where such a dispensation is granted, the offer document or offeree board circular (as appropriate), or any earlier document or announcement published during the offer period in which the profit forecast is referred to or first published, must include the directors' confirmations referred to in Rule 28.1(c)(i). Alternatively, in the case of a profit forecast which was published before the offer period commenced, the document or announcement may include a statement by the directors that the profit forecast is no longer valid and an explanation of why that is the case.

Except with the consent of the Panel, if, during the offer period (or in an announcement which commences an offer period), the offeree company or a securities exchange offeror either publishes for the first time or repeats a profit forecast for a future financial year, the document or announcement must include a corresponding profit forecast for the current financial year and for each intervening financial year. The requirements of Rule 28.1(a), (b) or (c)(i) (as appropriate) will apply to each such forecast for a financial year ending 15 months or less from the date on which it is, or was, first published and the requirements of Rule 28.2(a) will normally apply to each such forecast for a financial year ending more than 15 months from the date on which it is, or was, first published.

(*Rule 28.2*).

Compilation of profit forecasts and quantified financial benefits statements.

Any profit forecast or quantified financial benefits statement must be properly compiled and must be prepared with due care and consideration. The profit forecast or quantified financial benefits statement, and the assumptions on which it is based, are the responsibility of the relevant party to the offer and its directors.

A profit forecast (and the assumptions stated) or a quantified financial benefits statement (and the details included in accordance with Rule 28.6) must be:

(a) understandable: it must not be so complex or include such extensive disclosure that it cannot be readily understood;
(b) reliable: it must be supported by a thorough analysis of the offeree company's and/or the offeror's business and must represent factual and not hypothetical strategies, plans and risk analysis; and
(c) comparable (in the case of a profit forecast only): it should be capable of justification by comparison with outcomes in the form of historical financial information.

A forecast of profit before tax should disclose separately any nonrecurrent items and tax charges if they are expected to be abnormally high or low.

(*Rule 28.3*).

Assumptions and basis of beliefs.

When a profit forecast is included in any document or announcement published during an offer period (or in an announcement which commences an offer period), the document or announcement must include the principal assumptions on which the profit forecast is based.

The assumptions included for a profit forecast or bases of belief included for a quantified financial benefits statement should provide useful information as to its reasonableness and reliability. They must:

(a) be readily understandable;
(b) be specific and precise; and
(c) not relate to the general accuracy of the estimates underlying the profit forecast or the quantified financial benefits statement.

There must be a clear distinction between assumptions or bases of belief about factors which the directors (or other members of the company's management) can influence and those which they cannot

(*Rule 28.4*).

Profit estimates.

Rule 28.1 does not apply to a profit estimate included in:

(a) a preliminary statement of annual results which complies with the relevant provisions of the UKLA Rules;
(b) a half-yearly financial report which complies with the relevant provisions of the UKLA Rules, the AIM Rules for Companies or the ISDX Growth Market Rules for Issuers; or

(c) an interim management statement, or other interim financial information, which is published by virtue of a regulatory requirement and which has been prepared in accordance with the reporting framework set out in International Accounting Standard 34.

(*Rule 28.5*).

Disclosure requirements for quantified financial benefits statements.

When a quantified financial benefits statement is included in any document or announcement published during an offer period (or in an announcement which commences an offer period), the document or announcement must include:

(a) the bases of belief supporting the statement (identifying the principal assumptions and sources of information);
(b) an analysis, explanation and quantification of the constituent elements sufficient to enable the context and relative importance of those elements to be understood;
(c) a base figure where any comparison is made with historical financial performance or with existing cost bases and structures;
(d) details of any disbenefits expected to arise;
(e) in the case of a statement falling under paragraph (a) of the definition of a "quantified financial benefits statement", a statement that the expected financial benefits will accrue as a direct result of the success of the offer and could not be achieved independently of the offer;
(f) an indication of when the financial benefits are expected to be realised;
(g) an indication of whether the expected financial benefits will be recurring, clearly identifying any non-recurring benefit(s); and
(h) the recurring and non-recurring costs of realising the expected financial benefits.

(*Rule 28.6*).

Publication of investment analysts' forecast on website.

Where, during the offer period, the offeree company or a securities exchange offeror publishes on its website profit forecasts relating to it that are derived from investment analysts' forecasts, the forecasts on the website must be based on all forecasts provided by investment analysts who have published such forecasts, excluding:

(a) any forecasts which pre-date the publication of the company's latest preliminary statement of annual results or half-yearly financial report (as appropriate); and
(b) any forecasts by investment analysts whose employer is controlled by, controls or is under the same control as any party to the offer or a connected adviser to any party to the offer.

In addition to the exclusions in the preceding paragraph an investment analyst's forecast may exceptionally be excluded from the forecasts on the company's website if it is wholly anomalous or has been prepared on a wholly different basis from that of the other investment analysts.

Except with the consent of the Panel, the following requirements must be complied with (failing which, all investment analysts' forecasts must be removed from the website upon the commencement of the offer period):

(a) for each line in respect of which forecasts are published on the website, the highest and lowest figures forecast by any investment analyst must be stated, together with the arithmetic mean of all investment analysts' forecasts (a "*consensus forecast*");
(b) the name of each organisation whose forecasts have been included in the calculation of the consensus forecast, and the dates of the forecasts, must be stated;

(c) if any analyst's forecast has been excluded from the calculation of the consensus forecast, the name of the organisation, the date of the forecast and the reason for its exclusion, must be stated;
(d) during the offer period, the relevant section of the website must be kept up-to-date by including any new forecasts promptly after their publication and promptly excluding any forecasts which pre-date the publication of the latest preliminary statement of annual results or half-yearly financial report; and
(e) it must be prominently stated that the investment analysts' forecasts are not endorsed by the company and that they have not been reviewed or reported on in accordance with the requirements of Rule 28.1(a).

Subject to Rule 28.8, any reference to or quotation from a consensus or other third party forecast, other than publishing investment analysts' forecasts on a website in accordance with the requirements of this Rule 28.7, will be subject to Note 6 on Rule 28.1.

(*Rule 28.7*).

References to consensus forecasts relating to another party to the offer

Except with the consent of the Panel, if, during the offer period (or in an announcement which commences an offer period), a party to the offer ("party A") wishes to refer to investment analysts' forecasts relating to any other party to the offer ("party B"), party A must refer to either:

(a) a consensus forecast (see Rule 28.7(c)) published on party B's website in accordance with the requirements of Rule 28.7; or
(b) if no such consensus forecast has been published on party B's website, a consensus forecast compiled by party A in accordance with the requirements of Rule 28.7.

Where party A has referred to a consensus forecast relating to party B, any subsequent reference to that consensus forecast by party B will not be subject to Rule 28.1(a), provided that party B does not endorse the consensus forecast.

Any document or announcement which includes a reference by party A to a consensus forecast relating to party B must make clear whether or not the reference is being made with the agreement or approval of party B. Where the consensus forecast is referred to in any document or announcement which is published by party A with the agreement or approval of party B, or at a time when the offer is a recommended offer, the consensus forecast will be treated as having been endorsed and published by party B and Rule 28.1(a) will therefore apply.

(*Rule 28.8*).

Asset valuations

Rule 29

Valuations to be reported on if given in connection with an offer. When a valuation of assets is given in connection with an offer, it must be supported by the opinion of a named independent valuer.

- *Type of asset*
  This Rule applies not only to land, buildings and plant and equipment but also to other assets (eg contracts, stocks, intangible assets and individual parts of a business). Where such assets are involved, the Panel should be consulted in advance.

- *The valuer*
  In relation to land, buildings and plant and machinery, a valuer should be a corporate member of The Royal Institution of Chartered Surveyors or The Institute of Revenues Rating and Valuation or some other person approved by the Panel. In respect of other types of asset, the valuer should be an appropriately qualified person approved by the Panel. The valuer must be able to demonstrate that he meets any legal or regulatory requirements which apply in the circumstances in which the particular valuation is required and either
  (i) that he has, in respect of the particular type of property or asset, sufficient current local, national and international knowledge (as appropriate) of the particular market and the skills and understanding necessary to undertake the valuation competently; or
  (ii) where he satisfies (i) above, except that he has insufficient current knowledge, that he has the assistance of a person who has such knowledge and the skills and understanding necessary to provide the assistance required by the valuer.
- *In connection with an offer*. In certain cases, an offer document or defence circular includes a statement of assets reproducing directors' estimates of asset values published with the company's accounts in accordance with *Schedule 7, Part 1* of the *Large and Medium Sized Companies and Groups (Accounts and Reports) Regulations 2008*. The Panel will not regard such estimates as 'given in connection with an offer' unless asset values are a particularly significant factor in assessing the offer and the estimates are, accordingly, given considerably more prominence in the offer documents or circulars than merely being referred to in a note to a statement of assets in an appendix. In these circumstances, such estimates must be supported, subject to *Rule 29.2(e)*, by an independent valuer in accordance with this *Rule*.
- *Another party's assets*. A party to a takeover situation will not normally be permitted to issue a valuation, appraisal or calculation of worth of the assets owned by another party unless
  (i) it is supported by the unqualified opinion of a named independent valuer; and
  (ii) that valuer has had access to sufficient information to carry out a valuation, etc either in accordance with the Royal Institution of Chartered Surveyors' Appraisal and Valuation Standards ('*The Standards*') or in respect of assets other than land, buildings, plant and equipment, to appropriate standards approved by the Panel. Comments by one party about another party's valuation, appraisal or calculation of worth of its own assets may be permitted in exceptional circumstances. In all cases, the Panel must be consulted in advance.

(*Rule 29.1*).

Basis of valuation

(a) The basis of valuation must be clearly stated. Only in exceptional circumstances should it be qualified and in that event the valuer must explain the meaning of the words used. Similarly, special assumptions should not normally be made in a valuation but, if permitted by the Panel, they should be fully explained.
(b) In relation to valuations of land, buildings and plant and machinery, attention is drawn to The Standards.
(c) The basis of valuation will normally be market value as defined in The Standards.
(d) In the case of land currently being developed or with immediate development potential, in addition to giving the market value in the state existing at the date of valuation, the valuation should include
  (i) the value after the development has been completed;
  (ii) the value after the development has been completed and let;

(iii) the estimated total cost, including carrying charges, of completing the development and the anticipated dates of completion and of letting or occupation; and

(iv) a statement whether planning consent has been obtained and, if so, the date thereof and the nature of any conditions attaching to the consent which affect the value.

(e) In some exceptional cases, it will not be possible for a valuer to complete a full valuation of every property. The Panel may be prepared to regard the requirements of this *Rule* as met if the valuer carries out a valuation of a representative sample of properties and reports those valuations, with the directors taking sole responsibility for an estimate, based on the sample, to cover the remaining properties. This procedure will be available only where the portfolio as a whole is within the knowledge of the valuer, who must also certify the representative nature of the sample. Where this is done, the document sent to shareholders and persons with information rights should distinguish between properties valued professionally and those where the directors have made estimates on the basis of the sample valuation and should also compare such estimates with book values.

(*Rule 29.2*).

Potential tax liability. When a valuation is given in connection with an offer, there should normally be a statement regarding any potential tax liability which would arise if the assets were to be sold at the amount of the valuation, with an appropriate comment as to the likelihood of any such liability crystallizing.

(*Rule 29.3*).

Current valuation. A valuation must state the effective date as at which the assets were valued and the professional qualifications and address of the valuer. If a valuation is not current, the valuer must state that a current valuation would not be materially different. If this statement cannot be made, the valuation must be updated.

(*Rule 29.4*).

Opinion and consent letters

Publication of opinion. The opinion of value must be contained in the document containing the asset valuation.

Consent. The document must also state that the valuer has given and not withdrawn his consent to the publication of his valuation report.

Valuation certificate to be published on a website. Where a valuation of assets is given in any document published in connection with the offer , the valuation report must be published on a website in accordance with *Rule 26.3*, together with an associated report or schedule containing details of the aggregate valuation. Where the Panel is satisfied that such disclosure may be commercially disadvantageous to the company concerned, it will allow the report or schedule to appear in a summarised form. In certain cases, the Panel may require any of these documents to be reproduced in full in a document sent to shareholders and persons with information rights.

(*Rule 29.5*).

Waiver in certain circumstances. In exceptional cases, certain companies, in particular property companies, which are the subject of an unexpected offer may find difficulty in obtaining, within the time available, the opinion of an independent valuer to support an asset valuation, as required by this *Rule*, before the board's circular has to be published. In such cases, the Panel may be prepared exceptionally to waive strict compliance with this requirement.

(*Rule 29.6*).

Distribution of documentation during an offer

Rule 30 Publication of documents, announcements and information

If a document, an announcement or any information is required to be sent to any person, it will be treated as having been sent if it is:

(a) sent to the relevant person in hard copy form;
(b) sent to the relevant person in electronic form; or
(c) published on a website provided that the relevant person is sent a website notification no later than the date on which it is published on the website.

(*Rule 30.1*)

Right to receive copies of documents, announcements and information in hard copy form

(a) If a document, an announcement or any information is required to be sent to any person and it is:
  (i) sent to a person in electronic form; or
  (ii) published on a website and the person entitled to receive it is sent a website notification, that person may request a copy in hard copy form from the party which publishes it. Any such request must be made in accordance with the procedure specified in the document, announcement or information for the making of such requests and must provide an address to which the hard copy document, announcement or other information may be sent.
(b) A person entitled to receive a document, an announcement or any information may request that all future documents, announcements and information sent to that person in relation to an offer should be sent by the party which publishes it in hard copy form.
(c) If an offeror receives a request for copies of future documents, announcements and information sent to a person in connection with the offer to be sent in hard copy form, it must notify the offeree company as soon as possible and provide details of the address to which hard copy documents, announcements and information should be sent. If the offeree company receives a request for copies of future documents, announcements and information sent to a person in connection with the offer to be sent in hard copy form (either from the person concerned or from an offeror), it must provide the other parties to the offer with details of such requests at the same time as it provides them with updates to the company's register.
(d) If a request is made under (a) above for a hard copy of a document, an announcement or any information, the party which published it must ensure that it is sent to the relevant person as soon as possible and in any event within two business days of the request being received by that party.
(e) Any document, announcement or information that is sent to a person in electronic form or by means of being published on a website, and any related website notification, must contain a statement that the person to whom it is sent may request a copy of the document, announcement or information (and any information incorporated into it by reference to another source) in hard copy form and may also request that all future documents, announcements and information sent to that person in relation to the offer should be in hard copy form. Attention should be drawn to the fact that a hard copy of the document, announcement or information will not be sent to that person unless so requested and details

must be provided of how a hard copy may be obtained (including an address in the United Kingdom and a telephone number to which requests may be submitted).

(f) If a shareholder, person with information rights or other person is entitled to be sent a document, an announcement or any information and has elected in accordance with any applicable legal or regulatory provisions to receive communications from the offeree company in hard copy form (and such election has been made in respect of information generally and not only in respect of certain specific types of information), that election must be treated by each party to an offer as also applying to the form in which any document, announcement or information must be sent to that person in relation to the offer (see also Section 4 of Appendix 4). If a request is made under (b) above for copies of future documents, announcements and information to be sent in hard copy form, that request must be treated by each party to an offer as an election made in accordance with applicable legal or regulatory provisions to receive communications from the offeree company in hard copy form.

(Rule 30.2).

Distribution of documents, announcements and information to the Panel and other parties to an offer

(a) Before an offer document is published, a copy of the document in hard copy form and electronic form must be sent to the Panel. At the time of publication, a copy must also be sent in hard copy form and electronic form to the advisers to all other parties to the offer.

(b) Copies of all other documents, announcements and information published in connection with an offer by, or on behalf of, an offeror or the offeree company, including advertisements and any material released to the media (including any notes to editors), must at the time of publication or release be sent in electronic form to:
   (i) the Panel; and
   (ii) the advisers to all other parties to the offer.

   Documents must also be sent in hard copy form to the Panel and the advisers to all other parties to the offer at the time of publication. Such documents, announcements or information must not be released to the media under an embargo (see also Note 1 on *Rule 26*).

(c) If a party to an offer publishes a document, an announcement or any information outside normal business hours, that party must inform the advisers to all other parties to the offer of its publication immediately (if necessary by telephone). In such circumstances, special arrangements may need to be made to ensure that a copy of the document, announcement or information is sent directly to the relevant advisers and to the Panel. No party to an offer should be put at a disadvantage through a delay in the release of new information to it.

(*Rule 30.3*).

Rule 31 Timing of the offer

First closing date. An offer must initially be open for at least 21 days following the date on which the offer document is published.

(*Rule 31.1*).

Extension of offer. In any announcement of an extension of an offer, either

- the next closing date must be stated; or
- if the offer is unconditional as to acceptances, a statement may be made that the offer will remain open until further notice.

In the latter case, or if the offer will remain open for acceptances beyond the 70th day following publication of the offer document, at least 14 days' notice must be given, before the offer is closed, to those shareholders who have not accepted by sending a notification to offeree company shareholders and persons with information rights.

(*Rule 31.2*).

No obligation to extend. There is no obligation to extend an offer the conditions of which are not met by the first or any subsequent closing date.

(*Rule 31.3*).

Offer to remain open for 14 days after unconditional as to acceptances. After an offer has become or is declared unconditional as to acceptances, the offer must remain open for acceptance for not less than 14 days after the date on which it would otherwise have expired (see *Rules 33.1* and *33.2*). When, however, an offer is unconditional as to acceptances from the outset, a 14-day extension is not required but the position should be set out clearly and prominently in the offer document.

(*Rule 31.4*).

No extension statements. A 'no extension statement' is a statement that an offer will not be extended beyond a specified date unless it is unconditional as to acceptances. If an offeror (or its directors, officials or advisers) makes a no extension statement, and that statement is not withdrawn immediately if incorrect, the offeror will not be allowed subsequently to extend its offer beyond the stated date, except:

(i) where the right to do so in certain circumstances is specifically reserved at the time the no extension statement is made and those circumstances subsequently arise; or
(ii) in wholly exceptional circumstances.

If an offeror wishes to include a reservation to a no extension statement, the Panel must be consulted.

The provisions of Rule 31.4 will apply in any event.

(*Rule 31.5*).

Final day rule.

(a) Except with the consent of the Panel, an offer (whether revised or not) may not become or be declared unconditional as to acceptances after midnight on the 60th day after the day the initial offer document was published. The Panel's consent will normally only be given
  (i) if a competing firm offer has been announced;
  (ii) if the board of the offeree company consents to an extension;
  (iii) if there is a significant delay in the decision on whether there is to be a Phase 2 CMA reference or initiation of Phase 2 European Commission proceedings;
  (iv) as provided for in *Rule 31.9*;
  (v) if the offeror's receiving agent requests an extension for the purpose of complying with Note 7 on *Rule 10*; or
  (vi) when withdrawal rights are introduced under *Rule 13.6*.
(b) Any extension to which the Panel consents must be announced by the offeror in accordance with Rule 2.9. The Panel should be consulted as to whether a notification in respect of the extension should also be sent to offeree company shareholders and persons with information rights.
(c) For the purpose of the acceptance condition, the offeror may only take into account acceptances or purchases of shares in respect of which all relevant electronic instructions or documents are received by its receiving

agent before the last time for acceptance set out in the offeror's relevant document or announcement. This time must be no later than 1pm on the 60th day (or any other date beyond which the offeror has stated that its offer will not be extended). In the event of an extension with the consent of the Panel in circumstances other than those set out in paragraphs *(a)* (i) to (iii) above, acceptances or purchases in respect of which relevant electronic instructions or documents are received after 1 pm on the relevant date may only be taken into account with the agreement of the Panel, which will only be given in exceptional circumstances.

(d) Except with the consent of the Panel, on the 60th day (or any other date beyond which the offeror has stated that its offer will not be extended) an announcement should be made by 5pm as to whether the offer is unconditional as to acceptances or has lapsed. Such announcement should include, if possible, the details required by *Rule 17.1* but in any event must include a statement as to the current position in the count. The requirement to make an announcement by 5pm should not be reflected in the terms of the offer pursuant to *Rule 24.7*, but, if there is any question of a delay in the announcement, the Panel should be consulted as soon as practicable. Only in exceptional circumstances will the Panel agree to an offeror's request that this announcement may be made after 5pm.

(*Rule 31.6*).

Time for fulfilment of all other conditions. Except with the consent of the Panel, all conditions must be fulfilled or the offer must lapse within 21 days of the

- first closing date, or
- the date the offer becomes or is declared unconditional as to acceptances,

whichever is the later. The Panel's consent will normally only be granted if the outstanding condition involves a material official authorisation or regulatory clearance relating to the offer and it had not been possible to obtain an extension under *Rule 31.6*.

(*Rule 31.7*).

Settlement of consideration. Except with the consent of the Panel, the consideration must be sent to accepting shareholders within 14 days of the later of

- the first closing date of the offer;
- the date the offer becomes or is declared wholly unconditional; or
- the date of receipt of an acceptance complete in all respects.

(*Rule 31.8*).

Offeree company announcements after Day 39. The board of the offeree company should not, except with the consent of the Panel, announce any material new information (including trading results, profit or dividend forecasts, asset valuations and proposals for dividend payments or for any material acquisition or disposal) after the 39th day following the publication of the initial offer document. Where a matter which might give rise to such an announcement being made after the 39th day is known to the offeree company, every effort should be made to bring forward the date of the announcement, but, where this is not practicable or where the matter arises after that date, the Panel will normally give its consent to a later announcement. If an announcement of the kind referred to in this *Rule* is made after the 39th day, the Panel will normally be prepared to grant an extension to 'Day 46' (see *Rule 32.1(c)*) and/or 'Day 60' (see *Rule 31.6*) as appropriate.

(*Rule 31.9*).

Return of documents of title. If an offer lapses, all documents of title and other documents lodged with forms of acceptance must be returned as soon as practicable (and in any event within 14 days of the lapsing of the offer) and the receiving agent should immediately give instructions for the release of securities held in escrow.

(*Rule 31.10*).

Rule 32 Revision

Publication of revised offer document.

(a) If an offer is revised, a revised offer document, drawn up in accordance with *Rules 24* and *27*, must be sent to shareholders of the offeree company and persons with information rights. On the same day, the offeror must publish the offer document on a website in accordance with *Rule 30.4* and announce via a RIS that the offer document has been so published.

(b) At the same time, both the offeror and the offeree company must make the revised offer document readily available to their employee representatives or, where there are no employee representatives, to the employees themselves. The offeree company must also inform its employee representatives or employees of the right of employee representatives under *Rule 32.6* to have a separate opinion on the revised offer appended to any offeree board circular published in relation to the revised offer and of the offeree company's responsibility for the costs reasonably incurred by the employee representatives in obtaining advice required for the verification of the information contained in that opinion.

(c) The offer must be kept open for at least 14 days following the date on which the revised offer document is published. Therefore, no revised offer document may be published in the 14 days ending on the last day the offer is able to become unconditional as to acceptances.

(*Rule 32.1*).

No increase statements. If statements in relation to the value or type of consideration such as 'the offer will not be further increased' or 'our offer remains at xp per share and it will not be raised' are

- included in documents or announcements published in connection with an offer, or
- made by or on behalf of an offeror, its directors, officials or advisers,

and not withdrawn immediately if incorrect, only in wholly exceptional circumstances will the offeror be allowed subsequently to amend the terms of its offer in any way, except where the right to do so has been specifically reserved. This applies even if the amendment would not result in an increase of the value of the offer (eg the introduction of a lower paper alternative).

(*Rule 32.2*).

Entitlement to revised consideration. If an offer is revised, all shareholders who accepted the original offer must be entitled to the revised consideration.

(*Rule 32.3*).

New conditions for increased or improved offers. Subject to the prior consent of the Panel, and only to the extent necessary to implement an increased or improved offer, or to switch to or from a scheme of arrangement, the offeror may introduce new conditions (eg obtaining shareholders' approval or the admission to listing or admission to trading of new securities).

(*Rule 32.4*).

Competitive situations. If a competitive situation continues to exist in the later stages of the offer period, the Panel will normally require revised offers to be announced in accordance with an auction procedure, the terms of which will be determined by the Panel. This normally requires final revisions to competing offers to be announced by the 46th day following the publication of the competing offer document but enables an offeror to revise its offer within a set period in response to any revision announced by a competing offeror on or after the 46th day. The procedure will not normally require any revised offer document to be sent to the offeree company shareholders and persons with information rights before the expiry of a set period after the last revision to either offer is announced. The Panel will consider applying any alternative procedure which is agreed between competing offerors and the board of the offeree company.

(*Rule 32.5*).

The offeree board's opinion and the employee representatives' opinion.

(a) The board of the offeree company must send to the company's shareholders and persons with information rights a circular containing its opinion on the revised offer as required by *Rule 25.1(a)*, drawn up in accordance with *Rules 25* and *27*. and at the same time publish a circular on a website in accordance with Rule 30.4, announced via a RIS that the circular has been published and make it readily and promptly available to its employee representatives or where there are no employee representatives to the employees themselves.

(b) The board of the offeree company must append to its circular a separate opinion from its employee representatives on the effects of the revised offer on employment, provided such opinion is received in good time before publication of that circular. Where the opinion of the employee representatives is not received in good time before publication of the offeree board circular, the offeree company must promptly publish the employee representatives' opinion on a website and announce via a RIS that it has been so published, provided that it is received no later than 14 days after the date on which the offer becomes or is declared wholly unconditional.

(*Rule 32.6*, *Rider 32.7*).

Rule 33 Alternative offers

Timing and revision. In general, the provisions of *Rules 31* and *32* apply equally to alternative offers, including cash alternatives.

(*Rule 33.1*).

Shutting off cash underwritten alternatives. Where the value of a cash underwritten alternative provided by third parties is, at the time of announcement, more than half the maximum value of the offer, an offeror will not be obliged to keep that alternative open in accordance with *Rules 31.4* or *33.1* if it has sent a notification to offeree company shareholders and persons with information rights that it reserves the right to

- close it on a stated date, being not less than 14 days after the date on which the notification is published; or
- extend it on that stated date.

Notice under this *Rule* may not be given between the time when a competing offer has been announced and the end of the resulting competitive situation. See also *Rule 24.13*.

(*Rule 33.2*).

Reintroduction of alternative offers. Where a firm statement has been made that an alternative offer will not be extended or reintroduced and that alternative has ceased to be open for acceptance, neither that alternative, nor any substantially similar alternative, may be reintroduced. Where, however, such a statement has not been made and an alternative offer has closed for acceptance, an offeror will not be precluded from reintroducing that alternative at a later date. Reintroduction would constitute a revision of the offer and would, therefore, be subject to the requirements of, and only be permitted as provided in, *Rule 32*.

(*Rule 33.3*).

Rule 34 Right of withdrawal

When the right of withdrawal may be exercised

An accepting shareholder must be entitled to withdraw his acceptance from the date which is 21 days after the first closing date of the initial offer, if the offer has not by such date become or been declared unconditional as to acceptances. This entitlement to withdraw must be exercisable until the earlier of

- the time that the offer becomes or is declared unconditional as to acceptances; and
- the final time for lodgement of acceptances which can be taken into account in accordance with *Rule 31.6*.

(Rule 34.1)

An accepting shareholder must also be entitled to withdraw his acceptance if so determined by the Panel in accordance with *Rule 13.6*.

(Rule 34.2)

Return of documents of title

If a shareholder withdraws his acceptance, all documents of title and other documents lodged with the form of acceptance must be returned as soon as practicable following the receipt of the withdrawal (and in any event within 14 days) and the receiving agent should immediately give instructions for the release of securities held in escrow.

(*Rule 34.3*).

Restrictions following offers and possible offers

Rule 35

Delay of 12 months. Except with the consent of the Panel, where an offer has been

- announced or made but has not become or been declared wholly unconditional and has been withdrawn or has lapsed otherwise than pursuant to Rule 12.1,

neither the offeror, nor any person who acted in concert with the offeror in the course of the original offer, nor any person who is subsequently acting in concert with any of them, may within 12 months from the date on which such offer is withdrawn or lapses either

- announce an offer or possible offer for the offeree company (including a partial offer which could result in the offeror and persons acting in concert with it being interested in shares carrying 30% or more of the voting rights of the offeree company);

- acquire any interest in shares of the offeree company if the offeror or any such person would thereby become obliged under *Rule 9* to make an offer;
- acquire any interest in, or procure an irrevocable commitment in respect of, shares of the offeree company if the shares in which such person, together with any persons acting in concert with him, would be interested and the shares in respect of which he, or they, had acquired irrevocable commitments would in aggregate carry 30% or more of the voting rights of the offeree company;
- make any statement which raises or confirms the possibility that an offer might be made for the offeree company; or
- take any steps in connection with a possible offer for the offeree company where knowledge of the possible offer might be extended outside those who need to know in the offeror and its immediate advisers.

(*Rule 35.1*).

Partial offers. The restrictions in *Rule 35.1* will also apply following a partial offer

- which could result in the offeror and persons acting in concert with it being interested in shares carrying not less than 30% but not holding shares carrying more than 50% of the voting rights of the offeree company whether or not the offer has become or been declared wholly unconditional. When such an offer has become or been declared wholly unconditional, the period of 12 months runs from that date; and
- for more than 50% of the voting rights of the offeree company which has not become or been declared wholly unconditional.

The restrictions in *Rule 35.1* will not normally apply following a partial offer which could only result in the offeror and persons acting in concert with it being interested in shares carrying less than 30% of the voting rights of the offeree company.

(*Rule 35.2*).

Delay of six months before acquisitions above the offer value. Except with the consent of the Panel, if a person, together with any person acting in concert with him, holds shares carrying more than 50% of the voting rights of a company, neither that person nor any person acting in concert with him may, within six months of the closure of any previous offer made by him to the shareholders of that company which became or was declared wholly unconditional, make a second offer to any shareholder in that company, or acquire any interest in shares in that company, on more favourable terms than those made available under the previous offer See also *Rule 6.2(a)*. For this purpose the value of a securities exchange offer must be calculated as at the date the offer closed. In addition, special deals with favourable conditions attached may not be entered into during this six months period. See also *Rule 16*.

(*Rule 35.3*).

Restrictions on dealings by a competing offeror whose offer has lapsed. Except with the consent of the Panel, where an offer has been one of two or more competing offers and has lapsed, neither that offeror, nor any person acting in concert with that offeror, may acquire any interest in shares in the offeree company on more favourable terms than those made available under its lapsed offer until each of the competing offers has either been declared unconditional in all respects or has itself lapsed. For these purposes, the value of the lapsed offer must be calculated as at the day the offer lapsed.

(*Rule 35.4*).

Partial offers

Rule 36

Panel's consent required. The Panel's consent is required for any partial offer. Consent will normally be granted in the case of an offer which could not result in the offeror (and persons acting in concert with it) being interested in shares carrying 30% or more of the voting rights of a company.

(*Rule 36.1*).

Acquisitions before the offer. In the case of an offer which could result in the offeror (and persons acting in concert with it) being interested in shares carrying 30% or more but holding less than 100% of the voting rights of a company, the Panel's consent will not normally be granted if

- the offeror or persons acting in concert with it have acquired, selectively or in significant numbers, interests in shares in the offeree company during the 12 months preceding the application for consent; or
- interests in shares have been acquired at any time after the partial offer was reasonably in contemplation.

(*Rule 36.2*).

Acquisitions during and after the offer. The offeror (and persons acting in concert with it) may not acquire any interest in shares in the offeree company during the offer period. In addition, in the case of a successful partial offer,

- the offeror,
- any person who acted in concert with the offeror in the course of the partial offer, and
- any person who is subsequently acting in concert with any of them,

may not, except with the consent of the Panel, acquire any interest in such shares during a period of 12 months after the end of the offer period.

(*Rule 36.3*).

Offer for between 30% and 50%. When an offer is made which could result in the offeror (and persons acting in concert with it) being interested in shares carrying not less than 30% but not more than 50% of the voting rights of a company, the precise number of shares offered for must be stated and the offer may not be declared unconditional as to acceptances unless acceptances are received for not less than that number.

(*Rule 36.4*).

Approval of independent shareholders for offers of 30% or more. Any offer which could result in the offeror (and persons acting in concert with it) being interested in shares carrying 30% or more of the voting rights of a company must be conditional on approval of the offer (normally signified by means of a separate box on the form of acceptance) being given in respect of over 50% of the voting rights held by shareholders who are independent of the offeror (and persons acting in concert with it). This requirement may on occasion be waived if over 50% of the voting rights of the offeree company are held by one shareholder.

(*Rule 36.5*).

Warning about control position. In the case of a partial offer which could result in the offeror, either alone or with persons acting in concert with it, holding shares carrying over 50% of the voting rights of the offeree company, the offer document must contain specific and prominent reference to this and to the fact that, if the offer succeeds, the offeror or, where appropriate, the offeror and persons acting in concert with it, will be free, subject to *Rule 36.3* and, where relevant, to Note 4 on *Rule 9.1*, to acquire further interests in shares without incurring any obligation under *Rule 9* to make a general offer.

(*Rule 36.6*).

Scaling down. Partial offers must be made to all shareholders of the class and arrangements must be made for those shareholders who wish to do so to accept in full for the relevant percentage of their holdings. Shares tendered in excess of this percentage must be accepted by the offeror from each shareholder in the same proportion to the number tendered to the extent necessary to enable it to obtain the total number of shares for which it has offered.

(*Rule 36.7*).

Comparable offer. When an offer is made for a company with more than one class of equity share capital which could result in the offeror (and persons acting in concert with it) being interested in shares carrying 30% or more of the voting rights, a comparable offer must be made for each class.

(*Rule 36.8*).

Redemption or purchase by a company of its own securities

Rule 37

Possible requirement to make a mandatory offer. When a company redeems or purchases its own voting shares, any resulting increase in the percentage of shares carrying voting rights in which a person or group of persons acting in concert is interested will be treated as an acquisition for the purpose of *Rule 9*. Subject to prior consultation, the Panel will normally waive any resulting obligation to make a general offer if there is a vote of independent shareholders and a procedure on the lines of that set out in Appendix 1 to the Code is followed.

(*Rule 37.1*).

Limitation on subsequent acquisitions. Subsequent to the redemption or purchase by a company of its own voting shares, all persons will be subject, in acquiring further interests in shares in the company, to the provisions of *Rule 9.1*.

(*Rule 37.2*).

Redemption or purchase of securities by the offeree company

(a) *Shareholders' approval.* During the course of an offer, or even before the date of the offer if the board of the offeree company has reason to believe that a *bona fide* offer might be imminent, no redemption or purchase by the offeree company of its own shares may be effected without the approval of the shareholders at a general meeting. The notice convening the meeting must include information about the offer or anticipated offer. Where it is felt that the redemption or purchase is in pursuance of a contract entered into earlier or another pre-existing obligation, the Panel must be consulted and its consent to proceed without a shareholders' meeting obtained.
(b) *Public disclosure.* For the purpose of *Rule 8*, dealings in relevant securities include the redemption or purchase of, or taking or exercising an option over, any of its own relevant securities by the offeree company.
(c) *Disclosure in the offeree board circular.* Any offeree board circular published in connection with an offer must state the amount of relevant

securities of the offeree company which the offeree company has redeemed or purchased during the period commencing 12 months prior to the offer period and ending with the latest practicable date prior to the publication of the document. Details of any such redemptions and purchases must also be given, including dates and prices and the extent to which the shares redeemed or purchased were cancelled or held in treasury.

(*Rule 37.3*).

Redemption or purchase of securities by the offeror company.

(a) *Public disclosure.* For the purpose of *Rule 8*, dealings in relevant securities include the redemption or purchase of, or taking or exercising an option over, any of its own relevant securities by an offeror.

(b) *Disclosure in the offer document.* The offer document must state (in the case of a securities exchange offer only)

- the number of relevant securities of the offeror which the offeror has redeemed or purchased between the start of the offer period and the latest practicable date prior to the publication of the offer document; and
- details of any such redemptions and purchases, including dates and prices and the extent to which the shares redeemed or purchased were cancelled or held in treasury.

(*Rule 37.4*).

Dealings by connected exempt principal traders

Rule 38

Prohibited dealings. An exempt principal trader connected with an offeror or the offeree company must not carry out any dealings with the purpose of assisting the offeror or the offeree company, as the case may be.

(*Rule 38.1*).

Dealings between offerors and connected exempt principal traders. An offeror (and any person acting in concert with it) must not deal as principal with an exempt principal trader connected with the offeror in relevant securities of the offeree company during the offer period. It will generally be for the advisers to the offeror (including a corporate banker) to ensure compliance with this *Rule* rather than the principal trader. See also *Rule 4.2*.

(*Rule 38.2*).

Assenting securities and dealings in assented securities. An exempt principal trader connected with the offeror must not assent offeree company securities to the offer or purchase such securities in assented form until the offer is unconditional as to acceptances.

(*Rule 38.3*).

Voting. Securities owned by an exempt principal trader connected with an offeror or the offeree company must not be voted in the context of an offer.

(*Rule 38.4*).

Disclosure of dealings. Dealings in relevant securities, during the offer period, by an exempt principal trader connected with an offeror or the offeree company should be aggregated and disclosed to a RIS and the Panel not later than 12 noon on the business day following the date of the transactions, stating the following details.

- If the relevant trading desk has recognised intermediary status and is dealing in a client-serving capacity
  - (i) total acquisitions and disposals; and
  - (ii) the highest and lowest prices paid and received.
- If the relevant trading desk does not have recognised intermediary status, or if it does but is not dealing in a client-serving capacity, the details required under Note 5(a) on *Rule 8* (notes on public disclosures).

In each case, it should be stated whether the connection is with an offeror or the offeree company. In the case of dealings in options or derivatives, full details should be given so that the nature of the dealings can be fully understood.

(*Rule 38.5*).

Appendix 1 – Definitions

GENERAL DEFINITIONS

The following definitions apply for the purposes of this book.

Accounting reference date. See **2.18** ACCOUNTS (GENERAL) AND ACCOUNTING REFERENCE DATES AND PERIODS.

Accounting reference period. See **2.17** ACCOUNTS (GENERAL) AND ACCOUNTING REFERENCE DATES AND PERIODS.

Accounting standards. Accounting standards mean statements of standard accounting practice issued by prescribed bodies, and references to 'accounting standards applicable to a company's annual accounts' are to such standards as are, in accordance with their terms, relevant to the company's circumstances and to the accounts. [*CA 2006, s 464*]. The FRC is a prescribed body for these purposes. [*SI 2012 No 1471, Reg 23*].

Accounts meeting means (in relation to a public company) a general meeting of the company at which the company's annual accounts and reports are (or are to be) laid in accordance with *CA 2006, s 437*. [*CA 2006, s 437(3)*]

Annual accounts, mean

- any individual accounts prepared by the company for that year (see *CA 2006, s 394*); and
- any group accounts prepared by the company for that year

and include notes to the accounts giving information which is required by any provision of *CA 2006* or international accounting standards, and required or allowed by any such provision to be given in a note to company accounts.

This is subject to *CA 2006, s 408* (option to omit individual profit and loss account from annual accounts where information given in notes to the individual balance sheet , see **3.56** ACCOUNTS: LARGE COMPANIES).

[*CA 2006, ss 471(1), 472(2); SI 2012 No 2301, Reg 18; SI 2013 No 3008, Reg 7(3)*].

Annual accounts and reports. *In the case of an unquoted company*, its annual accounts and reports for a financial year are

- its annual accounts;
- the strategic report (if any) (see CHAPTER **2**)
- the directors' report, and
- the auditor's report on those accounts for financial years ending on or after 30 September 2013 on the strategic report (where this is covered by the auditor's report) (see CHAPTER **2**)) and the directors' report (unless the company is exempt from audit).

In the case of a quoted company, its annual accounts and reports for a financial year are

- its annual accounts;

- the directors' remuneration report, (for financial years ending on or after 30 September 2013 the strategic report (if any) (see CHAPTER 2))
- the directors' report; and
- the auditor's report on those accounts (for financial years ending on or after 30 September 2013 on the strategic report (where this is covered by the auditor's report) (see CHAPTER 2)) and the directors' report (unless the company is exempt from audit).

[*CA 2006, s 471(2)(3); SI 2013 No 1970, Schedule, para 18*].

Asset-locked body

- a CIC, a charity or (with effect from 1 October 2009, a permitted industrial and provident society); or
- a body established outside the UK that is equivalent to either of those.

Associated undertaking. See 3.62 ACCOUNTS: LARGE COMPANIES.

Balance sheet, includes notes to the accounts giving information which is required by any provision of *CA 2006* or international accounting standards, and required or allowed by any such provision to be given in a note to company accounts.

[*CA 2006, s 472(2)*].

BIS the Department for Business, Innovation and Skills

Body corporate includes a body incorporated outside the UK, but does not include

- a corporation sole; or
- a partnership that, whether or not a legal person, is not regarded as a body corporate under the law by which it is governed.

[*CA 2006, s 1173*].

Called-up share capital means so much of the share capital of a company as equals

- the aggregate amount of calls made on its shares (whether or not these calls have been paid);
- any share capital paid up without being called; and
- any share capital to be paid on a specified future date under the articles, under the terms of allotment of the relevant shares or under any other arrangements for payment of those shares.

[*CA 2006, s 547*].

Capital redemption reserve. See 34.18 PURCHASE OF OWN SHARES.

Class of shares. See 9.1 CLASS RIGHTS.

Companies Acts means

(a) the company law provisions of *CA 2006*;

(b) *C(AICE)A 2004, Pt 2* (community interest companies); and

(c) the provisions of *CA 1985* and the *CC(CP)A 1985* that remain in force.

Note that the provisions under (*b*) and (*c*) above are extended to Northern Ireland by *CA 2006, s 1284*.

[*CA 2006, s 2*].

Company means a company formed and registered under *CA 2006*, ie

- a company so formed and registered after the commencement of *CA 2006, Pt 1* (1 October 2009); or
- a company that immediately before that date
  - (i) was formed and registered under *CA 1985* or the *Companies (Northern Ireland) Order 1986 (SI 1986 No 1032)*, or
  - (ii) was an existing company for the purposes of that *Act* or that *Order*,

  (which is to be treated on commencement as if formed and registered under *CA 2006*).

[*CA 2006, s 1(1)*].

Constitution. Unless the context requires otherwise, references in the *Companies Acts* to a company's constitution include the company's articles and any resolutions or agreements to which *CA 2006, ss 29, 30* apply (see **14.10** CONSTITUTION – MEMORANDUM AND ARTICLES). [*CA 2006, s 17*]. Unless the context requires otherwise, references to a company's articles in any *CA 2006* provisions that were brought fully into force before 1 October 2009 include the company's memorandum.

[*SI 2007 No 2194, Sch 1 para 1*].

Contributory. In the Companies Acts, contributory means every person liable to contribute to the assets of the company in the event of it being wound up except for persons liable to contribute by virtue of a declaration by the court under *IA 1986, s 213* (fraudulent trading) or *IA 1986, s 214* (wrongful trading).

For the purposes of all proceedings for determining, and all proceedings prior to the final determination of, the persons who are to be deemed contributories, the expression includes any person alleged to be a contributory.

[*CA 2006, s 1170B*; *SI 2009 No 1941, Sch 1 para 260*].

Corporate governance statement means the statement required by the FCA Disclosure and Transparency Rules, paras 7.2.1 to 7.2.11. A 'separate' corporate governance statement means one that is not included in the directors' report. See **15.5** CORPORATE GOVERNANCE.

[*CA 2006, ss 472A, 538A; SI 2009 No 1581, Regs 5, 8*].

Corporation includes a body incorporated outside the UK, but does not include

- a corporation sole; or
- a partnership that, whether or not a legal person, is not regarded as a body corporate under the law by which it is governed.

[*CA 2006, s 1173*].

Court. Except as otherwise provided, the court means

- in England and Wales, the High Court or a county court;

- in Scotland, the Court of Session or sheriff court; and
- in Northern Ireland, the High Court.

[*CA 2006, s 1156(1)*].

Debenture includes debenture stock, bonds and any other securities of a company, whether or not constituting a charge on the assets of the company. [*CA 2006, s 738*]. See **17.6 Debt Finance–Debentures and Other Borrowing**.

Director. Director includes any person occupying the position of director by whatever name called.

[*CA 2006, s 250*].

Dormant company. A company is dormant during any period in which it has no 'significant accounting transaction'. A '*significant accounting transaction*' means a transaction which is required by *CA 2006, s 386* to be entered in the company's accounting records, but disregarding

(a) a transaction arising from the taking of shares in the company by a subscriber to the memorandum as a result of an undertaking of his in connection with the formation of the company; or

(b) a transaction consisting of the payment of

 (i) a fee to the Registrar of Companies on a change of name;

 (ii) a fee to the Registrar of Companies on the re-registration of a company;

 (iii) a penalty under *CA 2006, s 453* (penalty for failure to file accounts, see **2.10 Accounts: General**), or

 (iv) a fee to the Registrar of Companies for the registration of an annual return.

Any reference to a body corporate other than a company being dormant has a corresponding meaning.

[*CA 2006, s 1169*].

EEA state in relation to any time, means a state which at that time is a Member State or any other state which at that time is a party to the EEA agreement, ie the agreement on the European Economic Area signed at Oporto on 2 May 1992 (together with the Protocol adjusting that Agreement signed at Brussels on 17 March 1993, as modified or supplemented from time to time).

[*CA 2006, s 1170*].

The current Member States are Austria, Belgium, Bulgaria, Croatia, Cyprus, Czech Republic, Denmark, Estonia, Finland, France, Germany, Greece, Hungary, Iceland, Ireland, Italy, Latvia, Lichtenstein, Lithuania, Luxembourg, Malta, The Netherlands, Norway, Poland, Portugal, Romania, Slovakia , Slovenia, Spain, Sweden and the UK

EEA company and **EEA undertaking** mean a company or undertaking governed by the law of an EEA State.

[*CA 2006, s 1170*].

Electronic form. A document or information is sent or supplied in electronic form if it is sent or supplied

- by electronic means (eg by e-mail or fax); or
- by any other means while in an electronic form (eg sending a disk by post).

A document or information authorised or required to be sent or supplied in electronic form must be sent or supplied in a form, and by a means, that the sender or supplier reasonably considers will enable the recipient to read it and to retain a copy of it. A document or information can be read only if

- it can be read with the naked eye, or
- to the extent that it consists of images (eg photographs, pictures, maps, plans or drawings), it can be seen with the naked eye.

[*CA 2006, s 1168(3)(5)(6)(7)*].

Electronic means. A document or information is sent or supplied by electronic means if it is

- sent initially and received at its destination by means of electronic equipment for the processing (which expression includes digital compression) or storage of data; and
- entirely transmitted, conveyed and received by wire, by radio, by optical means or by other electromagnetic means.

[*CA 2006, s 1168(4)(7)*].

Employees' share scheme is a scheme for encouraging or facilitating the holding of shares or debentures of a company by or for the benefit of

- *bona fide* employees or former employees of the company, any subsidiary of the company, or the company's holding company or any subsidiary of the company's holding company; or
- the spouses, civil partners, surviving spouses, surviving civil partners or minor children or step-children of such employees or former employees.

[*CA 2006, s 1166*].

Equity share capital means a company's issued share capital excluding any part of that capital that does not carry any right (either as respects dividends or capital) to participate beyond a specified amount in a distribution.

[*CA 2006, s 548*].

Fellow subsidiary undertakings are undertakings which are 'subsidiary undertakings' of the same 'parent undertaking' but are not parent undertakings or subsidiary undertakings of each other.

[*CA 2006,s 1161(4)*].

Financial year. A company's first financial year begins with the first day of its first accounting reference period (see **2.17** Accounts (General) and Accounting Reference Dates and Periods) and ends with the last day of that period or such other date, not more than seven days before or after the end of that period, as the directors may determine.

Subsequent financial years begin with the day immediately following the end of the company's previous financial year and end with the last day of its next accounting reference period or such other date, not more than seven days before or after the end of that period, as the directors may determine.

The seven-day variation allows accounts either to be prepared for a 52-week period or always to end on a specific day of the week.

In relation to an undertaking which is not a company, a reference to its financial year is to any period in respect of which a profit and loss account of the undertaking is required to be made up (by its constitution or by the law under which it is established), whether that period is a year or not..

The directors of a parent company must secure that, except where in their opinion there are good reasons against it, the financial year of each of its subsidiary undertakings coincides with the company's own financial year.

[*CA 2006, s 390*].

Firm means any entity, whether or not a legal person, that is not an individual and includes a body corporate, a corporation sole and a partnership or other unincorporated association.

[*CA 2006, s 1173*].

Former Companies Acts means

- the 'Joint Stock Companies Acts', *Companies Act 1862*, *Companies (Consolidation) Act 1908*, *Companies Act 1929*, *Companies Act (Northern Ireland) 1932*, *Companies Acts 1948* to *1983*, *Companies Act (Northern Ireland) 1960*, *Companies (Northern Ireland) Order 1986* and *Companies Consolidation (Consequential Provisions) (Northern Ireland) Order 1986*, and
- the provisions of the *CA 1985* and the *CC(CP)A 1985* that are no longer in force.

For these purposes the *'Joint Stock Companies Acts'* means *Joint Stock Companies Act 1856*, *Joint Stock Companies Acts 1856, 1857*, *Joint Stock Banking Companies Act 1857*, and the *Act to enable Joint Stock Banking Companies to be formed on the principle of limited liability*, but does not include *Joint Stock Companies Act 1844*.

[*CA 2006, s 1171*].

The Gazette means

- as respects companies registered in England and Wales, the London Gazette;
- as respects companies registered in Scotland, the Edinburgh Gazette; and
- as respects companies registered in Northern Ireland, the Belfast Gazette.

[*CA 2006, s 1173*].

Group means a 'parent undertaking' and its 'subsidiary undertakings' (see below).

[*CA 2006, s 474(1)*].

Group undertaking in relation to an 'undertaking' means an undertaking which is

- a 'parent undertaking' or 'subsidiary undertaking' of that undertaking; or
- a subsidiary undertaking of any parent undertaking of that undertaking.

[*CA 2006, s 1161(5)*].

Hard copy. A document or information is sent or supplied in hard copy form if it is sent or supplied in a paper copy or similar form capable of being read. A document or information can be read only if

- it can be read with the naked eye; or
- to the extent that it consists of images (eg photographs, pictures, maps, plans or drawings), it can be seen with the naked eye.

[*CA 2006, s 1168(2)(6)(7)*].

Holding company. See, by implication, under definition of 'subsidiary' below.

IAS Regulation means EC Regulation No. 1606/2002 of the European Parliament and of the Council of 19 July 2002 on the application of international accounting standards.

[*CA 2006, s 474(1)*].

International accounting standards means the international accounting standards, within the meaning of the IAS Regulation (see above), adopted from time to time by the European Commission in accordance with that Regulation.

[*CA 2006, s 474(1)*].

Limited by guarantee. See 12 Company Formation and Types of Companies.

Limited by shares. See 12 Company Formation and Types of Companies.

Limited company. See 12 Company Formation and Types of Companies.

Members. The members of a company are

- the subscribers to the company's memorandum (who are deemed to have agreed to become members on subscribing their names and who become members on the company's registration); and
- every other person who agrees to become a member of the company and whose name is entered in the register of members.

[*CA 2006, s 112*].

MiFID investment firm means an investment firm within the meaning of *EC Directive 2004/39/EC, Art 4.1.1* other than

- a company to which that Directive does not apply by virtue of *Art 2* of that Directive;
- a company which is an exempt investment firm within the meaning of *SI 2007 No 126, Reg 4A(3)*;
- any other company which fulfils all the requirements set out in *SI 2007 No 126, Reg 4C(3)*; and
- in respect of a financial year beginning before, but ending on or after 1 November 2007 (the '*transitional financial year*'), any person who satisfies the following conditions.

  (a) Condition A is satisfies if, at any time that is within the transitional financial year and before 1 November 2007, the person would have been a MiFID investment firm if the Directive had had effect at that time.

  (b) Condition B is satisfied if the person

(i) was not, at any time that is within the transitional financial year and before 1 November 2007, an ISD investment firm within the meaning of *CA 1985, s 262* (as it had effect at that time); and

(ii) would not, at any time that is within the transitional financial year and is on or after 1 November 2007, have been such a firm if that section had had effect at that time as it had effect immediately before 1 November 2007.

[*CA 2006, ss 474, 539*].

Non-cash asset means any property or interest in property, other than cash (which includes foreign currency). Any reference to the transfer or acquisition of a non-cash asset includes

- the creation or extinction of an estate or interest in, or a right over, any property; and
- the discharge of a liability of any person, other than a liability for a liquidated sum.

[*CA 2006, s 1163*].

Officer in relation to a body corporate includes a director, manager or secretary.

[*CA 2006, s 1173*].

Old public company. An old public company is a company limited by shares, or a company limited by guarantee and having a share capital, which

- existed on 22 December 1980 (in Northern Ireland, 1 July 1983) or was incorporated after that date pursuant to an application made before that date;
- was not a private company within the meaning of *CA 1948, s 28* (in Northern Ireland, *CA (Northern Ireland) 1960, s 28*) on that date or, if later, on the day of the company's incorporation; and
- has not since that date or the day of the company's incorporation (as the case may be) either been re-registered as a public company or become a private company.

Subject to below, references in the Companies Acts to

- a public company, or
- a company other than a private company,

are to be read (unless the context otherwise requires) as including an old public company and references to a private company are to be read accordingly.

But this does not apply in relation to *CA 2006, Pt 7* (re-registration as a means of altering a company's status) and *CA 2006 662–669* (treatment of shares held by or for public company) and does not restrict the power to make provision by regulations under *CA 2006, s 65* (inappropriate use of indications of company type or legal form).

[*SI 2009 No 1941, Sch 3 paras 1, 2*].

Ordinary resolution. See **42.2** Resolutions and Meetings.

Overseas company means a company incorporated outside the UK.

[*CA 2006, ss 1044, 1173*].

Parent undertakings. See '*Meaning of 'parent' and 'subsidiary' undertaking*' below.

Participating interests. A participating interest means an 'interest in shares' held by an undertaking in another undertaking which it holds on a long-term basis for the purpose of securing a contribution to its activities by the exercise of control or influence arising from (or related to) that interest. Unless the contrary is shown, a holding of 20% or more of the shares of the undertaking is presumed to be a participating interest.

'*Interest in shares*' includes an interest which is convertible into an interest in shares and an option to acquire shares or any such interest (even if the relevant shares are, until the conversion or the exercise of the option, unissued).

An interest held on behalf of an undertaking is to be treated as held by it.

For the purposes of the expression 'participating interest'

- In the balance sheet and profit and loss formats set out in 3 ACCOUNTS: LARGE COMPANIES and 5 ACCOUNTS: SMALL COMPANIES, 'participating interest' does not include an interest in a group undertaking; and
- in those formats as they apply in relation to group accounts and in the definition of associated undertakings, the references above to the interest held by, and the purposes and activities of, the undertaking concerned are to be construed as references to the interest held by, and the purposes and activities of, the group.

[*SI 2008 No 409, Sch 8 para 8; SI 2008 No 410, Sch 10 para 11*].

Prescribed means prescribed (by Order or by Regulations) by the Secretary of State.

[*CA 2006, s 1167*].

Private company. See 12 COMPANY FORMATION AND TYPES OF COMPANIES.

Profit and loss account includes

- notes to the accounts giving information which is required by any provision of *CA 2006* or international accounting standards, and required or allowed by any such provision to be given in a note to company accounts; and
- in relation to a company that prepares IAS accounts, an income statement or other equivalent financial statement required to be prepared by international accounting standards.

In the case of an undertaking not trading for profit, any reference to a profit and loss account is to an income and expenditure account (and references to profit and loss and, in relation to group accounts, to a consolidated profit and loss account are construed accordingly).

[*CA 2006, ss 472(2), 474(1)(2)*].

Public company. See 12 COMPANY FORMATION AND TYPES OF COMPANIES.

Quoted company. A quoted company means a company whose equity share capital

- has been included in the official list in accordance with the provisions of *FSMA 2000, Part VI*;
- is officially listed in an EEA State; or

- is admitted to dealing on either the New York Stock Exchange or the exchange known as Nasdaq.

A company is a quoted company in relation to a financial year if it is a quoted company immediately before the end of the accounting reference period by reference to which that financial year was determined.

[*CA 2006, s 385(1)(2)*].

Receiver or manager (and certain related references). Any reference in the Companies Acts to a receiver or manager of the property of a company, or to a receiver of it, includes a receiver or manager or (as the case may be) a receiver of part only of that property and a receiver only of the income arising from the property or from part of it.

Any reference in the Companies Acts to the appointment of a receiver or manager under powers contained in an instrument includes an appointment made under powers that, by virtue of an enactment, are implied in and have effect as if contained in the instrument.

[*CA 2006, s 1170A*].

Redeemable shares. See **34.2 Purchase of Own Shares**.

Requirements of *CA 2006*. References in the company law provisions of *CA 2006* to the requirements of *CA 2006* include the requirements of Regulations and Orders made under it.

[*CA 2006, s 1172*].

Service address. A service address in relation to a person means an address at which documents may be effectively served on that person.

[*CA 2006, s 1141*].

Shadow director. See **18.1 Directors**.

Share means share in a company's share capital, and includes stock (except where a distinction between shares and stock is expressed or implied).

[*CA 2006, s 540(1)(4)*].

References to shares

- in relation to an undertaking with capital but no share capital, are to rights to share in the capital of the undertaking; and
- in relation to an undertaking without capital, are to interests
  (i) conferring any right to share in the profits, or liability to contribute to the losses, of the undertaking; or
  (ii) giving rise to an obligation to contribute to the debts or expenses of the undertaking in the event of a winding up.

[*CA 2006, s 1161(2)*].

Share premium account. See **46.1 Share Premium**.

Special notice (in relation to a resolution). See **42.18 Resolutions and Meetings**.

Special resolution. See **42.3 Resolutions and Meetings**.

Subsidiary

A company is a subsidiary of another company, (its holding company) in any of the following circumstances.

- If that other company holds a majority of the 'voting rights' in it.
- If that other company is a member of it and has the right to appoint or remove a majority of its board of directors, ie the right to appoint or remove directors holding a majority of the voting rights at meetings of the board on all, or substantially all, matters. For these purposes, a company is treated as having the right to appoint to a directorship if

  (i) a person's appointment to it follows necessarily from his appointment as director of the company; or

  (ii) the directorship is held by the company itself.

  A right to appoint or remove which is exercisable only with the consent or concurrence of another person is left out of account unless no other person has a right to appoint or, as the case may be, remove in relation to that directorship.
- If that other company is a member of it and controls alone, pursuant to an agreement with other members, a majority of the voting rights in it.
- If it is a subsidiary of a company which is itself a subsidiary of that other company.

'*Voting rights*' are rights conferred on shareholders in respect of their shares (or, in the case of a company not having a share capital, on members) to vote at general meetings of the company on all, or substantially all, matters.

For the above purposes,

(a) rights which are exercisable only in certain circumstances are taken into account only

- when the circumstances have arisen, and for so long as they continue to obtain; or
- when the circumstances are within the control of the person having the rights

and rights which are normally exercisable but are temporarily incapable of exercise continue to be taken into account;

(b) rights held by a person in a fiduciary capacity are treated as not held by him;

(c) rights held by a person as nominee for another are treated as held by the other; and rights are regarded as held as nominee if they are exercisable only on that other person's instructions or with his consent or concurrence;

(d) rights attached to shares held by way of security are treated as held by the person providing the security where

- apart from the right to exercise them to preserve the value of, or realise, the security, the rights are exercisable only in accordance with his instructions; or
- the shares are held in connection with the granting of loans as part of normal business activities and apart from the right to exercise them to preserve the value of, or realise, the security, the rights are exercisable only in his interests.

For these purposes, rights are treated as being exercisable in accordance with the instructions of, or in the interests of, a company if they are exercisable in accordance with the instructions of, or in the interests of, any subsidiary or holding company of that company or any subsidiary of a holding company of that company;

(e) rights are treated as held by a company if they are held by any of its subsidiaries and nothing in (*c*) or (*d*) above is to be construed as requiring rights held by a holding company to be treated as held by any of its subsidiaries; and

(f) voting rights in a company are reduced by any rights held by the company itself.

References in the provisions of (*b*) to (*f*) above to rights held by a person include rights falling to be treated as held by him by virtue of any other of those provisions but not rights which by virtue of any such provision are to be treated as not held by him.

[*CA 2006, ss 1159, 1160, Sch 6*].

Subsidiary undertakings. See '*Meaning of 'parent' and 'subsidiary' undertaking*' below.

Traded company. A traded company means a company any shares of which

- carry rights to vote at general meetings; and
- are admitted to trading on a regulated market in an EEA state by or with the consent of the company.

[*CA 2006, s 360C*].

Treasury shares. See **34.14 Purchase of Own Shares**.

Turnover, in relation to a company, means the amounts derived from the provision of goods and services falling within the company's ordinary activities, after deduction of trade discounts, value added tax and any other taxes based on the amounts so derived.

[*CA 2006, ss 474(1), 539(1)*].

UK-registered company means a company registered under *CA 2006* but does not include an overseas company that has registered particulars under *CA 2006, s 1046*.

[*CA 2006, ss 547, 1158*].

Undertaking (see also '*Meaning of 'parent' and 'subsidiary' undertaking*' below) means

- a body corporate or partnership, or
- an unincorporated association carrying on a trade or business, with or without a view to profit.

Where an undertaking is not a company, expressions appropriate to companies must be construed as references to the corresponding persons, officers, document or organs, as the case may be, appropriate to undertakings of that description.

[*CA 2006, s 1161(1)(3)*].

Unlimited company. See **12 Company Formation and Types of Companies**.

Unquoted company means a company that is not a quoted company (see above).

[*CA 2006, s 385(3)*].

Wholly-owned subsidiary. A company is a wholly-owned subsidiary of another company if it has no members except that other company and that other company's wholly-owned subsidiaries or persons acting on behalf of that other company or its wholly-owned subsidiaries. [*CA 2006, s 1159(2)*]. A similar definition applied under *CA 1985, s 736(2)*.

Working day, in relation to a company, means a day that is not a Saturday or Sunday, Christmas Day, Good Friday or any day that is a bank holiday under *Banking and Financial Dealings Act 1971* in the part of the UK where the company is registered.

[*CA 2006, s 1173*].

Written resolution. See **42.5** RESOLUTIONS AND MEETINGS.

MEANING OF 'PARENT' AND 'SUBSIDIARY' UNDERTAKING

An 'undertaking' is a '*parent undertaking*' in relation to another undertaking (a 'subsidiary undertaking') if

(a) it holds a majority of the 'voting rights' in the undertaking;

(b) it is a member of the undertaking and has the right to appoint or remove a majority of its board of directors;

(c) it has the right to exercise a dominant influence over the undertaking by virtue of

  (i) provisions in the undertaking's articles; or

  (ii) a 'control contract');

(d) it is a member of the undertaking and controls alone, pursuant to an agreement with other shareholders or members, a majority of the 'voting rights';

(e) it has the power to exercise, or actually exercises, dominant influence or control over it; or

(f) the two undertakings in question are managed on a unified basis.

For the above purposes, an undertaking is to be treated as a member of another undertaking if

- any of its subsidiary undertakings is a member of that undertaking; or
- any shares in that other undertaking are held by persons acting on behalf of the undertaking or any of its subsidiary undertakings.

A parent undertaking is treated as a parent undertaking of undertakings in relation to which any of its subsidiary undertakings are, or are treated as being, parent undertakings (and references to its subsidiary undertakings are construed accordingly).

References to shares are to allotted shares.

[*CA 2006, s 1162*].

Voting rights

'*Voting rights*' means the rights conferred on shareholders in respect of their shares (or, if the undertaking does not have a share capital, on members) to vote at general meetings of the undertaking on all (or substantially all) matters. In the case of an undertaking which does not have general meetings at which matters are decided by the exercise of voting rights, references to holding 'a majority of the voting rights' in the undertaking should be construed as having the right, under the constitution of the undertaking, to direct its overall policy or to alter the terms of its constitution.

[*CA 2006, Sch 7 para 2*].

Right to appoint or remove a majority of the directors

The reference to the right to appoint or remove a majority of the board of directors is to the right to appoint or remove directors holding a majority of the voting rights at board meetings on all (or substantially all) matters.

An undertaking is treated as having the right to appoint to a directorship if

- a person's appointment to it follows necessarily from his appointment as director of the undertaking; or
- the directorship is held by the undertaking itself.

No account is to be taken of a right to appoint (or remove) which can be exercised only with the consent or concurrence of another person, except where, in relation to that directorship, no-one else has the right to appoint (or remove).

[*CA 2006, Sch 7 para 3*].

Right to exercise dominant influence

An undertaking is not to be regarded as having the right to exercise a dominant influence over another undertaking unless it has the right to give directions, with respect to the operating and financial policies of that other undertaking, which its directors are obliged to comply with whether or not they are for the benefit of that other undertaking.

A '*control contract*' means a written contract, conferring a right to exercise a dominant influence, which

- is of a kind authorised by the articles of the undertaking in relation to which the right is exercisable; and
- is permitted by the law under which that undertaking is established.

[*CA 2006, Sch 7 para 4*].

General rules on 'rights'

The following rules apply for the purposes of 'rights' referred to above

(a) Rights exercisable only in certain circumstances are taken into account only

  (i) when the circumstances have arisen and for so long as they continue; or

  (ii) when the circumstances are within the control of the persons having the rights.

(b) Rights normally exercisable but temporarily incapable of being exercised must continue to be taken into account.

(c) Rights held by a person in a fiduciary capacity are treated as not held by him.

(d) Rights held by a person as nominee for another (ie rights exercisable only on the other's instructions or with his consent or concurrence) are treated as held by the other.

(e) Rights attached to shares held by way of security are treated as held by the person providing the security

(i) where the rights are exercisable only in accordance with that person's instructions (apart from the right to exercise them to preserve the value of, or realise, the security); and

(ii) if the shares are held in connection with the granting of loans as part of normal business activities, where the rights are exercisable only in that person's interests (apart from any right to exercise them to preserve the value of, or realise, the security).

Rights are treated as being exercisable in accordance with the instructions of, or in the interests of, an undertaking if they are exercisable in accordance with the instructions of, or in the interests of, any 'group undertaking'

(f) Rights are treated as held by a parent undertaking if they are held by any of its subsidiary undertakings.

(g) The voting rights in an undertaking must be reduced by any rights held by the undertaking itself.

Nothing in (*d*) or (*e*) above is to be construed as requiring rights held by a parent undertaking to be treated as held by any of its subsidiary undertakings.

References in (*c*) to (*g*) above to rights held by a person include rights falling to be treated as held by him, but exclude rights falling to be treated as not held by him, by virtue of any of these provisions.

[*CA 2006, Sch 7 paras 5–11*].

Appendix 2 – Forms

FORMS – GENERAL COMPANY USE

Companies are required to submit a variety of information on their business activities to the Registrar of Companies. All statutory forms are available on request and free of charge from Companies House Cardiff and from Companies House Edinburgh (see **39.1** Registrar of Companies). Forms can be obtained or submitted online or by post.

See **39.6** Registrar of Companies for use of forms and completion of forms generally.

The forms which are currently prescribed for *CA 2006* are divided into Webcheck (ie on line filing) and paper forms. Please see Companies House website for help in completing forms and for a complete list of forms. This Appendix does not include forms for LLPs, LPs, EEIGs, SEs, Cross Border Mergers, *Newspaper Libel and Registration Act*, UK companies not formed under *CA 2006*, pre 6 April 2013 mortgages, and those forms listed on Companies House website as *Companies Act 1985* paper forms.

CA 2006 forms

Online filing

AR01	Annual Return (£14 charge)
Annual Accounts	Audit Exempt Small Full Accounts (with Abbreviated Option)
Annual Accounts	Audit Exempt Abbreviated Accounts—Annual Accounts, Micro-entity accounts
AA01	Change of accounting reference date
AA02	Dormant Company Accounts
AD01	Change of registered office address
AP01	Appointment of Director
AP02	Appointment of Corporate Director
AP03	Appointment of Secretary
AP04	Appointment of Corporate Secretary
NM01	Change of company name (only file online if permission is not needed for the new company name)
TM01	Terminating appointment as Director
TM02	Terminating appointment as Secretary
CH01	Change of particulars for Director
CH02	Change of particulars for Corporate Director
CH03	Change of particulars for Secretary
CH04	Change of particulars for Corporate Secretary
AD02	Notification of single alternative inspection location (SAIL)
AD03	Change of location of the company records to the single alternative inspection location (SAIL)
AD04	Change of location of the company records to the registered office

Appendix 2 – Forms

***CA 2006* forms**	
IN01	Register a private company (only online if a private company and is limited by shares and is adopting model articles and permission is not needed for company name)
SH01	Return of Allotment of Shares
DS02	Withdrawal of application to strike off
MR01	Particulars of a charge
MR02	Particulars of a charge subject to which property has been acquired
MR04	Register a statement of satisfaction
MR05	Statement that part or whole of the property has been released
Postal filing	
AA01	Change of accounting reference date
AA02	Dormant Company Accounts (DCA)
AA03	Notice of resolution removing auditors from office
AA06	Statement of guarantee by a parent undertaking of a subsidiary company
RT01	Application for administrative restoration to the Register
AR01	Annual Return for returns made up to a date either before, on or after 1 October 2011 (select date)
AD01	Change of registered office address
AD02	Notification of single alternative inspection location (SAIL)
AD03	Change of location of the company records to the single alternative inspection location (SAIL)
AD04	Change of location of the company records to the registered office
AD05	Change situation of England and Wales or Welsh company
CC01	Notice of restriction on the company's articles
CC02	Notice of removal of restriction on the company's articles
CC03	Statement of compliance where amendment of articles restricted
CC04	Statement of company's objects
CC05	Change of constitution by enactment
CC06	Change of constitution by order of court or other authority
NE01	Exemption from requirement as to use of "limited" or "cyfyngedig" on change of name
NM01	Notice of change of name by resolution
NM02	Notice of change of name by conditional resolution
NM03	Notice confirming satisfaction of the conditional resolution for change of name
NM04	Notice of change of name by means provided for in the articles
NM05	Notice of change of name by resolution of directors
NM06	Request to seek comments of government department or other specified body on change of name
AP01	Appointment of director
AP02	Appointment of corporate director

CA 2006 forms

AP03	Appointment of secretary
AP04	Appointment of corporate secretary
TM01	Termination of appointment of director
TM02	Termination of appointment of secretary
CH01	Change of director's details
CH02	Change of corporate director's details
CH03	Change of secretary's details
CH04	Change of corporate secretary's details
DS01	Striking off application by a company
DS02	Withdrawal of striking off application by a company
IN01	Application to register a private or public company
Pro Forma Memorandum CA 2006 (with a share capital)	Pro Forma of CA 2006 Memorandum for a company with a share capital (notice of subscribers)
Pro Forma Memorandum CA 2006 (without a share capital)	Pro Forma of CA 2006 Memorandum for a company without a share capital (notice of subscribers)
IC01	Notice of intention to carry on business as an investment company
IC02	Notice that a company no longer wishes to be an investment company
RM01	Notice of appointment of an administrative receiver, receiver or manager
RM02	Notice of ceasing to act as an administrative receiver, receiver or manager
MR01	Particulars of a mortgage or charge (where date or creation of charge is on or after 6/4/2013)
MR02	Particulars of a charge subject to which property or undertaking has been acquired (where date or creation of charge is on or after 6/4/2013)
MR03	Particulars for the registration of a charge to secure a series of debentures (where date or creation of charge is on or after 6/4/2013)
MR04	Register a statement of satisfaction (where charge is created before, on or after 6/4/2013)
MR05	Statement that part (or the whole) of the property charged has been released from the charge (where charge is created before, on or after 6/4/2013)
MR06	Statement of company acting as trustee (where date or creation of charge is on or after 6/4/2013)
MR07	Particulars of alteration of charge (negative pledge)
MR08	Particulars of charge where there is no instrument (where date or creation of charge is on or after 6/4/2013)
MR09	Particulars of a charge subject to which property or undertaking has been acquired where there is no instrument (where date or creation of charge is on or after 6/4/2013)

Appendix 2 – Forms

CA 2006 forms	
MR10	Particulars for the registration of a charge to secure a series of debentures where there is no instrument (where date or creation of charge is on or after 6/4/2013)
AD06	Notice of opening of overseas branch register
AD07	Notice of discontinuance of overseas branch register
AP05	Appointment of a manager under Section 47 of the Companies (Audit, Investigations and Community Enterprise) Act 2004 or receiver and manager under Section 18 of the Charities Act 1993 or judicial factor (Scotland)
TMO3	Termination of appointment of manager under Section 47 of the Companies (Audit, Investigations and Community Enterprise) Act 2004 or receiver and manager under Section 18 of the Charities Act 1993 or judicial factor (Scotland)
CH05	Change of service address for manager appointed under Section 47 of the Companies (Audit, Investigations and Community Enterprise) Act 2004 or receiver and manager under Section 18 of the Charities Act 1993 or judicial factor (Scotland)
RP01	Replacement of document not meeting requirements for proper delivery
RP02A	Application for rectification by the Registrar of Companies
RP02B	Application for rectification of a registered office or a UK establishment address by the Registrar of Companies
RP03	Notice of an objection to a request for the Registrar of Companies to rectify the Register
RP04	Second filing of a document previously delivered
VT01	Certified voluntary translation of an original document that is or has been delivered to the Registrar of Companies
RR01	Application by a private company for re-registration as a public company
RR02	Application by a public company for re-registration as a private limited company
RR03	Notice by the company of application to the court for cancellation of resolution for re-registration
RR04	Notice by the applicants of application to the court for cancellation of resolution for re-registration
RR05	Application by a private limited company for re-registration as an unlimited company
Pro-Forma form of assent for re-registration of private company as unlimited	Pro-Forma form of assent for re-registration of private limited company as unlimited
RR06	Application by an unlimited company for re-registration as a private limited company
RR07	Application by a public company for re-registration as a private unlimited company

CA 2006 forms

Pro-Forma form of assent for re-registration of public company as private and unlimited	Pro-Forma form of assent for re-registration of public company as private and unlimited
RR08	Application by a public company for re-registration as a private limited company following a court order reducing capital
RR09	Application by a public company for re-registration as a private company following a cancellation of shares
Res CA2006	Special resolution on change of name
Written Res CA2006	Written special resolution on change of name
980(1)	Notice of takeover offer to non-assenting shareholders
980(dec)	Notice of declaration to non-assenting shareholders
984	Notice of takeover to non-assenting shareholders
SH01	Return of allotment of shares
SH02	Notice of consolidation, sub-division, redemption of shares or re-conversion of stock into shares
SH03	Return of purchase of own shares
SH04	Notice of sale or transfer of treasury shares
SH05	Notice of cancellation of treasury shares
SH06	Notice of cancellation of shares
SH07	Notice of cancellation of shares held by or for a public company
SH08	Notice of name or other designation of class of shares
SH09	Return of allotment by an unlimited company allotting new class of shares
SH10	Notice of particulars of variation of rights attached to shares
SH11	Notice of new class of members
SH12	Notice of particulars of variation of class rights
SH13	Notice of name or other designation of class of members
SH14	Notice of redenomination of shares
SH15	Notice of reduction of capital following redenomination
SH16	Notice by the applicants of application to court for cancellation of the special resolution approving a redemption or purchase of shares out of capital
SH17	Notice by the company of application to court for cancellation of the special resolution approving a redemption or purchase of shares out of capital
SH19	Statement of capital
SH50	Application for trading certificate for a public company
466	Particulars of an instrument of alteration to a floating charge created by a company registered in Scotland

Appendix 3 – Companies House Fees

1 Fees payable by companies
2 Fees payable by overseas companies
3 Fees payable by Community interest companies and other incorporations
4 Fees payable to companies

1 FEES PAYABLE BY COMPANIES

The Secretary of State may make provision, by Regulations, requiring the payment of fees to the Registrar of Companies in respect of the performance of his functions and services or facilities provided for purposes incidental to, or otherwise connected with, those functions.

[*CA 2006, s 1063*]

The following fees are payable to the Registrar of Companies as from 1 October 2012.

Company Incorporation & Registration	Web-Filed	Software	Paper
Incorporation (excludes CICs, Welsh companies filing in Welsh, Unlimited companies and s1040 companies)		£13.00	£40.00
Web incorporation	£15.00		
Same-day incorporation		£30.00	£100.00
Change of name	£8.00	£8.00	£10.00
Same-day change of name	£30.00	£30.00	£50.00
Same-day simultaneous re-registration and change of name			£100.00
Re-registration			£20.00
Same-day re-registration			£50.00
Annual document processing fee payable with Annual Return	£13.00	£13.00	£40.00
Voluntary Strike Off			£10.00
Mortgage charge registration	£10.00	£10.00	£13.00
Reduction of capital by solvency statement			£10.00
Same day reduction of capital by solvency statement			£50.00
Reduction of capital by court order			£10.00
Same day reduction of capital by court order			£50.00
Administrative Restoration			£100.00
Application to make an address unavailable for public inspection by an individual:			£55.00
Application to make an address unavailable for public inspection by the company: for any list of members (other than a long list) in hard copy form			£55.00*
Application to make an address unavailable for public inspection by the company: for any list of members (other than a long list) filed electronically			£55.00*
Application to make an address unavailable for public inspection by the company: for a long list of members delivered on CD-ROM or DVD-ROM			£55.00*

1 Appendix 3 – Companies House Fees

Company Incorporation & Registration	Web-Filed	Software	Paper
Application to make an address unavailable for public inspection by the company: for a long list of members in hard copy form			£55.00*
Application to make an address unavailable for public inspection by a person who registers a charge			£55.00*
Section 243 application to make protected usual residential address information unavailable to a Credit Reference Agency			£100.00
* Please note all fees are per document suppressed			

Companies House Direct	
Sign on	
Any Account	no charge
Monthly Subscription (per account per month)	£4.00
Monitor	
Monitor (Per company per annum)	no charge
Screen Charges	
Company indexes	no charge
Basic Company Details	no charge
History of Company Transactions	no charge
Register of Disqualified Directors	no charge
Insolvency Details	no charge
Company Appointments	no charge
Personal Appointments	£1.00
Full Mortgage Details	£1.00
Company Reports	
The Current Appointments Report	no charge
The Mortgage Statement	£1.00
The Company Record	£1.00
Document Images	
Download per document	£1.00
View and download per document	£1.00
Hard copy of company document **by post** or fax	£3.00
Document packages (up to 50 docs)	
By image download	£4.00
By post	£20.00
Certified copies	
Certified copy of document by post or collection	£20.00
Same day certified copy of document by post or collection	£60.00
Certificates of Incorporation	

Companies House Direct	
By post or collection	£20.00
Additional certificate (for same company) by post or collection	£10.00
Same day certificate of Incorporation by post or collection	£60.00
Additional faxed copy of same day certificate	no charge
Microfiche	
DVD copy of archive microfiche (to 31/12/2002) by post or collection	£20.00
Shareholder Lists	
DVD Bulk Shareholders list by post or collection	£20.00

Companies House Information Centre - CHIC	
Screen charges	
Online page print of document (per page)	£0.10
Company indexes	no charge
Basic Company Details	no charge
History of Company Transactions	no charge
Register of Disqualified Directors	no charge
Insolvency Details	no charge
Company Appointments	no charge
Personal Appointments	£1.00
Charge index	no charge
Full Charge details	£1.00
Company Reports	
The Current Appointments Report	no charge
The Mortgage Statement	£1.00
The Company Record	£1.00
Document images/orders	
View document image	£1.00
Print document (without viewing)	£1.00
Inspect original document	£6.00
Copy of a document	£3.00
Document Packages	
Print (up to 25 documents)	£7.00
Certified copies	
Certified copy of document (up to 10 pages) by post or collection at a CHIC	£20.00
— Each page thereafter by post or collection	£1.00

1 Appendix 3 – Companies House Fees

Companies House Information Centre - CHIC	
Same day certified copy of document by post or collection at a CHIC	£60.00
Certificates of Incorporation	
By post or collection	£20.00
Additional certificate (for same company) by post or collection	£10.00
Same day certificate of Incorporation by post or collection	£60.00
Additional faxed copy of same day certificate of Incorporation	no charge
Microfiche	
DVD copy of archive microfiche (to 31/12/2002) by post or collection	£20.00
Shareholder Lists	
DVD Bulk Shareholders list by post or collection	£20.00

Contact Centre: 0303 123 4500	
Registered Office address (per company) by telephone	no charge
Screen prints	
Alpha index, dissolved companies, former names (per page) by post, fax or email	£2.00
History screen and Registered office (per company) by post, fax or email	no charge
Company appointments by post, fax or email	£3.00
Mortgage details by post, fax or email	£3.00
Company Reports	
The current appointments report by post, fax or email	£3.00
The Mortgage Statement by post, fax or email	£3.00

Contact Centre: 0303 123 4500	
The company record by post, fax or email	£3.00
Document images	
Copy of company document by e-mail (post 1995 documents)	£3.00
Company documents by post or fax	
Copy of company document (other than long list of members) by post	£3.00
Copy of company document (other than long list of members) by fax	£3.00
Copy of company document (other than long list of members) by email	£3.00
Hard copy of document not on microfiche by post	£9.00
Paper copy bulk shareholder list - up to and Including 50th Page	£12.50
— Each additional page	£0.20
Certified copies	
Certified copy of document by post or collection at a CHIC	£20.00
Same day certified copy of document by post or collection at a CHIC	£60.00
Certificates of Incorporation	
By post or collection	£20.00
Additional certificate (for same company) by post or collection	£10.00
Same day certificate of Incorporation by post or collection	£60.00
Additional faxed copy of same day certificate of Incorporation	no charge
Microfiche	
DVD copy of archive microfiche (to 31/12/2002) by post or collection	£20.00
Shareholder Lists	
DVD Bulk Shareholders list by post or collection	£20.00
Archive search	
By post or telephone	£20.00

WebCheck	
Monitor	
Monitor (per company per annum)	no charge

1 Appendix 3 – Companies House Fees

WebCheck	
Company Reports:	
The Current Appointments Report	no charge
The Company Record	£1.00
Document images	
Download per document	£1.00

XML gateway search fees	
Note: plus 15% off total invoice value	
Sign on	
Monthly Subscription (per account)	£4.70
Data charges	
Personal Appointments	£1.00
Document images	
Download per document	£1.00

Extranet search fees	
Note: plus 15% off total invoice value	
Sign on	
Monthly Subscription (per account)	£4.70
Monitor	
Monitor (per company per annum)	no charge
Screen charges	
Personal Appointments	£1.00
Full mortgage details	£1.00
Company reports	
The Current Appointments Report	no charge
The Mortgage Statement	£1.00
The Company Record	£1.00
Document images	
Download per document	£1.00
Inspect and download per document	£1.00
Document packages	
Up to 50 documents - by image download	£4.00

2 FEES PAYABLE BY OVERSEAS COMPANIES

Registration of a UK establishment of an Overseas Company	£20.00
Same day registration of a UK establishment of an Overseas Company	£100.00
Change of corporate name or alternative name of an Overseas Company	£10.00
Same day change of corporate name or alternative name of an Overseas Company	£50.00
Annual document processing fee payable with the Overseas Company accounts	£20.00

3 FEES PAYABLE BY COMMUNITY INTEREST COMPANIES AND OTHER INCORPORATIONS

Fees payable by Community interest companies and other incorporations	
Registration of a Community Interest Company in accordance with section 36 of the Companies (Audit, Investigations and Community Enterprise) Act 2004	£20.00 Please submit a cheque or postal order for £35 payable to Companies House for the incorporation of a CIC to cover Companies House fee and the CIC Regulator's fee of £15
Registration of a company or LLP with constitutional documents in Welsh	£20.00
Registration of a company authorised to register in accordance with section 1040 of the Companies Act 2006	£20.00
Registration of an unlimited company in accordance with section 14 of the Companies Act 2006	£20.00

[*SI 2005 No 1788, Reg 36, Sch 5; SI 2009 No 1942, Reg 23; SI 2012 No 1907*].

4 FEES PAYABLE TO COMPANIES

The following *maximum* fees are payable to companies for inspection of, and copies of entries in, registers etc.

Fees payable to companies	
Inspection by *non-members* of	
• register and index of members' names under *CA 2006, s 116(1)(b)*	£3.50 for each hour (or part) of inspection
• register of directors under *CA 2006, s 162(5)(b)* or register of secretaries under *CA 2006, s 275(5)(b)* where inspection takes place after 30 September 2009	£3.50 for each hour (or part) of inspection
• register of directors and secretaries under *CA 1985, s 288(3)* where inspection takes place before 1 October 2009	£2.50 for each hour (or part) of inspection
• register of debenture holders under *CA 2006, s 744(1)(b)*	£3.50 for each hour (or part) of inspection
• instruments creating charges and register of charges under *CA 2006, s 877(4)(b)* (England and Wales and Northern Ireland) or *CA 2006, s 892(4)(b)* (Scotland)	£3.50 for each hour (or part) of inspection
• register of directors' interests in share and debentures under *CA 1985, s 325(5), Sch 13 para 25* where inspection takes place before 1 October 2009	£2.50 for each hour (or part) of inspection
Inspection is free to members.	
Copies of entries in	
• register of debenture holders under *CA 1985, s 191(2)* where the request is made before 6 April 2008;	
• register of directors' interests in shares and debentures under *CA 1985, s 325(5), Sch 13 para 26(1)*; or	
• register of members under *CA 1985, s 356(3)* where the request is made before 1 October 2007 or where, at the time of the request, the company is still obliged to submit an annual return made up to a date before 1 October 2008	
For the first 100 entries	£2.50
For the next 1,000 entries (or part)	£20.00
For every subsequent 1,000 entries (or part)	£15.00
Copies of entries in	
• register of debenture holders under *CA 2006, s 744(2)* where the request is made before on or after 6 April 2008;	

Fees payable to companies	
• register of members under *CA 2006, s 116(2)* where the request is made on or after 1 October 2007 and where, at the time of the request, the company is not still obliged to submit an annual return made up to a date before 1 October 2008; or	
• register of interests in shares disclosed under *CA 2006, s 811(2)*	
For the first 5 entries	£1.00
For the next 95 entries (or part)	£30.00
For the next 900 entries (or part)	£30.00
For the next 99,000 entries (or part)	£30.00
For the remainder of the entries in the register (or part)	£30.00
In addition, the company may charge reasonable costs incurred by it in delivering the copy of the entries to the person entitled to be provided with that copy	
Copies of	
• debenture trust deeds under *CA 1985, s 191(3)* where the request is made before 6 April 2008	10p per 100 words (or part)
• minutes under *CA 1985, s 383(3)* in respect of general meetings of the company held before 1 October 2007	10p per 100 words (or part)
Copies of	
• debenture trust deeds under *CA 2006, s 749(1)* where the request is made on or after 6 April 2008	10p per 500 words (or part) copies
• director's service contract (or memorandum setting out terms of that contract) under *CA 2006, s 229(2)*;	10p per 500 words (or part) copies
• director's qualifying indemnity provision under *CA 2006, s 238(2)*;	10p per 500 words (or part) copies
• records of resolutions and meetings under *CA 2006, s 358(4)*;	10p per 500 words (or part) copies
• report of the outcome of an investigation required by members about interests in the company's shares under *CA 2006, s 807(2)*	10p per 500 words (or part) copies
In addition, the company may charge reasonable costs incurred by it in delivering the copy of the company record to the person entitled to be provided with that copy	

[*SI 1991 No 1998; SI 2007 No 2612; SI 2007 No 3535; SI 2008 No 3007*].

Appendix 4 Standard Articles of association

(1) Companies Act 1985 Table A (SI 1985/805)
(2) Model articles: private companies limited by shares (SI 2008/3229, Sch 1). CA 2006
(3) Model articles: public companies (SI 2008/3229, Sch 3). CA 2006

COMPANIES ACT 1985 TABLE A (SI 1985/805) MODEL ARTICLES: COMPANIES LIMITED BY SHARES (SI 2008 NO 3229, SCH 1).

1	Regulations for management of a company limited by shares
2–5	Share Capital
6, 7	Share Certificates
8–11	Lien
12–22	Calls on shares and forfeiture
23–28	Transfer of shares
29–31	Transmission of shares
32–34	Alteration of share capital
35	Purchase of own shares
36, 37	General meetings
38, 39	Notice of general meetings
40–53	Proceedings at general meetings
54–63	Votes of members
64	Number of directors
65–69	Alternate directors
70, 71	Powers of directors
72	Delegation of directors' powers
73–80	Appointment and retirement of directors
81	Disqualification and removal of directors
82	Remuneration of directors
83	Directors' expenses
84–86	Directors' appointments and interests
87	Directors' gratuities and pensions
88–98	Proceedings of directors
99	Secretary
100	Minutes
101	The seal
102–108	Dividends
109	Accounts
110	Capitalisation of profits
111–116	Notices
117	Winding up
118	Indemnity

1 Regulations for management of a company limited by shares

In these regulations

"the Act" means the Companies Act 1985 including any statutory modification or re-enactment thereof for the time being in force [and any provisions of the Companies Act 2006 for the time being in force][2].

"the articles" means the articles of the company.

"clear days" in relation to the period of a notice means that period excluding the day when the notice is given or deemed to be given and the day for which it is given or on which it is to take effect.

["communication" means the same as in the Electronic Communications Act 2000.][1]

["electronic communication" means the same as in the Electronic Communications Act 2000.][1]

"executed" includes any mode of execution.

"office" means the registered office of the company.

"the holder" in relation to shares means the member whose name is entered in the register of members as the holder of the shares.

"the seal" means the common seal of the company.

"secretary" means the secretary of the company or any other person appointed to perform the duties of the secretary of the company, including a joint, assistant or deputy secretary.

"the United Kingdom" means Great Britain and Northern Ireland.

Unless the context otherwise requires, words or expressions contained in these regulations bear the same meaning as in the Act but excluding any statutory modification thereof not in force when these regulations become binding on the company.

Notes

---

1 Inserted by SI 2000 No 3373, art 32(1), Sch 1 para 1 with effect from 22 December 2000.

2 Inserted by SI 2007 No 2541, Reg 3 in relation to a company registered on or after 1 October 2007.

---

2 Share capital

Subject to the provisions of the Act and without prejudice to any rights attached to any existing shares, any share may be issued with such rights or restrictions as the company may by ordinary resolution determine.

3

Subject to the provisions of the Act, shares may be issued which are to be redeemed or are to be liable to be redeemed at the option of the company or the holder on such terms and in such manner as may be provided by the articles.

4

The company may exercise the powers of paying commissions conferred by the Act. Subject to the [provisions] of the Act, any such commission may be satisfied by the payment of cash or by the allotment of fully or partly paid shares or partly in one way and partly in the other.

Note

Word in square brackets substituted for the word 'provision' by SI 1985 No 1052 as from 1 August 1985.

5

Except as required by law, no person shall be recognised by the company as holding any share upon any trust and (except as otherwise provided by the articles or by law) the company shall not be bound by or recognise any interest in any share except an absolute right to the entirety thereof in the holder.

6 Share certificates

Every member, upon becoming the holder of any shares, shall be entitled without payment to one certificate for all the shares of each class held by him (and, upon transferring a part of his holding of shares of any class, to a certificate for the balance of such holding) or several certificates each for one or more of his shares of any class, to a certificate for the balance of such holding) or several certificates each for one or more of his shares upon payment for every certificate after the first of such reasonable sum as the directors may determine. Every certificate shall be sealed with the seal and shall specify the number, class and distinguishing numbers (if any) of the shares to which it relates and the amount or respective amounts paid up thereon. The company shall not be bound to issue more than one certificate for shares held jointly by several persons and delivery of a certificate to one joint holder shall be a sufficient delivery to all of them.

7

If a share certificate is defaced, worn-out, lost or destroyed, it may be renewed on such terms (if any) as to evidence and indemnity and payment of the expenses reasonably incurred by the company in investigating evidence as the directors may determine but otherwise free of charge, and (in the case of defacement or wearing-out) on delivery up of the old certificate.

8 Lien

The company shall have a first and paramount lien on every share (not being a fully paid share) for all moneys (whether presently payable or not) payable at a fixed time or called in respect of that share. The directors may at any time declare any share to be wholly or in part exempt from the provisions of this regulation. The company's lien on a share shall extend to any amount payable in respect of it.

9

The company may sell in such manner as the directors determine any shares on which the company has a lien if a sum in respect of which the lien exists is presently payable and is not paid within fourteen clear days after notice has been given to the holder of the share or to the person entitled to it in consequence of the death or bankruptcy of the holder, demanding payment and stating that if the notice is not complied with the shares may be sold.

10

To give effect to a sale the directors may authorise some person to execute an instrument of transfer of the shares sold to, or in accordance with the directions of, the purchaser. The title of the transferee to the shares shall not be affected by any irregularity in or invalidity of the proceedings in reference to the sale.

11

The net proceeds of the sale, after payment of the costs, shall be applied in payment of so much of the sum for which the lien exists as is presently payable, and any residue shall (upon surrender to the company for cancellation of the certificate for the shares sold and subject to a like lien for any moneys not presently payable as existed upon the shares before the sale) be paid to the person entitled to the shares at the date of the sale.

12 Calls on shares and forfeiture

Subject to the terms of allotment, the directors may make calls upon the members in respect of any moneys unpaid on their shares (whether in respect of nominal value or premium) and each member shall (subject to receiving at least fourteen clear days' notice specifying when and where payment is to be made) pay to the company as required by the notice the amount called on his shares. A call may be required to be paid by instalments. A call may, before receipt by the company of any sum due thereunder, be revoked in whole or part and payment of a call may be postponed in whole or part. A person upon whom a call is made shall remain liable for calls made upon him notwithstanding the subsequent transfer of the shares in respect whereof the call was made.

13

A call shall be deemed to have been made at the time when the resolution of the directors authorising the call was passed.

14

The joint holders of a share shall be jointly and severally liable to pay all calls in respect thereof.

15

If a call remains unpaid after it has become due and payable the person from whom it is due and payable shall pay interest on the amount unpaid from the day it became due and payable until it is paid at the rate fixed by the terms of allotment of the share or in the notice of the call or, if no rate is fixed, at the appropriate rate (as defined by the Act) but the directors may waive payment of the interest wholly or in part.

16

An amount payable in respect of a share on allotment or at any fixed date, whether in respect of nominal value or premium or as an instalment of a call, shall be deemed to be a call and if it is not paid the provisions of the articles shall apply as if that amount had become due and payable by virtue of a call.

17

Subject to the terms of allotment, the directors may make arrangements on the issue of shares for a difference between the holders in the amounts and times of payment of calls on their shares.

18

If a call remains unpaid after it has become due and payable the directors may give to the person from whom it is due not less than fourteen clear days' notice requiring payment of the amount unpaid together with any interest which may have accrued. The notice shall name the place where payment is to be made and shall state that if the notice is not complied with the shares in respect of which the call was made will be liable to be forfeited.

19

If the notice is not complied with any share in respect of which it was given may, before the payment required by the notice has been made, be forfeited by a resolution of the directors and the forfeiture shall include all dividends or other moneys payable in respect of the forfeited shares and not paid before the forfeiture.

20

Subject to the provisions of the Act, a forfeited share may be sold, re-alloted or otherwise disposed of on such terms and in such manner as the directors determine either to the person who was before the forfeiture the holder or to any other person and at any time before sale, re-allotment or other disposition, the forfeiture may be cancelled on such terms as the directors think fit. Where for the purposes of its disposal a forfeited share is to be transferred to any person the directors may authorise some person to execute an instrument of transfer of the share to that person.

21

A person any of whose shares have been forfeited shall cease to be a member in respect of them and shall surrender to the company for cancellation the certificate for the shares forfeited but shall remain liable to the company for all moneys which at the date of forfeiture were presently payable by him to the company in respect of those shares with interest at the rate at which interest was payable on those moneys before the forfeiture or, if no interest was so payable, at the appropriate rate (as defined in the Act) from the date of forfeiture until payment but the directors may waive payment wholly or in part or enforce payment without any allowance for the value of the shares at the time of forfeiture or for any consideration received on their disposal.

22

A statutory declaration by a director or the secretary that a share has been forfeited on a specified date shall be conclusive evidence of the facts stated in it as against all persons claiming to be entitled to the share and the declaration shall (subject to the execution of an instrument of transfer if necessary) constitute a good title to the share and the person to whom the share is disposed of shall not be bound to see to the application of the consideration, if any, nor shall his title to the share be affected by any irregularity in or invalidity of the proceedings in reference to the forfeiture or disposal of the share.

23 Transfer of shares

The instrument of transfer of a share may be in any usual form or in any other form which the directors may approve and shall be executed by or on behalf of the transferor and, unless the share is fully paid, by or on behalf of the transferee.

24

The directors may refuse to register the transfer of a share which is not fully paid to a person of whom they do not approve and they may refuse to register the transfer of a share on which the company has a lien. They may also refuse to register a transfer unless

(a) it is lodged at the office or at such other place as the directors may appoint and is accompanied by the certificate for the shares to which it relates and such other evidence as the directors may reasonably require to show the right of the transferor to make the transfer;

(b) it is in respect of only one class of shares; and

(c) it is in favour of not more than four transferees.

25

If the directors refuse to register a transfer of a share, they shall within two months after the date on which the transfer was lodged with the company send to the transferee notice of the refusal.

26

The registration of transfers of shares or of transfers of any class of shares may be suspended at such times and for such periods (not exceeding thirty days in any year) as the directors may determine.

27

No fee shall be charged for the registration of any instrument of transfer or other document relating to or affecting the title to any share.

28

The company shall be entitled to retain any instrument of transfer which is registered, but any instrument of transfer which the directors refuse to register shall be returned to the person lodging it when notice of the refusal is given.

29 Transmission of shares

If a member dies the survivor or survivors where he was a joint holder, and his personal representatives where he was a sole holder or the only survivor of joint holders, shall be the only persons recognised by the company as having any title to his interest; but nothing herein contained shall release the estate of a deceased member from any liability in respect of any share which had been jointly held by him.

30

A person becoming entitled to a share in consequence of the death or bankruptcy of a member may, upon such evidence being produced as the directors may properly require, elect either to become the holder of the share or to have some person nominated by him registered as the transferee. If he elects to become the holder he shall give notice to the company to that effect. If he elects to have another person registered he shall execute an instrument of transfer of the share to that person. All the articles relating to the transfer of shares shall apply to the notice or instrument of transfer as if it were an instrument of transfer executed by the member and the death or bankruptcy of the member had not occurred.

31

A person becoming entitled to a share in consequence of the death or bankruptcy of a member shall have the rights to which he would be entitled if he were the holder of the share, except that he shall not, before being registered as the holder of the share, be entitled in respect of it to attend or vote at any meeting of the company or at any separate meeting of the holders of any class of shares in the company.

32 Alteration of share capital

The company may by ordinary resolution

(a) increase its share capital by new shares of such amount as the resolution prescribes;

(b) consolidate and divide all or any of its share capital into shares of larger amount than its existing shares;

(c) subject to the provisions of the Act, sub-divide its shares, or any of them, into shares of smaller amount and the resolution may determine that, as between the shares resulting from the sub-division, any of them may have any preference or advantage as compared with the others; and

(d) cancel shares which, at the date of the passing of the resolution, have not been taken or agreed to be taken by any person and diminish the amount of its share capital by the amount of the shares so cancelled.

33

Whenever as a result of a consolidation of shares any members would become entitled to fractions of a share, the directors may, on behalf of those members, sell the shares representing the fractions for the best price reasonably obtainable to any person (including, subject to the provisions of the Act, the company) and distribute the net proceeds of sale in due proportion among those members, and the directors may authorise some person to execute an instrument of transfer of the shares to, or in accordance with the directions of, the purchaser. The transferee shall not be bound to see to the application of the purchase money nor shall his title to the shares be affected by any irregularity in or invalidity of the proceedings in reference to the sale.

34

Subject to the provisions of the Act, the company may by special resolution reduce its share capital, any capital redemption reserve and any share premium account in any way.

35 Purchase of own shares

Subject to the provisions of the Act, the company may purchase its own shares (including any redeemable shares) and, if it is a private company, make a payment in respect of the redemption or purchase of its own shares otherwise than out of distributable profits of the company or the proceeds of a fresh issue of shares.

36 General meetings

All general meetings other than annual general meetings shall be called extraordinary general meetings.

Note

This Article ceases to apply to a company registered on or after 1 October 2007. [*SI 2007 No 2541, Reg 4*].

37

The directors may call general meetings and, on the requisition of members pursuant to the provisions of the Act, shall forthwith proceed to convene an extraordinary general meeting for a date not later than eight weeks after receipt of the requisition. If there are not within the United Kingdom sufficient directors to call a general meeting, any director or any member of the company may call a general meeting.

Note

This article is amended by *SI 2007 No 2541, Reg 5* in relation to companies registered on or after 1 October 2007 as follows.

- For the words 'an extraordinary' substitute the word 'a'.

- For the words 'for a date not later than eight weeks after receipt of the requisition' substitute 'in accordance with the provisions of the Act'.

38 Notice of general meetings

An annual general meeting and an extraordinary general meeting called for the passing of a special resolution or a resolution appointing a person as a director shall be called by at least twenty-one clear days' notice. All other extraordinary general meetings shall be called by at least fourteen clear days' notice but a general meeting may be called by shorter notice if is so agreed

(a) in the case of an annual general meeting, by all the members entitled to attend and vote thereat; and

(b) in the case of any other meeting by a majority in number of the members having a right to attend and vote being a majority together holding not less than ninety-five per cent in nominal value of the shares giving that right.

The notice shall specify the time and place of the meeting and the general nature of the business to be transacted and, in the case of an annual general meeting, shall specify the meeting as such.

Subject to the provisions of the articles and to any restrictions imposed on any shares, the notice shall be given to all the members, to all persons entitled to a share in consequence of the death or bankruptcy of a member and to the directors and auditors.

Note

This Article is amended by *SI 2007 No 2541, Regs 9, 20* in relation to companies registered on or after 1 October 2007 as follows.

In relation to a private company limited by shares

- Omit the words 'An annual general meeting and an extraordinary general meeting called for the passing of a special resolution or a resolution appointing a person as a director shall be called by at least twenty-one clear days' notice. All other extraordinary'.
- Omit paragraph (a).
- In paragraph (b), omit the words 'in the case of any other meeting' and '– five'.
- Omit the words 'and, in the case of an annual general meeting, shall specify the meeting as such'.

In relation to public companies limited by shares

- After the words 'annual general meeting' omit the words 'and an extraordinary general meeting called for the passing of a special resolution or a resolution appointing a person as a director'.
- After the words 'All other' omit the word 'extraordinary'.

39

The accidental omission to give notice of a meeting to, or the non-receipt of notice of a meeting by, any person entitled to receive notice shall not invalidate the proceedings at that meeting.

40 Proceedings at general meetings

No business shall be transacted at any meeting unless a quorum is present. Two persons entitled to vote upon the business to be transacted, each being a member or a proxy for a member or a duly authorised representative of a corporation, shall be a quorum.

Note

This Article is amended by *SI 2007 No 2541, Reg 10* in relation to private companies limited by shares registered on or after 1 October 2007 as follows.

- At the beginning of the second sentence insert the words 'Save in the case of a company with a single member'.

41

If such a quorum is not present within half an hour from the time appointed for the meeting, or if during a meeting such a quorum ceases to be present, the meeting shall stand adjourned to the same day in the next week at the same time and place or [to] such time and place as the directors may determine.

Note

Word in square brackets substituted by *SI 1985 No 1052* with effect from 1 August 1985

42

The chairman, if any, of the board of directors or in his absence some other director nominated by the directors shall preside as chairman of the meeting, but if neither the chairman nor such other director (if any) be present within fifteen minutes after the time appointed for holding the meeting and willing to act, the directors present shall elect one of their number to be chairman and, if there is only one director present and willing to act, he shall be chairman.

43

If no director is willing to act as chairman, or if no director is present within fifteen minutes after the time appointed for holding the meeting, the members present and entitled to vote shall choose one of their number to be chairman.

44

A director shall, notwithstanding that he is not a member, be entitled to attend and speak at any general meeting and at any separate meeting of the holders of any class of shares in the company.

45

The chairman may, with the consent of a meeting at which a quorum is present (and shall if so directed by the meeting), adjourn the meeting from time to time and from place to place, but no business shall be transacted at an adjourned meeting other than business which might properly have been transacted at the meeting had the adjournment not taken place. When a meeting is adjourned for fourteen days or more, at least seven clear days' notice shall be given specifying the time and place of the adjourned meeting and the general nature of the business to be transacted. Otherwise it shall not be necessary to give any such notice.

46

A resolution put to the vote of a meeting shall be decided on a show of hands unless before, or on the declaration of the result of, the show of hands a poll is duly demanded. Subject to the provisions of the Act, a poll may be demanded

(a) by the chairman; or

(b) by at least two members having the right to vote at the meeting; or

(c) by a member or members representing not less than one-tenth of the total voting rights of all the members having the right to vote at the meeting; or

(d) by a member or members holding shares conferring a right to vote at the meeting being shares on which an aggregate sum has been paid up equal to not less than one-tenth of the total sum paid up on all the shares conferring that right;

and a demand by a person as proxy for a member shall be the same as a demand by the member.

47

Unless a poll is duly demanded a declaration by the chairman that a resolution has been carried or carried unanimously, or by a particular majority, or lost, or not carried by a particular majority and an entry to that effect in the minutes of the meeting shall be conclusive evidence of the fact without proof of the number or proportion of the votes recorded in favour of or against the resolution.

48

The demand for a poll may, before the poll is taken, be withdrawn but only with the consent of the chairman and a demand so withdrawn shall not be taken to have invalidated the result of a show of hands declared before the demand was made.

49

A poll shall be taken as the chairman directs and he may appoint scrutineers (who need not be members) and fix a time and place for declaring the result of the poll. The result of the poll shall be deemed to be the resolution of the meeting at which the poll was demanded.

50

In the case of an equality of votes, whether on a show of hands or on a poll, the chairman shall be entitled to a casting vote in addition to any other vote he may have.

Note

This Article ceases to have effect in relation to a company registered on or after 1 October 2007

[*SI 2007 No 2826, Reg 3*].

51

A poll demanded on the election of a chairman or on a question of adjournment shall be taken forthwith. A poll demanded on any other question shall be taken either forthwith or at such time and place as the chairman directs not being more than thirty days after the poll is demanded. The demand for a poll shall not prevent the continuance of a meeting for the transaction of any business other than the question on which the poll was demanded. If a poll is demanded before the declaration of the result of a show of hands and the demand is duly withdrawn, the meeting shall continue as if the demand had not been made.

52

No notice need be given of a poll not taken forthwith if the time and place at which it is to be taken are announced at the meeting at which it is demanded. In any other case at least seven clear days' notice shall be given specifying the time and place at which the poll is to be taken.

53

A resolution in writing executed by or on behalf of each member who would have been entitled to vote upon it if it had been proposed at a general meeting at which he was present shall be as effectual as if it had been passed at a general meeting duly convened and held and may consist of several instruments in the like form each executed by or on behalf of one or more members.

Note

This Article ceases to have effect in relation to a company registered on or after 1 October 2007.

[*SI 2007 No 2826, Reg 6*].

54 Votes of members

Subject to any rights or restrictions attached to any shares, on a show of hands every member who (being an individual) is present in person or (being a corporation) is present by a duly authorised representative, not being himself a member entitled to vote, shall have one vote and on a poll every member shall have one vote for every share of which he is the holder.

Note

This Article is amended by *SI 2007 No 2826, Reg 4* in relation to companies registered on or after 1 October 2007 as follows.

- After the words 'is present in person' insert the words 'or by proxy'.
- After the words 'is present by a duly authorised representative, insert the words 'or proxy'.
- Substitute for the words 'not being' the words 'unless the proxy (in either case) or the representative is'.

55

In the case of joint holders the vote of the senior who tenders a vote, whether in person or by proxy, shall be accepted to the exclusion of the votes of the other joint holders; and seniority shall be determined by the order in which the names of the holders stand in the register of members.

56

A member in respect of whom an order has been made by any court having jurisdiction (whether in the United Kingdom or elsewhere) in matters concerning mental disorder may vote, whether on a show of hands or on a poll, by his receiver, *curator bonis* or other person authorised in that behalf appointed by that court, and any such receiver, *curator bonis* or other person may, on a poll, vote by proxy. Evidence to the satisfaction of the directors of the authority of the person claiming to exercise the right to vote shall be deposited at the office, or at such other place as is specified in accordance with the articles for the deposit of instruments of proxy, not less than 48 hours before the time appointed for holding the meeting or adjourned meeting at which the right to vote is to be exercised and in default the right to vote shall not be exercisable.

Note

By virtue of the *Adults with Incapacity (Scotland) Act 2000, s 88(2), Sch 5, para 1* the references to a *curator bonis* shall be construed as references to a guardian with similar powers appointed under that Act.

57

No member shall vote at any general meeting or at any separate meeting of the holders of any class of shares in the company, either in person or by proxy, in respect of any share held by him unless all moneys presently payable by him in respect of that share have been paid.

58

No objection shall be raised to the qualification of any voter except at the meeting or adjourned meeting at which the vote objected to is tendered, and every vote not disallowed at the meeting shall be valid. Any objection made in due time shall be referred to the chairman whose decision shall be final and conclusive.

59

On a poll votes may be given either personally or by proxy. A member may appoint more than one proxy to attend on the same occasion.

60

[The appointment of][1] a proxy shall be [in writing][2] executed by or on behalf of the appointor and shall be in the following form (or in a form as near thereto as circumstances allow or in any other form which is usual or which the directors may approve)—

. . . . PLC/Limited

I/We, ... of . . . . , being a member/members of the above-named company, hereby appoint . . . . of . . . . , or failing him, ... of . . . . , as my/our proxy to vote in my/our names[s] and on my/our behalf at the annual/extraordinary general meeting of the company, to be held on . . . . 19 . . . . , and at any adjournment thereof.

Signed on .... 19.........."[3]

Notes

---

1 Substituted for the words 'An instrument appointing' by *SI 2000 No 3373, art 32(1), Sch 1 para 2* with effect from 22 December 2000.

2 Words in italics revoked by *SI 2000 No 3373, art 32(1), Sch 1 para 2* with effect from 22 December 2000.

3 This Article is amended by *SI 2007 No 2541, Regs 11, 21* in relation to companies registered on or after 1 October 2007 as follows.

In relation to a private company limited by shares

- After the words 'our behalf at the' omit the words 'annual/extraordinary'.

In relation to public companies limited by shares

- After the words 'our behalf at the annual/' omit the word 'extraordinary' and insert the words 'any other'.

61

Where it is desired to afford members an opportunity of instructing the proxy how he shall act the [appointment of][1] a proxy shall be in the following form (or in a form as near thereto as circumstances allow or in any other form which is usual or which the directors may approve)

. . . . PLC/Limited

I/We, ... of . . . . , being a member/members of the above-named company, hereby appoint . . . . of . . . . , or failing him, ... of . . . . , as my/our proxy to vote in my/our names[s] and on my/our behalf at the annual/extraordinary general meeting of the company, to be held on . . . . 19 . . . . , and at any adjournment thereof.

Signed on .... 19.........."

This form is to be used in respect of the resolutions mentioned below as follows:

Resolution No. 1 *for *against

Resolution No. 2 *for *against.

*Strike out whichever is not desired.

Unless otherwise instructed, the proxy may vote as he thinks fit or abstain from voting.
Signed this .... day of ...."

Notes

---

1 Substituted for the words 'instrument appointing' by *SI 2000 No 3373, art 32(1), Sch 1 para 3* with effect from 22 December 2000.

In relation to a private company limited by shares

- After the words 'our behalf at the' omit the words 'annual/extraordinary'.

In relation to public companies limited by shares

- After the words 'our behalf at the annual/' omit the word 'extraordinary' and insert the words 'any other'.

62

[The appointment of] a proxy and any authority under which it is executed or a copy of such authority certified notarially or in some other way approved by the directors may

(a) [in the case of an instrument in writing] be deposited at the office or at such other place within the United kingdom as is specified in the notice convening the meeting or in any instrument of proxy sent out by the company in relation to the meeting not less than 48 hours before the time for holding the meeting or adjourned meeting at which the person named in the instrument proposes to vote; or

[(aa) in the case of an appointment contained in an electronic communication, where an address has been specified for the purpose of receiving electronic communications

(i) in the notice convening the meeting, or

(ii) in any instrument of proxy sent out by the company in relation to the meeting, or

(iii) in any invitation contained in an electronic communication to appoint a proxy issued by the company in relation to the meeting,

be received at such address not less than 48 hours before the time for holding the meeting or adjourned meeting at which the person named in the appointment proposes to vote;]

(b) in the case of a poll taken more than 48 hours after it is demanded, be deposited [or received] as aforesaid after the poll has been demanded and not less than 24 hours before the time appointed for the taking of the poll; or

(c) where the poll is not taken forthwith but is taken not more than 48 hours after it was demanded, be delivered at the meeting at which the poll was demanded to the chairman or to the secretary or to any director;

[and an appointment of proxy which is not deposited, delivered or received] in a manner so permitted shall be invalid.

[In this regulation and the next, "address", in relation to electronic communications, includes any number or address used for the purposes of such communications.]

Note

Words 'The appointment of' substituted for the words 'The instrument appointing', words 'and an appointment of proxy which is not deposited, delivered or received' substituted for 'and an instrument of proxy which is not deposited or delivered', and other word in square brackets inserted by *SI 2000 No 3373, art 32(1), Sch 1 para 4* with effect from 22 December 2000.

63

A vote given or poll demanded by proxy or by the duly authorised representative of a corporation shall be valid notwithstanding the previous determination of the authority of the person voting or demanding a poll unless notice of the determination was received by the company at the office or at such other place at which the instrument of proxy was duly deposited [or, where the appointment of the proxy was contained in an electronic communication, at the address at which such appointment was duly received] before the commencement of the meeting or adjourned meeting at which the vote is given or the poll demanded or (in the case of a poll taken otherwise than on the same day as the meeting or adjourned meeting) the time appointed for taking the poll.

Note

Words in square brackets inserted by *SI 2000 No 3373, art 32(1), Sch 1 para 5* with effect from 22 December 2000.

64 Number of directors

Unless otherwise determined by ordinary resolution, the number of directors (other than alternate directors) shall not be subject to any maximum but shall be not less than two.

65 Alternate directors

Any director (other than an alternate director) may appoint any other director, or any other person approved by resolution of the directors and willing to act, to be an alternate director and may remove from office an alternate director so appointed by him.

66

An alternate director shall be entitled to receive notice of all meetings of directors and of all meetings of committees of directors of which his appointor is a member, to attend and vote at any such meeting at which the director appointing him is not personally present and generally to perform all the functions of his appointor as a director in his absence but shall not be entitled to receive any remuneration from the company for his services as an alternate director. But it shall not be necessary to give notice of such a meeting to an alternate director who is absent from the United Kingdom.

67

An alternate director shall cease to be an alternate director if his appointor ceases to be a director; but, if a director retires by rotation or otherwise but is reappointed or deemed to have been reappointed at the meeting at which he retires, any appointment of an alternate director made by him which was in force immediately prior to his retirement shall continue after his reappointment.

68

Any appointment or removal of an alternate director shall be by notice to the company signed by the director making or revoking the appointment or in any other manner approved by the directors.

69

Save as otherwise provided in the articles, an alternate director shall be deemed for all purposes to be a director and shall alone be responsible for his own acts and defaults and he shall not be deemed to be the agent of the director appointing him.

70 Powers of directors

Subject to the provisions of the Act, the memorandum and the articles and to any directions given by special resolution, the business of the company shall be managed by the directors who may exercise all the powers of the company. No alteration of the memorandum or articles and no such direction shall invalidate any prior act of the directors which would have been valid if that alteration had not been made or that direction had not been given. The powers given by this regulation shall not be limited by any special power given to the directors by the articles and a meeting of directors at which a quorum is present may exercise all powers exercisable by the directors.

71

The directors may, by power of attorney or otherwise, appoint any person to be the agent of the company for such purposes and on such conditions as they determine, including authority for the agent to delegate all or any of his powers.

72 Delegation of directors' powers

The directors may delegate any of their powers to any committee consisting of one or more directors. They may also delegate to any managing director or any director holding any other executive office such of their powers as they consider desirable to be exercised by him. Any such delegation may be made subject to any conditions the directors may impose, and either collaterally with or to the exclusion of their own powers and may be revoked or altered. Subject to any such conditions, the proceedings of a committee with two or more members shall be governed by the articles regulating the proceedings of directors so far as they are capable of applying.

73 Appointment and retirement of directors

At the first annual general meeting all the directors shall retire from office, and at every subsequent annual general meeting one-third of the directors who are subject to retirement by rotation or, if their number is not three or a multiple of three, the number nearest to one-third shall retire from office; but, if there is only one director who is subject to retirement by rotation, he shall retire.

Note

This Article ceases to have effect in relation to private companies limited by shares registered on or after 1 October 2007. [*SI 2007 No 2541, Reg 13*].

74

Subject to the provisions of the Act, the directors to retire by rotation shall be those who have been longest in office since their last appointment or reappointment, but as between persons who became or were last reappointed directors on the same day those to retire shall (unless they otherwise agree among themselves) be determined by lot.

Note

This Article ceases to have effect in relation to private companies limited by shares registered on or after 1 October 2007. [*SI 2007 No 2541, Reg 13*].

75

If the company, at the meeting at which a director retires by rotation, does not fill the vacancy the retiring director shall, if willing to act, be deemed to have been reappointed unless at the meeting it is resolved not to fill the vacancy or unless a resolution for the reappointment of the director is put to the meeting and lost.

Note

This Article ceases to have effect in relation to private companies limited by shares registered on or after 1 October 2007. [*SI 2007 No 2541, Reg 13*].

76

No person other than a director retiring by rotation shall be appointed or reappointed a director at any general meeting unless

(a) he is recommended by the directors; or

(b) not less than fourteen nor more than thirty-five clear days before the date appointed for the meeting, notice executed by a member qualified to vote at the meeting has been given to the company of the intention to propose that person for appointment or reappointment stating the particulars which would, if he were so appointed or reappointed, be required to be included in the company's register of directors together with notice executed by that person of his willingness to be appointed or reappointed.

Note

This Article is amended by *SI 2007 No 2541, Reg 14* in relation to private companies limited by shares registered on or after 1 October 2007 as follows.

- After the words 'No person' omit the words 'other than a director retiring by rotation'.

77

Not less than seven nor more than twenty-eight clear days before the date appointed for holding a general meeting notice shall be given to all who are entitled to receive notice of the meeting of any person (other than a director retiring by rotation at the meeting) who is recommended by the directors for appointment or reappointment as a director at the meeting or in respect of whom notice has been duly given to the company of the intention to propose him at the meeting for appointment or reappointment as a director. The notice shall give the particulars of that person which would, if he were so appointed or reappointed, be required to be included in the company's register of directors.

Note

This Article is amended by *SI 2007 No 2541, Reg 15* in relation to private companies limited by shares registered on or after 1 October 2007 as follows.

- After the words 'meeting of any person' omit the words '(other than a director retiring by rotation at the meeting)'.

78

Subject as aforesaid, the company may by ordinary resolution appoint a person who is willing to act to be a director either to fill a vacancy or as an additional director and may also determine the rotation in which any additional directors are to retire.

Note

This Article is amended by *SI 2007 No 2541, Reg 16* in relation to private companies limited by shares registered on or after 1 October 2007 as follows.

- Omit the words 'Subject as aforesaid,'.

79

The directors may appoint a person who is willing to act to be a director, either to fill a vacancy or as an additional director, provided that the appointment does not cause the number of directors to exceed any number fixed by or in accordance with the articles as the maximum number of directors. A director so appointed shall hold office only until the next following annual general meeting and shall not be taken into account in determining the directors who are to retire by rotation at the meeting. If not reappointed at such annual general meeting, he shall vacate office at the conclusion thereof.

Note

This Article is amended by *SI 2007 No 2541, Reg 17* in relation to private companies limited by shares registered on or after 1 October 2007 as follows.

- Omit the second and third sentences.

80

Subject as aforesaid, a director who retires at an annual general meeting may, if willing to act, be reappointed. If he is not reappointed, he shall retain office until the meeting appoints someone in his place, or if it does not do so, until the end of the meeting.

Note

This Article ceases to have effect in relation to private companies limited by shares registered on or after 1 October 2007. [*SI 2007 No 2541, Reg 18*].

81 Disqualification and removal of directors

The office of a director shall be vacated if

(a) he ceases to be a director by virtue of any provision of the Act or he becomes prohibited by law from being a director; or

(b) he becomes bankrupt or makes any arrangement or composition with his creditors generally; or

(c) he is, or may be, suffering from mental disorder and either

  (i) he is admitted to hospital in pursuance of an application for admission for treatment under the Mental Health Act 1983 or, in Scotland, an application for admission under the Mental Health (Scotland) Act 1960, or

  (ii) an order is made by a court having jurisdiction (whether in the United Kingdom or elsewhere) in matters concerning mental disorder for his detention or for the appointment of a receiver, curator bonis or other person to exercise powers with respect to his property or affairs; or

(d) he resigns his office by notice to the company; or

(e) he shall for more than six consecutive months have been absent without permission of the directors from meetings of directors held during that period and the directors resolve that his office be vacated.

Note

By virtue of the *Adults with Incapacity (Scotland) Act 2000, s 88(2), Sch 5, para 1* the references to a curator bonis shall be construed as references to a guardian with similar powers appointed under that Act.

82 Remuneration of directors

The directors shall be entitled to such remuneration as the company may by ordinary resolution determine and, unless the resolution provides otherwise, the remuneration shall be deemed to accrue from day to day.

83 Directors' expenses

The directors may be paid all travelling, hotel, and other expenses properly incurred by them in connection with their attendance at meetings of directors or committees of directors or general meetings or separate meetings of the holders of any class of shares or of debentures of the company or otherwise in connection with the discharge of their duties.

84 Directors' appointments and interests

Subject to the provisions of the Act, the directors may appoint one or more of their number to the office of managing director or to any other executive office under the company and may enter into an agreement or arrangement with any director for his employment by the company or for the provision by him of any services outside the scope of the ordinary duties of a director. Any such appointment, agreement or arrangement may be made upon such terms as the directors determine and they may remunerate any such director for his services as they think fit. Any appointment of a director to an executive office shall terminate if he ceases to be a director but without prejudice to any claim to damages for breach of the contract of service between the director and the company. A managing director and a director holding any other executive office shall not be subject to retirement by rotation.

85

Subject to the provisions of the Act, and provided that he has disclosed to the directors the nature and extent of any material interest of his, a director notwithstanding his office

(a) may be a party to, or otherwise interested in, any transaction or arrangement with the company or in which the company or in which the company is otherwise interested;

(b) may be a director or other officer of, or employed by, or a party to any transaction or arrangement with, or otherwise interested in, any body corporate promoted by the company or in which the company is otherwise interested; and

(c) shall not, by reason of his office, be accountable to the company for any benefit which he derives from any such office or employment or from any such transaction or arrangement or from any interest in any such body corporate and no such transaction or arrangement shall be liable to be avoided on the ground of any such interest or benefit.

86

For the purposes of regulation 85

(a) a general notice given to the directors that a director is to be regarded as having an interest of the nature and extent specified in the notice in any transaction or arrangement in which a specified person or class of persons is interested shall be deemed to be a disclosure that the director has an interest in any such transaction of the nature and extent so specified; and

(b) an interest of which a director has no knowledge and of which it is unreasonable to expect him to have knowledge shall not be treated as an interest of his.

87 Directors' gratuities and pensions

The directors may provide benefits, whether by the payment of gratuities or pensions or by insurance or otherwise, for any director who has held but no longer holds any executive office or employment with the company or with any body corporate which is or has been a subsidiary of the company or a predecessor in business of the company or of any such subsidiary, and for any member of his family (including a spouse and a former spouse) or any person who is or was dependent on him, and may (as well before as after he ceases to hold such office or employment) contribute to any fund and pay premiums for the purchase or provision of any such benefit.

88 Proceedings of directors

Subject to the provisions of the articles, the directors may regulate their proceedings as they think fit. A director may, and the secretary at the request of a director shall, call a meeting of the directors. It shall not be necessary to give notice of a meeting to a director who is absent from the United Kingdom. Questions arising at a meeting shall be decided by a majority of votes. In the case of an equality of votes, the chairman shall have a second or casting vote. A director who is also an alternate director shall be entitled in the absence of his appointor to a separate vote on behalf of his appointor in addition to his own vote.

89

The quorum for the transaction of the business of the directors may be fixed by the directors and unless so fixed at any other number shall be two. A person who holds office only as an alternate director shall, if his appointor is not present, be counted in the quorum.

90

The continuing directors or a sole continuing director may act notwithstanding any vacancies in their number, but, if the number of directors is less than the number fixed as the quorum, the continuing directors or director may act only for the purpose of filling vacancies or of calling a general meeting.

91

The directors may appoint one of their number to be the chairman of the board of directors and may at any time remove him from that office. Unless he is unwilling to do so, the director so appointed shall preside at every meeting of directors at which he is present. But if there is no director holding that office, or if the director holding it is unwilling to preside or is not present within five minutes after the time appointed for the meeting, the directors present may appoint one of their number to be chairman of the meeting.

92

All acts done by a meeting of directors, or of a committee of directors, or by a person acting as a director shall, notwithstanding that it be afterwards discovered that there was a defect in the appointment of any director or that any of them were disqualified from holding office, or had vacated office, or were not entitled to vote, be as valid as if every such person had been duly appointed and was qualified and had continued to be a director and had been entitled to vote.

93

A resolution in writing signed by all the directors entitled to receive notice of a meeting of directors or of a committee of directors shall be as valid and effectual as it if had been passed at a meeting of directors or (as the case may be) a committee of directors duly convened and held and may consist of several documents in the like form each signed by one or more directors; but a resolution signed by an alternate director need not also be signed by his appointor and, if it is signed by a director who has appointed an alternate director, it need not be signed by the alternate director in that capacity.

94

Save as otherwise provided by the articles, a director shall not vote at a meeting of directors or of a committee of directors on any resolution concerning a matter in which he has, directly or indirectly, an interest or duty which is material and which conflicts or may conflict with the interests of the company unless his interest or duty arises only because the case falls within one or more of the following paragraphs

- (a) the resolution relates to the giving to him of a guarantee, security, or indemnity in respect of money lent to, or an obligation incurred by him for the benefit of, the company or any of its subsidiaries;
- (b) the resolution relates to the giving to a third party of a guarantee, security, or indemnity in respect of an obligation of the company or any of its subsidiaries for which the director has assumed responsibility in whole or part and whether alone or jointly with others under a guarantee or indemnity or by the giving of security;

(c) his interest arises by virtue of his subscribing or agreeing to subscribe for any shares, debentures, or other securities of the company or any of its subsidiaries, or by virtue of his being, or intending to become, a participant in the underwriting or sub-underwriting of an offer of any such shares, debentures, or other securities by the company or any of its subsidiaries for subscription, purchase or exchange;

(d) the resolution relates in any way to a retirement benefits scheme which has been approved, or is conditional upon approval, by the Board of Inland Revenue for taxation purposes.

For the purposes of this regulation, an interest of a person who is, for any purpose of the Act (excluding any statutory modification thereof not in force when this regulation becomes binding on the company), connected with a director shall be treated as an interest of the director and, in relation to an alternate director, an interest of his appointor shall be treated as an interest of the alternate director without prejudice to any interest which the alternate director has otherwise.

95

A director shall not be counted in the quorum present at a meeting in relation to a resolution on which he is not entitled to vote.

96

The company may by ordinary resolution suspend or relax to any extent, either generally or in respect of any particular matter, any provision of the articles prohibiting a director from voting at a meeting of directors or of a committee of directors.

97

Where proposals are under consideration concerning the appointment of two or more directors to offices or employments with the company or any body corporate in which the company is interested the proposals may be divided and considered in relation to each director separately and (provided he is not for another reason precluded from voting) each of the directors concerned shall be entitled to vote and be counted in the quorum in respect of each resolution except that concerning his own appointment.

98

If a question arises at a meeting of directors or of a committee of directors as to the right of a director to vote, the question may, before the conclusion of the meeting, be referred to the chairman of the meeting and his ruling in relation to any director other than himself shall be final and conclusive.

99 Secretary

Subject to the provisions of the Act, the secretary shall be appointed by the directors for such term, at such remuneration and upon such conditions as they may think fit; and any secretary so appointed may be removed by them.

100 Minutes

The directors shall cause minutes to be made in books kept for the purpose

(a) of all appointments of officers made by the directors; and

(b) of all proceedings at meetings of the company, of the holders of any class of shares in the company, and of the directors, and of committees of directors, including the names of the directors present at each such meeting.

101 The seal

The seal shall only be used by the authority of the directors or of a committee of directors authorised by the directors. The directors may determine who shall sign any instrument to which the seal is affixed and unless otherwise so determined it shall be signed by a director and by the secretary or by a second director.

102 Dividends

Subject to the provisions of the Act, the company may by ordinary resolution declare dividends in accordance with the respective rights of the members, but no dividend shall exceed the amount recommended by the directors.

103

Subject to the provisions of the Act, the directors may pay interim dividends if it appears to them that they are justified by the profits of the company available for distribution. If the share capital is divided into different classes, the directors may pay interim dividends on shares which confer deferred or non-preferred rights with regard to dividend as well as on shares which confer preferential rights with regard to dividend, but no interim dividend shall be paid on shares carrying deferred or non-preferred rights if, at the time of payment, any preferential dividend is in arrear. The directors may also pay at intervals settled by them any dividend payable at a fixed rate if it appears to them that the profits available for distribution justify the payment. Provided the directors act in good faith they shall not incur any liability to the holders of shares conferring preferred rights for any loss they may suffer by the lawful payment of an interim dividend on any shares having deferred or non-preferred rights.

104

Except as otherwise provided by the rights attached to shares, all dividends shall be declared and paid according to the amounts paid up on the shares on which the dividend is paid. All dividends shall be apportioned and paid proportionately to the amounts paid up on the shares during any portion or portions of the period in respect of which the dividend is paid; but, if any share is issued on terms providing that it shall rank for dividend as from a particular date, that share shall rank for dividend accordingly.

105

A general meeting declaring a dividend may, upon the recommendation of the directors, direct that it shall be satisfied wholly or partly by the distribution of assets and, where any difficulty arises in regard to the distribution, the directors may settle the same and in particular may issue fractional certificates and fix the value for distribution of any assets and may determine that cash shall be paid to any member upon the footing of the value so fixed in order to adjust the rights of members and may vest any assets in trustees.

106

Any dividend or other moneys payable in respect of a share may be paid by cheque sent by post to the registered address of the person entitled or, if two or more persons are the holders of the share or are jointly entitled to it by reason of the death or bankruptcy of the holder, to the registered address of that one of those persons who is first named in the register of members or to such person and to such address as the person or persons entitled may in writing direct. Every cheque shall be made payable to the order of the person or persons entitled or to such other person as the person or persons entitled may in writing direct and payment of the cheque shall be a good discharge to the company. Any joint holder or other person jointly entitled to a share as aforesaid may give receipts for any dividend or other moneys payable in respect of the share.

107

No dividend or other moneys payable in respect of a share shall bear interest against the company unless otherwise provided by the rights attached to the share.

108

Any dividend which has remained unclaimed for twelve years from the date when it became due for payment shall, if the directors so resolve, be forfeited and cease to remain owing by the company.

109 Accounts

No member shall (as such) have any right of inspecting any accounting records or other book or document of the company except as conferred by statute or authorised by the directors or by ordinary resolution of the company.

110 Capitalisation of profits

The directors may with the authority of an ordinary resolution of the company

(a) subject as hereinafter provided, resolve to capitalise any undivided profits of the company not required for paying any preferential dividend (whether or not they are available for distribution) or any sum standing to the credit of the company's share premium account or capital redemption reserve;

(b) appropriate the sum resolved to be capitalised to the members who would have been entitled to it if it were distributed by way of dividend and in the same proportions and apply such sum on their behalf either in or towards paying up the amounts, if any, for the time being unpaid on any shares held by them respectively, or in paying up in full unissued shares or debentures of the company of a nominal amount equal to that sum, and allot the shares or debentures credited as fully paid to those members, or as they may direct, in those proportions, or partly in one way and partly in the other: but the share premium account, the capital redemption reserve, and any profits which are not available for distribution may, for the purposes of this regulation, only be applied in paying up unissued shares to be allotted to members credited as fully paid;

(c) make such provision by the issue of fractional certificates or by payment in cash or otherwise as they determine in the case of shares or debentures becoming distributable under this regulation in fractions; and

(d) authorise any person to enter on behalf of all the members concerned into an agreement with the company providing for the allotment to them respectively, credited as fully paid, of any shares or debentures to which they are entitled upon such capitalisation, any agreement made under such authority being binding on all such members.

[111 Notices

Any notice to be given to or by any person pursuant to the articles (other than a notice calling a meeting of the directors) shall be in writing or shall be given using electronic communications to an address for the time being notified for that purpose to the person giving the notice.

In this regulation, "address", in relation to electronic communications, includes any number or address used for the purposes of such communications.]

Note

Article 111 substituted by *SI 2000 No 3373, art 32(1), Sch 1 para 6* as from 22 December 2000. The text previously read 'Any notice to be given to or by any person pursuant to the articles shall be in writing except that a notice calling a meeting of the directors need not be in writing.'

112

The company may give any notice to a member either personally or by sending it by post in a prepaid envelope addressed to the member at his registered address or by leaving it at that address [or by giving it using electronic communications to an address for the time being notified to the company by the member]. In the case of joint holders of a share, all notices shall be given to the joint holder whose name stands first in the register of members in respect of the joint holding and notice so given shall be sufficient notice to all the joint holders. A member whose registered address is not within the United Kingdom and who gives to the company an address within the United Kingdom at which notices may be given to him[, or an address to which notices may be sent using electronic communications,] shall be entitled to have notices given to him at that address, but otherwise no such member shall be entitled to receive any notice from the company.

[In this regulation and the next, "address", in relation to electronic communications, includes any number or address used for the purposes of such communications.]

Note

Words in square brackets inserted by *SI 2000 No 3373, art 32(1), Sch 1 para 7* with effect from 22 December 2000.

113

A member present, either in person or by proxy, at any meeting of the company or of the holders of any class of shares in the company shall be deemed to have received notice of the meeting and, where requisite, of the purposes for which it was called.

114

Every person who becomes entitled to a share shall be bound by any notice in respect of that share which, before his name is entered in the register of members, has been duly given to a person from whom he derives his title.

115

Proof that an envelope containing a notice was properly addressed, prepaid and posted shall be conclusive evidence that that the notice was given. [Proof that a notice contained in an electronic communication was sent in accordance with guidance issued by the Institute of Chartered Secretaries and Administrators shall be conclusive evidence that the notice was given.] A notice shall, . . . be deemed to be given at the expiration of 48 hours after the envelope containing it was posted [or, in the case of a notice contained in an electronic communication, at the expiration of 48 hours after the time it was sent].

Note

Words in square brackets inserted by *SI 2000 No 3373, art 32(1), Sch 1 para 8* with effect from 22 December 2000.

116

A notice may be given by the company to the persons entitled to a share in consequence of the death or bankruptcy of a member by sending or delivering it, in any manner authorised by the articles for the giving of notice to a member, addressed to them by name, or by the title of representatives of the deceased, or trustee of the bankrupt or by any like description at the address, if any, within the United Kingdom supplied for that purpose by the persons claiming to be so entitled. Until such an address has been supplied, a notice may be given in any manner in which it might have been given if the death or bankruptcy had not occurred.

117 Winding up

If the company is wound up, the liquidator may, with the sanction of an extraordinary resolution of the company and any other sanction required by the Act, divide among the members in specie the whole or any part of the assets of the company and may, for that purpose, value any assets and determine how the division shall be carried out as between the members or different classes of members. The liquidator may, with the like sanction, vest the whole or any part of the assets in trustees upon such trusts for the benefit of the members as he with the like sanction determines, but no member shall be compelled to accept any assets upon which there is a liability.

Note

This Article is amended by *SI 2007 No 2541, Reg 7* in relation to companies registered on or after 1 October 2007 as follows.

- For the words 'an extraordinary' substitute the words 'a special'.

118 Indemnity

Subject to the provisions of the Act but without prejudice to any indemnity to which a director may otherwise be entitled, every director or other officer or auditor of the company shall be indemnified out of the assets of the company against any liability incurred by him in defending any proceedings, whether civil or criminal, in which judgment is given in his favour or in which he is acquitted or in connection with any application in which relief is granted to him by the court from liability for negligence, default, breach of duty or breach of trust in relation to the affairs of the company.

MODEL ARTICLES: PRIVATE COMPANIES LIMITED BY SHARES (SI 2008 NO 3229, SCH 1). COMPANIES ACT 2006 AS AMENDED BY THE MENTAL HEALTH DISCRIMINATION ACT 2013

INDEX

PART 1: INTERPRETATION AND LIMITATION OF LIABILITY

1. Defined terms
2. Liability of members

PART 2: DIRECTORS

Directors' powers and responsibilities

3. Directors' general authority
4. Shareholders' reserve power
5. Directors may delegate
6. Committees

Decision-making by directors

7. Directors to take decisions collectively
8. Unanimous decisions
9. Calling a directors' meeting
10. Participation in directors' meetings
11. Quorum for directors' meetings
12. Chairing of directors' meetings
13. Casting vote
14. Conflicts of interest
15. Records of decisions to be kept
16. Directors' discretion to make further rules

Appointment of directors

17. Methods of appointing directors
18. Termination of director's appointment
19. Directors' remuneration
20. Directors' expenses

PART 3: SHARES AND DISTRIBUTIONS

Shares

21. All shares to be fully paid up
22. Powers to issue different classes of share
23. Company not bound by less than absolute interests
24. Share certificates
25. Replacement share certificates
26. Share transfers
27. Transmission of shares
28. Exercise of transmittees' rights
29. Transmittees bound by prior notices

Dividends and other distributions

30. Procedure for declaring dividends
31. Payment of dividends and other distributions
32. No interest on distributions
33. Unclaimed distributions
34. Non-cash distributions
35. Waiver of distributions

Capitalisation of profits

36. Authority to capitalise and appropriation of capitalised sums

PART 4: DECISION-MAKING BY SHAREHOLDERS

Organisation of general meetings

37. Attendance and speaking at general meetings
38. Quorum for general meetings
39. Chairing general meetings
40. Attendance and speaking by directors and non-shareholders
41. Adjournment

Voting at general meetings

42. Voting: general
43. Errors and disputes
44. Poll votes
45. Content of proxy notices
46. Delivery of proxy notices
47. Amendments to resolutions

PART 5: ADMINISTRATIVE ARRANGEMENTS

48. Means of communication to be used
49. Company seals
50. No right to inspect accounts and other records
51. Provision for employees on cessation of business

Directors' indemnity and insurance

52. Indemnity
53. Insurance

PART 1: INTERPRETATION AND LIMITATION OF LIABILITY

1 Defined terms

In the articles, unless the context requires otherwise

"articles" means the company's articles of association;

"bankruptcy" includes individual insolvency proceedings in a jurisdiction other than England and Wales or Northern Ireland which have an effect similar to that of bankruptcy;

"chairman" has the meaning given in article 12;

"chairman of the meeting" has the meaning given in article 39;

"Companies Acts" means the Companies Acts (as defined in section 2 of the Companies Act 2006), in so far as they apply to the company;

"director" means a director of the company, and includes any person occupying the position of director, by whatever name called;

"distribution recipient" has the meaning given in article 31;

"document" includes, unless otherwise specified, any document sent or supplied in electronic form;

"electronic form" has the meaning given in section 1168 of the Companies Act 2006;

"fully paid" in relation to a share, means that the nominal value and any premium to be paid to the company in respect of that share have been paid to the company;

"hard copy form" has the meaning given in section 1168 of the Companies Act 2006;

"holder" in relation to shares means the person whose name is entered in the register of members as the holder of the shares;

"instrument" means a document in hard copy form;

"ordinary resolution" has the meaning given in section 282 of the Companies Act 2006;

"paid" means paid or credited as paid;

"participate", in relation to a directors' meeting, has the meaning given in article 10;

"proxy notice" has the meaning given in article 45;

"shareholder" means a person who is the holder of a share;

"shares" means shares in the company;

"special resolution" has the meaning given in section 283 of the Companies Act 2006;

"subsidiary" has the meaning given in section 1159 of the Companies Act 2006;

"transmittee" means a person entitled to a share by reason of the death or bankruptcy of a shareholder or otherwise by operation of law; and

"writing" means the representation or reproduction of words, symbols or other information in a visible form by any method or combination of methods, whether sent or supplied in electronic form or otherwise.

Unless the context otherwise requires, other words or expressions contained in these articles bear the same meaning as in the Companies Act 2006 as in force on the date when these articles become binding on the company.

2 Liability of members

The liability of the members is limited to the amount, if any, unpaid on the shares held by them.

PART 2: DIRECTORS

Directors' powers and responsibilities

3 Directors' general authority

Subject to the articles, the directors are responsible for the management of the company's business, for which purpose they may exercise all the powers of the company.

4 Shareholders' reserve power

(1) The shareholders may, by special resolution, direct the directors to take, or refrain from taking, specified action.

(2) No such special resolution invalidates anything which the directors have done before the passing of the resolution.

5 Directors may delegate

(1) Subject to the articles, the directors may delegate any of the powers which are conferred on them under the articles

(a) to such person or committee;

(b) by such means (including by power of attorney);

(c) to such an extent;

(d) in relation to such matters or territories; and

(e) on such terms and conditions;

as they think fit.

(2) If the directors so specify, any such delegation may authorise further delegation of the directors' powers by any person to whom they are delegated.

(3) The directors may revoke any delegation in whole or part, or alter its terms and conditions.

6 Committees

(1) Committees to which the directors delegate any of their powers must follow procedures which are based as far as they are applicable on those provisions of the articles which govern the taking of decisions by directors.

(2) The directors may make rules of procedure for all or any committees, which prevail over rules derived from the articles if they are not consistent with them.

Decision-making by directors

7 Directors to take decisions collectively

(1) The general rule about decision-making by directors is that any decision of the directors must be either a majority decision at a meeting or a decision taken in accordance with article 8.

(2) If

(a) the company only has one director, and

(b) no provision of the articles requires it to have more than one director,

the general rule does not apply, and the director may take decisions without regard to any of the provisions of the articles relating to directors' decision-making.

8 Unanimous decisions

(1) A decision of the directors is taken in accordance with this article when all eligible directors indicate to each other by any means that they share a common view on a matter.

(2) Such a decision may take the form of a resolution in writing, copies of which have been signed by each eligible director or to which each eligible director has otherwise indicated agreement in writing.

(3) References in this article to eligible directors are to directors who would have been entitled to vote on the matter had it been proposed as a resolution at a directors' meeting.

(4) A decision may not be taken in accordance with this article if the eligible directors would not have formed a quorum at such a meeting.

9 Calling a directors' meeting

(1) Any director may call a directors' meeting by giving notice of the meeting to the directors or by authorising the company secretary (if any) to give such notice.

(2) Notice of any directors' meeting must indicate

(a) its proposed date and time;

(b) where it is to take place; and

(c) if it is anticipated that directors participating in the meeting will not be in the same place,

how it is proposed that they should communicate with each other during the meeting.

(3) Notice of a directors' meeting must be given to each director, but need not be in writing.

(4) Notice of a directors' meeting need not be given to directors who waive their entitlement to notice of that meeting, by giving notice to that effect to the company not more than 7 days after the date on which the meeting is held. Where such notice is given after the meeting has been held, that does not affect the validity of the meeting, or of any business conducted at it.

10 Participation in directors' meetings

(1) Subject to the articles, directors participate in a directors' meeting, or part of a directors' meeting, when

(a) the meeting has been called and takes place in accordance with the articles, and

(b) they can each communicate to the others any information or opinions they have on any particular item of the business of the meeting.

(2) In determining whether directors are participating in a directors' meeting, it is irrelevant where any director is or how they communicate with each other.

(3) If all the directors participating in a meeting are not in the same place, they may decide that the meeting is to be treated as taking place wherever any of them is.

11 Quorum for directors' meetings

(1) At a directors' meeting, unless a quorum is participating, no proposal is to be voted on, except a proposal to call another meeting.

(2) The quorum for directors' meetings may be fixed from time to time by a decision of the directors, but it must never be less than two, and unless otherwise fixed it is two.

(3) If the total number of directors for the time being is less than the quorum required, the directors must not take any decision other than a decision

(a) to appoint further directors, or

(b) to call a general meeting so as to enable the shareholders to appoint further directors.

12 Chairing of directors' meetings

(1) The directors may appoint a director to chair their meetings.

(2) The person so appointed for the time being is known as the chairman.

(3) The directors may terminate the chairman's appointment at any time.

(4) If the chairman is not participating in a directors' meeting within ten minutes of the time at which it was to start, the participating directors must appoint one of themselves to chair it.

13 Casting vote

(1) If the numbers of votes for and against a proposal are equal, the chairman or other director chairing the meeting has a casting vote.

(2) But this does not apply if, in accordance with the articles, the chairman or other director is not to be counted as participating in the decision-making process for quorum or voting purposes.

14 Conflicts of interest

(1) If a proposed decision of the directors is concerned with an actual or proposed transaction or arrangement with the company in which a director is interested, that director is not to be counted as participating in the decision-making process for quorum or voting purposes.

(2) But if paragraph (3) applies, a director who is interested in an actual or proposed transaction or arrangement with the company is to be counted as participating in the decision-making process for quorum and voting purposes.

(3) This paragraph applies when

(a) the company by ordinary resolution disapplies the provision of the articles which would otherwise prevent a director from being counted as participating in the decision-making process;

(b) the director's interest cannot reasonably be regarded as likely to give rise to a conflict of interest; or

(c) the director's conflict of interest arises from a permitted cause.

(4) For the purposes of this article, the following are permitted causes

(a) a guarantee given, or to be given, by or to a director in respect of an obligation incurred by or on behalf of the company or any of its subsidiaries;

(b) subscription, or an agreement to subscribe, for shares or other securities of the company or any of its subsidiaries, or to underwrite, sub-underwrite, or guarantee subscription for any such shares or securities; and

(c) arrangements pursuant to which benefits are made available to employees and directors or former employees and directors of the company or any of its subsidiaries which do not provide special benefits for directors or former directors.

(5) For the purposes of this article, references to proposed decisions and decision-making processes include any directors' meeting or part of a directors' meeting.

(6) Subject to paragraph (7), if a question arises at a meeting of directors or of a committee of directors as to the right of a director to participate in the meeting (or part of the meeting) for voting or quorum purposes, the question may, before the conclusion of the meeting, be referred to the chairman whose ruling in relation to any director other than the chairman is to be final and conclusive.

(7) If any question as to the right to participate in the meeting (or part of the meeting) should arise in respect of the chairman, the question is to be decided by a decision of the directors at that meeting, for which purpose the chairman is not to be counted as participating in the meeting (or that part of the meeting) for voting or quorum purposes.

15 Records of decisions to be kept

The directors must ensure that the company keeps a record, in writing, for at least 10 years from the date of the decision recorded, of every unanimous or majority decision taken by the directors.

16 Directors' discretion to make further rules

Subject to the articles, the directors may make any rule which they think fit about how they take decisions, and about how such rules are to be recorded or communicated to directors.

Appointment of directors

17 Methods of appointing directors

(1) Any person who is willing to act as a director, and is permitted by law to do so, may be appointed to be a director

(a) by ordinary resolution, or

(b) by a decision of the directors.

(2) In any case where, as a result of death, the company has no shareholders and no directors, the personal representatives of the last shareholder to have died have the right, by notice in writing, to appoint a person to be a director.

(3) For the purposes of paragraph (2), where 2 or more shareholders die in circumstances rendering it uncertain who was the last to die, a younger shareholder is deemed to have survived an older shareholder.

18 Termination of director's appointment

A person ceases to be a director as soon as

(a) that person ceases to be a director by virtue of any provision of the Companies Act 2006 or is prohibited from being a director by law;

(b) a bankruptcy order is made against that person;

(c) a composition is made with that person's creditors generally in satisfaction of that person's debts;

(d) a registered medical practitioner who is treating that person gives a written opinion to the company stating that that person has become physically or mentally incapable of acting as a director and may remain so for more than three months;

(f) notification is received by the company from the director that the director is resigning from office, and such resignation has taken effect in accordance with its terms.

19 Directors' remuneration

(1) Directors may undertake any services for the company that the directors decide.

(2) Directors are entitled to such remuneration as the directors determine

(a) for their services to the company as directors, and

(b) for any other service which they undertake for the company.

(3) Subject to the articles, a director's remuneration may

(a) take any form, and

(b) include any arrangements in connection with the payment of a pension, allowance or gratuity, or any death, sickness or disability benefits, to or in respect of that director.

(4) Unless the directors decide otherwise, directors' remuneration accrues from day to day.

(5) Unless the directors decide otherwise, directors are not accountable to the company for any remuneration which they receive as directors or other officers or employees of the company's subsidiaries or of any other body corporate in which the company is interested.

20 Directors' expenses

The company may pay any reasonable expenses which the directors properly incur in connection with their attendance at

- (a) meetings of directors or committees of directors,
- (b) general meetings, or
- (c) separate meetings of the holders of any class of shares or of debentures of the company,

or otherwise in connection with the exercise of their powers and the discharge of their responsibilities in relation to the company.

PART 3: SHARES AND DISTRIBUTIONS

Shares

21 All shares to be fully paid up

(1) No share is to be issued for less than the aggregate of its nominal value and any premium to be paid to the company in consideration for its issue.

(2) This does not apply to shares taken on the formation of the company by the subscribers to the company's memorandum.

22 Powers to issue different classes of share

(1) Subject to the articles, but without prejudice to the rights attached to any existing share, the company may issue shares with such rights or restrictions as may be determined by ordinary resolution.

(2) The company may issue shares which are to be redeemed, or are liable to be redeemed at the option of the company or the holder, and the directors may determine the terms, conditions and manner of redemption of any such shares.

23 Company not bound by less than absolute interests

Except as required by law, no person is to be recognised by the company as holding any share upon any trust, and except as otherwise required by law or the articles, the company is not in any way to be bound by or recognise any interest in a share other than the holder's absolute ownership of it and all the rights attaching to it.

24 Share certificates

(1) The company must issue each shareholder, free of charge, with one or more certificates in respect of the shares which that shareholder holds.

(2) Every certificate must specify

- (a) in respect of how many shares, of what class, it is issued;
- (b) the nominal value of those shares;
- (c) that the shares are fully paid; and
- (d) any distinguishing numbers assigned to them.

(3) No certificate may be issued in respect of shares of more than one class.

(4) If more than one person holds a share, only one certificate may be issued in respect of it.

(5) Certificates must

- (a) have affixed to them the company's common seal, or
- (b) be otherwise executed in accordance with the Companies Acts.

25 Replacement share certificates

(1) If a certificate issued in respect of a shareholder's shares is

(a) damaged or defaced, or
(b) said to be lost, stolen or destroyed,

that shareholder is entitled to be issued with a replacement certificate in respect of the same shares.

(2) A shareholder exercising the right to be issued with such a replacement certificate

(a) may at the same time exercise the right to be issued with a single certificate or separate certificates;
(b) must return the certificate which is to be replaced to the company if it is damaged or defaced; and
(c) must comply with such conditions as to evidence, indemnity and the payment of a reasonable fee as the directors decide.

26 Share transfers

(1) Shares may be transferred by means of an instrument of transfer in any usual form or any other form approved by the directors, which is executed by or on behalf of the transferor.

(2) No fee may be charged for registering any instrument of transfer or other document relating to or affecting the title to any share.

(3) The company may retain any instrument of transfer which is registered.

(4) The transferor remains the holder of a share until the transferee's name is entered in the register of members as holder of it.

(5) The directors may refuse to register the transfer of a share, and if they do so, the instrument of transfer must be returned to the transferee with the notice of refusal unless they suspect that the proposed transfer may be fraudulent.

27 Transmission of shares

(1) If title to a share passes to a transmittee, the company may only recognise the transmittee as having any title to that share.

(2) A transmittee who produces such evidence of entitlement to shares as the directors may properly require

(a) may, subject to the articles, choose either to become the holder of those shares or to have them transferred to another person, and
(b) subject to the articles, and pending any transfer of the shares to another person, has the same rights as the holder had.

(3) But transmittees do not have the right to attend or vote at a general meeting, or agree to a proposed written resolution, in respect of shares to which they are entitled, by reason of the holder's death or bankruptcy or otherwise, unless they become the holders of those shares.

28 Exercise of transmittees' rights

(1) Transmittees who wish to become the holders of shares to which they have become entitled must notify the company in writing of that wish.

(2) If the transmittee wishes to have a share transferred to another person, the transmittee must execute an instrument of transfer in respect of it.

(3) Any transfer made or executed under this article is to be treated as if it were made or executed by the person from whom the transmittee has derived rights in respect of the share, and as if the event which gave rise to the transmission had not occurred.

29 Transmittees bound by prior notices

If a notice is given to a shareholder in respect of shares and a transmittee is entitled to those shares, the transmittee is bound by the notice if it was given to the shareholder before the transmittee's name has been entered in the register of members.

Dividends and other distributions

30 Procedure for declaring dividends

(1) The company may by ordinary resolution declare dividends, and the directors may decide to pay interim dividends.

(2) A dividend must not be declared unless the directors have made a recommendation as to its amount. Such a dividend must not exceed the amount recommended by the directors.

(3) No dividend may be declared or paid unless it is in accordance with shareholders' respective rights.

(4) Unless the shareholders' resolution to declare or directors' decision to pay a dividend, or the terms on which shares are issued, specify otherwise, it must be paid by reference to each shareholder's holding of shares on the date of the resolution or decision to declare or pay it.

(5) If the company's share capital is divided into different classes, no interim dividend may be paid on shares carrying deferred or non-preferred rights if, at the time of payment, any preferential dividend is in arrear.

(6) The directors may pay at intervals any dividend payable at a fixed rate if it appears to them that the profits available for distribution justify the payment.

(7) If the directors act in good faith, they do not incur any liability to the holders of shares conferring preferred rights for any loss they may suffer by the lawful payment of an interim dividend on shares with deferred or non-preferred rights.

31 Payment of dividends and other distributions

(1) Where a dividend or other sum which is a distribution is payable in respect of a share, it must be paid by one or more of the following means

(a) transfer to a bank or building society account specified by the distribution recipient either in writing or as the directors may otherwise decide;

(b) sending a cheque made payable to the distribution recipient by post to the distribution recipient at the distribution recipient's registered address (if the distribution recipient is a holder of the share), or (in any other case) to an address specified by the distribution recipient either in writing or as the directors may otherwise decide;

(c) sending a cheque made payable to such person by post to such person at such address as the distribution recipient has specified either in writing or as the directors may otherwise decide; or

(d) any other means of payment as the directors agree with the distribution recipient either in writing or by such other means as the directors decide.

In the articles, "the distribution recipient" means, in respect of a share in respect of which a dividend or other sum is payable

(a) the holder of the share; or

(b) if the share has two or more joint holders, whichever of them is named first in the register of members; or

(c) if the holder is no longer entitled to the share by reason of death or bankruptcy, or otherwise by operation of law, the transmittee.

32 No interest on distributions

The company may not pay interest on any dividend or other sum payable in respect of a share unless otherwise provided by

(a) the terms on which the share was issued, or

(b) the provisions of another agreement between the holder of that share and the company.

33 Unclaimed distributions

(1) All dividends or other sums which are

(a) payable in respect of shares, and

(b) unclaimed after having been declared or become payable,

may be invested or otherwise made use of by the directors for the benefit of the company until claimed.

(2) The payment of any such dividend or other sum into a separate account does not make the company a trustee in respect of it.

(3) If

(a) twelve years have passed from the date on which a dividend or other sum became due for payment, and

(b) the distribution recipient has not claimed it,

the distribution recipient is no longer entitled to that dividend or other sum and it ceases to remain owing by the company.

34 Non-cash distributions

(1) Subject to the terms of issue of the share in question, the company may, by ordinary resolution on the recommendation of the directors, decide to pay all or part of a dividend or other distribution payable in respect of a share by transferring non-cash assets of equivalent value (including, without limitation, shares or other securities in any company).

(2) For the purposes of paying a non-cash distribution, the directors may make whatever arrangements they think fit, including, where any difficulty arises regarding the distribution

(a) fixing the value of any assets;

(b) paying cash to any distribution recipient on the basis of that value in order to adjust the rights of recipients; and

(c) vesting any assets in trustees.

35 Waiver of distributions

Distribution recipients may waive their entitlement to a dividend or other distribution payable in respect of a share by giving the company notice in writing to that effect, but if

(a) the share has more than one holder, or

(b) more than one person is entitled to the share, whether by reason of the death or bankruptcy of one or more joint holders, or otherwise,

the notice is not effective unless it is expressed to be given, and signed, by all the holders or persons otherwise entitled to the share.

Capitalisation of profits

36 Authority to capitalise and appropriation of capitalised sums

(1) Subject to the articles, the directors may, if they are so authorised by an ordinary resolution

(a) decide to capitalise any profits of the company (whether or not they are available for distribution) which are not required for paying a preferential dividend, or any sum standing to the credit of the company's share premium account or capital redemption reserve; and

appropriate any sum which they so decide to capitalise (a "capitalised sum") to the persons who would have been entitled to it if it were distributed by way of dividend (the "persons entitled") and in the same proportions.

(2) Capitalised sums must be applied

(a) on behalf of the persons entitled, and

(b) in the same proportions as a dividend would have been distributed to them.

(3) Any capitalised sum may be applied in paying up new shares of a nominal amount equal to the capitalised sum which are then allotted credited as fully paid to the persons entitled or as they may direct.

(4) A capitalised sum which was appropriated from profits available for distribution may be applied in paying up new debentures of the company which are then allotted credited as fully paid to the persons entitled or as they may direct.

(5) Subject to the articles the directors may

(a) apply capitalised sums in accordance with paragraphs (3) and (4) partly in one way and partly in another;

(b) make such arrangements as they think fit to deal with shares or debentures becoming distributable in fractions under this article (including the issuing of fractional certificates or the making of cash payments); and

(c) authorise any person to enter into an agreement with the company on behalf of all the persons entitled which is binding on them in respect of the allotment of shares and debentures to them under this article.

PART 4: DECISION-MAKING BY SHAREHOLDERS

Organisation of general meetings

37 Attendance and speaking at general meetings

(1) A person is able to exercise the right to speak at a general meeting when that person is in a position to communicate to all those attending the meeting, during the meeting, any information or opinions which that person has on the business of the meeting.

(2) A person is able to exercise the right to vote at a general meeting when

(a) that person is able to vote, during the meeting, on resolutions put to the vote at the meeting, and

(b) that person's vote can be taken into account in determining whether or not such resolutions are passed at the same time as the votes of all the other persons attending the meeting.

(3) The directors may make whatever arrangements they consider appropriate to enable those attending a general meeting to exercise their rights to speak or vote at it.

(4) In determining attendance at a general meeting, it is immaterial whether any two or more members attending it are in the same place as each other.

(5) Two or more persons who are not in the same place as each other attend a general meeting if their circumstances are such that if they have (or were to have) rights to speak and vote at that meeting, they are (or would be) able to exercise them.

38 Quorum for general meetings

No business other than the appointment of the chairman of the meeting is to be transacted at a general meeting if the persons attending it do not constitute a quorum.

39 Chairing general meetings

(1) If the directors have appointed a chairman, the chairman shall chair general meetings if present and willing to do so.

(2) If the directors have not appointed a chairman, or if the chairman is unwilling to chair the meeting or is not present within ten minutes of the time at which a meeting was due to start

(a) the directors present, or

(b) (if no directors are present), the meeting,

must appoint a director or shareholder to chair the meeting, and the appointment of the chairman of the meeting must be the first business of the meeting.

(3) The person chairing a meeting in accordance with this article is referred to as "the chairman of the meeting".

40 Attendance and speaking by directors and non-shareholders

(1) Directors may attend and speak at general meetings, whether or not they are shareholders.

(2) The chairman of the meeting may permit other persons who are not

(a) shareholders of the company, or

(b) otherwise entitled to exercise the rights of shareholders in relation to general meetings,

to attend and speak at a general meeting.

41 Adjournment

(1) If the persons attending a general meeting within half an hour of the time at which the meeting was due to start do not constitute a quorum, or if during a meeting a quorum ceases to be present, the chairman of the meeting must adjourn it.

(2) The chairman of the meeting may adjourn a general meeting at which a quorum is present if

(a) the meeting consents to an adjournment, or

(b) it appears to the chairman of the meeting that an adjournment is necessary to protect the safety of any person attending the meeting or ensure that the business of the meeting is conducted in an orderly manner.

(3) The chairman of the meeting must adjourn a general meeting if directed to do so by the meeting.

(4) When adjourning a general meeting, the chairman of the meeting must

(a) either specify the time and place to which it is adjourned or state that it is to continue at a time and place to be fixed by the directors, and

(b) have regard to any directions as to the time and place of any adjournment which have been given by the meeting.

(5) If the continuation of an adjourned meeting is to take place more than 14 days after it was adjourned, the company must give at least 7 clear days' notice of it (that is, excluding the day of the adjourned meeting and the day on which the notice is given)

(a) to the same persons to whom notice of the company's general meetings is required to be given, and

(b) containing the same information which such notice is required to contain.

(6) No business may be transacted at an adjourned general meeting which could not properly have been transacted at the meeting if the adjournment had not taken place.

Voting at general meetings

42 Voting: general

A resolution put to the vote of a general meeting must be decided on a show of hands unless a poll is duly demanded in accordance with the articles.

43 Errors and disputes

(1) No objection may be raised to the qualification of any person voting at a general meeting except at the meeting or adjourned meeting at which the vote objected to is tendered, and every vote not disallowed at the meeting is valid.

(2) Any such objection must be referred to the chairman of the meeting, whose decision is final.

44 Poll votes

(1) A poll on a resolution may be demanded

(a) in advance of the general meeting where it is to be put to the vote, or

(b) at a general meeting, either before a show of hands on that resolution or immediately after the result of a show of hands on that resolution is declared.

(2) A poll may be demanded by

(a) the chairman of the meeting;

(b) the directors;

(c) two or more persons having the right to vote on the resolution; or

(d) a person or persons representing not less than one tenth of the total voting rights of all the shareholders having the right to vote on the resolution.

(3) A demand for a poll may be withdrawn if

(a) the poll has not yet been taken, and

(b) the chairman of the meeting consents to the withdrawal.

(4) Polls must be taken immediately and in such manner as the chairman of the meeting directs.

45 Content of proxy notices

(1) Proxies may only validly be appointed by a notice in writing (a "proxy notice") which

(a) states the name and address of the shareholder appointing the proxy;

(b) identifies the person appointed to be that shareholder's proxy and the general meeting in relation to which that person is appointed;

(c) is signed by or on behalf of the shareholder appointing the proxy, or is authenticated in such manner as the directors may determine; and

(d) is delivered to the company in accordance with the articles and any instructions contained in the notice of the general meeting to which they relate.

(2) The company may require proxy notices to be delivered in a particular form, and may specify different forms for different purposes.

(3) Proxy notices may specify how the proxy appointed under them is to vote (or that the proxy is to abstain from voting) on one or more resolutions.

(4) Unless a proxy notice indicates otherwise, it must be treated as

(a) allowing the person appointed under it as a proxy discretion as to how to vote on any ancillary or procedural resolutions put to the meeting, and

(b) appointing that person as a proxy in relation to any adjournment of the general meeting to which it relates as well as the meeting itself.

46 Delivery of proxy notices

(1) A person who is entitled to attend, speak or vote (either on a show of hands or on a poll) at a general meeting remains so entitled in respect of that meeting or any adjournment of it, even though a valid proxy notice has been delivered to the company by or on behalf of that person.

(2) An appointment under a proxy notice may be revoked by delivering to the company a notice in writing given by or on behalf of the person by whom or on whose behalf the proxy notice was given.

(3) A notice revoking a proxy appointment only takes effect if it is delivered before the start of the meeting or adjourned meeting to which it relates.

(4) If a proxy notice is not executed by the person appointing the proxy, it must be accompanied by written evidence of the authority of the person who executed it to execute it on the appointor's behalf.

47 Amendments to resolutions

(1) An ordinary resolution to be proposed at a general meeting may be amended by ordinary resolution if

(a) notice of the proposed amendment is given to the company in writing by a person entitled to vote at the general meeting at which it is to be proposed not less than 48 hours before the meeting is to take place (or such later time as the chairman of the meeting may determine), and

(b) the proposed amendment does not, in the reasonable opinion of the chairman of the meeting, materially alter the scope of the resolution.

(2) A special resolution to be proposed at a general meeting may be amended by ordinary resolution, if

(a) the chairman of the meeting proposes the amendment at the general meeting at which the resolution is to be proposed, and

(b) the amendment does not go beyond what is necessary to correct a grammatical or other non-substantive error in the resolution.

(3) If the chairman of the meeting, acting in good faith, wrongly decides that an amendment to a resolution is out of order, the chairman's error does not invalidate the vote on that resolution.

PART 5: ADMINISTRATIVE ARRANGEMENTS

48 Means of communication to be used

(1) Subject to the articles, anything sent or supplied by or to the company under the articles may be sent or supplied in any way in which the Companies Act 2006 provides for documents or information which are authorised or required by any provision of that Act to be sent or supplied by or to the company.

(2) Subject to the articles, any notice or document to be sent or supplied to a director in connection with the taking of decisions by directors may also be sent or supplied by the means by which that director has asked to be sent or supplied with such notices or documents for the time being.

(3) A director may agree with the company that notices or documents sent to that director in a particular way are to be deemed to have been received within a specified time of their being sent, and for the specified time to be less than 48 hours.

49 Company seals

(1) Any common seal may only be used by the authority of the directors.

(2) The directors may decide by what means and in what form any common seal is to be used.

(3) Unless otherwise decided by the directors, if the company has a common seal and it is affixed to a document, the document must also be signed by at least one authorised person in the presence of a witness who attests the signature.

(4) For the purposes of this article, an authorised person is

(a) any director of the company;

(b) the company secretary (if any); or

(c) any person authorised by the directors for the purpose of signing documents to which the common seal is applied.

50 No right to inspect accounts and other records

Except as provided by law or authorised by the directors or an ordinary resolution of the company, no person is entitled to inspect any of the company's accounting or other records or documents merely by virtue of being a shareholder.

51 Provision for employees on cessation of business

The directors may decide to make provision for the benefit of persons employed or formerly employed by the company or any of its subsidiaries (other than a director or former director or shadow director) in connection with the cessation or transfer to any person of the whole or part of the undertaking of the company or that subsidiary.

Directors' indemnity and insurance

52 Indemnity

(1) Subject to paragraph (2), a relevant director of the company or an associated company may be indemnified out of the company's assets against

(a) any liability incurred by that director in connection with any negligence, default, breach of duty or breach of trust in relation to the company or an associated company,

(b) any liability incurred by that director in connection with the activities of the company or an associated company in its capacity as a trustee of an occupational pension scheme (as defined in section 235(6) of the Companies Act 2006),

(c) any other liability incurred by that director as an officer of the company or an associated company.

(2) This article does not authorise any indemnity which would be prohibited or rendered void by any provision of the Companies Acts or by any other provision of law.

(3) In this article

(a) companies are associated if one is a subsidiary of the other or both are subsidiaries of the same body corporate, and

(b) a "relevant director" means any director or former director of the company or an associated company.

53 Insurance

(1) The directors may decide to purchase and maintain insurance, at the expense of the company, for the benefit of any relevant director in respect of any relevant loss.

(2) In this article

(a) a "relevant director" means any director or former director of the company or an associated company,

(b) a "relevant loss" means any loss or liability which has been or may be incurred by a relevant director in connection with that director's duties or powers in relation to the company, any associated company or any pension fund or employees' share scheme of the company or associated company, and

(c) companies are associated if one is a subsidiary of the other or both are subsidiaries of the same body corporate.

MODEL ARTICLES: PUBLIC COMPANIES (SI 2008 NO 3229, SCH 3). COMPANIES ACT 2006 AS AMENDED BY THE MENTAL HEALTH DISCRIMINATION ACT 2013

INDEX

PART 1: INTERPRETATION AND LIMITATION OF LIABILITY
1. Defined terms
2. Liability of members

PART 2: DIRECTORS

Directors' powers and responsibilities

3. Directors' general authority
4. Members' reserve power
5. Directors may delegate
6. Committees

Decision-making by directors

7. Directors to take decisions collectively
8. Calling a directors' meeting
9. Participation in directors' meetings
10. Quorum for directors' meetings
11. Meetings where total number of directors less than quorum
12. Chairing directors' meetings
13. Voting at directors' meetings: general rules
14. Chairman's casting vote at directors' meetings
15. Alternates voting at directors' meetings
16. Conflicts of interest
17. Proposing directors' written resolutions
18. Adoption of directors' written resolutions
19. Directors' discretion to make further rules

Appointment of directors

20. Methods of appointing directors
21. Retirement of directors by rotation
22. Termination of director's appointment
23. Directors' remuneration
24. Directors' expenses

Alternate directors

25. Appointment and removal of alternates
26. Rights and responsibilities of alternate directors
27. Termination of alternate directorship

PART 3: DECISION-MAKING BY MEMBERS

Organisation of general meetings

28. Members can call general meeting if not enough directors
29. Attendance and speaking at general meetings
30. Quorum for general meetings
31. Chairing general meetings
32. Attendance and speaking by directors and non-members
33. Adjournment

Voting at general meetings

34. Voting: general
35. Errors and disputes

36. Demanding a poll
37. Procedure on a poll
38. Content of proxy notices
39. Delivery of proxy notices
40. Amendments to resolutions

Restrictions on members' rights

41. No voting of shares on which money owed to company

Application of rules to class meetings

42. Class meetings

PART 4: SHARES AND DISTRIBUTIONS

Issue of shares

43. Powers to issue different classes of share
44. Payment of commissions on subscription for shares

Interests in shares

45. Company not bound by less than absolute interests

Share certificates

46. Certificates to be issued except in certain cases
47. Contents and execution of share certificates
48. Consolidated share certificates
49. Replacement share certificates

Shares not held in certificated form

50. Uncertificated shares
51. Share warrants

Partly paid shares

52. Company's lien over partly paid shares
53. Enforcement of the company's lien
54. Call notices
55. Liability to pay calls
56. When call notice need not be issued
57. Failure to comply with call notice: automatic consequences
58. Notice of intended forfeiture
59. Directors' power to forfeit shares
60. Effect of forfeiture
61. Procedure following forfeiture
62. Surrender of shares

Transfer and transmission of shares

63. Transfers of certificated shares
64. Transfer of uncertificated shares
65. Transmission of shares
66. Transmittees' rights
67. Exercise of transmittees' rights
68. Transmittees bound by prior notices

Consolidation of shares

69. Procedure for disposing of fractions of shares

Distributions

70. Procedure for declaring dividends
71. Calculation of dividends
72. Payment of dividends and other distributions
73. Deductions from distributions in respect of sums owed to the company
74. No interest on distributions

75. Unclaimed distributions
76. Non-cash distributions
77. Waiver of distributions

Capitalisation of profits

78. Authority to capitalise and appropriation of capitalised sums

PART 5: MISCELLANEOUS PROVISIONS

Communications

79. Means of communication to be used
80. Failure to notify contact details

Administrative arrangements

81. Company seals
82. Destruction of documents
83. No right to inspect accounts and other records
84. Provision for employees on cessation of business

Directors' indemnity and insurance

85. Indemnity
86. Insurance

PART 1: INTERPRETATION AND LIMITATION OF LIABILITY

1 Defined terms

In the articles, unless the context requires otherwise

"alternate" or "alternate director" has the meaning given in article 25;

"appointor" has the meaning given in article 25;

"articles" means the company's articles of association;

"bankruptcy" includes individual insolvency proceedings in a jurisdiction other than England and Wales or Northern Ireland which have an effect similar to that of bankruptcy;

"call" has the meaning given in article 54;

"call notice" has the meaning given in article 54;

"certificate" means a paper certificate (other than a share warrant) evidencing a person's title to specified shares or other securities;

"certificated" in relation to a share, means that it is not an uncertificated share or a share in respect of which a share warrant has been issued and is current;

"chairman" has the meaning given in article 12;

"chairman of the meeting" has the meaning given in article 31;

"Companies Acts" means the Companies Acts (as defined in section 2 of the Companies Act 2006), in so far as they apply to the company;

"company's lien" has the meaning given in article 52;

"director" means a director of the company, and includes any person occupying the position of director, by whatever name called;

"distribution recipient" has the meaning given in article 72;

"document" includes, unless otherwise specified, any document sent or supplied in electronic form;

"electronic form" has the meaning given in section 1168 of the Companies Act 2006;

"fully paid" in relation to a share, means that the nominal value and any premium to be paid to the company in respect of that share have been paid to the company;

"hard copy form" has the meaning given in section 1168 of the Companies Act 2006;

"holder" in relation to shares means the person whose name is entered in the register of members as the holder of the shares, or, in the case of a share in respect of which a share warrant has been issued (and not cancelled), the person in possession of that warrant;

"instrument" means a document in hard copy form;

"lien enforcement notice" has the meaning given in article 53;
"member" has the meaning given in section 112 of the Companies Act 2006;
"ordinary resolution" has the meaning given in section 282 of the Companies Act 2006;
"paid" means paid or credited as paid;
"participate", in relation to a directors' meeting, has the meaning given in article 9;
"partly paid" in relation to a share means that part of that share's nominal value or any premium at which it was issued has not been paid to the company;
"proxy notice" has the meaning given in article 38;
"securities seal" has the meaning given in article 47;
"shares" means shares in the company;
"special resolution" has the meaning given in section 283 of the Companies Act 2006;
"subsidiary" has the meaning given in section 1159 of the Companies Act 2006;
"transmittee" means a person entitled to a share by reason of the death or bankruptcy of a shareholder or otherwise by operation of law;
"uncertificated" in relation to a share means that, by virtue of legislation (other than section 778 of the Companies Act 2006) permitting title to shares to be evidenced and transferred without a certificate, title to that share is evidenced and may be transferred without a certificate; and
"writing" means the representation or reproduction of words, symbols or other information in a visible form by any method or combination of methods, whether sent or supplied in electronic form or otherwise.

Unless the context otherwise requires, other words or expressions contained in these articles bear the same meaning as in the Companies Act 2006 as in force on the date when these articles become binding on the company.

2 Liability of members

The liability of the members is limited to the amount, if any, unpaid on the shares held by them.

PART 2: DIRECTORS

Directors' powers and responsibilities

3 Directors' general authority

Subject to the articles, the directors are responsible for the management of the company's business, for which purpose they may exercise all the powers of the company.

4 Members' reserve power

(1)The members may, by special resolution, direct the directors to take, or refrain from taking, specified action.

(2) No such special resolution invalidates anything which the directors have done before the passing of the resolution.

5 Directors may delegate

(1) Subject to the articles, the directors may delegate any of the powers which are conferred on them under the articles

(a) to such person or committee;
(b) by such means (including by power of attorney);
(c) to such an extent;
(d) in relation to such matters or territories; and
(e) on such terms and conditions;

as they think fit.

(2) If the directors so specify, any such delegation may authorise further delegation of the directors' powers by any person to whom they are delegated.
(3) The directors may revoke any delegation in whole or part, or alter its terms and conditions.

6 Committees

(1) Committees to which the directors delegate any of their powers must follow procedures which are based as far as they are applicable on those provisions of the articles which govern the taking of decisions by directors.
(2) The directors may make rules of procedure for all or any committees, which prevail over rules derived from the articles if they are not consistent with them.

Decision-making by directors

7 Directors to take decisions collectively

Decisions of the directors may be taken

(a) at a directors' meeting, or

(b) in the form of a directors' written resolution.

8 Calling a directors' meeting

(1) Any director may call a directors' meeting.
(2) The company secretary must call a directors' meeting if a director so requests.
(3) A directors' meeting is called by giving notice of the meeting to the directors.
(4) Notice of any directors' meeting must indicate

(a) its proposed date and time;

(b) where it is to take place; and

(c) if it is anticipated that directors participating in the meeting will not be in the same place, how it is proposed that they should communicate with each other during the meeting.

(5) Notice of a directors' meeting must be given to each director, but need not be in writing.
(6) Notice of a directors' meeting need not be given to directors who waive their entitlement to notice of that meeting, by giving notice to that effect to the company not more than 7 days after the date on which the meeting is held. Where such notice is given after the meeting has been held, that does not affect the validity of the meeting, or of any business conducted at it.

9 Participation in directors' meetings

(1) Subject to the articles, directors participate in a directors' meeting, or part of a directors' meeting, when—

(a) the meeting has been called and takes place in accordance with the articles, and

(b) they can each communicate to the others any information or opinions they have on any particular item of the business of the meeting.

(2) In determining whether directors are participating in a directors' meeting, it is irrelevant where any director is or how they communicate with each other.
(3) If all the directors participating in a meeting are not in the same place, they may decide that the meeting is to be treated as taking place wherever any of them is.

10 Quorum for directors' meetings

(1) At a directors' meeting, unless a quorum is participating, no proposal is to be voted on, except a proposal to call another meeting.
(2) The quorum for directors' meetings may be fixed from time to time by a decision of the directors, but it must never be less than two, and unless otherwise fixed it is two.

11 Meetings where total number of directors less than quorum

(1) This article applies where the total number of directors for the time being is less than the quorum for directors' meetings.

(2) If there is only one director, that director may appoint sufficient directors to make up a quorum or call a general meeting to do so.

(3) If there is more than one director

(a) a directors' meeting may take place, if it is called in accordance with the articles and at least two directors participate in it, with a view to appointing sufficient directors to make up a quorum or calling a general meeting to do so, and

(b) if a directors' meeting is called but only one director attends at the appointed date and time to participate in it, that director may appoint sufficient directors to make up a quorum or call a general meeting to do so.

12 Chairing directors' meetings

(1) The directors may appoint a director to chair their meetings.

(2) The person so appointed for the time being is known as the chairman.

(3) The directors may appoint other directors as deputy or assistant chairmen to chair directors' meetings in the chairman's absence.

(4) The directors may terminate the appointment of the chairman, deputy or assistant chairman at any time.

(5) If neither the chairman nor any director appointed generally to chair directors' meetings in the chairman's absence is participating in a meeting within ten minutes of the time at which it was to start, the participating directors must appoint one of themselves to chair it.

13 Voting at directors' meetings: general rules

(1) Subject to the articles, a decision is taken at a directors' meeting by a majority of the votes of the participating directors.

(2) Subject to the articles, each director participating in a directors' meeting has one vote.

(3) Subject to the articles, if a director has an interest in an actual or proposed transaction or arrangement with the company

(a) that director and that director's alternate may not vote on any proposal relating to it, but

(b) this does not preclude the alternate from voting in relation to that transaction or arrangement on behalf of another appointor who does not have such an interest.

14 Chairman's casting vote at directors' meetings

(1) If the numbers of votes for and against a proposal are equal, the chairman or other director chairing the meeting has a casting vote.

(2) But this does not apply if, in accordance with the articles, the chairman or other director is not to be counted as participating in the decision-making process for quorum or voting purposes.

15 Alternates voting at directors' meetings

A director who is also an alternate director has an additional vote on behalf of each appointor who is

(a) not participating in a directors' meeting, and

(b) would have been entitled to vote if they were participating in it.

16 Conflicts of interest

(1) If a directors' meeting, or part of a directors' meeting, is concerned with an actual or proposed transaction or arrangement with the company in which a director is interested, that

director is not to be counted as participating in that meeting, or part of a meeting, for quorum or voting purposes.

(2) But if paragraph (3) applies, a director who is interested in an actual or proposed transaction or arrangement with the company is to be counted as participating in a decision at a directors' meeting, or part of a directors' meeting, relating to it for quorum and voting purposes.

(3) This paragraph applies when

(a) the company by ordinary resolution disapplies the provision of the articles which would otherwise prevent a director from being counted as participating in, or voting at, a directors' meeting;

(b) the director's interest cannot reasonably be regarded as likely to give rise to a conflict of interest; or

(c) the director's conflict of interest arises from a permitted cause.

(4) For the purposes of this article, the following are permitted causes

(a) a guarantee given, or to be given, by or to a director in respect of an obligation incurred by or on behalf of the company or any of its subsidiaries;

(b) subscription, or an agreement to subscribe, for shares or other securities of the company or any of its subsidiaries, or to underwrite, sub-underwrite, or guarantee subscription for any such shares or securities; and

(c) arrangements pursuant to which benefits are made available to employees and directors or former employees and directors of the company or any of its subsidiaries which do not provide special benefits for directors or former directors.

(5) Subject to paragraph (6), if a question arises at a meeting of directors or of a committee of directors as to the right of a director to participate in the meeting (or part of the meeting) for voting or quorum purposes, the question may, before the conclusion of the meeting, be referred to the chairman whose ruling in relation to any director other than the chairman is to be final and conclusive.

(6) If any question as to the right to participate in the meeting (or part of the meeting) should arise in respect of the chairman, the question is to be decided by a decision of the directors at that meeting, for which purpose the chairman is not to be counted as participating in the meeting (or that part of the meeting) for voting or quorum purposes.

17 Proposing directors' written resolutions

(1) Any director may propose a directors' written resolution.

(2) The company secretary must propose a directors' written resolution if a director so requests.

(3) A directors' written resolution is proposed by giving notice of the proposed resolution to the directors.

(4) Notice of a proposed directors' written resolution must indicate

(a) the proposed resolution, and

(b) the time by which it is proposed that the directors should adopt it.

(5) Notice of a proposed directors' written resolution must be given in writing to each director.

(6) Any decision which a person giving notice of a proposed directors' written resolution takes regarding the process of adopting that resolution must be taken reasonably in good faith.

18 Adoption of directors' written resolutions

(1) A proposed directors' written resolution is adopted when all the directors who would have been entitled to vote on the resolution at a directors' meeting have signed one or more copies of it, provided that those directors would have formed a quorum at such a meeting.

(2) It is immaterial whether any director signs the resolution before or after the time by which the notice proposed that it should be adopted.

(3) Once a directors' written resolution has been adopted, it must be treated as if it had been a decision taken at a directors' meeting in accordance with the articles.

(4) The company secretary must ensure that the company keeps a record, in writing, of all directors' written resolutions for at least ten years from the date of their adoption.

19 Directors' discretion to make further rules

Subject to the articles, the directors may make any rule which they think fit about how they take decisions, and about how such rules are to be recorded or communicated to directors.

Appointment of directors

20 Methods of appointing directors

Any person who is willing to act as a director, and is permitted by law to do so, may be appointed to be a director

(a) by ordinary resolution, or

(b) by a decision of the directors.

21 Retirement of directors by rotation

(1) At the first annual general meeting all the directors must retire from office.

(2) At every subsequent annual general meeting any directors

(a) who have been appointed by the directors since the last annual general meeting, or

(b) who were not appointed or reappointed at one of the preceding two annual general meetings,

must retire from office and may offer themselves for reappointment by the members.

22 Termination of director's appointment

A person ceases to be a director as soon as

(a) that person ceases to be a director by virtue of any provision of the Companies Act 2006 or is prohibited from being a director by law;

(b) a bankruptcy order is made against that person;

(c) a composition is made with that person's creditors generally in satisfaction of that person's debts;

(d) a registered medical practitioner who is treating that person gives a written opinion to the company stating that that person has become physically or mentally incapable of acting as a director and may remain so for more than three months;

(f) notification is received by the company from the director that the director is resigning from office as director, and such resignation has taken effect in accordance with its terms.

23 Directors' remuneration

(1) Directors may undertake any services for the company that the directors decide.

(2) Directors are entitled to such remuneration as the directors determine

(a) for their services to the company as directors, and

(b) for any other service which they undertake for the company.

(3) Subject to the articles, a director's remuneration may

(a) take any form, and

(b) include any arrangements in connection with the payment of a pension, allowance or gratuity, or any death, sickness or disability benefits, to or in respect of that director.

(4) Unless the directors decide otherwise, directors' remuneration accrues from day to day.

(5) Unless the directors decide otherwise, directors are not accountable to the company for any remuneration which they receive as directors or other officers or employees of the company's subsidiaries or of any other body corporate in which the company is interested.

24 Directors' expenses

The company may pay any reasonable expenses which the directors properly incur in connection with their attendance at

(a) meetings of directors or committees of directors,

(b) general meetings, or

(c) separate meetings of the holders of any class of shares or of debentures of the company,

or otherwise in connection with the exercise of their powers and the discharge of their responsibilities in relation to the company.

Alternate directors

25 Appointment and removal of alternates

(1) Any director (the "appointor") may appoint as an alternate any other director, or any other person approved by resolution of the directors, to

(a) exercise that director's powers, and

(b) carry out that director's responsibilities,

in relation to the taking of decisions by the directors in the absence of the alternate's appointor.

(2) Any appointment or removal of an alternate must be effected by notice in writing to the company signed by the appointor, or in any other manner approved by the directors.

(3) The notice must

(a) identify the proposed alternate, and

(b) in the case of a notice of appointment, contain a statement signed by the proposed alternate that the proposed alternate is willing to act as the alternate of the director giving the notice.

26 Rights and responsibilities of alternate directors

(1) An alternate director has the same rights, in relation to any directors' meeting or directors' written resolution, as the alternate's appointor.

(2) Except as the articles specify otherwise, alternate directors

(a) are deemed for all purposes to be directors;

(b) are liable for their own acts and omissions;

(c) are subject to the same restrictions as their appointors; and

(d) are not deemed to be agents of or for their appointors.

(3) A person who is an alternate director but not a director

(a) may be counted as participating for the purposes of determining whether a quorum is participating (but only if that person's appointor is not participating), and

(b) may sign a written resolution (but only if it is not signed or to be signed by that person's appointor).

No alternate may be counted as more than one director for such purposes.

(4) An alternate director is not entitled to receive any remuneration from the company for serving as an alternate director except such part of the alternate's appointor's remuneration as the appointor may direct by notice in writing made to the company.

27 Termination of alternate directorship

An alternate director's appointment as an alternate terminates

(a) when the alternate's appointor revokes the appointment by notice to the company in writing specifying when it is to terminate;

(b) on the occurrence in relation to the alternate of any event which, if it occurred in relation to the alternate's appointor, would result in the termination of the appointor's appointment as a director;

(c) on the death of the alternate's appointor; or

(d) when the alternate's appointor's appointment as a director terminates, except that an alternate's appointment as an alternate does not terminate when the appointor retires by rotation at a general meeting and is then re-appointed as a director at the same general meeting.

PART 3: DECISION-MAKING BY MEMBERS

Organisation of general meetings

28 Members can call general meeting if not enough directors

If

(a) the company has fewer than two directors, and

(b) the director (if any) is unable or unwilling to appoint sufficient directors to make up a quorum or to call a general meeting to do so,

then two or more members may call a general meeting (or instruct the company secretary to do so) for the purpose of appointing one or more directors.

29 Attendance and speaking at general meetings

(1) A person is able to exercise the right to speak at a general meeting when that person is in a position to communicate to all those attending the meeting, during the meeting, any information or opinions which that person has on the business of the meeting.

(2) A person is able to exercise the right to vote at a general meeting when

(a) that person is able to vote, during the meeting, on resolutions put to the vote at the meeting, and

(b) that person's vote can be taken into account in determining whether or not such resolutions are passed at the same time as the votes of all the other persons attending the meeting.

(3) The directors may make whatever arrangements they consider appropriate to enable those attending a general meeting to exercise their rights to speak or vote at it.

(4) In determining attendance at a general meeting, it is immaterial whether any two or more members attending it are in the same place as each other.

(5) Two or more persons who are not in the same place as each other attend a general meeting if their circumstances are such that if they have (or were to have) rights to speak and vote at that meeting, they are (or would be) able to exercise them.

30 Quorum for general meetings

No business other than the appointment of the chairman of the meeting is to be transacted at a general meeting if the persons attending it do not constitute a quorum.

31 Chairing general meetings

(1) If the directors have appointed a chairman, the chairman shall chair general meetings if present and willing to do so.

(2) If the directors have not appointed a chairman, or if the chairman is unwilling to chair the meeting or is not present within ten minutes of the time at which a meeting was due to start

(a) the directors present, or

(b) (if no directors are present), the meeting,

must appoint a director or member to chair the meeting, and the appointment of the chairman of the meeting must be the first business of the meeting.

(3) The person chairing a meeting in accordance with this article is referred to as "the chairman of the meeting".

32 Attendance and speaking by directors and non-members

(1) Directors may attend and speak at general meetings, whether or not they are members.

(2) The chairman of the meeting may permit other persons who are not

(a) members of the company, or

(b) otherwise entitled to exercise the rights of members in relation to general meetings,

to attend and speak at a general meeting.

33 Adjournment

(1) If the persons attending a general meeting within half an hour of the time at which the meeting was due to start do not constitute a quorum, or if during a meeting a quorum ceases to be present, the chairman of the meeting must adjourn it.

(2) The chairman of the meeting may adjourn a general meeting at which a quorum is present if

(a) the meeting consents to an adjournment, or

(b) it appears to the chairman of the meeting that an adjournment is necessary to protect the safety of any person attending the meeting or ensure that the business of the meeting is conducted in an orderly manner.

(3) The chairman of the meeting must adjourn a general meeting if directed to do so by the meeting.

(4) When adjourning a general meeting, the chairman of the meeting must

(a) either specify the time and place to which it is adjourned or state that it is to continue at a time and place to be fixed by the directors, and

(b) have regard to any directions as to the time and place of any adjournment which have been given by the meeting.

(5) If the continuation of an adjourned meeting is to take place more than 14 days after it was adjourned, the company must give at least 7 clear days' notice of it (that is, excluding the day of the adjourned meeting and the day on which the notice is given)

(a) to the same persons to whom notice of the company's general meetings is required to be given, and

(b) containing the same information which such notice is required to contain.

(6) No business may be transacted at an adjourned general meeting which could not properly have been transacted at the meeting if the adjournment had not taken place.

Voting at general meetings

34 Voting: general

A resolution put to the vote of a general meeting must be decided on a show of hands unless a poll is duly demanded in accordance with the articles.

35 Errors and disputes

(1) No objection may be raised to the qualification of any person voting at a general meeting except at the meeting or adjourned meeting at which the vote objected to is tendered, and every vote not disallowed at the meeting is valid.

(2) Any such objection must be referred to the chairman of the meeting whose decision is final.

36 Demanding a poll

(1) A poll on a resolution may be demanded

(a) in advance of the general meeting where it is to be put to the vote, or

(b) at a general meeting, either before a show of hands on that resolution or immediately after the result of a show of hands on that resolution is declared.

(2) A poll may be demanded by

(a) the chairman of the meeting;

(b) the directors;

(c) two or more persons having the right to vote on the resolution; or

(d) a person or persons representing not less than one tenth of the total voting rights of all the members having the right to vote on the resolution.

(3) A demand for a poll may be withdrawn if

(a) the poll has not yet been taken, and

(b) the chairman of the meeting consents to the withdrawal.

37 Procedure on a poll

(1) Subject to the articles, polls at general meetings must be taken when, where and in such manner as the chairman of the meeting directs.

(2) The chairman of the meeting may appoint scrutineers (who need not be members) and decide how and when the result of the poll is to be declared.

(3) The result of a poll shall be the decision of the meeting in respect of the resolution on which the poll was demanded.

(4) A poll on

(a) the election of the chairman of the meeting, or

(b) a question of adjournment,

must be taken immediately.

(5) Other polls must be taken within 30 days of their being demanded.

(6) A demand for a poll does not prevent a general meeting from continuing, except as regards the question on which the poll was demanded.

(7) No notice need be given of a poll not taken immediately if the time and place at which it is to be taken are announced at the meeting at which it is demanded.

(8) In any other case, at least 7 days' notice must be given specifying the time and place at which the poll is to be taken.

38 Content of proxy notices

(1) Proxies may only validly be appointed by a notice in writing (a "proxy notice") which

(a) states the name and address of the member appointing the proxy;

(b) identifies the person appointed to be that member's proxy and the general meeting in relation to which that person is appointed;

(c) is signed by or on behalf of the member appointing the proxy, or is authenticated in such manner as the directors may determine; and

(d) is delivered to the company in accordance with the articles and any instructions contained in the notice of the general meeting to which they relate.

(2) The company may require proxy notices to be delivered in a particular form, and may specify different forms for different purposes.

(3) Proxy notices may specify how the proxy appointed under them is to vote (or that the proxy is to abstain from voting) on one or more resolutions.

(4) Unless a proxy notice indicates otherwise, it must be treated as

(a) allowing the person appointed under it as a proxy discretion as to how to vote on any ancillary or procedural resolutions put to the meeting, and

(b) appointing that person as a proxy in relation to any adjournment of the general meeting to which it relates as well as the meeting itself.

39 Delivery of proxy notices

(1) Any notice of a general meeting must specify the address or addresses ("proxy notification address") at which the company or its agents will receive proxy notices relating to that meeting, or any adjournment of it, delivered in hard copy or electronic form.

(2) A person who is entitled to attend, speak or vote (either on a show of hands or on a poll) at a general meeting remains so entitled in respect of that meeting or any adjournment of it, even though a valid proxy notice has been delivered to the company by or on behalf of that person.

(3) Subject to paragraphs (4) and (5), a proxy notice must be delivered to a proxy notification address not less than 48 hours before the general meeting or adjourned meeting to which it relates.

(4) In the case of a poll taken more than 48 hours after it is demanded, the notice must be delivered to a proxy notification address not less than 24 hours before the time appointed for the taking of the poll.

(5) In the case of a poll not taken during the meeting but taken not more than 48 hours after it was demanded, the proxy notice must be delivered

(a) in accordance with paragraph (3), or

(b) at the meeting at which the poll was demanded to the chairman, secretary or any director.

(6) An appointment under a proxy notice may be revoked by delivering a notice in writing given by or on behalf of the person by whom or on whose behalf the proxy notice was given to a proxy notification address.

(7) A notice revoking a proxy appointment only takes effect if it is delivered before

(a) the start of the meeting or adjourned meeting to which it relates, or

(b) (in the case of a poll not taken on the same day as the meeting or adjourned meeting) the time appointed for taking the poll to which it relates.

(8) If a proxy notice is not signed by the person appointing the proxy, it must be accompanied by written evidence of the authority of the person who executed it to execute it on the appointor's behalf.

40 Amendments to resolutions

(1) An ordinary resolution to be proposed at a general meeting may be amended by ordinary resolution if

(a) notice of the proposed amendment is given to the company secretary in writing by a person entitled to vote at the general meeting at which it is to be proposed not less than 48 hours before the meeting is to take place (or such later time as the chairman of the meeting may determine), and

(b) the proposed amendment does not, in the reasonable opinion of the chairman of the meeting, materially alter the scope of the resolution.

(2) A special resolution to be proposed at a general meeting may be amended by ordinary resolution, if

(a) the chairman of the meeting proposes the amendment at the general meeting at which the resolution is to be proposed, and

(b) the amendment does not go beyond what is necessary to correct a grammatical or other non-substantive error in the resolution.

(3) If the chairman of the meeting, acting in good faith, wrongly decides that an amendment to a resolution is out of order, the chairman's error does not invalidate the vote on that resolution.

Restrictions on members' rights

41 No voting of shares on which money owed to company

No voting rights attached to a share may be exercised at any general meeting, at any adjournment of it, or on any poll called at or in relation to it, unless all amounts payable to the company in respect of that share have been paid.

Application of rules to class meetings

42 Class meetings

The provisions of the articles relating to general meetings apply, with any necessary modifications, to meetings of the holders of any class of shares.

PART 4: SHARES AND DISTRIBUTIONS

Issue of shares

43 Powers to issue different classes of share

(1) Subject to the articles, but without prejudice to the rights attached to any existing share, the company may issue shares with such rights or restrictions as may be determined by ordinary resolution.

(2) The company may issue shares which are to be redeemed, or are liable to be redeemed at the option of the company or the holder, and the directors may determine the terms, conditions and manner of redemption of any such shares.

44 Payment of commissions on subscription for shares

(1) The company may pay any person a commission in consideration for that person

(a) subscribing, or agreeing to subscribe, for shares, or

(b) procuring, or agreeing to procure, subscriptions for shares.

(2) Any such commission may be paid

(a) in cash, or in fully paid or partly paid shares or other securities, or partly in one way and partly in the other, and

(b) in respect of a conditional or an absolute subscription.

Interests in shares

45 Company not bound by less than absolute interests

Except as required by law, no person is to be recognised by the company as holding any share upon any trust, and except as otherwise required by law or the articles, the company is not in any way to be bound by or recognise any interest in a share other than the holder's absolute ownership of it and all the rights attaching to it.

Share certificates

46 Certificates to be issued except in certain cases

(1) The company must issue each member with one or more certificates in respect of the shares which that member holds.

(2) This article does not apply to

(a) uncertificated shares;

(b) shares in respect of which a share warrant has been issued; or

(c) shares in respect of which the Companies Acts permit the company not to issue a certificate.

(3) Except as otherwise specified in the articles, all certificates must be issued free of charge.
(4) No certificate may be issued in respect of shares of more than one class.
(5) If more than one person holds a share, only one certificate may be issued in respect of it.

47 Contents and execution of share certificates

(1) Every certificate must specify

(a) in respect of how many shares, of what class, it is issued;
(b) the nominal value of those shares;
(c) the amount paid up on them; and
(d) any distinguishing numbers assigned to them.

(2) Certificates must

(a) have affixed to them the company's common seal or an official seal which is a facsimile of the company's common seal with the addition on its face of the word "Securities" (a "securities seal"), or
(b) be otherwise executed in accordance with the Companies Acts.

48 Consolidated share certificates

(1) When a member's holding of shares of a particular class increases, the company may issue that member with

(a) a single, consolidated certificate in respect of all the shares of a particular class which that member holds, or
(b) a separate certificate in respect of only those shares by which that member's holding has increased.

(2) When a member's holding of shares of a particular class is reduced, the company must ensure that the member is issued with one or more certificates in respect of the number of shares held by the member after that reduction. But the company need not (in the absence of a request from the member) issue any new certificate if

(a) all the shares which the member no longer holds as a result of the reduction, and
(b) none of the shares which the member retains following the reduction,

were, immediately before the reduction, represented by the same certificate.

(3) A member may request the company, in writing, to replace

(a) the member's separate certificates with a consolidated certificate, or
(b) the member's consolidated certificate with two or more separate certificates representing such proportion of the shares as the member may specify.

(4) When the company complies with such a request it may charge such reasonable fee as the directors may decide for doing so.
(5) A consolidated certificate must not be issued unless any certificates which it is to replace have first been returned to the company for cancellation.

49 Replacement share certificates

(1) If a certificate issued in respect of a member's shares is

(a) damaged or defaced, or
(b) said to be lost, stolen or destroyed,

that member is entitled to be issued with a replacement certificate in respect of the same shares.

(2) A member exercising the right to be issued with such a replacement certificate

(a) may at the same time exercise the right to be issued with a single certificate or separate certificates;
(b) must return the certificate which is to be replaced to the company if it is damaged or defaced; and
(c) must comply with such conditions as to evidence, indemnity and the payment of a reasonable fee as the directors decide.

Shares not held in certificated form

50 Uncertificated shares

(1) In this article, "the relevant rules" means

(a) any applicable provision of the Companies Acts about the holding, evidencing of title to, or transfer of shares other than in certificated form, and

(b) any applicable legislation, rules or other arrangements made under or by virtue of such provision.

(2) The provisions of this article have effect subject to the relevant rules.

(3) Any provision of the articles which is inconsistent with the relevant rules must be disregarded, to the extent that it is inconsistent, whenever the relevant rules apply.

(4) Any share or class of shares of the company may be issued or held on such terms, or in such a way, that

(a) title to it or them is not, or must not be, evidenced by a certificate, or

(b) it or they may or must be transferred wholly or partly without a certificate.

(5) The directors have power to take such steps as they think fit in relation to

(a) the evidencing of and transfer of title to uncertificated shares (including in connection with the issue of such shares);

(b) any records relating to the holding of uncertificated shares;

(c) the conversion of certificated shares into uncertificated shares; or

(d) the conversion of uncertificated shares into certificated shares.

(6) The company may by notice to the holder of a share require that share

(a) if it is uncertificated, to be converted into certificated form, and

(b) if it is certificated, to be converted into uncertificated form,

to enable it to be dealt with in accordance with the articles.

(7) If

(a) the articles give the directors power to take action, or require other persons to take action, in order to sell, transfer or otherwise dispose of shares, and

(b) uncertificated shares are subject to that power, but the power is expressed in terms which assume the use of a certificate or other written instrument,

the directors may take such action as is necessary or expedient to achieve the same results when exercising that power in relation to uncertificated shares.

(8) In particular, the directors may take such action as they consider appropriate to achieve the sale, transfer, disposal, forfeiture, re-allotment or surrender of an uncertificated share or otherwise to enforce a lien in respect of it.

(9) Unless the directors otherwise determine, shares which a member holds in uncertificated form must be treated as separate holdings from any shares which that member holds in certificated form.

(10) A class of shares must not be treated as two classes simply because some shares of that class are held in certificated form and others are held in uncertificated form.

51 Share warrants

(1) The directors may issue a share warrant in respect of any fully paid share.

(2) Share warrants must be

(a) issued in such form, and

(b) executed in such manner,

as the directors decide.

(3) A share represented by a share warrant may be transferred by delivery of the warrant representing it.

(4) The directors may make provision for the payment of dividends in respect of any share represented by a share warrant.

(5) Subject to the articles, the directors may decide the conditions on which any share warrant is issued. In particular, they may

(a) decide the conditions on which new warrants are to be issued in place of warrants which are damaged or defaced, or said to have been lost, stolen or destroyed;

(b) decide the conditions on which bearers of warrants are entitled to attend and vote at general meetings;

(c) decide the conditions subject to which bearers of warrants may surrender their warrant so as to hold their shares in certificated or uncertificated form instead; and

(d) vary the conditions of issue of any warrant from time to time,

and the bearer of a warrant is subject to the conditions and procedures in force in relation to it, whether or not they were decided or specified before the warrant was issued.

(6) Subject to the conditions on which the warrants are issued from time to time, bearers of share warrants have the same rights and privileges as they would if their names had been included in the register as holders of the shares represented by their warrants.

(7) The company must not in any way be bound by or recognise any interest in a share represented by a share warrant other than the absolute right of the bearer of that warrant to that warrant.

Partly paid shares

52 Company's lien over partly paid shares

(1) The company has a lien ("the company's lien") over every share which is partly paid for any part of

(a) that share's nominal value, and

(b) any premium at which it was issued,

which has not been paid to the company, and which is payable immediately or at some time in the future, whether or not a call notice has been sent in respect of it.

(2) The company's lien over a share

(a) takes priority over any third party's interest in that share, and

(b) extends to any dividend or other money payable by the company in respect of that share and (if the lien is enforced and the share is sold by the company) the proceeds of sale of that share.

(3) The directors may at any time decide that a share which is or would otherwise be subject to the company's lien shall not be subject to it, either wholly or in part.

53 Enforcement of the company's lien

(1) Subject to the provisions of this article, if

(a) a lien enforcement notice has been given in respect of a share, and

(b) the person to whom the notice was given has failed to comply with it

the company may sell that share in such manner as the directors decide.

(2) A lien enforcement notice

(a) may only be given in respect of a share which is subject to the company's lien, in respect of which a sum is payable and the due date for payment of that sum has passed;

(b) must specify the share concerned;

(c) must require payment of the sum payable within 14 days of the notice;

(d) must be addressed either to the holder of the share or to a person entitled to it by reason of the holder's death, bankruptcy or otherwise; and

(e) must state the company's intention to sell the share if the notice is not complied with.

(3) Where shares are sold under this article

(a) the directors may authorise any person to execute an instrument of transfer of the shares to the purchaser or a person nominated by the purchaser, and

(b) the transferee is not bound to see to the application of the consideration, and the transferee's title is not affected by any irregularity in or invalidity of the process leading to the sale.

(4) The net proceeds of any such sale (after payment of the costs of sale and any other costs of enforcing the lien) must be applied

(a) first, in payment of so much of the sum for which the lien exists as was payable at the date of the lien enforcement notice,

(b) second, to the person entitled to the shares at the date of the sale, but only after the certificate for the shares sold has been surrendered to the company for cancellation or a suitable indemnity has been given for any lost certificates, and subject to a lien equivalent to the company's lien over the shares before the sale for any money payable in respect of the shares after the date of the lien enforcement notice.

(5) A statutory declaration by a director or the company secretary that the declarant is a director or the company secretary and that a share has been sold to satisfy the company's lien on a specified date

(a) is conclusive evidence of the facts stated in it as against all persons claiming to be entitled to the share, and

(b) subject to compliance with any other formalities of transfer required by the articles or by law, constitutes a good title to the share.

54 Call notices

(1) Subject to the articles and the terms on which shares are allotted, the directors may send a notice (a "call notice") to a member requiring the member to pay the company a specified sum of money (a "call") which is payable in respect of shares which that member holds at the date when the directors decide to send the call notice.

(2) A call notice

(a) may not require a member to pay a call which exceeds the total sum unpaid on that member's shares (whether as to the share's nominal value or any amount payable to the company by way of premium);

(b) must state when and how any call to which it relates is to be paid; and

(c) may permit or require the call to be paid by instalments.

(3) A member must comply with the requirements of a call notice, but no member is obliged to pay any call before 14 days have passed since the notice was sent.

(4) Before the company has received any call due under a call notice the directors may

(a) revoke it wholly or in part, or

(b) specify a later time for payment than is specified in the notice,

by a further notice in writing to the member in respect of whose shares the call is made.

55 Liability to pay calls

(1) Liability to pay a call is not extinguished or transferred by transferring the shares in respect of which it is required to be paid.

(2) Joint holders of a share are jointly and severally liable to pay all calls in respect of that share.

(3) Subject to the terms on which shares are allotted, the directors may, when issuing shares, provide that call notices sent to the holders of those shares may require them

(a) to pay calls which are not the same, or

(b) to pay calls at different times.

56 When call notice need not be issued

(1) A call notice need not be issued in respect of sums which are specified, in the terms on which a share is issued, as being payable to the company in respect of that share (whether in respect of nominal value or premium)

- (a) on allotment;
- (b) on the occurrence of a particular event; or
- (c) on a date fixed by or in accordance with the terms of issue.

(2) But if the due date for payment of such a sum has passed and it has not been paid, the holder of the share concerned is treated in all respects as having failed to comply with a call notice in respect of that sum, and is liable to the same consequences as regards the payment of interest and forfeiture.

57 Failure to comply with call notice: automatic consequences

(1) If a person is liable to pay a call and fails to do so by the call payment date

- (a) the directors may issue a notice of intended forfeiture to that person, and
- (b) until the call is paid, that person must pay the company interest on the call from the call payment date at the relevant rate.

(2) For the purposes of this article

- (a) the "call payment date" is the time when the call notice states that a call is payable, unless the directors give a notice specifying a later date, in which case the "call payment date" is that later date;
- (b) the "relevant rate" is
  - (i) the rate fixed by the terms on which the share in respect of which the call is due was allotted;
  - (ii) such other rate as was fixed in the call notice which required payment of the call, or has otherwise been determined by the directors; or
  - (iii) if no rate is fixed in either of these ways, 5 per cent per annum.

(3) The relevant rate must not exceed by more than 5 percentage points the base lending rate most recently set by the Monetary Policy Committee of the Bank of England in connection with its responsibilities under Part 2 of the Bank of England Act 1998(a).

(4) The directors may waive any obligation to pay interest on a call wholly or in part.

58 Notice of intended forfeiture

A notice of intended forfeiture

- (a) may be sent in respect of any share in respect of which a call has not been paid as required by a call notice;
- (b) must be sent to the holder of that share or to a person entitled to it by reason of the holder's death, bankruptcy or otherwise;
- (c) must require payment of the call and any accrued interest by a date which is not less than 14 days after the date of the notice;
- (d) must state how the payment is to be made; and
- (e) must state that if the notice is not complied with, the shares in respect of which the call is payable will be liable to be forfeited.

59 Directors' power to forfeit shares

If a notice of intended forfeiture is not complied with before the date by which payment of the call is required in the notice of intended forfeiture, the directors may decide that any share in respect of which it was given is forfeited, and the forfeiture is to include all dividends or other moneys payable in respect of the forfeited shares and not paid before the forfeiture.

60 Effect of forfeiture

(1) Subject to the articles, the forfeiture of a share extinguishes

(a) all interests in that share, and all claims and demands against the company in respect of it, and

(b) all other rights and liabilities incidental to the share as between the person whose share it was prior to the forfeiture and the company.

(2) Any share which is forfeited in accordance with the articles

(a) is deemed to have been forfeited when the directors decide that it is forfeited;

(b) is deemed to be the property of the company; and

(c) may be sold, re-allotted or otherwise disposed of as the directors think fit.

(3) If a person's shares have been forfeited

(a) the company must send that person notice that forfeiture has occurred and record it in the register of members;

(b) that person ceases to be a member in respect of those shares;

(c) that person must surrender the certificate for the shares forfeited to the company for cancellation;

(d) that person remains liable to the company for all sums payable by that person under the articles at the date of forfeiture in respect of those shares, including any interest (whether accrued before or after the date of forfeiture); and

(e) the directors may waive payment of such sums wholly or in part or enforce payment without any allowance for the value of the shares at the time of forfeiture or for any consideration received on their disposal.

(4) At any time before the company disposes of a forfeited share, the directors may decide to cancel the forfeiture on payment of all calls and interest due in respect of it and on such other terms as they think fit.

61 Procedure following forfeiture

(1) If a forfeited share is to be disposed of by being transferred, the company may receive the consideration for the transfer and the directors may authorise any person to execute the instrument of transfer.

(2) A statutory declaration by a director or the company secretary that the declarant is a director or the company secretary and that a share has been forfeited on a specified date

(a) is conclusive evidence of the facts stated in it as against all persons claiming to be entitled to the share, and

(b) subject to compliance with any other formalities of transfer required by the articles or by law, constitutes a good title to the share.

(3) A person to whom a forfeited share is transferred is not bound to see to the application of the consideration (if any) nor is that person's title to the share affected by any irregularity in or invalidity of the process leading to the forfeiture or transfer of the share.

(4) If the company sells a forfeited share, the person who held it prior to its forfeiture is entitled to receive from the company the proceeds of such sale, net of any commission, and excluding any amount which

(a) was, or would have become, payable, and

(b) had not, when that share was forfeited, been paid by that person in respect of that share,

but no interest is payable to such a person in respect of such proceeds and the company is not required to account for any money earned on them.

62 Surrender of shares

(1) A member may surrender any share

(a) in respect of which the directors may issue a notice of intended forfeiture;

(b) which the directors may forfeit; or

(c) which has been forfeited.

(2) The directors may accept the surrender of any such share.

(3) The effect of surrender on a share is the same as the effect of forfeiture on that share.

(4) A share which has been surrendered may be dealt with in the same way as a share which has been forfeited.

Transfer and transmission of shares

63 Transfers of certificated shares

(1) Certificated shares may be transferred by means of an instrument of transfer in any usual form or any other form approved by the directors, which is executed by or on behalf of

(a) the transferor, and

(b) (if any of the shares is partly paid) the transferee.

(2) No fee may be charged for registering any instrument of transfer or other document relating to or affecting the title to any share.

(3) The company may retain any instrument of transfer which is registered.

(4) The transferor remains the holder of a certificated share until the transferee's name is entered in the register of members as holder of it.

(5) The directors may refuse to register the transfer of a certificated share if

(a) the share is not fully paid;

(b) the transfer is not lodged at the company's registered office or such other place as the directors have appointed;

(c) the transfer is not accompanied by the certificate for the shares to which it relates, or such other evidence as the directors may reasonably require to show the transferor's right to make the transfer, or evidence of the right of someone other than the transferor to make the transfer on the transferor's behalf;

(d) the transfer is in respect of more than one class of share; or

(e) the transfer is in favour of more than four transferees.

(6) If the directors refuse to register the transfer of a share, the instrument of transfer must be returned to the transferee with the notice of refusal unless they suspect that the proposed transfer may be fraudulent.

64 Transfer of uncertificated shares

A transfer of an uncertificated share must not be registered if it is in favour of more than four transferees.

65 Transmission of shares

(1) If title to a share passes to a transmittee, the company may only recognise the transmittee as having any title to that share.

(2) Nothing in these articles releases the estate of a deceased member from any liability in respect of a share solely or jointly held by that member.

66 Transmittees' rights

(1) A transmittee who produces such evidence of entitlement to shares as the directors may properly require

(a) may, subject to the articles, choose either to become the holder of those shares or to have them transferred to another person, and

(b) subject to the articles, and pending any transfer of the shares to another person, has the same rights as the holder had.

(2) But transmittees do not have the right to attend or vote at a general meeting in respect of shares to which they are entitled, by reason of the holder's death or bankruptcy or otherwise, unless they become the holders of those shares

67 Exercise of transmittees' rights

(1) Transmittees who wish to become the holders of shares to which they have become entitled must notify the company in writing of that wish.

(2) If the share is a certificated share and a transmittee wishes to have it transferred to another person, the transmittee must execute an instrument of transfer in respect of it.

(3) If the share is an uncertificated share and the transmittee wishes to have it transferred to another person, the transmittee must

(a) procure that all appropriate instructions are given to effect the transfer, or

(b) procure that the uncertificated share is changed into certificated form and then execute an instrument of transfer in respect of it.

(4) Any transfer made or executed under this article is to be treated as if it were made or executed by the person from whom the transmittee has derived rights in respect of the share, and as if the event which gave rise to the transmission had not occurred.

68 Transmittees bound by prior notices

If a notice is given to a member in respect of shares and a transmittee is entitled to those shares, the transmittee is bound by the notice if it was given to the member before the transmittee's name has been entered in the register of members.

Consolidation of shares

69 Procedure for disposing of fractions of shares

(1) This article applies where

(a) there has been a consolidation or division of shares, and

(b) as a result, members are entitled to fractions of shares.

(2) The directors may

(a) sell the shares representing the fractions to any person including the company for the best price reasonably obtainable;

(b) in the case of a certificated share, authorise any person to execute an instrument of transfer of the shares to the purchaser or a person nominated by the purchaser; and

(c) distribute the net proceeds of sale in due proportion among the holders of the shares.

(3) Where any holder's entitlement to a portion of the proceeds of sale amounts to less than a minimum figure determined by the directors, that member's portion may be distributed to an organisation which is a charity for the purposes of the law of England and Wales, Scotland or Northern Ireland.

(4) The person to whom the shares are transferred is not obliged to ensure that any purchase money is received by the person entitled to the relevant fractions.

(5) The transferee's title to the shares is not affected by any irregularity in or invalidity of the process leading to their sale.

Distributions

70 Procedure for declaring dividends

(1) The company may by ordinary resolution declare dividends, and the directors may decide to pay interim dividends.

(2) A dividend must not be declared unless the directors have made a recommendation as to its amount. Such a dividend must not exceed the amount recommended by the directors.

(3) No dividend may be declared or paid unless it is in accordance with members' respective rights.

(4) Unless the members' resolution to declare or directors' decision to pay a dividend, or the terms on which shares are issued, specify otherwise, it must be paid by reference to each member's holding of shares on the date of the resolution or decision to declare or pay it.

(5) If the company's share capital is divided into different classes, no interim dividend may be paid on shares carrying deferred or non-preferred rights if, at the time of payment, any preferential dividend is in arrear.
(6) The directors may pay at intervals any dividend payable at a fixed rate if it appears to them that the profits available for distribution justify the payment.
(7) If the directors act in good faith, they do not incur any liability to the holders of shares conferring preferred rights for any loss they may suffer by the lawful payment of an interim dividend on shares with deferred or non-preferred rights.

71 Calculation of dividends

(1) Except as otherwise provided by the articles or the rights attached to shares, all dividends must be

(a) declared and paid according to the amounts paid up on the shares on which the dividend is paid, and

(b) apportioned and paid proportionately to the amounts paid up on the shares during any portion or portions of the period in respect of which the dividend is paid.

(2) If any share is issued on terms providing that it ranks for dividend as from a particular date, that share ranks for dividend accordingly.
(3) For the purposes of calculating dividends, no account is to be taken of any amount which has been paid up on a share in advance of the due date for payment of that amount.

72 Payment of dividends and other distributions

(1) Where a dividend or other sum which is a distribution is payable in respect of a share, it must be paid by one or more of the following means

(a) transfer to a bank or building society account specified by the distribution recipient either in writing or as the directors may otherwise decide;

(b) sending a cheque made payable to the distribution recipient by post to the distribution recipient at the distribution recipient's registered address (if the distribution recipient is a holder of the share), or (in any other case) to an address specified by the distribution recipient either in writing or as the directors may otherwise decide;

(c) sending a cheque made payable to such person by post to such person at such address as the distribution recipient has specified either in writing or as the directors may otherwise decide; or

(d) any other means of payment as the directors agree with the distribution recipient either in writing or by such other means as the directors decide.

(2) In the articles, "the distribution recipient" means, in respect of a share in respect of which a dividend or other sum is payable

(a) the holder of the share; or

(b) if the share has two or more joint holders, whichever of them is named first in the register of members; or

(c) if the holder is no longer entitled to the share by reason of death or bankruptcy, or otherwise by operation of law, the transmittee.

73 Deductions from distributions in respect of sums owed to the company

(1) If

(a) a share is subject to the company's lien, and

(b) the directors are entitled to issue a lien enforcement notice in respect of it,

they may, instead of issuing a lien enforcement notice, deduct from any dividend or other sum payable in respect of the share any sum of money which is payable to the company in respect of that share to the extent that they are entitled to require payment under a lien enforcement notice.

(2) Money so deducted must be used to pay any of the sums payable in respect of that share.

(3) The company must notify the distribution recipient in writing of

(a) the fact and amount of any such deduction;

(b) any non-payment of a dividend or other sum payable in respect of a share resulting from any such deduction; and

(c) how the money deducted has been applied.

74 No interest on distributions

The company may not pay interest on any dividend or other sum payable in respect of a share unless otherwise provided by

(a) the terms on which the share was issued, or

(b) the provisions of another agreement between the holder of that share and the company.

75 Unclaimed distributions

(1) All dividends or other sums which are

(a) payable in respect of shares, and

(b) unclaimed after having been declared or become payable,

may be invested or otherwise made use of by the directors for the benefit of the company until claimed.

(2) The payment of any such dividend or other sum into a separate account does not make the company a trustee in respect of it.

(3) If

(a) twelve years have passed from the date on which a dividend or other sum became due for payment, and

(b) the distribution recipient has not claimed it,

the distribution recipient is no longer entitled to that dividend or other sum and it ceases to remain owing by the company.

76 Non-cash distributions

(1) Subject to the terms of issue of the share in question, the company may, by ordinary resolution on the recommendation of the directors, decide to pay all or part of a dividend or other distribution payable in respect of a share by transferring non-cash assets of equivalent value (including, without limitation, shares or other securities in any company).

(2) If the shares in respect of which such a non-cash distribution is paid are uncertificated, any shares in the company which are issued as a non-cash distribution in respect of them must be uncertificated.

(3) For the purposes of paying a non-cash distribution, the directors may make whatever arrangements they think fit, including, where any difficulty arises regarding the distribution

(a) fixing the value of any assets;

(b) paying cash to any distribution recipient on the basis of that value in order to adjust the rights of recipients; and

(c) vesting any assets in trustees.

77 Waiver of distributions

Distribution recipients may waive their entitlement to a dividend or other distribution payable in respect of a share by giving the company notice in writing to that effect, but if

(a) the share has more than one holder, or

(b) more than one person is entitled to the share, whether by reason of the death or bankruptcy of one or more joint holders, or otherwise,

the notice is not effective unless it is expressed to be given, and signed, by all the holders or persons otherwise entitled to the share.

Capitalisation of profits

78 Authority to capitalise and appropriation of capitalised sums

(1) Subject to the articles, the directors may, if they are so authorised by an ordinary resolution

(a) decide to capitalise any profits of the company (whether or not they are available for distribution) which are not required for paying a preferential dividend, or any sum standing to the credit of the company's share premium account or capital redemption reserve; and

(b) appropriate any sum which they so decide to capitalise (a "capitalised sum") to the persons who would have been entitled to it if it were distributed by way of dividend (the "persons entitled") and in the same proportions.

(2) Capitalised sums must be applied

(a) on behalf of the persons entitled, and

(b) in the same proportions as a dividend would have been distributed to them.

(3) Any capitalised sum may be applied in paying up new shares of a nominal amount equal to the capitalised sum which are then allotted credited as fully paid to the persons entitled or as they may direct.

(4) A capitalised sum which was appropriated from profits available for distribution may be applied

(a) in or towards paying up any amounts unpaid on existing shares held by the persons entitled, or

(b) in paying up new debentures of the company which are then allotted credited as fully paid to the persons entitled or as they may direct.

(5) Subject to the articles the directors may

(a) apply capitalised sums in accordance with paragraphs (3) and (4) partly in one way and partly in another;

(b) make such arrangements as they think fit to deal with shares or debentures becoming distributable in fractions under this article (including the issuing of fractional certificates or the making of cash payments); and

(c) authorise any person to enter into an agreement with the company on behalf of all the persons entitled which is binding on them in respect of the allotment of shares and debentures to them under this article.

PART 5: MISCELLANEOUS PROVISIONS

Communications

79 Means of communication to be used

(1) Subject to the articles, anything sent or supplied by or to the company under the articles may be sent or supplied in any way in which the Companies Act 2006 provides for documents or information which are authorised or required by any provision of that Act to be sent or supplied by or to the company.

(2) Subject to the articles, any notice or document to be sent or supplied to a director in connection with the taking of decisions by directors may also be sent or supplied by the means by which that director has asked to be sent or supplied with such notices or documents for the time being.

(3) A director may agree with the company that notices or documents sent to that director in a particular way are to be deemed to have been received within a specified time of their being sent, and for the specified time to be less than 48 hours.

80 Failure to notify contact details

(1) If

(a) the company sends two consecutive documents to a member over a period of at least 12 months, and

(b) each of those documents is returned undelivered, or the company receives notification that it has not been delivered,

that member ceases to be entitled to receive notices from the company.

(2) A member who has ceased to be entitled to receive notices from the company becomes entitled to receive such notices again by sending the company

(a) a new address to be recorded in the register of members, or

(b) if the member has agreed that the company should use a means of communication other than sending things to such an address, the information that the company needs to use that means of communication effectively.

Administrative arrangements

81 Company seals

(1) Any common seal may only be used by the authority of the directors.

(2) The directors may decide by what means and in what form any common seal or securities seal is to be used.

(3) Unless otherwise decided by the directors, if the company has a common seal and it is affixed to a document, the document must also be signed by at least one authorised person in the presence of a witness who attests the signature.

(4) For the purposes of this article, an authorised person is

(a) any director of the company;

(b) the company secretary; or

(c) any person authorised by the directors for the purpose of signing documents to which the common seal is applied.

(5) If the company has an official seal for use abroad, it may only be affixed to a document if its use on that document, or documents of a class to which it belongs, has been authorised by a decision of the directors.

(6) If the company has a securities seal, it may only be affixed to securities by the company secretary or a person authorised to apply it to securities by the company secretary.

(7) For the purposes of the articles, references to the securities seal being affixed to any document include the reproduction of the image of that seal on or in a document by any mechanical or electronic means which has been approved by the directors in relation to that document or documents of a class to which it belongs.

82 Destruction of documents

(1) The company is entitled to destroy

(a) all instruments of transfer of shares which have been registered, and all other documents on the basis of which any entries are made in the register of members, from six years after the date of registration;

(b) all dividend mandates, variations or cancellations of dividend mandates, and notifications of change of address, from two years after they have been recorded;

(c) all share certificates which have been cancelled from one year after the date of the cancellation;

(d) all paid dividend warrants and cheques from one year after the date of actual payment; and

(e) all proxy notices from one year after the end of the meeting to which the proxy notice relates.

(2) If the company destroys a document in good faith, in accordance with the articles, and without notice of any claim to which that document may be relevant, it is conclusively presumed in favour of the company that

(a) entries in the register purporting to have been made on the basis of an instrument of transfer or other document so destroyed were duly and properly made;

(b) any instrument of transfer so destroyed was a valid and effective instrument duly and properly registered;

(c) any share certificate so destroyed was a valid and effective certificate duly and properly cancelled; and

(d) any other document so destroyed was a valid and effective document in accordance with its recorded particulars in the books or records of the company.

(3) This article does not impose on the company any liability which it would not otherwise have if it destroys any document before the time at which this article permits it to do so.

(4) In this article, references to the destruction of any document include a reference to its being disposed of in any manner.

83 No right to inspect accounts and other records

Except as provided by law or authorised by the directors or an ordinary resolution of the company, no person is entitled to inspect any of the company's accounting or other records or documents merely by virtue of being a member.

84 Provision for employees on cessation of business

The directors may decide to make provision for the benefit of persons employed or formerly employed by the company or any of its subsidiaries (other than a director or former director or shadow director) in connection with the cessation or transfer to any person of the whole or part of the undertaking of the company or that subsidiary.

Directors' indemnity and insurance

85 Indemnity

(1) Subject to paragraph (2), a relevant director of the company or an associated company may be indemnified out of the company's assets against

(a) any liability incurred by that director in connection with any negligence, default, breach of duty or breach of trust in relation to the company or an associated company,

(b) any liability incurred by that director in connection with the activities of the company or an associated company in its capacity as a trustee of an occupational pension scheme (as defined in section 235(6) of the Companies Act 2006),

(c) any other liability incurred by that director as an officer of the company or an associated company.

(2) This article does not authorise any indemnity which would be prohibited or rendered void by any provision of the Companies Acts or by any other provision of law.

(3) In this article

(a) companies are associated if one is a subsidiary of the other or both are subsidiaries of the same body corporate, and

(b) a "relevant director" means any director or former director of the company or an associated company.

86 Insurance

(1) The directors may decide to purchase and maintain insurance, at the expense of the company, for the benefit of any relevant director in respect of any relevant loss.

(2) In this article

(a) a "relevant director" means any director or former director of the company or an associated company,

(b) a "relevant loss" means any loss or liability which has been or may be incurred by a relevant director in connection with that director's duties or powers in relation to the company, any associated company or any pension fund or employees' share scheme of the company or associated company, and

(c) companies are associated if one is a subsidiary of the other or both are subsidiaries of the same body corporate.

Table of Statutes

A

Administration of Justice Act 1982
s 42 .... 18.1
Age of Legal Capacity (Scotland) Act 1991 .... 26.1

B

Banking and Financial Dealings Act 1971 .... App1
Bankruptcy and Diligence etc (Scotland) Act 2007
Pt 2 (ss 37–49) 43.2
s 46(1) 43.2
Bankruptcy (Scotland) Act 1985 .... 16.32, 42.16
s 57(1)(a) 48.14
58 .... 48.14
Building Societies Act 1986 .... 2.14
s 102C(1)(b) 34.23
Business Names Act 1985 .... 27.18
s 2(1) 27.21
7(6) 29.App

C

Charities Act 1960
s 22, 22A 18.1
Charities Act 1993
s 18 .... App1
24 .... 18.1
66 .... 18.66
Charities Act 2011 .... 8.29
s 76 .... 16.21
96 .... 18.1
100 .... 18.1
194(1) 16.13, 16.14
(2) 16.14
195 .... 16.13, 16.14
197 .... 14.5
198 .... 14.5, 14.6
201 .... 18.48, 18.53, 18.58, 18.59, 18.61, 18.62, 18.63
202 .... 18.48, 18.53, 18.58, 18.61, 18.62, 18.63
Charities Act (Northern Ireland) 1964
s 25 .... 18.1
Charities Act (Northern Ireland) 2013
s 5 .... 16.4
Charities and Trustee Investment (Scotland) Act 2005
s 7(2) 20.9
16 .... 14.5
Church Funds Investment Measure 1958
Schedule 18.1
Climate Change Act 2008
s 92 .... 20.17
93(2) 20.17
Commissioners for Oaths Act 1889
s 6 .... 30.App, App1
Communication Act 2003
Sch 17
para 83 .... 18.17
Companies Act 1862 .... App1
Companies Act 1929 .... App1
Companies Act 1948 .... App1
s 28 .... App1
Sch 1
Table A 26.8
Companies Act 1967 .... App1
s 13(1) 8.8
Companies Act 1976 .... App1
Companies Act 1980 .... 22.App, App1
Companies Act 1981 .... App1
Companies Act 1985 .... 1.2, 12.7, 14.1, 16.21, 21.2, 22.4, 28.1, 34.6, 34.7, 34.20, App1
s 1(1) 26.8
(3A) 26.8
6(1) 30.App
8(4) 14.4
10 .... 39.19
14(1), (2) 14.12
18 .... 14.13, 30.App
23(1) 26.7
24 .... 26.8
26 .... 30.App
28(1) 27.17
(6), (7) 27.17
29, 30 .... 30.App
31 .... 27.12
32 .... 27.16
35 .... 16.1
38 .... 16.6
52(7) 38.5
80, 80A 47.9
89 .... 33.25, 47.17
(1) 47.18
90–91 .... 47.17
95(1)–(2A) 47.18
96(1) 47.19
(3), (4) 47.19
120 .... 47.6
131, 132 .... 3.59
146(1)–(3) 34.23
151 .... 22.8, 22.App
153(4)(b), (c) 30.App
154 .... 22.App

Companies Act 1985 – *cont.*
s 155 .... 30.App
(2) 22.App
159–167 .... 22.App
168 .... 22.5, 22.App
169–181 .... 22.App
191(2) App3
192 .... 17.15
198–220 .... 24.1
Pt VII (221–262A) 30.App
s 224(2) 2.18
226–226B 22.App
227 .... 30.App
229 .... 30.App
233 .... 22.App
238 .... 30.App
(1) 22.App
239 .... 26.4
241 .... 42.30
(4) 30.App
245E(3) 29.App
245G(7) 29.App
252, 253 .... 30.App
258(1) 30.App
(4) 30.App
259 .... 30.App
Pt VIII (ss 263–281) 22.1
s 263(1)–(5) 22.App
264(1)–(4) 22.App
269–273 .... 22.App
274(1) 22.App
275(1)–(6) 22.App
276 .... 22.App
277(1)–(3) 22.App
278 .... 22.App
280(3) 22.App
281 .... 22.App
285 .... 18.7
288 .... 39.19
(1) 38.2
(2) 30.App
293(3) 18.6
308 .... 18.29
310 .... 8.40
317 .... 18.24, 18.55, 18.56
318(1) 18.54
(4), (5) 18.54
(7) 18.54
319 .... 18.53
320–322 .... 18.58
325(5) App3
356(3) App3
366, 366A 42.30
369(4) 42.14
378 .... 14.6, 42.1
386 .... 8.3
390A 8.3
394A(1) 29.App
Pt XII (ss 395–424) 30.64, 30.68
s 403 .... 30.70
405 .... 30.72

Companies Act 1985 – *cont.*
s 419 .... 30.70
424(3), (4) 25.2
425 .... 21.App
Pt XIIIA (428–430F) 48.10
Pt XIV (ss 431–453D) 25.1, 29.App, 30.14
s 431 .... 25.21
(1), (2) 25.2
432 .... 25.21
(1) 25.2, 25.9
(2)–(4) 25.2
433 .... 25.2, 25.7, 25.9, 25.10, 25.21
434 .... 25.3, 25.7, 25.18, 25.21
435 .... 25.18, 25.21
435B 25.18, 25.21
436 .... 25.3, 25.7, 25.18, 25.21
437 .... 18.15, 25.7, 25.18, 25.21, 26.10
(1), (1A) 25.4
(2), (2A) 25.4
(3) 25.2, 25.4
438 .... 25.18, 25.21
439 .... 25.5, 25.18, 25.21
440 .... 25.18, 25.21
441 .... 25.4, 25.18, 25.21, 30.App
442 .... 25.6, 25.7, 25.18, 25.21
(3) 25.9
443 .... 25.6, 25.7, 25.18, 25.21
444 .... 25.6, 25.7, 25.18, 25.21
445 .... 25.6, 25.7, 25.8, 25.18, 25.21, 25.23
446 .... 25.6, 25.18, 25.21
446A 25.6, 25.9, 25.18, 25.21
446B 25.6, 25.9, 25.10, 25.18, 25.21
446C, 446D 25.6, 25.10, 25.18, 25.21
446E 18.15, 25.6, 25.9, 25.18, 25.21
447 .... 18.15, 25.11, 25.12, 25.17, 25.18, 25.21, 26.10, 30.14
447A 25.11, 25.12, 25.21
448 .... 18.15, 25.11, 25.13, 25.21, 26.10, 29.5
448A 25.11, 25.14
449 .... 25.11, 25.15, 25.18, 25.21, 29.5
450 .... 25.11, 25.16, 25.21, 29.5
451 .... 25.11, 25.12, 25.17, 25.21, 29.5
451A 18.15, 25.11, 25.18
452 .... 25.21
453 .... 25.22
453A 18.15, 25.15, 25.18, 25.19, 29.5
(1), (2) 25.20
453B 25.20
453C 25.12, 25.20
453D 25.13, 25.15, 25.16, 25.17, 25.19
Pt XV (ss 454–457) 29.App, 42.38A
s 454 .... 24.6, 25.7, 25.8
(1) 25.23
(2), (3) 25.23, 25.24
455 .... 24.6, 25.7, 25.8, 25.24, 29.5
456 .... 24.6, 25.7, 25.8
(1)–(7) 25.25
457 .... 24.6, 25.7, 25.8, 25.25
459, 460 .... 26.10
462 .... 43.2

Companies Act 1985 – *cont.*
s 463 .... 43.3
464 .... 43.4
465(1) 43.2
(2) 43.4
466 .... 40.9A
(4), (4A) 43.5
486 .... 43.3, 43.4, 43.5
(1) 40.2A, 40.9A
651 .... 21.App
652 .... 21.10
(1)–(5) 21.App
(6)(a), (b) 21.App
652(7) 21.App
652A 21.10
A(1)–(6) 21.App
652B(1)–(8) 21.App
652C(1)–(7) 21.App
652D(1)–(4) 21.App
(8) 21.App
652E, 652F 21.App
653(1)–(2D) 21.App
(3) 21.App
Pt XXII (ss 695–690) App2
s 654, 655 .... 21.App
656 .... 21.App
(2) 21.7
(3)(a), (b) 21.7
657, 658 .... 21.App
690A, 690B 30.App
691 .... 39.19
(1)(b)(i) 30.App
692 .... 30.App, 39.19
(1) 30.App
692A(1)–(3) 30.App
693(1)(b)–(d) 30.App
(2)–(4) 30.App
694–696 .... 30.App
697(1)–(3) 30.App
698(2) 30.App
699 .... 30.App
699A 30.App
699AA 30.19, 30.App
699B 30.App
700 .... 30.19
(1)–(4) 30.App
702, 703 .... 30.App
703P, 703Q 30.App
705A(5) 30.App
710B App2
719 .... 14.6
721 .... 29.App
723B 18.67
(3)–(8) 30.15
723C–723E 18.67
725(1)–(3) 29.App
726 .... 29.App
(1), (2) 29.10
727 .... 8.40
(1)–(3) 29.App
730–734 .... 29.App

Companies Act 1985 – *cont.*
s 735B 30.15
744 .... 29.App, 30.App
Sch 4 .... 8.45
para 12(a) 22.App
20 .... 22.App
34(3)(a) 22.App
89 .... 22.App
Sch 7 .... 30.App
Sch 8
para 12(a) 22.App
20 .... 22.App
34(3)(a) 22.App
Sch 9
Pt I
para 19–26 .... 30.App
31 .... 30.App
Sch 10 .... 30.App
Sch 13
para 25 .... App3
26(1) App3
Sch 14
para 3 .... 38.7
Sch 15C 25.15
Sch 15D 25.15
Sch 20 .... 21.App
Sch 21A
para 1(1)(c) 30.App
(2)–(5) 30.App
2 .... 30.App, 39.19
3–7 .... 30.App
8 .... 30.8, 30.App
9 .... 30.App
Sch 21B
para 1, 2 .... 30.App
Sch 21C
para 2, 3 .... 30.37, 30.App
4–8 .... 30.App
9–15 .... 30.40, 30.App
Sch 21D
para 2(2) 30.App
3–6 .... 30.App
8, 9 .... 30.App
10(1) 30.App
11–13 .... 30.App
Sch 24 .... 21.App, 29.App, 30.App
Companies Act 1989
Pt II (ss 24–54) 8.8
31 .... 8.8
Pt III (ss 55–91) 25.1
s 62 .... 25.7
82 .... 30.14
83 .... 18.15
84 .... 25.18, 30.14
112(2) 43.6
(3)–(5) 16.4
(6)–(11) 43.7
120 .... 29.App
123 .... 29.App
137 .... 8.40
139 .... 18.16

Companies Act 1989 – *cont.*
s 141(4) 21.App
Pt VII (ss 154–191) 2.14
s 162 .... 14.5
211 .... 18.11
Sch 10
para 4–7 .... 22.App
10 .... 30.App
12, 13 .... 30.App
35 .... 18.12, 18.16
Sch 19
para 6 .... 30.App
17, 18 .... 29.App
Sch 24 .... 29.App
Companies Act 2006 ... 2.3, 2.13, 3.26, 3.35, 3.38, 3.41, 3.67, 5.28, 5.45, 10.1, 11.11, 11.13, 11.14, 12.6, 15.1, 15.2, 19.28, 19.29, 20.19, 20.20, 22.10, 25.4, 30.24, 32.20, 35.60, 39.2, 42.39, 45.3, 47.5, 47.60
Pt 1 (ss 1–6) .... 1.2, 28.1, Appl
s 1 .... 1.2
(1) .... 44.4, Appl
2 .... 1.2, 28.1, Appl
3 .... 12.7
4 .... 33.1
(2) 12.7
5 .... 12.7
6 .... 10.3, 12.7
Pt 2 (ss 7–16) 28.1
s 7 .... 12.2, 14.2, 26.8
8 .... 10.14, 14.2
9 .... 10.4, 12.3, 14.2, 37.1
10 .... 12.3, 14.2, 41.18
11 .... 12.3, 14.2
12 .... 12.3, 13.3, 14.2, 39.19
13, 14 .... 12.3
15 .... 12.4
16 .... 12.5
(6) 13.3
Pt 3 (ss 17–38) 28.1
s 17 .... 14.1, Appl
18 .... 10.4
19 .... 42.38A
20 .... 10.4, 12.3, 14.4
21 .... 14.5
22 .... 9.1, 9.4
(1), (2) 14.7
23, 24 .... 14.7
25 .... 14.9, 47.62
26 .... 14.6, 14.7
27 .... 14.8
28 .... 12.7, 14.2, 14.6, 26.9
29 ...... 14.1, 14.10, 14.11, 16.30, 18.24, 18.25, 18.56, 26.10, 34.7, 34.25, 35.5, 35.50, 39.13, 39.14, 41.6, 41.10, 41.16, 41.22, 47.9, 47.49, Appl

Companies Act 2006 – *cont.*
s 30 ...... 14.6, 14.10, 14.11, 16.30, 18.24, 18.25, 18.56, 26.10, 27.17, 34.7, 34.25, 35.5, 35.50, 39.13, 39.14, 41.6, 41.10, 41.16, 41.22, 47.9, 47.49, Appl
(1) 10.5
31 .... 16.1
(1) 14.2, 45.7
(2)(a) 10.14
32 .... 14.11
33 .... 14.12
34 .... 39.13
(1) 14.13
(2) 14.11, 14.13
(3)–(6) 14.13
35 .... 39.13
(1) 14.13
(2) 14.13
(a) 14.11
(3)–(5) 14.13
37 .... 12.7
38 .... 12.2
Pt 4 (ss 39–52) 28.1
s 39 .... 16.1, 17.2, 17.3, 18.52, 43.6
40 .... 16.3, 17.2, 17.3, 43.6
(1)–(4) 16.2
(5) 16.2, 45.7
(6) 16.2
41 .... 16.3, 17.3
42(1)–(4) 16.4
(4)(b) 16.4
43 .... 16.5, 30.59, 30.60
44 .... 16.6, 30.59, 30.61
45 .... 30.59
(1) 16.8
46 .... 16.6, 30.59, 30.61
47 .... 16.6, 30.59
48 .... 16.7, 30.59, 30.62
(2) 16.8
49 .... 16.9, 30.59
50 .... 16.10, 30.59
51 .... 12.1, 30.59, 30.63
52 .... 16.11
Pt 5 (ss 53–85) 28.1
s 53 .... 11.7, 27.4
54 .... 11.7, 27.7
(2) 30.14
55 .... 27.7
56(1) 27.7
57 .... 11.7, 27.8, 27.9, 30.11
58, 59 .... 27.2
60 .... 11.7, 16.14, 27.5
(1)(a)–(c) 27.2
(2), (3) 27.2
61(1)(a)(ii) 27.2
(b)(ii) 27.2
62 .... 27.2
63 .... 27.2
64 .... 27.12
65 .... 11.7, 27.5, Appl
66 .... 11.7, 21.11, 27.6

Companies Act 2006 – *cont.*
s 67, 68 ... 27.13
69 ... 27.14
75 ... 27.15
76 ... 27.16
77 ... 27.17
(1)(b) ... 14.6
78, 79 ... 27.17
80 ... 10.5, 10.30, 21.11, 27.12, 27.17
81 ... 21.11, 27.12, 27.17
82 ... 16.12, 16.14, 16.16
83 ... 16.16
84 ... 16.12
85 ... 16.13
Pt 6 (ss 86–88) ... 28.1
s 86 ... 37.1
87 ... 37.2
88 ... 37.3
(2) ... 39.13
Pt 7 (ss 89–111) ... 28.1, App1
s 89 ... 41.1
90 ... 10.27, 41.2
91 ... 41.3
(1) ... 11.6
92 ... 41.4
(3) ... 11.6
93 ... 41.5, 47.41
(2)(a) ... 11.6
94 ... 41.6
(2)(d) ... 39.13, 39.14
95 ... 41.6
96 ... 41.7
97 ... 10.27, 41.8, 47.57
98 ... 9.7, 34.1, 41.9, 47.46
99 ... 41.9
100 ... 41.10
101 ... 41.11
102 ... 10.27, 41.12
103 ... 41.13
104 ... 41.14
105 ... 41.15
106 ... 41.16
107 ... 41.17
108 ... 41.18
109 ... 41.19
110 ... 41.20
111 ... 41.21
Pt 8 (ss 112–144) ... 28.1
s 112 ... 26.1, App1
113 ... 18.16
(1)–(8) ... 38.5
114 ... 18.16
(1)–(6) ... 38.6
115(1)–(3) ... 38.5
(4) ... 38.6
(5), (6) ... 38.5
116 ... 38.6, 39.19
(1)(b) ... App3
(2) ... App3
117 ... 38.6
117 ... 39.19

Companies Act 2006 – *cont.*
s 118, 119 ... 38.6
120(1)–(4) ... 38.6
121 ... 38.5
122 ... 38.5
(3) ... 26.1
123(1)–(5) ... 38.5
124 ... 38.5
125 ... 38.5, 44.6, 44.7
126 ... 26.1, 38.5
127, 128 ... 38.5
129 ... 38.7
130(1)–(3) ... 38.7
131 ... 38.7
132(1)–(4) ... 38.7
133, 134 ... 38.7
135(1)–(5) ... 38.7
136, 137 ... 26.7
138–144 ... 26.7
Pt 9 (ss 145–153) ... 26.1, 28.1
s 145 ... 14.6, 26.1, 26.3
146 ... 2.12, 6.1, 14.6, 16.30, 19.31, 20.22, 26.1, 26.4
147 ... 26.4
148–150 ... 26.4
152 ... 26.1, 26.5, 42.4
153 ... 26.1, 26.6, 42.31, 42.35
Pt 10 (ss 154–259) ... 28.1
s 154–156 ... 18.2
156A ... 18.2
157–159 ... 18.6
160 ... 18.5, 18.7
161 ... 18.7
162 ... 18.16, 38.2
(5)(b) ... App3
163, 164 ... 7.2, 38.2
165 ... 18.16, 38.3
167 ... 18.2, 18.4, 18.16, 38.2, 38.3, 39.19
(1)(a) ... 10.21
168 ... 42.5
(1), (2) ... 18.9
(3), (4) ... 18.5
(5) ... 18.9, 18.52
169 ... 18.9
Pt 10, Ch 2 (ss 170–181) ... 18.16
s 170 ... 18.1, 18.23
(1) ... 26.11
171 ... 18.1, 18.24
172 ... 6.6, 18.1, 18.24, 26.12, 26.13
173 ... 18.1, 18.24, 18.30
174 ... 18.1, 18.24
175 ... 18.1, 18.24
(5)(a) ... 14.6
(6)(a), (b) ... 14.6
176 ... 18.1, 18.24
177 ... 18.1, 18.24, 18.55, 18.56
178 ... 18.1, 18.23
179 ... 18.1, 18.24
180 ... 18.1, 18.25, 18.55
181 ... 18.1, 18.26
182 ... 18.55

Companies Act 2006 – *cont.*
s 182(1) 18.56
(3) 18.56
183 .... 18.56
184, 185 .... 18.24, 18.56
186, 187 .... 18.56
188 .... 15.10, 18.1, 18.25, 18.53
189 .... 18.1, 18.25, 18.53
190 .... 18.1, 18.25, 18.58
(3) 18.59
191 .... 18.1, 18.25, 18.58
(3) App3
192–194 .... 18.1, 18.25, 18.58
195, 196 .... 18.1, 18.25, 18.58, 18.59
197–200 .... 18.1, 18.25, 18.61
201, 202 .... 18.1, 18.25, 18.62
203 .... 18.1, 18.25, 18.63
204–206 .... 18.1, 18.25, 18.64, 33.35
207–210 .... 18.1, 18.25, 18.64
211 .... 18.1, 18.25, 18.65
212 .... 18.1, 18.25
213, 214 .... 18.1, 18.25, 18.66
215 .... 5.42, 18.1, 18.25
(1), (2) 18.47
(3), (4) 18.48, 18.49, 18.50
216 .... 18.1, 18.25, 18.48, 18.49
217 .... 18.1, 18.25, 18.48, 18.51
218 .... 14.3, 18.1, 18.25, 18.48, 18.51
219 .. 5.41, 18.1, 18.25, 18.49, 18.51, 19.3
220, 221 .... 18.1, 18.25, 18.50
222 .... 18.1, 18.51
(3) 5.41
223 .... 18.48, 18.49, 18.53, 18.58, 18.61, 18.62, 18.63, 18.66
224 .... 18.48, 18.49, 18.53, 18.61, 18.62, 18.63
225 .... 18.47
226 .... 18.48, 18.53, 18.58, 18.59, 18.61, 18.62, 18.63, 18.66
226A–226F 18.25, 18.51A
227(1), (2) 18.52, 18.54
228 .... 18.54, 36.3
229 .... 18.54
(2) App3
230 .... 2.8, 18.54
231 .... 18.1, 18.57
232 .... 13.6, 18.43
233 .... 18.43
234 .... 18.43
235 .... 18.43
236 .... 18.43, 20.6
237 .... 18.43, 18.44, 36.3
238 .... 18.44
(2) App3
239 .... 18.45
240 .... 18.67
241 .... 18.68
242 .... 18.68
(1) 39.10
243 .... 12.3, 39.19, App3
(1), (2) 18.69

Companies Act 2006 – *cont.*
s 243(4)–(6) 18.70
(7) 18.69
244 .... 18.71
245, 246 .... 18.72, 38.2
247 .... 14.6, 18.30
248 .... 18.56, 42.40
249 .... 42.40
250 .... 18.1, App1
251(1) 18.1
252 .... 3.43, 16.3, 18.1, 33.47
253–255 .... 3.43, 18.1
256 .... 18.24, 18.43, 18.44, 18.50, 18.63, 18.64, 20.6
257 .... 14.1, 18.24, 18.25, 18.56
Pt 11 (ss 260–269) 28.1, 31.5
s 260–264 .... 26.12
265–269 .... 26.13
Pt 12 (ss 270–280) 28.1
s 270 .... 13.1
271 .... 13.1, 13.2
272, 273 .... 13.2
274 .... 13.5
275 .... 18.16, 38.2, 38.4
(5)(b) App3
276 .... 13.4, 18.16
(1) 38.4
277 .... 7.2, 38.4
278 .... 38.4
(1) 7.2
279 .... 38.4
280 .... 13.1, 18.3
Pt 13 (ss 281–361) 28.1, 42.12A
s 281 .... 14.6
(1)–(4) 42.1
282 .... 14.6, 42.2, 42.24
283 .... 14.6, 42.3
284 .... 42.4
285 .... 42.4
(2) 14.6
285A 14.6, 42.4
286, 287 .... 42.4
288 .... 42.5
(3) App3
289, 290 .... 42.6
291 .... 8.17, 26.3, 42.7
292 .... 26.3, 42.8
293 .... 8.17, 26.3, 42.8
294 .... 42.8
295 .... 42.8
296 .... 42.9
(4) 14.6
297 .... 42.9
(1) 36.2
298 .... 42.10
299 .... 42.11
300 .... 42.5
301 .... 42.12
302 .... 42.13
303 .... 14.6, 26.3, 42.13, 48.9
304, 305 .... 42.13, 42.19, 48.9

Companies Act 2006 – *cont.*
s 306 42.13
307 42.14
(3) 14.6
(6)(a) 14.6
307A 42.14
(6) 14.6
308 14.6, 42.15
309 14.6, 42.15
310 26.3, 42.16
(1), (2) 8.39
311(1), (2) 42.17
311(3) 42.17, 42.29
311A 42.17, 42.29, 42.31
312 42.18
313 42.19
314 26.3, 26.6, 42.20
315, 316 42.20
317 42.20
318 42.22, 42.29
319 42.23
319A 26.3, 42.17, 42.23A, 42.29
320 42.24
321 42.24, 42.29
322 42.24
322A 42.24
323 14.6, 35.2, 35.32, 34.46, 42.25
324 14.6, 26.3, 42.26
324A 42.26
325 26.4, 42.26
326 42.26
327(A1) 42.26, 42.29
(1)–(3) 14.6, 42.26
328 42.26
329(1) 42.26
(2) 42.24
330(A1) 42.26, 42.29
(1)–(5) 42.26
(6) 14.6, 42.26
(7) 42.26
331 42.26
332 42.27
333 14.6, 42.28
333A 42.28, 42.29
334, 335 42.29
336(1)–(4) 42.30
337 42.30
338, 338A 26.3, 26.6, 42.30, 42.31
339 42.19, 42.31
340–340B 42.31
341(1)–(6) 42.33
342 26.6, 42.35
343–346 42.35
347 42.34
348–350 42.36
351 42.37
352 42.38
353 42.33, 42.37
355, 356 42.41
357 42.42
358 42.43

Companies Act 2006 – *cont.*
s 358(4) App3
359 42.44
360 42.14, 42.18, 42.20, 42.30 42.31
360A 42.12A, 42.38A
360B(2) 42.17 42.33
360C App1
Pt 14 (ss 362–379) 28.1
s 362 31.1
363 31.1 39.19
364, 365 31.2
366–368 31.3
369 31.4
(4) 42.14
370, 371 31.5
372 31.6
373 31.7
374–378 31.8
379(1), (2) 31.2
Pt 15 (ss 380–474) 5.4, 28.1
s 381 5.2
382 5.2 20.15
383 5.2
(3) App3
384 5.3, 5.3B
384A 5.3A, 5.3B
384B 5.3B
385 2.4
(1) App1
(2) 8.27A, App1
(3) App1
386 18.16, 36.5, App1
387 36.5
388 18.16
(1)–(3) 36.6
(4), (5) 36.7
389(1), (2) 36.6
(3) 36.7
(4) 36.6, 36.7
390 30.25, 30.41, App1
(5) 3.57, 5.59
391 30.25, 30.41
(1) 2.17
(2)–(4) 2.18
(5), (6) 2.17
(7) 2.18
392 2.19, 30.25, 30.41, 30.App, 42.30, 42.31
393 2.16
(1) 8.33
(2A) 5.4
394 2.2, 3.2, 5.4, 18.16, 30.26, 30.42, App1
394A 2.2, 3.2
(2)(e) 39.8, 39.13, 39.14
395 22.4, 30.26, 30.42
(4A) 3.2, 5.4
396 3.2, 22.4, 22.7, 30.26, 30.42
(2) 5.4
397 3.2, 5.4, 22.4, 30.26, 30.42
398 5.3B, 5.56

Companies Act 2006 – *cont.*
s 399 ... 3.53, 18.16, 30.30, 30.46
400 ... 5.34, 5.36
(1) ... 3.54
(2) ... 3.54
(e) ... 39.13, 39.14
(3)–(6) ... 3.54
401 ... 5.34, 5.36
(1) ... 3.54
(2) ... 3.54
(f) ... 39.13, 39.14
(3)–(6) ... 3.54
402 ... 3.55, 5.57, 30.30, 30.46
402A ... 30.30, 30.46
403 ... 30.30, 30.46
(5A) ... 3.53, 5.56
404 ... 3.53, 5.56, 30.30, 30.46
405 ... 3.33, 3.55, 5.57, 30.31, 30.47
406 ... 3.53, 5.56, 30.30, 30.46
407(2)–(5) ... 3.2, 5.4
408 ... 3.56, 5.58, App1
409(3) ... 24.5
(4) ... 3.32, 5.31
(5) ... 3.32, 3.64, 5.31, 5.65
410 ... 3.32, 3.64, 5.31, 5.65
(3) ... 7.2
410A(1) ... 3.51
(2) ... 3.51
(b) ... 4.4
(3) ... 3.51
(4) ... 4.4
(5) ... 3.57
411 ... 3.56
(1)–(6) ... 3.49
(7) ... 3.57
412 ... 8.33
(1) ... 3.42, 5.40
(5), (6) ... 3.42, 5.40
413(1) ... 3.48, 5.44
(2) ... 3.74, 5.75
(3)–(7) ... 3.48, 3.74, 5.44, 5.75
414 ... 2.2, 18.16, 22.4, 30.33, 30.49
(1) ... 3.56, 5.58
414A ... 20.1
(5), (6) ... 6.1
414B ... 20.1
414C ... 20.2
(11) ... 20.1
414D ... 20.1
415 ... 20.1
415A ... 5.46, 20.4
416(1) ... 20.2
(1)(b) ... 20.3
(2) ... 20.3
(3) ... 20.4
(4) ... 6.6, 20.1
417(7) ... 4.3
418 ... 20.6
419 ... 10.16, 20.18
419A ... 2.2, 15.6
420 ... 19.1

Companies Act 2006 – *cont.*
s 420(4), (4A) ... 2.8
421 ... 8.33
(1)–(2) ... 19.2
(2A) ... 19.1
(3), (4) ... 19.1
422 ... 19.27
422A ... 2.8, 19.1, 19.27
423 ... 6.1, 8.2, 8.30, 10.16, 19.30, 19.31, 20.21, 20.22, 22.4, 26.3
(1)–(4) ... 2.6
(5) ... 2.6, 2.12
(6) ... 2.6
424 ... 2.6, 8.2, 10.16
425 ... 2.6, 10.16
426 ... 22.4
(1), (2) ... 6.1
(4) ... 6.1
426A ... 6.6, 33.29
(3) ... 6.1
428(3) ... 6.1, 6.6
430 ... 10.16, 18.51A
(2A) ... 2.8
431, 432 ... 2.7, 2.12, 10.16, 19.30, 20.21, 26.4
433 ... 2.4, 10.16, 18.16
434 ... 2.5
(3) ... 2.12
435 ... 2.5
436 ... 2.5, 10.16
437 ... 2.9, 2.12, 8.30, 10.16, 19.30, 20.21
(3) ... App1
438 ... 2.9, 10.16
439 ... 19.27
439A ... 18.51A, 19.5
440 ... 19.27
441 ... 2.10, 2.12, 10.16, 19.30, 20.21, 30.34, 30.50, 39.8, 39.14
442 ... 2.11, 6.2, 10.16, 30.34, 30.50
443 ... 2.11, 10.16
444 ... 4.5, 8.31
(1) ... 5.46, 10.16
(2), (3) ... 5.46
(3A), (3B) ... 2.10
(4), (5) ... 5.46
(6) ... 5.46, 10.16
(7) ... 5.46
444A ... 2.10, 4.5
(1) ... 10.16
445 ... 2.10, 8.31
(1) ... 4.5, 10.16
(2)–(4) ... 4.5
(5) ... 4.5, 10.16
(6), (7) ... 4.5
446 ... 2.10
(1) ... 10.16
(3) ... 10.16
447 ... 2.10
(1) ... 10.16
(3) ... 10.16
448(1)–(3) ... 12.7

Companies Act 2006 – *cont.*
s 448(4)(a), (b) 2.5
(5) 12.7
448A(2)(e) 39.8, 39.13, 39.14
449 .... 2.10, 4.5, 5.46, 8.31
(5) 2.5
450 .... 4.5, 5.46, 18.16
451 .... 2.10, 8.33, 10.16, 19.33, 20.24, 30.34, 30.50
452 . 2.10, 8.33, 10.16, 18.12, 19.33, 20.24
453 .. 2.10, 10.16, 21.9, 21.10, 39.7, App1
454 .... 10.16
(1), (2) 2.12
455 .... 2.14
456 .... 2.14, 8.22, 18.12
457 .... 2.14
458 .... 2.14, 29.5
459 .... 2.14
460 .... 2.14, 29.5
461 .... 2.14
463 .... 19.34, 20.25
(4) 8.38
(6) 8.38
464 .... App1
465 .... 4.2, 20.15
466 .... 4.2
467 .... 4.3
468 .... 48.11
469(1) 2.10, 3.3, 3.57, 5.5, 5.59
(2) 2.10, 5.59
(3) 2.10, 3.3, 3.57, 5.5, 5.59
(3A) 2.10, 5.5, 5.59
(4) 2.5
471(1)–(3) App1
472 .... 30.26, 30.29, 30.30, 30 32, 30.42, 30.45, 30.46, 30.48
(2) App1
472A App1
474(1) App1
(a) 5.4
(2) App1
Pt 16 (ss 475–539) .. 8.24, 8.28, 8.44, 20.5, 28.1
s 475, 476 .... 8.24
477 .... 8.25, 8.26
479 .... 8.27
479A 8.27A
(2)(e) 39.8, 39.13, 39.14
479B 8.27A
479C 8.27B
480 .... 3.16, 5.18, 5.55, 8.28
481 .... 8.28
482, 483 .... 8.29
485 .... 8.2
486 .... 8.6
487, 488 .... 8.3
489 .... 8.4
490 .... 8.6
491 .... 8.5
492 .... 8.15
493 .... 8.7

Companies Act 2006 – *cont.*
s 495 .... 6.2, 8.30
496 .... 6.2, 8.30
497 .... 6.2, 8.30, 19.2
497A 8.30
498 .... 8.33
(2), (3) 2.5
498A 8.30, 15.6
499 .... 10.20
(1)–(4) 8.36
500 .... 10.20
(1)–(5) 8.36
501 .... 10.20
(1)–(6) 8.36
502 .... 8.37
503–505 .... 8.34
506 .... 2.10, 4.5, 5.46, 8.34, 22.4
507–509 .... 8.35
510 .... 8.16, 42.5
511–513 .... 8.16
514 .... 8.17
515 .... 8.18
516, 517 .... 8.19
518 .... 8.20
519–521 .... 8.21
522–525 .... 8.22
526 .... 8.23
527 .... 26.6
(1)–(6) 8.45
528–530 .... 8.45
531 .... 8.45
532 .... 8.39
533 .... 8.40
534 .... 3.50, 8.41
535 .... 3.50, 8.42
536 .... 3.50, 8.43
537 .... 3.50, 8.44
538 .... 3.50, 8.41
538A App1
539 .... 8.30
(1) App1
Pt 17 (ss 540–657) 28.1
s 540 .... 47.1
(1) App1
(4) App1
541 .... 47.1
542(1), (2) 47.2
(4), (5) 47.2
543 .... 47.3
544 .... 44.3, 47.4
545, 546 .... 47.7
547, 548 .... 47.7, App1
549 .... 47.9
550 .... 14.6, 47.9
551 .... 14.6, 47.9, 47.18
552 .... 47.10
553(1)–(3) 47.10
554 .... 47.11
555, 556 .... 9.3, 47.12
557 .... 47.12
558, 559 .... 47.8

Companies Act 2006 – *cont.*
s 560 .... 47.13, 47.64
561 .... 33.25, 47.13, 47.18, 47.64
562 .... 47.14
563 .... 47.15, 47.64
564–566 .... 47.16, 47.64
567, 568 .... 47.17, 47.64
569 .... 47.18, 47.64
570 .... 33.23, 39.8, 47.64
3) 47.18
571 .... 33.23, 39.8, 47.64
(1)–(7) 47.18
572 .... 47.18, 47.64
573 .... 47.18, 47.64
574 .... 47.13, 47.64
575, 576 .... 47.19, 47.64
577 .... 47.13, 47.64
578(1)–(6) 47.20
579 .... 47.20
580 .... 47.24
581 .... 47.25
582 .... 47.23
(2) 47.62
583–586 .... 47.26
587(1)–(4) 47.26
588 .... 47.27
589(1)–(6) 47.28
590 .... 47.29
591 .... 47.30
592 .... 47.24, 47.26
593 .... 39.8
593 .... 35.21
(1) 47.32
(a), (b) 41.5
(2) 47.33
(3), (4) 47.32
594 .... 47.33
595 .... 47.33
596 .... 47.34
597 .... 47.35
598(1)–(5) 47.36
599 .... 47.36
600 .... 47.37
601 .... 47.36
602 .... 47.38
603 .... 47.39
604 .... 47.40
605 .... 47.43
606(1)–(6) 47.43
607 .... 47.44
608 .... 47.45
609 .... 47.32, 47.40
610 .... 46.1
(3) 47.63
611 .... 3.59, 5.61, 46.3
612 .... 3.59, 5.61, 46.2
613 .... 46.2
614 .... 46.1
615 .... 46.2, 46.3
616 .... 46.4
(1) 46.2

Companies Act 2006 – *cont.*
s 617(1)–(5) 47.46
618(1)–(4) 47.47
(5) 14.6, 47.47
619 .... 47.47
620, 621 .... 47.48
622 .... 14.6, 47.49
623 .... 39.8, 47.49
624 .... 47.49
625 .... 47.49
626 .... 39.13, 41.3, 47.50
627 .... 39.8, 47.50
628 .... 47.50
629 .... 9.1
630(2)–(6) 9.1
631(2)–(6) 9.4
632 .... 9.7
633(1)–(5) 9.2
634(1)–(5) 9.5
635 .... 9.5
636 .... 39.8
(1)–(3) 9.3
637 .... 39.8
(1)–(3) 9.3
638(1)–(3) 9.6
639(1)–(3) 9.6
640(1)–(3) 9.6
(6) 9.6
641 .... 14.6, 34.16, 34.21, 34.23, 47.51
(1)(a) 39.13
642 .... 14.6, 34.16, 34.21, 34.23, 47.52, 47.53
643 . 14.6, 34.16, 34.21, 34.23, 41.3, 47.53
644 .... 14.6, 34.16, 34.21, 34.23, 47.54
645 .... 34.16, 34.21, 34.23, 47.59
(1)–(4) 47.55
646, 647 .... 34.16, 34.21, 34.23, 47.55
648 .... 34.16, 34.21, 34.23, 41.3, 47.55
649 .... 34.16, 34.21, 34.23, 39.8, 47.56
650, 651 .... 34.16, 34.21, 34.23, 47.57
652 .... 34.16, 34.21, 34.23, 47.58
652A 21.9
653 .... 34.16, 34.21, 34.23, 47.58
655 .... 26.9
656 .... 47.63
Pt 18 (ss 658–737) 28.1
s 658(1)–(3) 34.1
659 .... 20.12, 34.1
(2)(c) 47.25
660 .... 34.22
661 .... 34.22
(3), (4) 18.43, 18.64
662 .... 34.23, 34.25, 39.13, 47.46, Appl
(1) 20.12
663 .... 34.24, Appl
664 .... 34.25, Appl
(1) 39.13
665, 666 .... 34.25, Appl
667 .... 34.26, Appl
668 .... 34.27, Appl
669 .... 34.28, Appl

Companies Act 2006 – *cont.*
s 670 .... 34.30
(2) 20.12
(4) 20.12
671–676 .... 34.29
677 .... 34.11, 34.20
678 .... 22.5, 22.8, 34.11, 45.2
(1) 34.20
(2) 34.21
(3) 34.20
(4) 34.21
(5) 34.20
679 .... 22.5, 22.8, 34.11
(1) 34.20
(2) 34.21
(3) 34.20
(4) 34.21
(5) 34.20
680 .... 34.11, 34.20
681 .... 34.11, 34.21
682 .... 34.11, 34.21
(2)(b)–(d) 3.25
683 .... 34.11, 34.21
Pt 18, Ch 3 (ss 684–689) 22.1
s 684 .... 34.2
685–689 .... 34.3
688(b) 34.18
689 .... 39.8
Pt 18, Ch 4 (ss 690–708) 22.1
s 690 .... 34.4
(1) 14.6
691(1) 34.4
(2) 34.5
692 .... 34.5
(1) 34.10
(1A) 34.10
(1ZA) 34.10
693(1)(a) 34.6
(b) 34.7
(2) 34.6
(3) 34.6
(b) 48.App
(4) 34.7
(5) 34.6, 34.7
693A 34.6
694(1)–(6) 34.6
695, 696 .... 34.6
697(1)–(5) 34.6
698, 699 .... 34.6
700(1)–(5) 34.6
701(1)–(8) 34.7
702, 703 .... 34.9
704 .... 34.6, 34.7
705 .... 22.5, 34.8
706 .... 34.5
(b)(ii) 34.18
707 .... 34.9
708 .... 34.9, 39.8
709, 710 .... 34.10
Pt 18, Ch 5 (ss 709–723) 22.1
s 711, 712 .... 34.11

Companies Act 2006 – *cont.*
s 713 .... 34.12, 34.12A
714–720 .... 34.12
720A 34.11, 34.12
(3), (4) 34.12A
720B 34.12A
(1) 34.9, 34.12A
(2)–(9) 34.12A
721 .... 34.12, 34.13
(6) 34.1, 47.46
722 .... 34.13
723 .... 34.12
724 .... 34.5, 34.9, 34.14
725(3) 34.14
726 .... 34.14
727, 728 .... 34.15
729 .... 34.9, 34.16
(4) 34.18
730 .... 34.16, 39.8
731 .... 34.15
732 .... 34.14, 34.17
733(2)–(4) 34.18
(5) 34.18, 47.63
(6) 34.18
734 .... 34.10
735 .... 34.19
736 .... 34.3, 34.5, 34.8, 34.10, 34.14
(2) App1
Pt 19 (ss 738–754) 28.1
s 738 .... 17.6, App1
739 .... 17.9
740 .... 17.10
741 .... 17.11
742 .... 17.17
743(1)–(6) 38.12
744(1)(b) App3
(2) App3
(6) 38.12
745–748 .... 38.12
749 .... 17.16
(1) App3
750, 751 .... 17.15
752 .... 17.12
753 .... 17.13
754 .... 17.14, 45.7
Pt 20 (ss 755–767) 28.1
s 755 .... 33.2, 34.25
(1)–(5) 47.21
756 .... 34.25, 47.21
757–758 .... 34.25, 47.22
759 .... 34.1, 34.25, 47.46
760 .... 34.25, 47.21
761 .... 12.5, 33.3, 47.36
762 .... 33.3. 39.8
763 .... 33.3
764–767 .... 33.3
Pt 21 (ss 768–790) 28.1
s 768 .... 44.1
769 .... 44.2
770 .... 44.6
771 .... 14.6 44.6

Companies Act 2006 – *cont.*
s 772 .... 44.6
773 .... 44.9
774 .... 44.9
775(1)–(4) 44.8
776, 777 .... 44.10
778 .... 44.2, 44.10
779 .... 19.3
(4) 44.12
780, 781 .... 44.12
782 .... 44.13
Pt 21A (ss 790A–790ZG) 38.14
Pt 22 (ss 791–828) 28.1, 42.38A
s 791 .... 24.1
792 .... 24.1
(2)(a) 24.2
793 .. 24.1, 33.6, 33.23, 33.47, 38.8, 38.10
(2)(b) 24.2
(3)–(7) 24.2
794 .... 24.1, 24.3, 24.6
795 .... 24.1, 24.3
796 .... 24.1, 24.2
797 .... 24.1, 24.6
798 .... 24.1, 24.7, 29.5
799, 800 .... 24.1, 24.8
801, 802 .... 24.1, 24.9
803, 804 .... 24.1, 24.4
805, 806 .... 24.1, 24.5
807 .... 24.1, 24.5
(2) App3
808 .... 24.1
(1)–(7) 38.8
809 .... 24.1
(1)–(5) 38.9
810 .... 24.1
(1)–(3) 38.8
(4) 38.9
(5), (6) 38.8, 38.9
811 .... 24.1, 38.9
(2) App3
812 .... 24.1, 38.9
813 .... 24.1, 38.9
814 .... 24.1, 38.9
815–817 .... 24.1, 38.10
818 .... 24.1, 38.8
819 .... 24.1
(1)–(3) 38.8
820 .... 24.1
(2)–(8) 24.2
821–823 .... 24.1, 24.2
824 .... 24.1, 24.2, 38.8
825 .... 24.1, 24.2
826 .... 24.1, 38.9
827 .... 24.1, 24.5, 38.8, 38.9
828 .... 24.1
Pt 23 (ss 829–853) 28.1, 47.59
s 829 .... 22.1
(2)(a) 47.63
830(1) 22.1
(2) 22.2, 47.63
(3) 22.2

Companies Act 2006 – *cont.*
s 831(1)–(6) 22.1
832–835 .... 22.1
836–839 .... 22.1, 22.4
840 .... 22.1, 22.5
841, 842 .... 22.1, 22.6
843 .... 22.1
844 .... 22.1, 22.3
845, 846 .... 22.1, 22.7
847 .... 22.1, 22.8
848 .... 22.1, 47.63
849 .... 22.1, 47.63
850 .... 22.1, 22.2
851 .... 22.1, 22.9
853(2) 22.2
(3) 22.1, 47.62
(4),(5) 22.2
(6) 22.7
853A–853L 7.5
Pt 24 (ss 854–859) 28.1
s 854 .... 7.1, 18.16
855 .... 7.2, 39.19
855A 7.2
856 .... 7.2
856A, 856B 7.2
858 .... 7.4
859 .... 40.8
859A 40.2A, 43.5
(3) 38.11, 40.8
(5) 40.8
859B 40.2A, 40.4, 43.5
(3), (4) 38.11, 40.8
(7) 40.8
859C 40.2A, 40.3
(3) 38.11, 40.8
859D 40.2A, 40.4
(1) 38.11
859E 40.2A
859F(3) 40.2A, 40.4, 40.8, 43.5
859G 40.2A
859H 40.2A
859I 43.5
859K 40.1, 40.10
859L 40.1, 40.8
859J 40.8
859M 39.7, 39.9, 43.5
859N 39.9, 43.5
859O 40.1, 40.9A
859P 38.11
859Q 38.11
Pt 25 (ss 860–894) 28.1, 38.11, 39.14, 39.19, 40.1, 40.2A, 40.9, 43.5, 46.2
s 860 .... 17.5, 18.16, 40.2
(4), (5) 45.7
861 .... 40.2
862 .... 40.3
863, 864 .... 40.4
865 .... 40.5
866(1), (2) 40.6
867 .... 40.6

Companies Act 2006 – *cont.*
s 868 .... 40.7
869 .... 40.8
870(1) 40.2
(2) 40.3
(3) 40.4
873 .... 40.9
(1), (2) 45.7
874 .... 40.2A, 45.6
(3) 45.7
875, 876 .... 38.11
877 .... 38.11
(4)(b) App3
878 .... 18.16, 40.11
879 .... 40.11
880 .... 40.12
881 .... 40.13
882, 883 .... 40.14
884 .... 40.15
885 .... 40.16
886(1) 40.11
(3) 40.14
887 .... 40.16
888 .... 40.17
(2) 40.12
889 .... 40.11
890, 891 .... 38.11
892 .... 38.11
(4)(b) App3
893 .... 40.18
Pt 26 (ss 895–901) . 9.7, 28.1, 33.14, 34.21, 41.5, 47.33, 47.47, 47.56
s 895 .... 21.3, 35.1
896 .... 35.2, 35.17
897(1)–(8) 35.2
898 .... 35.2
899 .... 14.11, 35.3, 35.56, 39.8
900 .... 14.11, 35.4, 39.8
901 .... 35.5
Pt 27 (ss 902–941) 28.1, 39.8
s 902, 903 .... 35.6
904 .... 35.7
905 .... 35.8
906 .... 35.8, 39.8
906A 35.8
(6) 35.30A
907 .... 35.9
908 .... 35.10, 35.17
909 .... 35.11, 35.17, 47.33
910 .... 35.12, 35.17
911 .... 35.13, 35.17
911A 35.13A
(4) 35.30A
911B 35.13B, 35.17
912 .... 35.14
913 .... 35.15
914 .... 35.16
915, 915A 35.17
916 .... 35.12, 35.17
(3B) 35.30A
(4B) 35.30A

Companies Act 2006 – *cont.*
s 917 .... 35.12, 35.17
(3B) 35.30A
(4B) 35.30A
918 .... 35.12, 35.17
(2B) 35.30A
(3B) 35.30A
918A 35.17
919 .... 35.18
920 .... 35.19
921 .... 35.19, 39.8
921A 35.19A
(6) 35.30A
922 .... 35.20
923 .... 35.21, 35.29
924 .... 35.22, 35.29, 47.33
925 .... 35.23, 35.29
926 .... 35.24, 35.29
926A 35.24A
(4) 35.30A
927 .... 35.25, 35.29
928 .... 35.26
929 .... 35.27
930 .... 35.28
931 .... 35.23, 35.29
(3B) 35.30A
(4B) 35.30A
932 .... 35.23, 35.29
(2B) 35.30A
(3B) 35.30A
933 .... 35.29
933A 35.29
934 .... 35.29
935–937 .... 35.31
938, 939 .... 35.32
940 .... 35.30
940A 35.30A
941 .... 35.7, 35.18, 35.25, 35.29, 35.30, 35.31, 35.32
Pt 28 (ss 942–992) 28.1, 48.1
Pt 28, Ch 1 (ss 942–965) 48.2
s 942(2) 48.1
943 .... 48.3
(1) 48.2, 48.9, 48.13
(2) 48.2
944(2)–(4) 48.2
945–948 .... 48.2
949 .... 29.5, 48.2
950 .... 48.2
951(1) 48.2
(3) 48.2
952 .... 48.2
953 .... 29.5, 48.3
954 .... 33.69, 48.2
955 .... 48.4
956 .... 48.8
962 .... 48.6
966, 967 .... 48.8
968 .... 48.9
969 .... 42.14, 48.9
970 .... 48.9

Companies Act 2006 – *cont.*
s 971 .... 48.9
972 .... 48.9
974 .... 48.10, 48.11, 48.15
975–978 .... 48.10, 48.11
979 .... 34.15, 48.10
(1)–(10) 48.12
(8), (9) 48.11
980 .... 48.10, 48.13
981, 982 .... 48.10, 48.14
983 .... 48.10
(1)–(8) 8.15
984 .... 48.10, 48.16
985 .... 48.10, 48.17
986 .... 48.10, 48.18
987 .... 48.10
(1)–(10) 48.19
988–990 .... 48.10, 48.11
991 .... 48.10
(1), (2) 48.11
Pt 29 (ss 993) 28.1
s 993 .... 16.18, 18.12
Pt 30 (ss 994–999) .. 9.7, 28.1, 47.22, 47.46
s 994, 995 .... 26.10, 34.1, 34.23, 34.27
996 .... 14.11, 26.10, 34.1, 34.23, 34.27
997 .... 34.1, 34.23, 34.27
998 .... 26.10, 34.1, 34.23, 34.27
999 .... 26.10, 34.1, 34.23, 34.27, 39.13
Pt 31 (ss 1000–1034) 28.1
s 1000(1)–(7) 21.1
1001, 1002 .... 21.1
1003 .... 10.25
(3)–(6) 21.2
1004 .... 21.2, 21.9
(1), (2) 21.3
(5)–(7) 21.3
1005 .... 21.2, 21.9
(1)–(6) 21.3
1006(1)–(7) 21.5
1007(1)–(7) 21.5
1008 .... 21.5
1009, 1010 .... 21.4
1011 .... 21.5
1012 .... 21.7, 21.12
1013–1022 .... 21.8
1024–1028 .... 21.9
1029–1032 .... 21.10
1033 .... 21.11, 27.17
1034 .... 21.12
Pt 32 (ss 1035–1039) 28.1
s 1035(5) 25.7
1036 .... 25.10
1039 .... 18.15
Pt 33 (ss 1040–1043) 28.1
s 1040 .... 11.1
1041 .... 11.1
1042 .... 11.2
1043 .... 12.7, 39.12
Pt 34 (ss 1044–1059) 28.1
s 1044 .... 30.1, App1

Companies Act 2006 – *cont.*
s 1046 .... 16.20, 16.21, 30.2, 30.56, 39.5, 39.9, 39.12, 39.19, App1
1047 .... 30.2, 30.11
1048 .... 30.11
1049 .... 30.18
1050 .... 30.35
1051 .... 30.51
1052 .... 39.19
1055, 1056 .... 30.2
1057 .... 30.58
1058 .... 30.2
1059 .... 30.3
1059A(5) 39.3
Pt 35 (ss 1060–1120) 28.1
s 1060 .... 39.1
1061 .... 39.3
1063 .... App3
1064, 1065 .... 39.4
1066, 1067 .... 39.5
1068 .... 39.15
(1)–(7) 39.6
1069–1071 .... 39.6
1072 .... 39.7
1073 .... 39.7, App1
1074–1076 .... 39.7
1077 .... 16.17, 39.8
1078 .... 39.8
1079 .... 14.8, 16.17
1080 .... 39.9
1081 .... 35.61, 39.9
1082–1084 .... 39.9
1085–1087 .... 39.10
1087A, 1087B 39.10
1088 .... 39.19, App3
1089–1091 .... 39.10
1093–1096 .... 39.11
1097 .... 39.9, 39.11
1097A 39.11
1098 .... 39.11
1099, 1100 .... 39.12
1102–1104 .... 35.61, 39.13
1105 .... 35.61, 38.11, 39.13
1106, 1107 .... 35.61, 39.13
1108–1110 .... 39.14
1111 .... 39.15
1112 .... 18.70, 30.14, 30.15, 35.61, 39.18, 39.19
1113 .... 18.12, 35.61, 39.16
1116 .... 39.17
Pt 36 (ss 1121–1133) 28.1
s 1121, 1122 .... 27.20, 27.22, 27.25, 27.27, 29.2, 35.61
1123 .... 27.20, 27.22, 27.25, 27.27, 29.2, 29.3, 35.61
1125 .... 27.20, 27.22, 27.25, 27.27, 29.1, 35.61
1126 .... 2.14, 27.20, 27.22, 27.25, 27.27, 29.5
1127 .... 27.20, 27.22, 27.25, 27.27, 29.4, 35.61

Companies Act 2006 – *cont.*
s 1128 .... 27.20, 27.22, 27.25, 27.27, 29.4, 35.61
1129 .... 27.20, 27.22, 27.25, 27.27, 29.3, 35.61
1130 .... 27.20, 27.22, 27.25, 27.27, 29.6, 35.61
1132 .... 29.7
1133 .... 29.App
Pt 37 (ss 1134–1157) 28.1
s 1134 .... 14.6, 36.1
1135 .... 36.1
(1)–(4) 38.1
(5) 38.12
1136 .... 18.44
(1), (2) 36.2
1138 .... 36.3
(1)–(3) 38.1
1139 .... 16.20
(2) 30.56
1140 .... 16.21, 30.56
1141 .... 16.19, Appl
1142 .... 16.19
1143 .... 14.6
(1)–(4) 16.22
1144 .... 14.6, 16.22
1145 . 14.6, 16.33, 26.4, 35.13, 35.24, 36.2
1146 .... 14.6
(2) 16.24
(3) 16.25
(4) 16.24, 16.25
1147 .... 14.6, 16.34
1148 .... 14.6
(1) 16.22, 16.25, 16.29, 16.32
(3) 16.22
1149 .... 47.41
1150(1)–(4) 47.41
1151, 1152 .... 47.41
1154(1)–(4) 10.22
1156 .... 29.8
(1) .... Appl
1157 .... 8.40, 18.42, 18.43, 18.64, 29.9
Pt 38 (ss 1158–1174) 28.1
s 1158 .... Appl
1159(2) .... Appl
1160 .... Appl
1161(1)–(5) .... Appl
1162, 1163 .... Appl
1166, 1167 .... Appl
1168(2)–(7) .... Appl
1169–1170B .... Appl
1171, 1172 .... Appl
1173 .... 13.6, Appl
Pt 39 (ss 1175–1181) 28.1
s 1175 .... 8.29
1177 .... 38.13
1182 .... 18.22
1184 .... 18.22
Pt 41 (ss 1192–1208) 28.1
s 1192 .... 27.19
1193, 1194 .... 27.20

Companies Act 2006 – *cont.*
s 1195(1) 27.20
(2)–(5) 27.23
1196 .... 27.20
1198 .... 27.22
1199 .... 27.21
1200 .... 27.24
1201–1203 .... 27.25
1204 .... 27.26
1205, 1206 .... 27.27
1207 .... 27.20, 27.22, 27.25, 27.27
1208 .... 27.19, 27.24
Pt 42 (ss 1209–1264) 2.14, 8.8
s 1209 .... 8.8
1212 .... 47.41
(1), (2) 8.8
1213 .... 8.10
1214 .... 8.9, 13.1
1215 .... 8.10
1216 .... 8.12
1217 .... 8.8
1219–1222 .... 8.8
1239 .... 8.13
1241(2) 8.14
1242–1247 .... 8.14
1248, 1249 .... 8.11
1252 .... 8.22
1260 .... 8.9
1261(2) 8.8
1265–1268 .... 33.48
1270 .... 33.48, 33.69
1271, 1272 .... 33.48
1277–1280 .... 42.45
Pt 45 (ss 1284–1287) 28.1
s 1284 .... 1.1, 1.2, 28.1, Appl
1285, 1286 .... 28.1
1287 .... 27.24, 28.1
Pt 46 (ss 1288–1297) 28.1
s 1293 .... 25.14
Pt 47 (ss 1298–1300) 28.1
s 1299 .... 1.1
Sch 2 .... 48.2
Sch 4
Pt 1
para 1 .... 16.23
2–4 .... 16.24
5–7 .... 16.25
8 .... 16.26
Pt 3
para 6 .... 14.6
Sch 5 .... 33.65, 35.13, 35.24
para 1 .... 16.27
2–4 .... 16.28
5–7 .... 16.29, 26.4
8–14 .... 16.30, 26.4
15 .... 16.31, 16.32
16 .... 16.32
Sch 6 .... Appl
Sch 7
para 2–4 .... Appl
Sch 9

Companies Act 2006 – *cont.*
Sch 9 – *cont.*
Pt. II 8.45
Sch 10
Pt.1 .... 8.8
Pt.2 .... 8.8
para 6, 7 .... 8.8
Pt.3 .... 8.8
para.23 .... 2.14
Sch 11
Pt.1 .... 8.8
Pt.2 .... 8.8
Sch 12 .... 8.14
Sch 15
para.3 .... 33.48
.6 .... 32.23, 33.70
.7 .... 33.47
.8 .... 32.24, 33.71
.10 .... 32.3, 33.48
Sch 16 .... 47.7
Companies Act (Northern Ireland) 1932 .... Appl
Companies Act (Northern Ireland) 1960
s 28 .... Appl
Companies (Consolidation) Act 1908 .... Appl
Companies (Audit Investigations and Community Enterprise) Act 2004
s 19 .... 8.40
Pt 2 (26–63) .... 1.2, 11.13, 28.1, Appl
s 26(1) 10.1
(2) 10.3
(3) 10.1
27 .... 10.17
28 .... 10.26
30 .... 10.7
32 .... 10.13
(6) 10.14
33 .... 10.15
34 .... 39.13
(1), (2) 10.16
(4) 10.16
35 .... 10.2
36(1), (2) 10.4
36A, 36B 10.4
37 .... 39.13
(1)–(4) 10.5
37A–37C 10.5
38, 38A 10.5
39 .... 10.6
40 .... 10.5
(3)–(9) 10.6
40A 10.6
41 .... 10.18
(4) 10.24
42 .... 10.19
43 .... 10.20
44 .... 10.30
45 .... 10.21, 10.30
46 .... 10.21
Companies (Audit Investigations and Community Enterprise) Act 2004 – *cont.*
s 46(3) 10.30
47 .... 10.22, 10.30, 16.21, App2
48 .... 10.23
(2) 10.30
49 .... 10.24
51 .... 10.25
52(2) 10.27
53 .... 10.28
54 .... 10.14
(1)–(4) 10.30
54A–54C 10.30
55, 55A 10.30
56 .... 10.31
59 .... 10.32
60 .... 10.33
Sch 2
para.5 .... 29.App
7–9 .... 29.App
16 .... 29.App
22–24 .... 29.App
28 .... 18.15
Sch 3 .... 10.17
para.5 .... 10.19
Sch 4 .... 10.26
Sch 7 .... 10.19
Companies Consolidation (Consequential Provisions) Act 1985 .. 1.2, 28.1, 29.App, Appl
Companies (Floating Charges and Receivers) (Scotland) Act 1972 .... 43.2, 43.4
Company Directors Disqualification Act 1986 .... 2.14
s 1(1) 18.11
1A 18.14, 18.15
(3) 18.11
2–5 .... 18.12
6, 7 .... 18.14
8 .... 25.4
(1)–(2A) 18.15
8A 18.15
(1) 18.14
8ZA(2)–(3) 18.15
8ZB–8ZE 18.15
9 .... 18.14, 18.16
(1A) 18.15
9A–9E 18.17
10 .... 18.18
11, 12 .... 18.19
12A, 12B 18.11
13 .... 18.20
14(1), (2) 18.20
15 .... 18.20
16(2) 18.12
18 .... 18.20
22A, 22B 18.11
22E 18.11
22(10) 18.11
Sch 1 .... 18.16, 18.17

Competition Act 1998
  s 25–30 .... 18.17
Consumer Credit Act 1974 .... 27.10
Conveyancing and Feudal Reform (Scotland) Act 1970
  s 9(8) 30.65, 40.11
Corporation Taxes Act 2010
  s 1122 .... 26.7
Court of Sessions Act 1988
  s 45 .... 8.11
Courts Act 2003
  Sch 8
    para 300 .... 18.12
Criminal Justice Act 1925
  s 33 .... 29.6
Criminal Justice Act 1982
  s 37 .... 29.App
Criminal Justice Act 1987
  s 2 .... 18.15
Criminal Justice Act 1991
  s 17 .... 29.1
Criminal Justice Act 1993 .... 23.1, 33.App, 48.App
  Part 5 (ss 52–64) 2.15
  s 52 .... 23.2
    53(1)–(3) 23.5
      (6) 23.5
    54 .... 23.3
    55(1)–(5) 23.3
    56(1), (2) 23.3
    57, 58 .... 23.3
    59 .... 23.2
    60(3), (4) 23.3
    61, 61A 23.4
    62 .... 23.2
    63(2) 23.4
  Sch 1
    para 1–3 .... 23.5
      4 .... 23.3
      5 .... 23.5
  Sch 2 .... 23.3
Criminal Justice Act 2003
  s 154(1) 10.19
Criminal Justice Act (Northern Ireland) Act 1945
  s 18 .... 29.6
Criminal Law (Consolidation) (Scotland) Act 1995
  s 28 .... 18.15
    44(1) 25.3
      (2) 10.19, 25.3, 25.12
Criminal Procedure (Consequential Provisions) (Scotland) Act 1995
  Sch 4
    para 56 .... 29.App
Criminal Procedure (Scotland) Act 1995
  s 70 .... 29.6
    136(3) 29.4
Criminal Procedure (Scotland) Act 1995 – *cont.*
  s 143 .... 29.6
Commonhold and Leasehold Reform Act 2002
  s 73 .... 27.5
Criminal Procedure (Scotland) Act 1975
  s 289B 29.1, 29.App
    289G 29.1, 29.App

D

Damages (Scotland) Act 1976 .... 21.10, 21.App
Data Protection Act 1998 .... 2.14, 25.15
  s 47 .... 30.14
Deregulation and Contracting Out Act 1994
  Sch 5 .... 21.App
  Sch 11
    para 6 .... 18.12
Disability Discrimination Act 1995
  .... 20.13

E

Employment Rights Act 1996
  Pt X (ss 94–134A) 35.58
Employment Act 2002
  s 204 .... 18.15, 18.17
    (3) 18.11
  Sch 17
    para 7, 8 .... 21.App
      18 .... 18.37
      40–42 .... 18.14
  Sch 21
    para 5 .... 18.19
  Sch 26 .... 17.14
Enterprise Act 2002 .... 45.5
  Pt 3 (ss 22–130) 35.33
Enterprise and Regulatory Reform Act 2013
  s 79(1) 19.1
      (2) 19.1, 19.27
    80 .... 18.51A
    81(10) 19.27

F

Fatal Accidents Act 1976 .... 21.10, 21.App
Finance Act 2004
  s 150(5) 18.43
    152 .... 19.18
    223(1)(b) 19.16
    229 .... 19.16
Financial Services and Markets Act 2000
  .... 2.14, 19.22, 23.1, 30.App, 33.6, 33.22, 48.App
  s 19 .... 33.55
  Pt IV (ss 40–55) 4.3, 33.55
  Pt VI (ss 72–103) 30.14, 32.1, 32.7, 32.13, 32.15, 32.16, 32.20, 32.23, 32.24, 33.4, 33.39, 33.71, 34.6, 34.7, App1

Financial Services and Markets Act 2000 – *cont.*
s 73A(1) ... 32.1, 33.4
(2) ... 33.4
(3) ... 33.39
(6) ... 33.48
74(1)–(3) ... 33.4
75(1)–(4) ... 33.4
(5), (6) ... 33.12
76(1)–(6) ... 33.12
77 ... 33.14
78, 78A ... 33.14
79 ... 33.4
80 ... 32.22, 33.9
81 ... 32.22, 33.11
82 ... 33.9, 33.10
85 ... 15.8, 32.1, 32.3, 32.15
(1) ... 32.4, 32.5
(2) ... 32.6
(5) ... 32.5
(6) ... 32.6
86(1)–(1B) ... 32.4
87 ... 32.7, 32.8
87A(1) ... 32.14
(2)–(6) ... 32.8, 32.14
(7) ... 32.10, 32.14
(9), (10) ... 32.14, 32.23
87B ... 32.12
87C ... 32.14, 32.15, 33.12
87D ... 32.14
87E, 87F ... 32.15
87FA, 87FB ... 32.15
87G ... 32.19
(1) ... 32.21
(2) ... 32.4
87H, 87I ... 32.15
87J ... 32.14
87K ... 32.15, 32.16, 32.23
87L ... 32.10, 32.15, 32.16
87M, 87N ... 32.16
87P ... 32.15
87Q ... 32.21
89A–89G ... 33.48
89H ... 33.48, 33.67
89I–89K ... 33.48
89L ... 32.23, 33.48, 33.70
90 ... 18.28, 32.22, 33.13, 33.69
90A ... 33.69
91, 92 ... 33.70
96B ... 33.47
(2) ... 33.App
96C ... 33.40
97 ... 32.24, 33.71
102 ... 32.25, 33.72
102A(3) ... 32.1
(6) ... 33.48
102B ... 32.3
102C ... 32.1
Pt VIII (ss 118–131A) ... 23.6
s 118 ... 33.App

Financial Services and Markets Act 2000 – *cont.*
s 118(1) ... 23.8, 23.9, 23.10, 23.11, 33.40, 33.41, 33.44
(a) ... 23.7
(2) ... 23.7
(3) ... 23.8
(4) ... 23.6
(5) ... 23.9
(6) ... 23.10
(7) ... 23.11
118A(1) ... 23.7, 23.8, 23.9, 23.10, 23.11
(4) ... 23.11
(5)(a)–(c) ... 23.12
118B, 118C ... 23.7
122–124 ... 23.13
126, 127 ... 23.13
130A(3) ... 23.7, 23.8, 23.9, 23.10, 23.11
131 ... 23.13
131A ... 23.12
144(1) ... 23.5
146 ... 30.14
Pt XI (ss 165–177) ... 26.10
s 165 ... 18.15
166 ... 30.14
167 ... 18.15, 25.18, 30.14
168 ... 18.15, 25.18
(3) ... 30.14
(5) ... 30.14
169 ... 18.15
(1)(b) ... 25.18
171 ... 18.15, 25.21
172 ... 18.15
173 ... 18.15, 25.21
175 ... 18.15
Pt XVII (ss 235–284) ... 44.4
s 237 ... 18.1
262(2)(k) ... 25.18
284 ... 18.15, 25.18, 30.14
Pt XVIII (ss 285–313) ... 3.20, 5.22, 34.6, 34.7
s 327 ... 33.55
381 ... 23.13
382 ... 33.69
384 ... 33.69
397 ... 23.6
Sch 1 ... 33.13
Sch 3
para 5(c) ... 33.55
(e) ... 33.55
Sch 10 ... 32.22
Sch 10A
para 2(4) ... 33.69
Sch 11A ... 32.5
Pt.1 ... 32.6
Fraud Act 2006
s 2 ... 30.14
Friendly Societies Act 1992
Sch 21
para.8 ... 18.11

G

Government of Wales Act 1998
s 96 .... 8.29
144 .... 8.29
Government Resources and Accounts Act 2000
s 25(6) 8.29

H

Human Rights Act 1998
s 6(1) 32.25, 33.72

I

Income and Corporation Taxes Act 1988
s 505(1) 10.30
Income Tax (Earnings and Pensions) Act 2003
s 393B(2) 19.3
Industrial and Provident Societies Act 1965
.... 39.12
s 53 .... 10.31
Industrial and Provident Societies Act (Northern Ireland) 1969 .... 39.12
Insolvency Act 1985
Sch 6
para 7 .... 29.App
47 .... 21.App
Insolvency Act 1986 .... 2.14, 10.29, 13.6, 30.53, 33.14, 35.1, 39.13, 45.3
Pt I (ss 1–7B) 18.12, 34.21
Pt II (s 8–27) 2.19, 18.12, 30.25, 30.41
Pt III (ss 28–72H) 18.12, 40.10, 43.2
s 41 .... 18.12
47 .... 18.16
51 .... 10.22
(1), (2) 30.72
53(1) 30.72
54(3) 30.72
66 .... 18.16
Pt IV (ss 73–219) 18.12, 43.3
s 74 .... 26.9
98, 99 .... 18.16
107 .... 45.7
109 .... 16.17
110 .... 34.21, 46.2, 47.33
123 .... 47.58
124 .... 26.9
131 .... 18.16
170 .... 18.12
175(2)(b) 45.5
(3) 45.5
176ZA 45.5, 45.7
176A 45.5
185 .... 43.3
206 .... 18.33, 18.34
207 .... 18.33, 18.35
208–211 .... 18.33, 18.36
212 .... 18.33, 18.37

Insolvency Act 1986 – *cont.*
s 213 .... 16.18, 18.18, 18.33, 18.38, App1
214 .... 18.18, 18.24, 18.33, 18.39, App1
215 .... 18.33
216, 217 .... 18.33, 18.40
218, 219 .... 18.41
Pt V (ss 220–229) 18.12
Pt VI (ss 230–246) 18.12, 18.19
s 234, 235 .... 18.16
238 .... 18.16, 45.2
239, 240 .... 18.16
242, 243 .... 18.16
Pt VII (ss 247–251) 18.12
s 248(1)(a), (b) 45.2
314 .... 44.9
388 .... 30.14
399 .... 30.14
411 .... 36.7
Pt XVI (ss 423–425) 18.16
Sch B1 .... 18.57
Sch 5 .... 44.9
Sch 6 .... 17.14
para 8–14 .... 45.5
Sch 10 .... 18.34, 18.35, 18.36
Sch 13 .... 21.App
Pt I 29.App
Insolvency Act 2000
s 5 .... 18.11
6 .... 18.14, 18.15
7(1) 18.11
10 .... 18.41
Sch 4
para 2 .... 18.11
3, 4 .... 18.12
5, 6 .... 18.14
7 .... 18.16
8–10 .... 18.20
11 .... 18.12

J

Joint Stock Banking Companies Act 1857
.... 11.1, App1
Joint Stock Companies Act 1844
.... 11.1, App1
Joint Stock Companies Act 1856
.... 11.1, App1
Joint Stock Companies Act 1857
.... 11.1, App1
Judgments Act 1838
s 17 .... 47.20

L

Land Registration (Scotland) Act 1979
.... 43.2
Law of Property Act 1925
s 53(1)(c) 45.7
Law of Property (Miscellaneous Provisions) Act 1989

Law of Property (Miscellaneous Provisions) Act 1989 – *cont.*
s 1(2)(b) 16.6, 30.61
2 .... 45.7
Law Reform (Miscellaneous Provisions) Act 1934
s 1(2)(c) 21.10, 21.App
Law Reform (Miscellaneous Provisions) Act 1934 (Northern Ireland)
s 14(2)(c) 21.10
Leasehold Reform, Housing and Urban Development Act 1993
s 4A 27.5
Legal Aid, Sentencing and Punishment of Offenders Act 2012
s 85(1)–(13) 29.1
(15)–(17) 29.1
86, 87 .... 29.1
Limitation Act 1980 .... 14.12
s 33 .... 21.App
Limited Liability Partnerships Act (Northern Ireland) 2002 .... 28.1
Limited Partnership Act 1907 . 27.19, 27.24, 28.1

M

Magistrates' Courts Act 1980
s 32 .... 29.1, 29.App
Sch 3 .... 29.6
Ministers of the Crown Act 1975 .... 18.1
Misrepresentation Act 1967 .... 33.69

N

Northern Ireland Act 1998
s 7(3) 48.8

O

Open-Ended Investment Companies Act (Northern Ireland) 2002 .... 28.1

P

Partnership Act 1890 .... 27.19, 27.24
Pension Schemes Act 1993
Pt III (ss 7–68) 34.29
s 61 .... 26.7, 34.29
Pension Schemes (Northern Ireland) Act 1993
Pt III (ss 3–64) 26.7, 34.29
s 57 .... 26.7, 34.29
Perjury Act 1911
s 2 .... 25.3
5 .... 10.19, 25.3, 25.12
Political Parties, Elections and Referendums Act 2000
Political Parties, Elections and Referendums Act 2000 – *cont.*
Pt II (ss 22–40) 31.1
Pt IV, Ch I (ss 50–53) 31.2
Public Finance and Accountability (Scotland) Act 2000
s 21 .... 8.29

R

Railway and Transport Safety Act 2003
Sch 2
para 19 .... 18.17
Requirements of Writing (Scotland) Act 1995 .... 16.9, 30.62, 44.1, 44.12
Sch 2
para 3 .... 16.7
Sch 4
para 55 .... 16.10
57 .... 16.10

S

Scotland Act 1998 .... 8.29
Small Business, Enterprise and Employment Act 2015 14.11, 19.3, 34.9, 34.12A, 34.16, 39.8, 41.18, 47.12, 47.47, 47.48, 47.49, 47.50, 47.54, 47.56
s 83 .... 38.9
84, 85 .... 14.5, 44.12
86 .... 44.12
87, 88 .... 18.2
89 .... 18.1, 18.23
90 .... 18.1
92 .... 7.5
94, 95 .... 38.14
96 .... 39.10
98 .... 41.6
99 .... 39.11
100 .... 12.3
104 .... 18.12
105 .... 18.15
164 .... 14.5, 18.23, 44.12
Sch 3 .... 38.14
Sch 4 .... 44.12
para 23 .... 38.5
Sch 5 .... 38.14
Stock Transfer Act 1963 .... 44.3, 47.4
s 1(1)–(4) 44.4
4(1) 44.4
Sch 1 .... 44.4
Stock Transfer Act 1982 .... 44.5
3 .... 44.10
Stock Transfer Act (Northern Ireland) 1963 .... 44.3, 44.4, 47.4

T

Theft Act 1968 .... 13.6
s 17 .... 35.8

Theft Act 1968 – *cont.*
s 19 .... 18.41
Trade Union and Labour Relations (Consolidation) Act 1992
s 1 .... 31.8
82(1)(a) 31.8
117(1) 8.26, 8.27A
122 .... 8.26, 8.27A
Tribunals, Courts and Enforcement Act 2007
Sch 16
para 5 .... 18.19
Sch 20
para 16 .... 18.19
Trustee Investments Act 1961
s 11 .... 18.1

U

Unfair Contract Terms Act 1977
s 2(2) 8.41
Unfair Contract Terms Act 1977 – *cont.*
s 3(2)(a) 8.41
16(1)(b) 8.41
17(1)(a) 8.41

W

Water Act 2003
Sch 7
para 25 .... 18.17
Welsh Language Act 1993
s 26 .... 39.13
30 .... 22.App

Table of Statutory Instruments

A

Accounting Standards (Prescribed Body) Regulations 2005, SI 2005/697 ... App1
Audit and Accountability (Northern Ireland) Order 2003, SI 2003/418
art 5(3) ... 8.29

B

Banking Consolidation Directive (Consequential Amendments) Regulations 2000, SI 2000/2952 ... 30.App
Business Names (Northern Ireland) Order 1986, SI 1986/1033 ... 28.1
art 4(1) ... 27.21

C

Capital Requirements Regulations 2013, SI 2013/3115
Sch 2
para 9 ... 32.4
Charities (Accounts and Reports) Regulations 2008, SI 2008/629 ... 8.30
Charities and Trustee Investment (Scotland) Act 2005 (Consequential Provisions and Modifications) Order 2006, SI 2006/242 ... 10.1, 10.6, 10.13
Schedule ... 43.6
Charities (Northern Ireland) Order 1987, SI 1987/2048
art 9 ... 14.5
Collective Investment in Transferable Securities (Contractual Scheme) Regulations 2013, SI 2013/1388
reg 4 ... 44.4
Community Interest Company Regulations 2005, SI 2005/1788
reg 1 ... 10.2
2 ... 10.2, 10.4, 10.5, 10.8, 10.9, 10.13
3–6 ... 10.2
7–10 ... 10.13
11 ... 10.4
12 ... 10.5
13–16 ... 10.14
17 ... 10.8
18–20 ... 10.9
21 ... 10.10
22 ... 10.9, 10.10
23 ... 10.29
24 ... 10.11
25 ... 10.12
Community Interest Company Regulations 2005, SI 2005/1788 – *cont.*
reg 26–29 ... 10.16
30–33 ... 10.22
36 ... App3
Sch 1 ... 10.13
Sch 2 ... 10.13
Sch 3 ... 10.13
Sch 4 ... 10.10
Sch 5 ... App3
Community Interest Company (Amendment) Regulations 2009, SI 2009/1942
reg 3 ... 10.13
5 ... 10.31
6–8 ... 10.13
19–22 ... 10.13
23 ... App3
Community Interest Company (Amendment) Regulations 2012, SI 2012/2335
reg 2 ... 10.16
Companies Act 1985 (Accounts of Small and Medium-sized Companies and Minor Accounting Amendments) Regulations 1997, SI 1997/220
reg 7 ... 22.App
Companies Act 2006 (Accounts, Reports and Audit) Regulations 2009, SI 2009/1581
reg 2 ... 2.2, 15.6
3(2), (3) ... 2.10
(6) ... 2.10
4(2), (3) ... 2.10
(6) ... 2.10
5 ... App1
6, 7 ... 8.30
7 ... 8.33
8 ... App1
10 ... 2.10
11, 12 ... 22.7
Companies Act 2006 (Amendment) (Accounts and Reports) Regulations 2008, SI 2008/393
reg 2 ... 4.2, 5.2
3 ... 5.2
4 ... 4.2
6 ... 5.46, 8.33, 20.4, 20.18
(1) ... 5.2
(6), (7) ... 2.10
(8) ... 2.10, 4.5
(9)(a) ... 2.10
7 ... 4.3
8 ... 3.51, 4.4
9 ... 3.2, 5.4
10 ... 3.56, 5.58
11 ... 3.57
12 ... 2.10, 5.46

Table of Statutory Instruments

Companies Act 2006 (Amendment) (Accounts and Reports) Regulations 2008, SI 2008/393 – *cont.*
reg 13 ..... 12.7
Companies Act 2006 (Amendment of Schedule 2) (No. 2) Order 2009, SI 2009/1208
..... 48.2
Companies Act 2006 (Amendment of Part 18) Regulations 2013, SI 2013/999
reg 3 ..... 34.5
4 ..... 34.5, 34.10
5 ..... 34.6
7 ..... 34.6
9 ..... 34.6
10 ..... 34.11
11 ..... 34.12
12 ..... 34.13
13 ..... 34.12
14 ..... 34.14
15 ..... 34.16
Companies Act 2006 (Amendment of Part 18) Regulations 2015, SI 2015/532
reg 3 ..... 34.10
4 ..... 34.9
5 ..... 34.10
7 ..... 34.14
9 ..... 34.10
Companies Act 2006 (Amendment of Part 25) Regulations 2013, SI 2013/600
..... 40.1
reg 3 ..... 40.8, 40.10
Sch 1 . 38.11, 40.2A, 40.3, 40.4, 40.8, 40.9, 40.9A, 40.10
Sch 2
para 1 ..... 43.5
3 ..... 39.8, 39.9, 39.13, 40.18
Companies Act 2006 and Limited Liability Partnerships (Transitional Provisions and Savings) (Amendment) Regulations 2009, SI 2009/2476 ..... 14.7, 21.7
Companies Act 2006 (Annual Return and Service Addresses) Regulations 2008, SI 2008/3000
reg 2–7 ..... 7.2
8 ..... 7.4
10 ..... 16.19
Sch 1 ..... 7.2
Sch 2 ..... 7.2
Companies Act 2006 (Annual Returns) Regulations 2011, SI 2011/1487
..... 7.2
Companies Act 2006 (Commencement No. 1, Transitional Provisions and Savings) Order 2006, SI 2006/3428
Sch 1
para 16 ..... 16.30
Sch 2 ..... 22.App
Companies Act 2006 (Commencement No. 1, Transitional Provisions and Savings) Order 2006, SI 2006/3428 – *cont.*
Sch 5
para 2 ..... 38.8
3 ..... 19.33
5 ..... 16.30
7 ..... 18.6
Companies Act 2006 (Commencement No. 2, Consequential Amendments, Transitional Provisions and Savings) Order 2007, SI 2007/1093
Sch 4
para 27 ..... 10.13
29 ..... 10.13
42–44 ..... 10.13
Companies Act 2006 (Commencement No. 3, Consequential Amendments, Transitional Provisions and Savings) Order 2007, SI 2007/2194
art 1 ..... 42.5
5 ..... 31.2
Sch 1
para 1 ..... 14.1, Appl
6 ..... 18.23
11 ..... 18.64
13 ..... 42.5
18 ..... 8.3
19 ..... 26.10
Sch 2 ..... 29.App
Sch 3
para 4 ..... 18.7
6 ..... 18.53
(2) 18.25
7 ..... 18.58
(2) 18.25
8(2) 18.25
12 ..... 18.43
(2) 18.25
13 ..... 18.54
14 ..... 18.57
21 ..... 26.13
23 ..... 14.6, 42.1
23A 42.24
26, 26A 42.14
28 ..... 42.19
44, 45 ..... 8.3
47 ..... 26.10
49 ..... 2.9
Sch 4
para 1 ..... 30.App
3 ..... 22.App
12 ..... 29.App
14–16 ..... 29.App
46 ..... 18.12
Companies Act 2006 (Commencement No. 5, Transitional Provisions and Savings) Order 2007, SI 2007/3495
art 3 ..... 38.5, 38.12

Companies Act 2006 (Commencement No. 5, Transitional Provisions and Savings) Order 2007, SI 2007/3495 – *cont.*
art 10 .... 18.23, 18.43, 18.64, 42.5
Sch 1
para 6 .... 5.46
14 .... 22.1
17, 18 .... 22.4
19 .... 22.5
20 .... 22.8
Sch 4
para 2, 3 .... 38.5
4 .... 13.1
11 .... 8.7
12 .... 8.30
13 .... 8.16
23 .... 38.12
35 .... 22.4
44 .... 29.App
46 .... 18.2
48 .... 18.24
49 .... 18.25
50 .... 18.56
Sch 5
para 2 .... 29.App
(5) 42.24

Companies Act 2006 (Commencement No. 6, Saving and Commencement Nos. 3 and 5 (Amendment) Order 2008, SI 2008/674
art 3 .... 8.29
Sch 3
para 1 .... 18.43, 18.64
2 .... 42.14
5 .... 18.43, 18.64

Companies Act 2006 (Commencement No. 7, Transitional Provisions and Savings) Order 2008, SI 2008/1886
art 2 .... 21.App

Companies Act 2006 (Commencement No. 8, Transitional Provisions and Savings) Order 2008, SI 2008/2860
art 5 .... 14.11
6 .. 5.46, 18.43, 18.64, 22.1, 22.4, 22.5, 22.8, 42.13
Sch 1 .... 29.10
Sch 2
para 4 .... 14.5
6 .... 14.8
9 .... 14.11
12 .... 14.13
17 .... 27.5, 27.6
19 .... 27.17
20 .... 27.12
21 .... 27.16
24 .... 26.8
25–29 .... 38.2
30 .... 38.3
33 .... 18.67
34 .... 18.68

Companies Act 2006 (Commencement No 8, Transitional Provisions and Savings) Order 2008, SI 2008/2860 – *cont.*
Sch 2 – *cont.*
para 35 .... 18.72
36 .... 18.63, 39.19
40 .... 18.30
42 .... 47.6
43–45 .... 47.9
49 .... 47.13
50 .... 47.17
52, 53 .... 47.18
54(1) 47.18
55 .... 47.18
73 .... 34.3
75 .... 34.6, 34.7
76 .... 34.6
88 .... 21.7
89 .... 21.App
90, 91 .... 21.10
92 .... 21.12
99 .... 39.6
100–102 .... 39.7
116 .... 29.App

Companies Act 2006 (Consequential Amendments etc) Order 2008, SI 2008/948
Sch 1
para 84 .... 30.App
86 .... 30.App
93, 94 .... 30.App
106 .... 18.11, 18.12, 18.16
242 .... 10.13
245, 246 .... 2.14
Sch 3
para 6 .... 43.7

Companies Act 2006 (Consequential Amendments and Transitional Provisions) Order 2011, SI 2011/1265
reg 28(2) 33.3

Companies Act 2006 (Consequential Amendments, Transitional Provisions and Savings) Order 2009, SI 2009/1941
art 2 .... 18.11, 18.20
11 .... 14.12
13 .... 29.10
Sch 1
para 85 .. 18.11, 18.12, 18.15, 18.16, 18.18, 18.19, 18.20
260 .... 22.4, 47.36, Appl
Sch 3
para 1, 2 .... Appl
3 .... 41.22
4–6 .... 42.23

Companies Act 2006 (Strategic Report and Directors' Report) Regulations 2013, SI 2013/1970 .... 2.3
reg 1(3) 2.12
3 .... 6.2, 20.1

Table of Statutory Instruments

Companies Act 2006 (Strategic Report and Directors' Report) Regulations 2013, SI 2013/1970 – *cont.*
reg 6 .... 20.3
7(3)(a) 20.1
(b) 20.1, 20.7, 20.9
(c) 20.1
(d) 20.1, 20.15
(e) 20.1
8(3) 20.12
9–11 .... 6.1
12 .... 6.6
13 .... 6.7
15 .... 20.17
Schedule
para 4 .... 2.7
6 .... 2.4
9 .... 2.10, 4.5
10, 11 .... 2.10
12(b), (c) 2.12
14 .... 2.14
16 .... 2.14
17 .... 19.34, 20.25
18 .... App1
21 .... 6.2, 8.30
22 .... 8.33
24 .... 30.18
25 .... 30.35

Companies Act 2006 (Extension of Takeover Panel Provisions) (Isle of Man) Order 2008, SI 2008/3122 .... 48.2

Companies Act 2006 (Part 35) (Consequential Amendments, Transitional Provisions and Savings) Order 2009, SI 2009/1802
Schedule 39.6, 39.7, 39.9, 39.11

Companies Act 1985 (Electronic Communications) Order 2000, SI 2000/3373
art 26 .... 30.App

Companies Act 1985 (International Accounting Standards and Other Accounting Amendments) Regulations 2004, SI 2004/2947
Sch 1
para 22 .... 22.App
25–28 .... 22.App
Sch 7
para 8 .... 22.App

Companies Act 1989 (Delegation) Order 2005, SI 2005/2337 .... 8.8

Companies Act 1985 (Power to Enter and Remain on Premises: Procedural) Regulations 2005, SI 2005/684
.... 25.20

Companies and Limited Liability Partnerships (Accounts and Audit Exemptions and Change of Accounting Framework) Regulations 2012, SI 2012/2301
reg 4 .... 8.25, 8.27

Companies and Limited Liability Partnerships (Accounts and Audit Exemptions and Change of Accounting Framework) Regulations 2012, SI 2012/2301 – *cont.*
reg 5 .... 8.27
6 .... 8.24
7 .... 8.27A, 8.27B
8 .... 2.2, 3.2
10 .... 2.10
12 .... 3.2
13 .... 5.4
15–17 .... 3.53, 5.56
18 .... App1
19 .... 39.8
21 .... 39.13, 39.14

Companies and Limited Liability Partnerships (Forms, etc) Amendment Regulations 2013, SI 2013/1947
reg 2 .... 39.6

Companies (Audit, Investigations and Community Enterprise) Order 2005, SI 2005/1967 .... 28.1

Companies (Authorised Minimum) Regulations 2008, SI 2008/729
reg 2 .... 33.3

Companies (Authorised Minimum) Regulations 2009, SI 2009/2425
reg 2 .... 33.3

Companies (Company Records) Regulations 2008, SI 2008/3006 .... 18.54, 38.2, 38.6
reg 3–5 .... 36.2
6(1), (2) 36.2
7–9 .... 36.2

Companies (Companies Authorised to Register) Regulations 2009, SI 2009/2437
.... 11.2
reg 3 .... 11.3
4 .... 11.4, 11.5, 11.6
5 .... 11.4, 11.5
6 .... 11.3, 11.4, 11.5
7, 8 .... 11.4, 11.5
9 .... 11.6
10 .... 11.7
12 .... 11.8
14 .... 11.9
15 .... 11.10
16 .... 11.11
17 .... 11.12
18, 19 .... 11.13
20 .... 11.11, 11.13
21 .... 11.14

Companies Consolidation (Consequential Provisions) (Northern Ireland) Order 1986, SI 1986/1035 .... 28.1, App1

Companies (Cross-Border Mergers) Regulations 2007, SI 2007/2974 .. 11.13, 35.35, 39.13
reg 2 .... 35.36
3(1)(b) 35.52
4 .... 35.61

Companies (Cross-Border Mergers) Regulations 2007, SI 2007/2974 – *cont.*
reg 5 .... 35.60
6 .... 35.37
7 .... 35.38
8(2A) 35.39
9 .... 35.40
10 .... 35.41
11 .... 35.46
12 .... 35.42
13 .... 35.43
14 .... 35.44
15 .... 35.45
16 .... 35.47
17 .... 35.48
18, 19 .... 35.49
20 .... 35.50
21 .... 35.51
22(1A) 35.52
23(4) 35.53
24, 25 .... 35.53
26(1)–(3) 35.53, 35.55
(4), (5) 35.53
27 .... 35.53
28 .... 35.54
29(2A) 35.54
30, 31 .... 35.54
32 .... 35.54
33 .... 35.55
34 .... 35.55, 35.58
35 .... 35.55
36 .... 35.56
37(2A) 35.56
38(5) 35.56
39, 40 .... 35.56
41, 42 .... 35.57
44–47 .... 35.58
49–51 .... 35.58
53–55 .... 35.59
Sch 1
para 3 .... 35.38
Sch 2
para 1 .... 35.53, 35.55
2 .... 35.53, 35.61
3 .... 35.54
4, 5 .... 35.57
6, 7 .... 35.58
9, 10 .... 35.58
12, 13 .... 35.59
Companies (Cross-Border Mergers) Regulations 2015, SI 2015/180
reg 2 .... 35.47
Companies (Defective Accounts and Directors' Reports) (Authorised Person) and Supervision of Accounts and Reports (Prescribed Body) Order 2008, SI 2008/623 .... 2.14
Companies (Disclosure of Auditor Remuneration and Liability Limitation Agreements) (Amendment) Regulations 2011, SI 2011/2198 .... 8.7
reg 2 .... 3.50
Companies (Disclosure of Auditor Remuneration and Liability Limitation Agreements) Regulations 2008, SI 2008/489 .... 8.8
reg 3 .... 3.50
4 .... 4.4, 5.45
5 .... 3.50
(1)(b) 3.57
6(1) 3.57
(2), (3) 3.50
7 .... 3.50
8 .... 3.50, 5.45
Sch 1 .... 3.50
Sch 2
para 10 .... 3.50
Companies (Disclosure of Address) Regulations 2009, SI 2009/214
reg 2–4 .... 18.69
5–8 .... 18.70
9, 10 .... 39.19
11 .... 39.19, App3
12, 13 .... 39.19
14–16 .... 18.70, 39.19
Sch 1 .... 18.69
Sch 2
para 1–11 .... 18.69
Companies (Disqualification Orders) Regulations 2009, SI 2009/2471 .... 18.20
Companies (Fees for Inspection and Copying of Company Records) (No.2) Regulations 2007, SI 2007/3535 .... App3
Companies (Fees for Inspection and Copying of Company Records) Regulations 2007, SI 2007/2612 .... App3
Companies (Fees for Inspection of Company Records) Regulations 2008, SI 2008/3007 .... App3
Companies (Forms) Regulations 1985, SI 1985/854
reg 6 .... App2
Companies (Forms) (Amendment) Regulations 1987, SI 1987/752
reg 4 .... 48.13, 48.16
Companies (Inspection and Copying of Registers, Indices and Documents) Regulations 1991, SI 1991/1998 .... App3
Companies (Late Filing Penalties) and Limited Liability Partnerships (Filing Periods and Late Filing Penalties) Regulations 2008, SI 2008/497 .... 2.11

Table of Statutory Instruments

Companies (Model Articles) Regulations 2008, SI 2008/3229
Sch 1 .... 14.3
art 1 .... **App4**
2 .... 14.6, 26.9, **App4**
3 .... 17.3, 18.29, 18.52, **App4**
4 .... 17.3, 26.9, **App4**
5 .... 18.8, 18.29, **App4**
6 .... 18.29, **App4**
7–13 .... 42.39, **App4**
14 .... 14.6, 42.39, **App4**
15 .... 42.40, **App4**
16 .... 14.6, 18.29, **App4**
17 .... 18.5, **App4**
18 .... 18.21, **App4**
19, 20 .... 18.46, **App4**
21 .... 47.25, **App4**
21.8 .... 14.7
22 .... 47.5, **App4**
23 .... 26.1, **App4**
24, 25 .... 44.11, **App4**
26 .... 44.4, 44.6, 44.7, **App4**
27, 28 .... 44.9, **App4**
29 .... **App4**
30–35 .... 22.10, **App4**
36 .... 47.62, 47.63, **App4**
37 .... 42.21, **App4**
38 .... 42.22, **App4**
39, 40 .... 42.23, **App4**
41 .... 42.27, **App4**
42 .... 42.24, **App4**
43 .... 42.4, **App4**
44 .... 42.24, **App4**
45, 46 .... 42.26, **App4**
47 .... 42.12, **App4**
48 .... 16.22, **App4**
49 .... 16.8, **App4**
50 .... 36.2, **App4**
51 .... 14.6, 18.30, **App4**
52, 53 .... 18.43, **App4**
Sch 2 .... 14.4
Sch 3 .... 14.3
art 2 .... 14.6, 26.9, **App4**
3 .... 17.3, 18.29, 18.52, **App4**
4 .... 17.3, 26.9, **App4**
5 .... 18.8, 18.29, **App4**
6 .... 18.29, **App4**
7–15 .... 42.39, **App4**
16 .... 14.6, 42.39, **App4**
17, 18 .... 42.39, **App4**
19 .... 18.29, **App4**
20, 21 .... 18.5, **App4**
22 .... 18.21, **App4**
23, 24 .... 18.46, **App4**
25 .... 18.1, 18.10, **App4**
26 .... 18.1, 18.10, **App4**
27 .... 18.1, 18.10
28 .... 18.2, **App4**
29 .... 42.21, **App4**
31, 32 .... 42.23, **App4**
33 .... 42.27

Companies (Model Articles) Regulations 2008, SI 2008/3229 – *cont.*
Sch 3 – *cont.*
art 34 .... 42.24, **App4**
35 .... 42.5, **App4**
36, 37 .... 42.24, **App4**
38 .... 42.22, 42.26, **App4**
39 .... 42.26, **App4**
40 .... 42.12, **App4**
41 .... 42.21, **App4**
43 .... 14.7, 47.5, **App4**
44 .... 47.10, **App4**
45 .... 26.1, **App4**
46 .... 44.10, **App4**
47–49 .... 44.11, **App4**
50 .... 44.14, **App4**
51 .... 44.12, **App4**
52–62 .... 47.25, **App4**
63, 64 .... 44.6, 44.7, **App4**
65–68 .... 44.9, **App4**
69 .... 47.47, **App4**
70–77 .... 22.10, **App4**
78 .... 47.62, 47.63, **App4**
79, 80 .... 16.22, **App4**
81 .... 16.8, **App4**
82 .... 36.4, **App4**
83 .... 36.2, **App4**
84 .... 14.6, 18.30, **App4**
85, 86 .... 18.43, **App4**

Companies (Northern Ireland) Order 1986, SI 1986/1032 .... 1.2, 17.15, 28.1, 30.App, App1
art 33(1) 26.7
40 .... 27.2
106(1) 47.19
(3), (4) 47.19
232(2) 2.18
440 .... 30.14
607(2) 21.7
(3)(a), (b) 21.7

Companies (Northern Ireland) Order 1990, SI 1990/593
art 5 .... 2.18
34 .... 8.8

Companies (Particulars of Company Charges) Regulations 2008, SI 2008/2996
reg 2 .... 40.2
3 .... 40.11
4 .... 40.3, 40.12

Companies (Particulars of Usual Residential Address) (Confidentiality Orders) Regulations 2002, SI 2002/912
Sch 2
para 2, 3 .... 30.App
5, 6 .... 30.App
8 .... 30.App
19 .... 30.App

Companies (Political Expenditure Exemption) Order 2007, SI 2007/2081 .... 31.8

Companies (Receipt of Accounts and Reports) Regulations 2013, SI 2013/1973
reg 4 ... 6.1
5 ... 6.2
6 ... 6.3
7 ... 6.4
8 ... 6.5
9 ... 6.4, 6.5
Companies (Reduction of Share Capital) Order 2008, SI 2008/1915
art 2 ... 47.53
3 ... 47.59
Companies (Registration) Regulations 2008, SI 2008/3014 ... 14.2
reg 5 ... 41.13
6 ... 41.20
Sch 3 ... 41.13
Sch 4 ... 41.20
Companies (Registrar, Languages and Trading Disclosures) Regulations 2006, SI 2006/3429
reg 2 ... 39.10
4, 5 ... 39.13
Companies (Reporting Requirements in Mergers and Divisions) Regulations 2011, SI 2011/1606
reg 9(2), (3) ... 35.12
10 ... 35.13
11 ... 35.13A
12 ... 35.13B
14 ... 35.17
15(2)–(4) ... 35.17
16(2)–(4) ... 35.17
17(2)–(4) ... 35.17
19(1), (2) ... 35.19
20 ... 35.19A
23(2) ... 35.23
25 ... 35.24
26 ... 35.25
27(2)–(4) ... 35.29
28(2)–(5) ... 35.29
29 ... 35.29
Companies (Revision of Defective Accounts and Reports) Regulations 2008, SI 2008/373
reg 2 ... 2.12
3(1)–(3) ... 2.12
(4) ... 20.19
4 ... 2.12
5 ... 20.20
6, 6A ... 19.29
7 ... 8.32
8, 9 ... 8.32
10 ... 2.12
11 ... 19.30, 20.21
12 ... 2.12, 19.31, 20.22
13 ... 2.12, 19.32, 20.23
14 ... 2.12, 19.33, 20.24
15, 16 ... 2.13
17 ... 6.7
Companies (Revision of Defective Accounts and Reports) Regulations 2008, SI 2008/373 – *cont.*
reg 18 ... 8.32
19(1) ... 2.12, 8.32
(2) ... 2.12
(3) ... 6.7
Companies (Revision of Defective Accounts and Reports) (Amendment) (No 2) Regulations 2013, SI 2013/2224
reg 5 ... 19.28, 20.19
7 ... 19.29
8, 9 ... 8.32
10 ... 19.30, 20.20, 20.21
11 ... 2.12, 19.31, 20.22
Companies (Share Capital and Acquisition by Company of its Own Shares) Regulations 2009, SI 2009/2022
reg 2 ... 47.14
3 ... 47.55
5 ... 34.14
Companies (Shares and Share Capital) Order 2009, SI 2009/388
art 2 ... 14.11, 34.9, 34.16, 34.24, 41.18, 47.12, 47.47, 47.48, 47.49, 47.50, 47.54, 47.56
3 ... 47.12
4 ... 34.15, 47.26
5 ... 34.12
Companies (Shareholders' Rights) Regulations 2009, SI 2009/1632
reg 8 ... 42.12A
20 ... 42.38A
22 ... 42.24
Companies (Tables A to F) Regulations 1985, SI 1985/805
Table A ... 14.1, 14.3, 14.4, 14.6
reg 1 ... **App4**
2 ... 47.5, **App4**
3 ... 14.6, **App4**
4 ... 47.10, **App4**
5 ... 26.1, **App4**
6, 7 ... 44.11, **App4**
8–11 ... 47.25, **App4**
12–16 ... 47.25, **App4**
17 ... 47.25, **App4**
18–22 ... 47.25, **App4**
23 ... 44.4, **App4**
24 ... 44.7, **App4**
25–28 ... 44.6, **App4**
29–31 ... 44.9, **App4**
32 ... 14.6, 47.47, **App4**
33 ... 47.47, **App4**
34 ... 14.6, 47.53, **App4**
35 ... **App4**
36 ... 14.6, **App4**
37 ... 43.13, **App4**
38 ... 14.6, 42.17, **App4**
39 ... 42.19, **App4**
40, 41 ... 42.22, **App4**

Companies (Tables A to F) Regulations 1985, SI 1985/805 – *cont.*
reg 42–44 .... 42.23, **App4**
45 .... 42.27, **App4**
46–48 .... 42.24, **App4**
49, 50 .... 42.24, **App4**
51 .... 42.24, **App4**
52 .... 42.24, **App4**
53 .... **App4**
54 .... 14.6, 42.4, **App4**
55–57 .... 42.4, **App4**
58 .... 42.4, **App4**
59 .... 42.4, 42.26, **App4**
60–63 .... 42.26, **App4**
64 .... 18.2, **App4**
65–69 .... 18.10, **App4**
70 .... 17.3, 18.29, 18.52, **App4**
71, 72 .... 18.29, **App4**
73–76 .... 14.6, 18.5, **App4**
77–80 .... 18.5, **App4**
81 .... 18.21, **App4**
82, 83 .... 18.46, **App4**
84 ...... 14.6, 18.5, 18.9, 18.52, **App4**
85 .... 14.6, **App4**
86 .... **App4**
87 .... 14.6, 18.46, **App4**
88–93 .... 42.39, **App4**
94 .... 14.6, 42.39, **App4**
95–98 .... 42.39, **App4**
99 .... 13.3, **App4**
100 .... 42.41, **App4**
101 .... 16.8, **App4**
102–108 .... 22.10, **App4**
109 .... 36.2, **App4**
110 .... 47.62, 47.63, **App4**
111 .... 14.6, 14.15, **App4**
112–116 .... 14.15, **App4**
117 .... 14.6, **App4**
118 .... 18.43, **App4**
Table C 14.4
D 14.4
E 14.4

Companies (Tables A to F) (Amendment) Regulations 2007, SI 2007/2541 .... 14.6, App4

Companies (Tables A to F) (Amendment) (No. 2) Regulations 2007, SI 2007/2826 .... 14.6, App4

Companies (Unfair Prejudice Applications) Proceedings Rules 2009, SI 2009/2469
r 1–6 .... 26.10

Companies Acts (Unregistered Companies) Regulations 2007, SI 2007/318 .... 12.7

Company and Business Names (Miscellaneous Provisions) Regulations 2009, SI 2009/1085
reg 1(3) 27.9
2(4) 27.9
10 .... 27.5

Company and Business Names (Miscellaneous Provisions) Regulations 2009, SI 2009/1085 – *cont.*
Sch 2 .... 27.5

Company Directors Disqualification (Northern Ireland) Order 2002, SI 2002/3150 .... 2.14, 18.11

Company, Limited Liability Partnership and Business (Names and Trading Disclosures) Regulations 2015, SI 2015/17 ..... 16.15, 27.2
reg 2 .... 27.8
4, 5 .... 27.5
7, 8 .... 27.6
12–15 .... 30.11
20 .... 16.13, 16.14
21–23 .... 16.13
24–26 .... 16.14
27 .... 16.15
28 .... 16.13, 16.14, 16.15
Sch 1 .... 27.8
Sch 2 .... 27.5
Sch 3 .... 27.6

Company, Limited Liability Partnership and Business Names (Sensitive Words and Expressions) Regulations 2014, SI 2014/3140 .... 27.7, 27.20

Courts-Martial Appeal (Amendment) Rules 2007, SI 2007/710
reg 5 .... 29.App

E

Electronic Money (Miscellaneous Amendments) Regulations 2002, SI 2002/765
reg 2 .... 30.App

Enterprise Act 2002 (Insolvency) Order 2003, SI 2003/2096
Sch 1
para 12 .... 18.16

European Communities (Recognition of Professional Qualifications) (First General System) Regulations 2005, SI 2005/18 .... 8.8

F

Fatal Accidents (Northern Ireland) Order 1977, SI 1944/1251 .... 21.10

Financial Services and Markets Act 2000 (Consequential Amendments and Repeals) Order 2001, SI 2001/3649
art 39 .... 18.15
341 .... 23.5

Financial Services and Markets Act 2000 (Market Abuse) Regulations 2005, SI 2005/381 ... 23.6, 23.7, 23.8, 23.9, 23.10, 23.11, 23.12, 33.40

Financial Services and Markets Act 2000 (Market Abuse) Regulations 2005, SI 2005/381 – *cont.*
reg 3 .... 23.5
Financial Services and Markets Act 2000 (Market Abuse) Regulations 2009, SI 2009/3128 .... 23.6
Financial Services and Markets Act 2000 (Market Abuse) Regulations 2011, SI 2011/2928 .... 23.6
Financial Services and Markets Act 2000 (Market Abuse) Regulations 2014, SI 2014/3081 .... 23.6
Financial Services and Markets Act 2000 (Markets in Financial Instruments) Regulations 2007, SI 2007/126
reg 4A(3) App1
4C(3) App1
Financial Services and Markets Act 2000 (Official Listing of Securities) Regulations 2001, SI 2001/2956
reg 6 .... 33.10
9 .... 33.10
Financial Services and Markets Act 2000 (Regulated Activities) Order 2001, SI 2001/544 .... 33.4

I

Industrial Relations (Northern Ireland) Order 1992, SI 1992/807
art 3 .... 31.8
4 .... 8.27A
57(2)(a) 31.8
Insider Dealing (Securities and Regulated Markets) Order 1994, SI 1994/187 .... 23.3
Insider Dealing (Securities and Regulated Markets) (Amendment) Order 1996, SI 1996/1561 .... 23.3
Insider Dealing (Securities and Regulated Markets) (Amendment) Order 2000, SI 2000/1923
art 2 .... 23.3
Insider Dealing (Securities and Regulated Markets) (Amendment) Order 2002, SI 2002/1874
art 2 .... 23.3
Insolvency Act 1986 (Prescribed Part) Order 2003, SI 2003/2097 .... 45.5
Insolvency (Northern Ireland) Order 1989, SI 1989/2405 . 2.14, 18.58, 30.53, 35.1, 39.13
art 3 .... 30.14
Pt II (arts 14–20) 34.21
Pt III (arts 21–39) 2.19, 30.25, 30.41
art 95 .... 16.17
96 .... 34.21, 41.5, 47.33
103 .... 47.58
Insolvency (Northern Ireland) Order 1989, SI 1989/2405 – *cont.*
art 359 .... 36.7
Insolvency Proceedings (Monetary Limits) Order 1986, SI 1986/1996 .... 18.34
Insolvent Companies (Reports on Conduct of Directors) Rules 1996, SI 1996/1909 .... 18.14
Insolvent Companies (Reports on Conduct of Directors) (Scotland) Rules 1996, SI 1996/1910 .... 18.14

J

Judgments Enforcement (Northern Ireland) Order 1981, SI 1981/226
art 46 .... 30.70, 40.7, 40.8
132(1) 40.7

L

Large and Medium-sized Companies and Groups (Accounts and Reports) (Amendment) Regulations 2013, SI 2013/1981
reg 2 .... 19.2, 19.27
3 .... 19.3, 19.4, 19.5, 19.6, 19.7, 19.8, ... 19.10, 19.17, 19.18, 19.19, 19.20, 19.21, 19.22, 19.23, 19.24, 19.25, 19.26
42, 43 .... 19.27
Schedule
Pt 4 .... 19.1
Large and Medium-sized Companies and Groups (Accounts and Reports) Regulations 2008, SI 2008/410 .... 3.2, 20.1, 24.5
reg 3(1) 3.3
(2) 3.56
4(1) 4.4, 4.5
(2) 3.3, 4.4
(3) 4.5
7 .... 3.32, 3.64
8 .... 3.41, 3.74
9(1) 3.57
11 .... 19.2
Sch 1 .... 3.57, 20.15
Pt 1
Section A
para 1–3 .... 3.3
4 .... 3.3
(1), (2) 3.60
5–9 .... 3.3
Section B
Format 1 (Balance sheet formats) **3.4**
Format 2 .... **3.4**
Format 1 (Profit and loss account format) **3.5**
Format 2 .... **3.5**

Large and Medium-sized Companies and Groups (Accounts and Reports) Regulations 2008, SI 2008/410 – *cont.*
Sch 1 – *cont.*
Format 3 .... 3.5
Format 4 .... 3.5
Pt 2
para 10–15 .... 3.6
16 .... 3.7
17–19 .... 3.8
20(1), (2) 3.8
21, 22 .... 3.8
23, 24 .... 3.9
25, 26 .... 3.10
27, 28 .... 3.11
29 .... 3.11, 3.25
30–33 .... 3.12
34 .... 3.13
35 .... 3.14
36–41 .... 3.15
42–44 .... 3.16
45 .... 3.16, 4.4
46 .... 3.17
47–50 .... 3.18
51–53 .... 3.19
54 .... 3.20
55–58 .... 3.21
59, 60 .... 3.22
61, 62 .... 3.23
63 .... 3.24
64 .... 3.25
65 .... 3.26, 3.56
66 .... 3.27, 3.56
67 .... 3.28, 3.56
68 .... 3.29, 3.56, 4.5
69 .... 3.30, 3.56
70, 71 .... 3.16
72 .... 3.31, 4.4
73 .... 3.24
Sch 2 .... 20.15
Sch 3 .... 20.15
Sch 4
para 1 .... 3.33, 3.65
2 .... 3.35, 3.67
3 .... 3.37, 3.68
4–6 .... 3.38, 3.71
7 .... 3.39, 3.72
8, 9 .... 3.40, 3.73
10 .... 3.33
11 .... 3.34
12 .... 3.36
13 .... 3.38
14 .... 3.34, 3.38
15 .... 3.64
16 .... 3.65
17 .... 3.66
18 .... 3.69
19 .... 3.70
20 .... 3.71
21 .... 3.72

Large and Medium-sized Companies and Groups (Accounts and Reports) Regulations 2008, SI 2008/410 – *cont.*
Sch 4 – *cont.*
para 22(2) 3.66, 3.70, 3.71
(3), (4) 3.64
24–27 .... 3.37, 3.68
Sch 5 .... 10.16
para 1 .... 3.43
2 .... 3.44
3 .... 3.45
4 .... 3.46
5 .... 3.47
6(1) 3.42
(2) 3.43, 3.44, 3.46
7(2)–(5) 3.43, 3.44, 3.45, 3.46, 3.47
(6) 3.42
8 .... 3.43, 3.44, 3.45, 3.46, 3.47
9 .... 3.43
10 .... 3.44
11, 12 .... 3.43, 3.44
13(1) 3.45
(2) 3.44
(3) 3.43
(4) 3.43, 3.44
(6), (7) 3.43, 3.44
14(1) 3.42
(2) 3.43, 3.46
15 .... 3.43, 3.44
(2) 3.45, 3.46, 3.47
Sch 6
para 1–5 .... 3.57
6 .... 3.58
7–16 .... 3.59
17 .... 3.60
18 .... 3.61
19–21 .... 3.62
22 .... 3.63
30(2) 39.13
Sch 7
Pt 1 .... 48.App
para 2 .... 20.7
3, 4 .... 20.8
5 .... 20.9
6 .... 20.10
7 .... 20.11
Pt 2 .... 33.28
para 8, 9 .... 20.12
Pt 3
para 10 .... 20.13
Pt 4
para 11 .... 20.14
Pt 5
para 12 .... 20.15
Pt 6
para 13 .... 20.16
14 .... 20.16
Sch 8
para 1 .... 19.6

Large and Medium-sized Companies and Groups (Accounts and Reports) Regulations 2008, SI 2008/410 – *cont.*
Sch 8 – *cont.*
para 2 .... 19.2
3 .... 19.15
4 .... 19.16
5 .... 19.16
6 .... 19.16
7 .... 19.16
8(1) 19.16
(2) 19.17
9 .... 19.17
10 .... 19.16, 19.17
11 .... 19.16
13 .... 19.18
14 .... 19.19
15 .... 19.20
16 .... 19.21
17 .... 19.22
18 .... 19.23
19 .... 19.24
20 .... 19.25
21 .... 19.5
22 .... 19.4
23 .... 19.26
Pt 4 .... 19.6, 19.27
para 24(1) 19.5
(2) 19.5, 19.27
(3) 19.5
(4) 19.27
25–28 .... 19.7
29 .... 19.8
30–32 .... 19.9
33–35 .... 19.10
36, 37 .... 19.11
38, 39 .... 19.12
40 .... 19.13
41 .... 19.2
42 .... 19.27
44 .... 19.16
44 .... 19.4
(3) 19.3
46–48 .... 19.3
45 .... 19.16
Sch 9
para 1 .... 34.11
(2) 3.5
2 .... 3.4, 3.22, 22.1, 22.4, 22.6, 34.11, 34.20
3 .... 34.20
4 .... 22.1, 34.11
7 .... 22.4
Sch 10
para 2, 3 .... 3.16
4 .... 3.4, 3.5, 3.8
5 .... 3.11
7 .... 3.19
8 .... 3.20
10 .... 3.3

Large and Medium-sized Companies and Groups (Accounts and Reports) Regulations 2008, SI 2008/410 – *cont.*
Sch 10 – *cont.*
para 11 .... Appl
12 .... 3.11
14 .... 3.5
15 .... 3.19

Legal Aid, Sentencing and Punishment of Offenders Act 2012 (Fines on Summary Conviction) Regulations 2015, SI 2015/664
Sch 3 ..... 2.9, 2.10, 8.10, 8.11, 8.19, 13.2, 18.2, 18.4, 18.72, 25.8, 27.2, 27.12, 29.1, 30.34, 30.50, 34.9, 34.15, 38.3, 39.11, 47.12, 47.35, 48.13, 48.16

M

Magistrates' Courts (Northern Ireland) Order1981, SI 1981/1675
art 166 .... 29.6
Sch 4 .... 29.6

Markets in Financial Instruments Directive (Consequential Amendments) Regulations 2007, SI 2007/2932
reg 3 .... 5.3

O

Open-Ended Investment Companies (Investment Companies with Variable Capital) Regulations 1996, SI 1996/2827
Sch 8
para 10 .... 18.16

Open-Ended Investment Companies Regulations 2001, SI 2001/1228
.... 44.4
reg 6 .... 12.7
30 .... 30.14
Sch 7
para 9 .... 18.16

Open-Ended Investment Companies Regulations (Northern Ireland) 2004, SI 2004/335
reg 22 .... 30.14

Oversea Companies (Accounts) (Modifications and Exemptions) Order 1990, SI 1990/440
art 2(1)(c) 30.App
(3) 30.App
Sch 1
para 3, 4 .... 30.App

Oversea Companies and Credit and Financial Institutions (Branch Disclosure) Regulations 1992, SI 1992/3179
reg 2 .... 30.App
3 .... 30.App
Sch 1 .... 30.App

Oversea Companies and Credit and Financial Institutions (Branch Disclosure) Regulations 1992, SI 1992/3179 – *cont.*
Sch 2
para 2 .... 30.App
3–9 .... 30.App
10–12 .... 30.App
13(3) 30.App
14 .... 30.App
16–18 .... 30.App
Sch 3
para 17 .... 30.App
Sch 4
para 5 .... 30.App
Overseas Companies (Execution of Documents and Registration of Charges) Regulations 2009, SI 2009/1917 .... 30.59
reg 2 .... 30.64
4 .... 30.60, 30.61, 34.6
5 .... 30.62
6 .... 30.63
Pt 3 (8–28) 39.13
reg 8 .... 30.64
9 .... 30.65, 30.67A
10–12 .... 30.66, 30.67A
13 .... 30.67, 30.67A
14–16 .... 30.67A, 30.68
17 .... 30.67A, 30.69
18 .... 30.67A, 30.70
19(1) 30.65
(2) 30.68
(3) 30.65
20 .... 30.67A, 30.72
21 .... 30.67A, 30.70
22 .... 30.67A, 30.71
23 .... 30.73
24 .... 30.73
(2A) 30.67A
25, 26 .... 30.73
27 .... 39.13, 39.19
Schedule
para 2 .... 30.64
3 .... 30.68
4 .... 30.64
6 .... 30.72
7 .... 30.70, 34.23, 34.27, 34.30
Overseas Companies (Execution of Documents and Registration of Charges) (Amendment) Regulations 2011, SI 2011/2194 .... 30.64
reg 2(1) 30.67A
(3) 30.67A, 30.68, 30.69, 30.70, 30.71, 30.72
(4), (5) 30.67A, 30.73
(6) 30.67A, 30.73
(7) 30.73
(8) 30.67A, 30.73
26A 30.73
Overseas Companies Regulations 2009, SI 2009/1801 .... 30.2
Overseas Companies Regulations 2009, SI 2009/1801 – *cont.*
reg 2 .... 30.4, 30.7, 30.8
Pt 2 (regs 3–11) 39.8
reg 3–7 .... 30.3
8, 9 .... 30.4, 39.13, 39.14
10 .... 30.5
11 .... 30.6
Pt 3 (regs 12–17) 39.8
reg 12, 13 .... 30.7
14 .... 30.7, 39.13, 39.14
15 .... 30.8, 39.13, 39.14
16 .... 30.9
17 .... 30.10
18, 19 .... 30.12
20, 21 .... 30.13
22–24 .... 30.14
25 .... 30.15
26 .... 30.16
27–29 .... 30.17
Pt 5 (regs 30–42) 39.8
reg 30 .... 30.19, 30.24
31 .... 30.19
32 .... 30.20, 39.13, 39.14
33 .... 30.21
34 .... 30.22
35 .... 30.23
36 .... 30.24
37 .... 30.25
38 .... 30.26, 30.30, 30.31
39 .... 30.33
40 .... 30.34, 39.13
41 .... 30.34
42 .... 30.26, 30.29, 30.30, 30.32
Pt 6 (regs 43–57) 39.8
reg 43 .... 30.36
Pt 6, Ch 2 (regs 44–50) 39.14
reg 44 .... 30.36
45, 46 .... 30.37, 39.13, 39.14
47 .... 30.38
48, 49 .... 30.37
50 .... 30.39
51 .... 30.40
52 .... 30.41
53 .... 30.42, 30.46, 30.47
54 .... 30.49
55 .... 30.50, 39.13
56 .... 30.50
57 .... 30.42, 30.45, 30.46, 30.48
58 .... 30.51
59 .... 30.52, 30.53
60, 61 .... 30.52
62–64 .... 30.53
65 .... 30.54
66 .... 30.55
67 .... 30.52, 30.53, 30.54
75 .... 16.21, 30.56
76 .... 39.8
77 .... 30.57, 39.8
78 .... 39.13

Overseas Companies Regulations 2009, SI 2009/1801 – *cont.*
Sch 1 .... 30.14
para 15–19 .... 30.29
Sch 2
para 1–11 .... 30.14
Sch 3 .... 30.15
Sch 4
para 1–9 .... 30.27
10–14 .... 30.28
20 .... 30.27
Sch 5 .... 30.32
Sch 6
para 1–9 .... 30.43
10–14 .... 30.44
15–19 .... 30.45
20 .... 30.43
Sch 7 .... 30.48
Sch 8
para 2 .... 30.App
3 .... 30.3, 30.4, 30.5
4, 5 .... 30.3
6, 7 .... 30.4
8 .... 30.5
9 .... 30.3, 30.4
10, 11 .... 30.3
12 .... 30.4
13 .... 30.5
(1)–(3) 30.3
14 .... 30.3, 30.4, 30.5
15, 16 .... 30.7
17 .... 30.8
19 .... 30.13
20 .... 30.17
21, 22 .... 30.15
23 .... 30.19
24 .... 30.24
25 .... 30.37
26 .... 30.40

P

Partnerships (Accounts) Regulations 2008, SI 2008/569
reg 7 .... 3.39, 3.72, 5.37, 5.73
17 .... 3.39, 5.37, 5.73
Payments to Governments and Miscellaneous Provisions Regulations 2014, SI 2014/3293
reg 2(1) 32.4
3 .... 32.15
Perjury (Northern Ireland) Order 1979, SI 1979/1714
art 7 .... 25.3
10 .... 10.19, 25.3, 25.12
Prospectus Regulations 2005, SI 2005/1433 ... 32.1, 32.3, 32.4, 32.5, 32.6, 32.7, 32.8, 32.10, 32.12, 32.14, 32.15, 32.16, 32.19, 32.21, 32.22, 32.23, 32.24
Prospectus Regulations 2011, SI 2011/1668 .... 32.4, 32.5
Public Bodies Act 2011 (Transitional Provision) Order 2012, SI 2012/1471
reg 23 .... App1
Prospectus Regulations 2012, SI 2012/1538
reg 2 .... 32.4, 32.8, 32.14
3 .... 32.4, 32.14
4 .... 32.8, 32.14
5 .... 32.15, 32.19
7 .... 32.22, 33.13
Prospectus Regulations 2013, SI 2013/1125
reg 2 .... 32.4
Public Bodies Act 2011 (Transitional Provision) Order 2012, SI 2012/1471
reg 23 .... App1

R

Recognised Auction Platform Regulations 2011, SI 2011/2699 .... 23.6
Registrar of Companies and Applications for Striking Off Regulations 2009, SI 2009/1803
reg 2 .... 21.2
3 .... 39.9
4, 5 .... 39.11
6, 7 .... 39.13
8 .... 39.14
Schedule 39.14
Registrar of Companies (Fees) (Companies, Overseas Companies and Limited Liability Partnerships) Regulations 2012, SI 2012/1907 .... App3
Regulatory Reform (Financial Services and Markets Act 2000) Order 200, SI 2007/1973 .... 33.14

S

Small Companies and Groups (Accounts and Directors' Report) Regulations 2008, SI 2008/409
reg 3 .... 5.4, 5.14
(2) 5.58
4 .... 5.4, 5.31
5 .... 5.4, 5.40
5A 5.4, 5.31, 5.40
6 .... 5.46
8 .... 5.59
9 .... 5.75
10 .... 5.64
11 .... 5.76
Sch 1 .... 5.7, 5.59
Pt 1
Section A
para 1(1A) 5.5
2, 3 .... 5.5

Table of Statutory Instruments

Small Companies and Groups (Accounts and Directors' Report) Regulations 2008, SI 2008/409 – *cont.*
Sch 1 – *cont.*
para 4 .... 5.5, 5.62
5–9 .... 5.5
Section B
Format 1 (Balance sheet formats) **5.6**
Item A 5.6
D 5.6
E(4) 5.6
H(4) 5.6
J 5.6
Format 2 .... **5.6**
Item C(II)(3) 5.6
(IV) 5.6
D 5.6
Format 1 (Profit and loss account format) **5.7**
Format 2 .... **5.7**
Item 7(a) 5.7
Format 3 .... **5.7**
Format 4 .... **5.7**
Item A(4)(a) 5.7
Pt 2 .... 5.5
para 10–15 .... 5.8
16 .... 5.9
17–19 .... 5.10
20(1), (2) 5.10
21, 22 .... 5.10
23, 24 .... 5.11
25, 26 .... 5.12
27, 28 .... 5.13
29 .... 5.13, 5.27
30–33 .... 5.14
34 .... 5.15
35 .... 5.16
36–41 .... 5.17
Pt 3
42 .... 5.19, 5.28
43, 44 .... 5.18
45 .... 5.19
46, 47 .... 5.20
48, 49 .... 5.21
50 .... 5.22
51–53 .... 5.23
54 .... 5.24
55, 56 .... 5.25
57 .... 5.26, 5.31, 5.40
58 .... 5.27
59 .... 5.28, 5.58
60 .... 5.29, 5.58
61 .... 5.30, 5.58
62, 63 .... 5.18
Sch 2
para 1 .... 5.32
2 .... 5.33
3 .... 5.34
4 .... 5.35, 5.46

Small Companies and Groups (Accounts and Directors' Report) Regulations 2008, SI 2008/409 – *cont.*
Sch 2 – *cont.*
para 5–7 .... 5.36
8 .... 5.37
9, 10 .... 5.38
11 .... 5.33, 5.36
12–17 .... 5.35, 5.69
Sch 3 .... 5.46, 5.76, 10.16
para 1 .... 5.41
2 .... 5.42
3 .... 5.43
4 .... 5.41, 5.42
(1) 5.40
5 .... 5.41, 5.42, 5.43
(6) 5.40
6–10 .... 5.41
11 .... 5.41
(1) 5.40
(2) 5.42
12 .... 5.41
Sch 4
para 1 .... 5.46, 5.47
2 .... 5.48
3 .... 5.49
4, 5 .... 5.50
6 .... 5.51
7 .... 5.52
8 .... 5.53
9 .... 5.54
10 .... 5.55
Sch 5
para 2, 3 .... 20.8
4 .... 20.9
5 .... 20.13
6 .... 20.12
Sch 6
para 1–5 .... 5.59
6 .... 5.60
7–16 .... 5.61
17 .... 5.62
18 .... 5.63
19, 20 .... 5.64
21 .... 5.65
22 .... 5.66
23 .... 5.67
24 .... 5.68
25 .... 5.69, 5.76
26 .... 5.70
27 .... 5.71
28–33 .... 5.72
34 .... 5.73
35, 36 .... 5.74
37(2) 5.67, 5.71, 5.72
(3), (4) 5.65
Sch 7
para 1(2) 5.7
2 .... 5.24, 22.4, 34.11, 34.20
3 .... 34.20

Small Companies and Groups (Accounts and Directors' Report) Regulations 2008, SI 2008/409 – *cont.*
Sch 7 – *cont.*
para 4 .... 34.11
5 .... 22.4
6 .... 22.6
Sch 8
para 1, 2 .... 5.17
3 .... 5.7, 5.10
5 .... 5.22
7 .... 5.5
8 .... App1
14 .... 5.7
Small Companies (Micro-Entities' Accounts) Regulations 2013, SI 2013/3008
reg 4 .... 5.3B
(2), (3) 5.2
(4) 5.3A
5 .... 2.16, 5.4
(4) 2.2
6 .... 2.10
7(2) 2.10, 5.5, 5.59
(3) App1
8 .... 8.30
9 .... 5.5
(5) 5.31, 5.40
10 .... 5.5, 5.6
(4) 5.7
11 .... 5.10, 5.12
13 .... 5.22
Statutory Auditors (Amendment of Companies Act 2006 and Delegation of Functions etc) Order 2012, SI 2012/1741 .... 8.14
reg 8 .... 8.22
15 .... 8.34
Statutory Auditors and Third Country Auditors Regulations 2007, SI 2007/3494
reg 4 .... 8.8
Statutory Auditors and Third Country Auditors Regulations 2007, SI 2007/3494 – *cont.*
reg 5 .... 8.8
17, 18 .... 8.8
29 .... 8.14
30 .... 8.13
31, 32 .... 8.14
34 .... 8.14
35(3A)(a) 8.14
36–39 .... 8.14
41 .... 8.22
42 .... 26.10
43 .... 8.14
Statutory Auditors and Third Country Auditors (Amendment) Regulations 2011, SI 2011/1856
reg 5 .... 8.8
7(6) 8.14
Statutory Auditors and Third Country Auditors (Amendment) (No. 2) Regulations 2008, SI 2008/2639 .... 8.14

U

Uncertificated Securities Regulations 2001, SI 2001/3755
reg 3(1) 44.14
4–20 .... 44.14
25 .... 44.14
28 .... 44.14
46 .... 44.14
Sch 1 .... 44.14
Uncertificated Securities (Amendment) Regulations 2013, SI 2013/632
.... 44.14
Unregistered Companies Regulations 2009, SI 2009/2436
Sch 1 .... 12.7
Sch 2 .... 12.7

Table of EU Legislation

Primary Legislation

Treaties Agreements and Conventions

Treaty establishing the European Community (Rome, 1957)
art 81, 82 .... 18.17

Conventions

European Convention of Human Rights and Fundamental Freedoms (Rome, 4 November 1950) (ECHR Convention) 25.3

Secondary Legislation

Directives

Commission Directive 2003/124/EC
art 2, 3 .... 33.39
Commission Directive 2004/72/EC
art 5, 6 .... 33.39
Council Directive 68/151/EEC
art 3 .. 35.42, 35.49, 35.51, 38.2, 38.4, 39.8
Council Directive 77/91/EEC
art 29 .... 33.23
Council Directive 78/660/EEC
.... 3.15, 5.17, 20.10
Council Directive 80/390/EEC
.... 32.6
Council Directive 83/349/EEC
.... 3.54, 8.27A, 20.10
Council Directive 85/611/EEC
.... 33.58
Council Directive 89/117/EEC
.... 30.App
Council Directive 89/666/EEC
.... 30.19, 30.64, 30.App
art 3 .... 30.3
Council Directive 91/674/EEC
art 2(1) 5.3B
European Parliament and Council Directive 94/19/EC 32.5
European Parliament and Council Directive 95/46/EC 30.14
European Parliament and Council Directive 2001/34/EC 32.6
Title IV 32.11
Title V 32.11
European Parliament and Council Directive 2002/12/EC
art 1(1)(a) 30.App
European Parliament and Council Directive 2003/6/EC 23.5, 23.6, 33.4
art 6 .... 33.39
European Parliament and Council Directive 2003/71/EC ... 32.4, 32.11, 32.15, 32.16, 32.23, 32.24, 33.4, 33.9, 33.70
art 2.1(m) 32.1
5(2) 32.6
(4)(b) 32.4
10 .... 33.47
14 .... 32.6
European Parliament and Council Directive 2004/25/EC 20.16
art 3 .... 48.App
(1) 48.2
4(1) 48.2
(2) 48.2
(c) 48.App
(e) 48.App
5 .... 48.2
6(1), (2) 48.2
(3) 48.2, 48.3
7 .... 48.2, 48.12
8 .... 48.2
9 .... 48.2, 48.9
9.5 .... 48.3
11 .... 48.7, 48.8, 48.19, 48.App
12 .... 48.7
13 .... 48.2
15, 16 .... 48.10
European Parliament and Council Directive 2004/39/EC .... 32.1, Appl
art 2 .... Appl
4.1 .... 33.58
4.1.1 .... Appl
4.1.14, 4.1.15 .... 33.69
4.1.18, 4.1.19 .... 33.69
6 .... 33.67
71(6) 32.4
Annex 11 .... 32.4
European Parliament and Council Directive 2004/109/EC ... 24.1, 33.4, 33.43, 33.49, 33.67, 33.70, 33.71
art 2.1(i) 33.69

Table of EU Legislation

European Parliament and Council Directive 2004/109/EC – *cont.*
art 13 .... 33.58
23.1 .... 33.64, 33.65
European Parliament and Council Directive 2005/56/EC 35.35
art 10.2 .... 35.37, 35.47
10.3 .... 35.43
11 .... 35.47, 35.48, 35.49
12, 13 .... 35.51
European Parliament and Council Directive 2005/60/EC 30.14
European Parliament and Council Directive 2006/48/EC
art 2 .... 5.3B
4 .... 5.3B
European Parliament and Council Directive 2013/34/EU
art 2(14), (15) 5.3B

Regulations

Commission Regulation (EC) 2273/2003 .... 23.5, 23.12
art 5(1) 33.36
Commission Regulation (EC) 809/2004 .... 32.1, 32.13, 32.15, 33.9
art 3–23 .... 32.10
26 .... 32.9

Commission Regulation (EC) 809/2004 – *cont.*
art 27 .... 32.20
29, 30 .... 32.17
34 .... 32.18
Annex I 32.10
Annex II 32.10
Annex III 32.10
Annex IV 32.10
Annex V 32.10
Annex VI 32.10
Annex VII 32.10, 33.9
Annex VIII 32.10, 33.9
Annex IX 32.10
Annex X 32.10, 33.9
Annex XI 32.10
Annex XII 32.10
Annex XIII 32.10
Annex XIV 32.10
Annex XV 32.10
Annex XVI 32.10, 33.9
Annex XVII 32.10
Annex XVIII 32.10
Council Regulation (EEC) 89/4064 .... 35.34
Council Regulation (EC) 139/2004 .... 35.34
art 8(3) 48.App
9(1) 48.App
Parliament and Council Regulation (EC) 1606/2002 .... 32.20, App1
art 4 .... 3.2, 3.53, 5.4, 5.56

Table of Cases

A

AE Green & Co v Central Advance and Discount Corpn Ltd (1920) 63 Acct LR 1 .... 8.38
Acatos & Hutcheson plc v Watson [1995] 1 BCLC 218, [1995] BCC 446 .... 34.1
Act Dampskib Hercules v Grand Trunk Pacific Rly Co [1912] 1 KB 222, 81 LJKB 189, 56 Sol Jo 51, 105 LT 695, 28 TLR 28, CA 30.App
Aerators Ltd v Tollitt [1902] 2 Ch 319, 71 LJ Ch 727, 10 Mans 95, 19 RPC 418, 53 WR 584, [1900–3] All ER Rep 564, 46 Sol Jo 451, 86 LT 651, 18 TLR 637 .... 26.13
Agnew v IRC [2001] UKPC 28, [2001] 2 AC 710, [2001] 3 WLR 454, [2001] Lloyd's Rep Bank 251, [2001] 2 BCLC 188, [2001] BCC 259, [2001] 5 LRC 478, [2001] All ER (D) 21 (Jun) 17.5, 45.4
Alabama, New Orleans, Texas and Pacific Junction Rly Co, Re [1891] 1 Ch 213, 60 LJ Ch 221, 2 Meg 377, 64 LT 127, 7 TLR 171, [1886–90] All ER Rep Ext 1143, CA 35.3
Allen v Gold Reefs of West Africa Ltd [1900] 1 Ch 656, 69 LJ Ch 266, 7 Mans 417, 48 WR 452, [1900–3] All ER Rep 746, 44 Sol Jo 261, 82 LT 210, 16 TLR 213, CA 14.5
Allen, Craig & Co (London) Ltd, Re [1934] Ch 483, 103 LJ Ch 193, 78 Sol Jo 223, 151 LT 323, 50 TLR 301, sub nom Allen, Craig [1934] All ER Rep 301 .... 8.30
Antwerp Waterworks Co Ltd, Re [1931] WN 186, 172 LT Jo 75, 72 L Jo 79 .... 47.55
Arctic Engineering Ltd (No 2), Re [1986] 2 All ER 346, [1986] 1 WLR 686, [1986] BCLC 253, [1986] PCC 1, 130 Sol Jo 429, [1986] LS Gaz R 1895 .... 18.12
Armagh Shoes Ltd, Re [1982] NI 59, [1984] BCLC 405 .... 45.4
Armour Hick Northern Ltd v Armour Trust Ltd [1980] 3 All ER 833, sub nom Armour Hick Northern Ltd v Whitehouse [1980] 1 WLR 1520, 124 Sol Jo 864 .... 34.20
Ashbury Railway Carriage and Iron Co Ltd v Riche (1875) LR 7 HL 653, 44 LJ Ex 185, 24 WR 794, 33 LT 450, [1874–80] All ER Rep Ext 2219, HL 16.1
A-G v Kitchin [1941] 2 All ER 735, CA 34.20
Atwool v Merryweather (1867) LR 5 Eq 464n, 37 LJ Ch 35 .... 26.11
Automatic Self-Cleansing Filter Syndicate Co Ltd v Cunninghame [1906] 2 Ch 34, 75 LJ Ch 437, 13 Mans 156, 50 Sol Jo 359, 94 LT 651, 22 TLR 378, CA 18.29
Aveling Barford Ltd v Perion Ltd [1989] BCLC 626, 5 BCC 677 .... 22.1, 22.7

B

B Johnson & Co (Builders) Ltd, Re [1955] Ch 634, [1955] 2 All ER 775, [1955] 3 WLR 269, 99 Sol Jo 490, CA 18.37
BML Group Ltd v Harman (1994) Times, 8 April, CA 42.13
Bahia and San Francisco Rly Co, Re (1868) LR 3 QB 584, 9 B & S 844, 37 LJQB 176, 16 WR 862, 18 LT 467 .... 44.1
Bairstow v Queens Moat Houses plc [2000] 1 BCLC 549, [2000] BCC 1025, [1999] All ER (D) 1378; sub nom Bairstow v Queens Moat Houses plc [2001] EWCA Civ 712, [2001] 2 BCLC 531, [2002] BCC 91, [2001] All ER (D) 211 (May) 22.8, 22.App
Bamford v Bamford [1970] Ch 212, [1968] 2 All ER 655, [1968] 3 WLR 317, 112 Sol Jo 416; affd [1970] Ch 212, [1969] 1 All ER 969, [1969] 2 WLR 1107, 113 Sol Jo 123, CA 47.9
Bank of Hindustan, China and Japan Ltd v Alison (1871) LR 6 CP 222, 40 LJCP 117, 19 WR 505, 23 LT 854, Ex Ch 47.6
Barnett Hoares & Co v South London Tramways Co (1887) 18 QBD 815, 56 LJQB 452, 35 WR 640, 57 LT 436, 3 TLR 611, CA 13.7
Bath Glass Ltd, Re [1988] BCLC 329, 4 BCC 130 .... 18.16
Beattie v E & F Beattie Ltd [1938] Ch 708, [1938] 3 All ER 214, 107 LJ Ch 333, 82 Sol Jo 521, 159 LT 220, 54 TLR 964, CA 14.12
Belmont Finance Corpn Ltd v Williams Furniture Ltd (No 2) [1980] 1 All ER 393, CA 22.8, 22.App, 34.20

Table of Cases

Birch v Cropper, Re Bridgewater Navigation Co Ltd (1889) 14 App Cas 525, 59 LJ Ch 122, 1 Meg 372, 38 WR 401, [1886–90] All ER Rep 628, 61 LT 621, 5 TLR 722, HL 47.5
Bird Precision Bellows Ltd, Re [1986] Ch 658, [1985] 3 All ER 523, [1986] 2 WLR 158, [1985] BCLC 493, [1986] PCC 25, 130 Sol Jo 51, [1986] LS Gaz R 36, CA 26.10
Black v Smallwood (1965) 117 CLR 52, [1966] ALR 744, 39 ALJR 405 (Aust HC), Aus HC 12.1
Bloomenthal v Ford [1897] AC 156, 66 LJ Ch 253, 4 Mans 156, 45 WR 449, 76 LT 205, 13 TLR 240, [1895–9] All ER Rep Ext 1845, HL 44.1
Bolton, Re, ex p North British Artificial Silk Ltd [1930] 2 Ch 48, 99 LJ Ch 209, [1929] B & CR 141, [1930] All ER Rep 628, 143 LT 425 .... 47.25
Borland's Trustee v Steel Bros & Co Ltd [1901] 1 Ch 279, 70 LJ Ch 51, 49 WR 120, 17 TLR 45 .... 47.1
Bradford Banking Co v Briggs, Son & Co Ltd (1886) 12 App Cas 29, 56 LJ Ch 364, 35 WR 521, 1 LDAB 75, 56 LT 62, 3 TLR 170, HL 47.25
Bradford Investments plc (No 2), Re [1991] BCLC 688, [1991] BCC 379 .... 47.28, 47.43
Brady v Brady [1989] AC 755, [1988] 2 All ER 617, [1988] 2 WLR 1308, [1988] BCLC 579, 4 BCC 390, 11 LDAB 112, 132 Sol Jo 820, HL 34.21
Brewery Assets Corpn, Re, Truman's Case [1894] 3 Ch 272, 63 LJ Ch 635, 1 Mans 359, 8 R 508, 43 WR 73, 38 Sol Jo 602, 71 LT 328 .... 47.9
Brightlife Ltd, Re [1987] Ch 200, [1986] 3 All ER 673, [1987] 2 WLR 197, [1986] BCLC 418, 2 BCC 99, 359, 131 Sol Jo 132, [1987] LS Gaz R 653 .... 17.5
British and American Trustee and Finance Corpn v Couper [1894] AC 399, 63 LJ Ch 425, 1 Mans 256, 6 R 146, 42 WR 652, [1891–4] All ER Rep 667, 70 LT 882, 10 TLR 415, HL 47.55
British India Steam Navigation Co v IRC (1881) 7 QBD 165, 50 LJQB 517, 29 WR 610, 44 LT 378 .... 17.6
Brown v British Abrasive Wheel Co [1919] 1 Ch 290, 88 LJ Ch 143, [1918–19] All ER Rep 308, 63 Sol Jo 373, 120 LT 529, 35 TLR 268 .... 14.5
Buchler v Talbot [2004] UKHL 9, [2004] 2 AC 298, [2004] 1 All ER 1289, [2004] 2 WLR 582, [2004] 1 BCLC 281, [2004] NLJR 381, (2004) Times, 5 March, 148 Sol Jo LB 299, [2004] 5 LRC 405, [2004] All ER (D) 89 (Mar), sub nom Leyland Daf Ltd, Re [2004] BCC 214 ...... 45.5
Buenos Ayres Great Southern Rly Co Ltd, Re, Buenos Ayres Great Southern Rly Co Ltd v Preston [1947] Ch 384, [1947] 1 All ER 729, [1948] LJR 131, 176 LT 468 .... 47.5
Bugle Press Ltd, Re, Re Houses and Estates Ltd [1961] Ch 270, [1960] 1 All ER 768, [1960] 2 WLR 658, 104 Sol Jo 289; affd [1961] Ch 270, [1960] 3 All ER 791, [1960] 3 WLR 956, 104 Sol Jo 1057, CA 48.18
Burland v Earle [1902] AC 83, 71 LJPC 1, 9 Mans 17, 50 WR 241, 85 LT 553, 18 TLR 41, [1900–3] All ER Rep Ext 1452, PC 22.10, 22.App, 26.11
Bushell v Faith [1970] AC 1099, [1970] 1 All ER 53, [1970] 2 WLR 272, 114 Sol Jo 54, HL 18.9
Byrne & Co v Leon Van Tienhoven & Co (1880) 5 CPD 344, 44 JP 667, 49 LJQB 316, 42 LT 371, [1874–80] All ER Rep Ext 1432, CPD 47.9

C

Candler v Crane Christmas & Co [1951] 2 KB 164, [1951] 1 All ER 426, 95 Sol Jo 171, [1951] 1 TLR 371, CA 8.38
Cannon v Trask (1875) LR 20 Eq 669, 44 LJ Ch 772 .... 42.17
Caparo Industries plc v Dickman [1990] 2 AC 605, [1990] 1 All ER 568, [1990] 2 WLR 358, [1990] BCLC 273, [1990] BCC 164, 11 LDAB 563, 134 Sol Jo 494, [1990] 12 LS Gaz R 42, [1990] NLJR 248, [1991] LRC (Comm) 460, HL 8.38, 34.12
Castiglione's Will Trusts, Re, Hunter v Mackenzie [1958] Ch 549, [1958] 1 All ER 480, [1958] 2 WLR 400, 102 Sol Jo 176 .... 34.1
Charterhouse Investment Trust Ltd v Tempest Diesels Ltd [1986] BCLC 1, 1 BCC 544 .... 34.20
Cheshire Banking Co, Re, Duff's Executors' Case (1886) 32 Ch D 301, 54 LT 558, 2 TLR 440, CA 44.9
City Equitable Fire Insurance Co Ltd, Re [1925] Ch 407, 94 LJ Ch 445, [1925] B & CR 109, [1924] All ER Rep 485, 133 LT 520, 40 TLR 853, CA 8.33, 18.31
City of Westminster Assurance Co Ltd v Registrar of Companies [1997] BCC 960, CA 21.App

Company, a (No 004475 of 1982), Re [1983] Ch 178, [1983] 2 All ER 36, [1983] 2 WLR 381, [1983] BCLC 126, 127 Sol Jo 153 .... 26.10
Company, a (No 002567 of 1982), Re [1983] 2 All ER 854, [1983] 1 WLR 927, [1983] BCLC 151, 127 Sol Jo 508, [1983] LS Gaz R 2133 .... 26.10
Conway v Petronius Clothing Co Ltd [1978] 1 All ER 185, [1978] 1 WLR 72, 122 Sol Jo 15 .... 36.2
Cooper (Gerald) Chemicals Ltd, Re [1978] Ch 262, [1978] 2 All ER 49, [1978] 2 WLR 866, 121 Sol Jo 848 .... 18.38
Cope (Benjamin) & Sons Ltd, Re, Marshall v Benjamin Cope & Sons Ltd [1914] 1 Ch 800, 83 LJ Ch 699, 21 Mans 254, 58 Sol Jo 432, 110 LT 905 .... 45.7
Cotter v National Union of Seamen [1929] 2 Ch 58, 98 LJ Ch 323, [1929] All ER Rep 342, 73 Sol Jo 206, 141 LT 178, 45 TLR 352, CA 26.11
Cousins v International Brick Co Ltd [1931] 2 Ch 90, 100 LJ Ch 404, [1931] All ER Rep 229, 145 LT 471, 47 TLR 217, CA 42.26
Crestjoy Products Ltd, Re [1990] BCLC 677, [1990] BCC 23 .... 18.14
Crossman, Re, Re Paulin. See IRC v Crossman
Cumbrian Newspapers Group Ltd v Cumberland and Westmorland Herald Newspaper and Printing Co Ltd [1987] Ch 1, [1986] 2 All ER 816, [1986] 3 WLR 26, [1986] BCLC 286, 2 BCC 99, 227, 130 Sol Jo 446, [1986] LS Gaz R 1719 .... 9.1

D

DHN Food Distributors Ltd v Tower Hamlets London Borough Council [1976] 3 All ER 462, [1976] 1 WLR 852, 74 LGR 506, 32 P & CR 240, 120 Sol Jo 215, 239 Estates Gazette 719, CA 12.6
DTC (CNC) Ltd v Gary Sargeant & Co (a firm) [1996] 2 All ER 369, [1996] 1 WLR 797, [1996] 1 BCLC 529 .... 36.5
Daimler Co Ltd v Continental Tyre and Rubber Co (Great Britain) Ltd [1916] 2 AC 307, 85 LJKB 1333, 22 Com Cas 32, [1916–17] All ER Rep 191, 60 Sol Jo 602, 114 LT 1049, 32 TLR 624, HL 12.6
Darby, Re, ex p Brougham [1911] 1 KB 95, 80 LJKB 180, 18 Mans 10 .... 12.6
David Payne & Co Ltd, Re, Young v David Payne & Co Ltd [1904] 2 Ch 608, 73 LJ Ch 849, 11 Mans 437, 48 Sol Jo 572, 91 LT 777, 20 TLR 590, [1904–7] All ER Rep Ext 1501, CA 17.2
De La Rue (Thomas) & Co Ltd and Reduced, Re [1911] 2 Ch 361, 81 LJ Ch 59, 19 Mans 71, 55 Sol Jo 715, 105 LT 542 .... 47.51
Deaduck Ltd (in liq), Re, Baker v Secretary of State for Trade and Industry [2000] 1 BCLC 148, [1999] All ER (D) 562 .... 18.14
Deverall v Grant Advertising Inc [1955] Ch 111, [1954] 3 All ER 389, [1954] 3 WLR 688, 98 Sol Jo 787, CA 30.56, 30.App
Dixon v Kennaway & Co [1900] 1 Ch 833, 69 LJ Ch 501, 7 Mans 446, 82 LT 527, 16 TLR 329 .... 44.1
Doloswella Rubber and Tea Estates Ltd and Reduced, Re [1917] 1 Ch 213, 86 LJ Ch 223, [1916–17] All ER Rep 769, 115 LT 853 .... 47.51
Dorman, Long & Co Ltd, Re, Re South Durham Steel and Iron Co Ltd [1934] Ch 635, 103 LJ Ch 316, [1933] All ER Rep 460, 78 Sol Jo 12, 151 LT 347 .... 35.2
Duomatic Ltd, Re [1969] 2 Ch 365, [1969] 1 All ER 161, [1969] 2 WLR 114, 112 Sol Jo 922 .... 42.1

E

EBM Co Ltd v Dominion Bank [1937] 3 All ER 555, 81 Sol Jo 814, PC 42.1
Ebrahimi v Westbourne Galleries Ltd [1973] AC 360, [1972] 2 All ER 492, [1972] 2 WLR 1289, 116 Sol Jo 412, HL 12.6
Edwards v Halliwell [1950] 2 All ER 1064, 94 Sol Jo 803, CA 26.11
Eley v Positive Government Security Life Assurance Co Ltd (1876) 1 Ex D 88, 34 LJQB 190, 45 LJQB 451, 24 WR 338, CA 14.12

Emma Silver Mining Co v Lewis & Son (1879) 4 CPD 396, 27 WR 836, 40 LT 749, CPD 12.1
English and Colonial Produce Co Ltd, Re [1906] 2 Ch 435, 75 LJ Ch 831, 13 Mans 387, 50 Sol Jo 595, 95 LT 580, 22 TLR 669, CA 12.1
Erlanger v New Sombrero Phosphate Co (1878) 3 App Cas 1218, 27 WR 65, [1874–80] All ER Rep 271, 39 LT 269, sub nom New Sombrero Phosphate Co v Erlanger 48 LJ Ch 73, HL 12.1
Eurostem Maritime Ltd, Re (1987) PCC 190 .... 18.1
Ewing v Buttercup Margarine Co Ltd [1917] 2 Ch 1, 86 LJ Ch 441, 34 RPC 232, [1916–17] All ER Rep 1012, 61 Sol Jo 443, 117 LT 67, 33 TLR 321, CA 26.13
Exchange Banking Co, Re, Flitcroft's Case (1882) 21 Ch D 519, 52 LJ Ch 217, 31 WR 174, 48 LT 86, CA 22.8, 22.App, 47.60
Exeter Trust Ltd v Screenways Ltd [1991] BCLC 888, [1991] BCC 477, 135 Sol Jo LB 12, CA 40.8
Express Engineering Works Ltd, Re [1920] 1 Ch 466, 89 LJ Ch 379, 122 LT 790, 36 TLR 275, [1920] All ER Rep Ext 850, CA 42.1

F

Florence Land and Public Works Co, Re, Nicol's Case, Tufnell and Ponsonby's Case (1883) 29 Ch D 421, 52 LT 933, 1 TLR 221, CA 47.8
Foss v Harbottle (1843) 2 Hare 461, 67 ER 189 .... 12.6, 26.11

G

George Barker (Transport) Ltd v Eynon [1974] 1 All ER 900, [1974] 1 WLR 462, [1974] 1 Lloyd's Rep 65, 118 Sol Jo 210, CA 17.7
Gibson v Barton (1875) LR 10 QB 329, 39 JP 628, 44 LJMC 81, 23 WR 858, 32 LT 396 .... 7.4
Gluckstein v Barnes [1900] AC 240, 69 LJ Ch 385, 7 Mans 321, 1 LDAB 303, 82 LT 393, 16 TLR 321, HL 12.1
Gold Coast Selection Trust Ltd v Humphrey (Inspector of Taxes) [1948] 2 All ER 379, [1948] AC 459 .... 46.1
Greenhalgh v Arderne Cinemas Ltd [1946] 1 All ER 512, 90 Sol Jo 248, CA 9.1
Greenhalgh v Arderne Cinemas Ltd [1951] Ch 286, [1950] 2 All ER 1120, 94 Sol Jo 855, CA 14.5

H

HR Harmer Ltd, Re [1958] 3 All ER 689, [1959] 1 WLR 62, 103 Sol Jo 73, CA 26.10
Hackney Pavilion Ltd, Re [1924] 1 Ch 276, 93 LJ Ch 193, [1923] All ER Rep 524, 130 LT 658 .... 44.7
Head (Henry) & Co Ltd v Ropner Holdings Ltd [1951] 2 All ER 994, [1952] Ch 124 .... 46.1
Hedley Byrne & Co Ltd v Heller & Partners Ltd [1964] AC 465, [1963] 2 All ER 575, [1963] 3 WLR 101, [1963] 1 Lloyd's Rep 485, 8 LDAB 155, 107 Sol Jo 454, HL 8.38, 34.12
Hellenic & General Trust Ltd, Re [1975] 3 All ER 382, [1976] 1 WLR 123, 119 Sol Jo 845 .... 35.1
Hely-Hutchinson v Brayhead Ltd [1968] 1 QB 549, [1967] 2 All ER 14 .... 18.56
Hickman v Kent or Romney Marsh Sheep-Breeders' Association [1915] 1 Ch 881, 84 LJ Ch 688, [1914–15] All ER Rep 900, 59 Sol Jo 478, 113 LT 159 .... 14.12
Holders Investment Trust Ltd, Re [1971] 2 All ER 289, [1971] 1 WLR 583, 115 Sol Jo 202 .... 9.2, 34.20
Holland v Revenue and Customs Comrs [2010] UKSC 51,[2011] 1 All ER 430 .... 18.1
Holwell Securities Ltd v Hughes [1974] 1 All ER 161, [1974] 1 WLR 155, 26 P & CR 544, 117 Sol Jo 912, CA 47.9
Hood Sailmakers Ltd v Axford [1996] 4 All ER 830, [1997] 1 WLR 625, [1997] 1 BCLC 721, [1977] BCC 263 .... 42.39

Horbury Bridge Coal, Iron and Waggon Co, Re (1879) 11 Ch D 109, 48 LJ Ch 341, 27 WR 433, 40 LT 353, CA ... 42.24
Houghton & Co v Nothard, Lowe and Wills Ltd [1928] AC 1, 97 LJKB 76, 4 LDAB 133, [1927] All ER Rep 97, 138 LT 210, 44 TLR 76, HL ... 29.App
House of Fraser plc v ACGE Investments Ltd [1987] AC 387, [1987] 2 WLR 1083, [1987] BCLC 478, 3 BCC 201, 131 Sol Jo 593, [1987] LS Gaz R 1491, 1987 SC (HL) 125, 1987 SLT 421, HL ... 9.1
Household Fire and Carriage Accident Insurance Co v Grant (1879) 4 Ex D 216, 44 JP 152, 48 LJQB 577, 27 WR 858, [1874–80] All ER Rep 919, 41 LT 298, CA ... 47.9

I

Illingworth v Houldsworth. See Yorkshire Woolcombers Association Ltd, Re, Houldsworth v Yorkshire Woolcombers Association Ltd
IRC v Crossman [1937] AC 26, [1936] 1 All ER 762, 80 Sol Jo 485, 52 TLR 415, sub nom Crossman, Re, Re Paulin 15 ATC 94, 105 LJKB 450, 154 LT 570, HL ... 47.1
IRC v Henry Ansbacher & Co [1963] AC 191, [1962] 3 All ER 843, [1962] 3 WLR 1292, 41 ATC 293, [1962] TR 281, 106 Sol Jo 899, sub nom IRC v Henry Ansbacher 8 LDAB 120, HL ... 17.6
IRC v Port of London Authority [1923] AC 507, 92 LJKB 655, 129 LT 365, 39 TLR 498, HL ... 17.1
Inverdeck Ltd, Re [1998] 2 BCLC 242, [1998] BCC 256 ... 44.6
Irvine v Union Bank of Australia (1877) 2 App Cas 366, 46 LJPC 87, 25 WR 682, 37 LT 176, LR 4 Ind App 86, PC ... 17.3
Isle of Thanet Electric Supply Co Ltd, Re [1950] Ch 161, [1949] 2 All ER 1060, 94 Sol Jo 32, CA ... 47.5
Itau BBA International Ltd, Re [2012] EWHC 1783 (Ch), [2013] Bus LR 490 ... 35.36

J

JEB Fasteners Ltd v Marks, Bloom & Co (a firm) [1983] 1 All ER 583, [1982] Com LR 226, CA ... 34.12
Jackson v Turquand (1869) LR 4 HL 305, 39 LJ Ch 11, HL ... 47.9
James v Boythorpe Colliery Co [1890] WN 28, 2 Meg 55 ... 45.7
John Shaw & Sons (Salford) Ltd v Shaw [1935] 2 KB 113, 104 LJKB 549, [1935] All ER Rep 456, 153 LT 245, CA ... 18.29
John Smith's Tadcaster Brewery Co Ltd, Re, John Smith's Tadcaster Brewery Co Ltd v Gresham Life Assurance Society Ltd [1953] Ch 308, [1953] 1 All ER 518, [1953] 2 WLR 516, 97 Sol Jo 150, CA ... 9.1
Jupiter House Investments (Cambridge) Ltd, Re [1985] 1 WLR 975, [1985] BCLC 222, 1 BCC 457, 129 Sol Jo 541, [1985] LS Gaz R 2817 ... 47.51

K

Keenan Bros Ltd, Re [1986] BCLC 242, 2 BCC 98, 970, [1985] IR 401, Ir SC ... 45.4
Kelner v Baxter (1866) LR 2 CP 174, 36 LJCP 94, 12 Jur NS 1016, 15 WR 278, 15 LT 213, [1861–73] All ER Rep Ext 2009 ... 12.1
Kingston Cotton Mill Co (No 2), Re [1896] 2 Ch 279, 65 LJ Ch 673, 3 Mans 171, 40 Sol Jo 531, 74 LT 568, 12 TLR 430, CA ... 8.33
Kirby v Wilkins [1929] 2 Ch 444, [1929] All ER Rep 356, 142 LT 16 ... 34.1
Kuala Pahi Rubber Estates Ltd v Mowbray (1914) 111 LT 1072, CA ... 17.10

L

Ladies' Dress Association Ltd v Pulbrook [1900] 2 QB 376, 69 LJQB 705, 7 Mans 465, 49 WR 6, CA ... 47.25

Land Credit Co of Ireland, Re, Weikersheim's Case (1873) 8 Ch App 831, 42 LJ Ch 435, 21 WR 612, 28 LT 653 ..... 26.1
Lands Allotment Co, Re [1894] 1 Ch 616, 63 LJ Ch 291, 1 Mans 107, 7 R 115, 42 WR 404, [1891–4] All ER Rep 1032, 38 Sol Jo 235, 70 LT 286, 10 TLR 234, CA 18.31
Lee v Lee's Air Farming Ltd [1961] AC 12, [1960] 3 All ER 420, [1960] 3 WLR 758, 104 Sol Jo 869, PC 12.6
Leeds Estate, Building and Investment Co v Shepherd (1887) 36 Ch D 787, 57 LJ Ch 46, 36 WR 322, 57 LT 684, 3 TLR 841 ..... 8.33
Leitch (William C) Bros Ltd, Re [1932] 2 Ch 71, 101 LJ Ch 380, [1932] All ER Rep 892, 148 LT 106 ..... 16.18, 18.38
Letts v IRC [1956] 3 All ER 588, [1957] 1 WLR 201, 35 ATC 367, 49 R & IT 782, [1956] TR 337, 101 Sol Jo 130 ..... 34.20
Leyland Daf Ltd, Re. See Buchler v Talbot
Littlewoods Mail Order Stores Ltd v IRC [1969] 3 All ER 855, [1969] 1 WLR 1241, 45 TC 519, 48 ATC 216, [1969] TR 215, 113 Sol Jo 488, CA 12.6
Lloyd Cheyham & Co Ltd v Littlejohn & Co [1987] BCLC 303, [1986] PCC 389, 2 PN 154 ..... 8.33
Lo-Line Electric Motors Ltd, Re [1988] Ch 477, [1988] 2 All ER 692, [1988] 3 WLR 26, [1988] BCLC 698, 4 BCC 415, 132 Sol Jo 851, [1988] 26 LS Gaz R 41, [1988] NLJR 119 ..... 18.1, 18.14, 18.16
London and General Bank (No 2), Re [1895] 2 Ch 673, 64 LJ Ch 866, 2 Mans 555, 12 R 502, 43 WR 481, 44 WR 80, 1 LDAB 221, [1895–9] All ER Rep 953, 39 Sol Jo 706, 73 LT 304, 11 TLR 573, CA 8.33
London and Northern Bank, Re, ex p Jones [1900] 1 Ch 220, 69 LJ Ch 24, 7 Mans 60, 81 LT 512 ..... 47.9
London Oil Storage Co Ltd v Seear Hasluck & Co (1904) 30 Acct LR 93 ..... 8.38
Longman v Bath Electric Tramways Ltd [1905] 1 Ch 646, 74 LJ Ch 424, 12 Mans 147, 53 WR 480, 92 LT 743, 21 TLR 373, CA 44.8
Lucania Temperance Billiard Halls (London) Ltd, Re [1966] Ch 98, [1965] 3 All ER 879, [1966] 2 WLR 5, 109 Sol Jo 933 ..... 47.55
Lyle & Scott Ltd v British Investment Trust Ltd [1959] AC 763, [1959] 2 All ER 661, [1959] 3 WLR 133, 103 Sol Jo 507, 1959 SC(HL) 64, 1959 SLT 198, HL 44.7
Lyle & Scott Ltd v Scott's Trustees [1959] AC 763, [1959] 2 All ER 661, [1959] 3 WLR 133, 103 Sol Jo 507, 1959 SC(HL) 64, 1959 SLT 198, HL 44.7

M

MB Group Ltd, Re [1989] BCLC 672, 5 BCC 684 ..... 47.57
Macaura v Northern Assurance Co Ltd [1925] AC 619, 94 LJPC 154, 31 Com Cas 10, [1925] All ER Rep 51, 69 Sol Jo 777, 133 LT 152, 41 TLR 447, HL 26.9
McCusker v McRae 1966 SC 253 ..... 36.2
Maidstone Buildings Provisions Ltd, Re [1971] 3 All ER 363, [1971] 1 WLR 1085, 115 Sol Jo 464 ..... 16.18
Mayfair Property Co, Re, Bartlett v Mayfair Property Co [1898] 2 Ch 28, 67 LJ Ch 337, 5 Mans 126, 46 WR 465, [1895–9] All ER Rep 738, 42 Sol Jo 430, 78 LT 302, 14 TLR 336, CA 47.6
Meyer v Scottish Textile and Manufacturing Co Ltd (or Scottish Co-operative Wholesale Society) 1954 SC 381, 1954 SLT 273, Ct of Sess 26.10
Monolithic Building Co, Re, Tacon v Monolithic Building Co [1915] 1 Ch 643, 84 LJ Ch 441, 21 Mans 380, [1914–15] All ER Rep 249, 59 Sol Jo 332, 112 LT 619, CA 40.2A, 40.11, 45.6
Moodie v W and J Shepherd Bookbinders) Ltd [1949] 2 All ER 1044, 94 Sol Jo 95, 1950 SC (HL) 60, HL 44.7
Morgan v Gray [1953] Ch 83, [1953] 1 All ER 213, [1953] 2 WLR 140, 97 Sol Jo 48 ..... 42.4
Morris v Hateley [1999] 13 LS Gaz R 31, (1999) Times, 10 March, CA 26.10
Morris v Kanssen [1946] AC 459, [1946] 1 All ER 586 ..... 18.7
Mosely v Koffyfontein Mines Ltd [1904] 2 Ch 108, 73 LJ Ch 569, 11 Mans 294, 53 WR 140, 48 Sol Jo 507, 91 LT 266, 20 TLR 557, CA 17.10
Musselwhite v C H Musselwhite & Son Ltd [1962] Ch 964, [1962] 1 All ER 201, [1962] 2 WLR 374, 106 Sol Jo 37 ..... 42.19

N

NFU (or National Farmers' Union) Development Trust Ltd, Re [1973] 1 All ER 135, [1972] 1 WLR 1548, 116 Sol Jo 679 .... 35.3
Natal Land and Colonization Co Ltd v Pauline Colliery and Development Syndicate [1904] AC 120, 73 LJPC 22, 11 Mans 29, 89 LT 678, [1900–3] All ER Rep Ext 1050, PC 12.1
National Dwellings Society v Sykes [1894] 3 Ch 159, 63 LJ Ch 906, 1 Mans 457, 8 R 758, 42 WR 696, 38 Sol Jo 601, 10 TLR 563 .... 42.27
National Telephone Co, Re [1914] 1 Ch 755, 83 LJ Ch 552, 21 Mans 217, 58 Sol Jo 12, 109 LT 389, 29 TLR 682 .... 47.5
National Westminster Bank plc v Spectrum Plus Ltd. See Spectrum Plus Ltd, Re; National Westminster Bank plc v Spectrum Plus Ltd
New Bullas Trading Ltd, Re [1994] 1 BCLC 485, [1994] BCC 36, 12 LDAB 569, 12 ACLC 3203, CA 45.4
New Sombrero Phosphate Co v Erlanger. See Erlanger v New Sombrero Phosphate Co
Newborne v Sensolid (Great Britain) Ltd [1954] 1 QB 45, [1953] 1 All ER 708, [1953] 2 WLR 596, 97 Sol Jo 209, CA 12.1
Newman (George) & Co, Re [1895] 1 Ch 674, 64 LJ Ch 407, 2 Mans 267, 12 R 228, 43 WR 483, 39 Sol Jo 346, 72 LT 697, 11 TLR 292, [1895–9] All ER Rep Ext 2160, CA 26.9
Newton v Birmingham Small Arms Co Ltd [1906] 2 Ch 378, 75 LJ Ch 627, 13 Mans 267, 54 WR 621, 2 LDAB 126, 50 Sol Jo 593, 95 LT 135, 22 TLR 664 .... 8.36
Nisbet v Shepherd [1994] 1 BCLC 300, [1994] BCC 91, CA 44.6

O

Ooregum Gold Mining Co of India v Roper [1892] AC 125, 61 LJ Ch 337, 41 WR 90, 36 Sol Jo 344, 66 LT 427, 8 TLR 436, HL 47.24
Oriel Ltd, Re [1985] 3 All ER 216, [1986] 1 WLR 180, [1985] BCLC 343, 10 LDAB 528, 129 Sol Jo 669, [1985] LS Gaz R 3446, CA 30.App

P

Panorama Developments (Guildford) Ltd v Fidelis Furnishing Fabrics Ltd [1971] 2 QB 711, [1971] 3 All ER 16, [1971] 3 WLR 440, 115 Sol Jo 483, CA 13.7
Parker & Cooper Ltd v Reading [1926] Ch 975, 96 LJ Ch 23, [1926] All ER Rep 323, 136 LT 117 .... 42.1
Patent File Co, Re, ex p Birmingham Banking Co (1870) 6 Ch App 83, 40 LJ Ch 190, 19 WR 193, 23 LT 484 .... 17.3
Patrick & Lyon Ltd, Re [1933] Ch 786, 102 LJ Ch 300, [1933] B & CR 151, [1933] All ER Rep 590, 77 Sol Jo 250, 149 LT 231, 49 TLR 372 .... 16.13, 18.38
Pender v Lushington (1877) 6 Ch D 70, 46 LJ Ch 317 .... 26.11
Pendleburys Ltd v Ellis Green & Co (1936) 80 Acct LR 39 .... 8.38
Perkins, Re, ex p Mexican Santa Barbara Mining Co (1890) 24 QBD 613, 59 LJQB 226, 2 Meg 197, 7 Morr 32, 38 WR 710, 6 TLR 203, CA 26.1
Peter's American Delicacy Co Ltd v Heath (1939) 61 CLR 457, Aus HC 14.5
Phonogram Ltd v Lane [1982] QB 938, [1981] 3 All ER 182, [1981] 3 WLR 736, [1982] 3 CMLR 615, [1981] Com LR 228, 125 Sol Jo 527, CA 12.1
Plaut v Steiner (1988) 5 BCC 352 .... 34.20
Poole v National Bank of China Ltd [1907] AC 229, 76 LJ Ch 458, 14 Mans 218, [1904–7] All ER Rep 138, 51 Sol Jo 513, 96 LT 889, 23 TLR 567, HL 47.55
Portbase Clothing Ltd, Re [1993] Ch 388, [1993] 3 All ER 829, [1993] 3 WLR 14, [1993] BCLC 796, [1993] BCC 96, 12 LDAB 332 .... 45.7
Potts' Executors v IRC [1951] AC 443, [1951] 1 All ER 76, 32 TC 211, 44 R & IT 136, [1950] TR 379, [1951] 1 TLR 152, L(TC) 1538, HL 17.1
Precision Dippings Ltd v Precision Dippings Marketing Ltd [1986] Ch 447, [1985] 3 WLR 812, [1985] BCLC 385, 129 Sol Jo 683, CA 22.4, 22.8 22.App
Priceland Ltd, Re, Waltham Forest London Borough Council v Registrar of Companies [1997] 1 BCLC 467, [1997] BCC 207 .... 21.App
Probe Data Systems Ltd (No 3), Re [1992] BCLC 405, [1992] BCC 110, CA 18.14

Prudential Assurance Co Ltd v Newman Industries Ltd (No 2) [1982] Ch 204, [1982] 1 All ER 354, [1982] 2 WLR 31, 126 Sol Jo 32, CA 26.9, 34.12

R

R v Brockley (1993) 99 Cr App Rep 385, [1994] Crim LR 671, [1994] 1 BCLC 606, [1994] BCC 131, 138 Sol Jo LB 5, CA 18.19
R v Campbell (1984) 78 Cr App Rep 95, [1984] BCLC 83, CA 18.11
R v Findlater [1939] 1 KB 594, [1939] 1 All ER 82, 27 Cr App Rep 24, 108 LJKB 289, 31 Cox CC 217, 83 Sol Jo 240, 160 LT 182, 55 TLR 330, CCA 17.6
R v Goodman [1993] 2 All ER 789, 97 Cr App Rep 210, 14 Cr App Rep (S) 147, [1994] 1 BCLC 349, [1992] BCC 625, CA 18.12
R v Holmes (1991) 13 Cr App Rep (S) 29, [1991] Crim LR 790, [1991] BCC 394 .... 18.11
Ramsgate Victoria Hotel Co v Montefiore (1866) LR 1 Exch 109, 4 H & C 164, 35 LJ Ex 90, 12 Jur NS 455, 14 WR 335, 13 LT 715, [1861–73] All ER Rep Ext 2232 .... 47.9
Ratners Group plc, Re [1988] BCLC 685, 4 BCC 293 .... 47.55
Rayfield v Hands [1960] Ch 1, [1958] 2 All ER 194, [1958] 2 WLR 851, 102 Sol Jo 348 .... 14.12
Richborough Furniture Ltd, Re [1996] 1 BCLC 507, [1996] BCC 155 .... 18.14
Robert Stephenson & Co Ltd, Re, Poole v Robert Stephenson & Co Ltd [1913] 2 Ch 201, 83 LJ Ch 121, 20 Mans 358, 56 Sol Jo 648, 107 LT 33, CA 45.7
Robson v Smith [1895] 2 Ch 118, 64 LJ Ch 457, 2 Mans 422, 13 R 529, 43 WR 632, 72 LT 559, 11 TLR 351 .... 17.7
Russell v Northern Bank Development Corpn Ltd [1992] 3 All ER 161, [1992] 1 WLR 588, [1992] BCLC 1016, [1992] BCC 578, [1992] 27 LS Gaz R 33, 136 Sol Jo LB 182, HL 14.5
Russell v Wakefield Waterworks Co (1875) LR 20 Eq 474, 44 LJ Ch 496, 23 WR 887, 32 LT 685, Ct of Ch 26.11

S

Salomon v A Salomon & Co Ltd [1897] AC 22, 66 LJ Ch 35, 4 Mans 89, 45 WR 193, 1 LDAB 240, [1895–9] All ER Rep 33, 41 Sol Jo 63, 75 LT 426, 13 TLR 46, HL 12.6
Saltdean Estate Co Ltd, Re [1968] 3 All ER 829, [1968] 1 WLR 1844, 112 Sol Jo 798 .... 9.1
Saunders v United Kingdom (Application 19187/91) (1996) 23 EHRR 313, [1998] 1 BCLC 362, [1997] BCC 872, 2 BHRC 358, ECtHR 25.3
Scottish Co-operative Wholesale Society Ltd v Meyer [1959] AC 324, [1958] 3 All ER 66, [1958] 3 WLR 404, 102 Sol Jo 617, 1958 SC (HL) 40, HL 26.10
Scottish Insurance Corpn Ltd v Wilsons & Clyde Coal Co Ltd [1949] AC 462, [1949] 1 All ER 1068, [1949] LJR 1190, 93 Sol Jo 423, 65 TLR 354, 1949 SC (HL) 90, 1949 SLT 230, HL 47.5
Secretary of State for Business, Innovation and Skills v Cathie [2012] EWCA Civ 739, [2012] All ER (D) 86 (Jun) 18.14
Selangor United Rubber Estates Ltd v Cradock [1967] 2 All ER 1255, [1967] 1 WLR 1168, 111 Sol Jo 633 .... 18.37
Selangor United Rubber Estates Ltd v Cradock (a bankrupt) (No 3) [1968] 2 All ER 1073, [1968] 1 WLR 1555, [1968] 2 Lloyd's Rep 289, 9 LDAB 66, 112 Sol Jo 744 ... 18.31, 22.8, 22.App
Short v Treasury Comrs [1948] 1 KB 116, [1947] 2 All ER 298, [1947] LJR 1463, 91 Sol Jo 482, 177 LT 338, 63 TLR 472, CA; affd [1948] AC 534, [1948] 2 All ER 509, [1949] LJR 143, 92 Sol Jo 573, 64 TLR 400, HL 26.9
Shuttleworth v Cox Bros & Co (Maidenhead) Ltd [1927] 2 KB 9, 96 LJKB 104, [1926] All ER Rep 498, 136 LT 337, 43 TLR 83, CA 14.5
Sidebottom v Kershaw, Leese & Co Ltd [1920] 1 Ch 154, 89 LJ Ch 113, 64 Sol Jo 114, 122 LT 325, 36 TLR 45, CA 14.5
Siebe Gorman & Co Ltd v Barclays Bank Ltd [1979] 2 Lloyd's Rep 142, 10 LDAB 94 .... 45.4
Simpson v Molson's Bank [1895] AC 270, 64 LJPC 51, 11 R 427, PC 26.1
Simpson v Westminster Palace Hotel Co (1860) 8 HL Cas 712, 6 Jur NS 985, 2 LT 707 .... 26.11
Slavenburg's Bank NV v Intercontinental Natural Resources Ltd [1980] 1 All ER 955, [1980] 1 WLR 1076, 124 Sol Jo 374 .... 17.6

Smith & Fawcett Ltd, Re [1942] Ch 304, [1942] 1 All ER 542, 111 LJ Ch 265, 86 Sol Jo 147, 166 LT 279, CA 44.7
South India Shipping Corpn Ltd v Export-Import Bank of Korea [1985] 2 All ER 219, [1985] 1 WLR 585, [1985] 1 Lloyd's Rep 413, [1985] FLR 106, [1985] BCLC 163, [1985] PCC 125, 129 Sol Jo 268, [1985] LS Gaz R 1005, CA 30.App
Southern Brazilian Rio Grande do Sul Rly Co Ltd, Re [1905] 2 Ch 78, 74 LJ Ch 392, 12 Mans 323, 53 WR 489, 49 Sol Jo 446, 92 LT 598, 21 TLR 451 .... 17.9
Southern Foundries (1926) Ltd v Shirlaw [1940] AC 701, [1940] 2 All ER 445, 109 LJKB 461, 84 Sol Jo 464, 164 LT 251, 56 TLR 637, HL 14.5
Sovereign Life Assurance Co v Dodd [1892] 2 QB 573, 62 LJQB 19, 4 R 17, 41 WR 4, [1891–4] All ER Rep 246, 36 Sol Jo 644, 67 LT 396, 8 TLR 684, CA 35.1
Spectrum Plus Ltd, Re, National Westminster Bank plc v Spectrum Plus Ltd [2005] UKHL 41, [2005] 2 AC 680, [2005] 4 All ER 209, [2005] 3 WLR 58, [2005] 2 Lloyd's Rep 275, [2005] 2 BCLC 269, [2005] NLJR 1045, (2005) Times, 1 July, [2006] 2 LRC 243, [2005] All ER (D) 368 (Jun), sub nom National Westminster Bank plc v Spectrum Plus Ltd [2005] BCC 694 .... 17.5
Stanhope Pension Trust Ltd v Registrar of Companies (1993) 69 P & CR 238, [1994] 1 BCLC 628, [1994] BCC 84, CA 21.App
Staples v Eastman Photographic Materials Co [1896] 2 Ch 303, 65 LJ Ch 682, 40 Sol Jo 513, 74 LT 479, 12 TLR 403, CA 47.5
Steen v Law [1964] AC 287, [1963] 3 All ER 770, [1963] 3 WLR 802, 107 Sol Jo 790, [1964] ALR 398, PC 34.21
Steinberg v Scala (Leeds) Ltd [1923] 2 Ch 452, 92 LJKB 944, [1923] All ER Rep 239, 67 Sol Jo 656, 129 LT 624, 39 TLR 542, CA 26.1
Sticky Fingers Restaurant Ltd, Re [1992] BCLC 84, [1991] BCC 754 .... 42.13
Sussex Brick Co, Re [1904] 1 Ch 598, 73 LJ Ch 308, 11 Mans 66, 52 WR 371, [1904–7] All ER Rep 673, 90 LT 426, CA 38.5

T

Temperance Loan Fund Ltd v Rose [1932] 2 KB 522, 101 LJKB 609, [1932] All ER Rep 690, 147 LT 330, CA 17.6
Tett v Phoenix Property and Investment Co Ltd [1984] BCLC 599; revsd [1986] BCLC 149, 2 BCC 99, 140, 129 Sol Jo 869, [1986] LS Gaz R 116, CA 44.7
Thomas Gerrard & Son Ltd, Re [1968] Ch 455, [1967] 2 All ER 525, [1967] 3 WLR 84, 111 Sol Jo 329 .... 8.33
Tiessen v Henderson [1899] 1 Ch 861, 68 LJ Ch 353, 6 Mans 340, 47 WR 459, 80 LT 483 .... 42.17
Topham v Greenside Glazed Fire-Brick Co (1887) 37 Ch D 281, 57 LJ Ch 583, 36 WR 464, 58 LT 274 .... 17.6
Trevor v Whitworth (1887) 12 App Cas 409, 57 LJ Ch 28, 36 WR 145, [1886–90] All ER Rep 46, 32 Sol Jo 201, 57 LT 457, 3 TLR 745, HL 34.1
Twycross v Grant (1877) 2 CPD 469, 46 LJQB 636, 25 WR 701, 36 LT 812, CA 12.1

U

Unisoft Group Ltd (No 3), Re [1994] 1 BCLC 609, [1994] BCC 766 .... 18.1

W

Wall v Exchange Investment Corpn [1926] Ch 143, 95 LJ Ch 132, [1925] All ER Rep 318, 134 LT 399, CA 42.4
Wall v London and Northern Assets Corpn [1899] 1 Ch 550, 68 LJ Ch 248, 6 Mans 312, 80 LT 70 .... 42.4
Wallersteiner v Moir [1974] 3 All ER 217, [1974] 1 WLR 991, 118 Sol Jo 464, CA 12.6, 22.8, 22.App, 34.20
Webb v Earle (1875) LR 20 Eq 556, 44 LJ Ch 608, 24 WR 46, Ct of Ch 47.5

Welton v Saffery [1897] AC 299, 66 LJ Ch 362, 4 Mans 269, 45 WR 508, [1895–9] All ER Rep 567, 41 Sol Jo 437, 76 LT 505, 13 TLR 340, HL 14.12, 47.24, 47.62
West Canadian Collieries Ltd, Re [1962] Ch 370, [1962] 1 All ER 26, [1961] 3 WLR 1416, 105 Sol Jo 1126 .... 42.19
Westburn Sugar Refineries Ltd, ex p [1951] AC 625, [1951] 1 All ER 881, 95 Sol Jo 317, [1951] 1 TLR 728, HL 47.51
Whaley Bridge Calico Printing Co v Green and Smith (1879) 5 QBD 109, 44 JP 185, 49 LJQB 326, 28 WR 351, 41 LT 674 .... 12.1
White v Bristol Aeroplane Co Ltd [1953] Ch 65, [1953] 1 All ER 40, [1953] 2 WLR 144, 97 Sol Jo 64, CA 9.1
Will v United Lankat Plantations Co Ltd [1914] AC 11, 83 LJ Ch 195, 21 Mans 24, [1911–13] All ER Rep 165, 58 Sol Jo 29, 109 LT 754, 30 TLR 37, HL 47.5
Wood v Odessa Waterworks Co (1889) 42 Ch D 636, 58 LJ Ch 628, 1 Meg 265, 37 WR 733, 5 TLR 596 .... 14.12, 22.10
Woodroffes (Musical Instruments) Ltd, Re [1986] Ch 366, [1985] 2 All ER 908, [1985] 3 WLR 543, [1985] BCLC 227, 10 LDAB 497, 129 Sol Jo 589, [1985] LS Gaz R 3170 .... 45.5
Workvale Ltd (in dissolution), Re [1992] 1 WLR 416, [1991] BCLC 528, [1992] BCC 349, CA 21.App

Y

Yorkshire Woolcombers Association Ltd, Re, Houldsworth v Yorkshire Woolcombers Association Ltd [1903] 2 Ch 284, 72 LJ Ch 635, 10 Mans 276, 88 LT 811, CA; affd sub nom Illingworth v Houldsworth [1904] AC 355, 73 LJ Ch 739, 12 Mans 141, 53 WR 113, 91 LT 602, 20 TLR 633, HL 17.5

Index

A

Abbreviated accounts,
balance sheet format, 5.47
group, 5.76
notes to the accounts, 5.48–5.55
requirements, 5.46
revised, 2.12
small companies, 2.10, 5.46–5.55
special auditor's report, 2.10, 8.31
statutory accounts, 2.5
Accounting policies,
disclosure, 3.16
Accounting principles,
accounts, in accordance with, 3.6, 5.8
Accounting records,
'company records', 16.13, 36.1
components, 36.5
criminal destruction, 36.8
directors' duty, 18.16, 18.27
duty to keep, 18.16, 36.5–36.8
form, 36.5
location and inspection, 36.6
preservation, 36.7
right to inspect, 36.2
statutory accounts, 2.5
strategic reports, 6.6
Accounting reference date,
alteration, 2.19
definition, 2.18
meaning, 2.17
notice to shorten or extend, 2.19
Accounting reference period,
definition, 2.17
determination, 2.17
financial year, 2.17
first, 2.17
Accounting standards,
definition, Appendix 1
disclosure, 2.15, 3.16
Financial Reporting Standards (FRSs), 2.15
International Accounting Standards (IASs), 2.15
International Financial Reporting Standards (IFRSs), 2.15
Statements of Standard Accounting Practice (SSAPs), 2.15
Accounting Standards Board (ASB),
standards issued, 2.15
Accounts,
abbreviated,
–generally, 2.5
–small companies, 2.10
–special auditor's report, 2.10
accounting standards, disclosure, 2.15
adoption of IAS standards, 2.15
'annual accounts', Appendix 1
approval, 2.2
auditor's report, 2.5
availability on website, 2.8
balance sheet,
–filing, 2.10
–introduction, 2.2
–signing, 2.4
–small company statement, 2.10
circulation,
–exceptions, 2.6
–method of sending, 16.28
–private company, 2.6
–public company, 2.6
–recipients, 2.6
–time allowed, 2.6
Companies House, filing, 2.11
delivery to Registrar of Companies, 2.5
directors' obligation, 2.2
euro translation, 2.10
filing,
–auditor's report, 2.10
–abbreviated, 2.10
–Companies House, 2.11
–deadline, 2.11
–euros, translation, 2.10
–failure, 2.10
–medium-sized companies, 2.10
–quoted companies, 2.10
–small companies, 2.10
–unquoted companies, 2.10
general meeting, 2.9
IAS accounts, and, 2.15
laying,
–deadline, 2.9
–general meeting, 2.9
–private companies, 2.9
–public companies, 2.9
medium-sized companies, 2.10
non-statutory,
–generally, 2.5
–statement on, 2.5

Index

Accounts, – *cont.*

overseas company,

–credit or financial institutions, 30.35–30.50

–filing, 30.34

–group, 30.30–30.32

–individual, 30.26–30.29

–introduction, 30.18

–parent law, 30.19–30.24

period for filing, 2.11

preparation, 2.2

private companies, 2.9

publication,

–generally, 2.3

–name of signatory, 2.4

–requirements, 2.5

quoted companies, 2.10

Registrar of companies, and, 2.5

revision of, 2.12

right to demand copies, 2.7

Secretary of State's powers, 2.14

signing,

–generally, 2.2

–name of signatory, 2.4

small companies, 2.2

strategic reports, 2.3

true and fair view, 2.16

website availability, 2.8

Accounts: large companies,

group,

–consistency of accounts within, 3.2

–parent undertaking, 3.40

group accounts,

–acquisition method of accounting, 3.59

–associated undertakings, 3.62, 3.70

–directors' remuneration and benefits, 3.74

–duty to prepare, 3.53–3.55

–elimination of group transactions, 3.58

–form and content, 3.57–3.63

–IAS group accounts, 3.53

–individual profit and loss account, 3.56

–joint ventures, 3.61, 3.69

–membership of certain undertakings, 3.72

–merger method of accounting, 3.59

–minority interests, 3.60

–other significant holdings, 3.71

–parent company is a subsidiary undertaking, 3.73

–related party transactions, 3.63

–related undertakings, 3.64–3.73

–subsidiary undertakings, 3.65–3.68

individual accounts,

–accounting policies, 3.16

–accounting principles, 3.6

–accounting standards 3.16

Accounts: large companies, – *cont.*

individual accounts, – *cont.*

–alternative accounting rules, 3.12–3.13

–auditor's liability limitation, 3.50

–auditor's remuneration, 3.50

–balance sheet formats, 3.4

–balance sheet, notes to the accounts, 3.16–3.24

–charitable company, 3.2

–current assets, 3.9

–debentures, 3.18

–depreciation rules, 3.12

–derivatives 3.15, 3.21

–directors' duty, 3.2

–directors' remuneration and benefits, 3.40–3.47

–disclosures, 3.16–3.31

–dividends, 3.16

–dormant companies, 3.16

–duty to prepare, 3.2

–employee numbers and costs, 3.49

–exceptional items, 3.30

–extraordinary items, 3.30

–fair value, 3.15, 3.21

–financial fixed assets 3.21

–financial instruments, 3.15, 3.21

–fixed assets, 3.8, 3.19

–fixed cumulative dividends, 3.22

–foreign currency translation, 3.16

–form and content, 3.3–3.31

–fungible assets 3.11

–guarantees and other financial commitments, 3.24

–historical cost accounting, 3.7

–IAS accounts, 3.2

–indebtedness, 3.23

–investment property, 3.15, 3.21

–investments, 3.20

–land and buildings, 3.19

–listed companies, 3.16

–living animals and plants, 3.15, 3.21

–loan interest, 3.27

–notes to the accounts, 3.16–3.31

–off-balance sheet arrangements, 3.51

–prior year adjustment, 3.30

–production cost, 3.11

–profit and loss account formats, 3.5

–profit and loss account, notes to the accounts, 3.26–3.31

–provisions, 3.22

–purchase price 3.11

–related party transactions, 3.31

–related undertakings, 3.32–3.40

–remuneration and benefits, 3.41–3.48

–reserves, 3.16, 3.22

Accounts: large companies, – *cont.*
individual accounts, – *cont.*
–revaluation reserve, 3.14
–share capital, 3.18
–significant holding, 3.38
–stock, 3.11
–subsidiary undertakings, 3.33–3.37
–tax, 3.28
–turnover, 3.29
meaning, 3.1
Accounts: medium-sized companies,
balance sheet total, 4.2
disclosures, not required, 4.1
excluded companies, 4.3
form and content, 4.4
group, 4.2
ineligible group, 4.3
meaning, 4.2
parent companies, 4.2
qualifying conditions, 4.2
Registrar of Companies, 4.5
signatory, 4.5
size, 4.2
strategic report, 4.5
Accounts: small companies,
abbreviated accounts, 2.5, 5.46–5.55
–format, 5.47
–group, 5.76
–notes to the accounts, 5.48–5.55
–Registrar of Companies, 5.46
group accounts,
–abbreviated, 5.76
–accounting framework, 5.56
–acquisition and merger accounting, 5.61
–associated undertakings, 5.64, 5.71
–directors' remuneration and benefits, 5.75
–elimination of group transactions, 5.60
–exclusion of subsidiaries, 5.57
–form and content, 5.59
–IAS group accounts, 5.56
–individual profit and loss account, 5.58
–joint ventures, 5.63, 5.70
–minority interests, 5.62
–notes to the accounts, 5.61
–parent undertaking drawing up, 5.38
–Registrar of Companies, 5.76
–related undertakings, 5.65
–subsidiary undertakings, 5.66–5.69
individual accounts,
–accounting principles, 5.8
–alternative accounting rules, 5.14–5.15
–auditor liability limitation agreement, 5.45
–auditor remuneration, 5.45
–balance sheet formats, 5.6
Accounts: small companies, – *cont.*
individual accounts, – *cont.*
–balance sheet, notes to the accounts, 5.19
–directors' remuneration and benefits, 5.39–5.44
–duty to prepare, 5.48
–dividends, 5.18
–exceptional items, 5.30
–excluded companies, 5 3
–extraordinary items, 5.30
–fair value, 5.18, 5.23
–financial commitments, 5.26
–financial instruments, 5.17, 5.23
–fixed assets, 5.21
–formats, 5.6–5.7
–form and content, 5.5
–guarantees, 5.26
–historical cost accounting, 5.9
–indebtedness, 5.24
–investment property, 5.23
–investments, 5.22
–IAS accounts, 5.4
–living animals and plants, 5.23
–notes to the accounts, 5.18–5.30
–prior year adjustments 5.30
–profit and loss account formats, 5.7
–provisions, 5.24
–related undertakings, 5.31–5.38
–reserves, 5.18, 5.24
–revaluation reserve, 5.16
–share capital, 5.20
–strategic report exemption, 20.1
–subsidiary undertakings, 5.32–5.35
–turnover, 5.29
notes to the accounts, 5.18–5.30, 5.61
–abbreviated, 5.48–5.55
–balance sheet, 5.19–5.27
–profit and loss account, 5.28–5.30
size,
–meaning, 5.2
–qualifying conditions, 5.2
Accounts: strategic reports,
conditions for sending out,
–ascertainment of wishes, 6.3
–consultation by notice, 6.4
–prohibitions, 6.2
–relevant consultation, 6.5
defective reports, 6.10
earnings per share, 33.29
form and content,
–directors' emoluments, 6.7
–group accounts, 6.9
–IAS accounts, 6.8
–individual accounts, 6.9

Index

Accounts: strategic reports, – *cont.*
form and content, – *cont.*
–parent company, 6.8
–requirements, 6.6
–summary balance sheet, 6.9
–summary profit and loss account, 6.8
listed companies, 33.29
recipients, 6.1
Acquisition of own shares,
general rule against, 34.1
–exceptions, 34.1
Acquisitions,
method of accounting, 3.59, 5.61
Address,
directors,
–overseas company, 30.12–30.17
–protection from disclosure, 18.67–18.73, 39.19
disclosure, 16.14
registered office,
–change, 37.2
–generally, 16.13–16.16
–requirement, 37.1
–Wales, 37.3
Registrar of Companies,
–application to make unavailable, 39.19
restricting disclosure,
–Companies House guidance booklet, 39.2
service, 16.19
AGM,
See Annual general meeting
AIM (Alternative Investment Market) companies
distributions, 22.16
Allotment of shares,
allowances, 47.10
certificates, 44.2
commissions, 47.10
discounts, 47.10
existing shareholders, 47.13
issue not fully subscribed, 47.20
power of directors, 47.9
pre-emption right,
–communication of pre-emption offers, 47.14
–disapplication, 47.18
–exclusion, 47.17
–exemptions, 47.16
–generally, 47.13
–liability for contravention, 47.15
–saving provisions, 47.19
private companies,
–prohibition of public offers, 47.21
public companies,
–issue not fully subscribed, 47.20
Allotment of shares, – *cont.*
registration, 47.11
return, 47.12
Alternate directors,
articles, 18.10
rights, 18.1
Amalgamations,
See also Reconstructions,
power of court to facilitate, 35.4
Announcements,
takeovers, 48 Appendix
Annual accounts,
See Accounts
Annual confirmation statements
generally, 7.5
Annual general meeting (AGM),
articles of association, 14.6
circulation of members' resolutions, 42.31
laying of accounts, 2.9
notice, 14.6, 42.30
private companies,
–requirement under articles, 2.9
–traded companies that are private, 42.30, 42.31
public companies, 42.30, 42.31
traded companies, 42.38A
Annual report,
financial, listed companies, 33.28
publication of, 2.3
Annual returns,
annual confirmation statements, 7.5
contents, 7.2
duty to deliver, 7.1
failure to deliver,
–generally 7.4
–offence, 29.1
method of filing, 7.3
reforms, 7.5
Registrar's Rules and Powers, 7.2
relevant market, 7.2
traded company, 7.2
Appointment,
auditors, 8.1–8.8
company secretary, 13.3
directors, 18.4–18.10
Approval of accounts,
offence, 2.2
revised accounts, 2.12
signing, 2.2
Approval of corporate governance statements,
signing, 2.2
Arrangements,
articles, 35.5

Arrangements, – *cont.*
court powers, 35.4
court sanction, 35.3
creditors' meetings, 35.2
members' meetings, 35.2
obligations, 35.5
Articles of association,
annual general meeting (AGM), 14.6
alteration,
–charitable company, 14.6
–effect on members, 14.9
–enactment, by, 14.13
–generally, 14.5–14.9
–legal aspects, 14.5
–order, by, 14.13
–practical issues, 14.6
–reconstruction, 35.5
charitable company, 14.4
community interest company, 10.13–10.14
companies not formed under the Companies Acts, 11.12
company name, 14.6
conflicting provisions of CA 2006, 14.6
directors,
–age restrictions, 14.6
–conflicts of interest, 14.6
–disqualification, 18.21
–meetings, 14.6
electronic communication, 14.6
employees, 14.6
enactment, 14.13
entrenched provisions, 14.7
filing requirements, 14.8
form and content, 14.4
general meetings,
–generally, 14.6
–private companies, removal of requirement, 2.9
–requirement, 2.9
guarantee, company limited by, 14.4
limitation of liability, 14.2
Model Articles, 14.6
nomination and information rights, 14.6
objects, 14.6
provisions for entrenchment, 14.7
proxies, 14.6
Registrar of Companies, 14.3, 14.7
requirement, 14.3
share capital,
–authorised, 14.6
–redenomination, 14.6
–reduction, 14.6
single alternate inspection location (SAIL), 7.2
standard, Appendix 4
Articles of association, – *cont.*
unlimited company, 14.4
Asset-locked body,
definition, Appendix 1
Assets,
current assets,
– accounts valuation, 3.9, 5.11
fair value accounting, 3.15, 5.17
fixed assets,
–accounts valuation, 3.8, 5.10
–directors' report disclosure, 20.7
–interests in land, 20.7
–notes to the accounts, disclosure, 3.19, 5.21
fungible, 3.11
historical cost accounting, 3.7, 3.12–3.13, 5.9, 5.14–5.15
Associated undertaking,
definition, 3.62
disclosure requirements, 3.62
takeovers, 48.11
Audit,
See also, Audit committee, Auditor; Auditor's report
corporate governance statement,
–consistency, 8.30
exemption, 2.5
–charitable companies, 8.29
–dormant companies, 8.28
–public sector, 8.29
–small companies, 8.25
–small companies: excluded from exemption, 8.26
–small companies: group, 8.27
–subsidiary companies, 8.27A
requirement, 8.24
second, 8.11
website, publication of concerns, 8.45
Audit committee,
Disclosure and Transparency Rules, 15.3
UK Corporate Governance Code, 15.8
Auditors,
See also Audit; Auditor's report
appointment,
–disclosure of remuneration, 8.7
–disclosure of terms, 8.7
–non-EEA, 8.14
–private companies, 8.2–8.3
–public companies, 8.4–8.5
–requirement, 8.1
–Secretary of State, default appointment, 8.6
–term of office, 8.3, 8.5
ceasing to hold office,
–notification, 8.22

Index

Auditors, – *cont.*
ceasing to hold office, – *cont.*
–statement, 8.21
directors' report,
–disclosure, 20.5
eligibility,
–appropriate qualification, 8.8
–independence, 8.9–8.10
–partnership, 8.12
–supervisory body, 8.8
joint, 8.23
liability,
–generally, 8.38
–indemnity for costs, 8.40
–liability limitation agreements, 8.41–8.44
–protection, 8.39
liability limitation agreements,
–auditors, and, 3.50
–authorisation by members, 8.43
–effect, 8.44
–generally, 8.41
–terms, 8.42
meetings, 8.37
offences, 8.35, 8.45
register of, 8.13
removal from office,
–generally, 8.16
–special notice, 8.18
–special procedure, 8.17
remuneration,
–disclosure, 3.50, 5.45
–fixing, 8.15
resignation of,
–generally, 8.19
–request directors to call general meeting, 8.20, 42.13
–rights, 8.20
resolutions, rights in relation to, 8.37
Auditor's report,
*See also*Audit; Auditor
abbreviated accounts, special report, 2.5, 8.31
ceasing to be exempt, 8.32
debenture holders, right to demand, 2.7
defective accounts or report, following, 8.32
directors' report, revised, 8.32
duties, in connection with, 8.33
filing, 2.10
medium-sized companies, 2.5
members, right to demand, 2.7
offences, 8.35
overseas company, 30.18
publication of accounts, 2.5
signature, 8.34
small companies, 2.5, 2.10
Auditor's report, – *cont.*
standard of care, case law, 8.33
Authorised share capital,
articles of association, 14.6
company formation, 47.6

B

Balance sheet,
definition, Appendix 1
formats,
–abbreviated, 5.47
–generally, 3.4
–small company, 5.6
name of signatory, 2.4
notes to the accounts, 3.17–3.25, 5.19
publication, 2.4
signing, 2.2
size of company,
–medium, 4.2
–small, 5.2
small companies, 2.10
–statement, 2.10
Bankruptcy,
disqualification as director, 18.19
Beneficial interest,
shares, in, 34.29
Bills of exchange,
endorsement, 16.11
Board of directors,
See also Chairman; Chief executive; Directors; Non-executive directors; Senior independent director
accounts,
–approval, 2.2
–name of signatory, 2.4
–signing, 2.2
composition, 15.14
corporate governance, 15.12
corporate governance statements,
–approval, 2.2
–signing, 2.2
diversity, 15.9, 15.14
Guidance on Board effectiveness, 15.13
matters reserved, 15.12
serving on other companies' remuneration committees, 15.14
Women on Boards report, 15.9
Bodies other than companies,
offences under the Companies Acts, 29.1
Body corporate,
meaning, Appendix 1

Bona vacantia,
property,
–dissolution, 21.7–21.8
–restoration, 21.12
Bonus issues,
funds available for, 47.63
procedure, 47.62
share premium account, 46.1
Borrowing,
authorisation, 17.3
charges,
–fixed charges, 45.4
–floating charges, 45.5
–mortgage contrasted with, 45.3
–priority, 45.7
–registration, 45.6
–validity, 45.7
debentures, 17.6–17.17
directors' powers, 17.3
financial assistance, 45.2
fixed charges, 17.5, 45.4
floating charges, 17.5, 45.5
meaning, 17.1
power to borrow, 17.2
'security', 17.5
types, 17.4
Branch register,
overseas branch, 38.7
Building societies,
disqualification of directors, 18.11
Business names,
application for, 27.23
business letters, inclusion, 16.14
company,
–articles of association, 14.6
–change of, compulsory, 27.11
–change of, voluntary, 27.17
–community interest, 10.15
–Companies House search, 27.10
–indication of type, 27.2
–insolvent liquidation, 18.40
–length of, 27.9
–not formed under the Companies Acts, 11.7
–permitted characters, 27.8
–prohibited, 27.3–27.7
–registration of, 27.10
–restoration, 21.11
disclosure requirement, 27.24–27.27
index, Registrar of Companies, 39.12
individuals,
–disclosure, 27.24–27.27
misleading indication of activities, 27.22
overseas company, 30.11
Business names, – *cont.*
partnerships,
–disclosure, 27.24–27.27
restricted and prohibited, 27.19–27.22
–exception for existing lawful business names, 27.21
–misleading indication of activities, 27.22
–sensitive words and expressions, 27.20
similarity to existing, 27.5–27.6, 27.13
Business premises,
disclosure required, 27.26

C

Called-up share capital,
*See also*Share capital
meaning, 47.6, Appendix 1
Calls,
payment for shares, 47.25
Capacity to act,
companies, 16.1
Capital,
See Share capital
Capital redemption reserve,
purchase of own shares, 34.18
Capitalisation,
profits, and, 22.1
Carbon dioxide,
directors' report disclosure, 20.17
Certificates of incorporation,
companies not formed under the Companies Acts, 11.8
details required, 12.4
Registrar of Companies, 39.4
re-registration, 41.7, 41.11, 41.14, 41.17, 41.21
Certification of securities,
share certificates, 44.1–44.13
–allotment, 44.2
–contents, 44.11
–court order to make good default, 44.13
–replacement, 44.11
–transfer, 44.10–44.11
Certified translations,
accounts, 30.4
constitution, 30.4
language requirements, 39.13
overseas companies, 30.4
Registrar of Companies, 39.7
Welsh companies, 39.13
Chairman,
chief executive, separate role, 15.1
corporate governance, 15.10–15.11, 15.13
meetings, 42.23–42.26

Index

Chairman, – *cont.*
Model Code, the, 33 Appendix
role, 18.1
standard Articles of association, Appendix 4
Change of name,
application, 27.17
compulsory, 27.12–27.16
voluntary, 27.17
Charges,
amendment, 40.9A
date of creation,
–after 6 April 2013, 40.2A
–before 6 April 2013, 40.2
debentures, 40.4–40.5
fixed charges, 17.5, 45.4
floating charges, 17.5, 17.14, 45.5
instruments creating, 38.11
meaning, 45.3
notification of addition to or amendment, 40.9A
overseas companies,
–appointment/cessation of receiver, 30.72
–copies of instruments, 30.73
–created on or after 1 October 2011, 30.67A
–debentures, 30.68–30.69
–duty to deliver particulars, 30.66
–ex facie absolute disposition (Scotland), 30.67
–introduction, 30.64
–register, entries of satisfaction and release, 30.70
–rectification of register by court, 30.71
–requiring registration, 30.65
priority, 45.7
public companies, own shares, 34.30
register,
–copies of instruments, 38.11
–entry details, 38.11
–Registrar of Companies, 40.8
–Scotland, 40.16
–special, 40.18
registration, England, Northern Ireland and Wales,
–appointment/cessation of receiver, 40.10
–applicable charges, 40.2
–certain charges affecting land, Northern Ireland, 40.7
–creation of a charge, 40.2
–debentures, 40.4
–endorsement of certificate on debentures, 40.5
–failure to register, 40.2
–introduction, 40.2
–property, 40.3

Charges, – *cont.*
registration, England, Northern Ireland and Wales, – *cont.*
–property situated outside the UK, 40.6
–register, rectification by court, 40.9
–Registrar of Companies, 40.8
registration of enforcement of security, 40.10
registration, property situated outside the UK, 40.6, 40.15
registration, Scotland,
–creation of charge, 40.11
–debentures, 40.14
–ex facie absolute disposition, 40.13
–failure to register, 40.11
–property acquired, 40.12
–property outside UK, 40.15
–rectification by court, 40.17
–register, 40.16
–Registrar of Companies, 40.16
validity, 45.7
Charitable companies,
accounts, 3.2
audit, 8.29
capacity, 16.4
community interest company, 10.6, 10.30
directors,
–duties, 18.26
–transactions, 18.63
model memorandum and articles, 14.4
name,
–disclosure on documents, 16.14
–display, 16.13
objects, 14.6
prospectus, exemption, 32.5
Scotland, 43.6–43.7
Charitable donations,
directors' report, 20.9
Chief executive,
chairman, separate role, 15.1
Model Code, the, 33 Appendix
remuneration committee proposals, 15.10
Circulation,
annual accounts and reports, 2.6
–private company, 2.6
–public company, 2.6
–recipients, 2.6
–time allowed, 2.6
City Code on Takeovers and Mergers,
Code, the, 48 Appendix
Civil penalty,
failure to file accounts and reports, 2.10
Class meeting,
provisions, 42.29
quoted companies, 42.38

Class of shares,
class rights, 9.1
Class rights,
court powers, 9.7
variation of, companies with share capital,
–generally, 9.1
–registration of particulars, 9.3
–right to object, 9.2
variation of, companies without shares, 9.4
–registration of particulars, 9.6
–right to object, 9.5
Code, The
City Code on Takeovers and Mergers, 48 Appendix
Model Code, 33 Appendix
UK Corporate Governance Code, 15.1–15.2
Combined Code
see UK Corporate Governance Code
Committee structure,
audit committee, 15.8
generally, 15.7
matters reserved to the board, 15.12
non-executive directors, 15.13
nomination committee, 15.9
remuneration committee, 15.10
risk committee, 15.11
Common seal,
authority to use, 16.8
engraving of name, 16.8
use abroad, 16.9
Communications,
deemed delivery, 16.34
electronic form,
–alteration of articles of association, 14.6
–by a company, 16.29
–deemed delivery, 16.34
–sent or supplied to company, 16.25
hard copy,
–by a company, 16.28
–deemed delivery, 16.34
–rights of members and debenture holders, 16.33
–sent or supplied to company, 16.24
registered name, and, 16.14
website, by means of, 16.30
Community Interest Companies (CIC),
articles of association,
–alteration of objects, 10.14
–requirement, 10.13
becoming, 10.3
cessation,
–becoming a charity, 10.30
–becoming an industrial and provident society, 10.31
–dissolution, 10.29
Community Interest Companies (CIC), – *cont.*
change of status, 10.27
charities, 10.6, 10.30
disclosure, 10.32
distribution restrictions,
–dividend cap, 10.9
–generally, 10.7
eligible companies, 10.2
excluded companies, 10.2
features, 10.1
fees, Appendix 3
industrial and provident society, 10.31
interest, and,
–generally, 10.7
–interest cap, 10.10
names, 10.15
objects, 10.14
offences, 10.33
Regulator,
–appeals, 10.26
–appointment and removal of directors, 10.21
–appointment and role, 10.17
–appointment of a manager, 10.22
–audit, 10.20
–conditions for exercising powers, 10.18
–dissolution and striking off, 10.25
–investigations, 10.19
–powers in relation to property, 10.23
–transfers of shares, 10.24
report on activities, 10.16
requirements, 10.4–10.5
restrictions on interest,
–generally, 10.7
–interest cap, 10.10
shares, 10.11
type of company, 12.7
Companies Act 2005 (CA2005),
accounting period beginning before date, 2
formation, 1.2
Companies Act 2006 (CA2006),
accounting period beginning after date, 2
individual accounts, 3.2
registration, 1.2
requirements,
Regulations and Orders inclusion, Appendix 1
territorial extent, 1.1
Companies Act individual accounts
See also Individual accounts
components, 3.2
duty to prepare, 3.2

Index

Companies Acts,
Acts referred to, 1.2
former, Appendix 1
meaning, Appendix 1
offences under, 29.1
Companies house,
*See also*Registrar of Companies
acceptance of accounts, 2.11
fees, Appendix 3
forms, Appendix 2
guidance booklets, 39.2
WebFiling, 39.20, Appendix 2
Companies not formed under the Companies Acts,
authorised to register, 11.1
consequences of registration,
–articles of association, 11.12
–capital structure, 11.14
–Companies Act, application of, 11.13
–constitution, 11.11
–deed of settlement, 11.12
–pending legal proceedings, 11.10
–transfer of property, rights and liabilities, 11.9
registration requirements,
–certificate of incorporation, 11.8
–companies other than joint stock companies, 11.4
–consent of members, 11.3
–joint stock company, 11.5
–name, 11.7
–registration as a public company, 11.6
–regulations, 11.2
Company,
definition, Appendix 1
listed, 2.4
meaning of, 1.2
medium-sized, 2.5
records, 16.13, 36.1
registered number, 39.5
service of documents, on, 16.20
small, 2.5
quoted, 2.4
unlimited, 2.5
unquoted, 2.4
Company communications,
deemed delivery, 16.34
electronic form,
–alteration of articles of association, 14.6
–by a company, 16.29
–deemed delivery, 16.34
–sent or supplied to company, 16.25
hard copy,
–by a company, 16.28
–deemed delivery, 16.34
Company communications, – ***cont.***
hard copy, – *cont.*
–rights of members and debenture holders, 16.33
–sent or supplied to company, 16.24
registered name, and, 16.14
website, by means of, 16.30
Company formation and types of companies,
articles of association, 14.3
community interest company, 12.7
formation,
–certificate, 12.4
–method, 12.2
–registration, 12.3, 12.5
guarantee, limited by, 12.7
limited, 12.7
open-ended investment company, 12.7
pre-incorporation contracts, 12.1
private, 12.7
promoters, 12.1
public, 12.7
separate legal person, 12.6
unlimited, 12.7
unregistered, 12.7
Company limited by guarantee,
articles of association, 14.4
meaning, 12.7
Company records,
meaning, 16.13, 36.1
Company seal,
authority to use, 16.8
engraving of name, 16.8
use abroad, 16.9
Company secretaries,
appointment, 13.3
dual capacity, 13.1
exclusion, 13.1
governance statements, signing, 2.2
liability, 13.6
officer, as, 13.6
powers, 13.7
private companies, 13.1
public companies, 13.2
removal, 13.3
service of documents, and, 16.21
status, 13.6
vacancy, 13.5
Compensation for loss of office,
directors, 18.47
Competition Commission (CC),
merger references, 35.33
Confidentiality of communications,
legal proceedings, 29.3

Conflicts of interest,
directors, 14.6
Connected persons,
director, with, 18.1
listed companies, 33.47
related party transactions,
–accounts disclosure, 3.31
–Listing Rules, 33.33
Consolidated accounts,
components, 3.53, 5.56
duty to prepare, 3.53, 5.56
Constitution,
alteration,
–enactment, by, 14.13
–order, by, 14.13
articles of association, 14.3
–alteration of, 14.5–14.9
–filing requirements, 14.8
–form and content, 14.4
–general meetings, 14.6
–objects, 14.6
–provisions for entrenchment, 14.7
definition, Appendix 1
limitation of liability, 14.2
members,
–documents to be provided to, 14.11
–effect of constitution, 14.12
memorandum of association, 14.2
resolutions, 14.10
Contracts,
directors,
–interests in, 18.55–18.57
–service, 18.52–18.54
formalities, 16.5
overseas companies, 30.59–30.63
Contributory,
persons liable to contribute, Appendix 1
Control contract,
right to exercise dominant influence, Appendix 1
Convertible securities,
takeovers, 48.11
Corporate governance,
see also Disclosure Rules; Listing Rules; Transparency Rules
audit committee, 15.8
chairman and chief executive, and, 15.1
company committees,
–audit committee, 15.8
–matters reserved to the board, 15.12
–non-executive directors, 15.13
–nomination committee, 15.9
–remuneration committee, 15.10
–risk committee, 15.11
–structure, 15.7
Corporate governance, – *cont.*
Davies Report, 15.9
Disclosure and Transparency Rules,
–generally 33.39–33.69
–introduction, 15.5
Financial Reporting Council (FRC), and, 15.1
Guidance on Board effectiveness, 15.13
introduction, 15.1
Listing Rules,
–generally, 33.4–33.38
–introduction, 15.4
matters reserved to the board, 15.12
meaning, 15.1
Model Code, the 33 Appendix 1
nomination committee, 15.9
non-executive directors (NEDs),
–generally, 15.13
–introduction, 18.1
regulatory framework,
–Companies Act 2006, 15.6
–Disclosure and Transparency Rules, 15.5
–Listing Rules, 15.4
–UK Corporate Governance Code, 15.2
–UK Stewardship Code, 15.3
remuneration committee, 15.10
risk committee, 15.11
risk management systems, 15.5, 15.11, 15.13
senior independent directors, 15.13
statement,
–approval, 2.2, 15.6
–consistency with accounts, 8.30
–filing, 2.10
–internal control, 15.5
–risk management systems, 15.5
–signing, 2.2, 15.6
Transparency Rules, 33.48–33.69
UK Corporate Governance Code, 15.2
UK regulatory framework, 15.2–15.6
UK Stewardship Code, 15.3
Women on Boards report, 15.9
Corporate Governance Code (The Code),
generally, 15.1–15.2
Corporate governance statement,
approval, 2.2, 15.6
consistency with accounts, 8.30
definition, Appendix 1
filing, 2.10
internal control, 15.5
risk management systems, 15.5
signing, 2.2, 15.6
Corporation,
bodies included as, Appendix 1
Costs,
legal proceedings, 29.9

Index

Court,
granting of relief, 29.9
jurisdictions,
–England and Wales, 29.8
–Northern Ireland, 29.8
–Scotland, 29.8
meaning, 29.8, Appendix 1
Credit institutions,
accounting documents,
–approval, 30.49
–duty to file, 30.37, 30.50
–financial year, 30.41
–group accounts, 30.46–30.48
–individual accounts, 30.42–30.45
–non-compliance, 30.39
–not required under parent law, 30.40
–required to prepare accounts under parent law, 30.36
–statement of details, 30.38
Credit transactions,
directors, 18.62
Creditors,
policy and practice, directors' report, 20.15
reconstructions and mergers, 35.2, 35.44
reduction of share capital,
–objections, 47.55
CREST,
distributions, 22.14
Stock Exchange share transfers, 44.14
Cross-border mergers,
approval of creditors, 35.44
approval of members, 35.43
CA 2006, application of certain provisions, 35.61
compliance and enforcement, 35.59
confidential information, 35.57
consequences of, 35.48
copies of order, 35.49
court approval, 35.47
directors' report, 35.39
documents to be circulated, 35.45
draft terms, 35.38
employee participation,
–confidential information, 35.57
–duty on merging company, 35.53
–election of special negotiating body, 35.55
–generally, 35.52
–negotiation of employee participation agreement, 35.54
–protection for employees and special negotiating body, 35.58
–rules of employee participation in transferee company, 35.56
–special negotiating body, 35.53
independent expert's report, 35.40
Cross-border mergers, – ***cont.***
inspection of documents, 35.41
meaning, 35.36
power of court, 35.46
public notice of receipt of registered documents, 35.42
Registrar of Companies, 35.51
requirements, 35.37
special negotiating body,
–duty on merging company, 35.53
–election of special negotiating body, 35.55
–generally, 35.52
–negotiation of employee participation agreement, 35.54
–protection for employees and special negotiating body, 35.58
independent expert's report, 35.40
transferee company's articles, 35.50
unregistered companies, 35.60
Current assets,
valuation, 3.9, 5.11

D

Deadline,
circulation of accounts, 2.6
directors' reports,
–voting rights, 20.16
filing of accounts, 2.11
keeping of accounting records, 36.7
keeping records of resolutions and meetings, 42.43
laying of accounts before general meeting, 2.9
legal proceedings, 29.4
merger references, 35.33
registration of allotment, 47.11
Dealing in own securities,
insider dealing, 23.7
listed companies, 33.36
Dealings with third parties,
bills of exchange, 16.11
capacity, 16.1–16.4
charitable companies,
– display of name, 16.13–16.14
–generally, 16.4
common seal, 16.8–16.10
company communication provisions, 16.22–16.34
contracts, 16.5
deeds, 16.6
directors,
–power to bind company, 16.2
–transactions involving, 16.3

Dealings with third parties, – *cont.*
display of registered name, 16.13
documents,
–deemed delivery, 16.34
–generally, 16.6–16.7
fraudulent trading, 16.18
promissory notes, 16.11
public notice, 16.17
registered name, 16.13–16.14
registered office, 16.13
seal, 16.8–16.10
service addresses, 16.19
service of documents, 16.20–16.21
trading disclosures, 16.12
Debenture holders,
entitlement to,
–accounts, 2.6–2.7
–auditors' report, 2.7
– copy of deed, 17.16
–directors' remuneration report, 2.7
–directors' report, 2.7
register, 38.12
Debentures,
accounts, disclosures, 3.18
bearer, to, 17.17
convertible, 17.8
debenture stock, 17.7
deposit of, secure advances, 17.13
floating charge, 17.14
irredeemable, 17.9
issue of, 17.10
meaning, Appendix 1
overseas companies, 30.68
perpetual, 17.9
power to re-issue, 17.12
redeemable, 17.12
registration of allotments, 17.11
registration of charges, 40.4
–endorsement of certificate, 40.5
–Scotland, 40.14
Scotland, 17.17, 40.14
secured, 17.14
trustees of, liabilities, 17.15
Debt finance,
borrowing
–authorisation, 17.3
–directors' powers, 17.3
–fixed charge, 17.5
–floating charge, 17.5
–meaning, 17.1
–power to, 17.2
–types of, 17.4
debentures, 17.6–17.17
–convertible, 17.8
Debt finance, – *cont.*
debentures, – *cont.*
–debenture stock, 17.7
–deposit of, secure advances, 17.13
–floating charge, 17.14
–holders, 17.16
–irredeemable, 17.9
–issue of, 17.10
–perpetual, 17.9
–power to re-issue, 17.12
–redeemable, 17.12
–registration of allotments, 17.11
–secured, 17.14
–trustees of, liabilities, 17.15
loan stock, 17.7
Deeds,
execution of, 16.6
De facto director,
meaning, 18.1
Deferred shares,
priority, 26.5
Definitions,
accounting reference date, 2.18
accounting reference period, 2.17
alternate director, 18.1
associated undertaking, 3.62
borrowing, 17.1
capitalisation, 22.1
chairman, 18.1
Companies Acts, 1.2
company, 1.2
company limited by guarantee, 12.7
debenture stock, 17.7
de facto director, 18.1
director, 18.1
directors' service contract, 18.52
distribution, 22.1
executive director, 18.1
financial year, 2.17
fixed charge, 17.5
floating charge, 17.5
glossary, Appendix 1
group, 2.5
guarantee company, 12.7
insider dealing provisions,
–acquire, 23.3
–company, 23.3
–dealing in securities, 23.3
limited company, 12.7
loan stock, 17.7
managing director, 18.1
market abuse, 23.6
medium-sized company, 4.2
members, 26.1

Definitions, – *cont.*
net assets, 22.1
non-executive director, 18.1
ordinary resolution, 42.2
ordinary shares, 47.5
overseas company, 30.1
political donation, 31.2
preference shares, 47.5
private company, 12.7
public company, 12.7
quoted company, 2.4
remuneration, 3.43, 3.50
reserve liability, 47.6
service contract, 18.52
shadow director, 18.1
share, 47.1
share capital,
–allotted, 47.6
–authorised, 47.6
–called-up, 47.6
–equity, 47.6
–issued, 47.6
–uncalled, 47.6
shareholder, 26.1
special resolution, 42.3
small company, 5.2
undistributable reserves, 22.1
unlimited company, 12.7
written resolution, 42.5
Depreciation,
accounting rules, 3.12, 5.10
Derivative claim,
proceedings by a member, 26.12–26.13
Derivatives,
fair value, 3.15
–disclosure, 3.21
–exceptions, 3.15
Development costs,
treatment,
–accounts, 3.8, 5.10
–distributions, 22.3
Directors,
See also Directors remuneration reports; Directors' reports
accounting records, duty, 18.16, 18.27
accounts,
–approval, 2.2
–corporate governance statements, 2.2
–duty to prepare, 2.2, 3.2
–fine, 2.2
–offence, 2.2
–signing, 2.2
address,
–overseas company, 30.12–30.17
Directors, – *cont.*
address, – *cont.*
–protection from disclosure, 18.67–18.73
–register, 38.3
age restrictions, 14.6, 18.6
alternate, 18.1, 18.10
appointment, 18.5
–age limits, 18.6
–restrictions on, 18.6
articles of association, 14.6
body corporate,
–connected with, 18.1
–controlling, 18.1
borrowing, power to authorise, 17.3
breaches, ratification, 18.45
chairman, 18.1
changes in, 18.4
conflicts of interest, 14.6
connected persons, 18.1
contracts with, 18.57
corporate governance statements,
–approval, 2.2
–signing, 2.2
credit transactions, 18.62
criminal liability, 18.41
–relief from, by court, 18.42
cross-border merger, 35.39
de facto, 18.1
declaration of interest, 18.56
delivery of accounts, 2.5
disqualification,
–articles, 18.21
–bankruptcy, 18.19
–competition infringements, 18.17
–contravention, 18.20
–determining unfitness, 18.16
–discretionary grounds, 18.15
–foreign, 18.22
–general misconduct, 18.12
–introduction, 18.11
–mandatory grounds, 18.14
–unfitness, 18.13
–wrongful trading, 18.18
dual capacity,
–company secretary as, 13.1
–limitations, 13.1
duties,
–charitable companies, 18.26
–disclosure of interests in contracts, 18.55
–general, 18.23–18.24
–loans, quasi-loans and credit transactions, 18.60
–not to accept benefits from third parties, 18.24

Directors, – *cont.*
duties, – *cont.*
–serious loss of capital, 47.61
–service contracts, 18.27
–substantial property transactions, 18.58
–to avoid conflicts of interest, 18.24
–to declare interest, 18.24
–to third parties, 18.28
employment, 18.46
executive, 18.1
exit pay, 15.14
fraudulent trading, 18.38
indemnification, 18.43–18.44
–pension scheme, 18.43
–standard articles, 18.43
insurance, 18.43
internal management, 18.27
interests,
–contracts, 18.55
–declaration of, 18.56
–register, 38.13–38.14
–shares, 18.1
–transactions, 18.55
liability, 18.31–18.45, 29.2
–criminal, 18.41
–fraud, 18.34–18.35
–fraudulent trading, 18.38
–indemnification, 18.43
–insurance, 18.43
–re-use of company name, 18.40
–shadow director, 29.2
–summary remedy, 18.37
–winding-up, misconduct in the course of, 18.36
–wrongful trading, 18.39
loans
–consequences of contravention, 18.66
–generally, 18.60
–members' approval, 18.61–18.64
–related arrangements, 18.63
–value, 18.65
managing director, 18.1
meaning of term, 18.1, Appendix 1
meetings, 42.23, 42.39
–articles of association, 14.6
–minutes, 42.40
mergers and divisions,
–explanatory report, 35.21
minimum age, 18.6
minimum number, 18.2
non-executive, 15.13, 18.1
number, 18.2
offences, 18.31–18.45, 29.2

Directors, – *cont.*
other companies' remuneration committees,
–serving on, 15.14
political donations,
–unauthorised, liability for, 31.4
payments for loss of office,
–generally, 18.47
–quoted companies, 18.51A
payments to directors,
–approval by members, 18.48
–legal liabilities, in discharge of, 18.50
–loss of office, for, 18.47, 18.51A
–small, 18.50
–takeover bids, 18.49
–without approval, 18.51
power to bind company, 16.2
powers of, 18.29–18.30
property transactions, 18.58–18.59
quasi-loans, 18.60–18.61
ratification of acts, 18.45
register,
–generally, 38.2
–particulars to be disclosed, 38.2
register of interests,
–generally, 38.13
–reforms, 38.14
Registrar of Companies, notification, 18.4
removal, 18.9
remuneration and benefits,
–accounts disclosure, 3.41–3.48, 3.74, 5.39–5.44
–approval by members, 18.48
–charitable companies, 18.48
–determined by, 18.46
–payment, 18.49
–payment for loss of office, 18.47, 18.51A
–reforms, 15.14
–resolutions, 18.49
–share transfer, 18.49
–shareholder power, and, 15.14
–takeover bids, 18.49
–without approval, 18.51
remuneration committees,
–serving on other companies', 15.14
remuneration report,
See also Directors' remuneration report
generally, 19.1–19.34
residential address,
–overseas company, 30 12–30.17
–protection from disclosure, 18.67–18.73
–register, 38.3
report,
–filing, 2.10
–signing, 2.4

Directors, – *cont.*
retirement, 18.5
rotation, 18.5
secretary, also acting as, 18.3
senior independent director, 15.13
service contracts, 18.52–18.54
–inspection of, 18.54
–long term, members' approval, 18.53
service of documents, on, 16.21
shadow, 18.1, 29.2
shareholder power, and, 15.14
substantial property transactions, 18.58–18.59
–contravention, 18.59
transactions involving, 16.3
true and fair view,
–duty in relation to, 2.16
UK Corporate Governance Code, 15.2
wrongful trading, 18.39
Directors' remuneration,
accounts disclosure, 3.41–3.48, 3.74, 5.39–5.44
approval by members, 18.48
charitable companies, 18.48
determined by, 18.46
payment, 18.49
payments for loss of office,
–generally, 18.47
–quoted companies, 18.51A
reforms, 15.14
resolution, voting on, 18.49
share transfer, 18.49
shareholder power, and, 15.14
takeover bids, 18.49
without approval, 18.51
Directors' remuneration policy,
See also Directors' remuneration reports
appointment package, 19.8
considerations,
–employment conditions, 19.12
–shareholder views, 19.13
contents,
–consideration of employment conditions, 19.12
–consideration of shareholder views, 19.13
–future policy table, 19.7
–illustrations of application, 19.10
–introduction, 19.6
–payment for loss of office, 19.11
–principles for package on appointment, 19.8
–service contracts, 19.9
defective policy, 19.28
employment conditions, 19.12
future table, 19.7
generally, 19.3
Directors' remuneration policy, – *cont.*
illustrations of application, 19.10
payment for loss of office, 19.11
service contracts, 19.9
shareholder views, 19.13
statement, 19.5
Directors' remuneration reports,
*See also*Directors' remuneration policy
auditor's responsibility, 8.33
'amounts to be shown', 19.3
approval, 19.27
compensation, 19.3
consideration of matters, 19.4
contents,
–introduction, 19.14
–payments for loss of office, 19.21
–payments to past directors, 19.20
–pensions, 19.18
–percentage change in remuneration of CEO, 19.24
–performance graph and table, 19.23
–relative importance of spend on pay, 19.25
–scheme interests, 19.19
–share interests, 19.22
–shareholdings, 19.22
–single total figure for each director, 19.16–19.17
–statement by chair of remuneration committee, 19.15
–statement of voting at general meeting, 19.26
debenture holders' right to demand, 2.7
defective reports, 19.28
definitions, 19.3
disclosure, 19.1
duty of directors, 19.1
false statements, 19.34
filing, 2.10
general provisions, 19.2
interpretation, 19.3
liability for false or misleading statements, 19.34
members,
–approval, 19.27
–right to demand, 2.7
misleading statements, 19.34
payments for loss of office, 19.21
payments to past directors, 19.20
pension scheme,
–definition, 19.3
–generally, 19.18
percentage change in remuneration of CEO, 19.24
performance graph, 19.23
'performance measure', 19.3

Directors' remuneration reports, – *cont.*
performance table, 19.23
'performance target', 19.3
preparation, 19.1
relative importance of spend on pay, 19.25
revision,
–approval, 19.29
–delivery to Registrar of Companies, 19.33
–effect, 19.30
–generally, 2.12
–introduction, 19.28
–laying, 19.32
–publication, 19.31
performance graph, 19.15
publication, 2.4
'qualifying services', 19.3
'retirement benefits', 19.3
revisions, 19.27
'scheme', 19.3
scheme interests, 19.19
share interests, 19.22
shareholdings, 19.22
signing, 19.27
single total figure for each director, 19.16–19.17
statement by chair of remuneration committee, 19.15
statement of voting at general meeting, 19.26
Directors' reports,
See also Directors; Directors' remuneration reports
approval, 20.18
charitable donations, 20.9
contents, 20.1–20.16
corporate governance statements, 20.16
creditors, policy and practice, 20.15
debenture holders' right to demand, 2.7
defective reports, 20.19
disabled persons, 20.13
disclosure of information to auditors, 20.5
dividends, 20.4
employee involvement, 20.14
failure to comply, 20.1
false statements, 20.25
filing, 2.10
financial instruments, 20.10
greenhouse gas emissions, 20.17
group accounts, 20.1
indemnity provisions, 20.6
interests in land, 20.7
liability for false statements, 20.25
listed companies, 20.1
medium-sized companies, 20.1
members' right to demand, 2.7
misleading statements, 20.25
Directors' reports, – *cont.*
names of directors, 20.2
overseas company, 30.18
penalties, 20.1
political donations, 20.8
principal activities, 20.3
publication, 2.4
qualifying indemnity provisions, 20.6
revision,
–approval, 20.20
–delivery to Registrar of Companies, 20.24
–effect, 20.21
–generally, 20.19
–laying, 20.23
–publication, 20.22
–signing, 20.20
right to demand, 2.7
Secretary of State's power, 2.14
securities traded on regulated market, 20.16
shares, own, 20.12
signing, 2.4, 20.18
small companies, 20.1
Disabled persons, employment of,
directors' report, 20.13
Disclosed interests,
public company shares register, 38.8–38.10
–location and inspection, 38.9
–removal of entries, 38.10
Disclosure,
business name, 27.24–27.27
charitable companies,
–fact that is company, 16.13, 16.14
community interest companies, 10.32
notes to the accounts,
–large companies, 3.16–3.31
–small companies, 5.18–5.30
registered name,
–generally, 16.14
–overseas companies, 30.12–30.17
trading information, 16.12–16.16
Disclosure Rules (listed companies),
audit committees, 15.8
corporate governance, 15.5
general provisions, 33.40
inside information,
–control, 33.45
–delaying disclosure, 33.44
insider lists, 33.46
modifying or dispensing with, 33.39
publication of information on the internet, 33.42
requirement to disclose, 33.41
synchronised release of information, 33.43

Disclosure Rules (listed companies), – *cont.*
transactions,
–connected persons, 33.47
–persons discharging managerial responsibilities, 33.47
Disqualification of directors,
articles, 18.21
bankruptcy, 18.19
competition infringements, 18.17
contravention, 18.20
determining unfitness, 18.16
discretionary grounds, 18.15
foreign, 18.22
general misconduct, 18.12
introduction, 18.11
mandatory grounds, 18.14
unfitness, 18.13
wrongful trading, 18.18
Dissolution,
Companies House guidance booklet, 39.2
notification of members, 21.5
property, 21.7–21.8
–bona vacantia, 21.8
–disclaimer, 21.8
striking off, 21.1–21.6
–objections to, 21.6
–voluntary, 21.2–21.6
Registrar of Companies, power, 21.1
Distributions,
accounting requirements,
–generally, 22.4–22.7
–interim accounts, 22.4
companies on LSE main market, 22.12
development costs, treatment of, 22.3
dividends,
–directors' report, 20.4
–fixed cumulative, disclosure, 3.22
–LSE main market, 22.12
–notes to the accounts, disclosure, 3.16
–payment of, 22.10
–small company, 5.18
–statement of, listed companies, 33.27
in kind, 22.7
listed companies,
–AIM companies, 22.16
–continuing obligations, 22.13
–CREST, 22.14
–introduction, 22.11
–LSE dividend procedure timetable, 22.15
–LSE main market, 22.12
–uncertified securities, 22.14
meaning, 22.1
procedures, 22.10
profits available for, 22.2–22.3
Distributions, – *cont.*
realised losses and profits, 22.6
restrictions on, 22.1, 22.9
revaluation, fixed assets, 22.6
successive, 22.5
unlawful, 22.8
Diversity in the boardroom,
corporate governance, 15.2
Women on Boards report, 15.9
Dividends,
See also Distributions
companies on LSE main market, 22.12
directors' report, 20.4
fixed cumulative, disclosure, 3.22
notes to the accounts, disclosure, 3.16
payment of, 22.10
small company, 5.18
statement of, listed companies, 33.27
Divisional restructuring,
allotment of shares restrictions, 35.28
approval of articles, 35.26
directors' explanatory report, 35.21
draft terms of scheme, 35.19
exceptions to rules, 35.29
expert's report, 35.22, 35.31
inspection of documents, 35.24
liability for defaults, 35.30
members' approval, 35.20
protection of holders with special rights, 35.27
report on material changes in assets, 35.25
supplementary accounting statement, 35.23
website, availability of documents, 35.24A
Documents,
business name, 27.25
charitable companies, 16.14
cross-border mergers, 35.45
delivery,
–manner, 39.6
–public notice of receipt, 39.8
–Registrar of Companies, 39.6
–requirements for proper, 39.7
execution of, 16.6, 30.59–30.62
forms, Appendix 2
investigations,
–destruction of documents, 25.16
–generally, 25.3, 25.17
meaning, 29.7
offence suspected,
–production and inspection, 29.7
particulars to be disclosed, 16.14
registered name, 16.14
service of, 30.56
–on company, 16.20
–on directors, 16.21

Documents, – *cont.*
service of, – *cont.*
–on secretaries, 16.21
takeovers, 48 Appendix
WebFiling, 39.20
website,
–divisions, 35.24A, 35.30A
–accounts, 2.8
–communication, 16.30
–mergers, 35.13A, 35.13B
–resolutions, 42.11
Dominion register,
overseas branch, 38.7
Dormant companies,
acting as agents, 3.16
audit exemption, 8.28
definition, Appendix 1

E

Earnings per share,
strategic reports, 33.29
EEA state,
definition, Appendix 1
European Economic Area, agreement on the, Appendix 1
non-EEA
–Disclosure and Transparency Rules, 33.68
Effectiveness,
Guidance on Board effectiveness, 15.13
Electronic form,
communications,
–alteration of articles of association, 14.6
–by a company, 16.29
–deemed delivery, 16.34
–sent or supplied to company, 16.25
documents, 42.10
meaning, Appendix 1
meetings and voting, 42.12A
notice of meeting, 42.15
WebFiling, 39.20
Electronic means,
deemed delivery, 16.34
definition, Appendix 1
Employees,
accounts, disclosure, 3.49
articles of association, 14.6
directors' report, 20.14
cross-border merger,
participation, 35.52–35.59
number of, size of company,
–medium, 4.2
–small, 5.2
Employees, – *cont.*
share scheme, Appendix 1
Entrenchment,
provisions, 14.7
Entry and search,
premises, 25.13, 25.19–25.20
Equity share capital,
classification of shares, 47.5
meaning, Appendix 1
European Community (EC),
member states, 2.19
European Economic Area (EEA),
states, 2.19, Appendix 1
Euros,
filing of accounts, 2.11
Exceptional items,
notes to the accounts disclosure, 3.30, 5.30
Executive director,
*See also*Directors,
role, 18.1
Executive remuneration,
reforms, 15.14
shareholder power, 15.14
Exemption,
audit, 2.5
Exit payments,
shareholder power, 15.14
Expenses,
power of court to grant relief, 29.9
security for costs (Scotland), 29.10
Extraordinary general meeting (EGM),
term not used in CA 2006, 14.6
Extraordinary item,
notes to the accounts disclosure, 3.30, 5.30
Extraordinary resolution,
term not used in CA 2006, 14.6,42.1

F

Fair value,
accounting, 3.15, 5.17
determination, 3.15
disclosure, 3.21, 5.23
Fair value reserve,
large companies, 3.15, 3.21
small companies, 5.17, 5.23
False statement,
offence, 39.18
Fees,
payable by companies/to companies, Appendix 3
Fellow subsidiary undertakings,
definition, Appendix 1

Index

Filing accounts,
abbreviated accounts, 2.10
–special auditor's report, 2.10
Companies House
–acceptance of accounts, 2.11
deadline, 2.11
euros, translation, 2.10
failure to file, 2.10
medium-sized companies, 2.10
–auditor's report, 2.10
–directors' report, 2.10
period for filing, 2.11
quoted companies, 2.10
–auditor's report, 2.10
–corporate governance statement, 2.10
–directors' remuneration report, 2.10
–directors' report, 2.10
small companies, 2.10
–auditor's report, 2.10
–balance sheet statement, 2.10
–directors' report, 2.10
time period allowed, 2.11
unquoted companies, 2.10
–auditor's report, 2.10
–corporate governance statement, 2.10
–directors' report, 2.10
WebFiling, 39.20
Filing obligations,
*See also*Registrar of Companies
accounts, 2.10
articles of association, 14.8
enforcement, 39.16
Financial assistance,
giving, 45.2
purchase of own shares, 34.20
Financial commitments,
accounts disclosure, 3.24, 5.26
Financial Conduct Authority (FCA),
*See also*Insider dealing and Market abuse
audit committees, 15.8
disclosure
–public company shares, 38.8
Financial Stability and Market Confidence Sourcebook (FINMAR), 23.13
listed companies,
–appointment of investigators, 33.71
–exemption from liability in damages, 33.72
Listing Rules, 33.4
prospectuses,
–application, 32.13
–appointment of investigators, 32.24
–approval by, 32.13–32.14
–exemption from liability, 32.25
–power to suspend, 32.16
Financial Conduct Authority (FCA), – *cont.*
suspending of listing, 33.14
Financial fixed assets,
fair value accounting, 3.21, 5.23
Financial instruments,
directors' report, 20.10
fair value accounting, 3.15, 3.21, 5.17, 5.23
Financial Reporting Council (FRC),
corporate governance responsibility, 15.1
Guidance on Board effectiveness, 15.13
UK Stewardship Code, 15.3
Financial Reporting Review Panel,
authorisation, 2.14
Financial Reporting Standards (FRSs),
disclosure, 2.15
Financial Services Authority (FSA),
*See*Financial Conduct Authority (FCA)
Financial statements,
*See*Accounts: large companies; Accounts: medium-sized companies; Accounts: small companies; Accounts: strategic reports
Financial year,
definition, Appendix 1
statutory accounts, for 2.5
Fines,
offences under the Companies Acts,
–standard scale, 29.1
–statutory maximum, 29.1
–summary conviction, removal of upper limit, 29.1
Firm,
meaning, Appendix 1
Fixed assets,
accounts,
–notes to the accounts, disclosure, 3.19, 5.21
–valuation, 3.8, 5.10
directors' report disclosure,
–interests in land, 20.7
Fixed charges,
debentures, 17.5
generally, 45.4
mortgage contrasted with, 45.3
priority, 45.7
registration, 45.6
validity, 45.7
Floating charges,
debentures, 17.5, 17.14
generally, 45.5
mortgage contrasted with, 45.3
priority, 45.7
registration, 45.6
Scotland,
–alteration, 43.5

Floating charges, – *cont.*
Scotland, – *cont.*
–introduction, 43.2
–priority, 43.4
–winding up, 43.3
validity, 45.7
Foreign currency translation,
accounts disclosure, 3.16
Formation of companies,
articles of association, 14.3
certificate, 12.4
memorandum of association, 14.2
method, 12.2
pre-incorporation contracts, 12.1
promoters, 12.1
registration, 12.3, 12.5
Formats,
balance sheet, 3.4
–abbreviated accounts, 5.47
–small company, 5.6
profit and loss account, 3.5
–small company, 5.7
Former Companies Acts,
meaning, Appendix 1
Forms,
general, Appendix 2
Fraud,
creditors, of, 18.35
trading, 16.18, 18.38
winding up, 18.36
–in anticipation of, 18.34
Fraudulent trading,
intent, 16.18
offence 16.18
FRC (Financial Reporting Council),
corporate governance responsibility, 15.1
Guidance on Board effectiveness, 15.13
Friendly societies,
disqualification of directors, 18.11
FSA (Financial Services Authority),
*See*Financial Conduct Authority (FCA)
Fungible assets,
valuation, 3.11

G

Gazette,
meaning, Appendix 1
publication in, 39.8
–alternative to, 39.17
General meetings,
articles, of association, 14.6
circulation of members' resolutions, 42.31
General meetings, – *cont.*
laying of accounts, 2.9
–deadline, 2.9
notice, 14.6,42.30
private companies,
–removal of requirement for, 2.9
–requirement under articles, 2.9
–traded companies that are private, 42.30, 42.31
public companies, 42.30, 42.31
traded companies, 42.38A
Goodwill,
accounts treatment, 3.8, 5.10
Governance,
*see*Corporate Governance
Greenhouse gas emissions,
directors' report disclosure, 20.17
Group,
directors' report, 20.1
meaning, 2.5, Appendix 1
size of group,
–medium, 4.2
–small, 5.2
Group accounts,
acquisition method of accounting, 3.59
associated undertakings,
–form and content, 3.62
–related undertakings, 3.70
consistency, 3.2
directors' remuneration and benefits, 3.74
duty to prepare, 3.53–3.55
elimination of group transactions, 3.58
form and content, 3.57–3.63
IAS group accounts, 3.53
individual profit and loss account, 3.56
joint ventures,
–form and content, 3.61
–related undertakings, 3.69
membership of certain undertakings, 3.72
merger method of accounting, 3.59
minority interests, 3.60
other significant holdings, 3.71
overseas companies, and, 30.30–30.32, 30.46–30.48
parent company is a subsidiary undertaking, 3.73
related party transactions, 3.63
related undertakings, 3.64–3.73
small companies and micro-entities, and,
–abbreviated, 5.76
–accounting framework, 5.56
–acquisition and merger accounting, 5.61
–associated undertakings, 5.64, 5.71
–directors' remuneration and benefits, 5.75
–elimination of group transactions, 5.60

Group accounts, – *cont.*
small companies and micro-entities, and, – *cont.*
–exclusion of subsidiaries, 5.57
–form and content, 5.59
–IAS group accounts, 5.56
–individual profit and loss account, 5.58
–joint ventures, 5.63, 5.70
–minority interests, 5.62
–notes to the accounts, 5.61
–parent undertaking drawing up, 5.38
–Registrar of Companies, 5.76
–related undertakings, 5.65
–subsidiary undertakings, 5.66–5.69
subsidiary undertakings, 3.65–3.68
Group reconstruction relief,
share premium, 46.3
Group undertakings,
meaning, Appendix 1
Guarantee companies
articles of association, 14.4
formation, 12.3
generally, 12.7
Guarantees,
accounts disclosure, 3.24, 5.26
Guidance booklets,
Companies House, 39.2

H

Half-yearly reports,
listed companies, 33.30
Hard copy form,
communications,
–by a company, 16.28
–deemed delivery, 16.34
–rights of members and debenture holders, 16.33
–sent or supplied to company, 16.24
meaning, Appendix 1
Higgs review,
non-executive directors, 15.13
Historical cost accounting,
alternative rules,
–disclosure, 3.13, 5.15
–generally, 3.12, 5.14
rules,
–current assets, 3.9, 5.11
–fixed assets, 3.8, 5.10
–production cost, 3.11, 5.13
–purchase price, 3.11, 5.13
HM Revenue and Customs (HMRC),
disclosure of tax information by, 2.14
Holding companies,
financial assistance, prohibited, 34.20
group reconstruction relief, 46.3
parent company, meaning, Appendix 1
overseas companies, 30.30
share premium, 46.2
subsidiary being member of, prohibition, 26.7

I

IAS (International Accounting Standards)
accounts, 2.15
compliance with, 2.2
group accounts, 3.53, 5.56
individual accounts, 3.2, 5.4
IAS accounts
changing from, 3.2, 3.53, 5.4, 5.56
group, 3.53, 5.56
individual, 3.2, 5.4
IAS Regulation,
meaning, Appendix 1
Income and expenditure account,
not trading for profit,
profit and loss account equivalent, Appendix 1
Income statement,
IAS accounts,
profit and loss account equivalent, Appendix 1
Incorporation,
articles of association, 14.3
certificate, 12.4
formation method, 12.2
registration, 12.3, 12.5
Indemnity,
directors' protection, 18.43–18.44
directors' report disclosure, 20.6
insurance, 18.43
Index of company names,
Registrar of Companies, 39.12
Indictments,
offences under Companies Acts, 29.1
Individual accounts,
components, 3.2
credit institutions, 30.42–30.45
duty to prepare, 3.2
financial institutions, 30.42–30.45
generally, 3.2
large companies,
–accounting policies, 3.16
–accounting principles, 3.6
–accounting standards 3.16
–alternative accounting rules, 3.12–3.13

Individual accounts, – *cont.*
large companies, – *cont.*
–auditor's liability limitation, 3.50
–auditor's remuneration, 3.50
–balance sheet formats, 3.4
–balance sheet, notes to the accounts, 3.16–3.24
–charitable company, 3.2
–current assets, 3.9
–debentures, 3.18
–depreciation rules, 3.12
–derivatives 3.15, 3.21
–directors' duty, 3.2
–directors' remuneration and benefits, 3.40–3.47
–disclosures, 3.16–3.31
–dividends, 3.16
–dormant companies, 3.16
–duty to prepare, 3.2
–employee numbers and costs, 3.49
–exceptional items, 3.30
–extraordinary items, 3.30
–fair value, 3.15, 3.21
–financial fixed assets 3.21
–financial instruments, 3.15, 3.21
–fixed assets, 3.8, 3.19
–fixed cumulative dividends, 3.22
–foreign currency translation, 3.16
–form and content, 3.3–3.31
–fungible assets 3.11
–guarantees and other financial commitments, 3.24
–historical cost accounting, 3.7
–IAS accounts, 3.2
–indebtedness, 3.23
–investment property, 3.15, 3.21
–investments, 3.20
–land and buildings, 3.19
–listed companies, 3.16
–living animals and plants, 3.15, 3.21
–loan interest, 3.27
–notes to the accounts, 3.16–3.31
–off-balance sheet arrangements, 3.51
–prior year adjustment, 3.30
–production cost, 3.11
–profit and loss account formats, 3.5
–profit and loss account, notes to the accounts, 3.26–3.31
–provisions, 3.22
–purchase price 3.11
–related party transactions, 3.31
–related undertakings, 3.32–3.40
–remuneration and benefits, 3.41–3.48
–reserves, 3.16, 3.22
–revaluation reserve, 3.14

Individual accounts, – *cont.*
large companies, – *cont.*
–share capital, 3.18
–significant holding, 3.38
–stock, 3.11
–subsidiary undertakings, 3.33–3.37
–tax, 3.28
–turnover, 3.29
small companies,
–accounting principles, 5.8
–alternative accounting rules, 5.14–5.15
–auditor liability limitation agreement, 5.45
–auditor remuneration, 5.45
–balance sheet formats, 5.6
–balance sheet, notes to the accounts, 5.19
–directors' remuneration and benefits, 5.39–5.44
–duty to prepare, 5.48
–dividends, 5.18
–exceptional items, 5.30
–excluded companies, 5.3
–extraordinary items, 5.30
–fair value, 5.18, 5.23
–financial commitments, 5.26
–financial instruments, 5.17, 5.23
–fixed assets, 5.21
–formats, 5.6–5.7
–form and content, 5.5
–guarantees, 5.26
–historical cost accounting, 5.9
–indebtedness, 5.24
–investment property, 5.23
–investments, 5.22
–IAS accounts, 5.4
–living animals and plants, 5.23
–notes to the accounts, 5.18–5.30
–prior year adjustments, 5.30
–profit and loss account formats, 5.7
–provisions, 5.24
–related undertakings, 5.31–5.38
–reserves, 5.18, 5.24
–revaluation reserve, 5.16
–share capital, 5.20
–strategic report exemption, 20.1
–subsidiary undertakings, 5.32–5.35
–turnover, 5.29
strategic reports, and, 6.9
Information,
investigations, 25.12–25.18, 25.21
–false, punishment, 25.17
privileged, 25.21
Information rights,
nomination of third party, 14.6

Index

Insider dealing,
control of inside information, 33.41
circumstances constituting, 23.2
defences, 23.5
definitions, 23.3
legislation, 23.1
market abuse, 23.7
market information, 23.3
penalties, 23.4
prevention, 33.41
price sensitive information, 23.3
securities, 23.3
Insolvent liquidation,
members, 26.11
unlawful distributions, 22.8
voluntary striking off, 21.2
wrongful trading, 18.39
Inspection of records,
availability for, 36.2
specified types, 36.2
Institutional investors,
exercise of voting rights, 42.45
Insurance,
directors, 18.43
Intangible assets,
accounting, 3.4, 3.12, 5.6
overseas companies, 30.29
Interests in public company shares,
investigation of, 24.2
members,
–investigation required by, 24.4
–report to, 24.5
notice to confirm, 24.2
–failure to comply, 24.3
obligation to disclose, 24.1
orders,
–for sale, 24.9
–restriction, 24.6–24.8
restriction orders, 24.6
–penalty for evasion, 24.7
–relaxation and removal of, 24.8
Internal control,
audit, 8.30
company committee structure, 15.7
corporate governance statements, 15.5
Internal management,
duties of directors, 18.27
International Accounting Standard Board (IASB),
standards issued, 2.15
International Accounting Standards (IAS),
accounts, 2.15
change of circumstance, 5.4, 5.56
compliance with, 2.2
International Accounting Standards (IAS), – *cont.*
IAS group accounts, 3.53, 5.4
IAS individual accounts, 3.2, 5.56
meaning, appendix 1
Internet,
WebFiling
–Companies House, 39.20
website,
–accounts availability, 2.8
–communication by means of, 16.30
–listed company, 33.42
–mergers, 35.13A–35.13B
–publication of audit concerns, 8.45
–publication of resolution, 42.11
–registered name, 16.14
–specified information, 16.14
Investigations,
company ownership, 25.7
documents,
–destruction, 25.16
–generally, 25.3, 25.17
expenses, 25.5
evidence, 25.3
information,
–disclosure, 25.18
–false, punishment for, 25.17
inspectors' 25.9
–reports, 25.4
interest in shares, 25.8
overseas companies, 25.22
premises, power to enter,
–generally, 25.13, 25.19–25.20
–procedure, 25.20
–written statement, 25.20
privileged information, 25.21
requisition and seizure of documents, 25.11–25.18
restrictions on shares, 25.23–25.25
Secretary of State powers, 25.1–25.25
Investment companies,
open-ended, 12.7
voting rights, 42.45
Investment property,
accounts
–disclosure, 3.21, 5.23
–valuation, 3.15, 5.17
Investments,
accounts disclosure, 3.20, 5.22
Investors,
See also Members
institutional, 42.45
prospectuses,
–generally, 32.22

Investors, – *cont.*
prospectuses, – *cont.*
–remedies, 32.21
Isle of Man,
takeovers, 48.2
Issued share capital,
See also Share capital
meaning, 47.6

J

Joint shareholders,
transmission of shares, 44.9
voting, 42.4
Joint stock company,
not formed under the Companies Acts, 11.5–11.6
Joint venture,
group accounts, 3.61, 5.63
disclosure, 3.69, 5.70

L

Land and buildings,
accounts disclosure, 3.19
directors' report, 20.7
Northern Ireland, registration of charges, 40.7
Language requirements,
accounts, 30.4
constitution, 30.4
Registrar of Companies,
–translation, 39.13
–transliteration, 39.14
Legal proceedings,
consent required, 29.5
court, the,
–granting of relief, 29.9
–jurisdictions, 29.8
directors' disqualification, 18.11–18.22
documents,
–production and inspection, 29.7
indictment, 29.1
legal professional privilege, 29.3
liability of officer, 29.2
Northern Ireland,
–court, the, 29.8
–unincorporated bodies, 29.6
punishment,
–indictment, 29.1
–standard scale, fines, 29.1
–summary conviction, 29.1
Legal proceedings, – *cont.*
Scotland,
–court, the, 29.8
–expenses, 29.10
–unincorporated bodies 29.6
summary conviction, 29.1
summary proceedings,
–time limit, 29.4
–venue, 29.4
unincorporated bodies,
–proceedings under Companies Acts, 29.6
Legal professional privilege,
confidentiality of communications, 29.3
refusal to disclose, 25.21, 29.3
Letters, business,
disclosure of information, 16.14
Liability,
bodies other than companies, 29.2
directors, 18.31–18.45, 29.2
–criminal, 18.41
–fraud, 18.34–18.35
–fraudulent trading, 18.38
–indemnification, 18.43
–insurance, 18.43
–re-use of company name, 18.40
–summary remedy, 18.37
–winding-up, misconduct in the course of, 18.36
–wrongful trading, 18.39
offences under the Companies Acts, 29.1–29.3
officer in default, 29.2
Liability limitation agreement,
auditors, and, 3.50
authorisation by members, 8.43
effect, 8.44
generally, 8.41
terms, 8.42
Lien,
accounting records, 36.5
shares, 47.25
standard articles of association, Appendix 4
Limitation of liability,
company's constitution, 14.2
Limited by guarantee,
meaning, 12.7
return of allotments, 47.12
Limited company,
meaning, 12.7
return of allotments, 47.12
Limited liability partnerships,
guidance, 39.2
Listed companies,
boardroom diversity, 15.2
corporate governance, 15.4

Listed companies, – *cont.*
directors, 18.5
directors' reports, 20.1
Disclosure Rules, 33.39–33.47
–connected persons, 33.47
–general provisions, 33.40
–inside information, 33.44, 33.45
–insider lists, 33.46
–modifying or dispensing with, 33.39
–persons discharging managerial responsibilities, 33.47
–publication of information on the internet, 33.42
–requirement to disclose, 33.41
–synchronised release of information, 33.43
distributions, 22.11
–AIM companies, 22.16
–continuing obligations, 22.13
–CREST, 22.14
–LSE dividend procedure timetable, 22.15
–LSE main market, 22.12
–uncertified securities, 22.14
FCA,
–appointment of investigators, 33.71
–exemption from liability in damages, 33.72
inside information, *see also* Insider dealing and market abuse
–control of, 33.41, 33.45
–delaying disclosure, 33.44
–publication on internet, 33.42
–synchronised release, 33.43
insider lists, 33.46
Listing Rules, *see also*Listing Rules 33.4–33.38
Model Code, The, 33 Appendix 1
penalties, 33.70
prospectuses, 32.3
quoted, definition as, 2.4
reverse takeovers, 33.31A
rights issues, 47.64–47.65
Transparency Rules, 33.48–33.69
–acquisition of major shareholdings, 33.55
–acquisition of own shares, 33.59
–aggregation of managed holdings, 33.58
–annual financial reports, 33.51
–categories of obligation, 33.48
–combined holdings, 33.61
–compensation for statements, 33.69
–direct and indirect holders, 33.56
–disclosure of information in a non-EEA State, 33.68
–disclosures by issuers, 33.60
–disposal of major shareholdings, 33.55
–disposal of own shares, 33.59
–dissemination of information, 33.67
–filing information, 33.63, 33.66

Listed companies, – *cont.*
Transparency Rules, – *cont.*
–financial instruments, 33.57
–general provisions, 33.49
–half-yearly financial reports, 33.52
–information requirements, 33.65
–issuers of shares and debt securities, 33.65
–language, 33.66
–major holdings, 33.55, 33.62
–non-EEA state issuers, 33.64
–notification rules, vote holder and issuer, 33.54–33.64
–periodic financial reporting, 33.50–33.53
Listing Rules,
application, 33.8
cancelling listing, 33.14
circulars,
–contents, 33.38
–premium listing, 33.37
compliance, 3.16
continuing obligations,
–annual financial report, 33.28
–half-yearly report, 33.30
–holders, 33.23
–introduction, 33.21–33.22
–notifications, 33.26
–preliminary statement of annual results, 33.27
–prior approval for share schemes, options, 33.24
–statement of dividends, 33.27
–strategic reports, 33.29
–transactions, 33.25
corporate governance, 15.4
dealing in own securities and treasury shares
–premium listing, 33.36
enforcement, 33.5
equity securities, 33.7A
FCA,
–appointment of investigators, 33.71
–exemption from liability in damages, 33.72
Listing Principles, 33.15
particulars where prospectus not required, 33.9
–approval and publication, 33.12
–compensation for statements, 33.13
–responsibility, 33.10
–supplementary, 33.11
penalties, 33.70
premium listing, 15.2
–circulars, 33.37
–related party transactions, 33.33
–significant transactions, 33.31
related party transactions,
–exempt transactions, 33.35

Listing Rules, – *cont.*
related party transactions, – *cont.*
–premium listing, 33.33
–requirements, 33.34
requirements, 33.6
–premium listing, 33.7A
–standard listing, 33.7B
restoring listing, 33.14
reverse takeovers, 33.31A
significant transactions,
–premium listing, 33.31
–notifying significant transactions, 33.32
sponsors,
–appointment, 33.17
–approval, 33.17
–dismissal, 33.17
–premium listing, 33.16
–principles, 33.19
–responsibilities, 33.18
–supervision, 33.20
suspending listing, 33.14
Loan interest,
accounts disclosure, 3.27
Loan stock,
use of term, 17.7
Loans and quasi-loans,
directors,
–consequences of contravention, 18.66
–generally, 18.60
–members' approval, 18.61–18.64
–related arrangements, 18.63
–value, 18.65
Location,
part of UK in which registered, disclosure, 16.14
LSE (London Stock Exchange) companies,
corporate transactions, 22.12
distributions, 22.11–22.16
dividend,
–inclusion of interest for this purpose, 22.12
–procedure timetable (DP timetable), 22.15

M

Management,
internal, duties, 18.27
Manager,
receiver, meaning Appendix 1
Managing director,
meaning, 18.1
Market abuse,
behaviour amounting to, 23.7
Market abuse, – *cont.*
dissemination, 23.11
exceptions, 23.12
improper disclosure, 23.8
legislation, 23.1
manipulating devices, 23.10
manipulating transactions, 23.9
penalties, 23.13
regulatory framework, 23.6
Medium-sized companies,
See also: Accounts: medium-sized companies
accounts,
–filing, 2.10
–revised, 2.13
–statutory, 2.5
directors' report 20.1
special auditor's report, 2.5
strategic report, 2.10
Meetings,
adjournment, 42.27
annual general meeting (AGM),
–articles, of association, 14.6
–circulation of members' resolutions, 42.31
–laying of accounts, 2.9
–notice, 14.6, 42.30
–private companies, 2.9
–public companies, 42.30, 42.31
–traded companies, 42.30, 42.31, 42.38A
articles of association, 14.6
calling, 42.13
chairman, 42.23
class, 42.29, 42.38
class of members, 42.44
directors, 42.23, 42.39
–minutes, 42.40
electronic documents, 42.28
electronic meetings, 42.12A
members' statements, 42.20
notice, 42.14, 42.30
–contents, 42.17
–failure to give, 42.19
–persons entitled to receive, 42.16
–special, 42.18
–ways of giving, 42.15
private companies,
–notice, 42.14
–traded, 42.30
procedure, 42.21
proxies, 42.26
public companies, AGM,
–circulation of resolutions, 42.31
–requirement to hold, 42.30
quorum, 42.22, 42.29

Index

Meetings, – *cont.*
quoted companies,
–independent assessor, 42.35–42.36
–independent report on poll, 42.34
–website publication of poll results, 42.33
records, 42.42
–inspection of, 42.43
resolutions, 42.1–42.4
–members' votes, 42.4
–ordinary, 42.2
–requirements for validity, 42.12
–special, 42.3
share capital,
–serious loss, 47.61
traded companies,
–circulation of members' matters, 42.31
–other matters included at AGM, 42.31
–participation, 42.38A
–questions, 42.23A
–requirement to hold AGM, 42.30
–website publication of poll results, 42.33
voting procedure, 42.24
written resolutions of private companies, 42.5–42.11
Members,
*See also*Meetings, Resolutions
articles of association,
–alteration, 14.9
calling meetings, 42.13
company, holding shares in another, 26.1
–subsidiaries, prohibition and exception, 26.7
definition, 26.1, Appendix 1
derivative claims, 26.11–26.13
–Scotland, 26.13
dissolution, notification, 21.5
documents to be provided to,
–annual accounts, 2.6–2.7
–auditors' report, 2.7
–constitutional documents, 14.11
–directors' remuneration report, 2.7
–directors' report, 2.7
exercise of rights, 26.2
information rights, 26.4
liabilities, 26.9
maximum, 26.8
minimum 26.8
minors, 26.1
nominees, 26.1
powers, 26.9
pre-emption right,
–communication of pre-emption offers, 47.14
–disapplication, 47.18
–exclusion, 47.17
Members, – *cont.*
pre-emption right, – *cont.*
–exemptions, 47.16
–generally, 47.13
–liability for contravention, 47.15
–saving provisions, 47.19
proceedings by, 26.11
reconstructions, meetings and approval, 35.2
–divisions, 35.20, 35.29
–mergers, 35.9, 35.43
register,
–location and inspection, 38.6
–overseas branch, 38.7
–particulars to be disclosed, 38.5
–single member companies, 38.5
relationship, with company and other members, 14.12
rights, 26.9–26.10
shares held on behalf of others, 26.5–26.6
statements, 42.20
trustees, 26.1
Memorandum of association,
charitable company, 14.4
objects, 14.2
share capital, 14.2
subscribers' statement, 14.2
Merger relief,
share premium, 46.2
Mergers,
articles, amendment, 35.50
City Code on Takeovers and Mergers, 48 Appendix
cross border,
–application of certain provisions CA 2006, 35.61
–approval of creditors, 35.44
–approval of members, 35.43
–compliance and enforcement, 35.59
–confidential information, 35.57
–consequences of, 35.48
–copies of order, 35.49
–court approval, 35.47
–directors' report, 35.39
–documents to be circulated, 35.45
–draft terms, 35.38
–employee participation, 35.52–35.58
–independent expert's report, 35.40
–inspection of documents, 35.41
–meaning, 35.36
–power of court, 35.46
–public notice of receipt of registered documents, 35.42
–Registrar of Companies, 35.51
–special negotiating body, 35.53–35.55
–requirements, 35.37

Mergers, – *cont.*
cross border, – *cont.*
–transferee company's articles, 35.50
–unregistered companies, 35.60
directors' explanatory report, 35.10
draft terms of scheme, 35.8
EC merger control regulations, 35.34
expert's report, 35.11, 35.22
holders' special rights, 35.15
inspection of documents, 35.13
members, approval, 35.9
Panel on Takeovers and Mergers,
–bid documentation rules, 48.3
–enforcement by the court, 48.4
–generally, 48.2–48.6, 48 Appendix
–liability in damages, exemption from, 48.6
–non-compliance with rules, 48.5
publication of documents on company website, 35.13A
powers of the court, 35.32, 35.46–35.47
public companies, 35.6–35.17
references, 35.33
Registrar of Companies, 35.42, 35.49, 35.51
supplementary accounting document, 35.12
transferee company,
–allotment of shares restrictions, 35.16
–approval of articles, 35.14
MiFID investment firm,
definition, Appendix 1
Minority interests,
group accounts, 3.60, 5.62
Minority shareholders,
takeovers,
–right to be bought out, 48.15
–right to buy out, 48.12
Minors,
members of company, 26.1
Minutes,
directors' meetings, 42.40
general meetings, 42.41
inspection, 42.43
years to be kept, 42.43
Model Code, The
listed companies, 33 Appendix 1
Mortgage,
charge, contrasted with, 45.3

N

Names and business names,
business,
–application for, 27.23
–disclosure requirement, 27.24–27.27
Names and business names, – *cont.*
business, – *cont.*
–generally, 27.18–27.27
–misleading indication of activities, 27.22
–prohibited 27.19
–restricted, 27.19–27.22
–sensitive words and expressions, 27.20
–similarity to existing, 27.13
charitable companies,
–disclosure of fact that is charity, 16.13
company,
–articles of association, 14.6
–change of, compulsory, 27.11–27.16
–change of, voluntary, 27.17
–community interest, 10.15
–Companies House search, 27.10
–indication of type, 27.2, 27.5
–insolvent liquidation, 18.40
–length of, 27.9
–not formed under the Companies Acts, 11.7
–offensive, 27.4
–permitted characters, 27.8
–prohibited 27.3–27.7
–registration of, 27.10
–restoration, 21.11
–same as existing name, 27.5–27.6
–sensitive words and expression, 27.7
–voluntary change of, 27.17
compulsory change of,
–ceasing to be entitled to exemption, 27.12
–misleading indication of activities, 27.16
–provision of misleading information, 27.15
–similarity to existing, 27.13–27.14
disclosure,
–failure to, 27.27
–generally, 27.24–27.25
index,
–Registrar of Companies, 39.12
individuals,
–disclosure, 27.24–27.27
opportunistic registration, 27.14
overseas company, 30.11
partnerships,
–disclosure, 27.24–27.27
NEDs (Non-executive directors),
challenge, 15.13
corporate governance, 15.13
Guidance on Board effectiveness, 15.13
Higgs Review, 15.13
risk, 15.13
role, 18.1
senior independent directors, 15.13

Nomination committee,
generally, 15.9
Nominees,
articles of association, 14.6
members of company, 26.1
purchase of own shares, held by, 34.22
Non-cash asset,
meaning, Appendix 1
Non-executive directors (NEDs),
See also Directors
challenge, 15.13
corporate governance, 15.13
Guidance on Board effectiveness, 15.13
Higgs Review, 15.13
liability, 15.13
risk, 15.13
role, 18.1
senior independent directors, 15.13
UK Corporate Governance Code, 15.2
Non-statutory accounts,
definition, 2.5
publication, 2.5
statement accompanying, 2.5
Northern Ireland,
accounting reference date, 2.18
community interest companies, 10.6
derivative claims, 26.12
extension of legislation to, 28.1
formation, 1.2
insider dealing, 23.4
legal proceedings,
–court, the, 29.8
–unincorporated bodies, 29.6
registration of charges,
–certain charges affecting land, 40.7
–generally, 40.2–40.10
Notes to the accounts,
balance sheet,
–abbreviated, 5.48–5.55
–generally, 3.17–3.25
–small company, 5.19–5.27
profit and loss account,
–generally, 3.26–3.31
–small company, 5.28–5.30
Notice of meetings,
contents of, 42.17
failure to give, 42.19
persons entitled to receive, 42.16
special, resolutions requiring, 42.18
ways of giving, 42.15
Number, registered,
disclosure, 16.14
Registrar of Companies, 39.5

O

Objects, company
charitable company, 14.6
community interest company, 10.14
memorandum and articles, 14.2, 14.6
Off-balance sheet arrangements,
accounts disclosure, 3.51
Offences,
See also Fines
annual return, failure to submit, 29.1
community interest companies, 10.33
consent required, 29.5
court, the
–granting of relief, 29.9
–jurisdictions, 29.8
directors,
–criminal, 18.41
–fraud, 18.34–18.35
–fraudulent trading, 18.38
–indemnification, 18.43
–insurance, 18.43
–re-use of company name, 18.40
–summary remedy, 18.37
–winding-up, misconduct in the course of, 18.36
–wrongful trading, 18.39
documents,
–production and inspection, 29.7
indictment, 29.1
insider dealing, 23.2–23.5
legal professional privilege, 29.3
liability of officer, 29.2
Northern Ireland,
–court, the, 29.8
–unincorporated bodies, 29.6
punishment, 29 Appendix
–indictment, 29.1
–standard scale, fines, 29.1
–summary conviction, 29.1
Scotland,
–court, the, 29.8
–security for costs, 29.10
–unincorporated bodies 29.6
summary conviction, 29.1
summary proceedings,
–time limit, 29.4
–venue, 29.4
unincorporated bodies,
–corporate bodies, proceedings as if, 29.6
–proceedings under Companies Acts, 29.6
Offers,
takeovers, 48 Appendix
Office of Fair Trading (OFT),
merger references, 35.33

Officer of the company,
company secretary, 13.6
liability, 2.4–2.5, 29.2
meaning, Appendix 1
Old public companies,
meaning, Appendix 1
re-registration, 41.22–41.23
Open-ended investment companies (OEIC),
disqualification of directors, 18.11
regulations, 12.7
Options,
share schemes, listed companies, 33.24
Orders,
requirements of CA 2006, Appendix 1
Ordinary resolution,
see also Resolutions
meaning, 42.2
Ordinary shares,
see also Shares
meaning, 47.5
Overseas branch,
register of members,
–branch register, 38.7
–dominion register, 38.7
Overseas companies,
accounts,
–credit or financial institutions, 30.35–30.50
–generally, 30.18–30.50
–individual, 30.26–30.29
–filing, 30.34
–group, 30.30–30.32
–parent law, 30.19–30.24
addresses, residential,
–disclosure, 30.12–30.17
–protection from disclosure, 30.12–30.13
alteration to registered particulars, 30.7–30.10
–non-compliance, penalty, 30.10
auditors' report, 30.18
certified translations,
–accounts, 30.4
–constitution, 30.4
charges, registration of,
–appointment/cessation of receiver, 30.72
–copies of instruments, 30.73
–created on or after 1 October 2011, 30.67A–30.72
–debentures, 30.68–30.69
–duty to deliver particulars, 30.66
–ex facie absolute disposition (Scotland), 30.67
–generally, 30.64–30.73
–rectification of register by court, 30.71
–register, entries of satisfaction and release, 30.70
–requiring registration, 30.65
Overseas companies, – *cont*
charges, registration of, – *cont.*
–Scotland, 30.67
contracts, 30.59–30.60
credit institutions, accounting documents,
–approval, 30.49
–duty to file, 30.37, 30.50
–financial year, 30.41
–generally, 30.35
–group accounts, 30.46–30.48
–individual accounts, 30.42–30.45
–non-compliance, 30.39
–not required under parent law, 30.40
–required to prepare accounts under parent law, 30.36
–statement of details, 30.38
cross-border mergers, 35.35–35.60
debentures, 30.68–30.69
definition, 30.1, Appendix 1
directors' report, 30.18
disclosure,
–confidentiality order, 30.15
–residential addresses, 30.12–30.17
documents,
–execution of, 30.61–30.63
–language, 39.13
–Scotland, 30.62
fees, Appendix 3
financial institutions, accounting documents,
–approval, 30.49
–duty to file, 30.37, 30.50
–financial year, 30.41
–generally, 30.35
–group accounts, 30.46–30.48
–individual accounts, 30.42–30.45
–non-compliance, 30.39
–not required under parent law, 30.40
–required to prepare accounts under parent law, 30.36
–statement of details, 30.38
investigations, 25.22
name,
–display, 30.52
–registered, 30.11
notice of closure, duty, 30.57
pre-incorporation, 30.63
prospectuses,
–transfer of approval, 32.15
provisions applying before 1 Oct 2009, 30 Appendix
Registrar, relevant,
–UK regions, 30.58
registration,
–generally, 30.2–30.10
–initial, 30.3

Overseas companies, – *cont.*
registration, – *cont.*
–particulars required, 30.3
–transitional provisions, 30.3
registration of charges, 40.6
service of documents, 30.56
strategic report, 30.18
trading disclosures,
–address for service, 30.54
–civil consequences of failure, 30.55
–display of name, 30.52
–documents, 30.53
–generally, 30.51–30.55
translations, certified,
–accounts, 30.4
–constitution, 30.4

P

Panel on Takeovers and Mergers,
documentation, 48.3
enforcement by the court, 48.4
liability in damages, exemption from, 48.6
non-compliance with, 48.5
Parent company,
directors' report, 20.1
group accounts, 3.40, 5.38
meaning, Appendix 1
Parent law
overseas companies, 30.19–30.24
Participating interests,
meaning, Appendix 1
Partnerships,
guidance, 39.2
members, 26.1
names, 27.19, 27.24
qualifying partnerships, accounts, 3.39, 3.72, 5.37, 5.73
Payment for loss of office,
directors, 18.47
Penalties,
costs, 29.9
directors disqualification, 18.12–18.22
indictment, 29.1
late filing guidance booklet, 39.2
market abuse, 23.13
offences under the Companies Acts, 29.1, 29 Appendix
officer in default, liability, 29.2
security for costs, Scotland, 29.10
standard scale, 29.1
statutory maximum, 29.1
summary conviction, 29.1
Penalties, – *cont.*
summary proceedings, 29.4
unincorporated bodies, 29.2, 29.6
Political donations,
authorisation required, 31.3
definition, 31.2
directors' report, 20.8
exemption 31.8
–amount, 31.8
–by order, 31.8
–trade unions, 31.8
sponsorship, 31.2
unauthorised donations,
–directors' liabilities, 31.4–31.7
–remedies, 31.4
–shareholder action, 31.5–31.7
Poll,
quoted companies, independent report on, 42.34
right to demand, 42.24
voting by proxy, 42.26
website publication of results, 42.33
Pre-emption right,
communication of offers, 47.14
disapplication, 47.18
exemptions, 47.16
exclusion, 47.17
liability for contravention, 47.15
provisions, 47.13
saving provisions, 47.19
Preference shares,
types of, 47.5
Pre-incorporation,
pre-incorporation contracts, 12.2
promoters, 12.1
Preliminary statement of annual results,
listed companies, 33.27
Premises,
entry and search of, 25.13,25.19–25.20
Prescribed,
meaning, Appendix 1
Price-sensitive information,
insider dealing, 23.3
Prior year adjustment,
accounts disclosure, 3.30, 5.30
Private companies,
circulation of accounts, 2.6
company secretary, 13.1
general meeting,
–laying of accounts, 2.9
–removal of requirement for, 2.9
public company,
–comparison with, 33.2
purchase of own shares, 34.10

Private companies, – *cont.*
records,
–availability for inspection, 36.2
redemption of shares, 34.10
re-registering as limited, 41.15–41.18
–application and accompanying documents, 41.16
–certificate of incorporation, 41.17
–conditions, 41.15
–Statement of capital, 41.18
re-registering as public, 41.2–41.7
–application and accompanying documents, 41.6
–certificate of incorporation, 41.7
–conditions, 41.2
–net asset requirements, 41.4
–recent allotment of shares, non-cash consideration, 41.5
–share capital requirements, 41.3
re-registering as unlimited, 41.12–41.14
–application and accompanying documents, 41.13
–certificate of incorporation, 41.14
–conditions, 41.12
share capital,
–purchase of own shares, 34.10
–reduction supported by solvency statement, 47.52–47.54
shares,
–allotment, 47.9
–prohibition of public offers, 47.21–47.22
written resolutions,
–agreeing, 42.9
–circulation date, 42.6
–directors, proposed by, 42.7
–eligible members, 42.6
–general provisions, 42.5
–members, proposed by, 42.8
–sending documents, 42.10
–website publication, 42.11
Privileged information,
obligation of confidence, 25.21, 29.3
Professional privilege,
legal proceedings,
–confidentiality of communications, 29.3
–refusal to disclose, 25.21, 29.3
Profit and loss account,
formats, 3.5
–small company, 5.7
meaning, Appendix 1
notes to the accounts, 3.26–3.31
Profit forecasts,
takeovers, 48 Appendix
Profits,
distribution of, 22.2–22.3
Promissory note,
endorsement, 16.11
Promoters,
pre-incorporation, 12.1
Property,
acquired,
–charges existing, 40.3
–Scotland, 40.12
bona vacantia,
–dissolution, 21.7–21.8
–restoration, 21.12
dissolved company, of, 21.7
Prospectuses,
advertisements, 32.18
annual information update. 32.20
application of rules, 32.1
drawing up, 32.8–32.12
election to have, 32.7
exempt offers, 32.4
exempt securities, 32.5–32.6
external management company, 32.2
filing, 32.17
format, 32.9
FCA,
–application to, 32.13
–appointment of investigators, 32.24
–approval by, 32.13–32 14
–exemption from liability, 32.25
–power to suspend, 32.16
FSA, *See*FCA
investors,
–generally, 32.22
–remedies, 32.21
infringement of rules, 32.16
Listing Rules, 32.3
minimum information, 32.10
need for, 32.3
omission of information, 32.12
overseas,
–languages, use of, 32.15
–transfer of approval, 32.15
penalties, 32.23
publication of, 32.17
responsibility for complying, 32.1–32.2
supplementary, 32.19
terms of reference, 32.11
Proxies,
articles of association, 14.6
listed companies, 42.26
voting by 42.26
Public companies,
accounts,
–period allowed for filing, 2.11
annual general meetings, 42.30

Public companies, – *cont.*
annual general meetings, – *cont.*
–notice of, 42.30
circulation of accounts, 2.6
company secretary, 13.2
definition, 12.7, 33.1
directors,
–number required, 18.2, 33.2
disclosed interests in shares,
–register, 38.8
FCA, Transparency rules, 38.8
general meeting,
–laying of accounts, 2.9
interests in shares,
–investigation of, 24.2
–members, 24.4–24.5
–notice to confirm, 24.2–24.3
–obligation to disclose, 24.1
–orders for restriction on, 24.6–24.8
–orders for sale, 24.9
joint stock company registering as, 11.6
meetings, 42.30–42.31
mergers and divisions, 35.6–35.32
name, 27.2
old company,
–re-registering, 41.22
–re-registering as private, 41.23
private companies
–comparison with, 33.2
records,
–availability for inspection, 36.2
regulatory provisions and corporate governance,
–Aim Rules, 33.2
–Disclosure Rules, 33.39
–Listing Rules, 33.4
–Model Code, The, 33 Appendix 1
–Prospectus Rules, 32.3
–Transparency Rules, 33.48
–UK Corporate Governance Code, 33.2
re-registering becoming private, 41.8–41.11
–application and accompanying documents, 41.10
–application to court to cancel resolution, 41.9
–certificate of incorporation, 41.11
–conditions, 41.8
re-registering becoming private and unlimited, 41.19–41.21
–application and accompanying documents, 41.20
–certificate of incorporation, 41.21
–conditions, 41.19
reverse takeovers, 33.31A

Public companies, – *cont.*
share capital
–authorised minimum, 33.3, 47.7
–reduction below authorised minimum, 47.57
shares,
–allotment, 47.9
–charges on own, 34.30
–duty to cancel, 34.23–34.28
–independent valuation of non-cash consideration, 47.31–47.45
–issue not fully subscribed, 47.20
–payment, 47.26
trading certificate, 33.3
Public notice,
events requiring, 16.17
Public sector,
audit, 8.29
Publication,
accounts, 2.3
–auditor's report, 2.5
–group accounts, 2.5
–requirements, 2.5
name of signatory, 2.4
Published,
document regarded as, 2.4
Punishment for offences,
directors disqualification, 18.12–18.22
indictment, 29.1
offences under the Companies Acts, 29.1, 29 Appendix
officer in default, liability, 29.2
standard scale, 29.1
statutory maximum, 29.1
summary conviction, 29.1
summary proceedings, 29.4
unincorporated bodies, 29.2, 29.6
Purchase of own shares,
authority, 34.6
beneficial interest, 34.29
capital, payment out of,
–private company, 34.10–34.13
capital redemption reserve, 34.18
charges, on own shares, 34.30
disclosure, 34.9
distributable profits,
–payments made out of, 34.8
duty to cancel shares, 34.23
effect of failure to, 34.19
employees' share scheme, 34.6A
financial assistance for, 34.20
–offences, 34.20
–prohibitions and exceptions, 34.20–34.21
financing, 34.5
general rule, 34.1

Purchase of own shares, – *cont.*
general rule, – *cont.*
–exceptions, 34.1
market purchase, 34.7
nominee,
–accounting treatment, 34.28
–shares held by, 34.22
off-market purchase, 34.6
payment for, 34.5
private company,
–redemption, 34.10–34.13
profits, purchase out of,
–capital redemption reserve, 34.18
public company,
–accounting treatment, 34.28
–charges on own shares, 34.30
–duty to cancel shares, 34.23
–notice of cancellation, 34.24
–offences, 34.26
–re-registration as private, 34.25
–re-registration as public, 34.27
redeemable shares, 34.2–34.3
redemption,
–available profits, 34.11
–employees' share scheme, 34.12A
–objections, 34.13
–out of capital, 34.10
–requirements, 34.12
Registrar of Companies,
–notification, 34.9
resolutions, 34.6
–voting rights, 34.6
treasury shares, 34.14–34.17
–cancellation of, 34.16
–disposal of, 34.15
–offences relating to, 34.17
treatment of shares, 34.5

Q

Qualifying indemnity provisions,
directors' report disclosure, 20.6
Quasi-loans,
directors,
–consequences of contravention, 18.66
–generally, 18.60
–members' approval, 18.61–18.64
–related arrangements, 18.63
–value, 18.65
Quorum,
class meetings, 42.29
meeting requirement, 42.22
Quoted companies,
accounts,
–availability of, 2.8
–filing, 2.10
balance sheet, 2.4
definition, 2.4, Appendix 1
directors' remuneration report 2.4
directors' report, 2.4
greenhouse gas emissions disclosure, 20.17
poll results,
–independent report, 42.34
–publication, 42.33
strategic report, 20.1
website,
–annual report availability, 2.8
–publication of poll results, 42.33

R

Realised profits and losses,
distributions, 22.6
Receiver,
appointment, 40.10
meaning, Appendix 1
Registrar of Companies, 40.10
Reconstructions,
amalgamations,
–power of court to facilitate, 35.4
arrangements, 35.1–35.5
–articles, 35.5
–court powers, 35.4
–court sanction, 35.3
–creditors' meetings, 35.2
–members' meetings, 35.2
–obligations, 35.5
divisions,
–allotment of shares, restrictions, 35.28
–articles, approval of, 35.26
–assets, report on material changes, 35.25
–directors' explanatory report, 35.21
–draft terms of scheme, 35.19
–exceptions to rules, 35.29
–expert's report, 35.22, 35.31
–inspection of documents, 35.24
–liability for defaults, 35.30
–members' approval, 35.20
–protection of holders with special rights, 35.27
–supplementary accounting statement, 35.23
–website, availability of documents, 35.24A, 35.30A
mergers, 35.6–35.61

Index

Reconstructions, – *cont.*
mergers, – *cont.*
–articles, amendment, 35.50
–cross border, 35.35–35.36, 35.47–35.48
–directors' explanatory report, 35.10
–draft terms of scheme, 35.8
–EC merger control regulations, 35.34
–employee participation, 35.52–35.59
–expert's report, 35.11, 35.22
–holders' special rights, 35.15
–inspection of documents, 35.13
–members, approval, 35.9
–powers of the court, 35.32, 35.46–35.47
–pre-merger requirements, 35.36–35.45
–public companies, 35.6–35.17
–publication of documents on website, 35.13A
–references, 35.33
–Registrar of Companies, 35.42, 35.49, 35.51
–supplementary accounting document, 35.12
–transferee company, allotment of shares, 35.16
–unregistered companies, 35.60
Records,
accounting records,
–components, 36.5
–destruction, criminal, 36.8
–duty to keep, 36.5–36.8
–form, 36.5
–location and inspection, 36.6
–preservation, 36.7
–statutory accounts, 2.5
– strategic reports, 6.6
audit, 8.24, 8.33
company records, meaning, 16.13, 36.1
directors' duty, 18.16, 18.27
duty to keep, 18.16, 36.5–36.8
falsification,
–duty to take precautions, 36.3
form of, 36.1
inspection, 36.2, 36.6, 42.43
length of time to be kept,
–accounting records, 36.7
–records of resolutions and meetings, 42.43
meetings, 42.41–42.44
preservation of, 36.4, 36.7
provision of copies, 36.2
resolutions, 42.41
right to inspect, 36.2
specified records, 36.2
Redeemable shares,
redemption provisions, 34.3
registrar of companies, notice to, 34.3
Reference date,
*See*Accounting reference date
Reference period,
*See*Accounting reference period
Registered name,
*See*Names and business names
Registered office,
change of address, 37.2
charitable companies, 16.13
directors' service contracts, availability, 18.54
registered name, display of, 16.13
requirement to have, 37.1
Wales, 37.3
Register of charges,
copies of instruments, 38.11
entry details, 38.11
Registrar of Companies, 40.8
Scotland, 40.16
Register of debenture holders,
provisions for when kept, 38.12
Register of directors,
particulars to be disclosed, 38.2
Register of directors' interests,
generally, 38.13
reform, 38.14
Register of directors' residential addresses,
requirement, 38.3
Register of disclosed interests in public company shares,
location and inspection, 38.9
removal of entries, 38.10
Register of members,
location and inspection, 38.6
overseas branch, 38.7
particulars to be disclosed, 38.5
share warrants, 38.5
single member companies, 38.5
Register of secretaries,
particulars to be disclosed, 38.4
Registered number,
Registrar of Companies, 39.5
Registered office,
company formation, 12.3
Registers,
charges, 38.11
–copies of instruments, 38.11
debenture holders,
–option to keep, 38.12
directors, 38.2
directors' interests,
–generally, 38.13
–reforms, 38.14
disclosed interests in public company shares,
–generally, 38.8

Registers, – *cont.*
disclosed interests in public company shares, – *cont.*
–location and inspection, 38.9
–removal of entries, 38.10
directors' residential addresses, 38.3
form in which kept, 38.1
members,
–generally, 38.5–38.7
–location and inspection, 38.6
–overseas branch, 38.7
secretaries, 38.4
Registrar of companies,
abbreviated accounts, 5.46, 5.76
accounting reference date, 2.18
–alteration of, 2.19
articles of association, 14.3, 14.8
certificates of incorporation, 39.4
certified translations, 39.13
charges, 45.6
Companies House,
acceptance of accounts, 2.11
Cardiff, Appendix 2
Edinburgh, Appendix 2
fees, Appendix 3
forms, Appendix 2
delivery of documents, 39.6
directors, changes in, 18.4
directors' remuneration reports, 2.10
directors' report, 2.10, 20.23
documents,
–generally, 39.6
–manner of delivery, 39.6
–public notice of receipt, 39.8
duties and powers,
–certification or verification, 39.15
–correction or removal of material, 39.11
–enforcement of filing obligations, 39.16
–generally, 39.3–39.11
–index of company names, 39.12
–inspection and copying of register, 39.10
–language requirements, translation, 39.13
–language requirements, transliteration, 39.14
–maintaining company records, 39.9
false statement, offence, 39.18
fees, Appendix 3
filing,
–accounts, 2.10
–articles of association, 14.8
forms, Appendix 2
Gazette,
–alternative to, 39.17
–meaning, Appendix 1

Registrar of companies, – *cont.*
Gazette, – *cont.*
–publication in, 39.8
guidance booklets, 39.2
incorporation, 39.4
–articles of association, 14.3
inspection, 39.10
–address unavailable, application, 39.19
interest in public company shares, 24.5
mergers, 35.42, 35.49, 35.51
offence, false statement, 39.18
overseas companies, 30.2, 30.58
protected information,
–permitted disclosure, 18.69–18.73
redemption of shares, 34.3
register of charges,
–generally, 38.11, 40.8
–Scotland, 40.16
register of debenture holders, 38.12
register of directors, 38.2
register of directors' residential addresses, 38.3
register of disclosed interests in public company shares, 38.9
register of members, 38.5
register of secretaries, 38.4
registered numbers, 39.5
registered office, 37.1–37.3
registrars, contact details, 39.1
restoration, application, 21.9
revised accounts, 2.12
Registrar's Rules and Powers booklet, 39.2
small companies, 2.10
statutory accounts, delivery 2.5
striking off, 24.1
WebFiling, 39.20, Appendix 2
Registrars,
contact details, 39.1
Registration of allotment,
time limit, 47.11
Registration of charges,
England, Northern Ireland and Wales, 40.2–40.10
–appointment/cessation of receiver, 40.10
–applicable charges, 40.2
–certain charges affecting land, Northern Ireland 40.7
–creation of a charge, 40.2
–debentures, 40.4
–endorsement of certificate on debentures, 40.5
–failure to register, 40.2
–property situated outside the UK, 40.6
–property, 40.3
–property situated outside the UK, 40.6

Index

Registration of charges, – *cont.*
England, Northern Ireland and Wales, – *cont.*
–register, rectification by court, 40.9
–Registrar of Companies, 40.8
other jurisdictions,
–property situated outside the UK, 40.6, 40.15
requirement, 40.1
Scotland, 40.11–40.17
–creation of charge, 40.11
–debentures, 40.14
–ex facie absolute disposition, 40.13
–failure to register, 40.11
–property acquired, 40.12
–property outside UK, 40.15
–rectification by court, 40.17
–register, 40.16
–Registrar of Companies, 40.16
special register, 40.18
Registration of company,
application for, 12.3
certificate, 12.4
overseas company, 30.2–30.10
re-registration, 34.25–34.27
Regulations,
EU Regulations, prospectuses, 32.1
large and medium sized companies and groups, 3.2
requirements of CA 2006, Appendix 1
Regulatory framework,
UK Corporate Governance Code, 15.2–15.6
Related party transactions,
accounts disclosure, 3.31
Listing Rules, 33.33
Related undertakings,
accounts disclosures, 3.32–3.40, 3.64–3.73, 5.31–5.38
Relevant market, trading on,
annual return, 7.2
Removal,
directors, 18.9
Remuneration,
auditor,
–disclosure, 3.50, 5.45
–fixing, 8.15
directors,
–accounts disclosure, 3.41–3.48, 3.74, 5.39–5.44
–approval by members, 18.48
–charitable companies, 18.48
–determined by, 18.46
–payment, 18.49
–payment for loss of office, 18.47
–resolution, voting on, 18.49
Remuneration, – *cont.*
directors, – *cont.*
–shareholder power, 15.14
directors' remuneration reports,
See also Directors' remuneration reports
–generally, 19.1–19.34
executive, reforms, 15.14
policy,
See also Directors' remuneration policy
–contents, 19.6
–generally, 19.3
Remuneration committee,
directors serving on other companies', 15.14
executive remuneration, 15.14
UK Corporate Governance Code, 15.10
Reports, annual,
financial, listed companies, 33.28
publication of, 2.3
Re-registration,
old public company,
–re-registering, 41.22
–re-registering as private, 41.23
possibilities requiring, 41.1
private company becoming public, 41.2–41.7
–application and accompanying documents, 41.6
–certificate of incorporation, 41.7
–conditions, 41.2
–net asset requirements, 41.4
–recent allotment of shares, non-cash consideration, 41.5
–share capital requirements, 41.3
private company becoming unlimited, 41.12–41.14
–application and accompanying documents, 41.13
–certificate of incorporation, 41.14
–conditions, 41.12
public company becoming private, 41.8–41.11
–application and accompanying documents, 41.10
–application to court to cancel resolution, 41.9
–certificate of incorporation, 41.11
–conditions, 41.8
public company becoming private and unlimited, 41.19–41.21
–application and accompanying documents, 41.20
–certificate of incorporation, 41.21
–conditions, 41.19
unlimited private company becoming limited, 41.15–41.18
–application and accompanying documents, 41.16

Re-registration, – *cont.*
unlimited private company becoming limited, – *cont.*
–certificate of incorporation, 41.17
–conditions, 41.15
–statement of capital, 41.18
Reserve liability,
historical meaning, 47.6
Reserves,
accounts disclosure, 3.16, 3.22, 5.18, 5.24
reduction of share capital, 47.59
types of,
–capital redemption reserve, 34.18
–revaluation reserve, 3.14, 5.16
–undistributable, 22.1
Residential addresses of directors,
overseas company, 30.12–30.17
protection from disclosure,
–generally, 18.67–18.73
–Registrar of Companies, application, 39.19
register, 38.3
Resolutions,
articles, entitlement to vote, 42.4
class of members, 42.44
constitutional matters, 14.10
directors' meetings, 42.39–42.40
extraordinary,
– term not used in CA 2006, 42.1
institutional investors, 42.45
meetings, at, 42.12–42.29
–adjourned meetings, 42.27
–conditions for validity, 42.12
–electronic meetings, 42.12A
–failure to give notice, 42.19
–notice, 42.14
–poll, demanding, 42.24
–proxies, 42.26
–special notice required, 42.18
–voting procedure, 42.24
members' votes, 42.4
ordinary, 42.2
poll taken at meeting, 42.4
private company, 42.1
proxies, 42.4
public companies: annual general meetings, 42.30–42.31
–circulation, 42.31
–notice, 42.30
public company, 42.1
quoted companies: additional requirements, 42.32–42.38
–independent assessor, 42.35–42.36
–independent report on poll, 42.34
–website, 42.33, 42.37

Resolutions, – *cont.*
records, 42.41–42.44
–inspection, 42.43
Registrar of Companies, forwarded to, 14.10
Secretary of State,
–information required, 42.45
show of hands, at meeting, 42.4
special, 42.3
traded companies: annual general meetings, 42.30–42.31
–circulation, 42.31
–independent assessor, 42.35–42.36
–independent report on poll, 42.34
–notice, 42.30
–questions, 42.23
–requirements for participating, 42.38
–website, 42.33, 42.37
Treasury, the,
–information required, 42.45
voting,
–joint holders, 42.4
–written resolutions, 42.4
written resolutions of private companies,
–agreeing, 42.9
–circulation date, 42.6
–directors, proposed by, 42.7
–eligible members, 42.6
–general provisions, 42.5
–members, proposed by, 42.8
–sending documents, 42.10
–website publication, 42.11
Restoration,
application
–to the court, 21.10
–to the Registrar, 21.9
Companies House guidance booklet, 39.2
name, 21.11
property, vested as bona vacantia, 21.12
Restructuring,
*See*Reconstructions
Retirement,
directors, 18.4–18.5
Return of allotments,
requirements, 47.12
Revaluation of fixed assets,
distributions, impact on, 22.6
Revaluation reserve,
use of, 3.14, 5.16
Reverse takeovers,
Listing Rules, 33.31A
Revised accounts,
contents, 2.11
laying of, 2.12

Rights,
general rules, Appendix 1
Rights issues,
listed companies, 47.65
procedure, 47.64
Risk committee,
UK Corporate Governance Code, 15.11
Risk management systems,
corporate governance, 15.5, 15.11, 15.13
corporate governance statements, 15.5

S

Scotland,
charitable companies, 43.6–43.7
community interest companies, charities, 10.6
Companies Acts,
–specific references, 43.1
Companies House Edinburgh,
forms Appendix 2
confidentiality of communications, 29.3
debentures to bearer, 17.17
derivative proceedings, 26.13
execution of documents, 16.7
floating charge,
–alteration, 43.5
–priority, 43.4
–winding up, 43.3
insider dealing, 23.4
legal proceedings,
–court, the, 29.8
–security for costs, 29.10
–unincorporated bodies 29.6
overseas companies,
–delivery of documents, 30.58
–execution of documents, 30.62
public sector companies, audit, 8.29
registration of charges, 40.11–40.17
–creation of charge, 40.11
–debentures, 40.14
–ex facie absolute disposition, 40.13
–failure to register, 40.11
–property acquired, 40.12
–property outside UK, 40.15
–rectification by court, 40.17
–register, 40.16
–Registrar of Companies, 40.16
Seal of company,
authority to use, 16.8
engraving of name, 16.8
use abroad, 16.9
Search,
premises, 25.13, 25.19–25.20
Secretary of State,
authorised person, acting on behalf of, 2.14
Financial Reporting Review Panel, 2.14
power,
–annual accounts, 2.14
–directors' report, 2.14
Secretary of the company,
See Company secretaries
Securities,
See also Shares
CREST, 22.14,44.14
insider dealing, 23.3
prospectuses,
–exempt, 32.5–32.6
–generally, 32.1–32.25
share certificates,
–allotment, 44.2
–contents, 44.11
–court order to make good default, 44.13
–generally, 44.1–44.13
–replacement, 44.11
–transfer, 44.10–44.11
share warrants, 44.12
Stock Exchange transfers, 44.14
transfers,
–certificates, 44.10–44.11
–certification of instrument, 44.8
–generally, 44.3
–registration, 44.6
–restrictions, 44.7
–Stock Exchange, 44.14
–Stock Transfer Act 1963, 44.4
–transferee, action by, 44.5
–transferor, action by, 44.5
transmission of shares, 44.9
Security for company borrowing,
charges,
–fixed, 45.4
–floating, 45.5
–generally, 45.3–45.7
–priority, 45.7
–registration, 45.6
–validity, 45.7
financial assistance, 45.2
security, definition, 45.2
Sell-out,
application to the court, 48.18
joint offers, 48.19
meaning, 48.10
notices,
–effect, 48.17
–giving, 48.16
right to be bought out, 48.15

Senior independent directors,
non-executive directors, 15.13
Separate legal person,
concept, 12.6
Service address,
meaning, Appendix 1
Service contracts,
directors, 18.52–18.54
directors' remuneration policy, 19.9
Service of documents,
overseas companies, 30.56
Shadow director,
definition, 18.1
liability, 29.2
Share capital,
*See also*Class Rights; Shares
accounts disclosure, 3.18, 5.20
allotted, 47.6
articles of association, 14.6
authorised, 14.6, 47.6
called-up, 47.6
equity, 47.6
issued, 47.6
maintenance, 47.60–47.61
memorandum of association, 14.2
minimum, 47.7
public companies,
–below authorised minimum, 47.57
–generally, 47.7
redenomination, 14.6, 47.49–47.50
reduction,
–below authorised minimum, 47.57
–confirmed by the court, 47.55–47.56
–effect, 47.58
–introduction, 47.51
–reserve arising from, 47.59
–supported by a solvency statement, 47.52–47.54
reserve liability, 47.6
serious loss, 47.61
uncalled, 47.6
upper limit,
–not required, 14.2
–redenomination, 47.49–47.50
–reduction, 47.51–47.59
–reserve liability, 47.6
–uncalled, 47.6
Share certificates,
allotment, 44.2
contents, 44.11
court order to make good default, 44.13
replacement, 44.11
transfer, 44.10–44.11
Shareholders,
see also Members
executive remuneration,
–exit payments, 15.14
–generally, 15.14
listed companies,
–notification of major transactions, 33.55
minority,
–takeovers, 48.12, 48.15
unauthorised political donations,
–action, 31.5–31.7
Share options,
listed companies, prior approval, 33.24
Share premium,
applications of, 46.1
group reconstruction relief 46.3
merger relief, 46.2
supplementary provisions, 46.4
transfers to, 46.1
Shares,
See also Class rights, Distributions, Interests in public company shares, Purchase of own shares
allotment,
–allowances, 47.10
–commissions, 47.10
–discounts, 47.10
–existing shareholders, 47.13
–generally, 47.6, 45.8–47.21
–power of directors, 47.9
–pre-emption right, 47.13–47.19
–private companies, prohibition of public offers, 47.21
–public companies, issue not fully subscribed, 47.20
–registration, 47.11
–return of, 47.12
alteration of share capital,
–generally, 47.46–47.50
–reconversion of stock, 47.48
–redenomination, 47.49–47.50
–sub-division or consolidation, 47.47
authorised, 47.6
bonus issues,
–funds available for, 47 63
–generally, 47.62
certificates,
–allotment, 44.2
–contents, 44.11
–court order to make good default, 44.13
–replacement, 44.11
–transfer, 44.10–44.11
classification, 47.5
deferred, 47.5

Shares, – *cont.*
directors,
–power to allot, 47.9
disclosed interests in public company,
–register, 38.8
employees, 47.5
equity, 47.5
forfeiture, 34.1, 47.25
founders, 47.5
held on behalf of others, 26.5–26.6
listed companies,
incentive plans, 33.24
management, 47.5
meaning, 47.1, Appendix 1
nature of, 47.1
nominal value, 47.2
non-cash consideration,
–contravention, 47.40, 47.44
–exceptions to the valuation requirement, 47.33
–generally, 47.32–47.35
–independent valuation requirements, 47.41
–non-cash assets, transfer, 47.36–47.40
–power of court to grant relief, 47.43
–Registrar of Companies, copy of report, 47.35, 47.38
–re-registering as a public company, 47.39
–subsequent holder, liability, 47.42
–undertakings to do work, 47.45
–valuation and reporting requirements, 47.34, 47.37
numbering, 47.3
offer to the public, 47.21
options, 33.24
order for sale of, 24.9
ordinary, 47.5
payment for,
–allotment at a discount not permitted, 47.24
–calls, 47.25
–generally, 47.23–47.30
–penalty for contravention, 47.29
–power of court to grant relief, 47.28
–public companies, 47.26
–subsequent holder, liability, 47.27
–undertakings to do work, 47.30
pre-emption right,
–communication of pre-emption offers, 47.14
–disapplication, 47.18
–exclusion, 47.17
–exemptions, 47.16
–generally, 47.13
–liability for contravention, 47.15
–saving provisions, 47.19

Shares, – *cont.*
preference, 47.5
private companies,
–prohibition of public offers, 47.21–47.22
public companies,
–issue not fully subscribed, 47.20
–non-cash consideration, independent valuation, 47.31–47.45
–payment, 47.26
redeemable, 47.5
reduction of share capital,
–confirmed by the court, 47.55–47.56
–effect of, 47.58
–private companies, supported by solvency statement, 47.52–47.54
–public company, reducing below authorised minimum, 47.57
–reserve arising from, 47.59
restrictions,
–generally, 24.6–24.8
–relaxation and removal, 25.23–25.25
rights issues,
–generally, 47.64
–listed companies, 47.65
risk 47.5
share capital,
–allotted, 47.6
–authorised, 47.6
–called-up, 47.6
–equity, 47.6
–generally, 47.6–47.7
–issued, 47.6
–maintenance, 47.60–47.61
–minimum, 33.3, 47.7
–public companies, 47.7
–redenomination, 47.49–47.50
–reduction, 47.51–47.59
–reserve liability, 47.6
–uncalled, 47.6
stock,
–inclusion, 47.1
–reconversion, 47.48
transferability, 47.4
transfers,
–certificates, 44.10–44.11
–certification of instrument, 44.8
–generally, 44.3
–registration, 44.6
–restrictions, 44.7
–Stock Exchange, 44.14
–Stock Transfer Act 1963, 44.4
–transferee, action by, 44.5
–transferor, action by, 44.5
workers 47.5

Share schemes,
listed companies, 33.24
Share warrants,
issue, 44.12
register of members, 38.5
Significant transactions,
listed companies, 33.31
Signing of accounts,
balance sheet, 2.2
revised accounts, 2.12
Single alternate inspection location (SAIL),
annual return, 7.2
Single member company,
register of members, statement, 38.5
Size of company,
qualifying conditions,
–medium, 4.2
–small, 5.2
Small companies,
See also Accounts: small companies
accounts,
–abbreviated, 2.5, 2.10
–contents, 2.10
–filing, 2.10
–revised, 2.12
audit exemption, 8.24–8.27
balance sheet statement, 2.2
directors' report, 20.1
special auditor's report, 2.5
Special notice,
resolutions requiring, 42.18
Special resolution,
meaning, 42.3, Appendix 1
removal of requirement,
–laying accounts in general meeting, 2.9
Sponsors,
listed companies, 33.16
Sponsorship,
political donations, 31.2
Squeeze-out,
take-overs,
–application to the court, 48.18
–joint offers, 48.19
–meaning, 48.10
–notice, effect of, 48.14
–notice, giving of, 48.13
–right to buy out, 48.12
Statements of Standard Accounting Practice (SSAPs),
Companies Act accounts, in accordance with, 2.15
Statutory accounts,
See also Accounts
abbreviated accounts, 2.5
definition, 2.5
Statutory accounts, – ***cont.***
delivery in euros, 2.5
publication, 2.5
Stewardship Code,
aim, 15.3
website disclosure, 15.3
Stock,
accounts valuation, 3.11
shares, as, 47.1
Stock Exchange,
see also Listed companies
CREST, 45.14
transfer of shares, 45.14
Strategic reports,
approval, 20.18
conditions for sending out,
–ascertainment of wishes, 6.3
–consultation by notice, 6.4
–prohibitions, 6.2
–relevant consultation, 6.5
defective reports,
–generally, 20.19
–introduction, 6.10
earnings per share, 33.29
false statements, 20.25
form and content,
–additional requirements for quoted companies, 20.1
–generally, 20.1
–introduction, 6.6
introduction, 20.1
listed companies, 33.29
misleading statements, 20.25
recipients, 6.1
revision,
–approval, 20.20
–delivery to Registrar of Companies, 20.24
–effect, 20.21
–generally, 20.19
–laying, 20.23
–publication, 20.22
–signing, 20.20
sending out,
–conditions, 6.2–6.4
–generally, 6.1
signing, 2.4, 20.18
supplementary material, 6.6
Striking off,
Companies House guidance booklet, 39.2
Registrar of Companies power, 24.1
voluntary, 21.2–21.6
Subsidiary undertakings,
accounts disclosure, 3.33–3.37, 5.32–5.35
audit exemption conditions, 8.27A

Subsidiary undertakings, – *cont.*
meaning, Appendix 1
member of holding company, 26.7
Summary conviction,
generally, 29.1
removal of upper limit for fines, 29.1
Summary financial statement (SFS),
See also Strategic reports
generally, 6.1
Summary proceedings,
time limit, 29.4
venue, 29.4

T

Takeovers,
announcements, 48 Appendix
background, 48.1
City Code on Takeovers and Mergers, 48 Appendix
definitions,
–associate, 48.11
–convertible securities, 48.11
–take-over offer, 48.11
impediments to,
–consequences of opting out, 48.9
–opting in and opting out, 48.8
offer, 48 Appendix
Panel on Takeovers and Mergers,
–bid documentation rules, 48.3
–enforcement by the court, 48.4
–generally, 48.2–48.6, 48 Appendix
–liability in damages, exemption from, 48.6
–non-compliance with rules, 48.5
restrictions on dealings, 48 Appendix
reverse, 33.31A
secrecy, 48 Appendix
sell-out,
–application to the court, 48.18
–joint offers, 48.19
–meaning, 48.10
–notice, effect of, 48.17
–notice, giving of, 48.16
–right to be bought out, 48.15
squeeze-out,
–application to the court, 48.18
–joint offers, 48.19
–meaning, 48.10
–notice, effect of, 48.14
–notice, giving of, 48.13
–right to buy out, 48.12
timing, 48 Appendix

Taxation,
accounts disclosure, 3.28
deferred tax, 3.22
disclosure of information by HMRC, 2.14
Third parties,
bills of exchange, 16.11
capacity, 16.1–16.4
charitable companies,
– display of name, 16.13–16.14
–generally, 16.4
common seal, 16.8–16.10
company communication provisions, 16.22–16.34
contracts, 16.5
deeds, 16.6
directors,
–power to bind company, 16.2
–transactions involving, 16.3
display of registered name, 16.13
documents,
–deemed delivery, 16.34
–generally, 16.6–16.7
fraudulent trading, 16.18
promissory notes, 16.11
public notice, 16.17
registered name, 16.13–16.14
registered office, 16.13
seal, 16.8–16.10
service addresses, 16.19
service of documents, 16.20–16.21
trading disclosures, 16.12
Time limit,
circulation of accounts, 2.6
filing of accounts, 2.11
keeping of accounting records, 36.7
keeping records of resolutions and meetings, 42.43
laying of accounts before general meeting, 2.9
legal proceedings, 29.4
registration of allotment, 47.11
registration of charges, 45.6
Trade unions,
exemption as political donation, 31.8
Traded companies,
annual return, 7.2
meaning, Appendix 1
meetings,
–circulation of members' matters, 42.31
–other matters included at AGM, 42.31
–participation, 42.38A
–questions, 42.23A
–requirement to hold AGM, 42.30
–website publication of poll results, 42.33
publication of poll result, 42.33

Trading,
fraudulent, 16.18, 18.38
wrongful, 18.39
Trading certificate,
issue, 33.3
penalties, 33.3
procedure, 33.3
Trading disclosures,
overseas companies, 30.51–30.55
registered name, 16.13–16.14, 16.16
registered office, 16.13, 16.15–16.16
Transfer of securities,
certificates, 44.10–44.11
certification of instrument, 44.8
registration, 44.6
restrictions, 44.7
Stock Exchange, 44.14
Stock Transfer Act 1963, 44.4
transferee, action by, 44.5
transferor, action by, 44.5
Translations, certified,
accounts, 30.4
constitution, 30.4
Transparency,
executive remuneration, 15.14
Transparency Rules (listed companies),
audit committees, 15.8
categories of obligation, 33.48
compensation for statements, 33.69
corporate governance, 15.5
disclosure of information in a non-EEA State, 33.68
dissemination of information, 33.67
filing information, 33.66
general provisions, 33.49
information requirements,
–issuers of shares and debt securities, 33.65
language, 33.66
notification rules, vote holder and issuer,
–acquisition of major shareholdings, 33.55
–acquisition of own shares, 33.59
–aggregation of managed holdings, 33.58
–combined holdings, 33.61
–direct and indirect holders, 33.56
–disclosures by issuers, 33.60
–disposal of major shareholdings, 33.55
–disposal of own shares, 33.59
–filing of information with the FSA, 33.63
–financial instruments, 33.57
–generally, 33.54
–major holdings, 33.55, 33.62
–non-EEA state issuers, 33.64
obligation,
–categories, 33.48
Transparency Rules (listed companies), – *cont.*
periodic financial reporting,
–annual financial reports, 33.51
–exemptions, 33.53
–generally, 33.50–33.53
–half-yearly financial reports, 33.52
Treasury shares,
dealing in,
–listed companies, 33.36
purchase of own shares,
–cancellation, 34.16
–disposal, 34.15
–generally, 34.14
–offences, 34.17
True and fair view,
Counsels' opinion on meaning, 2.16
directors' duty, 2.16
Trustees,
debenture, of, 17.15
members of company, 26.1
Trusts,
directors, interest in, 18.1
Turnover,
accounts disclosure, 3.29, 5.29
definition, Appendix 1
size of company,
–medium, 4.2
–small, 5.2
Types of company, 12.7
not formed under the Companies Acts, 11.1

U

UK Corporate Governance Code (The Code),
FRC, 15.1–15.2
UK-registered company,
definition, Appendix 1
UK regulatory framework,
generally, 15.2–15.6
UK Stewardship Code,
generally, 15.3
website disclosure, 15.3
Undertaking,
definition, Appendix 1
Undistributable reserves,
reserves comprising, 22.1
Unfair prejudice,
class rights, 9.2
protection of members, 26.10
Unincorporated bodies,
offence under Companies Acts, 29.6

Index

Unlimited companies,
articles of association, 14.4
meaning, 12.7
non-statutory accounts, 2.5
re-registering as limited,
–application and accompanying documents, 41.16
–certificate of incorporation, 41.17
–conditions, 41.15
–generally, 41.15–41.18
–statement of capital, 41.18
statutory accounts, 2.5
Unquoted companies,
accounts filing, 2.10
meaning, Appendix 1
Registrar of Companies,
–copies to, 2.10
signing,
–balance sheet, 2.4
–directors' report, 2.4
–strategic report, 2.4
Unregistered companies,
cross-border mergers, 35.60
meaning, 12.7

V

Variation of class rights,
companies without shares,
–conditions and consent, 9.4
–registration of particulars, 9.6
–right to object, 9.5
share capital,
–conditions and consent, 9.1
–registration of particulars, 9.3
–right to object, 9.2
Voting,
members, 42.4
poll, by, 42.24
procedure, 42.24
proxies, 42.4, 42.26
–listed companies, 42.26
Voting rights,
meaning, Appendix 1

W

Wales,
community interest company, 10.15
Wales, – *cont.*
Companies House Cardiff, forms, Appendix 2
derivative claims, 26.12
registered office, 37.3
registration of charges, 40.2–40.10
Welsh, documents delivered in, 39.13
WebFiling,
Companies House, 39.20
fees, Appendix 3
forms, Appendix 2
Website,
accounts, availability, 2.8
audit, publication of concerns, 8.45
communication by means of, 16.30
divisions, publication of documents, 35.24A, 35.30A
listed company, 33.42
mergers,
–publication of documents, 35.13A
–report on material changes of assets, 35.13B
resolutions, publication of, 42.11
registered name, 16.14
specified information, 16.14
Wholly-owned subsidiary,
definition, Appendix 1
Winding up,
dissolution, 21
–notification of members, 21.5
–property, bona vacantia, 21.8
–property, disclaimer, 21.8
–striking off, objections to, 21.6
–voluntary striking off, 21.2–21.6
–Registrar of Companies, power, 21.1
Scotland, floating charge, 43.3
Women on Boards report,
generally, 15.9
Working day,
meaning of, Appendix 1
Written resolution,
agreeing to, 42.9
meaning, 42.5
proposed by directors, 42.7
proposed by members, 42.8
special resolution, 42.3
Wrongful trading,
directors, 18.18
insolvency, 18.39